THE FIRST AMENDMENT

ASPEN SELECT SERIES

THE FIRST AMENDMENT

Cases and Theory

Third Edition

Ronald J. Krotoszynski, Jr.
John S. Stone Chair and Professor of Law
University of Alabama School of Law

Christina E. Wells
Enoch H. Crowder Professor of Law
University of Missouri School of Law

Lyrissa Barnett Lidsky
Dean and C.A. Leedy Professor of Law
University of Missouri School of Law

Caroline Mala Corbin
Professor of Law
University of Miami School of Law

Wolters Kluwer

About Wolters Kluwer Legal & Regulatory U.S.

Wolters Kluwer Legal & Regulatory U.S. delivers expert content and solutions in the areas of law, corporate compliance, health compliance, reimbursement, and legal education. Its practical solutions help customers successfully navigate the demands of a changing environment to drive their daily activities, enhance decision quality and inspire confident outcomes.

Serving customers worldwide, its legal and regulatory portfolio includes products under the Aspen Publishers, CCH Incorporated, Kluwer Law International, ftwilliam.com and MediRegs names. They are regarded as exceptional and trusted resources for general legal and practice-specific knowledge, compliance and risk management, dynamic workflow solutions, and expert commentary.

In addition to our individual dedications, set forth below, we also collectively dedicate this book to the memory of our good friend, colleague, and former co-author, Professor Steven G. Gey, the David & Deborah Fonvielle and Donald & Janet Hinkle Professor of Law at the Florida State University College of Law. Steve passed away in 2011 after waging a long and heroic battle with amyotrophic lateral sclerosis (ALS), commonly known as Lou Gehrig's disease.

Steve was a consummate scholar and also a highly gifted teacher. He was the author of literally dozens of books, law review articles, and essays, many appearing in the nation's most prestigious law reviews and law journals. His legal scholarship was—and will remain for many years to come—highly influential. No less important than his intellect and scholarly accomplishments, however, was Steve's grace, good humor, and warmth—he was unfailingly pleasant and collegial, an academic who could disagree with others without ever becoming disagreeable. The four of us miss Steve deeply. Nevertheless, we are comforted with the thought that students, teachers, lawyers, and judges using this third edition of *The First Amendment: Cases and Theory* will benefit from Steve's distinctive voice, which still resonates within the pages of this book.

Ronald J. Krotoszynski, Jr., Christina E. Wells, Lyrissa Barnett Lidsky, Caroline Mala Corbin

June 2017

———————————

For my mother, Barbara Carol Jamison Krotoszynski (1949-2013).

—*R.K.*

To my sons: Jordan, Benjamin, and Asher.

—*L.L.*

For Ellie who, though still finding her voice, always speaks her mind.

—*C.W.*

For Michael, with gratitude and love.

—*C.C.*

SUMMARY OF CONTENTS

CONTENTS

CHAPTER 19
THE ESTABLISHMENT CLAUSE AND PUBLIC SCHOOLS   889

CHAPTER 20
THE ESTABLISHMENT CLAUSE AND GOVERNMENT
ENDORSEMENT OF RELIGION   927

PREFACE

It may come as a surprise to many students entering law school that an entire course could be devoted to a single amendment of the United States Constitution. On the other hand, it may also come as a surprise to other students that most of the jurisprudence discussed in this casebook is of relatively recent vintage—much of it dating back to the Warren and Burger Courts. The Supreme Court devoted very little attention to the First Amendment prior to World War I. Since that time, however, the First Amendment has become one of the most frequently litigated components of the Constitution. In fact, during the current Roberts Court era, the First Amendment has become a powerful tool to challenge federal, state, and local regulations that affect communication in any conceivable way, including, for example, restrictions on the sale of physicians' prescription data and offering consumers discounts for cash purchases. From the modern perspective, the First Amendment has become such a central part of our social, political, and religious interaction in the United States that it is difficult to envision an American society without it. In an increasingly diverse culture, which is witnessing an explosion of new media through which conflicting opinions can be disseminated, the First Amendment will almost certainly remain an important—indeed central—focal point of constitutional litigation.

This casebook surveys a broad range of contemporary First Amendment jurisprudence, including cases relating to each of the major concerns of the modern amendment—freedom of speech, press, assembly, association, and religion. The right of petition, although one of the five main clauses of the First Amendment, has not (at least to date) played an important doctrinal or jurisprudential role in securing expressive and religious freedoms in the United States. The two modern cases that squarely address the meaning and scope of the Petition Clause both declined to articulate and apply a specific jurisprudence of the clause. *See* Borough of Duryea v. Guarnieri, 564 U.S. 379, 387-399 (2011) (holding that the Petition Clause does not confer any special protection on complaints by government employees about their treatment by their employers because "[p]etitions, no less than speech, can interfere with the efficient and effective operation of the government" and noting that the rights of petition and free speech "share substantial common ground"); McDonald v. Smith, 472 U.S. 479, 482, 485 (1985) (holding that the Petition Clause does not create any greater right of public comment that contains false factual assertions than do the Free Speech or Free Press Clauses because the Petition Clause is "cut from the same cloth" as these parallel rights). *But cf.* Adderley v. Florida, 385 U.S. 39, 52 (1966) (Douglas, J., dissenting) (arguing that the Petition Clause should be interpreted to provide enhanced access to government property, such as a county jail, when speech and assembly have a clear petitioning component). Indeed, the nontextual implied right to freedom of association plays a more central role in contemporary First Amendment law and theory. Accordingly, the Petition Clause does not receive independent treatment in this book. However, should the Petition Clause come to play a more meaningful role in securing expressive freedoms in the United States, the authors will certainly include dedicated coverage of this clause in a future edition.

This casebook is organized around substantial excerpts of the Supreme Court's most significant First Amendment decisions. We have edited the cases relatively lightly, in an effort to let the Justices' own words lead students through the doctrine. In addition to the main cases, notes after many of the cases provide short excerpts or summaries of other relevant Supreme Court decisions and important academic commentary, along with references to some lower court decisions regarding matters on which the Supreme Court has not yet spoken. The chapters all include Theory Applied Problems after major sections and subsections to help focus students' attention on the particular applications and internal conflicts of the doctrine. The Theory Applied Problems provide an easy and reliable way to assess students' mastery of the relevant governing legal rules, principles, and theory.

A few words about our approach to contextualizing First Amendment problems and jurisprudence are in order. First, we have made a conscious effort to address the interplay of historical and political events and First Amendment doctrine. In our view, consideration of the historical and political context of free speech and religious freedom cases helps to illuminate the concerns that can motivate judges to accept or reject constitutional claims. Second, in several important areas, we incorporate decisions from foreign constitutional courts because we believe that these materials provide a helpful contrast with the U.S. approach to common legal problems. Looking at a problem from a comparative perspective often yields useful insights into the (often unstated) policies and objectives of contemporary First Amendment jurisprudence. In sum, considering both history and how other nations address common legal problems can help to foster better understanding of contemporary U.S. First Amendment jurisprudence, and this book incorporates and reflects this point of view.

We have organized this casebook with the intention of first providing students with a general background of overriding First Amendment concepts before turning to more specific areas in which the Supreme Court has developed and applied specialized rules. Modern First Amendment law can be very frustrating for the uninitiated because the lines between the various specialized rules and standards are often unclear. Indeed, the Supreme Court's consistent drift from general, open-ended principles to frame and decide First Amendment cases toward a vast sea of three- and four-part tests that apply only in very specific, limited circumstances provides one of the larger themes of this casebook. As you explore these materials, you should consider whether highly context-specific, complex, multipronged balancing tests better secure fundamental liberties than would more general, open-ended tests.

In some respects, attempting to understand First Amendment law is like learning to play three-dimensional chess. In many situations raising First Amendment issues, more than one set of rules will seem to apply. Any given case may raise generalized First Amendment concerns (such as the rule that the government may almost never engage in content or viewpoint regulation), coupled with specific rules developed for particular factual scenarios (such as the rules regarding obscenity, fighting words, threats, or government-subsidized speech), which are further complicated by special procedural rules (such as the expedited litigation requirements of *Freedman v. Maryland*), special remedial rules (such as the Court's strong discouragement of injunctive prior restraints), and even special statutory-construction mandates (such as the Court's unusual willingness to consider facial overbreadth challenges to statutes impinging on free speech). The First Amendment even has special real estate rules for government property, which dictate when and how that property must be opened to speakers wishing to express themselves to other members of the public. Learning to navigate the often conflicting crosscurrents of First Amendment law is one of the student's main tasks in a First Amendment course, and this casebook is designed to make that task easier.

The basic organization of the book divides the discussion of the First Amendment between the Speech Clauses, which are covered in Part I (the first twelve chapters), and the Religion Clauses, which are covered in Part II (the next eight chapters). Within the speech chapters, the discussion moves from an overview of the general theory and structure of the First Amendment to the specific doctrines that apply to particular areas of speech. The first three chapters provide an overview of the history and theory of the First Amendment, along with a discussion of the basic rules regarding content and viewpoint regulation by the government. These chapters also provide a basic understanding of the government's role in regulating political expression, which is the topic that the Supreme Court addressed in its earliest First Amendment cases, and which remains at the heart of free speech jurisprudence. Chapters 4 and 5 provide a general discussion of content and viewpoint regulation, along with a consideration of the ways in which the government can regulate speech without regard to the content of that speech. These chapters also discuss the rules governing speech in public forums. Chapter 6 is a bridge chapter, discussing the general rules regarding compelled and anonymous speech, and also addressing the specific First Amendment doctrines relating to electoral speech. Chapter 6 also considers in some detail how regulations of political speech implicate both compelled speech and anonymous speech. Chapters 7 through 12 move from the general to the particular, discussing a variety of different First Amendment doctrines that relate to specific types of speech, including commercial speech, media regulation, defamation, group libel, fighting words, erotica, government employees, and government-subsidized speech.

Part II discusses the Religion Clauses. The first chapter is an introduction to both clauses. The next two chapters discuss the Free Exercise Clause, and the remaining five chapters examine the Establishment Clause. In Chapter 13, Part II opens with a general overview of the history and theory of the Establishment and Free Exercise Clauses. Chapter 14 then turns to the meaning of "free exercise" and considers whether the Free Exercise Clause should protect religiously-motivated conduct no less than it protects religious belief. This chapter also considers statutory enactments that convey individual exemptions from neutral laws of general applicability when such laws impede religiously motivated conduct. Chapter 15 examines the ability of religious entities, such as churches, temples, and mosques, to seek and obtain exemptions from generally applicable laws through doctrines such as the ministerial exemption.

Chapter 16 provides an introduction and overview to the Establishment Clause; this chapter considers the various general tests that the Supreme Court has deployed to prevent religious establishments. Chapter 17 examines how the Establishment Clause impacts efforts by the federal and state governments to accommodate religiously motivated beliefs and conduct. Chapter 18 discusses cases involving government financing of religion, including indirect financing of religious K-12 schools through voucher programs, as well as direct financing via government grants to religious organizations that provide social services. The distinct problems and issues associated with bringing religious beliefs and practices into the K-12 public schools receive sustained coverage in Chapter 19. Finally, Chapter 20 considers the constitutional limits applicable to government efforts to promote religion in other contexts.

As this brief summary indicates, the complexities of the interrelationships between the many First Amendment standards and doctrines are daunting. Fortunately, the entertainment value of cases raising First Amendment issues is quite high. The reader will find in the materials that follow a gallery of rogues and heroes, dissenters and visionaries, and more than a few simple oddballs. The cast of characters includes Communists and Ku Klux Klansmen, cross burners, funeral protestors, punk rock bands seeking edgy trademarks, draft-card burners and anti-war protestors, atheists and evangelicals, Eugene V. Debs and Richard Nixon, Larry Flynt and Catherine McKinnon, Reverend Fred Phelps and Madalyn Murray O'Hair, and devout Jehovah's Witnesses and the purveyors of violent video games. In one sense it is their First Amendment that this book discusses, but in a more important sense this colorful cast has helped the Court define the scope of expressive and religious freedom enjoyed by the entire society. The authors of this casebook believe that we have rendered the story of the First Amendment in a way that makes it both coherent and digestible. Whether we have succeeded in that task is for the reader to decide, but at the very least we feel certain that no one will find this material boring.

Ronald J. Krotoszynski, Jr.
Christina E. Wells
Lyrissa Barnett Lidsky
Caroline Mala Corbin

June 2017

ACKNOWLEDGMENTS

I have genuinely enjoyed working with my dedicated and talented co-authors, Chris Wells, Lyrissa Lidsky, and Caroline Mala Corbin; one could not ask for better collaborators on a project of this size and scope. Moreover, it has been wonderful to have a colleague as smart, thoughtful, and careful as Professor Caroline Mala Corbin, our new co-author on the third edition. It is commonplace, perhaps to the point of cliché, to say that working with one's co-authors has been a pleasure, but in this instance, the sentiment happens to be both genuine and heartfelt. I also must note that, even with the passage of time, I continue to miss the wise counsel and good humor of our former co-author, Steve Gey, who passed away in 2011. Over the years, I have learned much about the First Amendment from the scholarship of Professors Gey, Wells, Lidsky, and Corbin. This casebook is immeasurably stronger because of the synergy of our collective efforts. I acknowledge with gratitude the support of Dean Mark Brandon and the University of Alabama School of Law, which greatly facilitated my work on this project. I also should note the support of the University of Alabama Law School Foundation, which provided generous financial support for this project in the form of summer research grants. Finally, the four of us wish to acknowledge the thoughtful and constructive reviews provided by our First Amendment colleagues on various iterations of the casebook; the book has benefitted significantly from the insights and observations of our colleagues in the field who took the time and energy to provide feedback on both the first and second editions. Although we do not know your names (the Aspen Publishers review process is anonymous), we wish to thank you for your assistance—the third edition of this casebook will be a more effective pedagogical tool because of your labors. R.K.

Thanks to Corryn Hall for her invaluable research assistance and advice over the last two years. Without her, I could not have finished my portion of this edition. The University of Missouri Law School Foundation also provided valuable research support. I am also grateful simply to be allowed to work with Ron, Lyrissa, and Caroline. C.W.

Many thanks to Linda Riedemann Norbut for stellar research assistance and to Lauren Stucki for seemingly endless proofreading. L.L.

My deepest thanks to Ron, Lyrissa, and Chris for their vote of confidence in inviting me to join them. Thanks also to my research assistant Jean Phillip Shami for his cheerfulness and his eagle eyes. C.M.C.

Ronald J. Krotoszynski, Jr., Christina E. Wells, Lyrissa Barnett Lidsky, and Caroline Mala Corbin

June 2017

PART
I

Freedom of Expression

CHAPTER
1

The History, Values, and Content
of the First Amendment

TABLE OF CONTENTS

The First Amendment of the United States Constitution establishes that "Congress shall make no law . . . abridging the freedom of speech, or of the press; or the right of the people peaceably to assemble, and to petition the government for a redress of grievances." Although this language seems straightforward and uncompromising, little about the amendment has proven to be so easy. Despite Justice Black's famous claim that "[n]either as offered nor as adopted is the language of this Amendment anything less than absolute," *see* Hugo L. Black, *The Bill of Rights*, 35 N.Y.U. L. Rev. 865, 874 (1960), the Supreme Court has never treated the First Amendment as absolutely protecting expression.

Numerous laws restricting speech exist with the Court's approval. For example, the state can criminalize incitement of lawless activity, Brandenburg v. Ohio, 395 U.S. 444 (1969), and ban the distribution of obscenity, Miller v. California, 413 U.S. 15 (1973). It can also regulate the time and place of protest gatherings in public forums, like streets and parks, Cox v. New Hampshire, 312 U.S. 569 (1941), and impose even greater restrictions on expression taking place on other public property, such as libraries or prisons, Adderley v. Florida, 385 U.S. 39 (1966). On the other hand, the Court has held government officials may not ban advocacy of illegal action even if it ostensibly causes harm. *Brandenburg, supra.* Nor, as a general rule, can the state punish speech because it offends the listener. Cohen v. California, 403 U.S. 15 (1971). And although the state can regulate the time and place of public protests, it cannot charge protestors differential fees based upon possible expenses associated with keeping order. Forsyth County, Ga. v. Nationalist Movement, 505 U.S. 123 (1992).

How does the Court justify differential treatment of incitement and advocacy of illegal activity, or obscenity and offensive speech, or time, place, and manner regulations and fees imposed upon protests? Many factors influence the Court, including the possible harm resulting from particular speech, the state's purpose for restraining speech, the form of the state's regulation, the form of the speech, the historical context of the speech, and the cost to society of overly restrictive speech regulations. Unfortunately, the Court has never explained with clarity or consistency the relationship between these influences and its doctrinal rules, or even the relationship of one doctrinal rule to another. Over time, the Court's free speech doctrine has developed into "a vast Sargasso Sea of drifting and entangled values, theories, rules, exceptions [and] predilections . . . [requiring] determined interpretive effort to derive a useful set of constitutional principles by which to evaluate regulations of expression." Robert C. Post, *Racist Speech, Democracy, and the First Amendment*, 32 Wm. & Mary L. Rev. 267, 278 (1991).

To complicate matters, the Court has never clearly defined when activity is sufficiently expressive to warrant First Amendment protection. While the Court has acknowledged that "expressive conduct" falls within the auspices of the First Amendment, it struggles to define the parameters of such conduct. Burning a flag to protest government action counts, Texas v. Johnson, 491 U.S. 397 (1989), as does burning one's draft card to protest the Vietnam War, United States v. O'Brien, 391 U.S. 367 (1968). But nude dancing is only "marginally" within the parameters of the First Amendment. Barnes v. Glen Theatre, Inc., 501 U.S. 560 (1991). How does the Supreme Court arrive at such conclusions? Furthermore, a great deal of what one thinks of as "expression"—for example, proxy statements under the securities laws or requests that another person help one with a crime (that is, criminal solicitation)—never even receive First Amendment scrutiny. *See, e.g.,* Frederick Schauer, *The Boundaries of the First Amendment: A Preliminary Exploration of Constitutional Salience*, 117 Harv. L. Rev. 1765 (2004). Why? The Supreme Court has been remarkably silent about how and why it draws these "boundaries." *Id.*

That said, principles and themes emerge from the Court's jurisprudence that aid interpretation of its doctrine. This book identifies and discusses those principles and themes as it applies them to various areas of free speech doctrine. It begins in this chapter with overviews of the history associated with the First Amendment, the values underlying protection of expression, and certain doctrinal themes that consistently emerge in the Court's decisions.

A. THE HISTORY OF FREE EXPRESSION IN ENGLAND AND THE EARLY YEARS OF THE REPUBLIC

Consider the following hypothetical:

> You are a small internet service provider that has received a national security letter, an administrative subpoena issued by the FBI, seeking to gather all information about the internet activities of one of your customers that the FBI believes is "relevant to a foreign counter-intelligence investigation," including their complete web browsing activity, the IP addresses of everyone the customer has communicated with, and records of online purchases. Under federal law, you are required to turn over the information to the FBI. Furthermore, you are prohibited from challenging the subpoena in a court of law or from ever disclosing to any other person that you have received it. *See* The USA Patriot Act § 505, Pub. L. No. 107-56, 115 Stat. 272 (2001).

As you read the history below, consider how it bears on the above hypothetical. To what extent does the First Amendment prohibit or allow national security letters? How do the struggles over English licensing and the law of seditious libel in England and the early Republic reflect on the subpoena issue?

1. England

Prior to and including the late eighteenth century, English officials attempted to suppress "dangerous" or "offensive" speech, ostensibly for the preservation of the country or the welfare of its citizens. For example, libels of private persons were frequently punished as breaches of the peace. *See* 4 William Blackstone, *Commentaries on the Laws of England* *150. In addition, the Crown and Parliament also attempted to punish expression criticizing government officials, government policies, and religion. *See* Leonard W. Levy, *Emergence of a Free Press* 4-8 (1985). Two forms of regulation emerged as most effective—licensing and prosecutions for seditious libel.

a. Licensing

The fifteenth century invention of the printing press saw increased distribution of written literature and a concomitant rise in the Crown's interest in regulating the distribution of potentially "dangerous" publications. Medieval laws punishing treason, heresy, libel, and spreading "false news" against the king (Scandalum Magnatum) were already available to suppress pernicious expression. However, such laws allowed only piecemeal regulation and the Crown wanted a more unified mechanism of regulation. Beginning in the sixteenth century, the Crown claimed the authority to license printed materials as a matter of royal prerogative (powers vested in the monarch alone). Those wanting to publish printed materials had to submit their work to licensing authorities who could censor portions of it prior to granting a license. Publication without licensors' approval was punishable in the prerogative courts (those associated with the Crown). The Crown justified licensing because "the stability of the government and the peace of the realm demanded strict control" of published materials. Fredrick Seaton Siebert, *Freedom of the Press in England 1476-1776* at 22 (1952). However, few standards guided censors in their decisions, placing publishers at the mercy of government officials' arbitrary determinations.

Licensing laws were controversial. Many English libertarians argued against them, claiming they were detrimental to personal liberty and good government. The English Levellers (a radical democratic movement formed during the seventeenth century English civil wars) argued that a free press was "essential unto Freedom...for what may not be done to that people who may not speak or write, but at the pleasure of Licensers." "The Humble Petition of Firm and Constant Friends," in *Leveller Manifestoes of the Puritan Revolution* 326, 328 (Don M. Wolfe ed., 1944). Similarly, John Milton argued that licensing laws would discourage learning, prove fruitless in preventing the spread of "evil," and placed too much faith in the infallibility of licensors. John Milton, "Areopagitica," in *Areopagitica and Of Education* 5, 21 (George H. Sabine ed., 1951).

Licensing laws nonetheless remained the primary mechanism for suppressing printed expression through the seventeenth century. In 1694, Parliament did not renew the licensing laws upon their expiration, primarily because they were expensive, imposed an undue burden on printers, were often widely ignored, and were difficult to enforce systematically. In effect, licensing expired for "reasons of expediency rather than of conviction on moral or philosophical grounds" regarding the necessity of a free press. Siebert, *supra*, at 261.

b.   Seditious Libel

While licensing waned as a mechanism of enforcement in the seventeenth century, other legal instruments of suppression came to the fore. Government officials initially attempted to prosecute speech under the treason laws, which prohibited (1) imagining or plotting the death of the King, (2) making war against the King, or (3) aiding the King's enemies. By the end of the seventeenth century, judges found that writings and printings critical of the Crown could provide the "overt act" necessary for successful treason prosecutions. For example, citizens were tried for publishing materials arguing that the King should be accountable to his subjects.

While government officials initially believed that "constructive treason" prosecutions were appropriate methods of suppressing publications critical of the government, prosecutions were difficult for several reasons. Much anti-government literature was not extreme enough to be considered treasonable; juries believed the death penalty to be an unduly harsh punishment; and Parliament enacted a law substantially reforming the procedures used at treason trials, thus providing greater protection for those accused of the crime. For discussion, see Siebert, *supra*, at 264-269; Philip Hamburger, *The Development of the Law of Seditious Libel and the Control of the Press*, 37 Stan. L. Rev. 661, 666, 717-23 (1985).

The English government thus increasingly turned to seditious libel prosecutions. Such prosecutions had been available to the government for at least a century as a subset of libel and defamation prosecutions, which had developed to prevent breaches of the peace. In the late sixteenth and early seventeenth centuries, the government pursued seditious libel prosecutions primarily when they involved written statements that tended to injure a specific official's reputation. Consequently, such prosecutions were similar to those involving libels of private individuals.

In 1605, Attorney General Edward Coke's prosecution of Lewis Pickering for publishing a defamatory poem about two Archbishops of Canterbury marked a significant change regarding libel concerning government officials. In his report of the case, Coke noted the consequences of libels against private persons versus government officials:

> If it be against a private man it deserveth a severe punishment, for although the Libel be made against one, yet it inciteth all those of the same family, kindred or society to revenge, and so may be the cause [by consequence of] quarrels and breach of the peace, and may be the cause of shedding of blood and of great inconvenience; if it be against a Magistrate, or other public person, it is a greater offence; for it concerneth not onely the breach of the peace, but also the scandal of the government; for what greater scandal of government can there be than to have corrupt or wicked Magistrates to be appointed and constituted but the King to govern his Subjects under him? And greater imputation to the State cannot be, than to suffer such corrupt men to sit in the sacred seat of Justice, or to have any medling in or concerning the administration of Justice.

Case de Libellis Famosis, 5 Coke 125a, 125a (1605). The case also established that criminal libels such as the one involved need not be false in order to be punished nor did the victim need to be alive for the government to punish the libel. *Id.* at 125a-125b. Although the Pickering case was prosecuted as a straightforward libel, the case's central propositions (dispensing with truth as a defense and establishing that libel against government officials caused greater mischief than private libels) were important building blocks in the transformation of seditious libel as a crime.

During the seventeenth and early eighteenth centuries, prosecutions of seditious libel began to change. Government officials urged that any writing critical of government, not just writing aimed at specific officials, qualified as seditious libel. Eventually, the courts recognized officials' claims. In Queen v. Tutchin, the publisher of a periodical, *The Observator*, was prosecuted for publishing general accusations that national leaders took bribes of French gold and that military officials were corrupt. In response to defendant's argument that libel required statements about a particular person, Lord Holt declared it would be "a very strange doctrine: to say it is not a libel reflecting on the government[.] [E]ndeavouring to possess the people that the government is maladministered by corrupt persons…is certainly a reflection on the government." Queen v. Tutchin, 90 Eng. Rep. 1133 (Q.B. 1704). Lord Holt enlarged the definition of seditious libel, permanently bringing it out from under the auspices of traditional libel and making it a separate crime. His justification echoed Coke's reasons for distinguishing between private libels and libels of specific government officials:

> If people should not be called to account for possessing the people with an ill opinion of the government, no government can subsist; for it is very necessary for all governments that the people should have a good opinion of it. And nothing can be worse to any government than to endeavour to procure animosities as to the

management of it. This has been always looked upon as a crime, and no government can be safe without it be punished.

Id.

As with earlier versions of seditious libel, judges found the truth of the published matter immaterial to the charge of seditious libel. In addition, they implied the knowledge and malice required for the crime came from the statement's defamatory content. In other words, the courts assumed the defendants had the necessary bad intent simply from the fact that the statement was defamatory; no other proof of intent was required. Some publishers attempted to evade the law's requirements by publishing satires or ironical statements that did not explicitly criticize government officials. But the courts made clear that such writings could still be punished as seditious libel. *See* Queen v. Dr. Brown, 88 Eng. Rep. 911 (Q.B. 1706). However, a jury rather than a judge had to find ironic or satirical writing libelous since it was not clearly malicious.

Detractors argued that the law of seditious libel gave judges too much leeway to find simple criticism of the government dangerous. For example, John Trenchard and Thomas Gordon, writing under the pseudonym "Cato," argued that "[w]hen words used in their true and proper sense, and understood in their literal and natural meaning, import nothing that is criminal; then to strain their genuine signification to make them intend sedition (which possibly the author might intend too) is such a stretch of discretionary power, as must subvert all the principles of free government, and overturn every species of liberty." Cato, "Second Discourse Upon Libels," 3 *Cato's Letters* No. 101. Trenchard and Gordon acknowledged that "men ought to speak well of their governors . . . while their governors deserve to be well spoken of; but [for officials] to do public mischief, without hearing of it, is only the prerogative and felicity of tyranny. . . . The administration of government is nothing else, but the attendance of trustees of the people upon the interest and affairs of the people. . . . Only the wicked governors of men dread what is said of them." Cato, "Of Freedom of Speech: That the Same Is Inseparable from Publick Liberty," in 1 *Cato's Letters* No. 15.

Despite criticism of seditious libel law, it eventually became settled practice. In 1769, Blackstone summarized the state of freedom of the press in England:

> The liberty of the press is indeed essential to the nature of a free state; but this consists in laying no previous restraints upon publications, and not in freedom from censure for criminal matter when punished. . . . To subject the press to the restrictive power of a licenser, as was formerly done . . . is to subject all freedom of sentiment to the prejudices of one man, and make him the arbitrary and infallible judge of all controverted points in learning, religion, and government. But to punish (as the law does at present) any dangerous or offensive writings, which, when published, shall on a fair and impartial trial be adjudged of a pernicious tendency, is necessary for the preservation of peace and good order, of government and religion, the only solid foundations of civil liberty.

Blackstone, *supra*, at *151-152. Accordingly, although prior restraints in the form of licensing schemes were considered antithetical to free expression, laws imposing subsequent punishment, such as seditious libel laws, were not.

2. The Early American Republic

a. Generally

There is some debate as to whether Blackstone's view prevailed in the colonies when the First Amendment was adopted. Licensing in the colonies, as in England, was considered inconsistent with free expression. The law of seditious libel, however, was another matter. Like much of English common law, the law of seditious libel passed over to the colonies. However, here were few seditious libel prosecutions in eighteenth century America. The most famous of these—the prosecution of John Peter Zenger for publishing remarks critical of the Governor General of New York in 1735—was an important milestone in such prosecutions. Zenger's counsel argued, against all existing precedent at the time, that Zenger should not be convicted because his publications were based in fact. Although truth had never been a defense to libel and Zenger's publication was a classic example of words often punished as seditious libel, the jury returned a "not guilty" verdict. The *Zenger* verdict signaled the depth of popular opposition to seditious libel laws used to punish criticism of the government. Accordingly, elected assemblies more commonly used "breaches of parliamentary privilege" (essentially, the power to find people in contempt) to punish statements critical of the legislature and the government. But even that tool became ineffective due to popular opposition. *See generally* Levy, *supra*, at 16-61, David A. Anderson, *The Origins of the Press Clause*, 30 UCLA L. Rev. 455, 509-515 (1983).

Thus, the law allowed substantial punishment of seditious libel but its practical effect was unclear. During the eighteenth century, newspapers and publications frequently printed material critical of the government with few repercussions. Nevertheless, colonists were not always principled in their willingness to extend protection to speech they disliked, especially as the rift between England and the colonies grew. Speech criticizing the royalist government was widely tolerated while loyalist speech was not. *See* Levy, *supra*, at 173-183; Anderson, *supra*, at 495; David M. Rabban, *The Ahistorical Historian: Leonard Levy on Freedom of Expression in Early American History*, 37 Stan. L. Rev. 795, 842 (1985); Richard Buel, "Freedom of the Press in Revolutionary America: The Evolution of Libertarianism, 1760-1820," in *The Press and the American Revolution* 59, 71-72, 74-75 (Bernard Bailyn & John Hench eds., 1980).

b. The Adoption of the First Amendment

First Amendment scholars debate whether the Framers of the First Amendment intended to adopt the Blackstonian view regarding freedom of expression. Zechariah Chafee expressed the standard libertarian sentiment that the Framers "intended to wipe out the common law of sedition, and make further prosecutions for criticism of government, without any incitement to law-breaking, forever impossible in the United States of America." Zechariah Chafee, *Freedom of Speech in War Time*, 32 Harv. L. Rev. 932, 947 (1919). Chaffee argued that since licensing schemes had expired in England in 1695 and in the colonies by 1725, the Framers of the First Amendment intended to do more than simply prohibit prior restraints.

Legal historian Leonard Levy, however, substantially challenged Chafee's assumptions. He concluded from historical evidence that although the "Declaration of Independence severed the political connection with England[,]. . . the American states continued the English common-law system except as explicitly rejected by statute. If the revolution produced any radical libertarians on the meaning of freedom of speech and press, they were not at the Constitutional Convention or the First Congress, which drafted the Bill of Rights." Levy, *supra*, at xv. Thus, Levy concluded that the Framers' conception of freedom of expression meant to leave the law of seditious libel intact. There is much to support Levy's hypothesis. As noted above, seditious libel laws did exist and the Framers tolerated some seditious libel prosecutions. Furthermore, they never intended to abolish such prosecutions in the states. Although James Madison, the primary architect of the First Amendment, also proposed a free press clause explicitly applicable to the states, the First Congress rejected Madison's attempts to protect free expression from state restrictions. Instead, the First Amendment expressly applies only to Congress. *See* Anderson, *supra*, at 476-478, 483.[1]

Although most scholars agree that seditious libel played a greater role in the colonies and the framing of the First Amendment than Professor Chafee acknowledges, not everyone agrees with Professor Levy. Several commentators argue that Levy's thesis misses important historical subtleties regarding the Constitution and the First Amendment. Professor David Rabban, for example, has noted that numerous prominent colonial theorists argued that the government is the servant of the people. They understood the necessity of reforming, if not totally eliminating, seditious libel prosecutions to conform to notions of popular sovereignty. These scholars argued that the common law of seditious libel should require a showing of malicious intent, truth should be a defense, and juries rather than judges should be allowed to decide whether publications were seditious. Without such changes, they believed seditious libel prosecutions interfered with popular sovereignty because officials were punishing mere criticism of government conduct rather than truly dangerous speech. *See generally* Rabban, *supra*; Anderson, *supra*; William T. Mayton, *Seditious Libel and the Lost Guarantee of Freedom of Expression*, 84 Colum. L. Rev. 91 (1984).

3. *The Sedition Act of 1798*

Enacted less than a decade after the First Amendment's adoption, the Sedition Act of 1798 produced the first significant controversy regarding the scope of First Amendment protection. The Act was adopted amid growing hostilities toward ideas generated by the French Revolution, which sparked a bitter political divide between the Federalist and Republican parties. The Federalists believed in a strong central government whose purpose was to preserve security and property rights. They had little faith in the "common man's" ability to govern, believing that citizens could voice their opinions through elections but that elected officials were better suited to the responsibility of governing. Republicans, on the other hand, were strong believers in popular government and valued liberty over security. They argued for

---

[1] Eventually, the Supreme Court read the First Amendment's freedom of speech as among the liberties protected by the Fourteenth Amendment's Due Process Clause applicable to the states. *See* Gitlow v. New York, 268 U.S. 652 (1925).

decentralized authority over decision-making and a government directly responsive to its citizens. Federalists viewed the ideas generated by the French Revolution as a threat to the nation's security; Republicans viewed it as a continuation of American ideals of liberty and democracy.

Federalists, who were then in power, argued France would imminently attack the United States and that it was necessary to prepare for war. Republicans refused to cooperate. In congressional debates and partisan newspapers accusations flew between the two parties. Federalists accused Republicans of disloyalty and argued hostile foreign forces were sowing the seeds of subversion within the country. Republicans accused the Federalists of exaggerating the danger to further their political ends. To silence critics and ensure a united front at home, Federalist politicians pushed the Sedition Act of 1798, Act of July 14, 1798, 1 Stat. 596, through Congress. The Sedition Act prohibited

> writing, printing, publishing or uttering, any false, scandalous, and malicious . . . writings against the government of the United States, or either house of the Congress of the United States, or the President of the United States, with intent to defame [them]; or to bring them . . . into contempt or disrepute; or to excite against them . . . the hatred of the good people of the United States, or to stir up sedition within the United States, or to excite any unlawful combinations therein, for opposing or resisting any law of the United States, or any [lawful] act of the President of the United States.

Given earlier criticism of the law of seditious libel, the Act provided that truth *was* a defense to a charge of seditious libel, that malicious intent *was* a required element of the crime, and that *juries*, rather than judges, were to decide whether a writing was defamatory.

Republicans opposed the Act, arguing it violated the First Amendment. They argued that the people, as absolute sovereigns over the government, had a right to criticize their elected officials. The Sedition Act, they feared, would be used to suppress information critical to public decision-making and good government. This was true even with the improvements because it was simply too easy for government officials to find that an opinion criticizing the government was not true and therefore could be punished. Thus, the indeterminacy of such laws would lead to self-censorship or too much discretion in government officials to act in their self-interest. Federalists, in contrast, justified the law as necessary to preserving the nation. Although they acknowledged the government was based upon notions of popular sovereignty, they maintained that in order to govern effectively, elected officials must be protected from criticism. Some argued that there was even greater reason to protect government officials from criticism in a popular government than in a monarchy because "[t]o mislead the judgment of the people, where they have no power may produce no mischief [but to] mislead the judgment of the people where they have *all* the power . . . must produce the greatest possible mischief." Richard Buel, *Securing the Revolution* 256 (1972). They further argued that the technical improvements in the law provided sufficient protection for speech.

In fact, the Act was vigorously prosecuted only against Republican newspapers and other Republican supporters. In 1799, Federalist officials began an organized campaign to prosecute the leaders of all prominent Republican newspapers (timing that coincided with national elections). From 1798 through 1801, at least 25 Republicans were prosecuted under the Act. Prosecutions were based on criticism such as that found in a handbill distributed by Anthony Haswell in support of Matthew Lyon, a Republican already convicted under the Act. Haswell wrote that Lyon was held "by the oppressive hand of usurped power in a loathsome prison, suffering all the indignities which can be heaped upon him by a hard-hearted savage, who has, to the disgrace of Federalism, been elevated to a station where he can satiate his barbarity on the misery of his victims." *See* Geoffrey R. Stone, *Perilous Times, Free Speech in Wartime* 63 (2004). As was the case in many such prosecutions, the judge directed the jury to enter a guilty verdict, and truth, much as the Republicans feared, provided very little defense for such a nebulous statement. Thus, the technical improvements to the Sedition Act provided little protection for speech critical of the government.

The Supreme Court never directly ruled on the constitutionality of the Sedition Act but several Justices upheld its constitutionality while riding circuit in the lower courts. Most scholars agree that the unpopularity of the Act was at least partly responsible for the Federalist defeat in the 1800 elections. The Act expired in 1801, and President Thomas Jefferson eventually pardoned persons convicted under it (although, ironically, he tolerated common law and state law seditious libel prosecutions of his critics). For more in-depth discussion of the history of the Sedition Act, see Levy, *supra*, at 242-349; Stone, *supra*, at 15-78; Mayton, *supra*, at 112, 121-130; Rabban, *supra*, at 841-854.

4. *From the Sedition Act to World War I*

The expiration of the Sedition Act did not resolve the dispute over whether the Framers meant to adopt the Blackstonian view or a more speech-protective view of the First Amendment. Although many came to understand the Sedition Act as a misguided exercise of power, government officials resuscitated the crime of seditious libel with some regularity. During the Civil War, for example, although no federal sedition statute was enacted, military officials issued orders prohibiting speech that expressed sympathy for the enemy, criticized the Army, or "tended to bring the war policy of the Administration into disrepute." Michael Kent Curtis, *Lincoln, Vallandigham, and Anti-War Speech in the Civil War*, 7 Wm. & Mary B. Rt. J. 105, 119-120 (1998). Citizens and politicians were arrested for anti-war sentiments under the orders. *Id.*; *see also* Stone, *supra*, at 94-126.

The Supreme Court resolved few free speech issues during the Civil War, but disputes over the meaning of the First Amendment were evident in Patterson v. Colorado, 205 U.S. 454, 462 (1907). *Patterson* involved contempt prosecutions of the owner and publisher of two newspapers in Colorado that featured a series of editorials criticizing recent Colorado Supreme Court rulings as politically motivated. The Attorney General of Colorado instituted criminal contempt proceedings in the state supreme court on the basis that the editorials "were designed, intended, and calculated to hold up to public opprobrium and to incite public contempt for this court and certain of the justices thereof, and for the purpose of leading the people of this state to distrust the fairness and impartiality of the decisions of this court." People v. New Times Pblg. Co, 35 Colo. 253, 276 (1906). Patterson (the owner) was found guilty of contempt and appealed to the United States Supreme Court.

A few points in the Court's majority opinion, written by Justice Holmes, are notable. First, Justice Holmes refused to decide whether the First Amendment protected freedom of speech from abridgement by the states in addition to the federal government. This issue "was finally decided in favor of speakers decades later. *See supra* footnote 1. Second, the majority noted that even if the First Amendment restrained states, it did not prevent Patterson's contempt conviction because

> the main purpose of such constitutional provisions is "to prevent all such *previous restraints* upon publications as had been practised by other governments," and they do not prevent the subsequent punishment of such as may be deemed contrary to the public welfare. The preliminary freedom extends as well to the false as to the true; the subsequent punishment may extend as well to the true as to the false. This was the law of criminal libel apart from statute in most cases, if not in all.
>   . . . [T]he rule applied to criminal libels applies yet more clearly to contempts. A publication likely to reach the eyes of a jury, declaring a witness in a pending cause a perjurer, would be none the less a contempt that it was true. . . . The theory of our system is that the conclusions to be reached in a case will be induced only by evidence and argument in open court, and not by any outside influence, whether of private talk or public print. . . . [I]f a court regards [a] publication concerning a matter of law pending before it, as tending toward. . . . interference, it may punish it. . . .

205 U.S. at 458-463.

Justice Harlan dissented. He first noted that "when the 14th Amendment prohibited the states from impairing or abridging the privileges of citizens of the United States, it necessarily prohibited the states from impairing or abridging the constitutional rights of such citizens to free speech and a free press." *Id.* at 558. Justice Harlan further rejected the majority's argument that the main purpose of the First Amendment was to protect against prior restraints. "I cannot assent to that view," Justice Harlan wrote, "if it be meant that the legislature may impair or abridge the rights of a free press and of free speech whenever it thinks that the public welfare requires that to be done. The public welfare cannot override constitutional privileges, and if the rights of free speech and of a free press are, in their essence, attributes of national citizenship, as I think they are, then neither Congress nor any state, since the adoption of the 14th Amendment, can, by legislative enactments or by judicial action, impair or abridge them." *Id.* at 559.

The prosecution of speakers critical of the war effort during World War I forced the Court to revisit whether the First Amendment protected speech from statutes imposing criminal punishment. In Schenck v. United States, 249 U.S. 47 (1919), *infra* p. 30 Justice Holmes this time found that the First Amendment was not simply limited to preventing prior restraints. As Chapter 2 illustrates in greater detail, deriving a judicial standard with which to judge the constitutionality of criminal statutes is still far from easy.

B. FIRST AMENDMENT VALUES

Colonial defenders of free expression posited many theories supporting the broad protection of free speech. Thomas Jefferson argued that free debate would lead to truth: "[T]ruth is great and will prevail if left to herself[;]. . . . she is the proper and sufficient antagonist to error, and has nothing to fear from the conflict unless by

human interposition disarmed of her natural weapons, free argument and debate."
Thomas Jefferson, "A Bill for Establishing Religious Freedoms," in 2 *The Papers of Thomas Jefferson* 545, 546 (Julian P. Boyd ed., 1950). James Madison argued that freedom of the press was necessary in a democratic government where officials were servants of the people who were the ultimate sovereigns. James Madison, "Report Accompanying the Virginia Resolution," reprinted in 4 *The Debates in the Several State Conventions on the Adoption of the Federal Constitution* 569-570 (J. Elliott ed., 1836). The Continental Congress approved a declaration in 1774 stating that

> [t]he importance of [freedom of the press] consists, besides the advancement of truth, science, morality, and arts in general, in its diffusion of liberal sentiments on the administration of Government, in its ready communication of thoughts between subjects, and its consequential promotion of union among them, whereby oppressive officers are shamed or intimidated into more honourable and just modes of conducting affairs.

Address to the Inhabitants of Quebec (1774). Do these justifications along with historical events argue for or against protecting expression? Do they stand alone as justifications for protecting free expression?

Modern theorists have taken up these themes as well. As you read the following excerpts on modern free speech values, consider how they relate to statements made contemporaneous with the adoption of the First Amendment. Does any theory satisfactorily explain why we believe free expression should be protected? This section also briefly refers to Supreme Court cases that cite theoretical justifications for protecting speech. The Court has never relied on a single unified principle to justify its free speech jurisprudence; rather it has relied on many different theoretical justifications. Should we search for a single overarching principle to justify protection of expression?

Recall the national security letter hypothetical above. Do the values discussed below shed light on whether such subpoenas are consistent with the First Amendment?

1. Truth and the Marketplace of Ideas

John Stuart Mill first elaborated on the search for truth rationale in *On Liberty*:

> [T]he peculiar evil of silencing the expression of an opinion is, that it is robbing the human race; posterity as well as the existing generation; those who dissent from the opinion, still more who hold it. If the opinion is right, they are deprived of the opportunity of exchanging error for truth: if wrong, they lose, what is almost as great a benefit, the clearer perception and livelier impression of truth, produced by its collision with error. . . .
> First, if any opinion is compelled to silence, that opinion may, for aught we can certainly know, be true. To deny this is to assume our own infallibility.
> Second, though the silenced opinion be an error, it may and very commonly does, contain a portion of the truth; and since the general or prevailing opinion on any subject is rarely or never the whole truth, it is only by the collision of adverse opinions that the remainder of the truth has any chance of being supplied.
> Thirdly, even if the received opinion be not only true, but the whole truth; unless it is suffered to be, and actually is, vigorously and earnestly contested, it will, by most of those who receive it, be held in the manner of prejudice, with

little comprehension or feeling of its rational grounds. And not only this but, fourthly, the meaning of the doctrine itself will be in danger of being lost, or enfeebled, and deprived of its vital effect on the character and conduct: the dogma being a mere formal profession, inefficacious for good, but cumbering the ground, and preventing the growth of any real and heartfelt conviction, from reason or personal experience.

John Stuart Mill, *On Liberty* 87, 118 (David Bromwich & George Kale eds., 2003).

Justice Holmes picked up this thread in his dissenting opinion in Abrams v. United States, 250 U.S. 616 (1919), arguing that

[p]ersecution for the expression of opinions seems to me perfectly logical. If you have no doubt of your premises or your power and want a certain result with all your heart you naturally express your wishes in law and sweep away all opposition. To allow opposition by speech seems to indicate that you think the speech impotent, as when a man says that he has squared the circle, or that you do not care whole heartedly for the result, or that you doubt either your power or your premises. But when men have realized that time has upset many fighting faiths, they may come to believe even more than they believe the very foundations of their own conduct that the ultimate good desired is better reached by free trade in ideas—that the best test of truth is the power of the thought to get itself accepted in the competition of the market, and that truth is the only ground upon which their wishes safely can be carried out. That at any rate is the theory of our Constitution. It is an experiment, as all life is an experiment. Every year if not every day we have to wager our salvation upon some prophecy based upon imperfect knowledge.

Id. at 630.

NOTES AND QUESTIONS

1. *The meaning of truth.* Do Holmes's theory and Mills's vision of the truth differ? For discussion, see Kent Greenawalt, *Free Speech Justifications*, 89 Colum. L. Rev. 119 (1989); G. Edward White, *Justice Holmes and the Modernization of Free Speech Jurisprudence: The Human Dimension*, 80 Cal. L. Rev. 391, 439 (1992).
2. *"Objective" truth?* Does such a thing as objective "truth" exist? What does the controversy over the Sedition Act of 1798 suggest about the difficulty of ascertaining objective truth and using it as a basis for protecting speech?
3. *Protecting falsity.* On the other hand, what good does it serve to protect patently false speech like statements "The Holocaust did not occur" or "The earth is flat"?

2. Self-Governance

Alexander Meiklejohn is the most famous modern proponent of the self-governance rationale:

We Americans . . . believe in self-government. . . . When self-governing men demand freedom of speech they are not saying that every individual has an unalienable right to speak whenever, wherever, however, he chooses. . . . [T]he vital point . . . is that no suggestion of policy shall be denied a hearing because it is on one side of the issue rather than another. . . . [T]hough citizens may, on other grounds, be barred from speaking, they may not be barred because their views are thought to be false or dangerous. No plan of action shall be outlawed because someone in control thinks it unwise, unfair, un-American. . . . And the reason for this equality of status in the field of ideas lies deep in the very foundations of the self-governing process. When men govern themselves, it is they—and no one else—who must pass judgment upon unwisdom and unfairness and danger. . . . Just so far as, at any point, the citizens who are to decide an issue are denied acquaintance with information or opinion or doubt or disbelief or criticism which is relevant to that issue, just so far as the result must be ill-considered, ill-balanced planning for the general good. *It is the mutilation of the thinking process of the community against which the First Amendment to the Constitution is directed.* The principle of the freedom of speech springs from the necessities of the program of self-government.

Alexander Meiklejohn, *Free Speech and Its Relation to Self-Government* 15-16, 24-27 (1948) (emphasis in original).

The Supreme Court has emphasized the self-governance rationale in various cases. In reversing a conviction for violating a statute prohibiting the display of a red flag as a symbol of opposition to organized government, the Court in Stromberg v. California, 283 U.S. 359, 369 (1931), stated that

[t]he maintenance of the opportunity for free political discussion to the end that government may be responsive to the will of the people and that changes may be obtained by lawful means, an opportunity essential to the security of the Republic, is a fundamental principle of our constitutional system.

In reversing a libel verdict brought against the *New York Times* by an Alabama municipal official, the Court in New York Times v. Sullivan, 376 U.S. 254, 270 (1964), relied on "a profound national commitment to the principle that debate on public issues should be uninhibited, robust, and wide-open, and that it may well include vehement, caustic, and sometimes unpleasantly sharp attacks on government and public officials."

NOTES AND QUESTIONS

1. *The meaning of self-governance.* Does Meiklejohn's theory imply that only speech pertaining to public issues or public functions is protected by the First Amendment? *See* Zechariah Chafee, *Book Review*, 62 Harv. L. Rev. 891, 896 (1949) (arguing that Meiklejohn's theory ignored the Framers' interest in religious, scientific, poetic, artistic, and dramatic expression). Meiklejohn later wrote that his concept of self-governance was broader than Chafee claimed, noting that "[s]elf-government can exist only insofar as the voters acquire the intelligence, integrity, sensitivity, and generous devotion to the general welfare that, in theory, casting a ballot is assumed to express[.]" Alexander Meiklejohn, *The First Amendment Is an Absolute*, 1961 Sup. Ct. Rev. 245, 255-257. How does Meikeljohn's second statement distinguish speech from other human activities that "also form personality [and] teach and create attitudes?" Robert Bork, *Neutral Principles and Some First Amendment Problems*, 47 Ind. L.J. 1, 27 (1971).

2. *Self-Governance and the checking value.* Perhaps the self-governance rationale is somewhat different from Meiklejohn's conception. Professor Vince Blasi argues that "[t]he central premise of the checking value [of free speech] is that the abuse of official power is an especially serious evil [due to government's special] capacity to employ legitimized violence. . . . Under [this] view of democracy, the role of the ordinary citizen is not so much to contribute on a continuing basis to the formation of public policy as to retain a veto power to be employed when the decisions of officials pass certain bounds." Vincent Blasi, *The Checking Value in First Amendment Theory*, 1977 Am. B. Found. Research J. 521, 527-542. Does Blasi's thesis more or less satisfactorily support a self-governance rationale than Meiklejohn's?

3. *Autonomy/Self-Fulfillment*

Recall the Continental Congress's "Address to the Inhabitants of Quebec," *supra*, and its reference to the "advancement of truth, science, morality, and arts in general." Non-political justifications for protecting speech were rare in colonial times as free expression was discussed primarily in political terms. Some Justices, however, have occasionally invoked individual-centered or autonomy-centered rationales to justify protection of speech. Most famously, Justice Brandeis opined that "[t]hose who won our independence believed that the final end of the state was to make men free to develop their faculties, and that in its government the deliberative forces should prevail over the arbitrary. . . . They believed liberty to be the secret of happiness and courage to be the secret of liberty." Whitney v. California, 274 U.S. 357, 375 (1927) (Brandeis, J., concurring).

Autonomy, however, is a notoriously malleable concept. It can take on vastly different meanings depending on one's views. David Richards argues that

> the significance of free expression rests on the central human capacity to create and express symbolic systems, such as speech, writing, pictures, and music. Freedom of expression permits and encourages the exercise of these [capacities]. In so doing, it nurtures and sustains the self-respect of the mature person. . . . The value of free expression, in this view, rests on its deep relation to self-respect arising from autonomous self-determination without which the life of the spirit is meager and slavish.

David A.J. Richards, *Free Speech and Obscenity Law: Toward a Moral Theory of the First Amendment*, 123 U. Pa. L. Rev. 45, 62 (1974). Martin Redish, on the other hand, argues that

> the constitutional guarantee of free speech ultimately serves only one true value, which I have labeled "individual self-realization[.]". . . [Self-realization] can be interpreted to refer either to development of the individual's powers and abilities—an individual "realizes" his or her full potential—or to the individual's control of his or her own destiny through making life-affecting decisions—an individual "realizes" the goals in life that he or she has set. . . .
>
> That the first amendment serves only one ultimate value, however, does not mean that the majority of values thought by others to be fostered by free speech— the "political process," "checking," and "marketplace-of-ideas" values—are invalid. . . . [T]hese other values, though perfectly legitimate, are in reality subvalues of self-realization. To the extent that they are legitimate, each can be

explained by—and only by—reference to the primary value: individual self-realization.

Martin H. Redish, *The Value of Free Speech*, 130 U. Pa. L. Rev. 591, 593-594 (1982). Finally, Christina Wells claims that

> [a]utonomy . . . is not about atomistic individuals but about social creatures entitled to respect for their dignity. . . . [A system of free expression based upon such autonomy] would not focus on the rights of the speaker qua speaker but on the integrity of our thought processes as individuals and members of the community. Our thought processes are integral to our capacity for deliberation and self-governance. Ensuring their integrity is thus a necessary aspect of any system of laws built upon [this conception] of autonomy. Given that we develop our thought processes by communicating with others, and thereby our capacity for self-governance, protecting public expression is especially important. . . .
>
>   A system of free expression based on [this conception of autonomy], however, would not merely concern itself with protection against government suppression. Because the State's purpose is to preserve the dignity of its citizen, such a system would also ensure that citizens use speech consistently with autonomy. The State can and should regulate speech, that by attempting to override the thought processes of other individuals, disrespects their rational capacities. Such speech does not facilitate, but rather detracts from, the public exercise of reason and is therefore the proper subject of the State's coercive powers.

Christina E. Wells, Reinvigorating Autonomy: Freedom and Responsibility in the Supreme Court's First Amendment Jurisprudence, 32 Harv. C.R.-C.L. L. Rev. 159, 161, 169-170 (1997).

NOTES AND QUESTIONS

1. *Speaker versus audience.* Do these individual authors locate the autonomy rationale in the speaker or in the listener? Does it make a difference from a First Amendment perspective if we think of the right as a "speaker's" right or a "listener's" right?
2. *The Supreme Court's approach.* The Supreme Court has not been consistent in locating free speech as a speaker's or listener's right. Compare Bridges v. California, 314 U.S. 252, 270 (1941) (stating that "it is a prized American privilege to speak one's mind") and First National Bank v. Bellotti, 435 U.S. 765, 791 n.31 (1981) (stating that "[t]he First Amendment rejects the highly paternalistic approach of statutes...which restrict what people may hear").

4. Dissent

In the years surrounding the American Revolution, "dissent" played a large role in furthering revolutionary ideals. Dissenting churches that broke with the Church of England circulated religious literature with revolutionary themes while preachers gave revolutionary sermons. *See* Patricia U. Bonomi, "Religious Dissent and the Case for American Exceptionalism" at 31-55 in *Religion in a Revolutionary Age* (Ronald Hoffman & Peter J. Albert eds., 1994). Thomas Paine's *Common Sense,* which argued for freedom from British rule in language infused with dissenting Protestant beliefs, was the best-selling book of its kind at the time.

Professor Steven Shiffrin is the strongest proponent of the notion that "the value of dissent should be given greater prominence in free speech and press law." Steven H. Shiffrin, *The First Amendment, Democracy, and Romance* 100-101 (1990). According to Professor Shiffrin, "dissent and the threat of dissent make hierarchy less oppressive. Dissent communicates the fears, hopes, and aspirations of the less powerful to those in power. It sometimes chills the abuse of power; it sometimes paves the way for change by those in power or of those in power." *Id.* at 96. Such speech also fosters community engagement rather than atomistic individualism because "[d]issenters seek converts and colleagues." *Id.* at 91-93. Finally, Shiffrin argues that dissent fosters the emergence of truth even though "[d]issenters are often wrong." Nevertheless, because truth does not necessarily prevail in the marketplace of ideas, dissent is necessary to create "a robust, burgeoning marketplace." *Id.* at 95-96.

NOTES AND QUESTIONS

1. *The meaning of dissent.* Does dissent encompass the right to engage in "speech that criticizes existing customs, habits, traditions, institutions, or authorities" or only speech that is the "popularly disdained view"? *Id.* at 77. Steven H. Shiffrin, *Dissent, Injustice, and the Meanings of America* xi, 77 (1999). Or must dissent be "part of a social practice that challenges unjust hierarchies with the prospect of promoting progressive change"? *Id.* at 42. Do these definitions matter?
2. *Is dissent different?* Do the values of dissent identified above separate it from other theories of the First Amendment?

5.   *Anti-Theory*

Does a neutral, theoretical principle support the First Amendment, or are the values identified above really politics in disguise? Consider the following excerpt:

> [I]f you have *any* answer to the question ["What is the First Amendment for?"], *any* answer at all, you are necessarily implicated in a regime of censorship. . . . [W]hen you say the First Amendment is for something—perhaps for giving truth the chance to emerge, or for providing the minds of citizens with the materials necessary for growth or self-realization, or for keeping the marketplace of ideas open in a democratic society—it becomes not only possible but inevitable that at some point you will ask of some instance of speech whether it in fact serves its high purpose or whether it does the opposite, retarding the search for truth, stunting the growth of mature judgment, fouling the marketplace.
>
> Although free-speech values supposedly stand alone and are said to be independent of circumstance and political pressure, they only become thick enough to provide a direction for decisionmaking when definitions and distinctions borrowed from particular circumstances (and borrowed selectively in relation to some substantive agenda) are presupposed as to their content. You must determine what you mean by "expression" or what is and is not a "free flow" or what does and does not constitute "self-realization" in relation to what notion of the self before any of these so-called principles will have any bite. And since these are not determinations those principles can make for themselves, when they

do have bite, when invoking them actually gets you somewhere, it will be because inside them is the outside—substantive values, preferred outcomes, politics—from which they are rhetorically distinguished.

Stanley Fish, "The Dance of Theory," in *Eternally Vigilant: Free Speech in the Modern Era* 199, 223 (Lee C. Bollinger & Geoffrey R. Stone eds., 2002) (emphasis in original). Is Professor Fish saying that theoretical justifications for protecting speech are unhelpful, or is he simply saying that they are not—in and of themselves—"neutral"? How would recognition of their "non-neutrality" potentially advance discussion regarding the goals of the First Amendment?

C. IMPLEMENTING THE FREEDOM OF SPEECH

The previous readings involved the text, historical groundings, and philosophical discussion of the values supporting the First Amendment. How do those inform a doctrine *implementing* the First Amendment? This book will discuss in some detail the Supreme Court's complex and evolving rules involving free expression. This chapter, however, provides a brief overview of the overarching legal themes that have dominated the Court's attention—speech vs. conduct, content discrimination, access to public property, prior restraints, vague and overly broad laws, and problems associated with facial and as-applied challenges.

When reading through the next several subsections, recall the national security letter hypothetical above and consider how it might implicate the legal doctrines set forth below.

1. Speech vs. Conduct

The First Amendment bars the government from "abridg[ing]" the "freedom of speech." Does this mean First Amendment applies only to speech in the literal sense or does it extend to expressive conduct? At what point does speech become so like conduct that the First Amendment no longer protects it?

Professor Thomas Emerson noted the importance of answering these questions in constructing a definition of "freedom of expression":

> The first task is to formulate in detail the distinction between "expression" and "action." . . . [T]he whole theory and practice of freedom of expression—the realization of any of the values it attempts to secure—rests upon this distinction. Hence the starting point for any legal doctrine must be to fix this line of demarcation.

Thomas I. Emerson, *Toward a General Theory of the First Amendment* 60 (1966). Unfortunately, the Court's jurisprudence regarding when conduct is sufficiently expressive to trigger First Amendment scrutiny is thin at best. It is often not clear as a practical matter where the line is between speech and action. As Professor Emerson noted, that line "at many points . . . becomes obscure. Expression often takes place in a context of action, or is closely linked with it, or is equivalent in its impact." *Id.*

Despite this lack of clarity, the speech/conduct distinction permeates much of the discussion surrounding the First Amendment. Chapter 5 takes up in depth the thorny question of when conduct amounts to expression within the Court's jurisprudence. But the speech/conduct distinction also permeates the discussion of whether speech has passed the bounds of expression and into the realm of unprotected conduct. *See, e.g.,* Roth v. United States, 354 U.S. 476, 514 (1957) (Douglas, J., dissenting) (discussing speech that is "so closely brigaded with illegal action as to be an inseparable part of it"). Many of the cases in Chapters 2 and 3 involving advocacy of illegal activity, fighting words, and speech that causes a hostile audience response raise such issues. Here, as with cases involving expressive conduct, the Court and scholars refer to unprotected speech as "conduct," but it is more often a shorthand way of saying "unprotected" or "low value" than it is an attempt to distinguish conduct from literal speech.

As you read the following chapters, keep in mind the question of whether the distinction between speech and conduct is helpful in determining whether the First Amendment should extend to the expression at issue.

2.   *Content Discrimination*

According to the Supreme Court, the "government has no power to restrict expression because of its message, its ideas, its subject matter, or its content." Brown v. Entertainment Merchants Ass'n 131 S. Ct. 2729, 2733 (2011). Why is the Court so concerned about government regulation of content?

Chapters 2 and 3 discuss the Court's doctrine pertaining to content regulation. Initially, the Court used a test determining whether speech posed a "clear and present" danger of harm. Ultimately, however, it settled on a test that distinguished statutes based on whether they explicitly regulate speech because of its content (content-based laws) or whether they affect speech but do not regulate based on what the speech says (content-neutral laws). The former are subject to stringent review called "strict scrutiny" while the latter statutes are subject to less rigorous review called "intermediate scrutiny." Turner Broadcasting v. FCC, 512 U.S. 622 (1994).

As noted above, the Court allows content discrimination if the speech is "unprotected" or "low value." The Court has found only a few categories of speech to be "low value," which it loosely describes as speech that contributes "no essential part of any exposition of ideas." Chaplinsky v. New Hampshire, 315 U.S. 568, 572 (1942). Thus far, the Court recognizes as "low value" only incitement to violence, threats, fighting words, obscenity, defamation, fraud, child pornography, and speech integral to criminal conduct. *See* United States v. Stevens, 130 S. Ct. 1577, 1584 (2010); *Brown,* 131 S. Ct. at 2729. Nevertheless, arguments over whether regulated speech falls into an existing category or whether one can draw analogies to existing low value speech categories are still quite common because, if successful, they allow states to engage in permissible content discrimination.

3.   *Access to Public Property*

The right to speak has little meaning if individuals or groups do not have access to public property, especially large public spaces such as parks. Originally, the Court was unsympathetic to speakers' desire for access to public property, effectively giving the government the same rights as private property owners to exclude speakers. Ultimately, however, it found that streets, parks, and sidewalks have "immemorially been held in trust for the use of the public and, time out of mind, have been used for purposes of assembly, communicating thoughts between citizens, and discussing public questions." Hague v. CIO, 307 U.S. 496 (1939). Nevertheless, government officials may still have interests in regulating access based on neutral considerations of "time, place, and manner." Chapter 4 discusses these issues in more detail.

To what extent must government officials make available for expressive purposes other government property such as government offices, public libraries, or mailboxes? The Court has grappled, not altogether successfully, with the extent to which property other than streets, parks, and sidewalks must be available for expressive purposes. Chapter 4 also discusses this issue in greater depth.

4. Vague and Overly Broad Laws

Laws can violate the Constitution not simply because they suppress speech based on content but because they proscribe too much speech or do not give fair notice as to what they attempt to regulate. The Court's doctrines of overbreadth and vagueness are designed to assess whether such laws are consistent with the First Amendment.

a. Overbreadth

Overbreadth doctrine starts from the assumption that government officials may legitimately proscribe some speech—e.g., government officials may regulate "low value" speech. Nevertheless, the overbreadth doctrine allows courts to strike down laws that are "draft[ed] . . . so broadly that they prohibit, or could prohibit, substantial amounts of constitutionally protected expression." Alan K. Chen, *Statutory Speech Bubbles, First Amendment Overbreadth, and Improper Legislative Purpose*, 38 Harv. C.R.-C.L. L. Rev. 31, 40 (2003). Overbreadth doctrine allows a person whose speech could permissibly be regulated to challenge a law as overly broad because the law might chill the speech of third-party non-litigant speakers. *See* Members of City Council of City of Los Angeles v. Taxpayers for Vincent, 466 U.S. 789 (1984); Gooding v. Wilson, 405 U.S. 518 (1972). As the Court has explained:

> Many persons, rather than undertake the considerable burden (and sometimes risk) of vindicating their rights through case-by-case litigation, will choose simply to abstain from protected speech—harming not only themselves but society as a whole, which is deprived of an uninhibited marketplace of ideas. Overbreadth adjudication, by suspending all enforcement of an over inclusive law, reduces these social costs caused by the withholding of protected speech.

Virginia v. Hicks, 539 U.S. 113, 119 (2003).

In cases involving expressive conduct rather than pure speech, the Court requires a showing of "substantial" overbreadth before striking down a law. *Hicks*, 539 U.S. at 123-124. The overbreadth "must not only be real, but substantial as well, judged in relation to the statute's plainly legitimate sweep." *Taxpayers for Vincent*, 466 U.S. at 800. In all overbreadth challenges, the Court has been willing to uphold a law if the state's highest court has construed it narrowly enough so that it does not apply to protected speech. *See* Brockett v. Spokane Arcades, Inc., 472 U.S. 491 (1985).

b. Vagueness

An overly broad law can often also be challenged as vague. Such challenges are actually due process challenges with special consideration of free speech issues. Vague laws are problematic for several reasons:

> First, because we assume that man is free to steer between lawful and unlawful conduct, we insist that laws give the person of ordinary intelligence a reasonable opportunity to know what is prohibited, so that he may act accordingly. Vague laws may trap the innocent by not providing fair warning. Second, if arbitrary and discriminatory enforcement is to be prevented, laws must provide explicit standards for those who apply them. A vague law impermissibly delegates basic policy matters to policemen, judges, and juries for resolution on an ad hoc and subjective basis, with the attendant dangers of arbitrary and discriminatory application. Third, but related, where a vague statute "abut(s) upon sensitive areas of basic First Amendment freedoms," it "operates to inhibit the exercise of (those) freedoms." Uncertain meanings inevitably lead citizens to "steer far wider of the unlawful zone" . . . than if the boundaries of the forbidden areas were clearly marked.

Grayned v. City of Rockford, 408 U.S. 104, 108-109 (1972). The prevention of arbitrary and discriminatory enforcement of laws affecting speech is a consistent theme in the Court's discussion of the vagueness doctrine. *See* United States v. Williams, 535 U.S. 285 (2010); Holder v. Humanitarian Law Project, 561 U.S. 1 (2010); Smith v. Goguen, 415 U.S. 566 (1974).

As with overbreadth challenges, a state court can narrowly interpret a law to remove the vagueness problem. *See Williams*, 535 U.S. 285. Clear statutory definitions and settled legal meanings also may save an otherwise vague law. *Id.* at 306. Furthermore, a statute is not vague merely because one can envision a close case regarding speech that may fall within its scope. *Id.* at 305-306. "What renders a statute vague is not the possibility that it will sometimes be difficult to determine whether the incriminating fact it establishes has been proved; but rather the indeterminacy of precisely what that fact is." *Id.* at 306.

Unlike overbreadth challenges, an individual engaging in conduct a statute clearly proscribes cannot "complain of the vagueness of the law as applied to the conduct of others." *Humanitarian Law Project*, 130 S. Ct. at 2719. "[A] vagueness challenge does not turn on whether a law applies to a substantial amount of protected expression." *Id.*

c. Facial and As-Applied Challenges to Laws

As a procedural matter, individuals or entities wanting to challenge laws as violating the First Amendment have two possible approaches available to them. They can challenge the law as "facially" invalid or they can challenge the law "as applied" to their particular speech.

A facial challenge argues that the statute could *never* be applied in a valid manner. In the First Amendment context, this argument translates into a claim that the statute creates an unacceptable risk of the suppression of ideas. Thus, "[w]hen asserting a facial challenge, a party seeks to vindicate not only his own rights, but those of others who may also be adversely impacted by the statute in question." City of Chicago v. Morales, 527 U.S. 41, 55 n.22 (1999); *Taxpayers for Vincent*, 466 U.S. at 789. Parties raising an as-applied challenge to the statute, on the other hand, argue that it is unconstitutional as applied to the party's own conduct.

Both the vagueness and overbreadth doctrines give rise to facial attacks. Specifically, "the overbreadth doctrine permits the facial invalidation of laws that inhibit the exercise of First Amendment rights if the impermissible applications of the law are substantial." *Morales*, 527 U.S. at 53. Further, a statute is subject to facial invalidation if "it fails to establish standards for the police and public that are sufficient to guard against the arbitrary deprivation of liberty interests." *Id.* at 53. Thus, "[w]hen vagueness permeates that text of...a law, it is subject to facial attack." *Id.* at 55.

If there are some conceivable instances of constitutional application, courts are more likely to entertain an as-applied challenge, but it is not always easy to tell when each challenge should be used. "[T]he distinction between facial and as-applied challenges is not so well defined that it has some automatic effect or that it must always control the pleadings and disposition in every case involving a constitutional challenge." Citizens United v. FEC, 130 S. Ct. 876, 893 (2009).

5. *Prior Restraint*

Although the Court eventually found that the First Amendment applied to subsequent punishment of speech as well as prior restraints, see Schenck v. United States, 249 U.S. 47 (1919), it nevertheless maintains a special antipathy to regulations amounting to prior restraints. Such regulations are the "most serious and least tolerable infringement of First Amendment rights." Nebraska Press Ass'n v. Stuart, 427 U.S. 539, 559 (1976). We know that the unfettered licensing schemes of sixteenth and seventeenth century England amounted to prior restraints, *see supra* Part I.A.1, but the Court has extended the concept to other forms of regulation. "[A]dministrative and judicial orders forbidding certain communications when issued in advance of the time that such communications are to occur" generally amount to prior restraints. Alexander v. United States, 509 U.S. 544, 550 (1993). Arbitrary decision-making and chilling of protected speech are primary concerns of the prior restraint doctrine. *See* Citizens United v. FEC, 130 S. Ct. 876, 895-96 (2009). Chapter 4, *infra*, discusses these issues in greater depth.

Nevertheless, the Court does not find all administrative and judicial orders to be prior restraints. It has upheld licensing schemes requiring protestors to apply for permits prior to their activities as long as those schemes provide adequate criteria for officials; regulate only time, place, and manner of the protests; and are unrelated to content. *See* Cox v. New Hampshire, 312 U.S. 569 (1941); Thomas v. Chicago Park Dist., 534 U.S. 316 (2002). Similarly, the Court has upheld content-neutral injunctions that regulate only the time, place, and manner of speech rather than suppressing it altogether. *See* Madsen v. Women's Health Ctr., Inc., 512 U.S. 753 (1994).

As you read, consider why courts disfavor some licensing schemes and injunctions and not others. For commentary on the Court's doctrine, see Vincent Blasi, *Toward a Theory of Prior Restraint: The Central Linkage*, 66 Minn. L. Rev.

11, 35-43 (1981); William T. Mayton, *Toward a Theory of First Amendment Process: Injunctions Against Speech, Subsequent Punishment, and the Costs of the Prior Restraint Doctrine*, 67 Cornell L. Rev. 245, 275 (1982); Frederick Schauer, *Fear, Risk and the First Amendment: Unraveling the Chilling Effect*, 58 B.U. L. Rev. 685, 725-730 (1978).

6. *Extra-Doctrinal Influences on the Law*

Given the brevity of the First Amendment, much decision-making regarding its scope and content is left to the courts, and ultimately the Supreme Court, as to whether speech is protected or unprotected. What influences the Court's decisions?

On the one hand, we know that the Court's jurisprudence protects core political speech and also extends some protection to commercial speech, sexually explicit speech, libel, offensive speech, and advocacy of illegal conduct. Even speech that can be punished, such as threats, incitement, fighting words, and obscenity, must meet carefully laid out judicial standards prior to suppression or punishment. On the other hand, as Professor Frederick Schauer notes, the Court apparently ignores whole areas of expression or states, with little or no discussion, that they are outside the purview of the First Amendment:

> The history of the First Amendment is the history of its boundaries. . . . Once the First Amendment shows up, much of the game is over. But the question whether the First Amendment shows up at all is rarely addressed, and the answer is too often simply assumed. . . .
>
> Though many cases involve the First Amendment, many more do not. The acts, behaviors, and restrictions not encompassed by the First Amendment at all— the events that remain wholly untouched by the First Amendment—are the ones that are simply not covered by the First Amendment. It is not that the speech is not protected. Rather, the entire event—an event that often involves "speech" in the ordinary language sense of the word—does not present a First Amendment issue at all, and the government's action is consequently measured against no First Amendment standard whatsoever. The First Amendment just does not show up.
>
> When the First Amendment does show up, the full arsenal of First Amendment rules, principles, standards, distinctions, presumptions, tools, factors, and three-part tests becomes available to determine whether the particular speech will actually wind up being protected. . . . But the fact that the[se] tests…are the ones to be applied reflects the coverage of the First Amendment. . . .
>
> By contrast, no First Amendment-generated level of scrutiny is used to determine whether the content-based advertising restrictions of the Securities Act of 1933 are constitutional, whether corporate executives may be imprisoned under the Sherman Act for exchanging accurate information about proposed prices with their competitors, whether an organized crime leader may be prosecuted for urging that his subordinates murder a mob rival, or whether a chainsaw manufacturer may be held liable in a products liability action for injuries caused by mistakes in the written instructions accompanying the tool. Each of these examples involves some punishment for speech, and each involves liability based both on the content and on the communicative impact of the speech. And yet no First Amendment degree of scrutiny appears. In these and countless other instances, the permissibility of regulation—unlike the control of incitement, libel, and commercial advertising—is not measured against First Amendment-generated standards. . . . [Indeed], an argument from the First Amendment would be seen as an argument from the wrong area of law; and in which, consequently, no First

Amendment principle guards, even to a limited extent, against infringement. Questions about the boundaries of the First Amendment are not questions of strength—the degree of protection that the First Amendment offers—but rather are questions of scope—whether the First Amendment applies at all. . . .

Frederick Schauer, The Boundaries of the First Amendment: A Preliminary Exploration of Constitutional Salience, 117 Harv. L. Rev. 1765, 1766-71 (2004).

NOTES AND QUESTIONS

1. *Finding a methodology.* Is there any plausible explanation for why the Court has chosen to include certain things and not others within the boundaries of the First Amendment?
2. *Extra-legal factors.* Schauer argues that "political, social, cultural, historical, psychological, rhetorical, and economic forces" influence "which policy questions surface as constitutional issues and which do not." 117 Harv. L. Rev. at 1768. As you read the following cases, consider whether the many factors that may influence cases better explain the decisions than do doctrine or theory.
3. *Extra-legal factors and doctrine.* Is Schauer's argument limited to the "boundaries" of the First Amendment, or do extra-legal factors also affect the Court's resolution of whether speech within the parameters of the First Amendment is protected?

CHAPTER
2

Setting the Modern Stage—Incitement and the "Clear and Present Danger" Test

TABLE OF CONTENTS

In a series of cases involving speech that incites illegal actions, the United States Supreme Court faced many of the same questions regarding regulation of speech that government officials in England and the early American Republic faced (*see supra* Chapter 1.A). The Court wrestled with questions involving whether government officials can suppress "dangerous" speech to protect the security and safety of its citizens and the extent to which such a security rationale can be abused. Although incitement of illegal activity is only a small part of free speech doctrine, the principles involved are central to the Court's modern free speech doctrine. Furthermore, debate over the relationship between national security and free expression continues today.

The Supreme Court originally was reluctant to extend much protection to speech considered dangerous to the nation's security, allowing punishment of speech presenting a "clear and present danger" of possible harm. Schenck v. United States, 249 U.S. 47 (1919). Judges applied that standard deferentially to allow punishment of speech critical of government actions during and after World War I. Abrams v. United States, 250 U.S. 616 (1919); Gitlow v. New York, 268 U.S. 652 (1925); Whitney v. California, 274 U.S. 357 (1927). Justices Holmes and Brandeis, however, argued for a stricter test, fearing that judicial deference to government officials' claims of harm would lead to widespread suppression of unpopular viewpoints. *See Abrams*, 250 U.S. 616 (Holmes, J., dissenting); *Whitney*, 274 U.S. 357 (Brandeis, J., concurring). Stricter versions of the "clear and present danger" test took hold in other areas of free speech jurisprudence but in the first half of the twentieth century the Court never used a strict version of the test to judge speech deemed dangerous to national security. In Dennis v. United States, 341 U.S. 494 (1951), a case decided during the height of the Cold War and the McCarthy era, the Court applied an extremely deferential version of the test to uphold the convictions of domestic Communists for allegedly conspiring to advocate the overthrow of the United States government. More than a decade later, as national security concerns waned, the

Court in Brandenburg v. Ohio, 395 U.S. 444 (1969), finally moved away from lenient versions of the "clear and present danger" test and announced its strictest version of the test to date. The case, however, did not involve a distinct threat to national security, and it is unclear the extent to which it overruled or superseded earlier cases. Thus, the extent to which the "clear and present danger" test should or does play a role in modern free speech jurisprudence is still very much a legitimate question. As Holder v. Humanitarian Law Project, 561 U.S. 1 (2010) shows, the Court remains conflicted about the extent to which it should defer to national security interests, especially in the modern context of terrorism.

A. WORLD WAR I—THE BIRTH OF "CLEAR AND PRESENT DANGER"

The Supreme Court faced its first significant test involving "dangerous" speech during World War I. The War was unpopular with many Americans, which posed a significant problem for the Wilson administration. Several organizations, including pacifist groups, labor unions, progressive groups, and the Socialist Party of America, openly spoke against the War, calling for public opposition through protests, demonstrations, and petitions. Nathan Fine, *Labor and Farmer Parties in the United States, 1828-1928*, at 13-14 (1928). *See also* Robert Justin Goldstein, *Political Repression in Modern America: From 1870 to 1976*, at 105-108 (2001). Such organizations, though often radical in nature and not popular with Americans generally, saw substantial increases in membership during the War. Goldstein, *supra*, at 105. Opposition to the War, however, was not limited to radical organizations, as citizens in the Midwest and South were also hostile or apathetic to the War and the draft. *Id.* at 105, 107.

Concerned that vocal opposition to the draft would paralyze the War effort, the Wilson administration tried to quell anti-war sentiment. Through the Committee on Public Information, the administration produced propaganda designed to create support for the war, including portrayals of German spies and saboteurs as lurking within the United States and of Russian Bolsheviks as German agents. Such propaganda also attempted to persuade Americans that "conscription, bond sales, and 'liberty cabbage' were the greatest national blessings since the Bill of Rights." Harry N. Scheiber, *The Wilson Administration and Civil Liberties* 16 (1960); *see also* Geoffrey R. Stone, *Perilous Times, Free Speech in Wartime* 153-155 (2004). The President linked groups opposing the war (many of whose members were immigrants) to German spies although no evidence of such a connection existed. Christina E. Wells, *Discussing the First Amendment*, 101 Mich. L. Rev. 1566, 1580-1581 (2003). The Wilson administration also asked private citizens to report suspicious or disloyal activity directly to the Department of Justice; the program triggered thousands of accusations of disloyalty. Goldstein, *supra*, at 110-113; Stone, *supra*, at 156-157.

In June 1917, shortly after entering World War I, the administration successfully lobbied Congress to pass the Espionage Act of 1917. Among other things, the Act made it a crime, "when the United States is at war," for any person to (1) "make or convey false reports or false statements with intent to interfere with" the military success of the United States or to "promote the success of its enemies," or (2) "wilfully cause or attempt to cause insubordination, disloyalty, mutiny, [or] refusal of duty," in the United States military, or (3) "wilfully obstruct the recruiting or enlistment service of the United States." Violation of the Act was punishable by a fine of up to $10,000 and a prison sentence of up to 20 years. Act of June 15, 1917, ch. 30, tit. I., § 3, 40 Stat. 217, 219. The Espionage Act also gave the postmaster the power to exclude from the mails any matter that violated the Act. 40 Stat. at 230-231.

Less than a year later, the Wilson administration again lobbied Congress for more restrictive laws, claiming that the Espionage Act's requirements posed too onerous a burden on the government and that a law directed specifically at seditious utterances was necessary. Scheiber, *supra*, at 23-24. Congress passed the Sedition Act of 1918, which amended the Espionage Act of 1917 to make it a crime to (1) willfully utter, print, write, or publish any disloyal, profane, scurrilous, or abusive language about the form of government of the United States, the Constitution, the United States military, the United States flag, or the uniforms of the United States military; (2) to urge curtailment of production of materials necessary to the war effort; and (3) to support the cause of any country at war with the United States or oppose the cause of the United States. Act of May 16, 1918, ch. 75, § 1, 40 Stat. 553.

In the next several years, over 2,000 people were prosecuted under the Espionage and Sedition Acts, with more than half such prosecutions resulting in conviction. Lower courts generally dealt with such cases under the then-prevailing "bad tendency" test. The Supreme Court eventually resolved whether these prosecutions were consistent with the First Amendment.

Following are two cases. The first case represents a typical lower court case involving a prosecution under the Espionage Act and application of the "bad tendency" test. The second involves the Supreme Court's first decision involving the Espionage Act and its implications for the First Amendment. *To what extent are these tests different, if at all?*

SHAFFER v. UNITED STATES

255 F. 886 (9th Cir. 1919)

[The government prosecuted Shaffer for illegally mailing a book, *The Finished Mystery*, which allegedly contained "treasonous, disloyal and seditious utterances" in violation of the Espionage Act of 1917. Specifically, prosecutors pointed to the following passage:

> "Standing opposite to these Satan has placed three great untruths, human immortality, the Anti-Christ, and a certain delusion which is best described by the word patriotism, but which is in reality murder, the spirit of the very devil. It is this last and crowning feature of Satan's work that is mentioned first. . . . If you say it is a war of defense against wanton and intolerable aggression, I must reply that every blow which we have endured has been primarily a blow directed, not against ourselves, but against England, and that it has yet to be proved that Germany has any intention or desire of attacking us. . . . The war itself is wrong. Its prosecution will be a crime. There is not a question raised, an issue involved, a cause at stake, which is worth the life of one blue-jacket on the sea or one khaki-coat in the trenches."

The defendant was convicted. The U.S. Court of Appeals for the Ninth Circuit affirmed the conviction, reasoning as follows:]

. . . It is true that disapproval of war and the advocacy of peace are not crimes under the Espionage Act; but the question here is not whether the publication contained expressions only of opinion . . . it is whether the natural and probable tendency and effect of the words quoted therefrom are such as are calculated to produce the result condemned by the statute. . . . Printed matter may tend to obstruct the recruiting and enlistment service, even if it contains no mention of recruiting or enlistment, and no reference to the military service of the United States. It is sufficient if the words used and disseminated are adapted to produce the result condemned by the statute.

The service may be obstructed by attacking the justice of the cause for which the war is waged, and by undermining the spirit of loyalty which inspires men to enlist or to register for conscription in the service of their country. The greatest inspiration for entering into such service is patriotism, the love of country. To teach that patriotism is murder and the spirit of the devil, and that the war against Germany was wrong and its prosecution a crime, is to weaken patriotism and the purpose to enlist or to render military service in the war. . . .

It is argued that the evidence fails to show that the plaintiff in error committed the act willfully and intentionally. But there is enough in the evidence to show the hostile attitude of his mind against the prosecution of the war by the United States, and that the books were intentionally concealed on his premises. He must be presumed to have intended the natural and probable consequences of what he knowingly did. . . . The judgment is affirmed.

SCHENCK v. UNITED STATES

249 U.S. 47 (1919)

Mr. Justice HOLMES delivered the opinion of the Court.

[Schenck, who was secretary general of the Socialist party, was convicted of conspiracy to violate Section 3 of the Espionage Act of 1917 "by causing and attempting to cause insubordination" in the military and by attempting "to obstruct the recruiting and enlistment service of the United States, when the United States was at war with the German Empire." Specifically, Schenck was convicted for conspiring "to have printed and circulated to men who had been called and accepted for military service . . . a document set forth and alleged to be calculated to cause such insubordination and obstruction."] . . .

The document in question upon its first printed side recited the first section of the Thirteenth Amendment, said that the idea embodied in it was violated by the conscription act and that a conscript is little better than a convict. In impassioned language it intimated that conscription was despotism in its worst form and a monstrous wrong against humanity in the interest of Wall Street's chosen few. It said, "Do not submit to intimidation," but in form at least confined itself to peaceful measures such as a petition for the repeal of the act. The other and later printed side of the sheet was headed "Assert Your Rights." It stated reasons for alleging that any one violated the Constitution when he refused to recognize "your right to assert your opposition to the draft," and went on, "If you do not assert and support your rights, you are helping to deny or disparage rights which it is the solemn duty of all citizens and residents of the United States to retain." It described the arguments on the other side as coming from cunning politicians and a mercenary capitalist press, and even silent consent to the conscription law as helping to support an infamous conspiracy.

It denied the power to send our citizens away to foreign shores to shoot up the people of other lands, and added that words could not express the condemnation such cold-blooded ruthlessness deserves, etc., winding up, "You must do your share to maintain, support and uphold the rights of the people of this country." Of course the document would not have been sent unless it had been intended to have some effect, and we do not see what effect it could be expected to have upon persons subject to the draft except to influence them to obstruct the carrying of it out. The defendants do not deny that the jury might find against them on this point.

But it is said, suppose that that was the tendency of this circular, it is protected by the First Amendment to the Constitution. Two of the strongest expressions are said to be quoted respectively from well-known public men. It well may be that the prohibition of laws abridging the freedom of speech is not confined to previous restraints, although to prevent them may have been the main purpose, as intimated in *Patterson v. Colorado*, 205 U.S. 454, 462. We admit that in many places and in ordinary times the defendants in saying all that was said in the circular would have been within their constitutional rights. But the character of every act depends upon the circumstances in which it is done. The most stringent protection of free speech would not protect a man in falsely shouting fire in a theatre and causing a panic. . . . The question in every case is whether the words used are used in such circumstances and are of such a nature as to create a clear and present danger that they will bring about the substantive evils that Congress has a right to prevent. It is a question of proximity and degree. When a nation is at war many things that might be said in time of peace are such a hindrance to its effort that their utterance will not be endured so long as men fight and that no Court could regard them as protected by any constitutional right. It seems to be admitted that if an actual obstruction of the recruiting service were proved, liability for words that produced that effect might be enforced. The statute of 1917 in section 4 punishes conspiracies to obstruct as well as actual obstruction. If the act, (speaking, or circulating a paper,) its tendency and the intent with which it is done are the same, we perceive no ground for saying that success alone warrants making the act a crime. Goldman v. United States, 245 U.S. 474, 477. . . .

Judgments affirmed.

NOTES AND QUESTIONS

1. Shaffer *and "bad tendency."* How protective of expression is *Shaffer*'s approach? Would the following acts or statements violate the Espionage Act if a court applied the "bad tendency" approach to judge the speaker's actions?
    a. distributing a pamphlet teaching that "Christians should not kill in wars";
    b. stating that "men conscripted to Europe are virtually condemned to death and everyone knows it";
    c. circulating a pamphlet urging the re-election of a Congressman who had voted against conscription;
    For discussion of prosecutions for statements under the Espionage Act, see Wells, *supra*, at 1582-1583.
2. Schenck *and "clear and present danger."* Justice Holmes announced the "clear and present danger" test for the first time in *Schenck*. What do these terms mean?

3. *Intent and "clear and present danger."* What role does intent to bring about harm play in Justice Holmes's formulation of the test? What evidence of such intent is necessary?

4. *The origin of "clear and present danger."* Is the "clear and present danger" test different from the "bad tendency" test?

   a. How would the Espionage Act prosecutions referred to in Question 1 turn out under Holmes's "clear and present danger" test?

   b. Do the following cases decided within one week of *Schenck* reflect on the difference between the "bad tendency" and "clear and present danger" tests?

      Frohwerk v. United States, 249 U.S. 204 (1919): Jacob Frohwerk, a copy-editor/publisher of the *Missouri Staats-Zeitung* (a German-language newspaper), was convicted of violating the Espionage Act and sentenced to ten years in prison for attempting to cause "disloyalty" and "refusal of duty" by articles produced in his newspaper. Frohwerk's articles called the war "a monumental and inexcusable mistake," and stated that the deaths of American soldiers were "outright murder." Intending to "warn the American people," he wrote of Germany's "undiminished strength" and "unconquerable spirit." Frohwerk blamed involvement in the war on Wall Street, claiming that our soldiers have "sold our honor, our very souls," so "a few men and corporations might amass unprecedented fortunes." Frohwerk wrote against the draft riots in Oklahoma and elsewhere, but allegedly used "language that might be taken to convey an innuendo of a different sort." He called the legal remedies for opposing the draft "all very well for those . . . past the draft age and [without] boys to be drafted," and he questioned criminal convictions of those who followed "the first impulse of nature: self-preservation." He also made "a remark to the effect that when rulers scheme to use it for their own purposes, loyalty serves to perpetuate wrong." 249 U.S. at 207-208.

      Justice Holmes, writing for a unanimous Court, admitted that there appeared to be no "special effort [by the defendant] to reach men who were subject to the draft." He also acknowledged that "it may be that all this might be said or written even in time of war in circumstances that would not make it a crime." *Id.* at 208. Nevertheless, Holmes upheld the conviction. After noting *Schenck*'s applicability, he stated that "it is impossible to say that it might not have been found that the circulation of the paper was in quarters where a little breath would be enough to kindle a flame and that the fact was known and relied upon by those who sent the paper out." *Id.* at 209.

      Debs v. United States, 249 U.S. 211 (1919): Eugene Debs, leader of the Socialist party and presidential candidate, was convicted and sentenced to ten years in prison under the Espionage Act for obstructing or attempting to obstruct military recruitment as a result of a speech made in July 1918. In his speech, which focused primarily on "Socialism, its growth, and a prophecy of its ultimate success," Debs opposed the war, praised persons convicted of hindering the draft, and espoused his belief that capitalism caused the war. 249 U.S. at 212-215. He also stated that "he had to be prudent and not say all that he thought, thus intimating to his hearers that they might infer that he meant more." *Id.* at 214. He told his listeners that "you need to know you are fit for something better than slavery and cannon fodder." *Id.* Authorities focused their attention on Debs because he was a prominent public figure who played a major role in the Pullman strikes and ran with some success as a third-party candidate for president. Immediately prior to giving his speech, Debs had visited with inmates convicted of attempt to inhibit the draft.

Delivering the opinion of the court, Justice Holmes declared that *Schenck* had "disposed of" Debs' First Amendment claim. Holmes dismissed the idea that the defendant was punished for his views on Socialism. Rather, Holmes argued, "if a part of the manifest intent of the more general utterances was to encourage those present to obstruct the recruiting service and if in passages such encouragement was directly given, the immunity of the general theme may not be enough to protect the speech." *Id.* at 212-213. According to Justice Holmes, if the "probable effect" of "one purpose of the speech, whether incidental or not does not matter, was to oppose [the] war," the speech "would not be protected." *Id.* at 214-215. Holmes thus upheld the lower court's jury instruction, which allowed conviction if "the words used had, as their natural tendency and reasonably probable effect, to obstruct the recruiting service" and the defendant so intended. *Id.* at 216.

5. *The "fire in a crowded theater" analogy.* What principle is Justice Holmes trying to establish with his statement in *Schenck* that "the most stringent protection of free speech would not protect a man in falsely shouting fire in a theatre and causing a panic?" How analogous is this situation to *Schenk, Frohwerk* and *Debs?*

6. *Free speech in wartime.* Should we give less protection to criticism of the government's actions during periods of war or is wartime a period when government is most likely to suppress speech based on pretext? *See* Vincent Blasi, *The Pathological Perspective and the First Amendment*, 85 Colum. L. Rev. 449 (1985); Christina E. Wells, *Questioning Deference*, 69 Mo. L. Rev. 903 (2004).

ABRAMS v. UNITED STATES
250 U.S. 616 (1919)

Mr. Justice CLARKE delivered the opinion of the Court.

[Defendants were Russian immigrants to the United States who distributed both publicly and secretively leaflets criticizing the United States government's decision to send troops to Russia as part of the effort against Germany during World War I. Defendants perceived the United States government's actions to be an effort to put down the Russian Revolution. As a result of circulating two leaflets criticizing the government's actions and calling for a general strike, defendants were prosecuted for violating the Sedition Act of 1918, for publishing "disloyal, scurrilous and abusive language about the form of government of the United States," using language "intended to incite, provoke and encourage resistance to the United States" during the war, and conspiring "to urge, incite and advocate curtailment of production of things and products, to wit, ordnance and ammunition, necessary and essential to the prosecution of the war." The Supreme Court dismissed the argument that the defendants' speech was protected by the First Amendment citing *Schenck* and *Frohwerk.* The Court then considered the sufficiency of the evidence supporting the convictions.]...

The first of the two articles attached to the indictment is conspicuously headed, "The Hypocrisy of the United States and her Allies." After denouncing President Wilson as a hypocrite and a coward because troops were sent into Russia, it proceeds to assail our government in general, saying:

> His [the President's] shameful, cowardly silence about the intervention in Russia reveals the hypocrisy of the plutocratic gang in Washington and vicinity.

It continues:

> He [the President] is too much of a coward to come out openly and say: "We capitalistic nations [including the U.S.] cannot afford to have a proletarian republic in Russia."

. . . [T]he circular culminates in:

> The Russian Revolution cries: Workers of the World! Awake! Rise! Put down your enemy and mine! Yes friends, there is only one enemy of the workers of the world and that is CAPITALISM. . . .

The second of the articles was printed in the Yiddish language and in the translation is headed, "Workers—Wake Up." After referring to "his Majesty, Mr. Wilson, and the rest of the gang, dogs of all colors!" it continues:

> Workers, Russian emigrants, you who had the least belief in the honesty of [the U.S] government . . ., must now throw away all confidence, must spit in the face the false, hypocritic, military propaganda which has fooled you so relentlessly, calling forth your sympathy, your help, to the prosecution of the war. . . .

[T]the spirit [of the leaflet] becomes more bitter as it proceeds to declare that—

> America and her Allies have betrayed [the Workers]. Their robberish aims are clear to all men. The destruction of the Russian Revolution, that is the politics of the march to Russia. *Workers, our reply to the barbaric intervention has to be a general strike! An open challenge* only will let the government know that not only the Russian Worker fights for freedom, but also *here in America lives the spirit of Revolution.*

This is not an attempt to bring about a change of administration by candid discussion, for no matter what may have incited the outbreak on the part of the defendant anarchists, the manifest purpose of such a publication was to create an attempt to defeat the war plans of the government of the United States, by bringing upon the country the paralysis of a general strike, thereby arresting the production of all munitions and other things essential to the conduct of the war. . . .

These excerpts sufficiently show, that while the immediate occasion for this particular outbreak of lawlessness, on the part of the defendant alien anarchists, may have been resentment caused by our government sending troops into Russia as a strategic operation against the Germans on the eastern battle front, yet the plain purpose of their propaganda was to excite, at the supreme crisis of the war, disaffection, sedition, riots, and, as they hoped, revolution, in this country for the purpose of embarrassing and if possible defeating the military plans of the government in Europe. Thus it is clear not only that some evidence but that much persuasive evidence was before the jury tending to prove that the defendants were guilty as charged in both the third and fourth counts of the indictment and under the long established rule of law hereinbefore stated the judgment of the District Court must be affirmed.

Mr. Justice HOLMES, dissenting.

. . . With regard to [the allegation that the defendants intend to hinder the war effort] it seems too plain to be denied that the suggestion to workers in the ammunition factories that they are producing bullets to murder their dearest, and the further advocacy of a general strike, both in the second leaflet, do urge curtailment of production of things necessary to the prosecution of the war within the meaning of the [Espionage and Sedition Acts]. But to make the conduct criminal that statute requires that it should be "with intent by such curtailment to cripple or hinder the United States in the prosecution of the war." It seems to me that no such intent is proved.

I am aware of course that the word "intent" as vaguely used in ordinary legal discussion means no more than knowledge at the time of the act that the consequences said to be intended will ensue. . . . But, when words are used exactly, a deed is not done with intent to produce a consequence unless that consequence is the aim of the deed. It may be obvious, and obvious to the actor, that the consequence will follow, and he may be liable for it even if he regrets it, but he does not do the act with intent to produce it unless the aim to produce it is the proximate motive of the specific act, although there may be some deeper motive behind.

It seems to me that this statute must be taken to use its words in a strict and accurate sense. They would be absurd in any other. A patriot might think that we were wasting money on aeroplanes, or making more cannon of a certain kind than we needed, and might advocate curtailment with success, yet even if it turned out that the curtailment hindered and was thought by other minds to have been obviously likely to hinder the United States in the prosecution of the war, no one would hold such conduct a crime. . . .

I never have seen any reason to doubt that the questions of law that alone were before this Court in *Schenck, Frohwerk*, and *Debs* were rightly decided. . . . [T]he United States constitutionally may punish speech that produces or is intended to produce a clear and imminent danger that it will bring about forthwith certain substantive evils that the United States constitutionally may seek to prevent. The power undoubtedly is greater in time of war than in time of peace because war opens dangers that do not exist at other times.

But as against dangers peculiar to war, as against others, the principle of the right to free speech is always the same. It is only the present danger of immediate evil or an intent to bring it about that warrants Congress in setting a limit to the expression of opinion where private rights are not concerned. Congress certainly cannot forbid all effort to change the mind of the country. Now nobody can suppose that the surreptitious publishing of a silly leaflet by an unknown man, without more, would present any immediate danger that its opinions would hinder the success of the government arms or have any appreciable tendency to do so. Publishing those opinions for the very purpose of obstructing, however, might indicate a greater danger and at any rate would have the quality of an attempt. So I assume that the second leaflet if published for the purposes [of hindering the war effort] might be punishable. But it seems pretty clear to me that nothing less than that would bring these papers within the scope of this law.

I do not see how anyone can find the intent required by the statute in any of the defendant's words. The second leaflet is the only one that affords even a foundation for the charge, and there, without invoking the hatred of German militarism expressed in the former one, it is evident from the beginning to the end that the only object of the paper is to help Russia and stop American intervention there against the popular government—not to impede the United States in the war that it was carrying on. To say that two phrases taken literally might import a suggestion of conduct that would have interference with the war as an indirect and probably undesired effect seems to me by no means enough to show an attempt to produce that effect. . . .

In this case sentences of twenty years imprisonment have been imposed for the publishing of two leaflets that I believe the defendants had as much right to publish as the Government has to publish the Constitution of the United States now vainly invoked by them. Even if I am technically wrong and enough can be squeezed from these poor and puny anonymities to turn the color of legal litmus paper; I will add, even if what I think the necessary intent were shown; the most nominal punishment seems to me all that possibly could be inflicted, unless the defendants are to be made to suffer not for what the indictment alleges but for the creed that they avow[.]. . .

Persecution for the expression of opinions seems to me perfectly logical. If you have no doubt of your premises or your power and want a certain result with all your heart you naturally express your wishes in law and sweep away all opposition. To allow opposition by speech seems to indicate that you think the speech impotent, as when a man says that he has squared the circle, or that you do not care whole heartedly for the result, or that you doubt either your power or your premises. But when men have realized that time has upset many fighting faiths, they may come to believe even more than they believe the very foundations of their own conduct that the ultimate good desired is better reached by free trade in ideas—that the best test of truth is the power of the thought to get itself accepted in the competition of the market, and that truth is the only ground upon which their wishes safely can be carried out. That at any rate is the theory of our Constitution. It is an experiment, as all life is an experiment. Every year if not every day we have to wager our salvation upon some prophecy based upon imperfect knowledge. While that experiment is part of our system I think that we should be eternally vigilant against attempts to check the expression of opinions that we loathe and believe to be fraught with death, unless they so imminently threaten immediate interference with the lawful and pressing purposes of the law that an immediate check is required to save the country. I wholly disagree with the argument of the Government that the First Amendment left the common law as to seditious libel in force. History seems to me against the notion. I had conceived that the United States through many years had shown its repentance for the Sedition Act of 1798 (Act July 14, 1798, c. 73, 1 Stat. 596), by repaying fines that it imposed. Only the emergency that makes it immediately dangerous to leave the correction of evil counsels to time warrants making any exception to the sweeping command, 'Congress shall make no law abridging the freedom of speech.' Of course I am speaking only of expressions of opinion and exhortations, which were all that were uttered here, but I regret that I cannot put into more impressive words my belief that in their conviction upon this indictment the defendants were deprived of their rights under the Constitution of the United States.

[Justice Brandeis's concurring opinion is omitted.]

MASSES PUBLISHING CO. v. PATTEN

244 F. 535 (S.D.N.Y. 1917)

LEARNED HAND, District Judge.

[Plaintiff produced a monthly revolutionary journal called "The Masses," which it wanted to send through the U.S. Mail. The postmaster of New York argued the entire publication violated the Espionage Act because "it tended to produce a violation of the law, to encourage the enemies of the United States, and to hamper the government in the conduct of the war." The postmaster also specifically identified four cartoons and four portions of text that violated the Espionage Act. Plaintiff sought a preliminary injunction forbidding the postmaster from refusing to accept its publication.] . . .

The four cartoons are entitled respectively, "Liberty Bell," "Conscription," "Making the World Safe for Capitalism," "Congress and Big Business." The first is a picture of the Liberty Bell broken in fragments. The obvious implication, taking the cartoon in its context with the number as a whole, is that the origin, purposes, and conduct of the war have already destroyed the liberties of the country. It is a fair inference that the draft law is an especial instance of the violation of the liberty and fundamental rights of any free people.

The second cartoon shows a cannon to the mouth of which is bound the naked figure of a youth, to the wheel that of a woman, marked "Democracy," and upon the carriage that of a man, marked "Labor." On the ground kneels a draped woman marked "Motherhood" in a posture of desperation, while her infant lies on the ground. The import of this cartoon is obviously that conscription is the destruction of youth, democracy, and labor, and the desolation of the family. No one can dispute that it was intended to rouse detestation for the draft law. . . .

. . . The [postmaster's] position is that to arouse discontent and disaffection among the people with the prosecution of the war and with the draft tends to promote a mutinous and insubordinate temper among the troops [and, therefore, the identified material violates the provision of the Espionage Act prohibiting intentionally causing disloyalty in the military forces]. This . . . is true; men who become satisfied that they are engaged in an enterprise dictated by the unconscionable selfishness of the rich, and effectuated by a tyrannous disregard for the will of those who must suffer and die, will be more prone to insubordination than those who have faith in the cause and acquiesce in the means. Yet to interpret the word "cause" so broadly would . . . involve necessarily as a consequence the suppression of all hostile criticism, and of all opinion except what encouraged and supported the existing policies, or which fell within the range of temperate argument. It would contradict the normal assumption of democratic government that the suppression of hostile criticism does not turn upon the justice of its substance or the decency and propriety of its temper. . . . Yet there has always been a recognized limit to such expressions, incident indeed to the existence of any compulsive power of the state itself. One may not counsel or advise others to violate the law as it stands. Words are not only the keys of persuasion, but the triggers of action, and those which have no purport but to counsel the violation of law cannot by any latitude of interpretation be a part of that public opinion which is the final source of government in a democratic state. The defendant asserts not only that the magazine indirectly through its propaganda leads to a disintegration of loyalty and a disobedience of law, but that in addition it counsels and advises resistance to existing law, especially to the draft. . . . To counsel or advise a man to an act is to urge upon him either that it is his interest or his duty to do it. While, of course, this may be accomplished as well by indirection as expressly, since words carry the meaning that they impart, the definition is exhaustive, I think, and I shall use it. Political agitation, by the passions it arouses or the convictions it engenders, may in fact stimulate men to the violation of law. . . . Yet to assimilate agitation, legitimate as such, with direct incitement to violent resistance, is to disregard the tolerance of all methods of political agitation which in normal times is a safeguard of free government. . . . If one stops short of urging upon others that it is their duty or their interest to resist the law, it seems to me one should not be held to have attempted to cause its violation. If that be not the test, I can see no escape from the conclusion that under this section every political agitation which can be shown to be apt to create a seditious temper is illegal. I am confident that by such language Congress had no such revolutionary purpose in view. It seems to me, however, quite plain that none of the language and none of the cartoons in this paper can be thought directly to counsel or advise insubordination or mutiny, without a violation of their meaning quite beyond any tolerable understanding. . . .

It follows that the plaintiff is entitled to the usual preliminary injunction.

NOTES AND QUESTIONS

1. *Justice Holmes and the evolution of "clear and present danger."* Is Holmes's version of the "clear and present danger" test in *Abrams* different from that in *Schenck* decided earlier in 1919? Several prominent scholars and judges publicly and privately criticized his reasoning in *Schenck* and related cases. Most scholars believe Holmes's attitude changed as a result of this criticism and as he watched what he believed to be government and judicial excess with respect to suppression of expression. *See, e.g.,* David Rabban, *The Emergence of Modern First Amendment Doctrine,* 50 U. Chi. L. Rev. 1205 (1983); G. Edward White, *Justice Holmes and the Modernization of Free Speech Jurisprudence: The Human Dimension,* 80 Cal. L. Rev. 391 (1992). *But see* Zechariah Chafee, Jr., *Free Speech in the United States* 86 (1941).

2. *The requisite parts of "clear and present danger."* Justice Holmes's *Abrams* dissent adds an immediacy requirement to the "clear and present danger" test. What are the advantages for speakers of adding an "immediacy" requirement to the clear and present danger test? What does "immediacy" mean in this context?

3. *The marketplace of ideas.* Holmes's dissent is famous for its exposition of the marketplace of ideas principle. Does the marketplace of ideas or search for truth rationale support the "clear and present danger" test?

4. *The* Masses *decision.* Judge Hand disliked the "clear and present danger" test because he believed it allowed judges to be swayed by passion. *See* Gerald Gunther, *Learned Hand and the Origins of Modern First Amendment Doctrine: Some Fragments of History,* 27 Stan. L. Rev. 719, 749 (1975).

    a. Is it better to focus on the express words of incitement (as does Hand) or the possible effects of incitement (as does the "clear and present danger" test) when determining whether to punish speech?

    b. How would the speakers in Question 1 after *Schenck* have fared under Hand's approach in *Masses?*

c.   Hand's decision in *Masses* was overturned on appeal in an opinion stating that "this court does not agree that [Judge Hand's] test is the law." *Masses Publg. Co. v. Patton*, 246 F. 24 (2d Cir. 1917).

B.   THE RED SCARE CASES

Following World War I, the United States entered a period of intense anti-radicalism. The Russian Revolution sparked fears of a possible Communist revolution within the United States. At the same time, the Russian Revolution catalyzed growth in American radical movements, such as the Socialist Party, and in various labor organizations (some of which were associated with radical movements), thus increasing tensions between such movements and those fearing the spread of radicalism. In 1919-1920, a series of protests, strikes, and bombings or attempted bombings attributed to radical forces further increased fear and hysteria around the country. Americans began to call for greater security measures.

During 1919, at least 27 states passed "red flag" laws (laws barring the display of flags as a sign of opposition to organized government), 16 states passed criminal syndicalism laws (laws prohibiting advocacy of overthrow of the government), and 12 states passed anarchy and sedition laws. Approximately 1,400 people were arrested under such laws, resulting in about 300 convictions. The Red Scare also led to massive efforts to round up and deport aliens believed to pose a radical threat. State and federal officials staged raids of radical organizations around the country. In January 1920, the infamous Palmer Raids, named after Attorney General A. Mitchell Palmer, involved the arrests of between 5,000 and 10,000 people who were allegedly members of radical organizations. Those arrested included almost every local and national leader of these organizations, and included many American citizens although the raids were ostensibly targeted at aliens. Many citizens were turned over to officials for prosecution under criminal syndicalism laws, although most were eventually freed due to lack of evidence. For more discussion of the Red Scare, see Robert Justin Goldstein, *Political Repression in Modern America: From 1870 to 1976*, at 139-163 (2001); Geoffrey R. Stone, *Perilous Times: Free Speech in Wartime* 220-230 (2004); Zechariah Chafee, Jr., *Free Speech in the United States* 141-240 (1941); Robert Murray, *Red Scare: A Study in National Hysteria, 1919-1920* (1964).

The following two cases arose during the Red Scare and involve prosecutions under criminal syndicalism laws. As you read them, consider how the Court's approach differs in these cases from the previous cases. Is this difference justified by the different laws at issue in the cases, or should the "clear and present danger" test govern?

GITLOW v. NEW YORK

268 U.S. 652 (1925)

Mr. Justice SANFORD delivered the opinion of the Court.

[Benjamin Gitlow was indicted and convicted along with others for violating Section 161 of the New York Penal Code, which provides that any person who

1. By word of mouth or writing advocates, advises or teaches the duty, necessity or propriety of overthrowing or overturning organized government by force or violence, or by assassination of the executive head or of any of the executive officials of government, or by any unlawful means [is guilty of a felony.] . . .

The trial established Gitlow was a member of the Left Wing Section of the Socialist Party ("LWS"), a dissenting branch formed to oppose its policy of "moderate Socialism." . . . The LWS was organized nationally at a conference in June, 1919. The conference elected a National Council, including Gitlow as a member. The National Council adopted and published a "Manifesto." Gitlow arranged for the printing, publication, and circulation of the Manifesto and other communist literature. Gitlow also travelled to different parts of the State to speak to branches of the Socialist Party about the principles of the LWS and advocating for their adoption. Although the Manifesto clearly advocated for the necessity of accomplishing the "Communist Revolution" through a militant and revolutionary Socialism, there was no evidence at trial that publication and circulation of the Manifesto had any such effect.]

. . . The sole contention here is . . . that as there was no evidence of any concrete result flowing from the publication of the Manifesto or of circumstances showing the likelihood of such result, the statute as construed and applied by the trial court penalizes the mere utterance . . . of "doctrine" having no quality of incitement[.]. . . . [Because expression] is only punishable "in circumstances involving likelihood of substantive evil," the statute contravenes the due process clause of the Fourteenth Amendment. . . .

The statute does not penalize the utterance or publication of abstract "doctrine" or academic discussion having no quality of incitement to any concrete action. It is not aimed against mere historical or philosophical essays. It does not restrain the advocacy of changes in the form of government by constitutional and lawful means. What it prohibits is language advocating, advising or teaching the overthrow of organized government by unlawful means. These words imply urging to action. . . .

The Manifesto, plainly, is neither the statement of abstract doctrine nor, as suggested by counsel, mere prediction that industrial disturbances and revolutionary mass strikes will result spontaneously in an inevitable process of evolution in the economic system. It advocates and urges in fervent language mass action which shall progressively foment industrial disturbances and through political mass strikes and revolutionary mass action overthrow and destroy organized parliamentary government. It concludes with a call to action in these words: "The proletariat revolution and the Communist reconstruction of society—*the struggle for these*—is now indispensable. . . . The Communist International calls the proletariat of the world to the final struggle!" . . . . [T]he jury were warranted in finding that the Manifesto advocated not merely the abstract doctrine of overthrowing organized government by force, violence and unlawful means, but action to that end[.]

For present purposes we may and do assume that freedom of speech and of the press—which are protected by the First Amendment from abridgment by Congress—are among the fundamental personal rights and "liberties" protected by the due process clause of the Fourteenth Amendment from impairment by the States. . . .

It is a fundamental principle, long established, that the freedom of speech and of the press which is secured by the Constitution, does not confer an absolute right to speak or publish, without responsibility, whatever one may choose, or an unrestricted and unbridled license that gives immunity for every possible use of language and

prevents the punishment of those who abuse this freedom. *Schenck; Frohwerk; Debs.*
. . .

[A] State may punish utterances endangering the foundations of organized government and threatening its overthrow by unlawful means. These imperil its own existence as a constitutional State. . . .

By enacting the present statute the State has determined, through its legislative body, that utterances advocating the overthrow of organized government by force, violence and unlawful means, are so inimical to the general welfare and involve such danger of substantive evil that they may be penalized in the exercise of its police power. That determination must be given great weight. . . . [T]he case is to be considered "in the light of the principle that the State is primarily the judge of regulations required in the interest of public safety and welfare"; and that its police "statutes may only be declared unconstitutional where they are arbitrary or unreasonable attempts to exercise authority vested in the State in the public interest." [U]tterances inciting to the overthrow of organized government by unlawful means, . . . by their very nature, involve danger to the public peace and to the security of the State. They threaten breaches of the peace and ultimate revolution. And the immediate danger is none the less real and substantial, because the effect of a given utterance cannot be accurately foreseen. . . . It cannot be said that the State is acting arbitrarily or unreasonably when in the exercise of its judgment as to the measures necessary to protect the public peace and safety, it seeks to extinguish [a] spark without waiting until it has enkindled the flame or blazed into the conflagration. . . .

We cannot hold that the present statute is an arbitrary or unreasonable exercise of the police power of the State unwarrantably infringing the freedom of speech or press; and we must and do sustain its constitutionality.

This being so it may be applied to every utterance—not too trivial to be beneath the notice of the law—which is of such a character and used with such intent and purpose as to bring it within the prohibition of the statute. In other words, when the legislative body has determined generally, in the constitutional exercise of its discretion, that utterances of a certain kind involve such danger of substantive evil that they may be punished, the question whether any specific utterance coming within the prohibited class is likely, in and of itself, to bring about the substantive evil, is not open to consideration. It is sufficient that the statute itself be constitutional and that the use of the language comes within its prohibition.

It is clear that the question in such cases is entirely different from that involved in those cases where the statute merely prohibits certain acts involving the danger of substantive evil, without any reference to language itself, and it is sought to apply its provisions to language used by the defendant for the purpose of bringing about the prohibited results. . . . In such case it has been held that the general provisions of the statute may be constitutionally applied to the specific utterance of the defendant if its natural tendency and probable effect was to bring about the substantive evil which the legislative body might prevent. *Schenck; Debs.* And the general statement in *Schenck* that the "question in every case is whether the words used are used in such circumstances and are of such a nature as to create a clear and present danger that they will bring about the substantive evils,"—upon which great reliance is placed in the defendant's argument—was manifestly intended, as shown by the context, to apply only in cases of this class, and has no application to those like the present, where the legislative body itself has previously determined the danger of substantive evil arising from utterances of a specified character. . . .

Affirmed.

Mr. Justice HOLMES, dissenting.

. . . I think that the criterion sanctioned by the full Court in *Schenck* applies: "The question in every case is whether the words used are used in such circumstances and are of such a nature as to create a clear and present danger that they will bring about the substantive evils that [the State] has a right to prevent." . . . If what I think the correct test is applied it is manifest that there was no present danger of an attempt to overthrow the government by force on the part of the admittedly small minority who shared the defendant's views. It is said that this manifesto was more than a theory, that it was an incitement. Every idea is an incitement. It offers itself for belief and if believed it is acted on unless some other belief outweighs it or some failure of energy stifles the movement at its birth. The only difference between the expression of an opinion and an incitement in the narrower sense is the speaker's enthusiasm for the result. Eloquence may set fire to reason. But whatever may be thought of the redundant discourse before us it had no chance of starting a present conflagration. If in the long run the beliefs expressed in proletarian dictatorship are destined to be accepted by the dominant forces of the community, the only meaning of free speech is that they should be given their chance and have their way.

If the publication of this document had been laid as an attempt to induce an uprising against government at once and not at some indefinite time in the future it would have presented a different question. The object would have been one with which the law might deal, subject to the doubt whether there was any danger that the publication could produce any result, or in other words, whether it was not futile and too remote from possible consequences. But the indictment alleges the publication and nothing more.

NOTES AND QUESTIONS

1. *Incorporation.* Although the text of the First Amendment applies only to Congress, *Gitlow* assumed that the freedom of speech and press "are among the fundamental personal rights and 'liberties' protected by the Due Process Clause of the Fourteenth Amendment." Since that brief statement in 1925 the Court has repeatedly cited *Gitlow* as the foundational case finding that the First Amendment freedoms are "fundamental components of the liberty safeguarded by the Due Process Clause" and thus applicable against the states. *See, e.g.,* First Nat'l Bank v. Bellotti, 425 U.S. 765, 780 (1978); NAACP v. Alabama ex rel. Patterson, 357 U.S. 449, 460 (1958); Stromberg v. California, 283 U.S. 359, 368 (1931).

2. *Deference to legislative pronouncements of danger.* Do you agree with Justice Sanford's claims that the "clear and present danger" standard is inapplicable because the statute at issue is specifically directed at speech, unlike the statutes in *Schenck* and *Abrams*, which were aimed at conduct?

3. *More on Holmes's marketplace of ideas.* Justice Holmes states that "if in the long run the beliefs expressed in proletarian dictatorship are destined to be accepted by the dominant forces of the community, the only meaning of free speech is that they should be given their chance and have their way." How does this affect your view of Justice Holmes's marketplace rationale in *Abrams*?

4. *The marketplace of ideas and totalitarian ideologies.* Should the First Amendment protect totalitarian ideologies intolerant of democratic principles? For arguments, see Robert Bork, *Neutral Principles and Some First Amendment*

Problems, 47 Ind. L.J. 1 (1971); Steven D. Smith, *Radically Subversive Speech and the Authority of Law*, 94 Mich. L. Rev. 348 (1995).

WHITNEY v. CALIFORNIA

274 U.S. 357 (1927)

Mr. Justice SANFORD delivered the opinion of the Court.

[Anita Whitney was convicted of violating the California Criminal Syndicalism Act, which stated:

> Section 1. The term "criminal syndicalism" as used in this act is hereby defined as any doctrine or precept advocating, teaching or aiding and abetting the commission of crime, sabotage (which word is hereby defined as meaning willful and malicious physical damage or injury to physical property), or unlawful acts of force and violence or unlawful methods of terrorism as a means of accomplishing a change in industrial ownership or control or effecting any political change.
>
> Sec. 2. Any person who: . . . Organizes or assists in organizing, or is or knowingly becomes a member of, any organization, society, group or assemblage of persons organized or assembled to advocate, teach or aid and abet criminal syndicalism; . . . Is guilty of a felony and punishable by imprisonment.

Specifically, Whitney was charged with and convicted of organizing and assisting in organizing, and knowingly becoming a member of an organization that assembled to advocate or teach criminal syndicalism. At trial the evidence showed that Whitney was a member of the Oakland branch of the Socialist Party. At the national convention in 1919, the Socialist Party split and the Oakland delegation adhered to the "radical group, which separately formed the Communist Labor Party of America ("CLP"). The CLP adopted a platform that, among other things, called for organizing workers in a "revolutionary class struggle to conquer the capitalist state and for the overthrow of capitalist rule, ultimately to establish a Dictatorship of the Proletariat." Whitney became a member of the CLP and attended its national convention as a delegate later that year. She was a member of various committees and signed a resolution that recognized the need to develop political power by voting for CLP candidates in elections and urging workers to vote for such candidates. Although this resolution was rejected by the CLP, Whitney remained at the convention. However, she testified that she never intended for the CLP to be an instrument of terrorism or violence nor was it her purpose to violate any known law.]

[The] Syndicalism Act as applied in this case [is not] repugnant to the due process clause as a restraint of the rights of free speech, assembly, and association. . . . [*See Gitlow*.] . . . The essence of the offense denounced by the Act is the combining with others in an association for the accomplishment of the desired ends through the advocacy and use of criminal and unlawful methods. It partakes of the nature of a criminal conspiracy. . . . That such united and joint action involves even greater danger to the public peace and security than the isolated utterances and acts of individuals is clear. We cannot hold that, as here applied, the Act is an unreasonable or arbitrary exercise of the police power of the State, unwarrantably infringing any right of free speech, assembly or association, or that those persons are protected from punishment by the due process clause who abuse such rights by joining and furthering an organization thus menacing the peace and welfare of the State.

Affirmed.

Mr. Justice BRANDEIS, concurring.

. . . [T]he statute [under which Ms. Whitney is punished] create[s] . . . a crime very unlike the old felony of conspiracy or the old misdemeanor of unlawful assembly. The mere act of assisting in forming a society for teaching syndicalism, of becoming a member of it, or assembling with others for that purpose is given the dynamic quality of crime. . . . Thus the accused is to be punished, not for attempt, incitement or conspiracy, but for a step in preparation, which, if it threatens the public order at all, does so only remotely. The novelty in the prohibition introduced is that the statute aims, not at the practice of criminal syndicalism, nor even directly at the preaching of it, but at association with those who propose to preach it. . . .

[A]lthough the rights of free speech and assembly are fundamental, they are not in their nature absolute. Their exercise is subject to restriction, if the particular restriction proposed is required in order to protect the state from destruction or from serious injury, political, economic or moral. That the necessity which is essential to a valid restriction does not exist unless speech would produce, or is intended to produce, a clear and imminent danger of some substantive evil which the state constitutionally may seek to prevent has been settled. *See Schenck.*

It is said to be the function of the Legislature to determine whether at a particular time and under the particular circumstances the formation of, or assembly with, a society organized to advocate criminal syndicalism constitutes a clear and present danger of substantive evil; and that by enacting the law here in question the Legislature of California determined that question in the affirmative. *Compare Gitlow*. The Legislature must obviously decide, in the first instance, whether a danger exists which calls for a particular protective measure. But where a statute is valid only in case certain conditions exist, the enactment of the statute cannot alone establish the facts which are essential to its validity. . . .

This court has not yet fixed the standard by which to determine when a danger shall be deemed clear; how remote the danger may be and yet be deemed present; and what degree of evil shall be deemed sufficiently substantial to justify resort to abridgment of free speech and assembly as the means of protection. To reach sound conclusions on these matters, we must bear in mind why a state is, ordinarily, denied the power to prohibit dissemination of social, economic and political doctrine which a vast majority of its citizens believes to be false and fraught with evil consequence.

Those who won our independence believed that the final end of the state was to make men free to develop their faculties, and that in its government the deliberative forces should prevail over the arbitrary. They valued liberty both as an end and as a means. They believed liberty to be the secret of happiness and courage to be the secret of liberty. They believed that freedom to think as you will and to speak as you think are means indispensable to the discovery and spread of political truth; that without free speech and assembly discussion would be futile; that with them, discussion affords ordinarily adequate protection against the dissemination of noxious doctrine; that the greatest menace to freedom is an inert people; that public discussion is a political duty; and that this should be a fundamental principle of the American government.[1] They recognized the risks to which all human institutions are

---

[1] Compare Thomas Jefferson: "We have nothing to fear from the demoralizing reasonings of some, if others are left free to demonstrate their errors and especially when the law stands ready to punish the first criminal act produced by the false reasonings; these are safer corrections than the conscience of the judge." Quoted by Charles A. Beard, *The Nation*, July 7, 1926, Vol. 123, P. 8. Also in first Inaugural Address: "If there be any among us who would wish to dissolve this union or

subject. But they knew that order cannot be secured merely through fear of punishment for its infraction; that it is hazardous to discourage thought, hope and imagination; that fear breeds repression; that repression breeds hate; that hate menaces stable government; that the path of safety lies in the opportunity to discuss freely supposed grievances and proposed remedies; and that the fitting remedy for evil counsels is good ones. Believing in the power of reason as applied through public discussion, they eschewed silence coerced by law—the argument of force in its worst form. Recognizing the occasional tyrannies of governing majorities, they amended the Constitution so that free speech and assembly should be guaranteed.

Fear of serious injury cannot alone justify suppression of free speech and assembly. Men feared witches and burnt women. It is the function of speech to free men from the bondage of irrational fears. To justify suppression of free speech there must be reasonable ground to fear that serious evil will result if free speech is practiced. There must be reasonable ground to believe that the danger apprehended is imminent. There must be reasonable ground to believe that the evil to be prevented is a serious one. Every denunciation of existing law tends in some measure to increase the probability that there will be violation of it.[5] Condonation of a breach enhances the probability. Expressions of approval add to the probability. Propagation of the criminal state of mind by teaching syndicalism increases it. Advocacy of lawbreaking heightens it still further. But even advocacy of violation, however reprehensible morally, is not a justification for denying free speech where the advocacy falls short of incitement and there is nothing to indicate that the advocacy would be immediately acted on. The wide difference between advocacy and incitement, between preparation and attempt, between assembling and conspiracy, must be borne in mind. In order to support a finding of clear and present danger it must be shown either that immediate serious violence was to be expected or was advocated, or that the past conduct furnished reason to believe that such advocacy was then contemplated.

Those who won our independence by revolution were not cowards. They did not fear political change. They did not exalt order at the cost of liberty. To courageous, self-reliant men, with confidence in the power of free and fearless reasoning applied through the processes of popular government, no danger flowing from speech can be deemed clear and present, unless the incidence of the evil apprehended is so imminent that it may befall before there is opportunity for full discussion. If there be time to expose through discussion the falsehood and fallacies, to avert the evil by the processes of education, the remedy to be applied is more speech, not enforced silence. Only an emergency can justify repression. Such must be the rule if authority is to be reconciled with freedom. Such, in my opinion, is the command of the Constitution. It is therefore always open to Americans to challenge a law abridging free speech and assembly by showing that there was no emergency justifying it.

Moreover, even imminent danger cannot justify resort to prohibition of these functions essential to effective democracy, unless the evil apprehended is relatively serious. Prohibition of free speech and assembly is a measure so stringent that it would be inappropriate as the means for averting a relatively trivial harm to society. A police measure may be unconstitutional merely because the remedy, although effective as means of protection, is unduly harsh or oppressive. Thus, a state might,

---

change its republican form, let them stand undisturbed as monuments of the safety with which error of opinion may be tolerated where reason is left free to combat it."

[5] Compare Judge Learned Hand in *Masses Publishing Co. v. Patten*, 244 F. 535, 540.

in the exercise of its police power, make any trespass upon the land of another a crime, regardless of the results or of the intent or purpose of the trespasser. It might, also, punish an attempt, a conspiracy, or an incitement to commit the trespass. But it is hardly conceivable that this court would hold constitutional a statute which punished as a felony the mere voluntary assembly with a society formed to teach that pedestrians had the moral right to cross uninclosed, unposted, waste lands and to advocate their doing so, even if there was imminent danger that advocacy would lead to a trespass. The fact that speech is likely to result in some violence or in destruction of property is not enough to justify its suppression. There must be the probability of serious injury to the State. Among free men, the deterrents ordinarily to be applied to prevent crime are education and punishment for violations of the law, not abridgment of the rights of free speech and assembly....

Whenever the fundamental rights of free speech and assembly are alleged to have been invaded, it must remain open to a defendant to present the issue whether there actually did exist at the time a clear danger, whether the danger, if any, was imminent, and whether the evil apprehended was one so substantial as to justify the stringent restriction interposed by the Legislature.... [T]he statute was passed and was sustained by the highest court of the State, creates merely a rebuttable presumption that these conditions have been satisfied.

Whether in 1919, when Miss Whitney did the things complained of, there was in California such clear and present danger of serious evil, might have been made the important issue in the case. She might have required that the issue be determined either by the court or the jury. She claimed below that the statute as applied to her violated the federal Constitution; but she did not claim that it was void because there was no clear and present danger of serious evil, nor did she request that the existence of these conditions of a valid measure thus restricting the rights of free speech and assembly be passed upon by the court or a jury. On the other hand, there was evidence on which the court or jury might have found that such danger existed. I am unable to assent to the suggestion in the opinion of the court that assembling with a political party, formed to advocate the desirability of a proletarian revolution by mass action at some date necessarily far in the future, is not a right within the protection of the Fourteenth Amendment. In the present case, however, there was other testimony which tended to establish the existence of a conspiracy, on the part of members of the International Workers of the World, to commit present serious crimes, and likewise to show that such a conspiracy would be furthered by the activity of the society of which Miss Whitney was a member. Under these circumstances the judgment of the State court cannot be disturbed. . . .

Mr. Justice HOLMES joins in this opinion.

NOTES AND QUESTIONS

1. *Brandeis's* Whitney *concurrence and free speech values.* Justice Brandeis's justifications for protecting free speech are as well-known as are those in Justice Holmes's *Abrams* dissent.

   a. What point does Brandeis seem to be making about the essential link between political "truth" and self-governance? *See* Vincent Blasi, *The First Amendment and the Idea of Civic Courage*, 29 Wm. & Mary L. Rev. 653, 673-675 (1988).

b. What vision of autonomy does Brandeis hold with his statement that "[t]hose who won our independence believed that the final end of the state was to make men free to develop their faculties"? For discussion, see Vincent Blasi, *Free Speech and Good Character*, 46 UCLA L. Rev. 1567 (1999).

2. *Justice Brandeis and "clear and present danger."* What does Justice Brandeis's version of the test add to Holmes's discussion in *Abrams*?

3. *Brandeis's decision to concur.* Given the tenor of his opinion, Justice Brandeis's concurrence with the decision to uphold Anita Whitney's conviction is curious. Did Justice Brandeis concur for technical reasons, simply because Anita Whitney failed to raise arguments on appeal, or because there were substantive arguments supporting her conviction? *See Brandeis on Democracy* 238 (Philippa Strum ed., 1995); Ronald K.L. Collins & David M. Skover, *Curious Concurrence: Justice Brandeis's Vote in Whitney v. California*, 2005 Sup. Ct. Rev. 333 (2006).

4. Whitney *and association. Whitney* raises issues regarding associational rights. The California statute made it illegal for any person knowingly to be a member in an organization that advocated certain unlawful activity. The *Whitney* majority held that the Constitution did not protect knowing membership. Is "knowledge" the appropriate mental state, or should the court require that the defendant intend to further the organization's illegal aims? What kind of activity is sufficient to meet the "knowing membership" requirement?

5. *Locating association within the First Amendment.* Although the association right is not specifically mentioned in the First Amendment, post-*Whitney* cases have recognized its importance to free speech rights, noting that "[t]he right of peaceable assembly is a right cognate to those of free speech and free press and is equally fundamental." *DeJonge*, 299 U.S. at 364; *see also* NAACP v. Alabama, 357 U.S. 449, 460 (1958). Why is the right to associate so important to the right of free expression?

C. THE SMITH ACT PROSECUTIONS

Soon after *Gitlow* and *Whitney*, the "clear and present danger" test evolved into the speech protective test that Justices Holmes and Brandeis envisioned. The Court used it in a variety of cases. *See, e.g.*, Cantwell v. Connecticut, 310 U.S. 296 (1940); Thornhill v. Alabama, 310 U.S. 88 (1940); Bridges v. California, 314 U.S. 252 (1941); Schneiderman v. United States, 320 U.S. 118 (1943); Taylor v. Mississippi, 319 U.S. 583 (1943). During the Cold War, however, the Supreme Court again upheld repressive legislation aimed at domestic Communists, as it did during World War I. The most famous of these cases was Dennis v. United States, 341 U.S. 494 (1951), which involved prosecution of several leaders of the Communist Party USA (CPUSA) for conspiring to advocate overthrow of the government. The *Dennis* trial and subsequent Supreme Court decision took place during a time of extreme hostility toward domestic Communists and growing fear that they conspired with the Soviet Union to threaten the security of the United States and American ideals. Christina E. Wells, *Questioning Deference*, 69 Mo. L. Rev. 903, 918 (2004).

Whether such fear was justified is far less clear. A traditional view of domestic Communists was that they were "agents of the Soviet Union, . . . financed by the

USSR and completely under its control. They faithfully reflected its views and carried out its orders. [Domestic Communists], in this view, had no will of their own." William C. Wiecek, *The Legal Foundations of Domestic Anti-Communism: The Background of Dennis v. United States*, 2001 Sup. Ct. Rev. 375, 407. As a result, those who feared the very real threats posed by the Soviet Union automatically associated domestic Communists with such threats. However, "another, more recent perception of domestic Communists challenges such assumptions. In this interpretation, American Communists were indigenous, authentic domestic radicals who saw in Communism the only effective understanding of socialism. . . . These Communists, especially the young among them who joined the Party in the 1930s, were idealists committed to a struggle for justice at home and against fascism abroad." *Id.* at 408. This view holds that many domestic Communists did not automatically take orders from Moscow and prosecution of them amounted to witch trials. Ultimately the answer regarding the domestic Communists may lie somewhere in between these two poles. *See id.* at 409; Christina E. Wells, *Fear and Loathing in Constitutional Decision-Making*, 2005 Wis. L. Rev. 115, 133-141.

For more discussion of Cold War legal issues involving American Communists, see Michal R. Belknap, *Cold War Political Justice: The Smith Act, the Communist Party, and American Civil Liberties* (1977); Peter L. Steinberg, *The Great "Red Menace": United States Prosecution of American Communists, 1947–1952* (1984); Geoffrey R. Stone, *Perilous Times: Free Speech in Wartime* 311-426 (2004); Martin H. Redish, *The Logic of Persecution: Free Expression and the McCarthy Era* (2005); Wiecek, *supra*; Wells, *Fear and Loathing, supra*; David Bernstein, *The Red Menace, Revisited*, 100 Nw. U. L. Rev. 1295 (2006).

DENNIS v. UNITED STATES

341 U.S. 494 (1951)

Mr. Chief Justice VINSON announced the judgment of the Court and an opinion in which Mr. Justice REED, Mr. Justice BURTON and Mr. Justice MINTON join.

Petitioners were indicted in July, 1948, for violation of the conspiracy provisions of the Smith Act, during the period of April, 1945, to July, 1948. A verdict of guilty as to all the petitioners was returned by the jury on October 14, 1949. The Court of Appeals affirmed the convictions. . . .

Sections 2 and 3 of the Smith Act provide as follows:

> Sec. 2. (a) It shall be unlawful for any person . . . to knowingly or willfully advocate, abet, advise, or teach the duty, necessity, desirability, or propriety of overthrowing or destroying any government in the United States by force or violence, or by the assassination of any officer of any such government[.]. . .
> Sec. 3. It shall be unlawful for any person to attempt to commit, or to conspire to commit, any of the acts prohibited by the provisions of . . . this title.

The indictment charged the petitioners with wilfully and knowingly conspiring (1) to organize as the Communist Party of the United States of America a society, group and assembly of persons who teach and advocate the overthrow and destruction of the Government of the United States by force and violence, and (2) knowingly and wilfully to advocate and teach the duty and necessity of overthrowing and destroying the Government of the United States by force and violence. The indictment further alleged that sec. 2 of the Smith Act proscribes these acts and that any conspiracy to take such action is a violation of sec. 3 of the Act.

The trial of the case extended over nine months, six of which were devoted to the taking of evidence, resulting in a record of 16,000 pages. Our limited grant of the writ of certiorari has removed from our consideration any question as to the sufficiency of the evidence. . . . Whether on this record petitioners did in fact advocate the overthrow of the Government by force and violence is not before us, and we must base any discussion of this point upon the conclusions stated in the opinion of the Court of Appeals, which treated the issue in great detail. That court held that the record in this case amply supports the necessary finding of the jury that petitioners, the leaders of the Communist Party in this country, were unwilling to work within our framework of democracy, but intended to initiate a violent revolution whenever the propitious occasion appeared. . . .

The obvious purpose of the statute is to protect existing Government, not from change by peaceable, lawful and constitutional means, but from change by violence, revolution and terrorism. That it is within the power of the Congress to protect the Government of the United States from armed rebellion is a proposition which requires little discussion. . . . The question with which we are concerned here is not whether Congress has such power, but whether the means which it has employed conflict with the First and Fifth Amendments to the Constitution.

[Petitioners attack the statute as invalid because] it prohibits academic discussion of the merits of Marxism-Leninism, . . . stifles ideas and is contrary to all concepts of a free speech and a free press. . . .

The very language of the Smith Act negates the interpretation which petitioners would have us impose on that Act. It is directed at advocacy, not discussion. Thus, the trial judge properly charged the jury that they could not convict if they found that petitioners did "no more than pursue peaceful studies and discussions or teaching and advocacy in the realm of ideas." He further charged that it was not unlawful "to conduct in an American college and university a course explaining the philosophical theories set forth in the books which have been placed in evidence." Such a charge is in strict accord with the statutory language, and illustrates the meaning to be placed on those words....But [the statute's]...application in this case has resulted in convictions for the teaching and advocacy of the overthrow of the Government by force and violence, which, even though coupled with the intent to accomplish that overthrow, contains an element of speech. For this reason, we must pay special heed to the demands of the First Amendment. . . .

The rule we deduce from [previous] cases is that where an offense is specified by a statute in nonspeech or nonpress terms, a conviction relying upon speech or press as evidence of violation may be sustained only when the speech or publication created a "clear and present danger" of attempting or accomplishing the prohibited crime, e.g., interference with enlistment. . . .

[In *Gitlow* and *Whitney,*] a legislature had found that a certain kind of speech was, itself, harmful and unlawful. The constitutionality of such a state statute had to be adjudged by this Court just as it determined the constitutionality of any state statute, namely, whether the statute was "reasonable." . . . Justices Holmes and Brandeis refused to accept this approach, but insisted that wherever speech was the evidence of the violation, it was necessary to show that the speech created the "clear and present danger" of the substantive evil which the legislature had the right to prevent. . . .

Although no case subsequent to *Whitney* and *Gitlow* has expressly overruled the majority opinions in those cases, there is little doubt that subsequent opinions have inclined toward the Holmes-Brandeis rationale. . . . [But] neither Justice Holmes nor Justice Brandeis ever envisioned that a shorthand phrase should be crystallized into a rigid rule to be applied inflexibly without regard to the circumstances of each case. . . .

In this case we are squarely presented with the application of the "clear and present danger" test, and must decide what that phrase imports. . . .

Obviously, the words cannot mean that before the Government may act, it must wait until the putsch is about to be executed, the plans have been laid and the signal is awaited. If Government is aware that a group aiming at its overthrow is attempting to indoctrinate its members and to commit them to a course whereby they will strike when the leaders feel the circumstances permit, action by the Government is required. . . .

Certainly an attempt to overthrow the Government by force, even though doomed from the outset because of inadequate numbers or power of the revolutionists, is a sufficient evil for Congress to prevent. . . . In the instant case the trial judge charged the jury that they could not convict unless they found that petitioners intended to overthrow the Government "as speedily as circumstances would permit." This does not mean, and could not properly mean, that they would not strike until there was certainty of success. What was meant was that the revolutionists would strike when they thought the time was ripe. . . .

Chief Judge Learned Hand, writing for the majority below, interpreted the phrase as follows: "In each case (courts) must ask whether the gravity of the "evil," discounted by its improbability, justifies such invasion of free speech as is necessary to avoid the danger." We adopt this statement of the rule. . . .

Likewise, we are in accord with the court below, which affirmed the trial court's finding that the requisite danger existed. The mere fact that from the period 1945 to 1948 petitioners' activities did not result in an attempt to overthrow the Government by force and violence is of course no answer to the fact that there was a group that was ready to make the attempt. The formation by petitioners of such a highly organized conspiracy, with rigidly disciplined members subject to call when the leaders, these petitioners, felt that the time had come for action, coupled with the inflammable nature of world conditions, similar uprisings in other countries, and the touch-and-go nature of our relations with countries with whom petitioners were in the very least ideologically attuned, convince us that their convictions were justified on this score. And this analysis disposes of the contention that a conspiracy to advocate, as distinguished from the advocacy itself, cannot be constitutionally restrained, because it comprises only the preparation. It is the existence of the conspiracy which creates the danger. . . .

Affirmed.

Mr. Justice CLARK took no part in the consideration or decision of this case.

Mr. Justice FRANKFURTER, concurring in affirmance of the judgment.

. . . The demands of free speech in a democratic society as well as the interest in national security are better served by candid and informed weighing of the competing interests, within the confines of the judicial process, than by announcing dogmas too inflexible for the non-Euclidian problems to be solved.

But how are competing interests to be assessed? . . . Full responsibility for the choice cannot be given to the courts. Courts are not representative bodies. They are not designed to be a good reflex of a democratic society. Their judgment is best informed, and therefore most dependable, within narrow limits. Their essential quality is detachment, founded on independence. History teaches that the independence of the judiciary is jeopardized when courts become embroiled in the passions of the day and assume primary responsibility in choosing between competing political, economic and social pressures.

Primary responsibility for adjusting the interests which compete in the situation before us of necessity belongs to the Congress. The nature of the power to be exercised by this Court has been delineated in decisions not charged with the emotional appeal of situations such as that now before us. We are to set aside the judgment of those whose duty it is to legislate only if there is no reasonable basis for it. . . .

Free-speech cases are not an exception to the principle that we are not legislators, that direct policy-making is not our province. How best to reconcile competing interests is the business of legislatures, and the balance they strike is a judgment not to be displaced by ours, but to be respected unless outside the pale of fair judgment. . . .

Mr. Justice JACKSON, concurring.

. . . The Communist Party . . . does not seek its strength primarily in numbers. Its aim is a relatively small party whose strength is in selected, dedicated, indoctrinated, and rigidly disciplined members. . . . Their strategy of stealth precludes premature or uncoordinated outbursts of violence, except, of course, when the blame will be placed on shoulders other than their own. . . . [E]ither by accident or design, the Communist stratagem outwits the anti-anarchist pattern of statute aimed against "overthrow by force and violence" if qualified by the doctrine that only "clear and present danger" of accomplishing that result will sustain the prosecution.

I would save [the clear and present danger test], unmodified, for application as a "rule of reason" in the kind of case for which it was devised. When the issue is criminality of a hot-headed speech on a street corner, or circulation of a few incendiary pamphlets, or parading by some zealots behind a red flag, or refusal of a handful of school children to salute our flag, it is not beyond the capacity of the judicial process to gather, comprehend, and weigh the necessary materials for decision whether it is a clear and present danger of substantive evil or a harmless letting off of steam. . . . [But unless] we are to hold our Government captive in a judge-made verbal trap, we must approach the problem of a well-organized, nation-wide conspiracy, such as I have described, as realistically as our predecessors faced the trivialities that were being prosecuted until they were checked with a rule of reason. . . .

Mr. Justice BLACK, dissenting.

. . . At the outset I want to emphasize what the crime involved in this case is, and what it is not. These petitioners were not charged with an attempt to overthrow the Government. They were not charged with overt acts of any kind designed to overthrow the Government. They were not even charged with saying anything or writing anything designed to overthrow the Government. The charge was that they agreed to assemble and to talk and publish certain ideas at a later date: The indictment is that they conspired to organize the Communist Party and to use speech or newspapers and other publications in the future to teach and advocate the forcible overthrow of the Government. No matter how it is worded, this is a virulent form of prior censorship of speech and press, which I believe the First Amendment forbids. I would hold sec. 3 of the Smith Act authorizing this prior restraint unconstitutional on its face and as applied.

. . . [T]he other opinions in this case show that the only way to affirm these convictions is to repudiate directly or indirectly the established "clear and present danger" rule. This the Court does in a way which greatly restricts the protections afforded by the First Amendment. The opinions for affirmance indicate that the chief reason for jettisoning the rule is the expressed fear that advocacy of Communist doctrine endangers the safety of the Republic. Undoubtedly, a governmental policy of unfettered communication of ideas does entail dangers. To the Founders of this Nation, however, the benefits derived from free expression were worth the risk. . . .

Public opinion being what it now is, few will protest the conviction of these Communist petitioners. There is hope, however, that in calmer times, when present pressures, passions and fears subside, this or some later Court will restore the First Amendment liberties to the high preferred place where they belong in a free society.

Mr. Justice DOUGLAS, dissenting.

. . . So far as the present record is concerned, what petitioners did was to organize people to teach and themselves teach the Marxist-Leninist doctrine contained chiefly in four books:[3] *Foundations of Leninism* by Stalin (1924); *The Communist Manifesto* by Marx and Engels (1848); *State and Revolution* by Lenin (1917); *History of the Communist Party of the Soviet Union* (B.) (1939). . . .

The opinion of the Court does not outlaw these texts nor condemn them to the fire, as the Communists do literature offensive to their creed. But if the books themselves are not outlawed, if they can lawfully remain on library shelves, by what reasoning does their use in a classroom become a crime? It would not be a crime under the Act to introduce these books to a class, though that would be teaching what the creed of violent overthrow of the Government is. The Act, as construed, requires the element of intent—that those who teach the creed believe in it. The crime then depends not on what is taught but on who the teacher is. That is to make freedom of speech turn not on what is said, but on the intent with which it is said. Once we start down that road we enter territory dangerous to the liberties of every citizen. . . .

. . . The Court, however . . . says, "The formation by petitioners of such a highly organized conspiracy, with rigidly disciplined members subject to call when the leaders, these petitioners, felt that the time had come for action, coupled with the inflammable nature of world conditions,. . . convince us that their convictions were justified on this score."

That ruling is in my view not responsive to the issue in the case. We might as well say that the speech of petitioners is outlawed because Soviet Russia and her Red Army are a threat to world peace. The nature of Communism as a force on the world scene would, of course, be relevant to the issue of clear and present danger of petitioners' advocacy within the United States. But the primary consideration is the

---

[3] Other books taught were *Problems of Leninism* by Stalin, *Strategy and Tactics of World Communism* (H.R. Doc. No. 619, 80th Cong., 2d Sess.), and *Program of the Communist International.*

strength and tactical position of petitioners and their converts in this country. On that there is no evidence in the record. . . .

How it can be said that there is a clear and present danger that this advocacy will succeed is, therefore, a mystery. [In] America, [Communists] are miserable merchants of unwanted ideas; their wares remain unsold. The fact that their ideas are abhorrent does not make them powerful.

The political impotence of the Communists in this country does not, of course, dispose of the problem. Their numbers; their positions in industry and government; the extent to which they have in fact infiltrated the police, the armed services, transportation, stevedoring, power plants, munitions works, and other critical places—these facts all bear on the likelihood that their advocacy of the Soviet theory of revolution will endanger the Republic. But the record is silent on these facts. If we are to proceed on the basis of judicial notice, it is impossible for me to say that the Communists in this country are so potent or so strategically deployed that they must be suppressed for their speech. . . . Only those held by fear and panic could think otherwise. . . .

NOTES AND QUESTIONS

1. *Clear and present danger in* Dennis. How is the *Dennis* plurality's application of the "clear and present danger" test different from the Holmes/Brandeis version that had evolved in the previous decades? Why would Vinson announce such a dramatically different test while reaffirming the role of the "clear and present danger" test in free speech doctrine?

2. *Critique of the "clear and present danger" standard.* Does the Court's treatment of the "clear and present danger" test suggest much of what is wrong with it? Consider the following:

> The amorphous balancing required in the clear and present danger test made it particularly susceptible to [skewing]. . . . Even in its most protective form, the test does little more than restate a generalized definition of risk analysis requiring courts to assess the likelihood that speech will cause a particular event. Such a test is no guard against overestimation of an event's probability, especially one that supposedly involved violent overthrow of the government, an evil that was "as great as could be imagined." In fact, given what psychologists know about human nature, one could have predicted that some of the *Dennis* judges would overreact to the alleged dangerousness of the CPUSA when applying the clear and present danger test.

Christina E. Wells, *Fear and Loathing in Constitutional Decision-Making,* 2005 Wis. L. Rev. 115, 201-202. Can we alter the standard to avoid these problems?

3. *Judicial deference in times of crisis.* If judges are no better than anyone else at estimating the possible harms of speech during times of crisis, should they simply defer to government officials' because officials are better placed to make decisions regarding security? *See, e.g.*, William H. Rehnquist, *All the Laws But One: Civil Liberties in Wartime* 205 (1998). Or, to the contrary, should judges craft rigid legal rules that can withstand those periods of pathology? *See* Vincent

4. Blasi, *The Pathological Perspective and the First Amendment*, 85 Colum. L. Rev. 449, 474 (1985).

5. *The aftermath of* Dennis. In the years following *Dennis*, the federal government charged at least 126 Communists with violating the Smith Act. Most of these lesser CPUSA leaders were convicted, with their convictions affirmed by appellate courts. The Supreme Court was largely uninvolved in these cases. During this period, however, many of the events that led to anti-Communist sentiment in the 1940s and early 1950s began to reverse themselves. The Korean War ended. Tensions with the Soviet Union eased after Joseph Stalin's death. And Joseph McCarthy, the charismatic crusader against domestic Communism, had been disgraced. In this atmosphere of somewhat lessening tension, the Supreme Court decided two important cases involving CPUSA leaders.

    a. *Yates v. United States*, 354 U.S. 298 (1957): *Yates* involved the Smith Act convictions of 14 lesser leaders of the CPUSA for conspiracy to advocate overthrow of the government. The government's case in *Yates* proceeded along the same lines as *Dennis*. In fact, the charges and evidence in both cases were so similar that Justice Clark characterized the *Yates* defendants as "engaged in this conspiracy with the defendants in *Dennis*" and as having "served in the same army." 354 U.S. at 344-345 (Clark, J., dissenting). The *Yates* Court, however, *reversed* the defendants' convictions. Justice Harlan, writing for the majority, interpreted the Smith Act as prohibiting only incitement of violence and not "advocacy and teaching of forcible overthrow as an abstract principle divorced from any effort to instigate action to that end." 354 U.S. at 318. He concluded that the lower court's jury instructions did not adequately make that distinction. He also characterized *Dennis*'s essential holding as being "that indoctrination of a group in preparation for future violent action" and exhortation to immediate forcible overthrow is not protected when a "group is of sufficient size and cohesiveness, is sufficiently oriented towards action, and other circumstances are such" that they reasonably justify apprehension that the action will occur. *Id.* at 321. Like Justice Douglas in *Dennis*, Justice Harlan found the evidence of defendant's "advocacy of action" insufficient to sustain the convictions on that rationale, describing it as "almost completely overshadowed by the hundreds of instances in the record in which overthrow, if mentioned at all, occurs in the course of doctrinal disputation so remote from action as to be almost wholly lacking in probative value." *Id.* at 327-331.

        Did Justice Harlan merely interpret *Dennis,* or did he divert the doctrine in a different direction? *See* Gerald Gunther, *Learned Hand and the Origins of Modern First Amendment Doctrine: Some Fragments of History*, 27 Stan. L. Rev. 719, 753 (1975).

    b. *Scales v. United States*, 367 U.S. 203 (1961): In *Scales*, the defendant was prosecuted for violating the membership clause of the Smith Act, which criminalized knowingly being a member in an organization that advocated the violent overthrow of the United States. The defendant argued that the clause violated his right of association under the First Amendment. The Court rejected the defendant's challenge:

        It is, of course, true that quasi-political parties or other groups that may embrace both legal and illegal aims differ from a technical conspiracy, which is defined by its criminal purpose, so that all knowing association with the conspiracy is a proper subject for criminal proscription as far as First Amendment liberties are concerned. If there were a similar blanket prohibition of association with a group having both legal and illegal aims, there would indeed be a real danger that legitimate political expression or association would be impaired, but the membership clause, as here construed...does not make criminal all association with an organization which has been shown to engage in illegal advocacy. There must be clear proof that a defendant "specifically intend(s) to accomplish (the aims of the organization) by resort to violence." Thus the member for whom the organization is a vehicle for the advancement of legitimate aims and policies does not fall within the ban of the statute: he lacks the requisite specific intent "to bring about the overthrow of the government as speedily as circumstances would permit." Such a person may be foolish, deluded, or perhaps merely optimistic, but he is not by this statute made a criminal.

367 U.S. at 229-230. The Court upheld defendant's conviction based upon evidence that he was an active leader in the CPUSA, and engaged in such activities as indoctrinating new members in the inevitability and desirability of the eventual violent overthrow of the government and in training them in specific techniques to use in possibly violent situations, such as a picket line. Justices Black, Douglas, and Brennan dissented. Justice Douglas argued that

There is here no charge of conspiracy, no charge of any overt act to overthrow the Government by force and violence, no charge of any other criminal act. The charge is being a "member" of the Communist Party, "well-knowing" that it advocated the overthrow of the Government by force and violence, "said defendant intending to bring about such overthrow by force and violence as speedily as circumstances would permit." That falls far short of a charge of conspiracy. Conspiracy rests not in intention alone but in an agreement with one or more others to promote an unlawful project. No charge of any kind or sort of agreement hitherto embraced in the concept of a conspiracy is made here. . . . We legalize today guilt by association, sending a man to prison when he committed no unlawful act. . . . The case is not saved by showing that petitioner was an active member. None of the activity constitutes a crime.

Id. at 263-264 (Douglas, J., dissenting). Is the majority's approach to freedom of association in *Scales* markedly better than the approach in *Whitney*?

6. Scales *and civil liability.* The Court later relied *on Scales* to hold that "[c]ivil liability may not be imposed merely because an individual belonged to a group, some members of which committed acts of violence." NAACP v. Claiborne Hardware Co., 458 U.S. 886, 920 (1982). Accordingly, the Court reversed the imposition of a large damage award on the NAACP and individuals for boycotting businesses in Claiborne County, Mississippi, although there was evidence of violence and possibly threatening behavior as part of the boycott. As in *Scales*, the Court noted that "[f]or liability to be imposed by reason of association alone, it is necessary to establish that the group itself possessed unlawful goals and that the individual held a specific intent to further those illegal aims." *Id.* The Court also noted that this intent must be judged "'according to the strictest law,'" for "'otherwise there is a danger that one in

sympathy with the legitimate aims of such an organization, but not specifically intending to accomplish them by resort to violence, might be punished for his adherence to lawful and constitutionally protected purposes, because of other and unprotected purposes which he does not necessarily share.'" *Id.* (quoting *Noto v. United States,* 367 U.S. 290 (1961)).

D. THE MODERN DOCTRINE

BRANDENBURG v. OHIO

395 U.S. 444 (1969)

PER CURIAM.

The appellant, a leader of a Ku Klux Klan group, was convicted under the Ohio Criminal Syndicalism statute for "advocat(ing) . . . the duty, necessity, or propriety of crime, sabotage, violence, or unlawful methods of terrorism as a means of accomplishing industrial or political reform" and for "voluntarily assembl(ing) with any society, group, or assemblage of persons formed to teach or advocate the doctrines of criminal syndicalism." . . . He was fined $1,000 and sentenced to one to 10 years' imprisonment. . . .

The record shows that a man, identified at trial as the appellant, telephoned an announcer-reporter on the staff of a Cincinnati television station and invited him to come to a Ku Klux Klan "rally" to be held at a farm in Hamilton County. With the cooperation of the organizers, the reporter and a cameraman attended the meeting and filmed the events. Portions of the films were later broadcast on the local station and on a national network. . . .

One film showed 12 hooded figures, some of whom carried firearms. They were gathered around a large wooden cross, which they burned. No one was present other than the participants and the newsmen who made the film. Most of the words uttered during the scene were incomprehensible when the film was projected, but scattered phrases could be understood that were derogatory of Negroes and, in one instance, of Jews. Another scene on the same film showed the appellant, in Klan regalia, making a speech. The speech, in full, was as follows:

> This is an organizers' meeting. We have had quite a few members here today which are—we have hundreds, hundreds of members throughout the State of Ohio. I can quote from a newspaper clipping from the Columbus, Ohio Dispatch, five weeks ago Sunday morning. The Klan has more members in the State of Ohio than does any other organization. We're not a revengent organization, but if our President, our Congress, our Supreme Court, continues to suppress the white, Caucasian race, it's possible that there might have to be some revengeance taken.

> We are marching on Congress July the Fourth, four hundred thousand strong. From there we are dividing into two groups, one group to march on St. Augustine, Florida, the other group to march into Mississippi. Thank you.

The second film showed six hooded figures one of whom, later identified as the appellant, repeated a speech very similar to that recorded on the first film. The reference to the possibility of "revengeance" was omitted, and one sentence was added: "Personally, I believe the nigger should be returned to Africa, the Jew returned to Israel." Though some of the figures in the films carried weapons, the speaker did not. The Ohio Criminal Syndicalism Statute was enacted in 1919. From 1917 to 1920, identical or quite similar laws were adopted by 20 States and two territories. . . . In 1927, this Court sustained the constitutionality of California's Criminal Syndicalism Act, . . . the text of which is quite similar to that of the laws of Ohio. *Whitney.* The Court upheld the statute on the ground that, without more, "advocating" violent means to effect political and economic change involves such danger to the security of the State that the State may outlaw it. . . . But *Whitney* has been thoroughly discredited by later decisions. *See Dennis.* These later decisions have fashioned the principle that the constitutional guarantees of free speech and free press do not permit a State to forbid or proscribe advocacy of the use of force or of law violation except where such advocacy is directed to inciting or producing imminent lawless action and is likely to incite or produce such action.[2] As we said in *Noto v. United States*, 367 U.S. 290, 297 (1961), "the mere abstract teaching . . . of the moral propriety or even moral necessity for a resort to force and violence, is not the same as preparing a group for violent action and steeling it to such action." . . . A statute which fails to draw this distinction impermissibly intrudes upon the freedoms guaranteed by the First and Fourteenth Amendments. It sweeps within its condemnation speech which our Constitution has immunized from governmental control. Cf. *Yates.* Measured by this test, Ohio's Criminal Syndicalism Act cannot be sustained. The Act punishes persons who "advocate or teach the duty, necessity, or propriety" of violence "as a means of accomplishing industrial or political reform"; or who publish or circulate or display any book or paper containing such advocacy; or who "justify" the commission of violent acts "with intent to exemplify, spread or advocate the propriety of the doctrines of criminal syndicalism"; or who "voluntarily assemble" with a group formed "to teach or advocate the doctrines of criminal syndicalism." Neither the indictment nor the trial judge's instructions to the jury in any way refined the statute's bald definition of the crime in terms of mere advocacy not distinguished from incitement to imminent lawless action.

Accordingly, we are here confronted with a statute which, by its own words and as applied, purports to punish mere advocacy and to forbid, on pain of criminal punishment, assembly with others merely to advocate the described type of action. Such a statute falls within the condemnation of the First and Fourteenth Amendments. The contrary teaching of *Whitney v. California* cannot be supported, and that decision is therefore overruled.

Mr. Justice BLACK, concurring.

I agree with the views expressed by Mr. Justice Douglas in his concurring opinion in this case that the "clear and present danger" doctrine should have no place in the interpretation of the First Amendment. I join the Court's opinion, which, as I understand it, simply cites [*Dennis*] but does not indicate any agreement on the

---

[2] It was on the theory that the Smith Act embodied such a principle and that it had been applied only in conformity with it that this Court sustained the Act's constitutionality. *Dennis.* That this was the basis for *Dennis* was emphasized in *Yates*, in which the Court overturned convictions for advocacy of the forcible overthrow of the Government under the Smith Act, because the trial judge's instructions had allowed conviction for mere advocacy, unrelated to its tendency to produce forcible action.

Court's part with the "clear and present danger" doctrine on which *Dennis* purported to rely.

Mr. Justice DOUGLAS, concurring.

. . . I see no place in the regime of the First Amendment for any "clear and present danger" test, whether strict and tight as some would make it, or free-wheeling as the Court in *Dennis* rephrased it.

When one reads [past] opinions closely and sees when and how the "clear and present danger" test has been applied, great misgivings are aroused. First, the threats were often loud but always puny and made serious only by judges so wedded to the status quo that critical analysis made them nervous. Second, the test was so twisted and perverted in *Dennis* as to make the trial of those teachers of Marxism an all-out political trial which was part and parcel of the cold war that has eroded substantial parts of the First Amendment. . . .

The line between what is permissible and not subject to control and what may be made impermissible and subject to regulation is the line between ideas and overt acts. The example usually given by those who would punish speech is the case of one who falsely shouts fire in a crowded theatre.

This is, however, a classic case where speech is brigaded with action. They are indeed inseparable and a prosecution can be launched for the overt acts actually caused. Apart from rare instances of that kind, speech is, I think, immune from prosecution. Certainly there is no constitutional line between advocacy of abstract ideas as in *Yates* and advocacy of political action as in *Scales*. The quality of advocacy turns on the depth of the conviction; and government has no power to invade that sanctuary of belief and conscience.

NOTES AND QUESTIONS

1. Brandenburg*'s aftermath.* The Court reaffirmed *Brandenburg* in Hess v. Indiana, 414 U.S. 105 (1973), a case involving anti-war protestors during the Vietnam War. During an anti-war demonstration at which about 100 protestors blocked the streets, defendant shouted, "[w]e'll take the fucking streets later (or again)." The Court reversed the conviction, stating that "[a]t best, [the] statement could be taken as counsel for present moderation; at worst, it amounted to nothing more than advocacy of illegal action at some indefinite future time. . . . [S]ince there was no evidence, or rational inference from the import of the language, that [defendant's] words were intended to produce, and likely to produce, imminent disorder, those words could not be punished by the State on the ground that they had 'a tendency to lead to violence.'" *Id.* at 108-109.

2. Brandenburg*'s protectiveness.* The *Brandenburg* test seems to combine both the "clear and present danger" test's focus on likelihood of harm and Judge Hand's approach in *Masses* requiring express incitement, ultimately resulting in the most speech-protective version of the "clear and present danger" test announced thus far. What is it about this version of the test that results in greater protection for speech? *See, e.g.,* Vincent Blasi, *Reading Holmes Through the Lens of Schauer: The Abrams Dissent,* 72 Notre Dame L. Rev. 1343, 1358-1359 (1997); Christina E. Wells, *Fear and Loathing in Constitutional Decision-Making,* 2005 Wis. L. Rev. 115, 206.

3. Brandenburg's "reliance" on precedent. Is *Brandenburg* really true to the post-*Whitney* cases that it claims "fashioned the principle" it announced? Can *Dennis*, even as read through the lens of *Yates*, be stretched to support the standard announced in *Brandenburg*?

4. Brandenburg *and line drawing.* Does Brandenburg draw the appropriate lines?

   a. Is *Brandenburg* overprotective of the clever speaker who, like Marc Antony's eulogy to Julius Caesar, masks his or her words of incitement in seemingly innocent words? *See* David Crump, *Camouflaged Incitement: Freedom of Speech, Communicative Torts, and the Borderland of the* Brandenburg *Test*, 29 Ga. L. Rev. 1 (1994).

   b. Is *Brandenburg* underprotective of speech, as Justice Douglas's concurrence intimates, because "what is permissible and not subject to control and what may be made impermissible and subject to regulation is the line between ideas and overt acts . . ."?

5. *Extending* Brandenburg *beyond advocacy. Brandenburg* is the Supreme Court's attempt to separate protected political advocacy from speech that crosses the line into the area of "unprotected" incitement of illegal activity. To what extent should courts extend *Brandenburg*'s standard to expression that is not political advocacy but that might cause harm, such as entertainment or speech that provides information? Scholars disagree profoundly on this issue. For discussion, see Kent Greenawalt, *Speech, Crime, and the Uses of Language* (1989); Rodney A. Smolla, *Should the Brandenburg v. Ohio Incitement Test Apply in Media Violence Tort Cases?*, 27 N. Ky. L. Rev. 1 (2000); S. Elizabeth Wilborn Malloy & Ronald J. Krotoszynski, Jr., *Recalibrating the Cost of Harm Advocacy: Getting Beyond Brandenburg*, 41 Wm. & Mary L. Rev. 1159 (2000); David A. Anderson, *Incitement and Tort Law*, 37 Wake Forest L. Rev. 957 (2002); Eugene Volokh, *Crime-Facilitating Speech*, 57 Stan. L. Rev. 1095 (2005). Consider the following problems in light of these questions.

THEORY-APPLIED PROBLEMS

1. *Entertainment and "incited" suicide.* As part of a series about the pleasures and dangers of unusual and taboo sexual practices, *Hustler Magazine* printed "Orgasm of Death," an article discussing the practice of autoerotic asphyxia. This practice entails masturbation while "hanging" oneself in order to temporarily cut off the blood supply to the brain at the moment of orgasm. The article included details about how the act is performed and the kind of physical pleasure those who engage in it seek to achieve. The heading identified "Orgasm of Death" as part of a series on "Sexplay," discussions of "sexual pleasures [that] have remained hidden for too long behind the doors of fear, ignorance, inexperience and hypocrisy" and are presented "to increase [readers'] sexual knowledge, to lessen [their] inhibitions and—ultimately—to make [them] much better lover[s]."

   An editor's note, positioned on the page so that it was likely to be the first text the reader will read, stated: "Hustler emphasizes the often-fatal dangers of the practice of 'auto-erotic asphyxia,' and recommends that readers seeking unique forms of sexual release DO NOT ATTEMPT this method. The facts are presented here solely for an educational purpose." The magazine further had a lengthy discussion of the dangers of autoerotic asphyxiation and statistics regarding the number of people who die each year as a result of the practice.

A 14-year-old boy was found hanging in his closet with a copy of the *Hustler Magazine* article at his feet. The boy's mother sued *Hustler Magazine* for inciting the suicide and sought civil damages. For more information, see Herceg v. Hustler Magazine, 814 F.2d 1017 (5th Cir. 1987).

Does imposition of liability satisfy the requirements of *Brandenburg*? Should *Brandenburg* be applied at all? Should we alter *Brandenburg* in this context?

2. *"How-to" manuals.* Paladin Enterprises published a book, *Hitman: A Technical Manual for Independent Contractors*, which gave explicit and detailed instructions on how to solicit, prepare for, and commit murders (at least 130 pages of this information) without being caught. Several months after the book's publication, James Perry brutally murdered a woman and her two children. Perry was solicited to do so by the victims' husband/father. In carrying out the killings, Perry meticulously followed the directions in the book *Hitman*, which was found in his apartment at the time of his arrest. The estate of the victims sued Paladin Enterprises, the publisher of the book, for wrongful death, alleging that the publisher aided and abetted Perry in the murders. For more information, see Rice v. Paladin Enterprises, 128 F.3d 233 (4th Cir. 1997).

Should the First Amendment be a defense to this lawsuit? If so, should we alter *Brandenburg* in this context?

Compare the *"Hitman"* scenario to the following situation:

A website published an article on how to deceive fingerprint identification security systems. Ellen Gates, a member of an animal rights organization, used this information to bypass a security system at an animal testing lab and free the monkeys used for testing. This action caused substantial physical damage and monetary loss to the lab, which sued the website for damages (under an aiding and abetting theory similar to the Hitman lawsuit).

Same questions as above. Does your answer differ from that in *"Hitman"*? If so, why? Do differences in outcome suggest that we should apply *Brandenburg* differently or that one of these scenarios simply falls outside the boundaries of the First Amendment?

E. NATIONAL SECURITY RATIONALES POST-*BRANDENBURG*

Many view *Brandenburg* as an implicit rejection of the previous cases applying deferential versions of the "clear and present danger" test. *See, e.g.,* Harry Kalven, Jr., *A Worthy Tradition* 231, 234 (1988). But although *Brandenburg* is quite speech-protective, the Court did not overrule *Dennis*. In fact, it claimed *Dennis* and subsequent cases "fashioned the principle" that *Brandenburg* espoused. What does it mean that these two cases even theoretically coexist? Consider these questions when reading the next case.

HOLDER v. HUMANITARIAN LAW PROJECT

561 U.S. 1 (2010)

Chief Justice ROBERTS delivered the opinion of the Court.

Congress has prohibited the provision of "material support or resources" to certain foreign organizations that engage in terrorist activity. 18 U.S.C. § 2339B(a)(1). That prohibition is based on a finding that the specified organizations "are so tainted by their criminal conduct that any contribution to such an organization facilitates that conduct." [*See* 18 U.S.C. § 2339B (Findings and Purpose)]. The plaintiffs in this litigation seek to provide support to two such organizations. Plaintiffs claim that they seek to facilitate only the lawful, nonviolent purposes of those groups, and that applying the material-support law to prevent them from doing so violates the Constitution. . . .

I

This litigation concerns 18 U.S.C. § 2339B, which makes it a federal crime to "knowingly provid[e] material support or resources to a foreign terrorist organization." Congress has amended the definition of "material support or resources" periodically, but at present it is defined as follows:

> "[T]he term 'material support or resources' means any property, tangible or intangible, or service, including currency or monetary instruments or financial securities, financial services, lodging, training, expert advice or assistance, safehouses, false documentation or identification, communications equipment, facilities, weapons, lethal substances, explosives, personnel (1 or more individuals who may be or include oneself), and transportation, except medicine or religious materials." 18 U.S.C. § 2339A(b)(1).

The authority to designate an entity a "foreign terrorist organization" rests with the Secretary of State. 8 U.S.C. §§ 1189(a)(1), (d)(4). She may, in consultation with the Secretary of the Treasury and the Attorney General, so designate an organization upon finding that it is foreign, engages in "terrorist activity" or "terrorism," and thereby "threatens the security of United States nationals or the national security of the United States." §§ 1189(a)(1), (d)(4). "'[N]ational security' means the national defense, foreign relations, or economic interests of the United States." § 1189(d)(2). An entity designated a foreign terrorist organization may seek review of that designation before the D.C. Circuit within 30 days of that designation. § 1189(c)(1). . . .

[In 1977, the Secretary of State designated 30 groups as foreign terrorist organizations, including the Turkey's Kurdistan Workers' Party (PKK) and the Liberation Tigers of Tamil Eelam (LTTE) of Sri Lanka. Evidence was presented regarding both parties' political aims of creating independent states in their respective countries and of numerous, violent attacks by both parties, including attacks that harmed Americans. Individual U.S. citizens and domestic organizations, [including] the Humanitarian Law Project (HLP) (a human rights organization with consultative status to the United Nations), filed a lawsuit in federal court claiming that they wanted to provide support for the humanitarian and political activities of the PKK and LTTE in the form of monetary contributions, other tangible aid, legal training, and political advocacy, but that they could not do so for fear of prosecution under § 2339B.]

III

Plaintiffs claim . . . that we should interpret the material-support statute, when applied to speech, to require proof that a defendant intended to further a foreign terrorist organization's illegal activities. . . . We reject plaintiffs' interpretation of § 2339B because it is inconsistent with the text of the statute. . . . Congress plainly spoke to the necessary mental state for a violation of § 2339B, and it chose knowledge about the organization's connection to terrorism, not specific intent to further the organization's terrorist activities. . . .

Scales v. United States, 367 U.S. 203, 211 (1961), . . . is readily distinguishable. That case involved the Smith Act, which prohibited membership in a group advocating the violent overthrow of the government. The Court held that a person could not be convicted under the statute unless he had knowledge of the group's illegal advocacy and a specific intent to bring about violent overthrow. This action is different: Section 2339B does not criminalize mere membership in a designated foreign terrorist organization. It instead prohibits providing "material support" to such a group. Nothing about *Scales* suggests the need for a specific intent requirement in such a case. The Court in *Scales*, moreover, relied on both statutory text and precedent that had interpreted closely related provisions of the Smith Act to require specific intent. Plaintiffs point to nothing similar here. . . .

V

. . . Plaintiffs claim that Congress has banned their "pure political speech." It has not. Under the material-support statute, plaintiffs may say anything they wish on any topic. . . . As the Government states: "The statute does not prohibit independent advocacy or expression of any kind." Section 2339B also "does not prevent [plaintiffs] from becoming members of the PKK and LTTE or impose any sanction on them for doing so." Congress has not, therefore, sought to suppress ideas or opinions in the form of "pure political speech." Rather, Congress has prohibited "material support," which most often does not take the form of speech at all. And when it does, the statute is carefully drawn to cover only a narrow category of speech to, under the direction of, or in coordination with foreign groups that the speaker knows to be terrorist organizations. . . .

The Government, [however], is wrong that the only thing actually at issue in this litigation is conduct. . . . [Section] 2339B regulates speech on the basis of its content. Plaintiffs want to speak to the PKK and the LTTE, and whether they may do so under § 2339B depends on what they say. If plaintiffs' speech to those groups imparts a "specific skill" or communicates advice derived from "specialized knowledge"—for example, training on the use of international law or advice on petitioning the United Nations—then it is barred. . . . We accordingly applied more rigorous scrutiny. [The Court applied strict scrutiny, which requires that the government show that the law be necessary to meet a compelling interest.]* . . .

---

* See Chapter 3 for discussion of the Court's doctrine applying strict scrutiny to content-based regulations – EDS.

Everyone agrees that the Government's interest in combating terrorism is an urgent objective of the highest order. Plaintiffs' complaint is that the ban on material support, applied to what they wish to do, is not "necessary to further that interest." The objective of combating terrorism does not justify prohibiting their speech, plaintiffs argue, because their support will advance only the legitimate activities of the designated terrorist organizations, not their terrorism.

Whether foreign terrorist organizations meaningfully segregate support of their legitimate activities from support of terrorism is an empirical question. When it enacted § 2339B in 1996, Congress made specific findings regarding the serious threat posed by international terrorism. One of those findings explicitly rejects plaintiffs' contention that their support would not further the terrorist activities of the PKK and LTTE: "[F]oreign organizations that engage in terrorist activity are so tainted by their criminal conduct that *any contribution to such an organization facilitates that conduct.*" § 301(a)(7) (emphasis added). . . .

Material support meant to "promot[e] peaceable, lawful conduct" can further terrorism by foreign groups in multiple ways. . . . Such support frees up other resources within the organization that may be put to violent ends. It also importantly helps lend legitimacy to foreign terrorist groups—legitimacy that makes it easier for those groups to persist, to recruit members, and to raise funds all of which facilitate more terrorist attacks. . . . Providing foreign terrorist groups with material support in any form also furthers terrorism by straining the United States' relationships with its allies and undermining cooperative efforts between nations to prevent terrorist attacks. . . .

Our precedents, old and new, make clear that concerns of national security and foreign relations do not warrant abdication of the judicial role. We do not defer to the Government's reading of the First Amendment, even when such interests are at stake. . . . But when it comes to collecting evidence and drawing factual inferences in this area, "the lack of competence on the part of the courts is marked" and respect for the Government's conclusions is appropriate. . . . The Government, when seeking to prevent imminent harms in the context of international affairs and national security, is not required to conclusively link all the pieces in the puzzle before we grant weight to its empirical conclusions. . . .

We turn to the particular speech plaintiffs propose to undertake. First, plaintiffs propose to "train members of [the] PKK on how to use humanitarian and international law to peacefully resolve disputes." Congress can, consistent with the First Amendment, prohibit this direct training. It is wholly foreseeable that the PKK could use the "specific skill[s]" that plaintiffs propose to impart as part of a broader strategy to promote terrorism. The PKK could, for example, pursue peaceful negotiation as a means of buying time to recover from short-term setbacks, lulling opponents into complacency, and ultimately preparing for renewed attacks. A foreign terrorist organization introduced to the structures of the international legal system might use the information to threaten, manipulate, and disrupt. This possibility is real, not remote.

Second, plaintiffs propose to "teach PKK members how to petition various representative bodies such as the United Nations for relief." The Government acts within First Amendment strictures in banning this proposed speech because it teaches the organization how to acquire "relief," which plaintiffs never define with any specificity, and which could readily include monetary aid. . . . Money is fungible and Congress logically concluded that money a terrorist group such as the PKK obtains using the techniques plaintiffs propose to teach could be redirected to funding the group's violent activities. . . .

All this is not to say that any future applications of the material-support statute to speech or advocacy will survive First Amendment scrutiny. It is also not to say that any other statute relating to speech and terrorism would satisfy the First Amendment. In particular, we in no way suggest that a regulation of independent speech would pass constitutional muster, even if the Government were to show that such speech benefits foreign terrorist organizations. We also do not suggest that Congress could extend the same prohibition on material support at issue here to domestic organizations. We simply hold that, in prohibiting the particular forms of support that plaintiffs seek to provide to foreign terrorist groups, § 2339B does not violate the freedom of speech. . . .

The judgment of the United States Court of Appeals for the Ninth Circuit is affirmed in part and reversed in part, and the cases are remanded for further proceedings consistent with this opinion.

It is so ordered.

Justice BREYER, with whom Justices GINSBURG and SOTOMAYOR join, dissenting.

. . . [The] Court has previously held that a person who associates with a group that uses unlawful means to achieve its ends does not thereby necessarily forfeit the First Amendment's protection for freedom of association. [*See Scales.*] Rather, . . ." [i]f the persons assembling have committed crimes elsewhere . . ., they may be prosecuted for their . . . violation of valid laws. But it is a different matter when the State, instead of prosecuting them for such offenses, seizes upon mere participation in a peaceable assembly and a lawful public discussion as the basis for a criminal charge." *DeJonge v. Oregon,* 299 U.S. 353 (1937).

Not even the "serious and deadly problem" of international terrorism can require *automatic* forfeiture of First Amendment rights. . . . If the statute is constitutional in this context, it would have to come with a strong justification attached. . . .

The Government does identify a compelling countervailing interest, namely, the interest in protecting the security of the United States and its nationals from the threats that foreign terrorist organizations pose by denying those organizations financial and other fungible resources. I do not dispute the importance of this interest. But I do dispute whether the interest can justify the statute's criminal prohibition. To put the matter more specifically, precisely how does application of the statute to the protected activities before us *help achieve* that important security-related end?

The Government makes two efforts to answer this question. *First,* the Government says that the plaintiffs' support for these organizations is "fungible" in the same sense as other forms of banned support. Being fungible, the plaintiffs' support could, for example, free up other resources, which the organization might put to terrorist ends.

The proposition that the two very different kinds of "support" are "fungible," however, is not *obviously* true. There is no *obvious* way in which undertaking advocacy for political change through peaceful means or teaching the PKK and LTTE, say, how to petition the United Nations for political change is fungible with other resources that might be put to more sinister ends in the way that donations of money, food, or computer training are fungible. . . .

The Government has provided us with no empirical information that might convincingly support this claim. Instead, the Government cites only to evidence that Congress was concerned about the "fungible" nature in general of resources, predominately money and material goods. . . . The most one can say in the Government's favor about these statements is that they *might* be read as offering highly general support for its argument. The statements do not, however, explain in any detail how the *plaintiffs'* political-advocacy-related activities might actually be "fungible" and therefore capable of being diverted to terrorist use. . . .

Second, the Government says that the plaintiffs' proposed activities will "bolste[r] a terrorist organization's efficacy and strength in a community" and "undermin[e] this nation's efforts to *delegitimize and weaken* those groups." . . . [W]ere the law to accept a "legitimating" effect, in and of itself and without qualification, as providing sufficient grounds for imposing such a ban, the First Amendment battle would be lost in untold instances where it should be won. . . . The argument applies as strongly to "independent" as to "coordinated" advocacy. . . .

Nor can the Government overcome these considerations simply by narrowing the covered activities to those that involve *coordinated*, rather than *independent*, advocacy. . . . I am not aware of any form of words that might be used to describe "coordination" that would not, at a minimum, seriously chill not only the kind of activities the plaintiffs raise before us, but also the "independent advocacy" the Government purports to permit. And, as for the Government's willingness to distinguish *independent* advocacy from *coordinated* advocacy, the former is *more* likely, not *less* likely, to confer legitimacy than the latter. [The] distinction "coordination" makes is arbitrary in respect to furthering the statute's purposes. . . .

In my own view, the majority's arguments stretch the concept of "fungibility" beyond constitutional limits. Neither Congress nor the Government advanced these particular hypothetical claims. I am not aware of any case in this Court—not [*Gitlow*], not [*Schenck*], not [*Abrams*], not the later Communist Party cases decided during the heat of the Cold War—in which the Court accepted anything like a claim that speech or teaching might be criminalized lest it, *e.g.,* buy negotiating time for an opponent who would put that time to bad use. . . .

I believe that a construction [of the statute] that would avoid the constitutional problem is "fairly possible." In particular, I would read the statute as criminalizing First-Amendment-protected pure speech and association only when the defendant knows or intends that those activities will assist the organization's unlawful terrorist actions. Under this reading, the Government would have to show, at a minimum, that such defendants provided support that they knew was significantly likely to help the organization pursue its unlawful terrorist aims. . . .

This reading of the statute protects those who engage in pure speech and association ordinarily protected by the First Amendment. But it does not protect that activity where a defendant purposefully intends it to help terrorism or where a defendant knows (or willfully blinds himself to the fact) that the activity is significantly likely to assist terrorism. . . . *Cf. Brandenburg.* At the same time, this reading does not require the Government to undertake the difficult task of proving which, as between peaceful and nonpeaceful purposes, a defendant specifically preferred; knowledge is enough. . . .

Having interpreted the statute to impose the *mens rea* requirement just described, I would remand the cases so that the lower courts could consider more specifically the precise activities in which the plaintiffs still wish to engage and determine whether and to what extent a grant of declaratory and injunctive relief were warranted. . . .

That is why, with respect, I dissent.

NOTES AND QUESTIONS

1. *National security redux.* The majority applied strict scrutiny, which it commonly uses for statutes that regulate speech based on its content. *See* Chapter 3, *infra.* Typically, that standard is quite rigorous, yet the majority here found that its requirements were met. Do you agree or does *Humanitarian Law Project* revive *Dennis*-style deference in national security cases? Should the majority have relied on *Brandenburg* or *Scales* as relevant precedents?
2. *Independent versus coordinated activities.* What is the difference between expressive activities "coordinated" with a designated terrorist organization as opposed to "independent" speech on an organization's behalf? Would a person operating a website that posted translated, pro-jihadist videos be "coordinating" with terrorist organizations? What if the website maintained links to pro-jihadist websites?
3. *Terrorism and the internet.* Some contemporary terrorist organizations use the internet to lure and radicalize American citizens. Does this argue in favor of laws outlawing access to websites encouraging support for ISIS even if they are "independent?" See Eric Posner, *Isis Gives Us No Choice But to Consider Limits on Speech*, Slate.com, Dec. 15, 2015, available at http://www.slate.com/articles/news_and_politics/view_from_chicago/2015/12/isis_s_online_radicaliz ation_efforts_present_an_unprecedented_danger.single.html.

THEORY-APPLIED PROBLEM

The Animal Enterprise Terrorism Act, 18 U.S.C. § 43, is a federal law that creates the following federal crime:

> (a) Offense.—Whoever travels in interstate or foreign commerce, or uses or causes to be used the mail or any facility of interstate or foreign commerce—
> (1) for the purpose of damaging or interfering with the operations of an animal enterprise; and
> (2) in connection with such purpose—
> (A) intentionally damages or causes the loss of any real or personal property (including animals or records) used by an animal enterprise [roughly defined as a commercial or academic enterprise that uses or sells animal products, or any zoo, aquarium, pet store or other lawful competitive animal event], or any real or personal property of a person or entity having a connection to, relationship with, or transactions with an animal enterprise; . . . or
> (C) conspires or attempts to do so;
> shall be punished [with the imposition of fines and/or a possible jail sentence].

Consider the statute as applied in the following situation: "Stop Animal Cruelty" ("SAC") is an organization devoted to halting animal cruelty. SAC recently targeted the activities of Animal Research Labs ("ARL"), which performs testing for companies that want to bring their products to market and specifically does so on animals (including rats, mice, and guinea pigs). SAC engages in a variety of actions, both legal and illegal, as part of their campaign to stop ARL's testing. These have included legal actions, such as political protests and leafleting, and illegal actions, such as physically assaulting researchers and burglarizing ARL's research labs.

SAC maintains a central website where it posts information and discussion of its protest activities. Thus, it posts informational items describing past protests, break-ins, and harassment of ARL workers. It also hosts discussion at this website about past, present, and future actions. Comments are posted by anyone who wants to log into the discussion group. Through its website, SAC also invites its supporters to engage in "electronic civil disobedience" against ARL and other companies associated with it. Electronic civil disobedience is a coordinated campaign by many people to inundate websites, e-mail servers, and the telephone service of a company. SAC sponsors electronic civil disobedience campaigns on the first Monday of every month. SAC reminds its supporters that electronic civil disobedience is illegal, so supporters should participate only if they "are prepared to suffer potentially severe consequences."

Recently, Anna posted a "bulletin" on SAC's website calling for "direct action" against the CEO of LifeCorp, Inc., a business that contracted with ARL to test its product. The call for action further noted that "First Monday approaches. Don't let these schmucks get away with this stuff." That same day, Bart commented in the website's discussion group stating, "I am excited to see someone finally paying attention to the plight of these poor animals. Keep up the good work!" On the first Monday of the next month, LifeCorp's computers were jammed for several hours with resulting damage approximating about $10,000.

Assume that none of the following actors participated in the acts of electronic civil disobedience but that they are members of SAC. Anna is arrested for violating the federal law as a result of her post on the website. Does she have a First Amendment defense? Bart is arrested for his comments in the discussion group on the website. Does he have a First Amendment defense? How do *Brandenberg*, *Scales*, and *Holder* direct your arguments?

CHAPTER
3

Content-Based Discrimination

TABLE OF CONTENTS

The last chapter reflects the Supreme Court's difficulty in establishing an acceptable test for punishing speech that incites illegal conduct. This line-drawing problem extends beyond incitement to other types of speech as well. One manner of dealing with these difficult line-drawing problems is for a court to create bright-line or categorical rules. Thus, a court might carve out a specific category of speech, such as incitement or threats, as "unprotected." A court could also view certain kinds of government regulations of speech as presumptively unconstitutional. Such categorical approaches arguably avoid ad hoc decision making by judges and juries who otherwise must make decisions pertaining to controversial speech without adequate guidelines. The Supreme Court has engaged in both categorical approaches, finding some speech to be "low value," and thus entitled to lesser or no First Amendment protection, and in finding that content-based regulations of "high-value" speech are presumptively suspicious. This chapter explores the Court's attempts to develop methodologies in these areas.

The first part of this chapter takes up the Court's attempt to construct categories of low-value speech beyond incitement. It examines three specific areas closely related to political speech—threats, fighting words, and hostile audience situations. (Other categories of low- or lesser-value speech, such as commercial speech, libel, and obscenity, appear later in the book in Chapters 7, 9, and 11.) The cases and questions in this section reflect the Court's willingness (or lack thereof) to identify certain speech as low value, and thus deserving of little or no First Amendment protection. They also reflect the difficulty in maintaining a strict definition of low-value categories and judges' continuing problems in identifying whether speech falls into a particular category. Finally, this section considers the extent to which the Court has developed a particular methodology for identifying low-value speech categories and/or whether the categories already mentioned comprise the sum total of the Court's low-value speech approach.

The second part of the chapter looks at the Court's jurisprudence regarding content-based regulations of high-value speech, which reflects the second of the categorical approaches. The Court has maintained that "content-based regulations are presumptively invalid." R.A.V. v. City of St. Paul, 505 U.S. 377 (1992). As a result, such regulations are subject to strict scrutiny, which requires the government to show a compelling interest and that regulations are necessary to meet that interest. It is generally quite difficult for the government to meet this burden. In contrast, content-neutral laws, which regulate speech but are not based upon the content of the expression, are judged by a more lenient, intermediate scrutiny standard. Content-neutral laws need only be narrowly drawn to meet a significant state interest and leave open ample alternatives of expression. *See, e.g.*, Turner Broad. Sys., Inc. v. FCC, 512 U.S. 622 (1994). As with categories of low-value speech, however, attempts to build broadly protective walls around speech by creating categories of disfavored regulations can raise difficult questions: Why does the Court disfavor content-based regulations of speech? How does one discern when a regulation is content-based? The cases and notes in this section reflect the Court's attempts to answer these questions.

As you read these materials, keep in mind the following: Does categorization work, or do categories eventually break down as judges find exceptions to bright-line rules? Is categorization a better approach than balancing societal and free speech interests against one another?

A.   DRAWING LINES BETWEEN PROTECTED AND UNPROTECTED SPEECH—CREATING CATEGORIES OF LOW-VALUE SPEECH

In Chaplinsky v. New Hampshire, 315 U.S. 568 (1942), *see infra* p. 85, the Supreme Court first announced the "two-level" theory of the First Amendment. According to the Court, "[t]here are certain well-defined and narrowly limited classes of speech, the prevention and punishment of which has never been thought to raise any Constitutional problem." The following materials represent select areas in which the Court has identified or rejected categories of low-value speech. As in the incitement cases, this material reflects the Court's particular difficulty in creating and maintaining categories of low-value speech.

1.   Speech That Threatens

WATTS v. UNITED STATES
394 U.S. 705 (1969)

PER CURIAM.

After a jury trial in the United States District Court for the District of Columbia, petitioner was convicted of violating a 1917 statute [18 U.S.C. § 871(a)] which prohibits any person from "knowingly and willfully . . . (making) any threat to take the life of or to inflict bodily harm upon the President of the United States. . . ." The incident which led to petitioner's arrest occurred on August 27, 1966, during a public rally on the Washington Monument grounds. The crowd present broke up into small discussion groups and petitioner joined a gathering scheduled to discuss police brutality. Most of those in the group were quite young, either in their teens or early twenties. Petitioner, who himself was 18 years old, entered into the discussion after one member of the group suggested that the young people present should get more education before expressing their views. According to an investigator for the Army Counter Intelligence Corps who was present, petitioner responded: "They always holler at us to get an education. And now I have already received my draft classification as 1-A and I have got to report for my physical this Monday coming. I am not going. If they ever make me carry a rifle the first man I want to get in my sights is L.B.J." "They are not going to make me kill my black brothers." On the basis of this statement, the jury found that petitioner had committed a felony by knowingly and willfully threatening the President. The United States Court of Appeals for the District of Columbia Circuit affirmed by a two-to-one vote. We reverse.

At the close of the Government's case, petitioner's trial counsel moved for a judgment of acquittal. He contended that there was "absolutely no evidence on the basis of which the jury would be entitled to find that (petitioner) made a threat against the life of the President." He stressed the fact that petitioner's statement was made during a political debate, that it was expressly made conditional upon an event—induction into the Armed Forces—which petitioner vowed would never occur, and that both petitioner and the crowd laughed after the statement was made. He concluded, "Now actually what happened here in all this was a kind of very crude offensive method of stating a political opposition to the President. What he was saying, he says, I don't want to shoot black people because I don't consider them my enemy, and if they put a rifle in my hand it is the people that put the rifle in my hand, as symbolized by the President, who are my real enemy." We hold that the trial judge erred in denying this motion.

Certainly the statute under which petitioner was convicted is constitutional on its face. The Nation undoubtedly has a valid, even an overwhelming, interest in protecting the safety of its Chief Executive and in allowing him to perform his duties without interference from threats of physical violence. Nevertheless, a statute such as this one, which makes criminal a form of pure speech, must be interpreted with the commands of the First Amendment clearly in mind. What is a threat must be distinguished from what is constitutionally protected speech.

The judges in the Court of Appeals differed over whether or not the "willfullness" requirement of the statute implied that a defendant must have intended to carry out his "threat." Some early cases found the willfullness requirement met if the speaker voluntarily uttered the charged words with "an apparent determination to carry them into execution." The majority below seemed to agree. Perhaps this interpretation is correct, although we have grave doubts about it. But whatever the "willfullness" requirement implies, the statute initially requires the Government to prove a true "threat." We do not believe that the kind of political hyperbole indulged in by petitioner fits within that statutory term. For we must interpret the language Congress chose "against the background of a profound national commitment to the principle that debate on public issues should be uninhibited, robust, and wide open, and that it may well include vehement, caustic, and sometimes unpleasantly sharp attacks on government and public officials." *New York Times Co. v. Sullivan*, 376 U.S. 254, 270 (1964). The language of the political arena...is often vituperative, abusive, and inexact. We agree with petitioner that his only offense here was "a kind of very crude offensive method of stating a political opposition to the President." Taken in context, and regarding the expressly conditional nature of the statement and the reaction of the listeners, we do not see how it could be interpreted otherwise. . . . It is so ordered. Court of Appeals reversed and case remanded with instructions.

Justice DOUGLAS, concurring.

The charge in this case is of an ancient vintage.

The federal statute under which petitioner was convicted traces its ancestry to the Statute of Treasons (25 Edw. 3) which made it a crime to "compass or imagine the Death of . . . the King." Note, *Threats to Take the Life of the President*, 32 Harv. L. Rev. 724, 725 (1919).

. . . "Like the Statute of Treasons, section 871 was passed in a 'relatively calm peacetime spring,' but has been construed under circumstances when intolerance for free speech was much greater than it normally might be." Note, *Threatening the President: Protected Dissenter or Political Assassin*, 57 Geo. L.J. 553, 570 (1969). Convictions under 18 U.S.C. § 871 have been sustained for displaying posters urging passersby to "hang (President) Roosevelt" for declaring that "President Wilson ought to be killed. It is a wonder some one has not done it already. If I had an opportunity, I would do it myself"; [and] for declaring that "Wilson is a wooden-headed son of a bitch. I wish Wilson was in hell, and if I had the power I would put him there." In sustaining an indictment under the statute against a man who indicated that he would enjoy shooting President Wilson if he had the chance, [a] trial court explained the thrust of § 871:

> The purpose of the statute was undoubtedly not only the protection of the President, but also the prohibition of just such statements as those alleged in this indictment. The expression of such direful intentions and desires, not only indicates a spirit of disloyalty to the nation bordering upon treason, but is, in a very real sense, a menace to the peace and safety of the country. . . . It arouses resentment and concern on the part of patriotic citizens.

United States v. Jasick, 252 F. 939, 933 (E.D. Mich. 1918). Suppression of speech as an effective police measure is an old, old device, outlawed by our Constitution.

Justice STEWART would deny the petition for certiorari.

[Justice WHITE's dissenting opinion is omitted.]

NOTES AND QUESTIONS

1. *The interest in punishing threats. Watts* intimates that threats fall into a category of unprotected speech, a fact that later Supreme Court cases have reaffirmed. *See* R.A.V. v. City of St. Paul, 505 U.S. 377, 388 (1992) (*see infra* p. 540); Virginia v. Black, 538 U.S. 343 (2003) (*see infra*, p. 549). What interests are served by punishing threatening speech? Several interests have been identified, including protecting individuals from the fear of violence, protecting individuals from the disruption that fear engenders, and protecting people from the possibility that threatened violence will occur. *R.A.V.*, 505 U.S. at 388. Are these interests

sufficient to support restrictions of speech, or are they merely unpleasant feelings? For commentary, see Steven G. Gey, *The Nuremberg Files and the First Amendment Value of Threats*, 78 Tex. L. Rev. 541 (2000); Steven J. Heyman, *Righting the Balance: An Inquiry into the Foundations and Limits of Freedom of Expression*, 78 B.U. L. Rev. 1275, 1323 (1998); Kenneth L. Karst, *Threats and Meanings: How the Facts Govern First Amendment Doctrine*, 58 Stan. L. Rev. 1337 (2006); Frederick Schauer, *Intentions, Conventions, and the First Amendment: The Case of Cross-Burning*, 2003 Sup. Ct. Rev. 197, 210.

2. *What is a "true threat"?* Does the Court ever clearly tell us what a "true threat" is? Why were Watts's statements so obviously hyperbole rather than threats?

Often statutes penalizing threats require that the speaker intend to threaten another person. But when they do not, the question arises as to whether there is a constitutional requirement of such intent before the speaker can be punished. In *Virginia v. Black* (*see infra* p. 549), the Court defined "true threats" as "those statements where the speakers mean to communicate a serious expression of an intent to commit an act of unlawful violence to a particular individual or group of individuals [although the] speaker need not actually intend to carry out the threat." 538 U.S. at 359-360. Unfortunately, lower courts after *Black* took very different approaches to the meaning of this phrase. As a result of the continuing confusion, the Supreme Court agreed to hear *United States v. Elonis*. As you read *Elonis*, consider whether it resolves the uncertainty regarding the mens rea required for a statement to be a true threat.

ELONIS v. UNITED STATES

135 S. Ct. 2001 (2015)

Chief Justice Roberts delivered the opinion of the Court. . . .

I

A

. . . In May 2010, Elonis's wife of nearly seven years left him, taking with her their two young children. Elonis began "listening to more violent music" and posting self-styled "rap" lyrics inspired by the music [to Facebook]. Eventually, Elonis changed the user name on his Facebook page from his actual name to a rap-style nom de plume, "Tone Dougie," to distinguish himself from his "on-line persona." The lyrics Elonis posted as "Tone Dougie" included graphically violent language and imagery. This material was often interspersed with disclaimers that the lyrics were "fictitious," with no intentional "resemblance to real persons." Elonis posted an explanation to another Facebook user that "I'm doing this for me. My writing is therapeutic."

Elonis's co-workers and friends viewed the posts in a different light. Around Halloween of 2010, Elonis posted a photograph of himself and a co-worker at a "Halloween Haunt" event at the amusement park where they worked. In the photograph, Elonis was holding a toy knife against his co-worker's neck, and in the caption Elonis wrote, "I wish." Elonis was not Facebook friends with the co-worker and did not "tag" her, a Facebook feature that would have alerted her to the posting. But the chief of park security was a Facebook "friend" of Elonis, saw the photograph, and fired him.

In response, Elonis posted a new entry on his Facebook page:

> "Moles! Didn't I tell y'all I had several? Y'all sayin' I had access to keys for all the f***in' gates. That I have sinister plans for all my friends and must have taken home a couple. Y'all think it's too dark and foggy to secure your facility from a man as mad as me? You see, even without a paycheck, I'm still the main attraction. Whoever thought the Halloween Haunt could be so f***in' scary?"

This post became the basis for Count One of Elonis's subsequent indictment, threatening park patrons and employees.

Elonis's posts frequently included crude, degrading, and violent material about his soon-to-be ex-wife. Shortly after he was fired, Elonis posted an adaptation of a satirical sketch that he and his wife had watched together. In the actual sketch, called "It's Illegal to Say . . .," a comedian explains that it is illegal for a person to say he wishes to kill the President, but not illegal to explain that it is illegal for him to say that. When Elonis posted the script of the sketch, however, he substituted his wife for the President. The posting was part of the basis for Count Two of the indictment, threatening his wife:

> "Hi, I'm Tone Elonis.
> Did you know that it's illegal for me to say I want to kill my wife? . . .
> It's one of the only sentences that I'm not allowed to say. . . .
> Now it was okay for me to say it right then because I was just telling you that it's illegal for me to say I want to kill my wife. . . .
> Um, but what's interesting is that it's very illegal to say I really, really think someone out there should kill my wife. . . .
> But not illegal to say with a mortar launcher.
> Because that's its own sentence. . . .
> I also found out that it's incredibly illegal, extremely illegal to go on Facebook and say something like the best place to fire a mortar launcher at her house would be from the cornfield behind it because of easy access to a getaway road and you'd have a clear line of sight through the sun room. . . .
> Yet even more illegal to show an illustrated diagram. [diagram of the house]. . . ."

The details about the home were accurate. At the bottom of the post, Elonis included a link to the video of the original skit, and wrote, "Art is about pushing limits. I'm willing to go to jail for my Constitutional rights. Are you?"

After viewing some of Elonis's posts, his wife felt "extremely afraid for [her] life." A state court granted her a three-year [restraining] order against Elonis. Elonis referred to the order in another post on his "Tone Dougie" page, also included in Count Two of the indictment:

> "Fold up your [restraining order] and put it in your pocket
> Is it thick enough to stop a bullet?
> Try to enforce an Order
> that was improperly granted in the first place
> Me thinks the Judge needs an education
> on true threat jurisprudence
> And prison time'll add zeros to my settlement . . .

And if worse comes to worse
I've got enough explosives
to take care of the State Police and the Sheriff's Department."

At the bottom of this post was a link to the Wikipedia article on "Freedom of speech." Elonis's reference to the police was the basis for Count Three of his indictment, threatening law enforcement officers.

That same month, interspersed with posts about a movie Elonis liked and observations on a comedian's social commentary, Elonis posted an entry that gave rise to Count Four of his indictment:

"That's it, I've had about enough
I'm checking out and making a name for myself
Enough elementary schools in a ten mile radius to initiate the most heinous school shooting ever imagined
And hell hath no fury like a crazy man in a Kindergarten class
The only question is . . . which one?"

Meanwhile, park security had informed both local police and the Federal Bureau of Investigation about Elonis's posts, and FBI Agent Denise Stevens had created a Facebook account to monitor his online activity. After the post about a school shooting, Agent Stevens and her partner visited Elonis at his house. Following their visit, during which Elonis was polite but uncooperative, Elonis posted another entry on his Facebook page, called "Little Agent Lady," which led to Count Five:

"You know your s***'s ridiculous
when you have the FBI knockin' at yo' door
Little Agent lady stood so close
Took all the strength I had not to turn the b**** ghost
Pull my knife, flick my wrist, and slit her throat
Leave her bleedin' from her jugular in the arms of her partner
[laughter]
So the next time you knock, you best be serving a warrant
And bring yo' SWAT and an explosives expert while you're at it
Cause little did y'all know, I was strapped wit' a bomb
Why do you think it took me so long to get dressed with no shoes on?
I was jus' waitin' for y'all to handcuff me and pat me down
Touch the detonator in my pocket and we're all goin'
[BOOM!]
Are all the pieces comin' together?
S***, I'm just a crazy sociopath
that gets off playin' you stupid f***s like a fiddle
And if y'all didn't hear, I'm gonna be famous
Cause I'm just an aspiring rapper who likes the attention
who happens to be under investigation for terrorism
cause y'all think I'm ready to turn the Valley into Fallujah
But I ain't gonna tell you which bridge is gonna fall
into which river or road
And if you really believe this s***
I'll have some bridge rubble to sell you tomorrow
[BOOM!][BOOM!][BOOM!]"

B

A grand jury indicted Elonis for making threats to injure patrons and employees of the park, his estranged wife, police officers, a kindergarten class, and an FBI agent, all in violation of 18 U.S.C. § 875(c) [which makes it a crime to transmit in interstate commerce "any communication containing any threat . . . to injure the person of another."] . . . At trial, Elonis testified that his posts emulated the rap lyrics of the well-known performer Eminem, some of which involve fantasies about killing his ex-wife. In Elonis's view, he had posted "nothing . . . that hasn't been said already." The Government presented as witnesses Elonis's wife and co-workers, all of whom said they felt afraid and viewed Elonis's posts as serious threats.

Elonis requested a jury instruction that "the government must prove that he intended to communicate a true threat." The District Court denied that request. The jury instructions instead informed the jury that

> "A statement is a true threat when a defendant intentionally makes a statement in a context or under such circumstances wherein a reasonable person would foresee that the statement would be interpreted by those to whom the maker communicates the statement as a serious expression of an intention to inflict bodily injury or take the life of an individual."

. . . A jury convicted Elonis on four of the five counts against him, acquitting only on the charge of threatening park patrons and employees. Elonis was sentenced to three years, eight months' imprisonment and three years' supervised release.

Elonis renewed his challenge to the jury instructions in the Court of Appeals, contending that the jury should have been required to find that he intended his posts to be threats. The Court of Appeals disagreed, holding that the intent required by Section 875(c) is only the intent to communicate words that the defendant understands, and that a reasonable person would view as a threat.

We granted certiorari.

II

. . . [Section 875(c)] requires that a communication be transmitted and that the communication contain a threat. It does not specify that the defendant must have any mental state with respect to these elements. In particular, it does not indicate whether the defendant must intend that his communication contain a threat. . . .

The fact that the statute does not specify any required mental state, however, does not mean that none exists. We have repeatedly held that "mere omission from a criminal enactment of any mention of criminal intent" should not be read "as dispensing with it." *Morissette v. United States*, 342 U.S. 246, 250 (1952). . . . Although there are exceptions, the "general rule" is that a guilty mind is "a necessary element in the indictment and proof of every crime." *United States v. Balint*, 258 U.S. 250, 251 (1922). We therefore generally "interpret[ ] criminal statutes to include broadly applicable scienter requirements, even where the statute by its terms does not contain them." *United States v. X–Citement Video, Inc.*, 513 U.S. 64, 70 (1994).

This is not to say that a defendant must know that his conduct is illegal before he may be found guilty. The familiar maxim "ignorance of the law is no excuse" typically holds true. Instead, our cases have explained that a defendant generally must "know the facts that make his conduct fit the definition of the offense," *Staples v. United States*, 511 U.S. 600, 608 n.3 (1994), even if he does not know that those facts give rise to a crime. . . .

When interpreting federal criminal statutes that are silent on the required mental state, we read into the statute "only that *mens rea* which is necessary to separate wrongful conduct from 'otherwise innocent conduct.'" *Carter v. United States*, 530 U.S. 255, 269 (2000). . . .

Section 875(c), as noted, requires proof that a communication was transmitted and that it contained a threat. The "presumption in favor of a scienter requirement should apply to *each* of the statutory elements that criminalize otherwise innocent conduct." *X–Citement Video*, 513 U.S. at 72 (emphasis added). The parties agree that a defendant under Section 875(c) must know that he is transmitting a communication. But communicating *something* is not what makes the conduct "wrongful." Here "the crucial element separating legal innocence from wrongful conduct" is the threatening nature of the communication. The mental state requirement must therefore apply to the fact that the communication contains a threat.

Elonis's conviction, however, was premised solely on how his posts would be understood by a reasonable person. Such a "reasonable person" standard is a familiar feature of civil liability in tort law, but is inconsistent with "the conventional requirement for criminal conduct—*awareness* of some wrongdoing." *Staples.* Having liability turn on whether a "reasonable person" regards the communication as a threat—regardless of what the defendant thinks—"reduces culpability on the all-important element of the crime to negligence," *United States v. Jeffries*, 692 F.3d 473, 484 (6th Cir. 2012) (Sutton, J., *dubitante*), and we "have long been reluctant to infer that a negligence standard was intended in criminal statutes," *Rogers v. United States*, 422 U.S. 35 (1975) (Marshall, J., concurring). . . .

The Government is at pains to characterize its position as something other than a negligence standard, emphasizing that its approach would require proof that a defendant "comprehended [the] contents and context" of the communication. The Government gives two examples of individuals who, in its view, would lack this necessary mental state—a "foreigner, ignorant of the English language," who would not know the meaning of the words at issue, or an individual mailing a sealed envelope without knowing its contents. But the fact that the Government would require a defendant to actually know the words of and circumstances surrounding a communication does not amount to a rejection of negligence. Criminal negligence standards often incorporate "the circumstances known" to a defendant. Courts then ask, however, whether a reasonable person equipped with that knowledge, not the actual defendant, would have recognized the harmfulness of his conduct. That is precisely the Government's position here: Elonis can be convicted, the Government contends, if he himself knew the contents and context of his posts, and a reasonable person would have recognized that the posts would be read as genuine threats. That is a negligence standard.

In support of its position the Government relies most heavily on *Hamling v. United States*, 418 U.S. 87 (1974). In that case, the Court rejected the argument that individuals could be convicted of mailing obscene material only if they knew the "legal status of the materials" distributed. Absolving a defendant of liability because he lacked the knowledge that the materials were legally obscene "would permit the defendant to avoid prosecution by simply claiming that he had not brushed up on the law." It was instead enough for liability that "a defendant had knowledge of the contents of the materials he distributed, and that he knew the character and nature of the materials."

This holding does not help the Government. In fact, the Court in *Hamling* approved a state court's conclusion that requiring a defendant to know the character of the material incorporated a "vital element of scienter" so that "not innocent but *calculated purveyance* of filth . . . is exorcised." In this case, "calculated purveyance" of a threat would require that Elonis know the threatening nature of his communication. Put simply, the mental state requirement the Court approved in *Hamling* turns on whether a defendant knew the *character* of what was sent, not simply its contents and context. . . .

In light of the foregoing, Elonis's conviction cannot stand. The jury was instructed that the Government need prove only that a reasonable person would regard Elonis's communications as threats, and that was error. . . .

There is no dispute that the mental state requirement in Section 875(c) is satisfied if the defendant transmits a communication for the purpose of issuing a threat, or with knowledge that the communication will be viewed as a threat. In response to a question at oral argument, Elonis stated that a finding of recklessness would not be sufficient. Neither Elonis nor the Government has briefed or argued that point, and we accordingly decline to address it. Given our disposition, it is not necessary to consider any First Amendment issues. . . .

Justice Alito . . . suggests that we have not clarified confusion in the lower courts. That is wrong. Our holding makes clear that negligence is not sufficient to support a conviction under Section 875(c), contrary to the view of nine Courts of Appeals. . . .

We may be "capable of deciding the recklessness issue," but following our usual practice of awaiting a decision below and hearing from the parties would help ensure that we decide it correctly.

The judgment of the United States Court of Appeals for the Third Circuit is reversed, and the case is remanded for further proceedings consistent with this opinion.

It is so ordered.

Justice ALITO, concurring in part and dissenting in part. . . .

The Court's disposition of this case is certain to cause confusion and serious problems. . . . The Court holds that the jury instructions in this case were defective because they required only negligence in conveying a threat. But the Court refuses to explain what type of intent was necessary. . . .

There is no justification for the Court's refusal to provide an answer. The Court says that "[n]either Elonis nor the Government has briefed or argued" the question whether recklessness is sufficient. But in fact both parties addressed that issue. Elonis argued that recklessness is not enough, and the Government argued that it more than suffices. If the Court thinks that we cannot decide the recklessness question without additional help from the parties, we can order further briefing and argument. In my view, however, we are capable of deciding the recklessness issue, and we should resolve that question now.

. . .

There can be no real dispute that recklessness regarding a risk of serious harm is wrongful conduct. . . . Someone who acts recklessly with respect to conveying a threat necessarily grasps that he is not engaged in innocent conduct. He is not merely careless. He is aware that others could regard his statements as a threat, but he delivers them anyway.

Accordingly, I would hold that a defendant may be convicted under § 875(c) if he or she consciously disregards the risk that the communication transmitted will be interpreted as a true threat. Nothing in the Court's non-committal opinion prevents lower courts from adopting that standard.

There remains the question whether interpreting § 875(c) to require no more than recklessness with respect to the element at issue here would violate the First Amendment. Elonis contends that it would. I would reject that argument.

It is settled that the Constitution does not protect true threats. And there are good reasons for that rule: True threats inflict great harm and have little if any social value. A threat may cause serious emotional stress for the person threatened and those who care about that person, and a threat may lead to a violent confrontation. It is true that a communication containing a threat may include other statements that have value and are entitled to protection. But that does not justify constitutional protection for the threat itself.

Elonis argues that the First Amendment protects a threat if the person making the statement does not actually intend to cause harm [but, rather, made the threat for a "'therapeutic'" purpose.] . . . Some people may experience a therapeutic or cathartic benefit only if they know that their words will cause harm or only if they actually plan to carry out the threat, but surely the First Amendment does not protect them.

Elonis also claims his threats were constitutionally protected works of art. . . . To make this point, his brief includes a lengthy excerpt from the lyrics of a rap song in which a very well-compensated rapper imagines killing his ex-wife and dumping her body in a lake. . . . But context matters. "Taken in context," lyrics in songs that are performed for an audience or sold in recorded form are unlikely to be interpreted as a real threat to a real person. Statements on social media that are pointedly directed at their victims, by contrast, are much more likely to be taken seriously. . . .

There was evidence that Elonis made sure his wife saw his posts. And she testified that they made her feel "'extremely afraid'" and "'like [she] was being stalked.'" Considering the context, who could blame her? Threats of violence and intimidation are among the most favored weapons of domestic abusers, and the rise of social media has only made those tactics more commonplace. A fig leaf of artistic expression cannot convert such hurtful, valueless threats into protected speech.

It can be argued that § 875(c), if not limited to threats made with the intent to harm, will chill statements that do not qualify as true threats, *e.g.*, statements that may be literally threatening but are plainly not meant to be taken seriously. We have sometimes cautioned that it is necessary to "exten[d] a measure of strategic protection" to otherwise unprotected false statements of fact in order to ensure enough "'breathing space'" for protected speech. *Gertz v. Robert Welch, Inc.*, 418 U.S. 323, 342 (1974). A similar argument might be made with respect to threats. But we have also held that the law provides adequate breathing space when it requires proof that false statements were made with reckless disregard of their falsity. Requiring proof of recklessness is similarly sufficient here.

Finally, because the jury instructions in this case did not require proof of recklessness, I would vacate the judgment below and remand for the Court of Appeals to decide in the first instance whether Elonis's conviction could be upheld under a recklessness standard. . . .

Justice THOMAS, dissenting.

We granted certiorari to resolve a conflict in the lower courts over the appropriate mental state for threat prosecutions under 18 U.S.C. § 875(c). . . .

Rather than resolve the conflict, the Court casts aside the approach used in nine Circuits and leaves nothing in its place. Lower courts are thus left to guess at the appropriate mental state for § 875(c). All they know after today's decision is that a requirement of general intent will not do. But they can safely infer that a majority of this Court would not adopt an intent-to-threaten requirement, as the opinion carefully leaves open the possibility that recklessness may be enough.

This failure to decide throws everyone from appellate judges to everyday Facebook users into a state of uncertainty. This uncertainty could have been avoided had we simply adhered to the background rule of the common law favoring general intent. Although I am sympathetic to my colleagues' policy concerns about the risks associated with threat prosecutions, the answer to such fears is not to discard our traditional approach to state-of-mind requirements in criminal law. Because the Court of Appeals properly applied the general-intent standard, and because the communications transmitted by Elonis were "true threats" unprotected by the First Amendment, I would affirm the judgment below. . . .

Applying ordinary rules of statutory construction, I would read § 875(c) to require proof of general intent. To "know the facts that make his conduct illegal" under § 875(c), a defendant must know that he transmitted a communication in interstate or foreign commerce that contained a threat. Knowing that the communication contains a "threat"—a serious expression of an intention to engage in unlawful physical violence—does not, however, require knowing that a jury will conclude that the communication contains a threat as a matter of law. Instead, . . . a defendant prosecuted under § 875(c) must know only the words used in that communication, along with their ordinary meaning in context.

General intent divides those who know the facts constituting the *actus reus* of this crime from those who do not. For example, someone who transmits a threat who does not know English—or who knows English, but perhaps does not know a threatening idiom—lacks the general intent required under § 875(c). Likewise, the hapless mailman who delivers a threatening letter, ignorant of its contents, should not fear prosecution. A defendant like Elonis, however, who admits that he "knew that what [he] was saying was violent" but supposedly "just wanted to express [him]self," acted with the general intent required under § 875(c), even if he did not know that a jury would conclude that his communication constituted a "threat" as a matter of law. . . .

In light of my conclusion that Elonis was properly convicted under the requirements of § 875(c), I must address his argument that his threatening posts were nevertheless protected by the First Amendment.

Elonis does not contend that threats are constitutionally protected speech, nor could he: "From 1791 to the present, . . . our society . . . has permitted restrictions upon the content of speech in a few limited areas," true threats being one of them. *R.A.V.* Instead, Elonis claims that only *intentional* threats fall within this particular historical exception.

If it were clear that intentional threats alone have been punished in our Nation since 1791, I would be inclined to agree. But that is the not the case. Although the Federal Government apparently did not get into the business of regulating threats until 1917, the States have been doing so since the late 18th and early 19th centuries. And that practice continued even after the States amended their constitutions to include speech protections similar to those in the First Amendment. State practice thus provides at least some evidence of the original meaning of the phrase "freedom of speech" in the First Amendment.

[Justice Thomas's opinion here reviewed several colonial and English statutes and cases and ultimately concluded that there was "good reason to believe that States bound by their own Constitutions to protect freedom of speech long ago enacted general-intent threat statutes."] . . .

I respectfully dissent.

NOTES AND QUESTIONS

1. *Threats and mens rea.* Which opinion has the most persuasive argument regarding the appropriate mens rea for threats?
2. *Constitutional or statutory principles.* Does it matter that the majority approached the issue as a matter of statutory interpretation rather than First Amendment principles?
3. *Discerning true threats.* We know that content, context and a certain mens rea are important to finding a true threat but how does a court or jury determine that statements are made recklessly, or with knowledge or purpose to threaten? Determining the mens rea associated with an apparently threatening statement can become especially problematic if statements are made publicly, or on the internet to large groups of people, or in situations where they are not delivered directly to the recipient. Consider the following scenarios. Do any of them involve true threats?

THEORY-APPLIED PROBLEMS

1. Bruce is a member of a militia who has blogged about national and local politics, especially gun control, for several years. On August 15, 2017, Bruce was arrested and charged with threatening to assault and murder all of the state Supreme Court judges in a blog post. Angered by the state Supreme Court's split decision upholding a local handgun ban, Bruce wrote on August 1, "Let me be the first to say this plainly: These judges deserve to be killed. Their blood will replenish the tree of liberty. A small price to pay for America's freedom." The next day, Bruce updated the post to include the names, work addresses, phone numbers, and photographs of the judges who decided the case. He also added an internet hyperlink to a publicly available, detailed satellite map and street map of the outside of the state Supreme Court building. Bruce previously called for assaults on judges in general although no action appears to have resulted from that speech.
2. After arriving home from her job at a local bank, Billie received a telephone message on her answering machine. In the message, a man calmly informed her that his name was Larry, that he wanted to talk to her, and that he had already sent her an e-mail. Earlier that day, Larry left her a message on her voice mail at work insisting that he speak with her about a credit card dispute between Larry and the bank. After receiving the second message at home, Billie was sufficiently alarmed and notified a night supervisor at the bank. Upon arriving at work the next morning, Billie read Larry's e-mail, which contained her current and prior addresses, including the location of her parents' home. Larry also compared Billie to Chicago Judge Joan Lefkow and provided a Web link to information about the 2005 murder of Lefkow's mother and husband in their

home after a member of a neo-Nazi organization posted Lefkow's home address on the Web. Larry further wrote, "I have run out of patience with you and your smug attitude."

3. During a 1995 meeting marking the anniversary of *Roe v. Wade*, the American Coalition of Life Activists (ACLA) revealed a poster listing the names and home addresses of the "Deadly Dozen," a group of doctors who performed abortions. The poster declared them guilty of "crimes against humanity" and offered $5,000 for information leading to the "arrest, conviction and revocation of license to practice medicine." The poster further stated that abortion had been a choice for East European and Jewish women during the Nazi regime and was prosecuted during the Nuremberg Trials as a war crime. The poster was also published in an affiliated magazine, Life Advocate, and distributed at ACLA events.

Later in 1995, in front of the St. Louis federal courthouse, ACLA unveiled a second poster, targeting Dr. Robert Crist. The poster accused Crist of crimes against humanity and various acts of medical malpractice, including a botched abortion. The poster included Crist's home and work addresses and his photograph and offered $500 to "any ACLA organization that successfully persuades Crist to turn from his child killing through activities within ACLA guidelines."

In January 1996, at another *Roe* anniversary event honoring prisoners convicted of anti-abortion violence, ACLA unveiled the "Nuremburg Files," a series of dossiers it had compiled on doctors, clinic employees, politicians, judges, and other abortion rights supporters. They hoped to conduct Nuremberg-like war crimes trials using "perfectly legal courts once the tide of this nation's opinion turns against the wanton slaughter of God's children." Neal Horsley, an anti-abortion activist, posted the information on a Web site. The Web site marked the names of those already victimized by anti-abortion terrorists, striking through the names of those who had been murdered and graying out the names of the wounded. ACLA's name originally appeared on the Web site, but Horsley removed it after the initiation of the lawsuit described below. The posters and Web site did not contain explicit threats against the doctors. However, similar posters prepared by others had preceded clinic violence in the past, a fact of which the doctors were aware. As a result of the posters, the doctors began wearing bulletproof vests, drawing the curtains on the windows of their homes, and accepting the protection of U.S. Marshals.

Along with two Portland-based health centers, the doctors sued ACLA, 12 activists, and an affiliated organization, alleging that their threatening statements violated state and federal law, including the Freedom of Access to Clinic Entrances Act of 1994 (FACE), 18 U.S.C. § 2489, which gives aggrieved persons a right of action against whoever by "threat of force . . . intentionally . . . intimidates . . . any person because that person is or has been . . . providing reproductive health services." For more discussion, see Planned Parenthood v. American Coalition of Life Activists, 290 F.3d 1059 (9th Cir. 2002).

2. *Fighting Words*

In declaring the two-level theory of the First Amendment, Chaplinsky v. New Hampshire, 315 U.S. 568 (1942), stated that "epithets or personal abuse" could not "in any proper sense" be considered "communication of information or opinion safeguarded by the Constitution." Those words originally came from an earlier case, Cantwell v. Connecticut, 310 U.S. 296 (1940), in which, unlike *Chaplinsky*, the Supreme Court reversed the speaker's criminal conviction. How does the Court determine the content and parameters of the category of speech that has come to be known as "fighting words"? Consider both *Cantwell* and *Chaplinsky* in light of that question.

CANTWELL v. CONNECTICUT

310 U.S. 296 (1940)

Mr. Justice ROBERTS delivered the opinion of the Court.

[Jesse Cantwell, a Jehovah's Witness, was arrested and convicted of the common law offense of inciting a breach of the peace].

The facts which were held to support the conviction of Jesse Cantwell on the [breach of peace] count were that he stopped two men in the street, asked, and received, permission to play a phonograph record, and played the record "Enemies", which attacked the religion and church of the two men, who were Catholics. Both were incensed by the contents of the record and were tempted to strike Cantwell unless he went away. On being told to be on his way he left their presence. There was no evidence that he was personally offensive or entered into any argument with those he interviewed.

The court held that the charge was not assault or breach of the peace or threats on Cantwell's part, but invoking or inciting others to breach of the peace, and that the facts supported the conviction of that offense. . . .

Conviction on the fifth count was not pursuant to a statute evincing a legislative judgment that street discussion of religious affairs, because of its tendency to provoke disorder, should be regulated, or a judgment that the playing of a phonograph on the streets should in the interest of comfort or privacy be limited or prevented. Violation of an Act exhibiting such a legislative judgment and narrowly drawn to prevent the supposed evil, would pose a question differing from that we must here answer.[9] . . . Here, however, the judgment is based on a common law concept of the most general and undefined nature. . . .

The offense known as breach of the peace embraces a great variety of conduct destroying or menacing public order and tranquility. It includes not only violent acts but acts and words likely to produce violence in others. . . . When clear and present danger of riot, disorder, interference with traffic upon the public streets, or other immediate threat to public safety, peace, or order, appears, the power of the state to prevent or punish is obvious. Equally obvious is it that a state may not unduly suppress free communication of views, religious or other, under the guise of conserving desirable conditions. Here we have a situation analogous to a conviction under a statute sweeping in a great variety of conduct under a general and indefinite characterization, and leaving to the executive and judicial branches too wide a discretion in its application.

Having these considerations in mind, we note that [Cantwell] was upon a public street, where he had a right to be, and where he had a right peacefully to impart his views to others. There is no showing that his deportment was noisy, truculent, overbearing or offensive. He requested of two pedestrians permission to play to them

---

[9] Compare Gitlow v. New York, 268 U.S. 652, 670, 671; Thornhill v. Alabama, 310 U.S. 88.

a phonograph record. The permission was granted. It is not claimed that he intended to insult or affront the hearers by playing the record. It is plain that he wished only to interest them in his propaganda. The sound of the phonograph is not shown to have disturbed residents of the street, to have drawn a crowd, or to have impeded traffic. Thus far he had invaded no right or interest of the public or of the men accosted.

The record played by Cantwell embodies a general attack on all organized religious systems as instruments of Satan and injurious to man; it then singles out the Roman Catholic Church for strictures couched in terms which naturally would offend not only persons of that persuasion, but all others who respect the honestly held religious faith of their fellows. The hearers were in fact highly offended. One of them said he felt like hitting Cantwell and the other that he was tempted to throw Cantwell off the street. The one who testified he felt like hitting Cantwell said, in answer to the question "Did you do anything else or have any other reaction?" "No, sir, because he said he would take the victrola and he went." The other witness testified that he told Cantwell he had better get off the street before something happened to him and that was the end of the matter as Cantwell picked up his books and walked up the street.

Cantwell's conduct, in the view of the court below, considered apart from the effect of his communication upon his hearers, did not amount to a breach of the peace. One may, however, be guilty of the offense if he commit acts or make statements likely to provoke violence and disturbance of good order, even though no such eventuality be intended. Decisions to this effect are many, but examination discloses that, in practically all, the provocative language which was held to amount to a breach of the peace consisted of profane, indecent, or abusive remarks directed to the person of the hearer. Resort to epithets or personal abuse is not in any proper sense communication of information or opinion safeguarded by the Constitution[.]. . .

We find in the instant case no assault or threatening of bodily harm, no truculent bearing, no intentional discourtesy, no personal abuse. On the contrary, we find only an effort to persuade a willing listener to buy a book or to contribute money in the interest of what Cantwell, however misguided others may think him, conceived to be true religion. In the realm of religious faith, and in that of political belief, sharp differences arise. In both fields the tenets of one man may seem the rankest error to his neighbor. To persuade others to his own point of view, the pleader, as we know, at times, resorts to exaggeration, to vilification of men who have been, or are, prominent in church or state, and even to false statement. But the people of this nation have ordained in the light of history, that, in spite of the probability of excesses and abuses, these liberties are, in the long view, essential to enlightened opinion and right conduct on the part of the citizens of a democracy. . . .

Although the contents of the record not unnaturally aroused animosity, we think that, in the absence of a statute narrowly drawn to define and punish specific conduct as constituting a clear and present danger to a substantial interest of the State, the petitioner's communication, considered in the light of the constitutional guarantees, raised no such clear and present menace to public peace and order as to render him liable to conviction of the common law offense in question.

The judgment affirming the convictions on the third and fifth counts is reversed and the cause is remanded for further proceedings not inconsistent with this opinion. So ordered.

Reversed and remanded.

CHAPLINSKY v. NEW HAMPSHIRE

315 U.S. 568 (1942)

Mr. Justice MURPHY delivered the opinion of the Court.

. . . Chaplinsky [a member of the religious sect known as Jehovah's Witnesses] was distributing the literature of his sect on the streets of Rochester on a busy Saturday afternoon. Members of the local citizenry complained to the City Marshal, Bowering, that Chaplinsky was denouncing all religion as a "racket." Bowering told them that Chaplinsky was lawfully engaged, and then warned Chaplinsky that the crowd was getting restless. Some time later a disturbance occurred and the traffic officer on duty at the busy intersection started with Chaplinsky for the police station, but did not inform him that he was under arrest or that he was going to be arrested. On the way, they encountered Marshal Bowering who had been advised that a riot was under way and was therefore hurrying to the scene. Bowering repeated his earlier warning to Chaplinsky who then [said to him "You are a God damned racketeer" and "a damned Fascist and the whole government of Rochester are Fascists or agents of Fascists"].

Chaplinsky's version of the affair was slightly different. He testified that when he met Bowering, he asked him to arrest the ones responsible for the disturbance. In reply Bowering cursed him and told him to come along. Appellant admitted that he said the words charged in the complaint with the exception of the name of the Deity.

. . .

[Chaplinsky was charged with and convicted for violation of Chapter 378, Section 2, of the Public Laws of New Hampshire: "No person shall address any offensive, derisive or annoying word to any other person who is lawfully in any street or other public place, nor call him by any offensive or derisive name, nor make any noise or exclamation in his presence and hearing with intent to deride, offend or annoy him, or to prevent him from pursuing his lawful business or occupation."]

[I]t is well understood that the right of free speech is not absolute at all times and under all circumstances. There are certain well-defined and narrowly limited classes of speech, the prevention and punishment of which has never been thought to raise any Constitutional problem. These include the lewd and obscene, the profane, the libelous, and the insulting or "fighting" words—those which by their very utterance inflict injury or tend to incite an immediate breach of the peace. It has been well observed that such utterances are no essential part of any exposition of ideas, and are of such slight social value as a step to truth that any benefit that may be derived from them is clearly outweighed by the social interest in order and morality. "Resort to epithets or personal abuse is not in any proper sense communication of information or opinion safeguarded by the Constitution, and its punishment as a criminal act would raise no question under that instrument." *Cantwell.*

On the authority of its earlier decisions, the state court declared that the statute's purpose was to preserve the public peace, no words being "forbidden except such as have a direct tendency to cause acts of violence by the person to whom, individually, the remark is addressed." It was further said: "The word 'offensive' is not to be defined in terms of what a particular addressee thinks. . . . The test is what men of common intelligence would understand would be words likely to cause an average addressee to fight. . . . The English language has a number of words and expressions which by   general consent   are 'fighting words' when said without a disarming smile. . . . Such words, as ordinary men know, are likely to cause a fight. So are threatening, profane or obscene revilings. Derisive and annoying words can be taken as coming within the purview of the statute as heretofore interpreted only when they have this characteristic of plainly tending to excite the addressee to a breach of the peace. . . . The statute, as construed, does no more than prohibit the face-to-face words plainly likely to cause a breach of the peace by the addressee, words whose speaking constitute a breach of the peace by the speaker—including 'classical fighting words', words in current use less 'classical' but equally likely to cause violence, and other disorderly words, including profanity, obscenity and threats." . . .

A statute punishing verbal acts, carefully drawn so as not unduly to impair liberty of expression, is not too vague for a criminal law. . . .

Nor can we say that the application of the statute to the facts disclosed by the record substantially or unreasonably impinges upon the privilege of free speech. Argument is unnecessary to demonstrate that the appellations "damn racketeer" and "damn Fascist" are epithets likely to provoke the average person to retaliation, and thereby cause a breach of the peace. . . .

Affirmed.

NOTES AND QUESTIONS

1. Cantwell, *clear and present danger, and epithets.* Why is *Cantwell* so concerned with the defendant's demeanor if it is applying a "clear and present danger" standard? Does the Court believe that abusive epithets are more likely to cause a hostile or violent response by the audience or that such words have no communicative value?

2. Cantwell *and common law breach of the peace.* Should it matter that Cantwell involved a common law crime rather than a statute? Given the Court's approach to vague and overly broad laws, *see supra* Chapter 1, would it have been any less concerned about a statute prohibiting "diversions tending to a breach of the peace?" *See, e.g.,* Terminiello v. Chicago, 337 U.S. 1 (1949) (reversing defendant's conviction under a breach of the peace statute).

3. *What are fighting words? Chaplinsky* seems to intimate two different standards for judging fighting words—one that is contextual and one that is objective. Aren't these standards very different? Which one should the Court use?

4. *Fighting words as non-communication? Chaplinsky* states that "fighting words" are "no essential part of any exposition of ideas." Why? Are they more akin to a physical assault? What is it about such words that place them wholly outside the First Amendment? For commentary, see Alexander Bickel, *The Morality of Consent* 72 (1975); Stephen W. Gard, *Fighting Words as Free Speech,* 58 Wash. U. L.Q. 531, 542 (1980); Martin Redish, *The Value of Free Speech,* 130 U. Pa. L. Rev. 591, 626 (1982); Mark C. Rutzick, *Offensive Language and the Evolution of First Amendment Protection,* 9 Harv. C.R.-C.L. L. Rev. 1, 10 (1974).

5. *The police as "reasonable addressees."* Should police officers, such as Marshal Bowering, be expected to respond with less emotion to fighting words than the average citizen? *See* Rutzick, *supra,* at 10.

6. *Fighting words and "emotional injury."* Is the prevention of "inflict[ion of] injury" (presumably emotional injury) sufficient to justify punishment of speech? For discussion see Rutzick, *supra,* at 6.

*AN EXTENDED NOTE ON THE POST-*CHAPLINSKY
FIGHTING-WORDS DOCTRINE

Chaplinsky is the only Supreme Court case to uphold a fighting-words conviction and it has not been overruled. In fact, recent cases have reaffirmed the viability of the fighting-words category. *See* R.A.V. v. City of St. Paul, *infra* p. 540. But subsequent cases appear to have substantially narrowed *Chaplinsky*'s reach. These cases reflect the Court's attempt to craft a narrow definition of fighting words that still leaves ample room for a speaker who attempts to persuade others to her point of view, even when she "resorts to exaggeration, vilification... and even to false statement."

In Cohen v. California, 403 U.S. 15 (1971), *see infra* p. 523, the Court reversed the conviction of Paul Robert Cohen for wearing a jacket with the words "Fuck the Draft" across the back. Cohen had been tried and found guilty under a California statute prohibiting any person from "maliciously and willfully disturbing the peace or quiet of any neighborhood or person . . . by . . . offensive conduct." Citing *Chaplinsky*, the Court stated that "the States are free to ban the simple use, without a demonstration of additional justifying circumstances, of so-called 'fighting words,' those personally abusive epithets which, when addressed to the ordinary citizen, are, as a matter of common knowledge, inherently likely to provoke violent reaction." It further noted, however, that

> [w]hile the four-letter word displayed by Cohen in relation to the draft is not uncommonly employed in a personally provocative fashion, in this instance it was clearly not 'directed to the person of the hearer.' *Cantwell.* No individual actually or likely to be present could reasonably have regarded the words on appellant's jacket as a direct personal insult. Nor do we have here an instance of the exercise of the State's police power to prevent a speaker from intentionally provoking a given group to hostile reaction. *Cf.* Feiner v. New York, 340 U.S. 315 (1951); Terminiello v. Chicago, 337 U.S. 1 (1949). There is, as noted above, no showing that anyone who saw Cohen was in fact violently aroused or that appellant intended such a result.

403 U.S. at 20. With these considerations in mind, the Court thus identified the free speech issue in stark terms: "Against this background, the issue flushed by this case stands out in bold relief. It is whether California can excise, as 'offensive conduct,' one particular scurrilous epithet from the public discourse, either upon the theory of the court below that its use is inherently likely to cause violent reaction or upon a more general assertion that the States, acting as guardians of public morality, may properly remove this offensive word from the public vocabulary. The rationale of the California court is plainly untenable. At most it reflects an 'undifferentiated fear or apprehension of disturbance (which) is not enough to overcome the right to freedom of expression.'" *Id.* at 22-23.

In Gooding v. Wilson, 405 U.S. 518 (1972), *see infra* p. 528, the defendant, who was protesting the Vietnam War at an induction center, swore at police officers trying to remove him, saying, "White son of a bitch, I'll kill you," "You son of a bitch, I'll choke you to death," and "You son of a bitch, if you ever put your hands on me again, I'll cut you all to pieces." He was convicted under a Georgia statute providing: "Any person who shall, without provocation, use to [or in the presence of another] . . . opprobrious words or abusive language, tending to cause a breach of the peace . . . shall be guilty of a misdemeanor." The Supreme Court reversed his conviction, finding that the statute's term "tending to cause a breach of the peace" did not "define the standard of responsibility with requisite narrow specificity." The Court found that past applications of the statute resulted in convictions where there was no likelihood that the person addressed would make an immediate violent response, in violation of the fighting-words doctrine defined by *Chaplinsky.* Accordingly, the Court believed that the statute left "wide open the standard of responsibility, so that it [was] easily susceptible to improper application."

Finally in Texas v. Johnson, 491 U.S. 397 (1989), *see infra* p. 208, the defendant was arrested for burning a flag under a Texas law punishing anyone who desecrated a flag in a manner that would offend another person. The Court rejected the argument that the law was justified by the state's interest in preventing breaches of the peace. "[N]o disturbance of the peace actually occurred or threatened to occur because of Johnson's burning of the flag," the Court noted. The State's position, therefore, "amounts to a claim that an audience that takes serious offense at particular expression is necessarily likely to disturb the peace and that the expression may be prohibited on this basis. Our precedents do not countenance such a presumption. On the contrary, they recognize that a principal function of free speech under our system of government is to invite dispute." The Court concluded that Johnson's expressive conduct did not "fall within that small class of 'fighting words' that are 'likely to provoke the average person to retaliation, and thereby cause a breach of the peace.' No reasonable onlooker would have regarded Johnson's generalized expression of dissatisfaction with the policies of the Federal Government as a direct personal insult or an invitation to exchange fisticuffs." 489 U.S. at 408-409.

What is left of *Chaplinsky*'s version of the fighting-words doctrine after these cases? Professor Stephen Gard has suggested that cases since *Chaplinsky* establish four required elements before fighting words can be punished: (1) provocative personal insult, (2) direct tendency to cause immediate violence, (3) face-to-face utterance, (4) directed at an individual. Gard, *supra*, at 536. *See also* Rutzick, *supra*, at 27. Is this a fair assessment of the modern cases? In what circumstances are fighting-words prosecutions most likely to be successful?

Does the focus on violence ignore the possible other injuries that personal abuse and epithets might inflict? Wendy B. Reilly, Note, *Fighting the Fighting Words Standard: A Call for Its Destruction*, 52 Rutgers L. Rev. 947, 956 (2000) (arguing that focus on breach of peace renders verbal assaults "*not* regulable . . . when directed at someone of a more pacific bent," even though such words inflict significant psychic injury). Chapter 10 provides lengthier treatment of *Cohen* and subsequent cases in the context of government efforts to promote civility.

3. *Hostile Audiences, the Heckler's Veto, and Offensive Speech*

Hostile audience situations are related to fighting-words situations. Both involve a hostile reaction by the audience to the speaker's words. The fighting-words decisions involve a determination of whether words are abusive or so akin to an assault that they are likely to cause a violent response. The hostile audience situation involves a question of whether government officials can punish a speaker for causing a breach of the peace because the audience responds in a hostile manner to a speaker's *ideas.* *Cantwell, supra*, raised this issue, as the speaker was convicted of inciting a breach of the peace for expressing views that offended others. The Court reversed his conviction, however, because there was no discernible threat to public order and because he was merely attempting to persuade people regarding his views, albeit with "provocative language."

Should speech that invokes a hostile audience response, but which does not involve fighting words, be considered low value? With one notable exception, the Court has generally been suspicious of attempts to shut down speakers based upon the audience's negative reaction to their message. As you read the following, consider how these situations differ from the Court's current definition of fighting words (or incitement). To what extent do concerns about vague and overly broad laws come into play in these cases?

In Terminiello v. Chicago, 337 U.S. 1 (1949), the Supreme Court also reversed a defendant's conviction under an ordinance providing that anyone who "[made] or assist[ed] in making any improper noise, riot, disturbance, breach of the peace, or diversion tending to a breach of the peace, within the limits of the city . . . shall be deemed guilty of disorderly conduct." The defendant's conviction resulted from a speech given under the auspices of the Christian Veterans of America, in which he vigorously condemned Communism and various racial groups, ridiculed his opponents, and called them names, including "slimy scum" and "snakes." Terminiello delivered his speech before a capacity crowd of 800 people. Outside, a crowd of up to 1,000 people gathered in protest. In response to Terminiello's speech, some members of the crowd inside the auditorium responded negatively and cursed Terminiello. The crowd outside was "angry and turbulent," shouting epithets about those attending the meeting. There were several disturbances, including bricks thrown through windows and stink bombs, despite police attempts to keep order. The trial court instructed the jury that "'breach of the peace' consists of any 'misbehavior which violates the public peace and decorum'; and that the 'misbehavior may constitute a breach of the peace if it stirs the public to anger, invites dispute, brings about a condition of unrest, or creates a disturbance, or if it molests the inhabitants in the enjoyment of peace and quiet by arousing alarm.'" In finding the statute unconstitutional as applied to Terminiello, the Supreme Court found:

> [A] function of free speech under our system of government is to invite dispute. It may indeed best serve its high purpose when it induces a condition of unrest, creates dissatisfaction with conditions as they are, or even stirs people to anger. Speech is often provocative and challenging. It may strike at prejudices and preconceptions and have profound unsettling effects as it presses for acceptance of an idea. That is why freedom of speech, though not absolute is nevertheless protected against censorship or punishment, unless shown likely to produce a clear and present danger of a serious substantive evil that rises far above public inconvenience, annoyance, or unrest. There is no room under our Constitution for a more restrictive view. For the alternative would lead to standardization of ideas either by legislatures, courts, or dominant political or community groups. The ordinance as construed by the trial court seriously invaded this province. It permitted conviction of petitioner if his speech stirred people to anger, invited public dispute, or brought about a condition of unrest. A conviction resting on any of those grounds may not stand.

337 U.S. at 4-5.

When, if ever, does an offensive idea present a "clear and present danger" of harm? Was there no danger of serious harm in *Terminiello*? What role did the jury instruction play in the Court's decision?

Compare the decisions in *Cantwell* and *Terminiello* to *Feiner* below:

FEINER v. NEW YORK
340 U.S. 315 (1951)

Mr. Chief Justice VINSON delivered the opinion of the Court.

Petitioner was convicted of the offense of disorderly conduct, a misdemeanor under the New York penal laws. . . .

On the evening of March 8, 1949, petitioner Irving Feiner was addressing an open-air meeting at the corner of South McBride and Harrison Streets in the City of Syracuse. At approximately 6:30 p.m., the police received a telephone complaint concerning the meeting, and two officers were detailed to investigate. One of these officers went to the scene immediately, the other arriving some twelve minutes later. They found a crowd of about seventy-five or eighty people, both Negro and white, filling the sidewalk and spreading out into the street. Petitioner, standing on a large wooden box on the sidewalk, was addressing the crowd through a loud-speaker system attached to an automobile. Although the purpose of his speech was to urge his listeners to attend a meeting to be held that night in the Syracuse Hotel, in its course he was making derogatory remarks concerning President Truman, the American Legion, the Mayor of Syracuse, and other local political officials.

The police officers made no effort to interfere with petitioner's speech, but were first concerned with the effect of the crowd on both pedestrian and vehicular traffic. They observed the situation from the opposite side of the street, noting that some pedestrians were forced to walk in the street to avoid the crowd. Since traffic was passing at the time, the officers attempted to get the people listening to petitioner back on the sidewalk. . . .

At this time, petitioner was speaking in a "loud, high-pitched voice." He gave the impression that he was endeavoring to arouse the Negro people against the whites, urging that they rise up in arms and fight for equal rights. The statements before such a mixed audience "stirred up a little excitement." Some of the onlookers made remarks to the police about their inability to handle the crowd and at least one threatened violence if the police did not act. There were others who appeared to be favoring petitioner's arguments. Because of the feeling that existed in the crowd both for and against the speaker, the officers finally "stepped in to prevent it from resulting in a fight." One of the officers approached the petitioner, not for the purpose of arresting him, but to get him to break up the crowd. He asked petitioner to get down off the box, but the latter refused to accede to his request and continued talking. The officer waited for a minute and then demanded that he cease talking. Although the officer had thus twice requested petitioner to stop over the course of several minutes, petitioner not only ignored him but continued talking. During all this time, the crowd was pressing closer around petitioner and the officer. Finally, the officer told petitioner he was under arrest and ordered him to get down from the box, reaching up to grab him. Petitioner stepped down, announcing over the microphone that "the law has arrived, and I suppose they will take over now." In all, the officer had asked petitioner to get down off the box three times over a space of four or five minutes. Petitioner had been speaking for over a half hour.

On these facts, petitioner was specifically charged with violation of Section 722 of the Penal Law of New York, the pertinent part of which is set out in the margin.[1] . . .

We are not faced here with blind condonation by a state court of arbitrary police action. . . . The courts below recognized petitioner's right to hold a street meeting at this locality, to make use of loud-speaking equipment in giving his speech, and to make derogatory remarks concerning public officials and the American Legion. They found that the officers in making the arrest were motivated solely by a proper concern for the preservation of order and protection of the general welfare, and that there was no evidence which could lend color to a claim that the acts of the police were a cover for suppression of petitioner's views and opinions. Petitioner was thus neither arrested nor convicted for the making or the content of his speech. Rather, it was the reaction which it actually engendered.

The language of *Cantwell* is appropriate here. ". . . When clear and present danger of riot, disorder, interference with traffic upon the public streets, or other immediate threat to public safety, peace, or order, appears, the power of the State to prevent or punish is obvious." . . .

We are well aware that the ordinary murmurings and objections of a hostile audience cannot be allowed to silence a speaker, and are also mindful of the possible danger of giving overzealous police officials complete discretion to break up otherwise lawful public meetings. "A State may not unduly suppress free communication of views, religious or other, under the guise of conserving desirable conditions." *Cantwell.* But we are not faced here with such a situation. It is one thing to say that the police cannot be used as an instrument for the suppression of unpopular views, and another to say that, when as here the speaker passes the bounds of argument or persuasion and undertakes incitement to riot, they are powerless to prevent a breach of the peace. Nor in this case can we condemn the considered judgment of three New York courts approving the means which the police, faced with a crisis, used in the exercise of their power and duty to preserve peace and order. The findings of the state courts as to the existing situation and the imminence of greater disorder coupled with petitioner's deliberate defiance of the police officers convince us that we should not reverse this conviction in the name of free speech.

Affirmed.

Mr. Justice BLACK, dissenting.

The record before us convinces me that petitioner, a young college student, has been sentenced to the penitentiary for the unpopular views he expressed[1] on matters

---

[1] Section 722. Any person who with intent to provoke a breach of the peace, or whereby a breach of the peace may be occasioned, commits any of the following acts shall be deemed to have committed the offense of disorderly conduct:

  [1] Uses offensive, disorderly, threatening, abusive or insulting language, conduct or behavior;

  [2] Acts in such a manner as to annoy, disturb, interfere with, obstruct, or be offensive to others;

  [3] Congregates with others on a public street and refuses to move on when ordered by the police.

[1] The trial judge framed the question for decision as follows: "The question here, is what was said and what was done? . . . There are acts and conduct an individual can engage in when you don't even have to have a crowd gathered around which would justify a charge of disorderly conduct. The question is, what did this defendant say and do at that particular time and the Court must determine whether those facts, concerning what the defendant did or said, are sufficient to support the charge." There is no suggestion in the record that petitioner "did" anything other than

of public interest while lawfully making a street-corner speech in Syracuse, New York. . . .

The Court's opinion apparently rests on this reasoning: The policeman, under the circumstances detailed, could reasonably conclude that serious fighting or even riot was imminent; therefore he could stop petitioner's speech to prevent a breach of peace; accordingly, it was "disorderly conduct" for petitioner to continue speaking in disobedience of the officer's request. As to the existence of a dangerous situation on the street corner, it seems farfetched to suggest that the "facts" show any imminent threat of riot or uncontrollable disorder. It is neither unusual nor unexpected that some people at public street meetings mutter, mill about, push, shove, or disagree, even violently, with the speaker. Indeed, it is rare where controversial topics are discussed that an outdoor crowd does not do some or all of these things. Nor does one isolated threat to assault the speaker forebode disorder. . . .

Moreover, assuming that the "facts" did indicate a critical situation, I reject the implication of the Court's opinion that the police had no obligation to protect petitioner's constitutional right to talk. The police of course have power to prevent breaches of the peace. But if, in the name of preserving order, they ever can interfere with a lawful public speaker, they first must make all reasonable efforts to protect him. . . . Their duty was to protect petitioner's right to talk, even to the extent of arresting the man who threatened to interfere. Instead, they shirked that duty and acted only to suppress the right to speak. . . .

Here petitioner was "asked" then "told" then "commanded" to stop speaking, but a man making a lawful address is certainly not required to be silent merely because an officer directs it. Petitioner was entitled to know why he should cease doing a lawful act. Not once was he told. I understand that people in authoritarian countries must obey arbitrary orders. I had hoped that there was no such duty in the United States. . . .

[Justice FRANKFURTER's concurring opinion is omitted.]

[Justice DOUGLAS's dissenting opinion is omitted.]

NOTES AND QUESTIONS

1. *Incitement to riot.* Did Feiner "undertake incitement to riot"? Did Feiner's speech present a clear and present danger of any violence? Is there any difference in Feiner's situation that can account for the different outcome in *Terminiello*?
2. Feiner *and police discretion.* What possible dangers arise with giving police officers this kind of discretion?
3. *Speaker versus audience.* What steps does the First Amendment require police to take to protect a speaker from a hostile crowd? *See generally* Note, *Freedom of Speech and Assembly: The Problem of the Hostile Audience*, 49 Colum. L. Rev. 1118 (1949). How much audience heckling must the police allow before they can remove disruptive audience members? *See* Note, *Regulation of Demonstrations*, 80 Harv. L. Rev. 1773, 1775 (1967).

---

(1) speak and (2) continue for a short time to invite people to a public meeting after a policeman had requested him to stop speaking.

4. *The aftermath of* Feiner. Consider the following cases decided after *Feiner*. Do they return to the tone established in *Terminiello*?

  a. Edwards v. South Carolina, 372 U.S. 229 (1963): One hundred and eighty-seven black students protested racial discrimination by walking in groups of approximately 15 from a local church in Columbia, South Carolina, to the South Carolina State House grounds, an area that was open to the public. Approximately 30 police with advance knowledge of the protest accompanied the students, and approximately 200 to 300 onlookers gathered to watch as the students marched on the State House grounds in an orderly manner. Police protection was sufficient at all times to control the crowd. The demonstrators were told that if they did not disperse within 15 minutes, they would be arrested. They refused and became somewhat "boisterous" by singing patriotic and religious songs, stamping their feet, and clapping their hands. The students were arrested and convicted of causing a breach of the peace. The Supreme Court of South Carolina affirmed their convictions and described the offense of breach of the peace as "a violation of public order, a disturbance of the public tranquility, by any act or conduct inciting to violence. . . . It is not necessary that the peace be actually broken to lay the foundation for a prosecution for this offense. If what is done is unjustifiable and unlawful, tending with sufficient directness to break the peace, no more is required. Nor is actual personal violence an essential element in the offense."

  The Supreme Court reversed the students' convictions, noting that the situation involved "was a far cry from the situation in *Feiner*." Rather, the Court concluded that the students "were convicted upon evidence which showed no more than that the opinions which they were peaceably expressing were sufficiently opposed to the views of the majority of the community to attract a crowd and necessitate police protection. . . . The Fourteenth Amendment does not permit a State to make criminal the peaceful expression of unpopular views." *Terminiello*. Justice Clark dissented, arguing that the situation was much more dangerous than the majority would admit: "Here 200 youthful Negro demonstrators were being aroused to a 'fever pitch' before a crowd of some 300 people who undoubtedly were hostile. Perhaps their speech was not so animated but in this setting their actions, their placards reading 'You may jail our bodies but not our souls' and their chanting of 'I Shall Not Be Moved,' accompanied by stamping feet and clapping hands, created a much greater danger of riot and disorder. It is my belief that anyone conversant with the almost spontaneous combustion in some Southern communities in such a situation will agree that the City Manager's action may well have averted a major catastrophe."

  b. Cox v. Louisiana, 379 U.S. 536 (1965): In December 1961, 2,000 students in Baton Rouge, Louisiana, demonstrated outside of the courthouse to protest segregation and the previous arrest of student demonstrators who were then being held in jail on the third floor of the courthouse. Cox, a minister and active member of the Congress of Racial Equality, was partly responsible for overseeing the demonstration. The protestors engaged in a peaceful march to the courthouse. As they neared the courthouse, the police chief told the demonstrators they were to confine their protest to the sidewalk on the side of the street opposite the courthouse. About 100 to 300 onlookers (mostly white) gathered. Seventy-five to 80 police officers and other city workers were also present, stationed in between the protestors and the onlookers. Some of the protestors carried picket signs suggesting that people boycott certain stores during the Christmas shopping season. Others sang patriotic and religious songs, which caused the jailed students, who could hear them, to sing in response. Cox gave a speech protesting racial discrimination at lunch counters and urging students to sit at them as part of their rights as tax-paying members of the public. Some members of the audience responded to his speech with "muttering and grumbling." Viewing Cox's speech as "inflammatory," the Sheriff ordered the demonstration to break up. Cox and the demonstrators refused. Cox was convicted of violating Louisiana's breach of the peace statute, which criminalized congregating in a public place and failing to disperse when ordered to do so.

The Supreme Court reversed, holding that it could find "no conduct which the State had a right to prohibit as a breach of the peace." The Court rejected the trial judge's statement that it was "inherently dangerous and a breach of the peace to bring 1,500 people, colored people, down in the predominantly white business district in the City of Baton Rouge" to sing songs of racial solidarity. According to the Supreme Court, there were no signs of violence by members of the audience, police protection was adequate at all times, and there was no indication that the students were "hostile, aggressive, or unfriendly." As in *Edwards*, the *Cox* Court found the situation to be "a far cry from *Feiner* "and concluded that "constitutional rights may not be denied simply because of hostility to the assertion of their exercise."

c. Gregory v. City of Chicago, 394 U.S. 111 (1969): Eighty-five demonstrators marched in an orderly fashion from Chicago's city hall to the mayor's residence to protest segregation. They then marched around Mayor Daley's house, singing songs, criticizing the mayor, and chanting slogans. After 8:30 P.M., the protestors stopped singing but continued marching quietly. As they marched, a crowd of bystanders grew from 35 to more than 1,000 people. Over the course of the evening, the spectators grew increasingly hostile to the protestors, shouting racial epithets and throwing rocks and eggs. Around 9:30 P.M. the police informed Gregory, leader of the march, that the situation was "dangerous and becoming riotous" and requested that the group leave several times. When Gregory and other protestors refused, they were arrested for breach of the peace. Gregory was convicted for violating a Chicago ordinance prohibiting the "making [of] any improper noise, riot, disturbance, breach of the peace, or diversion tending to a breach of the peace" or the gathering "in bodies or crowds for unlawful purposes, or for any purpose, to the annoyance or disturbance of other persons."

The Supreme Court reversed the defendant's conviction, arguing that "[t]here is no evidence in this record that petitioners' conduct was disorderly. . . . [C]onvictions so totally devoid of evidentiary support violate due process." Furthermore, the Court concluded that the trial judge "permitted the jury to convict for acts clearly entitled to First Amendment protection." Justice Black concurred, arguing that the ordinance was too vague: "The average person charged with its violation is necessarily left uncertain as to what conduct and attitudes of mind would be enough to convict under it. Who, for example, could possibly foresee what kind of noise or protected speech would be held to be 'improper'? . . . The so-called 'diversion tending to a breach of the peace' here was limited entirely and exclusively to the fact that when the policeman in charge of the special police detail concluded that the hecklers observing the march were dangerously close to rioting and that the demonstrators and others were likely to be engulfed in that riot, he ordered Gregory and his demonstrators to leave, and Gregory—standing on what he deemed to be his constitutional rights—refused to do so. . . . But under our democratic system of government, lawmaking is not entrusted to the moment-to-moment judgment of the policeman on his beat. Laws, that is valid laws, are to be made by representatives chosen to make laws for the future, not by police officers whose duty is to enforce laws already enacted and to make arrests only for conduct already made criminal."

5. *Feiner versus later cases.* Are these cases different from *Feiner* because of these latter speakers' words or conduct, the audiences' response, or the police presence?

4.   Stevens, Alvarez, *and Low-Value Speech Methodology*

The Court's incitement, threats, and fighting-words cases reflect its struggle to distinguish low-value speech and political, albeit offensive or upsetting, speech. Yet, despite the importance of distinguishing between low-value speech and otherwise protected speech, the Court never developed a discernable method for determining when speech is "low value." The Court frequently quotes a passage from *Chaplinsky*:

> There are certain well-defined and narrowly limited classes of speech, the prevention and punishment of which has never been thought to raise any Constitutional problem. . . . It has been well observed that such utterances are no essential part of any exposition of ideas, and are of such slight social value as a step to truth that any benefit that may be derived from them is clearly outweighed by the social interest in order and morality.

Is this statement a methodology for determining when speech falls into a category of low-value speech? Is it even a good idea to weigh the "slight social value of speech as a step to truth" against the other "social interests" in regulating such speech?

The Court faced that question in United States v. Stevens, 559 U.S. 460 (2010), which involved a free speech challenge to a federal statute barring the knowing creation, sale, possession, or depiction of animal cruelty "with the intention of placing that depiction in interstate or foreign commerce for commercial gain." 18 U.S.C. § 48(a). The statute defined "animal cruelty" as any visual or auditory depiction of "conduct in which a living animal is intentionally maimed, mutilated, tortured, wounded, or killed, if such conduct is illegal under Federal law or the law of the State in which the creation, sale, or possession takes place." 18 U.S.C. § 48(c)(1). It also exempted "any depiction that has serious religious, political, scientific, educational, journalistic, historical, or artistic value." 18 U.S.C. § 48(b). The law's proponents argued that it was designed to bar the production, sale, and possession of "crush videos," which involve the intentional killing of helpless animals as part of a sexual fetish. The law had been applied, however, to an individual, Robert Stevens, who sold videos portraying dog fighting, which is illegal in all 50 states. Stevens challenged the federal statute as facially invalid because it was overly broad.

The government argued that the statute was constitutional because the speech involved was "categorically unprotected" by the First Amendment. "Whether a given category of speech enjoys First Amendment protection depends upon a categorical balancing of the value of the speech against its societal costs," the government claimed. 559 U.S. at 470. Using this analysis, the government argued that "illegal acts of animal cruelty" that are made and sold for commercial gain lack expressive value. *Id.* The Court rejected the government's argument. It acknowledged that "[f]rom 1791 to the present . . . the First Amendment has 'permitted restrictions upon the content of speech in a few limited areas,'" including obscenity, defamation, fraud, incitement, and speech integral to criminal conduct. 559 U.S. at 468. But it noted that such categories are "well-defined and narrowly limited." *Id.* (citing *Chaplinsky*). According to the Court, the government's "free-floating test for First Amendment coverage" was "startling and dangerous." *Id.* at 470.

> The First Amendment's guarantee of free speech does not extend only to categories of speech that survive an ad hoc balancing of relative social costs and benefits. The First Amendment itself reflects a judgment by the American people that the benefits of its restrictions on the Government outweigh the costs. Our Constitution forecloses any attempt to revise that judgment simply on the basis that some speech is not worth it. . . .
> Our decisions . . . cannot be taken as establishing a freewheeling authority to declare new categories of speech outside the scope of the First Amendment. Maybe there are some categories of speech that have been historically unprotected, but have not yet been specifically identified or discussed as such in our case law. But if so, there is no evidence that "depictions of animal cruelty" is among them. We need not foreclose the future recognition of such additional categories to reject the Government's highly manipulable balancing test as a means of identifying them.

Id. at 471-72.

The Court struck down the statute as overly broad because it reached speech that would otherwise qualify for First Amendment protection. The Court also noted that lack of value did not alone make speech unprotected:

> Most of what we say to one another lacks "religious, political, scientific, educational, journalistic, historical, or artistic value" (let alone serious value), but it is still sheltered from government regulation. Even "'[w]holly neutral futilities . . . come under the protection of free speech as fully as do Keats' poems or Donne's sermons.'" Thus, the protection of the First Amendment presumptively extends to many forms of speech that do not qualify for the serious-value exception of § 48(b), but nonetheless fall within the broad reach of § 48(c).

Id. at 479-80.

In United States v. Alvarez, 132 S. Ct. 2537 (2012), the Court once again took the categorical approach to low value speech. In *Alvarez* the Court struck down a statute imposing criminal punishment when an individual lies about receiving a Congressional Medal of Honor. Although the plurality opinion acknowledged that defamation and fraud were existing categories of low value speech involving false statements, it rejected the argument that lies generally were unprotected. *Id.* at 2545.

The Court further noted that defamation and fraud, along with existing laws punishing perjury, making false statements to officials, or falsely representing oneself as a government official, involved "targeted prohibitions" with a compelling interest to regulate beyond the mere falsity of the statement – for example, maintaining the integrity of the court system (perjury) or preventing financial loss (fraud). *Id.* at 2545-46. It thus rejected the government's argument that the law at issue was justified because false statements generally have no value. *Id.* at 2546-47. Referring to *Stevens*, the plurality opinion noted:

> [P]erhaps there exist "some categories of speech that have been historically unprotected . . . but have not yet been specifically identified or discussed . . . in our case law." Before exempting a category of speech from the normal prohibition on content-based restrictions, however, the Court must be presented with "persuasive evidence that a novel restriction on content is part of a long (if heretofore unrecognized) tradition of proscription," The Government has not demonstrated that false statements generally should constitute a new category of unprotected speech on this basis.

Id. at 2547. Does *Alvarez* intimate that the creation of low value speech categories requires specific harm to result from the speech? *See id.* at 2554 (Breyer, J. concurring in the judgment); Lyrissa Barnett Lidsky, *Where's the Harm?: Free Speech and the Regulation of Lies,* 65 Wash. & Lee L. Rev. 1091 (2008).

AN EXTENDED NOTE ON DEFINING PROTECTED SPEECH— POSSIBLE LESSONS FROM CANADA

The Canadian courts have defined the outer limits of protected expression quite broadly to include both threats of violence and child pornography. For example, in R. v. Sharpe, [2001] 1 S.C.R. 45 (Can.), the Supreme Court of Canada found that possession of child pornography was an expressive act protected by the Canadian Charter of Rights and Freedoms. Chief Justice McLachlin stated that

> [a]mong the most fundamental rights possessed by Canadians is freedom of expression. It makes possible our liberty, our creativity, and our democracy. . . .
> The values underlying the right to free expression include individual self-fulfillment, finding the truth through an open exchange of ideas, and the political discourse fundamental to democracy. While some types of expression, like political expression, lie closer to the core of the guarantee than others, all are vital to a free and democratic society. . . . [T]he guarantee "ensure[s] that everyone can manifest their thoughts, opinions, beliefs, indeed all expressions of the heart and mind, however unpopular, distasteful or contrary to the mainstream. Such protection . . . is "fundamental" because in a free, pluralistic and democratic society we prize a diversity of ideas and opinions for their inherent value both to the community and to the individual." . . .
> The law challenged in this appeal engages mainly the justification of self-fulfillment. Child pornography does not generally contribute to the search for truth or to Canadian social and political discourse. Some question whether it engages even the value of self-fulfillment, beyond the base aspect of sexual exploitation. The concern in this appeal, however, is that the law may incidentally catch forms of expression that more seriously implicate self-fulfillment and that do not pose a risk of harm to children.

As to the contention that prohibiting possession of expressive material does not raise free expression concerns, I cannot agree. The right conferred by s. 2(b) of the Charter embraces a continuum of intellectual and expressive freedom— "freedom of thought, belief, opinion, and expression." The right to possess expressive material is integrally related to the development of thought, belief, opinion, and expression. The possession of such material allows us to understand the thought of others or consolidate our own thought. Without the right to possess expressive material, freedom of thought, belief, opinion, and expression would be compromised. Thus the possession of expressive materials falls within the continuum of rights protected by s. 2(b) of the Charter.

Id. at 70-73. Writing in dissent, however, Justice L'Heureux-Dubé, joined by Justices Gonthier and Bastarache, rejected the argument that possession of child pornography constituted expressive conduct worthy of constitutional protection:

It is clear that s. 163.1(4) restricts expression if child pornography can be considered expression. While the Crown has conceded this latter question, it is important to recognize that the right to free expression in s. 2(b) has always been considered to protect only those activities which are communicative. . . .

From our jurisprudence, it is unclear whether the requirement that an activity convey or attempt to convey meaning excludes all activities which are not prima facie communicative from the scope of the right to free expression in s. 2(b). For example, this Court speculated that the parking of a car is not protected expression since it is not prima facie communicative activity. While it may be true that s. 2(b) guarantees the right to possess "material [that] allows us to understand the thought of others," the scope of the right . . . to create and possess self-authored works, especially those not intended for others, in order to "consolidate our own thought" is far from clear. Thus, in our view, it is unfortunate that the Crown conceded the right to free expression was violated in this appeal in all respects, thereby depriving the Court of the opportunity to fully explore the content and scope of s. 2(b) as it applies in this case.

Id. at 127-129 (L'Heureux-Dubé, J., dissenting).

Note that the Canadian approach links the scope of protected expression to a discussion of whether the expression serves the values underlying why we protect free expression. Is this a better way to approach the question of whether speech is protected or unprotected or does it just beg the question?

In Canada, finding that speech falls within the protection of section 2(b) of the Charter of Rights and Freedoms is only the first step in a two-step analysis. Section 1 of the Charter states, "[t]he *Canadian Charter of Rights and Freedoms* guarantees the rights and freedoms set out in it subject only to such reasonable limits prescribed by law as can be demonstrably justified in a free and democratic society." Canadian Charter of Rights and Freedoms, § 1. Consistent with section 1 of the Charter, courts should uphold laws that violate constitutionally protected speech if they are saved by application of section 1. See R. v. Oakes, [1986] S.C.R. 103 (applying a multi-factored balancing test to determine whether a statute that violates a Charter right is nevertheless valid and operative). Many laws found to violate section 2(b) are saved from invalidation by operation of section 1. Does this make the very broad interpretation of protected expression easier to understand? How does this approach differ from the United States Supreme Court's approach in *Stevens*?

B. CONTENT DISCRIMINATION AND HIGH-VALUE SPEECH

In addition to identifying categories of low-value speech, in recent decades the Court has increasingly relied upon content discrimination principles to determine the validity of speech regulations. As with low-value speech, the Court's content discrimination rules attempt to categorize. In this instance, however, the categories relate to the types of laws enacted and applied rather than the nature of the speech at issue. The Court's distinction between content-based regulations (which it views with suspicion and subjects to the most rigorous scrutiny) and content-neutral regulations (which it judges by more lenient, intermediate scrutiny) has become a linchpin of its jurisprudence. Although highly recognizable and seemingly easy to recite in a set of formulaic tests, understanding and applying the Court's content discrimination jurisprudence is not easy.

REED v. TOWN OF GILBERT

135 S. Ct. 2218 (2015)

Justice THOMAS delivered the opinion of the Court.

The town of Gilbert, Arizona (or Town), has adopted a comprehensive code governing the manner in which people may display outdoor signs. Gilbert, Ariz., Land Development Code (Sign Code or Code), ch. 1, § 4.402 (2005). . . .

I

A

The Sign Code prohibits the display of outdoor signs anywhere within the Town without a permit, but it then exempts 23 categories of signs from that requirement. These exemptions include everything from bazaar signs to flying banners. Three categories of exempt signs are particularly relevant here.

The first is "Ideological Sign[s]." This category includes any "sign communicating a message or ideas for noncommercial purposes that is not a Construction Sign, Directional Sign, Temporary Directional Sign Relating to a Qualifying Event, Political Sign, Garage Sale Sign, or a sign owned or required by a governmental agency." Of the three categories discussed here, the Code treats ideological signs most favorably, allowing them to be up to 20 square feet in area and to be placed in all "zoning districts" without time limits.

The second category is "Political Sign[s]." This includes any "temporary sign designed to influence the outcome of an election called by a public body." The Code treats these signs less favorably than ideological signs. The Code allows the placement of political signs up to 16 square feet on residential property and up to 32 square feet on nonresidential property, undeveloped municipal property, and "rights-of-way." These signs may be displayed up to 60 days before a primary election and up to 15 days following a general election.

The third category is "Temporary Directional Signs Relating to a Qualifying Event." This includes any "Temporary Sign intended to direct pedestrians, motorists, and other passersby to a 'qualifying event.'" A "qualifying event" is defined as any "assembly, gathering, activity, or meeting sponsored, arranged, or promoted by a religious, charitable, community service, educational, or other similar non-profit organization." The Code treats temporary directional signs even less favorably than political signs. Temporary directional signs may be no larger than six square feet. They may be placed on private property or on a public right-of-way, but no more than four signs may be placed on a single property at any time. And, they may be displayed no more than 12 hours before the "qualifying event" and no more than 1 hour afterward.

B

Petitioners Good News Community Church (Church) and its pastor, Clyde Reed, wish to advertise the time and location of their Sunday church services. The Church is a small, cash-strapped entity that owns no building, so it holds its services at elementary schools or other locations in or near the Town. In order to inform the public about its services, which are held in a variety of different locations, the Church began placing 15 to 20 temporary signs around the Town, frequently in the public right-of-way abutting the street. The signs typically displayed the Church's name, along with the time and location of the upcoming service. Church members would post the signs early in the day on Saturday and then remove them around midday on Sunday. The display of these signs requires little money and manpower, and thus has proved to be an economical and effective way for the Church to let the community know where its services are being held each week.

This practice caught the attention of the Town's Sign Code compliance manager, who twice cited the Church for violating the Code. The first citation noted that the Church exceeded the time limits for displaying its temporary directional signs. The second citation referred to the same problem, along with the Church's failure to include the date of the event on the signs. . . .

[After unsuccessfully trying to informally resolve the issue], petitioners filed a complaint in the United States District Court for the District of Arizona, arguing that the Sign Code abridged their freedom of speech in violation of the First and Fourteenth Amendments. The District Court denied the petitioners' motion for a preliminary injunction. The Court of Appeals for the Ninth Circuit affirmed[.] . . .

We granted certiorari and now reverse.

II

A

. . . Under [the First Amendment], a government, including a municipal government vested with state authority, "has no power to restrict expression because of its message, its ideas, its subject matter, or its content." *Police Dept. of Chicago v. Mosley*, 408 U.S. 92, 95 (1972). Content-based laws—those that target speech based on its communicative content—are presumptively unconstitutional and may be justified only if the government proves that they are narrowly tailored to serve compelling state interests.

Government regulation of speech is content based if a law applies to particular speech because of the topic discussed or the idea or message expressed. This commonsense meaning of the phrase "content based" requires a court to consider whether a regulation of speech "on its face" draws distinctions based on the message a speaker conveys. Some facial distinctions based on a message are obvious, defining regulated speech by particular subject matter, and others are more subtle, defining regulated speech by its function or purpose. Both are distinctions drawn based on the message a speaker conveys, and, therefore, are subject to strict scrutiny.

Our precedents have also recognized a separate and additional category of laws that, though facially content neutral, will be considered content-based regulations of speech: laws that cannot be "'justified without reference to the content of the regulated speech,'" or that were adopted by the government "because of disagreement with the message [the speech] conveys," *Ward v. Rock Against Racism*, 491 U.S. 781, 791 (1989). Those laws, like those that are content based on their face, must also satisfy strict scrutiny.

<h1 style="text-align:center">B</h1>

The Town's Sign Code is content based on its face. It defines "Temporary Directional Signs" on the basis of whether a sign conveys the message of directing the public to church or some other "qualifying event." It defines "Political Signs" on the basis of whether a sign's message is "designed to influence the outcome of an election." And it defines "Ideological Signs" on the basis of whether a sign "communicat[es] a message or ideas" that do not fit within the Code's other categories. It then subjects each of these categories to different restrictions.

The restrictions in the Sign Code that apply to any given sign thus depend entirely on the communicative content of the sign. . . .   On its face, the Sign Code is a content-based regulation of speech. We thus have no need to consider the government's justifications or purposes for enacting the Code to determine whether it is subject to strict scrutiny.

<h1 style="text-align:center">C</h1>

In reaching the contrary conclusion, the Court of Appeals offered several theories to explain why the Town's Sign Code should be deemed content neutral. None is persuasive.

<h1 style="text-align:center">1</h1>

The Court of Appeals first determined that the Sign Code was content neutral because the Town "did not adopt its regulation of speech [based on] disagree[ment] with the message conveyed," and its justifications for regulating temporary directional signs were "unrelated to the content of the sign." In its brief to this Court, the United States similarly contends that a sign regulation is content neutral—even if it expressly draws distinctions based on the sign's communicative content—if those distinctions can be "'justified without reference to the content of the regulated speech.'" Brief for United States as *Amicus Curiae* 20, 24.

But this analysis skips the crucial first step in the content-neutrality analysis: determining whether the law is content neutral on its face. A law that is content based on its face is subject to strict scrutiny regardless of the government's benign motive, content-neutral justification, or lack of "animus toward the ideas contained" in the regulated speech. *Cincinnati v. Discovery Network, Inc.*, 507 U.S. 410, 429 (1993).

We have thus made clear that "'[i]llicit legislative intent is not the *sine qua non* of a violation of the First Amendment,'" and a party opposing the government "need adduce 'no evidence of an improper censorial motive.'" Although "a content-based purpose may be sufficient in certain circumstances to show that a regulation is content based, it is not necessary." *Turner Broadcasting System, Inc. v. FCC*, 512 U.S. 622, 642 (1994). In other words, an innocuous justification cannot transform a facially content-based law into one that is content neutral.

That is why we have repeatedly considered whether a law is content neutral on its face *before* turning to the law's justification or purpose. . . . Because strict scrutiny applies either when a law is content based on its face or when the purpose and justification for the law are content based, a court must evaluate each question before it concludes that the law is content neutral and thus subject to a lower level of scrutiny.

The Court of Appeals and the United States misunderstand our decision in *Ward* as suggesting that a government's purpose is relevant even when a law is content based on its face. That is incorrect. *Ward* had nothing to say about facially content-based restrictions because it involved a facially content-*neutral* ban on the use, in a city-owned music venue, of sound amplification systems not provided by the city. In that context, we looked to governmental motive, including whether the government had regulated speech "because of disagreement" with its message, and whether the regulation was "'justified without reference to the content of the speech.'" But *Ward*'s framework "applies only if a statute is content neutral." Hill v. Colorado, 530 U.S. 703, 766, (2000) (Kennedy, J., dissenting). Its rules thus operate "to protect speech," not "to restrict it."

The First Amendment requires no less. Innocent motives do not eliminate the danger of censorship presented by a facially content-based statute, as future government officials may one day wield such statutes to suppress disfavored speech. That is why the First Amendment expressly targets the operation of the laws—*i.e.,* the "abridg[ement] of speech"—rather than merely the motives of those who enacted them. "'The vice of content-based legislation ... is not that it is always used for invidious, thought-control purposes, but that it lends itself to use for those purposes.'" *Hill* (Scalia, J., dissenting). . . .

2

The Court of Appeals next reasoned that the Sign Code was content neutral because it "does not mention any idea or viewpoint, let alone single one out for differential treatment." . . .

This analysis conflates two distinct but related limitations that the First Amendment places on government regulation of speech. Government discrimination among viewpoints—or the regulation of speech based on "the specific motivating ideology or the opinion or perspective of the speaker"—is a "more blatant" and "egregious form of content discrimination." *Rosenberger v. Rector and Visitors of Univ. of Va.*, 515 U.S. 819, 829 (1995). But it is well established that "[t]he First Amendment's hostility to content-based regulation extends not only to restrictions on particular viewpoints, but also to prohibition of public discussion of an entire topic." *Consolidated Edison Co. of N.Y. v. Public Serv. Comm'n of N. Y.*, 447 U.S. 530, 537 (1980).

Thus, a speech regulation targeted at specific subject matter is content based even if it does not discriminate among viewpoints within that subject matter. For example, a law banning the use of sound trucks for political speech—and only political speech—would be a content-based regulation, even if it imposed no limits on the political viewpoints that could be expressed. The Town's Sign Code likewise singles out specific subject matter for differential treatment, even if it does not target viewpoints within that subject matter. Ideological messages are given more favorable treatment than messages concerning a political candidate, which are themselves given more favorable treatment than messages announcing an assembly of like-minded individuals. That is a paradigmatic example of content-based discrimination.

3

Finally, the Court of Appeals characterized the Sign Code's distinctions as turning on "'the content-neutral elements of who is speaking through the sign and whether and when an event is occurring.'" That analysis is mistaken on both factual and legal grounds.

To start, the Sign Code's distinctions are not speaker based. The restrictions for political, ideological, and temporary event signs apply equally no matter who sponsors them. If a local business, for example, sought to put up signs advertising the Church's meetings, those signs would be subject to the same limitations as such signs placed by the Church. And if Reed had decided to display signs in support of a particular candidate, he could have made those signs far larger—and kept them up for far longer—than signs inviting people to attend his church services. If the Code's distinctions were truly speaker based, both types of signs would receive the same treatment.

In any case, the fact that a distinction is speaker based does not, as the Court of Appeals seemed to believe, automatically render the distinction content neutral. Because "[s]peech restrictions based on the identity of the speaker are all too often simply a means to control content," *Citizens United v. Federal Election Comm'n*, 558 U.S. 310, 340 (2010), we have insisted that "laws favoring some speakers over others demand strict scrutiny when the legislature's speaker preference reflects a content preference," *Turner*. Thus, a law limiting the content of newspapers, but only newspapers, could not evade strict scrutiny simply because it could be characterized as speaker based. . . . Characterizing a distinction as speaker based is only the beginning—not the end—of the inquiry.

Nor do the Sign Code's distinctions hinge on "whether and when an event is occurring." The Code does not permit citizens to post signs on any topic whatsoever within a set period leading up to an election, for example. Instead, come election time, it requires Town officials to determine whether a sign is "designed to influence the outcome of an election" (and thus "political") or merely "communicating a message or ideas for noncommercial purposes" (and thus "ideological"). That obvious content-based inquiry does not evade strict scrutiny review simply because an event (*i.e.*, an election) is involved.

And, just as with speaker-based laws, the fact that a distinction is event based does not render it content neutral. . . . A regulation that targets a sign because it conveys an idea about a specific event is no less content based than a regulation that targets a sign because it conveys some other idea. Here, the Code singles out signs bearing a particular message: the time and location of a specific event. . . .

III

Because the Town's Sign Code imposes content-based restrictions on speech, those provisions can stand only if they survive strict scrutiny, "'which requires the Government to prove that the restriction furthers a compelling interest and is narrowly tailored to achieve that interest,'" *Arizona Free Enterprise Club's Freedom Club PAC v. Bennett*, 131 S. Ct. 2806, 2817 (2011). Thus, it is the Town's burden to demonstrate that the Code's differentiation between temporary directional signs and other types of signs, such as political signs and ideological signs, furthers a compelling governmental interest and is narrowly tailored to that end.

The Town cannot do so. It has offered only two governmental interests in support of the distinctions the Sign Code draws: preserving the Town's aesthetic appeal and traffic safety. Assuming for the sake of argument that those are compelling governmental interests, the Code's distinctions fail as hopelessly underinclusive.

Starting with the preservation of aesthetics, temporary directional signs are "no greater an eyesore" than ideological or political ones. Yet the Code allows unlimited proliferation of larger ideological signs while strictly limiting the number, size, and duration of smaller directional ones. The Town cannot claim that placing strict limits on temporary directional signs is necessary to beautify the Town while at the same time allowing unlimited numbers of other types of signs that create the same problem.

The Town similarly has not shown that limiting temporary directional signs is necessary to eliminate threats to traffic safety, but that limiting other types of signs is not. The Town has offered no reason to believe that directional signs pose a greater threat to safety than do ideological or political signs. If anything, a sharply worded ideological sign seems more likely to distract a driver than a sign directing the public to a nearby church meeting.

In light of this underinclusiveness, the Town has not met its burden to prove that its Sign Code is narrowly tailored to further a compelling government interest. . . .

IV

Our decision today will not prevent governments from enacting effective sign laws. The Town asserts that an "'absolutist'" content-neutrality rule would render "virtually all distinctions in sign laws . . . subject to strict scrutiny," but that is not the case. Not "all distinctions" are subject to strict scrutiny, only *content-based* ones are. Laws that are *content neutral* are instead subject to lesser scrutiny.

The Town has ample content-neutral options available to resolve problems with safety and aesthetics. For example, its current Code regulates many aspects of signs that have nothing to do with a sign's message: size, building materials, lighting, moving parts, and portability. And on public property, the Town may go a long way toward entirely forbidding the posting of signs, so long as it does so in an evenhanded, content-neutral manner. . . .

We reverse the judgment of the Court of Appeals and remand the case for proceedings consistent with this opinion.

It is so ordered.

Justice BREYER, concurring in the judgment.

I join Justice Kagan's separate opinion. Like Justice Kagan I believe that categories alone cannot satisfactorily resolve the legal problem before us. The First Amendment requires greater judicial sensitivity both to the Amendment's expressive objectives and to the public's legitimate need for regulation than a simple recitation of categories, such as "content discrimination" and "strict scrutiny," would permit. In my view, the category "content discrimination" is better considered in many contexts, including here, as a rule of thumb, rather than as an automatic "strict scrutiny" trigger, leading to almost certain legal condemnation.

To use content discrimination to trigger strict scrutiny sometimes makes perfect sense. There are cases in which the Court has found content discrimination an unconstitutional method for suppressing a viewpoint. And there are cases where the Court has found content discrimination to reveal that rules governing a traditional public forum are, in fact, not a neutral way of fairly managing the forum in the interest of all speakers.

But content discrimination, while helping courts to identify unconstitutional suppression of expression, cannot and should not *always* trigger strict scrutiny. To say that it is not an automatic "strict scrutiny" trigger is not to argue against that concept's use. I readily concede, for example, that content discrimination, as a conceptual tool, can sometimes reveal weaknesses in the government's rationale for a rule that limits speech. If, for example, a city looks to litter prevention as the rationale for a prohibition against placing newsracks dispensing free advertisements on public property, why does it exempt other newsracks causing similar litter? I also concede that, whenever government disfavors one kind of speech, it places that speech at a disadvantage, potentially interfering with the free marketplace of ideas and with an individual's ability to express thoughts and ideas that can help that individual determine the kind of society in which he wishes to live, help shape that society, and help define his place within it.

Nonetheless, in these latter instances to use the presence of content discrimination automatically to trigger strict scrutiny and thereby call into play a strong presumption against constitutionality goes too far. That is because virtually all government activities involve speech, many of which involve the regulation of speech. Regulatory programs almost always require content discrimination. And to hold that such content discrimination triggers strict scrutiny is to write a recipe for judicial management of ordinary government regulatory activity. . . .

I recognize that the Court could escape the problem by watering down the force of the presumption against constitutionality that "strict scrutiny" normally carries with it. But, in my view, doing so will weaken the First Amendment's protection in instances where "strict scrutiny" should apply in full force.

The better approach is to generally treat content discrimination as a strong reason weighing against the constitutionality of a rule where a traditional public forum, or where viewpoint discrimination, is threatened, but elsewhere treat it as a rule of thumb, finding it a helpful, but not determinative legal tool, in an appropriate case, to determine the strength of a justification. I would use content discrimination as a supplement to a more basic analysis, which, tracking most of our First Amendment cases, asks whether the regulation at issue works harm to First Amendment interests that is disproportionate in light of the relevant regulatory objectives. Answering this question requires examining the seriousness of the harm to speech, the importance of the countervailing objectives, the extent to which the law will achieve those objectives, and whether there are other, less restrictive ways of doing so. *See, e.g.,*

United States v. Alvarez, 132 S. Ct. 2537, 2551–2553 (2012) (Breyer, J., concurring in judgment). Admittedly, this approach does not have the simplicity of a mechanical use of categories. But it does permit the government to regulate speech in numerous instances where the voters have authorized the government to regulate and where courts should hesitate to substitute judicial judgment for that of administrators.

Here, regulation of signage along the roadside, for purposes of safety and beautification is at issue. There is no traditional public forum nor do I find any general effort to censor a particular viewpoint. Consequently, the specific regulation at issue does not warrant "strict scrutiny." Nonetheless, for the reasons that Justice Kagan sets forth, I believe that the Town of Gilbert's regulatory rules violate the First Amendment. I consequently concur in the Court's judgment only.

Justice KAGAN, with whom Justice GINSBURG and Justice BREYER join, concurring in the judgment.

Countless cities and towns across America have adopted ordinances regulating the posting of signs, while exempting certain categories of signs based on their subject matter. . . .

Given the Court's analysis, many sign ordinances of that kind are now in jeopardy. . . . [A]lthough the majority holds out hope that some sign laws with subject-matter exemptions "might survive" [strict scrutiny], the likelihood is that most will be struck down. . . . To clear that high bar, the government must show that a content-based distinction "is necessary to serve a compelling state interest and is narrowly drawn to achieve that end." So on the majority's view, courts would have to determine that a town has a compelling interest in informing passersby where George Washington slept. And likewise, courts would have to find that a town has no other way to prevent hidden-driveway mishaps than by specially treating hidden-driveway signs. (Well-placed speed bumps? Lower speed limits? Or how about just a ban on hidden driveways?) The consequence—unless courts water down strict scrutiny to something unrecognizable—is that our communities will find themselves in an unenviable bind: They will have to either repeal the exemptions that allow for helpful signs on streets and sidewalks, or else lift their sign restrictions altogether and resign themselves to the resulting clutter.

Although the majority insists that applying strict scrutiny to all such ordinances is "essential" to protecting First Amendment freedoms, I find it challenging to understand why that is so. This Court's decisions articulate two important and related reasons for subjecting content-based speech regulations to the most exacting standard of review. The first is "to preserve an uninhibited marketplace of ideas in which truth will ultimately prevail." *McCullen v. Coakley*, 134 S. Ct. 2518, 2529 (2014). The second is to ensure that the government has not regulated speech "based on hostility—or favoritism—towards the underlying message expressed." *R.A.V. v. St. Paul*, 505 U.S. 377, 386 (1992). Yet the subject-matter exemptions included in many sign ordinances do not implicate those concerns. Allowing residents, say, to install a light bulb over "name and address" signs but no others does not distort the marketplace of ideas. Nor does that different treatment give rise to an inference of impermissible government motive.

We apply strict scrutiny to facially content-based regulations of speech, in keeping with the rationales just described, when there is any "realistic possibility that official suppression of ideas is afoot." *Davenport v. Washington Ed. Assn.*, 551 U.S. 177, 189 (2007). That is always the case when the regulation facially differentiates on the basis of viewpoint. It is also the case (except in non-public or limited public forums) when a law restricts "discussion of an entire topic" in public debate. *Consolidated Edison Co. of N.Y. v. Public Serv. Comm'n of N. Y.*, 447 U.S. 530, 537, 539–540 (1980). . . . Subject-matter regulation, in other words, may have the intent or effect of favoring some ideas over others. When that is realistically possible— when the restriction "raises the specter that the Government may effectively drive certain ideas or viewpoints from the marketplace"—we insist that the law pass the most demanding constitutional test.

But when that is not realistically possible, we may do well to relax our guard so that "entirely reasonable" laws imperiled by strict scrutiny can survive. . . .

And indeed we have done just that: Our cases have been far less rigid than the majority admits in applying strict scrutiny to facially content-based laws—including in cases just like this one. In *Members of City Council of Los Angeles v. Taxpayers for Vincent*, 466 U.S. 789 (1984), the Court declined to apply strict scrutiny to a municipal ordinance that exempted address numbers and markers commemorating "historical, cultural, or artistic event[s]" from a generally applicable limit on sidewalk signs. After all, we explained, the law's enactment and enforcement revealed "not even a hint of bias or censorship." See also *Renton v. Playtime Theatres, Inc.*, 475 U.S. 41, 48 (1986) (applying intermediate scrutiny to a zoning law that facially distinguished among movie theaters based on content because it was "designed to prevent crime, protect the city's retail trade, [and] maintain property values . . .," not to suppress the expression of unpopular views"). And another decision involving a similar law provides an alternative model. In *City of Ladue v. Gilleo*, 512 U.S. 43 (1994), the Court assumed *arguendo* that a sign ordinance's exceptions for address signs, safety signs, and for-sale signs in residential areas did not trigger strict scrutiny. We did not need to, and so did not, decide the level-of-scrutiny question because the law's breadth made it unconstitutional under any standard.

The majority could easily have taken *Ladue*'s tack here. The Town of Gilbert's defense of its sign ordinance—most notably, the law's distinctions between directional signs and others—does not pass strict scrutiny, or intermediate scrutiny, or even the laugh test. The Town, for example, provides no reason at all for prohibiting more than four directional signs on a property while placing no limits on the number of other types of signs. Similarly, the Town offers no coherent justification for restricting the size of directional signs to 6 square feet while allowing other signs to reach 20 square feet. The best the Town could come up with at oral argument was that directional signs "need to be smaller because they need to guide travelers along a route." Why exactly a smaller sign better helps travelers get to where they are going is left a mystery. The absence of any sensible basis for these and other distinctions dooms the Town's ordinance under even the intermediate scrutiny that the Court typically applies to "time, place, or manner" speech regulations. Accordingly, there is no need to decide in this case whether strict scrutiny applies to every sign ordinance in every town across this country containing a subject-matter exemption.

I suspect this Court and others will regret the majority's insistence today on answering that question in the affirmative. As the years go by, courts will discover that thousands of towns have such ordinances, many of them "entirely reasonable." And as the challenges to them mount, courts will have to invalidate one after the other. (This Court may soon find itself a veritable Supreme Board of Sign Review.) And courts will strike down those democratically enacted local laws even though no one—certainly not the majority—has ever explained why the vindication of First

Amendment values requires that result. Because I see no reason why such an easy case calls for us to cast a constitutional pall on reasonable regulations quite unlike the law before us, I concur only in the judgment.

[Justice ALITO's concurring opinion is omitted.]

NOTES AND QUESTIONS

1. *Content discrimination methodology.* The *Reed* majority states a methodology for determining content-based and content-neutral laws. First, facially content-based laws are content-based, even if, as the Court notes, the government is not attempting to suppress speech because of what the speaker says. Second, the Court notes that some facially content-neutral laws may be content-based if there is a content-based purpose behind their application. Classic examples of the latter are breach of the peace statutes, such as those in the fighting-words and hostile audience cases in Sections A.2 and A.3, *supra*. Breach of the peace laws do not facially regulate speech of a particular content, but the government's purpose in applying those laws in *Cohen, Cox, Edwards*, and *Gregory* turned on the audience's hostility to the speaker's expression. Thus, application of the laws in those cases is considered to be content-based. *See* Holder v. Humanitarian Law Project, 561 U.S. 1 (2010).

2. *The dangers of content-based regulations.* Why does the Court disfavor content-based regulations? For further discussion, see Geoffrey R. Stone, *Content Regulation and the First Amendment*, 25 Wm. & Mary L. Rev. 189, (1983); Martin H. Redish, *The Content Distinction in First Amendment Analysis*, 34 Stan. L. Rev. 113 (1981).

3. *Viewpoint-based versus subject-matter based restrictions.* The Court is particularly suspicious of viewpoint-based regulations of speech. Many of the laws involved in previous sections of the book, such as the Espionage Act or state syndicalism laws, were viewpoint-based. On the other hand, subject-matter restrictions aim at entire subjects rather than particular viewpoints—for example, a law regulating only signs with commercial content. *Reed* emphasizes that the ban on content-based restrictions extends to these as well.

   Do subject-matter-based regulations pose the same dangers as viewpoint-based regulations or are they more like content-neutral regulations in terms of the dangers they pose to free expression? Are the concurring justices in *Reed* right that a less rigid approach to content-based regulations might be appropriate? For a discussion of this issue, *see* Geoffrey R. Stone, *Restrictions of Speech Because of Its Content: The Peculiar Case of Subject-Matter Restrictions*, 46 U. Chi. L. Rev. 81 (1978); Daniel A. Farber, *Content Regulation and the First Amendment: A Revisionist View*, 68 Geo. L.J. 727 (1980). Perhaps, as Professor Stone has noted, subject-matter restrictions "exist in a middle world, sharing some characteristics with both of the more common forms of restrictions." Stone, *Subject-Matter Restrictions, supra*, at 115.

The next case involves a "speaker-based" restriction on speech. As *Reed* noted, such restrictions are not automatically content-based but depend on whether "the legislature's speaker preference reflects a content preference." Consider whether the law in the following case reflects a content preference.

TURNER BROADCASTING SYSTEM, INC. v. FCC
512 U.S. 622 (1994)

Justice KENNEDY announced the judgment of the Court and delivered the opinion of the Court.

Sections 4 and 5 of the Cable Television Consumer Protection and Competition Act of 1992 [the Act] require cable television systems to devote a portion of their channels to the transmission of local broadcast television stations. This case presents the question whether these provisions abridge the freedom of speech or of the press, in violation of the First Amendment. . . .

The role of cable television in the Nation's communications system has undergone dramatic change over the past 45 years. . . . The earliest cable systems were built in the late 1940's to bring clear broadcast television signals to remote or mountainous communities. The purpose was not to replace broadcast television but to enhance it. Modern cable systems do much more than enhance the reception of nearby broadcast television stations. With the capacity to carry dozens of channels and import distant programming signals via satellite or microwave relay, today's cable systems are in direct competition with over the air broadcasters as an independent source of television programming.

Broadcast and cable television are distinguished by the different technologies through which they reach viewers. Broadcast stations radiate electromagnetic signals from a central transmitting antenna. These signals can be captured, in turn, by any television set within the antenna's range. Cable systems, by contrast, rely upon a physical, point to point connection between a transmission facility and the television sets of individual subscribers. Cable systems make this connection much like telephone companies, using cable or optical fibers strung aboveground or buried in ducts to reach the homes or businesses of subscribers. The construction of this physical infrastructure entails the use of public rights of way and easements and often results in the disruption of traffic on streets and other public property. As a result, the cable medium may depend for its very existence upon express permission from local governing authorities.

Cable technology affords two principal benefits over broadcast. First, it eliminates the signal interference sometimes encountered in over the air broadcasting and thus gives viewers undistorted reception of broadcast stations. Second, it is capable of transmitting many more channels than are available through broadcasting, giving subscribers access to far greater programming variety. . . . Newer systems can carry hundreds of channels, and many older systems are being upgraded with fiber optic rebuilds and digital compression technology to increase channel capacity.

The cable television industry includes both cable operators (those who own the physical cable network and transmit the cable signal to the viewer) and cable programmers (those who produce television programs and sell or license them to cable operators). . . . Although cable operators may create some of their own programming, most of their programming is drawn from outside sources. . . . Once the cable operator has selected the programming sources, the cable system functions, in essence, as a conduit for the speech of others, transmitting it on a continuous and unedited basis to subscribers. . . .

In contrast to commercial broadcast stations, which transmit signals at no charge to viewers and generate revenues by selling time to advertisers, cable systems charge subscribers a monthly fee for the right to receive cable programming and rely to a lesser extent on advertising. In most instances, cable subscribers choose the stations they will receive by selecting among various plans, or "tiers," of cable service. In a typical offering, the basic tier consists of local broadcast stations plus a number of cable programming networks selected by the cable operator. . . .

Section 4 of [the Act] requires carriage of "local commercial television stations," defined to include all full power television broadcasters, other than those qualifying as "noncommercial educational" stations under § 5, that operate within the same television market as the cable system. Cable systems with more than 12 active channels, and more than 300 subscribers, are required to set aside up to one third of their channels for commercial broadcast stations that request carriage. Cable systems with more than 300 subscribers, but only 12 or fewer active channels, must carry the signals of three commercial broadcast stations.

. . . The broadcast signals carried under this provision must be transmitted on a continuous, uninterrupted basis and must be placed in the same numerical channel position as when broadcast over the air. Further, subject to a few exceptions, a cable operator may not charge a fee for carrying broadcast signals in fulfillment of its must-carry obligations.

Section 5 of the Act imposes similar requirements regarding the carriage of local public broadcast television stations, referred to in the Act as local "noncommercial educational television stations." . . . As with commercial broadcast stations, § 5 requires cable system operators to carry the program schedule of the public broadcast station in its entirety and at its same over the air channel position.

Taken together, therefore, §§ 4 and 5 subject all but the smallest cable systems nationwide to must carry obligations, and confer must carry privileges on all full power broadcasters operating within the same television market as a qualified cable system.

Congress enacted the 1992 Cable Act after conducting three years of hearings on the structure and operation of the cable television industry. The conclusions Congress drew from its fact finding process are recited in the text of the Act itself. In brief, Congress found that the physical characteristics of cable transmission, compounded by the increasing concentration of economic power in the cable industry, are endangering the ability of over the air broadcast television stations to compete for a viewing audience and thus for necessary operating revenues. Congress determined that regulation of the market for video programming was necessary to correct this competitive imbalance. . . .

In light of these technological and economic conditions, Congress concluded that unless cable operators are required to carry local broadcast stations, "[t]here is a substantial likelihood that . . . additional local broadcast signals will be deleted, repositioned, or not carried," the "marked shift in market share" from broadcast to cable will continue to erode the advertising revenue base which sustains free local broadcast television, and that, as a consequence, "the economic viability of free local broadcast television and its ability to originate quality local programming will be seriously jeopardized." . . .

At the heart of the First Amendment lies the principle that each person should decide for himself or herself the ideas and beliefs deserving of expression, consideration, and adherence. Our political system and cultural life rest upon this ideal. Government action that stifles speech on account of its message, or that requires the utterance of a particular message favored by the Government, contravenes this essential right. Laws of this sort pose the inherent risk that the Government seeks not to advance a legitimate regulatory goal, but to suppress unpopular ideas or information or manipulate the public debate through coercion rather than persuasion. These restrictions "rais[e] the specter that the Government may effectively drive certain ideas or viewpoints from the marketplace." *Simon & Schuster, Inc. v. Members of State Crime Victims Bd.*, 502 U.S. 105, 116 (1991).

For these reasons, the First Amendment, subject only to narrow and well-understood exceptions, does not countenance governmental control over the content of messages expressed by private individuals. Our precedents thus apply the most exacting scrutiny to regulations that suppress, disadvantage, or impose differential burdens upon speech because of its content. Laws that compel speakers to utter or distribute speech bearing a particular message are subject to the same rigorous scrutiny. In contrast, regulations that are unrelated to the content of speech are subject to an intermediate level of scrutiny, see *Clark v. Community for Creative Non-Violence*, 468 U.S. 288 (1984), because in most cases they pose a less substantial risk of excising certain ideas or viewpoints from the public dialogue.

Deciding whether a particular regulation is content based or content neutral is not always a simple task. We have said that the "principal inquiry in determining content neutrality... is whether the government has adopted a regulation of speech because of [agreement or] disagreement with the message it conveys." *Ward v. Rock Against Racism*, 491 U.S. 781 (1989). The purpose, or justification, of a regulation will often be evident on its face. But while a content-based purpose may be sufficient in certain circumstances to show that a regulation is content based, it is not necessary to such a showing in all cases. Nor will the mere assertion of a content-neutral purpose be enough to save a law which, on its face, discriminates based on content.

As a general rule, laws that by their terms distinguish favored speech from disfavored speech on the basis of the ideas or views expressed are content based. By contrast, laws that confer benefits or impose burdens on speech without reference to the ideas or views expressed are in most instances content neutral.

Insofar as they pertain to the carriage of full-power broadcasters, the must-carry rules, on their face, impose burdens and confer benefits without reference to the content of speech. Although the provisions interfere with cable operators' editorial discretion by compelling them to offer carriage to a certain minimum number of broadcast stations, the extent of the interference does not depend upon the content of the cable operators' programming. The rules impose obligations upon all operators, save those with fewer than 300 subscribers, regardless of the programs or stations they now offer or have offered in the past. Nothing in the Act imposes a restriction, penalty, or burden by reason of the views, programs, or stations the cable operator has selected or will select. The number of channels a cable operator must set aside depends only on the operator's channel capacity; hence, an operator cannot avoid or mitigate its obligations under the Act by altering the programming it offers to subscribers.

The must-carry provisions also burden cable programmers by reducing the number of channels for which they can compete. But, again, this burden is unrelated to content, for it extends to all cable programmers irrespective of the programming they choose to offer viewers. And finally, the privileges conferred by the must-carry provisions are also unrelated to content. The rules benefit all full power broadcasters who request carriage—be they commercial or noncommercial, independent or network affiliated, English or Spanish language, religious or secular. The aggregate effect of the rules is thus to make every full power commercial and noncommercial broadcaster eligible for must-carry, provided only that the broadcaster operates within the same television market as a cable system.

It is true that the must-carry provisions distinguish between speakers in the television programming market. But they do so based only upon the manner in which speakers transmit their messages to viewers, and not upon the messages they carry: Broadcasters, which transmit over the airwaves, are favored, while cable programmers, which do not, are disfavored. Cable operators, too, are burdened by the carriage obligations, but only because they control access to the cable conduit. So long as they are not a subtle means of exercising a content preference, speaker distinctions of this nature are not presumed invalid under the First Amendment.

That the must-carry provisions, on their face, do not burden or benefit speech of a particular content does not end the inquiry. Our cases have recognized that even a regulation neutral on its face may be content based if its manifest purpose is to regulate speech because of the message it conveys. *United States v. Eichman*, 496 U.S. 310, 315 (1990).

Appellants contend, in this regard, that the must-carry regulations are content based because Congress' purpose in enacting them was to promote speech of a favored content. We do not agree. Our review of the Act and its various findings persuades us that Congress' overriding objective in enacting must-carry was not to favor programming of a particular subject matter, viewpoint, or format, but rather to preserve access to free television programming for the 40 percent of Americans without cable.

In unusually detailed statutory findings, Congress explained that because cable systems and broadcast stations compete for local advertising revenue and because cable operators have a vested financial interest in favoring their affiliated programmers over broadcast stations, cable operators have a built-in "economic incentive…to delete, reposition, or not carry local broadcast signals." Congress concluded that absent a requirement that cable systems carry the signals of local broadcast stations, the continued availability of free local broadcast television would be threatened. Congress sought to avoid the elimination of broadcast television because, in its words, "[s]uch programming is . . . free to those who own television sets and do not require cable transmission to receive broadcast television signals," and because "[t]here is a substantial governmental interest in promoting the continued availability of such free television programming, especially for viewers who are unable to afford other means of receiving programming."

By preventing cable operators from refusing carriage to broadcast television stations, the must-carry rules ensure that broadcast television stations will retain a large enough potential audience to earn necessary advertising revenue—or, in the case of noncommercial broadcasters, sufficient viewer contributions—to maintain their continued operation. In so doing, the provisions are designed to guarantee the survival of a medium that has become a vital part of the Nation's communication system, and to ensure that every individual with a television set can obtain access to free television programming. . . .

The design and operation of the challenged provisions confirm that the purposes underlying the enactment of the must-carry scheme are unrelated to the content of speech. The rules, as mentioned, confer must-carry rights on all full power broadcasters, irrespective of the content of their programming. They do not require or prohibit the carriage of particular ideas or points of view. They do not penalize cable operators or programmers because of the content of their programming. They do not compel cable operators to affirm points of view with which they disagree. They do not produce any net decrease in the amount of available speech. And they leave cable operators free to carry whatever programming they wish on all channels not subject to must-carry requirements.

. . . We do not think . . . [that the Act's references to the values of broadcast programming] cast any material doubt on the content-neutral character of must-carry. That Congress acknowledged the local orientation of broadcast programming and the role that noncommercial stations have played in educating the public does not indicate that Congress regarded broadcast programming as *more* valuable than cable programming. Rather, it reflects nothing more than the recognition that the services provided by broadcast television have some intrinsic value and, thus, are worth preserving against the threats posed by cable.

The operation of the Act further undermines the suggestion that Congress' purpose in enacting must-carry was to force programming of a "local" or "educational" content on cable subscribers. The provisions, as we have stated, benefit all full power broadcasters irrespective of the nature of their programming. In fact, if a cable system were required to bump a cable programmer to make room for a broadcast station, nothing would stop a cable operator from displacing a cable station that provides all local- or education-oriented programming with a broadcaster that provides very little. Appellants do not even contend, moreover, that broadcast programming is any more "local" or "educational" than cable programming.

Justice O'CONNOR, with whom Justice SCALIA and Justice GINSBURG join, and with whom Justice THOMAS joins, concurring in part and dissenting in part.

. . . I agree with the Court that some speaker-based restrictions—those genuinely justified without reference to content—need not be subject to strict scrutiny. But looking at the statute at issue, I cannot avoid the conclusion that its preference for broadcasters over cable programmers is justified with reference to content. The findings, enacted by Congress as § 2 of the Act, and which I must assume state the justifications for the law, make this clear. "There is a substantial governmental and First Amendment interest in promoting a diversity of views provided through multiple technology media." "[P]ublic television provides educational and informational programming to the Nation's citizens, thereby advancing the Government's compelling interest in educating its citizens. A primary objective and benefit of our Nation's system of regulation of television broadcasting is the local origination of programming. There is a substantial governmental interest in ensuring its continuation. Broadcast television stations continue to be an important source of local news and public affairs programming and other local broadcast services critical to an informed electorate."

Similar justifications are reflected in the operative provisions of the Act. In determining whether a broadcast station should be eligible for must-carry in a particular market, the Federal Communications Commission (FCC) must "afford particular attention to the value of localism by taking into account such factors as . . . whether any other [eligible station] provides news coverage of issues of concern to such community or provides carriage or coverage of sporting and other events of interest to the community." In determining whether a low-power station is eligible for must-carry, the FCC must ask whether the station "would address local news and informational needs which are not being adequately served by full power television broadcast stations." . . . These provisions . . . are . . . strong evidence of the statute's justifications.

Preferences for diversity of viewpoints, for localism, for educational programming, and for news and public affairs all make reference to content. They may not reflect hostility to particular points of view, or a desire to suppress certain subjects because they are controversial or offensive. They may be quite benignly motivated. But benign motivation, we have consistently held, is not enough to avoid the need for strict scrutiny of content-based justifications. The First Amendment does more than just bar government from intentionally suppressing speech of which it disapproves. It also generally prohibits the government from excepting certain kinds of speech from regulation because it thinks the speech is especially valuable.

This is why the Court is mistaken in concluding that the interest in diversity—in "access to a multiplicity" of "diverse and antagonistic sources"—is content neutral. Indeed, the interest is not "related to the *suppression* of free expression," but that is not enough for content neutrality. The interest in giving a tax break to religious, sports, or professional magazines, is not related to the suppression of speech; the interest in giving labor picketers an exemption from a general picketing ban is not related to the suppression of speech. But they are both related to the *content* of speech—to its communicative impact. The interest in ensuring access to a multiplicity of diverse and antagonistic sources of information, no matter how praiseworthy, is directly tied to the content of what the speakers will likely say. . . .

NOTES AND QUESTIONS

1. *Speaker-based restrictions and content preferences.* Which opinion in *Turner* has the more compelling argument as to whether this speaker based restriction reflects a "content preference?"
2. *The dangers of content-neutral restrictions.* Both *Turner* and *Reed* note that content-neutral restrictions receive substantially lower scrutiny than content-based restrictions. Are content-neutral restrictions really less worrisome than content-based restrictions as the Court's doctrinal approach suggests? Consider the following:

> The most puzzling aspect of the distinction between content-based and content-neutral restrictions is that either restriction reduces the sum total of information or opinions disseminated. . . . Whatever rationale one adopts for the constitutional protection of speech, the goals behind the rationale are undermined by any limitation on expression, content-based or not. For example, if one adopts the principle that the purpose of the first amendment is to facilitate the democratic process by making individuals better informed voters, regulations that limit expression on content-neutral grounds should be as suspect as content-based regulations, since they may also undermine this value. . . .
>
> The content distinction is conceptually and pragmatically untenable and should therefore be abandoned. . . . Instead, the courts should subject all restrictions on expression to the same critical scrutiny traditionally reserved for regulations drawn in terms of content.

Redish, *The Content Distinction, supra,* at 128-129, 142.

How does the following case fit with the Court's methodology distinguishing between content-based and content-neutral regulations?

RENTON v. PLAYTIME THEATRES, INC.

475 U.S. 41 (1986)

Justice REHNQUIST delivered the opinion of the Court.

[The city of Renton, Washington, enacted a zoning ordinance that prohibited adult motion picture theaters—defined as those showing films with "specified sexual activities"—from locating within 1,000 feet of any residential zone, family dwelling, church, park, or school. Playtime Theatres, Inc. sought a declaratory judgment that the Renton ordinance violated the First and Fourteenth Amendments and an injunction against the ordinance's enforcement.]

. . . The Renton ordinance . . . does not ban adult theaters altogether, but merely provides that such theaters may not be located within 1,000 feet of any residential zone, single- or multiple-family dwelling, church, park, or school. The ordinance is therefore properly analyzed as a form of time, place, and manner regulation.

Describing the ordinance as a time, place, and manner regulation is, of course, only the first step in our inquiry. This Court has long held that regulations enacted for the purpose of restraining speech on the basis of its content presumptively violate the First Amendment. *See Police Dep't v. Mosley*, 408 U.S. 92 (1972). On the other hand, so-called "content-neutral" time, place, and manner regulations are acceptable so long as they are designed to serve a substantial governmental interest and do not unreasonably limit alternative avenues of communication.

At first glance, the Renton ordinance . . . does not appear to fit neatly into either the "content-based" or the "content-neutral" category. To be sure, the ordinance treats theaters that specialize in adult films differently from other kinds of theaters. Nevertheless, as the District Court concluded, the Renton ordinance is aimed not at the *content* of the films shown at "adult motion picture theatres," but rather at the *secondary effects* of such theaters on the surrounding community. The . . . City Council's "*predominate* concerns" were with the secondary effects of adult theaters, and not with the content of adult films themselves.

[This] finding as to "predominate" intent...is more than adequate to establish that the city's pursuit of its zoning interests here was unrelated to the suppression of free expression. The ordinance by its terms is designed to prevent crime, protect the city's retail trade, maintain property values, and generally "protec[t] and preserv[e] the quality of [the city's] neighborhoods, commercial districts, and the quality of urban life," not to suppress the expression of unpopular views. . . .

In short, the Renton ordinance is completely consistent with our definition of "content-neutral" speech regulations as those that "are *justified* without reference to the content of the regulated speech." The ordinance does not contravene the fundamental principle that underlies our concern about "content-based" speech regulations: that "government may not grant the use of a forum to people whose views it finds acceptable, but deny use to those wishing to express less favored or more controversial views." *Mosley*. . . .

The appropriate inquiry in this case, then, is whether the Renton ordinance is designed to serve a substantial governmental interest and allows for reasonable alternative avenues of communication. It is clear that the ordinance meets such a standard. . . . [A] city's "interest in attempting to preserve the quality of urban life is one that must be accorded high respect."

The Court of Appeals ruled, however, that because the Renton ordinance was enacted without the benefit of studies specifically relating to "the particular problems or needs of Renton," the city's justifications for the ordinance were "conclusory and speculative." We think the Court of Appeals imposed on the city an unnecessarily rigid burden of proof. The record in this case reveals that Renton relied heavily on the experience of, and studies produced by, the city of Seattle. In Seattle, as in Renton, the adult theater zoning ordinance was aimed at preventing the secondary effects caused by the presence of even one such theater in a given neighborhood. . . .

We hold that Renton was entitled to rely on the experiences of Seattle and other cities[.] . . . The First Amendment does not require a city, before enacting such an ordinance, to conduct new studies or produce evidence independent of that already generated by other cities, so long as whatever evidence the city relies upon is reasonably believed to be relevant to the problem that the city addresses. . . .

Finally, turning to the question whether the Renton ordinance allows for reasonable alternative avenues of communication, we note that the ordinance leaves some 520 acres, or more than five percent of the entire land area of Renton, open to use as adult theater sites. . . . Respondents argue, however, that some of the land in question is already occupied by existing businesses, that "practically none" of the undeveloped land is currently for sale or lease, and that in general there are no "commercially viable" adult theater sites within the 520 acres left open by the Renton ordinance. . . .

. . . That respondents must fend for themselves in the real estate market, on an equal footing with other prospective purchasers and lessees, does not give rise to a First Amendment violation. And although we have cautioned against the enactment of zoning regulations that have "the effect of suppressing, or greatly restricting access to, lawful speech," we have never suggested that the First Amendment compels the Government to ensure that adult theaters, or any other kinds of speech-related businesses for that matter, will be able to obtain sites at bargain prices. . . .

Reversed.

Justice BLACKMUN concurs in the result.

Justice BRENNAN, with whom Justice MARSHALL joins, dissenting.

. . . The Court asserts that the ordinance is "aimed not at the *content* of the films shown at 'adult motion picture theatres,' but rather at the *secondary effects* of such theaters on the surrounding community," and thus is simply a time, place, and manner regulation. This analysis is misguided. . . . The fact that adult movie theaters may cause harmful "secondary" land-use effects may arguably give Renton a compelling reason to regulate such establishments; it does not mean, however, that such regulations are content neutral.

The ordinance discriminates on its face against certain forms of speech based on content. Movie theaters specializing in "adult motion pictures" may not be located within 1,000 feet of any residential zone, single- or multiple-family dwelling, church, park, or school. Other motion picture theaters, and other forms of "adult entertainment," such as bars, massage parlors, and adult bookstores, are not subject to the same restrictions. This selective treatment strongly suggests that Renton was interested not in controlling the "secondary effects" associated with adult businesses, but in discriminating against adult theaters based on the content of the films they exhibit. The Court ignores this discriminatory treatment, declaring that Renton is free "to address the potential problems created by one particular kind of adult business," and to amend the ordinance in the future to include other adult enterprises. However, because of the First Amendment interests at stake here, this one-step-at-a-time analysis is wholly inappropriate. . . .

Even assuming that the ordinance should be treated like a content-neutral time, place, and manner restriction, I would still find it unconstitutional. . . . [R]espondents are not on equal footing with other prospective purchasers and lessees, but must conduct business under severe restrictions not imposed upon other establishments. . . . [R]espondents do not ask Renton to guarantee low-price sites for their businesses, but seek only a reasonable opportunity to operate adult theaters in the city. By denying them this opportunity, Renton can effectively ban a form of protected speech from its borders. The ordinance "greatly restrict[s] access to . . . lawful speech" and is plainly unconstitutional.

NOTES AND QUESTIONS

1. *Renton and Reed.* The *Renton* majority's treatment of the zoning ordinance is seemingly inconsistent with the *Reed* majority's discussion of content discrimination methodology; yet the *Reed* majority ignored *Renton* and certainly did not explicitly overrule it. On the other hand, Justice Kagan's opinion in *Reed* treated *Renton* as reflecting the Court's earlier flexibility in approaching content-based regulations. Whose approach to *Renton* is better?

2. *Secondary effects.* What dangers are associated with adopting the secondary effects rationale referred to in *Renton*? Consider the following:

> Restrictions on free expression are rarely defended on the ground that the state simply didn't like what the defendant was saying; reference will generally be made to some danger beyond the message, such as a danger of riot, unlawful action or violent overthrow of the government. Thus in *Brandenburg* the state's defense was not that the speech in question was distasteful, though it surely was, but rather that speeches of that sort were likely to induce people to take the law into their own hands.

John Hart Ely, *Flag Desecration: A Case Study in the Roles of Categorization and Balancing in First Amendment Analysis*, 88 Harv. L. Rev. 1482, 1496 (1975) *see also* David Hudson, Jr., *The Secondary Effects Doctrine: "The Evisceration of First Amendment Freedoms,"* 37 Washburn L.J. 55, 93 (1997).

3. *The reach of secondary effects.* The Court has not extended the secondary effects rationale beyond zoning or other similar laws pertaining to sexually explicit speech. *See* City of Cincinnati v. Discovery Network, Inc., 507 U.S. 410 (1993) (rejecting secondary effects analysis as inapplicable to law banning distribution of commercial news racks on public sidewalks); Boos v. Barry, 485 U.S. 312 (1988) (law banning offensive displays near foreign embassies was not aimed at secondary effects); R.A.V. v. City of St. Paul, 505 U.S. 377 (1992) (law prohibiting certain kinds of symbolic fighting words was not aimed at the secondary effects of speech), *see infra* Chapter 10. Perhaps these cases along with *Reed* suggest that the Court is simply willing to treat content-based restrictions of sexually explicit, non-obscene speech differently from regulations of other speech. *See* Kathleen Sullivan, *Sex, Money, and Groups, Free Speech, and Association Decisions in the October 1999 Term*, 28 Pepp. L. Rev. 723, 730 (2001). Litigants still raise the secondary effects argument—sometimes

successfully—outside of the sexually explicit speech context. *See, e.g.*, Phelps-Roper v. Heineman, 720 F. Supp. 2d 1090 (D. Neb.), *rev'd*, 662 F.3d 485 (8th Cir. 2011) (finding law prohibiting protests near funerals was justified by the secondary effects of such protests on mourners).

For cases involving secondary effects reasoning in the context of sexually explicit speech, *see Erie v. Pap's A.M. and Barnes v. Glen Theatre, infra* Chapter 11.C.

CHAPTER
4

Content Neutrality and the Regulation of Speech on Government Property

TABLE OF CONTENTS

Government officials have not relied solely on laws regulating the content of speech to restrain speakers. During the nineteenth and early twentieth centuries, many cities also enacted laws banning distribution of leaflets or requiring speakers to obtain permits before speaking on public property. Although these laws did not aim at the content of speech, in numerous instances they were motivated by animosity toward the speech of particular groups that were active in proselytizing, parading, and protesting, such as the Salvation Army or labor organizations. *See, e.g.,* Richard T. Pfohl, Hague v. CIO *and the Roots of the Public Forum Doctrine: Translating Limits of Powers into Individual Rights*, 28 Harv. C.R.-C.L. L. Rev. 533 (1993). In other instances, city officials enacted such laws to manage multiple uses of public property or to protect other important interests such as public order or aesthetics.

Although not directly aimed at speech with a particular viewpoint or subject matter, laws banning leafleting or requiring permits for parades or gatherings can nevertheless affect a speaker's ability to express his or her message. To what extent do "content-neutral" laws significantly limiting access to government property violate the First Amendment? The Supreme Court originally found that the First Amendment was no obstacle to government regulation in this area. In Commonwealth v. Davis, 162 Mass. 510 (1895), *aff'd sub nom.* Davis v. Massachusetts, 167 U.S. 43 (1897), Justice Holmes, then writing as a Judge for the Massachusetts Supreme Judicial Court, wrote that "[f]or the legislature absolutely or conditionally to forbid public speaking in a highway or public park is no more an infringement of the rights of a member of the public than for the owner of a private house to forbid it in his house. . . . [If] the legislature may end the right of the public to enter upon the public place by putting an end to the dedication to public uses[,][s]o it may take the less step of limiting the public use to certain purposes." 162 Mass. at 511. The Supreme Court affirmed, finding that the Constitution "does not destroy the power of the states to enact police regulations as to the subjects within their control and does not have the effect of creating a particular and personal right in the citizen to use public property in defiance of the constitution and laws of the state. . . . The [government's] right to absolutely exclude all right to use necessarily includes the authority to determine under what circumstances such use may be availed of, as the greater power contains the lesser." 167 U.S. at 47-48.

As the Supreme Court's modern doctrine began to mature, the Court revisited the issue of whether content-neutral regulations of speakers on public (and sometimes private) property violated the First Amendment. The Court seemed to reject the notion that government officials have complete authority over public property. *See* Hague v. CIO, 307 U.S. 496 (1939). Thus, it struck down several anti-leafleting and permitting schemes in a series of foundational opinions that set the stage for the Court's later decisions. *See, e.g.,* Lovell v. Griffin, 303 U.S. 444 (1938); *Hague,* 307 U.S. 496; Schneider v. State, 308 U.S. 147 (1939); Martin v. City of Struthers, 319 U.S. 141 (1943). Over time, the Court has applied distinct doctrines to implement these early decisions—the "public forum" doctrine regarding speakers' access to public property, Perry Education Ass'n v. Perry Local Educators' Ass'n 460 U.S. 37 (1983); the "prior restraint" doctrine when determining the constitutionality of permitting or licensing requirements, Cox v. New Hampshire, 312 U.S. 569 (1941); and the Court's requirement that the government enact only content-neutral "time, place, and manner" restrictions of speech, Ward v. Rock Against Racism, 491 U.S. 781, 791 (1989).

As you read this chapter, consider the development of the Court's doctrine as well as these questions: (1) Is access to public property necessary for effective expression? (2) Do the Court's cases adequately protect expression—either in the access cases (i.e., the public forum cases) or in the cases judging the validity of regulations restricting speech (i.e., the cases on time, place, and manner restrictions or permitting requirements)?

A.   FOUNDATIONAL CASES

HAGUE v. CIO
307 U.S. 496 (1939)

Mr. Justice ROBERTS delivered an opinion in which Mr. Justice BLACK concurred.[*] . . .

[Individual citizens and labor organizations sued officials of Jersey City, New Jersey, alleging that a city ordinance giving the Director of Public Safety the ability to grant or deny permits for gatherings on public land or in public buildings violated the First and Fourteenth Amendments. They argued that the ordinance was void and was enforced against them in a discriminatory manner because of their beliefs. The citizens and labor organizations sought an injunction barring enforcement of the ordinance. After trial on the merits the District Court ruled in favor of the citizens

---

[*] Justice Roberts delivered a plurality opinion joined by Justice Black. Justice Stone delivered a separate opinion in which Justice Reed concurred. Chief Justice Hughes also concurred. Justices McReynolds and Butler filed dissenting opinions. Justices Frankfurter and Douglas did not participate in the decision.—EDS.

and labor organizations. City officials petitioned the Supreme Court for a writ of certiorari.]

. . . The question now presented is whether freedom to disseminate information concerning the provisions of the National Labor Relations Act, to assemble peaceably for discussion of the Act, and of the opportunities and advantages offered by it, is a privilege or immunity of a citizen of the United States secured against State abridgment by Section 1 of the Fourteenth Amendment; and whether the Judicial Code affords redress in a federal court for such abridgment. . . .

Although it has been held that the Fourteenth Amendment created no rights in citizens of the United States, but merely secured existing rights against state abridgment, it is clear that the right peaceably to assemble and to discuss these topics, and to communicate respecting them, whether orally or in writing, is a privilege inherent in citizenship of the United States which the Amendment protects.
. . .

. . . [In] the light of the facts found, privileges and immunities of the individual respondents as citizens of the United States, were infringed by the petitioners, by virtue of their official positions, under color of ordinances of Jersey City, unless, as petitioners contend, the city's ownership of streets and parks is as absolute as one's ownership of his home, with consequent power altogether to exclude citizens from the use thereof, or unless, though the city holds the streets in trust for public use, the absolute denial of their use to the respondents is a valid exercise of the police power.

The findings of fact negative the latter assumption. In support of the former the petitioners rely upon *Davis v. Massachusetts*, 167 U.S. 43. . . . [*Davis*] seems to be grounded on the holding of the State court that the Common "was absolutely under the control of the legislature," and that it was thus "conclusively determined there was no right in the plaintiff in error to use the common except in such mode and subject to such regulations as the legislature, in its wisdom, may have deemed proper to prescribe." . . .

The ordinance there in question apparently had a different purpose from that of the one here challenged, for it was not directed solely at the exercise of the right of speech and assembly, but was addressed as well to other activities, not in the nature of civil rights, which doubtless might be regulated or prohibited as respects their enjoyment in parks. In the instant case the ordinance deals only with the exercise of the right of assembly for the purpose of communicating views entertained by speakers, and is not a general measure to promote the public convenience in the use of the streets or parks.

We have no occasion to determine whether, on the facts disclosed, the *Davis* case was rightly decided, but we cannot agree that it rules the instant case. Wherever the title of streets and parks may rest, they have immemorially been held in trust for the use of the public and, time out of mind, have been used for purposes of assembly, communicating thoughts between citizens, and discussing public questions. Such use of the streets and public places has, from ancient times, been a part of the privileges, immunities, rights, and liberties of citizens. The privilege of a citizen of the United States to use the streets and parks for communication of views on national questions may be regulated in the interest of all; it is not absolute, but relative, and must be exercised in subordination to the general comfort and convenience, and in consonance with peace and good order; but it must not, in the guise of regulation, be abridged or denied.

We think the court below was right in holding the ordinance . . . void upon its face. It does not make comfort or convenience in the use of streets or parks the standard of official action. It enables the Director of Safety to refuse a permit on his mere opinion that such refusal will prevent "riots, disturbances or disorderly assemblage." It can thus, as the record discloses, be made the instrument of arbitrary suppression of free expression of views on national affairs for the prohibition of all speaking will undoubtedly "prevent" such eventualities. But uncontrolled official suppression of the privilege cannot be made a substitute for the duty to maintain order in connection with the exercise of the right. . . .

As the ordinance is void, the respondents are entitled to a decree so declaring and an injunction against its enforcement by the petitioners. They are free to hold meetings without a permit and without regard to the terms of the void ordinance. . . .

[The concurring opinions of Justice STONE and Chief Justice HUGHES are omitted.]

[The dissenting opinions of Justices MCREYNOLDS and BUTLER are omitted.]

SCHNEIDER v. STATE

308 U.S. 147 (1939)

Mr. Justice ROBERTS delivered the opinion of the Court.

[Several cities, including Los Angeles, Milwaukee, and Worcester, Massachusetts, enacted ordinances prohibiting the distribution of handbills or leaflets in public. Irvington, New Jersey did not completely ban public "handbilling," but did enact onerous registration requirements. The cities justified the ordinances as means to deter crime, littering, and public nuisance. Citizens arrested under the ordinances alleged that the ordinances, while addressing municipal interests, abridged the freedoms of speech and press under the Fourteenth Amendment of the Constitution.]

Although a municipality may enact regulations in the interest of the public safety, health, welfare or convenience, these may not abridge the individual liberties secured by the Constitution to those who wish to speak, write, print or circulate information or opinion.

Municipal authorities, as trustees for the public, have the duty to keep their communities' streets open and available for movement of people and property, the primary purpose to which the streets are dedicated. So long as legislation to this end does not abridge the constitutional liberty of one rightfully upon the street to impart information through speech or the distribution of literature, it may lawfully regulate the conduct of those using the streets. For example, a person could not exercise this liberty by taking his stand in the middle of a crowded street, contrary to traffic regulations, and maintain his position to the stoppage of all traffic; a group of distributors could not insist upon a constitutional right to form a cordon across the street and to allow no pedestrian to pass who did not accept a tendered leaflet; nor does the guarantee of freedom of speech or of the press deprive a municipality of power to enact regulations against throwing literature broadcast in the streets. Prohibition of such conduct would not abridge the constitutional liberty since such activity bears no necessary relationship to the freedom to speak, write, print or distribute information or opinion.

This court has characterized the freedom of speech and that of the press as fundamental personal rights and liberties. The phrase is not an empty one and was not lightly used. It reflects the belief of the framers of the Constitution that exercise of the rights lies at the foundation of free government by free men. It stresses, as do many opinions of this court, the importance of preventing the restriction of enjoyment of these liberties.

In every case, therefore, where legislative abridgment of the rights is asserted, the courts should be astute to examine the effect of the challenged legislation. Mere legislative preferences or beliefs respecting matters of public convenience may well support regulation directed at other personal activities, but be insufficient to justify such as diminishes the exercise of rights so vital to the maintenance of democratic institutions. And so, as cases arise, the delicate and difficult task falls upon the courts to weigh the circumstances and to appraise the substantiality of the reasons advanced in support of the regulation of the free enjoyment of the rights. . . .

The Los Angeles, the Milwaukee, and the Worcester ordinances under review do not purport to license distribution but all of them absolutely prohibit it in the streets and, one of them, in other public places as well.

The motive of [this legislation] . . . is held by the courts below to be the prevention of littering of the streets and, although the alleged offenders were not charged with themselves scattering paper in the streets, their convictions were sustained upon the theory that distribution by them encouraged or resulted in such littering. We are of opinion that the purpose to keep the streets clean and of good appearance is insufficient to justify an ordinance which prohibits a person rightfully on a public street from handing literature to one willing to receive it. Any burden imposed upon the city authorities in cleaning and caring for the streets as an indirect consequence of such distribution results from the constitutional protection of the freedom of speech and press. This constitutional protection does not deprive a city of all power to prevent street littering. There are obvious methods of preventing littering. Amongst these is the punishment of those who actually throw papers on the streets. . . .

The judgment in each case is reversed and the causes are remanded for further proceedings not inconsistent with this opinion.

Reversed.

Mr. Justice MCREYNOLDS is of opinion that the judgment in each case should be affirmed.

MARTIN v. CITY OF STRUTHERS

319 U.S. 141 (1943)

Mr. Justice BLACK delivered the opinion of the Court. . . .

The appellant, espousing a religious cause in which she was interested—that of the Jehovah's Witnesses—went to the homes of strangers, knocking on doors and ringing doorbells in order to distribute to the inmates of the homes leaflets advertising a religious meeting. In doing so, she proceeded in a conventional and orderly fashion. For delivering a leaflet to the inmate of a home she was convicted in the Mayor's Court and was fined $10.00 on a charge of violating the following City ordinance:

> It is unlawful for any person distributing handbills, circulars or other advertisements to ring the door bell, sound the door knocker, or otherwise summon the inmate or inmates of any residence to the door for the purpose of

receiving such handbills, circulars or other advertisements they or any person with them may be distributing.

The appellant admitted knocking at the door for the purpose of delivering the invitation, but seasonably urged in the lower Ohio state court that the ordinance as construed and applied was beyond the power of the State because in violation of the right of freedom of press and religion as guaranteed by the First and Fourteenth Amendments. . . .

We are faced in the instant case with the necessity of weighing the conflicting interests of the appellant in the civil rights she claims, as well as the right of the individual householder to determine whether he is willing to receive her message, against the interest of the community which by this ordinance offers to protect the interests of all of its citizens, whether particular citizens want that protection or not. The ordinance does not control anything but the distribution of literature, and in that respect it substitutes the judgment of the community for the judgment of the individual householder. It submits the distributor to criminal punishment for annoying the person on whom he calls, even though the recipient of the literature distributed is in fact glad to receive it. In considering legislation which thus limits the dissemination of knowledge, we must "be astute to examine the effect of the challenged legislation" and must "weigh the circumstances and appraise the substantiality of the reasons advanced in support of the regulation." *Schneider.*

Ordinances of the sort now before us may be aimed at the protection of the householders from annoyance, including intrusion upon the hours of rest, and at the prevention of crime. . . . While door to door distributors of literature may be either a nuisance or a blind for criminal activities, they may also be useful members of society engaged in the dissemination of ideas in accordance with the best tradition of free discussion. The widespread use of this method of communication by many groups espousing various causes attests its major importance. "Pamphlets have proved most effective instruments in the dissemination of opinion. And perhaps the most effective way of bringing them to the notice of individuals is their distribution at the homes of the people." *Schneider.* . . . Door to door distribution of circulars is essential to the poorly financed causes of little people.

Freedom to distribute information to every citizen wherever he desires to receive it is so clearly vital to the preservation of a free society that, putting aside reasonable police and health regulations of time and manner of distribution, it must be fully preserved. The dangers of distribution can so easily be controlled by traditional legal methods, leaving to each householder the full right to decide whether he will receive strangers as visitors, that stringent prohibition can serve no purpose but that forbidden by the Constitution, the naked restriction of the dissemination of ideas.

Traditionally the American law punishes persons who enter onto the property of another after having been warned by the owner to keep off. . . . We know of no state which, as does the Struthers ordinance in effect, makes a person a criminal trespasser if he enters the property of another for an innocent purpose without an explicit command from the owners to stay away. The judgment below is reversed for further proceedings not inconsistent with this opinion.

Reversed.

[Justice FRANKFURTER'S concurring opinion is omitted.]

[Justice MURPHY'S concurring opinion is omitted.]

[Justice REED's dissenting opinion is omitted.]

NOTES AND QUESTIONS

1. Hague *and the foundations of public forum doctrine*. What kind of access to public property does *Hague* require?
2. Hague *and permits*. Why was the permit ordinance in *Hague* problematic? Is requiring speakers to obtain a permit always a problem or are there reasons why officials might want to use them?
3. Schneider *and balancing*. *Schneider* suggests that courts must engage in a balancing of interests to determine whether content-neutral regulations violate the First Amendment. How deferential is the balancing in *Schneider* (and also in *Martin*)? Is this balancing more akin to the strict or intermediate scrutiny introduced in the last chapter?
4. *Regulating particular "means" of communication*. What role does the means of communication play in the Court's balancing in the above cases? Why is it relevant in *Martin* that "[d]oor to door distribution of circulars is essential to the poorly financed causes of little people"?

   In Kovacs v. Cooper, 336 U.S. 77 (1949), the Court upheld an ordinance that prohibited the use of sound trucks or any other "loud speaker or sound amplifier" or any tool that emitted "loud or raucous noises" upon city streets or public places. The plurality held that the ordinance did not violate the First Amendment because "[t]here is no restriction upon the communication of ideas or discussion of issues" and "the need for reasonable protection in the homes or business houses from the distracting noises of vehicles equipped with such sound amplifying devices justifies the ordinance." Why does the regulation of noisy sound trucks upheld in *Kovacs* not seem to have the same effect on speakers' ability to disseminate their messages as did the regulation of leafleting in *Martin*? Why was the privacy rationale more important in *Kovacs* than in *Martin*?
5. *Content-neutrality rules outside the public forum*. *Martin* does not involve speech in a public forum—the ordinance regulated speakers while on private property. Nevertheless, the Court finds cases such as *Schneider* applicable. Should courts apply the same rules to speech that takes place on non-government property as they do to speech in the public forum?
6. *Bans on an entire medium*. To what extent is *Schneider* concerned with the fact that some of the laws amounted to complete bans of a particular medium (i.e., leafleting)? Why might the existence of alternatives means of communication, such as newspapers, television, and billboards, be insufficient when a particular medium is banned? *See* C. Edwin Baker, *Unreasoned Reasonableness: Mandatory Parade Permits and Time, Place and Manner Regulations*, 78 Nw. U. L. Rev. 937, 969 (1983); Susan Williams, *Content Discrimination and the First Amendment*, 139 U. Pa. L. Rev. 615, 637-638 (1991).

B.   TIME, PLACE, AND MANNER RESTRICTIONS—THE MODERN DOCTRINE

Schneider noted that speakers do not have complete license to exercise their rights by, for example, defying traffic regulations and standing in the middle of a crowded street or stopping traffic. It falls to "the courts to weigh the circumstances and to appraise the substantiality of the reasons advanced in support of the regulation of the free enjoyment of [speakers'] rights" when they conflict with other interests. *Schneider*, 308 U.S. at 161.

The Court's later cases have similarly tried to balance the government's needs against speakers' free speech rights. The most protective of the Court's doctrines in this regard involves its rules regarding regulation of speech in the "traditional public forum." As *Hague* noted, certain public property, such as streets, parks, and sidewalks, has from "time out of mind . . . been used for purposes of assembly, communicating thoughts between citizens, and discussing public questions." The Court's cases make clear that states and municipalities may enact laws regulating the "time, place, and manner" of speech in traditional public forums. But such regulations must be content-neutral, narrowly drawn to meet an important state interest and leave open ample alternatives of communication for the speaker. Ward v. Rock Against Racism, 491 U.S. 781, 791 (1989); Grayned v. City of Rockford, 408 U.S. 104, 115 (1972). In addition, if such laws involve permitting requirements, they cannot allow authorities to make arbitrary decisions granting or denying permits. Cox v. New Hampshire, 312 U.S. 569 (1941).

In Chapter 3, *Turner* and *Reed* noted that this approach to the review of content-neutral regulations involved "intermediate scrutiny." Despite this seemingly clear label, there remains confusion about the Court's application of intermediate scrutiny. When courts apply such scrutiny, it is unclear what government interests are necessary to sustain regulation, what evidence is required to support those interests, or how carefully tailored the government's regulations must be. As a result, the parameters of government authority to regulate speech in a traditional public forum are similarly unclear. These issues are raised in the cases below and the questions and notes that follow.

CLARK v. COMMUNITY FOR CREATIVE NON-VIOLENCE

468 U.S. 288 (1984)

Justice WHITE delivered the opinion of the Court.

The issue in this case is whether a National Park Service regulation prohibiting camping in certain parks violates the First Amendment when applied to prohibit demonstrators from sleeping in Lafayette Park and the Mall in connection with a demonstration intended to call attention to the plight of the homeless. We hold that it does not and reverse the contrary judgment of the Court of Appeals.

I

The Interior Department, through the National Park Service, is charged with responsibility for the management and maintenance of the National Parks and is authorized to promulgate rules and regulations for the use of the parks in accordance with the purposes for which they were established. . . . Lafayette Park is a roughly 7-acre square located across Pennsylvania Avenue from the White House. Although originally part of the White House grounds, President Jefferson set it aside as a park for the use of residents and visitors. It is a "garden park with a...formal landscaping of flowers and trees, with fountains, walks and benches." . . . The Mall is a stretch of land running westward from the Capitol to the Lincoln Memorial some two miles away. It includes the Washington Monument, a series of reflecting pools, trees, lawns, and other greenery. It is bordered by, inter alia, the Smithsonian Institution and the National Gallery of Art. Both the Park and the Mall were included in Major Pierre L'Enfant's original plan for the Capital. Both are visited by vast numbers of visitors from around the country, as well as by large numbers of residents of the Washington metropolitan area.

Under the regulations involved in this case, camping in National Parks is permitted only in campgrounds designated for that purpose. 36 CFR § 50.27(a) (1983). No such campgrounds have ever been designated in Lafayette Park or the Mall. . . . Demonstrations for the airing of views or grievances are permitted in the Memorial-core parks, but for the most part only by Park Service permits. . . . Temporary structures may be erected for demonstration purposes but may not be used for camping. . . .

In 1982, the Park Service issued a renewable permit to respondent Community for Creative Non-Violence (CCNV) to conduct a wintertime demonstration in Lafayette Park and the Mall for the purpose of demonstrating the plight of the homeless. The permit authorized the erection of two symbolic tent cities: 20 tents in Lafayette Park that would accommodate 50 people and 40 tents in the Mall with a capacity of up to 100. The Park Service, however, relying on the above regulations, specifically denied CCNV's request that demonstrators be permitted to sleep in the symbolic tents.

CCNV and several individuals then filed an action to prevent the application of the no-camping regulations to the proposed demonstration, which, it was claimed, was not covered by the regulation. . . . The District Court granted summary judgment in favor of the Park Service. The Court of Appeals, sitting en banc, reversed. . . .

II

We need not differ with the view of the Court of Appeals that overnight sleeping in connection with the demonstration is expressive conduct protected to some extent by the First Amendment. We assume for present purposes, but do not decide, that such is the case, *cf. United States v. O'Brien*, 391 U.S. 367 (1968), but this assumption only begins the inquiry. Expression, whether oral or written or symbolized by conduct, is subject to reasonable time, place, or manner restrictions. We have often noted that restrictions of this kind are valid provided that they are justified without reference to the content of the regulated speech, that they are narrowly tailored to serve a significant governmental interest, and that they leave open ample alternative channels for communication of the information.

It is also true that a message may be delivered by conduct that is intended to be communicative and that, in context, would reasonably be understood by the viewer to be communicative. . . . Symbolic expression of this kind may be forbidden or regulated if the conduct itself may constitutionally be regulated, if the regulation is narrowly drawn to further a substantial governmental interest, and if the interest is unrelated to the suppression of free speech. *O'Brien.*

Petitioners submit . . . the regulation forbidding sleeping is defensible either as a time, place, or manner restriction or as a regulation of symbolic conduct. We agree [that the regulations,] . . . including the ban on sleeping, are clearly limitations on the manner in which the demonstration could be carried out. . . .

[I]t is not disputed here that the prohibition on camping, and on sleeping specifically, is content-neutral and is not being applied because of disagreement with the message presented. Neither was the regulation faulted, nor could it be, on the ground that without overnight sleeping the plight of the homeless could not be communicated in other ways. The regulation otherwise left the demonstration intact, with its symbolic city, signs, and the presence of those who were willing to take their turns in a day-and-night vigil. Respondents do not suggest that there was, or is, any barrier to delivering to the media, or to the public by other means, the intended message concerning the plight of the homeless. . . .

It is also apparent to us that the regulation narrowly focuses on the Government's substantial interest in maintaining the parks in the heart of our Capital in an attractive and intact condition, readily available to the millions of people who wish to see and enjoy them by their presence. To permit camping . . . would be totally inimical to these purposes[.] . . .

. . . Absent the prohibition on sleeping, there would be other groups who would demand permission to deliver an asserted message by camping in Lafayette Park. Some of them would surely have as credible a claim in this regard as does CCNV, and the denial of permits to still others would present difficult problems for the Park Service. With the prohibition, however, as is evident in the case before us, at least some around-the-clock demonstrations lasting for days on end will not materialize, others will be limited in size and duration, and the purposes of the regulation will thus be materially served. Perhaps these purposes would be more effectively and not so clumsily achieved by preventing tents and 24-hour vigils entirely in the core areas. But the Park Service's decision to permit nonsleeping demonstrations does not, in our view, impugn the camping prohibition as a valuable, but perhaps imperfect, protection to the parks. . . .

[T]he foregoing analysis demonstrates that the Park Service regulation is sustainable under the four-factor standard of [*O'Brien*], for validating a regulation of expressive conduct, which, in the last analysis is little, if any, different from the standard applied to time, place, or manner restrictions.[8] . . .

We are unmoved by the Court of Appeals' view that the challenged regulation is unnecessary, and hence invalid, because there are less speech-restrictive alternatives that could have satisfied the Government interest in preserving park lands. There is no gainsaying that preventing overnight sleeping will avoid a measure of actual or threatened damage to Lafayette Park and the Mall. The Court of Appeals'

[8] Reasonable time, place, or manner restrictions are valid even though they directly limit oral or written expression. It would be odd to insist on a higher standard for limitations aimed at regulable conduct and having only an incidental impact on speech. Thus, if the time, place, or manner restriction on expressive sleeping, if that is what is involved in this case, sufficiently and narrowly serves a substantial enough governmental interest to escape First Amendment condemnation, it is untenable to invalidate it under *O'Brien* on the ground that the governmental interest is insufficient to warrant the intrusion on First Amendment concerns or that there is an inadequate nexus between the regulation and the interest sought to be served. . . .

suggestions that the Park Service minimize the possible injury by reducing the size, duration, or frequency of demonstrations would still curtail the total allowable expression in which demonstrators could engage, whether by sleeping or otherwise, and these suggestions represent no more than a disagreement with the Park Service over how much protection the core parks require or how an acceptable level of preservation is to be attained. We do not believe, however, that either [*O'Brien*] or the time, place, or manner decisions assign to the judiciary the authority to replace the Park Service as the manager of the Nation's parks or endow the judiciary with the competence to judge how much protection of park lands is wise and how that level of conservation is to be attained.

Accordingly, the judgment of the Court of Appeals is *reversed.*

Justice MARSHALL, with whom Justice BRENNAN joins, dissenting.

. . . Although sleep in the context of this case is symbolic speech protected by the First Amendment, it is nonetheless subject to reasonable time, place, and manner restrictions. I agree with the standard enunciated by the majority[.] . . . I conclude, however, that the regulations at issue in this case, as applied to respondents, fail to satisfy this standard. . . .

According to the majority, the significant Government interest advanced by denying respondents' request to engage in sleep-speech is the interest in "maintaining the parks in the heart of our capital in an attractive and intact condition, readily available to the millions of people who wish to see and enjoy them by their presence." . . . That interest is indeed significant. However, neither the Government nor the majority adequately explains how prohibiting respondents' planned activity will substantially further that interest. . . .

. . . The majority cites no evidence indicating that sleeping engaged in as symbolic speech will cause *substantial* wear and tear on park property. Furthermore, the Government's application of the sleeping ban in the circumstances of this case is strikingly underinclusive. The majority acknowledges that a proper time, place, and manner restriction must be "narrowly tailored." Here, however, the tailoring requirement is virtually forsaken inasmuch as the Government offers no justification for applying its absolute ban on sleeping yet is willing to allow respondents to engage in activities—such as feigned sleeping—that [are] no less burdensome. . . .

The disposition of this case impels me to make two additional observations. First, in this case, as in some others involving time, place, and manner restrictions, the Court has dramatically lowered its scrutiny of governmental regulations once it has determined that such regulations are content-neutral. The result has been the creation of a two-tiered approach to First Amendment cases: while regulations that turn on the content of the expression are subjected to a strict form of judicial review, regulations that are aimed at matters other than expression receive only a minimal level of scrutiny. . . .

Second, the disposition of this case reveals a mistaken assumption regarding the motives and behavior of government officials who create and administer content-neutral regulations. . . . The Court evidently assumes that the balance struck by officials is deserving of deference so long as it does not appear to be tainted by content discrimination. What the Court fails to recognize is that public officials have strong incentives to overregulate even in the absence of an intent to censor particular views. This incentive stems from the fact that of the two groups whose interests officials must accommodate—on the one hand, the interests of the general public and, on the other, the interests of those who seek to use a particular forum for First

Amendment activity—the political power of the former is likely to be far greater than that of the latter. . . .

For the foregoing reasons, I respectfully dissent.

[Chief Justice BURGER's concurring opinion is omitted.]

MEMBERS OF THE CITY COUNCIL OF THE CITY OF LOS ANGELES v. TAXPAYERS FOR VINCENT

466 U.S. 789 (1984)

Justice STEVENS delivered the opinion of the Court.

Section 28.04 of the Los Angeles Municipal Code prohibits the posting of signs on public property.[1] The question presented is whether that prohibition abridges appellees' freedom of speech within the meaning of the First Amendment.

In March 1979, Roland Vincent was a candidate for election to the Los Angeles City Council. A group of his supporters known as Taxpayers for Vincent (Taxpayers) entered into a contract with a political sign service company known as Candidates' Outdoor Graphics Service (COGS) to fabricate and post signs with Vincent's name on them. COGS produced 15 by 44-inch cardboard signs and attached them to utility poles at various locations by draping them over crosswires which support the poles and stapling the cardboard together at the bottom. The signs' message was: "Roland Vincent—City Council."

Acting under the authority of § 28.04 of the Municipal Code, employees of the city's Bureau of Street Maintenance routinely removed all posters attached to utility poles and similar objects covered by the ordinance, including the COGS signs. The weekly sign removal report covering the period March 1-March 7, 1979, indicated that among the 1,207 signs removed from public property during that week, 48 were identified as "Roland Vincent" signs. Most of the other signs identified in that report were apparently commercial in character. . . .

It is well settled that the state may legitimately exercise its police powers to advance esthetic values. . . . In this case, taxpayers and COGS do not dispute that it is within the constitutional power of the City to attempt to improve its appearance, or that this interest is basically unrelated to the suppression of ideas. Therefore the critical inquiries are whether that interest is sufficiently substantial to justify the effect of the ordinance on appellees' expression, and whether that effect is no greater than necessary to accomplish the City's purpose. . . .

Metromedia, Inc. v. San Diego, 453 U.S. 490 (1981), dealt with San Diego's prohibition of certain forms of outdoor billboards. There the Court considered the city's interest in avoiding visual clutter, and seven Justices explicitly concluded that this interest was sufficient to justify a prohibition of billboards. . . . We reaffirm the

---

[1] The ordinance reads as follows:

Sec. 28.04. Hand-bills, signs-public places and objects:

(a) No person shall paint, mark or write on, or post or otherwise affix, any hand-bill or sign to or upon any sidewalk, crosswalk, curb, curbstone, street lamp post, hydrant, tree, shrub, tree stake or guard, railroad trestle, electric light or power or telephone or telegraph or trolley wire pole, or wire appurtenance thereof or upon any fixture of the fire alarm or police telegraph system or upon any lighting system, public bridge, drinking fountain, life buoy, life preserver, life boat or other life saving equipment, street sign or traffic sign. . . .

conclusion of the majority in *Metromedia*. The problem addressed by this ordinance—the visual assault on the citizens of Los Angeles presented by an accumulation of signs posted on public property—constitutes a significant substantive evil within the City's power to prohibit. . . .

We turn to the question whether the scope of the restriction on appellees' expressive activity is substantially broader than necessary to protect the City's interest in eliminating visual clutter. The incidental restriction on expression which results from the City's attempt to accomplish such a purpose is considered justified as a reasonable regulation of the time, place, or manner of expression if it is narrowly tailored to serve that interest. . . .

It is true that the esthetic interest in preventing the kind of litter that may result from the distribution of leaflets on the public streets and sidewalks cannot support a prophylactic prohibition against the citizen's exercise of that method of expressing his views. In [*Schneider*], the Court held that ordinances that absolutely prohibited handbilling on the streets were invalid. The Court explained that cities could adequately protect the esthetic interest in avoiding litter without abridging protected expression merely by penalizing those who actually litter. . . .

The rationale of *Schneider* is inapposite in the context of the instant case. . . . In *Schneider*, an antilittering statute could have addressed the substantive evil without prohibiting expressive activity, whereas application of the prophylactic rule actually employed gratuitously infringed upon the right of an individual to communicate directly with a willing listener. Here, the substantive evil—visual blight—is not merely a possible by-product of the activity, but is created by the medium of expression itself. In contrast to *Schneider*, therefore, the application of the ordinance in this case responds precisely to the substantive problem which legitimately concerns the City. The ordinance curtails no more speech than is necessary to accomplish its purpose.

The Court of Appeals accepted the argument that a prohibition against the use of unattractive signs cannot be justified on esthetic grounds if it fails to apply to all equally unattractive signs wherever they might be located. . . . [However], the validity of the esthetic interest in the elimination of signs on public property is not compromised by failing to extend the ban to private property. The private citizen's interest in controlling the use of his own property justifies the disparate treatment. . . .

While the First Amendment does not guarantee the right to employ every conceivable method of communication at all times and in all places, a restriction on expressive activity may be invalid if the remaining modes of communication are inadequate. . . . The Los Angeles ordinance does not affect any individual's freedom to exercise the right to speak and to distribute literature in the same place where the posting of signs on public property is prohibited. To the extent that the posting of signs on public property has advantages over these forms of expression, . . . there is no reason to believe that these same advantages cannot be obtained through other means. . . .

Finally, Taxpayers and COGS argue that Los Angeles could have written an ordinance that would have had a less severe effect on expressive activity such as theirs, by permitting the posting of any kind of signs at any time on some types of public property, or by making a variety of other more specific exceptions to the ordinance: for signs carrying certain types of messages (such as political campaign signs), for signs posted during specific time periods (perhaps during political campaigns), for particular locations (perhaps for areas already cluttered by an excessive number of signs on adjacent private property), or for signs meeting design specifications (such as size or color). Plausible public policy arguments might well be made in support of any such exception, but it by no means follows that it is therefore constitutionally mandated, . . . nor is it clear that some of the suggested exceptions would even be constitutionally permissible. . . . To create an exception for appellees' political speech and not these other types of speech might create a risk of engaging in constitutionally forbidden content discrimination. . . . Moreover, the volume of permissible postings under such a mandated exemption might so limit the ordinance's effect as to defeat its aim of combating visual blight. . . .

The judgment of the Court of Appeals is reversed, and the case is remanded to that Court.

It is so ordered.

Justice BRENNAN, with whom Justice MARSHALL and Justice BLACKMUN join, dissenting.

. . . In deciding this First Amendment question, the critical importance of the posting of signs as a means of communication must not be overlooked. Use of this medium of communication is particularly valuable in part because it entails a relatively small expense in reaching a wide audience, allows flexibility in accommodating various formats, typographies, and graphics, and conveys its message in a manner that is easily read and understood by its reader or viewer. . . .

Nevertheless, the City of Los Angeles asserts that ample alternative avenues of communication are available. The City notes that, although the posting of signs on public property is prohibited, the posting of signs on private property and the distribution of handbills are not. But there is no showing that either of these alternatives would serve appellees' needs nearly as well as would the posting of signs on public property. First, there is no proof that a sufficient number of private parties would allow the posting of signs on their property. . . .

Similarly, the adequacy of distributing handbills is dubious, despite certain advantages of handbills over signs. . . . Particularly when the message to be carried is best expressed by a few words or a graphic image, a message on a sign will typically reach far more people than one on a handbill. The message on a posted sign remains to be seen by passersby as long as it is posted, while a handbill is typically read by a single reader and discarded. . . .

[A] reviewing court faces substantial difficulties determining whether the actual objective is related to the suppression of speech. The asserted interest in aesthetics may be only a facade for content-based suppression. . . . For example, in evaluating the ordinance before us in this case, the City might be pursuing either of two objectives, motivated by two very different judgments. One objective might be the elimination of "visual clutter," attributable in whole or in part to signs posted on public property. . . . A second objective might simply be the elimination of the messages typically carried by the signs. In that case, the aesthetic judgment would be that the signs' messages are themselves displeasing. The first objective is lawful, of course, but the second is not. Yet the City might easily mask the second objective by asserting the first and declaring that signs constitute visual clutter. In short, we must avoid unquestioned acceptance of the City's bare declaration of an aesthetic objective lest we fail in our duty to prevent unlawful trespasses upon First Amendment protections. . . .

In cases like this, where a total ban is imposed on a particularly valuable method of communication, a court should require the government to provide tangible proof of the legitimacy and substantiality of its aesthetic objective. Justifications for such restrictions articulated by the government should be critically examined to determine whether the government has committed itself to addressing the identified aesthetic problem.

In my view, such statements of aesthetic objectives should be accepted as substantial and unrelated to the suppression of speech only if the government demonstrates that it is pursuing an identified objective seriously and comprehensively and in ways that are unrelated to the restriction of speech. . . . Without such a demonstration, I would invalidate the restriction as violative of the First Amendment. . . .

I therefore dissent.

NOTES AND QUESTIONS

1. *Time, place, and manner restrictions.* In *Clark*, the Court relied on the four-part test from United States v. O'Brien, 391 U.S. 367 (1968), *see infra* page 201, to analyze the regulation prohibiting camping in national parks as applied to a protest group. That test is a form of intermediate scrutiny applicable to symbolic forms of expression. For more discussion of *O'Brien*, see *infra* Chapter 5.A.

   In Ward v. Rock Against Racism, 491 U.S. 781 (1989), the Court applied a similar version of intermediate scrutiny to purely expressive forms of communication: "Our cases make clear . . . that even in a public forum the government may impose reasonable restrictions on the time, place, or manner of protected speech, provided the restrictions 'are justified without reference to the content of the regulated speech, that they are narrowly tailored to serve a significant governmental interest, and that they leave open ample alternative channels for communication of the information.'" *Id.* (citing *Clark*, 468 U.S. at 293). The *Rock Against Racism* Court further "reaffirm[ed] . . . that a regulation of the time, place, or manner of protected speech must be narrowly tailored to serve the government's legitimate, content-neutral interests but that it need not be the least restrictive or least intrusive means of doing so. Rather, the requirement of narrow tailoring is satisfied 'so long as the . . . regulation promotes a substantial government interest that would be achieved less effectively absent the regulation.'" *Id.*

2. Clark *versus* Schneider. How rigorous is the *Clark* test, especially as interpreted in *Rock Against Racism*? Are the *Clark* dissenters correct that the majority "dramatically lowered its scrutiny of governmental regulations once it has determined that such regulations are content-neutral"? *See* G. Sidney Buchanan, *A Very Rational Court*, 30 Hous. L. Rev. 1509, 1548-1549 (1998); David S. Day, *The End of the Public Forum Doctrine*, 78 Iowa L. Rev. 143, 149 (1993).

3. *The government interest in* Clark. What government interest is at stake in *Clark*—the protection of the national parks in general? How do protestors and their desire to sleep in Lafayette Park for symbolic purposes threaten that interest?

4. Clark *and alternative means of communication.* Does the Park Service's willingness to allow demonstrators to remain in the park around the clock but not to camp with actual homeless persons provide a sufficient alternative means of communication given the nature of the protest?

5. Clark *and judicial deference.* Should judges defer to government officials who enact neutral time, place, and manner restrictions, or do such officials "have strong incentives to overregulate even in the absence of an intent to censor particular views"? *See* David Goldberger, *Judicial Scrutiny in Public Forum Cases: Misplaced Trust in the Judgment of Public Officials,* 32 Buff. L. Rev. 175, 207-208 (1983).

6. *Aesthetic interests.* Were Los Angeles's aesthetic interests in *Vincent* persuasive? Should we protect aesthetics independent of other harms or because they indirectly advance other interests, such as protection of property values? *See, e.g.,* John J. Costonis, *Law and Aesthetics: A Critique and a Reformulation of the Dilemmas,* 80 Mich. L. Rev. 355, 457 (1982).

7. *Is* Vincent *consistent with* Schneider*?* Is posting a sign on public property a particularly important form of expression such that leafleting and posting signs on private property are unreasonable alternatives?

CITY OF LADUE v. GILLEO
512 U.S. 43 (1994)

Justice STEVENS delivered the opinion of the Court.

[Respondent Margaret P. Gilleo owned a single-family home in Ladue, Missouri. In 1990, she placed on her front lawn 24- by 36-inch signs printed with the words, "Say No to War in the Persian Gulf, Call Congress Now." Upon complaining to police after these signs disappeared, she was told that such signs were prohibited in Ladue.

Ladue's ordinance prohibited all signs except those that fell within 1 of 10 exemptions. Thus, "residential identification signs" no larger than one square foot were allowed, as were signs advertising "that the property is for sale, lease or exchange" and identifying the owner or agent. Also exempted were signs "for churches, religious institutions, and schools," "[c]ommercial signs in commercially zoned or industrial zoned districts," and on-site signs advertising "gasoline filling stations." The ordinance's "Declaration of Findings, Policies, Interests, and Purposes" stated the reasons behind the law:

> [P]roliferation of an unlimited number of signs in private, residential, commercial, industrial, and public areas of the City of Ladue would create ugliness, visual blight and clutter, tarnish the natural beauty of the landscape as well as the residential and commercial architecture, impair property values, substantially impinge upon the privacy and special ambience of the community, and may cause safety and traffic hazards to motorists, pedestrians, and children.

Gilleo challenged the ordinance, which the District Court held unconstitutional.]

Relying on the plurality opinion in *Metromedia, Inc. v. San Diego,* 453 U.S. 490, the Court of Appeals held the ordinance invalid as a "content based" regulation because the City treated commercial speech more favorably than noncommercial speech and favored some kinds of noncommercial speech over others. Acknowledging that "Ladue's interests in enacting its ordinance are substantial," the Court of Appeals nevertheless concluded that those interests were "not sufficiently 'compelling' to support a content-based restriction." . . .

Under the Court of Appeals' content discrimination rationale, the City might theoretically remove the defects in its ordinance by simply repealing all of the exemptions. [But] Gilleo . . . is primarily concerned not with the scope of the exemptions available in other locations, such as commercial areas and on church property; she asserts a constitutional right to display an antiwar sign at her own home. Therefore, we first ask whether Ladue may properly *prohibit* Gilleo from displaying her sign, and then, only if necessary, consider the separate question whether it was improper for the City simultaneously to *permit* certain other signs. In examining the propriety of Ladue's near-total prohibition of residential signs, we will assume, *arguendo*, the validity of the City's submission that the various exemptions are free of impermissible content or viewpoint discrimination.[11] . . .

. . . Ladue's ordinance forbids Gilleo and other residents [from] display[ing] virtually any "sign" on their property. The ordinance defines that term sweepingly. A prohibition is not always invalid merely because it applies to a sizeable category of speech; the sign ban we upheld in *Vincent*, for example, was quite broad. But in *Vincent* we specifically noted that the category of speech in question—signs placed on public property—was not a "uniquely valuable or important mode of communication," and that there was no evidence that "appellees' ability to communicate effectively is threatened by ever-increasing restrictions on expression."

Here, in contrast, Ladue has almost completely foreclosed a venerable means of communication that is both unique and important. It has totally foreclosed that medium to political, religious, or personal messages. Signs that react to a local happening or express a view on a controversial issue both reflect and animate change in the life of a community. Often placed on lawns or in windows, residential signs play an important part in political campaigns, during which they are displayed to signal the resident's support for particular candidates, parties, or causes. They may not afford the same opportunities for conveying complex ideas as do other media, but residential signs have long been an important and distinct medium of expression.

Our prior decisions have voiced particular concern with laws that foreclose an entire medium of expression. Thus, we have held invalid ordinances that completely banned the distribution of pamphlets within the municipality, *Lovell v. City of Griffin*, 303 U.S. 444, 451-452 (1938); the door-to-door distribution of literature, *Martin*; *Schneider*; and live entertainment, *Schad v. Mount Ephraim*, 452 U.S. 61 (1981). Although prohibitions foreclosing entire media may be completely free of content or viewpoint discrimination, the danger they pose to the freedom of speech is readily apparent—by eliminating a common means of speaking, such measures can suppress too much speech.

Ladue contends, however, that its ordinance is a mere regulation of the "time, place, or manner" of speech because residents remain free to convey their desired messages by other means, such as *hand-held* signs, "letters, handbills, flyers, telephone calls, newspaper advertisements, bumper stickers, speeches, and neighborhood or community meetings." However, even regulations that do not foreclose an entire medium of expression, but merely shift the time, place, or manner of its use, must "leave open ample alternative channels for communication." *Clark*.

---

[11] Because we set to one side the content discrimination question, we need not address the City's argument that the ordinance, although speaking in subject-matter terms, merely targets the "undesirable secondary effects" associated with certain kinds of signs. *See Renton*, 475 U.S. at 49. The inquiry we undertake below into the adequacy of alternative channels of communication would also apply to a provision justified on those grounds. *See id.* at 50.

In this case, we are not persuaded that adequate substitutes exist for the important medium of speech that Ladue has closed off.

Displaying a sign from one's own residence often carries a message quite distinct from placing the same sign someplace else, or conveying the same text or picture by other means.

Residential signs are an unusually cheap and convenient form of communication. Especially for persons of modest means or limited mobility, a yard or window sign may have no practical substitute. *Cf. Vincent; Martin.* Even for the affluent, the added costs in money or time of taking out a newspaper advertisement, handing out leaflets on the street, or standing in front of one's house with a handheld sign may make the difference between participating and not participating in some public debate. Furthermore, a person who puts up a sign at her residence often intends to reach *neighbors*, an audience that could not be reached nearly as well by other means.

A special respect for individual liberty in the home has long been part of our culture and our law; that principle has special resonance when the government seeks to constrain a person's ability to *speak* there. Most Americans would be understandably dismayed, given that tradition, to learn that it was illegal to display from their window an 8- by 11-inch sign expressing their political views. Whereas the government's need to mediate among various competing uses, including expressive ones, for public streets and facilities is constant and unavoidable, see *Cox v. New Hampshire*, 312 U.S. 569 (1941), its need to regulate temperate speech from the home is surely much less pressing.

Our decision that Ladue's ban on almost all residential signs violates the First Amendment by no means leaves the City powerless to address the ills that may be associated with residential signs.[17] It bears mentioning that individual residents themselves have strong incentives to keep their own property values up and to prevent "visual clutter" in their own yards and neighborhoods—incentives markedly different from those of persons who erect signs on others' land, in others' neighborhoods, or on public property. Residents' self-interest diminishes the danger of the "unlimited" proliferation of residential signs that concerns the City of Ladue. We are confident that more temperate measures could in large part satisfy Ladue's stated regulatory needs without harm to the First Amendment rights of its citizens. As currently framed, however, the ordinance abridges those rights. Accordingly, the judgment of the Court of Appeals is

Affirmed.

[Justice O'CONNOR's concurring opinion is omitted.]

NOTES AND QUESTIONS

1. *Where does* Gilleo *fit?* Is *Gilleo* consistent with the Court's apparently lenient review when intermediate scrutiny is applied to content-neutral regulations, or is it more consistent with *Schneider* and *Martin*?

---

[17] Nor do we hold that every kind of sign must be permitted in residential areas. Different considerations might well apply, for example, in the case of signs (whether political or otherwise) displayed by residents for a fee, or in the case of off-site commercial advertisements on residential property. We also are not confronted here with mere regulations short of a ban.

2. *Inadequate Substitutes.* The *Gilleo* majority noted that it was "not persuaded that adequate substitutes exist[ed] for the important medium of speech that Ladue ha[d] closed off." Yet in *Vincent* the Court upheld a law banning posting signs on public property because there were other areas where speakers could disseminate their message. When does a medium become so important to a message that other means of dissemination are inadequate?

FRISBY v. SCHULTZ

487 U.S. 474 (1988)

Justice O'CONNOR delivered the opinion of the Court.

Brookfield, Wisconsin, has adopted an ordinance that completely bans picketing "before or about" any residence. This case presents a facial First Amendment challenge to that ordinance.

[Appellees] are individuals strongly opposed to abortion and wish to express their views on the subject by picketing on a public street outside the Brookfield residence of a doctor who apparently performs abortions at two clinics in neighboring towns. Appellees and others engaged in precisely that activity, assembling outside the doctor's home on at least six occasions between April 20, 1985, and May 20, 1985, for periods ranging from one to one and a half hours. The size of the group varied from 11 to more than 40. The picketing was generally orderly and peaceful; the town never had occasion to invoke any of its various ordinances prohibiting obstruction of the streets, loud and unnecessary noises, or disorderly conduct. Nonetheless, the picketing generated substantial controversy and numerous complaints. . . .

[O]n May 15, 1985, [the town enacted] the following flat ban on all residential picketing:

> It is unlawful for any person to engage in picketing before or about the residence
> or dwelling of any individual in the Town of Brookfield.

The ordinance itself recites the primary purpose of this ban: "the protection and preservation of the home" through assurance "that members of the community enjoy in their homes and dwellings a feeling of well-being, tranquility, and privacy." The Town Board believed that a ban was necessary because it determined that "the practice of picketing before or about residences and dwellings causes emotional disturbance and distress to the occupants . . . [and] has as its object the harassing of such occupants." . . . The ordinance also evinces a concern for public safety, noting that picketing obstructs and interferes with "the free use of public sidewalks and public ways of travel." . . .

Our prior holdings make clear that a public street does not lose its status as a traditional public forum simply because it runs through a residential neighborhood. . . .

[The] residential character of those streets may well inform the application of the relevant test, but it does not lead to a different test; the antipicketing ordinance must be judged against the stringent standards we have established for restrictions on speech in traditional public fora[.] . . .

[W]e accept the lower courts' conclusion that the Brookfield ordinance is content neutral. Accordingly, we turn to consider whether the ordinance is "narrowly tailored to serve a significant government interest" and whether it "leave[s] open ample alternative channels of communication." . . .

Because the last question is so easily answered, we address it first. Of course, before we are able to assess the available alternatives, we must consider more carefully the reach of the ordinance. The precise scope of the ban is not further described within the text of the ordinance, but in our view the ordinance is readily subject to a narrowing construction that avoids constitutional difficulties. Specifically, the use of the singular form of the words "residence" and "dwelling" suggests that the ordinance is intended to prohibit only picketing focused on, and taking place in front of, a particular residence. . . .

So narrowed, the ordinance permits the more general dissemination of a message. As appellants explain, the limited nature of the prohibition makes it virtually self-evident that ample alternatives remain: "Protestors have not been barred from the residential neighborhoods. They may enter such neighborhoods, alone or in groups, even marching. . . . They may go door-to-door to proselytize their views. They may distribute literature in this manner... or through the mails. They may contact residents by telephone, short of harassment."

We readily agree that the ordinance preserves ample alternative channels of communication and thus move on to inquire whether the ordinance serves a significant government interest. We find that such an interest is identified within the text of the ordinance itself: the protection of residential privacy. "The State's interest in protecting the well-being, tranquility, and privacy of the home is certainly of the highest order in a free and civilized society." *Carey v. Brown*, 447 U.S. 455, 471 (1980). . . . Although in many locations, we expect individuals simply to avoid speech they do not want to hear, *cf. Erznoznik v. City of Jacksonville*, 422 U.S. 205 (1975); *Cohen v. California*, 403 U.S. 15 (1971), the home is different. . . . [A] special benefit of the privacy all citizens enjoy within their own walls... is an ability to avoid intrusions. Thus, we have repeatedly held that individuals are not required to welcome unwanted speech into their own homes and that the government may protect this freedom. . . . There simply is no right to force speech into the home of an unwilling listener.

It remains to be considered, however, whether the Brookfield ordinance is narrowly tailored to protect only unwilling recipients of the communications. A statute is narrowly tailored if it targets and eliminates no more than the exact source of the "evil" it seeks to remedy. . . . A complete ban can be narrowly tailored, but only if each activity within the proscription's scope is an appropriately targeted evil. For example, in *Taxpayers for Vincent* we upheld an ordinance that banned all signs on public property because the interest supporting the regulation, an esthetic interest in avoiding visual clutter and blight, rendered each sign an evil. Complete prohibition was necessary because "the substantive evil—visual blight—[was] not merely a possible byproduct of the activity, but [was] created by the medium of expression itself."

The same is true here. The type of focused picketing prohibited by the Brookfield ordinance is fundamentally different from more generally directed means of communication that may not be completely banned in residential areas. . . . Here, in contrast, the picketing is narrowly directed at the household, not the public. The type of picketers banned by the Brookfield ordinance generally do not seek to disseminate a message to the general public, but to intrude upon the targeted resident, and to do so in an especially offensive way. Moreover, even if some such picketers have a broader communicative purpose, their activity nonetheless inherently and offensively intrudes on residential privacy. The devastating effect of targeted picketing on the quiet enjoyment of the home is beyond doubt. . . .

In this case, for example, appellees subjected the doctor and his family to the presence of a relatively large group of protesters on their doorstep in an attempt to force the doctor to cease performing abortions. But the actual size of the group is irrelevant; even a solitary picket can invade residential privacy. . . . The offensive and disturbing nature of the form of the communication banned by the Brookfield ordinance thus can scarcely be questioned. . . .

The First Amendment permits the government to prohibit offensive speech as intrusive when the "captive" audience cannot avoid the objectionable speech. . . . The target of the focused picketing banned by the Brookfield ordinance is just such a "captive." The resident is figuratively, and perhaps literally, trapped within the home, and because of the unique and subtle impact of such picketing is left with no ready means of avoiding the unwanted speech. . . . Thus, the "evil" of targeted residential picketing . . . is "created by the medium of expression itself." . . . Accordingly, the Brookfield ordinance's complete ban of that particular medium of expression is narrowly tailored.

Reversed.

Justice BRENNAN, with whom Justice MARSHALL joins, dissenting.

. . . The mere fact that speech takes place in a residential neighborhood does not automatically implicate a residential privacy interest. . . .

Without question there are many aspects of residential picketing that, if unregulated, might easily become intrusive or unduly coercive. Indeed, some of these aspects are illustrated by this very case. . . . [S]logan-shouting protesters regularly converged on Dr. Victoria's home and, in addition to protesting, warned young children not to go near the house because Dr. Victoria was a "baby killer." Further, the throng repeatedly trespassed onto the Victorias' property and at least once blocked the exits to their home. . . . Surely it is within the government's power to enact regulations as necessary to prevent such intrusive and coercive abuses. Thus, for example, the government could constitutionally regulate the number of residential picketers, the hours during which a residential picket may take place, or the noise level of such a picket. [S]ubstantial regulation is permitted to neutralize the intrusive or unduly coercive aspects of picketing around the home. But to say that picketing may be substantially regulated is not to say that it may be prohibited in its entirety. Once size, time, volume, and the like have been controlled to ensure that the picket is no longer intrusive or coercive, only the speech itself remains, conveyed perhaps by a lone, silent individual, walking back and forth with a sign. . . . Such speech, which no longer implicates the heightened governmental interest in residential privacy, is nevertheless banned by the Brookfield law. Therefore, the ordinance is not narrowly tailored. . . .

Justice STEVENS, dissenting.

"GET WELL CHARLIE—OUR TEAM NEEDS YOU."

In Brookfield, Wisconsin, it is unlawful for a fifth grader to carry such a sign in front of a residence for the period of time necessary to convey its friendly message to its intended audience. . . .

The picketing that gave rise to the ordinance enacted in this case was obviously intended to do more than convey a message of opposition to the character of the doctor's practice; it was intended to cause him and his family substantial psychological distress. . . . I do not believe that picketing for the sole purpose of imposing psychological harm on a family in the shelter of their home is constitutionally protected. I do believe, however, that the picketers have a right to communicate their strong opposition to abortion to the doctor, but after they have had a fair opportunity to communicate that message, I see little justification for allowing them to remain in front of his home and repeat it over and over again simply to harm the doctor and his family. Thus, I agree that the ordinance may be constitutionally applied to the kind of picketing that gave rise to its enactment.

On the other hand, the ordinance is unquestionably "overbroad" in that it prohibits some communication that is protected by the First Amendment. . . .

My hunch is that the town will probably not enforce its ban against friendly, innocuous, or even brief unfriendly picketing, and that the Court may be right in concluding that its legitimate sweep makes its overbreadth insubstantial. But there are two countervailing considerations that are persuasive to me. The scope of the ordinance gives the town officials far too much discretion in making enforcement decisions; while we sit by and await further developments, potential picketers must act at their peril. . . .

[Justice WHITE's opinion concurring in the judgment is omitted.]

NOTES AND QUESTIONS

1. *Targeted picketing and the privacy interest.* Does the government interest at stake in *Frisby* justify a complete ban of targeted picketing? Why can't the city use a narrower restriction such as a law regulating the time, size, or noise levels of demonstrations to protect against such picketing?

2. *The captive audience rationale.* The *Frisby* majority states that the First Amendment "permits the government to prohibit offensive speech as intrusive when the 'captive' audience cannot avoid the objectionable speech." Does the Court use the term "offensive" speech in the same way that it did in cases such as *Terminiello, Feiner, Chaplinsky,* and *Cohen, supra* Chapter 3?

AN EXTENDED NOTE ON REGULATING TARGETED PROTESTS OUTSIDE MEDICAL CLINICS—THE LAW LEADING UP TO McCULLEN v. COAKLEY

Would *Frisby*'s reasoning support bans on targeted protests that occur away from individual residences? In a series of cases from 1994 to 2003 the Court faced that question. The initial cases involved situations where medical clinics sought injunctions against anti-abortion protestors. Later, the Supreme Court dealt with issues involving statutes that created "bubble zones" around medical clinics regulating the areas in which protestors could operate.

In Madsen v. Women's Health Center, Inc., 512 U.S. 753 (1994), the Court answered both yes and no to the question of whether the First Amendment allowed regulation of targeted protests outside of non-residences. *Madsen* involved an injunction limiting anti-abortion protestors' expression around health clinics in order to protect the health and safety of women seeking medical services, keep public order, and protect medical privacy. Specifically, the injunction banned protestors from (1) picketing or demonstrating within 36 feet of the property line of the clinic; (2) "singing, chanting, whistling, shouting, yelling, [or use of] sound amplification equipment or other sounds or images observable to or within earshot of the patients inside the clinic" during its operating hours; (3) physically approaching a person using clinic services within 300 feet of the clinic without their manifested consent (the "no approach" zone); or (4) picketing or demonstrating within 300 feet of the residences of clinic staff.

A majority of the Supreme Court found that the injunction was a content-neutral regulation of expression. However, because of the dangers associated with injunctions, the majority found that the injunction deserved a slightly more stringent version of intermediate scrutiny. Applying this standard, the majority upheld the 36-foot buffer zone around the clinic because it aimed at preventing only focused picketing as in *Frisby* and because it was necessary to protect access to the clinic. In contrast, the Court struck down the 300-foot buffer zone around residences of clinic staff. That zone, the Court held, was far larger than the focused picketing regulation in *Frisby* and would ban "[g]eneral marching through residential neighborhoods, or even walking a route in front of an entire block of houses." *Id.* at 775.

The Court also upheld the noise restrictions, reasoning that "[n]oise control is particularly important around hospitals and medical facilities during surgery and recovery periods. . . . The First Amendment does not demand that patients at a medical facility undertake Herculean efforts to escape the cacophony of political protests." *Id.* at 772-773. The desire to protect patients emotionally, however, was insufficient to justify the "images observable" provision. Such a ban was too broad to support an interest in preventing threatening speech. Further, a patient inside the clinic who "found the expression contained in such images disagreeable" could simply ask "the clinic to pull its curtains . . . and no more is required to avoid seeing placards through the windows of the clinic." *Id.* at 773.

Finally, the Court found the "no approach" zone unconstitutional. Although acknowledging that the lower court was attempting to prevent stalking and harassment, the Court found that "a prohibition on *all* uninvited approaches of persons seeking the services of the clinic, regardless of how peaceful the contact may be," was overly broad. *Id.* at 774. "Absent evidence that the protesters' speech is independently proscribable (*i.e.*, 'fighting words' or threats), or is so infused with violence as to be indistinguishable from a threat of physical harm, this provision cannot stand." *Id.*

Three years later in Schenck v. Pro-Choice Network of Western New York, 519 U.S. 357 (1997), the Court again ruled on an injunction limiting the expressive activities of anti-abortion protestors outside medical clinics. A majority of the Court found that 15-foot buffer zones created around clinic property were constitutional under *Madsen* but invalidated a provision allowing zones that moved with persons entering and leaving the clinic in order to protect them. Such zones proved too difficult to comply with due to their constantly changing nature.

The *Schenck* majority also upheld a "cease and desist" provision requiring that sidewalk counselors within the fixed 15-foot buffer zone stop their activities if so requested although it rejected the lower court's reasoning that the provision was necessary "'to protect the right of the people approaching and entering the facilities to be left alone.'" *Id.* at 383. According to *Schenck*, the *Madsen* injunction was designed to protect access to clinics and was not some sort of generalized "'right to be left alone' on a public street or sidewalk." *Id.*

Hill v. Colorado, 530 U.S. 703 (2000), involved the constitutionality of a statute regulating protests within a 100-foot area of health clinics. Specifically, the statute prohibited anyone within the 100-foot area from knowingly approaching within eight feet of another person, without that person's consent, "for the purpose of passing a leaflet or handbill to, displaying a sign to, or engaging in oral protest, education, or counseling with such other person." In a badly split decision, the Court upheld the constitutionality of the statute.

Citing to *Madsen*, the majority noted that the state interest in protecting the health and welfare of its citizen might "justify a special focus on unimpeded access to health care facilities and the avoidance of potential trauma to patients associated with confrontational protests." 530 U.S. at 715. The majority acknowledged that much speech falling within the statutory zones occurred in traditional public forums. Nevertheless, it noted the importance of "recognize[ing] the significant difference between state restrictions on a speaker's right to address a willing audience and those that protect listeners from unwanted communication. This statute deals only with the latter." *Id.* at 715-16. According to the Court:

> The unwilling listener's interest in avoiding unwanted communication has been repeatedly identified in our cases. It is an aspect of the broader "right to be let alone" that one of our wisest Justices characterized as "the most comprehensive of rights and the right most valued by civilized men." Olmstead v. United States, 277 U.S. 438 (1928) (Brandeis, J., dissenting). The right to avoid unwelcome speech has special force in the privacy of the home and its immediate surroundings but can also be protected in confrontational settings. . . .
>
> We have . . . recognized that the "right to persuade" . . . is protected by the First Amendment. . . . Yet we have continued to maintain that "no one has a right to press even 'good' ideas on an unwilling recipient." None of our decisions has minimized the enduring importance of "a right to be free" from persistent "importunity, following and dogging" after an offer to communicate has been declined. . . .
>
> . . . We, of course, are not addressing whether there is [a "right to avoid unpopular speech in a public forum."] Rather, we are merely noting that our cases have repeatedly recognized the interests of unwilling listeners in situations where "the degree of captivity makes it impractical for the unwilling viewer or auditor to avoid exposure."

Id. at 716-18.

The majority also found the statute to be content-neutral because it (1) was not adopted as a result of disagreement with the message speech conveyed, (2) only regulated the places where speech occurred, and (3) the State's interests in protecting access and privacy were unrelated to the content of the protestors' speech. According to the majority, the statute "simply establishe[d] a minor place restriction on an extremely broad category of communications with unwilling listeners. . . . [T]he statute applies equally to used car salesman, animal rights activists, fundraisers, environmentalists, and missionaries." *Id.* at 723. Applying intermediate scrutiny, the majority found the statute constitutional in large part because protestors could easily still communicate with signs from across the eight-foot zone. The Court acknowledged that the zone might burden leafleters and those wanting to make oral statements but it noted that their task was not insurmountable since they could still reach their intended audience and comply with the law. *Id.* at 727.

Justice Scalia, joined by Justice Thomas, dissented, arguing that the statue was content-based. According to Justice Scalia, the majority's claim "that the statute poses no special threat to First Amendment freedoms . . . is a wonderful replication (except for its lack of sarcasm) of Anatole France's observation that '[t]he law, in its majestic equality, forbids the rich as well as the poor to sleep under bridges.' This Colorado law is no more targeted at used car salesmen, animal rights activists, fundraisers, environmentalists, and missionaries than French vagrancy law was targeted at the rich. We know what the Colorado legislators, by their careful selection of content . . . were taking aim at, for they set it forth in the statute itself: the "right to protest or counsel *against* certain medical procedures" on the sidewalks and streets surrounding health care facilities." *Id.* at 744 (Scalia, J. dissenting).

Justice Scalia also argued that the majority wrongly recognized a right to be let alone in public: "The Court . . . purports to derive from our cases a principle limiting the protection the Constitution affords the speaker's right to direct 'offensive messages' at 'unwilling' audiences in the public forum. There is no such principle. We have upheld limitations on a speaker's exercise of his right to speak on the public streets *when that speech intrudes into the privacy of the home. Frisby.* . . . The Court today elevates the abortion clinic to the status of the home." *Id.* at 752.

Justice Kennedy also dissented. He noted that the law required officials to examine the speaker's message to determine if they were picketing, counseling or educating, thus making the statute content-based. *Id.* at 766. Further, the law regulated only protest, education or counseling in "a special class of locations, which were likely to involve only a specific topic—abortion." Thus, he argued that the law was content-based in light of what and where it regulated speech. *Id.* at 767. Like Justice Scalia, Justice Kennedy also argued that the Court's past precedents recognized "that citizens usually bear the burden of disregarding unwelcome messages" when in public. *Id.* at 773. Accordingly, he viewed the majority's decision as "an unprecedented departure from this Court's teachings respecting unpopular speech in public fora." *Id.*

McCULLEN v. COAKLEY

134 S. Ct. 2518 (2014)

Chief Justice ROBERTS delivered the opinion of the Court.

. . .

I

[T]he Massachusetts Legislature amended [a] statute in 2007. The statute now provides:

> "No person shall knowingly enter or remain on a public way or sidewalk adjacent to a reproductive health care facility within a radius of 35 feet of any portion of an entrance, exit or driveway of a reproductive health care facility or within the area within a rectangle created by extending the outside boundaries of any entrance, exit or driveway of a reproductive health care facility in straight lines to the point where such lines intersect the sideline of the street in front of such entrance, exit or driveway."

A "reproductive health care facility," in turn, is defined as "a place, other than within or upon the grounds of a hospital, where abortions are offered or performed."

The 35–foot buffer zone applies only "during a facility's business hours," and the area must be "clearly marked and posted." In practice, facilities typically mark the zones with painted arcs and posted signs on adjacent sidewalks and streets. . . .

The Act exempts four classes of individuals: (1) "persons entering or leaving such facility"; (2) "employees or agents of such facility acting within the scope of their employment"; (3) "law enforcement, ambulance, firefighting, construction, utilities, public works and other municipal agents acting within the scope of their employment"; and (4) "persons using the public sidewalk or street right-of-way adjacent to such facility solely for the purpose of reaching a destination other than such facility." . . .

Some of the individuals who stand outside Massachusetts abortion clinics are fairly described as protestors, who express their moral or religious opposition to abortion through signs and chants or, in some cases, more aggressive methods such as face-to-face confrontation. Petitioners take a different tack. They attempt to engage women approaching the clinics in what they call "sidewalk counseling," which involves offering information about alternatives to abortion and help pursuing those options. . . . McCullen and the other petitioners consider it essential to maintain a caring demeanor, a calm tone of voice, and direct eye contact during these exchanges. Such interactions, petitioners believe, are a much more effective means of dissuading women from having abortions than confrontational methods such as shouting or brandishing signs, which in petitioners' view tend only to antagonize their intended audience. . . .

Petitioners at all three clinics claim that the buffer zones have considerably hampered their counseling efforts. Although they have managed to conduct some counseling and to distribute some literature outside the buffer zones—particularly at the Boston clinic—they say they have had many fewer conversations and distributed many fewer leaflets since the zones went into effect.

The second statutory exemption allows clinic employees and agents acting within the scope of their employment to enter the buffer zones. Relying on this exemption, the Boston clinic uses "escorts" to greet women as they approach the clinic, accompanying them through the zones to the clinic entrance. Petitioners claim that the escorts sometimes thwart petitioners' attempts to communicate with patients by blocking petitioners from handing literature to patients, telling patients not to "pay any attention" or "listen to" petitioners, and disparaging petitioners as "crazy."

In January 2008, petitioners sued Attorney General Coakley and other Commonwealth officials. They sought to enjoin enforcement of the Act, alleging that it violates the First and Fourteenth Amendments, both on its face and as applied to them. The District Court denied petitioners' facial challenge after a bench trial based on a stipulated record. The Court of Appeals for the First Circuit affirmed.

We granted certiorari.

II

By its very terms, the Massachusetts Act regulates access to "public way[s]" and "sidewalk[s]." Such areas occupy a "special position in terms of First Amendment protection" because of their historic role as sites for discussion and debate. *United States v. Grace*, 461 U.S. 171, 180 (1983).

It is no accident that public streets and sidewalks have developed as venues for the exchange of ideas. Even today, they remain one of the few places where a speaker can be confident that he is not simply preaching to the choir. With respect to other means of communication, an individual confronted with an uncomfortable message can always turn the page, change the channel, or leave the Web site. Not so on public streets and sidewalks. There, a listener often encounters speech he might otherwise tune out. . . . [T]his aspect of traditional public fora is a virtue, not a vice. . . .

Consistent with the traditionally open character of public streets and sidewalks, we have held that the government's ability to restrict speech in [traditional public forums] is "very limited." In particular, the guiding First Amendment principle that the "government has no power to restrict expression because of its message, its ideas, its subject matter, or its content" applies with full force in a traditional public forum. *Police Dept. of Chicago v. Mosley*, 408 U.S. 92, 95 (1972). As a general rule, in such a forum the government may not "selectively . . . shield the public from some kinds of speech on the ground that they are more offensive than others." *Erznoznik v. Jacksonville*, 422 U.S. 205, 209 (1975).

We have, however, afforded the government somewhat wider leeway to regulate features of speech unrelated to its content. "[E]ven in a public forum the government may impose reasonable restrictions on the time, place, or manner of protected speech, provided the restrictions 'are justified without reference to the content of the regulated speech, that they are narrowly tailored to serve a significant governmental interest, and that they leave open ample alternative channels for communication of the information.'" *Ward v. Rock Against Racism*, 491 U.S. 781, 791 (1989). . . .

III

. . .

The Act applies only at a "reproductive health care facility," defined as "a place, other than within or upon the grounds of a hospital, where abortions are offered or performed." Given this definition, petitioners argue, "virtually all speech affected by the Act is speech concerning abortion," thus rendering the Act content based.

We disagree. To begin, the Act does not draw content-based distinctions on its face. The Act would be content based if it required "enforcement authorities" to "examine the content of the message that is conveyed to determine whether" a violation has occurred. But it does not. Whether petitioners violate the Act "depends" not "on what they say" but simply on where they say it. Indeed, petitioners can violate the Act merely by standing in a buffer zone, without displaying a sign or uttering a word.

It is true, of course, that by limiting the buffer zones to abortion clinics, the Act has the "inevitable effect" of restricting abortion-related speech more than speech on other subjects. But a facially neutral law does not become content based simply because it may disproportionately affect speech on certain topics. On the contrary, "[a] regulation that serves purposes unrelated to the content of expression is deemed neutral, even if it has an incidental effect on some speakers or messages but not others." *Ward*. The question in such a case is whether the law is "'justified without reference to the content of the regulated speech.'" *Renton v. Playtime Theatres, Inc.*, 475 U.S. 41, 48 (1986).

The Massachusetts Act is. Its stated purpose is to "increase forthwith public safety at reproductive health care facilities." Respondents have articulated similar purposes before this Court—namely, "public safety, patient access to healthcare, and the unobstructed use of public sidewalks and roadways." It is not the case that "[e]very objective indication shows that the provision's primary purpose is to restrict speech that opposes abortion."

We have previously deemed the foregoing concerns to be content neutral. Obstructed access and congested sidewalks are problems no matter what caused them. A group of individuals can obstruct clinic access and clog sidewalks just as much when they loiter as when they protest abortion or counsel patients.

To be clear, the Act would not be content neutral if it were concerned with undesirable effects that arise from "the direct impact of speech on its audience" or "[l]isteners' reactions to speech." See *Boos v. Barry*, 485 U.S. 312 (1988). If, for example, the speech outside Massachusetts abortion clinics caused offense or made listeners uncomfortable, such offense or discomfort would not give the Commonwealth a content-neutral justification to restrict the speech. All of the problems identified by the Commonwealth here, however, arise irrespective of any listener's reactions. . . .

. . . [P]etitioners note that these interests "apply outside every building in the State that hosts any activity that might occasion protest or comment," not just abortion clinics. By choosing to pursue these interests only at abortion clinics, petitioners argue, the Massachusetts Legislature evinced a purpose to "single[ ] out for regulation speech about one particular topic: abortion."

We cannot infer such a purpose from the Act's limited scope. The broad reach of a statute can help confirm that it was not enacted to burden a narrower category of disfavored speech. At the same time, however, "States adopt laws to address the problems that confront them. The First Amendment does not require States to regulate for problems that do not exist." The Massachusetts Legislature amended the Act in 2007 in response to a problem that was, in its experience, limited to abortion clinics. . . . In light of the limited nature of the problem, it was reasonable for the Massachusetts Legislature to enact a limited solution. When selecting among various options for combating a particular problem, legislatures should be encouraged to choose the one that restricts less speech, not more. . . .

Petitioners also argue that the Act is content based because it exempts four classes of individuals, one of which comprises "employees or agents of [a reproductive healthcare] facility acting within the scope of their employment." This exemption, petitioners say, favors one side in the abortion debate and thus constitutes viewpoint discrimination—an "egregious form of content discrimination," . . .

There is nothing inherently suspect about providing some kind of exemption to allow individuals who work at the clinics to enter or remain within the buffer zones. In particular, the exemption cannot be regarded as simply a carve-out for the clinic escorts; it also covers employees such as the maintenance worker shoveling a snowy sidewalk or the security guard patrolling a clinic entrance.

Given the need for an exemption for clinic employees, the "scope of their employment" qualification simply ensures that the exemption is limited to its purpose of allowing the employees to do their jobs. . . . The limitation . . . makes clear . . . that exempted individuals are allowed inside the zones only to perform those acts authorized by their employers. There is no suggestion in the record that any of the clinics authorize their employees to speak about abortion in the buffer zones. . . .

It would be a very different question if it turned out that a clinic authorized escorts to speak about abortion inside the buffer zones. In that case, the escorts would not seem to be violating the Act because the speech would be within the scope of their employment. The Act's exemption for clinic employees would then facilitate speech on only one side of the abortion debate—a clear form of viewpoint discrimination that would support an as-applied challenge to the buffer zone at that clinic. But the record before us contains insufficient evidence to show that the exemption operates in this way at any of the clinics, perhaps because the clinics do not want to doom the Act by allowing their employees to speak about abortion within the buffer zones.

We thus conclude that the Act is neither content nor viewpoint based and therefore need not be analyzed under strict scrutiny.

IV

Even though the Act is content neutral, it still must be "narrowly tailored to serve a significant governmental interest." The tailoring requirement does not simply guard against an impermissible desire to censor. The government may attempt to suppress speech not only because it disagrees with the message being expressed, but also for mere convenience. Where certain speech is associated with particular problems, silencing the speech is sometimes the path of least resistance. But by demanding a close fit between ends and means, the tailoring requirement prevents the government from too readily "sacrific[ing] speech for efficiency."

For a content-neutral time, place, or manner regulation to be narrowly tailored, it must not "burden substantially more speech than is necessary to further the government's legitimate interests." *Ward.* Such a regulation, unlike a content-based restriction of speech, "need not be the least restrictive or least intrusive means of" serving the government's interests. But the government still "may not regulate expression in such a manner that a substantial portion of the burden on speech does not serve to advance its goals."

A

As noted, respondents claim that the Act promotes "public safety, patient access to healthcare, and the unobstructed use of public sidewalks and roadways." Petitioners do not dispute the significance of these interests. We have, moreover, previously recognized the legitimacy of the government's interests in "ensuring public safety and order, promoting the free flow of traffic on streets and sidewalks, protecting property rights, and protecting a woman's freedom to seek pregnancy-related services." *Schenck v. Pro–Choice Network of Western N.Y.,* 519 U.S. 357, 376 (1997). *See also Madsen v. Women's Health Center, Inc.,* 512 U.S. 753, 767–768 (1994). The buffer zones clearly serve these interests.

At the same time, the buffer zones impose serious burdens on petitioners' speech. At each of the three Planned Parenthood clinics where petitioners attempt to counsel patients, the zones carve out a significant portion of the adjacent public sidewalks, pushing petitioners well back from the clinics' entrances and driveways. The zones thereby compromise petitioners' ability to initiate the close, personal conversations that they view as essential to "sidewalk counseling."

For example, in uncontradicted testimony, McCullen explained that she often cannot distinguish patients from passersby outside the Boston clinic in time to initiate a conversation before they enter the buffer zone. And even when she does manage to begin a discussion outside the zone, she must stop abruptly at its painted border, which she believes causes her to appear "untrustworthy" or "suspicious." Given these limitations, McCullen is often reduced to raising her voice at patients from outside the zone—a mode of communication sharply at odds with the compassionate message she wishes to convey. . . .

The buffer zones have also made it substantially more difficult for petitioners to distribute literature to arriving patients. . . . In short, the Act operates to deprive petitioners of their two primary methods of communicating with patients.

The Court of Appeals and respondents are wrong to downplay these burdens on petitioners' speech. . . . [W]hile the First Amendment does not guarantee a speaker the right to any particular form of expression, some forms—such as normal conversation and leafletting on a public sidewalk—have historically been more closely associated with the transmission of ideas than others. . . . When the government makes it more difficult to engage in these modes of communication, it imposes an especially significant First Amendment burden.

Respondents also emphasize that the Act does not prevent petitioners from engaging in various forms of "protest"—such as chanting slogans and displaying signs—outside the buffer zones. That misses the point. Petitioners are not protestors. They seek not merely to express their opposition to abortion, but to inform women of various alternatives and to provide help in pursuing them. . . . It is thus no answer to say that petitioners can still be "seen and heard" by women within the buffer zones. If all that the women can see and hear are vociferous opponents of abortion, then the buffer zones have effectively stifled petitioners' message. . . .

B

The buffer zones burden substantially more speech than necessary to achieve the Commonwealth's asserted interests. . . .

. . . The Commonwealth's interests include ensuring public safety outside abortion clinics, preventing harassment and intimidation of patients and clinic staff, and combating deliberate obstruction of clinic entrances. The Act itself contains a separate provision . . . that prohibits much of this conduct. That provision subjects to criminal punishment "[a]ny person who knowingly obstructs, detains, hinders, impedes or blocks another person's entry to or exit from a reproductive health care facility." If Massachusetts determines that broader prohibitions along the same lines are necessary, it could enact legislation similar to the federal Freedom of Access to Clinic Entrances Act of 1994 (FACE Act), which subjects to both criminal and civil penalties anyone who "by force or threat of force or by physical obstruction, intentionally injures, intimidates or interferes with or attempts to injure, intimidate or interfere with any person because that person is or has been, or in order to intimidate such person or any other person or any class of persons from, obtaining or providing reproductive health services." Some dozen other States have done so. If the Commonwealth is particularly concerned about harassment, it could also consider an ordinance such as the one adopted in New York City that not only prohibits obstructing access to a clinic, but also makes it a crime "to follow and harass another person within 15 feet of the premises of a reproductive health care facility."

The Commonwealth points to a substantial public safety risk created when protestors obstruct driveways leading to the clinics. That is, however, an example of its failure to look to less intrusive means of addressing its concerns. Any such obstruction can readily be addressed through existing local ordinances. *See, e.g.,* Worcester, Mass., Revised Ordinances of 2008, ch. 12, § 25(b) ("No person shall stand, or place any obstruction of any kind, upon any street, sidewalk or crosswalk in such a manner as to obstruct a free passage for travelers thereon").

All of the foregoing measures are, of course, in addition to available generic criminal statutes forbidding assault, breach of the peace, trespass, vandalism, and the like. . . .

Respondents contend that the alternatives we have discussed suffer from two defects: First, given the "widespread" nature of the problem, it is simply not "practicable" to rely on individual prosecutions and injunctions. But far from being "widespread," the problem appears from the record to be limited principally to the Boston clinic on Saturday mornings. Moreover, by their own account, the police appear perfectly capable of singling out lawbreakers. . . .

The second supposed defect in the alternatives we have identified is that laws [we have identified] require a showing of intentional or deliberate obstruction, intimidation, or harassment, which is often difficult to prove. As Captain Evans predicted in his legislative testimony, fixed buffer zones would "make our job so much easier."

Of course they would. But that is not enough to satisfy the First Amendment. . . . A painted line on the sidewalk is easy to enforce, but the prime objective of the First Amendment is not efficiency. In any case, we do not think that showing intentional obstruction is nearly so difficult in this context as respondents suggest. To determine whether a protestor intends to block access to a clinic, a police officer need only order him to move. If he refuses, then there is no question that his continued conduct is knowing or intentional. . . .

The judgment of the Court of Appeals for the First Circuit is reversed, and the case is remanded for further proceedings consistent with this opinion.

It is so ordered.

Justice SCALIA, with whom Justice KENNEDY and Justice THOMAS join, concurring in the judgment. . . .

[P]etitioners maintain that the Act targets abortion-related—for practical purposes, abortion-opposing—speech because it applies outside abortion clinics only (rather than outside other buildings as well).

. . . It blinks reality to say, as the majority does, that a blanket prohibition on the use of streets and sidewalks where speech on only one politically controversial topic is likely to occur—and where that speech can most effectively be communicated—is not content based. Would the Court exempt from strict scrutiny a law banning access to the streets and sidewalks surrounding the site of the Republican National Convention? Or those used annually to commemorate the 1965 Selma–to–Montgomery civil rights marches? Or those outside the Internal Revenue Service? Surely not. . . .

Does a statute become "justified without reference to the content of the regulated speech" simply because the statute itself and those defending it in court *say* that it is? Every objective indication shows that the provision's primary purpose is to restrict speech that opposes abortion.

I begin, as suggested above, with the fact that the Act burdens only the public spaces outside abortion clinics. One might have expected the majority to defend the statute's peculiar targeting by arguing that those locations regularly face the safety and access problems that it says the Act was designed to solve. But the majority does not make that argument because it would be untrue. As the Court belatedly discovers in Part IV of its opinion, although the statute applies to all abortion clinics in Massachusetts, only one is known to have been beset by the problems that the statute supposedly addresses. The Court uses this striking fact (a smoking gun, so to speak) as a basis for concluding that the law is insufficiently "tailored" to safety and access concerns (Part IV) rather than as a basis for concluding that it is not *directed* to those concerns at all, but to the suppression of antiabortion speech. That is rather like invoking the eight missed human targets of a shooter who has killed one victim to prove, not that he is guilty of attempted mass murder, but that *he has bad aim*.

Whether the statute "restrict[s] more speech than necessary" in light of the problems that it allegedly addresses is, to be sure, relevant to the tailoring component of the First Amendment analysis (the shooter doubtless did have bad aim), but it is also relevant—powerfully relevant—to whether the law is really directed to safety and access concerns or rather to the suppression of a particular type of speech. Showing that a law that suppresses speech on a specific subject is so far-reaching that it applies even when the asserted non-speech-related problems are not present is persuasive evidence that the law is content based. In its zeal to treat abortion-related speech as a special category, the majority distorts not only the First Amendment but also the ordinary logic of probative inferences.

The structure of the Act also indicates that it rests on content-based concerns. The goals of "public safety, patient access to healthcare, and the unobstructed use of public sidewalks and roadways," are already achieved by an earlier-enacted subsection of the statute, which provides criminal penalties for "[a]ny person who knowingly obstructs, detains, hinders, impedes or blocks another person's entry to or exit from a reproductive health care facility." As the majority recognizes, that provision is easy to enforce. Thus, the speech-free zones carved out by subsection (b) add nothing to safety and access; what they achieve, and what they were obviously designed to achieve, is the suppression of speech opposing abortion. . . .

The provision at issue here was indisputably meant to serve the same interest [as in *Hill v. Colorado*] in protecting citizens' supposed right to avoid speech that they would rather not hear. . . . In concluding that the statute is content based and therefore subject to strict scrutiny, I necessarily conclude that *Hill* should be overruled. Reasons for doing so are set forth in the dissents in that case[.] . . . Protecting people from speech they do not want to hear is not a function that the First Amendment allows the government to undertake in the public streets and sidewalks. . . .

Petitioners [also] contend that the Act targets speech opposing abortion (and thus constitutes a presumptively invalid viewpoint-discriminatory restriction) for another reason as well: It exempts "employees or agents" of an abortion clinic "acting within the scope of their employment,"

It goes without saying that "[g]ranting waivers to favored speakers (or . . . denying them to disfavored speakers) would of course be unconstitutional." *Thomas v. Chicago Park Dist.*, 534 U.S. 316 (2002). The majority opinion sets forth a two-part inquiry for assessing whether a regulation is content based, but when it comes to assessing the exemption for abortion-clinic employees or agents, the Court forgets its own teaching. Its opinion jumps right over the prong that asks whether the provision "draw[s] . . . distinctions on its face" and instead proceeds directly to the purpose-related prong, asking whether the exemption "represent[s] a governmental attempt to give one side of a debatable public question an advantage in expressing its views to the people." . . .

Is there any serious doubt that *abortion-clinic employees or agents* "acting within the scope of their employment" near clinic entrances may—indeed, often will—speak in favor of abortion ("You are doing the right thing")? Or speak in opposition to the message of abortion opponents—saying, for example, that "this is a safe facility" to rebut the statement that it is not? The Court's contrary assumption is simply incredible. . . .

I concur only in the judgment that the statute is unconstitutional under the First Amendment.

[Justice ALITO'S opinion concurring in the judgment is omitted.]

NOTES AND QUESTIONS

1. *Content-based or content-neutral.* Is the statute in *McCullen* content-based or content-neutral? Which opinion has the better argument?
2. *Intermediate scrutiny.* How does *McCullen*'s application of intermediate scrutiny compare to earlier cases, such as *Clark, Vincent,* or even *Hill*?
3. *The continuing validity of "right to be let alone" in public.* Justice Scalia also argued the *McCullen* majority had already implicitly overruled *Hill* by acknowledging that the statute would be content-based if it considered the undesirable effects associated with listeners' reactions to speech. 134 S. Ct. at 2546 (Scalia, J. concurring). Does the right to be let alone, which was so much at the center of *Madsen, Schenck, and Hill,* survive *McCullen*?

Consider also Snyder v. Phelps, 562 U.S. 443 (2011), *see infra* p. 487, where the Supreme Court faced the question of whether protestors standing in a traditional public forum could be liable for the torts of invasion of privacy and intentional infliction of emotional distress as a result of their offensive signs. The protestors, members of a small religious sect, stood on the public sidewalks outside of the building where the deceased soldiers' memorial service was held. The protestors were not noisy or physically disruptive, and they stood several hundred feet away from the building. But they held extremely offensive signs with messages such as "Thank God for Dead Soldiers" and "God Hates Fags."

The Court rejected the claim by the soldier's father that the protests could be the subject of lawsuits for intentional infliction of emotional distress or invasion of privacy because they disrupted the funeral services. The Court first noted that the protestors spoke on matters of public concern although they did so in an extremely offensive matter. *Id.* at 454. Furthermore, church members conducted their picketing "peacefully . . . at a public place adjacent to a public street." Such space, the Court held, occupies a "special position in terms of First Amendment protection. We have repeatedly referred to public streets as the archetype of a traditional public forum." *Id.* at 456. Because the protestors "had the right to be where they were," had complied with all police requests, and were not otherwise unruly or violent, any attempt to claim distress or invasion of privacy turned on the content of their message rather than on actual disruption of the funeral, the Court concluded. *Id.* at 457.

The Court did not dismiss all possible regulation of funeral protests, however. Such protests are "'subject to reasonable time, place, or manner restrictions' that are consistent with the standards announced in this Court's precedents. [*See Clark.*]" The Court then cited as examples the numerous laws enacted since the church began actively protesting at funerals. *Id.* at 456-57.

Consider the following law in light of *Hill*, *McCullen* and the dictum in *Snyder*. Can funeral attendees claim a wider zone free from protests based on a privacy interest (i.e., the right to be let alone) after these cases? *See, e.g.*, Phelps-Roper v. City of Manchester, 697 F.3d 678 (8th Cir. 2012) (en banc).

THEORY-APPLIED PROBLEM—FUNERAL PROTESTS

Okla. Stat. Ann., tit. 21, Oklahoma Funeral Picketing § 1380. Act—Findings—Purposes—Definitions—Penalties—Damages

A. This section shall be known and may be cited as the "Oklahoma Funeral Picketing Act."

1. The Legislature finds that:

a. it is generally recognized that families have a substantial interest in organizing and attending funerals for deceased relatives,

b. the interests of families in privately and peacefully mourning the loss of deceased relatives are violated when funerals are targeted for picketing and other public demonstrations,

c. picketing of funerals causes emotional disturbance and distress to grieving families who participate in funerals, and

d. full opportunity exists under the terms and provisions of this section for the exercise of freedom of speech and other constitutional rights at times other than the period from two hours before the scheduled commencement of funeral services until two hours after the actual completion of the funeral services.

B. The purposes of this section are to:

1. Protect the privacy of grieving families during the period from two hours before the scheduled commencement of the funeral services until two hours after the actual completion of the funeral services; and

2. Preserve the peaceful character of cemeteries, mortuaries and churches from two hours before the scheduled commencement of funeral services until two hours after the actual completion of the funeral services.

C. As used in this section:

1. "Funeral" means the ceremonies, processions and memorial services held in connection with the burial or cremation of the dead; and

2. "Picketing" means protest activities engaged in by a person or persons within one thousand (1,000) feet of a cemetery, mortuary, church or other place where any portion of a funeral service is held during the period from two hours before the scheduled commencement of funeral services until two hours after the actual completion of the funeral services.

D. It is unlawful for any person to engage in picketing within one thousand (1,000) feet of any cemetery, church, mortuary or other place where any portion of a funeral service is held during the period from two hours before the scheduled commencement of funeral services until two hours after the actual completion of the funeral services.

E. Any person violating the provisions of this section shall be guilty of a misdemeanor and upon conviction thereof shall be punished by a fine of not more than Five Hundred Dollars ($500.00), or by imprisonment in the county jail not more than thirty (30) days, or by both such fine and imprisonment.

F. Notwithstanding the penalties provided in subsection E, any district court may enjoin conduct proscribed by this section and may in any such proceeding award damages, including punitive damages attorney fees or other appropriate relief against the persons found guilty of actions made unlawful by this section.

Is the law content-based or content-neutral? What are the government interests underlying the law? Are these legitimate interests in this context? Is the law narrowly tailored to meet the government interests?

C. MODES OF REGULATION IN THE PUBLIC FORUM— CONTINUING PROBLEMS WITH PERMITS AND POLICING

The legitimacy of time, place, and manner requirements also arises in the context of certain *mechanisms* for regulating expression in the public forum. This section discusses some of the different methods of regulation and related questions.

Permit Schemes. Courts have long recognized that cities may control speech so that speakers using public property do not unreasonably interfere with traffic flow and public safety, etc. *See Schneider, supra.* In order to gauge possible conflicts with other activities, impact on traffic, and need for law enforcement coverage, cities often require persons or groups wanting to engage in expression to obtain permits beforehand. Under what circumstances may a city grant or deny permits to speakers?

In Lovell v. Griffin, 303 U.S. 444 (1938), the Court struck down a city ordinance that prohibited the distribution of circulars or other literature "without first obtaining written permission from the City Manager." According to the Court,

> the ordinance is invalid on its face. Whatever the motive which induced its adoption, its character is such that it strikes at the very foundation of the freedom of the press by subjecting it to license and censorship. . . . While [the] freedom from previous restraint upon publication cannot be regarded as exhausting the guaranty of liberty, the prevention of that restraint was a leading purpose in the adoption of the constitutional provision. Legislation of the type of the ordinance in question would restore the system of license and censorship in its baldest form. . . . The ordinance cannot be saved because it relates to distribution and not to publication. "Liberty of circulating is as essential to that freedom as liberty of publishing; indeed, without the circulation, the publication would be of little value." As the ordinance is void on its face, it was not necessary for appellant to seek a permit under it. She was entitled to contest its validity in answer to the charge against her.

Id. at 451-453. *Hague, supra* p. 120, reached a similar conclusion when striking down a comparable permitting ordinance.

The permit systems in *Lovell* and *Hague* are considered to be a form of prior restraint but *why* are they so worrisome? The Court is apparently concerned that the lack of standards for granting or denying a license will cause speakers to self-censor.

See, e.g., City of Lakewood v. Plain Dealer Publg. Co., 486 U.S. 750, 757 (1988). Similarly, it has observed that the lack of standards allows officials to use post hoc justifications for essentially censorial decisions. *Id.* at 758; Cox v. Louisiana, 379 U.S. 536, 557 (1965). Numerous cases subsequent to *Lovell* and *Hague* reiterate the principle that standardless licensing systems amount to prior restraints. *See, e.g.,* Kunz v. New York, 340 U.S. 290 (1951); Shuttlesworth v. City of Birmingham, 394 U.S. 147 (1969); Thomas v. Chicago Park Dist., 534 U.S. 316 (2002). *See also* Elena Kagan, *Private Speech, Public Purpose: The Role of Governmental Motive in First Amendment Doctrine*, 63 U. Chi. L. Rev. 415, 459 (1996); Thomas I. Emerson, *The Doctrine of Prior Restraint*, 20 Law & Contemp. Probs. 648 (1955).

The Court has, however, approved licensing schemes that do not give officials arbitrary enforcement authority. In Cox v. New Hampshire, 312 U.S. 569 (1941), a group of Jehovah's Witnesses were convicted for violating a statute that prohibited parades and processions on public streets without first obtaining a license from the city officials or a special licensing committee. The Court upheld the statute against a First Amendment challenge, noting that the "authority of a municipality to impose regulations in order to assure the safety and convenience of the people in the use of public highways has never been regarded as inconsistent with civil liberties but rather as one of the means of safeguarding the good order upon which they ultimately depend. The control of travel on the streets of cities is the most familiar illustration of this recognition of social need. Where a restriction of the use of highways in that relation is designed to promote the public convenience in the interest of all, it cannot be disregarded by the attempted exercise of some civil right which in other circumstances would be entitled to protection." *Id.* at 574. *Cox* noted that the lower court had construed the statute to allow officials to take into account only "considerations of time, place and manner so as to conserve the public convenience." *Id.* at 575-576. Such a scheme gave "public authorities notice in advance so as to afford opportunity for proper policing." *Id.* at 576. Further, the neutral standards in the statute did not vest "the licensing board . . . with arbitrary power or an unfettered discretion; . . . its discretion must be exercised with 'uniformity of method of treatment upon the facts of each application, free from improper or inappropriate considerations and from unfair discrimination.' . . . [A] 'systematic, consistent and just order of treatment, with reference to the convenience of public use of the highways, is the statutory mandate.'" *Id.*

Cox supports the notion that licensing schemes can pass constitutional muster if official discretion to grant or deny the permit is sufficiently constrained by neutral criteria. What qualifies as a neutral "time, place, and manner" standard of decision in this context? It is apparently appropriate for an official to consider that the permit was not fully completed, that the permit contains material falsehoods, that the activity for which the permit is requested conflicts with another activity already planned for a particular location. *See Thomas,* 534 U.S. at 318 n.1 (upholding ordinance with similar criteria). What about a standard allowing officials to deny a permit because the proposed activity "would present an unreasonable danger to the health or safety" of others, including government employees or the public? *See id.* (upholding ordinance with similar standard). Is this standard consistent with *Hague?*

On the other hand, government officials cannot require permits for individuals who want to travel door-to-door to communicate or distribute literature individually rather than parade on public streets. *See* Watchtower Bible & Tract Soc'y v. Village of Stratton, 536 U.S. 150 (2002) (striking down an ordinance requiring such a permit, despite the city's legitimate interest in fraud/crime prevention and protection of privacy, because the ordinance discouraged spontaneous and anonymous speech and was not adequately tailored to the city's interests). Does *Watchtower Bible* also suggest that government officials cannot require permits of small groups who want to use the public forum for expressive purposes? *See* Berger v. City of Seattle, 569 F.3d 1029, 1039) (9th Cir. 2009) (noting that "single-speaker permitting requirements for speech in a public forum . . . [are] constitutionally suspect"); Cox v. City of Charleston, 416 F.3d 281, 285 (4th Cir. 2005) ("[U]nflinching application" of a permitting requirement "to groups as small as two or three renders it constitutionally infirm."); Douglas v. Brownell, 88 F.3d 1511, 1524 (8th Cir. 1996) ("[A]pplying the permit requirement to groups as small as ten persons compounds our conclusion that the parade permit ordinance is not narrowly tailored[.]").

Permit Fees. Is it permissible for government officials to charge a fee for use of the public forum? In *Cox v. New Hampshire, supra*, the licensing ordinance also contained a provision allowing the government to charge fees ranging up to $300. The Court upheld the provision, as construed by the lower court, which required the fee charged in any given instance to be no greater than required to "meet the expense incident to the administration of the act and to the maintenance of public order in the matter licensed." 312 U.S. at 577. Such provisions allow government officials to recoup the costs associated with expressive activity on public property but they raise free speech concerns. For example, can a state charge a fee regardless of the speaker's ability to pay? Should the government be able to charge such fees only to speakers and not to other users of streets and parks? How high can the fees go? *See* David Goldberger, *A Reconsideration of* Cox v. New Hampshire: *Can Demonstrators Be Required to Pay the Costs of Using America's Public Forums?*, 62 Tex. L. Rev. 403, 410-412 (1983).

In Forsyth Co. v. Nationalist Movement, 505 U.S. 123 (1992), the Court struck down another ordinance imposing a permit fee on speakers. The ordinance required payment of up to $1,000 for each day a parade or procession took place, and allowed government officials to adjust the amount of the fee "to meet the expense incident to the administration of the ordinance and to the maintenance of public order in the matter licensed." The Court believed that neither the ordinance nor county practice provided sufficiently defined, narrow standards. Rather, "[t]he decision how much to charge for police protection or administrative time—or even whether to charge at all—is left to the whim of the administrator." *Id.* at 133. The Court also noted that county officials interpreted the ordinance as allowing administrators the discretion to assess a fee covering "the cost of necessary and reasonable protection of persons participating in or observing [the expressive] activity." *Id.* at 134. The Court concluded that the county's interpretation was unconstitutionally content-based: "In order to assess accurately the cost of security for parade participants, the administrator must necessarily examine the content of the message that is conveyed, estimate the response of others to that content, and judge the number of police necessary to meet that response. The fee assessed will depend on the administrator's measure of the amount of hostility likely to be created by the speech based on its content. Those wishing to express views unpopular with bottle throwers, for example, may have to pay more for their permit." *Id.* After *Forsyth County*, would it be permissible for government officials to require insurance of speakers who want to use a public forum? *See generally* Eric Neisser, *Charging for Free Speech: User Fees and Insurance in the Marketplace of Ideas*, 74 Geo L.J. 257, 321-329 (1986).

Policing Protests. Many observers have argued that lower courts' deference to official decision-making regarding protests allows censorship in other ways. Some argue that lower courts apply the Court's time, place and manner restrictions so loosely as to effectively allow content-based regulation of speech:

> [C]aging or penning of protestors, establishment of no-protest zones (places where speech is excluded from a public forum) or free speech zones (places where speech is allowed), or heavy-handed policing of protestors are all tactics courts have considered narrowly-tailored to meet the government's interests in preserving security and preventing disorder. . . . Officials positing national security concerns to justify protestor "pens" or "cages" at presidential conventions inevitably raise them only against persons protesting candidate platforms; persons supporting candidates are rarely subjected to such indignities. This is not to say that officials consciously discriminate based on content but simply that protestors who seek change seem threatening; officials are more likely to see them as source of disorder.

Christina E. Wells, "The Promise and Peril of Protesting in the Internet Era," in *Free Speech in the Internet Era* 65 (2013). *See also* Ronald Krotoszynski, Jr., *Reclaiming the Petition Clause: Seditious Libel, "Offensive" Protest, and the Right to Petition the Government for Redress of Grievances* (2012). Accordingly, many have criticized the Court's "time, place and manner" requirements as providing insufficient guidance to cabin official discretion. Wells, *supra*; Krotoszynski, *supra*; Timothy Zick, *Speech and Spatial Tactics*, 84 Tex. L. Rev. 581 (2006).

Discretion is also exercised in other ways that can hurt protestors. Police use increasingly aggressive, sometimes militarized tactics to regulate generally peaceful protests. Arguably, such tactics chill speech by making protestors fear possible bodily harm. They also send the message that protests are more violent and less legitimate than they actually are. *See* Christina E. Wells, *Protest, Policing and the Petition Clause,* 66 Alabama Law Review 1159 (2015) (book review). Similarly, police arrest protestors for minor offenses such as trespassing or jaywalking, against which protestors rarely have a First Amendment defense. Sometimes, prosecutors attach conditions to dismissals of charges that require protestors/defendants to remain free of criminal charges or arrests for six months to a year. All such tactics have the potential to deter protestors from future speech out of fear of future arrests stemming from their protest actions. *Id.* How do we balance the police officers' legitimate need for discretion when making decisions and the rights of protestors?

THEORY-APPLIED PROBLEM

The city of Portland enacted the following ordinance: "It is unlawful for any person to conduct or participate in any organized entertainment, demonstration, or public gathering, or to make any address in a park without a written permit issued by the Parks Commissioner." Five individuals chose to protest a city decision to close a local elementary school. They decided to gather in a park in downtown Portland one weekend. The city had already issued an exclusive-use permit to an Art Show that weekend for the entire park. When a police officer discovered the protestors and that they did not have a permit, she asked them to leave. When they refused, she told them she would arrest them for violating the permit ordinance. They chose to stay, so she arrested them. Is the Portland ordinance constitutional, facially and as applied to the protestors?

D. FORUM ANALYSIS—WHEN SHOULD SPEAKERS HAVE ACCESS TO GOVERNMENT PROPERTY?

Recall *Hague v. CIO*'s statement that "[w]herever the title of streets and parks may rest, they have immemorially been held in trust for the use of the public and, time out of mind, have been used for purposes of assembly, communicating thoughts between citizens, and discussing public questions." *Hague* seems to make clear that certain government property must be available for expressive purposes. Surely this recognition is right, for "where if not in the public forum can public assembly occur?" Ashutosh Bhagwat, *Associational Speech*, 120 Yale L.J. 978, 1016 (2011). Nevertheless, it is unclear how meaningful the right of access is in *Hague*.

Observers have noted that *Hague* seemed to accept the view in *Commonwealth v. Davis* that traditional common law notions of property rights defined access to government property:

> [B]y focusing on the fact that parks and streets had historically been used for speech and assembly, instead of forthrightly recognizing that access to public property for speech purposes is essential to effective exercise of First Amendment rights, [Hague's] rationale created by implication two distinct classes of public property respecting public forum theory.

Geoffrey R. Stone, *Fora Americana*, 1974 Sup. Ct. Rev. 233, 238. This interpretation of *Hague*, seems to allow less access to government property that is not traditionally used for expressive purposes, such as libraries, courthouses, and prisons.

Professor Harry Kalven believed an approach focusing on tradition does not adequately account for the role of public spaces in individual and group expression. He argued that "in an open democratic society the streets, the parks, and other public places are an important facility for public discussion and political process. They are . . . a public forum that the citizen can commandeer; the generosity and empathy with which such facilities are made available is an index of freedom." Harry Kalven, *The Concept of the Public Forum: Cox v. Louisiana*, 1965 Sup. Ct. Rev. 1, 11-12. Professor Geoffrey Stone similarly argues that speakers' rights to use government property should turn on whether access to such property is essential for the effective exercise of their free speech rights. Stone, *supra*, at 251-252. Professor Timothy Zick argues that courts considering speakers' demands for access to public property should more carefully weigh the complex role that "place" has in expression. Timothy Zick, *Space, Place and Speech: The Expressive Topography*, 74 Geo. Wash. L. Rev. 439 (2006). Dean Robert Post, in contrast, defends differential treatment of public property:

> The object of the public forum . . . is the constitutional clarification and regulation of government authority over particular resources. Public forum cases require courts to decide whether a resource is subject to a kind of authority 'like' that characterized by the government's relationship to a newspaper editorial, which is to say like that involved in the governance of the general public, or whether it is subject to a kind of authority 'like' that characterized by the government's control over the internal management of its own institutions, which is to say to the authority of management.

Robert Post, *Between Governance and Management: The History and Theory of the Public Forum*, 34 UCLA L. Rev. 1713, 1782 (1987). Which of these arguments is more persuasive?

This section covers the Court's jurisprudence regarding whether and under what circumstances the government must make its property available for expressive purposes. The Court has struggled with this doctrine and individual justices have made arguments similar to those above to justify giving or denying access to speakers. As you read the following cases, consider whether a coherent theme emerges regarding speakers' rights of access to public property.

BROWN v. LOUISIANA

383 U.S. 131 (1966)

Mr. Justice FORTAS announced the judgment of the Court and an opinion in which THE CHIEF JUSTICE and Mr. Justice DOUGLAS join. . . .

The Audubon Regional Library is operated jointly by the Parishes of East Feliciana, West Feliciana, and St. Helena. It has three branches and two bookmobiles. The bookmobiles served 33 schools, both white and Negro, as well as "individuals." One of the bookmobiles was red, the other blue. The red bookmobile served only white persons. The blue bookmobile served only Negroes. It is a permissible inference that no Negroes used the branch libraries. . . .

Five young Negro males, all residents of East or West Feliciana Parishes, went into the adult reading or service room of the Audubon Regional Library at Clinton. . . . Petitioner Brown requested a book, "The Story of the Negro" by Arna Bontemps. Mrs. Reeves, [branch assistant,] checked the card catalogue, ascertained that the Branch did not have the book, so advised Mr. Brown, and told him that she would request the book from the State Library, that he would be notified upon its receipt and that "he could either pick it up or it would be mailed to him." She told him that "his point of service was a bookmobile or it could be mailed to him." Mrs. Reeves testified that she expected that the men would then leave; they did not, and she asked them to leave. They did not. Petitioner Brown sat down and the others stood near him. They said nothing; there was no noise or boisterous talking. Mrs. Reeves called Mrs. Perkins, the regional librarian, who was in another room. Mrs. Perkins asked the men to leave. They remained.

Neither Mrs. Reeves nor Mrs. Perkins had called the sheriff, but in "10 to 15 minutes" from the time of the arrival of the men at the library, the sheriff and deputies arrived. The sheriff asked the Negroes to leave. They said they would not. The sheriff then arrested them. The sheriff had been notified that morning that members of the Congress of Racial Equality "were going to sit-in" at the library. . . . When the sheriff arrived, there was no noise, no disturbance. He testified that he arrested them "for not leaving a public building when asked to do so by an officer." . . .

. . . There is no dispute that the library system was segregated, and no possible doubt that these petitioners were there to protest this fact. . . . There was [also] no violation of the statute which petitioners are accused of breaching [i.e., the same breach of peace statute involved in *Cox v. Louisiana, supra*, p. 93]; no disorder, no intent to provoke a breach of the peace and no circumstances indicating that a breach might be occasioned by petitioners' actions. . . .

. . . We are here dealing with an aspect of a basic constitutional right—the right under the First and Fourteenth Amendments guaranteeing freedom of speech and of assembly, and freedom to petition the Government for a redress of grievances. . . . As this Court has repeatedly stated, these rights are not confined to verbal expression. They embrace appropriate types of action which certainly include the right in a peaceable and orderly manner to protest by silent and reproachful presence, in a place where the protestant has every right to be, the unconstitutional segregation of public facilities. Accordingly, even if the accused action were within the scope of the statutory instrument, we would be required to assess the constitutional impact of its application, and we would have to hold that the statute cannot constitutionally be applied to punish petitioners' actions in the circumstances of this case. . . . The statute was deliberately and purposefully applied solely to terminate the reasonable, orderly, and limited exercise of the right to protest the unconstitutional segregation of a public facility. Interference with this right, so exercised, by state action is intolerable under our Constitution.

It is an unhappy circumstance that the locus of these events was a public library— a place dedicated to quiet, to knowledge, and to beauty. It is a sad commentary that this hallowed place in the Parish of East Feliciana bore the ugly stamp of racism. It is sad, too, that it was a public library which, reasonably enough in the circumstances, was the stage for a confrontation between those discriminated against and the representatives of the offending parishes. Fortunately, the circumstances here were such that no claim can be made that use of the library by others was disturbed by the demonstration. Perhaps the time and method were carefully chosen with this in mind. Were it otherwise, a factor not present in this case would have to be considered. Here, there was no disturbance of others, no disruption of library activities, and no violation of any library regulations. A State or its instrumentality may, of course, regulate the use of its libraries or other public facilities. But it must do so in a reasonable and nondiscriminatory manner, equally applicable to all and administered with equality to all. It may not do so as to some and not as to all. It may not provide certain facilities for whites and others for Negroes. And it may not invoke regulations as to use—whether they are ad hoc or general—as a pretext for pursuing those engaged in lawful, constitutionally protected exercise of their fundamental rights.

The decision below is *reversed.*

Mr. Justice BLACK, with whom Mr. Justice CLARK, Mr. Justice HARLAN, and Mr. Justice STEWART join dissenting. . . .

Contrary to the implications in the prevailing opinion it is incomprehensible to me that a State must measure disturbances in its libraries and on the streets with identical standards. Furthermore, the vice of discriminatory enforcement, which contaminates the "public street" phase of this statute, does not beset the statute's application to activity in public buildings. In the public building, unlike the street, peace and quiet is a fast and necessary rule, and as a result there is much less room for peace officers to abuse their authority in enforcing the "public building" part of the statute. . . .

[P]etitioners, as part of a plan, entered the library and once there stayed despite the librarians' protests until its normal activity was completely disrupted. To be sure, there were not "100 to 300 'grumbling' white onlookers" as there were in *Cox v. Louisiana,* but surely, in the prevailing opinion's futile effort to rely on *Cox,* it is not meant that 300 or 100 grumbling onlookers must be crowded into a library before Louisiana can maintain an action under this statute. A tiny parish branch library, staffed by two women, is not…a public thoroughfare as in *Edwards v. South Carolina*, and *Cox*. Short of physical violence, petitioners could not have more completely upset the normal, quiet functioning of the Clinton branch of the Audubon Regional Library….

[T]he conclusion that the statute was unconstitutionally applied because it interfered with the petitioners' so-called protest establishes a completely new constitutional doctrine….

Though the First Amendment guarantees the right of assembly and the right of petition along with the rights of speech, press, and religion, it does not guarantee to any person the right to use someone else's property, even that owned by government and dedicated to other purposes, as a stage to express dissident ideas….

I would affirm.

[Justice BRENNAN's opinion concurring in the judgment is omitted.]

[Justice WHITE's opinion concurring in the result is omitted.]

ADDERLEY v. FLORIDA

385 U.S. 39 (1966)

Mr. Justice BLACK delivered the opinion of the Court.

. . . Harriett Louise Adderley and 31 other persons[] were convicted . . . on a charge of "trespass with a malicious and mischievous intent" upon the premises of the county jail [in violation of Florida statute]. Petitioners, apparently all students of the Florida A. & M. University in Tallahassee, had gone from the school to the jail about a mile away . . . to "demonstrate" . . . their protests of arrests of other protesting students the day before, and perhaps to protest more generally against state and local policies and practices of racial segregation, including segregation of the jail….

Petitioners have insisted from the beginning of this case that it is controlled by and must be reversed because of our prior cases of *Edwards v. South Carolina*, 372 U.S. 229, and *Cox v. State of Louisiana*, 379 U.S. 536. We cannot agree.

. . . In *Edwards*, the demonstrators went to the South Carolina State Capital grounds to protest. In this case they went to the jail. Traditionally, state capitol grounds are open to the public. Jails, built for security purposes, are not. The demonstrators at the South Carolina Capital went in through a public driveway and as they entered they were told by state officials there that they had a right as citizens to go through the State House grounds as long as they were peaceful. Here the demonstrators entered the jail grounds through a driveway used only for jail purposes and without warning to or permission from the sheriff….

They went directly to the jail-door entrance where they were met by a deputy sheriff, evidently surprised by their arrival. He asked them to move back, claiming they were blocking the entrance to the jail and fearing that they might attempt to enter the jail. They moved back part of the way, where they stood or sat, singing, clapping and dancing on the jail driveway and on an adjacent grassy area upon the jail premises. This particular jail entrance and driveway were not normally used by the public, but by the sheriff's department for transporting prisoners to and from the courts several blocks away and by commercial concerns for servicing the jail. Even after their partial retreat, the demonstrators continued to block vehicular passage over this driveway up to the entrance of the jail. . . . [The sheriff] told them that they were trespassing upon jail property and that he would give them 10 minutes to leave or he would arrest them.

Neither of the leaders did anything to disperse the crowd, and one of them told the sheriff that they wanted to get arrested. . . . After about 10 minutes, the sheriff . . . told the demonstrators that . . . they were trespassing on county property in violation of the law, that they should all leave forthwith or he would arrest them[.] Some of the group then left. . . . In a few minutes, realizing that the remaining demonstrators had no intention of leaving, the sheriff ordered his deputies to surround those remaining on jail premises and placed them, 107 demonstrators, under arrest. . . .

The sheriff, as jail custodian, had power, as the state courts have here held, to direct that this large crowd of people get off the grounds. There is not a shred of evidence in this record that this power was exercised, . . . because the sheriff objected to what was being sung or said by the demonstrators or because he disagreed with the objectives of their protest. The record reveals that he objected only to their presence on that part of the jail grounds reserved for jail uses. There is no evidence at all that on any other occasion had similarly large groups of the public been permitted to gather on this portion of the jail grounds for any purpose. Nothing in the Constitution of the United States prevents Florida from even-handed enforcement of its general trespass statute against those refusing to obey the sheriff's order to remove themselves from what amounted to the curtilage of the jailhouse. The State, no less than a private owner of property, has power to preserve the property under its control for the use to which it is lawfully dedicated. For this reason there is no merit to the petitioners' argument that they had a constitutional right to stay on the property, over the jail custodian's objections, because this "area chosen for the peaceful civil rights demonstration was not only 'reasonable' but also particularly appropriate. . . . " Such an argument has as its major unarticulated premise the assumption that people who want to propagandize protests or views have a constitutional right to do so whenever and however and wherever they please. . . . We reject [that argument]. . . .

These judgments are

Affirmed.

Mr. Justice DOUGLAS, with whom THE CHIEF JUSTICE, Mr. Justice BRENNAN, and Mr. Justice FORTAS concur, dissenting. . . .

There is no question that petitioners had as their purpose a protest against the arrest of Florida A. & M. students for trying to integrate public theatres. . . . There was no violence; no threat of violence; no attempted jail break; no storming of a prison; no plan or plot to do anything but protest. The evidence is uncontradicted that the petitioners' conduct did not upset the jailhouse routine; . . . There was no shoving, no pushing, no disorder or threat of riot. It is said that some of the group blocked part of the driveway leading to the jail entrance. The chief jailer, to be sure, testified that vehicles would not have been able to use the driveway. Never did the students locate themselves so as to cause interference with persons or vehicles going to or coming from the jail. Indeed, it is undisputed that the sheriff and deputy sheriff, in separate cars, were able to drive up the driveway to the parking places near the entrance and that no one obstructed their path.

Further, it is undisputed that the entrance to the jail was not blocked. And whenever the students were requested to move they did so. If there was congestion, the solution was a further request to move to lawns or parking areas, not complete ejection and arrest. . . .

We do violence to the First Amendment when we permit this "petition for redress of grievances" to be turned into a trespass action. . . . Only the sheriff's fiat transformed lawful conduct into an unlawful trespass. . . .

The Court forgets that prior to this day our decisions have drastically limited the application of state statutes inhibiting the right to go peacefully on public property to exercise First Amendment rights. [*See Hague.*] . . .

There may be some public places which are so clearly committed to other purposes that their use for the airing of grievances is anomalous. There may be some instances in which assemblies and petitions for redress of grievances are not consistent with other necessary purposes of public property. A noisy meeting may be out of keeping with the serenity of the statehouse or the quiet of the courthouse. No one, for example, would suggest that the Senate gallery is the proper place for a vociferous protest rally. . . . But this is quite different from saying that all public places are off limits to people with grievances. . . . And it is farther yet from saying that the "custodian" of the public property in his discretion can decide when public places shall be used for the communication of ideas[.] . . . For to place such discretion in any public official, be he the "custodian" of the public property or the local police commissioner . . . is to place those who assert their First Amendment rights at his mercy. It gives him the awesome power to decide whose ideas may be expressed and who shall be denied a place to air their claims and petition their government. . . .

GREER v. SPOCK

424 U.S. 828 (1976)

Mr. Justice STEWART delivered the opinion of the Court.

The Fort Dix Military Reservation is a United States Army post located in a predominantly rural area of central New Jersey. Its primary mission is to provide basic combat training for newly inducted Army personnel. Accordingly, most of its 55 square miles are devoted to military training activities. The Federal Government exercises exclusive jurisdiction over the entire area within Fort Dix, including the state and county roads that pass through it. Civilian vehicular traffic is permitted on paved roads within the reservation, and civilian pedestrian traffic is permitted on both roads and footpaths. Military police regularly patrol the roads within the reservation, and they occasionally stop civilians and ask them the reason for their presence. Signs posted on the roads leading into the reservation state: "All vehicles are subject to search while on the Fort Dix Military Reservation" and "Soliciting prohibited unless approved by the commanding general." The main entrances to Fort Dix are not normally guarded, and a sign at one of the entrances says "Visitors Welcome." Civilians are freely permitted to visit unrestricted areas of the reservation.

Civilian speakers have occasionally been invited to the base to address military personnel. The subjects of their talks have ranged from business management to drug abuse. Visiting clergymen have, by invitation, participated in religious services at the base chapel. Theatrical exhibitions and musical productions have also been presented on the base. Speeches and demonstrations of a partisan political nature, however, are banned by Fort Dix Reg. 210-26 (1968), which provides that "[d]emonstrations, picketing, sit-ins, protest marches, political speeches and similar activities are prohibited and will not be conducted on the Fort Dix Military Reservation." The regulation has been rigidly enforced: Prior to this litigation, no political campaign speech had ever been given at Fort Dix. Restrictions are also placed on another type of expressive activity. Fort Dix Reg. 210-27 (1970) provides that "[t]he distribution or posting of any publication, including newspapers, magazines, handbills, flyers, circulars, pamphlets or other writings, issued, published or otherwise prepared by any person, persons, agency or agencies . . . is prohibited on the Fort Dix Military Reservation without prior written approval of the Adjutant General, this headquarters."

. . . Respondents Benjamin Spock and Julius Hobson were the candidates of the People's Party for the offices of President and Vice President of the United States, and Linda Jenness and Andrew Pulley were the candidates of the Socialist Workers Party for the same offices. On September 9, 1972, Spock, Hobson, Jenness, and Pulley wrote a joint letter to Major General Bert A. David, then commanding officer of Fort Dix, informing him of their intention to enter the reservation on September 23, 1972, for the purpose of distributing campaign literature and holding a meeting to discuss election issues with service personnel and their dependents. On September 18, 1972, General David rejected the candidates' request. . . .

On September 29, 1972, the respondents filed this suit in the United States District Court for the District of New Jersey to enjoin the enforcement of the Fort Dix regulations governing political campaigning and the distribution of literature, upon the ground that the regulations violated the First and Fifth Amendments of the Constitution. The District Court denied a preliminary injunction, but the Court of Appeals reversed that order and directed that preliminary injunctive relief be granted to the respondents. . . .

The Court of Appeals was mistaken in thinking that . . . whenever members of the public are permitted freely to visit a place owned or operated by the Government, then that place becomes a "public forum" for purposes of the First Amendment. Such a principle of constitutional law has never existed, and does not exist now. . . .

. . . [T]he business of a military installation like Fort Dix is to train soldiers, not to provide a public forum. . . . A necessary concomitant of the basic function of a military installation has been "the historically unquestioned power of [its] commanding officer summarily to exclude civilians from the area of his command." *Cafeteria Workers v. McElroy*, 367 U.S. 886 (1961). The notion that federal military reservations, like municipal streets and parks, have traditionally served as a place for free public assembly and communication of thoughts by private citizens is thus historically and constitutionally false.

The respondents, therefore, had no generalized constitutional right to make political speeches or distribute leaflets at Fort Dix, and it follows that Fort Dix Regs. 210-26 and 210-27 are not constitutionally invalid on their face. These regulations, moreover, were not unconstitutionally applied in the circumstances disclosed by the record in the present case.[10] . . .

[T]here is no claim that the military authorities discriminated in any way among candidates for public office based upon the candidates' supposed political views. . . .

---

[10] The fact that other civilian speakers and entertainers had sometimes been invited to appear at Fort Dix did not of itself serve to convert Fort Dix into a public forum or to confer upon political candidates a First or Fifth Amendment right to conduct their campaigns there. The decision of the military authorities that a civilian lecture on drug abuse, a religious service by a visiting preacher at the base chapel, or a rock musical concert would be supportive of the military mission of Fort Dix surely did not leave the authorities powerless thereafter to prevent any civilian from entering Fort Dix to speak on any subject whatever.

What the record shows, therefore, is a considered Fort Dix policy, objectively and evenhandedly applied, of keeping official military activities there wholly free of entanglement with partisan political campaigns of any kind. . . .

Such a policy is wholly consistent with the American constitutional tradition of a politically neutral military establishment under civilian control. . . .

For the reasons set out in this opinion the judgment is reversed.

It is so ordered.

Mr. Justice BRENNAN, with whom Mr. Justice MARSHALL concurs, dissenting.

. . . It bears special note that the notion of "public forum" has never been the touchstone of public expression, for a contrary approach blinds the Court to any possible accommodation of First Amendment values in this case. . . . Those cases permitting public expression without characterizing the locale involved as a public forum, together with those cases recognizing the existence of a public forum, albeit qualifiedly, evidence the desirability of a flexible approach to determining when public expression should be protected. Realizing that the permissibility of a certain form of public expression at a given locale may differ depending on whether it is asked if the locale is public forum or if the form of expression is compatible with the activities occurring at the locale, it becomes apparent that there is need for a flexible approach. Otherwise, with the rigid characterization of a given locale as not a public forum, there is the danger that certain forms of public speech at the locale may be suppressed, even though they are basically compatible with the activities otherwise occurring at the locale.

Not only does the Court's forum approach to public speech blind it to proper regard for First Amendment interests, but also the Court forecloses such regard by studied misperception of the nature of the inquiry. . . .

It is no answer to say that the commander of a military installation has the "historically unquestioned power . . . to exclude civilians from the area of his command." Where the interference with Fort functions by public expression does not differ from that presented by other activities in unrestricted areas, the Fort command may no more preclude such expression, than "'Congress may . . .' enact a regulation providing that no Republican, Jew or Negro shall be appointed to federal office." *McElroy.*

Similarly, it is no answer to say that the proposed activities in this case may be excluded because similar forms of expression have been evenhandedly excluded. An evenhanded exclusion of all public expression would no more pass constitutional muster than an evenhanded exclusion of all Roman Catholics. . . .

Mr. Justice MARSHALL, dissenting. . . .

The First Amendment infringement that the Court here condones is fundamentally inconsistent with the commitment of the Nation and the Constitution to an open society. That commitment surely calls for a far more reasoned articulation of the governmental interests assertedly served by the challenged regulations than is reflected in the Court's opinion. The Court, by its unblinking deference to the military's claim that the regulations are appropriate, has sharply limited one of the guarantees that makes this Nation so worthy of being defended. I dissent.

Mr. Justice STEVENS took no part in the consideration or decision of this case.

[Mr. Chief Justice BURGER's concurring opinion is omitted.]

NOTES AND QUESTIONS

1. *The meaning of* Brown. Under *Brown*, must officials allow speakers of all sorts to use libraries for expressive purposes, or only as long as speakers do not disrupt its normal functioning? Does *Brown* follow Professor Stone's reasoning, *supra*?

2. *The meaning of* Adderley. Why doesn't *Adderley* follow *Brown*'s reasoning? Are speakers inherently more disruptive of activities that take place on jailhouse grounds than in libraries? Consider Daniel A. Farber & John E. Nowak, *The Misleading Nature of Public Forum Analysis: Content and Context in First Amendment Adjudication*, 70 Va. L. Rev. 1219, 1234 (1984) ("Surely a government driveway is more like a public forum than a quiet library.").

3. *The role of "place" in speech.* Does *Adderley* give enough consideration to the speaker's choice and location of expression?

4. *Speech on military bases.* Would allowing the speakers in *Spock* to distribute literature and discuss political issues on military property generally open to the public have interfered with the operation of the military base? If not, why does the majority uphold their exclusion? Should the Court use a flexible approach to determining speakers' access to public property as Justice Brennan suggests?

5. *Additional early cases.* Other cases also began to flesh out the Court's principles regarding speech on public property. In Lehman v. City of Shaker Heights, 418 U.S. 298 (1974), the Court, in a 5-4 decision, upheld the city's rule banning political but not commercial advertisements on city-owned bus placards. Justice Blackmun, in the plurality opinion, rejected the argument that the placards were "public forums" for First Amendment purposes: "Although American constitutional jurisprudence, in the light of the First Amendment, has been jealous to preserve access to public places for purposes of free speech, the nature of the forum and the conflicting interests involved have remained important in determining the degree of protection afforded by the Amendment to the speech in question. Here, we have no open spaces, no meeting hall, park, street corner, or other public thoroughfare. Instead . . . [the placards], although incidental to the provision of public transportation, [are] a part of the commercial venture. In much the same way that a newspaper or periodical, or even a radio or television station, need not accept every proffer of advertising from the general public, a city transit system has discretion to develop and make reasonable choices concerning the type of advertising that may be displayed in its vehicles." *Id.* at 302-303.

    Justice Blackmun further found that the city's distinction between commercial and noncommercial advertisements was reasonable: "Revenue earned from long-term commercial advertising could be jeopardized by a requirement that short-term candidacy or issue-oriented advertisements be displayed on car cards. Users would be subjected to the blare of political propaganda. There could be lurking doubts about favoritism, and sticky administrative problems might arise in parceling out limited space to eager politicians. In these circumstances, the managerial decision to limit car card space to innocuous and less controversial commercial and service oriented advertising does not rise to the dignity of a First Amendment violation. Were we to hold to the contrary, display cases in public hospitals, libraries, office buildings, military compounds, and other public facilities immediately would become Hyde Parks open to every would-be pamphleteer and politician." *Id.* at 303-304.

Justice Brennan, joined by Justices Stewart, Marshall, and Powell, dissented, claiming that "the city created a forum for the dissemination of information and expression of ideas when it accepted and displayed commercial and public service advertisements on its rapid transit vehicles. Having opened a forum for communication, the city is barred by the First and Fourteenth Amendments from discriminating among forum users solely on the basis of message content." *Id.* at 310.

In Southeastern Promotions, Ltd. v. Conrad, 420 U.S. 546 (1975), the Court found that the directors of a municipal theater had violated the rights of a theatrical production company by refusing to allow it to perform the rock musical "Hair," which the directors understood might involve nudity and obscenity on stage. Justice Blackmun, writing for the Court, found that the directors' decision amounted to an unconstitutional prior restraint. Citing to *Adderley, Brown,* and *Lehman,* Justice Blackmun also noted that the theaters were public forums:

> Respondents' action was no less a prior restraint because the public facilities under their control happened to be municipal theaters. The Memorial Auditorium and the Tivoli were public forums designed for and dedicated to expressive activities. There was no question as to the usefulness of either facility for petitioner's production. There was no contention by the board that these facilities could not accommodate a production of this size. None of the circumstances qualifying as an established exception to the doctrine of prior restraint was present. . . . Nor was rejection of the application based on any regulation of time, place, or manner related to the nature of the facility or applications from other users. No rights of individuals in surrounding areas were violated by noise or any other aspect of the production. There was no captive audience.

Id. at 555-556.

Justice Rehnquist dissented, arguing that "public auditoriums" were not on par with streets and sidewalks in the Court's forum jurisprudence:

> [T]he apparent effect of the Court's decision is to tell the managers of municipal auditoriums that they may exercise no selective role whatsoever in deciding what performances may be booked. The auditoriums in question here have historically . . . accepted only productions not inappropriate for viewing by children so that the facilities might serve as a place for entertaining the whole family. Viewed apart from any constitutional limitations, such a policy would undoubtedly rule out much worthwhile adult entertainment. But if it is the desire of the citizens of Chattanooga, who presumably have paid for and own the facilities, that the attractions to be shown there should not be of the kind which would offend any substantial number of potential theatergoers, I do not think the policy can be described as arbitrary or unreasonable.

Id. at 571-572.

Do *Lehman* and *Southeastern Promotions* clarify the principles regarding speaker access to public property?

PERRY EDUCATION ASS'N v. PERRY LOCAL EDUCATORS' ASS'N
460 U.S. 37 (1983)

Justice WHITE delivered the opinion of the Court.

. . . The Metropolitan School District of Perry Township, Ind., operates a public school system of 13 separate schools. Each school building contains a set of mailboxes for the teachers. Interschool delivery by school employees permits messages to be delivered rapidly to teachers in the district. The primary function of this internal mail system is to transmit official messages among the teachers and between the teachers and the school administration. In addition, teachers use the system to send personal messages and individual school building principals have allowed delivery of messages from various private organizations.[2]

Prior to 1977, both the Perry Education Association (PEA) and the Perry Local Educators' Association (PLEA) represented teachers in the school district and apparently had equal access to the interschool mail system. In 1977, PLEA challenged PEA's status as *de facto* bargaining representative for the Perry Township teachers by filing an election petition with the Indiana Education Employment Relations Board (Board). PEA won the election and was certified as the exclusive representative, as provided by Indiana law.

. . . Following the election, PEA and the school district negotiated a labor contract in which the school board gave PEA "access to teachers' mailboxes in which to insert material" and the right to use the interschool mail delivery system to the extent that the school district incurred no extra expense by such use. The labor agreement noted that these access rights were being accorded to PEA "acting as the representative of the teachers" and went on to stipulate that [PEA would have exclusive access rights over other unions]. . . .

The exclusive access policy applies only to use of the mailboxes and school mail system. PLEA is not prevented from using other school facilities to communicate with teachers. PLEA may post notices on school bulletin boards; may hold meetings on school property after school hours; and may, with approval of the building principals, make announcements on the public address system. Of course, PLEA also may communicate with teachers by word of mouth, telephone, or the United States mail. . . .

. . . There is no question that constitutional interests are implicated by denying PLEA use of the interschool mail system. . . . The First Amendment's guarantee of free speech applies to teacher's [sic] mailboxes as surely as it does elsewhere within the school, *Tinker v. Des Moines School District*, 393 U.S. 503 (1969), and on sidewalks outside, *Police Department of Chicago v. Mosely*, 408 U.S. 92 (1972). But this is not to say that the First Amendment requires equivalent access to all parts of a school building in which some form of communicative activity occurs. . . . The existence of a right of access to public property and the standard by which limitations upon such a right must be evaluated differ depending on the character of the property at issue.

In places which by long tradition or by government fiat have been devoted to assembly and debate, the rights of the state to limit expressive activity are sharply

---

[2] Local parochial schools, church groups, YMCAs, and Cub Scout units have used the system. The record does not indicate whether any requests for use have been denied, nor does it reveal whether permission must separately be sought for every message that a group wishes delivered to the teachers.

circumscribed. At one end of the spectrum are streets and parks which "have immemorially been held in trust for the use of the public, and, time out of mind, have been used for purposes of assembly, communicating thoughts between citizens, and discussing public questions." *Hague v. CIO*. In these quintessential public forums, the government may not prohibit all communicative activity. For the state to enforce a content-based exclusion it must show that its regulation is necessary to serve a compelling state interest and that it is narrowly drawn to achieve that end. . . . The state may also enforce regulations of the time, place, and manner of expression which are content-neutral, are narrowly tailored to serve a significant government interest, and leave open ample alternative channels of communication. . . .

A second category consists of public property which the state has opened for use by the public as a place for expressive activity. The Constitution forbids a state to enforce certain exclusions from a forum generally open to the public even if it was not required to create the forum in the first place. *Widmar v. Vincent*, 454 U.S. 263 (1981) (university meeting facilities); *City of Madison Joint School District v. Wisconsin Public Employment Relations Comm'n*, 429 U.S. 167 (1976) (school board meeting); *Southeastern Promotions, Ltd. v. Conrad*, 420 U.S. 546 (1975) (municipal theater).[7] Although a state is not required to indefinitely retain the open character of the facility, as long as it does so it is bound by the same standards as apply in a traditional public forum. Reasonable time, place and manner regulations are permissible, and a content-based prohibition must be narrowly drawn to effectuate a compelling state interest.

Public property which is not by tradition or designation a forum for public communication is governed by different standards. We have recognized that the "First Amendment does not guarantee access to property simply because it is owned or controlled by the government." *United States Postal Service v. Greenburgh Civic Ass'n*, 453 U.S. 114, (1981). In addition to time, place, and manner regulations, the state may reserve the forum for its intended purposes, communicative or otherwise, as long as the regulation on speech is reasonable and not an effort to suppress expression merely because public officials oppose the speaker's view. . . .

The school mail facilities at issue here fall within this third category. . . . The internal mail system, at least by policy, is not held open to the general public. It is instead PLEA's position that the school mail facilities have become a "limited public forum" from which it may not be excluded because of the periodic use of the system by private non-school connected groups, and PLEA's own unrestricted access to the system prior to PEA's certification as exclusive representative.

Neither of these arguments is persuasive. The use of the internal school mail by groups not affiliated with the schools is no doubt a relevant consideration. If by policy or by practice the Perry School District has opened its mail system for indiscriminate use by the general public, then PLEA could justifiably argue a public forum has been created. This, however, is not the case. As the case comes before us, there is no indication in the record that the school mailboxes and interschool delivery system are open for use by the general public. Permission to use the system to communicate with teachers must be secured from the individual building principal. There is no court finding or evidence in the record which demonstrates that this permission has been granted as a matter of course to all who seek to distribute

---

[7] A public forum may be created for a limited purpose such as use by certain groups, e.g., *Widmar* (student groups), or for the discussion of certain subjects, e.g., *City of Madison Joint School District* (school board business).

material. We can only conclude that the schools do allow some outside organizations such as the YMCA, Cub Scouts, and other civic and church organizations to use the facilities. . . .

Moreover, even if we assume that by granting access to the Cub Scouts, YMCAs, and parochial schools, the school district has created a "limited" public forum, the constitutional right of access would in any event extend only to other entities of similar character. While the school mail facilities thus might be a forum generally open for use by the Girl Scouts, the local boys' club and other organizations that engage in activities of interest and educational relevance to students, they would not as a consequence be open to an organization such as PLEA, which is concerned with the terms and conditions of teacher employment. . . .

[PLEA also argues that the access policy in place prior to 1978] . . . converted the school mail facilities into a limited public forum generally open for use by employee organizations, and that once this occurred, exclusions of employee organizations thereafter must be judged by the constitutional standard applicable to public forums. The fallacy in the argument is that it is not the forum, but PLEA itself, which has changed. Prior to 1977, there was no exclusive representative for the Perry school district teachers. . . . Therefore the school district's policy of allowing both organizations to use the school mail facilities . . . was consistent with the school district's preservation of the facilities for school-related business, and did not constitute creation of a public forum. . . .

. . . In the Court of Appeals' view . . ., the access policy adopted by the Perry schools favors a particular viewpoint, that of the PEA, on labor relations, and consequently must be strictly scrutinized regardless of whether a public forum is involved. There is, however, no indication that the school board intended to discourage one viewpoint and advance another. We believe it is more accurate to characterize the access policy as based on the *status* of the respective unions rather than their views. Implicit in the concept of the nonpublic forum is the right to make distinctions in access on the basis of subject matter and speaker identity. . . . The touchstone for evaluating these distinctions is whether they are reasonable in light of the purpose which the forum at issue serves. . . .

The differential access provided PEA and PLEA is reasonable because it is wholly consistent with the district's legitimate interest in "preserv[ing] the property . . . for the use to which it is lawfully dedicated." *Postal Service*, 453 U.S. at 129-130. Use of school mail facilities enables PEA to perform effectively its obligations as exclusive representative of *all* Perry Township teachers. Conversely, PLEA does not have any official responsibility in connection with the school district and need not be entitled to the same rights of access to school mailboxes. . . .

Finally, the reasonableness of the limitations on PLEA's access to the school mail system is also supported by the substantial alternative channels that remain open for union-teacher communication to take place. . . . There is no showing here that PLEA's ability to communicate with teachers is seriously impinged by the restricted access to the internal mail system. . . .

The judgment of the Court of Appeals is

Reversed.

Justice BRENNAN, with whom Justice MARSHALL, Justice POWELL, and Justice STEVENS join, dissenting. . . .

. . . This case does not involve an "absolute access" claim. It involves an "equal access" claim. As such it does not turn on whether the internal school mail system is a "public forum." In focusing on the public forum issue, the Court disregards the First Amendment's central proscription against censorship, in the form of viewpoint discrimination, in any forum, public or nonpublic. . . .

Admittedly, this Court has not always required content neutrality in restrictions on access to government property. We upheld content-based exclusions in *Lehman v. City of Shaker Heights*, 418 U.S. 298 (1974), in *Greer v. Spock*, 424 U.S. 828 (1976), and in *Jones v. North Carolina Prisoners' Union*, 433 U.S. 119 (1977). All three cases involved an unusual forum, which was found to be nonpublic, and the speech was determined for a variety of reasons to be incompatible with the forum. These cases provide some support for the notion that the government is permitted to exclude certain subjects from discussion in nonpublic forums. They provide no support, however, for the notion that government, once it has opened up government property for discussion of specific subjects, may discriminate among viewpoints on those topics. . . .

. . . [I]t is clear that the exclusive access policy discriminates on the basis of viewpoint. The Court of Appeals found that "the access policy adopted by the Perry schools, in form a speaker restriction, favors a particular viewpoint on labor relations in the Perry [schools]: the teachers inevitably will receive from [the petitioner] self-laudatory descriptions of its activities on their behalf and will be denied the critical perspective offered by [the respondents]." This assessment of the effect of the policy is eminently reasonable. . . .

NOTES AND QUESTIONS

1. *The* Perry *categories. Perry* represents the Court's modern approach to forum analysis. As a general rule, courts try to determine into which of the forums—public, designated public, nonpublic (and now limited public)—particular government property falls before applying the relevant standard of review. How favorable is this approach to speakers? Can't the government usually construct "a plausible case that any new or non-traditional forum falls into the non-public category"? Steven G. Gey, *Reopening the Public Forum—From Sidewalks to Cyberspace*, 58 Ohio St. L.J. 1535, 1548 (1998).
2. Perry *and past cases*. Does *Perry* simply build on past cases, or does its "analysis mark[] a major doctrinal shift"? David S. Day, *The End of the Public Forum Doctrine*, 78 Iowa L. Rev. 143, 163 (1993). What is left of *Brown* after *Perry*?
3. *Creation of forums and government intent. Perry* focuses on the government's intent to open a forum in order to determine whether the forum's status is a designated forum or a nonpublic forum. What issues arise with focusing on government intent? What result in a situation where the government has already invited some speakers into the forum (as, for example, in *Greer v. Spock*)?
4. *Designated and/or limited forums*. Is *Perry*'s footnote 7 merely an explanation of how some designated forums operate, or does it somehow create yet another kind of forum—the "limited purpose" forum? Justices have occasionally referred to the limited and designated forums interchangeably but, increasingly, the Court has viewed designated and limited public forums as separate entities. *See, e.g.,* Christian Legal Society v. Martinez, 561 U.S. 661, 679 n.11 (2010), *infra* p. 185; Pleasant Grove City v. Summum, 555 U.S. 460, 469-70 (2009), *infra* p. 635. How meaningful is a "designated" public forum if the government is allowed to

exclude not only certain classes of speakers but also certain subject matters? Gey, *supra*, at 1548.

AN EXTENDED NOTE ON THE SUPREME COURT'S APPLICATION OF PERRY—CORNELIUS, KOKINDA, *AND* ROSENBERGER

The Court had several occasions to apply the *Perry* categories in the years following the decision. Consider whether the following cases clarify or confuse the Court's categories of forums. Just two years after *Perry*, the Court decided Cornelius v. NAACP Legal Defense & Education Fund, 473 U.S. 788 (1985), which did not involve physical property but, rather, a metaphysical forum. *Cornelius* concerned the Combined Federal Campaign (CFC), a voluntary fundraising drive aimed at federal employees and conducted during working hours. An executive order limited the CFC to "voluntary, tax-exempt, nonprofit charitable agencies that provide direct health and welfare services" and excluded legal defense and political advocacy groups. In determining the type of forum at issue, Justice O'Connor initially wrote that "[t]he government does not create a public forum by inaction or by permitting limited discourse, but only by intentionally opening a nontraditional forum for public discourse. Accordingly, the Court has looked to the policy and practice of the government to ascertain whether it intended to designate a place not traditionally open to assembly and debate as a public forum. The Court has also examined the nature of the property and its compatibility with expressive activity to discern the government's intent. . . . " *Id.* at 802-803.

Justice O'Connor rejected the argument that the government had "created a limited public forum for use by all charitable organizations to solicit funds from federal employees." *Id.* at 805. Neither the government's "practice nor its policy," Justice O'Connor wrote, "is consistent with an intent to designate the CFC as a public forum open to all tax-exempt organizations. The [government] developed extensive admission criteria to limit access to the Campaign to those organizations considered appropriate. Such selective access, unsupported by evidence of a purposeful designation for public use, does not create a public forum." *Id.* Justice O'Connor also found that the history and nature of the property at issue argued in favor of the CFC being a non-public forum: "The historical background indicates that the Campaign was designed to minimize the disruption to the workplace that had resulted from unlimited ad hoc solicitation activities by *lessening* the amount of expressive activity occurring on federal property. . . . [Further, the] federal workplace, like any place of employment, exists to accomplish the business of the employer. It follows that the Government has the right to exercise control over access to the federal workplace in order to avoid interruptions to the performance of the duties of its employees." *Id.*

Justice O'Connor then explained that "[c]ontrol over access to a nonpublic forum can be based on subject matter and speaker identity so long as the distinctions drawn are reasonable in light of the purpose served by the forum and are viewpoint neutral. Although a speaker may be excluded from a nonpublic forum if he wishes to address a topic not encompassed within the purpose of the forum, or if he is not a member of the class of speakers for whose especial benefit the forum was created, the government violates the First Amendment when it denies access to a speaker solely to suppress the point of view he espouses on an otherwise includible subject." *Id.* at 806.

According to Justice O'Connor, the exclusion of political advocacy and legal defense groups was reasonable because "the President could reasonably conclude that a dollar directly spent on providing food or shelter to the needy is more beneficial than a dollar spent on litigation that might or might not result in aid to the needy. Moreover, avoiding the appearance of political favoritism is a valid justification for limiting speech in a nonpublic forum." *Id.* at 809. Justice O'Connor further stated that the government could reasonably conclude that solicitations by political advocacy and legal defense groups might generate controversy. Thus, "the exclusion of respondents may reasonably be considered a means of 'insuring peace' in the federal workplace. . . . Although the avoidance of controversy is not a valid ground for restricting speech in a public forum, a nonpublic forum by definition is not dedicated to general debate or the free exchange of ideas. The First Amendment does not forbid a viewpoint-neutral exclusion of speakers who would disrupt a nonpublic forum and hinder its effectiveness for its intended purpose." *Id.* at 809-811. Noting, however, that "the purported concern to avoid controversy excited by particular groups may conceal a bias against the viewpoint advanced by the excluded speakers," the Court remanded to the lower court for a further determination that there had been no actual viewpoint discrimination. *Id.* at 812.

Justice Blackmun, joined by Justice Brennan, dissented, arguing that "[t]he Court's analysis empties the limited-public-forum concept of meaning and collapses the three categories of public forum, limited public forum, and nonpublic forum into two. The Court makes it *virtually* impossible to prove that a forum restricted to a particular class of speakers is a limited public forum. If the Government does not create a limited public forum unless it intends to provide an 'open forum' for expressive activity, and if the exclusion of some speakers is evidence that the Government did not intend to create such a forum, no speaker challenging denial of access will ever be able to prove that the forum is a limited public forum." *Id.* at 825.

In United States v. Kokinda, 497 U.S. 720 (1990), the Court returned to determining whether physical property involved a public forum—this time, considering whether the sidewalks around a United States Post Office were public forums. In *Kokinda*, members of a political advocacy organization set up a table on the sidewalk near the entrance to a post office in order to solicit donations and distribute literature. A postal service regulation prohibited the solicitation of contributions "on postal premises." Postal authorities asked the group to leave, were refused, and finally arrested members of the group. The free speech challenge arose out of these arrests.

Despite the common understanding after *Perry* that sidewalks are traditional public forums, Justice O'Connor, author of the plurality opinion, noted that "[t]he postal sidewalk at issue does not have the characteristics of public sidewalks traditionally open to expressive activity. The municipal sidewalk that runs parallel to the road in this case is a public passageway. The Postal Service's sidewalk is not such a thoroughfare. Rather, it leads only from the parking area to the front door of the post office. Unlike [a] public street . . ., which [is] 'continually open, often uncongested, and constitute[s] not only a necessary conduit in the daily affairs of a locality's citizens, but also a place where people [could] enjoy the open air or the company of friends and neighbors in a relaxed environment,' the postal sidewalk was constructed solely to provide for the passage of individuals engaged in postal business. The sidewalk leading to the entry of the post office is not the traditional public forum sidewalk referred to in *Perry*." *Id.* at 727.

Justice O'Connor further noted that "[t]he Postal Service has not expressly dedicated its sidewalks to any expressive activity. Indeed, postal property is expressly dedicated to only one means of communication: the posting of public notices on designated bulletin boards. No Postal Service regulation opens postal sidewalks to any First Amendment activity. To be sure, individuals or groups have been permitted to leaflet, speak, and picket on postal premises, but a regulation prohibiting disruption, and a practice of allowing some speech activities on postal property do not add up to the dedication of postal property to speech activities. We have held that '[t]he government does not create a public forum by . . . *permitting* limited discourse, but only by intentionally opening a nontraditional forum for public discourse. [*Cornelius*.]'" *Id.* at 730.

Justice O'Connor concluded that regulation of solicitation was reasonable and viewpoint-neutral. Although she acknowledged that solicitation was a form of protected speech, Justice O'Connor found the Postal Service's belief that "solicitation is inherently disruptive of the Postal Service's business" was reasonable given its history and experience. Further, the regulation was content-neutral since it applied to all groups regardless of viewpoint and was spurred not by a desire to suppress unpopular views but by the inherent disruptiveness of solicitation, regardless of the source.

Justice Kennedy concurred in the judgment but did not agree with Justice O'Connor's reasoning. Arguing against the need to apply traditional forum classifications, he would have upheld the regulation as a reasonable time, place and manner restriction under *Ward* and *Clark* (see *supra* Chapter 4.B). Justice Brennan dissented, joined by Justices Marshall, Stevens, and Blackmun (in part), arguing that the plurality's "wooden distinctions" between kinds of sidewalks had "no basis in prior cases." *Id.* at 744. "It is irrelevant," he continued, "that the sidewalk at issue may have been constructed only to provide access to the Bowie Post Office. Public sidewalks, parks, and streets have been reserved for public use as forums for speech even though government has not constructed them for expressive purposes. Parks are usually constructed to beautify a city and to provide opportunities for recreation, rather than to afford a forum for soapbox orators or leafleteers; streets are built to facilitate transportation, not to enable protesters to conduct marches; and sidewalks are created with pedestrians in mind, not solicitors. Hence, *why* the sidewalk was built is not salient. . . . The existence of a public forum does not turn on a particularized factual inquiry into whether a sidewalk serves one building or many or whether a street is a dead end or a major thoroughfare. . . . Rather, that the walkway at issue is a sidewalk open and accessible to the general public is alone sufficient to identify it as a public forum." *Id.* at 744-745.

In Rosenberger v. Rector & Visitors of the University of Virginia, 515 U.S. 819 (1995), the Court returned again to the metaphysical forum when it faced a challenge to a university's decision to deny payment of funds to a student newspaper. The University of Virginia had established a Student Activities Fund (SAF) from mandatory student fees assessed on each student. It used the funds to "support a broad range of extracurricular student activities that were 'related to the educational purpose of the University.'" *Id.* at 824. Eligible student groups could receive funds subject to certain criteria. However, even eligible groups could not receive funding or reimbursement for certain ineligible activities, including religious activities, philanthropic contributions and activities, political activities, activities that would jeopardize the University's tax-exempt status, those involving payment of honoraria, or social entertainment or related expenses. The University's guidelines defined the prohibition on "political activities" to include only electioneering and lobbying activities. They defined "religious activity," as including any activity that "primarily promotes or manifests a particular belief in or about a deity or an ultimate reality." *Id.* at 824-225.

Ronald Rosenberger formed Wide Awake Productions (WAP) on the university campus in 1990. WAP published a Christian magazine with a similar name. Rosenberger and the editors of the magazine envisioned its mission as "challeng[ing] Christians to live, in word and deed, according to the faith they proclaim and to encourage students to consider what a personal relationship with Jesus Christ means." *Id.* at 826. Although WAP was an eligible student organization, the university denied its request for reimbursement of the costs of printing its paper on the ground that the newspaper was a "religious activity" within the meaning of the university's guidelines.

A majority of the Court, led by Justice Kennedy, found that the SAF was a limited purpose public forum that was defined by reference to the speakers (incumbent university students) who could use it. Thus, the university could categorically deny access to any and all non-students, including local residents, faculty, or university staff. However, the university's exclusion of WAP's magazine constituted illegitimate viewpoint discrimination because WAP clearly fell within the scope of the forum's speaker-based limitation. The Court acknowledged that "the distinction is not a precise one. It is, in a sense, something of an understatement to speak of religious thought and discussion as just a viewpoint, as distinct from a comprehensive body of thought. The nature of our origins and destiny and their dependence upon the existence of a divine being have been subjects of philosophic inquiry throughout human history. We conclude, nonetheless, that...viewpoint discrimination is the proper way to interpret the University's objections to Wide Awake. By the very terms of the SAF prohibition, the University does not exclude religion as a subject matter but selects for disfavored treatment those student journalistic efforts with religious editorial viewpoints." *Id.* at 831.

Justice Souter, joined by three others, dissented. "The issue whether a distinction is based on viewpoint does not turn simply on whether a government regulation happens to be applied to a speaker who seeks to advance a particular viewpoint; the issue, of course, turns on whether the burden on speech is explained by reference to viewpoint. . . . Accordingly, the prohibition on viewpoint discrimination serves that important purpose of the Free Speech Clause, which is to bar the government from skewing public debate. . . . It is precisely this element of taking sides in a public debate that identifies viewpoint discrimination and makes it the most pernicious of all distinctions based on content." *Id.* at 893-895. The dissenters concluded that "[t]here is no viewpoint discrimination in the University's application of its guidelines to deny funding to Wide Awake. . . . If the guidelines were written or applied so as to limit only such Christian advocacy and no other evangelical efforts that might compete with it, the discrimination would be based on viewpoint. But . . . it applies to Muslim and Jewish and Buddhist advocacy as well as to Christian. And since it limits funding to activities promoting or manifesting a particular belief not only "in" but "about" a deity or ultimate reality, it applies to agnostics and atheists as well as it does to deists and theists. . . . As understood by their application to Wide Awake, [the guidelines] simply deny funding for hortatory speech that "primarily promotes or manifests" any view on the merits of religion; they deny funding for the entire subject matter of religious apologetics." *Id.* at 895-896.

Do these cases suggest a coherent approach to understanding when a forum is nonpublic (*Cornelius*) versus limited (*Rosenberger*)? Or when the exclusions from them are reasonable subject matter exclusions versus unreasonable viewpoint-based exclusions?

How speech-protective is the *Kokinda* Court's approach looking to the use for which property has been dedicated when the property is otherwise thought to be a traditional public forum? What does this do to the famous dictum on *Hague*?

The following cases and materials reflect the Court's continuing ambivalence and disagreement about the *Perry* trichotomy. To what extent has the Court's doctrine proven useful over time?

INTERNATIONAL SOCIETY FOR KRISHNA CONSCIOUSNESS, INC. v. LEE
505 U.S. 672 (1992)[*]

Chief Justice REHNQUIST delivered the opinion of the Court [in 91-155].

In this case we consider whether an airport terminal operated by a public authority is a public forum and whether a regulation prohibiting solicitation in the interior of an airport terminal violates the First Amendment.

The relevant facts in this case are not in dispute. Petitioner International Society for Krishna Consciousness, Inc. (ISKCON), is a not-for-profit religious corporation whose members perform a ritual known as *sankirtan*. The ritual consists of "'going into public places, disseminating religious literature and soliciting funds to support the religion.'"

Respondent Walter Lee, now deceased, was the police superintendent of the Port Authority of New York and New Jersey and was charged with enforcing the regulation at issue. The Port Authority owns and operates three major airports in the greater New York City area: John F. Kennedy International Airport (Kennedy), La Guardia Airport (La Guardia), and Newark International Airport (Newark). . . .

The airports are funded by user fees and operated to make a regulated profit. Most space at the three airports is leased to commercial airlines, which bear primary responsibility for the leasehold. The Port Authority retains control over unleased portions, including La Guardia's Central Terminal Building, portions of Kennedy's International Arrivals Building, and Newark's North Terminal Building (we refer to these areas collectively as the "terminals"). The terminals are generally accessible to the general public and contain various commercial establishments such as restaurants, snack stands, bars, newsstands, and stores of various types. Virtually all who visit the terminals do so for purposes related to air travel. . . .

The Port Authority has adopted a regulation forbidding within the terminals the repetitive solicitation of money or distribution of literature. . . . The regulation governs only the terminals; the Port Authority permits solicitation and distribution on

---

[*] In companion grants of certiorari, the Court split regarding the constitutionality of bans on solicitation and leafleting in an airport operated by the Port Authority of New York and New Jersey. A majority of the Court, in an opinion by Justice Rehnquist, found the ban on solicitation to be constitutional. A different majority found the ban on distribution of literature to be unconstitutional. The Justices also split rather badly on the forum analysis, as can be seen in the opinions.—EDS.

the sidewalks outside the terminal buildings. The regulation effectively prohibits ISKCON from performing *sankirtan* in the terminals. . . .

It is uncontested that the solicitation at issue in this case is a form of speech protected under the First Amendment. *Heffron v. International Soc. for Krishna Consciousness, Inc.*, 452 U.S. 640 (1981). But it is also well settled that the government need not permit all forms of speech on property that it owns and controls. *Postal Service v. Council of Greenburgh Civic Assns.*, 453 U.S. 114 (1981); *Greer*. . . .

These cases reflect, either explicitly or implicitly, a "forum based" approach for assessing restrictions that the government seeks to place on the use of its property. *Cornelius; Perry.* . . . The parties . . . disagree whether the airport terminals are public fora or nonpublic fora. . . . Like the Court of Appeals, we conclude that the terminals are nonpublic fora and that the regulation reasonably limits solicitation. . . .

Our recent cases provide additional guidance on the characteristics of a public forum. In *Cornelius* we noted that a traditional public forum is property that has as "a principal purpose . . . the free exchange of ideas." 473 U.S. at 800. Moreover, . . . the government does not create a public forum by inaction. Nor is a public forum created "whenever members of the public are permitted freely to visit a place owned or operated by the Government." The decision to create a public forum must instead be made "by intentionally opening a nontraditional forum for public discourse." *Cornelius.* Finally, we have recognized that the location of property also has bearing because separation from acknowledged public areas may serve to indicate that the separated property is a special enclave, subject to greater restriction. *United States v. Grace*, 461 U.S. 171 (1983).

These precedents foreclose the conclusion that airport terminals are public fora. . . . [G]iven the lateness with which the modern air terminal has made its appearance, it hardly qualifies for the description of having "immemorially . . . time out of mind" been held in the public trust and used for purposes of expressive activity. Moreover, even within the rather short history of air transport, it is only "[i]n recent years [that] it has become a common practice for various religious and non-profit organizations to use commercial airports as a forum for the distribution of literature, the solicitation of funds, the proselytizing of new members, and other similar activities." 45 Fed. Reg. 35314 (1980). Thus, the tradition of airport activity does not demonstrate that airports have historically been made available for speech activity. Nor can we say that these particular terminals, or airport terminals generally, have been intentionally opened by their operators to such activity; the frequent and continuing litigation evidencing the operators' objections belies any such claim . . . .

Petitioners attempt to circumvent the history and practice governing airport activity by pointing our attention to the variety of speech activity that they claim historically occurred at various "transportation nodes" such as rail stations, bus stations, wharves, and Ellis Island. Even if we were inclined to accept petitioner's historical account describing speech activity at these locations, an account respondent contests, we think that such evidence is of little import for two reasons. First, much of the evidence is irrelevant to *public* fora analysis, because sites such as bus and rail terminals traditionally have had *private* ownership. . . . The practices of privately held transportation centers do not bear on the government's regulatory authority over a publicly owned airport.

Second, the relevant unit for our inquiry is an airport, not "transportation nodes" generally. When new methods of transportation develop, new methods for accommodating that transportation are also likely to be needed. And with each new step, it therefore will be a new inquiry whether the transportation necessities are compatible with various kinds of expressive activity. To make a category of "transportation nodes," therefore, would unjustifiably elide what may prove to be critical differences of which we should rightfully take account. . . .

The differences among such facilities are unsurprising[.] . . . As commercial enterprises, airports must provide services attractive to the marketplace. In light of this, it cannot fairly be said that an airport terminal has as a principal purpose promoting "the free exchange of ideas." To the contrary, the record demonstrates that Port Authority management considers the purpose of the terminals to be the facilitation of passenger air travel, not the promotion of expression. Even if we look beyond the intent of the Port Authority to the manner in which the terminals have been operated, the terminals have never been dedicated (except under the threat of court order) to expression in the form sought to be exercised here: *i.e.*, the solicitation of contributions and the distribution of literature. . . .

Thus, we think that neither by tradition nor purpose can the terminals be described as satisfying the standards we have previously set out for identifying a public forum.

The restrictions here challenged, therefore, need only satisfy a requirement of reasonableness. We reiterate what we stated in *Kokinda:* The restriction "'need only be *reasonable*; it need not be the most reasonable or the only reasonable limitation.'" We have no doubt that under this standard the prohibition on solicitation passes muster.

We have on many prior occasions noted the disruptive effect that solicitation may have on business. . . . Passengers who wish to avoid the solicitor may have to alter their paths, slowing both themselves and those around them. The result is that the normal flow of traffic is impeded. . . . Delays may be particularly costly in this setting, as a flight missed by only a few minutes can result in hours worth of subsequent inconvenience.

In addition, face-to-face solicitation presents risks of duress that are an appropriate target of regulation. The skillful, and unprincipled, solicitor can target the most vulnerable, including those accompanying children or those suffering physical impairment and who cannot easily avoid the solicitation. The unsavory solicitor can also commit fraud through concealment of his affiliation or through deliberate efforts to shortchange those who agree to purchase. Compounding this problem is the fact that, in an airport, the targets of such activity frequently are on tight schedules. This in turn makes such visitors unlikely to stop and formally complain to airport authorities. As a result, the airport faces considerable difficulty in achieving its legitimate interest in monitoring solicitation activity to assure that travelers are not interfered with unduly.

The Port Authority has concluded that its interest in monitoring the activities can best be accomplished by limiting solicitation and distribution to the sidewalk areas outside the terminals. This sidewalk area is frequented by an overwhelming percentage of airport users. . . . Thus the resulting access of those who would solicit the general public is quite complete. [I]t would be odd to conclude that the Port Authority's terminal regulation is unreasonable despite the Port Authority having otherwise assured access to an area universally traveled.

The inconveniences to passengers and the burdens on Port Authority officials flowing from solicitation activity may seem small, but viewed against the fact that "pedestrian congestion is one of the greatest problems facing the three terminals," the Port Authority could reasonably worry that even such incremental effects would prove quite disruptive. Moreover, "[t]he justification for the Rule should not be measured by the disorder that would result from granting an exemption solely to ISKCON." For if ISKCON is given access, so too must other groups. . . . As a result, we conclude that the solicitation ban is reasonable.

For the foregoing reasons, the judgment of the Court of Appeals sustaining the ban on solicitation in Port Authority terminals is

*Affirmed.**

Justice O'CONNOR, concurring in No. 91-155 and concurring in the judgment in No. 91-339.

In the decision below, the Court of Appeals upheld a ban on solicitation of funds within the airport terminals operated by the Port Authority of New York and New Jersey, but struck down a ban on the repetitive distribution of printed or written material within the terminals. I would affirm both parts of that judgment.

I concur in the Court's opinion in No. 91-155, and agree that publicly owned airports are not public fora. Unlike public streets and parks, both of which our First Amendment jurisprudence has identified as "traditional public fora," airports do not count among their purposes the "free exchange of ideas[.]". . .

[W]e have consistently stated that restrictions on speech in nonpublic fora are valid only if they are "reasonable" and "not an effort to suppress expression merely because public officials oppose the speaker's view." The determination that airports are not public fora thus only begins our inquiry.

"The reasonableness of the Government's restriction [on speech in a nonpublic forum] must be assessed in light of the purpose of the forum and all the surrounding circumstances." . . . In this case, the "special attributes" and "surrounding circumstances" of the airports operated by the Port Authority are determinative. Not only has the Port Authority chosen *not* to limit access to the airports under its control, it has created a huge complex open to travelers and nontravelers alike. The airports house restaurants, cafeterias, snack bars, coffee shops, cocktail lounges, post offices, banks, telegraph offices, clothing shops, drug stores, food stores, nurseries, barber shops, currency exchanges, art exhibits, commercial advertising displays, bookstores, newsstands, dental offices, and private clubs. The International Arrivals Building at JFK Airport even has two branches of Bloomingdale's.

We have said that a restriction on speech in a nonpublic forum is "reasonable" when it is "consistent with the [government's] legitimate interest in 'preserv[ing] the property . . . for the use to which it is lawfully dedicated.'" *Perry.* . . . [T]he wide range of activities promoted by the Port Authority is no more directly related to facilitating air travel than are the types of activities in which the International Society for Krishna Consciousness, Inc. (ISKCON), wishes to engage. In my view, the Port Authority is operating a shopping mall as well as an airport. The reasonableness inquiry, therefore, is not whether the restrictions on speech are "consistent with... preserving the property" for air travel, but whether they are reasonably related to maintaining the multipurpose environment that the Port Authority has deliberately created. Applying that standard, I agree with the Court in No. 91-155 that the ban on solicitation is reasonable. . . .

In my view, however, the regulation banning leafletting—or, in the Port Authority's words, the "continuous or repetitive . . . distribution of . . . printed or

---

* This opinion applies also to No. 91-339, *Lee v. International Society for Krishna Consciousness, Inc.*, 505 U.S. 830.

written material"—cannot be upheld as reasonable on this record. I therefore concur in the judgment in No. 91-339, striking down that prohibition. . . . [W]e have expressly noted that leafletting does not entail the same kinds of problems presented by face-to-face solicitation. Specifically, "[o]ne need not ponder the contents of a leaflet or pamphlet in order mechanically to take it out of someone's hand. . . . 'The distribution of literature does not require that the recipient stop in order to receive the message the speaker wishes to convey; instead the recipient is free to read the message at a later time.'" With the possible exception of avoiding litter, *see Schneider v. State*, it is difficult to point to any problems intrinsic to the act of leafletting that would make it naturally incompatible with a large, multipurpose forum such as those at issue here. . . .

I would affirm the judgment of the Court of Appeals in both No. 91-155 and No. 91-339.

Justice KENNEDY, with whom Justice BLACKMUN, Justice STEVENS, and Justice SOUTER join, concurring in the judgments.

. . . Our public forum doctrine ought not to be a jurisprudence of categories rather than ideas or convert what was once an analysis protective of expression into one which grants the government authority to restrict speech by fiat. I believe that the Court's public forum analysis in these cases is inconsistent with the values underlying the Speech and Press Clauses of the First Amendment. . . .

The Court today holds that traditional public forums are limited to public property which have as "'a principal purpose . . . the free exchange of ideas,'" and that this purpose must be evidenced by a long-standing historical practice of permitting speech. The Court also holds that designated forums consist of property which the government intends to open for public discourse. All other types of property are, in the Court's view, nonpublic forums. . . and government-imposed restrictions of speech in these places will be upheld so long as reasonable and viewpoint neutral. Under this categorical view the application of public forum analysis to airport terminals seems easy. Airports are of course public spaces of recent vintage, and so there can be no time-honored tradition associated with airports of permitting free speech. And because governments have often attempted to restrict speech within airports, it follows *a fortiori* under the Court's analysis that they cannot be so-called "designated" forums. So, the Court concludes, airports must be nonpublic forums, subject to minimal First Amendment protection.

This analysis is flawed at its very beginning. It leaves the government with almost unlimited authority to restrict speech on its property by doing nothing more than articulating a nonspeech-related purpose for the area, and it leaves almost no scope for the development of new public forums absent the rare approval of the government. The Court's error lies in its conclusion that the public forum status of public property depends on the government's defined purpose for the property, or on an explicit decision by the government to dedicate the property to expressive activity. In my view, the inquiry must be an objective one, based on the actual, physical characteristics and uses of the property. The fact that in our public forum cases we discuss and analyze these precise characteristics tends to support my position. . . .

The Court's analysis rests on an inaccurate view of history. The notion that traditional public forums are properties that have public discourse as their principal purpose is a most doubtful fiction. The types of property that we have recognized as the quintessential public forums are streets, parks, and sidewalks. It would seem apparent that the principal purpose of streets and sidewalks, like airports, is to facilitate transportation, not public discourse, and we have recognized as much.

Similarly, the purpose for the creation of public parks may be as much for beauty and open space as for discourse. Thus under the Court's analysis, even the quintessential public forums would appear to lack the necessary elements of what the Court defines as a public forum.

The effect of the Court's narrow view of the first category of public forums is compounded by its description of the second purported category, the so-called "designated" forum. The requirements for such a designation are so stringent that I cannot be certain whether the category has any content left at all. In any event, it seems evident that under the Court's analysis today few, if any, types of property other than those already recognized as public forums will be accorded that status.

The Court's answer to these objections appears to be a recourse to history as justifying its recognition of streets, parks, and sidewalks, but apparently no other types of government property, as traditional public forums. The Court ignores the fact that the purpose of the public forum doctrine is to give effect to the broad command of the First Amendment to protect speech from governmental interference. The jurisprudence is rooted in historic practice, but it is not tied to a narrow textual command limiting the recognition of new forums. In my view the policies underlying the doctrine cannot be given effect unless we recognize that open, public spaces and thoroughfares that are suitable for discourse may be public forums, whatever their historical pedigree and without concern for a precise classification of the property. There is support in our precedents for such a view. See *Lehman* (plurality opinion); *Hague* (speaking of "streets and public places" as forums). . . .

. . . Under the proper circumstances I would accord public forum status to other forms of property, regardless of their ancient or contemporary origins and whether or not they fit within a narrow historic tradition. If the objective, physical characteristics of the property at issue and the actual public access and uses that have been permitted by the government indicate that expressive activity would be appropriate and compatible with those uses, the property is a public forum. The most important considerations in this analysis are whether the property shares physical similarities with more traditional public forums, whether the government has permitted or acquiesced in broad public access to the property, and whether expressive activity would tend to interfere in a significant way with the uses to which the government has as a factual matter dedicated the property. In conducting the last inquiry, courts must consider the consistency of those uses with expressive activities in general, rather than the specific sort of speech at issue in the case before it; otherwise the analysis would be one not of classification but rather of case-by-case balancing, and would provide little guidance to the State regarding its discretion to regulate speech. Courts must also consider the availability of reasonable time, place, and manner restrictions in undertaking this compatibility analysis. The possibility of some theoretical inconsistency between expressive activities and the property's uses should not bar a finding of a public forum, if those inconsistencies can be avoided through simple and permitted regulations. . . .

Under this analysis, it is evident that the public spaces of the Port Authority's airports are public forums. First, the District Court made detailed findings regarding the physical similarities between the Port Authority's airports and public streets. . . . Second, the airport areas involved here are open to the public without restriction. . . .

It is my view, however, that the Port Authority's ban on the "solicitation and receipt of funds" within its airport terminals should be upheld under the standards applicable to speech regulations in public forums. The regulation may be upheld as either a reasonable time, place, and manner restriction, or as a regulation directed at the nonspeech element of expressive conduct. . . .

If the Port Authority's solicitation regulation prohibited all speech that requested the contribution of funds, I would conclude that it was a direct, content-based restriction of speech in clear violation of the First Amendment. The Authority's regulation does not prohibit all solicitation, however; it prohibits the "solicitation and receipt of funds." I do not understand this regulation to prohibit all speech that solicits funds. . . . As I understand the restriction it is directed only at the physical exchange of money, which is an element of conduct interwoven with otherwise expressive solicitation. In other words, the regulation permits expression that solicits funds, but limits the manner of that expression to forms other than the immediate receipt of money. . . .

Justice SOUTER, with whom Justice BLACKMUN and Justice STEVENS join, concurring in the judgment in No. 91-339 and dissenting in No. 91-155.

From the Court's conclusion in No. 91-155...sustaining the total ban on solicitation of money for immediate payment, I respectfully dissent. . . .

[R]espondent comes closest to justifying the restriction as one furthering the government's interest in preventing coercion and fraud. The claim to be preventing coercion is weak to start with. While a solicitor can be insistent, a pedestrian on the street or airport concourse can simply walk away or walk on. . . . Since there is here no evidence of any type of coercive conduct, over and above the merely importunate character of the open and public solicitation, that might justify a ban, the regulation cannot be sustained to avoid coercion.

As for fraud, our cases do not provide government with plenary authority to ban solicitation just because it could be fraudulent. "Broad prophylactic rules in the area of free expression are suspect," and more than a laudable intent to prevent fraud is required to sustain the present ban. The evidence of fraudulent conduct here is virtually nonexistent. . . .

Accordingly, I would reverse the judgment of the Court of Appeals in No. 91-155 and strike down the ban on solicitation.

LEE v. INTERNATIONAL SOCIETY FOR KRISHNA CONSCIOUSNESS, INC.

505 U.S. 830 (1992)

PER CURIAM.

For the reasons expressed in the opinions of Justice O'Connor, Justice Kennedy, and Justice Souter, (see O'Connor, J., concurring in No. 91-155 and concurring in judgment in No. 91-339), (Kennedy, J., concurring in judgment), (Souter, J., concurring in judgment in No. 91-339 and dissenting in No. 91-155), the judgment of the Court of Appeals holding that the ban on distribution of literature in the Port Authority airport terminals is invalid under the First Amendment is

Affirmed.

Chief Justice REHNQUIST, with whom Justice WHITE, Justice SCALIA, and Justice THOMAS join, dissenting.

Leafletting presents risks of congestion similar to those posed by solicitation. It presents, in addition, some risks unique to leafletting. And of course, as with solicitation, these risks must be evaluated against a backdrop of the substantial congestion problem facing the Port Authority and with an eye to the cumulative impact that will result if all groups are permitted terminal access. Viewed in this light, I conclude that the distribution ban, no less than the solicitation ban, is reasonable. I therefore dissent from the Court's holding striking the distribution ban.

. . .

NOTES AND QUESTIONS

1. *Perry's continuing usefulness?* Is Justice Kennedy right that the Court's categories of forums have lost their usefulness? Consider Farber & Nowak, *supra*, at 1234-1235:

   > Classification of public places as various types of forums has only confused judicial opinions by diverting attention from the real first amendment issues involved in the cases. . . . Constitutional protection should depend not on labeling the speaker's physical location but on the first amendment values and governmental interests involved in the case. Of course, governmental interests are often tied to the nature of the case. . . . To this extent, the public forum doctrine is a useful heuristic device—a shorthand method of invoking [a] balanc[ing] of interests. But when the heuristic device becomes the exclusive method of analysis, only confusion and mistakes can result.

   Is there nothing to be said for Dean Post's notion, *supra*, that the government regulation of property can be classified according to whether the government primarily has managerial authority over it?
2. *The Kennedy alternative.* What are the advantages and disadvantages of Justice Kennedy's approach asking courts to engage in an inquiry "based on the actual, physical characteristics and uses of the property"? *See* Gey, *supra*, at 1566-1574.
3. *The consequences of Kennedy's approach.* Would Justice Kennedy's approach lead to intolerable results—for example, that a publicly owned cemetery is a public forum because it resembles a park in many respects and because distribution of literature would not be incompatible with the purpose of a cemetery? *See* Edward J. Neveril, Comment, *"Objective" Approaches to the Public Forum Doctrine: The First Amendment at the Mercy of Architectural Chicanery*, 90 Nw. U. L. Rev. 1185, 1240 (1996).

AN EXTENDED NOTE ON THE GOVERNMENT'S ABILITY TO TREAT PARKS AS SOMETHING OTHER THAN TRADITIONAL PUBLIC FORUMS

Lee v. ISKCON reflects a Court profoundly uncertain as to the application of its public forum principles. Most of that uncertainty arises when the Justices confront (and disagree about) the appropriate characterization of property as either designated, limited, or nonpublic forums. Such disagreement isn't terribly surprising given the variety of property that can fall into these categories and the fact-intensive nature of these inquiries. In contrast, numerous Supreme Court cases have reiterated that streets, parks, and sidewalks are quintessential traditional public forums from which speakers cannot be arbitrarily excluded. But how accurate is that rhetoric? The traditional public forum, as it turns out, is more complicated than it seems.

In Pleasant Grove City v. Summum, 555 U.S. 460 (2009), *infra* p. 635, the Supreme Court found public forum principles "out of place" in the context of a city's decision to exclude a privately-donated religious monument from a municipal park. The Court, in an opinion by Justice Alito, noted that "[t]he forum doctrine has been applied in situations in which government-owned property or a government program was capable of accommodating a large number of public speakers without defeating the essential function of the land or the program. For example, a park can accommodate many speakers and, over time, many parades and demonstrations. The Combined Federal Campaign [involved in *Cornelius*] permits hundreds of groups to solicit donations from federal employees. . . . By contrast, public parks can accommodate only a limited number of permanent monuments." *Id.* at 478. Justice Alito further noted that while "public parks have been used, 'time out of mind, . . . for purposes of assembly, communicating thoughts between citizens, and discussing public questions,' . . . one would be hard pressed to find a 'long tradition' of allowing people to permanently occupy public space with any manner of monuments." *Id.* at 478-479. As a result, the Court instead viewed the government's decision to exclude the monument as an instance of government speech (*see infra* Chapter 12), which gave the city greater leeway to exclude speech, even to the extent of promoting its own viewpoint.

Do *Summum* and *Kokinda, supra*, p. 172 indicate the Court's increased willingness to treat public parks or sidewalks as outside of the traditional public forum framework? In the aftermath of these decisions, lower courts have not been wholly consistent in their approach as to whether parks or sidewalks are outside of that framework.

Boardley v. U.S. Dep't of Interior, 615 F.3d 508 (D.C. Cir. 2010), involved National Park Service regulations pertaining to expressive activities in the nation's parks. First, the regulations called for park officials to designate "free speech areas" in each park that were available for free speech activities. Second, the regulations prohibited expressive activities without a permit. Park police stopped Michael Boardley as he attempted to distribute religious literature in a free speech area in Mount Rushmore National Park. He challenged the park's regulations as violating the First Amendment, relying in part on the argument that national parks were traditional public forums. The D.C. Circuit disagreed. "The protections of the First Amendment do not rise or fall depending on the characterization ascribed to a forum by the government," the court said. "Mount Rushmore does not become a public forum merely by being called a 'national park' any more than it would be transformed into a nonpublic forum if it were labeled a 'museum.' The dispositive question is not what the forum is *called*, but what *purpose* it serves, either by tradition or specific designation. What makes a park a traditional public forum is not its grass and trees, but the fact that it has 'immemorially been held in trust for the use of the public and, time out of mind, ha[s] been used for purposes of assembly, communicating thoughts between citizens, and discussing public questions.' Thus, to establish that a national park (in whole or part) is a traditional public forum, Boardley must show that, like a typical municipal park, it has been held open by the government for the purpose of public discourse." *Id.* at 515. The court found insufficient factual information to make a decision as to whether the parks themselves were traditional public forums, instead finding that the "free speech areas" within the parks amounted to designated public forums governed by the same rules as traditional public forums. The court then struck down the permitting requirement as an unconstitutional prior restraint because it applied to individuals and small groups, effectively inhibiting the exercise of their free speech rights. Under what circumstances will a national park ever be a public forum given the reasoning of *Boardley*? Is use of a "free speech area" within a traditional public forum a satisfactory substitute for free use of the public forum itself?

In contrast, the Ninth Circuit in Berger v. City of Seattle, 569 F.3d 1029 (9th Cir. 2009) (en banc), held that the Seattle Center was a public forum. The Seattle Center is a centrally located 80-acre public space that is home to the Space Needle, museums, sports arenas, theaters, a performance hall, and 23 acres of outdoor public park space. In 2002, the city of Seattle enacted regulations requiring outdoor street performers to obtain a permit, wear a badge displaying the permit, and perform only in designated areas. The regulations also prohibited all visitors to the Seattle Center from engaging in speech activities within 30 feet of "captive audiences"—roughly defined as people in eating areas, waiting in line for tickets or food, or in audiences watching performances. Michael Berger, a balloon artist, brought a facial challenge to the regulations alleging they violated the First Amendment. The Ninth Circuit agreed. "We begin our analysis," the court said, "with one bedrock principle: The protections afforded by the First Amendment are nowhere stronger than in streets and parks, both categorized for First Amendment purposes as traditional public fora." *Id.* at 1035-1036. Citing to *Hague*'s famous dictum, the court further noted that "among traditional public fora, public parks such as the Seattle Center are especially important locales for communication among the citizenry." *Id.* at 1036. Ultimately, the court struck down most of the regulations as either unconstitutional prior restraints or inconsistent with the Supreme Court's captive audience doctrine. Is it possible to distinguish *Berger* and *Boardley* for purposes of forum analysis? Is the distinction simply that *Berger* involved an open space in a city?

To what extent should we treat national monuments—usually located outdoors and under the National Park Service's auspices—as public forums? Many such monuments have been the sites of famous speeches and rallies, such as the Lincoln Memorial and Martin Luther King's "I Have a Dream" speech. In Oberwetter v. Hilliard, 639 F.3d 545 (D.C. Cir. 2011), the D.C. Circuit was unpersuaded that monuments are necessarily like parks for purposes of public forum analysis and ruled that the inside of the Jefferson Memorial in Washington, D.C., was a nonpublic forum. The issue arose when Mary Brooke Oberwetter and several others performed a silent, celebratory dance inside the Jefferson memorial near midnight on Jefferson's birthday. They were arrested for violating regulations prohibiting any and all "demonstrations" without a permit inside a national park or monument in the D.C. area. The regulation defined "demonstrations" to encompass "picketing, speechmaking, marching, holding vigils or religious services and all other like forms of conduct which involve the communication or expression of views or grievances . . . which has the effect, intent or propensity to draw a crowd of onlookers." The regulations also prohibited permits for certain areas, including the inside of the Jefferson Memorial.

Oberwetter sued claiming that the regulations as applied to her violated the First Amendment. In rejecting her claim, the D.C. Circuit, began with forum analysis. Although it started with "a working presumption that sidewalks, streets and parks are normally to be considered public forums," the court noted "that when government has dedicated property to a use inconsistent with conventional public assembly and debate . . . then the inconsistency precludes classification as a public forum." *Id.* at 552. Although it acknowledged that the Jefferson Memorial was within the National Park System, the court noted that national parks are unlike municipal parks in that they are widely varying in nature. Furthermore, "[n]ational memorials are places of public commemoration, not freewheeling forums for open expression, and thus the government may reserve them for purposes that preclude expressive activity. . . . In creating and maintaining the Jefferson Memorial in particular, the government has dedicated a space with a solemn commemorative purpose that is incompatible with the full range of free expression that is permitted in public forums." *Id.* Furthermore, the court noted that "outside the Jefferson Memorial . . . Oberwetter and her friends have always been free to dance to their hearts' content." *Id.* at 554. Because the Jefferson Memorial was a nonpublic forum, the government's desire to preserve a solemn atmosphere was reasonable, and there was no attempt to discriminate against a particular viewpoint, the Court found that Oberwetter's rights had not been violated. Under the logic of *Oberwetter*, can the federal government close all memorials in the D.C. area to all speech activity, provided that it does so on a viewpoint neutral basis?

Can you discern any coherent principle or treatment from these cases? Does the famous "time immemorial" dictum in *Hague* give clear guidance?

CHRISTIAN LEGAL SOCIETY v. MARTINEZ

561 U.S. 661 (2010)

Justice GINSBURG delivered the opinion of the Court.

[Hastings College of Law (Hastings or Law School) is a law school in the University of California public-school system. It encourages students to form extracurricular associations that "contribute to the Hastings community and experience." Hastings' "Registered Student Organization" (RSO) program officially recognizes student groups and extends them benefits, including eligibility to seek financial assistance from the Law School, use of Law School channels to communicate with students, participation in an annual Student Organizations Fair, and, with permission, use of the Law School's facilities for meetings and office space. Hastings also allows RSOs to use its name and logo. RSOs must also abide by certain conditions. In particular, this case involves the Law School's Policy on Nondiscrimination (Nondiscrimination Policy), which states:

"[Hastings] is committed to a policy against legally impermissible, arbitrary or unreasonable discriminatory practices. All groups, including administration, faculty, student governments, [Hastings]-owned student residence facilities and programs sponsored by [Hastings], are governed by this policy of nondiscrimination. [Hasting's] policy on nondiscrimination is to comply fully with applicable law.

"[Hastings] shall not discriminate unlawfully on the basis of race, color, religion, national origin, ancestry, disability, age, sex or sexual orientation. This nondiscrimination policy covers admission, access and treatment in Hastings-sponsored programs and activities."

Hastings interprets the Nondiscrimination Policy to mandate acceptance of all comers. In other words, RSOs must "allow any student to participate, become a member, or seek leadership positions in the organization, regardless of [her] status or beliefs."[1]

A student chapter of the Christian Legal Society (CLS) submitted to Hastings an application for RSO status. The Law School rejected the application because CLS's bylaws did not comply with the Nondiscrimination Policy. Specifically, CLS barred students based on religion and sexual orientation. CLS National does require members and officers to sign a "Statement of Faith" and to conduct their lives in accord with prescribed principles. Among those tenets is the belief that sexual activity should not occur outside of marriage between a man and a woman; CLS thus interprets its bylaws to exclude from affiliation anyone who engages in "unrepentant homosexual conduct." CLS also excludes students who hold religious convictions different from those in the Statement of Faith.

CLS filed suit claiming that Hastings violated CLS's First and Fourteenth Amendment rights to free speech, expressive association, and free exercise of religion. On cross-motions for summary judgment, the U.S. District Court for the Northern District of California ruled in favor of Hastings, finding that the Law School's all-comers condition on access to a limited public forum was both reasonable and viewpoint neutral. On appeal, the Ninth Circuit affirmed.]

III

A

In support of the argument that Hastings' all-comers policy treads on its First Amendment rights to free speech and expressive association, CLS draws on two lines of decisions. First, in a progression of cases, this Court has employed forum analysis to determine when a governmental entity, in regulating property in its charge, may place limitations on speech. Recognizing a State's right "to preserve the property under its control for the use to which it is lawfully dedicated," the Court has permitted restrictions on access to a limited public forum, like the RSO program here, with this key caveat: Any access barrier must be reasonable and viewpoint neutral, *e.g., Rosenberger; Perry.*[12]

Second, as evidenced by another set of decisions, this Court has rigorously reviewed laws and regulations that constrain associational freedom. In the context of public accommodations, we have subjected restrictions on that freedom to close scrutiny; such restrictions are permitted only if they serve "compelling state interests" that are "unrelated to the suppression of ideas—interests that cannot be advanced "through . . . significantly less restrictive [means]." *Roberts v. United States Jaycees,* 468 U.S. 609, 623 (1984). "Freedom of association," we have recognized, "plainly presupposes a freedom not to associate." Insisting that an

---

[1] "Th[is] policy," Hastings clarifies, "does not foreclose neutral and generally applicable membership requirements unrelated to 'status or beliefs.'" So long as all students have the *opportunity* to participate on equal terms, RSOs may require them, *inter alia,* to pay dues, maintain good attendance, refrain from gross misconduct, or pass a skill-based test, such as the writing competitions administered by law journals.

[12] Our decisions make clear, and the parties agree, that Hastings, through its RSO program, established a limited public forum.

organization embrace unwelcome members, we have therefore concluded, "directly and immediately affects associational rights." *Boy Scouts v. Dale*, 530 U.S. 640, 659 (2000).

CLS would have us engage each line of cases independently, but its expressive-association and free-speech arguments merge: *Who* speaks on its behalf, CLS reasons, colors *what* concept is conveyed. . . . [T]hree observations lead us to conclude that our limited-public-forum precedents supply the appropriate framework for assessing both CLS's speech and association rights.

First, the same considerations that have led us to apply a less restrictive level of scrutiny to speech in limited public forums as compared to other environments apply with equal force to expressive association occurring in limited public forums. . . . [S]peech and expressive-association rights are closely linked. When these intertwined rights arise in exactly the same context, it would be anomalous for a restriction on speech to survive constitutional review under our limited-public-forum test only to be invalidated as an impermissible infringement of expressive association. . . .

Second, . . . the strict scrutiny we have applied in some settings to laws that burden expressive association would, in practical effect, invalidate a defining characteristic of limited public forums—the State may "reserv[e][them] for certain groups." *Rosenberger*. An example sharpens the tip of this point: Schools, including Hastings, ordinarily, and without controversy, limit official student-group recognition to organizations comprising only students—even if those groups wish to associate with nonstudents. The same ground rules must govern both speech and association challenges in the limited-public-forum context, lest strict scrutiny trump a public university's ability to "confin[e] a [speech] forum to the limited and legitimate purposes for which it was created." *Rosenberger*.

Third, . . . CLS, in seeking what is effectively a state subsidy, faces only indirect pressure to modify its membership policies; CLS may exclude any person for any reason if it forgoes the benefits of official recognition. The expressive-association precedents on which CLS relies, in contrast, involved regulations that *compelled* a group to include unwanted members, with no choice to opt out. See, *e.g.*, *Dale*; *Roberts*. . . . Application of the less-restrictive limited-public-forum analysis better accounts for the fact that Hastings, through its RSO program, is dangling the carrot of subsidy, not wielding the stick of prohibition. . . .

We turn to the merits of the instant dispute, therefore, with the limited-public-forum decisions as our guide. . . .

C

We first consider whether Hastings' policy is reasonable taking into account the RSO forum's function and "all the surrounding circumstances." *Cornelius*.

Our inquiry is shaped by the educational context in which it arises: "First Amendment rights," we have observed, "must be analyzed in light of the special characteristics of the school environment." *Widmar v. Vincent*, 454 U.S. 263, 268 n.5 (1981). This Court is the final arbiter of the question whether a public university has exceeded constitutional constraints[.] . . . [H]owever, we have cautioned courts in various contexts to resist "substitut[ing] their own notions of sound educational policy for those of the school authorities which they review." . . .

With appropriate regard for school administrators' judgment, we review the justifications Hastings offers in defense of its all-comers requirement. First, the open-access policy "ensures that the leadership, educational, and social opportunities afforded by [RSOs] are available to all students." . . . RSOs, we count it significant, are eligible for financial assistance drawn from mandatory student-activity fees, the all-comers policy ensures that no Hastings student is forced to fund a group that would reject her as a member.

Second, the all-comers requirement helps Hastings police the written terms of its Nondiscrimination Policy without inquiring into an RSO's motivation for membership restrictions. . . . CLS proposes that Hastings permit exclusion because of *belief* but forbid discrimination due to *status*. But that proposal would impose on Hastings a daunting labor. How should the Law School go about determining whether a student organization cloaked prohibited status exclusion in belief-based garb? . . .

Third, the Law School reasonably adheres to the view that an all-comers policy, to the extent it brings together individuals with diverse backgrounds and beliefs, "encourages tolerance, cooperation, and learning among students." . . .

Fourth, Hastings' policy, which incorporates . . . state-law proscriptions on discrimination, conveys the Law School's decision "to decline to subsidize with public monies and benefits conduct of which the people of California disapprove.". . .

In sum, the several justifications Hastings asserts in support of its all-comers requirement are surely reasonable in light of the RSO forum's purposes.

The Law School's policy is all the more creditworthy in view of the "substantial alternative channels that remain open for [CLS-student] communication to take place." *Perry.* . . . [W]hen access barriers are viewpoint neutral, our decisions have counted it significant that other available avenues for the group to exercise its First Amendment rights lessen the burden created by those barriers. In this case, Hastings offered CLS access to school facilities to conduct meetings and the use of chalkboards and generally available bulletin boards to advertise events. Although CLS could not take advantage of RSO-specific methods of communication, the advent of electronic media and social-networking sites reduces the importance of those channels. . . . [Furthermore,] CLS . . . hosted a variety of activities the year after Hastings denied it recognition, and the number of students attending those meetings and events doubled.

CLS nevertheless deems Hastings' all-comers policy "frankly absurd." "There can be no diversity of viewpoints in a forum," it asserts, "if groups are not permitted to form around viewpoints." [But] the *advisability* of Hastings' policy does not control its *permissibility*. . . . [A] State's restriction on access to a limited public forum "need not be the most reasonable or the only reasonable limitation." *Cornelius.*

CLS also assails the reasonableness of the all-comers policy in light of the RSO forum's function by forecasting that the policy will facilitate hostile takeovers; if organizations must open their arms to all, CLS contends, saboteurs will infiltrate groups to subvert their mission and message. This supposition strikes us as more hypothetical than real. CLS points to no history or prospect of RSO-hijackings at Hastings. . . .

RSOs, moreover, in harmony with the all-comers policy, may condition eligibility for membership and leadership on attendance, the payment of dues, or other neutral requirements designed to ensure that students join because of their commitment to a group's vitality, not its demise. Several RSOs at Hastings limit their membership rolls and officer slates in just this way.

Hastings, furthermore, could reasonably expect more from its law students than the disruptive behavior CLS hypothesizes—and to build this expectation into its educational approach. A reasonable policy need not anticipate and preemptively close off every opportunity for avoidance or manipulation. If students begin to exploit an all-comers policy by hijacking organizations to distort or destroy their missions, Hastings presumably would revisit and revise its policy.

Finally, CLS asserts . . . that the Law School lacks any legitimate interest—let alone one reasonably related to the RSO forum's purposes—in urging "religious groups not to favor co-religionists for purposes of their religious activities." CLS's analytical error lies in focusing on the benefits it must forgo while ignoring the interests of those it seeks to fence out: Exclusion, after all, has two sides. Hastings, caught in the crossfire between a group's desire to exclude and students' demand for equal access, may reasonably draw a line in the sand permitting *all* organizations to express what they wish but *no* group to discriminate in membership.

D

We next consider whether Hastings' all-comers policy is viewpoint neutral.

[I]t is . . . hard to imagine a more viewpoint-neutral policy than one requiring *all* student groups to accept *all* comers. . . . " A regulation that serves purposes unrelated to the content of expression is deemed neutral, even if it has an incidental effect on some speakers or messages but not others." . . .

Hastings' requirement that student groups accept all comers, we are satisfied, "is justified without reference to the content [or viewpoint] of the regulated speech." *Ward*, 491 U.S. at 791. The Law School's policy aims at the *act* of rejecting would-be group members without reference to the reasons motivating that behavior: Hastings' "desire to redress th[e] perceived harms" of exclusionary membership policies "provides an adequate explanation for its [all-comers condition] over and above mere disagreement with [any student group's] beliefs or biases." *Wisconsin v. Mitchell*, 508 U.S. 476, 488 (1993). CLS's conduct—not its Christian perspective—is, from Hastings' vantage point, what stands between the group and RSO status. . . . CLS is simply confusing its *own* viewpoint-based objections to . . . nondiscrimination laws (which it is entitled to have and [to] voice) with viewpoint *discrimination*.

IV

In its reply brief, CLS contends that "[t]he peculiarity, incoherence, and suspect history of the all-comers policy all point to pretext." Neither the District Court nor the Ninth Circuit addressed an argument that Hastings selectively enforces its all-comers policy, and this Court is not the proper forum to air the issue in the first instance. On remand, the Ninth Circuit may consider CLS's pretext argument if, and to the extent, it is preserved.

For the foregoing reasons, we affirm the Court of Appeals' ruling that the all-comers policy is constitutional and remand the case for further proceedings consistent with this opinion.

It is so ordered.

Justice KENNEDY, concurring.

To be effective, a limited forum often will exclude some speakers based on their affiliation (*e.g.*, student versus nonstudent) or based on the content of their speech, interests, and expertise (*e.g.*, art professor not chosen as speaker for conference on public transit). When the government does exclude from a limited forum, however, other content-based judgments may be impermissible. . . .

In the instant case, however, if [CLS's] membership qualification were enforced, it would contradict a legitimate purpose for having created the limited forum in the first place. Many educational institutions, including respondent Hastings College of Law, have recognized that the process of learning occurs both formally in a classroom setting and informally outside of it. . . .

Law students come from many backgrounds and have but three years to meet each other and develop their skills. They do so by participating in a community that teaches them how to create arguments in a convincing, rational, and respectful manner and to express doubt and disagreement in a professional way. A law school furthers these objectives by allowing broad diversity in registered student organizations. But these objectives may be better achieved if students can act cooperatively to learn from and teach each other through interactions in social and intellectual contexts. A vibrant dialogue is not possible if students wall themselves off from opposing points of view. . . . A school quite properly may conclude that allowing an oath or belief-affirming requirement, or an outside conduct requirement, could be divisive for student relations and inconsistent with the basic concept that a view's validity should be tested through free and open discussion. The school's policy therefore represents a permissible effort to preserve the value of its forum.

. . . [If] it could be demonstrated that a school has adopted or enforced its policy with the intent or purpose of discriminating or disadvantaging a group on account of its views, petitioner also would have a substantial case on the merits if it were shown that the all-comers policy was either designed or used to infiltrate the group or challenge its leadership in order to stifle its views. But that has not been shown to be so likely or self-evident as a matter of group dynamics in this setting that the Court can declare the school policy void without more facts; and if there were a showing that in a particular case the purpose or effect of the policy was to stifle speech or make it ineffective, that, too, would present a case different from the one before us. . . .

Justice ALITO, with whom THE CHIEF JUSTICE, Justice SCALIA, and Justice THOMAS join, dissenting.

III

. . . . I am content to address the constitutionality of Hastings' actions under our limited public forum cases. . . . In this case, the forum consists of the RSO program. Once a public university opens a limited public forum, it "must respect the lawful boundaries it has itself set." *Rosenberger*. The university "may not exclude speech where its distinction is not 'reasonable in light of the purpose served by the forum.'" And the university must maintain strict viewpoint neutrality. . . .

This requirement of viewpoint neutrality extends to the expression of religious viewpoints. In an unbroken line of decisions analyzing private religious speech in limited public forums, we have made it perfectly clear that "[r]eligion is [a] viewpoint from which ideas are conveyed." . . . We have applied this analysis in cases in which student speech was restricted because of the speaker's religious viewpoint, and we have consistently concluded that such restrictions constitute viewpoint discrimination. We have also stressed that the rules applicable in a limited public forum are particularly important in the university setting, where "the State acts against a background of tradition of thought and experiment that is at the center of our intellectual and philosophic tradition." . . .

VI

. . .

A

. . . The accept-all-comers policy is antithetical to the design of the RSO forum for the same reason that a state-imposed accept-all-comers policy would violate the First Amendment rights of private groups if applied off campus. A group's First Amendment right of expressive association is burdened by the "forced inclusion" of members whose presence would "affec[t] in a significant way the group's ability to advocate public or private viewpoints." *Dale.* . . .

The Court first says that the accept-all-comers policy is reasonable because it helps Hastings to ensure that "'leadership, educational, and social opportunities'" are afforded to all students. The RSO forum, however, is designed to achieve these laudable ends in a very different way—by permitting groups of students, no matter how small, to form the groups they want. In this way, the forum multiplies the opportunity for students to serve in leadership positions; it allows students to decide which educational opportunities they wish to pursue through participation in extracurricular activities; and it permits them to create the "social opportunities" they desire by forming whatever groups they wish to create.

Second, the Court approves the accept-all-comers policy because it is easier to enforce than the Nondiscrimination Policy that it replaced. It would be "a daunting labor," the Court warns, for Hastings to try to determine whether a group excluded a member based on belief as opposed to status. This is a strange argument, since the Nondiscrimination Policy prohibits discrimination on substantially the same grounds as the antidiscrimination provisions of many States, including California, and except for the inclusion of the prohibition of discrimination based on sexual orientation, the Nondiscrimination Policy also largely tracks federal antidiscrimination laws. . . .

Nor is Hastings daunted by the labor of determining whether a club admissions exam legitimately tests knowledge or is a pretext for screening out students with disfavored beliefs. Asked at oral argument whether CLS could require applicants to pass a test on the Bible, Hastings' attorney responded: "If it were truly an objective knowledge test, it would be okay." The long history of disputes about the meaning of Bible passages belies any suggestion that it would be an easy task to determine whether the grading of such a test was "objective."

Third, the Court argues that the accept-all-comers policy, by bringing together students with diverse views, encourages tolerance, cooperation, learning, and the development of conflict-resolution skills. These are obviously commendable goals, but they are not undermined by permitting a religious group to restrict membership to persons who share the group's faith. . . .

Fourth, the Court observes that Hastings' policy "incorporates . . . state-law proscriptions on discrimination." Because the First Amendment obviously takes precedence over any state law, this would not justify the Hastings policy even if it were true—but it is not. The only Hastings policy considered by the Court—the accept-all-comers policy—goes far beyond any California antidiscrimination law. Neither Hastings nor the Court claims that California law demands that state entities must accept all comers. . . .

In sum, Hastings' accept-all-comers policy is not reasonable in light of the stipulated purpose of the RSO forum: to promote a diversity of viewpoints "*among*"—not within—"registered student organizations."

B

The Court is also wrong in holding that the accept-all-comers policy is viewpoint neutral. . . . The adoption of a facially neutral policy for the purpose of suppressing the expression of a particular viewpoint is viewpoint discrimination. A simple example illustrates this obvious point. Suppose that a hated student group at a state university has never been able to attract more than 10 members. Suppose that the university administration, for the purpose of preventing that group from using the school grounds for meetings, adopts a new rule under which the use of its facilities is restricted to groups with more than 25 members. Although this rule would be neutral on its face, its adoption for a discriminatory reason would be illegal.

Here, CLS has made a strong showing that Hastings' sudden adoption and selective application of its accept-all-comers policy was a pretext for the law school's unlawful denial of CLS's registration application under the Nondiscrimination Policy. [The dissent reviewed evidence involving what it saw as pretextual use of the policy to deny groups like CLS the ability to use exclusionary policies. EDS.] . . .

C

One final aspect of the Court's decision warrants comment. In response to the argument that the accept-all-comers-policy would permit a small and unpopular group to be taken over by students who wish to silence its message, the Court states that the policy would permit a registered group to impose membership requirements "designed to ensure that students join because of their commitment to a group's vitality, not its demise." With this concession, the Court tacitly recognizes that Hastings does not really have an accept-all-comers policy—it has an accept-some-dissident-comers policy—and the line between members who merely seek to change a group's message (who apparently must be admitted) and those who seek a group's "demise" (who may be kept out) is hopelessly vague. . . .

In the end, the Court refuses to acknowledge the consequences of its holding. A true accept-all-comers policy permits small unpopular groups to be taken over by students who wish to change the views that the group expresses. Rules requiring that members attend meetings, pay dues, and behave politely would not eliminate this threat.

The possibility of such takeovers, however, is by no means the most important effect of the Court's holding. There are religious groups that cannot in good conscience agree in their bylaws that they will admit persons who do not share their faith, and for these groups, the consequence of an accept-all-comers policy is marginalization.

[Justice STEVENS's concurring opinion is omitted.]

NOTES AND QUESTIONS

1. *Association versus public forum.* Does the Court satisfactorily explain why the association and public forum cases merge or why the public forum analysis is the more appropriate governing precedent? For discussion, see Toni M. Massarro, Christian Legal Society v. Martinez: *Six Frames*, 38 Hastings Con. L.Q. 569 (2011); John D. Inazu, *Justice Ginsberg and Religious Liberty*, 63 Hastings L.J. 1213 (2012). For a discussion of association rights, *see infra* Chapter 5.C.
2. *Limited public forum redux.* Many scholars had criticized as "nonsensical" the distinction between the limited public forum (*Perry*'s footnote 7) and the nonpublic forum. Does this decision shed light on the murky category of the limited public forum? For discussion, see Lyrissa Lidsky, *Public Forum 2.0*, 91 B.U. L. Rev. 1975, 1986-89 (2011).
3. *The all-comers policy.* Did the university have reasonable justifications for the all-comers policy?
4. *Viewpoint-neutrality.* Was Hastings' all-comers policy viewpoint neutral? Why isn't *Rosenberger* applicable here?

THEORY-APPLIED PROBLEMS

1. The General Services Administration (GSA) is a federal government agency that operates a Facebook page describing the mission of the GSA and issuing "status updates" about its actions and operations. Citizens can make comments on the Facebook page as long as they are linked to the topic of the status updates. What kind of forum is the GSA's Facebook page? To what extent can the GSA delete comments on its Facebook page?
2. Bland City has bi-weekly City Council meetings where issues on the agenda related to city governance are raised. Bland City recently adopted "rules of decorum" for city council meetings that forbade persons addressing the council from making "personal, impertinent, slanderous or profane remarks that disrupt, disturb or otherwise impede the orderly conduct of City Council meetings." Are such rules consistent with the forum created? Can Bland City remove a speaker from a meeting for giving the Nazi salute to a city official who has taken an action with which they are unhappy?

E. WHEN SHOULD SPEAKERS HAVE ACCESS TO PRIVATE PROPERTY?

In Marsh v. Alabama, 326 U.S. 501 (1946), the Court considered whether a state could "impose criminal punishment on a person who undertakes to distribute religious literature on the premises of a company-owned town contrary to the wishes of the town's management." The town, a suburb of Mobile, Alabama, known as Chickasaw, had the characteristics of other American towns, except that it was owned by the Gulf Shipbuilding Corporation. It had residential buildings, streets, sewers, and a business district. The town and its business district were accessible to and freely used by the public. The appellant in *Marsh*, a Jehovah's Witness, attempted to distribute religious literature on the town's sidewalks. She was told that distribution of literature violated company policy and was eventually arrested after refusing to leave company premises when requested.

The Court overturned the appellant's conviction in an opinion by Justice Black:

> Had the title to Chickasaw belonged not to a private but to a municipal corporation . . . it would have been clear that appellant's conviction must be reversed. Under our decision in Lovell v. Griffin . . . neither a state nor a municipality can completely bar the distribution of literature containing religious or political ideas on its streets, sidewalks and public places or make the right to distribute dependent on a flat license tax or permit to be issued by an official who could deny it at will. . . . The State urges in effect that the corporation's right to control the inhabitants of Chickasaw is coextensive with the right of a homeowner to regulate the conduct of his guests. We can not accept that contention. Ownership does not always mean absolute dominion. The more an owner, for his advantage, opens up his property for use by the public in general, the more do his rights become circumscribed by the statutory and constitutional rights of those who use it.

326 U.S. at 504-509.

Two decades later, in Amalgamated Food Employees v. Logan Valley Plaza, Inc., 391 U.S. 308 (1968), the Court considered whether a private shopping mall could exclude picketers or whether the mall fell within the principles enunciated in *Marsh*. The Court found unconstitutional a state court injunction prohibiting a union from picketing. According to the Court, "[t]he similarities between the business block in *Marsh* and the shopping center in the present case are striking. . . . The general public has unrestricted access to the mall property. The shopping center here is clearly the functional equivalent of the business district of Chickasaw involved in *Marsh*. . . . We see no reason why access to a business district in a company town for the purpose of exercising First Amendment rights should be constitutionally required, while access for the same purpose to property functioning as a business district should be limited simply because the property surrounding the 'business district' is not under the same ownership." *Id.* at 318-319.

The Court recognized, however, that the shopping mall's owners still retained the

> power to make reasonable regulations governing the exercise of First Amendment rights on their property. Certainly their rights to make such regulations are at the very least co-extensive with the powers possessed by States and municipalities, and recognized in many opinions of this Court, to control the use of public property. Thus where property is not ordinarily open to the public, this Court has held that access to it for the purpose of exercising First Amendment rights may be denied altogether. *See Adderley*. Even where municipal or state property is open to the public generally, the exercise of First Amendment rights may be regulated so as to prevent interference with the use to which the property is ordinarily put by the State. . . . In addition, the exercise of First Amendment rights may be regulated where such exercise will unduly interfere with the normal use of the public property by other members of the public with an equal right of access to it.

Id. at 320-321. The Court held that, unlike the above regulations, an injunction banning all trespass at the mall had the effect of prohibiting speech on the mall premises and was not consistent with the First Amendment. *Id.* at 323-334.

Just a few years later, however, the Court in Lloyd Corp. v. Tanner, 407 U.S. 551 (1972), distinguished *Logan Valley*, holding that exclusion of persons distributing leaflets from a largely enclosed shopping mall did not violate the First Amendment. *Lloyd* involved a challenge to the mall's complete ban on handbilling as applied to anti-war leafleters. The mall had strictly enforced its anti-handbilling policy against all groups. Some groups were allowed to use the mall's auditorium for expressive purposes although political groups were not. Charitable and civic organizations had also been allowed to solicit donations on mall property. Five people distributing anti-war leaflets were told to leave or they would be arrested for trespass. The individuals left the premises to avoid arrest but later brought a suit seeking to have the mall's policy declared invalid under the First Amendment. The lower courts, relying on *Marsh* and *Logan Valley* agreed with the leafleters. The Supreme Court reversed.

The majority opinion noted that "the facts of this case are significantly different" from *Logan Valley*. That case, the opinion noted, "extended *Marsh* to a shopping center situation in a different context from the company town setting, but it did so only in a context where the First Amendment activity was related to the shopping center's operations. . . . The opinion was carefully phrased to limit its holding to the picketing involved, where the picketing was 'directly related in its purpose to the use to which the shopping center property was being put' and where the store was located in the center of a large private enclave with the consequence that no other reasonable opportunities for the pickets to convey their message to their intended audience were available." *Id.* at 563-564.

The majority further rejected respondents' argument that the shopping mall's open nature created a First Amendment right of access: "The handbilling by respondents in the malls of Lloyd Center had no relation to any purpose for which the center was built and being used. It is nevertheless argued by respondents that, since the Center is open to the public, the private owner cannot enforce a restriction against handbilling on the premises. The thrust of this argument is considerably broader than the rationale of *Logan Valley*. It requires no relationship, direct or indirect, between the purpose of the expressive activity and the business of the shopping center. The message sought to be conveyed by respondents was directed to all members of the public, not solely to patrons of Lloyd Center or of any of its operations. Respondents could have distributed these handbills on any public street, on any public sidewalk, in any public park, or in any public building in the city of Portland." *Id.* at 564. Accordingly, the Court ruled against the respondents, concluding that "this Court has never held that a trespasser or an uninvited guest may exercise general rights of free speech on property privately owned." *Id.* at 568.

The dissent argued that *Logan Valley* and *Lloyd* were indistinguishable:

> For many persons who do not have easy access to television, radio, the major newspapers, and the other forms of mass media, the only way they can express themselves to a broad range of citizens on issues of general public concern is to picket, or to handbill, or to utilize other free or relatively inexpensive means of communication. The only hope that these people have to be able to communicate effectively is to be permitted to speak in those areas in which most of their fellow citizens can be found. One such area is the business district of a city or town or its

functional equivalent. And this is why respondents have a tremendous need to express themselves within Lloyd Center.

Id. at 580-581.

In Hudgens v. NLRB, 424 U.S. 507 (1976), the Court went beyond *Lloyd*'s attempt to merely distinguish *Logan Valley* on its facts and flatly stated that "the rationale of *Logan Valley* did not survive the Court's decision in the *Lloyd* case." *Id.* at 518. In rejecting the union picketers' claims of a right of access to shopping center property, the Court concluded that "under the present state of the law the constitutional guarantee of free expression has no part to play in a case such as this." *Id.* at 520. After *Hudgens*, can a mall owner exclude a patron because she does not like the message on the patron's T-shirt? *See, e.g.,* Nicole F. Barr, *T-shirt Redux, Charge to Be Dropped: Food Court Frenzy Protests Arrests,* The Enterprise (Albany), Mar. 6, 2003, at 1 (describing mall patron's arrest for trespass for refusing to remove "Give Peace a Chance" T-shirt).

Should owners of private property with characteristics of public forums (that is, quasi-public forums) have complete control over the decision regarding who has expressive access? Should it matter that private property with such characteristics takes up valuable open space and is often financed, in part, with public funds? *See Note, The Impermeable Life: Unsolicited Communications in the Marketplace of Ideas,* 118 Harv. L. Rev. 1314, 1324 (2005) (describing the Mall of America in Minneapolis, Minnesota, which covers "4.2 million square feet, attract[s] 37.5 million annual visitors, and [was] built with more than $100 million in public financing"). Should quasi-public forums be made available to speakers on matters of national interest and public concern? *See, e.g.,* Gregory P. Magarian, *The First Amendment, The Public-Private Distinction and Nongovernmental Suppression of Wartime Political Debate,* 73 Geo. Wash. L. Rev. 101, 103-104 (2004).

The advent of the internet raises issues pertaining to speakers' rights of access to private property. Must Google, Bing, or other powerful search engines refrain from discriminating against speakers much as the government does, or do they have they same rights as private property owners? For discussion, see Langdon v. Google, Inc., 474 F. Supp. 2d 622 (D. Del. 2007) (dismissing complaint alleging that internet search engines should be required to carry advertising because they are quasi-public forums).

Some states have attempted to give speakers greater access to quasi-public property under state constitutional provisions. PruneYard Shopping Center v. Robins, 447 U.S. 74 (1980), involved such a case. In PruneYard, high school students attempted to solicit signatures on shopping mall premises for a petition in opposition to an upcoming U.N. resolution against Zionism. The mall had a policy against allowing any speakers not associated with its commercial purposes. Accordingly, the students were asked to leave, which they did. They later filed a lawsuit challenging the mall's policy. The California Supreme Court held that the California Constitution protected "speech and petitioning, reasonably exercised, in shopping centers even when the centers are privately owned." 23 Cal. 3d 899 (1979).

In an opinion written by Justice Rehnquist, the Supreme Court rejected the mall's assertion that forcing it to allow speakers access somehow compelled it to associate with an unwanted message. Justice Rehnquist acknowledged the Court's decision in Wooley v. Maynard, 430 U.S. 705 (1977), *see infra* p. 248 in which it held that "a State may not constitutionally require an individual to participate in the dissemination of an ideological message by displaying it on his private property in a manner and for the express purpose that it be observed and read by the public." *Id.* at 86-87. However, he concluded that requiring PruneYard to provide speaker access did not amount to such a situation:

> [In] Wooley . . . the government itself prescribed the message, required it to be displayed openly on appellee's personal property that was used "as part of his daily life," and refused to permit him to take any measures to cover up the motto even though the Court found that the display of the motto served no important state interest. Here, by contrast, there are a number of distinguishing factors. Most important, the shopping center by choice of its owner is not limited to the personal use of appellants. It is instead a business establishment that is open to the public to come and go as they please. The views expressed by members of the public in passing out pamphlets or seeking signatures for a petition thus will not likely be identified with those of the owner. Second, no specific message is dictated by the State to be displayed on appellants' property. There consequently is no danger of governmental discrimination for or against a particular message. Finally, as far as appears here appellants can expressly disavow any connection with the message by simply posting signs in the area where the speakers or handbillers stand. Such signs, for example, could disclaim any sponsorship of the message and could explain that the persons are communicating their own messages by virtue of state law.

Id. at 87. Does *PruneYard* limit the effect of *Hudgens* in those states allowing a right of access under state constitutions?

CHAPTER
5

Symbolic Speech and Expressive Conduct

TABLE OF CONTENTS

A. INTRODUCTION

What counts as communication for purposes of the Free Speech Clause? Some cases are easy—so easy, in fact, that we never stop to consider whether the activity in question counts as speech: distributing leaflets, giving an address at a political rally, or showing a motion picture on environmental issues all count as obvious attempts at communication or "speech." Other acts lack any serious communicative element—chewing gum, taking out the garbage, or driving down an Interstate highway. Some physical acts, however, can be communicative or noncommunicative depending upon the context in which they occur. Burning a flag, for example, may be a simple act of vandalism or it may be an act of protest against government policies. *See* Texas v. Johnson, 491 U.S. 397 (1989); Spence v. Washington, 418 U.S. 405 (1974). Camping overnight in a park may be a recreational activity or a symbolic act of protest against homelessness, *see* Clark v. Community for Creative Non-Violence, 468 U.S. 288 (1984), or economic conditions, *see www.occupywallstreet.org.* The act of dancing may also be a recreational activity, *see* Dallas v. Stanglin, 490 U.S. 19 (1989), or it may be an expression of our innermost thoughts, *see, e.g.,* Barnes v. Glen Theatre, Inc., 501 U.S. 560 (1991) (finding nude dancing to be expressive conduct "marginally" within the "outer perimeters of the First Amendment"). Whether such acts are expressive largely depends on the speaker's intent to communicate a message.

Other potentially expressive conduct, however, poses more difficulties when it does not specifically communicate a particularized message. For example, are video games a form of expression that deserves First Amendment protection, or are they simply pure entertainment with no informational element? In *Brown v. Entertainment Merchants*, 131 S. Ct. 2729, 2733 (2011), *infra* p. 450, the Supreme Court stated that such games were expressive:

> Like the protected books, plays, and movies that preceded them, video games communicate ideas—and even social messages—through many familiar literary

devices (such as characters, dialogue, plot, and music) and through features distinctive to the medium (such as the player's interaction with the virtual world). That suffices to confer First Amendment protection. Under our Constitution, "esthetic and moral judgments about art and literature . . . are for the individual to make, not for the Government to decree, even with the mandate or approval of a majority."

Is it clear that all video games (or art and music, for that matter) communicate a message? Is a message truly necessary to protect all forms of communication under the First Amendment? Similar issues arise with computer code—such as encryption technology or computer algorithms. Do attempts to restrict dissemination of such code for security reasons raise First Amendment problems? *See* Universal City Studios, Inc. v. Corley, 273 F.3d 429 (2d Cir. 2001). As you read the following cases, consider whether courts should approach cases involving computer code and video games (or art and music) in the same manner as they do cases involving conduct in which the speaker intends to communicate a message.

Further complicating these questions is the issue of group expression. Does the mere act of joining a group express a message? Does assembling as a group express a message and may the group protect that message by excluding others who express inconsistent messages? The Court extends First Amendment protection to groups who associate for expressive purposes, but it generally does so using a different approach than in its symbolic speech cases involving individuals. *See* Roberts v. U.S. Jaycees, 468 U.S. 609 (1984); Hurley v. Irish-American Gay, Lesbian & Bisexual Group of Boston, 515 U.S. 557 (1995); Boy Scouts of Am. v. Dale, 530 U.S. 640 (2000). Why this is so and whether this is the right approach are questions the Court has largely left unanswered.

Finally, recall Professor Schauer's argument about the "boundaries" of the First Amendment, *supra* p. 25. Is there a point when expressive conduct, no matter what the speaker's intent, is simply beyond the limits of First Amendment protection? In theory, any act that seeks to send a message could be considered "speech." Under this approach, Timothy McVeigh's 1995 bombing of the Alfred P. Murrah Federal Building in Oklahoma City would count as "speech" because McVeigh intended his violent act as a protest against the federal government's actions at the Branch Davidian complex in Waco, Texas. McVeigh's claim of First Amendment protection would assuredly get nowhere in the federal courts. But why is it so clear that McVeigh's free speech claim would have no traction? Consider why courts draw the boundaries of the First Amendment where they do and where the outer limits of communication actually are or should be.

There is no single right answer to these questions. Courts in the United States take a particular approach to determining when conduct amounts to "speech" for purposes of the First Amendment although they do not always agree as to outcome under that approach. But the boundaries that our courts draw and the conclusions they reach are by no means self-evident.

B. SYMBOLIC SPEECH

The Court has long recognized that conduct short of pure speech can have an expressive component. Thus, marching in protest of segregation policies, *see, e.g.,*

Cox v. Louisiana, 379 U.S. 536 (1965), sit-ins to protest such policies, Brown v. Louisiana, 383 U.S. 131 (1966), or flying a flag to symbolize one's political views, Stromberg v. California, 283 U.S. 359, 369 (1931), have all been recognized as expression within the First Amendment. Earlier chapters raised expressive conduct issues. For example, Clark v. Community for Creative Non-Violence, *supra* p. 126, recognized that those who wanted to camp in Lafayette Park to protest homelessness engaged in expressive conduct triggering First Amendment scrutiny.

This chapter explores how the Court determines when conduct is sufficiently expressive to trigger First Amendment scrutiny and how it evaluates the validity of laws that regulate conduct, including expressive conduct. On the one hand, the Court could simply apply laws regulating conduct across the board. But such an approach would sweep in, and potentially punish, a large amount of valuable expressive conduct that violates the law—for example, protesting segregation with a sit-in that violates trespass laws. On the other hand, the Court could invalidate laws regulating conduct to the extent that they interfered with speakers' ability to express themselves. This, however, leads a court into difficult case-by-case inquiries regarding the circumstances necessary for adequate expression. Consider the following cases in which the Court identifies and applies a standard that allows the government to regulate conduct but also protects expressive conduct from regulations aimed at suppressing the expressive component of that conduct. Does the Court's standard work?

UNITED STATES v. O'BRIEN

391 U.S. 367 (1968)

Mr. Chief Justice WARREN delivered the opinion of the Court.

On the morning of March 31, 1966, David Paul O'Brien and three companions burned their Selective Service registration certificates on the steps of the South Boston Courthouse. A sizable crowd, including several agents of the Federal Bureau of Investigation, witnessed the event. . . .

For this act, O'Brien was indicted, tried, convicted, and sentenced in the United States District Court for the District of Massachusetts. He did not contest the fact that he had burned the certificate. He stated in argument to the jury that he burned the certificate publicly to influence others to adopt his antiwar beliefs, as he put it, "so that other people would reevaluate their positions with Selective Service, with the armed forces, and reevaluate their place in the culture of today, to hopefully consider my position."

The indictment upon which he was tried charged that he "willfully and knowingly did mutilate, destroy, and change by burning (his) Registration; in violation of [50 U.S.C. § 462(b)]." Section 462(b) is part of the Universal Military Training and Service Act of 1948. Section 462(b)(3) . . . was amended by Congress in 1965 . . . so that at the time O'Brien burned his certificate an offense was committed by any person, "who forges, alters, *knowingly destroys, knowingly mutilates*, or in any manner changes any such certificate. . . ." [The Court alternatively refers to the law as § 12(b)(3), which refers to the Act rather than the United States Code –EDS.]

[T]he Court of Appeals for the First Circuit held the 1965 Amendment unconstitutional as a law abridging freedom of speech. At the time the Amendment was enacted, a regulation of the Selective Service System required registrants to keep their registration certificates in their "personal possession at all times." Wilful violations of regulations promulgated pursuant to the Universal Military Training and Service Act were made criminal by statute. The Court of Appeals, therefore, was of the opinion that conduct punishable under the 1965 Amendment was already punishable under the nonpossession regulation, and consequently that the Amendment served no valid purpose; further, that in light of the prior regulation, the Amendment must have been "directed at public as distinguished from private destruction." On this basis, the court concluded that the 1965 Amendment ran afoul of the First Amendment by singling out persons engaged in protests for special treatment. . . .

We hold that the 1965 Amendment is constitutional both as enacted and as applied. We therefore vacate the judgment of the Court of Appeals and reinstate the judgment and sentence of the District Court. . . .

I

. . . We note at the outset that the 1965 Amendment plainly does not abridge free speech on its face, and we do not understand O'Brien to argue otherwise. Amended § 12(b)(3) on its face deals with conduct having no connection with speech. It prohibits the knowing destruction of certificates issued by the Selective Service System, and there is nothing necessarily expressive about such conduct. The Amendment does not distinguish between public and private destruction, and it does not punish only destruction engaged in for the purpose of expressing views. *Compare Stromberg v. California*, 283 U.S. 359 (1931). A law prohibiting destruction of Selective Service certificates no more abridges free speech on its face than a motor vehicle law prohibiting the destruction of drivers' licenses, or a tax law prohibiting the destruction of books and records.

O'Brien nonetheless argues that the 1965 Amendment is unconstitutional in its application to him, and is unconstitutional as enacted because what he calls the "purpose" of Congress was "to suppress freedom of speech." We consider these arguments separately.

II

O'Brien first argues that the 1965 Amendment is unconstitutional as applied to him because his act of burning his registration certificate was protected "symbolic speech" within the First Amendment. His argument is that the freedom of expression which the First Amendment guarantees includes all modes of "communication of ideas by conduct," and that his conduct is within this definition because he did it in "demonstration against the war and against the draft."

We cannot accept the view that an apparently limitless variety of conduct can be labeled "speech" whenever the person engaging in the conduct intends thereby to express an idea. However, even on the assumption that the alleged communicative element in O'Brien's conduct is sufficient to bring into play the First Amendment, it does not necessarily follow that the destruction of a registration certificate is constitutionally protected activity. This Court has held that when "speech" and "nonspeech" elements are combined in the same course of conduct, a sufficiently important governmental interest in regulating the nonspeech element can justify incidental limitations on First Amendment freedoms. To characterize the quality of the governmental interest which must appear, the Court has employed a variety of descriptive terms: compelling; substantial; subordinating; paramount; cogent; strong. Whatever imprecision inheres in these terms, we think it clear that a government regulation is sufficiently justified if it is within the constitutional power of the Government; if it furthers an important or substantial governmental interest; if the governmental interest is unrelated to the suppression of free expression; and if the incidental restriction on alleged First Amendment freedoms is no greater than is essential to the furtherance of that interest. We find that the 1965 Amendment to § 12(b)(3) of the Universal Military Training and Service Act meets all of these requirements, and consequently that O'Brien can be constitutionally convicted for violating it.

The constitutional power of Congress to raise and support armies and to make all laws necessary and proper to that end is broad and sweeping. . . . Pursuant to this power, Congress may establish a system of registration for individuals liable for training and service, and may require such individuals within reason to cooperate in the registration system. The issuance of certificates indicating the registration and eligibility classification of individuals is a legitimate and substantial administrative aid in the functioning of this system. And legislation to insure the continuing availability of issued certificates serves a legitimate and substantial purpose in the system's administration. . . .

Many . . . purposes [in addition to notification] would be defeated by the certificates' destruction or mutilation. Among these are:

1. The registration certificate serves as proof that the individual described thereon has registered for the draft. The classification certificate shows the eligibility classification of a named but undescribed individual. . . . Correspondingly, the availability of the certificates for such display relieves the Selective Service System of the administrative burden it would otherwise have in verifying the registration and classification of all suspected delinquents. . . .

2. The information supplied on the certificates facilitates communication between registrants and local boards, simplifying the system and benefiting all concerned. To begin with, each certificate bears the address of the registrant's local board, an item unlikely to be committed to memory. Further, each card bears the registrant's Selective Service number, and a registrant who has his number readily available so that he can communicate it to his local board when he supplies or requests information can make simpler the board's task in locating his file. . . .

3. Both certificates carry continual reminders that the registrant must notify his local board of any change of address, and other specified changes in his status. The smooth functioning of the system requires that local boards be continually aware of the status and whereabouts of registrants, and the destruction of certificates deprives the system of a potentially useful notice device.

4. The regulatory scheme involving Selective Service certificates includes clearly valid prohibitions against the alteration, forgery, or similar deceptive misuse of certificates. The destruction or mutilation of certificates obviously increases the difficulty of detecting and tracing abuses such as these. Further, a mutilated certificate might itself be used for deceptive purposes. . . .

We think it apparent that the continuing availability to each registrant of his Selective Service certificates substantially furthers the smooth and proper functioning of the system that Congress has established to raise armies. We think it also apparent that the Nation has a vital interest in having a system for raising armies that functions with maximum efficiency and is capable of easily and quickly responding to continually changing circumstances. For these reasons, the

Government has a substantial interest in assuring the continuing availability of issued Selective Service certificates.

It is equally clear that the 1965 Amendment specifically protects this substantial governmental interest. We perceive no alternative means that would more precisely and narrowly assure the continuing availability of issued Selective Service certificates than a law which prohibits their wilful mutilation or destruction. . . . The 1965 Amendment prohibits such conduct and does nothing more. In other words, both the governmental interest and the operation of the 1965 Amendment are limited to the noncommunicative aspect of O'Brien's conduct. The governmental interest and the scope of the 1965 Amendment are limited to preventing harm to the smooth and efficient functioning of the Selective Service System. When O'Brien deliberately rendered unavailable his registration certificate, he wilfully frustrated this governmental interest. For this noncommunicative impact of his conduct, and for nothing else, he was convicted.

The case at bar is therefore unlike one where the alleged governmental interest in regulating conduct arises in some measure because the communication allegedly integral to the conduct is itself thought to be harmful. In *Stromberg*, for example, this Court struck down a statutory phrase which punished people who expressed their "opposition to organized government" by displaying "any flag, badge, banner, or device." Since the statute there was aimed at suppressing communication it could not be sustained as a regulation of noncommunicative conduct. . . .

III

O'Brien finally argues that the 1965 Amendment is unconstitutional as enacted because what he calls the "purpose" of Congress was "to suppress freedom of speech." We reject this argument because under settled principles the purpose of Congress, as O'Brien uses that term, is not a basis for declaring this legislation unconstitutional.

It is a familiar principle of constitutional law that this Court will not strike down an otherwise constitutional statute on the basis of an alleged illicit legislative motive. . . .

Inquiries into congressional motives or purposes are a hazardous matter. When the issue is simply the interpretation of legislation, the Court will look to statements by legislators for guidance as to the purpose of the legislature, because the benefit to sound decision-making in this circumstance is thought sufficient to risk the possibility of misreading Congress' purpose. It is entirely a different matter when we are asked to void a statute that is, under well-settled criteria, constitutional on its face, on the basis of what fewer than a handful of Congressmen said about it. What motivates one legislator to make a speech about a statute is not necessarily what motivates scores of others to enact it, and the stakes are sufficiently high for us to eschew guesswork. We decline to void essentially on the ground that it is unwise legislation which Congress had the undoubted power to enact and which could be reenacted in its exact form if the same or another legislator made a "wiser" speech about it. . . .

There was little floor debate on this legislation in either House. Only Senator Thurmond commented on its substantive features in the Senate. After his brief statement, and without any additional substantive comments, the bill, H.R. 10306, passed the Senate. In the House debate only two Congressmen addressed themselves to the Amendment—Congressmen Rivers and Bray. The bill was passed after their statements without any further debate by a vote of 393 to 1. It is principally on the basis of the statements by these three Congressmen that O'Brien makes his congressional "purpose" argument. We note that if we were to examine legislative purpose in the instant case, we would be obliged to consider not only these statements but also the more authoritative reports of the Senate and House Armed Services Committees. The portions of those reports explaining the purpose of the Amendment are reproduced in the Appendix in their entirety. While both reports make clear a concern with the "defiant" destruction of so-called "draft cards" and with "open" encouragement to others to destroy their cards, both reports also indicate that this concern stemmed from an apprehension that unrestrained destruction of cards would disrupt the smooth functioning of the Selective Service System. . . .

[T]he Court of Appeals... should have affirmed the judgment of conviction entered by the District Court.

Mr. Justice MARSHALL took no part in the consideration or decision of these cases.

[Justice HARLAN's concurring opinion is omitted.]

[Justice DOUGLAS's dissenting opinion is omitted.]

It is so ordered.

NOTES AND QUESTIONS

1. *What is expressive conduct?* The *O'Brien* majority notes that it "cannot accept the view that an apparently limitless variety of conduct can be labeled 'speech' whenever the person engaging in the conduct intends thereby to express an idea." Is there any reason *not* to extend First Amendment analysis to all persons who clearly intend to express a message with their conduct? In Spence v. Washington, 418 U.S. 405, 410-411 (1974), the Court asked whether an "intent to convey a particularized message was present," and whether "in the surrounding circumstances the likelihood was great that the message would be understood by those who viewed it." Is the "intent plus audience" standard too expansive? Would a political assassin whom everyone understood to be sending a message with her act of violence fall within the boundaries of the First Amendment?

   The Supreme Court of Canada appears to have answered this last question in the affirmative insofar as its own Charter is concerned. Writing for the majority in R. v. Keegstra, [1990] 3 S.C.R. 697 (Can.), Chief Justice Dickson explained that

   > all activities conveying or attempting to convey meaning are considered expression for the purposes of s. 2(b); the content of expression is irrelevant in determining the scope of this Charter provision. Stated at its highest, an exception has been suggested where meaning is communicated directly via physical violence, the extreme repugnance of this form to free expression values justifying such an extraordinary step. Section 319(2) of the Criminal Code prohibits the communication of meaning that is repugnant, but the repugnance stems from the content of the message as opposed to its form.

> For this reason, I am of the view that hate propaganda is to be categorized as expression so as to bring it within the coverage of s. 2(b).

Id. at 732. Does this mean that in Canada threats of violence or perhaps acts of violence, if intended to convey a meaning, are constitutionally protected expression? Chief Justice Dickson suggests that threats of violence, and perhaps acts of violence, do enjoy protection as expressive conduct although other portions of the Canadian Charter may allow restrictions:

> While the line between form and content is not always easily drawn, in my opinion threats of violence can only be so classified by reference to the content of their meaning. As such, they do not fall within [any] exception . . ., and their suppression must be justified under s. 1. As I do not find threats of violence to be excluded from the definition of expression envisioned by s. 2(b), it is unnecessary to determine whether the threatening aspects of hate propaganda can be seen as threats of violence, or analogous to such threats, so as to deny it protection under s. 2(b).

Id. at 733. For more discussion, see Ronald J. Krotoszynski, Jr., *The First Amendment in Cross-Cultural Perspective: A Comparative Legal Analysis* 29-36 (2006).

2. *Protecting speech without an articulable message.* Much communication has no particularized message and would seem not to fit within the *Spence* test. The Court has maneuvered around this problem simply by saying that a "narrow, succinctly articulable message is not a condition of constitutional protection, which if confined to expressions conveying a 'particularized message,' would never reach the unquestionably shielded painting of Jackson Pollock, music of Arnold Schoenberg, or Jabberwocky verse of Lewis Carroll." Hurley v. Irish-American Gay, Lesbian & Bisexual Group of Boston, 515 U.S. 557, 569 (1995), *infra* p. 224. How are the examples in the above statement different from the situation in *Spence*?

3. *Questioning the speech/conduct distinction.* Is it possible to distinguish speech from conduct for First Amendment purposes? Consider the following positions by two eminent legal scholars. Who has the better argument?

> The guiding principle must be to determine which element is predominant in the conduct under consideration. Is expression the major element and the action only secondary? Or is the action the essence and the expression incidental? The answer, to a great extent, must be based on a common-sense reaction, made in light of the functions and operations of a system of freedom of expression.

Thomas I. Emerson, *The System of Freedom of Expression* 80 (1970).

> [B]urning a draft card to express opposition to the draft is an undifferentiated whole, 100% action and 100% expression. It involves no conduct that is not at the same time communication, and no communication that does not result from conduct. Attempts to determine which element 'predominates' will

therefore inevitably degenerate into question-begging judgments about whether the activity should be protected.

John Hart Ely, *Flag Desecration: A Case Study in the Roles of Categorization and Balancing in First Amendment Analysis*, 88 Harv. L. Rev. 1482, 1495 (1975).

4. *Application of the* O'Brien *factors in* O'Brien. Did the government meet its burden under the four-factor test in *O'Brien*? Are the government's interests "substantial" or "important" as you understand the meaning of those words, or were they "plausible but little more"? *See* Ely, *supra*, at 1486 n.17. Was the federal law "no greater than is essential" to further the government's interests? Note that in later years the Court, as with other intermediate scrutiny standards, has not required the government to use the least restrictive means available. Ward v. Rock Against Racism, 491 U.S. 781 (1989).

5. *Regulating means of expression.* Is it important that O'Brien specifically chose to burn his draft card as a means of protesting the draft? Does the fact that he could protest without burning his draft card mean that his right to express himself was unimpaired by the law? Compare this situation to Cohen v. California, 403 U.S. 15 (1971), *infra* p. 523, which arguably also involved a regulation of means (particular offensive words). In *Cohen*, the Court found that one could not suppress profanity without possibly suppressing certain views; thus, the government's actions were unconstitutional. Is the same possibly true in *O'Brien*, or are the situations distinguishable? For differing views, compare Dean Alfange, Jr., *Free Speech and Symbolic Conduct: The Draft-Card Burning Case*, 1968 Sup. Ct. Rev. 1, 17; Lawrence R. Velvel, *Freedom of Speech and the Draft Card Burning Cases*, 16 U. Kan. L. Rev. 149, 153 (1968).

6. *Motive versus purpose.* Was the legislature's reason for enacting the law in *O'Brien* "unrelated to free expression"? Note that the Court reaches this conclusion at least partly because it refuses to inquire into subjective legislative motivations. Recall that the Court obviously must inquire into government purpose when determining whether a law is content-based or content-neutral. *See* Turner Broad. Sys., Inc. v. FCC, 512 U.S. 622 (1994), *infra* p. 431. What does the Court look to in order to determine *those* purposes, and how are they different from subjective motivations? For discussion, see Robert Post, *Recuperating First Amendment Doctrine*, 47 Stan. L. Rev. 1249, 1268 (1995). Why is the Court so reluctant to inquire into the subjective motivation of legislators when it inquires into the motivation of administrative and executive decisions? *See, e.g.*, Yick Wo v. Hopkins, 118 U.S. 356 (1886).

O'Brien is one of many versions of intermediate scrutiny but it is aimed at a particular kind of content-neutral law—specifically a law regulating conduct. Prong 3 of the *O'Brien* test, however, acknowledges that government interests can be related to suppression of expression, thus making them potentially illegitimate and governed by different, much stricter standards of scrutiny. The following cases, which involve laws banning flag desecration, invoke this higher standard of scrutiny. As you read these cases, consider what it means for a law to "relate to the suppression of free expression" in such a way as to invoke this higher standard of scrutiny.

TEXAS v. JOHNSON
491 U.S. 397 (1989)

Justice BRENNAN delivered the opinion of the Court.
. . .

While the Republican National Convention was taking place in Dallas in 1984, respondent Johnson participated in a political demonstration dubbed the "Republican War Chest Tour." . . . The demonstration ended in front of Dallas City Hall, where Johnson unfurled the American flag, doused it with kerosene, and set it on fire. While the flag burned, the protestors chanted: "America, the red, white, and blue, we spit on you." After the demonstrators dispersed, a witness to the flag burning collected the flag's remains and buried them in his backyard. No one was physically injured or threatened with injury, though several witnesses testified that they had been seriously offended by the flag burning.

Of the approximately 100 demonstrators, Johnson alone was charged with a crime. The only criminal offense with which he was charged was the desecration of a venerated object in violation of Tex. Penal Code Ann. § 42.09(a)(3) (1989).[1]

After a trial, he was convicted, sentenced to one year in prison, and fined $2,000.
. . .

Johnson was convicted of flag desecration for burning the flag rather than for uttering insulting words. This fact somewhat complicates our consideration of his conviction under the First Amendment. We must first determine whether Johnson's burning of the flag constituted expressive conduct, permitting him to invoke the First Amendment in challenging his conviction. *See, e.g., Spence v. Washington*, 418 U.S. 405 (1974). If his conduct was expressive, we next decide whether the State's regulation is related to the suppression of free expression. *See, e.g., O'Brien.* If the State's regulation is not related to expression, then the less stringent standard we announced in *United States v. O'Brien* for regulations of no communicative conduct controls. If it is, then we are outside of *O'Brien*'s test, and we must ask whether this interest justifies Johnson's conviction under a more demanding standard. . . .

Especially pertinent to this case are our decisions recognizing the communicative nature of conduct relating to flags. Attaching a peace sign to the flag, *Spence*; refusing to salute the flag, *West Virginia State Board of Education v. Barnette*, 319 U.S. 624, 632 (1943); and displaying a red flag, *Stromberg v. California*, 283 U.S. 359 (1931), we have held, all may find shelter under the First Amendment. . . . That we have had little difficulty identifying an expressive element in conduct relating to flags should not be surprising. The very purpose of a national flag is to serve as a symbol of our country; it is, one might say, "the one visible manifestation of two hundred years of nationhood." *Smith v. Goguen*, 415 U.S. 566, 603 (1974).

---

[1] Texas Penal Code Ann. § 42.09 (1989) provides in full:

§ 42.09. Desecration of Venerated Object

    (a) A person commits an offense if he intentionally or knowingly desecrates:

        (1) a public monument;

        (2) a place of worship or burial; or

        (3) a state or national flag.

    (b) For purposes of this section, "desecrate" means deface, damage, or otherwise physically mistreat in a way that the actor knows will seriously offend one or more persons likely to observe or discover his action.

    (c) An offense under this section is a Class A misdemeanor.

We have not automatically concluded, however, that any action taken with respect to our flag is expressive. Instead, in characterizing such action for First Amendment purposes, we have considered the context in which it occurred. In *Spence*, for example, we emphasized that Spence's taping of a peace sign to his flag was "roughly simultaneous with and concededly triggered by the Cambodian incursion and the Kent State tragedy." . . .

The State of Texas conceded for purposes of its oral argument in this case that Johnson's conduct was expressive conduct, and this concession seems to us . . . prudent . . . . Johnson burned an American flag as part—indeed, as the culmination—of a political demonstration that coincided with the convening of the Republican Party and its renomination of Ronald Reagan for President. The expressive, overtly political nature of this conduct was both intentional and overwhelmingly apparent. . . .

In order to decide whether *O'Brien's* test applies here…we must decide whether Texas has asserted an interest in support of Johnson's conviction that is unrelated to the suppression of expression. If we find that an interest asserted by the State is simply not implicated on the facts before us, we need not ask whether *O'Brien*'s test applies. The State offers two separate interests to justify this conviction: preventing breaches of the peace and preserving the flag as a symbol of nationhood and national unity. We hold that the first interest is not implicated on this record and that the second is related to the suppression of expression. . . .

[The majority found that Texas's interest in preventing breaches of the peace did not justify Johnson's conviction for flag desecration. Neither the Court's incitement nor fighting-words doctrines supported the state's arguments. The Court stated that "no actual breach of the peace occurred at the time of the flagburning or in response to the flagburning." Furthermore, the Court's doctrine does not "countenance a presumption" that an audience member "that takes serious offense at particular expression is necessarily likely to disturb the peace and that the expression may be prohibited on this basis." Rather, the Court's precedents require "careful consideration of the actual circumstances" to determine whether a speaker's words meet the incitement or fighting-words standards of *Brandenburg* and *Chaplinsky. See supra* Chapters 2 and 3 for further discussion of these standards.—EDS.]

The State also asserts an interest in preserving the flag as a symbol of nationhood and national unity. . . .We are equally persuaded that this interest is related to expression in the case of Johnson's burning of the flag. The State, apparently, is concerned that such conduct will lead people to believe either that the flag does not stand for nationhood and national unity, but instead reflects other, less positive concepts, or that the concepts reflected in the flag do not in fact exist, that is, that we do not enjoy unity as a Nation. These concerns blossom only when a person's treatment of the flag communicates some message, and thus are related "to the suppression of free expression" within the meaning of *O'Brien*. We are thus outside of *O'Brien*'s test altogether.

It remains to consider whether the State's interest in preserving the flag as a symbol of nationhood and national unity justifies Johnson's conviction.

. . . Johnson was not . . . prosecuted for the expression of just any idea; he was prosecuted for his expression of dissatisfaction with the policies of this country, expression situated at the core of our First Amendment values.

Moreover, Johnson was prosecuted because he knew that his politically charged expression would cause "serious offense." If he had burned the flag as a means of disposing of it because it was dirty or torn, he would not have been convicted of flag desecration under this Texas law: federal law designates burning as the preferred means of disposing of a flag "when it is in such condition that it is no longer a fitting emblem for display," 36 U.S.C. § 176(k), and Texas has no quarrel with this means of disposal. The Texas law is thus not aimed at protecting the physical integrity of the flag in all circumstances, but is designed instead to protect it only against impairments that would cause serious offense to others. . . . Johnson's political expression was restricted because of the content of the message he conveyed. We must therefore subject the State's asserted interest in preserving the special symbolic character of the flag to "the most exacting scrutiny."

Texas argues that its interest in preserving the flag as a symbol of nationhood and national unity survives this close analysis. . . . [T]he State emphasizes the "'special place'" reserved for the flag in our Nation. The State's argument is not that it has an interest simply in maintaining the flag as a symbol of *something*, no matter what it symbolizes; indeed, if that were the State's position, it would be difficult to see how that interest is endangered by highly symbolic conduct such as Johnson's. Rather, the State's claim is that it has an interest in preserving the flag as a symbol of *nationhood* and *national unity*, a symbol with a determinate range of meanings. According to Texas, if one physically treats the flag in a way that would tend to cast doubt on either the idea that nationhood and national unity are the flag's referents or that national unity actually exists, the message conveyed thereby is a harmful one and therefore may be prohibited.[9]

If there is a bedrock principle underlying the First Amendment, it is that the government may not prohibit the expression of an idea simply because society finds the idea itself offensive or disagreeable. . . .[N]othing in our precedents suggests that a State may foster its own view of the flag by prohibiting expressive conduct relating to it. . . .

. . . To conclude that the government may permit designated symbols to be used to communicate only a limited set of messages would be to enter territory having no discernible or defensible boundaries. Could the government, on this theory, prohibit the burning of state flags? Of copies of the Presidential seal? Of the Constitution? In evaluating these choices under the First Amendment, how would we decide which symbols were sufficiently special to warrant this unique status? To do so, we would be forced to consult our own political preferences, and impose them on the citizenry, in the very way that the First Amendment forbids us to do.

There is, moreover, no indication—either in the text of the Constitution or in our cases interpreting it—that a separate juridical category exists for the American flag alone. . . . The First Amendment does not guarantee that other concepts virtually sacred to our Nation as a whole—such as the principle that discrimination on the basis of race is odious and destructive—will go unquestioned in the marketplace of ideas. We decline, therefore, to create for the flag an exception to the joust of principles protected by the First Amendment.

---

[9] Texas claims that "Texas is not endorsing, protecting, avowing or prohibiting any particular philosophy." If Texas means to suggest that its asserted interest does not prefer Democrats over Socialists, or Republicans over Democrats, for example, then it is beside the point, for Johnson does not rely on such an argument. He argues instead that the State's desire to maintain the flag as a symbol of nationhood and national unity assumes that there is only one proper view of the flag. Thus, if Texas means to argue that its interest does not prefer *any* viewpoint over another, it is mistaken; surely one's attitude toward the flag and its referents is a viewpoint.

It is not the State's ends, but its means, to which we object. It cannot be gainsaid that there is a special place reserved for the flag in this Nation, and thus we do not doubt that the government has a legitimate interest in making efforts to "preserv[e] the national flag as an unalloyed symbol of our country." *Spence.* . . . To say that the government has an interest in encouraging proper treatment of the flag, however, is not to say that it may criminally punish a person for burning a flag as a means of political protest. . . .

The way to preserve the flag's special role is not to punish those who feel differently about these matters. It is to persuade them that they are wrong. . . .

Johnson was convicted for engaging in expressive conduct. The State's interest in preventing breaches of the peace does not support his conviction because Johnson's conduct did not threaten to disturb the peace. Nor does the State's interest in preserving the flag as a symbol of nationhood and national unity justify his criminal conviction for engaging in political expression. The judgment of the Texas Court of Criminal Appeals is therefore

Affirmed.

Chief Justice REHNQUIST, with whom Justice WHITE and Justice O'CONNOR join, dissenting. . . .

The American flag . . . is not simply another "idea" or "point of view" competing for recognition in the marketplace of ideas. Millions and millions of Americans regard it with an almost mystical reverence regardless of what sort of social, political, or philosophical beliefs they may have. I cannot agree that the First Amendment invalidates the Act of Congress, and the laws of 48 of the 50 States, which make criminal the public burning of the flag. . . .

. . . [T]he public burning of the American flag by Johnson was no essential part of any exposition of ideas, and at the same time it had a tendency to incite a breach of the peace. Johnson was free to make any verbal denunciation of the flag that he wished; indeed, he was free to burn the flag in private. He could publicly burn other symbols of the Government or effigies of political leaders. He did lead a march through the streets of Dallas, and conducted a rally in front of the Dallas City Hall. He engaged in a "die-in" to protest nuclear weapons. He shouted out various slogans during the march, including: "Reagan, Mondale which will it be? Either one means World War III;" "Ronald Reagan, killer of the hour, Perfect example of U.S. power"; and "red, white and blue, we spit on you, you stand for plunder, you will go under." For none of these acts was he arrested or prosecuted; it was only when he proceeded to burn publicly an American flag stolen from its rightful owner that he violated the Texas statute. . . .

The result of the Texas statute is obviously to deny one in Johnson's frame of mind one of many means of "symbolic speech." Far from being a case of "one picture being worth a thousand words," flag burning is the equivalent of an inarticulate grunt or roar that, it seems fair to say, is most likely to be indulged in not to express any particular idea, but to antagonize others. . . . The Texas statute deprived Johnson of only one rather inarticulate symbolic form of protest—a form of protest that was profoundly offensive to many—and left him with a full panoply of other symbols and every conceivable form of verbal expression to express his deep disapproval of national policy. Thus, in no way can it be said that Texas is punishing him because his hearers—or any other group of people—were profoundly opposed to the message that he sought to convey. . . .

Justice STEVENS, dissenting.

. . . The statutory prohibition of flag desecration does not "prescribe what shall be orthodox in politics, nationalism, religion, or other matters of opinion or force citizens to confess by word or act their faith therein." *West Virginia Board of Education v. Barnette*, 319 U.S. 624, 642 (1943). . . . Nor does the statute violate "the government's paramount obligation of neutrality in its regulation of protected communication." *Young v. American Mini Theatres, Inc.*, 427 U.S. 50, 70 (1976) (plurality opinion). The content of respondent's message has no relevance whatsoever to the case. The concept of "desecration" does not turn on the substance of the message the actor intends to convey, but rather on whether those who view the *act* will take serious offense. Accordingly, one intending to convey a message of respect for the flag by burning it in a public square might nonetheless be guilty of desecration if he knows that others—perhaps simply because they misperceive the intended message—will be seriously offended. Indeed, even if the actor knows that all possible witnesses will understand that he intends to send a message of respect, he might still be guilty of desecration if he also knows that this understanding does not lessen the offense taken by some of those witnesses. . . . The case has nothing to do with "disagreeable ideas." It involves disagreeable conduct that, in my opinion, diminishes the value of an important national asset.

The Court is therefore quite wrong in blandly asserting that respondent "was prosecuted for his expression of dissatisfaction with the policies of this country, expression situated at the core of our First Amendment values." Respondent was prosecuted because of the method he chose to express his dissatisfaction with those policies. Had he chosen to spray-paint—or perhaps convey with a motion picture projector—his message of dissatisfaction on the facade of the Lincoln Memorial, there would be no question about the power of the Government to prohibit his means of expression. The prohibition would be supported by the legitimate interest in preserving the quality of an important national asset. Though the asset at stake in this case is intangible, given its unique value, the same interest supports a prohibition on the desecration of the American flag.[*]

[Justice KENNEDY's concurring opinion is omitted.]

---

[*] The Court suggests that a prohibition against flag desecration is not content neutral because this form of symbolic speech is only used by persons who are critical of the flag or the ideas it represents. In making this suggestion the Court does not pause to consider the far-reaching consequences of its introduction of disparate-impact analysis into our First Amendment jurisprudence. It seems obvious that a prohibition against the desecration of a gravesite is content neutral even if it denies some protesters the right to make a symbolic statement by extinguishing the flame in Arlington Cemetery where John F. Kennedy is buried while permitting others to salute the flame by bowing their heads. Few would doubt that a protester who extinguishes the flame has desecrated the gravesite, regardless of whether he prefaces that act with a speech explaining that his purpose is to express deep admiration or unmitigated scorn for the late President. Likewise, few would claim that the protester who bows his head has desecrated the gravesite, even if he makes clear that his purpose is to show disrespect. In such a case, as in a flag burning case, the prohibition against desecration has absolutely nothing to do with the content of the message that the symbolic speech is intended to convey.

UNITED STATES v. EICHMAN

496 U.S. 310 (1990)

[Soon after the Supreme Court handed down its 5-4 decision in *Texas v. Johnson*, Congress passed the Flag Protection Act of 1989, 18 U.S.C. § 700(a), which punished by fine and/or imprisonment anyone who "knowingly mutilates, defaces, physically defiles, burns, maintains on the floor or ground, or tramples upon any flag of the United States." 18 U.S.C. § 700(a)(1). The law exempted from punishment, however, "any conduct consisting of the disposal of a flag when it has become worn or soiled." 18 U.S.C. § 700(a)(2). Appellants in *Eichman* burned flags to protest the government's domestic and foreign policy, in one instance, and passage of the Flag Protection Act, in another. They were arrested for violating the Act in both instances, but the district courts found that the Act facially and as applied to them violated the First Amendment. The United States appealed to the Supreme Court.]

Mr. Justice BRENNAN delivered the opinion of the Court.

Although the Flag Protection Act contains no explicit content-based limitation on the scope of prohibited conduct, it is nevertheless clear that the Government's asserted *interest* is "related 'to the suppression of free expression,'" *Johnson*, and concerned with the content of such expression. The Government's interest in protecting the "physical integrity" of a privately owned flag rests upon a perceived need to preserve the flag's status as a symbol of our Nation and certain national ideals. But the mere destruction or disfigurement of a particular physical manifestation of the symbol, without more, does not diminish or otherwise affect the symbol itself in any way. For example, the secret destruction of a flag in one's own basement would not threaten the flag's recognized meaning. Rather, the Government's desire to preserve the flag as a symbol for certain national ideals is implicated "only when a person's treatment of the flag communicates [a] message" to others that is inconsistent with those ideals.

Moreover, the precise language of the Act's prohibitions confirms Congress' interest in the communicative impact of flag destruction. The Act criminalizes the conduct of anyone who "knowingly mutilates, defaces, physically defiles, burns, maintains on the floor or ground, or tramples upon any flag." Each of the specified terms—with the possible exception of "burns"—unmistakably connotes disrespectful treatment of the flag and suggests a focus on those acts likely to damage the flag's symbolic value. And the explicit exemption in § 700(a)(2) for disposal of "worn or soiled" flags protects certain acts traditionally associated with patriotic respect for the flag.

. . . Although Congress cast the Flag Protection Act of 1989 in somewhat broader terms than the Texas statute at issue in *Johnson*, the Act still suffers from the same fundamental flaw: It suppresses expression out of concern for its likely communicative impact. Despite the Act's wider scope, its restriction on expression cannot be "'justified without reference to the content of the regulated speech.'" The Act therefore must be subjected to "the most exacting scrutiny," and for the reasons stated in *Johnson*, the Government's interest cannot justify its infringement on First Amendment rights. We decline the Government's invitation to reassess this conclusion in light of Congress' recent recognition of a purported "national consensus" favoring a prohibition on flag burning. Even assuming such a consensus exists, any suggestion that the Government's interest in suppressing speech becomes more weighty as popular opposition to that speech grows is foreign to the First Amendment.

"'National unity as an end which officials may foster by persuasion and example is not in question.'" *Johnson*, 491 U.S. at 418. Government may create national symbols, promote them, and encourage their respectful treatment. But the Flag Protection Act of 1989 goes well beyond this by criminally proscribing expressive conduct because of its likely communicative impact.

We are aware that desecration of the flag is deeply offensive to many. But the same might be said, for example, of virulent ethnic and religious epithets, see *Terminiello v. Chicago*, 337 U.S. 1 (1949), vulgar repudiations of the draft, see *Cohen v. California*, 403 U.S. 15 (1971), and scurrilous caricatures, see *Hustler Magazine, Inc. v. Falwell*, 485 U.S. 46 (1988). "If there is a bedrock principle underlying the First Amendment, it is that the Government may not prohibit the expression of an idea simply because society finds the idea itself offensive or disagreeable." *Johnson*. Punishing desecration of the flag dilutes the very freedom that makes this emblem so revered, and worth revering.

The judgments of the District Courts are

Affirmed.

Justice STEVENS, with whom THE CHIEF JUSTICE, Justice WHITE, and Justice O'CONNOR join, dissenting.

The Court's opinion ends where proper analysis of the issue should begin. Of course "the Government may not prohibit the expression of an idea simply because society finds the idea itself offensive or disagreeable." None of us disagrees with that proposition. But it is equally well settled that certain methods of expression may be prohibited if (a) the prohibition is supported by a legitimate societal interest that is unrelated to suppression of the ideas the speaker desires to express; (b) the prohibition does not entail any interference with the speaker's freedom to express those ideas by other means; and (c) the interest in allowing the speaker complete freedom of choice among alternative methods of expression is less important than the societal interest supporting the prohibition.

Contrary to the position taken by counsel for the flag burners in *Johnson* it is now conceded that the Federal Government has a legitimate interest in protecting the symbolic value of the American flag. Obviously that value cannot be measured, or even described, with any precision. It has at least these two components: In times of national crisis, it inspires and motivates the average citizen to make personal sacrifices in order to achieve societal goals of overriding importance; at all times, it serves as a reminder of the paramount importance of pursuing the ideals that characterize our society.

The first question the Court should consider is whether the interest in preserving the value of that symbol is unrelated to suppression of the ideas that flag burners are trying to express. In my judgment the answer depends, at least in part, on what those ideas are. A flag burner might intend various messages. The flag burner may wish simply to convey hatred, contempt, or sheer opposition directed at the United States. . . . A flag burner may also, or instead, seek to convey the depth of his personal conviction about some issue, by willingly provoking the use of force against himself. . . . There is at least one further possibility: A flag burner may intend to make an accusation against the integrity of the American people who disagree with him. By burning the embodiment of America's collective commitment to freedom and equality, the flag burner charges that the majority has forsaken that commitment—that continued respect for the flag is nothing more than hypocrisy. . . .

The idea expressed by a particular act of flag burning is necessarily dependent on the temporal and political context in which it occurs. . . .

The Government's legitimate interest in preserving the symbolic value of the flag is, however, essentially the same regardless of which of many different ideas may have motivated a particular act of flag burning. . . .[T]he flag uniquely symbolizes the ideas of liberty, equality, and tolerance—ideas that Americans have passionately defended and debated throughout our history. The flag embodies the spirit of our national commitment to those ideals. The message thereby transmitted does not take a stand upon our disagreements, except to say that those disagreements are best regarded as competing interpretations of shared ideals. . . .

Thus, the Government may—indeed, it should—protect the symbolic value of the flag without regard to the specific content of the flag burners' speech. The prosecution in these cases does not depend upon the object of the defendants' protest. It is, moreover, equally clear that the prohibition does not entail any interference with the speaker's freedom to express his or her ideas by other means. It may well be true that other means of expression may be less effective in drawing attention to those ideas, but that is not itself a sufficient reason for immunizing flag burning. Presumably a gigantic fireworks display or a parade of nude models in a public park might draw even more attention to a controversial message, but such methods of expression are nevertheless subject to regulation.

These cases therefore come down to a question of judgment. Does the admittedly important interest in allowing every speaker to choose the method of expressing his or her ideas that he or she deems most effective and appropriate outweigh the societal interest in preserving the symbolic value of the flag? This question, in turn, involves three different judgments: (1) The importance of the individual interest in selecting the preferred means of communication; (2) the importance of the national symbol; and (3) the question whether tolerance of flag burning will enhance or tarnish that value. The opinions in *Texas v. Johnson* demonstrate that reasonable judges may differ with respect to each of these judgments.

. . . The freedom of expression protected by the First Amendment embraces not only the freedom to communicate particular ideas, but also the right to communicate them effectively. That right, however, is not absolute—the communicative value of a well-placed bomb in the Capitol does not entitle it to the protection of the First Amendment.

Burning a flag is not, of course, equivalent to burning a public building. . . . [W]hat makes these cases particularly difficult for me is what I regard as the damage to the symbol that has already occurred as a result of this Court's decision to place its stamp of approval on the act of flag burning. A formerly dramatic expression of protest is now rather commonplace. In today's marketplace of ideas, the public burning of a Vietnam draft card is probably less provocative than lighting a cigarette. Tomorrow flag burning may produce a similar reaction. There is surely a direct relationship between the communicative value of the act of flag burning and the symbolic value of the object being burned. . . .

Accordingly, I respectfully dissent.

NOTES AND QUESTIONS

1. *"Related to the suppression of free expression"*—Johnson *and communicative impact.* Given the wording of the statute, is the Texas law content-based or is the term "offend" neutral as to content?

    Or, alternatively, is the Texas statute content-based because of the way it was applied? In Holder v. Humanitarian Law Project, 561 U.S. 1, 28 (2010), *supra* p. 61, the Court noted:

    > Cohen . . . involved a generally applicable regulation of conduct, barring breaches of the peace. But when Cohen was convicted for wearing a jacket bearing an epithet, we did not apply *O'Brien*. Instead, we recognized that the generally applicable law was directed at Cohen because of what his speech communicated—he violated the breach of the peace statute because of the offensive content of his particular message. We accordingly applied more rigorous scrutiny and reversed his conviction.

    Does the concept of "communicative impact"—that is, attempts to regulate expressive conduct or speech based upon the message's impact on the audience—explain *Johnson*'s willingness to discard *O'Brien*'s framework?

2. *"Related to suppression of free expression"*—Eichman. Are the statutes in *Johnson* and *Eichman* equally problematic from a First Amendment perspective? Arguably, the *Johnson* statute was facially content-based or at the least applied in a content-based manner. But isn't the statute in *Eichman* facially neutral—instead focusing on "mutilation" or "defacement"? Should the Court have applied *O'Brien*'s four factors instead? Or is there something inherently content-based about those statutory terms, as the *Eichman* majority suggests?

3. *Related to suppression of free expression—symbolism.* Can one protect the flag's symbolic effect without interfering with the speaker's message? Consider the following argument:

    > [While attempts to protect symbolism] do not single out certain messages for proscription, they do single out one set of messages, namely the set of messages conveyed by the American flag, for protection. . . . Orthodoxy of thought can be fostered not simply by placing unusual restrictions on "deviant" expression but also by granting unusual protection to expression that is officially acceptable. An "improper use" statute, neutral respecting the messages it would inhibit though it may be, is not analogous to a law prohibiting the interruption of speeches. It is, at best, analogous to a law prohibiting the interruption of patriotic speeches, and that is a law that is hardly "unrelated to the suppression of free expression."

    Ely, *supra*, at 1506-1507.

4. *Protecting symbolism—government property.* In *Johnson*, Justice Stevens argues that the government can protect the flag from desecration just as it can protect memorials. Is Justice Stevens's analogy between the flag and the Lincoln Memorial persuasive? Would the analogy have been more or less strong if Justice Stevens had compared flag desecration to destroying the bald eagle (our national bird) for expressive purposes? *See* Geoffrey R. Stone, *Flagburning and the Constitution*, 75 Iowa L. Rev. 111 (1990).

5. *Speech or conduct.* Is Justice Rehnquist's reference in *Johnson* to flag burning as an "inarticulate grunt or roar" an argument that flag desecration is more like conduct than communication? Can one ban the conduct of flag desecration without having an impact on the speaker's message?

6. *A constitutional amendment?* Since *Eichman*, Congress has repeatedly attempted to pass a constitutional amendment prohibiting flag desecration. In 2006, an amendment reading, "The Congress shall have the power to prohibit the physical desecration of the flag of the United States," fell a single vote short of the necessary support needed in the Senate to send it to the states for ratification. The amendment passed the House of Representatives earlier in the year. Is the flag *sui generis* so that an exception should be made? Would such an amendment avoid litigation, or does the text of the above proposal still raise thorny interpretive issues?

C. EXCLUSION AS SPEECH AND FREE ASSOCIATION

The Court has long recognized the importance of associating with others for expressive purposes. For example, the Court in NAACP v. Alabama, 357 U.S. 449, 460 (1958), noted that "[i]t is beyond debate that freedom to engage in association for the advancement of beliefs and ideas is an inseparable aspect of the 'liberty' assured by the Due Process Clause of the Fourteenth Amendment, which embraces freedom of speech." Nevertheless, acknowledging that such freedom is protected and determining the parameters of that freedom are quite different things. For example, how should the Court determine that a group of people associates for expressive purposes and the extent of First Amendment protection afforded such groups? To what extent may groups exclude individuals whose beliefs or status are inconsistent with the group's expressive purpose? These are the questions that the Court takes up in the next several cases.

ROBERTS v. UNITED STATES JAYCEES
468 U.S. 609 (1984)

Justice BRENNAN delivered the opinion of the Court. . . .

The United States Jaycees (Jaycees), founded in 1920 as the Junior Chamber of Commerce, is a nonprofit membership corporation, incorporated in Missouri with national headquarters in Tulsa, Okla. The objective of the Jaycees, as set out in its bylaws, is to pursue

> such educational and charitable purposes as will promote and foster the growth and development of young men's civic organizations in the United States, designed to inculcate in the individual membership of such organization a spirit of genuine Americanism and civic interest, and as a supplementary education institution to provide them with opportunity for personal development and achievement and an avenue for intelligent participation by young men in the affairs of their community, state and nation, and to develop true friendship and understanding among young men of all nations. . . .

Regular membership is limited to young men between the ages of 18 and 35, while associate membership is available to individuals or groups ineligible for regular membership, principally women and older men. An associate member, whose dues are somewhat lower than those charged regular members, may not vote, hold local or national office, or participate in certain leadership training and awards programs. . . .

In 1974 and 1975, respectively, the Minneapolis and St. Paul chapters of the Jaycees began admitting women as regular members. Currently, the memberships and boards of directors of both chapters include a substantial proportion of women. As a result, the two chapters have been in violation of the national organization's bylaws for about 10 years. . . .

In December 1978, the president of the national organization advised both chapters that a motion to revoke their charters would be considered. . . . Shortly after receiving this notification, members of both chapters filed charges of discrimination with the Minnesota Department of Human Rights. The complaints alleged that the exclusion of women from full membership required by the national organization's bylaws violated the Minnesota Human Rights Act (Act), which provides in part:

> It is an unfair discriminatory practice: To deny any person the full and equal enjoyment of the goods, services, facilities, privileges, advantages, and accommodations of a place of public accommodation because of race, color, creed, religion, disability, national origin or sex.

Minn. Stat. § 363.03.

The term "place of public accommodation" is defined in the Act as "a business, accommodation, refreshment, entertainment, recreation, or transportation facility of any kind, whether licensed or not, whose goods, services, facilities, privileges, advantages or accommodations are extended, offered, sold, or otherwise made available to the public." § 363.01.

. . . [T]he national organization brought suit against various state officials, appellants here, in the United States District Court . . . [alleging that], by requiring the organization to accept women as regular members, application of the Act would violate the male members' constitutional rights of free speech and association. . . .

[T]he District Court entered judgment in favor of the state officials. On appeal, a divided Court of Appeals for the Eighth Circuit reversed. The Court of Appeals determined that, because "the advocacy of political and public causes, selected by the membership, is a not insubstantial part of what [the Jaycees organization] does," the organization's right to select its members is protected by the freedom of association guaranteed by the First Amendment. . . .

Our decisions have referred to constitutionally protected "freedom of association" in two distinct senses. In one line of decisions, the Court has concluded that choices to enter into and maintain certain intimate human relationships must be secured against undue intrusion by the State because of the role of such relationships in safeguarding the individual freedom that is central to our constitutional scheme. In this respect, freedom of association receives protection as a fundamental element of personal liberty. In another set of decisions, the Court has recognized a right to associate for the purpose of engaging in those activities protected by the First Amendment—speech, assembly, petition for the redress of grievances, and the exercise of religion. The Constitution guarantees freedom of association of this kind as an indispensable means of preserving other individual liberties.

The intrinsic and instrumental features of constitutionally protected association may, of course, coincide. . . . Still, the nature and degree of constitutional protection afforded freedom of association may vary depending on the extent to which one or the other aspect of the constitutionally protected liberty is at stake in a given case. We therefore find it useful to consider separately the effect of applying the Minnesota statute to the Jaycees on what could be called its members' freedom of intimate association and their freedom of expressive association.

The Court has long recognized that, because the Bill of Rights is designed to secure individual liberty, it must afford the formation and preservation of certain kinds of highly personal relationships a substantial measure of sanctuary from unjustified interference by the State. . . . Protecting these relationships from unwarranted state interference therefore safeguards the ability independently to define one's identity that is central to any concept of liberty.

The personal affiliations that exemplify these considerations, and that therefore suggest some relevant limitations on the relationships that might be entitled to this sort of constitutional protection, are those that attend the creation and sustenance of a family. . . . Family relationships, by their nature, involve deep attachments and commitments to the necessarily few other individuals with whom one shares not only a special community of thoughts, experiences, and beliefs but also distinctively personal aspects of one's life. . . . As a general matter, only relationships with these sorts of qualities are likely to reflect the considerations that have led to an understanding of freedom of association as an intrinsic element of personal liberty. Conversely, an association lacking these qualities—such as a large business enterprise—seems remote from the concerns giving rise to this constitutional protection. . . .

Between these poles, of course, lies a broad range of human relationships that may make greater or lesser claims to constitutional protection from particular incursions by the State. . . . We need not mark the potentially significant points on this terrain with any precision. We note only that factors that may be relevant include size, purpose, policies, selectivity, congeniality, and other characteristics that in a particular case may be pertinent. In this case, however, several features of the Jaycees clearly place the organization outside of the category of relationships worthy of this kind of constitutional protection.

The undisputed facts reveal that the local chapters of the Jaycees are large and basically unselective groups. . . . Apart from age and sex, neither the national organization nor the local chapters employ any criteria for judging applicants for membership, and new members are routinely recruited and admitted with no inquiry into their backgrounds. . . .

. . . Moreover, much of the activity central to the formation and maintenance of the association involves the participation of strangers to that relationship. Accordingly, we conclude that the Jaycees chapters lack the distinctive characteristics that might afford constitutional protection to the decision of its members to exclude women. We turn therefore to consider the extent to which application of the Minnesota statute to compel the Jaycees to accept women infringes the group's freedom of expressive association.

An individual's freedom to speak, to worship, and to petition the government for the redress of grievances could not be vigorously protected from interference by the State unless a correlative freedom to engage in group effort toward those ends were not also guaranteed. According protection to collective effort on behalf of shared goals is especially important in preserving political and cultural diversity and in shielding dissident expression from suppression by the majority. Consequently, we have long understood as implicit in the right to engage in activities protected by the First Amendment a corresponding right to associate with others in pursuit of a wide variety of political, social, economic, educational, religious, and cultural ends. In view of the various protected activities in which the Jaycees engages, that right is plainly implicated in this case.

Government actions that may unconstitutionally infringe upon this freedom can take a number of forms. Among other things, government may seek to impose penalties or withhold benefits from individuals because of their membership in a disfavored group; *Healy v. James,* 408 U.S. 169 (1972), it may attempt to require disclosure of the fact of membership in a group seeking anonymity; *Brown v. Socialist Workers '74 Campaign Committee,* 459 U.S. 87 (1982) and it may try to interfere with the internal organization or affairs of the group. By requiring the Jaycees to admit women as full voting members, the Minnesota Act works an infringement of the last type. There can be no clearer example of an intrusion into the internal structure or affairs of an association than a regulation that forces the group to accept members it does not desire. Such a regulation may impair the ability of the original members to express only those views that brought them together. Freedom of association therefore plainly presupposes a freedom not to associate.

The right to associate for expressive purposes is not, however, absolute. Infringements on that right may be justified by regulations adopted to serve compelling state interests, unrelated to the suppression of ideas, that cannot be achieved through means significantly less restrictive of associational freedoms. We are persuaded that Minnesota's compelling interest in eradicating discrimination against its female citizens justifies the impact that application of the statute to the Jaycees may have on the male members' associational freedoms.

On its face, the Minnesota Act does not aim at the suppression of speech, does not distinguish between prohibited and permitted activity on the basis of viewpoint, and does not license enforcement authorities to administer the statute on the basis of such constitutionally impermissible criteria. Nor does the Jaycees contend that the Act has been applied in this case for the purpose of hampering the organization's ability to express its views. Instead, as the Minnesota Supreme Court explained, the Act reflects the State's strong historical commitment to eliminating discrimination and assuring its citizens equal access to publicly available goods and services. That goal, which is unrelated to the suppression of expression, plainly serves compelling state interests of the highest order.

The Minnesota Human Rights Act at issue here is an example of public accommodations laws that were adopted by some States beginning a decade before enactment of their federal counterpart, the Civil Rights Act of 1875. . . .

A State enjoys broad authority to create rights of public access on behalf of its citizens. Minnesota has adopted a functional definition of public accommodations that reaches various forms of public, quasi-commercial conduct. . . . [I]n explaining its conclusion that the Jaycees local chapters are "place[s] of public accommodations" within the meaning of the Act, the Minnesota court noted the various commercial programs and benefits offered to members and stated that "[l]eadership skills are 'goods,'[and] business contacts and employment promotions are 'privileges' and 'advantages'. . . ." Assuring women equal access to such goods, privileges, and advantages clearly furthers compelling state interests.

In applying the Act to the Jaycees, the State has advanced those interests through the least restrictive means of achieving its ends. Indeed, the Jaycees has failed to demonstrate that the Act imposes any serious burdens on the male members' freedom of expressive association. . . . There is, however, no basis in the record for concluding that admission of women as full voting members will impede the organization's ability to engage in [its] protected [expressive] activities or to disseminate its preferred views. The Act requires no change in the Jaycees' creed of promoting the interests of young men, and it imposes no restrictions on the organization's ability to exclude individuals with ideologies or philosophies different from those of its existing members. . . .

[Furthermore, in] claiming that women might have a different attitude about such issues as the federal budget, school prayer, voting rights, and foreign relations, or that the organization's public positions would have a different effect if the group were not "a purely young men's association," the Jaycees relies solely on unsupported generalizations about the relative interests and perspectives of men and women. Although such generalizations may or may not have a statistical basis in fact with respect to particular positions adopted by the Jaycees, we have repeatedly condemned legal decisionmaking that relies uncritically on such assumptions. *See, e.g., Palmore v. Sidoti*, 466 U.S. 429, 433-434 (1984). . . .

In any event, even if enforcement of the Act causes some incidental abridgment of the Jaycees' protected speech, that effect is no greater than is necessary to accomplish the State's legitimate purposes. As we have explained, acts of invidious discrimination in the distribution of publicly available goods, services, and other advantages cause unique evils that government has a compelling interest to prevent—wholly apart from the point of view such conduct may transmit. Accordingly, like violence or other types of potentially expressive activities that produce special harms distinct from their communicative impact, such practices are entitled to no constitutional protection. In prohibiting such practices, the Minnesota Act therefore "responds precisely to the substantive problem which legitimately concerns" the State and abridges no more speech or associational freedom than is necessary to accomplish that purpose.

The judgment of the Court of Appeals is

Reversed.

THE CHIEF JUSTICE and Justice BLACKMUN took no part in the decision of this case.

Justice REHNQUIST concurs in the judgment.

Justice O'CONNOR, concurring in part and concurring in the judgment.
. . . The Court declares that the Jaycees' right of association depends on the organization's making a "substantial" showing that the admission of unwelcome members "will change the message communicated by the group's speech." I am not sure what showing the Court thinks would satisfy its requirement of proof of a membership-message connection, but whatever it means, the focus on such a connection is objectionable.

Imposing such a requirement, especially in the context of the balancing-of-interests test articulated by the Court, raises the possibility that certain commercial associations, by engaging occasionally in certain kinds of expressive activities, might improperly gain protection for discrimination. . . .

The Court's readiness to inquire into the connection between membership and message reveals a more fundamental flaw in its analysis. The Court pursues this inquiry as part of its mechanical application of a "compelling interest" test [but the] . . . Court entirely neglects to establish at the threshold that the Jaycees is an association whose activities or purposes should engage the strong protections that the First Amendment extends to expressive associations.

On the one hand, an association engaged exclusively in protected expression enjoys First Amendment protection of both the content of its message and the choice of its members. Protection of the message itself is judged by the same standards as protection of speech by an individual. Protection of the association's right to define its membership derives from the recognition that the formation of an expressive association is the creation of a voice, and the selection of members is the definition of that voice. . . .

On the other hand, there is only minimal constitutional protection of the freedom of commercial association. There are, of course, some constitutional protections of commercial speech—speech intended and used to promote a commercial transaction with the speaker. But the State is free to impose any rational regulation on the commercial transaction itself. . . .

Many associations cannot readily be described as purely expressive or purely commercial. No association is likely ever to be exclusively engaged in expressive activities[.] . . . And innumerable commercial associations also engage in some incidental protected speech or advocacy. . . .

In my view, an association should be characterized as commercial, and therefore subject to rationally related state regulation of its membership and other associational activities, when, and only when, the association's activities are not predominantly of the type protected by the First Amendment. It is only when the association is predominantly engaged in protected expression that state regulation of its membership will necessarily affect, change, dilute, or silence one collective voice that would otherwise be heard. . . .

Determining whether an association's activity is predominantly protected expression will often be difficult, if only because a broad range of activities can be expressive. It is easy enough to identify expressive words or conduct that [is] strident, contentious, or divisive, but protected expression may also take the form of quiet persuasion, inculcation of traditional values, instruction of the young, and community service. The purposes of an association, and the purposes of its members in adhering to it, are doubtless relevant in determining whether the association is primarily engaged in protected expression. Lawyering to advance social goals may be speech but ordinary commercial law practice is not. A group boycott or refusal to deal for political purposes may be speech, though a similar boycott for purposes of maintaining a cartel is not. Even the training of outdoor survival skills or participation in community service might become expressive when the activity is intended to develop good morals, reverence, patriotism, and a desire for self-improvement.

The considerations that may enter into the determination of when a particular association of persons is predominantly engaged in expression are therefore fluid and somewhat uncertain. But the Court has recognized the need to draw similar lines in the past. . . .

The State of Minnesota has a legitimate interest in ensuring nondiscriminatory access to the commercial opportunity presented by membership in the Jaycees. The members of the Jaycees may not claim constitutional immunity from Minnesota's antidiscrimination law by seeking to exercise their First Amendment rights through this commercial organization.

For these reasons, I agree with the Court that the Jaycees' First Amendment challenge to the application of Minnesota's public accommodations law is meritless. I therefore concur[.]

NOTES AND QUESTIONS

1. *Intimate association.* What role should the First Amendment play in protecting a right to intimate association? What types of groups or relationships is that right most likely to protect? *See* David A.J. Richards, *Constitutional Legitimacy and Constitutional Privacy*, 61 N.Y.U. L. Rev. 800, 845 (1986).

2. Roberts *and expressive association.* Is the *Roberts* Court wise to link a right to expressive association with an inquiry into whether the group has a message? Who has the better approach, the majority or Justice O'Connor? For commentary on both approaches, see Douglas O. Linder, *Freedom of Association After* Roberts v. United States Jaycees, 82 Mich. L. Rev. 1878 (1984); Seanna Valentine Shiffrin, *What Is Really Wrong with Compelled Association?*, 99 Nw. U. L. Rev. 839 (2005).

3. Roberts *and* O'Brien. *Roberts* bears a close relationship to *O'Brien.* Both cases require courts to identify state interests in regulating expressive conduct, determine whether those interests are unrelated to free expression, and whether the means to reach those interest is sufficiently tailored. *Roberts* is primarily concerned with whether the inclusion of a particular group of people will interfere with the association's expressive rights, while *O'Brien* is concerned with whether application of a general law will interfere with an individual's expression. *Roberts* also applies a much more stringent form of review than *O'Brien.* Both cases, however, require the Court to identify, at least on some level, a particularized message on behalf of the group or individual speaking. Are the two approaches so different that the *O'Brien* framework would have been inappropriate? Consider that question again when you read *Boy Scouts v. Dale, infra* p. 227.

4. *How far does* Roberts *reach?* Under the reasoning in *Roberts,* could an organization dedicated to eradicating women from the workplace exclude women, or must it accept women who adhere to that principle? What if the organization was more generally a "male supremacy" organization? Can the National Socialist Movement (a neo-Nazi group) be required to accept minorities and Jews? To what extent, if at all, does the focus in *Roberts* on the group's message allow status to be used as a proxy for message?

5. Roberts *in application.* In New York State Club Ass'n, Inc. v. City of New York, 487 U.S. 1 (1988), the Court upheld a New York City human rights ordinance that had the effect of banning discrimination based on race, creed, and sex in any private club that had more than "four hundred members, provide[d] regular meal service and regularly receive[d] payment . . . directly or indirectly from or on behalf of nonmembers for the furtherance of trade or business." *Id.* at 1. According to the Court, "[o]n its face, Local Law 63 does not affect 'in any significant way' the ability of individuals to form associations that will advocate public or private viewpoints. It does not require the clubs 'to abandon or alter' any activities that are protected by the First Amendment. If a club seeks to exclude individuals who do not share the views that the club's members wish to promote, the Law erects no obstacle to this end. Instead, the Law merely

prevents an association from using race, sex, and the other specified characteristics as shorthand measures in place of what the city considers to be more legitimate criteria for determining membership." *Id.* at 13.

HURLEY v. IRISH-AMERICAN GAY, LESBIAN & BISEXUAL GROUP OF BOSTON

515 U.S. 557 (1995)

Justice SOUTER delivered the opinion of the Court.

The issue in this case is whether Massachusetts may require private citizens who organize a parade to include among the marchers a group imparting a message the organizers do not wish to convey. We hold that such a mandate violates the First Amendment.

[In 1947, the City of Boston] granted authority to organize and conduct the St. Patrick's Day-Evacuation Day Parade to the petitioner South Boston Allied War Veterans Council, an unincorporated association of individuals elected from various South Boston veterans groups. Every year since that time, the Council has applied for and received a permit for the parade, which at times has included as many as 20,000 marchers and drawn up to 1 million watchers. No other applicant has ever applied for that permit. Through 1992, the city allowed the Council to use the city's official seal, and provided printing services as well as direct funding.

In 1992, a number of gay, lesbian, and bisexual descendants of the Irish immigrants joined together with other supporters to form the respondent organization, GLIB, to march in the parade as a way to express pride in their Irish heritage as openly gay, lesbian, and bisexual individuals[.] . . . Although the Council denied GLIB's application to take part in the 1992 parade, GLIB obtained a state-court order to include its contingent, which marched "uneventfully" among that year's 10,000 participants and 750,000 spectators.

In 1993, after the Council had again refused to admit GLIB to the upcoming parade, the organization and some of its members filed this suit against the Council, the individual petitioner John J. "Wacko" Hurley, and the city of Boston, alleging violations of . . . the state public accommodations law, which prohibits "any distinction, discrimination or restriction on account of . . . sexual orientation . . . relative to the admission of any person to, or treatment in any place of public accommodation, resort or amusement." . . .

If there were no reason for a group of people to march from here to there except to reach a destination, they could make the trip without expressing any message beyond the fact of the march itself. . . . Hence, we use the word "parade" to indicate marchers who are making some sort of collective point, not just to each other but to bystanders along the way. . . . Parades are thus a form of expression, not just motion, and the inherent expressiveness of marching to make a point explains our cases involving protest marches. [*See, e.g., Gregory*] . . .

The protected expression that inheres in a parade is not limited to its banners and songs, however, for the Constitution looks beyond written or spoken words as mediums of expression. Noting that "[s]ymbolism is a primitive but effective way of communicating ideas," *West Virginia Bd. of Ed. v. Barnette*, 319 U.S. 624, 632 (1943), our cases have recognized that the First Amendment shields such acts as saluting a flag (and refusing to do so), wearing an armband to protest a war, displaying a red flag, and even "[m]arching, walking or parading" in uniforms displaying the swastika, *National Socialist Party of America v. Skokie*, 432 U.S. 43 (1977). As some of these examples show, a narrow, succinctly articulable message is not a condition of constitutional protection, which if confined to expressions conveying a "particularized message," *cf. Spence*, would never reach the unquestionably shielded painting of Jackson Pollock, music of Arnold Schoenberg, or Jabberwocky verse of Lewis Carroll.

Not many marches, then, are beyond the realm of expressive parades, and the South Boston celebration is not one of them. . . . To be sure, we agree with the state courts that in spite of excluding some applicants, the Council is rather lenient in admitting participants. But a private speaker does not forfeit constitutional protection simply by combining multifarious voices, or by failing to edit their themes to isolate an exact message as the exclusive subject matter of the speech. Nor, under our precedent, does First Amendment protection require a speaker to generate, as an original matter, each item featured in the communication. Cable operators, for example, are engaged in protected speech activities even when they only select programming originally produced by others. *Turner Broadcasting System, Inc. v. FCC*, 512 U.S. 622, 636 (1994). For that matter, the presentation of an edited compilation of speech generated by other persons is a staple of most newspapers' opinion pages, which, of course, fall squarely within the core of First Amendment security, *Miami Herald Publishing Co. v. Tornillo*, 418 U.S. 241, 258 (1974), as does even the simple selection of a paid noncommercial advertisement for inclusion in a daily paper, see *New York Times v. Sullivan*, 376 U.S. 254 (1964). The selection of contingents to make a parade is entitled to similar protection.

Respondents' participation as a unit in the parade was equally expressive. GLIB was formed for the very purpose of marching in it, as the trial court found, in order to celebrate its members' identity as openly gay, lesbian, and bisexual descendants of the Irish immigrants, to show that there are such individuals in the community, and to support the like men and women who sought to march in the New York parade. . . . GLIB understandably seeks to communicate its ideas as part of the existing parade, rather than staging one of its own.

The Massachusetts public accommodations law . . . today prohibits discrimination on the basis of "race, color, religious creed, national origin, sex, sexual orientation . . . , deafness, blindness or any physical or mental disability or ancestry" in "the admission of any person to, or treatment in any place of public accommodation, resort or amusement." Mass. Gen. Laws § 272:98 (1992). Provisions like these are well within the State's usual power to enact when a legislature has reason to believe that a given group is the target of discrimination, and they do not, as a general matter, violate the First or Fourteenth Amendments.

In the case before us, however, the Massachusetts law has been applied in a peculiar way. Its enforcement does not address any dispute about the participation of openly gay, lesbian, or bisexual individuals in various units admitted to the parade. Petitioners disclaim any intent to exclude homosexuals as such, and no individual member of GLIB claims to have been excluded from parading as a member of any group that the Council has approved to march. Instead, the disagreement goes to the admission of GLIB as its own parade unit carrying its own banner. . . . Although the state courts spoke of the parade as a place of public accommodation, once the expressive character of both the parade and the marching GLIB contingent is understood, it becomes apparent that the state courts' application of the statute had the effect of declaring the sponsors' speech itself to be the public accommodation. Under this approach any contingent of protected individuals with a message would have the right to participate in petitioners' speech, so that the communication produced by the private organizers would be shaped by all those protected by the law who wished to join in with some expressive demonstration of their own. But this use of the State's power violates the fundamental rule of protection under the First Amendment, that a speaker has the autonomy to choose the content of his own message. . . .

Petitioners' claim to the benefit of this principle of autonomy to control one's own speech is as sound as the South Boston parade is expressive. Rather like a composer, the Council selects the expressive units of the parade from potential participants, and though the score may not produce a particularized message, each contingent's expression in the Council's eyes comports with what merits celebration on that day. Even if this view gives the Council credit for a more considered judgment than it actively made, the Council clearly decided to exclude a message it did not like from the communication it chose to make, and that is enough to invoke its right as a private speaker to shape its expression by speaking on one subject while remaining silent on another. . . .

Respondents argue that any tension between this rule and the Massachusetts law falls short of unconstitutionality, citing the most recent of our cases on the general subject of compelled access for expressive purposes, *Turner Broadcasting*. There we reviewed regulations requiring cable operators to set aside channels for designated broadcast signals, and applied only intermediate scrutiny. Respondents contend on this authority that admission of GLIB to the parade would not threaten the core principle of speaker's autonomy because the Council, like a cable operator, is merely "a conduit" for the speech of participants in the parade "rather than itself a speaker." But this metaphor is not apt here, because GLIB's participation would likely be perceived as having resulted from the Council's customary determination about a unit admitted to the parade, that its message was worthy of presentation and quite possibly of support as well. A newspaper, similarly, "is more than a passive receptacle or conduit for news, comment, and advertising," and we have held that "[t]he choice of material . . . and the decisions made as to limitations on the size and content . . . and treatment of public issues . . . —whether fair or unfair—constitute the exercise of editorial control and judgment" upon which the State can not intrude. . . .

In *Turner Broadcasting*, we found this problem absent in the cable context, because "[g]iven cable's long history of serving as a conduit for broadcast signals, there appears little risk that cable viewers would assume that the broadcast stations carried on a cable system convey ideas or messages endorsed by the cable operator." . . .

Parades and demonstrations, in contrast, are not understood to be so neutrally presented or selectively viewed. . . . Although each parade unit generally identifies itself, each is understood to contribute something to a common theme, and accordingly there is no customary practice whereby private sponsors disavow "any identity of viewpoint" between themselves and the selected participants. . . . Without deciding on the precise significance of the likelihood of misattribution, it nonetheless becomes clear that in the context of an expressive parade, as with a protest march, the parade's overall message is distilled from the individual presentations along the way, and each unit's expression is perceived by spectators as part of the whole. . . .

Our holding today rests not on any particular view about the Council's message but on the Nation's commitment to protect freedom of speech. Disapproval of a private speaker's statement does not legitimize use of the Commonwealth's power to compel the speaker to alter the message by including one more acceptable to others. Accordingly, the judgment of the Supreme Judicial Court is reversed, and the case is remanded for proceedings not inconsistent with this opinion.

It is so ordered.

BOY SCOUTS OF AMERICA v. DALE

530 U.S. 640 (2000)

Chief Justice REHNQUIST delivered the opinion of the Court.

Petitioners are the Boy Scouts of America and the Monmouth Council, a division of the Boy Scouts of America (collectively, Boy Scouts). The Boy Scouts is a private, not-for-profit organization engaged in instilling its system of values in young people. The Boy Scouts asserts that homosexual conduct is inconsistent with the values it seeks to instill. Respondent is James Dale, a former Eagle Scout whose adult membership in the Boy Scouts was revoked when the Boy Scouts learned that he is an avowed homosexual and gay rights activist. The New Jersey Supreme Court held that New Jersey's public accommodations law requires that the Boy Scouts readmit Dale. This case presents the question whether applying New Jersey's public accommodations law in this way violates the Boy Scouts' First Amendment right of expressive association. We hold that it does.

I

. . . Dale became a Boy Scout in 1981 and remained a Scout until he turned 18. By all accounts, Dale was an exemplary Scout. In 1988, he achieved the rank of Eagle Scout, one of Scouting's highest honors.

Dale applied for adult membership in the Boy Scouts in 1989. The Boy Scouts approved his application for the position of assistant scoutmaster of Troop 73. Around the same time, Dale left home to attend Rutgers University. After arriving at Rutgers, Dale first acknowledged to himself and others that he is gay. He quickly became involved with, and eventually became the copresident of, the Rutgers University Lesbian/Gay Alliance. In 1990, Dale attended a seminar addressing the psychological and health needs of lesbian and gay teenagers. A newspaper covering the event interviewed Dale about his advocacy of homosexual teenagers' need for gay role models. In early July 1990, the newspaper published the interview and Dale's photograph over a caption identifying him as the copresident of the Lesbian/Gay Alliance.

Later that month, Dale received a letter from Monmouth Council Executive James Kay revoking his adult membership. Dale wrote to Kay requesting the reason for Monmouth Council's decision. Kay responded by letter that the Boy Scouts "specifically forbid membership to homosexuals."

In 1992, Dale filed a complaint against the Boy Scouts in the New Jersey Superior Court. The complaint alleged that the Boy Scouts had violated New Jersey's public accommodations statute and its common law by revoking Dale's membership based solely on his sexual orientation. New Jersey's public accommodations statute prohibits, among other things, discrimination on the basis of sexual orientation in places of public accommodation.

The New Jersey Superior Court's Chancery Division granted summary judgment in favor of the Boy Scouts. . . . The New Jersey Superior Court's Appellate Division . . . reversed and . . . rejected the Boy Scouts' federal constitutional claims. The New Jersey Supreme Court affirmed the judgment of the Appellate Division. . . .

II

The forced inclusion of an unwanted person in a group infringes the group's freedom of expressive association if the presence of that person affects in a significant way the group's ability to advocate public or private viewpoints. *New York State Club Assn., Inc. v. City of New York*, 487 U.S. 1, 13 (1988). But the freedom of expressive association, like many freedoms, is not absolute. We have held that the freedom could be overridden "by regulations adopted to serve compelling state interests, unrelated to the suppression of ideas, that cannot be achieved through means significantly less restrictive of associational freedoms." *Roberts v. United States Jaycees*, 468 U.S. 609 (1984).

To determine whether a group is protected by the First Amendment's expressive associational right, we must determine whether the group engages in "expressive association." The First Amendment's protection of expressive association is not reserved for advocacy groups. But to come within its ambit, a group must engage in some form of expression, whether it be public or private. . . .

The Boy Scouts is a private, nonprofit organization. According to its mission statement:

> It is the mission of the Boy Scouts of America to serve others by helping to instill values in young people and, in other ways, to prepare them to make ethical choices over their lifetime in achieving their full potential.
>   The values we strive to instill are based on those found in the Scout Oath and Law:
>
> Scout Oath
>
> On my honor I will do my best
> To do my duty to God and my country
> and to obey the Scout Law;
> To help other people at all times;
> To keep myself physically strong,
> mentally awake, and morally straight.
>
> Scout Law
>
> A Scout is: Trustworthy, Obedient, Loyal, Cheerful, Helpful, Thrifty, Friendly, Brave, Courteous, Clean, Kind, Reverent.

Thus, the general mission of the Boy Scouts is clear: "[T]o instill values in young people." The Boy Scouts seeks to instill these values by having its adult leaders spend time with the youth members, instructing and engaging them in activities like camping, archery, and fishing. During the time spent with the youth members, the scoutmasters and assistant scoutmasters inculcate them with the Boy Scouts' values—both expressly and by example. It seems indisputable that an association that seeks to transmit such a system of values engages in expressive activity. . . .

Given that the Boy Scouts engages in expressive activity, we must determine whether the forced inclusion of Dale as an assistant scoutmaster would significantly affect the Boy Scouts' ability to advocate public or private viewpoints. This inquiry necessarily requires us first to explore, to a limited extent, the nature of the Boy Scouts' view of homosexuality. . . .

The Boy Scouts explains that the Scout Oath and Law provide "a positive moral code for living; they are a list of 'do's' rather than 'don'ts.'" The Boy Scouts asserts that homosexual conduct is inconsistent with the values embodied in the Scout Oath and Law, particularly with the values represented by the terms "morally straight" and "clean."

Obviously, the Scout Oath and Law do not expressly mention sexuality or sexual orientation. And the terms "morally straight" and "clean" are by no means self-defining. Different people would attribute to those terms very different meanings. . . .

The New Jersey Supreme Court analyzed the Boy Scouts' beliefs and found that the "exclusion of members solely on the basis of their sexual orientation is inconsistent with Boy Scouts' commitment to a diverse and 'representative' membership . . . [and] contradicts Boy Scouts' overarching objective to reach 'all eligible youth.'" The court concluded that the exclusion of members like Dale "appears antithetical to the organization's goals and philosophy." But our cases reject this sort of inquiry; it is not the role of the courts to reject a group's expressed values because they disagree with those values or find them internally inconsistent.

The Boy Scouts asserts that it "teach[es] that homosexual conduct is not morally straight," and that it does "not want to promote homosexual conduct as a legitimate form of behavior." We accept the Boy Scouts' assertion. We need not inquire further to determine the nature of the Boy Scouts' expression with respect to homosexuality. But because the record before us contains written evidence of the Boy Scouts' viewpoint, we look to it as instructive, if only on the question of the sincerity of the professed beliefs.

A 1978 position statement to the Boy Scouts' Executive Committee, signed by Downing B. Jenks, the President of the Boy Scouts, and Harvey L. Price, the Chief Scout Executive, expresses the Boy Scouts' "official position" with regard to "homosexuality and Scouting:"

Q: May an individual who openly declares himself to be a homosexual be a volunteer Scout leader?

A: No. The Boy Scouts of America is a private, membership organization and leadership therein is a privilege and not a right. We do not believe that homosexuality and leadership in Scouting are appropriate. We will continue to select only those who in our judgment meet our standards and qualifications for leadership.

Thus, at least as of 1978—the year James Dale entered Scouting—the official position of the Boy Scouts was that avowed homosexuals were not to be Scout leaders.

A position statement promulgated by the Boy Scouts in 1991 (after Dale's membership was revoked but before this litigation was filed) also supports its current view:

We believe that homosexual conduct is inconsistent with the requirement in the Scout Oath that a Scout be morally straight and in the Scout Law that a Scout be clean in word and deed, and that homosexuals do not provide a desirable role model for Scouts.

This position statement was redrafted numerous times but its core message remained consistent, [including in a 1993 position statement.] . . .

The Boy Scouts publicly expressed its views with respect to homosexual conduct by its assertions in prior litigation. For example, throughout a California case with similar facts filed in the early 1980's, the Boy Scouts consistently asserted the same position with respect to homosexuality that it asserts today. We cannot doubt that the Boy Scouts sincerely holds this view.

We must then determine whether Dale's presence as an assistant scoutmaster would significantly burden the Boy Scouts' desire to not "promote homosexual conduct as a legitimate form of behavior." As we give deference to an association's assertions regarding the nature of its expression, we must also give deference to an association's view of what would impair its expression. That is not to say that an expressive association can erect a shield against antidiscrimination laws simply by asserting that mere acceptance of a member from a particular group would impair its message. But here Dale, by his own admission, is one of a group of gay Scouts who have "become leaders in their community and are open and honest about their sexual orientation." Dale was the copresident of a gay and lesbian organization at college and remains a gay rights activist. Dale's presence in the Boy Scouts would, at the very least, force the organization to send a message, both to the youth members and the world, that the Boy Scouts accepts homosexual conduct as a legitimate form of behavior.

Hurley is illustrative on this point. [In *Hurley*, we] . . . noted that the parade organizers did not wish to exclude the GLIB members because of their sexual orientations, but because they wanted to march behind a GLIB banner. . . .

As the presence of GLIB in Boston's St. Patrick's Day parade would have interfered with the parade organizers' choice not to propound a particular point of view, the presence of Dale as an assistant scoutmaster would just as surely interfere with the Boy Scouts' choice not to propound a point of view contrary to its beliefs.

The New Jersey Supreme Court determined that the Boy Scouts' ability to disseminate its message was not significantly affected by the forced inclusion of Dale as an assistant scoutmaster because of the following findings:

> Boy Scout members do not associate for the purpose of disseminating the belief that homosexuality is immoral; Boy Scouts discourages its leaders from disseminating any views on sexual issues; and Boy Scouts includes sponsors and members who subscribe to different views in respect of homosexuality.

We disagree with the New Jersey Supreme Court's conclusion drawn from these findings.

First, associations do not have to associate for the "purpose" of disseminating a certain message in order to be entitled to the protections of the First Amendment. An association must merely engage in expressive activity that could be impaired in order to be entitled to protection. . . .

Second, even if the Boy Scouts discourages Scout leaders from disseminating views on sexual issues—a fact that the Boy Scouts disputes with contrary evidence—the First Amendment protects the Boy Scouts' method of expression. If the Boy

Scouts wishes Scout leaders to avoid questions of sexuality and teach only by example, this fact does not negate the sincerity of its belief discussed above.

Third, the First Amendment simply does not require that every member of a group agree on every issue in order for the group's policy to be "expressive association." The Boy Scouts takes an official position with respect to homosexual conduct, and that is sufficient for First Amendment purposes. . . .

Having determined that the Boy Scouts is an expressive association and that the forced inclusion of Dale would significantly affect its expression, we inquire whether the application of New Jersey's public accommodations law to require that the Boy Scouts accept Dale as an assistant scoutmaster runs afoul of the Scouts' freedom of expressive association. We conclude that it does.

State public accommodations laws were originally enacted to prevent discrimination in traditional places of public accommodation—like inns and trains. Over time, the public accommodations laws have expanded to cover more places. New Jersey's statutory definition of "'[a] place of public accommodation'" is extremely broad. . . . In this case, the New Jersey Supreme Court . . . applied its public accommodations law to a private entity without even attempting to tie the term "place" to a physical location. As the definition of "public accommodation" has expanded from clearly commercial entities, such as restaurants, bars, and hotels, to membership organizations such as the Boy Scouts, the potential for conflict between state public accommodations laws and the First Amendment rights of organizations has increased.

We recognized in [*Roberts*] that States have a compelling interest in eliminating discrimination against women in public accommodations. But . . . we went on to conclude that the enforcement of these statutes would not materially interfere with the ideas that the organization sought to express. In *Roberts*, we said "[i]ndeed, the Jaycees has failed to demonstrate . . . any serious burden on the male members' freedom of expressive association." . . .

Dale contends that we should apply the intermediate standard of review enunciated in *United States v. O'Brien*, 391 U.S. 367 (1968), to evaluate the competing interests. There the Court enunciated a four-part test for review of a governmental regulation that has only an incidental effect on protected speech—in that case the symbolic burning of a draft card. A law prohibiting the destruction of draft cards only incidentally affects the free speech rights of those who happen to use a violation of that law as a symbol of protest. But New Jersey's public accommodations law directly and immediately affects associational rights, in this case associational rights that enjoy First Amendment protection. Thus, *O'Brien* is inapplicable.

In *Hurley*, we applied traditional First Amendment analysis to hold that the application of the Massachusetts public accommodations law to a parade violated the First Amendment rights of the parade organizers. Although we did not explicitly deem the parade in *Hurley* an expressive association, the analysis we applied there is similar to the analysis we apply here. We have already concluded that a state requirement that the Boy Scouts retain Dale as an assistant scoutmaster would significantly burden the organization's right to oppose or disfavor homosexual conduct. The state interests embodied in New Jersey's public accommodations law do not justify such a severe intrusion on the Boy Scouts' rights to freedom of expressive association. That being the case, we hold that the First Amendment prohibits the State from imposing such a requirement through the application of its public accommodations law.[4] . . .

We are not, as we must not be, guided by our views of whether the Boy Scouts' teachings with respect to homosexual conduct are right or wrong; public or judicial disapproval of a tenet of an organization's expression does not justify the State's effort to compel the organization to accept members where such acceptance would derogate from the organization's expressive message. "While the law is free to promote all sorts of conduct in place of harmful behavior, it is not free to interfere with speech for no better reason than promoting an approved message or discouraging a disfavored one, however enlightened either purpose may strike the government." *Hurley*.

The judgment of the New Jersey Supreme Court is reversed, and the case is remanded for further proceedings not inconsistent with this opinion.

It is so ordered.

Justice STEVENS, with whom Justice SOUTER, Justice GINSBURG, and Justice BREYER join, dissenting. . . .

I

BSA's mission statement reads as follows: "It is the mission of the Boy Scouts of America to serve others by helping to instill values in young people and, in other ways, to prepare them to make ethical choices over their lifetime in achieving their full potential." Its federal charter declares its purpose is "to promote, through organization, and cooperation with other agencies, the ability of boys to do things for themselves and others, to train them in scoutcraft, and to teach them patriotism, courage, self-reliance, and kindred values, using the methods which were in common use by Boy Scouts on June 15, 1916." . . . In particular, the group emphasizes that "[n]either the charter nor the bylaws of the Boy Scouts of America permits the exclusion of any boy. . . .To meet these responsibilities we have made a commitment that our membership shall be representative of *all* the population in every community, district, and council." . . .

To bolster its claim that its shared goals include teaching that homosexuality is wrong, BSA directs our attention to two terms appearing in the Scout Oath and Law. The first is the phrase "morally straight," which appears in the Oath[.] [T]he second term is the word "clean," which appears in a list of 12 characteristics together constituting the Scout Law.

The Boy Scout Handbook defines "morally straight," as such:

> To be a person of strong character, guide your life with honesty, purity, and justice. Respect and defend the rights of all people. Your relationships with others should be honest and open. Be clean in your speech and actions, and faithful in

---

[4] We anticipated this result in *Hurley* when we illustrated the reasons for our holding in that case by likening the parade to a private membership organization. We stated: "Assuming the parade to be large enough and a source of benefits (apart from its expression) that would generally justify a mandated access provision, GLIB could nonetheless be refused admission as an expressive contingent with its own message just as readily as a private club could exclude an applicant whose manifest views were at odds with a position taken by the club's existing members." 515 U.S. at 580-81.

your religious beliefs. The values you follow as a Scout will help you become virtuous and self-reliant.

. . . As for the term "clean," the Boy Scout Handbook offers the following:

> A Scout is CLEAN. *A Scout keeps his body and mind fit and clean. He chooses the company of those who live by these same ideals. He helps keep his home and community clean.*
> You never need to be ashamed of dirt that will wash off. . . .
> There's another kind of dirt that won't come off by washing. It is the kind that shows up in foul language and harmful thoughts.
> Swear words, profanity, and dirty stories are weapons that ridicule other people and hurt their feelings. The same is true of racial slurs and jokes making fun of ethnic groups or people with physical or mental limitations. A Scout knows there is no kindness or honor in such mean-spirited behavior. He avoids it in his own words and deeds. He defends those who are targets of insults. . . .

It is plain as the light of day that neither one of these principles—"morally straight" and "clean"—says the slightest thing about homosexuality. Indeed, neither term in the Boy Scouts' Law and Oath expresses any position whatsoever on sexual matters.
. . .

More specifically, BSA has set forth a number of rules for Scoutmasters when these types of issues come up:

> You may have boys asking you for information or advice about sexual matters. . . .
> How should you handle such matters?
> Rule number 1: *You do not undertake to instruct Scouts, in any formalized manner, in the subject of sex and family life. The reasons are that it is not construed to be Scouting's proper area,* and that you are probably not well qualified to do this. . . .

In light of BSA's self-proclaimed ecumenism, furthermore, it is even more difficult to discern any shared goals or common moral stance on homosexuality. . . . "The BSA does not define what constitutes duty to God or the practice of religion. This is the responsibility of parents and religious leaders." In fact, many diverse religious organizations sponsor local Boy Scout troops. Because a number of religious groups do not view homosexuality as immoral or wrong and reject discrimination against homosexuals, it is exceedingly difficult to believe that BSA nonetheless adopts a single particular religious or moral philosophy when it comes to sexual orientation. . . .

II

The Court seeks to fill the void by pointing to a statement of "policies and procedures relating to homosexuality and Scouting," signed by BSA's President and Chief Scout Executive in 1978 and addressed to the members of the Executive Committee of the national organization. . . . [A]t most this letter simply adopts an exclusionary membership policy. But simply adopting such a policy has never been considered sufficient, by itself, to prevail on a right to associate claim.

Second, the 1978 policy was never publicly expressed—unlike, for example, the Scout's duty to be "obedient." It was an internal memorandum, never circulated beyond the few members of BSA's Executive Committee. . . . BSA's *public* posture—to the world and to the Scouts themselves—remained what it had always been: one of tolerance, welcoming all classes of boys and young men. . . .

The majority also relies on four other policy statements that were issued between 1991 and 1993. All of them were written and issued *after* BSA revoked Dale's membership. Accordingly, they have little, if any, relevance to the legal question before this Court. . . .

[A]t most the 1991 and 1992 statements declare only that BSA believed "homosexual *conduct* is inconsistent with the requirement in the Scout Oath that a Scout be morally straight and in the Scout Law that a Scout be clean in word and deed." But New Jersey's law prohibits discrimination on the basis of sexual *orientation.* And when Dale was expelled from the Boy Scouts, BSA said it did so because of his sexual orientation, not because of his sexual conduct.[8] . . .

III

[I]n *Jaycees,* we asked whether Minnesota's Human Rights Law requiring the admission of women "impose[d] any *serious burdens*" on the group's "collective effort on behalf of [its] *shared goals.*" Notwithstanding the group's obvious publicly stated exclusionary policy, we did not view the inclusion of women as a "serious burden" on the Jaycees' ability to engage in the protected speech of its choice. . . . The relevant question is whether the mere inclusion of the person at issue would "impose any serious burden," "affect in any significant way," or be "a substantial restraint upon" the organization's "shared goals," "basic goals," or "collective effort to foster beliefs." Accordingly, it is necessary to examine what, exactly, are BSA's shared goals and the degree to which its expressive activities would be burdened, affected, or restrained by including homosexuals.

The evidence before this Court makes it exceptionally clear that BSA has, at most, simply adopted an exclusionary membership policy and has no shared goal of disapproving of homosexuality. . . . In short, Boy Scouts of America is simply silent on homosexuality. There is no shared goal or collective effort to foster a belief about homosexuality at all—let alone one that is significantly burdened by admitting homosexuals. . . .

IV

The majority pretermits this entire analysis. It finds that BSA in fact "'teach[es] that homosexual conduct is not morally straight.'" This conclusion, remarkably, rests entirely on statements in BSA's briefs. Moreover, the majority insists that we must "give deference to an association's assertions regarding the nature of its expression" and "we must also give deference to an association's view of what would impair its expression." So long as the record "contains written evidence" to support a group's bare assertion, "[w]e need not inquire further." . . .

This is an astounding view of the law. . . . [N]othing in our cases calls for this Court to do any such thing. An organization can adopt the message of its choice, and

---

[8] At oral argument, BSA's counsel was asked: "[W]hat if someone is homosexual in the sense of having a sexual orientation in that direction but does not engage in any homosexual conduct?" Counsel answered: "[I]f that person also were to take the view that the reason they didn't engage in that conduct [was because] it would be morally wrong . . . that person would not be excluded."

it is not this Court's place to disagree with it. But we must inquire whether the group is, in fact, expressing a message (whatever it may be) and whether that message (if one is expressed) is significantly affected by a State's antidiscrimination law. . . .

There is, of course, a valid concern that a court's independent review may run the risk of paying too little heed to an organization's sincerely held views. But unless one is prepared to turn the right to associate into a free pass out of antidiscrimination laws, an independent inquiry is a necessity. . . .

In this case, no such concern is warranted. It is entirely clear that BSA in fact expresses no clear, unequivocal message burdened by New Jersey's law.

V

The majority's argument relies exclusively on *Hurley*. . . . Dale's inclusion in the Boy Scouts is nothing like the case in *Hurley*. His participation sends no cognizable message to the Scouts or to the world. Unlike GLIB, Dale did not carry a banner or a sign; he did not distribute any factsheet; and he expressed no intent to send any message. If there is any kind of message being sent, then, it is by the mere act of joining the Boy Scouts. Such an act does not constitute an instance of symbolic speech under the First Amendment.

It is true, of course, that some acts are so imbued with symbolic meaning that they qualify as "speech" under the First Amendment. See *United States v. O'Brien*, 391 U.S. 367 (1968). At the same time, however, "[w]e cannot accept the view that an apparently limitless variety of conduct can be labeled 'speech' whenever the person engaging in the conduct intends thereby to express an idea." Though participating in the Scouts could itself conceivably send a message on some level, it is not the kind of act that we have recognized as speech. Indeed, if merely joining a group did constitute symbolic speech; and such speech were attributable to the group being joined; and that group has the right to exclude that speech (and hence, the right to exclude that person from joining), then the right of free speech effectively becomes a limitless right to exclude for every organization, whether or not it engages in *any* expressive activities. That cannot be, and never has been, the law.

Furthermore, it is not likely that BSA would be understood to send any message, either to Scouts or to the world, simply by admitting someone as a member. . . . In 1992 over one million adults were active BSA members. The notion that an organization of that size and enormous prestige implicitly endorses the views that each of those adults may express in a non-Scouting context is simply mind boggling. . . .

VI

Unfavorable opinions about homosexuals "have ancient roots." *Bowers v. Hardwick*, 478 U.S. 186 (1986). Like equally atavistic opinions about certain racial groups, those roots have been nourished by sectarian doctrine. . . .

That such prejudices are still prevalent and that they have caused serious and tangible harm to countless members of the class New Jersey seeks to protect are established matters of fact that neither the Boy Scouts nor the Court disputes. That harm can only be aggravated by the creation of a constitutional shield for a policy that is itself the product of a habitual way of thinking about strangers. . . .

If we would guide by the light of reason, we must let our minds be bold. I respectfully dissent.

[Justice SOUTER's dissenting opinion is omitted.]

NOTES AND QUESTIONS

1. Roberts *and* Dale. Can *Dale* be squared with *Roberts*, or does it essentially change the rules? For discussion, see Dale Carpenter, *Expressive Association and Anti-Discrimination Law After Dale: A Tripartite Approach*, 85 Minn. L. Rev. 1515 (2001); Shiffrin, *supra*, at 846-847.
2. Hurley *and* Dale—*the analogy.* The *Dale* majority relied on *Hurley* to explain why including Dale interfered with the Boy Scouts' message. Is *Hurley* the appropriate comparison case? For discussion, see James P. Madigan, *Questioning the Coercive Effect of Self-Identifying Speech*, 87 Iowa L. Rev. 75 (2001); *Leading Cases—Boy Scouts of America v. Dale*, 114 Harv. L. Rev. 259, 265-266 (2001).
3. Dale's *implications.* Does *Dale*, if "applied correctly," mean that "Title VII is flatly unconstitutional" because it forces some people to send a message of equality that they oppose? Richard Epstein, *The Constitutional Perils of Moderation: The Case of the Boy Scouts*, 74 S. Cal. L. Rev. 119, 139-140 (2000); Jed Rubenfeld, *The First Amendment's Purpose*, 53 Stan. L. Rev. 767, 768-769 (2001).
4. *Was there an expressive group message?* After *Hurley* and *Dale*, how discernible must a group's expressive message be to qualify for protection under the Court's approach to freedom of association? Why doesn't the Court apply the *O'Brien* framework in *Dale*?
5. Dale *in light of subsequent events.* In 2015, the Boy Scouts ended its ban on gay leaders. See Erick Eckholm, *Mormons Assail Boy Scouts' Shift on Gay Leaders*, N.Y. Times, July 28, 2015, at A1. Does that policy change suggest that Justice Breyer was justified in his concern about the centrality of discrimination to the Boy Scouts?
6. *Expression or conduct?* Is excluding a person/group from a large diverse organization like the Boy Scouts expressive in the same way as excluding a person/group from a parade? Consider the following case as you think about your answer.

RUMSFELD v. FORUM FOR ACADEMIC & INSTITUTIONAL RIGHTS

547 U.S. 47 (2006)

ROBERTS, C.J., delivered the opinion of the Court.

When law schools began restricting the access of military recruiters to their students because of disagreement with the Government's policy on homosexuals in the military,[2] Congress responded by enacting the Solomon Amendment. That

---

[2] Under this policy, a person generally may not serve in the Armed Forces if he has engaged in homosexual acts, stated that he is a homosexual, or married a person of the same sex. Respondents do not challenge that policy in this litigation.

provision specifies that if any part of an institution of higher education denies military recruiters access equal to that provided other recruiters, the entire institution would lose certain federal funds. The law schools responded by suing, alleging that the Solomon Amendment infringed their First Amendment freedoms of speech and association.

Respondent Forum for Academic and Institutional Rights, Inc. (FAIR), is an association of law schools and law faculties. Its declared mission is "to promote academic freedom, support educational institutions in opposing discrimination and vindicate the rights of institutions of higher education." FAIR members have adopted policies expressing their opposition to discrimination based on, among other factors, sexual orientation. They would like to restrict military recruiting on their campuses because they object to the policy Congress has adopted with respect to homosexuals in the military. The Solomon Amendment, however, forces institutions to choose between enforcing their nondiscrimination policy against military recruiters in this way and continuing to receive specified federal funding.

FAIR argued that this forced inclusion and equal treatment of military recruiters violated the law schools' First Amendment freedoms of speech and association. According to FAIR, the Solomon Amendment was unconstitutional because it forced law schools to choose between exercising their First Amendment right to decide whether to disseminate or accommodate a military recruiter's message, and ensuring the availability of federal funding for their universities.

[We have recognized that] "judicial deference . . . is at its apogee" when Congress legislates under its authority to raise and support armies. Although Congress has broad authority to legislate on matters of military recruiting, it nonetheless chose to secure campus access for military recruiters indirectly, through its Spending Clause power. The Solomon Amendment gives universities a choice: Either allow military recruiters the same access to students afforded any other recruiter or forgo certain federal funds. Congress' decision to proceed indirectly does not reduce the deference given to Congress in the area of military affairs. Congress' choice to promote its goal by creating a funding condition deserves at least as deferential treatment as if Congress had imposed a mandate on universities.

The Solomon Amendment neither limits what law schools may say nor requires them to say anything. Law schools remain free under the statute to express whatever views they may have on the military's congressionally mandated employment policy, all the while retaining eligibility for federal funds. See Tr. of Oral Arg. 25 (Solicitor General acknowledging that law schools "could put signs on the bulletin board next to the door, they could engage in speech, they could help organize student protests"). As a general matter, the Solomon Amendment regulates conduct, not speech. It affects what law schools must *do*—afford equal access to military recruiters—not what they may or may not *say*.

In this case, accommodating the military's message does not affect the law schools' speech, because the schools are not speaking when they host interviews and recruiting receptions. Unlike a parade organizer's choice of parade contingents, a law school's decision to allow recruiters on campus is not inherently expressive. Law schools facilitate recruiting to assist their students in obtaining jobs. A law school's recruiting services lack the expressive quality of a parade, a newsletter, or the editorial page of a newspaper; its accommodation of a military recruiter's message is not compelled speech because the accommodation does not sufficiently interfere with any message of the school.

The Solomon Amendment does not violate law schools' freedom of speech, but the First Amendment's protection extends beyond the right to speak. We have recognized a First Amendment right to associate for the purpose of speaking, which we have termed a "right of expressive association." *See, e.g., Dale.* The reason we have extended First Amendment protection in this way is clear: The right to speak is often exercised most effectively by combining one's voice with the voices of others. *See Roberts.* If the government were free to restrict individuals' ability to join together and speak, it could essentially silence views that the First Amendment is intended to protect.

FAIR argues that the Solomon Amendment violates law schools' freedom of expressive association. According to FAIR, law schools' ability to express their message that discrimination on the basis of sexual orientation is wrong is significantly affected by the presence of military recruiters on campus and the schools' obligation to assist them. Relying heavily on our decision in *Dale*, the Court of Appeals agreed.

The Solomon Amendment, however, does not similarly affect a law school's associational rights. To comply with the statute, law schools must allow military recruiters on campus and assist them in whatever way the school chooses to assist other employers. Law schools therefore "associate" with military recruiters in the sense that they interact with them. But recruiters are not part of the law school. Recruiters are, by definition, outsiders who come onto campus for the limited purpose of trying to hire students—not to become members of the school's expressive association. This distinction is critical. Unlike the public accommodations law in *Dale*, the Solomon Amendment does not force a law school "'to accept members it does not desire.'" *Dale.*

NOTES AND QUESTIONS

1. How is the expressive conduct in *Spence* and *Hurley* different from the situation involved *FAIR*?
2. What does it mean for conduct to be "inherently expressive"? For discussion, see Caroline Mala Corbin, *Speech of Conduct? The Free Speech Claims of Wedding Vendors*, 65 Emory L.J. 241 (2015).
3. How does *FAIR* fit with *Roberts* and *Dale*? with *O'Brien*?

THEORY-APPLIED PROBLEMS

1. Thomas Hogue and Jason Wick are planning their wedding ceremony. They went to a locally-owned bakery—Sweets-For-the-Sweet—to order a cake. This bakery is widely known as the best baker of wedding cakes in town. However, Linda Mossman, the owner of Sweets (as it is locally known) refused to provide a cake for Hogue and Wick's wedding. She cited her sincerely held religious beliefs, which prevented her from being complicit in the sin of homosexuality. Hogue and Wick argue that Mossman's refusal amounts to discrimination under state laws that prevent discrimination in the provision of services based on race, gender, religion, sexual orientation and disability. Mossman argues that forcing her to provide a wedding cake amounts to a requirement that she endorse Hogue and Wick's lifestyle—i.e., that she express approval of their lifestyle through her

provision of services. Is Mossman's baking of a wedding cake expressive conduct that triggers First Amendment scrutiny?

2. Falun Gong ("The Practice of the Wheel of Law" in Chinese) is a "traditional Chinese spiritual discipline that includes exercise and meditation." Founded by Mr. Li Hongzhi in 1992, the organization enjoys thousands of members dispersed around the globe. Falun Gong features three main principles ("truth, compassion, and tolerance") and offers its adherents "better health, reduced stress, inner peace, and deepened morals." The organization promotes these benefits in part through the regular conduct of five meditation exercises, usually performed in a public place as part of a group.

   By 2016, Falun Gong made significant membership gains in Mississippi. In many of the larger cities, devotees of Falun Gong can be seen conducting their meditation exercises in public parks. Perhaps by happenstance, in March 2017, the Mississippi state legislature enacted a ban on group exercise in public parks. The new law provided that "no state, municipal or otherwise publicly owned park shall be used for group exercises, except for organized competitive sporting events, including, but not limited to, baseball, basketball, football, soccer, lacrosse, field hockey, and frisbee." The law applies to all "group exercises" that are not also "organized competitive sporting events." The Jackson, Mississippi chapter of Falun Gong received a letter from the City of Jackson Department of Parks and Recreation, asking that "your organization cease and desist from using any of the Jackson municipal parks for prohibited group exercise, including your 'meditation' practices." After receiving this letter, Falun Gong ceased meeting in the local municipal parks but initiated a section 1983 action seeking an injunction voiding the new Mississippi state law on free speech grounds. How should the district court rule?

3. In 2016, Falun Gong has generated a significant following in Jackson, Mississippi. Its members regularly use the local municipal parks to practice the organization's meditation exercises, which, to the uninitiated, look very much like pilates (a form of exercise focusing on flexibility and muscle strengthening). Pilates are also very popular in Jackson, Mississippi. In fact, the City of Jackson Department of Parks and Recreation ("Department"), which sponsors pilates classes in the evening at the main city recreational center, has found that demand for its classes far exceeds supply. The Department currently has a yearlong waiting list.

   Francine Jenkins, an associate at a large Jackson, Mississippi, law firm attempted to sign up for one of the Department's classes but was told that there was a one-year waiting list for the city-sponsored pilates program. Driving home from work, Jenkins noticed a group that exercises regularly in her neighborhood park in an area known as "The Meadow." The Department permits the reservation of "The Meadow" for group activities, including rallies, picnics, and concerts. Falun Gong reserves the Meadow on Wednesday evenings, from 7 P.M. to 8 P.M. for its meditation exercises. Jenkins, unable to join the city recreation center's pilates program, decided to join the Falun Gong group on Wednesdays. She was told, politely, but firmly, that she could not participate in the meditation exercises unless she became a member of Falun Gong. (These exercises are an integral aspect of Falun Gong's belief system as they promote its three main principles—"truth, compassion, and tolerance.") Jenkins refused because she did not subscribe to the group's beliefs. Wanting to participate in the exercises, which she thought looked interesting, Jenkins asked again if she could participate in the group's exercise period. The local chapter's leader again declined her request.

The City of Jackson enacted a comprehensive human rights ordinance in 2015 that prohibits discrimination based on "race, sex, national origin, ethnicity, religion, veteran's status, and sexual orientation" in "any place of public accommodation." The Mississippi Supreme Court has authoritatively construed the phrase "place of public accommodation" to include both physical places and organizations that generally solicit members from the public. Jenkins, irked at being excluded from yet another exercise class, filed a complaint with the City of Jackson Civil Rights Commission, alleging a violation of the nondiscrimination ordinance. The local chapter of Falun Gong asked the Commission to dismiss the complaint. The chapter claims that all adherents of Falun Gong are welcome to participate in the group exercises but that nonmembers who reject Falun Gong's teachings are not welcome. The chapter further asserts that Jenkins expressed interest only in the exercises and not in the organization's overall spiritual message. According to the chapter, such an attitude makes it quite impossible for the organization to welcome Jenkins to their devotions.

May the Civil Rights Commission rule in favor of Jenkins without violating the First Amendment?

4. The City of Richmond, facing a financial shortfall because tax receipts failed to equal estimated revenue used to prepare the annual budget, decided to increase the number of paid parking zones in the city. The Shockoe Bottom area of Richmond, a funky warehouse district featuring vintage clothing boutiques, nouveau cuisine eateries, and other upscale diversions, has traditionally featured free street parking in most zones and free street parking after 5 P.M. on weekdays and Saturdays in all legal street parking spots. As part of Richmond's effort to increase revenue, the city turned all legal street spaces in Shockoe Bottom into metered parking only, and applied the meters until midnight six nights a week (only Sunday was excepted).

The Shockoe Bottom Merchants Association (SBMA) opposed the city's decision to expand the times and locations of metered parking in the neighborhood. The SBMA organized a mass protest, encouraging all visitors to the neighborhood to "Stiff the Meter!" As part of the campaign, visitors to the area were encouraged to violate the new paid parking rules after 5 P.M. and in spaces that were formerly free parking. The SBMA also produced "Stiff the Meter!" magnetic stickers, which it encouraged visitors to place on the meters in lieu of paying for parking.

On May 16, 2017, the City of Richmond organized a massive parking enforcement dragnet operation, writing more than $3,452 in parking violation tickets. SBMA, on behalf of those who park in the neighborhood, appeared in municipal court to contest the charges, seeking class action status for all persons parked in Shockoe Bottom after 5 P.M. on May 16, 2017.

The SBMA argued that the violators were engaged in a mass protest of the city's outrageous and unfair new parking regulations in the neighborhood. The organization further argued that the enforcement effort was a viewpoint- and content-based effort to retaliate against persons who opposed the new parking rules. The city attorney, in formal filings, argued that the City of Richmond was simply attempting to enforce its entirely lawful parking regulations and that the citations should stand.

You sit as the municipal judge assigned to hear the contested parking tickets. How should you rule on the First Amendment defense to the citations?

CHAPTER
6

Compelled Speech
and Anonymous Speech

TABLE OF CONTENTS

A corollary of the First Amendment's right to speak is the right *not* to speak. The right not to speak encompasses a right to keep one's ideas to oneself and a right not to be compelled to voice the ideas of another. More controversially, the right not to speak may encompass a right not to pay for speech with which one disagrees. These negative rights flow from the First Amendment's concern with the protection of the autonomy and privacy of speakers. A speaker must be allowed to choose both whether to speak at all and what to say once she chooses to speak. Closely related to the right not to speak is the right to speak anonymously: the Supreme Court has recognized that, in some contexts, a speaker's identity is a component of her message that she may choose to include or omit at her option. The cases in this chapter demonstrate, however, that both the right not to speak and the right to speak anonymously are qualified rather than absolute rights.

A. THE RIGHT NOT TO SPEAK

World War II forms the historical backdrop to the opinion below, which was decided in 1943 and addressed the constitutionality of a West Virginia law requiring schoolchildren to "salute the flag" on a regular basis. The case below overturned a 1940 Supreme Court decision on the same subject.

WEST VIRGINIA STATE BOARD OF EDUCATION v. BARNETTE

319 U.S. 624 (1943)

Mr. Justice JACKSON delivered the opinion of the Court.

. . .

[On January 9, 1942, the West Virginia State Board of Education adopted a resolution requiring all students and teachers to participate on a regular basis in saluting the flag and reciting the Pledge of Allegiance. Appellees sought an injunction in district court to restrain enforcement against Jehovah's Witnesses.] The Witnesses are an unincorporated body teaching that the obligation imposed by law of God is superior to that of laws enacted by temporal government. Their religious beliefs include a literal version of Exodus, Chapter 20, verses 4 and 5, which says: "Thou shalt not make unto thee any graven image, or any likeness of anything that is in heaven above, or that is in the earth beneath, or that is in the water under the earth; thou shalt not bow down thyself to them nor serve them." They consider that the flag is an "image" within this command. For this reason they refuse to salute it.

Children of this faith have been expelled from school and are threatened with exclusion for no other cause. Officials threaten to send them to reformatories maintained for criminally inclined juveniles. Parents of such children have been prosecuted and are threatened with prosecutions for causing delinquency.

[The School Board moved to dismiss, and three judges of the District Court decided the case on the pleadings, restraining enforcement as to Jehovah's Witnesses. The Board appealed directly to the Supreme Court.]

. . .

The freedom asserted by these appellees does not bring them into collision with rights asserted by any other individual. It is such conflicts which most frequently require intervention of the State to determine where the rights of one end and those of another begin. But the refusal of these persons to participate in the ceremony does not interfere with or deny rights of others to do so. Nor is there any question in this case that their behavior is peaceable and orderly. The sole conflict is between authority and rights of the individual. The State asserts power to condition access to public education on making a prescribed sign and profession and at the same time to coerce attendance by punishing both parent and child. The latter stand on a right of self-determination in matters that touch individual opinion and personal attitude.

As the present Chief Justice said in dissent in the [*Minersville School District v.*] *Gobitis* case, the State may "require teaching by instruction and study of all in our history and in the structure and organization of our government, including the guaranties of civil liberty which tend to inspire patriotism and love of country." 310 U.S. at 604. Here, however, we are dealing with a compulsion of students to declare a belief. They are not merely made acquainted with the flag salute so that they may be informed as to what it is or even what it means. The issue here is whether this slow and easily neglected route to aroused loyalties constitutionally may be short-cut by substituting a compulsory salute and slogan. . . .

There is no doubt that, in connection with the pledges, the flag salute is a form of utterance. Symbolism is a primitive but effective way of communicating ideas. The use of an emblem or flag to symbolize some system, idea, institution, or personality, is a short cut from mind to mind. Causes and nations, political parties, lodges and ecclesiastical groups seek to knit the loyalty of their followings to a flag or banner, a color or design. . . . Associated with many of these symbols are appropriate gestures of acceptance or respect: a salute, a bowed or bared head, a bended knee. A person gets from a symbol the meaning he puts into it, and what is one man's comfort and inspiration is another's jest and scorn.

. . . Here it is the State that employs a flag as a symbol of adherence to government as presently organized. It requires the individual to communicate by word and sign his acceptance of the political ideas it thus bespeaks. Objection to this form of communication when coerced is an old one, well known to the framers of the Bill of Rights.

It is also to be noted that the compulsory flag salute and pledge requires affirmation of a belief and an attitude of mind. It is not clear whether the regulation contemplates that pupils forego any contrary convictions of their own and become unwilling converts to the prescribed ceremony or whether it will be acceptable if they simulate assent by words without belief and by a gesture barren of meaning. It is now a commonplace that censorship or suppression of expression of opinion is tolerated by our Constitution only when the expression presents a clear and present danger of action of a kind the State is empowered to prevent and punish. It would seem that involuntary affirmation could be commanded only on even more immediate and urgent grounds than silence. But here the power of compulsion is invoked without any allegation that remaining passive during a flag salute ritual creates a clear and present danger that would justify an effort even to muffle expression. To sustain the compulsory flag salute we are required to say that a Bill of Rights which guards the individual's right to speak his own mind, left it open to public authorities to compel him to utter what is not in his mind.

Whether the First Amendment to the Constitution will permit officials to order observance of ritual of this nature does not depend upon whether as a voluntary exercise we would think it to be good, bad or merely innocuous. Any credo of nationalism is likely to include what some disapprove or to omit what others think essential, and to give off different overtones as it takes on different accents or interpretations. If official power exists to coerce acceptance of any patriotic creed, what it shall contain cannot be decided by courts, but must be largely discretionary with the ordaining authority, whose power to prescribe would no doubt include power to amend.

. . . Free public education, if faithful to the ideal of secular instruction and political neutrality, will not be partisan or enemy of any class, creed, party, or faction. . . .

The Fourteenth Amendment, as now applied to the States, protects the citizen against the State itself and all of its creatures—Boards of Education not excepted. These have, of course, important, delicate, and highly discretionary functions, but none that they may not perform within the limits of the Bill of Rights. That they are educating the young for citizenship is reason for scrupulous protection of Constitutional freedoms of the individual, if we are not to strangle the free mind at its source and teach youth to discount important principles of our government as mere platitudes.

. . . The very purpose of a Bill of Rights was to withdraw certain subjects from the vicissitudes of political controversy, to place them beyond the reach of majorities and officials and to establish them as legal principles to be applied by the courts. One's right to life, liberty, and property, to free speech, a free press, freedom of worship and assembly, and other fundamental rights may not be submitted to vote; they depend on the outcome of no elections.

. . . . National unity as an end which officials may foster by persuasion and example is not in question. The problem is whether under our Constitution compulsion as here employed is a permissible means for its achievement.

Struggles to coerce uniformity of sentiment in support of some end thought essential to their time and country have been waged by many good as well as by evil men. Nationalism is a relatively recent phenomenon but at other times and places the ends have been racial or territorial security, support of a dynasty or regime, and particular plans for saving souls. As first and moderate methods to attain unity have failed, those bent on its accomplishment must resort to an ever-increasing severity. As governmental pressure toward unity becomes greater, so strife becomes more bitter as to whose unity it shall be. Probably no deeper division of our people could proceed from any provocation than from finding it necessary to choose what doctrine and whose program public educational officials shall compel youth to unite in embracing. Ultimate futility of such attempts to compel coherence is the lesson of every such effort from the Roman drive to stamp out Christianity as a disturber of its pagan unity, the Inquisition, as a means to religious and dynastic unity, the Siberian exiles as a means to Russian unity, down to the fast failing efforts of our present totalitarian enemies. Those who begin coercive elimination of dissent soon find themselves exterminating dissenters. Compulsory unification of opinion achieves only the unanimity of the graveyard.

It seems trite but necessary to say that the First Amendment to our Constitution was designed to avoid these ends by avoiding these beginnings. There is no mysticism in the American concept of the State or of the nature or origin of its authority. We set up government by consent of the governed, and the Bill of Rights denies those in power any legal opportunity to coerce that consent. Authority here is to be controlled by public opinion, not public opinion by authority.

The case is made difficult not because the principles of its decision are obscure but because the flag involved is our own. Nevertheless, we apply the limitations of the Constitution with no fear that freedom to be intellectually and spiritually diverse or even contrary will disintegrate the social organization. To believe that patriotism will not flourish if patriotic ceremonies are voluntary and spontaneous instead of a compulsory routine is to make an unflattering estimate of the appeal of our institutions to free minds. We can have intellectual individualism and the rich cultural diversities that we owe to exceptional minds only at the price of occasional eccentricity and abnormal attitudes. When they are so harmless to others or to the State as those we deal with here, the price is not too great. But freedom to differ is not limited to things that do not matter much. That would be a mere shadow of freedom. The test of its substance is the right to differ as to things that touch the heart of the existing order.

If there is any fixed star in our constitutional constellation, it is that no official, high or petty, can prescribe what shall be orthodox in politics, nationalism, religion, or other matters of opinion or force citizens to confess by word or act their faith therein. If there are any circumstances which permit an exception, they do not now occur to us.

We think the action of the local authorities in compelling the flag salute and pledge transcends constitutional limitations on their power and invades the sphere of intellect and spirit which it is the purpose of the First Amendment to our Constitution to reserve from all official control. [Affirming injunction against enforcement of the West Virginia Regulation.]

[Justice ROBERTS'S and Justice REED'S dissenting opinion is omitted.]

Justice BLACK and Justice DOUGLAS, concurring.

. . . Words uttered under coercion are proof of loyalty to nothing but self-interest. Love of country must spring from willing hearts and free minds, inspired by a fair administration of wise laws enacted by the people's elected representatives within the bounds of express constitutional prohibitions. These laws must, to be consistent with the First Amendment, permit the widest toleration of conflicting viewpoints consistent with a society of free men.

Neither our domestic tranquility in peace nor our martial effort in war depend on compelling little children to participate in a ceremony which ends in nothing for them but a fear of spiritual condemnation. If, as we think, their fears are groundless, time and reason are the proper antidotes for their errors. The ceremonial, when enforced against conscientious objectors, more likely to defeat than to serve its high purpose, is a handy implement for disguised religious persecution. As such, it is inconsistent with our Constitution's plan and purpose.

[Justice MURPHY'S concurring opinion is omitted.]

Justice FRANKFURTER, dissenting.

One who belongs to the most vilified and persecuted minority in history is not likely to be insensible to the freedoms guaranteed by our Constitution. Were my purely personal attitude relevant I should whole-heartedly associate myself with the general libertarian views in the Court's opinion, representing as they do the thought and action of a lifetime. But as judges we are neither Jew nor Gentile, neither Catholic nor agnostic. We owe equal attachment to the Constitution and are equally bound by our judicial obligations whether we derive our citizenship from the earliest or the latest immigrants to these shores. As a member of this Court I am not justified in writing my private notions of policy into the Constitution, no matter how deeply I may cherish them or how mischievous I may deem their disregard. . . .

. . . Saluting the flag suppresses no belief nor curbs it. Children and their parents may believe what they please, avow their belief and practice it. It is not even remotely suggested that the requirement for saluting the flag involves the slightest restriction against the fullest opportunity on the part both of the children and of their parents to disavow as publicly as they choose to do so the meaning that others attach to the gesture of salute. All channels of affirmative free expression are open to both children and parents. Had we before us any act of the state putting the slightest curbs upon such free expression, I should not lag behind any member of this Court in striking down such an invasion of the right to freedom of thought and freedom of speech protected by the Constitution.

NOTES AND QUESTIONS

1. *Identifying the harm.* In what manner are the children and their parents harmed by being forced to pledge allegiance to the flag? Is forcing children to salute the flag different from forcing them to take exams in which they must explain the theory of evolution rather than "intelligent design"?

2. *Is* Barnette *limited to its facts?* Is the fact that the children and their parents were subject to such severe sanctions for refusing to salute the flag a significant factor

in the decision? Would this case have come out differently if the objections to the pledge had stemmed from political rather than religious beliefs? Would this case have come out differently if a teacher had objected to being forced to lead the pledge of allegiance as part of her job responsibilities?

3. *The anti-orthodoxy principle.* Professor Jed Rubenfeld contends that the autonomy-based interest identified by Justice Robert Jackson in *Barnette*—the "anti-orthodoxy principle"—is the bedrock of the First Amendment. Rubenfeld observes that this principle is "absolutely incompatible with cost-benefit, balancing approaches to the First Amendment." Professor Rubenfeld concedes, however, that the anti-orthodoxy principle does not apply in all circumstances: "There is a kind of orthodoxy that government can and does enforce every day, even in the sense of prescribing what people must and must not say. I refer to the orthodoxy of true and false facts." *See* Jed Rubenfeld, *The First Amendment's Purpose,* 53 Stan. L. Rev. 767, 818-821 (2001). Is Rubenfeld correct that the government can always punish lies, even when those lies do no harm? What are the limits of the anti-orthodoxy principle? Does it only apply to "core" speech, such as political or religious speech?

AN EXTENDED NOTE REGARDING WOOLEY v. MAYNARD ("LIVE FREE OR DIE")

Wooley v. Maynard, 430 U.S. 705 (1977), involved a challenge by a Jehovah's Witness to a New Hampshire law prohibiting defacement of its "Live Free or Die" license plate, but *Wooley* was ultimately framed and decided by the Supreme Court as a compelled-speech case governed by the principle enunciated in *Barnette.* Chief Justice Burger, writing for the majority, explained:

> We begin with the proposition that the right of freedom of thought protected by the First Amendment against state action includes both the right to speak freely and the right to refrain from speaking at all. See Barnette. A system which secures the right to proselytize religious, political, and ideological causes must also guarantee the concomitant right to decline to foster such concepts. The right to speak and the right to refrain from speaking are complementary components of the broader concept of "individual freedom of mind." . . .
>
> . . . Here, as in Barnette, we are faced with a state measure which forces an individual, as part of his daily life—indeed constantly while his automobile is in public view—to be an instrument for fostering public adherence to an ideological point of view he finds unacceptable. In doing so, the State "invades the sphere of intellect and spirit which it is the purpose of the First Amendment to our Constitution to reserve from all official control."
>
> New Hampshire's statute in effect requires that appellees use their private property as a "mobile billboard" for the State's ideological message or suffer a penalty, as Maynard already has. As a condition to driving an automobile, a virtual necessity for most Americans, the Maynards must display "Live Free or Die" to hundreds of people each day. The fact that most individuals agree with the thrust of New Hampshire's motto is not the test; most Americans also find the flag salute acceptable. The First Amendment protects the right of individuals to hold a point of view different from the majority and to refuse to foster, in the way New Hampshire commands, an idea they find morally objectionable.

430 U.S. at 714-715.

The *Wooley* Court, however, did not consider this the end of the inquiry but instead went on to consider whether "the State's countervailing interest [was] sufficiently compelling to justify requiring appellees to display the state motto on their license plates" [citing United States v. O'Brien, 391 U.S. 367, 376-377 (1968)]. The Court held that the State interest underlying the defacement statute failed to outweigh the First Amendment interests of the Jehovah's Witness who did not wish to display the motto. The Court determined that the state's interest in vehicle identification could be achieved by "less drastic means" and that its interest in inculcating state pride was "not ideologically neutral." The Court explained that "where the State's interest is to disseminate an ideology, no matter how acceptable to some, such interest cannot outweigh an individual's First Amendment right to avoid becoming the courier for such message."

Is *Barnette* distinguishable from *Wooley*? Were other citizens likely to assume Mr. Maynard endorsed the state motto simply because it was on his license plate? What if the state motto were "Capitalism Sucks"? What if the state allowed a choice of several different license plates, including one that bore the words "Choose Life"? Would providing that option violate the First Amendment rights of citizens who hold "pro-choice" views?

B. THE RIGHT NOT TO PUBLISH
THE SPEECH OF OTHERS

The cases in this section present a slightly different issue than *Barnette* or *Wooley*, *supra*. Here, the government attempts to give one speaker a right of access to a publication owned and controlled by another speaker, typically asserting that access will foster desirable diversity in the marketplace of ideas. These cases pit the rights of one speaker against those of another speaker (and even of the public) in ways that *Barnette* and *Wooley* do not.

In examining the first case in this section, *Miami Herald v. Tornillo, infra*, it is important to be familiar with a particular strain of criticism of the marketplace of ideas as a First Amendment ideal. Certain critics contend that the concentration of mass media ownership has destroyed whatever marketplace of ideas might have existed when the First Amendment was adopted in 1791, and thus governmental intervention is necessary to bring marginalized voices back into the marketplace. One notable proponent of this view is Professor Jerome A. Barron, who contends that because the media themselves act as censors, effectively blocking public access to new and unpopular ideas, the government must provide access to mass media for ordinary citizens: "At the very minimum," Barron writes, "the creation of two remedies is essential—(1) a nondiscriminating right to purchase editorial advertisements in daily newspapers, and (2) a right of reply for public figures and public officers defamed in newspapers." Jerome A. Barron, *Freedom of the Press for Whom?* 6 (1973); *see also* Jerome A. Barron, *Access to the Press—A New First Amendment Right*, 80 Harv. L. Rev. 1641 (1967); Owen M. Fiss, *Why the State?*, 100 Harv. L. Rev. 781, 787-788 (1987) ("The state must put on the agenda issues that are systematically ignored and slighted and allow us to hear voices and viewpoints that would otherwise be silenced or muffled.").

Professor Barron had a chance to advocate his views in the Supreme Court. He represented Pat Tornillo, the litigant seeking access to the press, in the case that follows. As you read, consider whether *Miami Herald v. Tornillo* is a "right not to speak" case.

MIAMI HERALD v. TORNILLO

418 U.S. 241 (1974)

Mr. Chief Justice BURGER delivered the opinion of the Court.

The issue in this case is whether a state statute granting a political candidate a right to equal space to reply to criticism and attacks on his record by a newspaper, violates the guarantees of a free press.

I.

In the fall of 1972, appellee, Executive Director of the Classroom Teachers Association, apparently a teachers' collective-bargaining agent, was a candidate for the Florida House of Representatives. On September 20, 1972, and again on September 29, 1972, appellant printed editorials critical of appellee's candidacy. In response to these editorials appellee demanded that appellant print verbatim his replies, defending the role of the Classroom Teachers Association and the organization's accomplishments for the citizens of Dade County. Appellant declined to print the appellee's replies, and appellee brought suit in Circuit Court, Dade County, seeking declaratory and injunctive relief and actual and punitive damages in excess of $5,000. The action was premised on Florida Statute § 104.38 (1973), a "right of reply" statute. . . . [2]

[Appellant sought a declaratory judgment, and the Circuit Court held the right-of-reply section unconstitutional. The Florida Supreme Court reversed, holding that the statute furthered the "broad societal interest in the free flow of information to the public," and that it was not impermissibly vague. The court narrowed the statute by construing it to require "any reply" to be "wholly responsive to the charge made" and "neither libelous nor slanderous of the publication nor anyone else, nor vulgar nor profane." The case was remanded for further proceedings.]

---

[2] "104.38 *Newspaper Assailing Candidate in an Election; Space for Reply.* If any newspaper in its columns assails the personal character of any candidate for nomination or for election in any election, or charges said candidate with malfeasance or misfeasance in office, or otherwise attacks his official record, or gives to another free space for such purpose, such newspaper shall upon request of such candidate immediately publish free of cost any reply he may make thereto in as conspicuous a place and in the same kind of type as the matter that calls for such reply, provided such reply does not take up more space than the matter replied to. Any person or firm failing to comply with the provisions of this section shall be guilty of a misdemeanor of the first degree, punishable as provided in § 775.082 or § 775.083."[eft]

III.

[A.] The challenged statute creates a right to reply to press criticism of a candidate for nomination or election. The statute was enacted in 1913, and this is only the second recorded case decided under its provisions.

Appellant contends the statute is void on its face because it purports to regulate the content of a newspaper in violation of the First Amendment. Alternatively it is urged that the statute is void for vagueness since no editor could know exactly what words would call the statute into operation. It is also contended that the statute fails to distinguish between critical comment which is and which is not defamatory.

[B.][The Court summarized virtually every argument made by proponents of access to the media. The Court noted that access advocates argued that in 1791 "[a] true marketplace of ideas existed in which there was relatively easy access to the channels of communication." By 1973, however, concentration of ownership in the media industry, the "elimination of competing newspapers in most of our large cities," and other technological and economic developments had "place[d] in a few hands the power to inform the American people and shape public opinion." The increasing power and influence of the media had also deprived the public of meaningful participation in public debate. The Court further noted that access advocates had "urged that the claim of newspapers to be 'surrogates for the public' carries with it a concomitant fiduciary obligation to account for that stewardship." The only way to enforce such an obligation, however, would be "for government to take affirmative action."]

IV.

However much validity may be found in these arguments, at each point the implementation of a remedy such as an enforceable right of access necessarily calls for some mechanism, either governmental or consensual. If it is governmental coercion, this at once brings about a confrontation with the express provisions of the First Amendment and the judicial gloss on that Amendment developed over the years.

The Court foresaw the problems relating to government-enforced access as early as its decision in Associated Press v. United States. There it carefully contrasted the private "compulsion to print" called for by the Association's bylaws with the provisions of the District Court decree against appellants which "does not compel AP or its members to permit publication of anything which their 'reason' tells them should not be published." 326 U.S. [1, 20 n.18 (1945)]. In Branzburg v. Hayes, 408 U.S. 665, 681 (1972), we emphasized that the cases then before us "involve no intrusions upon speech or assembly, no prior restraint or restriction on what the press may publish, and no express or implied command that the press publish what it prefers to withhold." In Columbia Broadcasting System, Inc. v. Democratic National Committee, 412 U.S. 94, 117 (1973), the plurality opinion as to Part III noted:

> The power of a privately owned newspaper to advance its own political, social, and economic views is bounded by only two factors: first, the acceptance of a sufficient number of readers—and hence advertisers—to assure financial success; and, second, the journalistic integrity of its editors and publishers.

An attitude strongly adverse to any attempt to extend a right of access to newspapers was echoed by several Members of this Court in their separate opinions in that case. . . . [In a recent dissent,] Mr. Justice Stewart, joined by Mr. Justice Douglas, expressed the view that no "government agency—local, state, or federal—can tell a newspaper in advance what it can print and what it cannot."

We see that beginning with *Associated Press* the Court has expressed sensitivity as to whether a restriction or requirement constituted the compulsion exerted by government on a newspaper to print that which it would not otherwise print. The clear implication has been that any such a compulsion to publish that which "'reason' tells them should not be published" is unconstitutional. A responsible press is an undoubtedly desirable goal, but press responsibility is not mandated by the Constitution and like many other virtues it cannot be legislated.

Appellee's argument that the Florida statute does not amount to a restriction of appellant's right to speak because "the statute in question here has not prevented the Miami Herald from saying anything it wished" begs the core question. Compelling editors or publishers to publish that which "'reason' tells them should not be published" is what is at issue in this case. The Florida statute operates as a command in the same sense as a statute or regulation forbidding appellant to publish specified matter. Governmental restraint on publishing need not fall into familiar or traditional patterns to be subject to constitutional limitations on governmental powers. Grosjean v. American Press Co., 297 U.S. 233, 244-45 (1936). The Florida statute exacts a penalty on the basis of the content of a newspaper. The first phase of the penalty resulting from the compelled printing of a reply is exacted in terms of the cost in printing and composing time and materials and in taking up space that could be devoted to other material the newspaper may have preferred to print. It is correct, as appellee contends, that a newspaper is not subject to the finite technological limitations of time that confront a broadcaster but it is not correct to say that, as an economic reality, a newspaper can proceed to infinite expansion of its column space to accommodate the replies that a government agency determines or a statute commands the readers should have available.

Faced with the penalties that would accrue to any newspaper that published news or commentary arguably within the reach of the right-of-access statute, editors might well conclude that the safe course is to avoid controversy. Therefore, under the operation of the Florida statute, political and electoral coverage would be blunted or reduced. Government-enforced right of access inescapably "dampens the vigor and limits the variety of public debate," New York Times Co. v. Sullivan, supra, 376 U.S. at 279. The Court, in Mills v. Alabama, 384 U.S. 214, 218 (1966) stated that

> There is practically universal agreement that a major purpose of [the First] Amendment was to protect the free discussion of governmental affairs. This of course includes discussions of candidates. . . .

Even if a newspaper would face no additional costs to comply with a compulsory access law and would not be forced to forgo publication of news or opinion by the inclusion of a reply, the Florida statute fails to clear the barriers of the First Amendment because of its intrusion into the function of editors. A newspaper is more than a passive receptacle or conduit for news, comment, and advertising. The choice of material to go into a newspaper, and the decisions made as to limitations on the size and content of the paper, and treatment of public issues and public officials—whether fair or unfair—constitute the exercise of editorial control and judgment. It has yet to be demonstrated how governmental regulation of this crucial process can be exercised consistent with First Amendment guarantees of a free press as they have evolved to this time. Accordingly, the judgment of the Supreme Court of Florida is *Reversed.*

[Justices BRENNAN'S and REHNQUIST'S concurrence is omitted.]

Mr. Justice WHITE, concurring.

. . . A newspaper or magazine is not a public utility subject to "reasonable" governmental regulation in matters affecting the exercise of journalistic judgment as to what shall be printed. . . . We have learned, and continue to learn, from what we view as the unhappy experiences of other nations where government has been allowed to meddle in the internal editorial affairs of newspapers. Regardless of how beneficent-sounding the purposes of controlling the press might be, we prefer "the power of reason as applied through public discussion"—and remain intensely skeptical about those measures that would allow government to insinuate itself into the editorial rooms of this Nation's press.

. . . [T]his law runs afoul of the elementary First Amendment proposition that government may not force a newspaper to print copy which, in its journalistic discretion, it chooses to leave on the newsroom floor. . . .

NOTES AND QUESTIONS

1. *Basis of decision.* In what way does the right-of-reply statute "penalize" newspapers? Is the right-of-reply statute's interference with "the exercise of editorial control and judgment" an independent ground of decision? Could a newspaper be compelled to allow a candidate to purchase advertising at the prevailing rate to respond to an editorial "attack"?
2. *New media and right-of-reply statutes.* The internet gives millions of citizens, most of whom have no journalism training, access to a mass medium to publish their opinions, complaints, and harsh and sometimes defamatory criticisms of their fellow citizens. Would a right-of-reply statute directed at Web sites, blogs, or social media sites such as Facebook be unconstitutional?
3. *Right of access in other media.* The Supreme Court in *Tornillo* stressed that a newspaper is private property. Broadcasters may not use the airwaves without receiving a license from the government. Does the fact that the public in essence "owns the airwaves" mean that government regulators can compel the broadcast media—radio and television—to grant a right of reply to candidates or others criticized on the airwaves? Perhaps surprisingly, the answer is yes, for reasons you will see in Chapter 8, *infra. See* Red Lion Broad. Co. v. FCC, 395 U.S. 367 (1969).
4. *Is the election context special?* Is the argument for a right of reply stronger or weaker when it is limited to a pending election? Professor Cass Sunstein, who questions the outcome or at least the rationale in *Tornillo*, suggests that the Court may have suspected that the "special problem with [the statute] was that it was limited to candidates for office," which gave the Court reason "to suspect that the law was an effort by political candidates to insulate themselves from attack." Cass R. Sunstein, *Democracy and the Problem of Free Speech* 271 n.20 (1993).

Might incumbents reasonably think that they would benefit more from this type of statute than would challengers?

5. *Free press versus free speech?* Why isn't *Tornillo* clearly governed by *Barnette*? Is this a case that pits the First Amendment rights of the press against the rights of an individual speaker? Why do the First Amendment rights of the *Miami Herald* trump those of Pat Tornillo?

AN EXTENDED NOTE ON THE PACIFIC GAS & ELECTRIC CO. CASE

Pacific Gas & Electric. In Pacific Gas & Electric Co. v. Public Utilities Comm'n of California, 475 U.S. 1 (1986), the Supreme Court addressed the issue whether the state could compel a corporate speaker to "carry" the speech of a third party in its "newsletter," which consisted of information printed in the "extra space" in its billing statement. The corporate speaker in the case was a private utility company, PG&E, operating in a highly regulated environment. The third party who sought access to the public via the newsletter was a consumer group advocating utility rate normalization. California's Public Utility Commission had ordered PG&E to set aside some of the "extra space" in its billing envelope for use by the consumer group, reasoning that the "extra space" was the property of utility ratepayers and that ratepayers would "benefit more from exposure to a variety of views than they [would] from only that of PG&E."

In a plurality opinion by Justice Lewis Powell, the Court held that PG&E could not be forced to include speech with which it disagreed in its billing envelope. The plurality concluded that the compelled access provided by the order was both content-based and viewpoint-based, since the only groups that would be granted access would be those whose views on utility rates differed from PG&E's. Moreover, the order imposed an impermissible burden on PG&E's speech, since it might avoid speaking at all in order to avoid having to include the speech of its opponents in its newsletter. The order also compromised PG&E's "right to be free from government restrictions that abridge its own rights in order to 'enhance the relative voice' of its opponents. *Buckley v. Valeo*, 424 U.S. 1, 49 and n.55 (1976)."

Key to the plurality's opinion was its recognition that corporations, like individuals, may make valuable contributions to First Amendment discussion and debate:

> For corporations as for individuals, the choice to speak includes within it the choice of what not to say. And we have held that speech does not lose its protection because of the corporate identity of the speaker. Were the government freely able to compel corporate speakers to propound political messages with which they disagree, this protection would be empty, for the government could require speakers to affirm in one breath that which they deny in the next. . . . The danger that appellant will be required to alter its own message as a consequence of the government's coercive action is a proper object of First Amendment solicitude, because the message itself is protected. . . . Where, as in this case, the danger is one that arises from a content-based grant of access to private property, it is a danger that the government may not impose absent a compelling interest.

The plurality concluded that the Commission's order could not satisfy strict scrutiny. The State's interest in "fair and effective utility regulation" and specifically in "effective ratemaking proceedings" "may be compelling," but the State could not serve the interest by forcing PG&E to carry the speech of its opponents.

The plurality also found that the States interest "in promoting speech by making a variety of views available to [PG&E's] customers." However, the plurality found

> that this interest is not furthered by an order that is not content neutral. Moreover, the means chosen to advance variety tend to inhibit expression of appellant's views in order to promote [its opponents]. Our cases establish that the State cannot advance some points of view by burdening the expression of others. It follows that the Commission's order is not a narrowly tailored means of furthering this interest.
>
>   . . .
>
> We conclude that the Commission's order impermissibly burdens appellant's First Amendment rights because it forces appellant to associate with the views of other speakers, and because it selects the other speakers on the basis of their viewpoints. The order is not a narrowly tailored means of furthering a compelling state interest, and it is not a valid time, place, or manner regulation. [Vacated and remanded.]

Justice MARSHALL concurred in the judgment.

Justices REHNQUIST, WHITE and STEVENS dissented, distinguishing *Tornillo* on the grounds that the access granted in *PG&E* would not chill the utility's future speech, since it "cannot prevent the access by remaining silent or avoiding discussion of controversial subjects." The dissent identified the "more fundamental flaw" in the plurality decision as follows:

> [N]atural persons enjoy negative free speech rights because of their interest in self-expression; an individual's right not to speak or to associate with the speech of others is a component of the broader constitutional interest of natural persons in freedom of conscience. . . . Extension of the individual freedom of conscience decisions to business corporations strains the rationale of [our prior] cases beyond the breaking point. To ascribe to such artificial entities an "intellect" or "mind" for freedom of conscience purposes is to confuse metaphor with reality. Corporations generally have not played the historic role of newspapers as conveyers of individual ideas and opinion. . . .
>
>   . . . The right of access here constitutes an effort to facilitate and enlarge public discussion; it therefore furthers rather than abridges First Amendment values. Likewise, because the interest on which the constitutional protection of corporate speech rests is the societal interest in receiving information and ideas, the constitutional interest of a corporation in not permitting the presentation of other distinct views clearly identified as those of the speaker is de minimis. This is especially true in the case of PG&E, which is after all a regulated public utility. Any claim it may have had to a sphere of corporate autonomy was largely surrendered to extensive regulatory authority when it was granted legal monopoly status.

NOTES AND QUESTIONS

1. *Commercial speech and corporate speech.* As you will see in the following chapter, commercial speech receives fewer First Amendment protections than political speech. Commercial speech regulations typically are subject to

intermediate rather than strict constitutional scrutiny. *See* Central Hudson Gas & Elec. Corp. v. Public Service Comm'n, 447 U.S. 557 (1980) (holding that regulations of truthful and nonmisleading commercial speech are subject to intermediate scrutiny). In Zauderer v. Office of Disciplinary Counsel, 471 U.S. 626 (1985), the Supreme Court upheld compelled disclosures in commercial speech because they were "reasonably related to the State's interest in preventing deception to consumers," but indicated that "unjustified or unduly burdensome" disclosure requirements might be unconstitutional. *See also* Milavetz, Gallop & Milavetz v. U.S., 559 U.S. 229 (2010) (upholding disclosure requirement in a commercial speech case); Spirit Airlines v. U.S. Dep't of Transportation, 687 F.3d 403 (D.C. Cir. 2012), cert. denied, 133 S. Ct. 1723 (2013) (upholding a Department of Transportation rule that requires that the most prominent ticket price displayed on advertisements be the total price of tickets, including tax). Why doesn't the Court treat the PG&E case as involving a regulation of commercial speech? Why isn't all corporate speech inherently commercial speech, and therefore subject to (at most) intermediate scrutiny? Even if there are instrumental reasons for protecting corporate speech, why protect PG&E's speech in this case? Would the interest of the public in receiving information from a multiplicity of sources be better served by upholding the Commission decision?

2. *The basis for decision.* The plurality and the dissenters did not agree on the rationale for the decision in this case. The dissenters relied on PruneYard Shopping Center v. Robins, 447 U.S. 74 (1980), as the key precedent underpinning their decision. *PruneYard* held that California could constitutionally mandate the owner of a private shopping center to allow certain speakers access to its property, since allowing access did not constitute an "endorsement" of the message of the individual (as opposed to government) speakers, and the shopping center owner could in fact easily disavow agreement with the message of the speakers. The plurality opinion in this case, on the other hand, relied predominantly on *Tornillo* and *Wooley, supra.* What is the difference between the principle enunciated by *PruneYard* on the one hand and the principles in *Tornillo* and *Wooley* on the other? Why do you think Justice Marshall did not join the plurality opinion but concurred separately to stress that *PruneYard* provides an additional basis for the judgment in the case?

3. *Private property and First Amendment rights.* Whether something is or is not private property is largely a question of state law. Why should an individual's (or corporation's) First Amendment rights hinge so fundamentally on whether the speech takes place on private property or public property?

4. *Viewpoint neutrality and right of access.* PG&E operates under a state-granted monopoly, and it used its newsletter to foist its views on a captive audience of eight million utility consumers. One of the state's objectives in granting TURN a "right of access" to the "extra space" in the PG&E envelopes was to ensure that these consumers received information from a variety of viewpoints rather than just one. Is it possible to achieve this objective in a viewpoint-neutral fashion?

5. *Content-neutral compelled speech.* What if the state compels speech in a content-neutral manner? In Turner Broadcasting System, Inc. v. FCC, 512 U.S. 6222 (1994) (*Turner I*), the Court addressed the constitutionality of a federal statute requiring cable operators to carry the signals of over-the-air broadcasters; in essence, the law compelled cable operators to "carry" or subsidize the speech

of their broadcast competitors. The Court held that because the statute was not content-based, it should be subject only to intermediate scrutiny. The Court upheld the law in Turner Broadcasting System, Inc. v. FCC, 520 U.S. 180 (1997). For more on these cases, see Chapter 8, *infra*, p. 460.

6. *Physicians' speech and the right to know.* In Stuart v. Camnitz, 774 F.3d 238 (4th Cir. 2014), the Fourth Circuit struck down a portion of the North Carolina Woman's Right to Know Act, which required abortion doctors to perform an ultrasound and display the resulting sonogram while describing the image in real time to women seeking abortions. However, the Fifth and Eighth Circuits have upheld similar rules. Tex. Med. Providers Performing Abortion Servs. v. Lakey, 667 F.3d 570 (5th Cir. 2012); Planned Parenthood Minn., N.D., S.D. v. Rounds, 686 F.3d 889 (8th Cir. 2012). This circuit split is bound to cause confusion in other circuits where similar laws have been passed. Should courts see these as impermissible compelled speech rules, or as rules that advance a woman's right to know "truthful, non-misleading information relevant to [her] decision"?

C. THE RIGHT NOT TO PAY FOR THE SPEECH OF OTHERS

Thomas Jefferson once wrote: "To compel a man to subsidize with his taxes the propagation of ideas which he disbelieves and abhors is sinful and tyrannical." (Opening passage to the Virginia Statute for Religious Freedom (1786)). But is it also unconstitutional?

Many compelled speech cases in recent years have involved public-sector unions. Once a union is chosen by a majority of employees, the union collectively bargains with the employer on behalf of all employees over wages, benefits, and working conditions; unions also typically engage in lobbying and electioneering as well. But what about employees who did not vote for the union? They get the benefit of the union's collective bargaining on behalf of all employees even if they did not vote in favor of the union. Ordinarily, a union can charge even employees who do not support the union agency fees for the representation of their interests in collective bargaining, but may these dissenting employees also be forced to support the union's political advocacy? Must the union ask employees to "opt in" to support its political advocacy, or must it only give dissenting employees a right to opt out? These issues arise in the case below.

KNOX v. SERVICE EMPLOYEES INTERNATIONAL UNION, LOCAL 1000
132 S. Ct. 2277 (2012)

Mr. Justice ALITO delivered the opinion of the Court.

In this case, we decide whether the First Amendment allows a public-sector union to require objecting nonmembers to pay a special fee for the purpose of financing the union's political and ideological activities.

Under California law, public-sector employees in a bargaining unit may decide by majority vote to create an "agency shop" arrangement under which all the employees are represented by a union selected by the majority. While employees in the unit are not required to join the union, they must nevertheless pay the union an annual fee to cover the cost of union services related to collective bargaining (so-called chargeable expenses).

Our prior cases have recognized that such arrangements represent an "impingement" on the First Amendment rights of nonmembers. [ ] Thus, in *Abood v. Detroit Bd. of Ed.*, 431 U.S. 209 (1977), we held that a public-sector union, while permitted to bill nonmembers for chargeable expenses, may not require nonmembers to fund its political and ideological projects. And in [*Teachers v.*] *Hudson,* we identified procedural requirements that a union must meet in order to collect fees from nonmembers without violating their rights. 475 U.S. 292, 302–311 (1986). The First Amendment, we held, does not permit a public-sector union to adopt procedures that have the effect of requiring objecting nonmembers to lend the union money to be used for political, ideological, and other purposes not germane to collective bargaining. In the interest of administrative convenience, however, we concluded that a union "cannot be faulted" for calculating the fee that nonmembers must pay "on the basis of its expenses during the preceding year."

Hudson concerned a union's regular annual fees. The present case, by contrast, concerns the First Amendment requirements applicable to a special assessment or dues increase that is levied to meet expenses that were not disclosed when the amount of the regular assessment was set.

In June 2005, respondent, the Service Employees International Union, Local 1000 (SEIU), sent out its regular *Hudson* notice informing employees what the agency fee would be for the year ahead. The notice set monthly dues at 1% of an employee's gross monthly salary but capped monthly dues at $45. Based on the most recently audited year, the SEIU estimated that 56.35% of its total expenditures in the coming year would be dedicated to chargeable collective-bargaining activities. Thus, if a nonunion employee objected within 30 days to payment of the full amount of union dues, the objecting employee was required to pay only 56.35% of total dues. The SEIU's notice also [ ] stated that the agency fee was subject to increase at any time without further notice.

During this time, [the governor of California called a special election to consider two ballot propositions that would limit the power of public-sector unions]. The SEIU joined a coalition of public-sector unions in vigorously opposing these measures. . . .

On July 30, shortly after the end of the 30–day objection period for the June *Hudson* notice, the SEIU proposed [and implemented] a temporary 25% increase in employee fees, which it billed as an "Emergency Temporary Assessment to Build a Political Fight–Back Fund" . . . [to] be used "for a broad range of political expenses, including television and radio advertising, direct mail, voter registration, voter education, and get out the vote activities in our work sites and in our communities across California."

On August 31, the SEIU sent out a letter addressed to "Local 1000 Members and Fair Share Fee Payers," announcing that, for a limited period, their fees would be raised to 1.25% of gross monthly salary and the $45–per–month cap on regular dues would not apply. . . .

After receiving this letter, one of the plaintiffs in this case called the SEIU's offices to complain that the union was levying the special assessment for political purposes without giving employees a fair opportunity to object. [A union official explained that] those employees who had filed timely objections after the regular June *Hudson* notice were required to pay only 56.35% of the temporary increase.

Petitioners filed this class-action suit on behalf of 28,000 nonunion employees . . . . The District Court granted summary judgment for the petitioners, finding that the union "fully intended to use the 12 million additional dollars it anticipated to raise for political purposes." . . . A divided panel of the Ninth Circuit reversed. We granted certiorari.

Our cases have often noted the close connection between our Nation's commitment to self-government and the rights protected by the First Amendment. [ ]

The First Amendment creates "an open marketplace" in which differing ideas about political, economic, and social issues can compete freely for public acceptance without improper government interference. [ ] The government may not prohibit the dissemination of ideas that it disfavors, nor compel the endorsement of ideas that it approves. [ ] And the ability of like-minded individuals to associate for the purpose of expressing commonly held views may not be curtailed. See *Roberts v. United States Jaycees*, 468 U.S. 609, 623, 104 S. Ct. 3244 ("Freedom of association . . . plainly presupposes a freedom not to associate"); [ ].

Closely related to compelled speech and compelled association is compelled funding of the speech of other private speakers or groups. In *United States v. United Foods, Inc.*, 533 U.S. 405 (2001), we considered the constitutionality of a state scheme that compelled such funding. The subject of the speech at issue—promoting the sale of mushrooms—was not one that is likely to stir the passions of many, but the mundane commercial nature of that speech only highlights the importance of our analysis and our holding.

The federal Mushroom Promotion, Research, and Consumer Information Act required that fresh mushroom handlers pay assessments used primarily to fund advertisements promoting mushroom sales. A large producer objected to subsidizing these generic ads, and even though we applied the less demanding standard used in prior cases to judge laws affecting commercial speech, we held that the challenged scheme violated the First Amendment. We made it clear that compulsory subsidies for private speech are subject to exacting First Amendment scrutiny and cannot be sustained unless two criteria are met. First, there must be a comprehensive regulatory scheme involving a "mandated association" among those who are required to pay the subsidy. Such situations are exceedingly rare because, as we have stated elsewhere, mandatory associations are permissible only when they serve a "compelling state interes[t] . . . that cannot be achieved through means significantly less restrictive of associational freedoms."   Second, even in the rare case where a mandatory association can be justified, compulsory fees can be levied only insofar as they are a "necessary incident" of the "larger regulatory purpose which justified the required association."

When a State establishes an "agency shop" that exacts compulsory union fees as a condition of public employment, "[t]he dissenting employee is forced to support financially an organization with whose principles and demands he may disagree." Because a public-sector union takes many positions during collective bargaining that have powerful political and civic consequences, the compulsory fees constitute a form of compelled speech and association that imposes a "significant impingement on First Amendment rights." Our cases to date have tolerated this "impingement," and we do not revisit today whether the Court's former cases have given adequate recognition to the critical First Amendment rights at stake.

"The primary purpose" of permitting unions to collect fees from nonmembers, we have said, is "to prevent nonmembers from free-riding on the union's efforts, sharing the employment benefits obtained by the union's collective bargaining without sharing the costs incurred." Such free-rider arguments, however, are generally insufficient to overcome First Amendment objections. [For example, i]f a community association engages in a clean-up campaign or opposes encroachments by industrial development, no one suggests that all residents or property owners who benefit be required to contribute. . . .

Acceptance of the free-rider argument as a justification for compelling nonmembers to pay a portion of union dues represents something of an anomaly—one that we have found to be justified by the interest in furthering "labor peace." *Hudson.* But it is an anomaly nevertheless.

Similarly, requiring objecting nonmembers to opt out of paying the nonchargeable portion of union dues—as opposed to exempting them from making such payments unless they opt in—represents a remarkable boon for unions. Courts "do not presume acquiescence in the loss of fundamental rights." [ ] Once it is recognized, as our cases have, that a nonmember cannot be forced to fund a union's political or ideological activities, what is the justification for putting the burden on the nonmember to opt out of making such a payment? Shouldn't the default rule comport with the probable preferences of most nonmembers? And isn't it likely that most employees who choose not to join the union that represents their bargaining unit prefer not to pay the full amount of union dues? An opt-out system creates a risk that the fees paid by nonmembers will be used to further political and ideological ends with which they do not agree. . . .

Although the difference between opt-out and opt-in schemes is important, our prior cases have given surprisingly little attention to this distinction. Indeed, acceptance of the opt-out approach appears to have come about more as a historical accident than through the careful application of First Amendment principles.

. . . In [ ] cases such as *Abood* and *Hudson,* we assumed without any focused analysis [authorization of] the opt-out requirement as a constitutional matter. Thus in *Hudson* we did not take issue with the union's practice of giving employees annual notice and an opportunity to object to expected political expenditures. At the same time, however, we made it clear that the procedures used by a union to collect money from nonmembers must satisfy a high standard.

. . . Far from calling for a balancing of rights or interests, *Hudson* made it clear that any procedure for exacting fees from unwilling contributors must be "carefully tailored to minimize the infringement" of free speech rights. And to underscore the meaning of this careful tailoring, we followed that statement with a citation to cases holding that measures burdening the freedom of speech or association must serve a "compelling interest" and must not be significantly broader than necessary to serve that interest.

. . . The SEIU . . . asks us to approve a procedure under which (a) a special assessment billed for use in electoral campaigns was assessed without providing a new opportunity for nonmembers to decide whether they wished to contribute to this effort and (b) nonmembers who previously opted out were nevertheless required to pay more than half of the special assessment even though the union had said that the purpose of the fund was to mount a political campaign and that it would not be used for ordinary union expenses. This aggressive use of power by the SEIU to collect fees from nonmembers is indefensible.

First, we see no justification for the union's failure to provide a fresh *Hudson* notice. *Hudson* rests on the principle that nonmembers should not be required to fund a union's political and ideological projects unless they choose to do so after having "a fair opportunity" to assess the impact of paying for nonchargeable union activities.

Giving employees only one opportunity per year to make this choice is tolerable if employees are able at the time in question to make an informed choice. But a nonmember cannot make an informed choice about a special assessment or dues increase that is unknown when the annual notice is sent. When a union levies a special assessment or raises dues as a result of unexpected developments, the factors influencing a nonmember's choice may change. In particular, a nonmember may take special exception to the uses for which the additional funds are sought.

. . .

As *Hudson* held, procedures for collecting fees from nonmembers must be carefully tailored to minimize impingement on First Amendment rights, and the procedure used in this case cannot possibly be considered to have met that standard.

To respect the limits of the First Amendment, the union should have sent out a new notice allowing nonmembers to opt in to the special fee rather than requiring them to opt out. Our cases have tolerated a substantial impingement on First Amendment rights by allowing unions to impose an opt-out requirement at all. Even if this burden can be justified during the collection of regular dues on an annual basis, there is no way to justify the additional burden of imposing yet another opt-out requirement to collect special fees whenever the union desires.

The SEIU's treatment of nonmembers who opted out when the initial *Hudson* notice was sent also ran afoul of the First Amendment. The SEIU required these employees to pay 56.35% of the special assessment, just as they had been required to pay 56.35% of the regular annual dues. But the union proclaimed that the special assessment would be used to support an electoral campaign and would not be used for ordinary union expenses. Accordingly, there is no reason to suppose that 56.35% of the new assessment was used for properly chargeable expenses. On the contrary, if the union is to be taken at its word, virtually all of the money was slated for nonchargeable uses.

The procedure accepted in *Hudson* is designed for use when a union sends out its regular annual dues notices. The procedure is predicated on the assumption that a union's allocation of funds for chargeable and nonchargeable purposes is not likely to vary greatly from one year to the next. No such assumption is reasonable, however, when a union levies a special assessment or raises dues as a result of events that were not anticipated or disclosed at the time when a yearly *Hudson* notice was sent. Accordingly, use of figures based on an audit of the union's operations during an entire previous year makes no sense.

. . .

Unless it is possible to determine in advance with some degree of accuracy the percentage of union funds that will be used during an upcoming year for chargeable purposes—and the SEIU argues that this is not possible—there is at least a risk that, at the end of the year, unconsenting nonmembers will have paid either too much or too little. Which side should bear this risk?

The answer is obvious: the side whose constitutional rights are not at stake. "Given the existence of acceptable alternatives, [a] union cannot be allowed to commit dissenters' funds to improper uses even temporarily." *Ellis*, 466 U.S., at 444, 104 S. Ct. 1883. Thus, if unconsenting nonmembers pay too much, their First Amendment rights are infringed. On the other hand, if unconsenting nonmembers pay less than their proportionate share, no constitutional right of the union is violated because the union has no constitutional right to receive any payment from these employees. See *Davenport*, 551 U.S., at 185, 127 S. Ct. 2372. The union has simply lost for a few months the "extraordinary" benefit of being empowered to compel nonmembers to pay for services that they may not want and in any event have not agreed to fund.

As we have noted, by allowing unions to collect any fees from nonmembers and by permitting unions to use opt-out rather than opt-in schemes when annual dues are billed, our cases have substantially impinged upon the First Amendment rights of nonmembers. In the new situation presented here, we see no justification for any further impingement. The general rule—individuals should not be compelled to subsidize private groups or private speech—should prevail.

Public-sector unions have the right under the First Amendment to express their views on political and social issues without government interference. But employees who choose not to join a union have the same rights. The First Amendment creates a forum in which all may seek, without hindrance or aid from the State, to move public opinion and achieve their political goals. "First Amendment values [would be] at serious risk if the government [could] compel a particular citizen, or a discrete group of citizens, to pay special subsidies for speech on the side that [the government] favors." *United Foods*. Therefore, when a public-sector union imposes a special assessment or dues increase, the union must provide a fresh *Hudson* notice and may not exact any funds from nonmembers without their affirmative consent.

The judgment of the Ninth Circuit is *Reversed*, and the case is *Remanded* for further proceedings consistent with this opinion.

Justice SOTOMAYOR, with whom Justice GINSBURG joins, concurring in the judgment.

. . .

Justice BREYER, with whom Justice KAGAN joins, dissenting.

In *Teachers v. Hudson*, 475 U.S. 292, 106 S. Ct. 1066, 89 L.Ed.2d 232 (1986), this Court unanimously held that "the Union cannot be faulted for calculating its fee on the basis of its expenses during the preceding year." That is precisely what the union has done in this case. I see no reason to modify *Hudson*'s holding as here applied. I consequently dissent.

For the last 25 years unions and employers across the Nation have relied upon this Court's statements in *Hudson* in developing administratively workable systems that (1) allow unions to pay the costs of fulfilling their representational obligations to both members and nonmembers alike, while (2) simultaneously protecting the nonmembers' constitutional right not to support "'ideological causes not germane to [the union's] duties as collective-bargaining agent.'" [ ] The Court, in my view, should not depart, or create an exception, from *Hudson*'s framework here.

. . .

The Court also holds that, "when a public-sector union imposes a special assessment or dues increase," it "may not exact any funds from nonmembers without their affirmative consent." *Ante*, at 2296. In other words, the Court mandates an "opt-in" system in respect to the payment of special assessments.

Justice SOTOMAYOR's concurring opinion explains why the Court is wrong to impose this requirement. It runs directly contrary to precedent. No party asked that we do so. The matter has not been fully argued in this Court or in the courts below. I agree with her about this matter.

The decision is particularly unfortunate given the fact that each reason the Court offers in support of its "opt-in" conclusion seems in logic to apply, not just to special assessments, but to ordinary yearly fee charges as well. At least, its opinion can be so read. And that fact virtually guarantees that the opinion will play a central role in an ongoing, intense political debate.

The debate is generally about whether, the extent to which, and the circumstances under which a union that represents nonmembers in collective bargaining can require those nonmembers to help pay for the union's (constitutionally chargeable) collective-bargaining expenses. Twenty-three States have enacted "right to work" laws, which, in effect, prevent unions from requiring nonmembers to pay any of those costs. Other States have rejected the "right to work" approach and permit unions to require contributions from nonmembers, while protecting those nonmembers' right to opt out of supporting the union's political activities. Still others have enacted compromise laws that assume a nonmember does not wish to pay the nonchargeable portion of the fee unless he or she affirmatively indicates a desire to do so. The debate about public unions' collective-bargaining rights is currently intense.

The question of how a nonmember indicates a desire not to pay constitutes an important part of this debate. Must the union assume that the nonmember does not intend to pay unless he affirmatively indicates his desire to pay, by "opting in"? Or, may the union assume that the nonmember is willing to pay unless the nonmember indicates a desire not to pay, by "opting out"? Where, as here, nonchargeable political expenses are at issue, there may be a significant number of represented nonmembers who do not feel strongly enough about the union's politics to indicate a choice either way. That being so, an "opt-in" requirement can reduce union revenues significantly, a matter of considerable importance to the union, while the additional protection it provides primarily helps only those who are politically near neutral. See generally Sunstein & Thaler, Libertarian Paternalism is not an Oxymoron, 70 U. Chi. L.Rev. 1159, 1161 (2003) (explaining that default rules play an important role when individuals do not have "well-defined preferences"). Consequently, the Court, which held recently that the Constitution *permits* a State to impose an opt-in requirement [ ] has never said that it *mandates* such a requirement. There is no good reason for the Court suddenly to enter the debate, much less now to decide that the Constitution resolves it. . . .

NOTES AND QUESTIONS

1. *Involuntary association? Knox* did not end the debate about union charges to non-members. In 2016 the sudden death of Justice Antonin Scalia meant a 4-4 victory for labor unions in Friedrichs v. Cal. Teachers Ass'n, 136 S. Ct. 1083 (2016). In a per curiam opinion, an equally divided Court affirmed a Ninth Circuit decision allowing public-sector unions to collect fees from workers to pay for collective bargaining activities, even when those workers had chosen not to join and did not want to pay the fees. When the case was argued in front of the 9-justice Court, including the late Justice Scalia, at least five justices seemed inclined to say that forcing public workers to support unions they had declined to join violates the First Amendment. The case set no precedent and left open the opportunity for further challenges. Can you articulate the constitutional arguments on both sides of the issue? To what extent does the issue raise concerns about involuntary association in addition to compelled speech?

2. *The self-governance rationale*: Why does the Court lead off the opinion by stressing the importance of free speech to self-governance? What does *Knox*

have to do with self-governance? *See* Charlotte Garden, *Citizens, United and Citizens United: The Future of Labor Speech Rights?* 53 Wm. & Mary L. Rev. 1 (2011).

The following case addresses whether U.S. beef producers can be compelled to contribute to a government promotional campaign for beef. Does this case involve only commercial speech, which typically receives less First Amendment protection than political speech? Is the compelled-speech issue different in a case that involves commercial speech? Who is the speaker in this case?

JOHANNS v. LIVESTOCK MARKETING ASS'N

544 U.S. 550 (2005)

Justice SCALIA delivered the opinion of the Court.

For the third time in eight years, we consider whether a federal program that finances generic advertising to promote an agricultural product violates the First Amendment. In these cases, unlike the previous two, the dispositive question is whether the generic advertising at issue is the Government's own speech and therefore is exempt from First Amendment scrutiny.

The Beef Promotion and Research Act of 1985 (Beef Act or Act), 99 Stat. 1597, announces a federal policy of promoting the marketing and consumption of "beef and beef products," using funds raised by an assessment on cattle sales and importation. 7 U.S.C. § 2901(b). . . . [As authorized by the statute, the Secretary of Agriculture in 1986 issued a temporary Beef Promotion and Research Order, which imposed a $1-per-head assessment (or "checkoff") on all sales or importation of cattle and a comparable assessment on imported beef products. One purpose of checkoff was to fund a beef promotion campaign. The content of the promotion was proposed by an Operating Committee of the "Beef Board," a body appointed by the Secretary and comprised of "geographically representative" beef producers and importers. In 1986, a majority of U.S. beef producers voted to continue the beef promotion program.]

. . . [M]ore than $1 billion has been collected through the checkoff, and a large fraction of that sum has been spent on promotional projects authorized by the Beef Act—many using the familiar trademarked slogan "Beef. It's What's for Dinner." . . . Many promotional messages funded by the checkoff (though not all) bear the attribution "Funded by America's Beef Producers." Most print and television messages also bear a Beef Board logo, usually a check mark with the word "BEEF."

Respondents are two associations whose members collect and pay the checkoff, and several individuals who raise and sell cattle subject to the checkoff. [They sued the Department of Agriculture, the Secretary, and the Beef Board.] The District Court granted a limited preliminary injunction, which forbade the continued use of checkoff funds to laud the beef program or to lobby for governmental action relating to the checkoff.

While the litigation was pending, we held in United States v. United Foods, Inc., 533 U.S. 405 (2001), that a mandatory checkoff for generic mushroom advertising violated the First Amendment. Noting that the mushroom program closely resembles the beef program, respondents amended their complaint to assert a First Amendment challenge to the use of the beef checkoff for promotional activity. Respondents noted that the advertising promotes beef as a generic commodity, which, they contended, impedes their efforts to promote the superiority of, *inter alia*, American beef, grain-fed beef, or certified Angus or Hereford beef.

After a bench trial, the District Court ruled for respondents on their First Amendment claim. . . . The Court of Appeals for the Eighth Circuit affirmed. Unlike the District Court, the Court of Appeals did not dispute that the challenged advertising is government speech; instead, it held that government speech status is relevant only to First Amendment challenges to the speech's *content*, not to challenges to its compelled *funding*. Compelled funding of speech, it held, may violate the First Amendment even if the speech in question is the government's.

II.

We have sustained First Amendment challenges to allegedly compelled expression in two categories of cases: true "compelled-speech" cases, in which an individual is obliged personally to express a message he disagrees with, imposed by the government; and "compelled-subsidy" cases, in which an individual is required by the government to subsidize a message he disagrees with, expressed by a private entity. We have not heretofore considered the First Amendment consequences of government-compelled subsidy of the government's own speech.

We first invalidated an outright compulsion of speech in West Virginia Bd. of Ed. v. Barnette, 319 U.S. 624 (1943). . . . Likewise, in Wooley v. Maynard, 430 U.S. 705 (1977), we held that requiring a New Hampshire couple to bear the State's motto, "Live Free or Die," on their cars' license plates was an impermissible compulsion of expression. . . .

The reasoning of these compelled-speech cases has been carried over to certain instances in which individuals are compelled not to speak, but to subsidize a private message with which they disagree. Thus, although we have upheld state-imposed requirements that lawyers be members of the state bar and pay its annual dues, and that public school teachers either join the labor union representing their "shop" or pay "service fees" equal to the union dues, we have invalidated the use of the compulsory fees to fund speech on political matters. Keller v. State Bar of Cal., 496 U.S. 1 (1990); Abood v. Detroit Bd. of Ed., 431 U.S. 209 (1977). Bar or union speech with such content, we held, was not germane to the regulatory interests that justified compelled membership, and accordingly, making those who disagreed with it pay for it violated the First Amendment.

These latter cases led us to sustain a compelled-subsidy challenge to an assessment very similar to the beef checkoff, imposed to fund mushroom advertising. Deciding the case on the assumption that the advertising was private speech, not government speech, we concluded that *Abood* and *Keller* were controlling. As in those cases, mushroom producers were obliged by "law or necessity" to pay the checkoff; although *Abood* and *Keller* would permit the mandatory fee if it were "germane" to a "broader regulatory scheme," in *United Foods* the only regulatory purpose was the funding of the advertising.

In all of the cases invalidating exactions to subsidize speech, the speech was, or was presumed to be, that of an entity other than the government itself. Our compelled-subsidy cases have consistently respected the principle that "[c]ompelled support of a private association is fundamentally different from compelled support of government." *Abood* (Powell, J., concurring in judgment). "Compelled support of government"—even those programs of government one does not approve—is of course perfectly constitutional, as every taxpayer must attest. And some government programs involve, or entirely consist of, advocating a position. "The government, as a general rule, may support valid programs and policies by taxes or other exactions binding on protesting parties. Within this broader principle it seems inevitable that funds raised by the government will be spent for speech and other expression to advocate and defend its own policies." *Southworth,* 529 U.S., at 229. We have generally assumed, though not yet squarely held, that compelled funding of government speech does not alone raise First Amendment concerns.

III.

[A.] The Secretary of Agriculture does not write ad copy himself. Rather, the Beef Board's promotional campaigns are designed by the Beef Board's Operating Committee, only half of whose members are Beef Board members appointed by the Secretary. (All members of the Operating Committee are subject to *removal* by the Secretary.) Respondents contend that speech whose content is effectively controlled by a nongovernmental entity—the Operating Committee—cannot be considered "government speech." We need not address this contention, because we reject its premise: The message of the promotional campaigns is effectively controlled by the Federal Government itself.

The message set out in the beef promotions is from beginning to end the message established by the Federal Government. Congress has directed the implementation of a "coordinated program" of promotion, "including paid advertising, to advance the image and desirability of beef and beef products." 7 U.S.C. §§ 2901(b), 2902(13). Congress and the Secretary have also specified, in general terms, what the promotional campaigns shall contain, see, *e.g.,* § 2904(4)(B)(i) (campaigns "shall…take into account" different types of beef products), and what they shall not, see, *e.g.,* 7 CFR § 1260.169(d) (2004) (campaigns shall not, without prior approval, refer "to a brand or trade name of any beef product"). Thus, Congress and the Secretary have set out the overarching message and some of its elements, and they have left the development of the remaining details to an entity whose members are answerable to the Secretary (and in some cases appointed by him as well).

Moreover, the record demonstrates that the Secretary exercises final approval authority over every word used in every promotional campaign. . . . Officials of the Department also attend and participate in the open meetings at which proposals are developed.

. . . When, as here, the government sets the overall message to be communicated and approves every word that is disseminated, it is not precluded from relying on the government-speech doctrine merely because it solicits assistance from nongovernmental sources in developing specific messages.

[B.] Respondents also contend that the beef program does not qualify as "government speech" because it is funded by a targeted assessment on beef producers, rather than by general revenues. This funding mechanism, they argue, has two relevant effects: It gives control over the beef program not to politically accountable legislators, but to a narrow interest group that will pay no heed to respondents' dissenting views, and it creates the perception that the advertisements speak for beef producers such as respondents.

We reject the first point. The compelled-*subsidy* analysis is altogether unaffected by whether the funds for the promotions are raised by general taxes or through a targeted assessment. Citizens may challenge compelled support of private speech, but have no First Amendment right not to fund government speech. And that is no less true when the funding is achieved through targeted assessments devoted exclusively to the program to which the assessed citizens object. . . . The First Amendment does not confer a right to pay one's taxes into the general fund, because the injury of compelled funding (as opposed to the injury of compelled speech) does not stem from the Government's mode of accounting.

Some of our cases have justified compelled funding of government speech by pointing out that government speech is subject to democratic accountability. But our references to "traditional political controls," do not signify that the First Amendment duplicates the Appropriations Clause, U.S. Const., Art. I, § 9, cl. 7, or that every instance of government speech must be funded by a line item in an appropriations bill. Here, the beef advertisements are subject to political safeguards more than adequate to set them apart from private messages. The program is authorized and the basic message prescribed by federal statute, and specific requirements for the promotions' content are imposed by federal regulations promulgated after notice and comment. The Secretary of Agriculture, a politically accountable official, oversees the program, appoints and dismisses the key personnel, and retains absolute veto power over the advertisements' content, right down to the wording. And Congress, of course, retains oversight authority, not to mention the ability to reform the program at any time. No more is required.

[Respondents also] contend that crediting the advertising to "America's Beef Producers" impermissibly uses not only their money but also their seeming endorsement to promote a message with which they do not agree. Communications cannot be "government speech," they argue, if they are attributed to someone other than the government; and the person to whom they are attributed, when he is, by compulsory funding, made the unwilling instrument of communication, may raise a First Amendment objection.

We need not determine the validity of this argument—which relates to compelled *speech* rather than compelled *subsidy* with regard to respondents' facial challenge. Since neither the Beef Act nor the Beef Order requires attribution, neither can be the cause of any possible First Amendment harm. The District Court's order enjoining the enforcement of the Act and the Order thus cannot be sustained on this theory.

On some set of facts, this second theory might (again, we express no view on the point) form the basis for an as-applied challenge—if it were established, that is, that individual beef advertisements were attributed to respondents. The record, however, includes only a stipulated sampling of these promotional materials, and none of the exemplars provides any support for this attribution theory except for the tagline identifying the funding. Respondents apparently presented no other evidence of attribution at trial, and the District Court made no factual findings on the point. Indeed, in the only trial testimony on the subject that any party has identified, an employee of one of the respondent associations said he did *not* think the beef promotions would be attributed to his group. Whether the *individual* respondents who are beef producers would be associated with speech labeled as coming from "America's Beef Producers" is a question on which the trial record is altogether silent. We have only the funding tagline itself, a trademarked term that, standing alone, is not sufficiently specific to convince a reasonable factfinder that any particular beef producer, or all beef producers, would be tarred with the content of each trademarked ad. We therefore conclude that on the record before us an as-applied First Amendment challenge to the individual advertisements affords no basis on which to sustain the Eighth Circuit's judgment, even in part. [Vacated and remanded.]

Justice SOUTER, with whom Justice STEVENS and Justice KENNEDY join, dissenting.

. . . I take the view that if government relies on the government-speech doctrine to compel specific groups to fund speech with targeted taxes, it must make itself politically accountable by indicating that the content actually is a government message, not just the statement of one self-interested group the government is currently willing to invest with power. Sometimes, as in these very cases, government can make an effective disclosure only by explicitly labeling the speech as its own. Because the Beef Act fails to require the Government to show its hand, I would affirm the judgment of the Court of Appeals holding the Act unconstitutional, and I respectfully dissent from the Court's decision to condone this compelled subsidy.

. . . [W]hen government funds its speech with general tax revenue, as it usually does, no individual taxpayer or group of taxpayers can lay claim to a special, or even a particularly strong, connection to the money spent (and hence to the speech funded). Outrage is likely to be rare, and disagreement tends to stay temperate. But the relative palatability of a remote subsidy shared by every taxpayer is not to be found when the speech is funded with targeted taxes. For then, as here, the particular interests of those singled out to pay the tax are closely linked with the expression, and taxpayers who disagree with it suffer a more acute limitation on their presumptive autonomy as speakers to decide what to say and what to pay for others to say.

When a targeted assessment thus makes the First Amendment affront more galling, it does, or should, follow that greater care is required to assure that the political process can practically respond to limit the compulsion Jefferson inveighed against. . . . [T]argeted speech subsidies can be reviewed specifically for their susceptibility to response by the voters, and the intensity of the provocation experienced by the targeted group justifies just such scrutiny.

In these cases, the requirement of effective public accountability means the ranchers ought to prevail, it being clear that the Beef Act does not establish an advertising scheme subject to effective democratic checks. The reason for this is simple: the ads are not required to show any sign of being speech by the Government, and experience under the Act demonstrates how effectively the Government has masked its role in producing the ads. Most obviously, many of them include the tag line, "[f]unded by America's Beef Producers," which all but ensures that no one reading them will suspect that the message comes from the National Government. But the tag line just underscores the point that would be true without it, that readers would most naturally think that ads urging people to have beef for dinner were placed and paid for by the beef producers who stand to profit when beef is on the table. No one hearing a commercial for Pepsi or Levi's thinks Uncle Sam is the man talking behind the curtain. Why would a person reading a beef ad think Uncle Sam was trying to make him eat more steak? . . .

. . . . Nor is it any answer that resourceful taxpayers could discover the Government behind the beef ads by doing research on the implementation of the Beef Act. Of course a taxpayer could discover the facts by looking hard enough, but what would tip off the taxpayer to look? And even if a few taxpayers did unearth the truth it would not matter, for the First Amendment harm cannot be mitigated by the possibility that a few cognoscenti may actually understand how the scheme works. If the judiciary is justified in keeping hands off special assessments on dissenters from government speech, it is because there is a practical opportunity for political response; esoteric knowledge on the part of a few will not do.

In sum, the First Amendment cannot be implemented by sanctioning government deception by omission (or by misleading statement) of the sort the Court today condones, and expression that is not ostensibly governmental, which government is not required to embrace as publicly as it speaks, cannot constitute government speech sufficient to justify enforcement of a targeted subsidy to broadcast it. . . .

NOTES AND QUESTIONS

1. *Simply economic regulation?* Justice Breyer and Justice Ginsburg would have validated the beef promotion subsidies as "a form of economic regulation." What is the difference between an "economic regulation" and a compelled subsidy of speech?

2. *Mixed government messages.* The dissent pointed out that the promotional ads for beef conflicted with government recommendations that Americans should consume limited amounts of saturated fats, such as those found in beef. Should it have been relevant to the outcome of *Johanns* that the government was speaking out of both sides of its mouth?

3. *Statutory limits on government speech. Johanns* suggested that government speech need not be labeled as such. Why can't the government simply pay reporters to write editorials lauding new government initiatives? In fact, the Department of Education tried to do just that. In 2005, the Government Accountability Office issued a report concluding that the Education Department broke the law when it surreptitiously paid conservative commentator Armstrong Williams $241,000 for promoting its "No Child Left Behind" program. The payment violated a 2003 statutory ban on "covert propaganda" because Williams did not disclose the arrangement, effectively masking the government's role as creator. Similarly, a $38,421 promotional video on the No Child Left Behind program, designed to appear as a news report, violated the covert propaganda ban because it failed to disclose the government as the video's author. *See* Christopher Lee, *GAO Issues Mixed Ruling on Payments to Commentator,* Wash. Post, Oct. 1, 2005, at A10.

4. *Misidentification.* If the government wishes to participate in the marketplace of ideas, should it be required to do so in a transparent fashion? See Helen Norton, Government Speech 2.0, 87 Denv. U. L. Rev. 899 (2010) (arguing that the government does not have the same right to participate anonymously or pseudonymously that individuals do); see also Lyrissa Barnett Lidsky, Public Forum 2.0, 91 B.U. L. Rev. 1975 (2011) (arguing that government use of interactive social media should be governed by First Amendment principles applicable to public forums).

D. ANONYMOUS SPEECH AND
COMPELLED DISCLOSURES

Can the government compel a speaker to provide his audience with information necessary to enable proper interpretation of the speaker's message? If the audience knows, for instance, that a speaker will gain financially from successfully advocating a particular policy, the audience may be more skeptical of the speaker's message or may discount it entirely. One might therefore argue that knowledge of the speaker's financial motive is necessary to allow the audience to interpret his speech correctly; in this circumstance, one might reasonably contend that a disclosure requirement imposed on the speaker would foster First Amendment values. The Supreme Court has accepted this argument in some, but not all, contexts, as you will see below.

A similar argument for disclosure arises when a speaker chooses to speak without disclosing his true identity. In many instances, knowledge of an author's identity will assist the audience in interpreting the author's message, and yet the Supreme Court has recognized a qualified right to speak anonymously. What First Amendment values are furthered by depriving the audience of information that would help them properly interpret a speaker's message? In the cases below, the government asserts that audiences will benefit from having more information about the speaker or her motives. As you read the cases, pay careful attention to the strength of the government interest required to overcome a speaker's interest in controlling the presentation of her message: Must the government's interest be "compelling" or "important" or "substantial" or merely "legitimate" before the First Amendment interests at stake can be overcome?

1. Disclosure of Speaker Identity or Motive

Meese v. Keene, below, deals with the constitutionality of a federal statute aimed at policing "political propaganda" by requiring foreign films to carry a disclaimer. The Court found the statute constitutional by a 5-3 vote, with Justice Scalia not participating.

MEESE v. KEENE

481 U.S. 465 (1987)

Justice STEVENS delivered the opinion of the Court.

The Foreign Agents Registration Act of 1938, 52 Stat. 631-633, as amended in 1942 and 1966, 22 U.S.C. §§ 611-621 (Act), uses the term "political propaganda," as defined in the Act, to identify those expressive materials that must comply with the Act's registration, filing, and disclosure requirements. The constitutionality of those underlying requirements and the validity of the characteristics used to define the regulated category of expressive materials are not at issue in this case. The District Court concluded, however, that Congress violated the First Amendment by using the term "political propaganda" as the statutory name for the regulated category of expression.

[The appellee, a member of the California State Senate, wanted to exhibit three Canadian movies dealing with nuclear war and acid rain. He sued in district court and obtained a preliminary injunction against application of the Act to the three films. The district court later granted summary judgment and a permanent injunction "against enforcement of any portion of the Act which incorporates the term 'political propaganda.'" The Supreme Court noted probable jurisdiction over the Attorney General's appeal under 28 U.S.C. § 1252 and reversed.]

I.

The statute. . . was enacted: "[T]o protect the national defense, internal security, and foreign relations of the United States by requiring public disclosure by persons engaging in propaganda activities and other activities for or on behalf of foreign governments, foreign political parties, and other foreign principals so that the Government and the people of the United States may be informed of the identity of such persons and may appraise their statements and actions in the light of their associations and activities." 56 Stat. 248-249.

. . . The statute classifies the three films produced by the Film Board as "political propaganda" because they contain political material intended to influence the foreign policies of the United States, or may reasonably be adapted to be so used.

When the agent of a foreign principal disseminates any "political propaganda" in the United States mails or in the channels of interstate commerce, he or she must also provide the Attorney General with a copy of the material and with a report describing the extent of the dissemination. In addition, he or she must provide the recipient of the material with a disclosure statement on a form prescribed by the Attorney General. . . . The standard form to be used with films reads as follows:

> This material is prepared, edited, issued or circulated by (name and address of registrant) which is registered with the Department of Justice, Washington, D.C. under the Foreign Agents Registration Act as an agent of (name and address of foreign principal). Dissemination reports on this film are filed with the Department of Justice where the required registration statement is available for public inspection. Registration does not indicate approval of the contents of this material by the United States Government.

It should be noted that the term "political propaganda" does not appear on the form. The statutory definition of that term reads as follows:

> (j) The term 'political propaganda' includes any oral, visual, graphic, written, pictorial, or other communication or expression by any person (1) which is reasonably adapted to, or which the person disseminating the same believes will, or which he intends to, prevail upon, indoctrinate, convert, induce, or in any other way influence a recipient or any section of the public within the United States with reference to the political or public interests, policies, or relations of a government or a foreign country or a foreign political party or with reference to the foreign policies of the United States or promote in the United States racial, religious, or social dissensions, or (2) which advocates, advises, instigates, or promotes any racial, social, political, or religious disorder, civil riot, or other conflict involving the use of force or violence in any other American republic or the overthrow of any government or political subdivision of any other American republic by any means involving the use of force or violence. § 611(j).

II.

. . . [Keene establishes a cognizable injury for standing purposes by showing not merely a "subjective chill," but also that]" if he were to exhibit the films while they bore such characterization, his personal, political, and professional reputation would suffer and his ability to obtain re-election and to practice his profession would be impaired."

III.

We begin our examination of the District Court's ruling on the First Amendment issue by noting that the term "political propaganda" has two meanings. In popular parlance many people assume that propaganda is a form of slanted, misleading speech that does not merit serious attention and that proceeds from a concern for advancing the narrow interests of the speaker rather than from a devotion to the truth. []. Casualty reports of enemy belligerents, for example, are often dismissed as nothing more than "propaganda." As defined in the Act, the term political propaganda includes misleading advocacy of that kind. But it also includes advocacy materials that are completely accurate and merit the closest attention and the highest respect. Standard reference works include both broad, neutral definitions of the word "propaganda" that are consistent with the way the word is defined in this statute, and also the narrower, pejorative definition.

. . . [The District Court found that] the denigration of speech to which the label "political propaganda" has been attached constitutes "a conscious attempt to place a whole category of materials beyond the pale of legitimate discourse," and is therefore an unconstitutional abridgment of that speech. We find this argument unpersuasive, indeed, untenable, for three reasons.

First, the term "political propaganda" does nothing to place regulated expressive materials "beyond the pale of legitimate discourse." . . . Congress did not prohibit, edit, or restrain the distribution of advocacy materials in an ostensible effort to protect the public from conversion, confusion, or deceit.

To the contrary, Congress simply required the disseminators of such material to make additional disclosures that would better enable the public to evaluate the import of the propaganda. The statute does not prohibit appellee from advising his audience that the films have not been officially censured in any way. Disseminators of propaganda may go beyond the disclosures required by statute and add any further information they think germane to the public's viewing of the materials. By compelling some disclosure of information and permitting more, the Act's approach recognizes that the best remedy for misleading or inaccurate speech contained within materials subject to the Act is fair, truthful, and accurate speech. See generally *Whitney v. California,* 274 U.S. 357, 377 (1927) (Brandeis, J., concurring) ("If there be time to expose through discussion the falsehood and fallacies, to avert the evil by the processes of education, the remedy to be applied is more speech, not enforced silence"). The prospective viewers of the three films at issue may harbor an unreasoning prejudice against arguments that have been identified as the "political propaganda" of foreign principals and their agents, but the Act allows appellee to combat any such bias simply by explaining—before, during, or after the film, or in a wholly separate context—that Canada's interest in the consequences of nuclear war and acid rain does not necessarily undermine the integrity or the persuasiveness of its advocacy.

Ironically, it is the injunction entered by the District Court that withholds information from the public. The suppressed information is the fact that the films fall within the category of materials that Congress has judged to be "political propaganda." A similar paternalistic strategy of protecting the public from information was followed by the Virginia Assembly, which enacted a ban on the advertising of prescription drug prices by pharmacists. See *Virginia Pharmacy Bd. v. Virginia Citizens Consumer Council, Inc.*, 425 U.S. 748 (1976). The State sought to justify the ban as a means of preventing "the aggressive price competition that will result from unlimited advertising" and the "loss of stable pharmacist-customer relationships" that would result from comparison shopping on the basis of price. We wholly rejected these justifications, finding that the ban was predicated upon assumptions about the reactions the public would have if they obtained the "wrong" kind of information. . . .

Likewise, despite the absence of any direct abridgment of speech, the District Court in this case assumed that the reactions of the public to the label "political propaganda" would be such that the label would interfere with freedom of speech. In *Virginia Pharmacy Bd.*, we squarely held that a zeal to protect the public from "too much information" could not withstand First Amendment scrutiny: "There is, of course, an alternative to this highly paternalistic approach. That alternative is to assume that this information is not in itself harmful, that people will perceive their own best interests if only they are well enough informed, and that the best means to that end is to open the channels of communication rather than to close them. . . . It is precisely this kind of choice, between the dangers of suppressing information, and the dangers from its misuse if it is freely available, that the First Amendment makes for us."

Second, the reasoning of the District Court is contradicted by history. The statutory definition of "political propaganda" has been on the books for over four decades. We should presume that the people who have a sufficient understanding of the law to know that the term "political propaganda" is used to describe the regulated category also know that the definition is a broad, neutral one rather than a pejorative one. . . . There is a risk that a partially informed audience might believe that a film that must be registered with the Department of Justice is suspect, but there is no evidence that this suspicion—to the degree it exists—has had the effect of Government censorship.

Third, Congress' use of the term "political propaganda" does not lead us to suspend the respect we normally owe to the Legislature's power to define the terms that it uses in legislation. We have no occasion here to decide the permissible scope of Congress' "right to speak"; we simply view this particular choice of language, statutorily defined in a neutral and evenhanded manner, as one that no constitutional provision prohibits the Congress from making. . . . Congress' use of the term "propaganda" in this statute, as indeed in other legislation, has no pejorative connotation. As judges it is our duty to construe legislation as it is written, not as it might be read by a layman, or as it might be understood by someone who has not even read it. If the term "political propaganda" is construed consistently with the neutral definition contained in the text of the statute itself, the constitutional concerns voiced by the District Court completely disappear. [Reversed and remanded.]

Justice BLACKMUN, with whom Justice BRENNAN and Justice MARSHALL join, dissenting in part.

. . . . The Act grew out of the investigations of the House Un-American Activities Committee, formed in 1934 to investigate Nazi propaganda activities in the United States and the dissemination of subversive propaganda controlled by foreign countries attacking the American form of government. . . .

In 1942, Congress revised the Act at the request of the Department of Justice in order to strengthen the Government's "chief instrument. . . for controlling foreign agent activity in the theater of political propaganda." Hearings on H.R. 6045 before Subcommittee No. 4 of the House Committee on the Judiciary, 77th Cong., 1st Sess., Ser. No. 9, p. 24 (1941) (1941 Hearings) (statement of Lawrence M.C. Smith, Chief, Special Defense Unit, Department of Justice). The amendments included the definition of propaganda in addition to labeling and reporting requirements virtually identical to those imposed under the current version of the Act. . . .

Even if Congress had enacted the "propaganda" designation at issue here with a completely neutral purpose, that would not be sufficient for the First Amendment inquiry, for the Court has "long recognized that even regulations aimed at proper governmental concerns can restrict unduly the exercise of rights protected by the First Amendment." []. . . .

A definition chosen by Congress is controlling as to the scope of the statute, but the Court has never held that Congress' choice of a definition precludes an independent determination of a statute's constitutionality based upon its *actual* effect. . . .

. . . It simply strains credulity for the Court to assert that "propaganda" is a neutral classification.

NOTES AND QUESTIONS

1. *Content-based disclosure requirement.* Why isn't the disclosure requirement in *Meese* invalid as a content-based restriction on speech? Does the majority believe the statute is not content-based, or that even if it is content-based, it does not violate the First Amendment?

2. *The informational rationale.* Can disclosure requirements imposed on speech always be justified on the grounds that disclosures provide audiences with additional information and thus further First Amendment values? The majority contends that it is paternalistic to assume an audience will not be able to "discount" the political propaganda label, but is it more paternalistic to assume that the audience needs the label? Assume that a federal statute requires all diet books not written by doctors to be labeled in large red letters on the cover with the words: ALERT! THIS BOOK WAS NOT WRITTEN BY A DOCTOR. Would this statute violate the First Amendment? Why or why not? You should reevaluate your answer after reading the remaining materials in this chapter.

3. *Native advertising.* What happens when the line between advertising and editorial content becomes blurred? Advertisers who disguise their ads as news, product reviews, or entertainment, without including a clear disclosure of sponsorship, could find themselves in trouble with the Federal Trade Commission. Retailer Lord & Taylor settled with the FTC for charges that the clothing company deceived consumers by paying for an Instagram post and an article in an online publication without disclosing that the posts actually were

paid promotions for the company's new clothing line. In the Matter of Lord & Taylor, LLC, 2016 FTC LEXIS 73 (F.T.C. May 20, 2016).

Is requiring an author to disclose his credentials different from requiring him to reveal his identity? The Supreme Court has held that the First Amendment protects anonymous speech, but the scope of that protection is unclear. You should carefully contrast the treatment of anonymous speech in *McIntyre v. Ohio Elections Commission*, below, with the treatment of anonymous speech in *Citizens United v. FEC*, which appears in the following section of this chapter, which deals specifically with disclosure requirements in the electoral context.

McINTYRE v. OHIO ELECTIONS COMMISSION

514 U.S. 334 (1995)

Justice STEVENS delivered the opinion of the Court.

. . . On April 27, 1988, Margaret McIntyre distributed leaflets to persons attending a public meeting at the Blendon Middle School in Westerville, Ohio. At this meeting, the superintendent of schools planned to discuss an imminent referendum on a proposed school tax levy. The leaflets expressed Mrs. McIntyre's opposition to the levy. There is no suggestion that the text of her message was false, misleading, or libelous. She had composed and printed it on her home computer and had paid a professional printer to make additional copies. Some of the handbills identified her as the author; others merely purported to express the views of "CONCERNED PARENTS AND TAX PAYERS." . . .

While Mrs. McIntyre distributed her handbills, an official of the school district, who supported the tax proposal, advised her that the unsigned leaflets did not conform to the Ohio election laws. . . .

. . . Five months later, the same school official filed a complaint with the Ohio Elections Commission charging that Mrs. McIntyre's distribution of unsigned leaflets violated § 599.09(A) of the Ohio Code, [which provided that any publication promoting a ballot issue was required to include the "name and residence" of the person "who issues, makes, or is responsible therefor." The Commission fined McIntyre $100. She appealed, and when the case reached the Ohio Supreme Court, the court affirmed, holding that the minor burden the election law posed on speakers was more than offset by the state interest in helping voters assess the "validity" of campaign literature and identifying disseminators of fraud, libel or false advertising.]

II.

Ohio maintains that the statute under review is a reasonable regulation of the electoral process. The State does not suggest that all anonymous publications are pernicious or that a statute totally excluding them from the marketplace of ideas would be valid. This is a wise (albeit implicit) concession, for the anonymity of an author is not ordinarily a sufficient reason to exclude her work product from the protections of the First Amendment.

"Anonymous pamphlets, leaflets, brochures and even books have played an important role in the progress of mankind." *Talley v. California*, 362 U.S., at 64. Great works of literature have frequently been produced by authors writing under assumed names. Despite readers' curiosity and the public's interest in identifying the creator of a work of art, an author generally is free to decide whether or not to disclose his or her true identity. The decision in favor of anonymity may be motivated by fear of economic or official retaliation, by concern about social ostracism, or merely by a desire to preserve as much of one's privacy as possible. Whatever the motivation may be, at least in the field of literary endeavor, the interest in having anonymous works enter the marketplace of ideas unquestionably outweighs any public interest in requiring disclosure as a condition of entry. Accordingly, an author's decision to remain anonymous, like other decisions concerning omissions or additions to the content of a publication, is an aspect of the freedom of speech protected by the First Amendment.

The freedom to publish anonymously extends beyond the literary realm. In *Talley*, the Court held that the First Amendment protects the distribution of unsigned handbills urging readers to boycott certain Los Angeles merchants who were allegedly engaging in discriminatory employment practices. 362 U.S. at 60. Writing for the Court, Justice Black noted that "[p]ersecuted groups and sects from time to time throughout history have been able to criticize oppressive practices and laws either anonymously or not at all." Justice Black recalled England's abusive press licensing laws and seditious libel prosecutions, and he reminded us that even the arguments favoring the ratification of the Constitution advanced in the Federalist Papers were published under fictitious names. On occasion, quite apart from any threat of persecution, an advocate may believe her ideas will be more persuasive if her readers are unaware of her identity. Anonymity thereby provides a way for a writer who may be personally unpopular to ensure that readers will not prejudge her message simply because they do not like its proponent. Thus, even in the field of political rhetoric, where "the identity of the speaker is an important component of many attempts to persuade," *City of Ladue v. Gilleo*, 512 U.S. 43, 56 (1994), the most effective advocates have sometimes opted for anonymity. The specific holding in *Talley* related to advocacy of an economic boycott, but the Court's reasoning embraced a respected tradition of anonymity in the advocacy of political causes. This tradition is perhaps best exemplified by the secret ballot, the hard-won right to vote one's conscience without fear of retaliation.

III.

. . . *Talley* does not necessarily control the disposition of this case. We must, therefore, decide whether and to what extent the First Amendment's protection of anonymity encompasses documents intended to influence the electoral process.

. . . [T]he Ohio Code does not control the mechanics of the electoral process. It is a regulation of pure speech. Moreover, even though this provision applies evenhandedly to advocates of differing viewpoints, it is a direct regulation of the content of speech. Every written document covered by the statute must contain "the name and residence or business address of the chairman, treasurer, or secretary of the organization issuing the same, or the person who issues, makes, or is responsible therefor." Ohio Rev. Code Ann. § 3599.09(A) (1988). Furthermore, the category of covered documents is defined by their content—only those publications containing speech designed to influence the voters in an election need bear the required markings. Consequently, we are not faced with an ordinary election restriction; this case "involves a limitation on political expression subject to exacting scrutiny." . . .

Indeed, as we have explained on many prior occasions, the category of speech regulated by the Ohio statute occupies the core of the protection afforded by the First Amendment: "Discussion of public issues and debate on the qualifications of candidates are integral to the operation of the system of government established by our Constitution. The First Amendment affords the broadest protection to such political expression in order 'to assure [the] unfettered interchange of ideas for the bringing about of political and social changes desired by the people.' *Roth v. United States,* 354 U.S. 476, 484 (1957). Although First Amendment protections are not confined to 'the exposition of ideas,' . . ., 'there is practically universal agreement that a major purpose of that Amendment was to protect the free discussion of governmental affairs, . . . of course includ[ing] discussions of candidates. . . . '*Mills v. Alabama,* 384 U.S. 214, 218 (1966). . . . In a republic where the people are sovereign, the ability of the citizenry to make informed choices among candidates for office is essential, for the identities of those who are elected will inevitably shape the course that we follow as a nation. As the Court observed in *Monitor Patriot Co. v. Roy,* 401 U.S. 265, 272 (1971), 'it can hardly be doubted that the constitutional guarantee has its fullest and most urgent application precisely to the conduct of campaigns for political office.'" . . .

Of course, core political speech need not center on a candidate for office. The principles enunciated in *Buckley* extend equally to issue-based elections such as the school tax referendum that Mrs. McIntyre sought to influence through her handbills. Indeed, the speech in which Mrs. McIntyre engaged—handing out leaflets in the advocacy of a politically controversial viewpoint—is the essence of First Amendment expression. That this advocacy occurred in the heat of a controversial referendum vote only strengthens the protection afforded to Mrs. McIntyre's expression: Urgent, important, and effective speech can be no less protected than impotent speech, lest the right to speak be relegated to those instances when it is least needed. No form of speech is entitled to greater constitutional protection than Mrs. McIntyre's.

When a law burdens core political speech, we apply "exacting scrutiny," and we uphold the restriction only if it is narrowly tailored to serve an overriding state interest. Our precedents thus make abundantly clear that the Ohio Supreme Court applied a significantly more lenient standard than is appropriate in a case of this kind.

IV.

Nevertheless, the State argues that, even under the strictest standard of review, the disclosure requirement in § 3599.09(A) is justified by two important and legitimate state interests. Ohio judges its interest in preventing fraudulent and libelous statements and its interest in providing the electorate with relevant information to be sufficiently compelling to justify the anonymous speech ban. These two interests necessarily overlap to some extent, but it is useful to discuss them separately.

Insofar as the interest in informing the electorate means nothing more than the provision of additional information that may either buttress or undermine the argument in a document, we think the identity of the speaker is no different from other components of the document's content that the author is free to include or exclude. We have already held that the State may not compel a newspaper that prints editorials critical of a particular candidate to provide space for a reply by the candidate. *Tornillo.* . . . The simple interest in providing voters with additional relevant information does not justify a state requirement that a writer make statements or disclosures she would otherwise omit. Moreover, in the case of a handbill written by a private citizen who is not known to the recipient, the name and address of the author add little, if anything, to the reader's ability to evaluate the document's message. Thus, Ohio's informational interest is plainly insufficient to support the constitutionality of its disclosure requirement.

The state interest in preventing fraud and libel stands on a different footing. We agree with Ohio's submission that this interest carries special weight during election campaigns when false statements, if credited, may have serious adverse consequences for the public at large. Ohio does not, however, rely solely on § 3599.09(A) to protect that interest. Its Election Code includes detailed and specific prohibitions against making or disseminating false statements during political campaigns. These regulations apply both to candidate elections and to issue-driven ballot measures. Thus, Ohio's prohibition of anonymous leaflets plainly is not its principal weapon against fraud. Rather, it serves as an aid to enforcement of the specific prohibitions and as a deterrent to the making of false statements by unscrupulous prevaricators. Although these ancillary benefits are assuredly legitimate, we are not persuaded that they justify § 3599.09(A)'s extremely broad prohibition.

As this case demonstrates, the prohibition encompasses documents that are not even arguably false or misleading. It applies not only to the activities of candidates and their organized supporters, but also to individuals acting independently and using only their own modest resources. It applies not only to elections of public officers, but also to ballot issues that present neither a substantial risk of libel nor any potential appearance of corrupt advantage. It applies not only to leaflets distributed on the eve of an election, when the opportunity for reply is limited, but also to those distributed months in advance. It applies no matter what the character or strength of the author's interest in anonymity. Moreover, as this case also demonstrates, the absence of the author's name on a document does not necessarily protect either that person or a distributor of a forbidden document from being held responsible for compliance with the Election Code. Nor has the State explained why it can more easily enforce the direct bans on disseminating false documents against anonymous authors and distributors than against wrongdoers who might use false names and addresses in an attempt to avoid detection. We recognize that a State's enforcement interest might justify a more limited identification requirement, but Ohio has shown scant cause for inhibiting the leafletting at issue here.

V.

Finally, Ohio vigorously argues that our opinions in *First Nat. Bank of Boston v. Bellotti*, 435 U.S. 765 (1978), and *Buckley v. Valeo*, 424 U.S. 1 (1976) (per curiam), amply support the constitutionality of its disclosure requirement. Neither case is controlling: The former concerned the scope of First Amendment protection afforded to corporations; The relevant portion of the latter concerned mandatory disclosure of campaign-related expenditures. Neither case involved a prohibition of anonymous campaign literature.

. . . A written election-related document—particularly a leaflet—is often a personally crafted statement of a political viewpoint. Mrs. McIntyre's handbills surely fit that description. As such, identification of the author against her will is particularly intrusive; it reveals unmistakably the content of her thoughts on a controversial issue. Disclosure of an expenditure and its use, without more, reveals far less information. It may be information that a person prefers to keep secret, and undoubtedly it often gives away something about the spender's political views. Nonetheless, even though money may "talk," its speech is less specific, less personal, and less provocative than a handbill—and as a result, when money supports an unpopular viewpoint it is less likely to precipitate retaliation.

Not only is the Ohio statute's infringement on speech more intrusive than the *Buckley* disclosure requirement [on campaign expenditures], but it rests on different and less powerful state interests. The Federal Election Campaign Act of 1971, at issue in *Buckley*, regulates only candidate elections, not referenda or other issue-based ballot measures; and we construed "independent expenditures" to mean only those expenditures that "expressly advocate the election or defeat of a clearly identified candidate." . . . In candidate elections, the Government can identify a compelling state interest in avoiding the corruption that might result from campaign expenditures. Disclosure of expenditures lessens the risk that individuals will spend money to support a candidate as a *quid pro quo* for special treatment after the candidate is in office. Curriers of favor will be deterred by the knowledge that all expenditures will be scrutinized by the Federal Election Commission and by the public for just this sort of abuse. Moreover, the federal Act contains numerous legitimate disclosure requirements for campaign organizations; the similar requirements for independent expenditures serve to ensure that a campaign organization will not seek to evade disclosure by routing its expenditures through individual supporters. In short, although *Buckley* may permit a more narrowly drawn statute, it surely is not authority for upholding Ohio's open-ended provision.

VI.

Under our Constitution, anonymous pamphleteering is not a pernicious, fraudulent practice, but an honorable tradition of advocacy and of dissent. Anonymity is a shield from the tyranny of the majority. See generally J. Mill, On Liberty and Considerations on Representative Government 1, 3-4 (R. McCallum ed. 1947). It thus exemplifies the purpose behind the Bill of Rights, and of the First Amendment in particular: to protect unpopular individuals from retaliation—and their ideas from suppression—at the hand of an intolerant society. The right to remain anonymous may be abused when it shields fraudulent conduct. But political speech by its nature will sometimes have unpalatable consequences, and, in general, our society accords greater weight to the value of free speech than to the dangers of its misuse. Ohio has not shown that its interest in preventing the misuse of anonymous election-related speech justifies a prohibition of all uses of that speech. The State may, and does, punish fraud directly. But it cannot seek to punish fraud indirectly by indiscriminately outlawing a category of speech, based on its content, with no necessary relationship to the danger sought to be prevented. . . .

Justice SCALIA, with whom THE CHIEF JUSTICE joins, dissenting.
    . . . Preferring the views of the English utilitarian philosopher John Stuart Mill to the considered judgment of the American people's elected representatives from coast to coast, the Court discovers a hitherto unknown right-to-be-unknown while engaging in electoral politics. I dissent from this imposition of free-speech

imperatives that are demonstrably not those of the American people today, and that there is inadequate reason to believe were those of the society that begat the First Amendment or the Fourteenth.

. . . The law at issue here. . . forbids the expression of no idea, but merely requires identification of the speaker when the idea is uttered in the electoral context. It is at the periphery of the First Amendment. . . .

. . . [T]he usefulness of a signing requirement lies not only in promoting observance of the law against campaign falsehoods (though that alone is enough to sustain it). It lies also in promoting a civil and dignified level of campaign debate—which the State has no power to command, but ample power to encourage by such undemanding measures as a signature requirement. . . .

. . . We have approved much more onerous disclosure requirements in the name of fair elections. In *Buckley v. Valeo,* 424 U.S. 1 (1976), we upheld provisions of the Federal Election Campaign Act that required private individuals to report to the Federal Election Commission independent expenditures made for communications advocating the election or defeat of a candidate for federal office. Our primary rationale for upholding this provision was that it served an "informational interest" by "increas[ing] the fund of information concerning those who support the candidates." The provision before us here serves the same informational interest, as well as more important interests, which I have discussed above. . . . If *Buckley* remains the law, this is an easy case. . . .

NOTES AND QUESTIONS

1. *Right of expressive association.* In NAACP v. Alabama ex rel. Patterson, 357 U.S. 449 (1958), the Supreme Court held that the First Amendment prohibited Alabama from requiring the NAACP to disclose the names and addresses of its members. The Court characterized the NAACP as a nonprofit corporation dedicated to furthering the shared political beliefs of its members through expressive activities. The Court declared that "freedom to engage in association for the advancement of beliefs and ideas is an inseparable aspect of the 'liberty' assured by the Due Process Clause of the Fourteenth Amendment, which embraces freedom of speech." The Court also recognized the "vital relationship between freedom to associate and privacy in one's associations." Therefore, the Court held that compelled disclosure of the NAACP's membership lists would violate the First Amendment because it would subject its members "to economic reprisal, loss of employment, threat of physical coercion, and other manifestations of public hostility." The Court reached this conclusion in the face of ample evidence regarding the state of Alabama's attempts to harass and intimidate the NAACP. (Remember, this case came out in 1958.) What state interest would justify compelled disclosure of membership information for a particular organization? Would the government's generalized suspicion that a group might be aiding potential terrorists be enough to justify compelling the group to turn over its membership information?

2. *Was the handbill misleading?* Why did the Court ignore the fact that the handbill was attributed to "Concerned Parents and Taxpayers" even though Margaret McIntyre was the only one responsible for the handbill's content? Is it because most readers of the handbill would not be misled because they would read the handbill critically—taking into account that anyone could claim to be

"Concerned Parents and Taxpayers" and that the handbill contained grammatical errors, an unsophisticated graphic design, and an obvious bias on a local political issue? Is the Court's faith in the audience justified?

3. *Disclosure requirements and electoral speech.* The majority in *McIntyre* stresses that Ohio is attempting to regulate "pure speech" rather than "the mechanics of the electoral process." Justice Scalia's dissent, on the other hand, notes that the Court has previously "approved much more onerous disclosure requirements [than the one at issue in *McIntyre*] in the name of fair elections." You should reevaluate this claim after reading the cases in the next section.

4. *More anonymous speech issues in the Supreme Court. McIntyre* is not the Supreme Court's only, or even its last, word on the right to speak anonymously. In Talley v. California, 362 U.S. 60, 80 (1960), the Court struck down an ordinance prohibiting *all* anonymous handbilling, finding the ordinance insufficiently tailored to the state interest in preventing fraud. In Watchtower Bible & Tract Society of New York, Inc. v. Stratton, 536 U.S. 150 (2002), the Court struck down an ordinance prohibiting door-to-door canvassing without a permit from the mayor's office, holding that the ordinance was overbroad and insufficiently tailored to protect privacy or prevent fraud and crime. In Buckley v. American Constitutional Law Foundation, Inc., 525 U.S. 182, 199-200 (1999), the Court struck down a state law requiring people circulating petitions regarding issue referenda to wear identification badges.

THEORY-APPLIED PROBLEMS—ANONYMITY AND ACCOUNTABILITY

1. *Mask ordinances.* Assume a state passes a law forbidding the wearing of a mask in public. Would such a statute be constitutional as a means to protect public safety? Would a statute that forbids the wearing of a mask in any building owned or leased by the state be constitutional? *Compare* Church of the Am. Knights of the Ku Klux Klan v. Kerid, 356 F.3d 197, 206-207 (2d Cir. 2004) (ordinance upheld), *with* American Knights of the Ku Klux Klan v. City of Goshen, 50 F. Supp. 2d 835, 840-842 (N.D. Ind. 1999) (ordinance struck down).

2. *Internet anonymity.* The internet has made it easier for citizens to speak anonymously or pseudonymously. Would a federal statute making it a crime to knowingly initiate an anonymous internet communication with the "intent to annoy, abuse, threaten, or harass any person who receives the communication" be likely to withstand a First Amendment challenge? For more on the topic of internet anonymity, see Lyrissa Barnett Lidsky & Thomas F. Cotter, *Authorship, Audiences, and Anonymous Speech*, 82 Notre Dame L. Rev. 1537 (2007); Lee Tien, *Who's Afraid of Anonymous Speech? McIntyre and the Internet*, 75 Or. L. Rev. 117, 120 (1996). For more discussion regarding online harassment, see Danielle Keats Citron, Hate Crimes in Cyberspace (2014).

DOE v. REED

561 U.S. 186 (2010)

Chief Justice ROBERTS delivered the opinion of the Court.

The State of Washington allows its citizens to challenge state laws by referendum. Roughly four percent of Washington voters must sign a petition to place such a referendum on the ballot. That petition, which by law must include the names and addresses of the signers, is then submitted to the government for verification and canvassing, to ensure that only lawful signatures are counted. The Washington Public Records Act (PRA) authorizes private parties to obtain copies of government documents, and the State construes the PRA to cover submitted referendum petitions.

This case arises out of a state law extending certain benefits to same-sex couples, and a corresponding referendum petition to put that law to a popular vote. Respondent intervenors invoked the PRA to obtain copies of the petition, with the names and addresses of the signers. Certain petition signers and the petition sponsor objected, arguing that such public disclosure would violate their rights under the First Amendment.

The course of this litigation, however, has framed the legal question before us more broadly. The issue at this stage of the case is not whether disclosure of this particular petition would violate the First Amendment, but whether disclosure of referendum petitions in general would do so. We conclude that such disclosure does not as a general matter violate the First Amendment, and we therefore affirm the judgment of the Court of Appeals. We leave it to the lower courts to consider in the first instance the signers' more focused claim concerning disclosure of the information on this particular petition, which is pending before the District Court. . . .

III

[A.] The compelled disclosure of signatory information on referendum petitions is subject to review under the First Amendment. An individual expresses a view on a political matter when he signs a petition under Washington's referendum procedure. In most cases, the individual's signature will express the view that the law subject to the petition should be overturned. Even if the signer is agnostic as to the merits of the underlying law, his signature still expresses the political view that the question should be considered "by the whole electorate." In either case, the expression of a political view implicates a First Amendment right. The State, having "cho[sen] to tap the energy and the legitimizing power of the democratic process, . . . must accord the participants in that process the First Amendment rights that attach to their roles."

Respondents counter that signing a petition is a legally operative legislative act and therefore "does not involve any significant expressive element." It is true that signing a referendum petition may ultimately have the legal consequence of requiring the secretary of state to place the referendum on the ballot. But we do not see how adding such legal effect to an expressive activity somehow deprives that activity of its expressive component, taking it outside the scope of the First Amendment. Respondents themselves implicitly recognize that the signature expresses a particular viewpoint, arguing that one purpose served by disclosure is to allow the public to engage signers in a debate on the merits of the underlying law.

Petition signing remains expressive even when it has legal effect in the electoral process. But that is not to say that the electoral context is irrelevant to the nature of our First Amendment review. We allow States significant flexibility in implementing their own voting systems. To the extent a regulation concerns the legal effect of a particular activity in that process, the government will be afforded substantial latitude to enforce that regulation. Also pertinent to our analysis is the fact that the PRA is not a prohibition on speech, but instead a disclosure requirement. "[D]isclosure requirements may burden the ability to speak, but they...do not prevent anyone from speaking." Citizens United v. Federal Election Comm'n [*infra* p. 308].

We have a series of precedents considering First Amendment challenges to disclosure requirements in the electoral context. These precedents have reviewed such challenges under what has been termed "exacting scrutiny." See, e.g., Buckley v. Valeo, 424 U.S. 1, 64 (1976) [discussed *infra* p. 304] . . . That standard "requires a 'substantial relation' between the disclosure requirement and a 'sufficiently important' governmental interest." To withstand this scrutiny, "the strength of the governmental interest must reflect the seriousness of the actual burden on First Amendment rights."

[B.] Respondents assert two interests to justify the burdens of compelled disclosure under the PRA on First Amendment rights: (1) preserving the integrity of the electoral process by combating fraud, detecting invalid signatures, and fostering government transparency and accountability; and (2) providing information to the electorate about who supports the petition. Because we determine that the State's interest in preserving the integrity of the electoral process suffices to defeat the argument that the PRA is unconstitutional with respect to referendum petitions in general, we need not, and do not, address the State's "informational" interest.

The State's interest in preserving the integrity of the electoral process is undoubtedly important. "States allowing ballot initiatives have considerable leeway to protect the integrity and reliability of the initiative process, as they have with respect to election processes generally." The State's interest is particularly strong with respect to efforts to root out fraud, which not only may produce fraudulent outcomes, but has a systemic effect as well: It "drives honest citizens out of the democratic process and breeds distrust of our government." . . .

But the State's interest in preserving electoral integrity is not limited to combating fraud. That interest extends to efforts to ferret out invalid signatures caused not by fraud but by simple mistake, such as duplicate signatures or signatures of individuals who are not registered to vote in the State. That interest also extends more generally to promoting transparency and accountability in the electoral process, which the State argues is "essential to the proper functioning of a democracy." Plaintiffs contend that the disclosure requirements of the PRA are not "sufficiently related" to the interest of protecting the integrity of the electoral process [because the secretary of state engages in a publicly observable verification and canvassing process and there are criminal laws addressing fraud in the petition process]. . . .

But the secretary's verification and canvassing will not catch all invalid signatures: The job is large and difficult (the secretary ordinarily checks "only 3 to 5% of signatures," and the secretary can make mistakes, too. Public disclosure can help cure the inadequacies of the verification and canvassing process.

Disclosure also helps prevent certain types of petition fraud otherwise difficult to detect, such as outright forgery and "bait and switch" fraud, in which an individual signs the petition based on a misrepresentation of the underlying issue. The signer is in the best position to detect these types of fraud, and public disclosure can bring the issue to the signer's attention.

Public disclosure thus helps ensure that the only signatures counted are those that should be, and that the only referenda placed on the ballot are those that garner enough valid signatures. Public disclosure also promotes transparency and accountability in the electoral process to an extent other measures cannot. In light of the foregoing, we reject plaintiffs' argument and conclude that public disclosure of referendum petitions in general is substantially related to the important interest of preserving the integrity of the electoral process.

[C.] Plaintiffs' more significant objection is that "the strength of the governmental interest" does not "reflect the seriousness of the actual burden on First Amendment rights." According to plaintiffs, the objective of those seeking disclosure of the R-71 petition is not to prevent fraud, but to publicly identify those who had validly signed and to broadcast the signers' political views on the subject of the petition. Plaintiffs allege, for example, that several groups plan to post the petitions in searchable form on the Internet and then encourage other citizens to seek out the R-71 signers.

Plaintiffs explain that once on the Internet, the petition signers' names and addresses "can be combined with publicly available phone numbers and maps," in what will effectively become a blueprint for harassment and intimidation. To support their claim that they will be subject to reprisals, plaintiffs cite examples from the history of a similar proposition in California, and from the experience of one of the petition sponsors in this case.

In related contexts, we have explained that those resisting disclosure can prevail under the First Amendment if they can show "a reasonable probability that the compelled disclosure [of personal information] will subject them to threats, harassment, or reprisals from either Government officials or private parties." [Buckley v. Valeo.] The question before us, however, is not whether PRA disclosure violates the First Amendment with respect to those who signed the R-71 petition, or other particularly controversial petitions. The question instead is whether such disclosure in general violates the First Amendment rights of those who sign referendum petitions.

The problem for plaintiffs is that their argument rests almost entirely on the specific harm they say would attend disclosure of the information on the R-71 petition, or on similarly controversial ones. But typical referendum petitions "concern tax policy, revenue, budget, or other state law issues." Voters care about such issues, some quite deeply—but there is no reason to assume that any burdens imposed by disclosure of typical referendum petitions would be remotely like the burdens plaintiffs fear in this case.

Plaintiffs have offered little in response. They have provided us scant evidence or argument beyond the burdens they assert disclosure would impose on R-71 petition signers or the signers of other similarly controversial petitions. Indeed, what little plaintiffs do offer with respect to typical petitions in Washington hurts, not helps: Several other petitions in the State "have been subject to release in recent years," plaintiffs tell us, but apparently that release has come without incident.

Faced with the State's unrebutted arguments that only modest burdens attend the disclosure of a typical petition, we must reject plaintiffs' broad challenge to the PRA. In doing so, we note—as we have in other election law disclosure cases—that upholding the law against a broad-based challenge does not foreclose a litigant's success in a narrower one. [P]laintiffs may press the narrower challenge in Count II of their complaint in proceedings pending before the District Court.

[Affirmed.]

[In separate concurring opinions, Justices Stevens, Breyer, Sotomayor, and Ginsburg expressed doubt that an as-applied challenge could succeed because in their view any burdens imposed on speech by disclosure of the signers' names would be inadequate to justify a holding that the First Amendment required secrecy. Justice Alito thought the plaintiffs would have a strong case for relief against the statute as applied to the Referendum 71 petition because they would be able to cite evidence of widespread intimidation and harassment accompanying a ballot proposition in California to ban gay marriage. Only Justice Scalia argued that the plaintiffs lacked any cognizable First Amendment interest. "Our Nation's longstanding traditions of legislating and voting in public refute the claim that the First Amendment accords a right to anonymity in the performance of an act with governmental effect."]

Justice THOMAS, dissenting.

Just as "[c]onfidence in the integrity of our electoral processes is essential to the functioning of our participatory democracy," [] so too is citizen participation in those processes, which necessarily entails political speech and association under the First Amendment. In my view, compelled disclosure of signed referendum and initiative petitions under the Washington Public Records Act (PRA), Wash. Rev. Code § 42.56.001, et seq. (2008), severely burdens those rights and chills citizen participation in the referendum process. Given those burdens, I would hold that Washington's decision to subject all referendum petitions to public disclosure is unconstitutional because there will always be a less restrictive means by which Washington can vindicate its stated interest in preserving the integrity of its referendum process. I respectfully dissent. . . .

NOTES AND QUESTIONS

1. *Strict scrutiny, or something else?* Is the "exacting scrutiny" applied by the majority equivalent to what courts have called "strict scrutiny" in other contexts?
2. *Freedom from disclosure as constitutional interest?* If the public's interest in who is seeking a referendum is not an interest protected by the First Amendment, is it anomalous to hold that the interests of the public officials or the petition signers in resisting disclosure *do* require First Amendment protection?

2. Disclosure of Political Campaign Contributions and Expenditures

Some background information (quite a bit, actually) is required to understand the Supreme Court's complex jurisprudence regarding disclosure requirements in the electoral context. One key distinction that must be appreciated is that between campaign expenditures and campaign contributions. The importance of this distinction arises from the Court's 1976 decision in Buckley v. Valeo, 424 U.S. 1 (1976).

Buckley addressed the constitutionality of certain provisions of the Federal Election Campaign Act (FECA), as amended in 1974. The FECA contained a provision forbidding any person from giving more than $1,000 in a year to the campaign of a candidate for federal office (the contribution limit), or from spending more than $1,000 in a year to advocate the election or defeat of a candidate (the expenditure or spending limit). The Court upheld the FECA's *contribution* limit, finding that its "*limited effect* upon First Amendment freedoms" was justified by the government interest in "limit[ing] the actuality and appearance of corruption resulting from large individual financial contributions." (Emphasis added.)

Yet the Court struck down the FECA's *expenditure* limit, finding the speech at issue to be core political speech: "Advocacy of the election or defeat of candidates for federal office is no less entitled to protection under the First Amendment than the discussion of political policy generally or advocacy of the passage or defeat of legislation." The government asserted that the "primary purpose" of the expenditure limit was to prevent corruption and the appearance of corruption and "to prevent circumvention of the contribution limitation." The government contended, moreover, an "ancillary" interest in "equalizing the relative ability of individuals and groups to influence the outcome of elections." The Court found that the expenditure limitations did not adequately serve the government's primary interests, and it rejected the government's ancillary interest on the grounds that the First Amendment forbids the government from "restrict[ing] the speech of some elements of our society in order to enhance the relative voice of others."

In essence, *Buckley* found that the expenditure limit violated the First Amendment because it equated the spending of money on advocating a candidate with actually speaking in favor of that candidate. Moreover, the *Buckley* Court viewed the limit on expenditures "relative to a clearly identified candidate" as "preclud[ing] most associations from effectively amplifying the voice of their adherents, the original basis for the recognition of First Amendment protection of the freedom of association." The Court cited *NAACP v. Alabama*, which had recognized a right of expressive association, in support of this proposition.

In addition to the contribution and expenditure limits at issue in *Buckley*, the FECA contained disclosure requirements requiring reporting of contributions and expenditures (and the identities of those behind them) to the Federal Election Commission. The Supreme Court applied "exacting scrutiny" to these disclosure requirements because "compelled disclosure has the potential for substantially infringing the exercise of First Amendment rights." However, the Court upheld the disclosure requirements, finding them to be "the least restrictive means" of achieving the government's compelling interests in informing the electorate about how campaigns are financed, preventing corruption and the appearance of corruption, and detecting violations of the contributions limits. How can this holding be reconciled with the Court's decision in *McIntyre*, which recognized a qualified First Amendment right to speak anonymously in support of a ballot referendum measure? How did the state interests asserted to justify the disclosure requirements in *McIntyre* differ from the state interests asserted in *Buckley*? Is there a difference between speaking in favor of an issue, like Margaret McIntyre did, and speaking in favor of a candidate?

Buckley gave federal candidates for political office, as well as their supporters and detractors, plenty of avenues for circumventing the FECA's regulations. The contribution limits upheld in *Buckley* did not apply to "soft money"—money given to political parties or other political organizations and not used to directly advocate the election or defeat of specific candidates. Eventually such funds, raised primarily from corporations and labor unions, made the FECA's contribution limits largely ineffectual. In the Bipartisan Campaign Reform Act of 2002 (BCRA) (better known as the McCain-Feingold Act, after its sponsors), Congress amended the Federal Election Campaign Act to eliminate loopholes, particularly the soft-money loophole. *See* Pub. L. No. 107-155, 116 Stat. 81 (codified in scattered sections of 2 and 47 U.S.C.). The Supreme Court upheld a facial challenge to the new restrictions on soft money in an extremely lengthy and complex decision in McConnell v. Federal

Election Comm'n, 540 U.S. 93 (2003). As part of this decision, the Court also upheld several new disclosure requirements imposed on election-related speech.

The BCRA's disclosure requirements were a response to perceived circumvention of the disclosure requirements upheld in *Buckley* in 1976. At that time, the FECA required sponsors of political ads *expressly* advocating election or defeat of a candidate to disclose their names to the Federal Election Commission (FEC). The FEC construed the disclosure provision to apply only when an election ad contained "magic words" such as "Elect John Smith" or "Vote Against Jane Doe." Unless the ad contained the "magic words," it was designated an "issue ad" and did not have to comply with the disclosure requirements (or the spending limitations) of the FECA. The "magic words" construction and the marked differential in treatment of express advocacy versus issue advocacy was not arbitrary: it was an attempt to protect the First Amendment rights of individuals or organizations to speak out regarding political *issues*, because this speech arguably does not pose the same dangers to the electoral process as speech regarding a candidate. Nonetheless, the express advocacy versus issue advocacy distinction was easy to exploit. Anyone who wanted to avoid the disclosure requirements only had to be slightly clever or subtle to produce an ad supporting or attacking a candidate that did not contain the "magic words."

Congress tried to eliminate this perceived end-run around the FECA's disclosure requirements by redefining the category of ads subject to the requirements. Instead of distinguishing between express ads and issue ads, the BCRA broadened the FECA's disclosure requirements to apply to a new category of ads knows as "electioneering communications." Electioneering communications are "'broadcast, cable, or satellite communication[s]' that refer to a candidate for federal office in the sixty days prior to the general election or the thirty days prior to the primary." 2 U.S.C.A. § 434(f)(3)(A)(i) (West Supp. IV 2004) (amending section 304 of the FECA). Section 203 of the BCRA made it a federal crime for corporations or unions to use general treasury funds to pay for "electioneering communications," *and* section 201 subjected this new category of electioneering communications to "significant disclosure requirements." 2 U.S.C. § 441b(b)(2); McConnell v. FEC, 540 U.S. 93, 190 (2003).

The Supreme Court upheld the new restrictions on "electioneering communications," including the disclosure provisions, against a facial challenge in *McConnell.* The majority opinion expressed hostility to anonymous political speech and, in the process, cast doubt on the scope of the right to speak anonymously that the Court had recognized in McIntyre v. Ohio, *supra.* The Court agreed with Congress that "sham issue ads"—ads that advocated the support or defeat of a candidate without using the "magic words"—were tainting the electoral process. The Court criticized the sponsors of these *"so-called* issue ads," observing that they "often used misleading names to conceal their identity." *Id.* at 128 (emphasis added). Moreover, the Court specifically criticized the ad sponsors' choice to speak anonymously, characterizing their actions as attempting to "hide themselves from the scrutiny of the voting public." The Court accepted the argument that this would impair the public's ability "to make informed choices in the political marketplace."

The Court branded the anonymous ads as "dubious and misleading" in part because the pseudonyms used by their sponsors suggested broad support for their message. As an example, the Court cited an ad run by "Republicans for Clean Air" in the 2000 presidential primary. "Republicans for Clean Air" was actually sponsored by two (rather wealthy) individuals rather than an organization. The Court credited evidence that "mysterious groups" ran ads under "misleading names" in order to boost the effectiveness of the ads. Thus, the Court essentially treated the decision to remain anonymous as a dirty campaign trick, and it viewed the anonymous ads as contributing little, if any, to political discourse.

These assumptions led the Court to uphold the BCRA's various disclosure requirements on their face. The Court's discussion of BCRA § 201 is illustrative. Section 201 amended the FECA to require anyone who disburses or makes a contract to disburse $10,000 or more per calendar year on electioneering communications to file a statement with the FEC. This statement must identify, among other things, all those who contributed $1,000 or more to the disbursement. The Court recognized that, *as applied*, this requirement might interfere with the First Amendment right of association; however, it stated that the disclosure requirement "does not prevent anyone from speaking." *Id.* at 197-198. The Court also found the disclosure requirements amply supported by three "important state interests," namely, providing more information to the electors, deterring corruption and the appearance of corruption, and providing data necessary to enforce other campaign finance restrictions.

The Supreme Court addressed disclosure requirements in the election context once again in its 2010 decision in Citizens United v. Federal Election Comm'n, 558 U.S. 310 (2010), which is excerpted below to illustrate both the Court's current thinking with regard to disclosure and disclaimer provisions in the electoral context as well as its much more controversial application of First Amendment principles to corporate participation in the electoral process. Pay special attention to both issues as you read the opinion below.

Factually, the *Citizens United* case involved a highly critical and partisan documentary about the Democratic presidential candidate Hillary Clinton. The documentary was sponsored by Citizens United, a nonprofit corporation devoted to advancing conservative causes. Citizens United planned to offer the movie on a pay-per-view or "video-on-demand" basis in the weeks preceding the 2008 presidential primary, but the Federal Election Commission found that the movie was an "electioneering communication" under the BCRA. The BCRA prohibited corporations and unions from making independent expenditures from general treasury funds for "electioneering communications," defined as publicly distributed "broadcast, cable or satellite communication[s]" referring to a "clearly identified candidate" for federal elective office, within 30 days of a primary or 60 days of a general election. The BCRA allowed corporations and unions to make electioneering communications or engage in express advocacy for or against candidates, but only if they established "separate segregated funds" limited to donations from the corporation's employees or stockholders or the union's members. Relatively few took advantage of this provision, however, because of the difficulty of establishing such funds.

The district court granted summary judgment for the FEC, denying Citizens United's request for declaratory and injunctive relief. The Supreme Court granted certiorari, and held by a 5-4 margin that the BCRA's ban on electioneering communications by corporations and unions was unconstitutional and that the government may not prevent them from tapping into their general treasury funds to support or oppose candidates for federal elective office, so long as the expenditures of funds are not coordinated with candidates. In other words, the decision not only allowed corporations to engage in electioneering communications; it also allowed them to engage in political speech during elections on an equal footing with individual citizens by allowing for payments for political advertisements from general treasury funds. In reaching its broad holding, the Court overturned two prior cases: McConnell v. Federal Election Comm'n, 540 U.S. 93 (2003), which had upheld the principal features of the BCRA, and Austin v. Michigan Chamber of Commerce, 494 U.S. 652 (1990), which had supported banning independent expenditures by corporations and unions to support or oppose candidates.

In addition to banning electioneering communications by corporations and unions, another provision of the BCRA imposed disclosure and disclaimer obligations on *anyone* making electioneering communications. *Citizens United* also challenged the constitutionality of these disclosure and disclaimer provisions, which the Supreme Court upheld by an 8-1 margin.

CITIZENS UNITED v. FEDERAL ELECTION COMMISSION

558 U.S. 310 (2010)

KENNEDY, J., delivered the opinion of the Court.
[The facts and procedural history of the case are summarized above.]

III.

The First Amendment provides that "Congress shall make no law. . . bridging the freedom of speech." Laws enacted to control or suppress speech may operate at different points in the speech process. The following are just a few examples of restrictions that have been attempted at different stages of the speech process-all laws found to be invalid: restrictions requiring a permit at the outset, *Watchtower Bible & Tract Soc. of N.Y., Inc. v. Village of Stratton,* 536 U.S. 150, 153 (2002); imposing a burden by impounding proceeds on receipts or royalties, *Simon & Schuster, Inc. v. Members of N.Y. State Crime Victims Bd.,* 502 U.S. 105, 108, 123 (1991); seeking to exact a cost after the speech occurs; and subjecting the speaker to criminal penalties, *Brandenburg v. Ohio,* 395 U.S. 444, 445 (1969) *(per curiam).*

The law before us is an outright ban, backed by criminal sanctions. Section 441b makes it a felony for all corporations—including nonprofit advocacy corporations— either to expressly advocate the election or defeat of candidates or to broadcast electioneering communications within 30 days of a primary election and 60 days of a general election. Thus, the following acts would all be felonies under § 441b: The Sierra Club runs an ad, within the crucial phase of 60 days before the general election, that exhorts the public to disapprove of a Congressman who favors logging in national forests; the National Rifle Association publishes a book urging the public to vote for the challenger because the incumbent U.S. Senator supports a handgun ban; and the American Civil Liberties Union creates a Web site telling the public to vote for a Presidential candidate in light of that candidate's defense of free speech. These prohibitions are classic examples of censorship.

Section 441b is a ban on corporate speech notwithstanding the fact that a PAC created by a corporation can still speak. [] A PAC is a separate association from the corporation. So the PAC exemption from § 441b's expenditure ban, § 441b(b)(2), does not allow corporations to speak. Even if a PAC could somehow allow a corporation to speak—and it does not—the option to form PACs does not alleviate the First Amendment problems with § 441b. PACs are burdensome alternatives; they are expensive to administer and subject to extensive regulations. . . .

. . . This might explain why fewer than 2,000 of the millions of corporations in this country have PACs. [] PACs, furthermore, must exist before they can speak. Given the onerous restrictions, a corporation may not be able to establish a PAC in time to make its views known regarding candidates and issues in a current campaign.

Section 441b's prohibition on corporate independent expenditures is thus a ban on speech. As a "restriction on the amount of money a person or group can spend on political communication during a campaign," that statute "necessarily reduces the quantity of expression by restricting the number of issues discussed, the depth of their exploration, and the size of the audience reached." *Buckley v. Valeo*[]. Were the Court to uphold these restrictions, the Government could repress speech by silencing certain voices at any of the various points in the speech process. []. If § 441b applied to individuals, no one would believe that it is merely a time, place, or manner restriction on speech. Its purpose and effect are to silence entities whose voices the Government deems to be suspect.

Speech is an essential mechanism of democracy, for it is the means to hold officials accountable to the people. [] The right of citizens to inquire, to hear, to speak, and to use information to reach consensus is a precondition to enlightened self-government and a necessary means to protect it. The First Amendment "'has its fullest and most urgent application' to speech uttered during a campaign for political office." []

For these reasons, political speech must prevail against laws that would suppress it, whether by design or inadvertence. Laws that burden political speech are "subject to strict scrutiny," which requires the Government to prove that the restriction "furthers a compelling interest and is narrowly tailored to achieve that interest." []. While it might be maintained that political speech simply cannot be banned or restricted as a categorical matter [], the quoted language from *WRTL* provides a sufficient framework for protecting the relevant First Amendment interests in this case. We shall employ it here.

Premised on mistrust of governmental power, the First Amendment stands against attempts to disfavor certain subjects or viewpoints. []. Prohibited, too, are restrictions distinguishing among different speakers, allowing speech by some but not others. []. As instruments to censor, these categories are interrelated: Speech restrictions based on the identity of the speaker are all too often simply a means to control content.

Quite apart from the purpose or effect of regulating content, moreover, the Government may commit a constitutional wrong when by law it identifies certain preferred speakers. By taking the right to speak from some and giving it to others, the Government deprives the disadvantaged person or class of the right to use speech to strive to establish worth, standing, and respect for the speaker's voice. The Government may not by these means deprive the public of the right and privilege to determine for itself what speech and speakers are worthy of consideration. The First Amendment protects speech and speaker, and the ideas that flow from each.

. . . [I]t is inherent in the nature of the political process that voters must be free to obtain information from diverse sources in order to determine how to cast their votes. . . .

We find no basis for the proposition that, in the context of political speech, the Government may impose restrictions on certain disfavored speakers. Both history and logic lead us to this conclusion.

[A.1.] The Court has recognized that First Amendment protection extends to corporations. [].

This protection has been extended by explicit holdings to the context of political speech. []. Under the rationale of these precedents, political speech does not lose First Amendment protection "simply because its source is a corporation." *Bellotti* []; see *Pacific Gas & Elec. Co. v. Public Util. Comm'n of Cal.,* [] (plurality opinion). The Court has thus rejected the argument that political speech of corporations or other associations should be treated differently under the First Amendment simply because such associations are not "natural persons." []

In *Buckley,* the Court addressed various challenges to the Federal Election Campaign Act of 1971 (FECA) as amended in 1974. [*Buckley* upheld limits on direct contributions to candidates based on prevention of corruption and the appearance of corruption, since large contributions could be used to "secure a political quid pro quo"; however, *Buckley* struck down limits on independent expenditures because they did not serve the government's anti-corruption interests. Buckley failed to address the FECA's ban on independent expenditures by corporations and unions, which was recodified] at 2 U.S.C. § 441b four months after *Buckley* was decided. Section 441b is the independent expenditure restriction challenged here.

Less than two years after *Buckley, Bellotti* reaffirmed the First Amendment principle that the Government cannot restrict political speech based on the speaker's corporate identity. *Bellotti* could not have been clearer when it struck down a state-law prohibition on corporate independent expenditures related to referenda issues[.] .

. . [*Bellotti*] rested on the principle that the Government lacks the power to ban corporations from speaking.

Bellotti did not address the constitutionality of the State's ban on corporate independent expenditures to support candidates. In our view, however, that restriction would have been unconstitutional under *Bellotti*'s central principle: that the First Amendment does not allow political speech restrictions based on a speaker's corporate identity.

Thus the law stood until *Austin. Austin* "uph[eld] a direct restriction on the independent expenditure of funds for political speech for the first time in [this Court's] history." 494 U.S., at 695 (Kennedy, J., dissenting). There, the Michigan Chamber of Commerce sought to use general treasury funds to run a newspaper ad supporting a specific candidate. Michigan law, however, prohibited corporate independent expenditures that supported or opposed any candidate for state office. A violation of the law was punishable as a felony. The Court sustained the speech prohibition.

To bypass *Buckley* and *Bellotti,* the *Austin* Court identified a new governmental interest in limiting political speech: an antidistortion interest. *Austin* found a compelling governmental interest in preventing "the corrosive and distorting effects of immense aggregations of wealth that are accumulated with the help of the corporate form and that have little or no correlation to the public's support for the corporation's political ideas."

[B.] The Court is thus confronted with conflicting lines of precedent: a pre-*Austin* line that forbids restrictions on political speech based on the speaker's corporate identity and a post-*Austin* line that permits them. No case before *Austin* had held that Congress could prohibit independent expenditures for political speech based on the speaker's corporate identity. Before *Austin* Congress had enacted legislation for this purpose, and the Government urged the same proposition before this Court. See *MCFL, supra,* at 257, 107 S. Ct. 616 []. In neither of these cases did the Court adopt the proposition.

In its defense of the corporate-speech restrictions in § 441b, the Government notes the antidistortion rationale on which *Austin* and its progeny rest in part, yet it all but abandons reliance upon it. It argues instead that two other compelling interests support *Austin*'s holding that corporate expenditure restrictions are constitutional: an anticorruption interest, and a shareholder-protection interest. We consider the three points in turn.

If the First Amendment has any force, it prohibits Congress from fining or jailing citizens, or associations of citizens, for simply engaging in political speech. If the antidistortion rationale were to be accepted, however, it would permit Government to ban political speech simply because the speaker is an association that has taken on the corporate form. The Government contends that *Austin* permits it to ban corporate expenditures for almost all forms of communication stemming from a corporation. If *Austin* were correct, the Government could prohibit a corporation from expressing political views in media beyond those presented here, such as by printing books. The Government responds "that the FEC has never applied this statute to a book," and if it did, "there would be quite [a] good as-applied challenge." Tr. of Oral Arg. 65 (Sept. 9, 2009). This troubling assertion of brooding governmental power cannot be reconciled with the confidence and stability in civic discourse that the First Amendment must secure.

Political speech is "indispensable to decisionmaking in a democracy, and this is no less true because the speech comes from a corporation rather than an individual." *Bellotti*. . . . *Buckley* rejected the premise that the Government has an interest "in equalizing the relative ability of individuals and groups to influence the outcome of elections." *Buckley* was specific in stating that "the skyrocketing cost of political campaigns" could not sustain the governmental prohibition. The First Amendment's protections do not depend on the speaker's "financial ability to engage in public discussion."

. . . The rule that political speech cannot be limited based on a speaker's wealth is a necessary consequence of the premise that the First Amendment generally prohibits the suppression of political speech based on the speaker's identity.

. . . It is irrelevant for purposes of the First Amendment that corporate funds may "have little or no correlation to the public's support for the corporation's political ideas." []. All speakers, including individuals and the media, use money amassed from the economic marketplace to fund their speech. The First Amendment protects the resulting speech, even if it was enabled by economic transactions with persons or entities who disagree with the speaker's ideas. []

Austin's antidistortion rationale would produce the dangerous, and unacceptable, consequence that Congress could ban political speech of media corporations. [] Media corporations are now exempt from § 441b's ban on corporate expenditures. []. Yet media corporations accumulate wealth with the help of the corporate form, the largest media corporations have "immense aggregations of wealth," and the views expressed by media corporations often "have little or no correlation to the public's support" for those views. Thus, under the Government's reasoning, wealthy media corporations could have their voices diminished to put them on par with other media entities. . . .

The media exemption discloses further difficulties with the law now under consideration. There is no precedent supporting laws that attempt to distinguish between corporations which are deemed to be exempt as media corporations and those which are not. "We have consistently rejected the proposition that the institutional press has any constitutional privilege beyond that of other speakers."[]

With the advent of the Internet and the decline of print and broadcast media, moreover, the line between the media and others who wish to comment on political and social issues becomes far more blurred.

. . . *Austin* interferes with the "open marketplace" of ideas protected by the First Amendment. [] It permits the Government to ban the political speech of millions of associations of citizens. See Statistics of Income 2 (5.8 million for-profit corporations filed 2006 tax returns). Most of these are small corporations without large amounts of wealth. See Supp. Brief for Chamber of Commerce of the United States of America as *Amicus Curiae* 1, 3 (96% of the 3 million businesses that belong to the U.S. Chamber of Commerce have fewer than 100 employees); M. Keightley, Congressional Research Service Report for Congress, Business Organizational Choices: Taxation and Responses to Legislative Changes 10 (2009) (more than 75% of corporations whose income is taxed under federal law, see 26 U.S.C. § 301, have less than $1 million in receipts per year). This fact belies the Government's argument that the statute is justified on the ground that it prevents the "distorting effects of immense aggregations of wealth." [] It is not even aimed at amassed wealth.

The censorship we now confront is vast in its reach. The Government has "muffle[d] the voices that best represent the most significant segments of the economy." []. And "the electorate [has been] deprived of information, knowledge and opinion vital to its function." []. By suppressing the speech of manifold corporations, both for-profit and nonprofit, the Government prevents their voices and viewpoints from reaching the public and advising voters on which persons or entities are hostile to their interests. Factions will necessarily form in our Republic, but the remedy of "destroying the liberty" of some factions is "worse than the disease." The Federalist No. 10, p. 130 (B. Wright ed. 1961) (J. Madison). Factions should be checked by permitting them all to speak, and by entrusting the people to judge what is true and what is false.

The purpose and effect of this law is to prevent corporations, including small and nonprofit corporations, from presenting both facts and opinions to the public. . . . References to massive corporate treasuries should not mask the real operation of this law. Rhetoric ought not obscure reality.

Even if § 441b's expenditure ban were constitutional, wealthy corporations could still lobby elected officials, although smaller corporations may not have the resources to do so. And wealthy individuals and unincorporated associations can spend unlimited amounts on independent expenditures. *See, e.g., WRTL*, 551 U.S., at 503-504 (opinion of Scalia, J.) ("In the 2004 election cycle, a mere 24 individuals contributed an astounding total of $142 million to [26 U.S.C. § 527 organizations]"). Yet certain disfavored associations of citizens—those that have taken on the corporate form—are penalized for engaging in the same political speech.

When Government seeks to use its full power, including the criminal law, to command where a person may get his or her information or what distrusted source he or she may not hear, it uses censorship to control thought. This is unlawful. The First Amendment confirms the freedom to think for ourselves.

What we have said also shows the invalidity of other arguments made by the Government. For the most part relinquishing the antidistortion rationale, the Government falls back on the argument that corporate political speech can be banned in order to prevent corruption or its appearance. . . . [But l]imits on independent expenditures, such as § 441b, have a chilling effect extending well beyond the Government's interest in preventing *quid pro quo* corruption. . . .

. . . . When *Buckley* identified a sufficiently important governmental interest in preventing corruption or the appearance of corruption, that interest was limited to *quid pro quo* corruption. []. The fact that speakers may have influence over or access to elected officials does not mean that these officials are corrupt:

> Favoritism and influence are not...avoidable in representative politics. It is in the nature of an elected representative to favor certain policies, and, by necessary corollary, to favor the voters and contributors who support those policies. It is well understood that a substantial and legitimate reason, if not the only reason, to cast a vote for, or to make a contribution to, one candidate over another is that the candidate will respond by producing those political outcomes the supporter favors. Democracy is premised on responsiveness. McConnell, 540 U.S., at 297 (opinion of Kennedy, J.).

Reliance on a "generic favoritism or influence theory . . . is at odds with standard First Amendment analyses because it is unbounded and susceptible to no limiting principle."

The appearance of influence or access, furthermore, will not cause the electorate to lose faith in our democracy. By definition, an independent expenditure is political speech presented to the electorate that is not coordinated with a candidate. []. The fact that a corporation, or any other speaker, is willing to spend money to try to persuade voters presupposes that the people have the ultimate influence over elected officials. . . .

. . . . If elected officials succumb to improper influences from independent expenditures; if they surrender their best judgment; and if they put expediency before principle, then surely there is cause for concern. We must give weight to attempts by Congress to seek to dispel either the appearance or the reality of these influences. The remedies enacted by law, however, must comply with the First Amendment; and, it is our law and our tradition that more speech, not less, is the governing rule. An outright ban on corporate political speech during the critical preelection period is not a permissible remedy. Here Congress has created categorical bans on speech that are asymmetrical to preventing *quid pro quo* corruption.

The Government contends further that corporate independent expenditures can be limited because of its interest in protecting dissenting shareholders from being compelled to fund corporate political speech. This asserted interest, like *Austin*'s antidistortion rationale, would allow the Government to ban the political speech even of media corporations. . . . . There is, furthermore, little evidence of abuse that cannot be corrected by shareholders "through the procedures of corporate democracy."[].

. . . . For the reasons above, it must be concluded that *Austin* was not well reasoned. . . . *Austin* is undermined by experience since its announcement. Political speech is so ingrained in our culture that speakers find ways to circumvent campaign finance laws. See, *e.g., McConnell*, 540 U.S., at 176-177, 124 S. Ct. 619 ("Given BCRA's tighter restrictions on the raising and spending of soft money, the incentives . . . to exploit [26 U.S.C. § 527] organizations will only increase"). Our Nation's speech dynamic is changing, and informative voices should not have to circumvent onerous restrictions to exercise their First Amendment rights. Speakers have become adept at presenting citizens with sound bites, talking points, and scripted messages that dominate the 24-hour news cycle. Corporations, like individuals, do not have monolithic views. On certain topics corporations may possess valuable expertise, leaving them the best equipped to point out errors or fallacies in speech of all sorts, including the speech of candidates and elected officials.

Rapid changes in technology—and the creative dynamic inherent in the concept of free expression—counsel against upholding a law that restricts political speech in certain media or by certain speakers. Today, 30-second television ads may be the most effective way to convey a political message. Soon, however, it may be that Internet sources, such as blogs and social networking Web sites, will provide citizens with significant information about political candidates and issues. Yet, § 441b would seem to ban a blog post expressly advocating the election or defeat of a candidate if that blog were created with corporate funds. The First Amendment does not permit Congress to make these categorical distinctions based on the corporate identity of the speaker and the content of the political speech.

. . . *Austin* should be and now is overruled. We return to the principle established in *Buckley* and *Bellotti* that the Government may not suppress political speech on the basis of the speaker's corporate identity. No sufficient governmental interest justifies limits on the political speech of nonprofit or for-profit corporations. . . .

IV.

[A.] Citizens United next challenges BCRA's disclaimer and disclosure provisions as applied to *Hillary* [its partisan documentary about 2008 Democratic presidential candidate Hillary Clinton] and the three advertisements for the movie. Under [Section 311 of the Bipartisan Campaign Reform Act of 2002 (BCRA)], televised electioneering communications funded by anyone other than a candidate must include a disclaimer that "'is responsible for the content of this advertising.'" The required statement must be made in a "clearly spoken manner," and displayed on the screen in a "clearly readable manner" for at least four seconds. It must state that the communication "is not authorized by any candidate or candidate's committee"; it must also display the name and address (or Web site address) of the person or group that funded the advertisement. Under BCRA § 201, any person who spends more than $10,000 on electioneering communications within a calendar year must file a disclosure statement with the FEC. That statement must identify the person making the expenditure, the amount of the expenditure, the election to which the communication was directed, and the names of certain contributors.

Disclaimer and disclosure requirements may burden the ability to speak, but they "impose no ceiling on campaign-related activities," *Buckley*[], and "do not prevent anyone from speaking," *McConnell* []. The Court has subjected these requirements to "exacting scrutiny," which requires a "substantial relation" between the disclosure requirement and a "sufficiently important" governmental interest.

In *Buckley*, the Court explained that disclosure could be justified based on a governmental interest in "provid[ing] the electorate with information" about the sources of election-related spending. The *McConnell* Court applied this interest in rejecting facial challenges to BCRA §§ 201 and 311. There was evidence in the record that independent groups were running election-related advertisements "while hiding behind dubious and misleading names." The Court therefore upheld BCRA §§ 201 and 311 on the ground that they would help citizens 'make informed choices in the political marketplace.

Although both provisions were facially upheld, the Court acknowledged that as-applied challenges would be available if a group could show a "reasonable probability" that disclosure of its contributors' names "will subject them to threats, harassment, or reprisals from either Government officials or private parties."

For the reasons stated below, we find the statute valid as applied to the ads for the movie and to the movie itself.

[B.] Citizens United argues that the disclaimer requirements in § 311 are unconstitutional as applied to its ads [promoting the *Hillary* documentary]. It contends that the governmental interest in providing information to the electorate does not justify requiring disclaimers for any commercial advertisements, including the ones at issue here. We disagree. The ads fall within BCRA's definition of an "electioneering communication." They referred to then-Senator Clinton by name shortly before a primary and contained pejorative references to her candidacy. The disclaimers required by § 311 "provid[e] the electorate with information" [] and "insure that the voters are fully informed" about the person or group who is speaking []. At the very least, the disclaimers avoid confusion by making clear that the ads are not funded by a candidate or political party.

. . . [D]isclosure is a less restrictive alternative to more comprehensive regulations of speech. In *Buckley*, the Court upheld a disclosure requirement for independent expenditures even though it invalidated a provision that imposed a ceiling on those expenditures. In *McConnell*, three Justices who would have found § 441b to be unconstitutional nonetheless voted to uphold BCRA's disclosure and disclaimer requirements. And the Court has upheld registration and disclosure requirements on lobbyists, even though Congress has no power to ban lobbying itself. *United States v. Harriss*, 347 U.S. 612, 625 (1954). . . .

Citizens United also disputes that an informational interest justifies the application of § 201 to its ads, which only attempt to persuade viewers to see the film. Even if it disclosed the funding sources for the ads, Citizens United says, the information would not help viewers make informed choices in the political marketplace. This is similar to the argument rejected above with respect to disclaimers. Even if the ads only pertain to a commercial transaction, the public has an interest in knowing who is speaking about a candidate shortly before an election. . . .

Last, Citizens United argues that disclosure requirements can chill donations to an organization by exposing donors to retaliation. Some *amici* point to recent events in which donors to certain causes were blacklisted, threatened, or otherwise targeted for retaliation. In *McConnell*, the Court recognized that § 201 would be unconstitutional as applied to an organization if there were a reasonable probability that the group's members would face threats, harassment, or reprisals if their names were disclosed. The examples cited by *amici* are cause for concern. Citizens United, however, has offered no evidence that its members may face similar threats or reprisals. To the contrary, Citizens United has been disclosing its donors for years and has identified no instance of harassment or retaliation.

. . . A campaign finance system that pairs corporate independent expenditures with effective disclosure has not existed before today. . . . With the advent of the Internet, prompt disclosure of expenditures can provide shareholders and citizens with the information needed to hold corporations and elected officials accountable for their positions and supporters. Shareholders can determine whether their corporation's political speech advances the corporation's interest in making profits, and citizens can see whether elected officials are "'in the pocket' of so-called moneyed interests." 540 U.S., at 259 (opinion of Scalia, J.); [] The First Amendment protects political speech; and disclosure permits citizens and shareholders to react to the speech of corporate entities in a proper way. This transparency enables the electorate to make informed decisions and give proper weight to different speakers and messages.

[C.] For the same reasons we uphold the application of BCRA §§ 201 and 311 [the disclosure and disclaimer provisions] to the ads, we affirm their application to *Hillary.* We find no constitutional impediment to the application of BCRA's disclaimer and disclosure requirements to a movie broadcast via video-on-demand. And there has been no showing that, as applied in this case, these requirements would impose a chill on speech or expression.

NOTES AND QUESTIONS

1. *Mistrust of government as the basis for* Citizens United. Is the Court correct in stating that the First Amendment is "premised on mistrust of government"? What is the basis of this mistrust: government fallibility, government tyranny, or something else? Does this mistrust adequately justify the result in the case?

2. *Level of scrutiny.* What level of scrutiny does the majority apply in *Citizens United?* To the ban on corporate and union speech? To the disclosure and disclaimer requirements?

3. *No special constitutional protection for media corporations.* The Court states that there is no constitutional basis for giving nonmedia corporations fewer speech rights than media corporations. Is the Court correct? What does this statement suggest about whether the Court believes that the Press Clause gives special rights to the media not accorded to other speakers? You should revisit this question after studying the materials in Chapter 8, *infra.*

4. *The chilling effect of fear of harassment.* Should the *possibility* of harassment of speakers, standing alone, be a sufficient basis for invalidating the disclosure and disclaimer requirements of the BCRA? In his dissent from the portion of the *Citizens United* opinion upholding the BCRA's disclosure and disclaimer requirements, Justice Thomas noted that "the 'advent of the Internet' enables 'prompt disclosure of expenditures,' which 'provide[s]' political opponents 'with the information needed' to intimidate and retaliate against their foes." He therefore stated: "I cannot endorse a view of the First Amendment that subjects citizens of this nation to death threats, ruined careers, damaged or defaced property, or pre-emptive and threatening warning letters as a price for engaging in 'core political speech, the primary object of First Amendment protection.'" 558 U.S. at 485.

5. *Disclosure and the Federal Election Commission.* In *Citizens United,* the Supreme Court suggested it would look favorably on the imposition of additional disclosure requirements, and it seemed to view transparency as the cure for any harms that might flow from "electioneering speech" by corporations or unions. As of 2012, however, no additional disclosure requirements had been imposed.

6. *Aggregate limits on campaign contributions.* In McCutcheon v. Federal Election Commission, 572 U.S. ___, 134 S. Ct. 1434 (2014), the Supreme Court struck down the aggregate limits on the amount of money an individual could donate in a two-year election cycle. The four-justice plurality held the limits violated the First Amendment by restricting citizens' participation in the democratic process, while not furthering the government's stated interest in preventing quid pro quo corruption or the appearance of such corruption.

7. *Harassment as a basis for exemption from compelled disclosure laws.* In
   Buckley v. Valeo, 424 U.S. 1 (1976), the Supreme Court suggested that speakers
   might be exempted from compelled disclosure laws if they could show a
   "reasonable probability" that disclosure would subject speakers to "threats,
   harassment, or reprisals." Brown v. Socialist Workers' 74 Campaign Committee
   (Ohio), 459 U.S. 87 (1982), illustrates how speakers might make an as-applied
   challenge on this basis. *Brown* addressed the constitutionality of applying an
   Ohio law requiring political parties to report the names of campaign contributors
   and recipients of campaign disbursements to the Socialist Workers Party
   ("SWP"), a minor political party. The Court held that application of the Ohio law
   to the Party was unconstitutional. As applied, the law interfered with the Party's
   First Amendment interests in association and impaired its ability "to operate
   effectively" and disseminate its ideas. *Id.* at 98. The Party, which advocated the
   "abolition of capitalism and the establishment of a workers' government to
   achieve socialism," provided evidence of harassment by both private parties and
   the government. *Id.* at 88. For example, the Party showed that in the four years
   before trial, it had received "threatening phone calls and hate mail, the burning of
   SWP literature, the destruction of SWP members' property, police harassment of
   a party candidate, and the firing of shots at an SWP office. There was also
   evidence that in the 12-month period before trial 22 SWP members, including 4
   in Ohio, were fired because of their party membership." *Id.* at 99. In holding that
   the Party has shown a reasonable probability of harassment, the Court also relied
   on evidence presented at trial that the FBI had engaged in "massive" surveillance
   of the Party and had "conducted a counterintelligence program" designed to
   interfere with its recruiting efforts. "This program included 'disclosing to the
   press the criminal records of SWP candidates, and sending anonymous letters to
   SWP members, supporters, spouses, and employers.'" *Id.* Is "massive"
   government surveillance of an organization, standing alone, enough to constitute
   harassment—even where such surveillance is lawful? Would infiltration of the
   organization by government agents constitute harassment? Does it matter
   whether the government believes the organization's aims are unlawful or merely
   unwise? Professors Geoffrey R. Stone and William P. Marshall have observed
   that "*Brown* poses an intriguing question: In what circumstances, if any, does the
   First Amendment compel the government to exempt particular speakers from an
   otherwise constitutional law of general application?" *Brown v. Socialist
   Workers: Inequality as a Command of the First Amendment,* 1983 Sup. Ct. Rev.
   583, 583 (1983). How would you answer this question?
8. *Electoral anonymity and corruption.* Does public disclosure of the names of
   those who contribute to candidates for office or those who receive election-
   related expenditures truly inhibit electoral corruption? How do voters receive
   this information? How much significance do they give it?

CHAPTER
7

Commercial Speech

TABLE OF CONTENTS

To what extent should advertising enjoy serious First Amendment protection as "speech"? Before answering this question, consider the fact that prior to the 1970s, the Supreme Court routinely rejected efforts to extend free speech protection to commercial solicitations or advertisements, instead amalgamating such materials with commerce itself. For an example of this, see Railway Express Agency, Inc. v. New York City, 336 U.S. 106 (1949) (excerpted below in Section A). Indeed, Railway Express did not even attempt to litigate a First Amendment claim, resting its challenge to a ban on certain commercial advertising on the doctrine of substantive due process, on the Equal Protection Clause, and on the Interstate Commerce Clause. Thus, as late as 1949, the idea that advertising enjoys any protection as "speech" was utterly implausible—indeed, it was more plausible to raise a dormant Commerce Clause preemption argument against New York City's panel truck advertising ban!

The Supreme Court began to move away from its position that advertising does not have any free speech value (and hence protection) in the 1970s. The first major case involved advertising of a service that itself enjoyed serious constitutional protection: abortion. *See* Bigelow v. Virginia, 421 U.S. 809 (1975) (excerpted below in Section B). Because a targeted advertising ban against promotion of abortion services could be seen as a burden on the underlying substantive liberty (the due process liberty interest in terminating a pregnancy), it was not clear if the speech would have enjoyed protection if the subject matter were more mundane (for example, the sale of groceries). By the 1980s, however, it was clear that the Supreme Court had experienced a change of heart; commercial advertising no longer existed outside the protection of the Free Speech Clause.

Over time, the Supreme Court continued to expand the protection of commercial speech.

One of the most protective lines of the Supreme Court's commercial speech jurisprudence prohibits the regulation of commercial speech when direct regulations would be equally effective at advancing the government's purpose. Thus, even if the government could ban the sale of alcohol, it cannot regulate the advertising of alcohol as a means of discouraging consumption. Similarly, regulation of commercial speech cannot be more burdensome than the regulation of noncommercial speech, unless commercial speech as a class causes the particular social problem to be remedied. In fact, the Supreme Court's protection of commercial speech seemed even more aggressive—at least in the 1980s and 1990s—than its willingness to protect noncommercial speech in public forums.

This chapter begins by considering the historical exclusion of commercial speech from free speech protections and the Supreme Court's subsequent change of heart. It considers the special rules that limit government burdens on commercial speech. Finally, the chapter examines the problem of defining "commercial" speech. For a concept of such sweeping importance to First Amendment law, the Supreme Court has not been particularly helpful in defining precisely what makes speech "commercial" rather than "noncommercial."

A. THE HISTORICAL APPROACH

Valentine represents the classic pre-1970s statement on the exclusion of commercial speech from serious First Amendment protection. *Railway Express* is illustrative of how the legal community generally accepted the complete exclusion of advertising from the free speech project.

VALENTINE v. CHRESTENSEN

316 U.S. 52 (1942)

Mr. Justice ROBERTS delivered the opinion of the Court.

The respondent, a citizen of Florida, owns a former United States Navy submarine which he exhibits for profit. In 1940 he brought it to New York City and moored it at a State pier in the East River. He prepared and printed a handbill advertising the boat and soliciting visitors for a stated admission fee. On his attempting to distribute the bill in the city streets, he was advised by the petitioner, as Police Commissioner, that this activity would violate § 318 of the Sanitary Code, which forbids distribution in the streets of commercial and business advertising matter, but was told that he might freely distribute handbills solely devoted to "information or a public protest."

Respondent thereupon prepared and showed to the petitioner, in proof form, a double-faced handbill. On one side was a revision of the original, altered by the removal of the statement as to admission fee but consisting only of commercial advertising. On the other side was a protest against the action of the City Dock Department in refusing the respondent wharfage facilities at a city pier for the exhibition of his submarine, but no commercial advertising. The Police Department advised that distribution of a bill containing only the protest would not violate § 318, and would not be restrained, but that distribution of the double-faced bill was prohibited. The respondent, nevertheless, proceeded with the printing of his proposed bill and started to distribute it. He was restrained by the police.

Respondent then brought this suit to enjoin the petitioner from interfering with the distribution. [The district court ruled in favor of Chrestensen, and the Second Circuit affirmed.]

The question is whether the application of the ordinance to the respondent's activity was, in the circumstances, an unconstitutional abridgement of the freedom of the press and of speech.

1. This court has unequivocally held that the streets are proper places for the exercise of the freedom of communicating information and disseminating opinion and that, though the states and municipalities may appropriately regulate the privilege in the public interest, they may not unduly burden or proscribe its employment in these public thoroughfares. We are equally clear that the Constitution imposes no such restraint on government as respects purely commercial advertising. Whether, and to what extent, one may promote or pursue a gainful occupation in the streets, to what extent such activity shall be adjudged a derogation of the public right of user, are matters for legislative judgment. The question is not whether the legislative body may interfere with the harmless pursuit of a lawful business, but whether it must permit such pursuit by what it deems an undesirable invasion of, or interference with, the full and free use of the highways by the people in fulfillment of the public use to which streets are dedicated. If the respondent was attempting to use the streets of New York by distributing commercial advertising, the prohibition of the code provision was lawfully invoked against his conduct.

2. The respondent contends that, in truth, he was engaged in the dissemination of matter proper for public information, none the less so because there was inextricably attached to the medium of such dissemination commercial advertising matter. The court below appears to have taken this view, since it adverts to the difficulty of apportioning, in a given case, the contents of the communication as between what is of public interest and what is for private profit. We need not indulge nice appraisal based upon subtle distinctions in the present instance nor assume possible cases not now presented. It is enough for the present purpose that the stipulated facts justify the conclusion that the affixing of the protest against official conduct to the advertising circular was with the intent, and for the purpose, of evading the prohibition of the ordinance. If that evasion was successful, every merchant who desires to broadcast advertising leaflets in the streets need only append a civic appeal, or a moral platitude, to achieve immunity from the law's command.

The decree is

Reversed.

RAILWAY EXPRESS AGENCY, INC. v. NEW YORK

336 U.S. 106 (1949)

Mr. Justice DOUGLAS delivered the opinion of the Court.

Section 124 of the Traffic Regulations of the City of New York promulgated by the Police Commissioner provides:

"No person shall operate, or cause to be operated, in or upon any street an advertising vehicle; provided that nothing herein contained shall prevent the putting of business notices upon business delivery vehicles, so long as such vehicles are engaged in the usual business or regular work of the owner and not used merely or mainly for advertising."

Appellant is engaged in a nation-wide express business. It operates about 1,900 trucks in New York City and sells the space on the exterior sides of these trucks for advertising. That advertising is for the most part unconnected with its own business. It was convicted in the magistrate's court and fined. The judgment of conviction was sustained in the Court of Special Sessions. The Court of Appeals affirmed without opinion by a divided vote. The case is here on appeal. . . .

The Court of Special Sessions concluded that advertising on vehicles using the streets of New York City constitutes a distraction to vehicle drivers and to pedestrians alike and therefore affects the safety of the public in the use of the streets. We do not sit to weigh evidence on the due process issue in order to determine whether the regulation is sound or appropriate; nor is it our function to pass judgment on its wisdom. See *Olsen v. Nebraska*, 313 U.S. 236. We would be trespassing on one of the most intensely local and specialized of all municipal problems if we held that this regulation had no relation to the traffic problem of New York City. It is the judgment of the local authorities that it does have such a relation. And nothing has been advanced which shows that to be palpably false.

The question of equal protection of the laws is pressed more strenuously on us. . . .

[The court rejected the Equal Protection Clause argument.]

It is finally contended that the regulation is a burden on interstate commerce in violation of Art. I, § 8 of the Constitution. Many of these trucks are engaged in delivering goods in interstate commerce from New Jersey to New York. Where traffic control and the use of highways are involved and where there is no conflicting federal regulation, great leeway is allowed local authorities, even though the local regulation materially interferes with interstate commerce.

Affirmed.

NOTES AND QUESTIONS

1. *Commercial or noncommercial speech?* Was Chrestensen engaged in commercial or noncommercial speech? His revised leaflets included a complaint and remonstrance against the City Dock Department for refusing to rent him wharfage facilities for his submarine. If a commercial message is joined to a noncommercial message, should the speech be deemed "commercial"? Is Justice Roberts correct to assume that any other approach would effectively end regulation of commercial speech?

2. *The absence of a First Amendment claim.* Why did Railway Express not challenge a flat ban on speech? The New York City ordinance had the effect of prohibiting all speech on panel trucks, unless the speech related to the owner's business. The law was little different than a ban on political buttons or yard signs, in that it foreclosed the use of private property for speech. Does this suggest that the exclusion of commercial speech was deeply ingrained in the 1940s?

3. *Entertainment as commerce rather than speech.* In the early twentieth century, the Supreme Court emphatically rejected the contention that motion pictures, as well as "the theatre, the circus, and all other shows and spectacles, and their

performances" enjoy *any* First Amendment protection. Mutual Film Corp. v. Industrial Comm'n, 236 U.S. 230, 243 (1915). Writing for a unanimous Supreme Court, Justice McKenna explained that "[w]e immediately feel that the argument is wrong or strained which extends the guaranties of free opinion and speech to the multitudinous shows which are advertised on the bill-boards of our cities and towns . . . and which seeks to bring motion pictures and other spectacles into practical and legal similitude to a free press and liberty of opinion." *Id.* at 243-244. "The judicial sense supporting the common sense of the country is against the contention." *Id.* at 244. Thus, not only commercial speech, but also motion pictures, theater performances, and other public "spectacles" fell outside "the freedom of speech" safeguarded by the First Amendment. The profit-seeking motive of theater operators plainly informed the Supreme Court's decision to deny First Amendment protection to motion picture exhibitors: "It cannot be put out of view that the exhibition of moving pictures is a business pure and simple, originated and conducted for profit, like other spectacles, not to be regarded, nor intended to be regarded by the Ohio constitution, we think, as part of the press of the country or as organs of public opinion." *Id. Mutual Film Corp.* thus incorporates and reflects the *Valentine* view that speech associated with commercial activity has no claim on the First Amendment.

4. *Commercial speech as ordinary commerce.* Until the 1970s, the Supreme Court's view was that advertising was not "speech" but rather an aspect of "commerce." After its repudiation of the *Lochner* doctrine, see Lochner v. New York, 198 U.S. 45 (1908), the Supreme Court generally sustained any regulation of commerce that, at least in theory, possessed a rational relationship to a legitimate state interest. Accordingly, during this period any regulation of commercial speech was constitutional if it had any possible rational basis (whether real or merely theoretical). In light of this, raising a free speech objection to the New York City ordinance regulating ads on panel trucks would have been utterly futile.

B. THE NEW UNDERSTANDING

In 1975, the Supreme Court took a major step away from its traditional view that advertising had no call on free speech protections. By 1980, the turn was complete and the Supreme Court had declared advertising and other forms of commercial speech to be protected speech activity. The Court never really fashioned a compelling rationale for this change of policy, other than the law and economics rationale that some listeners valued advertising as much or more than other forms of speech (whether political, artistic, literary, or scientific). The Court seemed to be taking the view that it had no business establishing consumer preferences in the marketplace of ideas, and that categorically excluding commercial speech from protection could not be justified by the "low value" of such speech activity.

The Supreme Court did suggest that the transfer of information, regardless of its content, from a willing speaker to a willing listener fell within the scope of the Free Speech Clause. In other words, if speakers and listeners acted as if commercial speech has social value, then such speech must have social value. The Justices never attempted to ground their commercial speech doctrine in the original understanding of the Free Speech Clause (that is, did Madison think commercial speech enjoyed First Amendment protection?), perhaps because such an argument was untenable in light of consistent holdings over time that amalgamated commercial speech with commerce itself. Nor did they embrace a marketplace conception of the value of speech in other areas, such as sexually explicit speech, where consumers of speech might prefer modes of speech deemed offensive or harmful to the general community.

BIGELOW v. VIRGINIA
421 U.S. 809 (1975)

Mr. Justice BLACKMUN delivered the opinion of the Court.

An advertisement carried in appellant's newspaper led to his conviction for a violation of a Virginia statute that made it a misdemeanor, by the sale or circulation of any publication, to encourage or prompt the procuring of an abortion. The issue here is whether the editor-appellant's First Amendment rights were unconstitutionally abridged by the statute. The First Amendment, of course, is applicable to the States through the Fourteenth Amendment. *Schneider v. State*, 308 U.S. 147, 160 (1939).

The Virginia Weekly was a newspaper published by the Virginia Weekly Associates of Charlottesville. It was issued in that city and circulated in Albemarle County, with particular focus on the campus of the University of Virginia. Appellant, Jeffrey C. Bigelow, was a director and the managing editor and responsible officer of the newspaper.

On February 8, 1971, the Weekly's Vol. V, No. 6, was published and circulated under the direct responsibility of the appellant. On page 2 of that issue was the following advertisement:

"UNWANTED PREGNANCYLET US HELP YOU
Abortions are now legal in New York.
There are no residency requirements.
FOR IMMEDIATE PLACEMENT IN ACCREDITED
HOSPITALS AND CLINICS AT LOW COST

Contact

WOMEN'S PAVILION
515 Madison Avenue
New York, N.Y. 10022

or call any time

[(212) 371-6670 or (212) 371-6650
AVAILABLE 7 DAYS A WEEK
STRICTLY CONFIDENTIAL.
We will make all arrangements for you and help you with information and
counseling." . . .

On May 13 Bigelow was charged with violating Va. Code Ann. § 18.1-63 (1960). [The statute prohibited publication of any materials that could "encourage or prompt the procuring of abortion."]

Appellant was first tried and convicted. . . . The court rejected appellant's claim that the statute was unconstitutional and adjudged him guilty. He was sentenced to pay a fine of $500, with $350 thereof suspended "conditioned upon no further violation" of the statute.

The Supreme Court of Virginia granted review and by a 4-2 vote, affirmed Bigelow's conviction. . . .

The central assumption made by the Supreme Court of Virginia was that the First Amendment guarantees of speech and press are inapplicable to paid commercial advertisements. Our cases, however, clearly establish that speech is not stripped of First Amendment protection merely because it appears in that form.

The fact that the particular advertisement in appellant's newspaper had commercial aspects or reflected the advertiser's commercial interests did not negate all First Amendment guarantees. The State was not free of constitutional restraint merely because the advertisement involved sales or "solicitations," or because appellant was paid for printing it, or because appellant's motive or the motive of the advertiser may have involved financial gain. The existence of "commercial activity, in itself, is no justification for narrowing the protection of expression secured by the First Amendment." *Ginzburg v. United States*, 383 U.S. 463, 474 (1966).

Although other categories of speech—such as fighting words, *Chaplinsky v. New Hampshire*, 315 U.S. 568, 572 (1942), or obscenity, *Roth v. United States*, 354 U.S. 476, 481-485 (1957), *Miller v. California*, 413 U.S. 15, 23 (1973), or libel, *Gertz v. Robert Welch, Inc.*, 418 U.S. 323 (1974), or incitement, *Brandenburg v. Ohio*, 395 U.S. 444 (1969)—have been held unprotected, no contention has been made that the particular speech embraced in the advertisement in question is within any of these categories.

The appellee, as did the Supreme Court of Virginia, relies on *Valentine v. Chrestensen*, 316 U.S. 52 (1942), where a unanimous Court, in a brief opinion, sustained an ordinance which had been interpreted to ban the distribution of a handbill advertising the exhibition of a submarine. . . . But the holding is distinctly a limited one: the ordinance was upheld as a reasonable regulation of the manner in which commercial advertising could be distributed. The fact that it had the effect of banning a particular handbill does not mean that *Chrestensen* is authority for the proposition that all statutes regulating commercial advertising are immune from constitutional challenge. The case obviously does not support any sweeping proposition that advertising is unprotected *per se*. . . .

Viewed in its entirety, the advertisement conveyed information of potential interest and value to a diverse audience—not only to readers possibly in need of the services offered, but also to those with a general curiosity about, or genuine interest in, the subject matter or the law of another State and its development, and to readers seeking reform in Virginia. The mere existence of the Women's Pavilion in New York City, with the possibility of its being typical of other organizations there, and the availability of the services offered, were not unnewsworthy. Also, the activity advertised pertained to constitutional interests. See *Roe v. Wade*, 410 U.S. 113 (1973), and *Doe v. Bolton*, 410 U.S. 179 (1973). Thus, in the case, appellant's First Amendment interests coincided with the constitutional interests of the general public.

Moreover, the placement services advertised in appellant's newspaper were legally provided in New York at that time. The Virginia Legislature could not have regulated the advertiser's activity in New York, and obviously could not have proscribed the activity in that State.

A State does not acquire power or supervision over the internal affairs of another State merely because the welfare and health of its own citizens may be affected when they travel to that State. It may seek to disseminate information so as to enable its citizens to make better informed decisions when they leave. But it may not, under the guise of exercising internal police powers, bar a citizen of another State from disseminating information about an activity that is legal in that State.

We conclude, therefore, that the Virginia courts erred in their assumptions that advertising, as such, was entitled to no First Amendment protection and that appellant Bigelow had no legitimate First Amendment interest. We need not decide in this case the precise extent to which the First Amendment permits regulation of advertising that is related to activities the State may legitimately regulate or even prohibit. . . .

If application of this statute were upheld under these circumstances, Virginia might exert the power sought here over a wide variety of national publications or interstate newspapers carrying advertisements similar to the one that appeared in Bigelow's newspaper or containing articles on the general subject matter to which the advertisement referred. Other States might do the same. The burdens thereby imposed on publications would impair, perhaps severely, their proper functioning. We know from experience that "liberty of the press is in peril as soon as the government tries to compel what is to go into a newspaper." 2 Z. Chafee, Government and Mass Communications 633 (1947). The policy of the First Amendment favors dissemination of information and opinion, and "[t]he guarantees of freedom of speech and press were not designed to prevent 'the censorship of the press merely, but any action of the government by means of which it might prevent such free and general discussion of public matters as seems absolutely essential . . .' 2 Cooley, Constitutional Limitations 886 (8th ed.)." *Curtis Publishing Co. v. Butts*, 388 U.S. 130, 150 (1967) (opinion of Harlan, J.).

We conclude that Virginia could not apply Va. Code Ann. § 18.1-63 (1960), as it read in 1971, to appellant's publication of the advertisement in question without unconstitutionally infringing upon his First Amendment rights. The judgment of the Supreme Court of Virginia is therefore reversed.

It is so ordered.

Mr. Justice REHNQUIST, with whom Mr. Justice WHITE joins, dissenting.

The Court's opinion does not confront head-on the question which this case poses, but makes contact with it only in a series of verbal sideswipes. The result is the fashioning of a doctrine which appears designed to obtain reversal of this judgment, but at the same time to save harmless from the effects of that doctrine the many prior cases of this Court which are inconsistent with it. . . .

If the Court's decision does, indeed, turn upon its conclusion that the advertisement here in question was protected by the First and Fourteenth Amendments, the subject of the advertisement ought to make no difference. It will not do to say, as the Court does, that this advertisement conveyed information about the "subject matter or the law of another State and its development" to those "seeking reform in Virginia," and that it related to abortion, as if these factors somehow put it on a different footing from other commercial advertising. This was a proposal to furnish services on a commercial basis, and since we have always refused to distinguish for First Amendment purposes on the basis of content, it is no different from an advertisement for a bucket shop operation or a Ponzi scheme which has its headquarters in New York. If Virginia may not regulate advertising of commercial abortion agencies because of the interest of those seeking to reform Virginia's abortion laws, it is difficult to see why it is not likewise precluded from regulating advertising for an out-of-state bucket shop on the ground that such information might be of interest to those interested in repealing Virginia's "blue sky" laws. . . .

Assuming *arguendo* that this advertisement is something more than a normal commercial proposal, I am unable to see why Virginia does not have a legitimate public interest in its regulation. . . .

Since the statute in question is a "reasonable regulation that serves a legitimate public interest," *ante*, at 826, I would affirm the judgment of the Supreme Court of Virginia.

NOTES AND QUESTIONS

1. *Commercial or noncommercial speech?* Did the advertisement enjoy protection because it was about abortion or because it conveyed truthful, useful information to a willing recipient? In other words, is *Bigelow* really an abortion case rather than a free speech case?

2. *Is advertising different from other kinds of speech?* Does Justice Rehnquist have a point? Does Justice Blackmun adequately address the larger question that the case presents? Outside the specific context of abortion, may a state government limit or ban advertising in order to discourage activities or behaviors that, although legal, the state government thinks to be harmful?

3. *Subsequent doctrinal developments.* If *Bigelow* had been about abortion, rather than commercial speech more generally, its doctrinal impact would have been limited. Subsequent cases, however, generalized the right to convey and receive commercial information.

VIRGINIA STATE BOARD OF PHARMACY v. VIRGINIA CITIZENS CONSUMER COUNCIL, INC.

425 U.S. 748 (1976)

Mr. Justice BLACKMUN delivered the opinion of the Court.

The plaintiff-appellees in this case attack, as violative of the First and Fourteenth Amendments, that portion of § 54-524.35 of Va. Code Ann. (1974), which provides that a pharmacist licensed in Virginia is guilty of unprofessional conduct if he "(3) publishes, advertises or promotes, directly or indirectly, in any manner whatsoever, any amount, price, fee, premium, discount, rebate or credit terms...for any drugs which may be dispensed only by prescription." The three-judge District Court declared the quoted portion of the statute "void and of no effect" and enjoined the defendant-appellants, the Virginia State Board of Pharmacy and the individual members of that Board, from enforcing it. We noted probable jurisdiction of the appeal.

Since the challenged restraint is one that peculiarly concerns the licensed pharmacist in Virginia, we begin with a description of that profession as it exists under Virginia law. . . .

Inasmuch as only a licensed pharmacist may dispense prescription drugs in Virginia, § 54-524.48, advertising or other affirmative dissemination of prescription drug price information is effectively forbidden in the State. Some pharmacies refuse even to quote prescription drug prices over the telephone. The Board's position, however, is that this would not constitute an unprofessional publication. It is clear, nonetheless, that all advertising of such prices, in the normal sense, is forbidden. The prohibition does not extend to nonprescription drugs, but neither is it confined to prescriptions that the pharmacist compounds himself. Indeed, about 95% of all prescriptions now are filled with dosage forms prepared by the pharmaceutical manufacturer.

This is not the first challenge to the constitutionality of § 54-524.35 and what is now its third-numbered phrase. Shortly after the phrase was added to the statute in 1968, a suit seeking to enjoin its operation was instituted by a drug retailing company and one of its pharmacists. Although the First Amendment was invoked, the challenge appears to have been based primarily on the Due Process and Equal Protection Clauses of the Fourteenth Amendment. In any event, the prohibition on drug price advertising was upheld. The three-judge court did find that the dispensation of prescription drugs "affects the public health, safety and welfare." No appeal was taken.

The present, and second, attack on the statute is one made not by one directly subject to its prohibition, that is, a pharmacist, but by prescription drug consumers who claim that they would greatly benefit if the prohibition were lifted and advertising freely allowed. The plaintiffs are an individual Virginia resident who suffers from diseases that require her to take prescription drugs on a daily basis, and two nonprofit organizations. Their claim is that the First Amendment entitles the user of prescription drugs to receive information that pharmacists wish to communicate to them through advertising and other promotional means, concerning the prices of such drugs. . . .

The question first arises whether, even assuming that First Amendment protection attaches to the flow of drug price information, it is a protection enjoyed by the appellees as recipients of the information, and not solely, if at all, by the advertisers themselves who seek to disseminate that information.

Freedom of speech presupposes a willing speaker. But where a speaker exists, as is the case here, the protection afforded is to the communication, to its source and to its recipients both. This is clear from the decided cases. . . . If there is a right to advertise, there is a reciprocal right to receive the advertising, and it may be asserted by these appellees.

The appellants contend that the advertisement of prescription drug prices is outside the protection of the First Amendment because it is "commercial speech." There can be no question that in past decisions the court has given some indication that commercial speech is unprotected. . . .

Last Term, in *Bigelow v. Virginia*, 421 U.S. 809 (1975), the notion of unprotected "commercial speech" all but passed from the scene. . . .

Some fragment of hope for the continuing validity of a "commercial speech" exception arguably might have persisted because of the subject matter of the advertisement in *Bigelow*. . . .

Here, in contrast [to *Bigelow*], the question whether there is a First Amendment exception for "commercial speech" is squarely before us. Our pharmacist does not wish to editorialize on any subject, cultural, philosophical, or political. He does not wish to report any particularly newsworthy fact, or to make generalized observations even about commercial matters. The "idea" he wishes to communicate is simply this: "I will sell you the X prescription drug at the Y price." Our question, then, is whether this communication is wholly outside the protection of the First Amendment.

We begin with several propositions that already are settled or beyond serious dispute. It is clear, for example, that speech does not lose its First Amendment protection because money is spent to project it, as in a paid advertisement of one form or another. . . . Speech likewise is protected even though it is carried in a form that is "sold" for profit . . . and even though it may involve a solicitation to purchase or otherwise pay or contribute money.

If there is a kind of commercial speech that lacks all First Amendment protection, therefore, it must be distinguished by its content. Yet the speech whose content deprives it of protection cannot simply be speech on a commercial subject. No one would contend that our pharmacist may be prevented from being heard on the subject of whether, in general, pharmaceutical prices should be regulated, or their advertisement forbidden. . . .

Our question is whether speech which does "no more than propose a commercial transaction," is so removed from any "exposition of ideas," and from "'truth, science, morality, and arts in general, in its diffusion of liberal sentiments on the administration of Government,'" that it lacks all protection. Our answer is that it is not.

Focusing first on the individual parties to the transaction that is proposed in the commercial advertisement, we may assume that the advertiser's interest is a purely economic one. That hardly disqualifies him from protection under the First Amendment. . . .

As to the particular consumer's interest in the free flow of commercial information, that interest may be as keen, if not keener by far, than his interest in the day's most urgent political debate. Appellees' case in this respect is a convincing one. Those whom the suppression of prescription drug price information hits the hardest are the poor, the sick, and particularly the aged. A disproportionate amount of their income tends to be spent on prescription drugs; yet they are the least able to learn, by shopping from pharmacist to pharmacist, where their scarce dollars are best spent. When drug prices vary as strikingly as they do, information as to who is charging what becomes more than a convenience. It could mean the alleviation of physical pain or the enjoyment of basic necessities.

Generalizing, society also may have a strong interest in the free flow of commercial information. Even an individual advertisement, though entirely "commercial," may be of general public interest. . . . Obviously, not all commercial messages contain the same or even a very great public interest element. There are few to which such an element, however, could not be added. Our pharmacist, for example, could cast himself as a commentator on store-to-store disparities in drug prices, giving his own and those of a competitor as proof. We see little point in requiring him to do so, and little difference if he does not.

Moreover, there is another consideration that suggests that no line between publicly "interesting" or "important" commercial advertising and the opposite kind could ever be drawn. Advertising, however tasteless and excessive it sometimes may seem, is nonetheless dissemination of information as to who is producing and selling what product, for what reason, and at what price. So long as we preserve a predominantly free enterprise economy, the allocation of our resources in large measure will be made through numerous private economic decisions. It is a matter of public interest that those decisions, in the aggregate, be intelligent and well informed.

To this end, the free flow of commercial information is indispensable. And if it is indispensable to the proper allocation of resources in a free enterprise system, it is also indispensable to the formation of intelligent opinions as to how that system ought to be regulated or altered. Therefore, even if the First Amendment were thought to be primarily an instrument to enlighten public decisionmaking in a democracy, we could not say that the free flow of information does not serve that goal. . . .

The challenge now made, however, is based on the First Amendment. This casts the Board's justifications in a different light, for on close inspection it is seen that the State's protectiveness of its citizens rests in large measure on the advantages of their being kept in ignorance. The advertising ban does not directly affect professional standards one way or the other. It affects them only through the reactions it is assumed people will have to the free flow of drug price information. There is no claim that the advertising ban in any way prevents the cutting of corners by the pharmacist who is so inclined. That pharmacist is likely to cut corners in any event. The only effect the advertising ban has on him is to insulate him from price competition and to open the way for him to make a substantial, and perhaps even excessive, profit in addition to providing an inferior service. The more painstaking pharmacist is also protected but, again, it is a protection based in large part on public ignorance.

It appears to be feared that if the pharmacist who wishes to provide low cost, and assertedly low quality, services is permitted to advertise, he will be taken up on his offer by too many unwitting customers. They will choose the low-cost, low-quality service and drive the "professional" pharmacist out of business. They will respond only to costly and excessive advertising, and end up paying the price. They will go from one pharmacist to another, following the discount, and destroy the pharmacist-customer relationship. They will lose respect for the profession because it advertises. All this is not in their best interests, and all this can be avoided if they are not permitted to know who is charging what.

There is, of course, an alternative to this highly paternalistic approach. That alternative is to assume that this information is not in itself harmful, that people will perceive their own best interests if only they are well enough informed, and that the best means to that end is to open the channels of communication rather than to close them. If they are truly open, nothing prevents the "professional" pharmacist from marketing his own assertedly superior product, and contrasting it with that of the low-cost, high-volume prescription drug retailer. But the choice among these alternative approaches is not ours to make or the Virginia General Assembly's. It is precisely this kind of choice, between the dangers of suppressing information, and the dangers of its misuse if it is freely available, that the First Amendment makes for us. . . .

In concluding that commercial speech, like other varieties, is protected, we of course do not hold that it can never be regulated in any way. Some forms of commercial speech regulation are surely permissible. We mention a few only to make clear that they are not before us and therefore are not foreclosed by this case.

There is no claim, for example, that the prohibition on prescription drug price advertising is a mere time, place, and manner restriction. . . .

Nor is there any claim that prescription drug price advertisements are forbidden because they are false or misleading in any way. . . .

Also, there is no claim that the transactions proposed in the forbidden advertisements are themselves illegal in any way. . . .

What is at issue is whether a State may completely suppress the dissemination of concededly truthful information about entirely lawful activity, fearful of that information's effect upon its disseminators and its recipients. Reserving other questions, we conclude that the answer to this one is in the negative.

The judgment of the District Court is affirmed.

It is so ordered.

Mr. Chief Justice BURGER, concurring.

. . . I doubt that we know enough about evaluating the quality of medical and legal services to know which claims of superiority are "misleading" and which are justifiable. Nor am I sure that even advertising the price of certain professional services is not inherently misleading, since what the professional must do will vary greatly in individual cases. It is important to note that the Court wisely leaves these issues to another day.

Mr. Justice STEWART, concurring.

. . . Today the Court ends the anomalous situation created by *Chrestensen* and holds that a communication which does no more than propose a commercial transaction is not "wholly outside the protection of the First Amendment." But since it is a cardinal principle of the First Amendment that "government has no power to restrict expression because of its message, its ideas, its subject matter, or its content," the Court's decision calls into immediate question the constitutional legitimacy of every state and federal law regulating false or deceptive advertising. I write separately to explain why I think today's decision does not preclude such governmental regulation.

Mr. Justice REHNQUIST, dissenting.

The logical consequences of the Court's decision in this case, a decision which elevates commercial intercourse between a seller hawking his wares and a buyer seeking to strike a bargain to the same plane as has been previously reserved for the free marketplace of ideas, are far reaching indeed. Under the Court's opinion the way will be open not only for dissemination of price information but for active promotion of prescription drugs, liquor, cigarettes, and other products the use of which it has previously been thought desirable to discourage. Now, however, such promotion is protected by the First Amendment so long as it is not misleading or does not promote an illegal product or enterprise. In coming to this conclusion, the Court has overruled a legislative determination that such advertising should not be allowed and has done so on behalf of a consumer group which is not directly disadvantaged by the statute in question. This effort to reach a result which the court obviously considers desirable is a troublesome one, for two reasons. It extends standing to raise First Amendment claims beyond the previous decisions of this Court. It also extends the protection of that Amendment to purely commercial endeavors which its most vigorous champions on this Court had thought to be beyond its pale.

NOTES AND QUESTIONS

1. *A clear rule: commercial speech enjoys constitutional protection.* In *Bigelow*, it was far from clear whether commercial speech enjoyed significant First Amendment protection or whether commercial speech related to a fundamental

right (the liberty interest in terminating a pregnancy) enjoyed significant constitutional protection. *Virginia State Board of Pharmacy* clarifies the meaning and scope of *Bigelow* by establishing that commercial speech has categorical protection under the Free Speech Clause, regardless of the particular good or service being hawked. Thus, unlike *Bigelow*, *Virginia State Board of Pharmacy* is not ambiguous about the scope of the ruling: commercial speech has some claim on the Free Speech Clause. Even so, many important questions remain to be addressed.

2. *Regulating commercial speech.* First, to what extent, if any, may government regulate commercial speech? Are such regulations subject to the same restrictions applicable to noncommercial speech (such as content-neutral, reasonable time, place, and manner restrictions if the speech takes place on public property)? If not, precisely what rules govern regulations that fall short of a total ban on commercial speech? Moreover, is the subject matter of the speech entirely irrelevant? For example, could advertising about alcohol or tobacco be regulated more aggressively than advertising about laundry detergents?

3. *The lack of a general test for commercial speech regulations.* Even though Justice Blackmun's majority opinion does not set forth a categorical test for evaluating regulations of commercial speech, it does offer some general guiding principles. For commercial speech to be protected, it must be truthful and non-misleading. Moreover, it appears that a state could ban advertising of illegal activities or transactions. Assuming that the advertising is truthful and relates to a lawful product, are any restrictions consistent with the First Amendment?

4. *The greater includes the lesser argument.* If government can regulate the underlying activity, up to and including a flat ban, why can't government take the "lesser step" of regulating advertising to discourage consumption? Thus, if government can ban commercial gambling activities, shouldn't the First Amendment tolerate the regulation of promotional advertising instead? Doesn't the greater power to ban include the lesser power to regulate? Or does this misperceive the values at stake?

The following case, *Central Hudson*, provides a generic test for evaluating the constitutionality of commercial speech restrictions; the decision brought much needed doctrinal clarity to an area that had developed impressionistically up to this point.

CENTRAL HUDSON GAS & ELECTRIC CORP. v. PUBLIC SERVICE COMMISSION OF NEW YORK

447 U.S. 557 (1980)

Mr. Justice POWELL delivered the opinion of the Court.

This case presents the question whether a regulation of the Public Service Commission of the State of New York violates the First and Fourteenth Amendments because it completely bans promotional advertising by an electrical utility.

In December 1973, the Commission, appellee here, ordered electric utilities in New York State to cease all advertising that "promot[es] the use of electricity." The order was based on the Commission's finding that "the interconnected utility system in New York State does not have sufficient fuel stocks or sources of supply to continue furnishing all customer demands for the 1973-1974 winter."

[After reviewing its policies on advertising in a rulemaking proceeding], the Commission declared all promotional advertising contrary to the national policy of conserving energy. It acknowledged that the ban is not a perfect vehicle for conserving energy. . . . Still, the Commission adopted the restriction because it was deemed likely to "result in some dampening of unnecessary growth" in energy consumption.

Appellant challenged the order in state court, arguing that the Commission had restrained commercial speech in violation of the First and Fourteenth Amendments. The Commission's order was upheld by the trial court and at the intermediate appellate level. The New York Court of Appeals affirmed. . . .

The Commission's order restricts only commercial speech, that is, expression related solely to the economic interests of the speaker and its audience. The First Amendment, as applied to the States through the Fourteenth Amendment, protects commercial speech from unwarranted governmental regulation. Commercial expression not only serves the economic interest of the speaker, but also assists consumers and furthers the societal interest in the fullest possible dissemination of information. In applying the First Amendment to this area, we have rejected the "highly paternalistic" view that government has complete power to suppress or regulate commercial speech. . . .

Nevertheless, our decisions have recognized "the 'common-sense' distinction between speech proposing a commercial transaction, which occurs in an area traditionally subject to government regulation, and other varieties of speech." . . . The Constitution therefore accords a lesser protection to commercial speech than to other constitutionally guaranteed expression. The protection available for particular commercial expression turns on the nature both of the expression and of the governmental interests served by its regulation.

The First Amendment's concern for commercial speech is based on the informational function of advertising. Consequently, there can be no constitutional objection to the suppression of commercial messages that do not accurately inform the public about lawful activity. The government may ban forms of communication more likely to deceive the public than to inform it, or commercial speech related to illegal activity.[6]

If the communication is neither misleading nor related to unlawful activity, the government's power is more circumscribed. The State must assert a substantial interest to be achieved by restrictions on commercial speech. Moreover, the regulatory technique must be in proportion to that interest. The limitation on expression must be designed carefully to achieve the State's goal. Compliance with this requirement may be measured by two criteria. First, the restriction must directly advance the state interest involved; the regulation may not be sustained if it provides only ineffective or remote support for the government's purpose. Second, if the

---

[6] In most other contexts, the First Amendment prohibits regulation based on the content of the message. Two features of commercial speech permit regulation of its content. First, commercial speakers have extensive knowledge of both the market and their products. Thus, they are well situated to evaluate the accuracy of their messages and the lawfulness of the underlying activity. In addition, commercial speech, the offspring of economic self-interest, is a hardy breed of expression that is not "particularly susceptible to being crushed by overbroad regulation."

governmental interest could be served as well by a more limited restriction on commercial speech, the excessive restrictions cannot survive.

Under the first criterion, the Court has declined to uphold regulations that only indirectly advance the state interest involved. . . .

The second criterion recognizes that the First Amendment mandates that speech restrictions be "narrowly drawn." The regulatory technique may extend only as far as the interest it serves. The State cannot regulate speech that poses no danger to the asserted state interest, nor can it completely suppress information when narrower restrictions on expression would serve its interest as well. . . .

In commercial speech cases, then, a four-part analysis has developed. At the outset, we must determine whether the expression is protected by the First Amendment. For commercial speech to come within that provision, it at least must concern lawful activity and not be misleading. Next, we ask whether the asserted governmental interest is substantial. If both inquiries yield positive answers, we must determine whether the regulation directly advances the governmental interest asserted, and whether it is not more extensive than is necessary to serve that interest.

We now apply this four-step analysis for commercial speech to the Commission's arguments in support of its ban on promotional advertising.

The Commission offers two state interests as justifications for the ban on promotional advertising. The first concerns energy conservation. Any increase in demand for electricity—during peak or off-peak periods—means greater consumption of energy. The Commission argues, and the New York court agreed, that the State's interest in conserving energy is sufficient to support suppression of advertising designed to increase consumption of electricity. In view of our country's dependence on energy resources beyond our control, no one can doubt the importance of energy conservation. Plainly, therefore, the state interest asserted is substantial. . . .

Next, we focus on the relationship between the State's interests and the advertising ban. Under this criterion, the Commission's laudable concern over the equity and efficiency of appellant's rates does not provide a constitutionally adequate reason for restricting protected speech. The link between the advertising prohibition and appellant's rate structure is, at most, tenuous. The impact of promotional advertising on the equity of appellant's rates is highly speculative. Advertising to increase off-peak usage would have to increase peak usage, while other factors that directly affect the fairness and efficiency of appellant's rates remained constant. Such conditional and remote eventualities simply cannot justify silencing appellant's promotional advertising.

In contrast, the State's interest in energy conservation is directly advanced by the Commission order at issue here. There is an immediate connection between advertising and demand for electricity. Central Hudson would not contest the advertising ban unless it believed that promotion would increase its sales. Thus, we find a direct link between the state interest in conservation and the Commission's order.

We come finally to the critical inquiry in this case: whether the Commission's complete suppression of speech ordinarily protected by the First Amendment is no more extensive than necessary to further the State's interest in energy conservation. The Commission's order reaches all promotional advertising, regardless of the impact of the touted service on overall energy use. But the energy conservation rationale, as important as it is, cannot justify suppressing information about electric devices or services that would cause no net increase in total energy use. In addition, no showing has been made that a more limited restriction on the content of promotional advertising would not serve adequately the State's interests. . . .

The Commission's order prevents appellant from promoting electric services that would reduce energy use by diverting demand from less efficient sources, or that would consume roughly the same amount of energy as do alternative sources. In neither situation would the utility's advertising endanger conservation or mislead the public. To the extent that the Commission's order suppresses speech that in no way impairs the State's interest in energy conservation, the Commission's order violates the First and Fourteenth Amendments and must be invalidated.

Accordingly, the judgment of the New York Court of Appeals is

Reversed.

Mr. Justice BLACKMUN, with whom Mr. Justice BRENNAN joins, concurring in the judgment.

I agree with the Court that the Public Service Commission's ban on promotional advertising of electricity by public utilities is inconsistent with the First and Fourteenth Amendments. I concur only in the Court's judgment, however, because I believe the test now evolved and applied by the Court is not consistent with our prior cases and does not provide adequate protection for truthful, nonmisleading, noncoercive commercial speech. . . .

I seriously doubt whether suppression of information concerning the availability and price of a legally offered product is ever a permissible way for the State to "dampen" demand for or use of the product. Even though "commercial" speech is involved, such a regulatory measure strikes at the heart of the First Amendment. This is because it is a covert attempt by the State to manipulate the choices of its citizens, not by persuasion or direct regulation, but by depriving the public of the information needed to make a free choice. As the Court recognizes, the State's policy choices are insulated from the visibility and scrutiny that direct regulation would entail and the conduct of citizens is molded by the information that government chooses to give them. . . .

It appears that the Court would permit the State to ban all direct advertising of air conditioning, assuming that a more limited restriction on such advertising would not effectively deter the public from cooling its homes. In my view, our cases do not support this type of suppression. If a governmental unit believes that use or overuse of air conditioning is a serious problem, it must attack that problem directly, by prohibiting air conditioning or regulating thermostat levels. Just as the Commonwealth of Virginia may promote professionalism of pharmacists directly, so too New York may *not* promote energy conservation "by keeping the public in ignorance."

Mr. Justice STEVENS, with whom Mr. Justice BRENNAN joins, concurring in the judgment.

Because "commercial speech" is afforded less constitutional protection than other forms of speech, it is important that the commercial speech concept not be defined too broadly lest speech deserving of greater constitutional protection be inadvertently suppressed. The issue in this case is whether New York's prohibition on the promotion of the use of electricity through advertising is a ban on nothing but commercial speech.

In my judgment one of the two definitions the Court uses in addressing that issue is too broad and the other may be somewhat too narrow. . . .

In sum, I concur in the result because I do not consider this to be a "commercial speech" case.

Mr. Justice REHNQUIST, dissenting.

. . . Given what seems to me full recognition of the holding of *Virginia Pharmacy Board* that commercial speech is entitled to some degree of First Amendment protection, I think the Court is nonetheless incorrect in invalidating the carefully considered state ban on promotional advertising in light of pressing national and state energy needs.

NOTES AND QUESTIONS

1. *The* Central Hudson *test.* Central Hudson adopts a four-part test for determining the constitutionality of a government regulation burdening commercial speech: The speech must relate to a lawful product and must not be false or misleading; if the speech meets this prerequisite, the government must proffer a "substantial" reason for the regulation, the regulation must directly advance the substantial government interest, and the regulation cannot be more extensive than necessary to achieve that interest.

2. *Is commercial speech distinguishable from other kinds of speech?* Why should commercial speech be a dispreferred stepsister of noncommercial speech? Justice Powell suggests, in footnote 6 of *Central Hudson*, that commercial speech can be more highly regulated because "commercial speakers have extensive knowledge of both the market and their products" and accordingly can "evaluate the accuracy of their messages and the lawfulness of the underlying activity." Moreover, he posits that "commercial speech, the offspring of economic self-interest, is a hardy breed of expression" that is not easily squelched. Even if both of these observations are perfectly true, that does not justify second-class status for commercial speech in theoretical terms. If people care more about the Macy's Labor Day Sale than the candidates for city council, should the government be able to suppress one category of speech simply because the government believes political speech is more important? For an argument that commercial speech should receive equal treatment, see Alex Kozinski & Stuart Banner, *Who's Afraid of Commercial Speech?*, 76 Va. L. Rev. 627 (1990).

3. *Does the* Central Hudson *test work?* Does Justice Powell's four-part test do a good job of formalizing the test for determining whether regulations of commercial speech are constitutionally permissible? The first prong seems entirely sensible and flows directly from *Virginia State Board of Pharmacy.* To be protected, commercial speech must be truthful and must relate to a lawful good or service. These inquiries are fairly objective as well, making this part of the test relatively easy to apply. What about the last three factors—whether the regulation "directly advances" the government's "substantial" interest in way that "is not more extensive than necessary"? Are these aspects of the test easily applied? Objective?

4. *The substantial government interest prong.* Is it very likely that government would adopt and enforce regulations for a problem that it deems insubstantial? Or that, objectively viewed, is "insubstantial"? As you might predict, this prong does not fence out many commercial speech claims.

5. *The direct advancement prong.* The question of direct advancement is capable of
    easy manipulation. How perfect does the means/end fit have to be in order to
    satisfy this prong? A reviewing court does not have to strain very much to find
    this criterion met—or not. The third prong of the test, accordingly, is a major
    front in commercial speech battles. Similarly, whether a restriction is "more
    extensive than necessary" is hardly an objective inquiry. To some extent, the
    social value of the product being advertised, as perceived by a judge, will
    prefigure the degree to which a regulation goes too far. Limits on advertising
    cars, on the one hand, might, on a de facto basis, be harder to sustain than
    regulations on the sale of alcohol or racy books. If one views the underlying
    product as lacking social merit, it is unlikely that one will find that a regulation
    of commercial speech regarding that product "goes too far" in light of the social
    benefits obtained.

THEORY-APPLIED PROBLEM

The state of Indiana, concerned about the prevalence of teenagers and children
using tobacco products unlawfully, enacts a statute that bans "the use or depiction of
cartoon or cartoon-like characters in tobacco advertisements, whether in print, over
broadcast outlets, on billboards, signs, or on packaging for tobacco products."
Violations are punishable with a fine of up to $10,000, with each item bearing a
prohibited cartoon or cartoon-like figure constituting an independent violation of the
law. The law seeks to prohibit the use of characters, like Joe Camel, who empirical
studies show make smoking more appealing to children. Indeed, a study published in
the *Journal of the American Medical Association* finds that five- and six-year olds
are better able to identify Joe Camel than either Mickey Mouse or Fred Flintstone.

Before the new law's effective date, R.J. Reynolds Corporation, the maker of
Camel brand cigarettes, brings suit in federal district court in Indianapolis, Indiana,
seeking a declaratory judgment that the new ban on cartoon or cartoon-like
characters to promote tobacco products violates the First Amendment and seeking an
injunction against its enforcement. At the time, tobacco products are lawful in
Indiana but may only be sold to and possessed by persons at least 18 years of age.
How should the district court rule?

AN EXTENDED NOTE ON POSADAS *AND THE USE OF COMMERCIAL SPEECH REGULATIONS IN LIEU OF DIRECT REGULATIONS*

In Posadas de Puerto Rico Associates v. Tourism Co., 478 U.S. 328 (1986), the
Supreme Court sustained a ban on casino advertising aimed at encouraging local
citizens to gamble. Because gambling could be prohibited entirely, Justice Rehnquist
reasoned, the Commonwealth of Puerto Rico could take the less burdensome
approach of discouraging patronage of casinos by regulating promotional advertising.
He explained that

> [a]ppellant also makes the related argument that, having chosen to legalize casino
> gambling for residents of Puerto Rico, the legislature is prohibited by the First
> Amendment from using restrictions on advertising to accomplish its goal of
> reducing demand for such gambling. We disagree. In our view, appellant has the
> argument backwards. As we noted in the preceding paragraph, it is precisely

because the government could have enacted a wholesale prohibition of the underlying conduct that it is permissible for the government to take the less intrusive step of allowing the conduct, but reducing the demand through restrictions on advertising. It would surely be a Pyrrhic victory for casino owners such as appellant to gain recognition of a First Amendment right to advertise their casinos to the residents of Puerto Rico, only to thereby force the legislature into banning casino gambling by residents altogether. It would just as surely be a strange constitutional doctrine which would concede to the legislature the authority to totally ban a product or activity, but deny to the legislature the authority to forbid the stimulation of demand for the product or activity through advertising on behalf of those who would profit from such increased demand. Legislative regulation of products or activities deemed harmful, such as cigarettes, alcoholic beverages, and prostitution, has varied from outright prohibition on the one hand, see, e.g., Cal. Penal Code Ann. § 647(b) (West Supp. 1986) (prohibiting soliciting or engaging in act of prostitution), to legalization of the product or activity with restrictions on stimulation of its demand on the other hand, see, e.g., Nev. Rev. Stat. §§ 244.345(1), (8) (1986) (authorizing licensing of houses of prostitution except in counties with more than 250,000 population), §§ 201.430, 201.440 (prohibiting advertising of houses of prostitution "[in] any public theater, on the public streets of any city or town, or on any public highway," or "in [a] place of business"). To rule out the latter, intermediate kind of response would require more than we find in the First Amendment.

Id. at 346-347.

In dissent, Justice Brennan rejected the "greater includes the lesser" argument, suggesting that a regulation of commercial speech presented First Amendment issues that a ban on casino gambling would not:

The Court reasons that because Puerto Rico could legitimately decide to prohibit casino gambling entirely, it may also take the "less intrusive step" of legalizing casino gambling but restricting speech. According to the Court, it would "surely be a strange constitutional doctrine which would concede to the legislature the authority to totally ban [casino gambling] but deny to the legislature the authority to forbid the stimulation of demand for [casino gambling]" by banning advertising. I do not agree that a ban on casino advertising is "less intrusive" than an outright prohibition of such activity. A majority of States have chosen not to legalize casino gambling, and we have never suggested that this might be unconstitutional. However, having decided to legalize casino gambling, Puerto Rico's decision to ban truthful speech concerning entirely lawful activity raises serious First Amendment problems. Thus, the "constitutional doctrine" which bans Puerto Rico from banning advertisements concerning lawful casino gambling is not so strange a restraint—it is called the First Amendment.

Id. at 354 n.4 (Brennan, J., dissenting).

A decade later, in 44 Liquormart v. Rhode Island, 517 U.S. 484 (1996), a plurality of the Supreme Court squarely rejected the "greater includes the lesser" view that regulations (up to and including targeted bans) of commercial speech could serve as fungible substitutes for direct regulations of conduct. Writing for the plurality, Justice Stevens observed that "[f]urther consideration persuades us that the 'greater-includes-the-lesser' argument should be rejected" because "it is inconsistent with both logic and well-settled doctrine." *Id.* at 511. Justice Stevens explained the Court's reasoning as follows:

> Although we do not dispute the proposition that greater powers include lesser ones, we fail to see how that syllogism requires the conclusion that the State's power to regulate commercial activity is "greater" than its power to ban truthful, nonmisleading commercial speech. Contrary to the assumption made in Posadas, we think it quite clear that banning speech may sometimes prove far more intrusive than banning conduct. As a venerable proverb teaches, it may prove more injurious to prevent people from teaching others how to fish than to prevent fish from being sold. Similarly, a local ordinance banning bicycle lessons may curtail freedom far more than one that prohibits bicycle riding within city limits. In short, we reject the assumption that words are necessarily less vital to freedom than actions, or that logic somehow proves that the power to prohibit an activity is necessarily "greater" than the power to suppress speech about it.

Id. Thus, "[t]he text of the First Amendment makes clear that the Constitution presumes that attempts to regulate speech are more dangerous than attempts to regulate conduct." *Id.* at 512. Justice Stevens emphasized that this "presumption accords with the essential role that the free flow of information plays in a democratic society." *Id.* And, "[a]s a result, the First Amendment directs that government may not suppress speech as easily as it may suppress conduct, and that speech restrictions cannot be treated as simply another means that the government may use to achieve its ends." *Id.*

Because Justice Stevens only garnered four votes for his complete rejection of the *Posadas*" greater includes the lesser" reasoning, however, the question remained open as to whether government could regulate commercial speech as a proxy for regulation of the underlying substantive activity. Three years later, in *Greater New Orleans Broadcasting Association* (*infra* p. 320, a majority of the Supreme Court essentially endorsed Justice Stevens's position and rejected the "greater includes the lesser" syllogism.

NOTES AND QUESTIONS

1. *The "lesser" power to regulate commercial speech and* Posadas. If commercial speech is really "low value" speech and is more robust than other forms of speech, should government be permitted to regulate it in lieu of adopting direct regulations? Did the *Posadas* approach have a certain logic? As between banning gambling and banning advertising of gambling, isn't the net freedom of citizens enhanced, rather than reduced, by permitting the speech regulations?

2. *Is regulating commercial speech really the same as regulating conduct?* On the other hand, perhaps speech regulations really *are* totally different in kind than direct regulations of behavior. The First Amendment does not require a state government to permit or prohibit commercial gambling, but it does limit the ability of a state government to regulate, much less ban, speech. Thus, perhaps Justice Stevens has the better of the argument that a ban on speech is *not* simply a lesser included power. Isn't there something troubling about government attempting to trick citizens into virtuous behavior? And, if government thinks a particular behavior is socially harmful (but not harmful enough to justify a ban), government remains free to share its views in the marketplace of ideas.

3. *Growing skepticism toward commercial speech regulations.* Over time, the Supreme Court has become increasingly demanding of commercial speech restrictions and has required government to establish that targeted speech

restrictions are part of a consistent larger program of regulation in order to find the third and fourth prongs of *Central Hudson* have been met. In this regard, consider the following case.

GREATER NEW ORLEANS BROADCASTING ASS'N, INC. v. UNITED STATES
527 U.S. 173 (1999)

Justice STEVENS delivered the opinion of the Court.

Federal law prohibits some, but by no means all, broadcast advertising of lotteries and casino gambling. In *United States v. Edge Broadcasting Co.*, 509 U.S. 418 (1993), we upheld the constitutionality of 18 U.S.C. § 1304 as applied to broadcast advertising of Virginia's lottery by a radio station located in North Carolina, where no such lottery was authorized. Today we hold that § 1304 may not be applied to advertisements of private casino gambling that are broadcast by radio or television stations located in Louisiana, where such gambling is legal.

Through most of the 19th and the first half of the 20th centuries, Congress adhered to a policy that not only discouraged the operation of lotteries and similar schemes, but forbade the dissemination of information concerning such enterprises by use of the mails, even when the lottery in question was chartered by a state legislature. Consistent with this Court's earlier view that commercial advertising was unprotected by the First Amendment, see *Valentine v. Chrestensen*, 316 U.S. 52, 54 (1942), we found that the notion that "lotteries . . . are supposed to have a demoralizing influence upon the people" provided sufficient justification for excluding circulars concerning such enterprises from the federal postal system, *Ex parte Jackson*, 96 U.S. 727, 736-737 (1878). We likewise deferred to congressional judgment in upholding the similar exclusion for newspapers that contained either lottery advertisement or prize lists. The current versions of the early anti-lottery statutes are now codified at 18 U.S.C. §§ 1301-1303.

Congress extended its restrictions on lottery-related information to broadcasting as communications technology made that practice both possible and profitable. . . .

Petitioners are an association of Louisiana broadcasters and its members who operate FCC-licensed radio and television stations in the New Orleans metropolitan area. But for the threat of sanctions pursuant to § 1304 and the FCC's companion regulation, petitioners would broadcast promotional advertisements for gaming available at private, for-profit casinos that are lawful and regulated in both Louisiana and neighboring Mississippi. According to an FCC official, however, "[u]nder appropriate conditions, some broadcast signals from Louisiana broadcasting stations may be heard in neighboring states including Texas and Arkansas," where private casino gambling is unlawful.

Petitioners brought this action against the United States and the FCC in the District Court for the Eastern District of Louisiana, praying for a declaration that § 1304 and the FCC's regulation violate the First Amendment as applied to them, and for an injunction preventing enforcement of the statute and the rule against them. After noting that all the parties agreed that the case should be decided on their cross-motions for summary judgment, the District Court ruled in favor of the Government. . . . A divided panel of the Court of Appeals for the Fifth Circuit agreed with the District Court's application of *Central Hudson*, and affirmed the grant of summary judgment to the Government. . . .

We now reverse.

In a number of cases involving restrictions on speech that is "commercial" in nature, we have employed *Central Hudson*'s four-part test to resolve First Amendment challenges. . . . In this analysis, the Government bears the burden of identifying a substantial interest and justifying the challenged restriction.

The four parts of the *Central Hudson* test are not entirely discrete. All are important and, to a certain extent, interrelated: Each raises a relevant question that may not be dispositive to the First Amendment inquiry, but the answer to which may inform a judgment concerning the other three. Partly because of these intricacies, petitioners as well as certain judges, scholars, and *amici curiae* have advocated repudiation of the *Central Hudson* standard and implementation of a more straightforward and stringent test for assessing the validity of governmental restrictions on commercial speech. As the opinions in *44 Liquormart* demonstrate, reasonable judges may disagree about the merits of such proposals. It is, however, an established part of our constitutional jurisprudence that we do not ordinarily reach out to make novel or unnecessarily broad pronouncements on constitutional issues when a case can be fully resolved on a narrower ground. In this case, there is no need to break new ground. *Central Hudson*, as applied in our more recent commercial speech cases, provides an adequate basis for decision.

All parties to this case agree that the messages petitioners wish to broadcast constitute commercial speech, and that these broadcasts would satisfy the first part of the *Central Hudson* test: Their content is not misleading and concerns lawful activities, *i.e.*, private casino gambling in Louisiana and Mississippi. As well, the proposed commercial messages would convey information—whether taken favorably or unfavorably by the audience—about an activity that is the subject of intense public debate in many communities. In addition, petitioners' broadcasts presumably would disseminate accurate information as to the operation of market competitors, such as pay-out ratios, which can benefit listeners by informing their consumption choices and fostering price competition. Thus, even if the broadcasters' interest in conveying these messages is entirely pecuniary, the interests of, and benefit to, the audience may be broader.

The second part of the *Central Hudson* test asks whether the asserted governmental interest served by the speech restriction is substantial. . . .

No one seriously doubts that the Federal Government may assert a legitimate and substantial interest in alleviating the societal ills [associated with gambling], or in assisting like-minded States to do the same. But in the judgment of both the Congress and many state legislatures, the social costs that support the suppression of gambling are offset, and sometimes outweighed, by countervailing policy considerations, primarily in the form of economic benefits. . . .

Even though the Government has identified substantial interests, when we consider both their quality and the information sought to be suppressed, the crosscurrents in the scope and application of § 1304 become more difficult for the Government to defend.

The third part of the *Central Hudson* test asks whether the speech restriction directly and materially advances the asserted government interest. . . . We have observed that "this requirement is critical; otherwise, 'a State could with ease restrict commercial speech in the service of other objectives that could not themselves justify a burden on commercial expression.'" *Rubin*, 514 U.S., at 487, quoting *Edenfield*, 507 U.S., at 771.

The fourth part of the test complements the direct-advancement inquiry of the third, asking whether the speech restriction is not more extensive than necessary to serve the interests that support it. The Government is not required to employ the least restrictive means conceivable, but it must demonstrate narrow tailoring of the challenged regulation to the asserted interest—"a fit that is not necessarily perfect, but reasonable; that represents not necessarily the single best disposition but one whose scope is in proportion to the interest served."

As applied to petitioners' case, § 1304 cannot satisfy these standards. With regard to the first asserted interest—alleviating the social costs of casino gambling by limiting demand—the Government contends that its broadcasting restrictions directly advance that interest because "promotional" broadcast advertising concerning casino gambling increases demand for such gambling, which in turn increases the amount of casino gambling that produces those social costs. Additionally, the Government believes that compulsive gamblers are especially susceptible to the pervasiveness and potency of broadcast advertising. Assuming the accuracy of this causal chain, it does not necessarily follow that the Government's speech ban has directly and materially furthered the asserted interest. While it is no doubt fair to assume that more advertising would have some impact on overall demand for gambling, it is also reasonable to assume that much of that advertising would merely channel gamblers to one casino rather than another. More important, any measure of the effectiveness of the Government's attempt to minimize the social costs of gambling cannot ignore Congress' simultaneous encouragement of tribal casino gambling, which may well be growing at a rate exceeding any increase in gambling or compulsive gambling that private casino advertising could produce. . . .

We need not resolve the question whether any lack of evidence in the record fails to satisfy the standard of proof under *Central Hudson*, however, because the flaw in the Government's case is more fundamental: The operation of § 1304 and its attendant regulatory regime is so pierced by exemptions and inconsistencies that the Government cannot hope to exonerate it. . . .

The FCC's interpretation and application of §§ 1304 and 1307 underscore the statute's infirmity. Attempting to enforce the underlying purposes and policy of the statute, the FCC has permitted broadcasters to tempt viewers with claims of "Vegas-style excitement" at a commercial "casino," if "casino" is part of the establishment's proper name and the advertisement can be taken to refer to the casino's amenities, rather than directly promote its gaming aspects. While we can hardly fault the FCC in view of the statute's focus on the suppression of certain types of information, the agency's practice is squarely at odds with the governmental interests asserted in this case.

From what we can gather, the Government is committed to prohibiting accurate product information, not commercial enticements of all kinds, and then only when conveyed over certain forms of media and for certain types of gambling—indeed, for only certain brands of *casino* gambling—and despite the fact that messages about the availability of such gambling are being conveyed over the airwaves by other speakers. . . .

The second interest asserted by the Government—the derivative goal of "assisting" States with policies that disfavor private casinos—adds little to its case. We cannot see how this broadcast restraint, ambivalent as it is, might directly and adequately further any *state* interest in dampening consumer demand for casino gambling if it cannot achieve the same goal with respect to the similar *federal* interest. . . .

Accordingly, respondents cannot overcome the presumption that the speaker and the audience, not the Government, should be left to assess the value of accurate and nonmisleading information about lawful conduct. Had the Federal Government adopted a more coherent policy, or accommodated the rights of speakers in States that have legalized the underlying conduct, this might be a different case. But under current federal law, as applied to petitioners and the messages that they wish to convey, the broadcast prohibition in 18 U.S.C. § 1304 and 47 CFR § 73.1211 (1998) violates the First Amendment. The judgment of the Court of Appeals is therefore

Reversed.

Chief Justice REHNQUIST, concurring.

Title 18 U.S.C. § 1304 regulates broadcast advertising of lotteries and casino gambling. I agree with the Court that "[t]he operation of § 1304 and its attendant regulatory regime is so pierced by exemptions and inconsistencies" that it violates the First Amendment. . . . Were Congress to undertake substantive regulation of the gambling industry, rather than simply the manner in which it may broadcast advertisements, "exemptions and inconsistencies" such as those in § 1304 might well prove constitutionally tolerable.

Justice THOMAS, concurring in the judgment.

I continue to adhere to my view that "[i]n cases such as this, in which the government's asserted interest is to keep legal users of a product or service ignorant in order to manipulate their choices in the marketplace," the *Central Hudson* test should not be applied because "such an 'interest' is *per se* illegitimate and can no more justify regulation of 'commercial speech' than it can justify regulation of 'noncommercial' speech." *44 Liquormart, Inc. v. Rhode Island*, 517 U.S. 484, 518 (1996) (opinion concurring in part and concurring in judgment). Accordingly, I concur only in the judgment.

NOTES AND QUESTIONS

1. *Applying* Central Hudson. *Greater New Orleans Broadcasting Association.* presents a routine application of *Central Hudson*. Clearly, even if government has the power to restrict—or prohibit—the underlying good or service, this greater power *does not* imply that government can use speech restrictions to discourage consumption of a good or service. *See* 44 Liquormart v. Rhode Island, 517 U.S. 484, 509-510 (1994). Even though Louisiana and the federal government remain free to criminalize commercial gambling operations, they cannot discourage gambling by restricting advertising of it on broadcast television and radio stations. Another lesson of *Greater New Orleans Broadcasting* is the notion that a partial ban on commercial speech stands a lesser chance of meeting the "direct advancement" and "narrow tailoring" prongs of *Central Hudson* than would a complete ban.

2. *Burdening commercial speech.* Should government be required to adopt commercial speech restrictions as part of a comprehensive and internally consistent regulatory program to satisfy the third and fourth prongs of *Central Hudson*? Normally, government is permitted to address a social problem in a piecemeal fashion—not so here. If a government regulatory scheme contains numerous exceptions or provisos, it appears that restrictions on commercial

speech are less likely to survive judicial review. Just as government cannot use a ban on commercial speech (in lieu of direct regulations) to discourage the sale of a good or service, so too government cannot place relatively greater weight on commercial speech restrictions (rather than direct regulations) as part of a comprehensive regulatory effort.

3. *Even more robust protection for commercial speech.* Does Justice Thomas have the better view? Should a presumption exist that a flat ban on truthful, non-misleading information about a lawful good or service violates the Free Speech Clause? If government is not regulating commercial speech, but banning it, would the adoption of a per se rule help to clarify the proper free speech analysis? Or is Justice Stevens correct to insist that *Central Hudson* always provides the proper means of analysis? If the results in concrete cases work more or less just like a per se rule, wouldn't it make sense for the Supreme Court to acknowledge this fact?

4. *A dead letter?* Is anything left of the *Posadas* "lesser includes the greater" approach? Consider the case of government-mandated gruesome tobacco warning labels. The FDA ordered cigarette manufacturers to place graphic warning labels on cigarette packaging. See Ellen P. Goodman, *Visual Gut Punch: Persuasion, Emotion and the Constitutional Meaning of Graphic Disclosure*, 99 Cornell L. Rev. 513 (2014). The FDA claimed that the labels were necessary to help consumers make well-informed choices about the health risks associated with the use of tobacco products; the tobacco companies argued that the FDA was trying to scare consumers into quitting smoking by using emotionally manipulative graphic images. Two U.S. Courts of Appeals considered challenges to the graphic visual labels and reached conflicting results. *Compare* Discount Tobacco City & Lottery Inc. v. U.S., 674 F.3d 509, 529-30 (6th Cir. 2012) (rejecting a facial challenge to the FDA's graphic labeling requirements and explaining that "the color graphics requirement materially advances the government's stated interest in counteracting the informational deficit regarding health hazards") *with* R.J. Reynolds Tobacco Co. v. FDA, 696 F.3d 1205, 1214 (D.C. Cir. 2012) (invalidating the FDA's graphic labeling regulations, on an as-applied basis, as unconstitutional compelled speech and holding that "a disclosure requirement is only appropriate if the government shows that, absent a warning, there is a self-evident—or at least 'potentially real'—danger that an advertisement will mislead consumers"). Did the government's power to ban tobacco altogether perhaps influence the Sixth Circuit—leading that court to uphold the graphic warning requirement? Or is *Discount Tobacco City* simply an example of a lower court applying the first prong of *Central Hudson* (commercial speech must be truthful and non-misleading)? Moreover, if tobacco companies intentionally misled consumers about the adverse health effects of tobacco consumption, may government require them to correct consumer information deficits that they helped to create? For a thoughtful analysis and a doctrinal proposal that government efforts to "inform" consumers cannot constitutionally extend to lobbying consumers to refrain from engaging in a lawful activity, see Jennifer M. Keighley, *Can You Handle the Truth? Compelled Commercial Speech and the First Amendment*, 15 U. Pa. J. Const. L. 539 (2012).

SORRELL v. IMS HEALTH INC.

564 U.S. 552 (2011)

Justice KENNEDY delivered the opinion of the Court.

Vermont law restricts the sale, disclosure, and use of pharmacy records that reveal the prescribing practices of individual doctors. Vt. Stat. Ann., Tit. 18, § 4631 (Supp. 2010). Subject to certain exceptions, the information may not be sold, disclosed by pharmacies for marketing purposes, or used for marketing by pharmaceutical manufacturers. Vermont argues that its prohibitions safeguard medical privacy and diminish the likelihood that marketing will lead to prescription decisions not in the best interests of patients or the State. It can be assumed that these interests are significant. Speech in aid of pharmaceutical marketing, however, is a form of expression protected by the Free Speech Clause of the First Amendment. As a consequence, Vermont's statute must be subjected to heightened judicial scrutiny. The law cannot satisfy that standard. . . .

Pharmacies, as a matter of business routine and federal law, receive prescriber-identifying information when processing prescriptions. See 21 U.S.C. § 353(b); see also Vt. Bd. of Pharmacy Admin. Rule 9.1 (2009); Rule 9.2. Many pharmacies sell this information to "data miners," firms that analyze prescriber identifying information and produce reports on prescriber behavior. Data miners lease these reports to pharmaceutical manufacturers subject to nondisclosure agreements. Detailers, who represent the manufacturers, then use the reports to refine their marketing tactics and increase sales.

In 2007, Vermont enacted the Prescription Confidentiality Law. The measure is also referred to as Act 80. It has several components. The central provision of the present case is § 4631(d).

> "A health insurer, a self-insured employer, an electronic transmission intermediary, a pharmacy, or other similar entity shall not sell, license, or exchange for value regulated records containing prescriber-identifiable information, nor permit the use of regulated records containing prescriber-identifiable information for marketing or promoting a prescription drug, unless the prescriber consents. . . . Pharmaceutical manufacturers and pharmaceutical marketers shall not use prescriber-identifiable information for marketing or promoting a prescription drug unless the prescriber consents. . . ."

[Vermont's law sought to restrict access to prescription data as part of an effort to thwart "detailing," the use of high-pressure in-office marketing visits by pharmaceutical company representatives aimed at increasing the "detailed" physician's prescribing rate for the company's proprietary drugs. The state argued that detailing has adverse affects on the cost of heath care in the state, by encouraging physicians to prescribe more-expensive proprietary drugs rather than less-expensive generic equivalents. By generally prohibiting the sale of prescription data by third parties, like pharmacies, Vermont hoped to curtail the health care costs associated with successful "detailing."]

[A group of data miners, sellers of aggregated prescription data from pharmacies, and an association of pharmaceutical manufacturers, initiated a challenge to the new law, arguing that it violated the First Amendment's Free Speech Clause. Following a bench trial, the district court rejected the plaintiffs' claims and held the law to be constitutional. On appeal, the U.S. Court of Appeals for the Second Circuit reversed on First Amendment grounds, holding that Vermont's ban on the sale of prescription data for the purpose of detailing unduly restricted lawful commercial speech. The Supreme Court granted review to resolve a circuit split on this question.]

[T]he opening clause of § 4631(d) prohibits pharmacies, health insurers, and similar entities from selling prescriber-identifying information, subject to the statutory exceptions set out at § 4631(e). Under that reading, pharmacies may sell the information to private or academic researchers, see § 4631(e)(1), but not, for example, to pharmaceutical marketers. There is no dispute as to the remainder of § 4631(d). It prohibits pharmacies, health insurers, and similar entities from disclosing or otherwise allowing prescriber-identifying information to be used for marketing. And it bars pharmaceutical manufacturers and detailers from using the information for marketing. The questions now are whether § 4631(d) must be tested by heightened judicial scrutiny and, if so, whether the State can justify the law.

On its face, Vermont's law enacts content-and speaker-based restrictions on the sale, disclosure, and use of prescriber-identifying information. The provision first forbids sale subject to exceptions based in large part on the content of a purchaser's speech. For example, those who wish to engage in certain "educational communications," § 4631(e)(4), may purchase the information. The measure then bars any disclosure when recipient speakers will use the information for marketing. Finally, the provision's second sentence prohibits pharmaceutical manufacturers from using the information for marketing. The statute thus disfavors marketing, that is, speech with a particular content. More than that, the statute disfavors specific speakers, namely pharmaceutical manufacturers. As a result of these content-and speaker-based rules, detailers cannot obtain prescriber-identifying information, even though the information may be purchased or acquired by other speakers with diverse purposes and viewpoints. Detailers are likewise barred from using the information for marketing, even though the information may be used by a wide range of other speakers. For example, it appears that Vermont could supply academic organizations with prescriber-identifying information to use in countering the messages of brand-name pharmaceutical manufacturers and in promoting the prescription of generic drugs. But § 4631(d) leaves detailers no means of purchasing, acquiring, or using prescriber-identifying information. The law on its face burdens disfavored speech by disfavored speakers.

Any doubt that § 4631(d) imposes an aimed, content-based burden on detailers is dispelled by the record and by formal legislative findings. . . .

Act 80 is designed to impose a specific, content-based burden on protected expression. It follows that heightened judicial scrutiny is warranted. See *Cincinnati v. Discovery Network, Inc.*, 507 U.S. 410, 418 (1993) (applying heightened scrutiny to "a categorical prohibition on the use of newsracks to disseminate commercial messages"). . . .

The First Amendment requires heightened scrutiny whenever the government creates "a regulation of speech because of disagreement with the message it conveys." . . . A government bent on frustrating an impending demonstration might pass a law demanding two years' notice before the issuance of parade permits. Even if the hypothetical measure on its face appeared neutral as to content and speaker, its purpose to suppress speech and its unjustified burdens on expression would render it unconstitutional. Commercial speech is no exception. A "consumer's concern for the free flow of commercial speech often may be far keener than his concern for urgent political dialogue." *Bates v. State Bar of Ariz.*, 433 U.S. 350, 364 (1977). That reality has great relevance in the fields of medicine and public health, where information can save lives. . . .

The State asks for an exception to the rule that information is speech, but there is no need to consider that request in this case. The State has imposed content- and speaker-based restrictions on the availability and use of prescriber-identifying information. So long as they do not engage in marketing, many speakers can obtain and use the information. But detailers cannot. Vermont's statute could be compared with a law prohibiting trade magazines from purchasing or using ink. Cf. *Minneapolis Star*, 460 U.S. 575. Like that hypothetical law, § 4631(d) imposes a speaker- and content-based burden on protected expression, and that circumstance is sufficient to justify application of heightened scrutiny. As a consequence, this case can be resolved even assuming, as the State argues, that prescriber-identifying information is a mere commodity.

In the ordinary case it is all but dispositive to conclude that a law is content-based and, in practice, viewpoint-discriminatory. The State argues that a different analysis applies here because, assuming § 4631(d) burdens speech at all, it at most burdens only commercial speech. As in previous cases, however, the outcome is the same whether a special commercial speech inquiry or a stricter form of judicial scrutiny is applied. For the same reason there is no need to determine whether all speech hampered by § 4631(d) is commercial, as our cases have used that term.

Under a commercial speech inquiry, it is the State's burden to justify its content-based law as consistent with the First Amendment. To sustain the targeted, content-based burden § 4631(d) imposes on protected expression, the State must show at least that the statute directly advances a substantial governmental interest and that the measure is drawn to achieve that interest. There must be a "fit between the legislature's ends and the means chosen to accomplish those ends." As in other contexts, these standards ensure not only that the State's interests are proportional to the resulting burdens placed on speech but also that the law does not seek to suppress a disfavored message.

The State's asserted justifications for § 4631(d) come under two general headings. First, the State contends that its law is necessary to protect medical privacy, including physician confidentiality, avoidance of harassment, and the integrity of the doctor-patient relationship. Second, the State argues that § 4631(d) is integral to the achievement of policy objectives—namely, improved public health and reduced healthcare costs. Neither justification withstands scrutiny. . . .

The State contends that § 4631(d) advances important public policy goals by lowering the costs of medical services and promoting public health. If prescriber-identifying information were available for use by detailers, the State contends, then detailing would be effective in promoting brand-name drugs that are more expensive and less safe than generic alternatives. This logic is set out at length in the legislative findings accompanying § 4631(d). Yet at oral argument here, the State declined to acknowledge that § 4631(d)'s objective purpose and practical effect were to inhibit detailing and alter doctors' prescription decisions. The State's reluctance to embrace its own legislature's rationale reflects the vulnerability of its position.

While Vermont's stated policy goals may be proper, § 4631(d) does not advance them in a permissible way. As the Court of Appeals noted, the "state's own explanation of how" § 4631(d) "advances its interests cannot be said to be direct." 630 F.3d, at 277. The State seeks to achieve its policy objectives through the indirect means of restraining certain speech by certain speakers—that is, by diminishing detailers' ability to influence prescription decisions. Those who seek to censor or burden free expression often assert that disfavored speech has adverse effects. But the "fear that people would make bad decisions if given truthful information" cannot justify content-based burdens on speech. "The First Amendment directs us to be especially skeptical of regulations that seek to keep people in the dark for what the government perceives to be their own good." *44 Liquormart, supra*, at 503 (opinion of Stevens, J.); see also *Linmark Associates, Inc. v. Willingboro*, 431 U.S. 85, 97 (1977). These precepts apply with full force when the audience, in this case prescribing physicians, consists of "sophisticated and experienced" consumers. . . .

Vermont may be displeased that detailers who use prescriber-identifying information are effective in promoting brand-name drugs. The State can express that view through its own speech. See *Linmark*, 431 U.S., at 97; cf. § 4622(a)(1) (establishing a prescription drug educational program). But a State's failure to persuade does not allow it to hamstring the opposition. The State may not burden the speech of others in order to tilt public debate in a preferred direction. "The commercial marketplace, like other spheres of our social and cultural life, provides a forum where ideas and information flourish. Some of the ideas and information are vital, some of slight worth. But the general rule is that the speaker and the audience, not the government, assess the value of the information presented." . . .

The capacity of technology to find and publish personal information, including records required by the government, presents serious and unresolved issues with respect to personal privacy and the dignity it seeks to secure. In considering how to protect those interests, however, the State cannot engage in content-based discrimination to advance its own side of a debate.

If Vermont's statute provided that prescriber-identifying information could not be sold or disclosed except in narrow circumstances then the State might have a stronger position. Here, however, the State gives possessors of the information broad discretion and wide latitude in disclosing the information, while at the same time restricting the information's use by some speakers and for some purposes, even while the State itself can use the information to counter the speech it seeks to suppress. Privacy is a concept too integral to the person and a right too essential to freedom to allow its manipulation to support just those ideas the government prefers.

When it enacted § 4631(d), the Vermont Legislature found that the "marketplace for ideas on medicine safety and effectiveness is frequently one-sided in that brand-name companies invest in expensive pharmaceutical marketing campaigns to doctors." 2007 Vt. Laws No. 80, § 1(4). "The goals of marketing programs," the legislature said, "are often in conflict with the goals of the state." § 1(3). The text of § 4631(d), associated legislative findings, and the record developed in the District Court establish that Vermont enacted its law for this end. The State has burdened a form of protected expression that it found too persuasive. At the same time, the State has left unburdened those speakers whose messages are in accord with its own views. This the State cannot do.

The judgment of the Court of Appeals is affirmed.

It is so ordered.

Justice BREYER, with whom Justice GINSBURG and Justice KAGAN join, dissenting.

The Vermont statute before us adversely affects expression in one, and only one, way. It deprives pharmaceutical and data-mining companies of data, collected pursuant to the government's regulatory mandate, that could help pharmaceutical companies create better sales messages. In my view, this effect on expression is inextricably related to a lawful governmental effort to regulate a commercial enterprise. The First Amendment does not require courts to apply a special "heightened" standard of review when reviewing such an effort. And, in any event, the statute meets the First Amendment standard this Court has previously applied when the government seeks to regulate commercial speech. For any or all of these reasons, the Court should uphold the statute as constitutional. . . .

There are several reasons why the Court should review Vermont's law "under the standard appropriate for the review of economic regulation," not "under a heightened standard appropriate for the review of First Amendment issues." *Glickman,* 521 U.S., at 469. For one thing, Vermont's statute neither forbids nor requires anyone to say anything, to engage in any form of symbolic speech, or to endorse any particular point of view, whether ideological or related to the sale of a product.

For another thing, the same First Amendment standards that apply to Vermont here would apply to similar regulatory actions taken by other States or by the Federal Government acting, for example, through Food and Drug Administration (FDA) regulation. (And the Federal Government's ability to preempt state laws that interfere with existing or contemplated federal forms of regulation is here irrelevant.)

Further, the statute's requirements form part of a traditional, comprehensive regulatory regime. Cf. *United Foods, supra,* at 411 [U.S. v. United Foods, 533 U.S. 405, 411 (2001)]. The pharmaceutical drug industry has been heavily regulated at least since 1906. See Pure Food and Drugs Act, 34 Stat. 768. Longstanding statutes and regulations require pharmaceutical companies to engage in complex drug testing to ensure that their drugs are both "safe" and "effective." 21 U.S.C. §§ 355(b)(1), 355(d). Only then can the drugs be marketed, at which point drug companies are subject to the FDA's exhaustive regulation of the content of drug labels and the manner in which drugs can be advertised and sold. § 352(f)(2); 21 CFR pts. 201-203 (2010).

Finally, Vermont's statute is directed toward information that exists only by virtue of government regulation. Under federal law, certain drugs can be dispensed only by a pharmacist operating under the orders of a medical practitioner. 21 U.S.C. § 353(b). Vermont regulates the qualifications, the fitness, and the practices of pharmacists themselves, and requires pharmacies to maintain a "patient record system" that, among other things, tracks who prescribed which drugs. Vt. Stat. Ann., Tit. 26, §§ 2041(a), 2022(14) (Supp. 2010); Vt. Bd. of Pharmacy Admin. Rules (Pharmacy Rules) 9.1, 9.24(e) (2009). But for these regulations, pharmacies would have no way to know who had told customers to buy which drugs (as is the case when a doctor tells a patient to take a daily dose of aspirin). . . .

If the Court means to create constitutional barriers to regulatory rules that might affect the *content* of a commercial message, it has embarked upon an unprecedented task—a task that threatens significant judicial interference with widely accepted regulatory activity. Nor would it ease the task to limit its "heightened" scrutiny to regulations that only affect certain speakers. As the examples that I have set forth illustrate, many regulations affect only messages sent by a small class of regulated speakers, for example, electricity generators or natural gas pipelines.

The Court also uses the words "aimed" and "targeted" when describing the relation of the statute to drug manufacturers. But, for the reasons just set forth, to require "heightened" scrutiny on this basis is to require its application early and often when the State seeks to regulate industry. Any statutory initiative stems from a legislative agenda. Any administrative initiative stems from a regulatory agenda. The related statutes, regulations, programs, and initiatives almost always reflect a point of view, for example, of the Congress and the administration that enacted them and ultimately the voters. And they often aim at, and target, particular firms that engage in practices about the merits of which the Government and the firms may disagree. Section 2 of the Sherman Act, 15 U.S.C. § 2, for example, which limits the truthful, nonmisleading speech of firms that, due to their market power, can affect the competitive landscape, is directly aimed at, and targeted at, monopolists.

In short, the case law in this area reflects the need to ensure that the First Amendment protects the "marketplace of ideas," thereby facilitating the democratic creation of sound government policies without improperly hampering the ability of government to introduce an agenda, to implement its policies, and to favor them to the exclusion of contrary policies. To apply "heightened" scrutiny when the regulation of commercial activities (which often involve speech) is at issue is unnecessarily to undercut the latter constitutional goal. The majority's view of this case presents that risk. . . .

[I] believe that the statute before us satisfies the "intermediate" standards this Court has applied to restrictions on commercial speech. *A fortiori* it satisfies less demanding standards that are more appropriately applied in this kind of commercial regulatory case—a case where the government seeks typical regulatory ends (lower drug prices, more balanced sales messages) through the use of ordinary regulatory means (limiting the commercial use of data gathered pursuant to a regulatory mandate). The speech-related consequences here are indirect, incidental, and entirely commercial.

The Court reaches its conclusion through the use of important First Amendment categories—"content-based," "speaker-based," and "neutral"—but without taking full account of the regulatory context, the nature of the speech effects, the values these First Amendment categories seek to promote, and prior precedent. At best the Court opens a Pandora's Box of First Amendment challenges to many ordinary regulatory practices that may only incidentally affect a commercial message. At worst, it reawakens *Lochner*'s pre-New Deal threat of substituting judicial for democratic decisionmaking where ordinary economic regulation is at issue. See *Central Hudson*, 447 U.S., at 589 (Rehnquist, J., dissenting).

Regardless, whether we apply an ordinary commercial speech standard or a less demanding standard, I believe Vermont's law is consistent with the First Amendment. And with respect, I dissent.

NOTES AND QUESTIONS

1. *Ordinary commercial transactions as speech.* After *Sorrell*, are any and all commercial transactions potentially constitutionally protected commercial speech? For example, would government efforts to regulate chewing gum sales in convenience stores be subject to intermediate scrutiny, to the extent that the regulations affect the ability of a store to market chewing gum to potential customers? What about regulations of deceptive or unfair marketing practices? Or would such regulations be sustained on the first prong of *Central Hudson*, that is, the speech must be truthful and non-misleading to enjoy constitutional protection? But, if aggressive marketing techniques, like detailing, pressure physicians into prescribing more expensive yet no more effective drugs, why is such a practice not akin to a form of fraud? Is the ability of a physician to simply close his office to detailers a sufficient response? But wouldn't this also be true of consumers with respect to deceptive marketing techniques? For a thoughtful

discussion of paternalism as a basis for regulating commercial speech, see
Tamara R. Piety, *Brandishing the First Amendment: Commercial Expression in
America* (2012).

2. *Content- and viewpoint-discrimination revisited.* Justice Kennedy, writing for
the majority, clearly frames the primary issue in *Sorrell* as involving both
content- and viewpoint-based discrimination: "On its face, Vermont's law enacts
content- and speaker-based restrictions on the sale, disclosure, and use of
prescriber-identifying information." This is certainly true; yet any regulation
regarding the marketing or sale of a good or service raises the same issues. For
example, the Securities and Exchange Commission regulates the speech
associated with initial public offerings of securities, such as shares of common
stock; it disallows some speech and mandates other speech, including mandatory
information that a seller must disclose to would-be buyers. Should such
regulations be subject to heightened scrutiny under the First Amendment? Or
does Justice Breyer have the stronger view here, that is, that government as an
administrative regulator generally does not have to answer for the First
Amendment effects of otherwise permissible regulatory programs? Does either
approach adequately address the problems and shortcomings that would arise
from adopting it? Or is a proverbial "third way" needed to address such cases? If
so, how should courts articulate the governing test when deciding when to treat a
regulatory regime that regulates commercial speech as triggering heightened
First Amendment scrutiny?

3. *The difficulty in setting boundaries.* These boundary issues arise frequently and
in myriad circumstances, yet the Supreme Court largely has failed to address
them; instead, it seems to know when the First Amendment provides the relevant
framework (and when it doesn't). For a very useful discussion of the problem,
see Frederick Schauer, *The Boundaries of the First Amendment: A Preliminary
Exploration of Constitutional Salience*, 117 Harv. L. Rev. 1765 (2004).

4. *Secondary effects and the First Amendment.* Should the First Amendment mean
that the federal and state governments are simply powerless to regulate markets
in information when those markets cause externalities, such as higher health care
costs? In the context of nude dancing, for example, the Supreme Court has
embraced the invocation of "secondary effects" as a basis for regulating—and
even banning—speech (erotic dance, for example). See *supra* Chapter 4 and
infra Chapter 11, Part C. Why should the secondary effects of nude dancing
justify content-based speech restrictions when the secondary effects of
pharmaceutical representatives' aggressive marketing techniques do not justify a
content-based ban on the sale of prescription data?

5. *Is data collection speech?* If Vermont's regulation of a physician's prescription
data is a content-based speech restriction, does this mean that any and all
government regulations of the use of data are content-based speech restrictions
too? And, accordingly, must survive strict judicial scrutiny under the First
Amendment? For an argument that the answer to this question is "yes," see Jane
Bambauer, *Is Data Speech?*, 66 Stan. L. Rev. 57 (2014). Professor Bambauer
posits that "[t]he First Amendment is, in many ways, an experiment that hinders
the government from deciding what speech, and what thoughts, are good, even if
most level-headed people could agree on the matter. After all, a benevolent
dictator is still a dictator." *Id.* at 118; *see id.* at 60 (arguing that "the freedom of
speech carries an implicit right to create knowledge" and that government

regulation that substantially interferes with knowledge creation, including data collection, is "presumptively illegitimate and must withstand judicial scrutiny"). Consistent with these views, she argues that "[t]he sanctity of a freely made mind requires protection not only for speech, but also for the digestion of raw facts," *id.* at 120, meaning that data collection and data mining constitute forms of protected First Amendment activity. Do you find these arguments persuasive? Or should data collection and data mining be characterized as antecedent activities to speech?

6. *Privacy and the commercial speech doctrine.* Does the protection of personal privacy not constitute a sufficiently important government objective to sustain restrictions on the sale of a person's medical history or a doctor's prescribing habits? Moreover, after *Sorrell* is there any room left for the federal or state governments to enact statutory privacy protections? *See* Ashutosh Bhagwat, Sorrell v. IMS Health: *Details, Detailing, and the Death of Privacy*, 36 Vt. L. Rev. 855, 856 (2012) (arguing that *Sorrell* might have "dramatic, and extremely troubling, implications for a broad range of existing and proposed rules that seek to control disclosure of personal information in order to protect privacy"). Or did Vermont simply enact a poorly drafted statute, given the highly targeted nature of the ban on selling prescription data to third parties? As an alternative to regulating information markets in physician prescription data, could Vermont instead create a statutory *property interest* in prescription data and require affirmative, direct consent from the patient receiving the medications and/or the physician prescribing the medications before a pharmacy or insurance company could sell the information to a third party? In other words, would a statute that more directly and more completely advances an interest in data privacy stand a better chance of surviving judicial review against a First Amendment challenge?

C. LIMITATIONS ON THE ABILITY OF GOVERNMENT TO REGULATE COMMERCIAL SPEECH BECAUSE OF ITS COMMERCIAL NATURE

The Supreme Court, even as it extended protection to commercial speech in cases like *Virginia State Board of Pharmacy* and *Central Hudson*, maintained that such speech stands on the lower rung of the hierarchy of First Amendment free speech values. It has sufficient value to merit protection as "free speech" but is ostensibly not as central to the free speech project as political speech, or even artistic, literary, or scientific speech. If this is so, may government then single out commercial speech for special regulatory burdens? The answer appears to be a qualified no. Even so, cases involving the Federal Trade Commission's do-not-call registry suggest that targeted bans of commercial speech might in fact be consistent with the Free Speech Clause.

1.   The Rule Against Discrimination Against Commercial Speech as Such

CITY OF CINCINNATI v. DISCOVERY NETWORK, INC.

507 U.S. 410 (1993)

Justice STEVENS delivered the opinion of the Court.

Motivated by its interest in the safety and attractive appearance of its streets and sidewalks, the city of Cincinnati has refused to allow respondents to distribute their commercial publications through freestanding newsracks located on public property. The question presented is whether this refusal is consistent with the First Amendment. In agreement with the District Court and the Court of Appeals, we hold that it is not.

Respondent Discovery Network, Inc. is engaged in the business of providing adult educational, recreational, and social programs to individuals in the Cincinnati area. It advertises those programs in a free magazine that it publishes nine times a year. Although these magazines consist primarily of promotional material pertaining to Discovery's courses, they also include some information about current events of general interest. Approximately one-third of these magazines are distributed through the 38 newsracks that the city authorized Discovery to place on public property in 1989.

Respondent Harmon Publishing Company, Inc., publishes and distributes a free magazine that advertises real estate for sale at various locations throughout the United States. The magazine contains listings and photographs of available residential properties in the greater Cincinnati area, and also includes some information about interest rates, market trends, and other real estate matters. In 1989, Harmon received the city's permission to install 24 newsracks at approved locations. About 15% of its distribution in the Cincinnati area is through those devices.

In March 1990, the city's Director of Public Works notified each of the respondents that its permit to use dispensing devices on public property was revoked, and ordered the newsracks removed within 30 days. Each notice explained that respondent's publication was a "commercial handbill" within the meaning of § 714-1-C of the Municipal Code and therefore § 714-23 of the code prohibited its distribution on public property. [The city and publishers agreed to seek a judicial determination of the constitutionality of the city's newsrack policy.] Respondents then commenced this litigation in the United States District Court for the Southern District of Ohio.

After an evidentiary hearing the District Court concluded that "the regulatory scheme advanced by the City of Cincinnati completely prohibiting the distribution of commercial handbills on the public right of way violates the First Amendment." [T]he Court of Appeals agreed with the District Court that the burden placed on speech "cannot be justified by the paltry gains in safety and beauty achieved by the ordinance." . . .

There is no claim in this case that there is anything unlawful or misleading about the contents of respondents' publications. Moreover, respondents do not challenge their characterization as "commercial speech." Nor do respondents question the substantiality of the city's interest in safety and esthetics. It was, therefore, proper for the District Court and the Court of Appeals to judge the validity of the city's prohibition under the standards we set forth in *Central Hudson* and *Fox*. It was the city's burden to establish a "reasonable fit" between its legitimate interests in safety and esthetics and its choice of a limited and selective prohibition of newsracks as the means chosen to serve those interests.

There is ample support in the record for the conclusion that the city did not "establish the reasonable fit we require." The ordinance on which it relied was an outdated prohibition against the distribution of any commercial handbills on public property. It was enacted long before any concern about newsracks developed. Its apparent purpose was to prevent the kind of visual blight caused by littering, rather than any harm associated with permanent, freestanding dispensing devices. The fact that the city failed to address its recently developed concern about newsracks by regulating their size, shape, appearance, or number indicates that it has not "carefully calculated" the costs and benefits associated with the burden on speech imposed by its prohibition. The benefit to be derived from the removal of 62 newsracks while about 1,500-2,000 remain in place was considered "minute" by the District Court and "paltry" by the Court of Appeals. We share their evaluation of the "fit" between the city's goal and its method of achieving it.

In seeking reversal, the city argues that it is wrong to focus attention on the relatively small number of newsracks affected by its prohibition, because the city's central concern is with the overall number of newsracks on its sidewalks, rather than with the unattractive appearance of a handful of dispensing devices. It contends, first, that a categorical prohibition on the use of newsracks to disseminate commercial messages burdens no more speech than is necessary to further its interest in limiting the number of newsracks; and, second, that the prohibition is a valid "time, place, and manner" regulation because it is content neutral and leaves open ample alternative channels of communication. We consider these arguments in turn.

The city argues that there is a close fit between its ban on newsracks dispensing "commercial handbills" and its interests in safety and esthetics because every decrease in the number of such dispensing devices necessarily effects an increase in safety and an improvement in the attractiveness of the cityscape. In the city's view, the prohibition is thus *entirely* related to its legitimate interests in safety and esthetics.

We accept the validity of the city's proposition, but consider it an insufficient justification for the discrimination against respondents' use of newsracks that are no more harmful than the permitted newsracks, and have only a minimal impact on the overall number of newsracks on the city's sidewalks. The major premise supporting the city's argument is the proposition that commercial speech has only a low value. Based on that premise, the city contends that the fact that assertedly more valuable publications are allowed to use newsracks does not undermine its judgment that its esthetic and safety interests are stronger than the interest in allowing commercial speakers to have similar access to the reading public.

We cannot agree. In our view, the city's argument attaches more importance to the distinction between commercial and noncommercial speech than our cases warrant and seriously underestimates the value of commercial speech.

This very case illustrates the difficulty of drawing bright lines that will clearly cabin commercial speech in a distinct category. For respondents' publications share important characteristics with the publications that the city classifies as "newspapers." Particularly, they are "commercial handbills" within the meaning of § 714-1-C of the city's code because they contain advertising, a feature that apparently also places ordinary newspapers within the same category. Separate provisions in the code specifically authorize the distribution of "newspapers" on the public right of way, but that term is not defined. Presumably, respondents' publications do not qualify as newspapers because an examination of their content discloses a higher ratio of advertising to other text, such as news and feature stories, than is found in the exempted publications. Indeed, Cincinnati's City Manager has determined that publications that qualify as newspapers and therefore *can* be distributed by newsrack are those that are published daily and/or weekly and "*primarily* presen[t] coverage of, and commentary on, current events."

The absence of a categorical definition of the difference between "newspapers" and "commercial handbills" in the city's code is also a characteristic of our opinions considering the constitutionality of regulations of commercial speech. Fifty years ago, we concluded that the distribution of a commercial handbill was unprotected by the First Amendment, even though half of its content consisted of political protest. *Valentine v. Chrestensen*, 316 U.S. 52 (1942). A few years later, over Justice Black's dissent, we held that the "commercial feature" of door-to-door solicitation of magazine subscriptions was a sufficient reason for denying First Amendment protection to that activity. *Breard v. Alexandria*, 341 U.S. 622 (1951). Subsequent opinions, however, recognized that important commercial attributes of various forms of communication do not qualify their entitlement to constitutional protection. . . . We then held that even speech that does no more than propose a commercial transaction is protected by the First Amendment. . . .

[F]or the purpose of deciding this case, we assume that all of the speech barred from Cincinnati's sidewalks is what we have labeled "core" commercial speech and that no such speech is found in publications that are allowed to use newsracks. We nonetheless agree with the Court of Appeals that Cincinnati's actions in this case run afoul of the First Amendment. Not only does Cincinnati's categorical ban on commercial newsracks place too much importance on the distinction between commercial and noncommercial speech, but in this case, the distinction bears no relationship *whatsoever* to the particular interests that the city has asserted. It is therefore an impermissible means of responding to the city's admittedly legitimate interests.

The city has asserted an interest in esthetics, but respondent publishers' newsracks are no greater an eyesore than the newsracks permitted to remain on Cincinnati's sidewalks. Each newsrack, whether containing "newspapers" or "commercial handbills" is equally unattractive. . . .

In the absence of some basis for distinguishing between "newspapers" and "commercial handbills" that is relevant to an interest asserted by the city, we are unwilling to recognize Cincinnati's bare assertion that the "low value" of commercial speech is a sufficient justification for its selective and categorical ban on newsracks dispensing "commercial handbills." Our holding, however, is narrow. As should be clear from the above discussion, we do not reach the question whether, given certain facts and under certain circumstances, a community might be able to justify differential treatment of commercial and noncommercial newsracks. We simply hold that on this record Cincinnati has failed to make such a showing. Because the distinction Cincinnati has drawn has absolutely no bearing on the interests it has asserted, we have no difficulty concluding, as did the two courts below, that the city has not established the "fit" between its goals and its chosen means that is required by our opinion in *Fox*. It remains to consider the city's argument that its prohibition is a permissible time, place, and manner regulation. . . .

[T]he city's newsrack policy is neither content neutral nor, as demonstrated in Part III, *supra*, "narrowly tailored." Thus, regardless of whether or not it leaves open ample alternative channels of communication, it cannot be justified as a legitimate time, place, or manner restriction on protected speech.

The judgment of the Court of Appeals is

Affirmed.

Justice BLACKMUN, concurring.

I agree that Cincinnati's ban on commercial newsracks cannot withstand scrutiny under *Central Hudson Gas & Electric Corp. v. Public Serv. Comm'n of N.Y.*, 447 U.S. 557 (1980), and *Board of Trustees of State University of N.Y. v. Fox*, 492 U.S. 469 (1989), and I therefore join the Court's opinion. I write separately because I continue to believe that the analysis set forth in *Central Hudson* and refined in *Fox* afford insufficient protection for truthful, noncoercive commercial speech concerning lawful activities. . . .

I am heartened by the Court's decision today to reject the extreme extension of *Central Hudson*'s logic, and I hope the Court ultimately will come to abandon *Central Hudson*'s analysis entirely in favor of one that affords full protection for truthful, noncoercive commercial speech about lawful activities.

Chief Justice REHNQUIST, with whom Justice WHITE and Justice THOMAS join, dissenting.

Concerned about the safety and esthetics of its streets and sidewalks, the city of Cincinnati decided to do something about the proliferation of newsracks on its street corners. Pursuant to an existing ordinance prohibiting the distribution of "commercial handbills" on public property, the city ordered respondents Discovery Newswork, Inc., and Harmon Publishing Company, Inc., to remove their newsracks from its sidewalks within 30 days. Respondents publish and distribute free of charge magazines that consist principally of commercial speech. Together their publications account for 62 of the 1,500-2,000 newsracks that clutter Cincinnati's street corners. Because the city chose to address its newsrack problem by banning only those newsracks that disseminate commercial handbills, rather than regulating all newsracks (including those that disseminate traditional newspapers) alike, the Court holds that its actions violate the First Amendment to the Constitution. I believe this result is inconsistent with prior precedent. . . .

[D]espite the fact that we have consistently distinguished between commercial and noncommercial speech for the purpose of determining whether the regulation of speech is permissible, the Court holds that in attempting to alleviate its newsrack problem Cincinnati may not choose to proceed incrementally by burdening only commercial speech first. Based on the different levels of protection we have accorded commercial and noncommercial speech, we have previously said that localities may not favor commercial over noncommercial speech in addressing similar urban problems, see *Metromedia, Inc. v. San Diego, supra*, at 513 (plurality opinion), but before today we have never even suggested that the converse holds true. It is not surprising, then, that the Court offers little in the way of precedent supporting its new rule. . . .

If (as I am certain) Cincinnati may regulate newsracks that disseminate commercial speech based on the interests it has asserted, I am at a loss as to why its scheme is unconstitutional because it does not also regulate newsracks that disseminate noncommercial speech. One would have thought that the city, perhaps even following the teachings of our commercial speech jurisprudence, could have decided to place the burden of its regulatory scheme on less protected speech (*i.e.,* commercial handbills) without running afoul of the First Amendment. Today's decision, though, places the city in the position of having to decide between restricting more speech—fully protected speech—and allowing the proliferation of newsracks on its street corners to continue unabated. It scarcely seems logical that the First Amendment compels such a result. . . .

NOTES AND QUESTIONS

1. *Prohibiting discrimination against commercial speech. Discovery Network* is an important, indeed landmark, commercial speech decision. Justice Stevens appears to say that regulations targeting commercial speech for adverse treatment vis-à-vis noncommercial speech are valid *only* if commercial speech contributes in a non-general way to the problem being addressed. If too many newsracks litter fair Cincinnati's streets, the problem is clutter, not the clutter created by newspapers and magazines featuring predominantly commercial speech (viz., *Harmon Homes, Thrifty Nickel*).

2. *The potential virtues of differential treatment.* Why shouldn't government be able to disprefer commercial speech when attempting to mitigate a genuine aesthetic concern? Recall that in *Railway Express Agency*, the Supreme Court permitted New York City to ban third-party advertisements on panel trucks, even though the city permitted advertisements associated with the owner's business on panel trucks. Justice Douglas suggested that the Constitution permitted New York City to address the problem of visual blight in a piecemeal fashion. If, as Justice Powell observed in *Central Hudson*, commercial speech is more robust and less socially valuable than other kinds of speech, why shouldn't government have a freer hand in regulating it?

3. *The baby and the bath water objection.* Paradoxically, does *Discovery Network* mean—as it seems to say—that free speech values would be advanced more effectively if Cincinnati banned all newsracks on city property? That would lead to an even greater burden on the marketplace of ideas, wouldn't it? Does Chief Justice Rehnquist's dissent have a point? For an argument that *Discovery Network* has the potential to do more harm than good precisely because it invites the adoption of broader speech restrictions targeting both commercial and noncommercial speech, see William W. Van Alstyne, *Remembering Melville Nimmer: Some Cautionary Notes on Commercial Speech*, 43 UCLA L. Rev. 1635 (1996).

4. *Is commercial speech less protected than noncommercial speech?* After *Discovery Network*, what, if anything, remains of the idea that commercial speech stands on a lesser free speech footing than noncommercial speech?

2.   Discovery Network *Applied?: Offensive Trademarks and Off-Label Rx Drug Marketing*

Discovery Network holds that government may not treat commercial speech less favorably than non-commercial speech, unless the commercial speech presents social harms that the unregulated non-commercial speech of the same kind or character does not. But when does commercial speech present a sufficiently particularized threat to justify regulating or proscribing it—but not non-commercial speech of a similar stripe? The examples of offensive trademarks and off-label prescription drug marketing help to shed some light on this important question.

The Lantham Act is a federal law that permits individuals and businesses to register trademarks and, after registration, grants the holder of the trademark the exclusive right to use the trademark when associated with a particular good, service, or activity. However, the Lantham Act prohibits the Patent and Trademark Office (PTO) from registering "scandalous, disparaging, or immoral" trademarks. *See* 15 U.S.C. § 1052(a). For many years, the federal courts, notably including the U.S. Court of Appeals for the Federal Circuit, upheld this statutory limitation on trademarks and the PTO's associated policy of refusing to register trademarks that feature offensive language, sexually-explicit content, or offensive racial stereotypes. *See In re Tam*, 808 F.3d 1321, 1330 (Fed. Cir. 2015) (en banc), *cert. granted*, 137 S. Ct. 30 (2016) (providing illustrative disallowed trademarks, including "Redskins," "AmishHomo," "Christian Prostitute," "Wet Bac," and "2 Dyke Minimum"). Prior to *Tam*, the lower federal courts uniformly had rejected First Amendment challenges to trademark denials because refusals to register a trademark did not prohibit use of the trademark; instead, such decisions simply denied the user the right to prevent others from also using the trademark. *See In re Fox*, 702 F. 3d 633, 635 (Fed. Cir. 2012); In re Boulevard Entm't, Inc., 334 F.3d 1336, 1343 (Fed. Cir. 2003).

The Federal Circuit abrubtly changed course in 2015, holding that the government's ban on offensive trademarks constituted not merely a content-based restriction on speech, but a viewpoint-based speech regulation. *In Re Tam*, 808 F.3d at 1334-37. The case involved the PTO's denial of a trademark for a rock band called "The Slants," fronted by lead singer Simon Shiao Tam. By choosing the name "The Slants" for his band, Tam sought "to make a statement about racial and cultural issues." *Id.* at 1327-28. More specifically, the band's name reflected an effort "to 'reclaim' and 'take ownership' of Asian stereotypes." *Id.* at 1331. The PTO declined to register "The Slants" for a trademark because the proposed trademark was "likely disparaging to 'persons of Asian descent' under § 2(a)." *Id.* A three-judge panel, applying binding circuit precedent, affirmed the PTO's refusal to register the proposed trademark. *See id.* at 1331-33.

The full court, on its own motion, decided to rehear the case en banc and reversed the panel's decision. The en banc court held that section 2(a) constituted an impermissible form of viewpoint discrimination, explaining that it "stifle[d] the use of certain disfavored messages." *Id.* at 1339. Judge Kimberly Moore added that "[s]trict scrutiny therefore governs [the court's] First Amendment assessment—and no argument has been made that the measure survives such scrutiny." *Id.* The government argued that because trademarks are commercial in nature, strict scrutiny should not apply, even if section 2(a) constitutes a viewpoint-based speech regulation. However, the Federal Circuit squarely rejected this argument, holding instead that section 2(a) "regulates expressive speech, not commercial speech, and therefore strict scrutiny is appropriate." *Id.* at 1355.

The en banc *Tam* Court also found that denials of registration for offensive or disparaging trademarks would not pass muster under *Central Hudson*—even if offensive or disparaging trademarks are properly viewed as commercial, rather than non-commercial, speech—because the regulation does not regulate "false or misleading" speech and failed to advance a substantial government interest. *See id.* at 1355-57. The court explained that "the case law does not recognize a substantial [government] interest in discriminatorily regulating private speech to try to reduce racial intolerance" by "burden[ing] speech it finds offensive." *Id.* at 1557. Thus, "[w]ith no substantial government interests, the disparagement provision of § 2(a) cannot satisfy the *Central Hudson* test." *Id.*

Was the *Tam* majority correct to find that trademarks are non-commerical speech? And does the government clearly lack a substantial interest in refusing to grant trademark protection to offensive or stigmatizing commercial trademarks? Doesn't the government's issuance of a trademark suggest its tacit approval of the message that the trademark conveys? And could offensive trademarks be viewed as "false and misleading" commercial speech? Or are arguments of this sort simply a means of opening the door to government censorship of commercial speech based on the viewpoint of the speaker? On the other hand, however, could *Discovery Network* be understood to permit a targeted regulation of this sort precisely because the government has a substantial interest in refusing to lend its support to offensive or degrading trademarks—just as it has a parallel interest in not giving tax benefits to racially discriminatory colleges and universities? *See* Bob Jones Univ. v. U.S., 461 U.S. 574 (1983) (upholding the IRS's decision to strip Bob Jones University of its section 501(c)(3) status because of the university's racially discriminatory policies). Even if government cannot proscribe racist or scatological language more generally in society (see *infra* Chapter 10), must it facilitate commercial speech of this sort? And don't trademarks featuring racial stereotypes, with the government's active assistance, cause obvious social harms? See *In Re* Tam, 808 F.3d at 1363-64, 1372-73 (Dyk, J., concurring in part and dissenting in part) (arguing that the PTO should have registered Tam's proposed trademark but rejecting the broader argument that section 2(a) is generally unconstitutional because the government need not lend its support to offensive and disparaging trademarks that lack any legitimate "informational function"). Or does the PTO's inconsistent enforcement of section 2(a) doom the whole project? After all, the PTO allowed trademarks for "Aunt Jemima," "Uncle Ben," and the "Frito Bandito." See Brian D. Behnken & Gregory D. Smithers, Racism in American Popular Media: From Aunt Jemima to the Frito Bandito (2015). Given that the PTO has registered racially problematic trademarks in the past, is the real problem with section 2(a) a long-term pattern of inconsistent and selective enforcement, i.e., viewpoint discrimination? Alternatively, could one characterize Tam's proposed trademark as non-commercial in nature—and therefore meriting more vigorous First Amendment protection than more typical trademarks? *See Tam*, 808 F.3d at 1373-74 (Dyk, J., concurring in part and dissenting in part) (finding that section 2(a) is generally valid but that the PTO violated the First Amendment by denying Tam's trademark application because it constituted political speech). Another potential mode of First Amendment analysis: Is section 2(a) arguably void for undue vagueness? *See id.* at 1361-62 (O'Malley, J., concurring) (arguing that section 2(a)'s "disparagement" standard is too vague to survive First Amendment scrutiny); *see supra* Chapter 1. The Supreme Court is expected to resolve this question in its 2016-2017 Term.

The Food and Drug Administration's (FDA) ban against off-label prescription drug marketing efforts by drug manufacturers provides another context in which to test *Discovery Network*'s rule that government may regulate commercial speech, but not non-commercial speech, only when commercial speech presents an identifiable social harm that identical non-commercial speech does not. For many years, the federal courts routinely sustained the FDA's ban against such marketing efforts. However, the enhanced scope of protection afforded to commercial speech over time placed increasing pressure on the FDA's ban against off-label marketing by drug makers. If one views commercial speech by a drug maker as presenting a more serious risk of being false and misleading, then a targeted ban on commercial speech of this sort, by this subset of speakers, might be consistent with *Discovery Network* because it constitutes a particularized threat that non-commercial speech about off-label drug applications would not. *United States v. Caronia*, 703 F.3d 149 (2012), casts serious doubt on this analysis and suggests that drug makers have a First Amendment right to actively promote off-label uses of FDA-approved drugs.

In order to sell a prescription medicine, a drug manufacturer must prove its efficacy to the FDA through a series of highly demanding clinical trials. *See* Food, Drug, and Cosmetic Act (FDCA), 21 U.S.C. §§ 331, 352, 355 (prohibiting the sale or promotion of "misbranded" drugs and requiring a pharmaceutical company to prove the efficacy of a drug for a particular condition and to label a drug consistently with the drug's established efficacy). Once approved based on demonstrated clinical efficacy, the drug's manufacturer may lawfully market that drug for its demonstrated purpose. However, the FDA has taken the position that a drug manufacturer may not *itself* market a prescription drug for "off-label" purposes, even though *physicians* are entirely free to prescribe prescription drugs for off-label uses. Thus, drug makers may not affirmatively advertise or promote an FDA-approved drug for such off-label uses—even if such uses are widely-accepted within the medical community.

For many years, federal courts sustained the FDA's ban against pharmaceutical companies marketing prescription drugs for off-label use—even though this constituted a speech restriction in a circumstance where the underlying speech was accurate and truthful and where it was also perfectly lawful for a physician to prescribe the drug for the off-label use to a patient. Moreover, anyone other than the drug's maker would have been quite free to promote an off-label use of an FDA-approved drug; only the drug's maker could run afoul the FDA's "misbranding" regulations. Misbranding of drugs, including promotion of off-label uses, exposed pharmaceutical companies and their marketing staff to both civil and criminal sanctions.

In 2012, however, following the Supreme Court's decision in *Sorrell*, the U.S. Court of Appeals for the Second Circuit invalidated the FDA's efforts to prohibit pharmaceutical companies from promoting the off-label use of FDA-approved prescription drugs. *See Caronia*, 703 F.3d at 166-69. Writing for the panel majority, Judge Denny Chin explained that "[t]he government's construction of the FDCA's misbranding provisions to prohibit and criminalize the promotion of off-label drug use by pharmaceutical manufacturers is content- and speaker-based, and, therefore, subject to heightened scrutiny." *Id.* at 164-65. Turning to the *Central Hudson* four-part test, Judge Chin easily found the first and second prongs were satisfied: Caronia's speech was truthful and non-misleading and related to a lawful product and the government possessed a substantial interest in preventing misleading or inaccurate drug marketing efforts by drug makers. *Id.* at 165-66. However, the government could not meet the third and fourth prongs of *Central Hudson* because the ban against promoting off-label uses did not directly advance the government's interest in avoiding misbranded prescription drugs nor was it narrowly tailored. *See id.* at 166-69.

The key to both holdings is the fact that it is perfectly legal to prescribe FDA-approved drugs for off-label uses. As Judge Chin explained, "off-label drug usage is not unlawful, and the FDA's drug approval process generally contemplates that approved drugs will be used in off-label ways." *Id.* at 166. Thus, "even if pharmaceutical manufacturers are barred from off-label promotion, physicians can prescribe, and patients can use, drugs for off-label purposes." *Id.* Thus, because off-label drug use is legal, "it does not follow that prohibiting the truthful promotion of off-label drug usage by a particular class of speakers would directly further the government's goals of preserving the efficacy and integrity of the FDA's drug approval process and reducing patient exposure to unsafe and ineffective drugs." *Id.* at 166.

Only if one views speech about off-label uses of prescription drugs as inherently "false and misleading" could the FDA's speech ban have survived constitutional scrutiny. And, in terms of *Discovery Network*, false and misleading commercial speech about prescription drugs would at least arguably constitute a particular evil that would justify targeted regulation. Because drug makers have a strong financial incentive to promote the widest possible use of their products, drug makers have a powerful financial incentive to push toward the outer limits of plausibility in making new claims about their products that other potential speakers do not. In this sense, then, a pharmaceutical company's speech promoting off-label uses of its FDA-approved drugs presents social risks that identical speech by others does not.

However, this logic only holds true if one accepts the view that *any* effort to promote off-label uses of prescription drugs presents an unacceptable risk of self-dealing by drug makers. As Dean Rodney Smolla has argued, "[t]he arguments advanced by the FDA to defend its ban on off-label drug promotion . . . are all deeply flawed when measured against modern First Amendment principles" because "[t]hose principles no longer permit the FDA to exert its near-absolute ban on truthful, non-misleading promotional and marketing information by pharmaceutical companies and their agents regarding the off-label uses of drugs." Rodney A. Smolla, *Off Label Drug Advertising and the First Amendment*, 50 Wake Forest L. Rev. 81, 91 (2015). Accordingly, "to the extent that drug companies seek to share information about the prescribing habits of other doctors and extant medical literature regarding off-label uses, the companies, even if sharing this information for a commercial purpose, appear to be trafficking in scientific data regarding prescription habits analytically indistinguishable from the information held protected by the First Amendment in *Sorrell*." *Id.* at 103. *But cf.* David Orentlicher, *Off-Label Drug Marketing, The First Amendment, and Federalism*, 50 Wash. U. J.L. & Pol'y 89, 103 (2016) ("First Amendment concerns should not block regulation of off-label marketing. A company's off-label promotional speech provides probative evidence of illicit conduct—the distribution of misbranded drugs—and therefore restrictions of off-label promotion should not trigger First Amendment protection.").

The FDA declined to seek Supreme Court review of the Second Circuit's *Caronia* decision but has indicated that it will continue to initiate prosecutions for "false and misleading" promotion of off-brand use of prescription drugs. *See* Marc J. Scheineson & Guillermo Cuevas, United States v. Caronia, *The Increasing Strength of Commercial Free Speech and Potential New Emphasis on Classifying Off-Label Promotion as "False and Misleading"*, 68 Food & Drug L.J. 201, 211-12 (2013). Even if other federal and state courts find *Caronia* persuasive, serious questions remain to be addressed regarding what constitutes "truthful" off-label drug advertising. *See* Kathryn Bi, Comment, *What Is "False or Misleading" Off-Label Promotion?*, 82 U. Chi. L. Rev. 975 (2015) (noting that "[t]hough off-label promotion is at the center of numerous active lawsuits and a national policy debate, courts have not yet addressed what constitutes 'false or misleading' off-label speech" and proposing a theoretical and doctrinal framework for addressing this lacuna in existing law). For a thoughtful debate on the merits of *Caronia*, see Stephanie M. Greene & Lars Noah, *Debate: Off Label Drug Promotion and the First Amendment*, 162 U. Pa. L. Rev. Online 239 (2014).

THEORY-APPLIED PROBLEM

In 2017, the Federal Trade Commission considers adopting a "do-not-track" registry, largely modeled on its do-not-call registry; the new program would require all commercial Web site operators to offer a do-not-track option to persons who visit their Web sites. The incumbent chair of the FTC explains that "despite some good actors, self-regulation of privacy has not worked adequately and is not working adequately for American consumers." The chair adds that "[w]e would like to see companies work a lot faster to make consumer choice easier." Under the new regulations, all commercial Web sites (defined as "websites that seek to sell goods or services to the general public") must have an easy-to-find and easy-to-use do-not-track function that completely disables any and all tracking software or protocols from saving the visitor's data "for marketing or other commercial purposes." You work as an assistant general counsel for Boogle, a large and highly diversified Web services company that in part generates revenue by bundling, processing, and selling data obtained from third-party commercial Web sites. The proposed FTC regulation would interrupt the supply of Web site visitors' data, and thereby the data being analyzed, bundled, and sold to advertisers. Boogle's general counsel asks you to advise her on whether any valid First Amendment objections would potentially exist to the FTC's proposed mandatory do-not-track regulations. How do you advise her? Would such a challenge likely succeed in federal court? Moreover, does the commercial speech doctrine provide the only potential First Amendment objection to such a regulation? What other First Amendment issues might be raised in litigation?

D. THE PROBLEM OF DEFINING COMMERCIAL SPEECH

One distinct problem with the Supreme Court's commercial speech doctrine is the failure of the Justices to define with any precision exactly what constitutes "commercial" as opposed to "noncommercial" speech. Does any communication from a business or corporation count as commercial speech? What if the speaker has a financial motive for speaking but the speech itself does not solicit the sale of a good or service? Should the constitutional status of speech be measured by the identity of the speaker? The following three cases take up the problem of defining precisely when speech or speakers are "commercial" in nature.

BOLGER v. YOUNGS DRUG PRODUCTS CORP.

463 U.S. 60 (1983)

Justice MARSHALL delivered the opinion of the Court.

Title 39 U.S.C. § 3001(e)(2) prohibits the mailing of unsolicited advertisements for contraceptives. The District Court held that, as applied to appellee's mailings, the statute violates the First Amendment. We affirm.

Section 3001(e)(2) states that "[a]ny unsolicited advertisement of matter which is designed, adapted, or intended for preventing conception is nonmailable matter, shall not be carried or delivered by mail, and shall be disposed of as the Postal Service directs. . . . " As interpreted by Postal Services regulations, the statutory provision does not apply to unsolicited advertisements in which the mailer has no commercial interest. In addition to the civil consequences of a violation of § 3001(e)(2), 18 U.S.C. § 1461 makes it a crime knowingly to use the mails for anything declared by § 3001(e) to be nonmailable.

Appellee Youngs Drug Products Corp. (Youngs) is engaged in the manufacture, sale, and distribution of contraceptives. Youngs markets its products primarily through sales to chain warehouses and wholesale distributors, who in turn sell contraceptives to retail pharmacists, who then sell those products to individual customers. Appellee publicizes the availability and desirability of its products by various methods. This litigation resulted from Youngs' decision to undertake a campaign of unsolicited mass mailings to members of the public. In conjunction with its wholesalers and retailers, Youngs seeks to mail to the public on an unsolicited basis three types of materials:

- multi-page, multi-item flyers promoting a large variety of products available at a drugstore, including prophylactics;
- flyers exclusively or substantially devoted to promoting prophylactics;
- informational pamphlets discussing the desirability and availability of prophylactics in general or Youngs' products in particular.

In 1979 the Postal Service traced to a wholesaler of Youngs' products an allegation of an unsolicited mailing of contraceptive advertisements. The Service warned the wholesaler that the mailing violated 39 U.S.C. § 3001(e)(2). Subsequently, Youngs contacted the Service and furnished it with copies of Youngs' three types of proposed mailings, stating its view that the statute could not constitutionally restrict the mailings. The Service rejected Youngs' legal argument and notified the company that the proposed mailings would violate § 3001(e)(2). Youngs then brought this action for declaratory and injunctive relief in the United States District Court for the District of Columbia. It claimed that the statute, as applied to its proposed mailings, violated the First Amendment and that Youngs and its wholesaler were refraining from distributing the advertisements because of the Service's warning. [The federal district court agreed with Youngs Drug that § 3001(e)(2) violated the company's free speech rights. A direct appeal to the Supreme Court followed.]

Beginning with *Bigelow v. Virginia*, 421 U.S. 809 (1975), this Court extended the protection of the First Amendment to commercial speech. Nonetheless, our decisions have recognized "the 'common-sense' distinction between speech proposing a commercial transaction, which occurs in an area traditionally subject to government regulation, and other varieties of speech." Thus, we have held that the Constitution accords less protection to commercial speech than to other constitutionally safeguarded forms of expression. . . .

Because the degree of protection afforded by the First Amendment depends on whether the activity sought to be regulated constitutes commercial or noncommercial speech, we must first determine the proper classification of the mailings at issue here. Appellee contends that its proposed mailings constitute "fully protected" speech, so that § 3001(e)(2) amounts to an impermissible content-based restriction on such expression. Appellants argue, and the District Court held, that the proposed mailings are all commercial speech. The application of § 3001(e)(2) to appellee's proposed mailings must be examined carefully to ensure that speech deserving of greater constitutional protection is not inadvertently suppressed.

Most of appellee's mailings fall within the core notion of commercial speech— "speech which does 'no more than propose a commercial transaction.'" Youngs' informational pamphlets, however, cannot be characterized merely as proposals to engage in commercial transactions. Their proper classification as commercial or noncommercial speech thus presents a closer question. The mere fact that these pamphlets are conceded to be advertisements clearly does not compel the conclusion that they are commercial speech. Similarly, the reference to a specific product does not by itself render the pamphlets commercial speech. Finally, the fact that Youngs has an economic motivation for mailing the pamphlets would clearly be insufficient by itself to turn the materials into commercial speech.

The combination of all these characteristics, however, provides strong support for the District Court's conclusion that the informational pamphlets are properly characterized as commercial speech. The mailings constitute commercial speech notwithstanding the fact that they contain discussions of important public issues such as venereal disease and family planning. We have made clear that advertising which "links a product to a current public debate" is not thereby entitled to the constitutional protection afforded noncommercial speech. A company has the full panoply of protections available to its direct comments on public issues, so there is no reason for providing similar constitutional protection when such statements are made in the context of commercial transactions. Advertisers should not be permitted to immunize false or misleading product information from government regulation simply by including references to public issues.

We conclude, therefore, that all of the mailings in this case are entitled to the qualified but nonetheless substantial protection accorded to commercial speech.

[The Court applied the four-part *Central Hudson* test and found § 3001(e)(2) to be overbroad because the means selected (a complete ban) were not proportionate to the advancement of the government's substantial interest in protecting minors from information about birth control.]

We thus conclude that the justifications offered by appellants are insufficient to warrant the sweeping prohibition on the mailing of unsolicited contraceptive advertisements. As applied to appellee's mailings, § 3001(e)(2) is unconstitutional. The judgment of the District Court is therefore

Affirmed.

Justice REHNQUIST, with whom Justice O' CONNOR joins, concurring in the judgment.

I agree that the judgment should be affirmed, but my reasoning differs from that of the Court. The right to use the mails is undoubtedly protected by the First

Amendment, *Blount v. Rizzi*, 400 U.S. 410 (1971). But because the home mailbox has features which distinguish it from a public hall or public park, where it may be assumed that all who are present wish to hear the views of the particular speaker then on the rostrum, it cannot be totally assimilated for purposes of analysis with these traditional public forums. . . .

The questions whether § 3001(e)(2) directly advances these interests, and whether it is more extensive than necessary, are more problematic [than whether the government possessed a substantial reason for the ban].

Thus, under this Court's cases the intrusion generated by Youngs' proposed advertising is relatively small, and the restriction imposed by § 3001(e)(2) is relatively large. Although this restriction directly advances weighty governmental interests, it is somewhat more extensive than is necessary to serve those interests. On balance I conclude that this restriction on Youngs' commercial speech has not been adequately justified. Section 3001(e)(2) therefore violates the First Amendment as applied to Youngs and to material of the type Youngs has indicated that it plans to send, and I agree that the judgment of the District Court should be affirmed.

Justice STEVENS, concurring in the judgment.

Two aspects of the Court's opinion merit further comment: (1) its conclusion that all of the communications at issue are properly classified as "commercial speech" (*ante*, at 68); and (2) its virtually complete rejection of offensiveness as a possibly legitimate justification for the suppression of speech. My views are somewhat different from the Court's on both of these matters.

Even if it may not intend to do so, the Court's opinion creates the impression that "commercial speech" is a fairly definite category of communication that is protected by a fairly definite set of rules that differ from those protecting other categories of speech. That impression may not be wholly warranted. . . .

NOTES AND QUESTIONS

1. *The problem of defining "commercial speech." Youngs Drug* is a hard case: At least some of the flyers in question made no effort to sell goods or services. "Condoms and Human Sexuality" and "Plain Talk About Venereal Disease" would undoubtedly be fully protected speech if distributed by a chapter of Planned Parenthood rather than Youngs Drug Products Corporation. Does the commercial motive of Youngs Drug render the speech commercial in nature? If not, what precise factor leads Justice Marshall to declare all the materials to constitute commercial speech?

2. *A distinction without a difference?* If a subjective commercial motivation (as objectively determined by a reviewing court) defines "commercial speech," is the *New York Times* or *ABC World News Tonight* commercial speech? Certainly the parent corporations of both the *New York Times* and *ABC World News Tonight* hope to make money by distributing newspapers and news programs. Moreover, the content exists in part to support the sale of advertising—printed ads in the case of a newspaper and commercial air time in the case of a broadcast network. Yet, if the New York Times and ABC World News Tonight both constitute commercial speech, what is left of the residual category of "noncommercial" speech? Suppose a politician running for Congress supports increased defense spending, in part because local industrial facilities within her

congressional district contract with the Pentagon for the design and construction of weapons systems. Is the candidate's speech "commercial speech" because she hopes that, if elected, she will increase the net amount of economic activity in the community?

3. *The relevant factors and the governing test.* *Youngs Drug* relies on three factors to make the commercial speech determination: (1) the speaker's concession in court that the pamphlets were advertisements, (2) reference to Youngs Drug products (even if generically) in the pamphlets, and (3) an economic motivation for mailing the pamphlets. Should these factors be dispositive? *See* Ronald J. Krotoszynski, Jr., *Into the Woods: Broadcasters, Bureaucrats, and Children's Television Programming,* 45 Duke L.J. 1193 (1996) (arguing that the Supreme Court's attempts to define commercial speech have failed and would lead to incoherent results if followed consistently).

4. *False and misleading commercial speech.* Justice Marshall says that "[a]dvertisers should not be able to immunize false or misleading product information from government regulation simply by including references to public issues." Is this a kind of return to *Chrestensen*'s holding that mixing commercial and noncommercial speech does not have the effect of bringing the full weight of the Free Speech Clause to bear? Consider this question in light of the following case.

CONSOLIDATED EDISON CO. v. PUBLIC SERVICE COMMISSION

447 U.S. 530 (1980)

Mr. Justice POWELL delivered the opinion of the Court.

The question in this case is whether the First Amendment, as incorporated by the Fourteenth Amendment, is violated by an order of the Public Service Commission of the State of New York that prohibits the inclusion in monthly electric bills of inserts discussing controversial issues of public policy.

The Consolidated Edison Company of New York, appellant in this case, placed written material entitled "Independence Is Still a Goal, and Nuclear Power Is Needed To Win the Battle" in its January 1976 billing envelope. The bill insert stated Consolidated Edison's views on "the benefits of nuclear power," saying that they "far outweigh any potential risk" and that nuclear power plants are safe, economical, and clean. The utility also contended that increased use of nuclear energy would further this country's independence from foreign energy sources.

In March 1976, the Natural Resources Defense Council, Inc. (NRDC), requested Consolidated Edison to enclose a rebuttal prepared by NRDC in its next billing envelope. When Consolidated Edison refused, NRDC asked the Public Service Commission of the State of New York to open Consolidated Edison's billing envelopes to contrasting views on controversial issues of public importance.

On February 17, 1977, the Commission, appellee here, denied NRDC's request, but prohibited "utilities from using bill inserts to discuss political matters, including the desirability of future development of nuclear power." The Commission explained its decision in a Statement of Policy on Advertising and Promotional Practices of Public Utilities issued on February 25, 1977. The Commission concluded that Consolidated Edison customers who receive bills containing inserts are a captive audience of diverse views who should not be subjected to the utility's beliefs. Accordingly, the Commission barred utility companies from including bill inserts that express "their opinions or viewpoints on controversial issues of public policy." The Commission did not, however, bar utilities from sending bill inserts discussing topics that are not "controversial issues of public policy." The Commission later denied petitions for rehearing filed by Consolidated Edison and other utilities.

Consolidated Edison sought review of the Commission's order in the New York state courts. The [state trial court] held the order unconstitutional. . . . The Court of Appeals [New York's highest state court] held that the order did not violate the Constitution because it was a valid time, place, and manner regulation designed to protect the privacy of Consolidated Edison's customers. We reverse.

The restriction on bill inserts cannot be upheld on the ground that Consolidated Edison is not entitled to freedom of speech. In *First National Bank of Boston v. Bellotti*, 435 U.S. 765 (1978), we rejected the contention that a State may confine corporate speech to specified issues. That decision recognized that "[t]he inherent worth of the speech in terms of its capacity for informing the public does not depend upon the identity of its source, whether corporation, association, union, or individual." Because the state action limited protected speech, we concluded that the regulation could not stand absent a showing of a compelling state interest.

This Court has emphasized that the First Amendment "embraces at the least the liberty to discuss publicly and truthfully all matters of public concern. . . ." In the mailing that triggered the regulation at issue, Consolidated Edison advocated the use of nuclear power. The Commission has limited the means by which Consolidated Edison may participate in the public debate on this question and other controversial issues of national interest and importance. Thus, the Commission's prohibition of discussion of controversial issues strikes at the heart of the freedom to speak.

The Commission's ban on bill inserts is not, of course, invalid merely because it imposes a limitation upon speech. We must consider whether the State can demonstrate that its regulation is constitutionally permissible. The Commission's arguments require us to consider three theories that might justify the state action. We must determine whether the prohibition is (i) a reasonable time, place, or manner restriction, (ii) a permissible subject-matter regulation, or (iii) a narrowly tailored means of serving a compelling state interest. . . .

The Commission does not pretend that its action is unrelated to the content or subject matter of bill inserts. Indeed, it has undertaken to suppress certain bill inserts precisely because they address controversial issues of public policy. The Commission allows inserts that present information to consumers on certain subjects, such as energy conservation measures, but it forbids the use of inserts that discuss public controversies. The Commission, with commendable candor, justifies its ban on the ground that consumers will benefit from receiving "useful" information, but not from the prohibited information. The Commission's own rationale demonstrates that its action cannot be upheld as a content-neutral time, place, or manner regulation.

The Commission next argues that its order is acceptable because it applies to all discussion of nuclear power, whether pro or con, in bill inserts. The prohibition, the Commission contends, is related to subject matter rather than to the views of a particular speaker. Because the regulation does not favor either side of a political controversy, the Commission asserts that it does not unconstitutionally suppress freedom of speech.

The First Amendment's hostility to content-based regulation extends not only to restrictions on particular viewpoints, but also to prohibition of public discussion of an entire topic. As a general matter, "the First Amendment means that government has no power to restrict expression because of its message, its ideas, its subject matter, or its content." . . . To allow a government the choice of permissible subjects for public debate would be to allow that government control over the search for political truth. . . .

Where a government restricts the speech of a private person, the state action may be sustained only if the government can show that the regulation is a precisely drawn means of serving a compelling state interest. The Commission argues finally that its prohibition is necessary (i) to avoid forcing Consolidated Edison's views on a captive audience, (ii) to allocate limited resources in the public interest, and (iii) to ensure that ratepayers do not subsidize the cost of the bill inserts.

The State Court of Appeals largely based its approval of the prohibition upon its conclusion that the bill inserts intrude upon individual privacy. The court stated that the Commission could act to protect the privacy of the utility's customers because they have no choice whether to receive the insert and the views expressed in the insert may inflame their sensibilities. But the Court of Appeals erred in its assessment of the seriousness of the intrusion.

Even if a short exposure to Consolidated Edison's views may offend the sensibilities of some consumers, the ability of government "to shut off discourse solely to protect others from hearing it [is] dependent upon a showing that substantial privacy interests are being invaded in an essentially intolerable manner."*Cohen v. California*, 403 U.S., at 21. A less stringent analysis would permit a government to slight the First Amendment's role "in affording the public access to discussion, debate, and the dissemination of information and ideas." Where a single speaker communicates to many listeners, the First Amendment does not permit the government to prohibit speech as intrusive unless the "captive" audience cannot avoid objectionable speech. . . .

The Commission's suppression of bill inserts that discuss controversial issues of public policy directly infringes the freedom of speech protected by the First and Fourteenth Amendments. The state action is neither a valid time, place, or manner restriction, nor a permissible subject-matter regulation, nor a narrowly drawn prohibition justified by a compelling state interest. Accordingly, the regulation is invalid. *First National Bank of Boston v. Bellotti*, 435 U.S., at 795.

The decision of the New York Court of Appeals is

Reversed.

Mr. Justice MARSHALL, concurring.

I join the Court's opinion. I write separately to emphasize that our decision today in no way addresses the question whether the Commission may exclude the costs of bill inserts from the rate base, nor does it intimate any view on the appropriateness of any allocation of such costs the Commission might choose to make.

Mr. Justice STEVENS, concurring in the judgment.

Any student of history who has been reprimanded for talking about the World Series during a class discussion of the First Amendment knows that it is incorrect to state that a "time, place, or manner restriction may not be based upon either the content or subject matter of speech." And every lawyer who has read our Rules, or our cases upholding various restrictions on speech with specific reference to subject matter must recognize the hyperbole in the dictum: "But, above all else, the First Amendment means that government has no power to restrict expression because of its message, its ideas, its subject matter, or its content." . . .

There are, in fact, many situations in which the subject matter, or indeed, even the point of view of the speaker, may provide a justification for a time, place, and manner regulation. . . .

Instead of trying to justify our conclusion by reasoning from honeycombed premises, I prefer to identify the basis of decision in more simple terms. A regulation of speech that is motivated by nothing more than a desire to curtail expression of a particular point of view on controversial issues of general interest is the purest example of a "law . . . abridging the freedom of speech, or of the press." A regulation that denies one group of persons the right to address a selected audience on "controversial issues of public policy" is plainly such a regulation. . . .

Accordingly, I concur in the judgment of the Court.

Mr. Justice BLACKMUN, with whom Mr. Justice REHNQUIST as to Parts I and II joins, dissenting.

My dissent in this case in no way indicates any disapprobation on my part of the precious rights of free speech (so carefully catalogued by the Court in its opinion) that are protected by the First and Fourteenth Amendments against repression by the State. . . .

But I cannot agree with the Court that the New York Public Service Commission's ban on the utility bill insert somehow deprives the utility of its First and Fourteenth Amendment rights. Because of Consolidated Edison's monopoly status and its rate structure, the use of the insert amounts to an exaction from the utility's customers by way of forced aid for the utility's speech. And, contrary to the Court's suggestion, an allocation of the insert's cost between the utility's shareholders and the ratepayers would not eliminate this coerced subsidy.

NOTES AND QUESTIONS

1. *Corporations as speakers.* Why doesn't Justice Powell treat the flyers as commercial speech and apply *Central Hudson*'s four-part test? The cases came down the same term and Justice Powell authored the majority opinions in both. Clearly, Consolidated Edison has a financial motivation for advocating the construction and operation of nuclear power plants. Indeed, in this respect, how is Consolidated Edison any different from Youngs Drug?

2. *Corporations and noncommercial speech.* Should all corporate speech be deemed "commercial" in nature? Why would a corporation seek to communicate a message with the general public, except to advance the entity's economic interests? The raison d'être of a corporation is ostensibly to maximize shareholder wealth; this being so, why doesn't the majority even address the question of whether to characterize the bill inserts as "commercial" versus "noncommercial" speech?

3. *A rigorous test.* Justice Powell applies the strongest test known to modern constitutional law, the compelling state interest test, because the PSC adopted a content-based regulation. Would the case come out differently under *Central Hudson*'s four-part test? Is that why he does not address the status of the speech as possibly "commercial" in nature?

4. *Should a profit motive matter?* Even the concurring and dissenting Justices do
    not quibble with affording Consolidated Edison's speech full First Amendment
    protection. Thus, it seems to be the case that if a corporation speaks about a
    controversial issue of the day, and does not directly seek to promote its own
    products (although even this proposition is debatable in *Consolidated Edison*),
    the fact that a corporation is speaking does not automatically make the speech
    "commercial" in nature. Even so, *should* government have the power to regulate
    corporate speech more aggressively than noncorporate speech? Isn't corporate
    speech, like commercial speech more generally, likely to be more robust because
    of the commercial motivation of the speaker? Consider these questions in light of
    the following case.

FIRST NATIONAL BANK OF BOSTON v. BELLOTTI

435 U.S. 765 (1978)

Mr. Justice POWELL delivered the opinion of the Court.

In sustaining a state criminal statute that forbids certain expenditures by banks
and business corporations for the purpose of influencing the vote on referendum
proposals, the Massachusetts Supreme Court held that the First Amendment rights of
a corporation are limited to issues that materially affect its business, property, or
assets. The court rejected appellants' claim that the statute abridges freedom of
speech in violation of the First and Fourteenth Amendments. The issue presented in
this context is one of first impression in this Court. We now reverse.

The statute at issue [§ 8] prohibits appellants, two national banking associations
and three business corporations, from making contributions or expenditures "for the
purpose of . . . influencing or affecting the vote on any question submitted to the
voter, other than one materially affecting any of the property, business or assets of
the corporation." The statute further specifies that "[n]o question submitted to the
voters solely concerning the taxation of the income, property or transactions of
individuals shall be deemed materially to affect the property, business or assets of the
corporation." A corporation that violates § 8 may receive a maximum fine of
$50,000; a corporate officer, director, or agent who violates the section may receive a
maximum fine of $10,000 or imprisonment for up to one year, or both.

Appellants wanted to spend money to publicize their views on a proposed
constitutional amendment that was to be submitted to the voters as a ballot question
at a general election on November 2, 1976. The amendment would have permitted
the legislature to impose a graduated tax on the income of individuals. After
appellee, the Attorney General of Massachusetts, informed appellants that he
intended to enforce § 8 against them, they brought this action seeking to have the
statute declared unconstitutional. . . .

Appellants argued that § 8 violates the First Amendment, the Due Process and
Equal Protection Clauses of the Fourteenth Amendment, and similar provisions of
the Massachusetts Constitution. They prayed that the statute be declared
unconstitutional on its face and as it would be applied to their proposed expenditures.
[The Supreme Judicial Court of Massachusetts rejected these objections and
sustained § 8 as applied to the plaintiffs.]

The court below framed the principal question in this case as whether and to what
extent corporations have First Amendment rights. We believe that the court posed the
wrong question. The Constitution often protects interests broader than those of the

party seeking their vindication. The First Amendment, in particular, serves significant societal interests. The proper question therefore is not whether corporations "have" First Amendment rights and, if so, whether they are coextensive with those of natural persons. Instead, the question must be whether § 8 abridges expression that the First Amendment was meant to protect. We hold that it does.

The speech proposed by appellants is at the heart of the First Amendment's protection. . . . The referendum issue that appellants wish to address falls squarely within [the protection of the Free Speech Clause]. In appellants' view, the enactment of a graduated personal income tax, as proposed to be authorized by constitutional amendment, would have a seriously adverse effect on the economy of the State. The importance of the referendum issue to the people and government of Massachusetts is not disputed. Its merits, however, are the subject of sharp disagreement. . . .

The court below nevertheless held that corporate speech is protected by the First Amendment only when it pertains directly to the corporation's business interests. In deciding whether this novel and restrictive gloss on the First Amendment comports with the Constitution and the precedents of this court, we need not survey the outer boundaries of the Amendment's protection of corporate speech, or address the abstract question whether corporations have the full measure of rights that individuals enjoy under the First Amendment. The question in this case, simply put, is whether the corporate identity of the speaker deprives this proposed speech of what otherwise would be its clear entitlement to protection. We turn now to that question.

The court below found confirmation of the legislature's definition of the scope of a corporation's First Amendment rights in the language of the Fourteenth Amendment. Noting that the First Amendment is applicable to the States through the Fourteenth, and seizing upon the observation that corporations "cannot claim for themselves the liberty which the Fourteenth Amendment guarantees," *Pierce v. Society of Sisters*, 268 U.S. 510, 535 (1925), the court concluded that a corporation's First Amendment rights must derive from its property rights under the Fourteenth.

This is an artificial mode of analysis, untenable under decisions of this Court. . . . [The Court went on to find that corporate speech makes a valuable contribution to the marketplace of ideas.]

Nor do our recent commercial speech cases lend support to appellee's business interest theory. They illustrate that the First Amendment goes beyond protection of the press and the self-expression of individuals to prohibit government from limiting the stock of information from which members of the public may draw. A commercial advertisement is constitutionally protected not so much because it pertains to the seller's business as because it furthers the societal interest in the "free flow of commercial information."

We thus find no support in the First or Fourteenth Amendment, or in the decisions of this Court, for the proposition that speech that otherwise would be within the protection of the First Amendment loses that protection simply because its source is a corporation that cannot prove, to the satisfaction of a court, a material effect on its business or property. The "materially affecting" requirement is not an identification of the boundaries of corporate speech etched by the Constitution itself. Rather, it amounts to an impermissible legislative prohibition of speech based on the identity of the interests that spokesmen may represent in public debate over controversial issues and a requirement that the speaker have a sufficiently great interest in the subject to justify communication.

Section 8 permits a corporation to communicate to the public its views on certain referendum subjects—those materially affecting its business—but not others. It also singles out one kind of ballot question—individual taxation—as a subject about which corporations may never make their ideas public. The legislature has drawn the line between permissible and impermissible speech according to whether there is a sufficient nexus, as defined by the legislature, between the issue presented to the voters and the business interests of the speaker.

In the realm of protected speech, the legislature is constitutionally disqualified from dictating the subjects about which persons may speak and the speakers who may address a public issue. . . .

The constitutionality of § 8's prohibition of the "exposition of ideas" by corporations turns on whether it can survive the exacting scrutiny necessitated by a state-imposed restriction of freedom of speech. Especially where, as here, a prohibition is directed at speech itself and the speech is intimately related to the process of governing, "the State may prevail only upon showing a subordinating interest which is compelling," "and the burden is on the government to show the existence of such an interest." Even then, the State must employ means "closely drawn to avoid unnecessary abridgement." . . .

The Supreme Judicial Court did not subject § 8 to "the critical scrutiny demanded under accepted First Amendment and equal protection principles" because of its view that the First Amendment does not apply to appellants' proposed speech. For this reason the court did not even discuss the State's interests in considering appellants' First Amendment argument. [Justice Powell rejected the justifications that the state offered in support of the law.]

Because that portion of § 8 challenged by appellants prohibits protected speech in a manner unjustified by a compelling state interest, it must be invalidated. The judgment of the Supreme Judicial Court is

Reversed.

Mr. Chief Justice BURGER, concurring.

I join the opinion and judgment of the Court but write separately to raise some questions likely to arise in this area in the future. . . .

Because the First Amendment was meant to guarantee freedom to express and communicate ideas, I can see no difference between the right of those who seek to disseminate ideas by way of a newspaper and those who give lectures or speeches and seek to enlarge the audience by publication and wide dissemination. "[T]he purpose of the Constitution was not to erect the press into a privileged institution but to protect all persons in their right to print what they will as well as to utter it. '. . . the liberty of the press is no greater and no less . . .' than the liberty of every citizen of the Republic." *Pennekamp v. Florida*, 328 U.S. 331, 364 (1946) (Frankfurter, J., concurring).

In short, the First Amendment does not "belong" to any definable category of persons or entities: It belongs to all who exercise its freedoms.

Mr. Justice WHITE, with whom Mr. Justice BRENNAN and Mr. Justice MARSHALL join, dissenting.

The Massachusetts statute challenged here forbids the use of corporate funds to publish views about referenda issues having no material effect on the business, property, or assets of the corporation. The legislative judgment that the personal income tax issue, which is the subject of the referendum out of which this case arose, has no such effect was sustained by the Supreme Judicial Court of Massachusetts and is not disapproved by this Court today. Hence, as this case comes to us, the issue is whether a State may prevent corporate management from using the corporate treasury to propagate views having no connection with the corporate business. The Court commendably enough squarely faces the issue but unfortunately errs in deciding it. The Court invalidates the Massachusetts statute and holds that the First Amendment guarantees corporate managers the right to use not only their personal funds, but also those of the corporation, to circulate fact and opinion irrelevant to the business placed into their charge and necessarily representing their own personal or collective views about political and social questions. I do not suggest for a moment that the First Amendment requires a State to forbid such use of corporate funds, but I do strongly disagree that the First Amendment forbids state interference with managerial decisions of this kind. . . .

I would affirm the judgment of the Supreme Judicial Court for the Commonwealth of Massachusetts.

Mr. Justice REHNQUIST, dissenting.
[Justice Rehnquist's dissenting opinion is omitted.]

NOTES AND QUESTIONS

1. *The identity of the speaker and commercial speech.* Should the identity of the speaker be dispositive? In this respect, both *Consolidated Edison* and *Bellotti* are surprising cases. In neither case does the commercial motive for the speech affect—at all—the fully protected status of the speech. Writing for the majority in both cases, Justice Powell seems simply to assume that the speech at issue was noncommercial in nature, presumably because the speech did not attempt to sell directly a good or service. Yet, ConEd's speech directly related to business objectives—the building and operation of nuclear power plants in New York State. Similarly, the First National Bank of Boston was engaged in advocacy regarding a referendum issue to advance its commercial interests. Indeed, both *Consolidated Edison* and *Bellotti* apply strict scrutiny to the laws at issue—the strictest test known to contemporary constitutional law.

2. *The relevance of* Youngs Drug. How can the outcome—and standard of review—applied in *Youngs Drug* be reconciled with the more demanding standard of review applied in *Consolidated Edison* and *Bellotti?* Indeed, Justice Powell references the commercial speech doctrine in *Bellotti* but never seems to consider applying *Central Hudson* to the Massachusetts ban on corporate advocacy regarding a pending state referendum.

3. *Should the* Central Hudson *test apply?* At a minimum, if corporate speech is, by definition, "commercial speech," should state and federal limits on corporate speech be tested under the more generous standards of *Central Hudson?* Would *Bellotti* be decided differently if the Court had applied *Central Hudson?*

4. *A relevant distinction?* Given the robust protection that the Supreme Court has afforded commercial speech, and the sometimes parsimonious protection afforded political speech in traditional public forums (under the rubric of the time, place, and manner doctrine; *see, e.g.,* Ward v. Rock Against Racism, *supra,* page 133), does the definitional question ultimately matter?

AN EXTENDED NOTE ON COMMERCIAL VERSUS NON-COMMERCIAL USE OF A CELEBRITY'S PERSONA WITHOUT PERMISSION OR CONSENT

In Jordan v. Jewel Food Stores, Inc., 743 F. 3d 509 (2014), Jewel Food Stores, Inc. (Jewel), a company that operates the Jewel-Osco grocery store chain in Chicago, Illinois, agreed to buy advertising space in *Sports Illustrated*; in exchange for the advertising buy, Jewel Food Stores received a full page in a special commemorative edition of *Sports Illustrated* celebrating Michael Jordan's induction into the Basketball Hall of Fame. Jewel's copy in this special edition featured a pair of sneakers emblazoned with Jordan's jersey number (23) and text reading "A Shoe In! After six NBA championships, scores of rewritten record books and numerous buzzer beaters, Michael Jordan's elevation in the Basketball Hall of Fame was never in doubt! Jewel-Osco salutes #23 on his many accomplishments as we honor a fellow Chicagoan who was 'just around the corner' for so many years." *Id.* at 512. The full page display, which appeared on the inside back cover of the special issue, also prominently featured Jewel-Osco's logo and slogan. Michael Jordan sued Jewel after publication of the special issue, seeking $5 million in compensatory damages, as well as additional exemplary damages, alleging a violation of federal trademark law as well as an Illinois right of publicity statute. Jewel moved for summary judgment, arguing that both Jordan's federal and state claims were precluded by the First Amendment. *Id.* at 512-13. The district court accepted Jewel's characterization of its copy as constitutionally protected non-commercial speech and entered summary judgment in the company's favor; Jordan appealed this decision.

The Seventh Circuit reversed, finding that the copy constituted commercial, rather than noncommercial, speech. Writing for the panel majority, Judge Diane Sykes observed that "[i]t's clear that the textual focus of Jewel's ad is a congratulatory salute to Jordan on his induction into the Hall of Fame" and, accordingly, "[i]f the literal import of the words were all that mattered, this celebratory tribute would be noncommercial." *Id.* at 517. However, "evaluating the text requires consideration of its context, and this truism has special force when applying the commercial-speech doctrine." *Id.* This is so because "[m]odern commercial advertising is enormously varied in form and style." *Id.* at 517-18.

On the facts presented, the copy had two functions: congratulating Jordan and promoting Jewel-Osco grocery stores. Thus, "considered in context, and without the rose-colored glasses, Jewel's ad has an unmistakable commercial function: enhancing the Jewel-Osco brand in the minds of consumers." Moreover, "[t]his commercial message is implicit but easily inferred, and is the dominant one." In consequence, the copy in the special edition constituted commercial speech. *See id.* at 519 (noting that "the ad's commercial nature is readily apparent" even though "[i]t may be generic and implicit"). Thus, the Seventh Circuit used an objective analysis to ascertain the probable subjective intent of the speaker; on the facts presented, Jewel's copy constituted "a form of image advertising aimed at promoting goodwill for the Jewel-Osco brand by exploiting public affection for Jordan at an auspicious moment in his career." *Id.*

Are you persuaded by this analysis? By way of contrast, could the University of North Carolina use Michael Jordan's image without his consent in promotional materials touting the success of its student athletes? Or would this use constitute "commercial" speech, potentially engendering trademark and right of personality liability for the university, if the university were trying to exploit Jordan's image as part of it general marketing and recruiting efforts? The *Jewel Food Stores* court observed that "[n]othing we say here is meant to suggest that a company cannot use its graphic logo or slogan in an otherwise noncommercial way without thereby transforming the communication into commercial speech." *Id.* at 520. But when a for-profit company includes the image of a public figure in corporate promotional materials, won't it be very hard pressed to prove that its motives did not encompass "image advertising"? Clearly, simply avoiding the inclusion of "an outright sales pitch," *id.*, is not enough to alter the essentially commercial nature of corporate promotional material. But what would be?

Under this broad reasoning, what, if anything, could Jewel have done to avoid having its effort to publicly congratulate Michael Jordan on his election to the Hall of Fame engender a multi-million dollar trademark and right of personality liability? Would an express disclaimer in the copy—"This Is Not an Advertisement"—have worked for Jewel? Or should we be concerned about the ability of a publicly-traded corporation to appropriate a celebrity's image without incurring liability of this sort? After all, what precisely is the social value of Jewel's speech? And should this affect the balancing of the relevant interests? Could the Chicago public school district have run the same ad, in precisely the same way, without it being considered commercial speech? Why or why not? Should we generally assume that corporate speakers engage in commercial speech —at least in close cases—on the theory that most of the time, corporations act to maximize shareholder wealth?

THEORY-APPLIED PROBLEM

Perhaps, like Justice Stewart and obscenity, the Justices "know [commercial speech] when they see it." Is the definition of commercial speech simply a matter of intuition? If so, consider the following hypotheticals and analyze whether the speech is "commercial" or "noncommercial."

1. Philip Morris sponsors a traveling exhibit on the Constitution and Bill of Rights. To promote this exhibit, the company takes out large full-page ads in local papers, stating "Philip Morris Supports Freedom, You Should, Too!"
2. Absolut Vodka places print ads in a variety of magazines, featuring an Absolut vodka bottle wrapped in bright red tape, with the phrase "Absolut DC" underneath the bottle.
3. Andy Warhol creates a series of silk-screen images of Campbell's soup cans and seeks to exhibit them in a local Pittsburgh, Pennsylvania, public gallery space. The city government rejects the submission for the exhibit "because of the commercial nature of the art." Campbell's Soup, enamored of the Warhol prints, reproduces them in a variety of newspaper and magazine spreads, with "Campbell's M'm! M'm! Good!" beneath the prints.

AN EXTENDED NOTE ON CITIZENS UNITED v. FEC

In Citizens United v. FEC, 558 U.S. 310 (2010) (excerpted *supra* p. 289), the Supreme Court reaffirmed and extended its prior holdings that corporations are entitled to the full protection of the First Amendment when engaging in political speech. Writing for the majority, Justice Kennedy explained that

> [p]remised on mistrust of governmental power, the First Amendment stands against attempts to disfavor certain subjects or viewpoints. See, e.g., United States v. Playboy Entertainment Group, Inc., 529 U.S. 803, 813 (2000) (striking down content-based restriction). Prohibited, too, are restrictions distinguishing among different speakers, allowing speech by some but not others. See First Nat. Bank of Boston v. Bellotti, 435 U.S. 765, 784 (1978). As instruments to censor, these categories are interrelated: Speech restrictions based on the identity of the speaker are all too often simply a means to control content.
>
> Quite apart from the purpose or effect of regulating content, moreover, the Government may commit a constitutional wrong when by law it identifies certain preferred speakers. By taking the right to speak from some and giving it to others, the Government deprives the disadvantaged person or class of the right to use speech to strive to establish worth, standing, and respect for the speaker's voice. The Government may not by these means deprive the public of the right and privilege to determine for itself what speech and speakers are worthy of consideration. The First Amendment protects speech and speaker, and the ideas that flow from each.

558 U.S. at 340-41. Justice Kennedy concluded that "[w]e find no basis for the proposition that, in the context of political speech, the Government may impose restrictions on certain disfavored speakers." *Id.* at 341.

The importance of protecting core political speech from government censorship plainly serves as the linchpin of the *Citizens United* majority's logic:

> When Government seeks to use its full power, including the criminal law, to command where a person may get his or her information or what distrusted source he or she may not hear, it uses censorship to control thought. This is unlawful. The First Amendment confirms the freedom to think for ourselves.

Id. at 908.

Yet, with respect to for-profit, publicly traded corporations, the entity exists for one and only one purpose, namely, to maximize shareholder wealth. We can place to one side nonprofit entities, such as the NRA or Planned Parenthood, that use a corporate form to harness the energy of a large, broad-based membership base to influence public policy regarding matters such as gun control or family planning. Companies such as General Motors or Walmart, however, do not exist for the purpose of doing anything more than returning a profit to their investors. In what respect, then, can the "political" speech of a for-profit enterprise be deemed anything but "commercial speech"? Can speech by a for-profit corporation ever be truly noncommercial? Isn't the concept of "corporate political speech," at least with respect to for-profit enterprises, an oxymoron?

If the animating purpose of the speech is to facilitate the sale of goods or services, then the fact that the content might otherwise constitute noncommercial speech should be of no moment whatsoever. *See Youngs Drug, supra* p. 368. *Citizens United*, like *Bellotti* before it, completely elides this point and appears simply to assume that speech by for-profit corporations related to candidates and elections can and does constitute noncommercial speech, entitled to the fullest protection of the First Amendment. *See Citzens United*, 558 U.S. at 319 ("The government may regulate *corporate political speech* through disclaimer and disclosure requirements, but it may not suppress that speech altogether." (emphasis added)).

Does—or should—the profit motive affect the potential value of political speech sponsored by for-profit corporations? Alternatively, should the protected status of corporate political communications depend on the precise context and content of the speech? The identity of the speaker? Both? Neither? Or does *Citizens United* suggest that the commercial or noncommercial character of speech is not to be gleaned from the intent or purpose of the *speaker* in communicating the message but rather on the potential value and purpose of the information to the *intended audience*? Under this approach, the listener, rather than the speaker, would determine the nature of the speech as either commercial or noncommercial. But, if this is so, where does this leave *Youngs Drug*'s approach of considering the motive of the speaker in assessing how to characterize the nature of the speech being regulated?

On the other hand, in the context of *Citizens United*, would characterization of speech by for-profit corporations as "commercial speech" rather than "political speech" affect the probable outcome of a First Amendment challenge to the federal government's flat ban on such communications? In other words, would a flat ban on corporate political speech pass muster under *Central Hudson*'s four-part test? If not, then the question of whether a for-profit corporation may ever engage in noncommercial speech might be less important than it seemed upon first consideration.

Suppose, however, that the federal government sought to regulate political advertising by for-profit corporations rather than simply ban it outright, perhaps by requiring that shareholders specifically approve any such expenditures from the corporation's treasury. With respect to something short of a complete ban, the characterization of the speech being regulated as "commercial" or "noncommercial" might well prefigure the validity of the regulation.

If corporate political speech were characterized as commercial speech, however, interesting questions would immediately arise regarding how to apply the *Central Hudson* test—and particularly the first prong of the test, namely that the speech must be "truthful and non-misleading." When a 30-second television or radio spot says, "Jane Doe would be a great U.S. Senator and far better than the present incumbent," how does one assess whether the speech is "truthful and non-misleading"? Would the government itself get to make this determination? Or would this task be left to the federal courts? Or does the difficulty of ascertaining the truth or falsity of political speech mean that it is best to simply leave the question up to the marketplace to resolve? *See, e.g.*, United States v. Alvarez, 567 U.S. 709 (2012).

To date, the Supreme Court has simply assumed that speech that appears to be political in nature, even if disseminated by a for-profit corporation, is fully and completely "political speech" rather than "commercial speech." The question of how to properly characterize such speech, however, seems significantly more complicated than the Justices have acknowledged. In sum, important issues remain and seem to require a fuller exposition than they have received to date.

THEORY-APPLIED PROBLEM

Acme Cigarettes has developed "Fred the Fox" as its corporate logo. Fred the Fox appears in a wide variety of mail, print, and billboard advertisements for Acme's cigarettes. Children's advocates claim that Fred the Fox is a thinly veiled effort to market cigarettes to children, who cannot lawfully purchase, possess, or consume them. Many of the advertisements appear in California. Acme issues a press release stating that "Fred the Fox does not encourage underage smoking—empirical evidence proves this to be true." It also purchases newspaper advertising space and broadcast radio and television ads defending Fred the Fox. The Smoke-Free Children's Alliance brings a suit under the California Unfair Competition Law, alleging that Acme has intentionally misled consumers in an effort to increase sales.

Is the speech at issue "commercial" or "noncommercial"? Should it be subject to suppression in the same fashion as speech that misstates the gas mileage of a truck or claims that sugar pills cure cancer? Does *Central Hudson*'s first prong provide the answer: Such speech can be regulated because it is "false and misleading"? If so, then the characterization of the speech as "commercial" rather than "noncommercial" could well prove to be outcome determinative.

CHAPTER
8

Regulation of the Mass Media

TABLE OF CONTENTS

The First Amendment to the U.S. Constitution protects both freedom of speech and freedom of the press, but the Supreme Court typically treats them as merely different facets of a more general right to freedom of expression. In interpreting the First Amendment's Press Clause, the Court has often stated that the press is entitled to no greater First Amendment protection than the general public, and most First Amendment decisions involving the media are grounded at least as much in the Free Speech Clause of the First Amendment as in the Press Clause.

That said, members of the mass communications media have litigated a number of seminal First Amendment cases before the Supreme Court, and the resulting jurisprudence often reflects their interests. The focus of this chapter, therefore, is on the body of case law most directly affecting the media. As you read these cases, you should pay special attention to the following questions. First, does "the press" receive special First Amendment protections under the Press Clause not accorded to other speakers under the Free Speech Clause? A second question is intertwined with the first: If "the press" receives special First Amendment protections, what is "the press"? This question has become more difficult to answer since the advent of the Internet, which provides most American citizens with the ability to distribute their views through a medium of mass communication. A third question is whether newsgathering activities receive the same level of First Amendment protection as publication of the news. Finally, to what extent is the First Amendment's protection "medium-specific"? As you will see, most First Amendment principles apply equally to all media—broadcasting, print, Internet publishers, satellite, and cable programmers and operators—but a few apply differently, particularly when it comes to broadcasting, due to the special characteristics of the medium.

The Framers of the First Amendment left very little indication of whether "freedom of the press" was meant to protect the press as an institution that plays a "structural" role in enabling democratic self-governance, or whether it merely was meant to protect speech when widely disseminated by means of the printing press. If the latter is the case, anyone who "functions" as the press by distributing his or her speech to a mass audience should be able to claim protection under the Press Clause of the First Amendment as well as the Free Speech Clause. Scholars have debated whether the structural or functional definition of the press is consistent with the Framer's intent.

Leading media law scholar David Anderson has argued that the Framers were influenced by contemporary state constitutions protecting freedom of the press and that the Framers saw the Press Clause as necessary to protect the role of the press as a check on governmental abuses of power; in contrast, the protection of freedom of speech seems to have reflected concern for individual autonomy. *See generally* David A. Anderson, *The Origin of the Press Clause*, 30 UCLA L. Rev. 455, 534 (1983). Professor Eugene Volokh, on the other hand, contends that the Speech Clause of the First Amendment protects spoken words and the Press Clause protects printed words, that is, words that can be broadly disseminated. He looks to how the word "press" was defined both around 1791, when the First Amendment was drafted, and in 1868, when the Fourteenth Amendment was ratified, and contends that the text was understood to protect a "technology," not an industry or institution. *See generally* Eugene Volokh, *Freedom for the Press as an Industry, or the Press as a Technology? From the Framing to Today*, 160 U. Pa. L. Rev. 1 (2011).

The conception of the Press Clause as a structural protection for the press as an institution was famously advocated by Justice Potter Stewart. Justice Stewart's structural account of the Press Clause led him to argue for special First Amendment privileges for the institutional press. For example, Justice Stewart contended that the press (but not individuals) have a First Amendment privilege not to disclose confidential news sources to a grand jury. He also contended that the press (but not individuals) deserved special protections against being held liable for defamation of public officials. See generally Potter Stewart, Or of the Press, 26 Hastings L.J. 631 (1975). Justice Stewart's view has never been adopted by the Court, and, indeed, in Citizens United v. Federal Elections Comm'n, 558 U.S. 50 (2010), the Court expressly stated that the "institutional press" has no "constitutional privilege beyond that of other speakers." But see id. at 431 n.57 (Stevens, J., concurring in part and dissenting in part) (suggesting that the press "might be able to claim special First Amendment status" under the Press Clause).

There are powerful pragmatic reasons that the Court has tended to embrace a functional account of the Press Clause, typically extending protection to anyone who publishes to a mass audience. This functional account avoids the difficult problem of defining which members of the press qualify for special privileges, a problem that has been compounded as first the Internet and now mobile-based technologies have turned millions of ordinary citizens into publishers. That said, many of the Supreme Court's most important First Amendment decisions are shaped by the needs and interests of the institutional press, one of the few repeat players in First Amendment litigation.

A. REGULATION OF THE PRESS

As noted above, the press has been a frequent litigant in First Amendment cases in the Supreme Court. Much of this litigation has addressed the press's ability to gather and disseminate news and information. The case below, however, involves a state law imposing a limit on the press's ability to advocate for or against a government policy by publishing an election-day editorial. As you read it, consider whether the case would have come out differently if the law had been applied against an individual speaker rather than a member of the institutional press.

MILLS v. ALABAMA
384 U.S. 214 (1966)

Mr. Justice BLACK delivered the opinion of the Court.

[The Alabama Corrupt Practices Act made it a crime to solicit votes for or against any ballot proposition on election day. The Birmingham Post-Herald carried an election-day editorial urging voters to support a ballot proposition replacing their existing city commission with a mayor-council system. Editor James E. Mills was arrested for violating the statute. The trial court granted a demurrer on the criminal complaint, but the Alabama Supreme Court reversed, holding that the law was a reasonable restriction imposing only a minor limitation on the press.]

I.

[The Court rejected the argument that there was no final judgment because Mills had not yet been convicted.]

II.

We come now to the merits. The First Amendment, which applies to the States through the Fourteenth, prohibits laws "abridging the freedom of speech, or of the press." The question here is whether it abridges freedom of the press for a State to punish a newspaper editor for doing no more than publishing an editorial on election day urging people to vote a particular way in the election. We should point out at once that this question in no way involves the extent of a State's power to regulate conduct in and around the polls in order to maintain peace, order and decorum there. The sole reason for the charge that Mills violated the law is that he wrote and published an editorial on election day urging Birmingham voters to cast their votes in favor of changing their form of government.

Whatever differences may exist about interpretations of the First Amendment, there is practically universal agreement that a major purpose of that Amendment was to protect the free discussion of governmental affairs. This of course includes discussions of candidates, structures and forms of government, the manner in which government is operated or should be operated, and all such matters relating to political processes. The Constitution specifically selected the press, which includes not only newspapers, books, and magazines, but also humble leaflets and circulars, see Lovell v. City of Griffin, 303 U.S. 444, to play an important role in the discussion of public affairs. Thus the press serves and was designed to serve as a powerful antidote to any abuses of power by governmental officials and as a constitutionally chosen means for keeping officials elected by the people responsible to all the people whom they were selected to serve. Suppression of the right of the press to praise or criticize governmental agents and to clamor and contend for or against change, which is all that this editorial did, muzzles one of the very agencies the Framers of our Constitution thoughtfully and deliberately selected to improve our society and keep it free. The Alabama Corrupt Practices Act by providing criminal penalties for publishing editorials such as the one here silences the press at a time it can be most effective. . . . [T]he Alabama Supreme Court nevertheless sustained the constitutionality of the law on the ground that the restrictions on the press were only 'reasonable restrictions' or at least 'within the field of reasonableness.' The court reached this conclusion because it thought the law imposed only a minor limitation on the press-restricting it only on election days-and because the court thought the law served a good purpose. It said:

> 'It is a salutary legislative enactment that protects the public from confusive last-minute charges and countercharges and the distribution of propaganda in an effort to influence voters on an election day; when as a practical matter, because of lack of time, such matters cannot be answered or their truth determined until after the election is over.' [ ]

This argument, even if it were relevant to the constitutionality of the law, has a fatal flaw. The state statute leaves people free to hurl their campaign charges up to the last minute of the day before election. The law held valid by the Alabama Supreme Court then goes on to make it a crime to answer those 'last-minute' charges on election day, the only time they can be effectively answered. Because the law prevents any adequate reply to these charges, it is wholly ineffective in protecting the electorate 'from confusive last-minute charges and countercharges.' We hold that no test of reasonableness can save a state law from invalidation as a violation of the First Amendment when that law makes it a crime for a newspaper editor to do no more than urge people to vote one way or another in a publicly held election.

The judgment of the Supreme Court of Alabama is reversed and the case is remanded for further proceedings not inconsistent with this opinion.

. . .

Mr. Justice DOUGLAS, with whom Mr. Justice BRENNAN joins, concurring.

. . .

The decision of the Alabama Supreme Court approved a law which, in my view, is a blatant violation of freedom of the press. The threat of penal sanctions has, we are told, already taken its toll in Alabama: the Alabama Press Association and the Southern Newspaper Publishers Association, as amici curiae, tell us that since November 1962 editorial comment on election day has been nonexistent in Alabama. The chilling effect of this prosecution is thus anything but hypothetical; it is currently being experienced by the newspapers and the people of Alabama.

We deal here with the rights of free speech and press in a basic form: the right to express views on matters before the electorate. In light of appellant's concession that he has no other defense to offer should the case go to trial, [ ] and considering the importance of the First Amendment rights at stake in this litigation, it would require regard for some remote, theoretical interests of federalism to conclude that this Court lacks jurisdiction because of the unlikely possibility that a jury might disregard a trial judge's instructions and acquit.

Indeed, even had appellant been unwilling to concede that he has no defense—apart from the constitutional question—to the charges against him, we would be warranted in reviewing this case. That result follows a fortiori from our holdings that where First Amendment rights are jeopardized by a state prosecution which, by its very nature, threatens to deter others from exercising their First Amendment rights, a federal court will take the extraordinary step of enjoining the state prosecution. Dombrowski v. Pfister, 380 U.S. 479; Cameron v. Johnson, 381 U.S. 74. As already noted, this case has brought editorial comment on election day to a halt throughout the State of Alabama.

. . .

For these reasons, and for the reasons stated in the opinion of the Court, I conclude that the judgment is final.

[Justice Harlan would have dismissed the appeal for want of a final judgment.]

NOTES AND QUESTIONS

1. *Non-press Speakers.* Justice Black describes the statute as a "flagrant abridgment of the constitutionally guaranteed freedom of the press," and his opinion emphasizes the press's constitutional role in the discussion of public affairs. Does that indicate that this is a press clause decision that would not necessarily apply to a non-press speaker? For example, would *Mills* preclude enforcement of a statute that forbade candidates from making last-minute accusations about their opponents?

2. *Strict scrutiny?* What test does the Supreme Court apply to resolve this case? Does the Court hold the statute unconstitutional because it is a content-based regulation of speech?

3. *Generally applicable laws.* Like other businesses, the media are subject to generally applicable laws. For example, they must obey employment laws, municipal ordinances, and pay taxes. The government does not violate the First Amendment by subjecting the media to these laws, though even generally applicable laws may be subject to enhanced scrutiny when they appear to disproportionately target or affect the press. For example, given that the power to tax is the power to destroy and that the government may attempt to use its taxing power to silence or punish those with whom it disagrees, the Supreme Court has applied heightened First Amendment scrutiny where taxes singled out the media for a burden place on no other speakers, where they disproportionately affect a small number of media, or where the tax burden is based on the content of the publication. See Leathers v. Medlock, 499 U.S. 439 (1990).

B. MEDIA NEWSGATHERING AND ACCESS RIGHTS

In order to report on important events, the media must be able to gather information. The media's need to gather information gives rise to two distinct First Amendment claims. First, the media sometimes claim that the First Amendment gives them a right to be free from government interference with their information-gathering efforts. Thus, in *Branzburg v. Hayes*, below, the media claimed that a qualified privilege protected reporters from being forced to testify about the identity of their confidential sources when subpoenaed to testify before grand juries. The claim to a constitutional "reporter's privilege," in essence, is a claim that the First Amendment gives the media a right to be free from government interference with confidential source relationships.

Yet this is not the only First Amendment claim that the media make on behalf of their need to gather information. At times, the media also claim a right to receive access to information possessed or controlled by the government. The media, for example, have claimed a First Amendment right of access to criminal trials, government institutions, and civil discovery documents. The materials in this chapter deal only with First Amendment claims of access, but bear in mind that both federal and state statutes give the media access to a wide variety of government information. For example, the federal Freedom of Information Act gives citizens a right of access to a wide array of information in the hands of executive agencies. Similar legislation at the state level gives citizens access to various types of government meetings and government documents. These statutory claims should not be confused with the constitutional claims discussed below.

1. Reporter's Privilege Against Compelled Disclosure of Confidential Sources

BRANZBURG v. HAYES

408 U.S. 665 (1972)

(Together with In re Pappas and United States v. Caldwell)
WHITE, J., wrote the opinion of the Court, in which BURGER, C.J., and BLACKMUN, POWELL, and REHNQUIST, JJ., joined.

[This case involved four consolidated cases in which reporters were subpoenaed to testify before criminal grand juries. Branzburg, a reporter for the Courier-Journal, a Louisville, Kentucky newspaper, was involved in two of the cases. One of the cases involved a story Branzburg wrote regarding the production of hashish; the story was based on his personal observations of two local residents of Jefferson County, Kentucky, synthesizing hashish from marijuana. Shortly after this story ran in the Courier-Journal, Branzburg was subpoenaed by a Jefferson County grand jury. He appeared but refused to identify anyone involved in making hashish. The state trial court ordered him to identify them and rejected his claim that the state reporters' privilege statute, the First Amendment to the U.S. Constitution, or the Kentucky Constitution protected him from having to reveal the information. He sought writs of prohibition and mandamus, which were denied by the Kentucky Court of Appeals, which also denied his writs of prohibition and mandamus in a second, similar case.]

In re Pappas [involved a reporter who gained entrance to the police-barricaded headquarters of the Black Panthers in New Bedford, Massachusetts]. As a condition of entry, Pappas agreed not to disclose anything he saw or heard inside the store except an anticipated police raid. . . . [The raid never took place, but the reporter was subpoenaed to testify before a grand jury. He] refused to answer any questions about what had taken place inside headquarters while he was there, claiming that the First Amendment afforded him a privilege to protect confidential informants and their information. A second summons was then served upon him, [but the trial judged denied his motion to quash because Massachusetts had no statutory reporter's privilege. The Supreme Judicial Court of Massachusetts affirmed.]

United States v. Caldwell . . . arose from subpoenas issued by a federal grand jury in the Northern District of California to respondent Earl Caldwell, a reporter for the New York Times assigned to cover the Black Panther Party and other black militant groups. [Caldwell was served with a subpoena that ordered him to testify before a grand jury investigating the Black Panther Party.] Respondent and his employer, the New York Times, moved to quash on the ground that the unlimited breadth of the subpoenas and the fact that Caldwell would have to appear in secret before the grand jury would destroy his working relationship with the Black Panther Party and "suppress vital First Amendment freedoms . . . by driving a wedge of distrust and silence between the news media and the militants." . . .

[The District Court denied Respondent's motion to quash, and upon Caldwell's refusal to testify, ordered him jailed for contempt. The Court of Appeals reversed the contempt order based on a qualified First Amendment privilege. The Supreme Court then granted certiorari.]

II

. . . Although the newsmen in these cases do not claim an absolute privilege against official interrogation in all circumstances, they assert that the reporter should not be forced either to appear or to testify before a grand jury or at trial until and unless sufficient grounds are shown for believing that the reporter possesses information relevant to a crime the grand jury is investigating, that the information the reporter has is unavailable from other sources, and that the need for the information is sufficiently compelling to override the claimed invasion of First Amendment interests occasioned by the disclosure. . . . The heart of the claim is that the burden on news gathering resulting from compelling reporters to disclose confidential information outweighs any public interest in obtaining the information.

We do not question the significance of free speech, press, or assembly to the country's welfare. Nor is it suggested that news gathering does not qualify for First Amendment protection; without some protection for seeking out the news, freedom of the press could be eviscerated. But these cases involve no intrusions upon speech or assembly, no prior restraint or restriction on what the press may publish, and no express or implied command that the press publish what it prefers to withhold. No exaction or tax for the privilege of publishing, and no penalty, civil or criminal, related to the content of published material is at issue here. The use of confidential sources by the press is not forbidden or restricted; reporters remain free to seek news from any source by means within the law. No attempt is made to require the press to publish its sources of information or indiscriminately to disclose them on request.

The sole issue before us is the obligation of reporters to respond to grand jury subpoenas as other citizens do and to answer questions relevant to an investigation into the commission of crime. Citizens generally are not constitutionally immune from grand jury subpoenas; and neither the First Amendment nor any other constitutional provision protects the average citizen from disclosing to a grand jury information that he has received in confidence. The claim is, however, that reporters are exempt from these obligations because if forced to respond to subpoenas and identify their sources or disclose other confidences, their informants will refuse or be reluctant to furnish newsworthy information in the future. This asserted burden on news gathering is said to make compelled testimony from newsmen constitutionally suspect and to require a privileged position for them.

It is clear that the First Amendment does not invalidate every incidental burdening of the press that may result from the enforcement of civil or criminal statutes of general applicability. Under prior cases, otherwise valid laws serving substantial public interests may be enforced against the press as against others, despite the possible burden that may be imposed. The Court has emphasized that "the publisher of a newspaper has no special immunity from the application of general laws. He has no special privilege to invade the rights and liberties of others." *Associated Press v. NLRB*, 301 U.S. 103, 132-133 (1937). It was there held that the Associated Press, a news-gathering and disseminating organization, was not exempt from the requirements of the National Labor Relations Act. . . .

It has generally been held that the First Amendment does not guarantee the press a constitutional right of special access to information not available to the public generally. In *Zemel v. Rusk*, for example, [a ban on travel to Cuba] was held constitutional, for "the right to speak and publish does not carry with it the unrestrained right to gather information."

Despite the fact that news gathering may be hampered, the press is regularly excluded from grand jury proceedings, our own conferences, the meetings of other official bodies gathered in executive session, and the meetings of private organizations. Newsmen have no constitutional right of access to the scenes of crime or disaster when the general public is excluded, and they may be prohibited from attending or publishing information about trials if such restrictions are necessary to assure a defendant a fair trial before an impartial tribunal. . . .

It is thus not surprising that the great weight of authority is that newsmen are not exempt from the normal duty of appearing before a grand jury and answering questions relevant to a criminal investigation. . . .

The prevailing constitutional view of the newsman's privilege is very much rooted in the ancient role of the grand jury that has the dual function of determining if there is probable cause to believe that a crime has been committed and of protecting citizens against unfounded criminal prosecutions. Grand jury proceedings are constitutionally mandated for the institution of federal criminal prosecutions for capital or other serious crimes, and "its constitutional prerogatives are rooted in long centuries of Anglo-American history." The Fifth Amendment provides that "no person shall be held to answer for a capital, or otherwise infamous crime, unless on a presentment or indictment of a Grand Jury." The adoption of the grand jury "in our Constitution as the sole method for preferring charges in serious criminal cases shows the high place it held as an instrument of justice." . . . Because its task is to inquire into the existence of possible criminal conduct and to return only well-founded indictments, its investigative powers are necessarily broad. . . . Hence, the grand jury's authority to subpoena witnesses is not only historic, but essential to its task. . . .

A number of States have provided newsmen a statutory privilege of varying breadth, but the majority have not done so, and none has been provided by federal statute. Until now the only testimonial privilege for unofficial witnesses that is rooted in the Federal Constitution is the Fifth Amendment privilege against compelled self-incrimination. We are asked to create another by interpreting the First Amendment to grant newsmen a testimonial privilege that other citizens do not enjoy. This we decline to do. Fair and effective law enforcement aimed at providing security for the person and property of the individual is a fundamental function of government, and the grand jury plays an important, constitutionally mandated role in this process. On the records now before us, we perceive no basis for holding that the public interest in law enforcement and in ensuring effective grand jury proceedings is insufficient to override the consequential, but uncertain, burden on news gathering that is said to result from insisting that reporters, like other citizens, respond to relevant questions put to them in the course of a valid grand jury investigation or criminal trial.

This conclusion itself involves no restraint on what newspapers may publish or on the type or quality of information reporters may seek to acquire, nor does it threaten the vast bulk of confidential relationships between reporters and their sources. Grand juries address themselves to the issues of whether crimes have been committed and who committed them. Only where news sources themselves are implicated in crime or possess information relevant to the grand jury's task need they or the reporter be concerned about grand jury subpoenas. Nothing before us indicates that a large number or percentage of *all* confidential news sources falls into either category and would in any way be deterred by our holding that the Constitution does not, as it never has, exempt the newsman from performing the citizen's normal duty of appearing and furnishing information relevant to the grand jury's task.

The preference for anonymity of those confidential informants involved in actual criminal conduct is presumably a product of their desire to escape criminal prosecution, and this preference, while understandable, is hardly deserving of constitutional protection. It would be frivolous to assert—and no one does in these cases—that the First Amendment, in the interest of securing news or otherwise, confers a license on either the reporter or his news sources to violate valid criminal laws. Although stealing documents or private wiretapping could provide newsworthy information, neither reporter nor source is immune from conviction for such conduct, whatever the impact on the flow of news. Neither is immune, on First Amendment grounds, from testifying against the other, before the grand jury or at a criminal trial. . . .

Thus, we cannot seriously entertain the notion that the First Amendment protects a newsman's agreement to conceal the criminal conduct of his source, or evidence thereof, on the theory that it is better to write about crime than to do something about it. . . .

The argument that the flow of news will be diminished by compelling reporters to aid the grand jury in a criminal investigation is not irrational, nor are the records before us silent on the matter. But we remain unclear how often and to what extent informers are actually deterred from furnishing information when newsmen are forced to testify before a grand jury. The available data indicate that some newsmen rely a great deal on confidential sources and that some informants are particularly sensitive to the threat of exposure and may be silenced if it is held by this Court that, ordinarily, newsmen must testify pursuant to subpoenas, but the evidence fails to demonstrate that there would be a significant constriction of the flow of news to the public if this Court reaffirms the prior common-law and constitutional rule regarding the testimonial obligations of newsmen. Estimates of the inhibiting effect of such subpoenas . . . are widely divergent and to a great extent speculative. . . . Reliance by the press on confidential informants does not mean that all such sources will in fact dry up because of the later possible appearance of the newsman before a grand jury. The reporter may never be called and if he objects to testifying, the prosecution may not insist. Also, the relationship of many informants to the press is a symbiotic one which is unlikely to be greatly inhibited by the threat of subpoena: quite often, such informants are members of a minority political or cultural group that relies heavily on the media to propagate its views, publicize its aims, and magnify its exposure to the public. Moreover, grand juries characteristically conduct secret proceedings, and law enforcement officers are themselves experienced in dealing with informers, and have their own methods for protecting them without interference with the effective administration of justice. There is little before us indicating that informants whose interest in avoiding exposure is that it may threaten job security, personal safety, or peace of mind, would in fact be in a worse position, or would think they would be, if they risked placing their trust in public officials as well as reporters. We doubt if the informer who prefers anonymity but is sincerely interested in furnishing evidence of crime will always or very often be deterred by the prospect of dealing with those public authorities characteristically charged with the duty to protect the public interest as well as his.

. . . [W]e cannot accept the argument that the public interest in possible future news about crime from undisclosed, unverified sources must take precedence over the public interest in pursuing and prosecuting those crimes reported to the press by informants and in thus deterring the commission of such crimes in the future.

We note first that the privilege claimed is that of the reporter, not the informant, and that if the authorities independently identify the informant, neither his own reluctance to testify nor the objection of the newsman would shield him from grand jury inquiry, whatever the impact on the flow of news or on his future usefulness as a secret source of information. More important, it is obvious that agreements to conceal information relevant to commission of crime have very little to recommend them from the standpoint of public policy. . . . Such conduct deserves no encomium, and we decline now to afford it First Amendment protection by denigrating the duty of a citizen, whether reporter or informer, to respond to grand jury subpoena and answer relevant questions put to him.

. . .

Neither are we now convinced that a virtually impenetrable constitutional shield, beyond legislative or judicial control, should be forged to protect a private system of informers operated by the press to report on criminal conduct, a system that would be unaccountable to the public, would pose a threat to the citizen's justifiable expectations of privacy, and would equally protect well-intentioned informants and those who for pay or otherwise betray their trust to their employer or associates. . . .

We are admonished that refusal to provide a First Amendment reporter's privilege will undermine the freedom of the press to collect and disseminate news. But this is not the lesson history teaches us. . . . From the beginning of our country the press has operated without constitutional protection for press informants, and the press has flourished. . . . The obligation to testify in response to grand jury subpoenas will not threaten [] sources not involved with criminal conduct and without information relevant to grand jury investigations, and we cannot hold that the Constitution places the sources in these two categories either above the law or beyond its reach.

The argument for such a constitutional privilege rests heavily on those cases holding that the infringement of protected First Amendment rights must be no broader than necessary to achieve a permissible governmental purpose. We do not deal, however, with a governmental institution that has abused its proper function. . . . [Moreover, t]he requirements of those cases [holding] that a State's interest must be "compelling" or "paramount" to justify even an indirect burden on First Amendment rights...are also met here. . . .

The privilege claimed here is conditional, not absolute; given the suggested preliminary showings and compelling need, the reporter would be required to testify. Presumably, such a rule would reduce the instances in which reporters could be required to appear, but predicting in advance when and in what circumstances they could be compelled to do so would be difficult. Such a rule would also have implications for the issuance of compulsory process to reporters at civil and criminal trials and at legislative hearings. If newsmen's confidential sources are as sensitive as they are claimed to be, the prospect of being unmasked whenever a judge determines the situation justifies it is hardly a satisfactory solution to the problem. For them, it would appear that only an absolute privilege would suffice.

We are unwilling to embark the judiciary on a long and difficult journey to such an uncertain destination. The administration of a constitutional newsman's privilege would present practical and conceptual difficulties of a high order. Sooner or later, it would be necessary to define those categories of newsmen who qualified for the privilege, a questionable procedure in light of the traditional doctrine that liberty of the press is the right of the lonely pamphleteer who uses carbon paper or a mimeograph just as much as of the large metropolitan publisher who utilizes the latest photocomposition methods. Freedom of the press is a "fundamental personal right" which "is not confined to newspapers and periodicals. It necessarily embraces pamphlets and leaflets. . . . The press in its historic connotation comprehends every sort of publication which affords a vehicle of information and opinion." . . . The informative function asserted by representatives of the organized press in the present cases is also performed by lecturers, political pollsters, novelists, academic researchers, and dramatists. Almost any author may quite accurately assert that he is contributing to the flow of information to the public, that he relies on confidential sources of information, and that these sources will be silenced if he is forced to make disclosures before a grand jury. . . .

[I]n the end, by considering whether enforcement of a particular law served a "compelling" governmental interest, the courts would be inextricably involved in distinguishing between the value of enforcing different criminal laws. By requiring testimony from a reporter in investigations involving some crimes but not in others, they would be making a value judgment that a legislature had declined to make, since in each case the criminal law involved would represent a considered legislative judgment, not constitutionally suspect, of what conduct is liable to criminal prosecution. The task of judges, like other officials outside the legislative branch, is not to make the law but to uphold it in accordance with their oaths.

At the federal level, Congress has freedom to determine whether a statutory newsman's privilege is necessary and desirable and to fashion standards and rules as narrow or broad as deemed necessary to deal with the evil discerned and, equally important, to refashion those rules as experience from time to time may dictate. There is also merit in leaving state legislatures free, within First Amendment limits, to fashion their own standards in light of the conditions and problems with respect to the relations between law enforcement officials and press in their own areas. . . .

In addition, there is much force in the pragmatic view that the press has at its disposal powerful mechanisms of communication and is far from helpless to protect itself from harassment or substantial harm. . . .

Finally, as we have earlier indicated, news gathering is not without its First Amendment protections, and grand jury investigations if instituted or conducted other than in good faith, would pose wholly different issues for resolution under the First Amendment. Official harassment of the press undertaken not for purposes of law enforcement but to disrupt a reporter's relationship with his news sources would have no justification. Grand juries are subject to judicial control and subpoenas to motions to quash. We do not expect courts will forget that grand juries must operate within the limits of the First Amendment as well as the Fifth. [The Court then reversed *Caldwell*, affirmed *Branzburg v. Hayes* and *Branzburg v. Meigs*, and held that as to *In re Pappas*, petitioner was required to testify subject] to the supervision of the presiding judge as to "the propriety, purposes, and scope of the grand jury inquiry and the pertinence of the probable testimony."

Mr. Justice POWELL, concurring.

I add this brief statement to emphasize what seems to me to be the limited nature of the Court's holding. The Court does not hold that newsmen, subpoenaed to testify before a grand jury, are without constitutional rights with respect to the gathering of news or in safeguarding their sources. Certainly, we do not hold, as suggested in Mr. Justice Stewart's dissenting opinion, that state and federal authorities are free to "annex" the news media as "an investigative arm of government." The solicitude repeatedly shown by this Court for First Amendment freedoms should be sufficient assurance against any such effort, even if one seriously believed that the media—properly free and untrammeled in the fullest sense of these terms—were not able to protect themselves.

As indicated in the concluding portion of the opinion, the Court states that no harassment of newsmen will be tolerated. If a newsman believes that the grand jury investigation is not being conducted in good faith he is not without remedy. Indeed, if the newsman is called upon to give information bearing only a remote and tenuous relationship to the subject of the investigation, or if he has some other reason to believe that his testimony implicates confidential source relationships without a legitimate need of law enforcement, he will have access to the court on a motion to quash and an appropriate protective order may be entered. The asserted claim to privilege should be judged on its facts by the striking of a proper balance between freedom of the press and the obligation of all citizens to give relevant testimony with respect to criminal conduct. The balance of these vital constitutional and societal interests on a case-by-case basis accords with the tried and traditional way of adjudicating such questions.[*]

In short, the courts will be available to newsmen under circumstances where legitimate First Amendment interests require protection.

---

[*] It is to be remembered that Caldwell asserts a constitutional privilege not even to appear before the grand jury unless a court decides that the Government has made a showing that meets the three preconditions specified in the dissenting opinion of Mr. Justice Stewart. To be sure, this would require a "balancing" of interests by the court, but under circumstances and constraints significantly different from the balancing that will be appropriate under the court's decision. The newsman witness, like all other witnesses, will have to appear; he will not be in a position to litigate at the threshold the State's very authority to subpoena him. Moreover, . . . , the court—when called upon to protect a newsman from improper or prejudicial questioning—would be free to balance the competing interests on their merits in the particular case. The new constitutional rule endorsed by th[e] dissenting opinion would, as a practical matter, defeat such a fair balancing and the essential societal interest in the detection and prosecution of crime would be heavily subordinated.

Mr. Justice DOUGLAS, dissenting in *United States v. Caldwell*.

. . . A reporter is no better than his source of information. Unless he has a privilege to withhold the identity of his source, he will be the victim of governmental intrigue or aggression. If he can be summoned to testify in secret before a grand jury, his sources will dry up and the attempted exposure, the effort to enlighten the public, will be ended. If what the Court sanctions today becomes settled law, then the reporter's main function in American society will be to pass on to the public the press releases which the various departments of government issue. . . .

Mr. Justice STEWART, with whom Mr. Justice BRENNAN and Mr. Justice MARSHALL join, dissenting.

The Court's crabbed view of the First Amendment reflects a disturbing insensitivity to the critical role of an independent press in our society. The question whether a reporter has a constitutional right to a confidential relationship with his source is of first impression here, but the principles that should guide our decision are as basic as any to be found in the Constitution. While Mr. Justice Powell's enigmatic concurring opinion gives some hope of a more flexible view in the future, the Court in these cases holds that a newsman has no First Amendment right to protect his sources when called before a grand jury. The Court thus invites state and federal authorities to undermine the historic independence of the press by attempting to annex the journalistic profession as an investigative arm of government. Not only will this decision impair performance of the press' constitutionally protected functions, but it will, I am convinced, in the long run harm rather than help the administration of justice.

I

The reporter's constitutional right to a confidential relationship with his source stems from the broad societal interest in a full and free flow of information to the public. . . .

. . . A corollary of the right to publish must be the right to gather news. . . . News must not be unnecessarily cut off at its source, for without freedom to acquire information the right to publish would be impermissibly compromised. Accordingly, a right to gather news, of some dimensions, must exist. . . .

The right to gather news implies, in turn, a right to a confidential relationship between a reporter and his source. This proposition follows as a matter of simple logic once three factual predicates are recognized: (1) newsmen require informants to gather news; (2) confidentiality—the promise or understanding that names or certain aspects of communications will be kept off the record—is essential to the creation and maintenance of a news-gathering relationship with informants; and (3) an unbridled subpoena power—the absence of a constitutional right protecting, in *any* way, a confidential relationship from compulsory process—will either deter sources from divulging information or deter reporters from gathering and publishing information. . . .

[II.] Posed against the First Amendment's protection of the newsman's confidential relationships in these cases is society's interest in the use of the grand jury to administer justice fairly and effectively. The grand jury serves two important functions: "to examine into the commission of crimes" and "to stand between the prosecutor and the accused, and to determine whether the charge was founded upon credible testimony or was dictated by malice or personal ill will." . . . And to perform these functions the grand jury must have available to it every man's relevant evidence.

Yet the longstanding rule making every person's evidence available to the grand jury is not absolute. The rule has been limited by the Fifth Amendment, the Fourth Amendment, and the evidentiary privileges of the common law. . . .

Such an interest must surely be the First Amendment protection of a confidential relationship. [T]his protection does not exist for the purely private interests of the newsman or his informant, nor even, at bottom, for the First Amendment interests of either partner in the news-gathering relationship. Rather, it functions to insure nothing less than democratic decisionmaking through the free flow of information to the public, and it serves, thereby, to honor the "profound national commitment to the principle that debate on public issues should be uninhibited, robust, and wide-open." *New York Times Co. v. Sullivan*, 376 U.S. at 270.

In striking the proper balance between the public interest in the efficient administration of justice and the First Amendment guarantee of the fullest flow of information, we must begin with the basic proposition that because of their "delicate and vulnerable" nature, *NAACP v. Button*, 371 U.S., at 433, and their transcendent importance for the just functioning of our society, First Amendment rights require special safeguards.

[A.] This Court has erected such safeguards when government, by legislative investigation or other investigative means, has attempted to pierce the shield of privacy inherent in freedom of association. In no previous case have we considered the extent to which the First Amendment limits the grand jury subpoena power. . . .

The established method of "carefully" circumscribing investigative powers is to place a heavy burden of justification on government officials when First Amendment rights are impaired. . . .

Thus, when an investigation impinges on First Amendment rights, the government must not only show that the inquiry is of "compelling and overriding importance" but it must also "convincingly" demonstrate that the investigation is "substantially related" to the information sought.

Governmental officials must, therefore, demonstrate that the information sought is *clearly* relevant to a *precisely* defined subject of governmental inquiry. They must demonstrate that it is reasonable to think the witness in question has that information. And they must show that there is not any means of obtaining the information less destructive of First Amendment liberties. . . .

Accordingly, when a reporter is asked to appear before a grand jury and reveal confidences, I would hold that the government must (1) show that there is probable cause to believe that the newsman has information that is clearly relevant to a specific probable violation of law; (2) demonstrate that the information sought cannot be obtained by alternative means less destructive of First Amendment rights; and (3) demonstrate a compelling and overriding interest in the information.

This is not to say that a grand jury could not issue a subpoena until such a showing were made, and it is not to say that a newsman would be in any way privileged to ignore any subpoena that was issued. Obviously, before the government's burden to make such a showing were triggered, the reporter would have to move to quash the subpoena, asserting the basis on which he considered the particular relationship a confidential one.

[B.] The crux of the Court's rejection of any newsman's privilege is its observation that only "where news sources themselves are implicated in crime or possess information *relevant* to the grand jury's task need they or the reporter be concerned about grand jury subpoenas." But this is a most misleading construct. For it is obviously not true that the only persons about whom reporters will be forced to testify will be those "confidential informants involved in actual criminal conduct" and those having "information suggesting illegal conduct by others." As noted above, given the grand jury's extraordinarily broad investigative powers and the weak standards of relevance and materiality that apply during such inquiries, reporters, if they have no testimonial privilege, will be called to give information about informants who have neither committed crimes nor have information about crime. It is to avoid deterrence of such sources and thus to prevent needless injury to First Amendment values that I think the government must be required to show probable cause that the newsman has information that is clearly relevant to a specific probable violation of criminal law.

NOTES AND QUESTIONS

1. *Sources and privilege.* Will confidential sources "dry up" without a privilege? How much do sources rely on the existence, or absence, of a reporter's privilege in deciding whether to provide information to the media? Should this matter to the outcome of the decision? Is it subject to empirical proof?

2. *Is* Branzburg *a plurality opinion?* An important part of understanding Supreme Court decisions is "counting heads." Four members of the Court would recognize a constitutional reporter's privilege. Would Justice Powell also recognize a constitutional privilege in some circumstances? Why did Justice Powell decide to write a separate concurrence after joining the majority (five votes) decision?

3. *A surprising twist.* Many state and federal courts read *Branzburg* to create a constitutional reporter's privilege. How? By reading Justice Powell's concurrence together with the dissent, the court found five votes for creating some form of qualified constitutional privilege. Is this an honest reading of *Branzburg*? Several federal appellate courts have said no, noting that Powell joined in Justice White's opinion, and arguing that his concurrence only addresses abuse of the subpoena power rather than routine use. *See, e.g.*, United States v. Smith, 135 F.3d 963 (5th Cir. 1998); In re Grand Jury Proceedings, 5 F.3d 397 (9th Cir. 1993); In re Grand Jury Proceedings, 810 F.2d 580 (6th Cir. 1987); *see also* In re WTHR-TV, 693 N.E.2d 1 (Ind. 1998).

4. *Privilege variables.* Reporters possess valuable information that is sought in a variety of contexts other than grand jury proceedings. Reporters may be subpoenaed to testify at criminal trials and at civil trials, and their testimony may be sought by legislative committees or administrative tribunals. The government or private litigants may seek information that is confidential or nonconfidential, published or unpublished, eyewitness observations or hearsay. Moreover, disclosure may be sought when reporters themselves are parties to litigation (as in defamation actions). Which of these variables should weigh in favor of disclosure? Jurisdictions vary in answering this question.

5. *Shield statutes and other sources of privilege.* Before *Branzburg*, 17 states had shield statutes (that is, statutorily enacted reporters' privileges) in place. In 2015, the National Law Journal reported that forty-nine states and the District of Columbia had shield laws. Tony Mauro, *Formerly Jailed Journalists Push for*

Federal Shield Law, Nat'l. L.J., June 2, 2015. Although more than 100 bills to enact a shield law have been filed at the federal level, none has passed both houses of Congress. Many bills failed because the media could not agree as to the terms of such legislation. Statutes are not the only source of privilege law. Some courts have interpreted their state constitutions or their common law to create a reporter's privilege to protect confidential sources. In addition, federal courts sometimes suggest that federal common law may be a source of privilege. Rule 501 of the Federal Rules of Evidence provides that privilege issues in federal courts "shall be governed by the principles of the common law as they may be interpreted by the courts of the United States in the light of reason and experience." However, state privilege law controls "with respect to an element of a claim or defense as to which State law supplies the rule of decision." The courts that turn to federal common law as the source for privilege rely on the same policies as those that turn to the First Amendment as the source. It should be obvious from this account of the sources of privilege that different jurisdictions enact and apply their reporter's privilege with varying degrees of fervor. These variations make the law of reporter's privilege quite complex.

6. *Reconsidering a substantive press clause*. Might the press lose something from a substantive press clause—that is, one that gives the press special rights not available to individuals under the Free Speech Clause? Several commentators have worried that if the media gain special rights because of their status as the public's eyes and ears, special responsibilities might follow. For example, special rights, such as a reporter's privilege, might come with an enforceable responsibility to provide the public with full and fair coverage of important issues. *See* Anthony Lewis, *A Preferred Position for Journalism?*, 7 Hofstra L. Rev. 595, 605 (1979); William W. Van Alstyne, *The Hazards to the Press of Claiming a "Preferred Position,"* 28 Hastings L.J. 761 (1977). Professor David Anderson has worried that the extension of special *constitutional* rights to the press might lead to the elimination of the many special *nonconstitutional* rights the press receives under existing law. Anderson concludes: "The paradox of the Press Clause is this: giving the press special constitutional protection inevitably diminishes the ability to give the press special protection by nonconstitutional means." If the Supreme Court recognizes special constitutional press rights that must be accorded to anyone who meets the definition of press, other government entities may forgo creating statutory or administrative protections because fighting over who gets them is too difficult or too costly: "The prospect of litigating these issues, or just the burden of devising policies to avoid litigation, might dissuade agencies from attempting to accommodate the press when doing so entails the exclusion of someone else." *See* David A. Anderson, *Freedom of the Press*, 80 Tex. L. Rev. 429, 511-512 (2002); *but see* Sonja R. West, *Awakening the Press Clause*, 58 UCLA L. Rev. 1025, 1027-1029 (2011) (contending that the Press Clause should provide protection for the press as an institution).

AN EXTENDED NOTE ON GOVERNMENT SECRECY, SUBPOENAS, AND THE INVESTIGATION OF LEAKS

After the terrorist attacks on the United States on September 11, 2001, federal and state governments began to fear that terrorists might use publicly available information to plan and carry out further attacks. In response, the government began to invoke security concerns as a basis for withholding information from the public and pursuing and punishing those who leaked classified information. The federal government's campaign against "leaks" during that period resulted in a dramatic increase in subpoenas to journalists. Indeed, under President Barack Obama, the Justice Department prosecuted more government officials for leaking classified information than had any previous administration. The Obama administration initiated at least eleven Espionage Act prosecutions against government officials accused of leaking national security information. Leak cases raise difficult issues. In some cases involving leaks, the leak itself is the crime; thus, the reporter who receives the leaked information possesses direct evidence of the commission of a crime. Yet leaks from every echelon of government are common, and many important stories would be lost without them.

One high-profile leaks case illustrates some of the difficulties such cases pose. The case involved a prosecution brought against Jeffrey Sterling, a former member of the CIA's Iran Task Force. The government suspected that Sterling was a source for an account in journalist James Risen's book "State of War" about a botched CIA attempt to sabotage Iranian nuclear research.

The government subpoenaed Risen, on the basis that his testimony was essential to prove the case against Sterling. A district judge quashed the government's subpoena insofar as it required Risen to identify his source, U.S. v. Sterling, 818 F. Supp. 2d 945 (E.D. Va. 2011), but the Fourth Circuit reversed. U.S. v. Sterling, 724 F.3d 482 (4th Cir. 2013).

Citing *Branzburg*, the court held: "There is no First Amendment testimonial privilege, absolute or qualified, that protects a reporter from being compelled to testify by the prosecution or the defense in criminal proceedings about criminal conduct that the reporter personally witnessed or participated in, absent a showing of bad faith, harassment, or other such non-legitimate motive, even though the reporter promised confidentiality to his source." The court rejected the argument that Justice Powell's *Branzburg* concurrence had "tacit[ly] endorsed" the dissenting opinion of Justice Stewart. The court further noted that the Supreme Court "has never varied from" *Branzburg*'s holding since it was decided, and thus it was the only court authorized to recognize a reporter's privilege based in the First Amendment.

The court concluded that Risen "has 'direct information . . . concerning the commission of serious crimes.' [ ] Indeed, he can provide the *only* first-hand account of the commission of a most serious crime indicted by the grand jury—the illegal disclosure of classified, national security information by one who was entrusted by our government to protect national security, but who is charged with endangering it instead." The court also concluded that the there was no evidence that the government subpoenaed Risen's testimony in bad faith or for purposes of harassment. Instead, the government was "seek[ing] to compel evidence that Risen alone possesses—evidence that goes to the heart of the prosecution."

The court refused to recognize a reporter's privilege rooted in federal common law, again citing *Branzburg* as clear authority on the issue. The court concluded: "If Risen is to be protected from being compelled to testify and give what evidence of crime he possesses, in contravention of every citizen's duty to do so, we believe that decision should rest with the Supreme Court, which can revisit *Branzburg* and the policy arguments it rejected, or with Congress, which can more effectively and comprehensively weigh the policy arguments for and against adopting a privilege and define its scope."

Judge Roger Gregory, dissenting, argued that Risen's testimony should have been shielded by both a qualified First Amendment privilege and a federal common law privilege tailored specifically to the context of national security leaks. In order to overcome the qualified privilege, the government would have to show that the subpoenaed information was "highly material and relevant, necessary or critical to the maintenance of the claim, and not obtainable from other sources." To this inquiry, the judge would add in national security cases "consideration of two additional factors: the harm caused by the public dissemination of the information, and the newsworthiness of the information conveyed." Consideration of these additional factors would allow the privilege to be overridden in "matters of national security" in the face of "pressing governmental interests."

Applying this test in *Sterling*, the judge would have quashed the government's subpoena seeking Risen's testimony. After summarizing the evidence against Sterling in detail, the judge concluded that the government had failed to show a compelling interest in obtaining Risen's testimony regarding his confidential sources, because this testimony would be superfluous in light of the other strong evidence available to the government. Moreover, the information was available from other means.

Turning to the newsworthiness and harm inquiries, the judge found the information concluded that the information published by Risen concerning "the United States intelligence community's efforts concerning the development of the Iranian nuclear program" to be highly newsworthy. Indeed, Risen's book suggested that the efforts were so misguided that they "may have helped Iran advance its nuclear program." Globally, the information "portends to inform the reader of a blundered American intelligence mission in Iran," an especially important topic in the wake of the U.S. invasion of Iraq based on flawed intelligence information.

The judge, however, did not assess the harm caused by the leak of the classified information but instead would have remanded to the district court, because "the Government has not clearly articulated the nature, extent, and severity of the harm resulting from the leak. Without such evidence, it is impossible for a reviewing court to determine whether the First Amendment interest in presenting newsworthy information to the public—if indeed the district court finds the information newsworthy—is outweighed by the consequences of the leak." The judge conceded that this balancing might be difficult, but "[t]he First Amendment interest in informed popular debate does not simply vanish at the invocation of the words 'national security.'" (citing United States v. Morison, 844 F.2d 1057, 1081 (4th Cir. 1988) (Wilkinson, J., concurring)).

Risen's seven-year battle not to testify ended after Attorney General Eric Holder announced prosecutors would end attempts to compel his testimony. Matt Apuzzo, *Times Reporter Will Not Be Called to Testify in Leak Case*, N.Y. Times, Jan. 12, 2015. Jeffrey Sterling was sentenced to three and half years in prison.

Does the modified balancing test tip the scales toward the Government's interest in protecting classified information or against it? To what extent would application of the modified balancing test lead to enhanced protection of confidential sources in leaks cases? To what extent would it allow federal judges to usurp the role of the legislative and executive branches?

THEORY-APPLIED PROBLEM—SUBPOENA OF TELEPHONE RECORDS

Can the federal government avoid First Amendment issues involved in subpoenaing reporters to testify about leaks simply by obtaining their telephone records from third-party companies? What arguments can you make on both sides of this issue? The question is not a hypothetical one. In a 2013 leaks investigation, the Justice Department secretly subpoenaed two months' worth of records from twenty of the Associated Press' phone lines. Mark Sherman, *Gov't Obtains Wide AP Phone Records in Probe*, Assoc. Press, May 13, 2013. Also in 2013, the Federal Bureau of Investigation obtained a search warrant for the contents of the personal email of Fox News correspondent James Rosen in 2010. (James Risen, mentioned above, and James Rosen are two separate journalists.) The search warrant issued based on an assertion that the government had probable cause to believe the reporter had violated the Espionage Act by soliciting a State Department official to leak classified information. Ann E. Marimow, *A Rare Peek Into a Justice Department Leak Probe*, Wash. Post, May 19, 2013. Although the government has prosecuted leakers of government information under the Espionage Act, it has not previously prosecuted a journalist for soliciting such leaks. Then-Attorney General Eric Holder explained to a House judiciary committee that the government did not necessarily plan to proceed against Rosen; instead, the allegations of aiding and abetting allowed the government to sidestep the federal Privacy Protection Act's prohibition against government searches of newsrooms in criminal investigations. Ann E. Marimow, *Justice Department's Scrutiny of Fox News Reporter James Rosen in Leak Case Draws Fire*, Wash. Post, May 20, 2013. *See also* New York Times Co. v. Gonzales, 382 F. Supp. 2d 457 (S.D.N.Y. 2005), (holding that reporters enjoyed a qualified privilege both under the First Amendment and under federal common law that prevented the government from obtaining their telephone records, particularly when it could check its own telephone records to try to uncover the leak), vacated and remanded in New York Times Co. v. Gonzales, 459 F.3d 160, 163 (2d Cir. 2006) (holding that whatever privilege might exist had been overcome as a matter of law under the facts of the case).

2. Access to Courtrooms

RICHMOND NEWSPAPERS, INC. v. VIRGINIA
448 U.S. 555 (1980)

Mr. Chief Justice BURGER announced the judgment of the Court and delivered an opinion, in which Mr. Justice WHITE and Mr. Justice STEVENS joined.

[In 1977, the Virginia Supreme Court reversed Stevenson's conviction of second-degree murder because the trial court had improperly admitted a bloodstained shirt purportedly belonging to Stevenson into evidence. Stevenson's case was retried, but his second trial ended in a mistrial. So did his third.] It appears that the mistrial may have been declared because a prospective juror had read about Stevenson's previous trials in a newspaper and had told other prospective jurors about the case before the retrial began. Stevenson was tried in the same court for a fourth time beginning on September 11, 1978. Present in the courtroom when the case was called were appellants Wheeler and McCarthy, reporters for appellant Richmond Newspapers,

Inc. Before the trial began, counsel for the defendant moved that it be closed to the public. . . .

[The prosecutor did not object, and the trial judge entered an order excluding the public and the press from the courtroom. Appellants moved to vacate and asked for a hearing.] At the closed hearing, counsel for appellants observed that no evidentiary findings had been made by the court prior to the entry of its closure order and pointed out that the court had failed to consider any other, less drastic measures within its power to ensure a fair trial. . . . [The court denied the motion to vacate, the closed trial continued, and the defendant was acquitted. The Virginia Supreme Court denied the newspaper's appeal.]

II

We begin consideration of this case by noting that the precise issue presented here has not previously been before this Court for decision. In *Gannett Co. v. DePasquale* the Court was not required to decide whether a right of access to *trials*, as distinguished from hearings on pretrial motions, was constitutionally guaranteed. The Court held that the Sixth Amendment's guarantee to the accused of a public trial gave neither the public nor the press an enforceable right of access to a pretrial suppression hearing. . . .

[H]ere for the first time the Court is asked to decide whether a criminal trial itself may be closed to the public upon the unopposed request of a defendant, without any demonstration that closure is required to protect the defendant's superior right to a fair trial, or that some other overriding consideration requires closure.

[A.] The origins of the proceeding which has become the modern criminal trial in Anglo-American justice can be traced back beyond reliable historical records. We need not here review all details of its development, but a summary of that history is instructive. What is significant for present purposes is that throughout its evolution, the trial has been open to all who cared to observe.

[The opinion traced a tradition of open public trials in England from "the days before the Norman Conquest" to the present day and then turned to the tradition of open public trials in America.]

We have found nothing to suggest that the presumptive openness of the trial, which English courts were later to call "one of the essential qualities of a court of justice" was not also an attribute of the judicial systems of colonial America. . . .

[B.][T]he historical evidence demonstrates conclusively that at the time when our organic laws were adopted, criminal trials both here and in England had long been presumptively open. This is no quirk of history; rather, it has long been recognized as an indispensable attribute of an Anglo-American trial. Both Hale in the 17th century and Blackstone in the 18th saw the importance of openness to the proper functioning of a trial; it gave assurance that the proceedings were conducted fairly to all concerned, and it discouraged perjury, the misconduct of participants, and decisions based on secret bias or partiality.

. . . The early history of open trials in part reflects the widespread acknowledgment, long before there were behavioral scientists, that public trials had significant community therapeutic value. Even without such experts to frame the concept in words, people sensed from experience and observation that, especially in the administration of criminal justice, the means used to achieve justice must have the support derived from public acceptance of both the process and its results.

When a shocking crime occurs, a community reaction of outrage and public protest often follows. Thereafter the open processes of justice serve an important prophylactic purpose, providing an outlet for community concern, hostility, and emotion. Without an awareness that society's responses to criminal conduct are underway, natural human reactions of outrage and protest are frustrated and may manifest themselves in some form of vengeful "self-help," as indeed they did regularly in the activities of vigilante "committees" on our frontiers.

. . . To work effectively, it is important that society's criminal process "satisfy the appearance of justice," . . ., and the appearance of justice can best be provided by allowing people to observe it. . . .

People in an open society do not demand infallibility from their institutions, but it is difficult for them to accept what they are prohibited from observing. When a criminal trial is conducted in the open, there is at least an opportunity both for understanding the system in general and its workings in a particular case. . . .

In earlier times, both in England and America, attendance at court was a common mode of "passing the time." . . . Yet "[it] is not unrealistic even in this day to believe that public inclusion affords citizens a form of legal education and hopefully promotes confidence in the fair administration of justice." . . . Instead of acquiring information about trials by firsthand observation or by word of mouth from those who attended, people now acquire it chiefly through the print and electronic media. In a sense, this validates the media claim of functioning as surrogates for the public. While media representatives enjoy the same right of access as the public, they often are provided special seating and priority of entry so that they may report what people in attendance have seen and heard. This "[contributes] to public understanding of the rule of law and to comprehension of the functioning of the entire criminal justice system. . . ." *Nebraska Press Assn. v. Stuart*, 427 U.S., at 587 (Brennan, J., concurring in judgment).

[C.] From this unbroken, uncontradicted history, supported by reasons as valid today as in centuries past, we are bound to conclude that a presumption of openness inheres in the very nature of a criminal trial under our system of justice.

III

[A.] . . . The Bill of Rights was enacted against the backdrop of the long history of trials being presumptively open. Public access to trials was then regarded as an important aspect of the process itself; the conduct of trials "before as many of the people as chuse to attend" was regarded as one of "the inestimable advantages of a free English constitution of government." . . . In guaranteeing freedoms such as those of speech and press, the First Amendment can be read as protecting the right of everyone to attend trials so as to give meaning to those explicit guarantees. . . . Free speech carries with it some freedom to listen. "In a variety of contexts this Court has referred to a First Amendment right to 'receive information and ideas.'" *Kleindienst v. Mandel*, 408 U.S. 753, 762 (1972). What this means in the context of trials is that the First Amendment guarantees of speech and press, standing alone, prohibit government from summarily closing courtroom doors which had long been open to the public at the time that Amendment was adopted. . . .

It is not crucial whether we describe this right to attend criminal trials to hear, see, and communicate observations concerning them as a "right of access," . . . [11] or a "right to gather information," for we have recognized that "without some protection for seeking out the news, freedom of the press could be eviscerated." *Branzburg v. Hayes*, 408 U.S. 665, 681 (1972). The explicit, guaranteed rights to speak and to publish concerning what takes place at a trial would lose much meaning if access to observe the trial could, as it was here, be foreclosed arbitrarily.

[B.] The right of access to places traditionally open to the public, as criminal trials have long been, may be seen as assured by the amalgam of the First Amendment guarantees of speech and press; and their affinity to the right of assembly is not without relevance. . . . Subject to the traditional time, place, and manner restrictions, see, *e.g., Cox v. New Hampshire*, 312 U.S. 569 (1941), streets, sidewalks, and parks are places traditionally open, where First Amendment rights may be exercised, . . .; a trial courtroom also is a public place where the people generally—and representatives of the media—have a right to be present, and where their presence historically has been thought to enhance the integrity and quality of what takes place.

[C.] We hold that the right to attend criminal trials[17] is implicit in the guarantees of the First Amendment; without the freedom to attend such trials, which people have exercised for centuries, important aspects of freedom of speech and "of the press could be eviscerated." *Branzburg*, 408 U.S., at 681.

[D.] Having concluded there was a guaranteed right of the public under the First and Fourteenth Amendments to attend the trial of Stevenson's case, we return to the closure order challenged by appellants. The Court in *Gannett [v. DePasquale]* made clear that although the Sixth Amendment guarantees the accused a right to a public trial, it does not give a right to a private trial. Despite the fact that this was the fourth trial of the accused, the trial judge made no findings to support closure; no inquiry was made as to whether alternative solutions would have met the need to ensure fairness; there was no recognition of any right under the Constitution for the public or press to attend the trial. In contrast to the pretrial proceeding dealt with in *Gannett*, there exist in the context of the trial itself various tested alternatives to satisfy the constitutional demands of fairness. See, *e.g., Nebraska Press Assn. v. Stuart*, 427 U.S., at 563-565; *Sheppard v. Maxwell*, 384 U.S., at 357-362. There was no suggestion that any problems with witnesses could not have been dealt with by their exclusion from the courtroom or their sequestration during the trial. Nor is there anything to indicate that sequestration of the jurors would not have guarded against their being subjected to any improper information. All of the alternatives admittedly present difficulties for trial courts, but none of the factors relied on here was beyond

---

[11] *Procunier* and *Saxbe* are distinguishable in the sense that they were concerned with penal institutions which, by definition, are not "open" or public places. Penal institutions do not share the long tradition of openness, although traditionally there have been visiting committees of citizens, and there is no doubt that legislative committees could exercise plenary oversight and "visitation rights." *Saxbe*, 417 U.S., at 849, noted that "limitation on visitations is justified by what the Court of Appeals acknowledged as 'the truism that prisons are institutions where public access is generally limited.' 161 U. S. App. D. C., at 80, 494 F.2d, at 999. See *Adderley v. Florida*, 385 U.S. 39, 41 (1966) [jails]." See also *Greer v. Spock*, 424 U.S. 828 (1976) (military bases).

[17] Whether the public has a right to attend trials of civil cases is a question not raised by this case, but we note that historically both civil and criminal trials have been presumptively open.

the realm of the manageable. Absent an overriding interest articulated in findings, the trial of a criminal case must be open to the public.

Mr. Justice POWELL took no part in the consideration or decision of this case.

Mr. Justice BRENNAN, with whom Mr. Justice MARSHALL joins, concurring in the judgment.
    . . . Because I believe that the First Amendment—of itself and as applied to the States through the Fourteenth Amendment—secures...a public right of access [to criminal trial], I agree with those of my Brethren who hold that, without more, agreement of the trial judge and the parties cannot constitutionally close a trial to the public.
    While freedom of expression is made inviolate by the First Amendment, and, with only rare and stringent exceptions, may not be suppressed, . . . the First Amendment has not been viewed by the Court in all settings as providing an equally categorical assurance of the correlative freedom of access to information.[2] Yet the Court has not ruled out a public access component to the First Amendment in every circumstance. Read with care and in context, our decisions must therefore be understood as holding only that any privilege of access to governmental information is subject to a degree of restraint dictated by the nature of the information and countervailing interests in security or confidentiality. . . .
    The Court's approach in right-of-access cases simply reflects the special nature of a claim of First Amendment right to gather information. Customarily, First Amendment guarantees are interposed to protect communication between speaker and listener. When so employed against prior restraints, free speech protections are almost insurmountable. . . . But the First Amendment embodies more than a commitment to free expression and communicative interchange for their own sakes; it has a *structural* role to play in securing and fostering our republican system of self-government. Implicit in this structural role is not only "the principle that debate on public issues should be uninhibited, robust, and wide-open," *New York Times Co. v. Sullivan*, 376 U.S. 254, 270 (1964), but also the antecedent assumption that valuable public debate—as well as other civic behavior—must be informed. The structural model links the First Amendment to that process of communication necessary for a democracy to survive, and thus entails solicitude not only for communication itself, but also for the indispensable conditions of meaningful communication.
    However, . . . "[there] are few restrictions on action which could not be clothed by ingenious argument in the garb of decreased data flow." *Zemel v. Rusk.* An assertion of the prerogative to gather information must accordingly be assayed by considering the information sought and the opposing interests invaded.
    This judicial task is as much a matter of sensitivity to practical necessities as it is of abstract reasoning. But at least two helpful principles may be sketched. First, the

---

[2] A conceptually separate, yet related, question is whether the media should enjoy greater access rights than the general public. See, *e.g., Saxbe v. Washington Post Co.,* 417 U.S., at 850; *Pell v. Procunier,* 417 U.S., at 834-835. But no such contention is at stake here. Since the media's right of access is at least equal to that of the general public, see *ibid.,* this case is resolved by a decision that the state statute unconstitutionally restricts public access to trials. As a practical matter, however, the institutional press is the likely, and fitting, chief beneficiary of a right of access because it serves as the "agent" of interested citizens, and funnels information about trials to a large number of individuals.

case for a right of access has special force when drawn from an enduring and vital tradition of public entree to particular proceedings or information. Such a tradition commands respect in part because the Constitution carries the gloss of history. More importantly, a tradition of accessibility implies the favorable judgment of experience. Second, the value of access must be measured in specifics. Analysis is not advanced by rhetorical statements that all information bears upon public issues; what is crucial in individual cases is whether access to a particular government process is important in terms of that very process.

To resolve the case before us, therefore, we must consult historical and current practice with respect to open trials, and weigh the importance of public access to the trial process itself.

[The opinion cited numerous historical sources indicating that both English common law and American colonial law had recognized a right of public trial. It then noted that the "overwhelming majority of States secure the right to public trials."]

III

Publicity serves to advance several of the particular purposes of the trial (and, indeed, the judicial) process. Open trials play a fundamental role in furthering the efforts of our judicial system to assure the criminal defendant a fair and accurate adjudication of guilt or innocence. But, as a feature of our governing system of justice, the trial process serves other, broadly political, interests, and public access advances these objectives as well. To that extent, trial access possesses specific structural significance.

The trial is a means of meeting "the notion, deeply rooted in the common law, that 'justice must satisfy the appearance of justice.'" . . . One major function of the trial, hedged with procedural protections and conducted with conspicuous respect for the rule of law, is to make that demonstration.

Secrecy is profoundly inimical to this demonstrative purpose of the trial process. Open trials assure the public that procedural rights are respected, and that justice is afforded equally. Closed trials breed suspicion of prejudice and arbitrariness, which in turn spawns disrespect for law. Public access is essential, therefore, if trial adjudication is to achieve the objective of maintaining public confidence in the administration of justice.

But the trial is more than a demonstrably just method of adjudicating disputes and protecting rights. It plays a pivotal role in the entire judicial process, and, by extension, in our form of government. Under our system, judges are not mere umpires, but, in their own sphere, lawmakers—a coordinate branch of *government*. While individual cases turn upon the controversies between parties, or involve particular prosecutions, court rulings impose official and practical consequences upon members of society at large. Moreover, judges bear responsibility for the vitally important task of construing and securing constitutional rights. Thus, so far as the trial is the mechanism for judicial factfinding, as well as the initial forum for legal decision making, it is a genuine governmental proceeding.

It follows that the conduct of the trial is pre-eminently a matter of public interest. See *Cox Broadcasting Corp. v. Cohn*, 420 U.S., at 491-492. More importantly, public access to trials acts as an important check, akin in purpose to the other checks and balances that infuse our system of government. . . .

Finally, with some limitations, a trial aims at true and accurate factfinding. Of course, proper factfinding is to the benefit of criminal defendants and of the parties in civil proceedings. But other, comparably urgent, interests are also often at stake. A miscarriage of justice that imprisons an innocent accused also leaves a guilty party at large, a continuing threat to society. Also, mistakes of fact in civil litigation may inflict costs upon others than the plaintiff and defendant. Facilitation of the trial factfinding process, therefore, is of concern to the public as well as to the parties. . . .

Popular attendance at trials, in sum, substantially furthers the particular public purposes of that critical judicial proceeding. In that sense, public access is an indispensable element of the trial process itself. Trial access, therefore, assumes structural importance in our "government of laws," *Marbury v. Madison*, 1 Cranch 137, 163 (1803).

IV

. . . With regard to the case at hand, our ingrained tradition of public trials and the importance of public access to the broader purposes of the trial process, tip the balance strongly toward the rule that trials be open. What countervailing interests might be sufficiently compelling to reverse this presumption of openness need not concern us now, for the statute at stake here authorizes trial closures at the unfettered discretion of the judge and parties. [Reversed.]

Mr. Justice STEWART, concurring in the judgment.
    . . . In conspicuous contrast to a military base, . . . or a prison, . . . a trial courtroom is a public place. Even more than city streets, sidewalks, and parks as areas of traditional First Amendment activity, a trial courtroom is a place where representatives of the press and of the public are not only free to be, but where their presence serves to assure the integrity of what goes on.

But this does not mean that the First Amendment right of members of the public and representatives of the press to attend civil and criminal trials is absolute. Just as a legislature may impose reasonable time, place, and manner restrictions upon the exercise of First Amendment freedoms, so may a trial judge impose reasonable limitations upon the unrestricted occupation of a courtroom by representatives of the press and members of the public. Much more than a city street, a trial courtroom must be a quiet and orderly place. Moreover, every courtroom has a finite physical capacity, and there may be occasions when not all who wish to attend a trial may do so.[3] And while there exist many alternative ways to satisfy the constitutional demands of a fair trial, those demands may also sometimes justify limitations upon the unrestricted presence of spectators in the courtroom.

Since in the present case the trial judge appears to have given no recognition to the right of representatives of the press and members of the public to be present at the Virginia murder trial over which he was presiding, the judgment under review must be reversed.

[Justice STEVENS'S concurrence and Justice REHNQUIST'S dissent are omitted.]

---

[3] In such situations, representatives of the press must be assured access. *Houchins v. KQED, Inc.*, 438 U.S. 1, 16 (opinion concurring in judgment).

NOTES AND QUESTIONS

1. *Value of openness as a limit on the access right.* Can it be argued that openness plays a positive role in almost every type of governmental meeting or proceeding? Should the right of access extend broadly to other types of governmental proceedings? Federal courts have recognized a right of access to civil trials. *See, e.g.,* Publicker Indus., Inc. v. Cohen, 733 F.2d 1059 (3d Cir. 1984).

2. *History of openness as a limit on the access right.* How valuable is a constitutional right of access that depends on historical recognition for its existence?

3. *Distinguishing* Gannett. Is *Richmond Newspapers* truly distinguishable from *Gannett v. DePasquale*, which is discussed several times in the case?

4. *Free press versus fair trial.* The conflict between a criminal defendant's Sixth Amendment right to a fair trial and the press's and public's First Amendment right to information about that trial comes up in a variety of contexts. The Supreme Court has recognized that trial publicity can, in certain circumstances, violate a criminal defendant's due process rights. Sheppard v. Maxwell, 384 U.S. 333 (1966) (involving a high-profile trial in which the trial judge allowed "newsmen" to take over the courtroom, resulting in "bedlam" and depriving the defendant "of that 'judicial serenity and calm to which [he] was entitled'" by the Due Process Clause). To safeguard the rights of the criminal defendant, the Court has encouraged trial judges to employ procedures to reduce the effect of prejudicial pretrial publicity on a defendant's fair trial right, including change of venue, postponement, extensive and searching voir dire of prospective jurors, clear instructions regarding publicity, sequestration of the jury, and restraining the comments of trial participants. One option that the trial judge does not have (except perhaps in the rarest of cases) is to put a prior restraint on what the press may publish in order to protect the Sixth Amendment rights of a criminal defendant. Later in this chapter, we examine Nebraska Press Ass'n v. Stuart, 427 U.S. 539 (1976), which establishes stringent constitutional standards that a trial judge must satisfy in order to enjoin publication of prejudicial pretrial publicity.

5. *Equal rights or special rights?* The logic of *Richmond Newspapers* is premised on the notion that the public has a constitutional right to attend criminal trials, and therefore so does the press. In other words, the press receives no greater right to attend criminal trials than does the general public. Does Justice Stewart's concurrence, which suggests that the press should receive preferential seating when space is limited, turn an "equal" right of the press and the public to attend criminal trials into a "special" right of the press?

AN EXTENDED NOTE ON EXPANSION OF THE RIGHT OF ACCESS *AFTER* RICHMOND NEWSPAPERS

The Supreme Court expanded the right of access in a series of opinions after *Richmond Newspapers* and in the process diluted the requirement that a "history of openness" must underpin any constitutional right of access.

In Globe Newspaper Co. v. Superior Court, 457 U.S. 596 (1982), the Court struck down a state statute requiring automatic closure of the courtroom during the trial testimony of minor victims of sexual offenses. The Court held that the key inquiry was not the history of openness of a particular type of trial—such as a sex offense trial. Rather the key inquiry was whether the state could show that closure was "necessitated by a compelling governmental interest" and that its statute was "narrowly tailored to serve that interest." The Court held that mandatory closure was not justified despite the fact that protecting minors is a compelling state interest. Instead, the Court held that a trial judge must make a case-by-case determination that closure is necessary to protect this interest.

In Press-Enterprise Co. v. Superior Court, 464 U.S. 501 (1984) (*Press-Enterprise I*), the Court held that there is a constitutional right of access to attend the voir dire portion of a criminal trial. In that case, the trial judge closed all but three days of a six-week voir dire in a case involving a black defendant charged with raping and murdering a white teenager. The trial judge believed closure was necessary to protect prospective jurors' privacy. The judge not only closed the voir dire but also refused to release transcripts of voir dire after the criminal trial was over. The Supreme Court unanimously reversed. The Court acknowledged that a juror may sometimes have a compelling interest in privacy, but the Court stated that the interest could be protected by questioning the juror with regard to private matters in chambers. The Court refined the constitutional test applied in *Richmond Newspapers* and *Globe Newspaper*, stating: "The presumption of openness may be overcome only by an overriding interest based on findings that closure is essential to preserve higher values and is narrowly tailored to serve that interest. The interest is to be articulated along with findings specific enough that a reviewing court can determine whether the closure order was properly entered." How difficult will this standard be for a trial judge to satisfy? Is ensuring juror candor a more compelling interest than protecting juror privacy?

Finally, in Press-Enterprise Co. v. Superior Court, 478 U.S. 1 (1986) (*Press-Enterprise II*), the Supreme Court held that the press and public have a constitutional right of access to pretrial hearings in criminal cases. *Press-Enterprise II* involved a claim of access to a preliminary probable cause hearing in a California criminal trial; the particular type of preliminary hearing at issue appears to have been unique to California procedure as it existed in 1986. (The procedure was modified by voter initiative in 1990, making it less attractive to defendants in some cases and unavailable to them in others.) Obviously, then, the Court did not put much emphasis on the "historical tradition of openness" of this type of proceeding, instead noting only that most states provide for open preliminary hearings in criminal trials. Instead, the Court focused on "whether public access to preliminary hearings as they are conducted in California plays a significant positive role in the actual functioning of the process." The Court emphasized that the preliminary hearing is the final step in many criminal cases, and it therefore found openness of the preliminary hearing would foster most of the same positive goals as in the trial itself. The Court concluded that a qualified right of access attached to the preliminary hearing, and that the trial judge had not made the requisite findings—that "closure is essential to preserve higher values and is narrowly tailored to serve that interest"—to justify closure. It is worth noting that in both *Press-Enterprise I* and *Press-Enterprise II* the media sought access to transcripts of the proceedings. The Court decided that there was a right to attend the proceedings themselves, and, by extension, that there is a right of access to the records of open proceedings.

An additional access case is worth noting, though it deals with access to documents rather than access to a proceeding and deals with a civil rather than a criminal trial. In Seattle Times Co. v. Rhinehart, 467 U.S. 20 (1984), plaintiff

Rhinehart and a religious group he headed sued two newspapers for libel. During discovery in the libel case, the newspapers sought information about the religious group's membership and fundraising. The trial court ordered the plaintiffs to produce the information but issued a protective order to prevent the newspapers from publishing it or otherwise disclosing it. The newspapers claimed that the protective order violated their First Amendment right to disseminate the information. The Supreme Court held, however, that "where, as in this case, a protective order is entered upon a showing of good cause as required by Rule 26(c) [of the Federal Rules of Civil Procedure], is limited to the context of pretrial civil discovery, and does not restrict the dissemination of the information if gained from other sources, it does not offend the First Amendment." Would a contrary result have given media litigants an unfair advantage in civil litigation? Why did the Court believe that the protective order here was "not the kind of classic prior restraint that requires exacting First Amendment scrutiny"?

Lower courts have not always faithfully applied the stringent constitutional standards that govern courtroom closure. In Presley v. Georgia, 558 U.S. 209 (2010), a defendant fought all the way to the Supreme Court to have his right to a public trial upheld in a per curiam decision, even though the Supreme Court had clearly recognized the right for a quarter of a century. In *Presley*, a trial court ordered courtroom closure during voir dire of prospective jurors, explaining that "it's up to the individual judge to decide what's comfortable." The judge did not articulate any "overriding interest" in closure beyond a generic risk that the defendant's uncle, who wished to be present, might sit near prospective jurors; nor did the judge consider alternatives to closure. Nonetheless, the Georgia Court of Appeals and the Georgia Supreme Court upheld closure. The Georgia Supreme Court found that "the trial court certainly had an overriding interest in ensuring that potential jurors heard no inherently prejudicial remarks from observers during voir dire," and held that the trial court was not required *sua sponte* to consider alternatives to closure, such as holding the voir dire in a bigger courtroom so that the public and prospective jurors need not be seated together. The U.S. Supreme Court reversed, holding that a criminal defendant's "Sixth Amendment right to a public trial extends to the voir dire of prospective jurors." The Court reminded lower courts that the high burden of justifying closure lies with the trial court and not with the criminal defendant: "Trial courts are obligated to take every reasonable measure to accommodate public attendance at criminal trials." Given that few litigants have the persistence or resources to appeal their cases all the way to the U.S. Supreme Court, what signal does *Presley* send to a trial judge who wishes to order closure of a criminal proceeding? See Daniel Levitas, Scaling Waller: How Courts Have Eroded the Sixth Amendment Public Trial Right, 59 Emory L.J. 493 (2009) (observing that appellate courts have upheld courtroom closures even when trial courts have not applied the appropriate constitutional standards to justify closure nor made the requisite findings prior to closure).

THEORY-APPLIED PROBLEM—CLOSURE TO PROTECT CHILDREN

Assume that a tabloid newspaper publishes a story alleging that the minor child of a celebrity suffers from severe depression and is addicted to drugs. Suit is brought on the child's behalf for the tort of defamation, and the case proceeds to trial. At trial, the child's attorney requests the trial judge to close the courtroom to outside observers, contending that the trial is likely to involve testimony about the minor child's psychological and physical health and that closure is essential to protect the child's privacy. The attorney for the tabloid does not object, and the trial judge states on the record: "Closure of the courtroom is essential to protect the minor child's privacy and to prevent him from being traumatized by subsequent publication of matters of a private nature to the public at large." Is the closure order likely to be constitutional? Why or why not?

3. Access to Government Institutions

In *Richmond Newspapers* and its progeny, the Supreme Court struggled to reach an accommodation between a First Amendment right of access to criminal trials and the Sixth Amendment rights of criminal defendants. A different accommodation must be struck in cases in which the press has asserted a right of access to governmental institutions such as prisons. Namely, the First Amendment interests must be balanced against the government's need to administer prisons to protect the safety and privacy of inmates, maintain order and discipline, and protect the security of the public.

The first cases dealing with prison access were Pell v. Procunier, 417 U.S. 817 (1974), and Saxbe v. Washington Post Co., 417 U.S. 843 (1974). *Pell* and *Saxbe* involved a ban on media interviews with specific inmates in the California prisons and in federal prisons respectively. Justice Stewart wrote for the Court in both cases, upholding the ban. Justice Stewart viewed the case as governed by the principle that the First Amendment does not "impose[] upon government the affirmative duty to make available to journalists sources of information not available to members of the public generally." The prison regulation at issue treated the press no worse than members of the general public, and it did not foreclose other avenues of gaining information about the prison system. Reporters could tour the prisons and "speak about any subject to any inmates whom they might encounter." They could also interview randomly selected inmates. Significantly, Justice Stewart noted that the ban was "not part of an attempt by the State to conceal the conditions of its prisons or to frustrate the press investigation and reporting of those conditions." Thus, the ban on individual interviews was upheld.

Four Justices dissented in *Pell* and *Saxbe*. Justice Powell, joined by Justices Brennan and Marshall, wrote in *Saxbe* that he could not "follow the Court in concluding that *any* government restriction on press access to information, so long as it is nondiscriminatory, falls outside the purview of First Amendment concern. . . . At some point official restraints on access to news sources, even though not directed solely at the press, may so undermine the function of the First Amendment that it is both appropriate and necessary to require the Government to justify such regulations in terms more compelling than discretionary authority and administrative convenience." Justice Douglas also dissented. *Pell* and *Saxbe* were 5-4 decisions. Would they have come out differently if the government had placed extensive, rather than limited, restrictions on press and public access to prisons? The case below addresses that question. Note that only seven Justices took part in the decision.

HOUCHINS v. KQED, INC.

438 U.S. 1 (1978)

Mr. Chief Justice BURGER announced the judgment of the Court and delivered an opinion, in which Mr. Justice WHITE and Mr. Justice REHNQUIST joined.

The question presented is whether the news media have a constitutional right of access to a county jail, over and above that of other persons, to interview inmates and make sound recordings, films, and photographs for publication and broadcasting by newspapers, radio, and television.

Petitioner Houchins, as Sheriff of Alameda County, Cal., controls all access to the Alameda County Jail at Santa Rita. Respondent KQED operates licensed television and radio broadcasting stations which have frequently reported newsworthy events relating to penal institutions in the San Francisco Bay Area. On March 31, 1975, KQED reported the suicide of a prisoner in the Greystone portion of the Santa Rita jail. The report included a statement by a psychiatrist that the conditions at the Greystone facility were responsible for the illnesses of his patient-prisoners there, and a statement from petitioner denying that prison conditions were responsible for the prisoners' illnesses.

KQED requested permission to inspect and take pictures within the Greystone facility. After permission was refused, KQED and the Alameda and Oakland branches of the National Association for the Advancement of Colored People (NAACP) filed suit under 42 U.S.C. § 1983. [They sought an injunction to prevent the sheriff from violating their First Amendment rights by excluding them. Shortly thereafter, the sheriff instituted a new prison tour program open to the public and the press.]

Each tour was limited to 25 persons and permitted only limited access to the jail. The tours did not include the disciplinary cells or the portions of the jail known as "Little Greystone," the scene of alleged rapes, beatings, and adverse physical conditions. Photographs of some parts of the jail were made available, but no cameras or tape recorders were allowed on the tours. Those on the tours were not permitted to interview inmates, and inmates were generally removed from view.

. . . [Respondents continued to seek wider access. In response to their request for a preliminary injunction, the sheriff contended] that unregulated access by the media would infringe inmate privacy, and tend to create "jail celebrities," who in turn tend to generate internal problems and undermine jail security. He also contended that unscheduled media tours would disrupt jail operations.

. . . After considering the testimony, affidavits, and documentary evidence presented by the parties, the District Court preliminarily enjoined petitioner from denying KQED news personnel and "responsible representatives" of the news media access to the Santa Rita facilities, including Greystone, "at reasonable times and hours" and "from preventing KQED news personnel and responsible representatives of the news media from utilizing photographic and sound equipment or from utilizing inmate interviews in providing full and accurate coverage of the Santa Rita facilities."

The District Court rejected petitioner's contention that the media policy then in effect was necessary to protect inmate privacy or minimize security and administrative problems. It found that the testimony of officials involved with other jails indicated that a "more flexible press policy at Santa Rita [was] both desirable and attainable." [The Court of Appeals affirmed.]

II

Notwithstanding our holding in *Pell v. Procunier*, respondents assert that the right recognized by the Court of Appeals flows logically from our decisions construing the First Amendment. They argue that there is a constitutionally guaranteed right to gather news under *Pell v. Procunier* and *Branzburg v. Hayes*, 408 U.S. 665, 681, 707 (1972). From the right to gather news and the right to receive information, they argue for an implied special right of access to government-controlled sources of information. This right, they contend, compels access as a *constitutional* matter. . . . Respondents contend that public access to penal institutions is necessary to prevent officials from concealing prison conditions from the voters and impairing the public's right to discuss and criticize the prison system and its administration.

III

We can agree with many of the respondents' generalized assertions; conditions in jails and prisons are clearly matters "of great public importance." *Pell v. Procunier.* Penal facilities are public institutions which require large amounts of public funds, and their mission is crucial in our criminal justice system. Each person placed in prison becomes, in effect, a ward of the state for whom society assumes broad responsibility. It is equally true that with greater information, the public can more intelligently form opinions about prison conditions. Beyond question, the role of the media is important; acting as the "eyes and ears" of the public, they can be a powerful and constructive force, contributing to remedial action in the conduct of public business. They have served that function since the beginning of the Republic, but like all other components of our society media representatives are subject to limits.

The media are not a substitute for or an adjunct of government and, like the courts, they are "ill equipped" to deal with problems of prison administration. We must not confuse the role of the media with that of government; each has special, crucial functions, each complementing—and sometimes conflicting with—the other.

The public importance of conditions in penal facilities and the media's role of providing information afford no basis for reading into the Constitution a right of the public or the media to enter these institutions, with camera equipment, and take moving and still pictures of inmates for broadcast purposes. This Court has never intimated a First Amendment guarantee of a right of access to all sources of information within government control. Nor does the rationale of the decisions upon which respondents rely lead to the implication of such a right.

Grosjean v. American Press Co., supra, and *Mills v. Alabama, supra*, emphasized the importance of informed public opinion and the traditional role of a free press as a source of public information. But an analysis of those cases reveals that the Court was concerned with the freedom of the media to *communicate* information once it is obtained; neither case intimated that the Constitution *compels* the government to provide the media with information or access to it on demand. . . .

Branzburg v. Hayes offers even less support for the respondents' position. Its observation, in dictum, that "news gathering is not without its First Amendment protections," in no sense implied a constitutional right of access to news sources. That observation must be read in context; it was in response to the contention that forcing a reporter to disclose to a grand jury information received in confidence would violate the First Amendment by deterring news sources from communicating information. There is an undoubted right to gather news "from any source by means within the law," but that affords no basis for the claim that the First Amendment compels others—private persons or governments—to supply information.

. . . . The right to *receive* ideas and information is not the issue in this case. The issue is a claimed special privilege of access which the Court rejected in *Pell* and *Saxbe*, a right which is not essential to guarantee the freedom to communicate or publish.

IV

The respondents' argument is flawed, not only because it lacks precedential support and is contrary to statements in this Court's opinions, but also because it invites the Court to involve itself in what is clearly a legislative task which the Constitution has left to the political processes. Whether the government should open penal institutions in the manner sought by respondents is a question of policy which a legislative body might appropriately resolve one way or the other.

A number of alternatives are available to prevent problems in penal facilities from escaping public attention. . . . Citizen task forces and prison visitation committees continue to play an important role in keeping the public informed on deficiencies of prison systems and need for reforms. Grand juries, with the potent subpoena power— not available to the media—traditionally concern themselves with conditions in public institutions; a prosecutor or judge may initiate similar inquiries, and the legislative power embraces an arsenal of weapons for inquiry relating to tax-supported institutions. In each case, these public bodies are generally compelled to publish their findings and, if they default, the power of the media is always available to generate public pressure for disclosure. But the choice as to the most effective and appropriate method is a policy decision to be resolved by legislative decision. We must not confuse what is "good," "desirable," or "expedient" with what is constitutionally commanded by the First Amendment. To do so is to trivialize constitutional adjudication.

Unarticulated but implicit in the assertion that media access to the jail is essential for informed public debate on jail conditions is the assumption that media personnel are the best qualified persons for the task of discovering malfeasance in public institutions. But that assumption finds no support in the decisions of this Court or the First Amendment. . . .

There is no discernible basis for a constitutional duty to disclose, or for standards governing disclosure of or access to information. Because the Constitution affords no guidelines, absent statutory standards, hundreds of judges would, under the Court of Appeals' approach, be at large to fashion ad hoc standards, in individual cases, according to their own ideas of what seems "desirable" or "expedient." We, therefore, reject the Court of Appeals' conclusory assertion that the public and the media have a First Amendment right to government information regarding the conditions of jails and their inmates and presumably all other public facilities such as hospitals and mental institutions.

. . . Petitioner cannot prevent respondents from learning about jail conditions in a variety of ways, albeit not as conveniently as they might prefer. Respondents have a First Amendment right to receive letters from inmates criticizing jail officials and reporting on conditions. Respondents are free to interview those who render the legal assistance to which inmates are entitled. They are also free to seek out former inmates, visitors to the prison, public officials, and institutional personnel, as they sought out the complaining psychiatrist here.

Moreover, California statutes currently provide for a prison Board of Corrections that has the authority to inspect jails and prisons and *must* provide a public report at regular intervals. Health inspectors are required to inspect prisons and provide reports to a number of officials, including the State Attorney General and the Board of Corrections. Fire officials are also required to inspect prisons. Following the reports of the suicide at the jail involved here, the County Board of Supervisors called for a report from the County Administrator; held a public hearing on the report, which was open to the media; and called for further reports when the initial report failed to describe the conditions in the cells in the Greystone portion of the jail.

Neither the First Amendment nor the Fourteenth Amendment mandates a right of access to government information or sources of information within the government's control. Under our holdings in *Pell v. Procunier*, and *Saxbe v. Washington Post Co.*, until the political branches decree otherwise, as they are free to do, the media have no special right of access to the Alameda County Jail different from or greater than that accorded the public generally. [Reversed and remanded.]

Mr. Justice STEWART, concurring in the judgment.

. . . The First and Fourteenth Amendments do not guarantee the public a right of access to information generated or controlled by government, nor do they guarantee the press any basic right of access superior to that of the public generally. The Constitution does no more than assure the public and the press equal access once government has opened its doors. Accordingly, I agree substantially with what the opinion of The Chief Justice has to say on that score.

We part company, however, in applying these abstractions to the facts of this case. Whereas he appears to view "equal access" as meaning access that is identical in all respects, I believe that the concept of equal access must be accorded more flexibility in order to accommodate the practical distinctions between the press and the general public.

When on assignment, a journalist does not tour a jail simply for his own edification. He is there to gather information to be passed on to others, and his mission is protected by the Constitution for very specific reasons. . . . Our society depends heavily on the press for that enlightenment. . . .

That the First Amendment speaks separately of freedom of speech and freedom of the press is no constitutional accident, but an acknowledgment of the critical role played by the press in American society. The Constitution requires sensitivity to that role, and to the special needs of the press in performing it effectively. A person touring Santa Rita jail can grasp its reality with his own eyes and ears. But if a television reporter is to convey the jail's sights and sounds to those who cannot personally visit the place, he must use cameras and sound equipment. In short, terms of access that are reasonably imposed on individual members of the public may, if they impede effective reporting without sufficient justification, be unreasonable as applied to journalists who are there to convey to the general public what the visitors see.

. . . I agree that the judgment of the Court of Appeals affirming the District Court's order must be reversed [as overbroad based on the available record]. But I would not foreclose the possibility of further relief for KQED on remand. In my view, the availability and scope of future permanent injunctive relief must depend upon the extent of access then permitted the public, and the decree must be framed to accommodate equitably the constitutional role of the press and the institutional requirements of the jail.

Mr. Justice STEVENS, with whom Mr. Justice BRENNAN and Mr. Justice POWELL join, dissenting.

. . . In this case, the record demonstrates that both the public and the press had been consistently denied any access to the inner portions of the Santa Rita jail, that there had been excessive censorship of inmate correspondence, and that there was no valid justification for these broad restraints on the flow of information. . . . An official prison policy of concealing such knowledge from the public by arbitrarily cutting off the flow of information at its source abridges the freedom of speech and of the press protected by the First and Fourteenth Amendments to the Constitution.

NOTES AND QUESTIONS

1. *Reconciling* Richmond Newspapers. Is this decision consistent with *Richmond Newspapers*? Could the test applied in that case be applied here to reach the same result?

2. *Justice Stewart's Press Clause.* What is the significance of Justice Stewart's decision? Recall that only seven Justices participated in deciding this case. On what points do Justice Stewart and the plurality opinion agree? Is an independent right of access arising under the Press Clause necessary to the decision of these cases?

3. *Choosing the relevant precedent to resolve other access issues.* Do the media have a First Amendment right of access to battlefields? Which is the relevant precedent, *Richmond Newspapers* and the Court's other courtroom access precedents, or *Houchins*? See Flynt v. Rumsfeld, 355 F.3d 697 (D.C. Cir. 2004) (refusing to apply *Richmond Newspapers* to a claim asserting First Amendment right of access by the media to accompany U.S. troops into combat). Access issues can crop up in more surprising venues. In Leigh v. Salazar, 668 F.3d 1126 (9th Cir. 2012), a panel of the U.S. Court of Appeals for the Ninth Circuit reversed and remanded for reconsideration a trial court's denial of a preliminary injunction to a photojournalist seeking unrestricted access to a "horse gather," or roundup, of wild horses by the Bureau of Land Management. Roundups are statutorily authorized to remedy overpopulation. During a roundup, the agency allowed daily public viewings of the gathered horses. A photojournalist for Horseback magazine observed the gathered horses, but she was restricted to "designated viewing areas" and required to sit down and stay quiet. The Ninth Circuit held that the relevant precedent for judging her claim of access were the Supreme Court's *courtroom* access cases; therefore, it directed the lower court to consider on remand whether there was a historical tradition of access to the horse gathers and whether access would play a positive role in the functioning of the gathers. If these test were met, the government could still overcome the access right by establishing an "overriding interest" served by restrictions "narrowly tailored" to serve the interest.

C. PRIOR RESTRAINTS

1. *The Presumption of Unconstitutionality*

The classic prior restraint is a licensing law—a law that forbids a person from publishing his ideas without first receiving the permission, or "license," of a government official. The first licensing laws were a response to the spread of printing presses in the late fifteenth century. As this medium of mass communication spread, so did government attempts to control it.

In England, the government initially prohibited publishers from printing works without first receiving a license from government officials, who had the power to censor or to ban works at will. However, English licensing laws eventually came to be seen as a threat to press freedom, and they were not renewed in England after 1693. By the eighteenth century, William Blackstone's famous treatise on the English common law articulated the objection to licensing as follows:

> The liberty of the press is indeed essential to the nature of a free state; but this consists in laying no previous restraints on publications, and not in freedom from censure for criminal matter when published. Every freeman has an undoubted right to lay what sentiments he pleases before the public; to forbid this is to destroy the freedom of the press; but if he publishes what is improper, mischievous or illegal, he must take the consequences of his own temerity.

4 William Blackstone, Commentaries *151, *152 (1769).

The common law prohibition on prior restraints also was in effect in the American colonies in the eighteenth century, providing a backdrop to the adoption of the First Amendment in 1791. Indeed, the first major controversy over the meaning of the First Amendment was not about whether it prohibited prior restraints; rather, it was over whether it prohibited prior restraints as well as seditious libel—that is, criminal punishment of citizens who criticize the government.

The first controversy over the meaning of the First Amendment began just seven years after its adoption, when the Federalist Party enacted the Sedition Act of 1798. The Sedition Act was the Federalists' attempt to silence Republican newspapers and prevent Republicans from taking control of Congress and the Presidency in the election of 1800. The Sedition Act made it a crime to publish false, malicious, or scandalous items about the federal government, Congress, or the President. Conspicuously, the Sedition Act did not criminalize criticism of then-Vice President Thomas Jefferson, a Republican. Moreover, the Federalists hedged their bets against a Republican sweep of the elections of 1800 by making the Sedition Act expire in 1801. Although the Sedition Act was enforced vigorously against Republican newspapers, virtually silencing them, Thomas Jefferson won the presidency and his party took control of Congress. The Sedition Act expired and was not renewed.

Passage of the Sedition Act triggered a national debate on the meaning of press freedom. As leaders of this debate, both James Madison and Thomas Jefferson wrote extended discourses on press freedom in which they argued that the First Amendment deprived the federal government of power to punish seditious libel. Whether or not their expansive conceptions of the First Amendment were shared by a majority of Framers, they were a tremendous influence on the shape of subsequent First Amendment doctrine. (Virginia adopted Madison's arguments as "The Virginia

Report of 1799-80," and Kentucky adopted Jefferson's as "The Kentucky Resolutions of 1798." Both are excerpted in Leonard Levy, *Freedom of the Press from Zenger to Jefferson* (Leonard Levy ed., 1966).)

The Supreme Court has never questioned that the First Amendment forbids prior restraints. But what is a prior restraint? Blackstone had used the term to mean a group of government officials with authority to censor or ban works prior to publication. But with the expansion of equity jurisdiction, judicial restraints on publication in the form of injunctions became more common. The Supreme Court was forced to decide whether such injunctions—often called gag orders—were also "prior restraints" forbidden by the First Amendment.

Near v. Minnesota, 283 U.S. 697 (1931), is sometimes called the Supreme Court's first great press case, and it involved just such a judicial restraint on publication. *Near v. Minnesota* was a 5-4 decision. As you read it, try to imagine what First Amendment jurisprudence would look like today if it had gone the other way.

NEAR v. MINNESOTA

283 U.S. 697 (1931)

[An unusual Minnesota law authorized abatement, as a public nuisance, of a "malicious, scandalous and defamatory newspaper, or other periodical." A Minnesota prosecutor sought abatement of The Saturday Press after it published several stories alleging "that a Jewish gangster was in control of gambling, bootlegging and racketeering in Minneapolis" with the complicity of law enforcement. The Minnesota state court concluded that The Saturday Press had "made serious accusations against the public officials named. . . ." Although the abatement statute provided a defense "that the truth was published with good motives and for justifiable ends," the publisher of The Saturday Press did not assert this defense. Instead, he asserted that the abatement statute was unconstitutional. The Minnesota court nonetheless "abated" The Saturday Press as a public nuisance and entered a permanent injunction forbidding the defendants from circulating "any publication whatsoever which is a malicious, scandalous or defamatory newspaper." The Minnesota Supreme Court affirmed, concluding that the injunction did not prevent defendants "from operating a newspaper in harmony with the public welfare, to which all must yield."]

Mr. Chief Justice HUGHES delivered the opinion of the Court.

. . . If we cut through mere details of procedure, the operation and effect of the statute in substance is that public authorities may bring the owner or publisher of a newspaper or periodical before a judge upon a charge of conducting a business of publishing scandalous and defamatory matter—in particular that the matter consists of charges against public officers of official dereliction—and, unless the owner or publisher is able and disposed to bring competent evidence to satisfy the judge that the charges are true and are published with good motives and for justifiable ends, his newspaper or periodical is suppressed and further publication is made punishable as a contempt. This is of the essence of censorship.

The question is whether a statute authorizing such proceedings in restraint of publication is consistent with the conception of the liberty of the press as historically conceived and guaranteed. In determining the extent of the constitutional protection, it has been generally, if not universally, considered that it is the chief purpose of the guaranty to prevent previous restraints upon publication. The struggle in England, directed against the legislative power of the licenser, resulted in renunciation of the censorship of the press. The liberty deemed to be established was thus described by Blackstone: "The liberty of the press is indeed essential to the nature of a free state; but this consists in laying no previous restraints upon publications, and not in freedom from censure for criminal matter when published. . . ." 4 Bl. Com. 151, 152. . . . The distinction was early pointed out between the extent of the freedom with respect to censorship under our constitutional system and that enjoyed in England. Here, as Madison said, "the great and essential rights of the people are secured against legislative as well as against executive ambition. They are secured, not by laws paramount to prerogative, but by constitutions paramount to laws. This security of the freedom of the press requires that it should be exempt not only from previous restraint by the Executive, as in Great Britain, but from legislative restraint also." Report on the Virginia Resolutions, Madison's Works, vol. IV, p. 543. . . .

The criticism upon Blackstone's statement has not been because immunity from previous restraint upon publication has not been regarded as deserving of special emphasis, but chiefly because that immunity cannot be deemed to exhaust the conception of the liberty guaranteed by State and Federal Constitutions. . . . [I]t is recognized that punishment for the abuse of the liberty accorded to the press is essential to the protection of the public, and that the common-law rules that subject the libeler to responsibility for the public offense, as well as for the private injury, are not abolished by the protection extended in our Constitutions. The law of criminal libel rests upon that secure foundation. . . . For whatever wrong the appellant has committed or may commit, by his publications, the state appropriately affords both public and private redress by its libel laws. As has been noted, the statute in question does not deal with punishments; it provides for no punishment, except in case of contempt for violation of the court's order, but for suppression and injunction—that is, for restraint upon publication.

The objection has also been made that the principle as to immunity from previous restraint is stated too broadly, if every such restraint is deemed to be prohibited. That is undoubtedly true; the protection even as to previous restraint is not absolutely unlimited. But the limitation has been recognized only in exceptional cases. "When a nation is at war many things that might be said in time of peace are such a hindrance to its effort that their utterance will not be endured so long as men fight and that no Court could regard them as protected by any constitutional right." Schenck v. United States, 249 U. S. 47, 52. No one would question but that a government might prevent actual obstruction to its recruiting service or the publication of the sailing dates of transports or the number and location of troops. On similar grounds, the primary requirements of decency may be enforced against obscene publications. The security of the community life may be protected against incitements to acts of violence and the overthrow by force of orderly government. The constitutional guaranty of free speech does not "protect a man from an injunction against uttering words that may have all the effect of force." Gompers v. Buck's Stove & Range Co., 221 U.S. 418. . . . These limitations are not applicable here. Nor are we now concerned with questions as to the extent of authority to prevent publications in order to protect private rights according to the principles governing the exercise of the jurisdiction of courts of equity.

. . . The fact that for approximately one hundred and fifty years there has been almost an entire absence of attempts to impose previous restraints upon publications relating to the malfeasance of public officers is significant of the deep-seated conviction that such restraints would violate constitutional right. Public officers, whose character and conduct remain open to debate and free discussion in the press, find their remedies for false accusations in actions under libel laws providing for redress and punishment, and not in proceedings to restrain the publication of newspapers and periodicals. The general principle that the constitutional guaranty of the liberty of the press gives immunity from previous restraints has been approved in many decisions under the provisions of state constitutions.

The importance of this immunity has not lessened. While reckless assaults upon public men, and efforts to bring obloquy upon those who are endeavoring faithfully to discharge official duties, exert a baleful influence and deserve the severest condemnation in public opinion, it cannot be said that this abuse is greater, and it is believed to be less, than that which characterized the period in which our institutions took shape. Meanwhile, the administration of government has become more complex, the opportunities for malfeasance and corruption have multiplied, crime has grown to most serious proportions, and the danger of its protection by unfaithful officials and of the impairment of the fundamental security of life and property by criminal alliances and official neglect, emphasizes the primary need of a vigilant and courageous press, especially in great cities. The fact that the liberty of the press may be abused by miscreant purveyors of scandal does not make any the less necessary the immunity of the press from previous restraint in dealing with official misconduct. Subsequent punishment for such abuses as may exist is the appropriate remedy, consistent with constitutional privilege.

In attempted justification of the statute, it is said that it deals not with publication per se, but with the "business" of publishing defamation. If, however, the publisher has a constitutional right to publish, without previous restraint, an edition of his newspaper charging official derelictions, it cannot be denied that he may publish subsequent editions for the same purpose. He does not lose his right by exercising it. If his right exists, it may be exercised in publishing nine editions, as in this case, as well as in one edition. If previous restraint is permissible, it may be imposed at once; indeed, the wrong may be as serious in one publication as in several. Characterizing the publication as a business, and the business as a nuisance, does not permit an invasion of the constitutional immunity against restraint. . . .

. . . The statute in question cannot be justified by reason of the fact that the publisher is permitted to show, before injunction issues, that the matter published is true and is published with good motives and for justifiable ends. If such a statute, authorizing suppression and injunction on such a basis, is constitutionally valid, it would be equally permissible for the Legislature to provide that at any time the publisher of any newspaper could be brought before a court, or even an administrative officer (as the constitutional protection may not be regarded as resting on mere procedural details), and required to produce proof of the truth of his publication, or of what he intended to publish and of his motives, or stand enjoined. If this can be done, the Legislature may provide machinery for determining in the complete exercise of its discretion what are justifiable ends and restrain publication accordingly. And it would be but a step to a complete system of censorship. . . .

Justice BUTLER, dissenting[,with whom Justices VAN DEVANTER, REYNOLDS, and SUTHERLAND concur].

. . . The Minnesota statute does not operate as a previous restraint on publication within the proper meaning of that phrase. It does not authorize administrative control in advance such as was formerly exercised by the licensers and censors, but prescribes a remedy to be enforced by a suit in equity. In this case there was previous publication made in the course of the business of regularly producing malicious, scandalous, and defamatory periodicals. The business and publications unquestionably constitute an abuse of the right of free press. The statute denounces the things done as a nuisance on the ground, as stated by the state Supreme Court, that they threaten morals, peace, and good order. There is no question of the power of the state to denounce such transgressions. The restraint authorized is only in respect of continuing to do what has been duly adjudged to constitute a nuisance. . . . There is nothing in the statute purporting to prohibit publications that have not been adjudged to constitute a nuisance. It is fanciful to suggest similarity between the granting or enforcement of the decree authorized by this statute to prevent further publication of malicious, scandalous, and defamatory articles and the previous restraint upon the press by licensers as referred to by Blackstone and described in the history of the times to which he alludes. . . .

NOTES AND QUESTIONS

1. *Defining prior restraint.* Why are prior restraints considered worse than subsequent punishment of speech? What is the essence of a prior restraint? The Supreme Court rejected an attempt to characterize a restriction on speech as a prior restraint in Alexander v. United States, 509 U.S. 544 (1993). Alexander was convicted of engaging in the business of selling obscene material and of transporting four obscene magazines and three obscene videos in interstate commerce. This formed the basis for a forfeiture action under the Racketeer Influenced and Corrupt Organizations Act (RICO), which allowed the government to seize Alexander's 31 businesses, confiscate $9 million in profits, and destroy millions of dollars' worth of books and videos found in Alexander's stores. Although the Supreme Court remanded the case for determination whether the forfeiture was an "excessive fine" under the Eighth Amendment, the Court rejected the argument that the forfeiture operated as a prior restraint. The Court instead found the forfeiture to be a valid subsequent punishment akin to a prison term and fine. Chief Justice Rehnquist, writing for the Court, explained:

> Petitioner's proposed definition of the term "prior restraint" would undermine the time-honored distinction barring speech in the future and penalizing past speech. . . . Because we have interpreted the First Amendment as providing greater protection from prior restraints than from subsequent punishments, it is important for us to delineate with some precision the defining characteristics of a prior restraint. To hold that the forfeiture order in this case constituted a prior restraint would have the opposite effect: it would blur the line separating prior restraints from subsequent punishments to such a degree that it would be impossible to determine with any certainty whether a particular measure is a prior restraint or not.

Despite Justice's Rehnquist's admonition about defining prior restraints with precision, his opinion for the Court provided no more guidance than what is given in the quoted paragraph. Justice Kennedy, joined by Justices Blackmun and Stevens, dissented in *Alexander*, contending that the forfeiture scheme, like the abatement statute in *Near*, had the "operation and effect" of a prior restraint and raised the same dangers of "state censorship and the unacceptable chilling of protected speech." For further reading regarding prior restraints, see Martin Redish, *The Proper Role of the Prior Restraint Doctrine in First Amendment Theory*, 70 Va. L. Rev. 53 (1984); Jeffrey A. Smith, *Prior Restraint: Original Intentions and Modern Interpretations*, 28 Wm. & Mary L. Rev. 439 (1987).

2. *The collateral bar.* Most jurisdictions have a "collateral bar" rule, which prohibits a person who violates an injunction from challenging its constitutionality. The purpose of the collateral bar rule is to ensure that individuals comply with judicial orders unless they are invalidated through judicial process. Failure to comply with an injunction may result in a conviction of criminal contempt. The collateral bar rule is the reason that the media are not free to ignore injunctions against publication, even injunctions that are almost certainly unconstitutional. The collateral bar rule may have serious consequences for free speech: an injunction may delay publication long enough so that the information loses its value, or it may prevent publication by one source even though another source is free to publish.

3. *Prior restraints versus subsequent punishments.* Professor John Jeffries contends that "there is only one respect in which injunctions plausibly can be claimed to have a First Amendment impact significantly greater than the threat of subsequent punishment. That argument is based on the traditional rule that the legality of an injunction may not be challenged by disobeying its terms. In its most uncompromising form, the traditional approach would declare that the invalidity or even unconstitutionality of a court order would be no defense in a contempt proceeding based on violation of that order." *Rethinking Prior Restraints*, 92 Yale L.J. 409, 426-433 (1983). Jeffries argues, however, that "a properly limited collateral bar rule would not be destructive of our system of freedom of expression." Courts have in fact carefully confined the collateral bar rule in cases involving prior restraints on expression, as discussed below.

4. *The transparently invalid exception to the collateral bar.* First Amendment concerns have led some courts to develop an exception to the collateral bar rule for "transparently invalid" injunctions. Most notable is In re Providence Journal Co., 820 F.2d 1354 (1st Cir. 1987) (en banc). A newspaper, the Providence Journal, obtained FBI surveillance logs of alleged mobster Raymond Patriarca, who had recently died. At the request of Patriarca's son, a trial judge temporarily enjoined publication pending a hearing to determine whether the surveillance information had been wrongfully released under the Freedom of Information Act. Despite the temporary restraining order, the Providence Journal published information from the logs. The trial judge then appointed a special prosecutor to press criminal contempt against the newspaper and its editor. They were convicted. The judge suspended an 18-month jail sentence on condition that the editor perform 200 hours of community service. The newspaper was fined $100,000. On appeal, a panel of First Circuit judges reversed. The panel relied on dicta in Walker v. City of Birmingham, 388 U.S. 307 (1967), which had affirmed contempt convictions against Martin Luther King, Jr. and others for violating an injunction against parading without a permit; however, *Walker* had acknowledged that defendants may ignore a "transparently invalid" injunction. The panel held that the injunction against the Providence Journal was transparently invalid because there was no indication that the heavy presumption

of unconstitutionality could be overcome, it was not authorized by statute, and it was not likely to be effective since the FBI had distributed the same information to others. The case was reheard en banc by the First Circuit, which did not vacate the panel's opinion, but which did modify it, stating that "finer tuning is available to minimize the disharmony between respect for court orders and respect for free speech." Thus, the court stated: "It is not asking much, beyond some additional expense and time, to require a publisher, even when it thinks it is the subject of a transparently unconstitutional order of a prior restraint, to make a good-faith effort to seek emergency relief from the appellate court. If timely access to the appellate court is not available or if timely decision is not forthcoming, the publisher may then proceed to publish and challenge the constitutionality of the order in contempt proceedings." What advice would you give to a publisher who had been enjoined by a Rhode Island court in light of this decision? What if the appellate court grants review, but not expedited review? *See also* United States v. Dickinson, 465 F.2d 496 (5th Cir. 1972) ("[I]n the absence of strong indications that the appellate process is being deliberately stalled—certainly not so in this record—violation with impunity does not occur simply because immediate decision is not forthcoming, even though the communication enjoined is 'news.'"); Procter & Gamble Co. v. Bankers Trust Co., 78 F.3d 219 (6th Cir. 1996) (determining that a permanent injunction on publication was "patently invalid").

2.   *The National Security Exception*

The first test of whether a prior restraint could be justified in the name of national security came in the so-called "Pentagon Papers" case, excerpted below. In the midst of the Vietnam War, the New York Times obtained a classified government document detailing U.S. involvement in Vietnam. The document consisted of 47 volumes (the "Pentagon Papers"), many of which gave the historical backdrop to U.S. involvement. After several months of studying the volumes, the New York Times published the first in a planned series of articles about the Pentagon Papers. The Justice Department sought an injunction. A New York district judge temporarily enjoined publication, and the Second Circuit granted the injunction. In the meanwhile, the Washington Post began publishing material from the Pentagon Papers. The Justice Department again asked for an injunction, but the district judge and the Court of Appeals for the District of Columbia Circuit denied the motion. The Supreme Court issued stays to prevent either newspaper from publishing, heard oral argument, and issued the following decision five days later. Although the Court's opinion is per curiam, every Justice wrote a separate opinion.

NEW YORK TIMES CO. v. UNITED STATES
("Pentagon Papers" Case)
403 U.S. 713 (1971)

PER CURIAM.

We granted certiorari in these cases in which the United States seeks to enjoin the New York Times and the Washington Post from publishing the contents of a classified study entitled "History of U.S. Decision-Making Process on Viet Nam Policy."

"Any system of prior restraints of expression comes to this Court bearing a heavy presumption against its constitutional validity." Bantam Books, Inc. v. Sullivan, 372 U.S. 58, 70 (1963); see also Near v. Minnesota ex rel. Olson, 283 U.S. 697 (1931). The Government "thus carries a heavy burden of showing justification for the imposition of such a restraint." . . . . The District Court for the Southern District of New York in the New York Times case, and the District Court for the District of Columbia and the Court of Appeals for the District of Columbia Circuit in the Washington Post case held that the Government had not met that burden. We agree.

The judgment of the Court of Appeals for the District of Columbia Circuit is therefore affirmed. The order of the Court of Appeals for the Second Circuit is reversed, and the case is remanded with directions to enter a judgment affirming the judgment of the District Court for the Southern District of New York. The stays entered June 25, 1971, by the Court are vacated. The judgments shall issue forthwith.

NOTES AND QUESTIONS

1. *The Pentagon Papers and executive power.* As noted above, every member of the Court wrote a separate opinion in the Pentagon Papers case. Three justices would have barred the newspapers from further publication. Justice John Marshall Harlan, writing for himself, Chief Justice Warren Burger, and Justice Harry Blackmun, contended that federal courts owe deference to the executive branch in foreign affairs and that review should be limited to determining whether the dispute was with the "proper compass of the President's foreign relations power." Was the Court correct in "second-guessing" the executive branch's determination that disclosure of the Pentagon Papers could "irreparably impair national security?" Does the First Amendment demand that the Court do so?

2. *The importance of statutory authorization.* Several of the Justices wrote that they might have been willing to issue an injunction if statutory authorization were present. Why does statutory authorization matter? In his 1992 book, *Free Speech in an Open Society*, Professor Rodney Smolla explains: "The exercise of a prior restraint is such an anathema in the American First Amendment tradition that only the combined authority of the legislative and executive branch, after review by the judiciary, should be enough to sustain it."

3. *Permissible prior restraints.* Injunctions are authorized by section 502 of the Copyright Act, and are commonly granted as a remedy in copyright infringement cases. Injunctions are also commonly granted to prevent publication of trade secrets. Although courts have tended to grant injunctions in copyright and trade secret cases without applying much, if any, First Amendment scrutiny, scholars have begun to argue that courts should apply the same standards before granting preliminary injunctions in intellectual property cases that they do before granting them in defamation cases. See Mark A. Lemley & Eugene Volokh, *Freedom of Speech and Injunctions in Intellectual Property Cases*, 48 Duke L.J. 147 (1998). *See also* State ex rel. Sports Mgmt. News, Inc. v. Nachtigal, 921 P.2d 1304 (Or. 1996) (applying traditional prior restraint analysis in a trade secrets case).

AN EXTENDED NOTE ON THE PROGRESSIVE CASE

In United States v. The Progressive, Inc. 467 F. Supp. 990 (W.D. Wis. 1979), a district judge upheld a prior restraint after the government sought an injunction under the Atomic Energy Act, 42 U.S.C. §§ 2011 et seq., prohibiting The Progressive magazine from publishing an article called, "The H-bomb secret: How we got it— why we're telling it." The magazine asserted that it had assembled the information about how to make an H-bomb from publicly available information. Its ostensible purpose in publishing the information was to "alert the people of this country to the false illusion of security created by the government's futile efforts at secrecy." The magazine contended that the article did not pose an imminent threat because the production of an H-bomb requires materials, facilities, and technicians that no individuals and few nations possessed. The government questioned the assertion that all of the information the magazine relied on came from the public domain and asserted that even if it did, the publication of the article might aid enemies who would not be able to pull all of the information together. The government submitted affidavits from the Secretary of State and Secretary of Defense to substantiate its claim that the article would irreparably harm national security. The district judge granted the injunction against publication, though not without reservations. Here's an excerpt from his thoughtful opinion:

> A mistake in ruling against The Progressive will seriously infringe cherished First Amendment rights. If a preliminary injunction is issued, it will constitute the first instance of a prior restraint against a publication in this fashion in the history of this country, to this Court's knowledge. . . . It will curtail defendants' First Amendment rights in a drastic and substantial fashion. It will infringe upon our right to know and to be informed as well.
>
> A mistake in ruling against the United States could pave the way for thermonuclear annihilation for us all. In that event, our right to life is extinguished and the right to publish becomes moot.
>
> In the Near case, the Supreme Court recognized that publication of troop movements in time of war would threaten national security and could therefore be restrained. Times have changed significantly since 1931 when Near was decided. Now war by foot soldiers has been replaced in large part by war by machines and bombs. No longer need there be an advance warning or any preparation time before a nuclear war could be commenced.
>
> In light of these factors, the Court concludes that publication of the technical information on the hydrogen bomb contained in the article is analogous to publication of troop movements or locations in time of war and falls within the narrow exception to the rule against prior restraints.

While the magazine's appeal was pending, a Wisconsin newspaper published a letter containing the very information The Progressive had been enjoined not to publish. The Chicago Tribune also announced its intention to publish the information. The government withdrew its complaint, and the case was dismissed. *See* 467 F. Supp. 990 (W.D. Wis.), *dismissed as moot*, 610 F.2d 819 (7th Cir. 1979).

THEORY-APPLIED PROBLEM—A NATIONAL SECURITY HYPOTHETICAL

It is easy to imagine terrorists using information about weaknesses in our critical infrastructure or about chemical or biological weapons to kill hundreds of thousands of people. Assume that a magazine plans to run an article with a "map" of the U.S. fiber-optic network, assembled from publicly available documents. Government officials learn of the article and seek an injunction on the grounds that terrorists could use the information to cripple the business and industrial sector of the U.S. economy. How should a court rule? (The government chose to "classify" the dissertation of George Mason University graduate student Sean Gorman for precisely this reason. *See* Sean Gorman, *9/11 Turned Thesis into Time Bomb*, Pittsburgh Post-Gazette, July 13, 2003, at A11.)

AN EXTENDED NOTE ON "SUBSEQUENT PUNISHMENT" OF LEAKERS

If it is almost impossible to enjoin publication of government secrets, why not preserve them by prosecuting disclosures? Can the media be prosecuted under the Espionage Act for disclosing information related to the national defense? In United States v. Rosen, 445 F. Supp. 2d 602 (E.D. Va. 2006), a district judge rejected the First Amendment arguments of two former lobbyists charged with illegally receiving classified security information and disclosing it to Israeli officials and reporters. The defendants were lobbyists for the American Israel Public Affairs Committee (AIPAC). They allegedly received information about classified matters involving U.S. Middle East strategy from a Pentagon analyst and passed it along to Israeli officials and journalists. They were charged with violations of 18 U.S.C. § 793, which makes it a crime to willfully communicate information "relating to the national defense which information the possessor has reason to believe could be used to the injury of the United States or to the advantage of any foreign nation" to "any person not entitled to receive it." The defendants moved to dismiss the indictments, arguing that the Espionage Act was intended to apply to government employees and others for whom disclosure would be a breach of trust, and that applying it to outsiders who owed no special obligation to help keep the government's secrets would violate the First Amendment. The trial judge concluded that application of the Espionage Act to outsiders would be constitutional in "situations in which national security is genuinely at risk." He therefore construed the definition of national defense information to mean "information potentially damaging to the United States or useful to an enemy of the United States." He also rejected the defendants' overbreadth and vagueness challenges to the statute. The government dropped the charges against two of the defendants in 2009, after the Fourth Circuit ruled that the government would have to disclose certain classified information to proceed. See United States v. Rosen, 557 F.3d 192 (4th Cir. 2009). [Another had pled guilty in 2005.] Jerry Markon, *U.S. Drops Case Against Ex-Lobbyists: Former AIPAC Employees Faced Espionage Charges*, Washington Post, May 2, 2009, at *http://www.washingtonpost.com/wpdyn/content/article/2009/05/01/AR200905010131 0.html*.

If the lobbyists in *Rosen* could be prosecuted for disclosing classified information "leaked" by a government official, what would prevent the government from prosecuting reporters for publishing similar information? Is the potential for harm to national security less in the case of media publication? For a discussion of the dearth of First Amendment precedents to prevent such prosecutions, see William E. Lee, *Probing Secrets: The Press and Inchoate Liability for Newsgathering Crimes*, 36 Am. J. of Crim L. 129 (2009).

Although the government has not yet prosecuted journalists under the Espionage Act, it has used the Act as the basis for obtaining a warrant to search a journalist's emails. In 2010 the FBI obtained a search warrant for the personal email of Fox News correspondent James Rosen based on showing probable cause that he had violated the Espionage Act by soliciting classified information from State Department official Stephen Jin-Woo Kim. Ann E. Marimow, *A Rare Peek Into a Justice Department Leak Probe*, Wash. Post, May 19, 2013. After the warrant's existence came to light in May 2013, the Justice Department indicated it had little interest in actually prosecuting Rosen but had instead used the search warrant merely to bolster its investigation of the source of the leak. Ann E. Marimow, *Justice Department's Scrutiny of Fox News Reporter James Rosen in Leak Case Draws Fire*, Wash. Post, May 20, 2013. Stephen Jin-Woo Kim pleaded guilty to sharing national security information with Rosen. Merrill Knox, *Former State Dept. Adviser Pleads Guilty in James Rosen Leak Case*, MediaBistro, Feb. 7, 2014. Mr. Rosen stated that the incident "marked, by all accounts, the first time in American history that a reporter had been designated a criminal by the United States government simply for doing his job." Grant Pender, *Journalist James Rosen Speaks About Press Freedoms Under Obama Administration*, The Daily Northwestern, Apr. 12, 2015.

THEORY-APPLIED PROBLEM—WIKILEAKS

In 2010 WikiLeaks.org, an online "publisher" of leaked documents, released some 400,000 secret U.S. government documents on its Web site. The Guardian newspaper in England and the New York Times published some of these documents, too, which they had obtained through an arrangement with WikiLeaks founder Julian Assange. The documents included diplomatic cables, intelligence assessments, and confidential military information that Assange allegedly received from U.S. intelligence analyst Pfc. Bradley Manning. A Pentagon official called the release of classified material by WikiLeaks a boon to "terrorist organizations" and said the release "put at risk the lives of our troops." John F. Burns and Ravi Somaiya, *WikiLeaks Founder Gets Support in Rebuking U.S. on Whistleblowers*, Oct. 23, 2010, at *http://www.nytimes.com/2010/10/24/world/24london.html*. The U.S. government began a criminal investigation of Julian Assange, and a grand jury reportedly returned an indictment against him. Then-Secretary of State Hillary Clinton called the disclosures "an attack against the international community." Should the government have sought an injunction against WikiLeaks, The Guardian, and/or the New York Times to prevent them from disclosing the secret and allegedly damaging documents? Why or why not? Could the New York Times editors responsible for publishing the leaked documents be prosecuted under the Espionage Act of 1917? Could the U.S. government prosecute Mr. Assange, who is not a U.S. citizen and who did not release any leaked documents within the United States, if it finds that he encouraged or assisted Pfc. Bradley Manning to leak the documents? See Charlie Savage, *U.S. Tries to Build Case for Conspiracy by WikiLeaks*, N.Y. Times, Dec. 15, 2010, at *http://www.nytimes.com/2010/12/16/world/16wiki.html*. [You may want to return to this question after reading Bartnicki v. Vopper, 532 U.S. 514 (2001) (holding that the First Amendment prevented imposing liability on media for broadcasting the audio recording of a conversation of public concern that was illegally intercepted by a third party, independent of any media involvement), *supra* Chapter 9.] Does the First Amendment prevent the U.S. government from pressuring American companies to stop hosting WikiLeaks.org on their Internet servers? See Doug Gross, *WikiLeaks Cut Off from Amazon Servers*, CNN, Dec. 1, 2010, at *http://articles.cnn.com/2010-12-01/us/wikileaks.amazon_1_julian-assange-wikileaks -amazon-officials?_s=PM:US*. Does it prevent the government from pressuring American credit card companies—Bank of America, Visa, MasterCard, PayPal, Western Union—to block donations by American credit card holders to support WikiLeaks.org, a nonprofit company? See *WikiLeaks Bypasses Financial Blockade with Bitcoin*, Forbes, Aug. 8, 2012, at *http://www.forbes.com/sites/jonmatonis /2012/08/20/wikileaks-bypasses-financial-blockade-with-bitcoin/*. Does the First Amendment prevent the U.S. government from "hacking" WikiLeaks' Internet servers to prevent release of leaked documents? See *WikiLeaks Hacked by "Very Skilled" Attackers Prior to Iraq Doc. Release*, Forbes, Oct. 22, 2010, at *http://www.forbes.com/sites/andygreenberg/2010/10/22/wikileaks-hacked-by-very- ski lled-attackers/*. For more on the legal issues surrounding disclosures by WikiLeaks, see Christina E. Wells, *Contextualizing Disclosure's Effects: WikiLeaks, Balancing, and the First Amendment*, 97 Iowa L. Rev. Bulletin 51 (2012).

THEORY APPLIED PROBLEM—INJUNCTIONS AS REMEDIES FOR DEFAMATION?

Can a court issue a post-trial injunction requiring a defendant to remove from his website statements he made that a civil jury has found to be defamatory? What are the arguments for and against the issues of such an injunction? In Kinney v. Barnes, 443 S.W.3d 87 (Tx. 2014), the Texas Supreme Court rejected the arguments of a plaintiff who had won a defamation judgment at trial that the defendant should be permanently enjoined from making future statements *similar* to those that a jury had determined to be defamatory. The court reasoned that the speech on the defendant's website that had been adjudicated defamatory by the jury fell into the category of speech unprotected by the First Amendment, and therefore an injunction requiring removal of that speech was not an unconstitutional prior restraint. By contrast, an injunction against future, similar speech runs the risk of chilling constitutionally protected expression: "Given the inherently contextual nature of defamatory speech, even the most narrowly crafted of injunctions risks enjoining protected speech because the same statement made at a different time and in a different context may no longer be actionable. Untrue statements may later become true; unprivileged statements may later become privileged." Noting that the U.S. Supreme Court had never "definitively addressed" the issue, the Texas Supreme Court cited the Texas Constitution as the basis for its holding regarding injunctions against future speech. What are the implications of this decision? Can a court issue a post-trial injunction requiring a defendant to remove information that has been found to invade privacy? What about a criminal record that has been expunged? What about ordering a review website to take down a review that a jury has determined to be defamatory? What about ordering a review website to take down a review after a default judgment in favor of a defamation plaintiff?

3. *Free Press/Fair Trial*

Prejudicial publicity can deprive a criminal defendant of his or her Sixth Amendment right to a fair trial. In Sheppard v. Maxwell, 384 U.S. 333 (1966), the Supreme Court reversed the conviction of a criminal defendant on this ground and recommended a number of steps trial judges should take to control prejudicial publicity in high-profile cases. These steps included, for example, sequestration of the trial, change of venue, searching voir dire of jurors exposed to publicity, orders to participants not to reveal information prior to trial, and so forth. Perhaps naturally, some judges took the direct route and began imposing restraints on the publication of prejudicial information about the criminal defendant prior to trial. That practice ended because of the following case.

NEBRASKA PRESS ASS'N v. STUART

427 U.S. 539 (1976)

Chief Justice BURGER delivered the opinion of the Court.

The respondent State District Judge entered an order restraining the petitioners from publishing or broadcasting accounts of confessions or admission made by the accused or facts "strongly implicative" of the accused in a widely reported murder of six persons. We granted certiorari to decide whether the entry of such an order on the showing made before the state court violated the constitutional guarantee of freedom of the press.

On the evening of October 18, 1975, local police found the six members of the Henry Kellie family murdered in their home in Sutherland, Neb., a town of about 850 people. Police released the description of a suspect, Erwin Charles Simants, to the reporters who had hastened to the scene of the crime. Simants was arrested and arraigned in Lincoln County Court the following morning, ending a tense night for this small rural community.

The crime immediately attracted widespread news coverage, by local, regional, and national newspapers, radio and television stations. [Four days after the crime, the County Court, at the request of the prosecutor and defense attorney, entered an order restricting the release of information about the case.]

Simants' preliminary hearing was held the same day, open to the public but subject to the order. The County Court bound over the defendant for trial to the State District Court. The charges, as amended to reflect the autopsy findings, were that Simants had committed the murders in the course of a sexual assault.

[Petitioners moved to vacate the County Court order. After a hearing, the District Court entered a narrower restrictive order, based on his finding of] "a clear and present danger that pre-trial publicity could impinge upon the defendant's right to a fair trial." The order applied only until the jury was impaneled, and specifically prohibited petitioners from reporting five [specified] subjects. . . .

[Petitioners sought expedited appeal in the Nebraska Supreme Court, which] modified the District Court's order to accommodate the defendant's right to a fair trial and the petitioners' interest in reporting pretrial events. The order as modified prohibited reporting of only three matters: (a) the existence and nature of any confessions or admissions made by the defendant to law enforcement officers, (b) any confessions or admissions made to any third parties, except members of the press, and (c) other facts "strongly implicative" of the accused. . . . After construing

Nebraska law to permit closure in certain circumstances, the court remanded the case to the District Judge for reconsideration of the issue whether pretrial hearings should be closed to the press and public.

We granted certiorari to address the important issues raised by the District Court order as modified by the Nebraska Supreme Court, but we denied the motion to expedite review or to stay entirely the order of the State District Court pending Simants' trial. We are informed by the parties that since we granted certiorari, Simants has been convicted of murder and sentenced to death. His appeal is pending in the Nebraska Supreme Court.

[The Court held that the case was not moot, since it was "capable of repetition, yet evading review."]

III

The problems presented by this case are almost as old as the Republic. Neither in the Constitution nor in contemporaneous writings do we find that the conflict between these two important rights was anticipated, yet it is inconceivable that the authors of the Constitution were unaware of the potential conflicts between the right to an unbiased jury and the guarantee of freedom of the press. The unusually able lawyers who helped write the Constitution and later drafted the Bill of Rights were familiar with the historic episode in which John Adams defended British soldiers charged with homicide for firing into a crowd of Boston demonstrators; they were intimately familiar with the clash of the adversary system and the part that passions of the populace sometimes play in influencing potential jurors. They did not address themselves directly to the situation presented by this case; their chief concern was the need for freedom of expression in the political arena and the dialogue in ideas. But they recognized that there were risks to private rights from an unfettered press. . . .

The trial of Aaron Burr in 1807 presented Mr. Chief Justice Marshall, presiding as a trial judge, with acute problems in selecting an unbiased jury. Few people in the area of Virginia from which jurors were drawn had not formed some opinions concerning Mr. Burr or the case, from newspaper accounts and heightened discussion both private and public. The Chief Justice conducted a searching voir dire of the two panels eventually called, and rendered a substantial opinion on the purposes of voir dire and the standards to be applied. See 1 Causes Celebres, Trial of Aaron Burr for Treason 404-427, 473-481 (1879); United States v. Burr, 25 Fed. Cas. No. 14,692g, p. 49 (CC Va. 1807). Burr was acquitted, so there was no occasion for appellate review to examine the problem of prejudicial pretrial publicity. Mr. Chief Justice Marshall's careful voir dire inquiry into the matter of possible bias makes clear that the problem is not a new one.

The speed of communication and the pervasiveness of the modern news media have exacerbated these problems, however, as numerous appeals demonstrate. The trial of Bruno Hauptmann in a small New Jersey community for the abduction and murder of the Charles Lindberghs' infant child probably was the most widely covered trial up to that time, and the nature of the coverage produced widespread public reaction. Criticism was directed at the "carnival" atmosphere that pervaded the community and the courtroom itself. Responsible leaders of press and the legal profession including other judges pointed out that much of this sorry performance could have been controlled by a vigilant trial judge and by other public officers subject to the control of the court. . . .

The excesses of press and radio and lack of responsibility of those in authority in the Hauptmann case and others of that era led to efforts to develop voluntary guidelines for courts, lawyers, press, and broadcasters. The effort was renewed in 1965 when the American Bar Association embarked on a project to develop standards for all aspects of criminal justice, including guidelines to accommodate the right to a fair trial and the rights of a free press. The resulting standards, approved by the Association in 1968, received support from most of the legal profession. . . . In the wake of these efforts, the cooperation between bar associations and members of the press led to the adoption of voluntary guidelines like Nebraska's.

In practice, of course, even the most ideal guidelines are subjected to powerful strains when a case such as Simants' arises, with reporters from many parts of the country on the scene. Reporters from distant places are unlikely to consider themselves bound by local standards. They report to editors outside the area covered by the guidelines, and their editors are likely to be guided only by their own standards. To contemplate how a state court can control acts of a newspaper or broadcaster outside its jurisdiction, even though the newspapers and broadcasts reach the very community from which jurors are to be selected, suggests something of the practical difficulties of managing such guidelines. . . .

IV

. . . In the overwhelming majority of criminal trials, pretrial publicity presents few unmanageable threats to this important right. But when the case is a "sensational" one tensions develop between the right of the accused to trial by an impartial jury and the rights guaranteed others by the First Amendment. The relevant decisions of this Court, even if not dispositive, are instructive by way of background.

. . . In Sheppard v. Maxwell, 384 U.S. 333, 86 S. Ct. 1507, 16 L. Ed. 2d 600 (1966), the Court focused sharply on the impact of pretrial publicity and a trial court's duty to protect the defendant's constitutional right to a fair trial. With only Mr. Justice Black dissenting, and he without opinion, the Court ordered a new trial for the petitioner, even though the first trial had occurred 12 years before. Beyond doubt the press had shown no responsible concern for the constitutional guarantee of a fair trial; the community from which the jury was drawn had been inundated by publicity hostile to the defendant. But the trial judge "did not fulfill his duty to protect (the defendant) from the inherently prejudicial publicity which saturated the community and to control disruptive influences in the courtroom." The Court noted that "unfair and prejudicial news comment on pending trials has become increasingly prevalent," and issued a strong warning:

> Due process requires that the accused receive a trial by an impartial jury free from outside influences. . . . [W]here there is a reasonable likelihood that prejudicial news prior to trial will prevent a fair trial, the judge should continue the case until the threat abates, or transfer it to another county not so permeated with publicity. In addition, sequestration of the jury was something the judge should have raised sua sponte with counsel. If publicity during the proceedings threatens the fairness of the trial, a new trial should be ordered. But we must remember that reversals are but palliatives; the cure lies in those remedial measures that will prevent the prejudice at its inception. . . . Neither prosecutors, counsel for defense, the accused, witnesses, court staff nor enforcement officers coming under the jurisdiction of the court should be permitted to frustrate its function. Collaboration

between counsel and the press as to information affecting the fairness of a criminal trial is not only subject to regulation, but is highly censurable and worthy of disciplinary measures. . . .

Because the trial court had failed to use even minimal efforts to insulate the trial and the jurors from the "deluge of publicity," the Court vacated the judgment of conviction and a new trial followed, in which the accused was acquitted. . . .

The state trial judge in the case before us acted responsibly, out of a legitimate concern, in an effort to protect the defendant's right to a fair trial. What we must decide is not simply whether the Nebraska courts erred in seeing the possibility of real danger to the defendant's rights, but whether in the circumstances of this case the means employed were foreclosed by another provision of the Constitution.

V

The First Amendment provides that "Congress shall make no law . . . abridging the freedom . . . of the press," and it is "no longer open to doubt that the liberty of the press and of speech, is within the liberty safeguarded by the due process clause of the Fourteenth Amendment from invasion by state action." [*Near.*] The Court has interpreted these guarantees to afford special protection against orders that prohibit the publication or broadcast of particular information or commentary orders that impose a "previous" or "prior" restraint on speech. None of our decided cases on prior restraint involved restrictive orders entered to protect a defendant's right to a fair and impartial jury, but the opinions on prior restraint have a common thread relevant to this case.

. . . The thread running through [our prior] cases is that prior restraints on speech and publication are the most serious and the least tolerable infringement on First Amendment rights. A criminal penalty or a judgment in a defamation case is subject to the whole panoply of protections afforded by deferring the impact of the judgment until all avenues of appellate review have been exhausted. Only after judgment has become final, correct or otherwise, does the law's sanction become fully operative.

A prior restraint, by contrast and by definition, has an immediate and irreversible sanction. If it can be said that a threat of criminal or civil sanctions after publication "chills" speech, prior restraint "freezes" it at least for the time.

The damage can be particularly great when the prior restraint falls upon the communication of news and commentary on current events. Truthful reports of public judicial proceedings have been afforded special protection against subsequent punishment. See Cox Broadcasting Corp. v. Cohn, 420 U.S. 469, 492-493 (1975). For the same reasons the protection against prior restraint should have particular force as applied to reporting of criminal proceedings, whether the crime in question is a single isolated act or a pattern of criminal conduct. . . .

The extraordinary protections afforded by the First Amendment carry with them something in the nature of a fiduciary duty to exercise the protected rights responsibly, a duty widely acknowledged but not always observed by editors and publishers. It is not asking too much to suggest that those who exercise First Amendment rights in newspapers or broadcasting enterprises direct some effort to protect the rights of an accused to a fair trial by unbiased jurors.

Of course, the order at issue like the order requested in New York Times does not prohibit but only postpones publication. Some news can be delayed and most commentary can even more readily be delayed without serious injury, and there often is a self-imposed delay when responsible editors call for verification of information. But such delays are normally slight and they are self-imposed. Delays imposed by governmental authority are a different matter. . . .

As a practical matter, moreover, the element of time is not unimportant if press coverage is to fulfill its traditional function of bringing news to the public promptly.

The authors of the Bill of Rights did not undertake to assign priorities as between First Amendment and Sixth Amendment rights, ranking one as superior to the other. In this case, the petitioners would have us declare the right of an accused subordinate to their right to publish in all circumstances. But if the authors of these guarantees, fully aware of the potential conflicts between them, were unwilling or unable to resolve the issue by assigning to one priority over the other, it is not for us to rewrite the Constitution by undertaking what they declined to do. It is unnecessary, after nearly two centuries, to establish a priority applicable in all circumstances. Yet it is nonetheless clear that the barriers to prior restraint remain high unless we are to abandon what the Court has said for nearly a quarter of our national existence and implied throughout all of it. . . .

VI

We turn now to the record in this case to determine whether, as Learned Hand put it, "the gravity of the 'evil,' discounted by its improbability, justifies such invasion of free speech as is necessary to avoid the danger." United States v. Dennis, 183 F.2d 201, 212 (CA2 1950), aff'd, 341 U.S. 494(1951); see also L. Hand, The Bill of Rights 58-61 (1958). To do so, we must examine the evidence before the trial judge when the order was entered to determine (a) the nature and extent of pretrial news coverage; (b) whether other measures would be likely to mitigate the effects of unrestrained pretrial publicity; and (c) how effectively a restraining order would operate to prevent the threatened danger. The precise terms of the restraining order are also important. We must then consider whether the record supports the entry of a prior restraint on publication, one of the most extraordinary remedies known to our jurisprudence.

[A.] In assessing the probable extent of publicity, the trial judge had before him newspapers demonstrating that the crime had already drawn intensive news coverage, and the testimony of the County Judge, who had entered the initial restraining order based on the local and national attention the case had attracted. The District Judge was required to assess the probable publicity that would be given these shocking crimes prior to the time a jury was selected and sequestered. He then had to examine the probable nature of the publicity and determine how it would affect prospective jurors.

Our review of the pretrial record persuades us that the trial judge was justified in concluding that there would be intense and pervasive pretrial publicity concerning this case. He could also reasonably conclude, based on common man experience, that publicity might impair the defendant's right to a fair trial. He did not purport to say more, for he found only "a clear and present danger that pre-trial publicity *could* impinge upon the defendant's right to a fair trial." (Emphasis added.) His conclusion as to the impact of such publicity on prospective jurors was of necessity speculative, dealing as he was with factors unknown and unknowable.

[B.] We find little in the record that goes to another aspect of our task, determining whether measures short of an order restraining all publication would have insured the defendant a fair trial. Although the entry of the order might be read as a judicial determination that other measures would not suffice, the trial court made no express findings to that effect; the Nebraska Supreme Court referred to the issue only by implication.

Most of the alternatives to prior restraint of publication in these circumstances were discussed with obvious approval in Sheppard v. Maxwell: (a) change of trial venue to a place less exposed to the intense publicity that seemed imminent in Lincoln County; (b) postponement of the trial to allow public attention to subside; (c) searching questioning of prospective jurors...to screen out those with fixed opinions as to guilt or innocence; (d) the use of emphatic and clear instructions on the sworn duty of each juror to decide the issues only on evidence presented in open court. Sequestration of jurors is, of course, always available. Although that measure insulates jurors only after they are sworn, it also enhances the likelihood of dissipating the impact of pretrial publicity and emphasizes the elements of the jurors' oaths.

. . . We have noted earlier that pretrial publicity, even if pervasive and concentrated, cannot be regarded as leading automatically and in every kind of criminal case to an unfair trial. The decided cases "cannot be made to stand for the proposition that juror exposure to information about a state defendant's prior convictions or to news accounts of the crime with which he is charged alone presumptively deprives the defendant of due process." Murphy v. Florida, 421 U.S., at 799, 95 S. Ct., at 2036. . . .

We have . . . examined this record to determine the probable efficacy of the measures short of prior restraint on the press and speech. There is no finding that alternative measures would not have protected Simants' rights, and the Nebraska Supreme Court did no more than imply that such measures might not be adequate. Moreover, the record is lacking in evidence to support such a finding.

[C.] We must also assess the probable efficacy of prior restraint on publication as a workable method of protecting Simants' right to a fair trial, and we cannot ignore the reality of the problems of managing and enforcing pretrial restraining orders. The territorial jurisdiction of the issuing court is limited by concepts of sovereignty, see, . . .; Pennoyer v. Neff, 95 U.S. 714 (1878). The need for *in personam* jurisdiction also presents an obstacle to a restraining order that applies to publication at large as distinguished from restraining publication within a given jurisdiction.

The Nebraska Supreme Court narrowed the scope of the restrictive order, and its opinion reflects awareness of the tensions between the need to protect the accused as fully as possible and the need to restrict publication as little as possible. The dilemma posed underscores how difficult it is for trial judges to predict what information will in fact undermine the impartiality of jurors, and the difficulty of drafting an order that will effectively keep prejudicial information from prospective jurors. When a restrictive order is sought, a court can anticipate only part of what will develop that may injure the accused. But information not so obviously prejudicial may emerge, and what may properly be published in these "gray zone" circumstances may not violate the restrictive order and yet be prejudicial.

Finally, we note that the events disclosed by the record took place in a community of 850 people. It is reasonable to assume that, without any news accounts being printed or broadcast, rumors would travel swiftly by word of mouth. One can only speculate on the accuracy of such reports, given the generative propensities of rumors; they could well be more damaging than reasonably accurate news accounts. But plainly a whole community cannot be restrained from discussing a subject intimately affecting life within it.

Given these practical problems, it is far from clear that prior restraint on publication would have protected Simants' rights.

[D.] Finally, another feature of this case leads us to conclude that the restrictive order entered here is not supportable. At the outset the County Court entered a very broad restrictive order, the terms of which are not before us; it then held a preliminary hearing open to the public and the press. There was testimony concerning at least two incriminating statements made by Simants to private persons; the statement—evidently a confession that he gave to law enforcement officials— was also introduced. The State District Court's later order was entered after this public hearing and, as modified by the Nebraska Supreme Court, enjoined reporting of[, among other things, any confession or confessions made by Simants.]

To the extent that this order prohibited the reporting of evidence adduced at the open preliminary hearing, it plainly violated settled principles: "(T)here is nothing that proscribes the press from reporting events that transpire in the courtroom." Sheppard v. Maxwell, 384 U.S., at 362-363. See also Cox Broadcasting Corp. v. Cohn, 420 U.S. 469 (1975). The County Court could not know that closure of the preliminary hearing was an alternative open to it until the Nebraska Supreme Court so construed state law; but once a public hearing had been held, what transpired there could not be subject to prior restraint.

The third prohibition of the order was defective in another respect as well. As part of a final order, entered after plenary review, this prohibition regarding "implicative" information is too vague and too broad to survive the scrutiny we have given to restraints on First Amendment rights. . . .

[E.] Our analysis ends as it began, with a confrontation between prior restraint imposed to protect one vital constitutional guarantee and the explicit command of another that the freedom to speak and publish shall not be abridged. We reaffirm that the guarantees of freedom of expression are not an absolute prohibition under all circumstances, but the barriers to prior restraint remain high and the presumption against its use continues intact. We hold that, with respect to the order entered in this case prohibiting reporting or commentary on judicial proceedings held in public, the barriers have not been overcome; to the extent that this order restrained publication of such material, it is clearly invalid. To the extent that it prohibited publication based on information gained from other sources, we conclude that the heavy burden imposed as a condition to securing a prior restraint was not met. . . .

Justice WHITE, concurring.

Technically there is no need to go farther than the Court does to dispose of this case, and I join the Court's opinion. I should add, however, that for the reasons which the Court itself canvasses there is grave doubt in my mind whether orders with respect to the press such as were entered in this case would ever be justifiable. . . .

Justice BRENNAN, with whom Justice STEWART and Justice MARSHALL join, concurring in the judgment.

. . . The right to a fair trial by a jury of one's peers is unquestionably one of the most precious and sacred safeguards enshrined in the Bill of Rights. I would hold, however, that resort to prior restraints on the freedom of the press is a constitutionally impermissible method for enforcing that right; judges have at their disposal a broad spectrum of devices for ensuring that fundamental fairness is accorded the accused without necessitating so drastic an incursion on the equally fundamental and salutary constitutional mandate that discussion of public affairs in a free society cannot depend on the preliminary grace of judicial censors.

. . . Recognition of any judicial authority to impose prior restraints on the basis of harm to the Sixth Amendment rights of particular defendants, especially since that harm must remain speculative, will thus inevitably interject judges at all levels into censorship roles that are simply inappropriate and impermissible under the First Amendment. Indeed, the potential for arbitrary and excessive judicial utilization of any such power would be exacerbated by the fact that judges and committing magistrates might in some cases be determining the propriety of publishing information that reflects on their competence, integrity, or general performance on the bench.

[Justice STEVENS'S concurring opinion is omitted.]

NOTES AND QUESTIONS

1. *Distinguishing* Near. Why doesn't the majority opinion simply apply the presumption of unconstitutionality from *Near* or the Pentagon Papers case? Although the *Nebraska Press* standard seems lower, is it really? Can a prior restraint on the press ever comply with the stringent guidelines set forth in *Nebraska Press*?

2. *Restraints on trial participants.* One alternative to restraints on the media to prevent prejudicial publicity is to impose restraints on trial participants, such as attorneys, police, and witnesses. Most states have rules limiting what attorneys involved in pending proceedings may say. The Supreme Court addressed the constitutionality of those rules in Gentile v. State Bar of Nevada, 501 U.S. 1030 (1991), which held that states may regulate attorney speech to protect the fair trial rights of criminal defendants based on a showing of a "substantial likelihood of material prejudice."

3. *Media standing.* Courts have held that the media have standing to challenge gag orders on trial participants, such as lawyers. It is not clear, however, what standard should be applied to such challenges. The Second Circuit, for example, upheld a restraint on trial participants in the face of a media challenge upon a showing of a "reasonable likelihood" that pretrial publicity would prejudice the fair trial rights of the defendants. Application of Dow Jones & Co., 842 F.2d 603 (2d Cir. 1988). The Ninth Circuit also uses that test, *see* Radio & Television News Ass'n v. U.S. Dist. Court, 781 F.2d 1443 (9th Cir. 1986), but the Sixth Circuit applies a clear and present danger standard, CBS, Inc. v. Young, 522 F.2d 234 (6th Cir. 1975).

THEORY-APPLIED PROBLEM—PROTECTING THE FAIR TRIAL RIGHT

A court martial is a military court that tries cases involving crimes committed by members of the armed forces, as defined by the Uniform Code of Military Justice. Courts martial may be conducted in secret. Assume the federal Congress, disturbed by the degree of pretrial publicity given to the case of Sergeant Bowe Bergdahl, a

U.S. soldier accused of desertion who spent five years as a hostage of the Taliban, passes a law called the Courts Martial Fair Trial Act. The act provides that a newspaper, broadcaster, or cable television station may not publish information concerning the existence or contents of a confession allegedly made to law enforcement officers, military officials, or others by a defendant who is to be tried by a court martial, unless the publisher first gives notice to the defendant via his attorney of the intent to publish the contents of the confession, and simultaneously publishes any statement of the defendant or his attorney regarding the alleged confession. The publisher is required to publish the response in full, provided it does not exceed the column space or air time devoted to reporting the alleged confession. Failure to comply with the act will subject the publisher to a criminal fine not to exceed $5,000. Is the act constitutional? Why or why not? What precedent applies to resolve this issue?

D. REGULATION OF BROADCASTERS

We have considered whether the press might be treated differently than other speakers for some First Amendment purposes. We now consider whether different media might warrant differential treatment under the First Amendment. Before beginning, it is worth emphasizing that the vast majority of First Amendment protections apply equally to all media. For example, a prior restraint is presumptively unconstitutional whether it is deployed against a broadcaster, a newspaper, or an Internet Web site. The constitutional restrictions on the tort of defamation apply whether the defendant is a provider of cable programming, a provider of broadcast programming, or a magazine publisher. However, there are some situations in which a particular medium of expression (usually broadcasting) is subject to regulation that would be unconstitutional if applied to another medium.

Broadcasting is the medium most commonly singled out for differential treatment under the First Amendment, and this differential treatment is typically justified by the technical characteristics of the electromagnetic spectrum employed by broadcasters. However, the argument that the technological features of different media justify differential First Amendment treatment has arisen in the contexts of the Internet, cable, and direct broadcast satellite. We begin with the status of broadcasting.

The electromagnetic spectrum is a unique natural resource. Utilization does not use it up or wear it out. It does not require maintenance. It is subject to pollution (interference), but once the interference is removed, the pollution and its effects disappear. It is intangible, unable to be seen or touched, and it is everywhere, in the sense that it surrounds us whether we are in a building or outside. In many ways the airwaves are like a public resource, in the sense that they are omnipresent and can be used by many people. On the other hand, the airwaves are like private property in that they can be occupied to the exclusion of others.

Five properties determine the use of the spectrum: space, time, frequency, power, and antenna height. Two broadcasters can broadcast on the same frequency at the same time if they are far enough apart, operating at low enough power, or their antennae are sufficiently low or separated by mountains that are sufficiently high. Where two users of the spectrum are not sufficiently separated by space, time, frequency, power, or antenna height, they interfere with each other. A particularly powerful signal may drown out a weaker one or, as is more commonly the case, the signals will be of less quality or even unintelligible as a result of their interference with each other.

Historically, these technological characteristics led the government to regulate broadcast media differently than other media, and history goes far toward explaining the unique First Amendment status of broadcasting. During the 1920s, technology advanced to the point where hundreds of radio stations could begin broadcasting to the public. At first, there was little or no government oversight of these broadcasters. The Supreme Court described the situation thus: "the allocation of frequencies was left entirely to the private sector, and the result was chaos." Red Lion Broad. Co. v. FCC, 395 U.S. 367 (1969). Competing stations broadcast at the same frequency in the same geographic location, and signal interference made it impossible for them to reach their listeners. It soon became apparent that governmental regulation was essential for the broadcasting system to function. Both broadcasters and government regulators turned to Congress for help.

Congress responded with the Radio Act of 1927. The Act created the Federal Radio Commission (FRC), which became the Federal Communications Commission (FCC) in 1934. The FRC (later the FCC) was responsible for allocating the electromagnetic spectrum available for commercial and public broadcasting in a manner "consistent with the public interest, convenience [and] necessity." Broadcast licenses were issued for a limited term, and licenses were to be granted and renewed as dictated by "public interest, convenience, or necessity." Broadcast licensees that carried the advertisements of one political candidate were required to give or sell equal time to opposing candidates. The Act forbade censorship of broadcast programming, while it banned obscene, indecent, or profane language.

Even though the Communications Act of 1934 soon replaced the Radio Act, the new Act retained most of the provisions governing broadcasters. The 1934 Communications Act centralized federal authority over common carriers (telephone and telegraph operators) and broadcasters in the Federal Communications Commission. Even though the Communications Act was substantially amended by the Telecommunications Competition and Deregulation Act of 1996, the FCC today continues to issue licenses to broadcasters, renew licenses periodically, ensure that broadcasters comply with technical and operations rules, and develop rules to regulate broadcasting. The FCC's exercise of its regulatory authority has given rise to a host of litigation addressing the scope of First Amendment rights of broadcasters.

Red Lion. One of the most important of cases concerning the First Amendment rights of broadcasters was Red Lion Broad. Co. v. FCC, 395 U.S. 367 (1969). In *Red Lion,* the FCC proposed to make a rule—the "personal attack" rule—out of its common law practice of insisting that when "during the presentation of views on a controversial issue of public importance, an attack is made upon the honesty, character, integrity or like personal qualities of an identified person or group, the licensee shall, within a reasonable time, [no longer than a week] after the attack" send that person or group a script or tape of the attack and "an offer of a reasonable opportunity to respond over the licensee's facilities." During the mid-1960s two cases arose challenging the "personal attack" rule. The Supreme Court addressed both cases in *Red Lion* and unanimously upheld the rule.

Justice White, writing for the Court, began by noting that each medium of communication warranted individual legal treatment:

Just as the Government may limit the use of sound-amplifying equipment potentially so noisy that it drowns out civilized private speech, so may the Government limit the use of broadcast equipment. The risk of free speech of a broadcaster, the user of a sound truck, or any other individual does not embrace a right to snuff out the free speech of others.

When two people converse face to face, both should not speak at once if either is to be clearly understood. But the range of the human voice is so limited that there could be meaningful communications if half the people in the United States were talking and the other half listening. Just as clearly, half the people might publish and the other half read. But the reach of radio signals is incomparably greater than the range of the human voice and the problem of interference is a massive reality. The lack of know-how and equipment may keep many from the air, but only a tiny fraction of those with resources and intelligence can hope to communicate by radio at the same time if intelligible communication is to be had, even if the entire radio spectrum is utilized in the present state of commercially acceptable technology.

The Court noted that it was this chaos in the early days that led Congress to develop a licensing system. Then, the Court concluded that the First Amendment must bend to the realities of the broadcast medium:

Where there are substantially more individuals who want to broadcast than there are frequencies to allocate, it is idle to posit an unabridgeable First Amendment right to broadcast comparable to the right of every individual to speak, write, or publish. If 100 persons want broadcast licenses but there are only 10 frequencies to allocate, all of them may have the same "right" to a license; but if there is to be any effective communication by radio, only a few can be licensed and the rest must be barred from the airwaves. It would be strange if the First Amendment, aimed at protecting and furthering communications, prevented the Government from making radio communication possible by requiring licenses to broadcast and by limiting the number of licenses so as not to overcrowd the spectrum.

. . . By the same token, as far as the First Amendment is concerned those who are licensed stand no better than those to whom licenses are refused. A license permits broadcasting, but the licensee has no constitutional right to be the one who holds the license or to monopolize a radio frequency to the exclusion of his fellow citizens. There is nothing in the First Amendment which prevents the Government from requiring a licensee to share his frequency with others and to conduct himself as a proxy or fiduciary with obligations to present those views and voices which are representative of his community and which would otherwise, by necessity, be barred from the airwaves.

This is not to say that the First Amendment is irrelevant to public broadcasting. On the contrary, it has a major role to play as the Congress itself recognized in [section] 326 [of the Communications Act], which forbids FCC interference with "the right of free speech by means of radio communication." Because of the scarcity of radio frequencies, the Government is permitted to put restraints on licensees in favor of others whose views should be expressed on this unique medium. But the people as a whole retain their interest in free speech by radio and their collective right to have the medium function consistently with the ends and purposes of the First Amendment. It is the right of the viewers and listeners, not the right of the broadcasters, which is paramount. . . . It is the purpose of the First Amendment to preserve an uninhibited marketplace of ideas in which truth will ultimately prevail, rather than to countenance monopolization of that market, whether it be by the Government itself or a private licensee . . .; [Times v. Sullivan]; Abrams v. United States, 250 U.S. 616, 630 (1919) (Holmes,

J., dissenting). "[S]peech concerning public affairs is more than self-expression; it is the essence of self-government." [Garrison v. Louisiana]. . . . It is the right of the public to receive suitable access to social, political, esthetic, moral, and other ideas and experiences which is crucial here. That right may not constitutionally be abridged either by Congress or by the FCC.

The Court then turned to the specific constraint applied to broadcasters in the case. Justice White observed that the "Government could surely have decreed that each frequency should be shared among all or some of those who wish to use it, each being assigned a portion of the broadcast day or the broadcast week." Nor could the "personal attack" rule be distinguished from the requirement that broadcasters must give or sell time to political candidates if the station has given or sold time to their opponents—a provision that had never been questioned:

> Nor can we say that it is inconsistent with the First Amendment goal of producing an informed public capable of conducting its own affairs to require a broadcaster to permit answers to personal attacks occurring in the course of discussing controversial issues, or to require that the political opponents of those endorsed by the station be given a chance to communicate with the public. Otherwise, station owners and a few networks would have unfettered power to make time available only to the highest bidders, to communicate only their own views on public issues, people and candidates, and to permit on the air only those with whom they agreed. There is no sanctuary in the First Amendment for unlimited private censorship operating in a medium not open to all.

The Court next rejected the claim that if this type of obligation is imposed, licensees will eliminate coverage of important political issues. The opinion noted that broadcasters had not aired bland programming in the past and observed:

> . . . [E]ven now they do not assert that they intend to abandon their efforts in this regard. It would be better if the FCC's encouragement were never necessary to induce the broadcasters to meet the responsibility. And if experience with the administration of those doctrines indicates that they have the net effect of reducing rather than enhancing the volume and quality of coverage, there will be time enough to reconsider the constitutional implications. The fairness doctrine in the past has had no such overall effect.
>
> . . . [Moreover, if licensees] should suddenly prove timorous, the Commission is not powerless to insist that they give adequate and fair attention to public issues. It does not violate the First Amendment to treat licensees given the privilege of using scarce radio frequencies as proxies for the entire community, obligated to give suitable time and attention to matters of great public concern. . . . Congress need not stand idly by and permit those with licenses to ignore the problems which beset the people or to exclude from the airways anything but their own views of fundamental questions. The statute, long administrative practice, and cases are to this effect.

After rejecting claims of "vagueness," the Court also rejected the claim that even if past scarcity justified this rule, current conditions no longer did so:

> Scarcity is not entirely a thing of the past. Advances in technology, such as microwave transmission, have led to more efficient utilization of the frequency spectrum, but uses for that spectrum have also grown apace. Portions of the spectrum must be reserved for vital uses unconnected with human

communication, such as radio-navigational aids used by aircraft and vessels. Conflicts have even emerged between such vital functions as defense preparedness and experimentation in methods of averting midair collisions through radio warning devices. "Land mobile services" such as police, ambulance, fire department, public utility, and other communications systems have been occupying an increasingly crowded portion of the frequency spectrum and there are, apart from licensed amateur radio operators' equipment, 5,000,000 transmitters operated on the "citizens' band" which is also increasingly congested. Among the various uses for radio frequency space, including marine, aviation, amateur, military, and common carrier users, there are easily enough claimants to permit use of the whole with an even smaller allocation to broadcast radio and television uses than now exists.

. . . The rapidity with which technological advances succeed one another to create more efficient use of spectrum space on the one hand, and to create new uses for that space by ever growing numbers of people on the other, makes it unwise to speculate on the future allocation of that space. It is enough to say that the resource is one of considerable and growing importance whose scarcity impelled its regulation by an agency authorized by Congress. Nothing in this record, or in our own researches, convinces us that the resource is no longer one for which there are more immediate and potential uses than can be accommodated, and for which wise planning is essential. This does not mean, of course, that every possible wavelength must be occupied at every hour by some vital use in order to sustain the congressional judgment.

Even where gaps in coverage existed, Justice White's opinion for the Court noted:

[E]xisting broadcasters have often attained their present position because of their initial government selection in competition with others before new technological advances opened new opportunities for further uses. Long experience in broadcasting, confirmed habits of listeners and viewers, network affiliation, and other advantages in program procurement give existing broadcasters a substantial advantage over new entrants, even where new entry is technologically possible. These advantages are the fruit of a preferred position conferred by the Government. Some present possibility for new entry by competing stations is not enough, in itself, to render unconstitutional the Government's effort to assure that a broadcaster's programming ranges widely enough to serve the public interest.

In view of the scarcity of broadcast frequencies, the Government's role in allocating those frequencies, and the legitimate claims of those unable without governmental assistance to gain access to those frequencies for expression of their views, we hold the regulations and ruling at issue here are both authorized by statute and constitutional.

NOTES AND QUESTIONS

1. *Reconciling* Tornillo. In Miami Herald Publishing Co. v. Tornillo, which is excerpted in Chapter 6, *supra*, the Supreme Court struck down a Florida statute that purported to give a political candidate a "right of reply" when "any newspaper in its column assails the personal character" of the candidate. The Court held that the right-of-reply statute violated the First Amendment because it interfered with the editorial discretion of newspaper publishers and penalized the publication of particular types of content. Although the Court decided *Tornillo* five years after *Red Lion*, the Court did not mention *Red Lion* or attempt to

distinguish it. Can you reconcile the two cases? Don't both cases involve "government-enforced access" to a medium of mass communication in the name of promoting diversity in the marketplace of ideas?

2. *Demise of the personal attack rule. Red Lion* remains an important case defining the First Amendment rights of broadcasters, but the personal attack rule is no longer in effect. *See* Radio-Television News Directors Ass'n v. FCC, 229 F.3d 269 (D.C. Cir. 2000) (issuing writ of mandamus vacating the personal attack and political editorial rules). However, the paradigm of broadcast regulation outlined in *Red Lion* continues to have validity. For now, the important point is to see how differently the Court treated broadcasting in 1969 (*Red Lion*) and print media in 1974 (*Tornillo*).

3. *Criticism of the scarcity rationale.* The scarcity rationale for broadcast regulation has received intense criticism. Many commentators, including the FCC, the U.S. Court of Appeals for the District of Columbia Circuit, scholars, and several Supreme Court Justices, have argued that the scarcity doctrine no longer justifies special constitutional treatment of government restrictions on broadcast expression. *See* Columbia Broad. Sys., Inc. v. Democratic Natl. Comm'n, 412 U.S. 94, 144 (1973) (Stewart, J., concurring); *id.* at 149 (Douglas, J., concurring); Telecommunications Research & Action Ctr. v. FCC, 801 F.2d 501 (D.C. Cir. 1986); In re Complaint of Syracuse Peace Council Against Television Station WTVH Syracuse, N.Y., 2 FCC Rec. 5043, 5048 (1987) (mem. opinion and order); Lee C. Bollinger, *Images of a Free Press* 87-90 (1991); Lucas A. Powe, *American Broadcasting and the First Amendment* 197-209 (1987); Fred H. Cate, *The First Amendment and the National Information Infrastructure*, 30 Wake Forest L. Rev. 1 (1995); Mark S. Fowler & Daniel L. Brenner, *A Marketplace Approach to Broadcast Regulation*, 60 Tex. L. Rev. 207 (1982); David L. Bazelon, *FCC Regulation of the Telecommunications Press*, 1975 Duke L.J. 213; Ronald Coase, *The Federal Communications Commission*, 2 J.L. & Econ. 1, 12-27 (1959).

4. *Is scarcity a thing of the past?* Even if physical scarcity was once a feature of the electromagnetic spectrum, technology is quickly making it a thing of the past. *See* Christopher S. Yoo, *The Rise and Demise of the Technology-Specific Approach to the First Amendment*, 91 Geo. L.J. 245 (2003); Kevin D. Werbach, *Supercommons: Toward A Unified Theory of Wireless Communication*, 82 Tx. L. Rev. (2004). Technology has both expanded the broadcast spectrum and erased lines between broadcasters and other media. Even the FCC has conceded "the dramatic transformation in the telecommunications marketplace provides a basis for the [Supreme] Court to reconsider its application of diminished First Amendment protection to the electronic media." In re Complaint of Syracuse Peace Council, 2 FCC Rec. 5043, 5058 (1987) (citing FCC v. League of Women Voters, 468 U.S. 364 (1984)).

5. *Justifications for broadcast regulation.* In *Red Lion*, the Court focused on the scarcity of electromagnetic spectrum as a justification for treating broadcast media differently from print media. A related justification is that the public retains ownership of the airwaves, and broadcasters are merely licensed to use them in the public interest. The Telecommunications Act of 1996, Pub. L. No. 104-104, 110 Stat. 56 (1996), 47 U.S.C. § 309(1) (2000), revised the licensing criteria employed by the FCC but still required the FCC to base license renewal in part on the public interest. The Supreme Court invoked the FCC's "'broad'

mandate to assure broadcasters operate in the public interest" as a justification for a requirement that broadcasters maintain records of "politically related broadcasting requests" to aid the government in policing campaign finance restrictions. McConnell v. Federal Elections Comm'n, 540 U.S. 93, 232, 124 S. Ct. 619, 712 (2003). Scarcity and public ownership are not the only justifications advanced for regulation of broadcasting, as you will see in the case below. As you read it, consider the distinctive characteristics of the broadcast medium that allow the FCC to "channel" and censure indecent content on the airwaves.

FCC v. PACIFICA FOUNDATION

438 U.S. 726 (1978)

Mr. Justice STEVENS delivered the opinion of the Court (Parts I, II, III, and IV-C) and an opinion in which THE CHIEF JUSTICE and Mr. Justice REHNQUIST joined (Parts IV-A and IV-B).

This case requires that we decide whether the Federal Communications Commission has any power to regulate a radio broadcast that is indecent but not obscene.

A satiric humorist named George Carlin recorded a 12-minute monologue entitled "Filthy Words" before a live audience in a California theater. He began by referring to his thoughts about "the words you couldn't say on the public, ah, airwaves, um, the ones you definitely wouldn't say, ever." He proceeded to list those words and repeat them over and over again in a variety of colloquialisms. The transcript of the recording, which is appended to this opinion, indicates frequent laughter from the audience.

At about 2 o'clock in the afternoon on Tuesday, October 30, 1973, a New York radio station, owned by respondent Pacifica Foundation, broadcast the "Filthy Words" monologue. A few weeks later a man, who stated that he had heard the broadcast while driving with his young son, wrote a letter complaining to the Commission. . . .

On February 21, 1975, the Commission issued a declaratory order granting the complaint and holding that Pacifica "could have been the subject of administrative sanctions." . . .

The Commission characterized the language used in the Carlin monologue as "patently offensive," though not necessarily obscene, and expressed the opinion that it should be regulated by principles analogous to those found in the law of nuisance where the "law generally speaks to *channeling* behavior more than actually prohibiting it. . . . [The] concept of 'indecent' is intimately connected with the exposure of children to language that describes, in terms patently offensive as measured by contemporary community standards for the broadcast medium, sexual or excretory activities and organs, at times of the day when there is a reasonable risk that children may be in the audience." [The D.C. Circuit Court of Appeals reversed, and the Supreme Court granted certiorari.]

. . .

[Before reaching the First Amendment question, the Court addressed several preliminary questions. One of these was whether the FCC had statutory authority to regulate indecency. The Court concluded that it did. After analyzing the text and legislative history of § 326 of the Communications Act of 1934, the Court concluded that the statutory provision did give the Commission "authority to impose sanctions on licensees who engage in obscene, indecent, or profane broadcasting." The Court then turned to a second statutory question.]

The only other statutory question presented by this case is whether the afternoon broadcast of the "Filthy Words" monologue was indecent within the meaning of § 1464. . . .

. . . Pacifica does not quarrel with the conclusion that this afternoon broadcast was patently offensive. Pacifica's claim that the broadcast was not indecent within the meaning of the statute rests entirely on the absence of prurient appeal.

The plain language of the statute does not support Pacifica's argument. The words "obscene, indecent, or profane" are written in the disjunctive, implying that each has a separate meaning. Prurient appeal is an element of the obscene, but the normal definition of "indecent" merely refers to nonconformance with accepted standards of morality.

. . . [T]here is no basis for disagreeing with the Commission's conclusion that indecent language was used in this broadcast.

IV[*]

[A][Pacifica] argues that the Commission's construction of the statutory language broadly encompasses so much constitutionally protected speech that reversal is required even if Pacifica's broadcast of the "Filthy Words" monologue is not itself protected by the First Amendment. . . . Th[is] argument fails because our review is limited to the question whether the Commission has the authority to proscribe this particular broadcast. . . .

. . . It is true that the Commission's order may lead some broadcasters to censor themselves. At most, however, the Commission's definition of indecency will deter only the broadcasting of patently offensive references to excretory and sexual organs and activities. While some of these references may be protected, they surely lie at the periphery of First Amendment concern. . . . Invalidating any rule on the basis of its hypothetical application to situations not before the Court is "strong medicine" to be applied "sparingly and only as a last resort." . . . We decline to administer that medicine to preserve the vigor of patently offensive sexual and excretory speech.

[B.] When the issue is narrowed to the facts of this case, the question is whether the First Amendment denies government any power to restrict the public broadcast of indecent language in any circumstances. For if the government has any such power, this was an appropriate occasion for its exercise.

. . . The classic exposition of the proposition that both the content and the context of speech are critical elements of First Amendment analysis is Mr. Justice Holmes' statement for the Court in Schenck v. United States, 249 U.S. 47, 52:

> "We admit that in many places and in ordinary times the defendants in saying all that was said in the circular would have been within their constitutional rights. But the character of every act depends upon the circumstances in which it is done. . . . The most stringent protection of free speech would not protect a man in falsely shouting fire in a theatre and causing a panic. It does not even protect a man from an injunction against uttering words that may have all the effect of force. . . . The question in every case is whether the words used are used in such circumstances

---

[*] [Editor's Note: Make sure you count the votes supporting IV.A. and IV.B.!]

and are of such a nature as to create a clear and present danger that they will bring about the substantive evils that Congress has a right to prevent."

Other distinctions based on content have been approved in the years since *Schenck*. The government may forbid speech calculated to provoke a fight. . . . It may pay heed to the "'commonsense differences' between commercial speech and other varieties." . . . It may treat libels against private citizens more severely than libels against public officials. . . . Obscenity may be wholly prohibited. . . .

The question in this case is whether a broadcast of patently offensive words dealing with sex and excretion may be regulated because of its content. Obscene materials have been denied the protection of the First Amendment because their content is so offensive to contemporary moral standards. But the fact that society may find speech offensive is not a sufficient reason for suppressing it. Indeed, if it is the speaker's opinion that gives offense, that consequence is a reason for according it constitutional protection. For it is a central tenet of the First Amendment that the government must remain neutral in the marketplace of ideas. If there were any reason to believe that the Commission's characterization of the Carlin monologue as offensive could be traced to its political content—or even to the fact that it satirized contemporary attitudes about four-letter words—First Amendment protection might be required. But that is simply not this case. These words offend for the same reasons that obscenity offends. Their place in the hierarchy of First Amendment values was aptly sketched by Mr. Justice Murphy when he said: "[Such] utterances are no essential part of any exposition of ideas, and are of such slight social value as a step to truth that any benefit that may be derived from them is clearly outweighed by the social interest in order and morality." *Chaplinsky v. New Hampshire*, 315 U.S., at 572.

. . . [C.] We have long recognized that each medium of expression presents special First Amendment problems. And of all forms of communication, it is broadcasting that has received the most limited First Amendment protection. Thus, although other speakers cannot be licensed except under laws that carefully define and narrow official discretion, a broadcaster may be deprived of his license and his forum if the Commission decides that such an action would serve "the public interest, convenience, and necessity." Similarly, although the First Amendment protects newspaper publishers from being required to print the replies of those whom they criticize [*Tornillo*], it affords no such protection to broadcasters; on the contrary, they must give free time to the victims of their criticism [*Red Lion*].

The reasons for these distinctions are complex, but two have relevance to the present case. First, the broadcast media have established a uniquely pervasive presence in the lives of all Americans. Patently offensive, indecent material presented over the airwaves confronts the citizen, not only in public, but also in the privacy of the home, where the individual's right to be left alone plainly outweighs the First Amendment rights of an intruder. Because the broadcast audience is constantly tuning in and out, prior warnings cannot completely protect the listener or viewer from unexpected program content. To say that one may avoid further offense by turning off the radio when he hears indecent language is like saying that the remedy for an assault is to run away after the first blow. One may hang up on an indecent phone call, but that option does not give the caller a constitutional immunity or avoid a harm that has already taken place.

Second, broadcasting is uniquely accessible to children, even those too young to read. Although Cohen's written message might have been incomprehensible to a first grader [referring to Cohen v. California, 403 U.S. 15 (1971), in which the Supreme Court defended the First Amendment right to wear a "Fuck the Draft" jacket], Pacifica's broadcast could have enlarged a child's vocabulary in an instant. Other forms of offensive expression may be withheld from the young without restricting the expression at its source. Bookstores and motion picture theaters, for example, may be prohibited from making indecent material available to children. We held in *Ginsberg v. New York*, 390 U.S. 629, that the government's interest in the "well-being of its youth" and in supporting "parents' claim to authority in their own household" justified the regulation of otherwise protected expression. The ease with which children may obtain access to broadcast material, coupled with the concerns recognized in *Ginsberg*, amply justify special treatment of indecent broadcasting.

It is appropriate, in conclusion, to emphasize the narrowness of our holding. This case does not involve a two-way radio conversation between a cab driver and a dispatcher, or a telecast of an Elizabethan comedy. We have not decided that an occasional expletive in either setting would justify any sanction or, indeed, that this broadcast would justify a criminal prosecution. The Commission's decision rested entirely on a nuisance rationale under which context is all-important. The concept requires consideration of a host of variables. The time of day was emphasized by the Commission. The content of the program in which the language is used will also affect the composition of the audience, and differences between radio, television, and perhaps closed-circuit transmissions, may also be relevant. As Mr. Justice Sutherland wrote, a "nuisance may be merely a right thing in the wrong place—like a pig in the parlor instead of the barnyard." . . . We simply hold that when the Commission finds that a pig has entered the parlor, the exercise of its regulatory power does not depend on proof that the pig is obscene.

Mr. Justice POWELL, with whom Mr. Justice BLACKMUN joins, concurring in part and concurring in the judgment.

. . . During most of the broadcast hours, both adults and unsupervised children are likely to be in the broadcast audience, and the broadcaster cannot reach willing adults without also reaching children. This, as the Court emphasizes, is one of the distinctions between the broadcast and other media to which we often have adverted as justifying a different treatment of the broadcast media for First Amendment purposes. In my view, the Commission was entitled to give substantial weight to this difference in reaching its decision in this case.

A second difference, not without relevance, is that broadcasting—unlike most other forms of communication—comes directly into the home, the one place where people ordinarily have the right not to be assaulted by uninvited and offensive sights and sounds. . . . Although the First Amendment may require unwilling adults to absorb the first blow of offensive but protected speech when they are in public before they turn away, a different order of values obtains in the home. . . .

. . . As the foregoing demonstrates, my views are generally in accord with what is said in Part IV-C of Mr. Justice Stevens' opinion. I therefore join that portion of his opinion. I do not join Part IV-B, however, because I do not subscribe to the theory that the Justices of this Court are free generally to decide on the basis of its content which speech protected by the First Amendment is most "valuable" and hence deserving of the most protection, and which is less "valuable" and hence deserving of less protection.

Mr. Justice BRENNAN, with whom Mr. Justice MARSHALL joins, dissenting.

. . . [N]either of the factors relied on by both the opinion of my Brother Powell and the opinion of my Brother Stevens—the intrusive nature of radio and the presence of children in the listening audience—can, when taken on its own terms, support the FCC's disapproval of the Carlin monologue. These two asserted justifications are further plagued by a common failing: the lack of principled limits on their use as a basis for FCC censorship. No such limits come readily to mind, and neither of the opinions constituting the Court serve to clarify the extent to which the FCC may assert the privacy and children-in-the-audience rationales as justification for expunging from the airways protected communications the Commission finds offensive. Taken to their logical extreme, these rationales would support the cleansing of public radio of any "four-letter words" whatsoever, regardless of their context. The rationales could justify the banning from radio of a myriad of literary works, novels, poems, and plays by the likes of Shakespeare, Joyce, Hemingway, Ben Jonson, Henry Fielding, Robert Burns, and Chaucer; they could support the suppression of a good deal of political speech, such as the Nixon tapes; and they could even provide the basis for imposing sanctions for the broadcast of certain portions of the Bible.

NOTES AND QUESTIONS

1. *Self-help as remedy.* Why isn't turning off the radio or TV an adequate remedy against broadcast indecency? Is an Internet user just as likely to encounter offensive material unexpectedly?
2. *Safe harbors.* After *Pacifica*, the FCC ordered broadcasters to channel indecent programming during late-night hours when children were less likely to be in the audience. Action for Children's Television v. FCC, 58 F.3d 654 (D.C. Cir. 1995), *cert. denied*, 516 U.S. 1072 (1996), upheld the FCC's designation of "safe harbors" (10 P.M. to 6 A.M.) for indecent content on the grounds that government has a compelling interest in protecting children from indecent broadcasts and that channeling indecency into late-night hours was not an undue burden on First Amendment rights of broadcasters.

In 2003 the FCC changed its prior standard regarding broadcast indecency, which had permitted isolated uses of expletives, and began imposing indecency fines (forfeitures) on broadcasters for the airing of even a single use of an expletive. The FCC's "fleeting expletive" rule was invalidated as "arbitrary and capricious" by the Second Circuit Court of Appeals in 2007. Fox Television Stations, Inc. v. FCC, 489 F. 3d 444 (2d Cir. 2007), *rev'd*, 556 U.S. 502 (2009), but the Supreme Court reversed on administrative law grounds and remanded. On remand, the Second Circuit struck down the FCC's indecency policy in its entirety on First Amendment grounds. The Supreme Court again granted certiorari and reversed the Second Circuit in the opinion below. Note that in doing so, the Court avoids the invitation to revisit the constitutionality of its "medium-specific" approach to broadcast indecency regulation and instead decides the case on due process grounds.

FEDERAL COMMUNICATIONS COMMISSION v.
FOX TELEVISION STATIONS, INC.

567 U.S. ___ , 132 S. Ct. 2307 (2012)

Justice KENNEDY delivered the opinion of the Court.

In FCC v. Fox Television Stations, Inc., 556 U.S. 502, 529 (2009) *(Fox I)*, the Court held that the Federal Communication Commission's decision to modify its indecency enforcement regime to regulate so-called fleeting expletives was neither arbitrary nor capricious. The Court then declined to address the constitutionality of the policy, however, because the United States Court of Appeals for the Second Circuit had yet to do so. On remand, the Court of Appeals found the policy was vague and, as a result, unconstitutional. 613 F.3d 317 (2010). The case now returns to this Court for decision upon the constitutional question.

I

. . . [A.] Title 18 U.S.C. § 1464 provides that "[w]hoever utters any obscene, indecent, or profane language by means of radio communication shall be fined . . . or imprisoned not more than two years, or both." The Federal Communications Commission (Commission) has been instructed by Congress to enforce § 1464 between the hours of 6 A.M. and 10 P.M. []. And the Commission has applied its regulations to radio and television broadcasters alike, []. Although the Commission has had the authority to regulate indecent broadcasts under § 1464 since 1948 (and its predecessor commission, the Federal Radio Commission, since 1927), it did not begin to enforce § 1464 until the 1970's. []

This Court first reviewed the Commission's indecency policy in FCC v. Pacifica Foundation, 438 U.S. 726 (1978). In *Pacifica*, the Commission determined that George Carlin's "Filthy Words" monologue was indecent. It contained "'language that describes, in terms patently offensive as measured by contemporary community standards for the broadcast medium, sexual or excretory activities and organs, at times of the day when there is a reasonable risk that children may be in the audience.'" *Id.*, at 732 (quoting 56 F.C.C. 2d 94, 98 (1975)). This Court upheld the Commission's ruling. The broadcaster's statutory challenge was rejected. The Court held the Commission was not engaged in impermissible censorship . . . and that § 1464's definition of indecency was not confined to speech with an appeal to the prurient interest, []. Finding no First Amendment violation, the decision explained the constitutional standard under which regulations of broadcasters are assessed. It observed that "broadcast media have established a uniquely pervasive presence in the lives of all Americans," [], and that "broadcasting is uniquely accessible to children, even those too young to read," []. In light of these considerations, "broadcasting . . . has received the most limited First Amendment protection." []. Under this standard the Commission's order passed constitutional scrutiny. The Court did note the narrowness of its holding, explaining that it was not deciding whether "an occasional expletive . . . would justify any sanction." []; see also *id.*, at 760–761 (Powell, J., concurring in part and concurring in judgment) ("[C]ertainly the Court's holding . . . does not speak to cases involving the isolated use of a potentially offensive word in the course of a radio broadcast, as distinguished from the verbal shock treatment administered by respondent here").

From 1978 to 1987, the Commission did not go beyond the narrow circumstances of *Pacifica* and brought no indecency enforcement actions. []. Recognizing that *Pacifica* provided "no general prerogative to intervene in any case where words similar or identical to those in *Pacifica* are broadcast over a licensed radio or television station," the Commission distinguished between the "repetitive occurrence of the 'indecent' words" (such as in the Carlin monologue) and an "isolated" or "occasional" expletive, that would not necessarily be actionable. [].

In 1987, the Commission determined it was applying the *Pacifica* standard in too narrow a way. It stated that in later cases its definition of indecent language would "appropriately includ[e] a broader range of material than the seven specific words at issue in [the Carlin monologue]." [] Thus, the Commission indicated it would use the "generic definition of indecency" articulated in its 1975 *Pacifica* order, [] and assess the full context of allegedly indecent broadcasts rather than limiting its regulation to a "comprehensive index . . . of indecent words or pictorial depictions" [].

 . . . In 2001, the Commission issued a policy statement intended "to provide guidance to the broadcast industry regarding [its] caselaw interpreting 18 U.S.C. § 1464 and [its] enforcement policies with respect to broadcast indecency." [] In that document the Commission restated that for material to be indecent it must depict sexual or excretory organs or activities and be patently offensive as measured by contemporary community standards for the broadcast medium. []. Describing the framework of what it considered patently offensive, the Commission explained that three factors had proved significant:

"(1) [T]he explicitness or graphic nature of the description or depiction of sexual or excretory organs or activities; (2) whether the material dwells on or repeats at length descriptions of sexual or excretory organs or activities; (3) whether the material appears to pander or is used to titillate, or whether the material appears to have been presented for its shock value." []

As regards the second of these factors, the Commission explained that "[r]epetition of and persistent focus on sexual or excretory material have been cited consistently as factors that exacerbate the potential offensiveness of broadcasts. In contrast, where sexual or excretory references have been made once or have been passing or fleeting in nature, this characteristic has tended to weigh against a finding of indecency." []. The Commission then gave examples of material that was not found indecent because it was fleeting and isolated, [citing one FCC ruling finding "a fleeting and isolated utterance" in the context of live and spontaneous programming not actionable and another finding that fleeting language referring to sexual activity with a child was patently offensive].

[B.] It was against this regulatory background that the three incidents of alleged indecency at issue here took place. First, in the 2002 Billboard Music Awards, broadcast by respondent Fox Television Stations, Inc., the singer Cher exclaimed during an unscripted acceptance speech: "I've also had my critics for the last 40 years saying that I was on my way out every year. Right. So f*** 'em." []. Second, Fox broadcast the Billboard Music Awards again in 2003. There, a person named Nicole Richie made the following unscripted remark while presenting an award: "Have you ever tried to get cow s*** out of a Prada purse? It's not so f***ing simple." []. The third incident involved an episode of NYPD Blue, a regular television show broadcast by respondent ABC Television Network. The episode broadcast on February 25, 2003, showed the nude buttocks of an adult female character for approximately seven seconds and for a moment the side of her breast. During the scene, in which the character was preparing to take a shower, a child portraying her boyfriend's son entered the bathroom. A moment of awkwardness followed. [].

After these incidents, but before the Commission issued Notices of Apparent Liability to Fox and ABC, the Commission issued a decision sanctioning NBC for a comment made by the singer Bono during the 2003 Golden Globe Awards. Upon winning the award for Best Original Song, Bono exclaimed: "'This is really, really, f***ing brilliant. Really, really great.'" []. Reversing a decision by its enforcement bureau, the Commission found the use of the F-word actionably indecent. []. The Commission held that the word was "one of the most vulgar, graphic and explicit descriptions of sexual activity in the English language," and thus found "any use of that word or a variation, in any context, inherently has a sexual connotation." []. Turning to the isolated nature of the expletive, the Commission reversed prior rulings that had found fleeting expletives not indecent. The Commission held "the mere fact that specific words or phrases are not sustained or repeated does not mandate a finding that material that is otherwise patently offensive to the broadcast medium is not indecent." [].

[C.][The Commission did not impose penalties on Fox or NBC on the ground that they did not have sufficient notice that such broadcasts would violate FCC policy regarding fleeting expletives, but imposed forfeitures of $27,500 on each of the 45 ABC affiliates that carried the NYPD Blue episode on the ground that the policy against nudity was sufficiently clear.]

[Fox appealed the FCC decision arguing, among other things, that the government may not punish broadcast speech that in any other medium would be protected by the First Amendment. Fox and other networks argued that changes in the media landscape, especially the growth of cable and the Internet, had made the rationale of *Pacifica* untenable. The Second Circuit did not decide the constitutional question, but vacated the rulings against Fox on the ground the Commission's reversal of policy violated the Administrative Procedures Act. In *Fox I* the Supreme Court reversed that decision and did not consider the constitutional question because it had not been decided by the court of appeals. On remand from *Fox I*, the court of appeals again held the Commission's indecency policy unconstitutional, this time on the ground that the policy failed to give broadcasters sufficient notice of what would be considered indecent. The court of appeals found the vagueness inherent in the policy had forced broadcasters to "choose between not airing . . . controversial programs [or] risking massive fines or possibly even loss of their licenses." The Second Circuit then vacated the forfeiture order against ABC.]

The Government sought review of both judgments. . . .

II

A fundamental principle in our legal system is that laws which regulate persons or entities must give fair notice of conduct that is forbidden or required. []. This requirement of clarity in regulation is essential to the protections provided by the Due Process Clause of the Fifth Amendment. [] It requires the invalidation of laws that are impermissibly vague. A conviction or punishment fails to comply with due process if the statute or regulation under which it is obtained "fails to provide a person of ordinary intelligence fair notice of what is prohibited, or is so standardless that it authorizes or encourages seriously discriminatory enforcement." []. As this Court has explained, a regulation is not vague because it may at times be difficult to prove an incriminating fact but rather because it is unclear as to what fact must be proved. [].

Even when speech is not at issue, the void for vagueness doctrine addresses at least two connected but discrete due process concerns: first, that regulated parties should know what is required of them so they may act accordingly; second, precision and guidance are necessary so that those enforcing the law do not act in an arbitrary or discriminatory way. [] When speech is involved, rigorous adherence to those requirements is necessary to ensure that ambiguity does not chill protected speech.

These concerns are implicated here because, at the outset, the broadcasters claim they did not have, and do not have, sufficient notice of what is proscribed. And leaving aside any concerns about facial invalidity, they contend that the lengthy procedural history set forth above shows that the broadcasters did not have fair notice of what was forbidden. Under the 2001 Guidelines in force when the broadcasts occurred, a key consideration was "'whether the material dwell[ed] on or repeat[ed] at length'" the offending description or depiction. []. In the 2004 *Golden Globes* Order, issued after the broadcasts, the Commission changed course and held that fleeting expletives could be a statutory violation. *Fox I*, []. In the challenged orders now under review the Commission applied the new principle promulgated in the *Golden Globes* Order and determined fleeting expletives and a brief moment of indecency were actionably indecent. This regulatory history, however, makes it apparent that the Commission policy in place at the time of the broadcasts gave no notice to Fox or ABC that a fleeting expletive or a brief shot of nudity could be actionably indecent; yet Fox and ABC were found to be in violation. The Commission's lack of notice to Fox and ABC that its interpretation had changed so the fleeting moments of indecency contained in their broadcasts were a violation of § 1464 as interpreted and enforced by the agency "fail[ed] to provide a person of ordinary intelligence fair notice of what is prohibited." []. This would be true with respect to a regulatory change this abrupt on any subject, but it is surely the case when applied to the regulations in question, regulations that touch upon "sensitive areas of basic First Amendment freedoms," [].

The Government raises two arguments in response, but neither is persuasive. As for the two fleeting expletives, the Government concedes [in its brief] that "Fox did not have reasonable notice at the time of the broadcasts that the Commission would consider non-repeated expletives indecent." The Government argues, nonetheless, that Fox "cannot establish unconstitutional vagueness on that basis . . . because the Commission did not impose a sanction where Fox lacked such notice." []. As the Court observed when the case was here three Terms ago, it is true that the Commission declined to impose any forfeiture on Fox, [], and in its order the Commission claimed that it would not consider the indecent broadcasts either when considering whether to renew stations' licenses or "in any other context," []. This "policy of forbearance," as the Government calls it, does not suffice to make the issue moot. Though the Commission claims it will not consider the prior indecent broadcasts "in any context," it has the statutory power to take into account "any history of prior offenses" when setting the level of a forfeiture penalty. [] Just as in the First Amendment context, the due process protection against vague regulations "does not leave [regulated parties] . . . at the mercy of *noblesse oblige*." [] Given that the Commission found it was "not inequitable to hold Fox responsible for [the 2003 broadcast]," [], and that it has the statutory authority to use its finding to increase any future penalties, the Government's assurance it will elect not to do so is insufficient to remedy the constitutional violation.

In addition, when combined with the legal consequence described above, reputational injury provides further reason for granting relief to Fox. . . . [F]indings of wrongdoing can result in harm to a broadcaster's "reputation with viewers and advertisers." . . . [The challenged FCC orders] describe in strongly disapproving terms the indecent material broadcast by Fox, [] (noting the "explicit, graphic, vulgar, and shocking nature of Ms. Richie's comments"), and Fox's efforts to protect children from being exposed to it, [] (finding Fox had failed to exercise "'reasonable judgment, responsibility, and sensitivity to the public's needs and tastes to avoid [a] patently offensive broadcas[t]'"). Commission sanctions on broadcasters for indecent material are widely publicized. []. The challenged orders could have an adverse impact on Fox's reputation that audiences and advertisers alike are entitled to take into account.

With respect to ABC, the Government with good reason does not argue no sanction was imposed. The fine against ABC and its network affiliates for the seven seconds of nudity was nearly $1.24 million. []. The Government argues instead that ABC had notice that the scene in NYPD Blue would be considered indecent in light of a 1960 decision where the Commission declared that the "televising of nudes might well raise a serious question of programming contrary to 18 U.S.C. § 1464." []. This argument does not prevail. An isolated and ambiguous statement from a 1960 Commission decision does not suffice for the fair notice required when the Government intends to impose over a $1 million fine for allegedly impermissible speech. The Commission, furthermore, had released decisions before sanctioning ABC that declined to find isolated and brief moments of nudity actionably indecent. [The court cited an FCC decision finding full frontal nudity in Schindler's List not indecent.] This is not to say, of course, that a graphic scene from Schindler's List involving nude concentration camp prisoners is the same as the shower scene from NYPD Blue. It does show, however, that the Government can point to nothing that would have given ABC affirmative notice that its broadcast would be considered actionably indecent. It is likewise not sufficient for the Commission to assert, as it did in its order, that though "the depiction [of nudity] here is not as lengthy or repeated" as in some cases, the shower scene nonetheless "does contain more shots or lengthier depictions of nudity" than in other broadcasts found not indecent. []. This broad language fails to demonstrate that ABC had fair notice that its broadcast could be found indecent. In fact, a Commission ruling prior to the airing of the NYPD Blue episode had deemed 30 seconds of nude buttocks "very brief" and not actionably indecent in the context of the broadcast. []. In light of this record of agency decisions, and the absence of any notice in the 2001 Guidance that seven seconds of nude buttocks would be found indecent, ABC lacked constitutionally sufficient notice prior to being sanctioned.

The Commission failed to give Fox or ABC fair notice prior to the broadcasts in question that fleeting expletives and momentary nudity could be found actionably indecent. Therefore, the Commission's standards as applied to these broadcasts were vague, and the Commission's orders must be set aside.

III

It is necessary to make three observations about the scope of this decision. First, because the Court resolves these cases on fair notice grounds under the Due Process Clause, it need not address the First Amendment implications of the Commission's indecency policy. It is argued that this Court's ruling in *Pacifica* (and the less rigorous standard of scrutiny it provided for the regulation of broadcasters, []) should be overruled because the rationale of that case has been overtaken by technological change and the wide availability of multiple other choices for listeners and viewers. []. The Government for its part maintains that when it licenses a conventional broadcast spectrum, the public may assume that the Government has its own interest in setting certain standards. []. These arguments need not be addressed here. In light of the Court's holding that the Commission's policy failed to provide fair notice it is unnecessary to reconsider *Pacifica* at this time.

This leads to a second observation. Here, the Court rules that Fox and ABC lacked notice at the time of their broadcasts that the material they were broadcasting could be found actionably indecent under then-existing policies. Given this disposition, it is unnecessary for the Court to address the constitutionality of the current indecency policy as expressed in the *Golden Globes* Order and subsequent adjudications. The Court adheres to its normal practice of declining to decide cases not before it. []

Third, this opinion leaves the Commission free to modify its current indecency policy in light of its determination of the public interest and applicable legal requirements. And it leaves the courts free to review the current policy or any modified policy in light of its content and application.

The judgments of the United States Court of Appeals for the Second Circuit are vacated, and the cases are remanded for further proceedings consistent with the principles set forth in this opinion.

Justice GINSBURG, concurring in the judgment

In my view, the Court's decision in FCC v. Pacifica Foundation, [], was wrong when it issued. Time, technological advances, and the Commission's untenable rulings in the cases now before the Court show why *Pacifica* bears reconsideration. Cf. FCC v. Fox Television Stations, Inc., 556 U. S. 502-535 (2009) (Thomas, J., concurring).

Justice SOTOMAYOR took no part in the consideration or decision of these cases.

NOTES AND QUESTIONS

1. *The chilling effect of uncertainty?* Whether the First Amendment permits the FCC to punish the broadcast of fleeting expletives remains unresolved almost 30 years after the Commission announced its intention to do so. As the opinion points out, the FCC is still free to enforce an indecency policy that provides sufficient notice to broadcasters. The vagueness problem as described by the Second Circuit was that it "forced broadcasters to 'choose between not airing . . . controversial programs [or] risking massive fines or possibly even loss of their licenses.'" Is the uncertainty as to whether the Commission has any power to regulate broadcast indecency any less likely to put broadcasters to such a choice?

At some point, does the Court's "normal practice of declining to decide cases not before it" become a First Amendment issue in itself? Note that the Court did not affirm the Second Circuit decisions, but vacated and remanded. Presumably the networks can renew their First Amendment challenge there.

2. *Vagueness, overbreadth, and the need for flexibility.* Can the FCC cure the vagueness problem by decreeing that any use of certain words, or any nude depiction of certain body parts, is a violation? Is there a more nuanced solution that would pass muster?

3. *The wardrobe malfunction case.* The Supreme Court declined to hear the FCC's appeal of a Third Circuit decision vacating the Commission's $550,000 fine against CBS for airing a brief glimpse of Janet Jackson's bare breast during a "wardrobe malfunction" at the 2004 Super Bowl halftime show. FCC v. CBS Corp., 567 U.S.___, 132 S. Ct. 2677 (2012).

4. Fox *as forgone opportunity to revisit* Pacifica. Why did the Supreme Court forgo the opportunity, presented in the *Fox* cases above, to revisit *Pacifica* and the broader issue whether broadcasters receive less First Amendment protection from content-based regulation than do other media? Some commentators have speculated that Justice Sonia Sotomayor's recusal may have left the Court split 4-4 on whether to overturn *Pacifica*, and the Court ruled narrowly to avoid issuing an opinion that would not bring unanimity or clarity. *See, e.g.,* Eugene Volokh, FCC v. Fox Television *Decided Narrowly on Lack-of-Fair-Notice Grounds,* VOLOKH CONSPIRACY (June 21, 2012), http://www. volokh.com/2012/06/21/fcc-v-fox-television-decided-narrowly-on-lack-of-fair-notice-grounds (speculating that Justices Ginsburg, Thomas, Kennedy, and Kagan might have favored overruling *Pacifica*, and that Justices Scalia, Alito, Breyer, and Roberts favored upholding it); Joe Flint & David Savage, *Justices Decline to Address Bid to Overturn FCC Indecency Rules,* L.A. TIMES (Jun. 22, 2012), *available at* http://articles.latimes.com/2012/jun/22/business/la-fi-ct-court-indecency-20120622. When a 4-4 deadlock occurs, the case is not deemed precedential; the Court simply announces that the Court is evenly divided and affirms the lower court decision under review. The affirmance is issued to afford finality for the litigants in that particular case. In the event of such a tie, the court typically issues a *per curiam* decision. *See, e.g.,* Comment, *Supreme Court No-Clear-Majority Decisions: A Study in Stare Decisis,* 24 U. CHI. L. REV. 99 (1956) (analyzing various types of no-clear-majority decisions and considering their treatment by subsequent courts). Regardless, the Court's narrow decision leaves the FCC free to regulate indecency as long as its policy for doing so provides constitutionally sufficient notice of the prohibited conduct. After the Court issued its ruling, commissioners of the FCC announced that they would continue to regulate broadcast indecency, within First Amendment parameters announced by the Court.

E.   REGULATION OF CABLE SYSTEM OPERATORS

The following case, Turner Broadcasting System Inc. v. FCC, 512 U.S. 622 (1994), is known as *Turner I* because the same case later went back to the Supreme Court as *Turner II*, 520 U.S. 180 (1997). *Turner I* illustrates the importance of the distinction between content-based versus content-neutral regulations on speech, but the case is used here primarily to illustrate the Court's resolution of whether the First Amendment applies in a "medium-specific" fashion to cable operators or programmers.

Both *Turner I* and *Turner II* address the constitutionality of "must-carry" provisions in the Cable Act of 1992. The must-carry provisions require cable operators to carry the signals of local over-the-air broadcasters. These provisions were a response to the perceived negative effects of deregulation of the cable industry by the Cable Communications Policy Act of 1984. After the 1984 Act took effect, cable providers began to increase subscription rates, shift broadcasters to less desirable channels, and deny access to competitors. In response to this, and to the lobbying of a coalition of broadcasters and consumer activists, Congress passed the Cable Act of 1992 (Cable Television Consumer Protection and Competition Act of 1992). President George H.W. Bush vetoed it, but his veto was overridden.

The main issue that *Turner I* addresses is what constitutional standard applies to must-carry provisions. *Turner I* concludes that the must-carry rules are content-neutral and subject to intermediate scrutiny. It then vacates and remands to the district court for additional fact-finding and application of the standard. The case returns to the Supreme Court as *Turner II*, at which point the Supreme Court *applies* intermediate scrutiny to the must-carry provisions and deems them constitutional. In the course of reaching these issues, the Court provides its most extensive analysis to date of whether the unique characteristics of cable as a medium justify applying to it the regulatory paradigm outlined in *Red Lion*. As you read, consider what it tells you about how far the government can go in regulating cable to enhance diversity in the marketplace of ideas.

TURNER BROADCASTING SYSTEM, INC. v. FCC
("Turner I")
512 U.S. 622 (1994)

Justice KENNEDY announced the judgment of the Court and delivered the opinion of the Court, except as to Part III-B.

. . . [A.] The role of cable television in the Nation's communications system has undergone dramatic change over the past 45 years. Given the pace of technological advancement and the increasing convergence between cable and other electronic media, the cable industry today stands at the center of an ongoing telecommunications revolution with still undefined potential to affect the way we communicate and develop our intellectual resources.

The earliest cable systems were built in the late 1940's to bring clear broadcast television signals to remote or mountainous communities. The purpose was not to replace broadcast television but to enhance it. Modern cable systems do much more than enhance the reception of nearby broadcast television stations. With the capacity to carry dozens of channels and import distant programming signals via satellite or microwave relay, today's cable systems are in direct competition with over-the-air broadcasters as an independent source of television programming.

Broadcast and cable television are distinguished by the different technologies through which they reach viewers. Broadcast stations radiate electromagnetic signals from a central transmitting antenna. These signals can be captured, in turn, by any television set within the antenna's range. Cable systems, by contrast, rely upon a physical, point-to-point connection between a transmission facility and the television sets of individual subscribers. Cable systems make this connection much like telephone companies, using cable or optical fibers strung aboveground or buried in ducts to reach the homes or businesses of subscribers. The construction of this physical infrastructure entails the use of public rights-of-way and easements and often results in the disruption of traffic on streets and other public property. As a result, the cable medium may depend for its very existence upon express permission from local governing authorities.

Cable technology affords two principal benefits over broadcast. First, it eliminates the signal interference sometimes encountered in over-the-air broadcasting and thus gives viewers undistorted reception of broadcast stations. Second, it is capable of transmitting many more channels than are available through broadcasting, giving subscribers access to far greater programming variety. More than half of the cable systems in operation today have a capacity to carry between 30 and 53 channels. 1994 Television and Cable Factbook I-69. And about 40 percent of cable subscribers are served by systems with a capacity of more than 53 channels. Newer systems can carry hundreds of channels, and many older systems are being upgraded with fiber optic rebuilds and digital compression technology to increase channel capacity.

The cable television industry includes both cable operators (those who own the physical cable network and transmit the cable signal to the viewer) and cable programmers (those who produce television programs and sell or license them to cable operators). In some cases, cable operators have acquired ownership of cable programmers, and vice versa. Although cable operators may create some of their own programming, most of their programming is drawn from outside sources. These outside sources include not only local or distant broadcast stations, but also the many national and regional cable programming networks that have emerged in recent years, such as CNN, MTV, ESPN, TNT, C-Span, The Family Channel, Nickelodeon, Arts and Entertainment, Black Entertainment Television, CourtTV, The Discovery Channel, American Movie Classics, Comedy Central, The Learning Channel, and The Weather Channel. Once the cable operator has selected the programming sources, the cable system functions, in essence, as a conduit for the speech of others, transmitting it on a continuous and unedited basis to subscribers.

In contrast to commercial broadcast stations, which transmit signals at no charge to viewers and generate revenues by selling time to advertisers, cable systems charge subscribers a monthly fee for the right to receive cable programming and rely to a lesser extent on advertising. . . .

[B.] . . . . At issue in this case is the constitutionality of the so-called must-carry provisions, contained in §§ 4 and 5 of the Act, which require cable operators to carry the signals of a specified number of local broadcast television stations.

Section 4 requires carriage of "local commercial television stations," defined to include all full power television broadcasters, other than those qualifying as "noncommercial educational" stations under § 5, that operate within the same television market as the cable system. Cable systems with more than 12 active channels, and more than 300 subscribers, are required to set aside up to one-third of their channels for commercial broadcast stations that request carriage. Cable systems with more than 300 subscribers, but only 12 or fewer active channels, must carry the signals of three commercial broadcast stations.

. . . . The broadcast signals carried under this provision must be transmitted on a continuous, uninterrupted basis, and must be placed in the same numerical channel position as when broadcast over the air. Further, subject to a few exceptions, a cable operator may not charge a fee for carrying broadcast signals in fulfillment of its must-carry obligations.

Section 5 of the Act imposes similar requirements regarding the carriage of local public broadcast television stations, referred to in the Act as local "noncommercial educational television stations." . . .

[C.] Congress enacted the 1992 Cable Act after conducting three years of hearings on the structure and operation of the cable television industry. The conclusions Congress drew from its factfinding process are recited in the text of the Act itself. In brief, Congress found that the physical characteristics of cable transmission, compounded by the increasing concentration of economic power in the cable industry, are endangering the ability of over-the-air broadcast television stations to compete for a viewing audience and thus for necessary operating revenues. Congress determined that regulation of the market for video programming was necessary to correct this competitive imbalance.

. . . In light of these technological and economic conditions, Congress concluded that unless cable operators are required to carry local broadcast stations, "there is a substantial likelihood that . . . additional local broadcast signals will be deleted, repositioned, or not carried"; the "marked shift in market share" from broadcast to cable will continue to erode the advertising revenue base which sustains free local broadcast television; and that, as a consequence, "the economic viability of free local broadcast television and its ability to originate quality local programming will be seriously jeopardized."

II

There can be no disagreement on an initial premise: Cable programmers and cable operators engage in and transmit speech, and they are entitled to the protection of the speech and press provisions of the First Amendment. Leathers v. Medlock, 499 U.S. 439, 444 (1991). Through "original programming or by exercising editorial discretion over which stations or programs to include in its repertoire," cable programmers and operators "seek to communicate messages on a wide variety of topics and in a wide variety of formats." . . . By requiring cable systems to set aside a portion of their channels for local broadcasters, the must-carry rules regulate cable speech in two respects: The rules reduce the number of channels over which cable operators exercise unfettered control, and they render it more difficult for cable programmers to compete for carriage on the limited channels remaining. Nevertheless, because not every interference with speech triggers the same degree of scrutiny under the First Amendment, we must decide at the outset the level of scrutiny applicable to the must-carry provisions.

[A.] We address first the Government's contention that regulation of cable television should be analyzed under the same First Amendment standard that applies to regulation of broadcast television. It is true that our cases have permitted more intrusive regulation of broadcast speakers than of speakers in other media. But the rationale for applying a less rigorous standard of First Amendment scrutiny to broadcast regulation, whatever its validity in the cases elaborating it, does not apply in the context of cable regulation.

The justification for our distinct approach to broadcast regulation rests upon the unique physical limitations of the broadcast medium. As a general matter, there are more would-be broadcasters than frequencies available in the electromagnetic spectrum. And if two broadcasters were to attempt to transmit over the same frequency in the same locale, they would interfere with one another's signals, so that neither could be heard at all. The scarcity of broadcast frequencies thus required the establishment of some regulatory mechanism to divide the electromagnetic spectrum and assign specific frequencies to particular broadcasters. In addition, the inherent physical limitation on the number of speakers who may use the broadcast medium has been thought to require some adjustment in traditional First Amendment analysis to permit the Government to place limited content restraints, and impose certain affirmative obligations, on broadcast licensees. . . .

Although courts and commentators have criticized the scarcity rationale since its inception, we have declined to question its continuing validity as support for our broadcast jurisprudence, and see no reason to do so here. The broadcast cases are inapposite in the present context because cable television does not suffer from the inherent limitations that characterize the broadcast medium. Indeed, given the rapid advances in fiber optics and digital compression technology, soon there may be no practical limitation on the number of speakers who may use the cable medium. Nor is there any danger of physical interference between two cable speakers attempting to share the same channel. In light of these fundamental technological differences between broadcast and cable transmission, application of the more relaxed standard of scrutiny adopted in *Red Lion* and the other broadcast cases is inapt when determining the First Amendment validity of cable regulation. . . .

This is not to say that the unique physical characteristics of cable transmission should be ignored when determining the constitutionality of regulations affecting cable speech. They should not. But whatever relevance these physical characteristics may have in the evaluation of particular cable regulations, they do not require the alteration of settled principles of our First Amendment jurisprudence.

Although the Government acknowledges the substantial technological differences between broadcast and cable, it advances a second argument for application of the *Red Lion* framework to cable regulation. It asserts that the foundation of our broadcast jurisprudence is not the physical limitations of the electromagnetic spectrum, but rather the "market dysfunction" that characterizes the broadcast market. Because the cable market is beset by a similar dysfunction, the Government maintains, the *Red Lion* standard of review should also apply to cable. While we agree that the cable market suffers certain structural impediments, the Government's argument is flawed in two respects. First, as discussed above, the special physical characteristics of broadcast transmission, not the economic characteristics of the broadcast market, are what underlies our broadcast jurisprudence. Second, the mere assertion of dysfunction or failure in a speech market, without more, is not sufficient to shield a speech regulation from the First Amendment standards applicable to non-broadcast media.

By a related course of reasoning, the Government and some appellees maintain that the must-carry provisions are nothing more than industry-specific antitrust legislation, and thus warrant rational basis scrutiny under this Court's "precedents governing legislative efforts to correct market failure in a market whose commodity is speech." . . . This contention is unavailing. [W]hile the enforcement of a generally applicable law may or may not be subject to heightened scrutiny under the First Amendment, [ ] , laws that single out the press, or certain elements thereof, for special treatment "pose a particular danger of abuse by the State," and so are always subject to at least some degree of heightened First Amendment scrutiny. Because the must-carry provisions impose special obligations upon cable operators and special burdens upon cable programmers, some measure of heightened First Amendment scrutiny is demanded.

[B.] [T]he First Amendment, subject only to narrow and well-understood exceptions, does not countenance governmental control over the content of messages expressed by private individuals. [*R.A.V.*]; Texas v. Johnson, 491 U.S. 397, 414 (1989). Our precedents thus apply the most exacting scrutiny to regulations that suppress, disadvantage, or impose differential burdens upon speech because of its content. [ ]. Laws that compel speakers to utter or distribute speech bearing a particular message are subject to the same rigorous scrutiny. [ ]. In contrast, regulations that are unrelated to the content of speech are subject to an intermediate level of scrutiny, [ ], because in most cases they pose a less substantial risk of excising certain ideas or viewpoints from the public dialogue.

Deciding whether a particular regulation is content based or content neutral is not always a simple task. We have said that the "principal inquiry in determining content neutrality . . . is whether the government has adopted a regulation of speech because of [agreement or] disagreement with the message it conveys." [ ] See *R.A.V.* [ ] ("The government may not regulate [speech] based on hostility—or favoritism—towards the underlying message expressed"). The purpose, or justification, of a regulation will often be evident on its face. [ ] But while a content-based purpose may be sufficient in certain circumstances to show that a regulation is content based, it is not necessary to such a showing in all cases. [ ] Nor will the mere assertion of a content-neutral purpose be enough to save a law which, on its face, discriminates based on content. [ ]

As a general rule, laws that by their terms distinguish favored speech from disfavored speech on the basis of the ideas or views expressed are content based. [ ] By contrast, laws that confer benefits or impose burdens on speech without reference to the ideas or views expressed are in most instances content neutral. [ ]

[C.] Insofar as they pertain to the carriage of full power broadcasters, the must-carry rules, on their face, impose burdens and confer benefits without reference to the content of speech. Although the provisions interfere with cable operators' editorial discretion by compelling them to offer carriage to a certain minimum number of broadcast stations, the extent of the interference does not depend upon the content of the cable operators' programming. The rules impose obligations upon all operators, save those with fewer than 300 subscribers, regardless of the programs or stations they now offer or have offered in the past. Nothing in the Act imposes a restriction, penalty, or burden by reason of the views, programs, or stations the cable operator has selected or will select. The number of channels a cable operator must set aside depends only on the operator's channel capacity; hence, an operator cannot avoid or mitigate its obligations under the Act by altering the programming it offers to subscribers. Cf. *Miami Herald Publishing Co. v. Tornillo*, 418 U.S. at 256-257 (newspaper may avoid access obligations by refraining from speech critical of political candidates).

The must-carry provisions also burden cable programmers by reducing the number of channels for which they can compete. But, again, this burden is unrelated to content, for it extends to all cable programmers irrespective of the programming they choose to offer viewers. And finally, the privileges conferred by the must-carry provisions are also unrelated to content. The rules benefit all full power broadcasters who request carriage—be they commercial or noncommercial, independent or network-affiliated, English or Spanish language, religious or secular. The aggregate effect of the rules is thus to make every full power commercial and noncommercial broadcaster eligible for must-carry, provided only that the broadcaster operates within the same television market as a cable system.

It is true that the must-carry provisions distinguish between speakers in the television programming market. But they do so based only upon the manner in which speakers transmit their messages to viewers, and not upon the messages they carry: Broadcasters, which transmit over the airwaves, are favored, while cable programmers, which do not, are disfavored. Cable operators, too, are burdened by the carriage obligations, but only because they control access to the cable conduit. So long as they are not a subtle means of exercising a content preference, speaker distinctions of this nature are not presumed invalid under the First Amendment.

That the must-carry provisions, on their face, do not burden or benefit speech of a particular content does not end the inquiry. Our cases have recognized that even a regulation neutral on its face may be content-based if its manifest purpose is to regulate speech because of the message it conveys.

. . . Our review of the Act and its various findings persuades us that Congress' overriding objective in enacting must-carry was not to favor programming of a particular subject matter, viewpoint, or format, but rather to preserve access to free television programming for the 40 percent of Americans without cable.

In unusually detailed statutory findings Congress explained that because cable systems and broadcast stations compete for local advertising revenue, and because cable operators have a vested financial interest in favoring their affiliated programmers over broadcast stations, cable operators have a built-in "economic incentive . . . to delete, reposition, or not carry local broadcast signals." Congress concluded that absent a requirement that cable systems carry the signals of local broadcast stations, the continued availability of free local broadcast television would be threatened. Congress sought to avoid the elimination of broadcast television because, in its words, "such programming is . . . free to those who own television sets and do not require cable transmission to receive broadcast television signals," and because "there is a substantial governmental interest in promoting the continued availability of such free television programming, especially for viewers who are unable to afford other means of receiving programming."

By preventing cable operators from refusing carriage to broadcast television stations, the must-carry rules ensure that broadcast television stations will retain a large enough potential audience to earn necessary advertising revenue—or, in the case of noncommercial broadcasters, sufficient viewer contributions, see § 2(a)(8)(B)—to maintain their continued operation. In so doing, the provisions are designed to guarantee the survival of a medium that has become a vital part of the Nation's communication system, and to ensure that every individual with a television set can obtain access to free television programming.

. . . [O]ur precedents have held that "protecting noncable households from loss of regular television broadcasting service due to competition from cable systems," is not only a permissible governmental justification, but an "important and substantial federal interest."

The design and operation of the challenged provisions confirm that the purposes underlying the enactment of the must-carry scheme are unrelated to the content of speech. The rules, as mentioned, confer must-carry rights on all full power broadcasters, irrespective of the content of their programming. They do not require or prohibit the carriage of particular ideas or points of view. They do not penalize cable operators or programmers because of the content of their programming. They do not compel cable operators to affirm points of view with which they disagree. They do not produce any net decrease in the amount of available speech. And they leave cable operators free to carry whatever programming they wish on all channels not subject to must-carry requirements.

Appellants and the dissent make much of the fact that, in the course of describing the purposes behind the Act, Congress referred to the value of broadcast programming. In particular, Congress noted that broadcast television is "an important source of local news[,] public affairs programming and other local broadcast services critical to an informed electorate," and that noncommercial television "provides educational and informational programming to the Nation's citizens." We do not think, however, that such references cast any material doubt on the content-neutral character of must-carry. That Congress acknowledged the local orientation of broadcast programming and the role that noncommercial stations have played in educating the public does not indicate that Congress regarded broadcast programming as *more* valuable than cable programming. Rather, it reflects nothing more than the recognition that the services provided by broadcast television have some intrinsic value and, thus, are worth preserving against the threats posed by cable.

The operation of the Act further undermines the suggestion that Congress' purpose in enacting must-carry was to force programming of a "local" or "educational" content on cable subscribers. The provisions, as we have stated, benefit all full power broadcasters irrespective of the nature of their programming. In fact, if a cable system were required to bump a cable programmer to make room for a broadcast station, nothing would stop a cable operator from displacing a cable station that provides all local- or education-oriented programming with a broadcaster that provides very little. Appellants do not even contend, moreover, that broadcast programming is any more "local" or "educational" than cable programming. Cf. *Leathers v. Medlock. . . .*

. . . We likewise reject the suggestion, advanced by appellants and by Judge Williams in dissent, that the must-carry rules are content-based because the preference for broadcast stations "*automatically* entails content requirements." It is true that broadcast programming, unlike cable programming, is subject to certain limited content restraints imposed by statute and FCC regulation. But it does not follow that Congress mandated cable carriage of broadcast television stations as a means of ensuring that particular programs will be shown, or not shown, on cable systems.

As an initial matter, the argument exaggerates the extent to which the FCC is permitted to intrude into matters affecting the content of broadcast programming. The FCC is forbidden by statute from engaging in "censorship" or from promulgating any regulation "which shall interfere with the [broadcasters'] right of free speech." 47 U.S.C. § 326. . . . In particular, the FCC's oversight responsibilities do not grant it the power to ordain any particular type of programming that must be offered by broadcast stations; for although "the Commission may inquire of licensees what they have done to determine the needs of the community they propose to serve, the Commission may not impose upon them its private notions of what the public ought to hear." . . .

. . . In a regime where Congress or the FCC exercised more intrusive control over the content of broadcast programming, an argument similar to appellants' might carry greater weight. But in the present regulatory system, those concerns are without foundation. . . .

III

[A.] In sum, the must-carry provisions do not pose such inherent dangers to free expression, or present such potential for censorship or manipulation, as to justify application of the most exacting level of First Amendment scrutiny. [T]he appropriate standard by which to evaluate the constitutionality of must-carry is the intermediate level of scrutiny applicable to content-neutral restrictions that impose an incidental burden on speech. See United States v. O'Brien, 391 U.S. 367 (1968).

Under *O'Brien*, a content-neutral regulation will be sustained if

> it furthers an important or substantial governmental interest; if the governmental interest is unrelated to the suppression of free expression; and if the incidental restriction on alleged First Amendment freedoms is no greater than is essential to the furtherance of that interest. Id. at 377.

To satisfy this standard, a regulation need not be the least speech-restrictive means of advancing the Government's interests. "Rather, the requirement of narrow tailoring is satisfied 'so long as the . . . regulation promotes a substantial government interest that would be achieved less effectively absent the regulation.'" Narrow tailoring in this context requires, in other words, that the means chosen do not "burden substantially more speech than is necessary to further the government's legitimate interests."

Congress declared that the must-carry provisions serve three interrelated interests: (1) preserving the benefits of free, over-the-air local broadcast television, (2) promoting the widespread dissemination of information from a multiplicity of sources, and (3) promoting fair competition in the market for television programming. None of these interests is related to the "suppression of free expression," or to the content of any speakers' messages. And viewed in the abstract, we have no difficulty concluding that each of them is an important governmental interest.

. . . [A]ssuring that the public has access to a multiplicity of information sources is a governmental purpose of the highest order, for it promotes values central to the First Amendment. Indeed, "'it has long been a basic tenet of national communications policy that "the widest possible dissemination of information from diverse and antagonistic sources is essential to the welfare of the public."'" . . . Finally, the Government's interest in eliminating restraints on fair competition is always substantial, even when the individuals or entities subject to particular regulations are engaged in expressive activity protected by the First Amendment.

[B.] That the Government's asserted interests are important in the abstract does not mean, however, that the must-carry rules will in fact advance those interests.

. . . The Government's assertion that the must-carry rules are necessary to protect the viability of broadcast television rests on two essential propositions: (1) that unless cable operators are compelled to carry broadcast stations, significant numbers of broadcast stations will be refused carriage on cable systems; and (2) that the broadcast stations denied carriage will either deteriorate to a substantial degree or fail altogether.

. . . [W]e hold that the District Court erred in granting summary judgment in favor of the Government. Because of the unresolved factual questions, the importance of the issues to the broadcast and cable industries, and the conflicting conclusions that the parties contend are to be drawn from the statistics and other evidence presented, we think it necessary to permit the parties to develop a more thorough factual record, and to allow the District Court to resolve any factual disputes remaining, before passing upon the constitutional validity of the challenged provisions. [Vacated and remanded.]

Justice O'CONNOR, with whom Justice SCALIA and Justice GINSBURG join, and with whom Justice THOMAS joins as to Parts I and III, concurring in part and dissenting in part.

    . . . Preferences for diversity of viewpoints, for localism, for educational programming, and for news and public affairs all make reference to content. . . . The First Amendment does more than just bar government from intentionally suppressing speech of which it disapproves. It also generally prohibits the government from excepting certain kinds of speech from regulation because it thinks the speech is especially valuable. . . . The interest in ensuring access to a multiplicity of diverse and antagonistic sources of information, no matter how praiseworthy, is directly tied to the content of what the speakers will likely say.

NOTES AND QUESTIONS

1. *Content-neutral or content-based?* Does Congress's desire to preserve the "benefits of free, over-the-air local broadcasting" reflect a preference for particular content? How can one consider the benefits without considering the content?

2. *Distinguishing* Tornillo. Why doesn't *Miami Herald v. Tornillo* govern this case? After all, the must-carry rules certainly interfere with the editorial discretion of cable operators. The Court suggested that one distinction is that "the cable operator exercises far greater control over access to the relevant medium." Can you think of any other distinctions between this case and *Tornillo*?

3. *Counting the votes.* Justice Stevens thought the must-carry rules should be upheld without further proceedings, but he provided the fifth vote for remand in order to provide a disposition.

4. *Turner II.* Upon remand of *Turner I*, the U.S. District Court for the District of Columbia conducted extensive fact-finding and then voted 2-1 to uphold the must-carry rules. The Supreme Court took the case on direct review and affirmed. Turner Broad. Sys., Inc. v. FCC, 520 U.S. 180 (1997) (*"Turner II"*). The Justices were again sharply divided, even though Justice Breyer had replaced Justice Blackmun in the interim between the two decisions. The five Justices in the majority held that the must-carry provisions satisfied *O'Brien*'s intermediate scrutiny test and were therefore constitutional. Although *Turner I* rejected the broadcast paradigm of regulation, the outcome of the *Turner* cases arguably depends on the unique characteristics of cable as medium. Justice Breyer, partially concurring in *Turner II*, made this point particularly explicit:

> [I] note (and agree) that a cable system, physically dependent upon the availability of space along city streets, at present (perhaps less in the future) typically faces little competition, that it therefore constitutes a kind of bottleneck that controls the range of viewer choice (whether or not it uses any consequent economic power for economically predatory purposes), and

that *some* degree—at least a limited degree—of governmental intervention and control through regulation can prove appropriate when justified under *O'Brien* (at least when not "content based"). . . . I agree further that the burden the statute imposes upon the cable system, potential cable programmers, and cable viewers is limited and will diminish as typical cable system capacity grows over time.

Id. at 228. Would a must-carry provision for newspapers, even a content-neutral one designed to preserve a multiplicity of voices in the marketplace of ideas, survive constitutional scrutiny?

AN EXTENDED NOTE ON INDECENCY ON CABLE TELEVISION

In 1992 Congress passed the Cable Television Consumer Protection and Competition Act, 47 U.S.C. § 532(h), (j), and note following § 531. The purpose of the Act was to regulate indecent material on cable television. In Denver Area Educational Telecommunications Consortium, Inc. v. FCC, 518 U.S. 727 (1996), the Court addressed the constitutionality of three provisions of the Act. The Court struck down, 6-3, section 10(b) of the Act, which required "cable system operators to segregate certain 'patently offensive' programming, to place it on a single channel, and to block that channel from viewer access unless the viewer requests access in advance and in writing." The government contended that this so-called "segregate and block" should be judged according to the principles announced in the Court's opinion in *Pacifica*, which "does not require that regulations of indecency on television be subject to the strictest" First Amendment "standard of review." The Court refused to address this argument directly, stating:

Nor need we here determine whether, or the extent to which, Pacifica does, or does not, impose some lesser standard of review where indecent speech is at issue. That is because once one examines this governmental restriction, it becomes apparent that, not only is it not a "least restrictive alternative" and is not "narrowly tailored" to meet its legitimate objective, it also seems considerably "more extensive than necessary." That is to say, it fails to satisfy this Court's formulations of the First Amendment's "strictest," as well as its somewhat less "strict," requirements. The provision before us does not reveal the caution and care that the standards underlying these various verbal formulas impose upon laws that seek to reconcile the critically important interest in protecting free speech with very important, or even compelling, interests that sometimes warrant restrictions.

The Court believed that the "segregate and block" provision was overly restrictive in several different respects. For example, the provision "force[d] the viewer to receive (for days or weeks at a time) all 'patently offensive' programming or none," and it "automatically place[d] the viewer's name on a special list." The Court also held that the provision was not narrowly tailored to protect children, a concededly compelling interest, because less restrictive means such as scrambling laws and "lockboxes"—used by parents to block particular channels—were available.

Despite striking down the "segregate and block" provision of the Act, the Court upheld section 10(a) of the Act, which granted cable system operators the discretion to block programming believed to be indecent on leased access channels—that is, a channel set aside by federal law for lease by third parties unaffiliated with the cable system. The Court held that this provision was "a sufficiently tailored response to an extraordinarily important problem," and Justice Thomas, writing for three others, noted that "[i]t is one thing to compel an operator to carry leased and public access speech, in apparent violation of *Tornillo*, but it is another thing altogether to say that the First Amendment forbids Congress to give back part of the operators' editorial discretion, which all recognize as fundamentally protected, in favor of a broader access right."

Finally, the Justices struck down section 10(c) of the Act, which gave cable operators discretion to block programming on *public* access channels that they believe to be indecent. Five Justices agreed on this result, but not on the explanation for it. Justice Breyer and three others found several differences between leased access channels and public access channels, emphasizing that "public programming control systems currently in place" can already minimize the exposure of children to indecent programming on public access channels. They concluded that section 10(c) was neither "necessary to protect children" nor "appropriately tailored to secure that end." Justice Kennedy and Ginsburg would have struck down the provision as a content-based restriction imposed on a public forum—that is, the public access channels—that failed to satisfy strict scrutiny.

The Telecommunications Act of 1996, 47 U.S.C. § 561, attempted once more to address indecent and obscene cable programming. Section 505 of the Act gave cable operators two options. One option was to "fully scramble" or "fully block" audio and video portions of any "sexually explicit adult programming or other programming that is indecent on any channel of its service primarily dedicated to sexually-oriented programming." The other option was to limit their transmission to the hours between 10 P.M. and 6 A.M. Most cable operators chose the "time channeling" option rather than the complete scrambling option. Playboy Entertainment Group brought the following suit challenging the constitutionality of the scrambling requirement. The following decision struck down the requirement by a 5-4 vote.

UNITED STATES v. PLAYBOY ENTERTAINMENT GROUP, INC.

529 U.S. 803 (2000)

Justice KENNEDY delivered the opinion of the Court.

This case presents a challenge to § 505 of the Telecommunications Act of 1996, Pub. L. 104-104, 110 Stat. 136, 47 U.S.C. § 561 (1994 ed., Supp. III). Section 505 requires cable television operators who provide channels "primarily dedicated to sexually-oriented programming" either to "fully scramble or otherwise fully block" those channels or to limit their transmission to hours when children are unlikely to be viewing, set by administrative regulation as the time between 10 P.M. and 6 A.M. Even before enactment of the statute, signal scrambling was already in use. Cable operators used scrambling in the regular course of business, so that only paying customers had access to certain programs. Scrambling could be imprecise, however; and either or both audio and visual portions of the scrambled programs might be heard or seen, a phenomenon known as "signal bleed." The purpose of § 505 is to shield children from hearing or seeing images resulting from signal bleed.

To comply with the statute, the majority of cable operators adopted the second, or "time channeling," approach. The effect of the widespread adoption of time channeling was to eliminate altogether the transmission of the targeted programming outside the safe harbor period in affected cable service areas. In other words, for two-thirds of the day no household in those service areas could receive the programming, whether or not the household or the viewer wanted to do so.

Appellee Playboy Entertainment Group, Inc, challenged the statute as unnecessarily restrictive content-based legislation violative of the First Amendment. After a trial, a three-judge District Court concluded that a regime in which viewers could order signal blocking on a household-by-household basis presented an effective, less restrictive alternative to § 505. Finding no error in this conclusion, we affirm.

I

Playboy Entertainment Group owns and prepares programs for adult television networks, including Playboy Television and Spice. Playboy transmits its programming to cable television operators, who retransmit it to their subscribers, either through monthly subscriptions to premium channels or on a so-called "pay-per-view" basis. Cable operators transmit Playboy's signal, like other premium channel signals, in scrambled form. The operators then provide paying subscribers with an "addressable converter," a box placed on the home television set. The converter permits the viewer to see and hear the descrambled signal. It is conceded that almost all of Playboy's programming consists of sexually explicit material as defined by the statute. . . .

II

. . . The speech in question is defined by its content; and the statute which seeks to restrict it is content based. Section 505 applies only to channels primarily dedicated to "sexually explicit adult programming or other programming that is indecent." The statute is unconcerned with signal bleed from any other channels. . . . The overriding justification for the regulation is concern for the effect of the subject matter on young viewers. . . .

Not only does § 505 single out particular programming content for regulation, it also singles out particular programmers. . . . [T]he statutory disability applies only to channels "primarily dedicated to sexually-oriented programming." One sponsor of the measure even identified appellee by name. See 141 Cong. Rec. 15587 (1995) (statement of Sen. Feinstein) (noting the statute would apply to channels "such as the Playboy and Spice channels"). Laws designed or intended to suppress or restrict the expression of specific speakers contradict basic First Amendment principles. Section 505 limited Playboy's market as a penalty for its programming choice, though other channels capable of transmitting like material are altogether exempt.

The effect of the federal statute on the protected speech is now apparent. . . . According to the District Court, "30 to 50% of all adult programming is viewed by households prior to 10 P.M.," when the safe-harbor period begins. To prohibit this much speech is a significant restriction of communication between speakers and willing adult listeners, communication which enjoys First Amendment protection. It is of no moment that the statute does not impose a complete prohibition. The distinction between laws burdening and laws banning speech is but a matter of degree. . . .

Since § 505 is a content-based speech restriction, it can stand only if it satisfies strict scrutiny. If a statute regulates speech based on its content, it must be narrowly tailored to promote a compelling Government interest. If a less restrictive alternative would serve the Government's purpose, the legislature must use that alternative. To do otherwise would be to restrict speech without an adequate justification, a course the First Amendment does not permit.

Our precedents teach these principles. Where the designed benefit of a content-based speech restriction is to shield the sensibilities of listeners, the general rule is that the right of expression prevails, even where no less restrictive alternative exists. We are expected to protect our own sensibilities "simply by averting [our] eyes." [*Cohen v. California; Erzoznik*.] Here, of course, we consider images transmitted to some homes where they are not wanted and where parents often are not present to give immediate guidance. Cable television, like broadcast media, presents unique problems, which inform our assessment of the interests at stake, and which may justify restrictions that would be unacceptable in other contexts. See [*DAETC; Pacifica*]. No one suggests the Government must be indifferent to unwanted, indecent speech that comes into the home without parental consent. The speech here, all agree, is protected speech; and the question is what standard the Government must meet in order to restrict it. As we consider a content-based regulation, the answer should be clear: The standard is strict scrutiny. This case involves speech alone; and even where speech is indecent and enters the home, the objective of shielding children does not suffice to support a blanket ban if the protection can be accomplished by a less restrictive alternative.

    . . . There is, moreover, a key difference between cable television and the broadcasting media, which is the point on which this case turns: Cable systems have the capacity to block unwanted channels on a household-by-household basis. The option to block reduces the likelihood, so concerning to the Court in *Pacifica*, that traditional First Amendment scrutiny would deprive the Government of all authority to address this sort of problem. The corollary, of course, is that targeted blocking enables the Government to support parental authority without affecting the First Amendment interests of speakers and willing listeners—listeners for whom, if the speech is unpopular or indecent, the privacy of their own homes may be the optimal place of receipt. Simply put, targeted blocking is less restrictive than banning, and the Government cannot ban speech if targeted blocking is a feasible and effective means of furthering its compelling interests. This is not to say that the absence of an effective blocking mechanism will in all cases suffice to support a law restricting the speech in question; but if a less restrictive means is available for the Government to achieve its goals, the Government must use it.

III

    . . . When a student first encounters our free speech jurisprudence, he or she might think it is influenced by the philosophy that one idea is as good as any other, and that in art and literature objective standards of style, taste, decorum, beauty, and esthetics are deemed by the Constitution to be inappropriate, indeed unattainable. Quite the opposite is true. The Constitution no more enforces a relativistic philosophy or moral nihilism than it does any other point of view. The Constitution exists precisely so that opinions and judgments, including esthetic and moral judgments about art and literature, can be formed, tested, and expressed. What the Constitution says is that these judgments are for the individual to make, not for the Government to decree, even with the mandate or approval of a majority. Technology expands the capacity to choose; and it denies the potential of this revolution if we assume the Government is best positioned to make these choices for us.

. . . There is little hard evidence of how widespread or how serious the problem of signal bleed is. Indeed, there is no proof as to how likely any child is to view a discernible explicit image, and no proof of the duration of the bleed or the quality of the pictures or sound. To say that millions of children are subject to a risk of viewing signal bleed is one thing; to avoid articulating the true nature and extent of the risk is quite another. Under § 505, sanctionable signal bleed can include instances as fleeting as an image appearing on a screen for just a few seconds. The First Amendment requires a more careful assessment and characterization of an evil in order to justify a regulation as sweeping as this. . . .

In addition, market-based solutions such as programmable televisions, VCR's, and mapping systems (which display a blue screen when tuned to a scrambled signal) may eliminate signal bleed at the consumer end of the cable. . . .

. . . The Government also failed to prove [that voluntary blocking at the request of the cable subscriber, available under § 504] would be an ineffective alternative to § 505. . . . There is no evidence that a well-promoted voluntary blocking provision would not be capable at least of informing parents about signal bleed (if they are not yet aware of it) and about their rights to have the bleed blocked (if they consider it a problem and have not yet controlled it themselves).

. . . It is no response that voluntary blocking requires a consumer to take action, or may be inconvenient, or may not go perfectly every time. A court should not assume a plausible, less restrictive alternative would be ineffective; and a court should not presume parents, given full information, will fail to act. If unresponsive operators are a concern, moreover, a notice statute could give cable operators ample incentive, through fines or other penalties for noncompliance, to respond to blocking requests in prompt and efficient fashion.

[The Government then contended voluntary blocking was insufficient because "[t]here would certainly be parents—perhaps a large number of parents—who out of inertia, indifference, or distraction, simply would take no action to block signal bleed, even if fully informed of the problem and even if offered a relatively easy solution."]

Even upon the assumption that the Government has an interest in substituting itself for informed and empowered parents, its interest is not sufficiently compelling to justify this widespread restriction on speech. The Government's argument stems from the idea that parents do not know their children are viewing the material on a scale or frequency to cause concern, or if so, that parents do not want to take affirmative steps to block it and their decisions are to be superseded. The assumptions have not been established; and in any event the assumptions apply only in a regime where the option of blocking has not been explained. The whole point of a publicized § 504 would be to advise parents that indecent material may be shown and to afford them an opportunity to block it at all times, even when they are not at home and even after 10 P.M. Time channeling does not offer this assistance. The regulatory alternative of a publicized § 504, which has the real possibility of promoting more open disclosure and the choice of an effective blocking system, would provide parents the information needed to engage in active supervision. The Government has not shown that this alternative, a regime of added communication and support, would be insufficient to secure its objective, or that any overriding harm justifies its intervention.

. . . Basic speech principles are at stake in this case. When the purpose and design of a statute is to regulate speech by reason of its content, special consideration or latitude is not accorded to the Government merely because the law can somehow be described as a burden rather than outright suppression. We cannot be influenced, moreover, by the perception that the regulation in question is not a major one because the speech is not very important. The history of the law of free expression is one of vindication in cases involving speech that many citizens may find shabby, offensive, or even ugly. It follows that all content-based restrictions on speech must give us more than a moment's pause. If television broadcasts can expose children to the real risk of harmful exposure to indecent materials, even in their own home and without parental consent, there is a problem the Government can address. It must do so, however, in a way consistent with First Amendment principles. Here the Government has not met the burden the First Amendment imposes. . . .

Justice BREYER, with whom THE CHIEF JUSTICE, Justice O'CONNOR, and Justice SCALIA join, dissenting.

The majority first concludes that the Government failed to prove the seriousness of the problem—receipt of adult channels by children whose parents did not request their broadcast. This claim is flat-out wrong. For one thing, the parties concede that basic RF scrambling does not scramble the audio portion of the program. For another, Playboy itself conducted a survey of cable operators who were asked: "Is your system in full compliance with Section 505 (no discernible audio or video bleed)?" To this question, 75% of cable operators answered "no." . . .

I would add to this empirical evidence the majority's own statement that "*most cable operators had 'no practical choice but to curtail'*" adult programming by switching to nighttime only transmission of adult channels. *If signal bleed is not a significant empirical problem, then why, in light of the cost of its cure, must so many cable operators switch to night time hours?* There is no realistic answer to this question. I do not think it realistic to imagine that signal bleed occurs just enough to make cable operators skittish, without also significantly exposing children to these images.

. . . The majority's second claim—that the Government failed to demonstrate the absence of a "less restrictive alternative"—presents a closer question. The specific question is whether § 504's "opt-out" amounts to a "less restrictive," but *similarly* practical and *effective*, way to accomplish § 505's child-protecting objective. . . .

. . . Unlike the majority, I believe the record makes clear that § 504's opt-out is not a similarly effective alternative. Section 504 (opt-out) and § 505 (opt-in) work differently in order to achieve very different legislative objectives. Section 504 gives parents the power to tell cable operators to keep any channel out of their home. Section 505 does more. Unless parents explicitly consent, it inhibits the transmission of adult cable channels to children whose parents may be unaware of what they are watching, whose parents cannot easily supervise television viewing habits, whose parents do not know of their § 504 "opt-out" rights, or whose parents are simply unavailable at critical times. In this respect, § 505 serves the same interests as the laws that deny children access to adult cabarets or X-rated movies. These laws, and § 505, all act in the absence of direct parental supervision.

This legislative objective is perfectly legitimate. Where over 28 million school age children have both parents or their only parent in the work force, where at least 5 million children are left alone at home without supervision each week, and where children may spend afternoons and evenings watching television outside of the home with friends, § 505 offers independent protection for a large number of families. . . . [G]overnment has a compelling interest in helping parents by preventing minors from accessing sexually explicit materials in the absence of parental supervision.

NOTES AND QUESTIONS

1. *Evidentiary support.* How much more evidence would Congress need about the problem of signal bleed in order to justify § 505?
2. *Opt out/opt in.* Will a provision allowing audience members to "opt out" of receiving offensive speech always be constitutionally preferable to a provision forcing audience members who wish to receive the speech to "opt in"?
3. *Cable as medium.* How much of this decision rests on the distinct technological features of cable as a medium?
4. *Regulating "bad" parenting.* Why isn't the government allowed to regulate to protect children in the face of parental indifference or inertia? If, as the evidence indicates, "fewer than 0.5% of cable subscribers requested full blocking" under § 504, does this mean that signal bleed was not a significant problem? That few parents cared about signal bleed? Or that few parents knew that full blocking was available upon request? Is the interpretation of the evidence relevant to the constitutional analysis?

F.   REGULATION OF THE INTERNET AND NEW MEDIA

The Telecommunications Act of 1996 attempted to regulate indecency not merely on cable systems but on the Internet as well. Title V of the Telecommunications Act is called the Communications Decency Act (CDA). The constitutionality of two provisions of the CDA was at issue in *Reno v. ACLU*, below. However, in addressing the constitutionality of the CDA provisions, the Court also addressed a more fundamental jurisprudential issue, namely, whether the broadcast paradigm of indecency regulation laid out in *Pacifica* also applied to the Internet.

<u>RENO v. ACLU</u>
521 U.S. 844 (1997)

Justice STEVENS delivered the opinion of the Court.

At issue is the constitutionality of two statutory provisions enacted to protect minors from "indecent" and "patently offensive" communications on the Internet. Notwithstanding the legitimacy and importance of the congressional goal of protecting children from harmful materials, we agree with the three-judge District Court that the statute abridges "the freedom of speech" protected by the First Amendment.

[The Court began its opinion by reiterating some of the district court's extensive factual findings about the nature of the Internet, comparing it to "a vast library including millions of readily available and indexed publications and a sprawling mall offering goods and services." The Court also noted that "[f]rom the publishers' point of view, it constitutes a vast platform from which to address and hear from a world-wide audience of millions of readers, viewers, researchers, and buyers. Any person or organization with a computer connected to the Internet can 'publish' information." The Court then turned to the challenged provisions of the CDA: the "indecent transmission" provision and the "patently offensive display" provision. The first, § 223(a), prohibited knowing transmission of obscene or indecent messages to any recipient under 18 years of age. The second provision, § 223(d), prohibited knowing sending or displaying of patently offensive messages in a manner available to a person under 18 years of age. That section defined such messages as "any comment, request, suggestion, proposal, image, or other communication that, in context, depicts or describes, in terms patently offensive as measured by contemporary community standards, sexual or excretory activities or organs, regardless of whether the user of such service placed the call or initiated the communication." It then provided for affirmative defenses for those who take good-faith measure to restrict access by minors and for those who restrict access through certain age or credit card verification systems.]

In *Ginsberg*, we upheld the constitutionality of a New York statute that prohibited selling to minors under 17 years of age material that was considered obscene as to them even if not obscene as to adults. . . . [W]e relied not only on the State's independent interest in the well-being of its youth, but also on our consistent recognition of the principle that "the parents' claim to authority in their own household to direct the rearing of their children is basic in the structure of our society." In four important respects, the statute upheld in *Ginsberg* was narrower than the CDA. First, we noted in *Ginsberg* that "the prohibition against sales to minors does not bar parents who so desire from purchasing the magazines for their children." Under the CDA, by contrast, neither the parents' consent—nor even their participation—in the communication would avoid the application of the statute. Second, the New York statute applied only to commercial transactions, whereas the CDA contains no such limitation. Third, the New York statute cabined its definition of material that is harmful to minors with the requirement that it be "utterly without redeeming social importance for minors." The CDA fails to provide us with any definition of the term "indecent" as used in § 223(a)(1) and, importantly, omits any requirement that the "patently offensive" material covered by § 223(d) lack serious literary, artistic, political, or scientific value. Fourth, the New York statute defined a minor as a person under the age of 17, whereas the CDA, in applying to all those under 18 years, includes an additional year of those nearest majority.

In *Pacifica*, we . . . concluded that the ease with which children may obtain access to broadcasts, "coupled with the concerns recognized in *Ginsberg*," justified special treatment of indecent broadcasting.

As with the New York statute at issue in *Ginsberg*, there are significant differences between the order upheld in *Pacifica* and the CDA. First, the order in *Pacifica*, issued by an agency that had been regulating radio stations for decades, targeted a specific broadcast that represented a rather dramatic departure from traditional program content in order to designate when—rather than whether—it would be permissible to air such a program in that particular medium. The CDA's broad categorical prohibitions are not limited to particular times and are not dependent on any evaluation by an agency familiar with the unique characteristics of the Internet. Second, unlike the CDA, the Commission's declaratory order was not punitive; we expressly refused to decide whether the indecent broadcast "would justify a criminal prosecution." Finally, the Commission's order applied to a medium which as a matter of history had "received the most limited First Amendment protection," in large part because warnings could not adequately protect the listener from unexpected program content. The Internet, however, has no comparable history. Moreover, the District Court found that the risk of encountering indecent material by accident is remote because a series of affirmative steps is required to access specific material.

. . . In Southeastern Promotions, Ltd. v. Conrad, 420 U.S. 546, 557, 43 L. Ed. 2d 448, 95 S. Ct. 1239 (1975), we observed that "each medium of expression . . . may present its own problems." Thus, some of our cases have recognized special justifications for regulation of the broadcast media that are not applicable to other speakers. In these cases, the Court relied on the history of extensive government regulation of the broadcast medium; the scarcity of available frequencies at its inception; and its "invasive" nature.

Those factors are not present in cyberspace. Neither before nor after the enactment of the CDA have the vast democratic fora of the Internet been subject to the type of government supervision and regulation that has attended the broadcast industry. Moreover, the Internet is not as "invasive" as radio or television. The District Court specifically found that "communications over the Internet do not 'invade' an individual's home or appear on one's computer screen unbidden. Users seldom encounter content 'by accident.'" It also found that "almost all sexually explicit images are preceded by warnings as to the content," and cited testimony that "'odds are slim' that a user would come across a sexually explicit sight by accident."

. . . . [U]nlike the conditions that prevailed when Congress first authorized regulation of the broadcast spectrum, the Internet can hardly be considered a "scarce" expressive commodity. It provides relatively unlimited, low-cost capacity for communication of all kinds. The Government estimates that "as many as 40 million people use the Internet today, and that figure is expected to grow to 200 million by 1999." This dynamic, multifaceted category of communication includes not only traditional print and news services, but also audio, video, and still images, as well as interactive, real-time dialogue. Through the use of chat rooms, any person with a phone line can become a town crier with a voice that resonates farther than it could from any soapbox. Through the use of Web pages, mail exploders, and newsgroups, the same individual can become a pamphleteer. As the District Court found, "the content on the Internet is as diverse as human thought." We agree with its conclusion that our cases provide no basis for qualifying the level of First Amendment scrutiny that should be applied to this medium.

. . . The breadth of the CDA's coverage is wholly unprecedented. Unlike the regulations upheld in Ginsberg and Pacifica, the scope of the CDA is not limited to commercial speech or commercial entities. Its open-ended prohibitions embrace all nonprofit entities and individuals posting indecent messages or displaying them on their own computers in the presence of minors. The general, undefined terms "indecent" and "patently offensive" cover large amounts of nonpornographic material with serious educational or other value. Moreover, the "community standards" criterion as applied to the Internet means that any communication available to a nation-wide audience will be judged by the standards of the community most likely to be offended by the message. The regulated subject matter includes any of the seven "dirty words" used in the Pacifica monologue, the use of which the Government's expert acknowledged could constitute a felony. It may also extend to discussions about prison rape or safe sexual practices, artistic images that include nude subjects, and arguably the card catalogue of the Carnegie Library.

. . . Under the CDA, a parent allowing her 17-year-old to use the family computer to obtain information on the Internet that she, in her parental judgment, deems appropriate could face a lengthy prison term. See 47 U.S.C. A. § 223(a)(2) (Supp. 1997). Similarly, a parent who sent his 17-year-old college freshman information on birth control via e-mail could be incarcerated even though neither he, his child, nor anyone in their home community, found the material "indecent" or "patently offensive," if the college town's community thought otherwise.

The breadth of this content-based restriction of speech imposes an especially heavy burden on the Government to explain why a less restrictive provision would not be as effective as the CDA. It has not done so. . . . Particularly in the light of the absence of any detailed findings by the Congress, or even hearings addressing the special problems of the CDA, we are persuaded that the CDA is not narrowly tailored if that requirement has any meaning at all.

. . . We agree with the District Court's conclusion that the CDA places an unacceptably heavy burden on protected speech, and that the defenses do not constitute the sort of "narrow tailoring" that will save an otherwise patently invalid unconstitutional provision. In *Sable*, we remarked that the speech restriction at issue there amounted to "'burning the house to roast the pig.'" The CDA, casting a far darker shadow over free speech, threatens to torch a large segment of the Internet community.

Justice O'CONNOR, with whom THE CHIEF JUSTICE joins, concurring in the judgment in part and dissenting in part. [Omitted.]

NOTES AND QUESTIONS

1. *Defining minors.* Is one of the problems with the CDA provisions that they make no distinctions between 17-year olds and 7-year olds? If so, how should Congress remedy this problem?
2. *A medium-specific First Amendment.* Is the First Amendment "medium specific"? Or is there one set of First Amendment standards for broadcasters and a different set of standards for all other media? Is "intrusiveness" (in the sense that one can be subjected to indecent material without warning or consent) still a valid rationale for tolerating more regulation of a medium than might otherwise be allowed?
3. *Protecting minors by restricting adults.* How much may a regulation designed to protect children infringe upon nonobscene speech before it is declared invalid?
4. *Community standards and the internet.* Is the application of a "community standards" criterion to define indecency inherently unconstitutional when applied to the Internet, which crosses all geographical boundaries?
5. *Mobile access and invasiveness.* Today many children have access to smart phones, iPads, or other mobile devices that offer instant Web access and browsing capability. As of 2009, 77 percent of teens had mobile phones. See Implementation of the Child Safe Viewing Act: Examination of Parental Control Technologies for Video or Audio Programming, 24 F.C.C.R. 11,413, 11,414 & n.5. Does this make the Internet as invasive as radio or television?

6. *Video games as medium.* In Brown v. Entertainment Merchants Ass'n, 564 U.S. 786 (2011), the Supreme Court rejected the argument that the medium of video games should receive a reduced level of First Amendment protection. The case involved a constitutional challenge to a California statute prohibiting sale or rental of violent video games to minors. The state argued that the interactive graphic nature of such games justified the prohibition, but the Court struck down the California law as a content-based restriction on speech. The Court's opinion conceded that video games have little to do with protection of discourse on public matters, but the Court granted full First Amendment protection, stating: "[W]e have long recognized that it is difficult to distinguish politics from entertainment, and dangerous to try." The Court found no relevant distinction between the video games and the "books, plays, and moves that preceded them.": "video games communicate ideas—and even social messages—through many familiar literary devices (such as characters, dialogue, plot, and music) and through features distinctive to the medium (such as the player's interaction with the virtual world)." The opinion further rejected the notion that violent speech fell into a category of low-value or unprotected speech, even when aimed at children. As Justice Scalia noted in his opinion for the Court, many of the classics of children's literature "contain no shortage of gore. Grimm's Fairy Tales, for example, are grim indeed." Thus, without compelling evidence showing that violent video games cause actual harm to minors, the California law failed strict scrutiny. For further discussion of the Roberts Court's lack of receptiveness to arguments for "medium-specific" First Amendment protections, see Lyrissa Barnett Lidsky, Not A Free Press Court?, 2012 B.Y.Y.L. Rev. 1819 (2012). For discussion of government attempts to regulate "gruesome speech," ostensibly to protect children, and the constitutional obstacles to doing so, see Eugene Volokh, Gruesome Speech, 100 Cornell L. Rev. 901(2015).

7. *Medium-specific standards applied to video-on-demand?* In Citizens United v. Federal Elections Commission, 558 U.S. 310 (2010), excerpted in Chapter 6, the Court refused to apply different First Amendment standards to "movies shown through video-on-demand" than it applied to "television ads" simply because users must take affirmative steps to obtain video-on-demand. The Court stated:

> While some means of communication may be less effective than others at influencing the public in different contexts, any effort by the Judiciary to decide which means of communications are to be preferred for the particular type of message and speaker would raise questions as to the courts' own lawful authority. Substantial questions would arise if courts were to begin saying what means of speech should be preferred or disfavored. And in all events, those differentiations might soon prove to be irrelevant or outdated by technologies that are in rapid flux. []
>
> Courts, too, are bound by the First Amendment. We must decline to draw, and then redraw, constitutional lines based on the particular media or technology used to disseminate political speech from a particular speaker.

AN EXTENDED NOTE ON THE PROTECTION OF CHILDREN FROM INDECENT INTERNET CONTENT

Congress responded to the Court's decision in Reno v. ACLU by enacting the Child Online Protection Act (COPA), 47 U.S.C. § 231(a), which represented a more limited attempt to regulate Internet indecency. COPA imposed criminal penalties for the knowing posting, for "commercial purposes," of Internet content "harmful to minors," § 231(a), which it defined as

> any communication . . . that is obscene or that—
>   (A) the average person, applying contemporary community standards, would find, taking the material as a whole and with respect to minors, is designed to appeal to, or is designed to pander to, the prurient interest;
>   (B) depicts, describes, or represents, in a manner patently offensive with respect to minors, an actual or simulated sexual act or sexual contact, an actual or simulated normal or perverted sexual act, or a lewd exhibition of the genitals or post-pubescent female breast; and
>   (C) taken as a whole, lacks serious literary, artistic, political, or scientific value for minors."

The statute provided an affirmative defense to those who took steps to prevent minors from gaining access to the prohibited materials. Before COPA could take effect, Internet providers and civil liberties groups successfully sought a preliminary injunction against enforcement. The Supreme Court granted certiorari, vacated the judgment of the Court of Appeals, and remanded. The Court held that the community standards language of COPA did not, standing alone, render it unconstitutional. *See* Ashcroft v. ACLU (*"Ashcroft I"*), 535 U.S. 564 (2002). On remand, the Third Circuit again affirmed the district court's grant of the preliminary injunction. The Supreme Court again granted certiorari and in Ashcroft v. American Civil Liberties (*"Ashcroft II"*), 542 U.S. 656 (2004), again enjoined enforcement of COPA and remanded to the district court for trial. The Court held that the government had failed to show that proposed alternatives, such as filtering, would not be as effective as COPA's content-based restrictions on speech. The Court also concluded that there were

> important practical reasons to let the injunction stand pending a full trial on the merits. First, the potential harms from reversing the injunction outweigh those of leaving it in place by mistake. . . .
>   Second, there are substantial factual disputes remaining in the case. As mentioned above, there is a serious gap in the evidence as to the effectiveness of filtering software. . . .
>   Third, and on a related point, the factual record does not reflect current technological reality—a serious flaw in any case involving the Internet. The technology of the Internet evolves at a rapid pace. Yet the factfindings of the District Court were entered in February 1999, over five years ago. Since then, certain facts about the Internet are known to have changed. . . . It is reasonable to assume that other technological developments important to the First Amendment analysis have also occurred during that time. More and better filtering alternatives may exist than when the District Court entered its findings. Indeed, we know that after the District Court entered its factfindings, a congressionally appointed commission issued a report that found that filters are more effective than verification screens.
>   Delay between the time that a district court makes factfindings and the time that a case reaches this Court is inevitable, with the necessary consequence that there will be some discrepancy between the facts as found and the facts at the time the appellate court takes up the question. . . . By affirming the preliminary injunction and remanding for trial, we allow the parties to update and supplement the factual record to reflect current technological realities.

Justice Stevens and Justice Ginsburg wrote a separate concurrence, objecting to the application of community standards in defining the prohibited content, since it would "penalize speakers for making available to the general World Wide Web audience that which the least tolerant communities in America deem unfit for their children's consumption, and consider that principle a sufficient basis for deciding this case."

Justices Breyer, Scalia, O'Connor, and the Chief Justice dissented, noting that Congress had invested "eight years of legislative effort" trying to address the problem and had endeavored valiantly to respond to the Court's criticism in Reno of the predecessor.

On remand, the district court again concluded that COPA was unconstitutionally vague, overbroad, and not narrowly tailored and, as a result, the court permanently enjoined the Attorney General from enforcing the statute. ACLU v. Gonzales, 478 F. Supp. 2d 775 (E.D. Pa. 2007). The Third Circuit affirmed. ACLU v. Mukasey, 534 F.3d 181 (3d Cir. 2008), *cert. denied*, 555 U.S. 1137 (2009). What would you advise Congress to do in response to *Ashcroft II*? Remember that this was a 5-4 decision, with Justices Scalia, O'Connor, Breyer, and Rehnquist dissenting. Chief Justice Roberts and Justice Alito replaced Chief Justice Rehnquist and Justice O'Connor after *Ashcroft II* was decided. Justice Antonin Scalia has since died.

How should the government legislate to protect children when technological solutions, like filtering software, are rapidly evolving? Do technological problems evolve just as rapidly? As spam filters become better at identifying spam, senders of spam become better at evading spam filters. Do the providers of indecent content have the same incentive to evade filters?

The Supreme Court in 2008 upheld the constitutionality of a statute criminalizing virtual child pornography in United States v. Williams, 553 U.S. 285 (2008). After the Court's 2002 decision in Ashcroft v. Free Speech Coalition, striking down Congress's initial attempt to ban technologically created child pornography, Congress passed a new statute making it a crime to distribute or promote "purported material . . . . that reflects the belief, or is intended to cause another to believe" that it is a "visual depiction of an actual minor engaging in sexually explicit conduct." *See* 18 U.S.C. § 2252A(a)(3)(B). The respondent in Williams was charged with pandering virtual child pornography under this statute after he uploaded child pornography to the Internet that he explicitly labeled "REAL." The Supreme Court held that the statute was neither substantially overbroad nor vague. The Court construed the statute narrowly, limiting it to portrayals that would necessarily cause a reasonable viewer to believe that the actors actually engaged in sexual conduct on camera; the Court excluded from the statute's reach materials billed as virtual child pornography or "sex between youthful-looking adult actors." In dissent, Justices Souter and Ginsburg said the statute attempted to evade the First Amendment protection of virtual child pornography by punishing proposals to transact in it rather than the virtual child pornography itself.

AN EXTENDED NOTE ON NET NEUTRALITY

Existing technology gives broadband providers the ability to control various aspects of subscribers' access to the Internet—for example, what websites and applications they can access, and the speed and reliability of various connections. In ?w instances they have used this power to slow peer-to-peer communications or to levy surcharges on certain users. Congress and the FCC have been urged to adopt regulations to prevent providers from discriminating among subscribers who have paid for the same level of access. The goal of such regulations is known colloquially as "network neutrality," although there is little agreement as to exactly how much neutrality this should require. Providers say they need freedom to engage in such discrimination to make efficient use of their networks' capacities. Critics say the providers want to control the architecture of broadband, give preferential treatment to sites and services in which they have a financial interest, and emulate the model of the cable television industry's multiple tiers of service for which the subscriber pays extra fees.

Embedded in this controversy are many questions about the appropriate regulatory model (if any). The clearest nondiscrimination model is common carrier regulation. Traditional telephone companies, for example, are treated as common carriers who must offer service to all similarly situated customers on the same terms and at the same rates. Cable television offers another model; cable systems are required to offer a certain basic level of content (as we saw in *Turner I*), but beyond that they have considerable freedom to choose what to offer their customers, how to package it, and how to price it. As users of the electromagnetic spectrum (and possibly by virtue of their pervasiveness and intrusiveness), broadband providers might be thought to be subject to the broadcasting model of regulation. Or they might be thought to be as immune from regulation as booksellers or newspapers.

The FCC attempted to regulate net neutrality to ensure an "open Internet," but its efforts to do so were twice rebuffed by the U.S. Court of Appeals for the D.C. Circuit on jurisdictional grounds. Comcast Corp. v. FCC, 600 F.3d 642 (D.C. Cir. 2010) (holding that FCC lacked ancillary jurisdiction to enforce net neutrality); Verizon v. FCC, 740 F.3d 623 (D.C. Cir. 2014).

In response, the FCC began rulemaking proceedings and sought public comment "on how best to protect and promote an open Internet." These proceedings resulted in the 2015 Open Internet Order, 80 Fed. Reg. 19,738 (Apr. 13, 2015), which took effect on June 12, 2015. In a press release on its website, the FCC asserted that the Open Internet rules will "protect and maintain open, uninhibited access to legal online content without broadband Internet access providers being allowed to block, impair, or establish fast/slow lanes to lawful content." The FCC grounded its authority to promulgate the rules on Title II of the Communications Act and Section 706 of the Telecommunications Act of 1996; in other words, the FCC voted to treat broadband Internet like telecommunications services rather than information services but agreed to refrain or "forbear" from enforcing certain common carrier obligations on broadband providers, such as price-setting. The FCC asserted that broadband providers are "conduits, not speakers, with respect to broadband Internet access services." The FCC further asserted that the rules "are tailored to the important government interest in maintaining an open Internet as a platform for expression, among other things."

In United States Telecom. Ass'n v. FCC, 825 F.3d 674 (D.C. Cir. 2016), the D.C. Circuit held that the FCC had statutory authority to reclassify broadband as a telecommunications service/utility and that its decision to do so was not arbitrary and capricious. The broadband providers had contended that the reclassification violated their First Amendment rights by forcing them "to transmit speech with which they might disagree." But the D.C. Circuit held that the requirement that "broadband providers [ ] offer a standardized service that transmits data on a non-discriminatory basis" had "long been imposed on [other common carriers such as] "telephone companies, railroads, and postal services, without raising any First Amendment issue." The court held that because the providers "merely facilitate the transmission of the speech of others rather than engage in speech in their own right," their First Amendment concerns were without merits. In other words, the court credited the FCC's findings that the broadband providers acted as conduits for the speech of others and neither intended to convey a message nor exercised "editorial intervention." Of course, insofar as a broadband provider might offer its own *content*—such as a news or weather site—separate from its internet access service, the provider would receive the same protection under the First Amendment as other producers of internet content. But the challenged rules apply only to the provision of internet access as common carriage, as to which equal access and nondiscrimination mandates present no First Amendment problem. A dissenting judge would have held that the reclassification was arbitrary and capricious in violation of the Administrative Procedure Act.

Despite this victory, statements made by the then-new FCC Chairman Ajit Pai and by President Donald J. Trump in 2016 cast the fate of net neutrality into doubt.

CHAPTER
9

Tort Law and the First Amendment

TABLE OF CONTENTS

Tort law implicates First Amendment values when it attempts to impose liability on those who make or publish statements that allegedly harm the reputation, privacy, or emotional tranquility of others. This chapter first examines the interaction between First Amendment law and torts that impose liability for harms caused by publication, including the torts of defamation, intentional infliction of emotional distress, and public disclosure of private facts. The chapter then examines the interaction between the First Amendment and the so-called "newsgathering torts."

A. FIRST AMENDMENT LIMITATIONS ON THE TORT OF DEFAMATION

The term *defamation* encompasses the twin torts of libel and slander. As a rule of thumb, defamation in written or any other relatively permanent form is libel; defamation in spoken or other "impermanent" form is slander. Libel and slander are civil actions, allowing private litigants who have been defamed to recover monetary damages for harm to their reputations. Defamation, therefore, is concerned with policing the boundaries of free expression and forcing speakers to pay for harm caused by their speech. For obvious reasons, the press is a common target of defamation actions, and fear of tort liability shapes many editorial decisions.

Until 1964, the tort of defamation was purely a matter of state law: defamatory speech, like fighting words and obscenity, was deemed to be outside the scope of First Amendment protection. As in 1964, the common law of most states today requires plaintiffs seeking recovery for defamation to prove the existence of (1) a defamatory communication by the defendant, (2) "of and concerning" the plaintiff, and (3) publication by the defendant to at least one third party. Note that the common law typically does not require a libel plaintiff to prove actual harm to his or her reputation,[1] but instead allows juries to award "presumed damages" based on the nature of the defamatory statement made by the defendant. This unusual feature of the common law tort is justified by the difficulty of proving harm to reputation. Reputation is a sociological construct. In other words, one's reputation is defined by how one is perceived by others. Therefore, the tort defines a defamatory communication as one that "tends to harm" an individual's reputation in the eyes of his or her community. In order to be defamatory, a communication must go beyond mere name-calling and actually call into question a plaintiff's moral fiber. Hence, it is ordinarily defamatory to call an individual an adulterer, a domestic abuser, or a murderer, but it is not defamatory to call him a jerk or a neat freak or even to state falsely that he has died.

Because this is a First Amendment casebook rather than a Torts casebook, we will not dwell on the intricacies of tort law, but instead will focus on the Supreme Court's "constitutionalization" of defamation law since 1964. You should be aware, nonetheless, that defendants often are able to defeat defamation cases based on tort law alone, without reference to the First Amendment. Even before the Supreme Court began to constitutionalize defamation law, tort law had developed a variety of privileges designed to protect freedom of expression. For example, although one who repeats the defamatory statement of another will ordinarily be liable as if he had originated it (this is known as the "republication rule"), the common law recognizes a privilege that protects a person who repeats or "republishes" a defamatory statement made by someone else in the course of an official government proceeding. Even today, the media often rely on this tort privilege—the "fair and accurate report privilege"—to avoid liability for defamation when reporting on governmental affairs. Moreover, by 1964, tort law provided that a defendant could defend against a defamation action by establishing the truth of his publication. In fact, the defendant did not ordinarily have to prove that each and every fact in his publication was literally true. So long as the defendant could establish "substantial truth"—that the gist or sting of the slightly inaccurate statement was the same as the true facts—the defendant could evade defamation liability. In considering the Supreme Court's seminal decision in *New York Times v. Sullivan,* you should consider why the Supreme Court determined that tort law did not do enough to protect press freedom. You should also consider *Sullivan* in the context of the civil rights movement and consider what would have been the fate of that movement if the half-million-dollar defamation verdict imposed against the New York Times by the Alabama courts had been allowed to survive.

---

[1] Slander plaintiffs typically must be able to put an actual dollar figure on their losses unless they show that the slander falls into one of four categories known as slander per se. The four categories concern allegations of lack of chastity, unfitness for one's business or profession, having a loathsome disease, and commission of a crime.

1. *Defamation of Public Officials*

NEW YORK TIMES CO. v. SULLIVAN

376 U.S. 254 (1964)

Justice BRENNAN delivered the opinion of the Court.

We are required in this case to determine for the first time the extent to which the constitutional protections for speech and press limit a State's power to award damages in a libel action brought by a public official against critics of his official conduct. . . .

[L.B. Sullivan, a city commissioner in Montgomery, Alabama, sued the New York Times Company and four African-American clergymen for libel based on a full-page advertisement published in the New York Times in 1960. The ad asked readers to help fund the civil rights movement and decried an "unprecedented wave of terror" in the South. The ad listed the names of 64 persons, including the clergymen, who purportedly endorsed its content. Sullivan's libel claim focused on two of the ad's ten paragraphs:]

> "In Montgomery, Alabama, after students sang 'My Country, 'Tis of Thee' on the State Capitol steps, their leaders were expelled from school, and truckloads of police armed with shotguns and tear-gas ringed the Alabama State College Campus. When the entire student body protested to state authorities by refusing to re-register, their dining hall was padlocked in an attempt to starve them into submission."
>
> . . .
>
> "Again and again the Southern violators have answered Dr. King's peaceful protests with intimidation and violence. They have bombed his home almost killing his wife and child. They have assaulted his person. They have arrested him seven times—for 'speeding,' 'loitering' and similar 'offenses.' And now they have charged him with 'perjury'—a felony under which they could imprison him for ten years. . . . "

[Sullivan contended that the ad accused him of overseeing a campaign of violence in his capacity as supervisor of the police. His witnesses testified that they understood the ad to refer to him, and he showed that he had not participated in the events attributed to the police. He did not put on evidence establishing pecuniary losses resulting from the libel, but instead sought recovery of presumed damages. The Times conceded that the ad contained inaccuracies: the students sang the National Anthem rather than "My Country, 'Tis of Thee"; nine students were expelled for demanding service at a lunch counter in the county courthouse, not for leading a demonstration; the police never literally "ringed" the campus; and Dr. King had been arrested four times, not seven. The trial judge instructed the jury that the statements in the ad were libelous per se (that is, libelous on their face) and not privileged. He also instructed that the jury could impose liability if it found petitioners had published the statements "of and concerning" Sullivan. The judge also told jury members they could award presumed and punitive damages even if no actual damages were shown and punitive damages could be awarded if they found "evidence of actual malice or malice in fact." The jury returned a verdict of $500,000, and the judge did not require the jury to designate which portion, if any, of the award constituted punitive damages. The Supreme Court of Alabama affirmed.]

I

We may dispose at the outset of two grounds asserted to insulate the judgment of the Alabama courts from constitutional scrutiny. The first is the proposition relied on by the State Supreme Court—that "The Fourteenth Amendment is directed against State action and not private action." That proposition has no application to this case. Although this is a civil lawsuit between private parties, the Alabama courts have applied a state rule of law which petitioners claim to impose invalid restrictions on their constitutional freedoms of speech and press. . . . The second contention is that the constitutional guarantees of freedom of speech and of the press are inapplicable here, at least so far as the Times is concerned, because the allegedly libelous statements were published as part of a paid, "commercial" advertisement. . . . The publication here was not a "commercial" advertisement. . . . It communicated information, expressed opinion, recited grievances, protested claimed abuses, and sought financial support on behalf of a movement whose existence and objectives are matters of the highest public interest and concern. . . . Any other conclusion would discourage newspapers from carrying "editorial advertisements" of this type, and so might shut off an important outlet for the promulgation of information and ideas by persons who do not themselves have access to publishing facilities—who wish to exercise their freedom of speech even though they are not members of the press. . . .

II

. . .

The question before us is whether [Alabama libel law], as applied to an action brought by a public official against critics of his official conduct, abridges the freedom of speech and of the press that is guaranteed by the First and Fourteenth Amendments.

Respondent relies heavily, as did the Alabama courts, on statements of this Court to the effect that the Constitution does not protect libelous publications. Those statements do not foreclose our inquiry here. None of the cases sustained the use of libel laws to impose sanctions upon expression critical of the official conduct of public officials. . . . Like insurrection, contempt, advocacy of unlawful acts, breach of the peace, obscenity, solicitation of legal business, and the various other formulae for the repression of expression that have been challenged in this Court, libel can claim no talismanic immunity from constitutional limitations. It must be measured by standards that satisfy the First Amendment.

. . .

[W]e consider this case against the background of a profound national commitment to the principle that debate on public issues should be uninhibited, robust, and wide-open, and that it may well include vehement, caustic, and sometimes unpleasantly sharp attacks on government and public officials. See *Terminiello v. Chicago*, 337 U.S. 1, 4. . . . The present advertisement, as an expression of grievance and protest on one of the major public issues of our time, would seem clearly to qualify for the constitutional protection. The question is whether it forfeits that protection by the falsity of some of its factual statements and by its alleged defamation of respondent. Authoritative interpretations of the First Amendment guarantees have consistently refused to recognize an exception for any test of truth—whether administered by judges, juries, or administrative officials—

and especially one that puts the burden of proving truth on the speaker. The constitutional protection does not turn upon "the truth, popularity, or social utility of the ideas and beliefs which are offered." *N.A.A.C.P. v. Button*, 371 U.S. 415, 445. As Madison said, "Some degree of abuse is inseparable from the proper use of every thing; and in no instance is this more true than in that of the press." 4 Elliot's Debates on the Federal Constitution (1876), p. 571....

[E]rroneous statement is inevitable in free debate, and . . . it must be protected if the freedoms of expression are to have the "breathing space" that they "need . . . to survive. . . . [As the Circuit Court of Appeals for the District of Columbia wrote in *Sweeney v. Patterson*, 128 F.2d 457, 458 (D.C. Cir.), *cert. denied*, 317 U.S. 67 (1942)]:

> "Cases which impose liability for erroneous reports of the political conduct of officials reflect the obsolete doctrine that the governed must not criticize their governors. . . . The interest of the public here outweighs the interest of appellant or any other individual. The protection of the public requires not merely discussion, but information. Political conduct and views which some respectable people approve, and others condemn, are constantly imputed to Congressmen. Errors of fact, particularly in regard to a man's mental states and processes, are inevitable. . . . Whatever is added to the field of libel is taken from the field of free debate."

Injury to official reputation affords no more warrant for repressing speech that would otherwise be free than does factual error. Where judicial officers are involved, this Court has held that concern for the dignity and reputation of the courts does not justify the punishment as criminal contempt of criticism of the judge or his decision. *Bridges v. California*, 314 U.S. 252. This is true even though the utterance contains "half-truths" and "misinformation." Such repression can be justified, if at all, only by a clear and present danger of the obstruction of justice. If judges are to be treated as "men of fortitude, able to thrive in a hardy climate," surely the same must be true of other government officials, such as elected city commissioners. Criticism of their official conduct does not lose its constitutional protection merely because it is effective criticism and hence diminishes their official reputations.

If neither factual error nor defamatory content suffices to remove the constitutional shield from criticism of official conduct, the combination of the two elements is no less inadequate. This is the lesson to be drawn from the great controversy over the Sedition Act of 1798, which first crystallized a national awareness of the central meaning of the First Amendment. . . .

Although the Sedition Act was never tested in this Court, the attack upon its validity has carried the day in the court of history. Fines levied in its prosecution were repaid by Act of Congress on the ground that it was unconstitutional. . . . The invalidity of the Act has also been assumed by Justices of this Court. These views reflect a broad consensus that the Act, because of the restraint it imposed upon criticism of government and public officials, was inconsistent with the First Amendment.

. . . What a State may not constitutionally bring about by means of a criminal statute is likewise beyond the reach of its civil law of libel. The fear of damage awards under a rule such as that invoked by the Alabama courts here may be markedly more inhibiting than the fear of prosecution under a criminal statute. Alabama, for example, has a criminal libel law which subjects to prosecution "any person who speaks, writes, or prints of and concerning another any accusation falsely and maliciously importing the commission by such person of a felony, or any other indictable offense involving moral turpitude," and which allows as punishment upon conviction a fine not exceeding $500 and a prison sentence of six months. Presumably a person charged with violation of this statute enjoys ordinary criminal-law safeguards such as the requirements of an indictment and of proof beyond a reasonable doubt. These safeguards are not available to the defendant in a civil action. The judgment awarded in this case—without the need for any proof of actual pecuniary loss—was one thousand times greater than the maximum fine provided by the Alabama criminal statute, and one hundred times greater than that provided by the Sedition Act. And since there is no double-jeopardy limitation applicable to civil lawsuits, this is not the only judgment that may be awarded against petitioners for the same publication.[18] Whether or not a newspaper can survive a succession of such judgments, the pall of fear and timidity imposed upon those who would give voice to public criticism is an atmosphere in which the First Amendment freedoms cannot survive. . . .

The state rule of law is not saved by its allowance of the defense of truth. . . . Allowance of the defense of truth, with the burden of proving it on the defendant, does not mean that only false speech will be deterred. Even courts accepting this defense as an adequate safeguard have recognized the difficulties of adducing legal proofs that the alleged libel was true in all its factual particulars. Under such a rule, would-be critics of official conduct may be deterred from voicing their criticism, even though it is believed to be true and even though it is in fact true, because of doubt whether it can be proved in court or fear of the expense of having to do so. They tend to make only statements which "steer far wider of the unlawful zone." *Speiser v. Randall*, 357 U.S. at 526. The rule thus dampens the vigor and limits the variety of public debate. It is inconsistent with the First and Fourteenth Amendments.

The constitutional guarantees require, we think, a federal rule that prohibits a public official from recovering damages for a defamatory falsehood relating to his official conduct unless he proves that the statement was made with "actual malice"—that is, with knowledge that it was false or with reckless disregard of whether it was false or not. An oft-cited statement of a like rule, which has been adopted by a number of state courts, is found in the Kansas case of *Coleman v. MacLennan*, 78 Kan. 711, 98 P. 281 (1908). . . .

Such a privilege for criticism of official conduct is appropriately analogous to the protection accorded a public official when *he* is sued for libel by a private citizen. In *Barr v. Matteo*, 360 U.S. 564, 575, this Court held the utterance of a federal official to be absolutely privileged if made "within the outer perimeter" of his duties. The States accord the same immunity to statements of their highest officers, although some differentiate their lesser officials and qualify the privilege they enjoy. But all hold that all officials are protected unless actual malice can be proved. The reason for the official privilege is said to be that the threat of damage suits would otherwise "inhibit the fearless, vigorous, and effective administration of policies of government" and "dampen the ardor of all but the most resolute, or the most irresponsible, in the unflinching discharge of their duties." Analogous considerations

---

[18] The Times states that four other libel suits based on the advertisement have been filed against it by others who have served as Montgomery City Commissioners and by the Governor of Alabama; that another $500,000 verdict has been awarded in the only one of these cases that has yet gone to trial; and that the damages sought in the other three total $2,000,000.

support the privilege for the citizen-critic of government. It is as much his duty to criticize as it is the official's duty to administer. As Madison said, "the censorial power is in the people over the Government, and not in the Government over the people." It would give public servants an unjustified preference over the public they serve, if critics of official conduct did not have a fair equivalent of the immunity granted to the officials themselves.

We conclude that such a privilege is required by the First and Fourteenth Amendments.

III

We hold today that the Constitution delimits a State's power to award damages for libel in actions brought by public officials against critics of their official conduct. Since this is such an action, the rule requiring proof of actual malice is applicable. While Alabama law apparently requires proof of actual malice for an award of punitive damages, where general damages are concerned malice is "presumed." Such a presumption is inconsistent with the federal rule. . . . Since the trial judge did not instruct the jury to differentiate between general and punitive damages, it may be that the verdict was wholly an award of one or the other. But it is impossible to know, in view of the general verdict returned. Because of this uncertainty, the judgment must be reversed and the case remanded.

Since respondent may seek a new trial, we deem that considerations of effective judicial administration require us to review the evidence in the present record to determine whether it could constitutionally support a judgment for respondent. This Court's duty is not limited to the elaboration of constitutional principles; we must also in proper cases review the evidence to make certain that those principles have been constitutionally applied. This is such a case, particularly since the question is one of alleged trespass across "the line between speech unconditionally guaranteed and speech which may legitimately be regulated." *Speiser.* In cases where that line must be drawn, the rule is that we "examine for ourselves the statements in issue and the circumstances under which they were made to see . . . whether they are of a character which the principles of the First Amendment, as adopted by the Due Process Clause of the Fourteenth Amendment, protect." *Pennekamp v. Florida,* 328 U.S. 331, 335. We must "make an independent examination of the whole record," so as to assure ourselves that the judgment does not constitute a forbidden intrusion on the field of free expression.

Applying these standards, we consider that the proof presented to show actual malice lacks the convincing clarity which the constitutional standard demands, and hence that it would not constitutionally sustain the judgment for respondent under the proper rule of law. The case of the individual petitioners requires little discussion. Even assuming that they could constitutionally be found to have authorized the use of their names on the advertisement, there was no evidence whatever that they were aware of any erroneous statements or were in any way reckless in that regard. The judgment against them is thus without constitutional support.

As to the Times, we similarly conclude that the facts do not support a finding of actual malice. . . . The Times' failure to retract upon respondent's demand, although it later retracted upon the demand of Governor Patterson, is . . . not adequate evidence of malice for constitutional purposes. Whether or not a failure to retract may ever constitute such evidence, there are two reasons why it does not here. *First,* the letter written by the Times reflected a reasonable doubt on its part as to whether the advertisement could reasonably be taken to refer to respondent at all. *Second*, it was not a final refusal, since it asked for an explanation on this point—a request that respondent chose to ignore. . . . It may be doubted that a failure to retract which is not itself evidence of malice can retroactively become such by virtue of a retraction subsequently made to another party. But in any event that did not happen here, since the explanation given by the Times' Secretary for the distinction drawn between respondent and the Governor was a reasonable one, the good faith of which was not impeached.

Finally, there is evidence that the Times published the advertisement without checking its accuracy against the news stories in the Times' own files. The mere presence of the stories in the files does not, of course, establish that the Times "knew" the advertisement was false, since the state of mind required for actual malice would have to be brought home to the persons in the Times' organization having responsibility for the publication of the advertisement. With respect to the failure of those persons to make the check, the record shows that they relied upon their knowledge of the good reputation of many of those whose names were listed as sponsors of the advertisement, and upon the letter from A. Philip Randolph, known to them as a responsible individual, certifying that the use of the names was authorized. . . .

We also think the evidence was constitutionally defective in another respect: it was incapable of supporting the jury's finding that the allegedly libelous statements were made "of and concerning" respondent. Respondent relies on the words of the advertisement and the testimony of six witnesses to establish a connection between it and himself. . . . There was no reference to respondent in the advertisement, either by name or official position. . . . [Moreover, the statements about the police] were false only in that the police had been "deployed near" the campus but had not actually "ringed" it and had not gone there in connection with the State Capitol demonstration, and in that Dr. King had been arrested only four times [rather than seven]. The ruling that these discrepancies between what was true and what was asserted were sufficient to injure respondent's reputation may itself raise constitutional problems, but we need not consider them here. Although the statements may be taken as referring to the police, they did not on their face make even an oblique reference to respondent as an individual. Support for the asserted reference must, therefore, be sought in the testimony of respondent's witnesses. But none of them suggested any basis for the belief that respondent himself was attacked in the advertisement beyond the bare fact that he was in overall charge of the Police Department and thus bore official responsibility for police conduct. . . . [Thus, proof that the ad pertained to Sullivan relied]"on the bare fact of respondent's official position."

This proposition has disquieting implications for criticism of governmental conduct. For good reason, "no court of last resort in this country has ever held, or even suggested, that prosecutions for libel on government have any place in the American system of jurisprudence." . . . The present proposition would sidestep this obstacle by transmuting criticism of government, however impersonal it may seem on its face, into personal criticism, and hence potential libel, of the officials of whom the government is composed. There is no legal alchemy by which a State may thus create the cause of action that would otherwise be denied for a publication which, as respondent himself said of the advertisement, "reflects not only on me but on the other Commissioners and the community." Raising as it does the possibility that a good-faith critic of government will be penalized for his criticism, the proposition relied on by the Alabama courts strikes at the very center of the constitutionally protected area of free expression. We hold that such a proposition may not constitutionally be utilized to establish that an otherwise impersonal attack on governmental operations was a libel of an official responsible for those operations. Since it was relied on exclusively here, and there was no other evidence to connect the statements with respondent, the evidence was constitutionally insufficient to support a finding that the statements referred to respondent.

The judgment of the Supreme Court of Alabama is reversed and the case is remanded to that court for further proceedings not inconsistent with this opinion.

Justice BLACK, with whom Justice DOUGLAS joins, concurring.

. . . I vote to reverse exclusively on the ground that the Times and the individual defendants had an absolute, unconditional constitutional right to publish in the Times advertisement their criticisms of the Montgomery agencies and officials. . . .

The half-million-dollar verdict does give dramatic proof, however, that state libel laws threaten the very existence of an American press virile enough to publish unpopular views on public affairs and bold enough to criticize the conduct of public officials. The factual background of this case emphasizes the imminence and enormity of that threat. . . . [B]riefs before us show that in Alabama there are now pending eleven libel suits by local and state officials against the Times seeking $5,600,000, and five such suits against the Columbia Broadcasting System seeking $1,700,000. Moreover, this technique for harassing and punishing a free press—now that it has been shown to be possible—is by no means limited to cases with racial overtones; it can be used in other fields where public feelings may make local as well as out-of-state newspapers easy prey for libel verdict seekers. . . .

Justice GOLDBERG, with whom Justice DOUGLAS joins, concurring in the result.

. . . In my view, the First and Fourteenth Amendments to the Constitution afford to the citizen and to the press an absolute, unconditional privilege to criticize official conduct despite the harm which may flow from excesses and abuses. . . .

NOTES AND QUESTIONS

1. *The effect of presumed damages.* The New York Times had a very small circulation in Alabama in 1960. Fewer than 400 copies of the edition with the allegedly libelous advertisement circulated in Alabama, only 35 of which were circulated in Montgomery County. Should this have been relevant to Sullivan's damages? What damages do you think Sullivan actually suffered? Would it have been possible to provide adequate breathing room for First Amendment interests simply by capping the amount of damages recoverable in libel actions or by abolishing the doctrine of presumed damages?

2. *Does false speech have constitutional value?* In a footnote, the majority opinion cited John Stuart Mill's *On Liberty* for the proposition that "[e]ven a false statement may be deemed to make a valuable contribution to public debate, since it brings about 'the clearer perception and livelier impression of truth, produced by its collision with error.'" What other rationales justify protecting false speech? Why does the Court refuse to give absolute protection to false speech about public officials? In Garrison v. Louisiana, 379 U.S. 64 (1964), the Court

held that the actual malice standard also applied when the State attempted to punish libel as a criminal offense. There, the Court stated that "the use of the known lie as a tool is at once at odds with the premises of democratic government and with the orderly manner in which economic, social, or political change is to be effected."

3. *Shifting the burden of proof of falsity to plaintifffs?* Does the Court's holding—that plaintiffs who are public officials must prove actual malice—implicitly shift the burden of proof on falsity to the plaintiff? Many lower courts believed so, and in Philadelphia Newspapers, Inc. v. Hepps, 475 U.S. 767 (1986), the Supreme Court made it clear that the plaintiff must indeed prove falsity as part of a prima facie case of defamation in all cases involving matters of public concern.

4. *Constitutionalizing the identification element?* Was the Court's determination that the advertisement was not "of and concerning" Sullivan an intrusion into the fact-finding function of the jury? Why or why not? Tort law traditionally assigns the jury the job of determining whether the allegedly defamatory statement made by the defendant actually referred to the plaintiff. The identification element is not an obstacle when the defendant identifies the plaintiff by name, but sometimes the defendant identifies the plaintiff only by physical or other personal characteristics, and the plaintiff must show that some audience members would reasonably understand the defamatory statement to refer to the plaintiff. Plaintiffs may also face problems in proving the identification element when the defendant makes a defamatory statement about a group of which the plaintiff is a part. A defamatory statement about a small group may defame every member of that group, but a defamatory statement about a large group will not be deemed to "identify" each member of that group, because the defamatory "sting" will be too diffuse to attach to each member as an individual.

5. *Hate speech and group libel.* Although hate speech is not a constitutional category, some states have statutes that make it a crime to defame a class of people because of their race or religion. Although the Supreme Court, 5-4, upheld the constitutionality of a "group libel" statute in Beauharnais v. Illinois, 343 U.S. 250 (1952), subsequent decisions such as R.A.V. v. City of St. Paul, 505 U.S. 377 (1992) make the constitutionality of such statutes highly suspect.

6. *State action.* In an omitted portion of the opinion, the Court stated: "[T]he Alabama courts have applied a state rule of law which petitioners claim to impose invalid restrictions on their constitutional freedoms of speech and press. It matters not that that law has been applied in a civil action and that it is common law only, though supplemented by statute. The test is not the form in which state power has been applied but, whatever the form, whether such power has in fact been exercised." Where (or what) was the state action here?

7. *Procedural protection for defamation defendants (convincing clarity /independent review).* Although the substantive protections of *Sullivan*, particularly the actual malice rule, are obviously important, the procedural protections are critical as well. The requirement that the plaintiff prove actual malice with convincing clarity (rather than the usual preponderance) tilts the scales in favor of defendants. At least in cases under the Federal Rules of Civil Procedure, the convincing clarity requirement means that a judge must determine at summary judgment "whether the evidence in the record could support a reasonable jury finding either that the plaintiff has shown actual malice by clear and convincing evidence or that the plaintiff has not." Anderson v. Liberty

Lobby, Inc., 477 U.S. 242 (1986). Moreover, the requirement that appellate courts "independently review the record as a whole" to ensure that actual malice has been proved with convincing clarity further tilts the scale toward defendants. This requirement stems from Bose Corp. v. Consumers Union, 466 U.S. 485 (1984). The Supreme Court explained that the requirement that appellate courts independently review the record to support the finding of actual malice "reflects a deeply held conviction that judges —and particularly members of this Court—must exercise such review in order to preserve the precious liberties established and ordained by the Constitution. The question whether the evidence in the record in a defamation case is of the convincing clarity required to strip the utterance of First Amendment protection is not merely a question for the trier of fact. Judges, as expositors of the Constitution, must independently decide whether the evidence in the record is sufficient to cross the constitutional threshold that bars the entry of any judgment that is not supported by clear and convincing proof of 'actual malice.'"

8. *Proving actual malice.* In order for a plaintiff to establish actual malice, the Supreme Court has said that "[t]here must be sufficient evidence to permit the conclusion that the defendant in fact entertained serious doubts as to the truth of his publication." St. Amant v. Thompson, 390 U.S. 727 (1968). In other words, actual malice focuses on the mental state of the defendant at the time of publication, especially his subjective awareness of falsity. Actual malice may be found, for example, where the defendant invents a story, bases it on "an unverified anonymous telephone call," publishes information "so inherently improbable that only a reckless man would have put [it] in circulation," or where the defendant publishes despite "obvious reasons to doubt the veracity of [an] informant or the accuracy of his reports." On the other hand, the Supreme Court has held that actual malice may not be based merely on evidence that the defendant failed to investigate fully before publication; however, "the purposeful avoidance of the truth is in a different category." Harte-Hanks Communs, Inc. v. Connaughton, 491 U.S. 657 (1989). In addition, a plaintiff cannot show actual malice by showing only that the defendant acted out of bad motive, ill will, or spite (that is, common law malice), though these can be relevant to show knowledge or reckless disregard for falsity when coupled with other evidence. By the same token, the defendant's lack of objectivity, the adoption of a sarcastic tone, the reliance on a single source, or the misinterpretation of available data will not, by themselves, be enough to establish actual malice. Time, Inc. v. Pape, 401 U.S. 279 (1971). Finally, the plaintiff may not show actual malice by establishing that the defendant knew of a mere technical falsehood in the publication. Thus, even a showing that a reporter deliberately altered a direct quotation by the plaintiff is not a showing of actual malice, unless the material meaning is changed in a way that is defamatory. Masson v. New Yorker Magazine, 501 U.S. 496 (1991). As these examples make clear, mere professional negligence or neglect of good journalistic practices does not equate with actual malice. In fact, the Supreme Court has said that actual malice cannot be shown by proof of even "highly unreasonable conduct constituting an extreme departure from the standards of investigation and reporting ordinarily adhered to by responsible publishers." Curtis Publg. Co. v. Butts, 388 U.S. 130 (1967).

9. *Who is a public official?* After *Sullivan*, a plaintiff who is determined to be a public official will rarely be able to surmount the constitutional obstacles

necessary to prevail in a libel suit. Therefore, the determination of whether a plaintiff is a public official is a critical one. The Supreme Court has defined the category of public officials to apply "at the very least to those among the hierarchy of government employees who have, or appear to the public to have, substantial responsibility for or control over the conduct of governmental affairs." Rosenblatt v. Baer, 383 U.S. 75 (1966). A person will be deemed a public official "[w]here [that person's] position in government has such apparent importance that the public has an independent interest in the qualifications and performance of the person who holds it, beyond the general public interest in the qualifications and performance of all government employees." A low-level government employee does not become a public official simply because a news story about him attracts public attention; he must be a public official by virtue of his position of potential influence over governmental policy. Is a police officer a public official? (Typically yes.) What about a fireman or a school principal? (Sometimes yes and sometimes no.)

2.   Defamation of Public Figures: The Extension of the Sullivan Rules

In 1967 the Supreme Court extended *Sullivan*'s protections to cases involving public figures suing for libel. Curtis Publishing Co. v. Butts and Associated Press v. Walker, decided together, 388 U.S. 130 (1967), both involved plaintiffs who had gained prominence in their selected spheres of influence. Wally Butts was the athletic director and former coach of the University of Georgia. In fact, it was this prominent position that made the ensuing defamatory newspaper story about him newsworthy, for the story stated that he had "fixed" a football game by telling a rival coach his secret plays. Walker, on the other hand, was prominent partly by virtue of his former position as an Army general, but more pertinently by virtue of his political activism. Walker resigned from the military to protest federal intervention in the South to support civil rights. Walker sued for defamation after a news wire report stated that he had instigated and participated in a riot against the federal marshals supporting the registration of African-American student James Meredith at the University of Mississippi. The question before the Supreme Court was whether the *Sullivan* actual malice rule should apply to Butts and Walker. In a fractured opinion, a majority of the Court said yes.

Chief Justice Warren, joined by four other justices, justified application of the actual malice rule to public figures by pointing to the significant public interest in both of the plaintiffs. Warren further explained that "what we have commonly considered to be the private sector" has become increasingly powerful and has even taken over some governmental functions. This shift of power to the private sector means that "many who do not hold public office at the moment are nevertheless intimately involved in the resolution of important public questions or, by reason of their fame, shape events in areas of concern to society at large."

The political power and influence wielded by public figures gives the public a "legitimate and substantial interest in the[ir] conduct." This alone might justify treating them like public officials for purposes of defamation law. Yet the Court also reasoned that it was fair to subject public figures to the actual malice rule because public figures, like public officials, have "ready access" to the media "both to influence policy and to counter criticism of their views and activities." In other words, public figures have tools other than tort law to deal with defamatory falsehoods. Moreover, public scrutiny of public figures may be even more important than public scrutiny of public officials, precisely because public figures are not subject to the political process. Thus, the proper balance between protecting "uninhibited debate" about public figures and safeguarding an individual's reputation is properly struck by adoption of the actual malice rule.

The Court did more than extend the actual malice rule to public figures; it also extended the other procedural protections of press freedom developed in *Sullivan*. Public figures, like public officials, must both prove actual malice by clear and convincing evidence and prove falsity. And courts must independently review cases in which public figures are involved to ensure the plaintiff has adduced adequate evidence of actual malice to justify a judgment in his or her favor. As we shall see in the following sections, application of these procedural safeguards has dramatically reduced defamation recoveries for a broad class of plaintiffs.

3. *Defamation of Private Figures Involved in Matters of Public Concern*

Once the *Sullivan* rules extended to public-figure plaintiffs, there was increasing pressure to extend them to all cases involving matters of public concern. In other words, there was pressure to shift emphasis from the status of the plaintiff to the subject matter discussed in the allegedly defamatory publication. Although the Supreme Court in Rosenbloom v. Metromedia, Inc., 403 U.S. 29 (1971), initially appeared to endorse this approach, it firmly rejected it in *Gertz*, below. As you read *Gertz*, pay attention to the passages defining the different types of public figures and explaining why public figures and private figures deserve different legal treatment. Private figures, like the plaintiff in *Gertz*, are defined by *not* being public figures.

GERTZ v. ROBERT WELCH, INC.
418 U.S. 323 (1974)

Justice POWELL delivered the opinion of the Court.

. . . [Petitioner Elmer Gertz represented the Nelson family in civil litigation against Nuccio, a Chicago policeman convicted of murdering their son.]

Respondent publishes American Opinion, a monthly outlet for the views of the John Birch Society. . . . [T]he managing editor of American Opinion commissioned an article on the murder trial of Officer Nuccio. . . . In March 1969 respondent published the resulting article under the title "FRAME-UP: Richard Nuccio And The War On Police." The article purports to demonstrate that [Nuccio's] prosecution was part of the Communist campaign against the police.

. . . Notwithstanding petitioner's remote connection with the prosecution of Nuccio, respondent's magazine portrayed him as an architect of the "frame-up." According to the article, the police file on petitioner took "a big, Irish cop to lift." The article stated that petitioner had been an official of the "Marxist League for Industrial Democracy, originally known as the Intercollegiate Socialist Society, which has advocated the violent seizure of our government." It labeled Gertz a "Leninist" and a "Communist-fronter." . . .

The implication that petitioner had a criminal record was false. . . . There was also no basis for the charge that petitioner was a "Leninist" or a "Communist-fronter."

And he had never been a member of the "Marxist League for Industrial Democracy" or the "Intercollegiate Socialist Society."

The managing editor of American Opinion made no effort to verify or substantiate the charges against petitioner. Instead, he appended an editorial introduction stating that the author had "conducted extensive research into the Richard Nuccio Case." . . .

Petitioner filed a diversity action for libel. [Following a jury verdict for petitioner of $50,000, the district court entered a J.N.O.V. on the ground that *Sullivan*'s actual malice rule applied to "discussion of any public issue," and the Seventh Circuit affirmed.]

The principal issue in this case is whether a newspaper or broadcaster that publishes defamatory falsehoods about an individual who is neither a public official nor a public figure may claim a constitutional privilege against liability for the injury inflicted by those statements. . . .

We begin with the common ground. Under the First Amendment there is no such thing as a false idea. However pernicious an opinion may seem, we depend for its correction not on the conscience of judges and juries but on the competition of other ideas. But there is no constitutional value in false statements of fact. Neither the intentional lie nor the careless error materially advances society's interest in "uninhibited, robust, and wide-open" debate on public issues. They belong to that category of utterances which "are no essential part of any exposition of ideas, and are of such slight social value as a step to truth that any benefit that may be derived from them is clearly outweighed by the social interest in order and morality." *Chaplinsky v. New Hampshire*, []. . .

Although the erroneous statement of fact is not worthy of constitutional protection, it is nevertheless inevitable in free debate. . . . Our decisions recognize that a rule of strict liability that compels a publisher or broadcaster to guarantee the accuracy of his factual assertions may lead to intolerable self-censorship. . . .

The need to avoid self-censorship by the news media is, however, not the only societal value at issue. If it were, this Court would have embraced long ago the view that publishers and broadcasters enjoy an unconditional and indefeasible immunity from liability for defamation. Such a rule would, indeed, obviate the fear that the prospect of civil liability for injurious falsehood might dissuade a timorous press from the effective exercise of First Amendment freedoms. Yet absolute protection for the communications media requires a total sacrifice of the competing value served by the law of defamation.

The legitimate state interest underlying the law of libel is the compensation of individuals for the harm inflicted on them by defamatory falsehood. We would not lightly require the State to abandon this purpose, for, as Mr. Justice Stewart has reminded us, the individual's right to the protection of his own good name "reflects no more than our basic concept of the essential dignity and worth of every human being—a concept at the root of any decent system of ordered liberty. . . ."

The *New York Times* standard defines the level of constitutional protection appropriate to the context of defamation of a public person. Those who, by reason of the notoriety of their achievements or the vigor and success with which they seek the public's attention, are properly classed as public figures and those who hold governmental office may recover for injury to reputation only on clear and convincing proof that the defamatory falsehood was made with knowledge of its falsity or with reckless disregard for the truth. This standard administers an extremely powerful antidote to the inducement to media self-censorship of the common-law rule of strict liability for libel and slander. And it exacts a correspondingly high price from the victims of defamatory falsehood. . . . For the reasons stated below, we conclude that the state interest in compensating injury to the reputation of private individuals requires that a different rule should obtain with respect to them.

Theoretically, of course, the balance between the needs of the press and the individual's claim to compensation for wrongful injury might be struck on a case-by-case basis. . . . But this approach would lead to unpredictable results and uncertain expectations, and it could render our duty to supervise the lower courts unmanageable. Because an *ad hoc* resolution of the competing interests at stake in each particular case is not feasible, we must lay down broad rules of general application. . . .

With that caveat we have no difficulty in distinguishing among defamation plaintiffs. The first remedy of any victim of defamation is self-help—using available opportunities to contradict the lie or correct the error and thereby to minimize its adverse impact on reputation. Public officials and public figures usually enjoy significantly greater access to the channels of effective communication and hence have a more realistic opportunity to counteract false statements than private individuals normally enjoy.[18] Private individuals are therefore more vulnerable to injury, and the state interest in protecting them is correspondingly greater.

More important than the likelihood that private individuals will lack effective opportunities for rebuttal, there is a compelling normative consideration underlying the distinction between public and private defamation plaintiffs. An individual who decides to seek governmental office must accept certain necessary consequences of that involvement in public affairs. He runs the risk of closer public scrutiny than might otherwise be the case. And society's interest in the officers of government is not strictly limited to the formal discharge of official duties. As the Court pointed out in *Garrison v. Louisiana*, the public's interest extends to "anything which might touch on an official's fitness for office. . . . Few personal attributes are more germane to fitness for office than dishonesty, malfeasance, or improper motivation, even though these characteristics may also affect the official's private character."

Those classed as public figures stand in a similar position. Hypothetically, it may be possible for someone to become a public figure through no purposeful action of his own, but the instances of truly involuntary public figures must be exceedingly rare. For the most part those who attain this status have assumed roles of special prominence in the affairs of society. Some occupy positions of such persuasive power and influence that they are deemed public figures for all purposes. More commonly, those classed as public figures have thrust themselves to the forefront of particular public controversies in order to influence the resolution of the issues involved. In either event, they invite attention and comment.

Even if the foregoing generalities do not obtain in every instance, the communications media are entitled to act on the assumption that public officials and public figures have voluntarily exposed themselves to increased risk of injury from defamatory falsehood concerning them. No such assumption is justified with respect to a private individual. He has not accepted public office or assumed an "influential

---

[18] Of course, an opportunity for rebuttal seldom suffices to undo harm of defamatory falsehood. Indeed, the law of defamation is rooted in our experience that the truth rarely catches up with a lie. But the fact that the self-help remedy of rebuttal, standing alone, is inadequate to its task does not mean that it is irrelevant to our inquiry.

role in ordering society." He has relinquished no part of his interest in the protection of his own good name, and consequently he has a more compelling call on the courts for redress of injury inflicted by defamatory falsehood. Thus, private individuals are not only more vulnerable to injury than public officials and public figures; they are also more deserving of recovery.

For these reasons we conclude that the States should retain substantial latitude in their efforts to enforce a legal remedy for defamatory falsehood injurious to the reputation of a private individual. . . . We hold that, so long as they do not impose liability without fault, the States may define for themselves the appropriate standard of liability for a publisher or broadcaster of defamatory falsehood injurious to a private individual. . . . [This approach] recognizes the strength of the legitimate state interest in compensating private individuals for wrongful injury to reputation, yet shields the press and broadcast media from the rigors of strict liability for defamation. At least this conclusion obtains where, as here, the substance of the defamatory statement "makes substantial danger to reputation apparent." . . .

[W]e endorse this approach in recognition of the strong and legitimate state interest in compensating private individuals for injury to reputation. But this countervailing state interest extends no further than compensation for actual injury. For the reasons stated below, we hold that the States may not permit recovery of presumed or punitive damages, at least when liability is not based on a showing of knowledge of falsity or reckless disregard for the truth.

The common law of defamation is an oddity of tort law, for it allows recovery of purportedly compensatory damages without evidence of actual loss. Under the traditional rules pertaining to actions for libel, the existence of injury is presumed from the fact of publication. Juries may award substantial sums as compensation for supposed damage to reputation without any proof that such harm actually occurred. The largely uncontrolled discretion of juries to award damages where there is no loss unnecessarily compounds the potential of any system of liability for defamatory falsehood to inhibit the vigorous exercise of First Amendment freedoms. Additionally, the doctrine of presumed damages invites juries to punish unpopular opinion rather than to compensate individuals for injury sustained by the publication of a false fact. More to the point, the States have no substantial interest in securing for plaintiffs such as this petitioner gratuitous awards of money damages far in excess of any actual injury.

We would not, of course, invalidate state law simply because we doubt its wisdom, but here we are attempting to reconcile state law with a competing interest grounded in the constitutional command of the First Amendment. It is therefore appropriate to require that state remedies for defamatory falsehood reach no farther than is necessary to protect the legitimate interest involved. It is necessary to restrict defamation plaintiffs who do not prove knowledge of falsity or reckless disregard for the truth to compensation for actual injury. We need not define "actual injury," as trial courts have wide experience in framing appropriate jury instructions in tort actions. Suffice it to say that actual injury is not limited to out-of-pocket loss. Indeed, the more customary types of actual harm inflicted by defamatory falsehood include impairment of reputation and standing in the community, personal humiliation, and mental anguish and suffering. Of course, juries must be limited by appropriate instructions, and all awards must be supported by competent evidence concerning the injury, although there need be no evidence which assigns an actual dollar value to the injury.

We also find no justification for allowing awards of punitive damages against publishers and broadcasters held liable under state-defined standards of liability for defamation. . . . [P]unitive damages are wholly irrelevant to the state interest that justifies a negligence standard for private defamation actions. They are not compensation for injury. Instead, they are private fines levied by civil juries to punish reprehensible conduct and to deter its future occurrence. In short, the private defamation plaintiff who establishes liability under a less demanding standard than that stated by *New York Times* may recover only such damages as are sufficient to compensate him for actual injury.

[R]espondent contends that we should affirm the judgment below on the ground that petitioner is either a public official or a public figure. There is little basis for the former assertion. [Respondent] argues that petitioner's appearance at the coroner's inquest rendered him a "de facto public official." Our cases recognize no such concept. Respondent's suggestion would sweep all lawyers under the *New York Times* rule as officers of the court and distort the plain meaning of the "public official" category beyond all recognition. We decline to follow it.

Respondent's characterization of petitioner as a public figure raises a different question. . . . Petitioner has long been active in community and professional affairs. He has served as an officer of local civic groups and of various professional organizations, and he has published several books and articles on legal subjects. Although petitioner was consequently well known in some circles, he had achieved no general fame or notoriety in the community. None of the prospective jurors called at the trial had ever heard of petitioner prior to this litigation, and respondent offered no proof that this response was atypical of the local population. We would not lightly assume that a citizen's participation in community and professional affairs rendered him a public figure for all purposes. Absent clear evidence of general fame or notoriety in the community, and pervasive involvement in the affairs of society, an individual should not be deemed a public personality for all aspects of his life. It is preferable to reduce the public-figure question to a more meaningful context by looking to the nature and extent of an individual's participation in the particular controversy giving rise to the defamation.

In this context it is plain that petitioner was not a public figure. He played a minimal role at the coroner's inquest, and his participation related solely to his representation of a private client. He took no part in the criminal prosecution of Officer Nuccio. Moreover, he never discussed either the criminal or civil litigation with the press and was never quoted as having done so. He plainly did not thrust himself into the vortex of this public issue, nor did he engage the public's attention in an attempt to influence its outcome. We are persuaded that the trial court did not err in refusing to characterize petitioner as a public figure for the purpose of this litigation.

We therefore conclude that the *New York Times* standard is inapplicable to this case and that the trial court erred in entering judgment for respondent. Because the jury was allowed to impose liability without fault and was permitted to presume damages without proof of injury, a new trial is necessary. We reverse and remand for further proceedings in accord with this opinion.

Justice DOUGLAS, dissenting.

. . . The standard announced today leaves the States free to "define for themselves the appropriate standard of liability for a publisher or broadcaster" in the circumstances of this case. This of course leaves the simple negligence standard as an option, with the jury free to impose damages upon a finding that the publisher failed to act as "a reasonable man." With such continued erosion of First Amendment protection, I fear that it may well be the reasonable man who refrains from speaking.

NOTES AND QUESTIONS

1. *Rejecting the public concern test?* Why did the majority in *Gertz* reject a rule that would focus on the status of the speech (that is, whether the speech was of public concern) rather than the status of the plaintiff (whether the plaintiff is a public or private figure)?

2. *Who is a public figure?* Public figures come in three different types, all of which have additional defining criteria. The three types are (1) "general" public figures, who have achieved such pervasive fame or notoriety that they are public figures "for all purposes and in all contexts"; (2) limited-purpose public figures, who are public figures only for purposes of discussion of a particular controversy in which they have become involved; and (3) "involuntary" public figures, who are thrust into a controversy through no action of their own and become public figures only for purposes of discussion of that controversy.

3. *What is an "actual injury"?* The best guidance on this issue comes from Time, Inc. v. Firestone, 424 U.S. 448 (1976). There the plaintiff relied on the testimony of her minister, physician, attorney, and friends to establish that she had suffered mental anguish, but she did not provide any evidence of reputational harm. The Supreme Court held that *Gertz* did not forbid recovery, even absent evidence of pecuniary injury to reputation. Does *Firestone* suggest that the requirement that private-figure plaintiffs like Gertz must prove actual injury (if they do not prove actual malice) is not that onerous?

4. *Establishing negligence.* Must the plaintiff establish that the defendant failed to behave as a "reasonable publisher or broadcaster" or merely that the defendant failed to behave as a reasonable person? Does it matter whether the standard is professional negligence or ordinary care?

5. *Setting a constitutional "floor."* It is important to remember that *Gertz* sets a First Amendment minimum and that states are free to impose a fault standard greater than negligence if they choose. New York, for example, requires private plaintiffs to show that the publisher "acted in a grossly irresponsible manner," at least where the defamation concerns a matter of "legitimate public concern." Chapadeau v. Utica Observer-Dispatch, Inc., 341 N.E.2d 569 (N.Y. 1975); Gaeta v. New York News, Inc., 465 N.E.2d 802 (N.Y. 1984).

6. *The outcome of* Gertz. When the *Gertz* case was retried, the plaintiff proved actual malice, and a jury award of $100,000 in compensatory damages and $300,000 in punitive damages was affirmed on appeal. Gertz v. Robert Welch, Inc., 680 F.2d 527 (7th Cir. 1982).

7. *Proof of falsity.* At common law truth was a defense to libel, to be pleaded and proved by the defendant. The Supreme Court in Philadelphia Newspapers, Inc. v. Hepps, 475 U.S. 767 (1986), clarified that public officials and public figures must prove falsity in order to recover for defamation. More surprisingly, the Court held that private-figure plaintiffs suing over speech on a matter of public concern must also prove falsity. In other words, in the common situation where such speech cannot be proved true or false, the plaintiff will lose. The rationale for putting the burden of proving falsity on the plaintiff was that where the

evidence is ambiguous as to whether particular speech is true or false, the balance should tip "in favor of protecting true speech." Thus, the media will not be chilled from publishing speech on matters of public concern just because they fear they will not be able to later prove its truth to a jury's satisfaction.

8. *Applying* Gertz *to bloggers.* In Obsidian Financial Group LLC v. Cox, 740 F.3d 1284 (9th Cir. 2014), the Ninth Circuit, falling in line with other circuits, held that the requirements of *Gertz* apply to lawsuits against bloggers no less than lawsuits against traditional media. The defendant blogger in the case maintained a site called obsidianfinancesucks.com, which was devoted to "one-sided" and hyperbolic criticism of the plaintiff Obsidian Finance. Nonetheless, the court concluded that "[t]he protections of the First Amendment do not turn on whether the journalist was a trained journalist, formally affiliated with traditional news entities, engaged in conflict-of-interest disclosure, went beyond just assembling others' writings, or tried to get both sides of the story." The court noted that every other circuit to address the issue had held that First Amendment protections in libel cases apply equally to the institutional press and individual speakers. It cited cases from the Second, Third, Fourth, Eighth, Tenth, and D.C. Circuits. For discussion of how social-media cases are reshaping libel doctrine, see Lyrissa Barnett Lidsky & RonNell Andersen Jones, *Of Reasonable Readers and Unreasonable Speakers: Libel Law in a Networked World*, 23 Va. J. Soc. Pol'y & L. 155 (2016).

4.   *Defamation of Private Figures Involved in Matters of Private Concern*

In Dun & Bradstreet v. Greenmoss Builders, 472 U.S. 749 (1985), the Supreme Court held, in a plurality decision, that not all defamation actions are subject to First Amendment limitations. In *Dun & Bradstreet*, a construction contractor sued for defamation after five of its creditors received a false credit report stating that the contractor had filed for bankruptcy. The defamation occurred because a 17-year-old employee of the credit-reporting agency, who had been paid to review state bankruptcy petitions, mistakenly attributed the bankruptcy of one of the plaintiff's former employees to the plaintiff itself. The credit-reporting agency made no attempt to verify the information before reporting it to five subscribers of its credit report, who were contractually bound not to reveal the contents to anyone else. The plaintiff won a verdict of $50,000 in compensatory or presumed damages and $300,000 in punitive damages on its defamation claim. The defendant Dun & Bradstreet moved for a new trial on the grounds that the trial court did not properly instruct the jury that punitive damages could not be awarded without proof of actual malice. In other words, the basis for the motion was that the constitutional requirements set forth in *Gertz v. Robert Welch, Inc.*, had not been met.

   In a plurality decision, the United States Supreme Court agreed that Dun & Bradstreet was not entitled to the protections of *Gertz*. The Court based its decision on the conclusion that the case involved "speech on matters of purely *private* concern," and distinguished *Gertz* as involving a matter of undoubted *public* concern. In a case involving a private-figure plaintiff and a matter of merely private concern, the plurality opinion held that "permitting recovery of presumed and punitive damages . . . absent a showing of 'actual malice' does not violate the First Amendment."

The plurality's rationale was that a different balance must be struck in cases where the type of speech involves only matters of private concern. The speech at issue in these cases is "less important" from a First Amendment standpoint than speech on matters of public concern: Private-concern speech is less essential to the "free and robust debate of public issues" or to a "meaningful dialogue of ideas concerning self-government." On the other side of the balance, the state interest in awarding presumed and punitive damages as an "effective" remedy for defamation is higher in cases involving matters of private concern, given the difficulties plaintiffs face in proving actual damages even where "'it is all but certain that serious harm has resulted in fact.'"

Although the plurality did not spell out the practical implications of this decision, its reasoning suggested that states may impose strict liability on defendants who defame private plaintiffs concerning matters of private concern. In other words, the *Dun & Bradstreet* decision may mean that in a limited class of cases, the states may simply require a plaintiff to prove the traditional common law elements of defamation—the publication of a defamatory statement of and concerning the plaintiff—without regard to fault.

However, the reach of the Court's decision is limited because its analysis indicated that cases involving purely private-concern speech will be rare. The Court indicated that "content, form and context" are determinative in deciding whether speech is of public concern or of private concern. Based on these factors, Dun & Bradstreet's credit report was private because it was "solely in the individual interest of the speaker and its specific business audience." Almost by definition, the credit report made no contribution to "the free flow of commercial information" because the audience for the speech consisted only of the five paid subscribers who were contractually bound not to disseminate the information more widely. The Court also emphasized that the speech deserved no special constitutional protection due to the allegedly "hardy" nature of commercial speech in general. Because credit-reporting agencies will have powerful market incentives to continue publishing and to verify the accuracy of reports, they will presumably not be unduly chilled by the imposition of defamation liability for false reports. For further clarification on what constitutes a matter of public concern, see the discussion in *Snyder v. Phelps*, excerpted later in this chapter.

5. The Constitutional "Privilege" Protecting Opinion

What if a plaintiff seeks to recover damages for the publication of material that is neither true nor false? In *Gertz v. Robert Welch*, the Supreme Court stated in dicta that "[u]nder the First Amendment there is no such thing as a false idea." Many lower courts interpreted this dictum as creating a privilege against defamation liability for anything that might be labeled opinion. In the following case, the Supreme Court chastises the lower courts for providing too much protection for opinion and set parameters for the so-called opinion privilege. The key inquiry, according to the Court, is whether a publication implies an assertion of objective fact. As you read, make sure to discern what two categories of statements the Court identifies as not implying an assertion of objective fact.

MILKOVICH v. LORAIN JOURNAL CO.

497 U.S. 1 (1990)

Chief Justice REHNQUIST delivered the opinion of the Court.

. . . This lawsuit is before us for the third time in an odyssey of litigation spanning nearly 15 years. Petitioner Milkovich, now retired, was the wrestling coach at Maple Heights High School in Maple Heights, Ohio. In 1974, his team was involved in an altercation at a home wrestling match with a team from Mentor High School. Several people were injured. In response to the incident, the Ohio High School Athletic Association (OHSAA) held a hearing at which Milkovich and H. Don Scott, the Superintendent of Maple Heights Public Schools, testified. Following the hearing, OHSAA placed the Maple Heights team on probation for a year and declared the team ineligible for the 1975 state tournament. OHSAA also censured Milkovich for his actions during the altercation. Thereafter, several parents and wrestlers sued OHSAA in the Court of Common Pleas of Franklin County, Ohio, seeking a restraining order against OHSAA's ruling on the grounds that they had been denied due process in the OHSAA proceeding. Both Milkovich and Scott testified in that proceeding. The court overturned OHSAA's probation and ineligibility orders on due process grounds.

The day after the court rendered its decision, respondent [Ted] Diadiun's column appeared in the News-Herald, a newspaper which circulates in Lake County, Ohio, and is owned by respondent Lorain Journal Co. The column bore the heading "Maple beat the law with the 'big lie,'" beneath which appeared Diadiun's photograph and the words "TD Says." The carryover page headline announced ". . . Diadiun says Maple told a lie." The column contained the following passages:

> "'. . . [A] lesson was learned (or relearned) yesterday by the student body of Maple Heights High School, and by anyone who attended the Maple-Mentor wrestling meet of last Feb. 8.
> "'A lesson which, sadly, in view of the events of the past year, is well they learned early.
> "'It is simply this: If you get in a jam, lie your way out.
> "'If you're successful enough, and powerful enough, and can sound sincere enough, you stand an excellent chance of making the lie stand up, regardless of what really happened.
> "'The teachers responsible were mainly head Maple wrestling coach, Mike Milkovich, and former superintendent of schools H. Donald Scott.
> . . . "'Anyone who attended the meet, whether he be from Maple Heights, Mentor, or impartial observer, knows in his heart that Milkovich and Scott lied at the hearing after each having given his solemn oath to tell the truth.
> "'But they got away with it.
> "'Is that the kind of lesson we want our young people learning from their high school administrators and coaches?
> "'I think not.'"

Petitioner commenced a defamation action against respondents in the Court of Common Pleas of Lake County, Ohio, alleging that the headline of Diadiun's article and the nine passages quoted above "accused plaintiff of committing the crime of perjury, an indictable offense in the State of Ohio, and damaged plaintiff directly in his life-time occupation of coach and teacher, and constituted libel per se." The action proceeded to trial, and the court granted a directed verdict to respondents on the ground that the evidence failed to establish the article was published with "actual malice" as required by *New York Times Co. v. Sullivan.* [While Milkovich's appeals were ongoing, the Ohio Supreme Court upheld a grant of summary judgments against Principal Scott, on the grounds that Diadiun's column was constitutionally protected opinion. Subsequently, the Ohio Court of Appeals upheld a grant of summary judgment against Milkovich, concluding that it was bound by the Ohio Supreme Court's analysis in Scott's case. The U.S. Supreme Court granted certiorari and reversed.]

. . . Respondents would have us recognize . . . still another First-Amendment-based protection for defamatory statements which are categorized as "opinion" as opposed to "fact." For this proposition they rely principally on the following dictum from our opinion in *Gertz:*

> "Under the First Amendment there is no such thing as a false idea. However pernicious an opinion may seem, we depend for its correction not on the conscience of judges and juries but on the competition of other ideas. But there is no constitutional value in false statements of fact."

Judge Friendly appropriately observed that this passage "has become the opening salvo in all arguments for protection from defamation actions on the ground of opinion, even though the case did not remotely concern the question." *Cianci v. New Times Publishing Co.,* 639 F.2d 54, 61 (2d Cir. 1980). Read in context, though, the fair meaning of the passage is to equate the word "opinion" in the second sentence with the word "idea" in the first sentence. Under this view, the language was merely a reiteration of Justice Holmes' classic "marketplace of ideas" concept. See *Abrams v. United States,* 250 U.S. 616, 630 (1919) (dissenting opinion) ("The ultimate good desired is better reached by free trade in ideas— . . . the best test of truth is the power of the thought to get itself accepted in the competition of the market").

Thus, we do not think this passage from *Gertz* was intended to create a wholesale defamation exemption for anything that might be labeled "opinion." . . . Not only would such an interpretation be contrary to the tenor and context of the passage, but it would also ignore the fact that expressions of "opinion" may often imply an assertion of objective fact.

If a speaker says, "In my opinion John Jones is a liar," he implies a knowledge of facts which lead to the conclusion that Jones told an untruth. Even if the speaker states the facts upon which he bases his opinion, if those facts are either incorrect or incomplete, or if his assessment of them is erroneous, the statement may still imply a false assertion of fact. Simply couching such statements in terms of opinion does not dispel these implications; and the statement, "In my opinion Jones is a liar," can cause as much damage to reputation as the statement, "Jones is a liar." As Judge Friendly aptly stated: "[It] would be destructive of the law of libel if a writer could escape liability for accusations of [defamatory conduct] simply by using, explicitly or implicitly, the words 'I think.'" It is worthy of note that at common law, even the privilege of fair comment did not extend to "a false statement of fact, whether it was expressly stated or implied from an expression of opinion." *Restatement (Second) of Torts, § 566,* Comment *a* (1977).

Apart from their reliance on the *Gertz* dictum, respondents do not really contend that a statement such as, "In my opinion John Jones is a liar," should be protected by a separate privilege for "opinion" under the First Amendment. But they do contend that in every defamation case the First Amendment mandates an inquiry into whether a statement is "opinion" or "fact," and that only the latter statements may be actionable. They propose that a number of factors developed by the lower courts (in what we hold was a mistaken reliance on the *Gertz* dictum) be considered in deciding which is which. But we think the "'breathing space'" which "'freedoms of expression require in order to survive,'" is adequately secured by existing constitutional doctrine without the creation of an artificial dichotomy between "opinion" and fact.

Foremost, we think [*Philadelphia Newspapers, Inc. v.*] *Hepps* stands for the proposition that a statement on matters of public concern must be provable as false before there can be liability under state defamation law, at least in situations, like the present, where a media defendant is involved. Thus, unlike the statement, "In my opinion Mayor Jones is a liar," the statement, "In my opinion Mayor Jones shows his abysmal ignorance by accepting the teachings of Marx and Lenin," would not be actionable. *Hepps* ensures that a statement of opinion relating to matters of public concern which does not contain a provably false factual connotation will receive full constitutional protection.

Next, the *Bresler-Letter Carriers-Falwell* line of cases provides protection for statements that cannot "reasonably [be] interpreted as stating actual facts" about an individual. *Falwell*, 485 U.S. at 50. This provides assurance that public debate will not suffer for lack of "imaginative expression" or the "rhetorical hyperbole" which has traditionally added much to the discourse of our Nation.

The *New York Times-Butts-Gertz* culpability requirements further ensure that debate on public issues remains "uninhibited, robust, and wide-open." *New York Times*, 376 U.S. at 270. Thus, where a statement of "opinion" on a matter of public concern reasonably implies false and defamatory facts regarding public figures or officials, those individuals must show that such statements were made with knowledge of their false implications or with reckless disregard of their truth. Similarly, where such a statement involves a private figure on a matter of public concern, a plaintiff must show that the false connotations were made with some level of fault as required by *Gertz*. Finally, the enhanced appellate review required by *Bose Corp.* provides assurance that the foregoing determinations will be made in a manner so as not to "constitute a forbidden intrusion of the field of free expression." *Bose Corp.*, 466 U.S. at 499 (quotation omitted).

We are not persuaded that, in addition to these protections, an additional separate constitutional privilege for "opinion" is required to ensure the freedom of expression guaranteed by the First Amendment. The dispositive question in the present case then becomes whether a reasonable factfinder could conclude that the statements in the Diadiun column imply an assertion that petitioner Milkovich perjured himself in a judicial proceeding. We think this question must be answered in the affirmative. As the Ohio Supreme Court itself observed: "The clear impact in some nine sentences and a caption is that [Milkovich]'lied at the hearing after . . . having given his solemn oath to tell the truth.'" This is not the sort of loose, figurative, or hyperbolic language which would negate the impression that the writer was seriously maintaining that petitioner committed the crime of perjury. Nor does the general tenor of the article negate this impression.

We also think the connotation that petitioner committed perjury is sufficiently factual to be susceptible of being proved true or false. A determination whether petitioner lied in this instance can be made on a core of objective evidence by comparing, *inter alia*, petitioner's testimony before the OHSAA board with his subsequent testimony before the trial court. . . .

The numerous decisions discussed above establishing First Amendment protection for defendants in defamation actions surely demonstrate the Court's recognition of the Amendment's vital guarantee of free and uninhibited discussion of public issues. But there is also another side to the equation; we have regularly acknowledged the "important social values which underlie the law of defamation," and recognized that "society has a pervasive and strong interest in preventing and redressing attacks upon reputation." *Rosenblatt v. Baer*, 383 U.S. 75 (1966). [Reversed and remanded.]

Justice BRENNAN, with whom Justice MARSHALL joins, dissenting.

. . . Although I agree with the majority that statements must be scrutinized for implicit factual assertions, the majority's scrutiny in this case does not "hold the balance true," between protection of individual reputation and freedom of speech. The statements complained of neither state nor imply a false assertion of fact, and, under the rule the Court reconfirms today, they should be found not libel "as a matter of constitutional law." Readers of Diadiun's column are signaled repeatedly that the author does not actually know what Milkovich said at the court hearing and that the author is surmising, from factual premises made explicit in the column, that Milkovich must have lied in court.

NOTES AND QUESTIONS

1. *The role of context.* In *Milkovich*, the Supreme Court failed to specify what role, if any, context plays in determining whether an allegedly defamatory statement "implies an assertion of objective fact." Must lower courts consider context in deciding whether a statement "cannot reasonably be interpreted as stating actual facts"? In deciding whether it is "provably false"? For more on the role of context in determining whether an allegedly defamatory statement is protected "opinion" under the First Amendment, see Jerry J. Phillips, *Opinion and Defamation: The Camel in the Tent*, 57 Tenn. L. Rev. 647 (1990), and Lyrissa Barnett Lidsky, *Silencing John Doe: Defamation and Discourse in Cyberspace*, 49 Duke L.J. 855 (2000) (dealing with the difficulties of applying the opinion privilege to allegedly defamatory statements made on Internet message boards).
2. *The media/nonmedia distinction in the age of the Internet.* The Court in *Milkovich* again "reserved judgment" on the question of whether the protection for statements that are not provably false applies to nonmedia defendants. 497 U.S. at 20 n.6. Does the logic of *Milkovich* suggest that its protections should extend only to media defendants? Why? Does the media/nonmedia distinction deserve re-examination in light of the growth of blogs and other novel forms of communication that blur the line between media and nonmedia speakers?
3. *Do false statement of fact have constitutional value?* In United States v. Alvarez, 567 U.S. ___ (2012), 132 S. Ct 2537, the Supreme Court struck down the Stolen Valor Act, a federal statute making it a crime for a person to falsely claim that she received a military decoration authorized by Congress. The decision affirmed that the government lacks the power to censor lies—even highly offensive ones—absent a showing of significant harm. Six justices concluded that the false statements prohibited by the Stolen Valor Act were not "in a general category that is presumptively unconstitutional." A plurality of four justices applied strict scrutiny to reach this result. Although "[t]he Government's interest in protecting

the integrity of the Medal of Honor is beyond question," the government could not show the Act was "actually necessary" to achieve that interest. The government showed no evidence that lies about military awards would dilute their meaning, and "counterspeech" could easily be deployed against false claims. In addition, "[a] Government-created database" listing soldiers who received medals or honors was a less restrictive alternative to criminalization of speech. The two justices who joined the plurality in invalidating the Act differed as to the appropriate level of constitutional scrutiny of restrictions on false speech such as lies about military honors: they applied "intermediate scrutiny" or "proportionality" analysis and determined that the harm to speech interests was "disproportionate" to the Act's advancement of the government's interest in upholding the integrity of its military awards.

4. *Online review sites.* In Seaton v. TripAdvisor, 728 F.3d 592 (6th Cir. 2013), plaintiff Kenneth Seaton, the sole owner of Grand Resort Hotel and Convention, sued TripAdvisor for defamation, false light, and invasion of privacy for placing his hotel on its "2011 Dirtiest Hotels List." TripAdvisor filed a motion to dismiss, asserting that its placement of the Grand Resort on the list constituted non-actionable opinion. The district court granted TripAdvisor's motion to dismiss. The Sixth Circuit affirmed, holding that TripAdvisor's placement of Seaton's hotel on its dirtiest hotels list was "not capable of being understood as defamatory." The court based this conclusion, first, on the fact that the "superlative" adjective "dirtiest" was "loose, hyperbolic language." Second, the court looked at the "general tenor" of the list, which billed itself as a product of user reviews rather than "scientific study," with the user reviews being full of hyperbole and subjective accounts of travelers' experiences. Finally, the court placed the TripAdvisor list in the "broader context" of online rankings. TripAdvisor's compilation of user comments was part of broader online trend: "[T]op ten" lists and the like appear with growing frequency on the web." Thus, "a reasonable observer understands that placement on and ranking within the bulk of such lists constitutes opinion, not a provable fact." Although the plaintiff contended that TripAdvisor employed a flawed methodology for ranking user comments, the court found that "the subjective weighing of factors cannot be proven false and therefore cannot be the basis of a defamation claim." Indeed, the court's opinion repeatedly stressed the subjectivity of such rankings as a basis for affirming dismissal of plaintiff's claim.

5. *An injunction remedy for online defamation?* In Kinney v. Barnes, 443 S.W.3d 87 (Tex. 2014), *cert. denied*, 135 S. Ct. 1164 (2015), the Texas Supreme Court held that a court may issue a post-trial injunction requiring a defendant to remove from his website statements he made that a civil jury has found to be defamatory. However, the court held that an injunction on future speech of a similar nature was an unconstitutional prior restraint that ran the risk of chilling constitutionally protected expression. The court cited the "inherently contextual nature of defamatory speech" as problematic, explaining "even the most narrowly crafted of injunctions risks enjoining protected speech because the same statement made at a different time and in a different context may no longer be actionable. Untrue statements may later become true; unprivileged statements may later become privileged." In sum, this case stands for the general recognition that "the appropriate remedy for defamation is damages, not injunctive relief." What are implications of this decision? Can a court issue a

post-trial injunction requiring a defendant to remove information that has been found to invade privacy? What about a criminal record that has been expunged?

6. *Libel and the Press Clause.* What do the libel cases discussed in this chapter suggest about whether the Press Clause of the First Amendment provides "special rights" to the press not already provided by the Speech Clause? Is this message consistent with that expressed in the line of cases developed in Chapter 8, which dealt with mass media and the First Amendment?

7. *Statutory modifications of the "republication rule" in the Internet age.* For purposes of defamation law, a defendant "publishes" a statement when he originates or repeats defamatory material to at least one third person. Publication can be accomplished by written, oral, broadcast, photographic, printed, or other means. A person is liable for the "republication"—that is, the repetition—of another's defamatory statement as if he originated it. For example, a newspaper that publishes a defamatory letter to the editor can be sued for defamation for the contents of that letter. The rationale for the republication rule is that otherwise media and others could defame at will merely by finding someone to whom they can attribute a defamatory statement. The "republication rule" is sometimes modified to protect those who repeat (or "publish") the statements of others. For example, a tort privilege protects the media when they fairly and accurate report on open public meetings, and the actual malice rule acts as a constitutional privilege protecting one who repeats information learned from others as long as he or she does not knowingly or recklessly disregard the falsity of the repeated information.

    The "republication rule" is deeply at odds with the practices of Internet communications. The Internet has developed a culture of more or less uninhibited repetition of information originated by others. Early on, Congress recognized that defamation lawsuits threatened to stifle free speech in this then-new medium, and it stepped in to insulate Internet service providers from defamation and other tort liability when they act merely as intermediaries allowing the "republication" of speech originated by others. Congress provided, in Section 230 of the Communications Decency Act (CDA), that: "No provider or user of an interactive computer service shall be treated as the publisher or speaker of any information provided by another information content provider." 47 U.S.C. § 230(c)(1). As interpreted by courts, Section 230 broadly bars lawsuits seeking to hold any Internet service provider liable for "publishing" or refusing to remove content originated by other speakers. *See, e.g.,* Zeran v. America Online, Inc., 129 F.3d 327 (4th Cir. 1997) (barring lawsuit against AOL for delay in removing defamatory messages posted by unidentified third party).

    A few courts have attempted to limit the broad scope of Section 230 immunity. In Fair Housing Council of San Fernando Valley v. Roommates.com LLC, 521 F.3d 1157, 36 Med. L. Rptr. 1545 (9th Cir. 2008) (en banc), for example, the U.S. Court of Appeals for the Ninth Circuit held, 8-3, that a Web site's active involvement in soliciting the content supplied by its users deprived the Web site's operators of CDA immunity in a housing discrimination action. The Web site offered a "roommate-matching" service and required users of the service to answer questionnaires with information about gender, sexual preference, and whether children would be living in the user's household. The Ninth Circuit held that three aspects of the Roommates.com Web site deprived it of CDA immunity. First, requiring users to answer questions about their sex, family status, and sexual orientation made Roommates.com an "information content provider" rather than a conduit for information supplied by third parties. Second, the creation of user profiles based on answers to the required questionnaire made Roommates.com an information "developer" rather than a "passive transmitter of information provided by others." Third, the creation of a search engine that allowed "discriminatory filtering" by users—that is, filtering based on gender and other illegal criteria—made Roommates.com "forfeit any immunity to which it was otherwise entitled." The court distinguished the search engine function of Roommates.com from search engines functions such as Google's, which "provide neutral tools to carry out what may be unlawful or illicit searches." The court also stressed that "an editor's minor changes to the spelling, grammar and length of third-party content do not strip him of Section 230 immunity." For other cases expressing dissatisfaction with the broad scope of Section 230 immunity in cases like *Zeran*, see Doe v. GTE Corp., 347 F.3d 655 (7th Cir. 2003); Chicago Lawyers' Committee for Civil Rights Under the Law, Inc. v. Craigslist, Inc., 519 F.3d 666 (7th Cir. 2008). What are the implications of this case for defamation law? What about sites that solicit online gossip, like TheDirty.com? Other cases applying § 230 include Klayman v. Zuckerberg, 753 F.3d 1354 (D.C. Cir. 2014) (applying 230 immunity); Jones v. Dirty World Entertainment, 755 F.3d 398 (6th Cir. 2014) (granting immunity); J.S. v. Village Voice Media Holdings, 359 P.3d 714 (Wash. 2015) (rejecting blanket immunity); Doe v. Backpage.com 2016 U.S. App. Lexis 4671 (1st Cir. Mar. 14, 2016).

8. *Libel law abroad.* Libel laws in other countries are less favorable—often far less favorable—to defendants than those of the United States. The Supreme Court of Canada recently reduced the disparity with its decision in Grant v. Torstar Corp. (Can.), [2009] 3 S.C.R. 640. The *Torstar* decision makes a new defense available to Canadian libel defendants publishing in both traditional and new media. The defense protects "responsible communication on matters of public interest." In determining whether publication was "responsible," courts examine how diligently the defendant has attempted to verify the defamatory statement prior to publishing. Factors include the "seriousness of the allegation"; the "public importance of the matter"; "urgency"; the "status and reliability of the source"; "whether the plaintiff's side of the story was sought and accurate reported"; whether "inclusion of the defamatory statement was justifiable"; whether the statement was reported for "the fact that it was made" as opposed to its truth; and "any other relevant circumstances." The Canadian Supreme Court explicitly rejected the "American approach of protecting all statements about public figures, unless the plaintiff can show malice" and instead adopted the "middle road . . . chosen by courts in Australia, New Zealand, South Africa and the United Kingdom." The Court believed this "middle road" "represents a reasonable and proportionate response to the need to protect reputation while sustaining the public exchange of information that is vital to modern Canadian society."

THEORY-APPLIED PROBLEM—A RESTAURANT REVIEW

Assume that a restaurant critic for the Ohio Post reviews a new steakhouse called Chops. The critic pans the restaurant, stating that "my strip steak was miserably tough and fatty." The owner of Chops sues for libel. Rate the owner's chances of success in light of *Milkovich*. What if the owner can prove that the critic ordered a steak sandwich made with flank steak, an inferior cut, rather than a strip steak? What if the owner can prove that on the date the critic claims to have eaten the strip steak the critic actually ordered only salmon?

THEORY-APPLIED PROBLEM—EXTENDING MILKOVICH TO OTHER TORTS?

Are the First Amendment protections *Milkovich* identifies only relevant in defamation cases? In what other contexts might *Milkovich*'s principle come into play? Could the government pass a statute barring candidates for elective office from employing parodies targeted at their opponents?

THEORY-APPLIED PROBLEM—HASHTAG LIBEL

A company named Able Business Co. sues a competitor for libel, based on the competitor's social media posts that say: "We support the USA 100 percent. We encourage you to ask our competitor, Able Business Co., about its support. #MADEINCHINA #RedDragon." Is this statement defamatory? Is it protected by the constitutional privilege for opinion, assuming that Able Business Co. is a registered U.S. corporation with its principal place of business and the overwhelming majority of its supplier in the U.S.? See AvePoint, Inc. v. Power Tools, Inc., 981 F. Supp. 2d 496 (W.D. Va. 2013).

AN EXTENDED NOTE ON JURISDICTION AND LIBEL TOURISM

The First Amendment does not exempt libel defendants from general rules regarding jurisdiction in distant places. *See* Keeton v. Hustler Magazine, Inc., 465 U.S. 770 (1984). For example, in Calder v. Jones, 465 U.S. 783 (1984), the Supreme Court held that the National Enquirer magazine was subject to specific jurisdiction in California even though the reporter and editor worked at the magazine's headquarters in Florida. The Court held that jurisdiction was proper because the effects of an allegedly defamatory article in the magazine were felt in California. The article was about an actor who lived in California and concerned her activities there; 600,000 copies of the magazine were sold in California, and the intentional acts of the publishers "were expressly aimed at California" because they "knew that the brunt of [reputational] injury would be felt" there.

The Supreme Court again addressed personal jurisdiction analysis in Walden v. Fiore, 134 S. Ct. 1115 (2014). There, the Court clarified that "[t]he crux of Calder was that the reputation-based 'effects' of the alleged libel connected the defendants to California, not just to the plaintiff. The strength of that connection was largely a function of the libel tort. However scandalous a newspaper might be, it can lead to a loss of reputation only if communicated to (and read and understood by) third persons." The effect on the California audience, coupled with the California focus of the article, "connected the defendants' conduct to California, not just to a plaintiff who lived there."

Many countries have jurisdictional rules that allow foreign defendants to be sued in their courts and under their law. Material posted on the Internet can be accessed in any country and therefore is arguably "published" there and thus subject to jurisdiction in any country in which it is received. See, for example, Dow Jones & Co. v. Gutnick (2002) 210 C.L.R. 575, in which the Australian High Court held that the New York publisher of Barron's magazine could be sued in Australia for statements made on its Web site about an Australian businessman, even it had no physical presence in Australia and very few Australian subscribers.

Other countries' defamation laws are considerably less protective of defendants than those of the United States. The term "libel tourism" is sometimes used to describe plaintiffs' attempt to forum-shop for a jurisdiction with the most favorable libel laws. Ordinarily, unless the defendant has assets in the forum jurisdiction, a plaintiff who wins a libel case abroad can collect it only by having a U.S. court enforce the foreign judgment. Congress passed the SPEECH Act in 2010 to protect U.S. citizens from the threat of foreign libel judgments. See Securing the Protection of our Enduring and Established Constitutional Heritage Act, 28 U.S.C. §§ 4101-4105 (2010). The Act provides, among other things, that U.S. courts may not enforce foreign judgments unless (1) the law applied in the foreign court provided at least as much protection to free expression as U.S. law, or (2) the speech would have subjected the speaker to liability for defamation under U.S. law, even if the foreign jurisdiction's law was not as protective of expression as U.S. law.

B. FIRST AMENDMENT LIMITATIONS ON INTENTIONAL INFLICTION OF EMOTIONAL DISTRESS

Typically intentional infliction of emotional distress is actionable when a defendant, through "outrageous" conduct, intentionally or recklessly inflicts severe emotional distress on the plaintiff. *See Restatement (Second) of Torts* § 46. In the following case, a public-figure plaintiff based his claim of intentional infliction on an outrageous parody advertisement.

HUSTLER MAGAZINE, INC. v. FALWELL
485 U.S. 46 (1989)

Chief Justice REHNQUIST delivered the opinion of the Court.

. . . Respondent Jerry Falwell, a nationally known minister who has been active as a commentator on politics and public affairs, sued petitioner [Hustler Magazine] and its publisher, petitioner Larry Flynt, to recover damages for invasion of privacy, libel, and intentional infliction of emotional distress. The District Court directed a verdict against respondent on the privacy claim, and submitted the other two claims to a jury. The jury found for petitioners on the defamation claim, but found for respondent on the claim for intentional infliction of emotional distress and awarded damages [or $100,000 in compensatory damages and $50,000 in punitives against each petitioner]. We now consider whether this award is consistent with the First and Fourteenth Amendments of the United States Constitution.

The inside front cover of the November 1983 issue of Hustler Magazine featured a "parody" of an advertisement for Campari Liqueur that contained the name and picture of respondent and was entitled "Jerry Falwell talks about his first time." This parody was modeled after actual Campari ads that included interviews with various celebrities about their "first times." Although it was apparent by the end of each interview that this meant the first time they sampled Campari, the ads clearly played on the sexual double entendre of the general subject of "first times." Copying the form and layout of these Campari ads, Hustler's editors chose respondent as the featured celebrity and drafted an alleged "interview" with him in which he states that his "first time" was during a drunken incestuous rendezvous with his mother in an outhouse. The Hustler parody portrays respondent and his mother as drunk and immoral, and suggests that respondent is a hypocrite who preaches only when he is drunk. In small print at the bottom of the page, the ad contains the disclaimer, "ad parody—not to be taken seriously." . . .

. . . The jury . . . found against respondent on the libel claim, specifically finding that the ad parody could not "reasonably be understood as describing actual facts about [respondent] or actual events in which [he] participated." . . . The jury ruled for respondent on the intentional infliction of emotional distress claim. . . . On appeal, the United States Court of Appeals for the Fourth Circuit affirmed the judgment against petitioners. . . .

This case presents us with a novel question involving First Amendment limitations upon a State's authority to protect its citizens from the intentional infliction of emotional distress. We must decide whether a public figure may recover damages for emotional harm caused by the publication of an ad parody offensive to him, and doubtless gross and repugnant in the eyes of most. Respondent would have us find that a State's interest in protecting public figures from emotional distress is sufficient to deny First Amendment protection to speech that is patently offensive and is intended to inflict emotional injury, even when that speech could not reasonably have been interpreted as stating actual facts about the public figure involved. This we decline to do.

At the heart of the First Amendment is the recognition of the fundamental importance of the free flow of ideas and opinions on matters of public interest and concern. "The freedom to speak one's mind is not only an aspect of individual liberty—and thus a good unto itself—but also is essential to the common quest for truth and the vitality of society as a whole." . . . We have therefore been particularly vigilant to ensure that individual expressions of ideas remain free from governmentally imposed sanctions. . . .

The sort of robust political debate encouraged by the First Amendment is bound to produce speech that is critical of those who hold public office or those public figures who are "intimately involved in the resolution of important public questions or, by reason of their fame, shape events in areas of concern to society at large." . . . Justice Frankfurter put it succinctly in *Baumgartner v. United States*, . . . , when he said that "one of the prerogatives of American citizenship is the right to criticize public men and measures." Such criticism, inevitably, will not always be reasoned or moderate; public figures as well as public officials will be subject to "vehement, caustic, and sometimes unpleasantly sharp attacks." . . .

Of course, this does not mean that any speech about a public figure is immune from sanction in the form of damages. Since *New York Times Co. v. Sullivan*, we have consistently ruled that a public figure may hold a speaker liable for the damage to reputation caused by publication of a defamatory falsehood, but only if the statement was made "with knowledge that it was false or with reckless disregard of whether it was false or not." . . . False statements of fact are particularly valueless; they interfere with the truth-seeking function of the marketplace of ideas, and they cause damage to an individual's reputation that cannot easily be repaired by counterspeech, however persuasive or effective. But even though falsehoods have little value in and of themselves, they are "nevertheless inevitable in free debate" . . ., and a rule that would impose strict liability on a publisher for false factual assertions would have an undoubted "chilling" effect on speech relating to public figures that does have constitutional value. . . . [B]reathing space is provided by a constitutional rule that allows public figures to recover for libel or defamation only when they can prove both that the statement was false and that the statement was made with the requisite level of culpability.

Respondent argues, however, that a different standard should apply in this case because here the State seeks to prevent not reputational damage, but the severe emotional distress suffered by the person who is the subject of an offensive publication. In respondent's view . . ., so long as the utterance was intended to inflict emotional distress, was outrageous, and did in fact inflict serious emotional distress, it is of no constitutional import whether the statement was a fact or an opinion, or whether it was true or false. It is the intent to cause injury that is the gravamen of the tort, and the State's interest in preventing emotional harm simply outweighs whatever interest a speaker may have in speech of this type.

Generally speaking the law does not regard the intent to inflict emotional distress as one which should receive much solicitude, and it is quite understandable that most if not all jurisdictions have chosen to make it civilly culpable where the conduct in question is sufficiently "outrageous." But in the world of debate about public affairs, many things done with motives that are less than admirable are protected by the First Amendment. In *Garrison v. Louisiana*, we held that even when a speaker or writer is motivated by hatred or ill-will his expression was protected by the First Amendment. . . . [W]hile such a bad motive may be deemed controlling for purposes of tort liability in other areas of the law, we think the First Amendment prohibits such a result in the area of public debate about public figures.

Were we to hold otherwise, there can be little doubt that political cartoonists and satirists would be subjected to damages awards without any showing that their work falsely defamed its subject. Webster's defines a caricature as "the deliberately distorted picturing or imitating of a person, literary style, etc. by exaggerating features or mannerisms for satirical effect." . . . The appeal of the political cartoon or caricature is often based on exploration of unfortunate physical traits or politically embarrassing events—an exploration often calculated to injure the feelings of the subject of the portrayal. The art of the cartoonist is often not reasoned or evenhanded, but slashing and one-sided. One cartoonist expressed the nature of the art in these words:

> "The political cartoon is a weapon of attack, of scorn and ridicule and satire; it is least effective when it tries to pat some politician on the back. It is usually as welcome as a bee sting and is always controversial in some quarters." Long, The Political Cartoon: Journalism's Strongest Weapon, The Quill, 56, 57 (Nov. 1962).

Several famous examples of this type of intentionally injurious speech were drawn by Thomas Nast, probably the greatest American cartoonist to date, who was associated for many years during the post-Civil War era with Harper's Weekly. In the pages of that publication Nast conducted a graphic vendetta against William M. "Boss" Tweed and his corrupt associates in New York City's "Tweed Ring." It has been described by one historian of the subject as "a sustained attack which in its passion and effectiveness stands alone in the history of American graphic art." . . . Another writer explains that the success of the Nast cartoon was achieved "because of the emotional impact of its presentation. It continuously goes beyond the bounds of good taste and conventional manners." . . .

Despite their sometimes caustic nature, from the early cartoon portraying George Washington as an ass down to the present day, graphic depictions and satirical cartoons have played a prominent role in public and political debate. Nast's castigation of the Tweed Ring, Walt McDougall's characterization of presidential candidate James G. Blaine's banquet with the millionaires at Delmonico's as "The Royal Feast of Belshazzar," and numerous other efforts have undoubtedly had an effect on the course and outcome of contemporaneous debate. Lincoln's tall, gangling posture, Teddy Roosevelt's glasses and teeth, and Franklin D. Roosevelt's jutting jaw and cigarette holder have been memorialized by political cartoons with an effect that could not have been obtained by the photographer or the portrait artist. From the viewpoint of history it is clear that our political discourse would have been considerably poorer without them.

Respondent contends, however, that the caricature in question here was so "outrageous" as to distinguish it from more traditional political cartoons. There is no doubt that the caricature of respondent and his mother published in Hustler is at best a distant cousin of the political cartoons described above, and a rather poor relation at that. If it were possible by laying down a principled standard to separate the one from the other, public discourse would probably suffer little or no harm. But we doubt that there is any such standard, and we are quite sure that the pejorative description "outrageous" does not supply one. "Outrageousness" in the area of political and social discourse has an inherent subjectiveness about it which would allow a jury to impose liability on the basis of the jurors' tastes or views, or perhaps on the basis of their dislike of a particular expression. An "outrageousness" standard thus runs afoul of our longstanding refusal to allow damages to be awarded because the speech in question may have an adverse emotional impact on the audience. . . .

We conclude that public figures and public officials may not recover for the tort of intentional infliction of emotional distress by reason of publications such as the one here at issue without showing in addition that the publication contains a false statement of fact which was made with "actual malice," i.e., with knowledge that the statement was false or with reckless disregard as to whether or not it was true. This is not merely a "blind application" of the *New York Times* standard; it reflects our considered judgment that such a standard is necessary to give adequate "breathing space" to the freedoms protected by the First Amendment.

Here it is clear that respondent Falwell is a "public figure" for purposes of First Amendment law. The jury found against respondent on his libel claim when it decided that the Hustler ad parody could not "reasonably be understood as describing actual facts about [respondent] or actual events in which [he] participated." . . . The Court of Appeals interpreted the jury's finding to be that the ad parody "was not reasonably believable," and in accordance with our custom we accept this finding. Respondent is thus relegated to his claim for damages awarded by the jury for the intentional infliction of emotional *distress* by "outrageous" conduct. But for reasons heretofore stated this claim cannot, consistently with the First Amendment, form a basis for the award of damages when the conduct in question is the publication of a caricature such as the ad parody involved here. The judgment of the Court of Appeals is accordingly

Reversed.

Justice KENNEDY took no part in the consideration or decision of this case.

NOTES AND QUESTIONS

1. *First Amendment protection for satire, hyperbole, parody. Falwell* held narrowly that public figures must prove actual malice to recover for intentional infliction based on the publication of allegedly outrageous material. But the Supreme Court's later opinion in Milkovich v. Lorain Journal, 497 U.S. 1 (1990), which is excerpted in Section A.5 of this chapter, interpreted *Falwell* as protecting statements that cannot "reasonably be interpreted as stating actual facts" about an individual. The Court reasoned that such statements must be protected so that "public debate will not suffer for lack of 'imaginative expression' or the 'rhetorical hyperbole' which has traditionally added much to the discourse of our nation." Does this rationale apply only to speech about public figures?

2. *Newsgathering and emotional distress.* May a public-figure plaintiff bring a claim for intentional infliction of emotional distress if a reporter uses intrusive methods to gather information about the plaintiff?

In the case below, the plaintiff sues for intentional infliction and other torts after the defendants protest outside his son's funeral holding signs with highly offensive messages. What does the plaintiff contend is "outrageous" about the defendants' conduct in this case: the content of defendants' speech, the setting, or both?

SNYDER v. PHELPS

562 U.S. 443 (2011)

Chief Justice ROBERTS delivered the opinion of the Court.

. . . Fred Phelps founded the Westboro Baptist Church in Topeka, Kansas, in 1955. The church's congregation believes that God hates and punishes the United States for its tolerance of homosexuality, particularly in America's military. . . . [T]hey have picketed nearly 600 funerals [to spread their message, including the funeral of Marine Lance Corporal Matthew Snyder, who was killed in the line of duty in Iraq.]

Phelps became aware of Matthew Snyder's funeral and decided to travel to Maryland with six other Westboro Baptist parishioners (two of his daughters and four of his grandchildren) to picket. On the day of the memorial service, the Westboro congregation members picketed on public land adjacent to public streets near the Maryland State House, the United States Naval Academy, and Matthew Snyder's funeral. The Westboro picketers carried signs [stating:] "God Hates the USA/Thank God for 9/11," "America is Doomed," "Don't Pray for the USA," "Thank God for IEDs," "Thank God for Dead Soldiers," "Pope in Hell," "Priests Rape Boys," "God Hates Fags," "You're Going to Hell," and "God Hates You."

[The picketing took place 1,000 feet from the church. Snyder's father, the plaintiff in this tort action against Westboro, could not see what was written on the picket signs on his way to the funeral, but he saw them while watching a news broadcast of the protest later that night. He sued Phelps, his daughters, and Westboro for defamation, publicity given to private life, intentional infliction of emotional distress, intrusion upon seclusion, and civil conspiracy. A federal district court granted summary judgment for Westboro on the defamation and publicity claims. A jury found for Snyder on the intentional infliction, intrusion, and civil conspiracy claims and awarded him $2.9 million in compensatory and $8 million in punitive damages. The punitive were remitted to $2.1 million. The Court of Appeals reversed on First Amendment grounds, and the Supreme Court granted certiorari.]

Whether the First Amendment prohibits holding Westboro liable for its speech in this case turns largely on whether that speech is of public or private concern, as determined by all the circumstances of the case. "[S]peech on 'matters of public concern' . . . is 'at the heart of the First Amendment's protection.'" *Dun & Bradstreet, Inc. v. Greenmoss Builders, Inc.*, 472 U.S. 749, 758-759 (1985) (opinion of Powell, J.). . . .

. . . [W]here matters of purely private significance are at issue, First Amendment protections are often less rigorous. *Hustler.* That is because restricting speech on purely private matters does not implicate the same constitutional concerns as limiting speech on matters of public interest: "[T]here is no threat to the free and robust debate of public issues; there is no potential interference with a meaningful dialogue of ideas"; and the "threat of liability" does not pose the risk of "a reaction of self-censorship" on matters of public import. *Dun & Bradstreet.*

We noted a short time ago, in considering whether public employee speech addressed a matter of public concern, that "the boundaries of the public concern test are not well defined." *San Diego v. Roe*, 543 U.S. 77 (2004) (per curiam). Although that remains true today, we have articulated some guiding principles, principles that accord broad protection to speech to ensure that courts themselves do not become inadvertent censors.

Speech deals with matters of public concern when it can "be fairly considered as relating to any matter of political, social, or other concern to the community," *Connick* [v. Myers, 461 U.S. 138 (1983)], or when it "is a subject of legitimate news interest; that is, a subject of general interest and of value and concern to the public," *San Diego.* The arguably "inappropriate or controversial character of a statement is irrelevant to the question whether it deals with a matter of public concern." [].

[W]e concluded in *San Diego v. Roe* that, in the context of a government employer regulating the speech of its employees, videos of an employee engaging in sexually explicit acts did not address a public concern; the videos "did nothing to inform the public about any aspect of the [employing agency's] functioning or operation." 543 U.S., at 84.

Deciding whether speech is of public or private concern requires us to examine the "'content, form, and context'" of that speech, "'as revealed by the whole record.'" *Dun & Bradstreet* (quoting *Connick*). As in other First Amendment cases, the court is obligated "to 'make an independent examination of the whole record' in order to make sure that 'the judgment does not constitute a forbidden intrusion on the field of free expression.'" In considering content, form, and context, no factor is dispositive, and it is necessary to evaluate all the circumstances of the speech, including what was said, where it was said, and how it was said.

The "content" of Westboro's signs plainly relates to broad issues of interest to society at large, rather than matters of "purely private concern." . . . While the [] messages [on Westboro's signs] may fall short of refined social or political commentary, the issues they highlight—the political and moral conduct of the United States and its citizens, the fate of our Nation, homosexuality in the military, and scandals involving the Catholic clergy—are matters of public import. The signs certainly convey Westboro's position on those issues, in a manner designed . . . to reach as broad a public audience as possible. And even if a few of the signs—such as "You're Going to Hell" and "God Hates You"—were viewed as containing messages related to Matthew Snyder or the Snyders specifically, that would not change the fact that the overall thrust and dominant theme of Westboro's demonstration spoke to broader public issues.

Apart from the content of Westboro's signs, Snyder contends that the "context" of the speech—its connection with his son's funeral—makes the speech a matter of private rather than public concern. The fact that Westboro spoke in connection with a funeral, however, cannot by itself transform the nature of Westboro's speech. . . .

. . . Westboro had been actively engaged in speaking on the subjects addressed in its picketing long before it became aware of Matthew Snyder, and there can be no serious claim that Westboro's picketing did not represent its "honestly believed" views on public issues. There was no pre-existing relationship or conflict between Westboro and Snyder that might suggest Westboro's speech on public matters was intended to mask an attack on Snyder over a private matter. []

. . . Westboro's choice to convey its views in conjunction with Matthew Snyder's funeral made the expression of those views particularly hurtful to many, especially to Matthew's father. The record makes clear that the applicable legal term—"emotional distress"—fails to capture fully the anguish Westboro's choice added to Mr. Snyder's already incalculable grief. But Westboro conducted its picketing peacefully on matters of public concern at a public place adjacent to a public street. Such space occupies a "special position in terms of First Amendment protection." *United States v. Grace,* 461 U.S. 171, 180 (1983). "[W]e have repeatedly referred to public streets as the archetype of a traditional public forum," noting that "'[t]ime out of mind' public streets and sidewalks have been used for public assembly and debate." *Frisby v. Schultz,* 487 U.S. 474, 480 (1988).

. . . Maryland now has a law imposing restrictions on funeral picketing, Md. Crim. Law Code Ann. § 10-205 (Lexis Supp. 2010), as do 43 other States and the Federal Government. To the extent these laws are content neutral, they raise very different questions from the tort verdict at issue in this case. Maryland's law, however, was not in effect at the time of the events at issue here. . . .

Simply put, the church members had the right to be where they were. Westboro alerted local authorities to its funeral protest and fully complied with police guidance on where the picketing could be staged. The picketing was conducted under police supervision some 1,000 feet from the church, out of the sight of those at the church. The protest was not unruly; there was no shouting, profanity, or violence.

The record confirms that any distress occasioned by Westboro's picketing turned on the content and viewpoint of the message conveyed, rather than any interference with the funeral itself. A group of parishioners standing at the very spot where Westboro stood, holding signs that said "God Bless America" and "God Loves You," would not have been subjected to liability. It was what Westboro said that exposed it to tort damages.

. . . The jury here was instructed that it could hold Westboro liable for intentional infliction of emotional distress based on a finding that Westboro's picketing was "outrageous." "Outrageousness," however, is a highly malleable standard with "an inherent subjectiveness about it which would allow a jury to impose liability on the basis of the jurors' tastes or views, or perhaps on the basis of their dislike of a particular expression." *Hustler*. . . . What Westboro said, in the whole context of how and where it chose to say it, is entitled to "special protection" under the First Amendment, and that protection cannot be overcome by a jury finding that the picketing was outrageous.

. . . Westboro believes that America is morally flawed; many Americans might feel the same about Westboro. Westboro's funeral picketing is certainly hurtful and its contribution to public discourse may be negligible. But Westboro addressed matters of public import on public property, in a peaceful manner, in full compliance with the guidance of local officials. The speech was indeed planned to coincide with Matthew Snyder's funeral, but did not itself disrupt that funeral, and Westboro's choice to conduct its picketing at that time and place did not alter the nature of its speech.

Speech is powerful. It can stir people to action, move them to tears of both joy and sorrow, and—as it did here—inflict great pain. On the facts before us, we cannot react to that pain by punishing the speaker. As a Nation we have chosen a different course—to protect even hurtful speech on public issues to ensure that we do not stifle public debate. That choice requires that we shield Westboro from tort liability for its picketing in this case. [Affirmed.]

NOTES AND QUESTIONS

1. *A personal assault?* In dissent, Justice Samuel Alito labeled Westboro's speech a "vicious verbal assault" and a "brutal attack." Is Justice Alito correct that there is no need to protect the speech of the Westboro protestors here because they have "almost limitless opportunities" to voice their opinions on "moral, religious, and political issues" in other contexts? Is there a First Amendment right to convey your message in the format or context where it is most likely to be heard or seen? Should the majority have given more weight to the argument that the Westboro protestors were exploiting the funeral of a private citizen to attract public attention to their repugnant views? Does it matter whether the picketing was directed to "society at large" or to the family of Matthew Snyder? *See* Steven J. Heyman, *To Drink the Cup of Fury: Funeral Picketing, Public Discourse and the First Amendment*, 45 Conn. L. Rev. 101 (2012).

2. *The constitutionality of funeral protest statutes.* Is the Court majority encouraging states to pass funeral protest statutes? The Court suggests content-neutral laws imposing reasonable time, place, and manner restrictions on funeral picketing would not violate the First Amendment. At least 41 states and the federal govern have passed statutes restricting funeral protests. *See* Christina E. Wells, *Privacy and Funeral Protest*, 87 N.C. L. Rev. 151, 158 (2008) (discussing the constitutionality of these statutes).

THEORY-APPLIED PROBLEM—FUNERAL PROTESTS

A state law makes it a misdemeanor to engage in "violent, abusive, indecent, profane, boisterous, unreasonably loud or otherwise disorderly conduct" within 500 feet of a funeral service within the hour preceding such service, during such service, or within the hour immediately following the conclusion of such service. Is this law constitutional? Why or why not? Would the law be constitutional if it were limited by adding the requirement that the conduct "tends to cause or provoke a disturbance"?

THEORY-APPLIED PROBLEM—INTENTIONAL INFLICTION AND PUBLIC CONCERN

Assume a high school student creates a Web site called "My Teacher Sux." On the site, he ridicules the teaching style, appearance, and intelligence of his math teacher. The site includes a page captioned, "Why Should My Math Teacher Die? [Joke!]" and asks visitors to the site for contributions of $20 to hire a hit man. Many of the students in the teacher's class learn of and visit the site, and one of them brings it to the teacher's attention. The teacher becomes so severely distressed he must take medical leave and cannot finish the school year. He sues the student for intentional infliction of emotional distress. Is the First Amendment a bar to recovery? The facts of this problem are based loosely on J.S. v. Bethlehem Area Sch. Dist., 807 A.2d 803 (Pa. 2002).

C. FIRST AMENDMENT LIMITATIONS ON IMPOSING LIABILITY FOR PUBLISHING TRUE INFORMATION

The previous cases in this chapter dealt with First Amendment limits on torts that impose liability on publishers of information alleged to be false or at least not provably true. A harder issue is presented when states attempt to impose liability based on the publication of truthful but private information. Many states recognize the tort of public disclosure of private facts, which is defined by the *Restatement (Second) of Torts § 652D* as being actionable when a defendant gives publicity to private facts about a plaintiff, the disclosure is highly offensive to a reasonable person, and the disclosure is not of public concern. Because the tort developed in the twentieth century, the tort elements reflect an attempt to accommodate the publication of newsworthy information. However, the constitutionality of the tort is cast into doubt by the following case. Can you see why?

THE FLORIDA STAR v. B. J. F.

491 U.S. 524 (1989)

Justice MARSHALL delivered the opinion of the Court.

Florida Stat. § 794.03 (1987) makes it unlawful to "print, publish, or broadcast . . . in any instrument of mass communication" the name of the victim of a sexual offense. Pursuant to this statute, appellant The Florida Star was found civilly liable for publishing the name of a rape victim which it had obtained from a publicly released police report. The issue presented here is whether this result comports with the First Amendment. We hold that it does not.

I

. . . On October 20, 1983, appellee B. J. F. reported to the Duval County, Florida, Sheriff's Department (Department) that she had been robbed and sexually assaulted by an unknown assailant. The Department prepared a report on the incident which identified B. J. F. by her full name. The Department then placed the report in its pressroom. The Department does not restrict access either to the pressroom or to the reports made available therein.

[The Florida Star, a Jacksonville newspaper, sent a "reporter-trainee" to the pressroom. The trainee copied the police report, including B. J. F.'s full name.] A Florida Star reporter then prepared a one-paragraph article about the crime, derived entirely from the trainee's copy of the police report. The article included B. J. F.'s full name. It appeared in the "Police Reports" section on October 29, 1983, one of 54 police blotter stories in that day's edition. . . . In printing B. J. F.'s full name, The Florida Star violated its internal policy of not publishing the names of sexual offense victims.

On September 26, 1984, B. J. F. [sued] the Department and the Florida Star, alleging that these parties negligently violated § 794.03. Before trial, the Department settled with B. J. F. for $2,500. . . .

[At trial,] B. J. F. testified that . . . she had heard about the article from fellow workers and acquaintances; that her mother had received several threatening phone calls from a man who stated that he would rape B. J. F. again; and that these events had forced B. J. F. to change her phone number and residence, to seek police protection, and to obtain mental health counseling. In defense, The Florida Star put forth evidence indicating that the newspaper had learned B. J. F.'s name from the incident report . . . , and that the newspaper's violation of its internal rule against publishing the names of sexual offense victims was inadvertent.

[The trial judge] ruled from the bench that § 794.03 was constitutional [and] directed [a] verdict on the issue of negligence, finding the newspaper *per se* negligent based upon its violation of § 794.03. This ruling left the jury to consider only the questions of causation and damages. The jury awarded B. J. F. $75,000 in compensatory damages and $25,000 in punitive damages. [The District Court of Appeal affirmed and the Florida Supreme Court denied review.]

II

. . . The parties to this case frame their contentions in light of a trilogy of cases which have presented, in different contexts, the conflict between truthful reporting and state-protected privacy interests. In Cox Broadcasting Corp. v. Cohn, 420 U.S. 469 (1975), we found unconstitutional a civil damages award entered against a television station for broadcasting the name of a rape-murder victim which the station had obtained from courthouse records. In Oklahoma Publishing Co. v. Oklahoma County District Court, 430 U.S. 308 (1977), we found unconstitutional a state court's pretrial order enjoining the media from publishing the name or photograph of an 11-year-old boy in connection with a juvenile proceeding involving that child which reporters had attended. Finally, in Smith v. Daily Mail Publishing Co., 443 U.S. 97 (1979), we found unconstitutional the indictment of two newspapers for violating a state statute forbidding newspapers to publish, without written approval of the juvenile court, the name of any youth charged as a juvenile offender. The papers had learned about a shooting by monitoring a police band radio frequency and had obtained the name of the alleged juvenile assailant from witnesses, the police, and a local prosecutor. . . .

We conclude that imposing damages on appellant for publishing B. J. F.'s name violates the First Amendment. . . . Despite the strong resemblance this case bears to *Cox Broadcasting*, that case cannot fairly be read as controlling here. The name of the rape victim in that case was obtained from courthouse records that were open to public inspection, a fact which Justice White's opinion for the Court repeatedly noted. That role is not directly compromised where, as here, the information in question comes from a police report prepared and disseminated at a time at which not only had no adversarial criminal proceedings begun, but no suspect had been identified.

Nor need we accept appellant's invitation to hold broadly that truthful publication may never be punished consistent with the First Amendment. Our cases have carefully eschewed reaching this ultimate question, mindful that the future may bring scenarios which prudence counsels our not resolving anticipatorily. Indeed, in *Cox Broadcasting*, we pointedly refused to answer even the less sweeping question "whether truthful publications may ever be subjected to civil or criminal liability" for invading "an area of privacy" defined by the State. Respecting the fact that press freedom and privacy rights are both "plainly rooted in the traditions and significant concerns of our society," we instead focused on the less sweeping issue "whether the State may impose sanctions on the accurate publication of the name of a rape victim obtained from public records—more specifically, from judicial records which are maintained in connection with a public prosecution and which themselves are open to public inspection." We continue to believe that the sensitivity and significance of the interests presented in clashes between First Amendment and privacy rights counsel relying on limited principles that sweep no more broadly than the appropriate context of the instant case.

In our view, this case is appropriately analyzed with reference to [the] limited First Amendment principle . . . articulated in *Daily Mail* . . . : "[I]f a newspaper lawfully obtains truthful information about a matter of public significance then state officials may not constitutionally punish publication of the information, absent a need to further a state interest of the highest order." According the press the ample protection provided by that principle is supported by at least three separate considerations, in addition to, of course, the overarching "'public interest, secured by the Constitution, in the dissemination of truth.'" The cases on which the *Daily Mail* synthesis relied demonstrate these considerations.

First, because the *Daily Mail* formulation only protects the publication of information which a newspaper has "lawfully obtain[ed]," the government retains ample means of safeguarding significant interests upon which publication may impinge, including protecting a rape victim's anonymity. To the extent sensitive information rests in private hands, the government may under some circumstances forbid its nonconsensual acquisition, thereby bringing outside of the *Daily Mail* principle the publication of any information so acquired. To the extent sensitive information is in the government's custody, it has even greater power to forestall or mitigate the injury caused by its release. The government may classify certain information, establish and enforce procedures ensuring its redacted release, and extend a damages remedy against the government or its officials where the government's mishandling of sensitive information leads to its dissemination. Where information is entrusted to the government, a less drastic means than punishing truthful publication almost always exists for guarding against the dissemination of private facts.

A second consideration undergirding the *Daily Mail* principle is the fact that punishing the press for its dissemination of information which is already publicly available is relatively unlikely to advance the interests in the service of which the State seeks to act. It is not, of course, always the case that information lawfully acquired by the press is known, or accessible, to others. But where the government has made certain information publicly available, it is highly anomalous to sanction persons other than the source of its release. . . .

A third and final consideration is the "timidity and self-censorship" which may result from allowing the media to be punished for publishing certain truthful information. *Cox Broadcasting* noted this concern with overdeterrence in the context of information made public through official court records, but the fear of excessive media self-suppression is applicable as well to other information released, without qualification, by the government. A contrary rule, depriving protection to those who rely on the government's implied representations of the lawfulness of dissemination, would force upon the media the onerous obligation of sifting through government press releases, reports, and pronouncements to prune out material arguably unlawful for publication. This situation could inhere even where the newspaper's sole object was to reproduce, with no substantial change, the government's rendition of the event in question.

Applied to the instant case, the *Daily Mail* principle clearly commands reversal. The first inquiry is whether the newspaper "lawfully obtain[ed] truthful information about a matter of public significance." It is undisputed that the news article describing the assault on B. J. F. was accurate. In addition, appellant lawfully obtained B. J. F.'s name. Appellee's argument to the contrary is based on the fact that under Florida law, police reports which reveal the identity of the victim of a sexual offense are not among the matters of "public record" which the public, by law, is entitled to inspect. But the fact that state officials are not required to disclose such reports does not make it unlawful for a newspaper to receive them when furnished by the government. Nor does the fact that the Department apparently failed to fulfill its obligation under § 794.03 not to "cause or allow to be . . . published" the name of a sexual offense victim make the newspaper's ensuing receipt of this information unlawful. Even assuming the Constitution permitted a State to proscribe *receipt* of information, Florida has not taken this step. It is clear, furthermore, that the news article concerned "a matter of public significance," in the sense in which the *Daily Mail* synthesis of prior cases used that term. That is, the article generally, as opposed to the specific identity contained within it, involved a matter of paramount public import: the commission, and investigation, of a violent crime which had been reported to authorities.

The second inquiry is whether imposing liability on appellant pursuant to § 794.03 serves "a need to further a state interest of the highest order." Appellee argues that a rule punishing publication furthers three closely related interests: the privacy of victims of sexual offenses; the physical safety of such victims, who may be targeted for retaliation if their names become known to their assailants; and the goal of encouraging victims of such crimes to report these offenses without fear of exposure. . . .

At a time in which we are daily reminded of the tragic reality of rape, it is undeniable that these are highly significant interests, a fact underscored by the Florida Legislature's explicit attempt to protect these interests by enacting a criminal statute prohibiting much dissemination of victim identities. We accordingly do not rule out the possibility that, in a proper case, imposing civil sanctions for publication of the name of a rape victim might be so overwhelmingly necessary to advance these interests as to satisfy the *Daily Mail* standard. For three independent reasons, however, imposing liability for publication under the circumstances of this case is too precipitous a means of advancing these interests to convince us that there is a "need" within the meaning of the *Daily Mail* formulation for Florida to take this extreme step. . . .

First is the manner in which appellant obtained the identifying information in question. As we have noted, where the government itself provides information to the media, it is most appropriate to assume that the government had, but failed to utilize, far more limited means of guarding against dissemination than the extreme step of punishing truthful speech. That assumption is richly borne out in this case. B. J. F.'s identity would never have come to light were it not for the erroneous, if inadvertent, inclusion by the Department of her full name in an incident report made available in a pressroom open to the public. . . . Where, as here, the government has failed to police itself in disseminating information, it is clear under *Cox Broadcasting, Oklahoma Publishing*, and *Landmark Communications* that the imposition of damages against the press for its subsequent publication can hardly be said to be a narrowly tailored means of safeguarding anonymity. Once the government has placed such information in the public domain, "reliance must rest upon the judgment of those who decide what to publish or broadcast," and hopes for restitution must rest upon the willingness of the government to compensate victims for their loss of privacy and to protect them from the other consequences of its mishandling of the information which these victims provided in confidence.

That appellant gained access to the information in question through a government news release makes it especially likely that, if liability were to be imposed, self-censorship would result. Reliance on a news release is a paradigmatically "routine newspaper reporting techniqu[e]." The government's issuance of such a release, without qualification, can only convey to recipients that the government considered dissemination lawful, and indeed expected the recipients to disseminate the information further. . . .

A second problem with Florida's imposition of liability for publication is the broad sweep of the negligence *per se* standard applied under the civil cause of action implied from § 794.03. Unlike claims based on the common-law tort of invasion of privacy, civil actions based on § 794.03 require no case-by-case findings that the disclosure of a fact about a person's private life was one that a reasonable person would find highly offensive. [L]iability follows automatically from publication. This is so regardless of whether the identity of the victim is already known throughout the community; whether the victim has voluntarily called public attention to the offense; or whether the identity of the victim has otherwise become a reasonable subject of public concern—because, perhaps, questions have arisen whether the victim fabricated an assault by a particular person. Nor is there a scienter requirement of any kind under § 794.03, engendering the perverse result that truthful publications challenged pursuant to this cause of action are less protected by the First Amendment than even the least protected defamatory falsehoods: those involving purely private figures, where liability is evaluated under a standard, usually applied by a jury, of ordinary negligence. . . .

Third, and finally, the facial underinclusiveness of § 794.03 raises serious doubts about whether Florida is, in fact, serving, with this statute, the significant interests which appellee invokes in support of affirmance. Section 794.03 prohibits the publication of identifying information only if this information appears in an "instrument of mass communication," a term the statute does not define. Section 794.03 does not prohibit the spread by other means of the identities of victims of sexual offenses. An individual who maliciously spreads word of the identity of a rape victim is thus not covered, despite the fact that the communication of such information to persons who live near, or work with, the victim may have consequences as devastating as the exposure of her name to large numbers of strangers....

When a State attempts the extraordinary measure of punishing truthful publication in the name of privacy, it must demonstrate its commitment to advancing this interest by applying its prohibition evenhandedly, to the smalltime disseminator as well as the media giant. Where important First Amendment interests are at stake, the mass scope of disclosure is not an acceptable surrogate for injury. A ban on disclosures effected by "instrument[s] of mass communication" simply cannot be defended on the ground that partial prohibitions may effect partial relief. Without more careful and inclusive precautions against alternative forms of dissemination, we cannot conclude that Florida's selective ban on publication by the mass media satisfactorily accomplishes its stated purpose. . . .

Justice SCALIA, concurring in part and concurring in the judgment.

I think it sufficient to decide this case to rely upon the third ground set forth in the Court's opinion: that a law cannot be regarded as protecting an interest "of the highest order," and thus as justifying a restriction upon truthful speech, when it leaves appreciable damage to that supposedly vital interest unprohibited. In the present case, I would anticipate that the rape victim's discomfort at the dissemination of news of her misfortune among friends and acquaintances would be at least as great as her discomfort at its publication by the media to people to whom she is only a name. Yet the law in question does not prohibit the former in either oral or written form. Nor is it at all clear, as I think it must be to validate this statute, that Florida's general privacy law would prohibit such gossip. Nor, finally, is it credible that the interest meant to be served by the statute is the protection of the victim against a rapist still at large—an interest that arguably would extend only to mass publication. There would be little reason to limit a statute with that objective to rape alone; or to extend it to all rapes, whether or not the felon has been apprehended and confined. In any case, the instructions here did not require the jury to find that the rapist was at large.

Justice WHITE, joined by Chief Justice REHNQUIST and Justice O'CONNOR, dissenting.

At issue in this case is whether there is any information about people, which—though true—may not be published in the press. By holding that only "a state interest of the highest order" permits the State to penalize the publication of truthful information, and by holding that protecting a rape victim's right to privacy is not among those state interests of the highest order, the Court accepts appellant's invitation, . . . to obliterate one of the most noteworthy legal inventions of the 20th century: the tort of the publication of private facts. . . . Even if the Court's opinion does not say as much today, such obliteration will follow inevitably from the Court's conclusion here. If the First Amendment prohibits wholly private persons (such as B. J. F.) from recovering for the publication of the fact that she was raped, I doubt that there remain any "private facts" which persons may assume will not be published in the newspapers or broadcast on television.

NOTES AND QUESTIONS

1. *Plaintiff must defend state's interests and means.* The Supreme Court's application of the *Daily Mail* test meant that the burden was on B. J. F. to defend the state of Florida's choice of § 794.03 as a means of protecting her privacy. Did her tort action fail because the state interests underlying the statute were not "of the highest order," or because the statute was not narrowly tailored to achieve the state interests?

2. *Implications for the public disclosure privacy tort.* What are the implications of the decision for plaintiffs who sue defendants in tort for public disclosure of private facts? When, if ever, can tort liability be imposed for the publication of truthful information about a matter of public concern?

3. *Right to be forgotten.* Personal privacy receives markedly more protection in Europe than in the United States, and First Amendment limitations provide no shield there for global media companies. For example, a 2014 decision by the European Court of Justice (the EU's highest court) recognized a privacy right unknown in the U.S, which is commonly referred to as the right to be forgotten. The court held that search engines like Google must remove certain privacy-invading links from their search results. The case arose in Spain, where a man complained that a Google search of his name turned up a 12-year-old newspaper story about proceedings against him for debt. He contended that the story, although accurate, was no longer relevant because the matter had been fully resolved. He demanded that Google remove the link that pulled up the story when users entered his name in a Google search. The Court held that the 1995 Data Protection Directive of the European Parliament gives individuals a right to insist on removal of data that are "inadequate, irrelevant, or no longer relevant, or excessive in relation to the purposes for which they were processed and in the light of the time that has elapsed Case C-131/12, Google Spain SL, Google Inc. v. Agencia Española de Protectión de Datos (AEPD), Mario Costeja Gonzáles, Court of Justice (Grand Chamber), 13 May 2014. The court concluded that the individual's privacy rights "override, as a rule, not only the economic interest of the operator of the search engine but also the interest of the general public in having access to that information," unless "the role played by the data subject in public life" justifies the interference with his privacy rights. Search engines are not required to remove a link until the subject makes a request. Even then they need not do so until the courts of the member country determine that maintaining the link would be contrary to the Directive as interpreted by this decision. There is no strong overall jurisprudential or legislative shift toward a similar right in the United States. In January 2015, for example, the Second Circuit, for example, ruled that a woman who had been arrested in 2010 and whose arrest had later been nullified could not order the arrest removed from websites. She had argued that the information was now false and defamatory and, therefore, should be erased under Connecticut's Erasure Statute, one that mandates that government records be erased after a nullifying prosecutorial decision, but the court found that no "amount of wishing can undo [the] historical truth" of the arrest. Martin v. Hearst Corp., 777 F.3d 546 (2d Cir. 2015).

AN EXTENDED NOTE ON DEFINING "UNLAWFULLY OBTAINED"

In Bartnicki v. Vopper, 532 U.S. 514 (2001), the Supreme Court addressed the question whether information is "unlawfully obtained" by a broadcaster who receives the information from a third party who obtained it in violation of wiretap laws. In *Bartnicki*, the chief negotiator for a local teacher's union was recorded while speaking on her cell phone to the union's president about a proposed teacher's strike. In the course of their conversation, the union president stated in regard to the school board with whom they were negotiating: "If they're not gonna move for three percent, we're gonna have to go to their, their homes. . . . To blow off their front porches, we'll have to do some work on some of those guys. (PAUSES) Really, um, really and truthfully because this is, you know, this is bad news. (UNDECIPHERABLE.)" The person who illegally intercepted and recorded this conversation was never identified, but an opponent of the union came into possession of the tape and turned it over to a local radio talk show host who broadcasted it on his show. It was also broadcast by another station and published by local newspapers. The union negotiator and union president sued the talk show host, his radio station, and other members of the media, alleging that each one "knew or had reason to know" that recording their private telephone conversation was a violation of Pennsylvania and federal wiretap law. The federal wiretap statute made it a crime to "intentionally disclose [], or endeavor [] to disclose, to any other person the contents of any wire, oral, or electronic communication, knowing or having reason to know that the information was obtained through the interception of a wire, oral, or electronic communication. . . ." 18 U.S.C. § 2511(1)(a). Pennsylvania's statute was similar. Both statutes authorized suits for damages. The U.S. Court of Appeals for the Third Circuit held that the wiretap statutes were content-neutral. Bartnicki v. Vopper, 200 F.3d 109 (1999). Applying intermediate scrutiny, the Third Circuit held that the statutes were invalid because they deterred more speech than necessary to protect the privacy interests at stake. The Supreme Court reached the same result by a different route. Although the Court conceded that the wiretap statutes were "content-neutral law[s] of general applicability," the Court analyzed "the [statutes'] naked prohibition against disclosures" as "a regulation of pure speech." The Court therefore applied the same exacting constitutional test that it had applied in *B.J.F.*, holding, 6-3, that as to the broadcaster, the information contained on the intercepted recording was not unlawfully obtained. The government asserted that the statute served an interest in deterring illegal interceptions of private conversations and remedying the harm caused by illegal interception. The Court, however, stated that these interests could be adequately served by punishing the person who illegally intercepted the conversation in the first place rather than "punishing disclosures of lawfully obtained information of public interest by one not involved in the initial illegality." Despite the breadth of this language, the Court emphasized that *Bartnicki* involved a narrow set of facts: Specifically, it involved public-figure plaintiffs whose illegally recorded conversations involved "truthful information of public concern." Indeed, the concurring Justices Breyer and O'Connor, whose votes were essential to make the 6-3 majority, wrote separately to emphasize that the Court's "narrow" holding rested on "special circumstances" present in the case: The fact that the broadcasters acted lawfully prior to disclosure, and the fact that the "information publicized involved a matter of *unusual* public concern, namely, a threat of potential physical harm to others" (emphasis added). The Court's decision, they wrote, did not create a broad, general "'public interest' exception" to the application of wiretap laws to members of the media. For a high-profile test case regarding the scope of the *Bartnicki* decision, *see* Boehner v. McDermott, 484 F.3d 573 (D.C. Cir. 2007). See also Dahlstrom v. Sun-Times Media, LLC., 777 F.3d 937 (7th Cir. 2015).

D. FIRST AMENDMENT LIMITATIONS ON IMPOSING LIABILITY BASED ON NEWSGATHERING METHODS

Sometimes plaintiffs bring tort actions based on the methods by which the media (or others) obtain information rather than based on the publication of that information. For example, plaintiffs may sue when reporters engage in trespass, fraud, or intrusions in an effort to gather information for publication. While publication receives full First Amendment protection, the Supreme Court in Cohen v. Cowles Media, which appears immediately below, held that "generally applicable laws do not offend the First Amendment simply because their enforcement against the press has incidental effects on its ability to gather the news." As you read *Cohen*, which deals with the law of promissory estoppel rather than tort law, you should attempt to reconcile it with the cases you've studied previously in this chapter.

COHEN v. COWLES MEDIA CO.

501 U.S. 663 (1991)

[Cohen was a consultant working on a Republican gubernatorial campaign. He offered to provide reporters with court documents showing that the Democratic candidate for lieutenant governor had previously been convicted of shoplifting, but only on condition that Cohen not be identified as the source. Reporters from two different newspapers took the information from Cohen on his terms, but their editors included Cohen's name in the resulting story. Cohen lost his job as a result, and he sued both newspapers. The Minnesota Supreme Court held that (1) the reporters' arrangement with Cohen did not amount to a contract, (2) he might have a cause of action for breach of the promise of confidentiality on a theory of promissory estoppel, but (3) permitting such a judgment would violate the First Amendment. Cohen appealed.]

Justice WHITE delivered the opinion of the Court.
. . . Respondents rely on the proposition that "if a newspaper lawfully obtains truthful information about a matter of public significance then state officials may not constitutionally punish publication of the information, absent a need to further a state interest of the highest order." That proposition is unexceptionable, and it has been applied in various cases that have found insufficient the asserted state interests in preventing publication of truthful, lawfully obtained information. See, e.g., *Florida Star v. B.J.F.* . . .
This case, however, is not controlled by this line of cases but, rather, by the equally well-established line of decisions holding that generally applicable laws do not offend the First Amendment simply because their enforcement against the press has incidental effects on its ability to gather and report the news. As the cases relied on by respondents recognize, the truthful information sought to be published must

have been lawfully acquired. The press may not with impunity break and enter an office or dwelling to gather news. Neither does the First Amendment relieve a newspaper reporter of the obligation shared by all citizens to respond to a grand jury subpoena and answer questions relevant to a criminal investigation, even though the reporter might be required to reveal a confidential source. *Branzburg v. Hayes. . . .* The press, like others interested in publishing, may not publish copyrighted material without obeying the copyright laws. . . . Similarly, the media must obey the National Labor Relations Act . . . and the Fair Labor Standards Act . . .; may not restrain trade in violation of the antitrust laws . . .; and must pay non-discriminatory taxes. . . . It is, therefore, beyond dispute that "[t]he publisher of a newspaper has no special immunity from the application of general laws. He has no special privilege to invade the rights and liberties of others." . . . Accordingly, enforcement of such general laws against the press is not subject to stricter scrutiny than would be applied to enforcement against other persons or organizations.

There can be little doubt that the Minnesota doctrine of promissory estoppel is a law of general applicability. It does not target or single out the press. Rather, insofar as we are advised, the doctrine is generally applicable to the daily transactions of all the citizens of Minnesota. The First Amendment does not forbid its application to the press.

Justice Blackmun suggests that applying Minnesota promissory estoppel doctrine in this case will "punish" respondents for publishing truthful information that was lawfully obtained. . . . This is not strictly accurate because compensatory damages are not a form of punishment. . . . If the contract between the parties in this case had contained a liquidated damages provision, it would be perfectly clear that the payment to petitioner would represent a cost of acquiring newsworthy material to be published at a profit, rather than a punishment imposed by the State. The payment of compensatory damages in this case is constitutionally indistinguishable from a generous bonus paid to a confidential news source. In any event, as indicated above, the characterization of the payment makes no difference for First Amendment purposes when the law being applied is a general law and does not single out the press. Moreover, Justice Blackmun's reliance on cases like *Florida Star v. B.J.F.* and *Smith v. Daily Mail* is misplaced. In those cases, the State itself defined the content of publications that would trigger liability. Here, by contrast, Minnesota law simply requires those making promises to keep them. The parties themselves, as in this case, determine the scope of their legal obligations, and any restrictions that may be placed on the publication of truthful information are self-imposed.

Also, it is not at all clear that respondents obtained Cohen's name "lawfully" in this case, at least for purposes of publishing it. Unlike the situation in *Florida Star,* where the rape victim's name was obtained through lawful access to a police report, respondents obtained Cohen's name only by making a promise that they did not honor. The dissenting opinions suggest that the press should not be subject to any law, including copyright law for example, which in any fashion or to any degree limits or restricts the press' right to report truthful information. The First Amendment does not grant the press such limitless protection.

Nor is Cohen attempting to use a promissory estoppel cause of action to avoid the strict requirements for establishing a libel or defamation claim. . . . Cohen is not seeking damages for injury to his reputation or his state of mind. He sought damages in excess of $50,000 for breach of a promise that caused him to lose his job and lowered his earning capacity. Thus, this is not a case like *Hustler Magazine, Inc. v. Falwell,* where we held that the constitutional libel standards apply to a claim alleging that the publication of a parody was a state-law tort of intentional infliction of emotional distress.

Respondents and amici argue that permitting Cohen to maintain a cause of action for promissory estoppel will inhibit truthful reporting because news organizations will have legal incentives not to disclose a confidential source's identity even when that person's identity is itself newsworthy. Justice Souter makes a similar argument. But if this is the case, it is no more than the incidental, and constitutionally insignificant, consequence of applying to the press a generally applicable law that requires those who make certain kinds of promises to keep them. . . . [The Court remanded to the Minnesota Supreme Court, which affirmed an award to Cohen of $200,000 on his promissory estoppel claim.]

Justice BLACKMUN, with whom Justice MARSHALL and Justice SOUTER join, dissenting.

. . . I regard our decision in *Hustler Magazine, Inc. v. Falwell* . . . to be precisely on point. . . . There was no doubt that Virginia's tort of intentional infliction of emotional distress was "a law of general applicability" unrelated to the suppression of speech. . . . As in *Hustler*, the operation of Minnesota's doctrine of promissory estoppel in this case cannot be said to have a merely "incidental" burden on speech; the publication of important political speech is the claimed violation. Thus, as in *Hustler*, the law may not be enforced to punish the expression of truthful information or opinion. In the instant case, it is undisputed that the publication at issue was true.

To the extent that truthful speech may ever be sanctioned consistent with the First Amendment, it must be in furtherance of a state interest "of the highest order." Because the Minnesota Supreme Court's opinion makes clear that the State's interest in enforcing its promissory estoppel doctrine in this case was far from compelling . . . I would affirm that court's decision.

[Justice Souter also dissented, in an opinion in which Justice Marshall, Justice Blackmun, and Justice O'Connor joined. He argued that "the State's interest in enforcing a newspaper's promise of confidentiality [is] insufficient to outweigh the interest in unfettered publication of the information revealed in this case. . . ."]

NOTES AND QUESTIONS

1. *Reconciling* Bartnicki. Did the reporters "unlawfully obtain" Cohen's name? Cohen offered to "leak" the negative documents concerning the Democratic candidate only if the reporters promised him confidentiality. The reporters promised confidentiality, but their editors reneged on the promise because they believed Cohen's name was part of what made the story newsworthy. What makes the reporters' method of obtaining the information unlawful? Is it clearly unlawful in a way that accepting information known to have been obtained by a third party in violation of federal law is not?

2. *Laws of general application.* Why isn't defamation a law of general application that does not offend the First Amendment when applied to the press? Is it because it is a law that directly affects publication, as opposed to newsgathering?

CHAPTER
10

The Conflict Between Free Speech and Promoting Equality, Civility, and Mutual Respect

TABLE OF CONTENTS

To what extent can government restrict speech in order to advance other (constitutional) interests, such as social equality (or even mere civility) between the races, the sexes, and various religious groups? Does the First Amendment, properly read and applied, completely bar government efforts to promote social harmony in an increasingly pluralistic society by imposing limits on "hate speech"? Or, in the alternative, should free speech principles give way when necessary to protect equality and human dignity? What about baseline notions of civility in public discourse? Should government be utterly powerless to enact regulations aimed at securing these values?

Since the 1970s (and arguably since the late 1960s), the Supreme Court of the United States generally has invalidated most government efforts aimed at promoting equality, dignity, and civility, in the name of safeguarding freedom of speech. The Justices have never suggested that hate speech has any particular social value but instead have emphasized that the danger of empowering the government to censor even highly offensive speech clearly outweighs the value of creating a more civil marketplace of ideas. Justice Kennedy, for example, has noted that "[t]he Nation well knows that one of the costs of the First Amendment is that it protects the speech we detest as well as the speech we embrace." United States v. Alvarez, 567 U.S. 709 (2012). *Alvarez* involved intentional false claims about military honors, a kind of speech obviously lacking much (any?) objective social value. Even "[t]hough few might find [Alvarez's] statements anything but contemptible, his right to make those statements is protected by the Constitution's guarantee of freedom of speech and expression." *Id.* The Supreme Court's approach to hate speech consistently has followed this logic.

The contemporary U.S. approach advances free speech at the cost of protecting social equality, dignity, and civility. The protection of such speech undoubtedly imposes serious social costs. *See* Jeremy Waldron, *The Harm in Hate Speech* (2012) (arguing that hate speech marginalizes its victims within the political community, reduces the vibrancy and vitality of public discourse, and positing that the harms hate speech causes cannot be effectively addressed by counter speech). The United States Supreme Court's approach, however, reflects an assumption that counter speech often can serve as an effective antidote to racist, sexist, homophobic, or otherwise bigoted speech. Moreover, even if this does not hold true in all cases, hate speech should still enjoy constitutional protection "not because we doubt the speech inflicts harm, but because we fear the censorship more." Michael W. McConnell, *You Can't Say That*, N.Y. Times, June 24, 2012, BR14 (book review).

Alternative approaches to the regulation of hate speech not only exist but flourish in other industrial democracies, such as Canada and Germany. In other words, the U.S. approach of privileging hate speech in order to ensure full and robust political dialogue is not the only way to address the problem, even in a society generally committed to protecting freedom of expression. Some First Amendment scholars have questioned whether U.S. law adequately advances equality values when free speech and equality collide. *See, e.g.*, Richard Delgado, *Campus Anti-racism Rules: Constitutional Narratives in Collision*, 85 Nw. U. L. Rev. 343 (1991); Mari Matsuda, *Public Response to Racist Speech: Considering the Victim's Story*, 87 Mich. L. Rev. 2320 (1989). Other scholars, while acknowledging the importance of the equality project, question whether speech codes are an effective (let alone constitutionally permissible) response, particularly in light of the inevitably content- and viewpoint-based nature of such speech restrictions. *See, e.g.*, Steven G. Gey, *The Case Against Post-Modern Censorship Theory*, 145 U. Pa. L. Rev. 193 (1996).

The modern rule against civility codes aimed at improving social relations masks a more complicated historical picture. The U.S. Supreme Court relatively recently sustained statutes and regulations facially aimed at securing a modicum of civility in public communications. Cases like *Beauharnais*, decided in 1952, reflect a very different sensibility than cases like *Cohen* and *Gooding*. Moreover, even in the contemporary United States, the commitment to protecting free speech is not absolute. For example, Title VII prohibits the creation of "hostile work environments" based on race, gender, or religion; the creation of such an environment generally involves speech that reflects animus or hostility based on race, sex, or religion. Yet, most judges, legal academics, and practitioners do not view Title VII as impermissibly trenching on the First Amendment. *Cf.* Kinsley R. Browne, *Title VII as Censorship: Hostile-Environment Harassment and the First Amendment*, 52 Ohio St. L.J. 481 (1991); Eugene Volokh, *Freedom of Speech and Workplace Harassment*, 39 UCLA L. Rev. 1791 (1992).

This chapter considers the problem of "group libel": speech that attacks a particular group based on race, gender, religion, or other characteristics generally thought to be inappropriate bases for public or private discrimination. It then examines in some detail Title VII and cases sustaining the application of Title VII on facts that strongly implicate free speech principles. Finally, the chapter reviews major cases invalidating government efforts to promote equality, human dignity, and civility in the United States but sustaining such laws in Canada. These cases reflect the fact that the Supreme Court of Canada views legislative efforts to promote equality via speech restrictions more sympathetically than does the contemporary Supreme Court of the United States. In Canada, fear that the government will abuse the power to censor particularly noxious forms of hate speech has not prevented the creation and enforcement of bans against hate speech, notwithstanding a strong constitutional free speech guarantee.

This chapter does not seek to persuade the reader that one approach is inherently superior to another, or that a decent and just society must adopt or must not adopt particular rules or regulatory regimes. Rather, the point is to establish the fact of the conflicts between freedom of speech and the equality project, and also between free speech and efforts to secure a modicum of civility in public discourse. Any polity committed to free speech, equality, and civility will have to deal with resolving inevitable conflicts between a commitment to a full and free marketplace of ideas and a strong commitment to equal access to political, social, and economic opportunities without regard to race, sex, religion, national origin, or sexual orientation.

A.   THE ANCIEN RÉGIME: GROUP LIBEL REGULATIONS AND THE FIRST AMENDMENT

As late as 1952, the Supreme Court sustained a content- and viewpoint-based Illinois law that prohibited "group libel" of persons based on "race, color, creed, or religion." Invoking a history of toxic race relations in Illinois, the Supreme Court held (by a 5-4 vote) that Illinois had a legitimate interest in promoting social peace among a diverse population. Reasoning that group libel simply represented an extension of well-settled tort defamation principles applicable to individual citizens, the majority found the Illinois law sufficiently important to trump free speech principles. As later cases will make clear, the *Beauharnais* approach has not withstood the test of time. Even so, it represents a very different baseline for evaluating the consistency of hate speech regulations with the Free Speech Clause of the First Amendment.

<u>BEAUHARNAIS v. ILLINOIS</u>

343 U.S. 250 (1952)

Mr. Justice FRANKFURTER delivered the opinion of the Court.

The petitioner was convicted upon information in the Municipal Court of Chicago of violating § 224a of the Illinois Criminal Code, Ill. Rev. Stat., 1949, c. 38, Div. 1, § 471. He was fined $200. The section provides:

> "It shall be unlawful for any person, firm or corporation to manufacture, sell, or offer for sale, advertise or publish, present or exhibit in any public place in this state any lithograph, moving picture, play, drama or sketch, which publication or exhibition portrays depravity, criminality, unchastity, or lack of virtue of a class of citizens, of any race, color, creed or religion which said publication or exhibition exposes the citizens of any race, color, creed or religion to contempt, derision, or obloquy or which is productive of breach of the peace or riots. . . ."

Beauharnais challenged the statute as violating the liberty of speech and of the press guaranteed as against the States by the Due Process Clause of the Fourteenth Amendment, and as too vague, under the restrictions implicit in the same Clause, to support conviction for crime. The Illinois courts rejected these contentions and sustained defendant's conviction. We granted certiorari in view of the serious questions raised concerning the limitations imposed by the Fourteenth Amendment on the power of a State to punish utterances promoting friction among racial and religious groups.

The information, cast generally in the terms of the statute, charged that Beauharnais "did unlawfully . . . exhibit in public places lithographs, which publications portray depravity, criminality, unchastity or lack of virtue of citizens of Negro race and color and which exposes [*sic*] citizens of Illinois of the Negro race and color to contempt, derision, or obloquy. . . ." The lithograph complained of was a leaflet setting forth a petition calling on the Mayor and City Council of Chicago "to halt the further encroachment, harassment and invasion of white people, their property, neighborhoods and persons, by the Negro. . . ." Below was a call for "One million self respecting white people in Chicago to unite. . ." with the statement added that "If persuasion and the need to prevent the white race from becoming mongrelized by the negro will not unite us, then the aggressions . . . rapes, robberies, knives, guns and marijuana of the negro, surely will." This, with more language, similar if not so violent, concluded with an attached application for membership in the White Circle League of America, Inc.

The testimony at the trial was substantially undisputed. From it the jury could find that Beauharnais was president of the White Circle League; that, at a meeting on January 6, 1950, he passed out bundles of the lithographs in question, together with other literature, to volunteers for distribution on downtown Chicago street corners the following day; that he carefully organized that distribution, giving detailed instructions for it; and that the leaflets were in fact distributed on January 7 in accordance with his plan and instructions. The court, together with other charges on burden of proof and the like, told the jury "if you find . . . that the defendant, Joseph Beauharnais, did . . . manufacture, sell, or offer for sale, advertise or publish, present or exhibit in any public place the lithograph . . . then you are to find the defendant guilty . . . "[.] He refused to charge the jury, as requested by the defendant, that in order to convict they must find "that the article complained of was likely to produce a clear and present danger of a serious substantive evil that rises far above public inconvenience, annoyance or unrest." Upon this evidence and these instructions, the jury brought in the conviction here for review. . . .

[T]oday, every American jurisdiction—the forty-eight States, the District of Columbia, Alaska, Hawaii and Puerto Rico—punish libels directed at individuals. "There are certain well-defined and narrowly limited classes of speech, the prevention and punishment of which have never been thought to raise any Constitutional problem. These include the lewd and obscene, the profane, the libelous, and the insulting or "fighting" words—those which by their very utterance inflict injury or tend to incite an immediate breach of the peace. It has been well observed that such utterances are no essential part of any exposition of ideas, and are of such slight social value as a step to truth that any benefit that may be derived from them is clearly out-weighed by the social interest in order and morality." . . .

No one will gainsay that it is libelous falsely to charge another with being a rapist, robber, carrier of knives and guns, and user of marijuana. The precise question before us, then, is whether the protection of "liberty" in the Due Process Clause of the Fourteenth Amendment prevents a State from punishing such libels—as criminal libel has been defined, limited and constitutionally recognized time out of mind—directed at designated collectivities and flagrantly disseminated. There is even authority, however dubious, that such utterances were also crimes at common law. It is certainly clear that some American jurisdictions have sanctioned their punishment under ordinary criminal libel statutes. We cannot say, however, that the question is concluded by history and practice. But if an utterance directed at an individual may be the object of criminal sanctions, we cannot deny to a State power to punish the same utterance directed at a defined group, unless we can say that this is a wilful [*sic*] and purposeless restriction unrelated to the peace and well-being of the State.

Illinois did not have to look beyond her own borders or await the tragic experience of the last three decades to conclude that wilful purveyors of falsehood concerning racial and religious groups promote strife and tend powerfully to obstruct the manifold adjustments required for free, ordered life in a metropolitan, polyglot community. From the murder of the abolitionist Lovejoy in 1837 to the Cicero riots of 1951, Illinois has been the scene of exacerbated tension between races, often flaring into violence and destruction. In many of these outbreaks, utterances of the character here in question, so the Illinois legislature could conclude, played a significant part. The law was passed on June 29, 1917, at a time when the State was struggling to assimilate vast numbers of new inhabitants, as yet concentrated in discrete racial or national or religious groups—foreign-born brought to it by the crest of the great wave of immigration, and Negroes attracted by jobs in war plants and allurements of northern claims. Nine years earlier, in the very city where the legislature sat, what is said to be the first northern race riot had cost the lives of six people, left hundreds of Negroes homeless and shocked citizens into action far beyond the borders of the State. Less than a month before the bill was enacted, East St. Louis had seen a day's rioting, prelude to an outbreak, only four days after the bill became law, so bloody that it led to Congressional investigation. A series of bombings had begun which was to culminate two years later in the awful race riot which held Chicago in its grip for seven days in summer of 1919. Nor has the tension and violence between the groups defined in the statute been limited in Illinois to clashes between whites and Negroes.

In the face of this history and its frequent obligato of extreme racial and religious propaganda, we would deny experience to say that the Illinois legislature was without reason in seeking ways to curb false or malicious defamation of racial and religious groups, made in public places and by means calculated to have a powerful emotional impact on those to whom it was presented. . . .

It may be argued, and weightily, that this legislation will not help matters; that tension and on occasion violence between racial and religious groups must be traced to causes more deeply embedded in our society than the ranting of modern Know-Nothings. Only those lacking responsible humility will have a confident solution for problems as intractable as the frictions attributable to differences of race, color or religion. This being so, it would be out of bounds for the judiciary to deny the legislature a choice of policy, provided it is not unrelated to the problem and not forbidden by some explicit limitation on the State's power. That the legislative remedy might not in practice mitigate the evil, or might itself raise new problems, would only manifest once more the paradox of reform. . . .

We are warned that the choice open to the Illinois legislature here may be abused, that the law may be discriminatorily enforced; prohibiting libel of a creed or of a racial group, we are told, is but a step from prohibiting libel of a political party.[18]

---

[18] It deserves emphasis that there is no such attempt in this statute. The rubric "race, color, creed or religion" which describes the type of group libel of which is punishable, has attained too fixed a meaning to permit political groups to be brought within it. If a statute sought to outlaw libels of political parties, quite different problems not now before us would be raised. For one thing, the whole doctrine of fair comment as indispensable to the democratic political process

Every power may be abused, but the possibility of abuse is a poor reason for denying Illinois the power to adopt measures against criminal libels sanctioned by centuries of Anglo-American law. "While this Court sits" it retains and exercises authority to nullify action which encroaches on freedom of utterance under the guise of punishing libel. Of course discussion cannot be denied and the right, as well as the duty, of criticism must not be stifled. . . .

Libelous utterances not being within the area of constitutionally protected speech, it is unnecessary, either for us or for the State courts, to consider the issues behind the phrase "clear and present danger." Certainly no one would contend that obscene speech, for example, may be punished only upon a showing of such circumstances. Libel, as we have seen, is in the same class.

We find no warrant in the Constitution for denying to Illinois the power to pass the law here under attack. But it bears repeating—although it should not—that our finding that the law is not constitutionally objectionable caries no implication of approval of the wisdom of the legislation or of its efficacy. These questions may raise doubts in our minds as well as in others. It is not for us, however, to make the legislative judgment. We are not at liberty to erect those doubts into fundamental law.

Affirmed.

Mr. Justice BLACK, with whom Mr. Justice DOUGLAS concurs, dissenting.

This case is here because Illinois inflicted criminal punishment on Beauharnais for causing the distribution of leaflets in the city of Chicago. The conviction rests on the leaflet's contents, not on the time, manner or place of distribution. Beauharnais is head of an organization that opposes amalgamation and favors segregation of white and colored people. After discussion, an assembly of his group decided to petition the mayor and council of Chicago to pass laws for segregation. Volunteer members of the group agreed to stand on street corners, solicit signers to petitions addressed to city authorities, and distribute leaflets giving information about the group, its beliefs and its plans. In carrying out this program a solicitor handed out a leaflet which was the basis of this prosecution. . . .

Today's case degrades First Amendment freedoms to the "rational basis" level. It is now a certainty that the new "due process" coverall offers far less protection to liberty than would adherence to our former cases compelling states to abide by the unequivocal First Amendment command that its defined freedoms shall not be abridged. . . .

This Act sets up a system of state censorship which is at war with the kind of free government envisioned by those who forced adoption of our Bill of Rights. The motives behind the state law may have been to do good. But the same can be said about most laws making opinions punishable as crimes. History indicates that urges to do good have led to the burning of books and even to the burning of "witches." . . .

If there be minority groups who hail this holding as their victory, they might consider the possible relevancy of this ancient remark:

"Another such victory and I am undone."

---

would come into play. See *People v. Fuller*, [238 Ill. 116, 125,] 87 N.E. 338-39 [(1909)]; *Commonwealth v. Pratt*, 208 Mass. 553, 559, 95 N.E. 105, 106 [(1911)]. Political parties, like public men, are, as it were, public property.

Mr. Justice REED, with whom Mr. Justice DOUGLAS joins, dissenting.
[Opinion omitted.]

Mr. Justice DOUGLAS, dissenting.

Hitler and his Nazis showed how evil a conspiracy could be which was aimed at destroying a race by exposing it to contempt, derision, and obloquy. I would be willing to concede that such conduct directed at a race or group in this country could be made an indictable offense. For such a project would be more than the exercise of free speech. Like picketing, it would be free speech plus.

I would also be willing to concede that even without the element of conspiracy there might be times and occasions when the legislative or executive branch might call a halt to inflammatory talk, such as the shouting of "fire" in a school or a theater.

My view is that in any case other public interests are to override the plain command of the First Amendment, the peril of speech must be clear and present, leaving no room for argument, raising no doubts as to the necessity of curbing speech in order to prevent disaster. . . .

Mr. Justice JACKSON, dissenting.

[Justice Jackson objected to the procedures used to enforce the Illinois group libel statute.]

NOTES AND QUESTIONS

1. *The problem of discretionary enforcement of hate speech regulations.* Is the *Beauharnais* majority naive to believe that a group libel statute will be enforced consistently and in an even-handed fashion? And, if a "well fixed star in our constitutional constellation" mandates that government may not generally "prescribe what shall be orthodox in politics, nationalism, religion, or other matters of opinion" in the words of Justice Jackson in West Virginia State Board of Education v. Barnette, 319 U.S. 624, 642 (1942), how does one distinguish a mandatory pledge from a rule against racist speech? Don't both involve government efforts to create and enforce "orthodoxy"? Perhaps ironically, in *Beauharnais*, the same Justice Jackson, although dissenting, nevertheless seems quite sympathetic to the ends, if not the means, that the Illinois state legislature sought to advance. How can one reconcile the seemingly inconsistent results reached in *Beauharnais* and *Barnette*?

2. *No such thing as "free" speech?* Professor Stanley Fish has famously asserted that there really is no such thing as "free speech," if by "free speech" one means speech that does not impose social costs of some sort. *See* Stanley Fish, *There's No Such Thing as Free Speech, and It's a Good Thing, Too* 102-133 (1994). If this is so, is it reasonable for a state government to attempt to redistribute some of the social costs of speech activity? Suppose empirical studies show that racist stereotypes, perpetuated in part by materials of the sort that Beauharnais sought to distribute in Chicago, lead to persistent discrimination against people of color in a wide variety of contexts. If government shows clearly that such speech demonstrably causes social, economic, and political discrimination against minorities, would that justify the enactment and enforcement of a group libel

law? Why should minorities bear the social cost of racist speech? Are they really the least cost avoiders?

3. *A global perspective.* On the other hand, one would do well to consider the success (or lack thereof) of hate speech codes in places that maintain and enforce them, like Canada and Germany. Germany has maintained not only comprehensive speech codes that prohibit incitement to racial hatred but also laws that protect personal honor and dignity. *See* Ronald J. Krotoszynski, Jr., *The First Amendment in Cross-Cultural Perspective: A Comparative Legal Analysis of the Freedom of Speech* 118-130 (2006) (discussing hate speech regulations in Germany). Even so, the problem of racist hate speech, after more than 60 years of aggressive enforcement of these laws, has not gone away. *Id.* at 130-131, 135-137. As a means of preventing the dissemination of hate speech and combating the social evils of racism, speech codes do not seem to be particularly effective at achieving their larger purposes.

4. *The dangers of government censorship.* Does Justice Black's dissent make an important point? Can government be trusted to prohibit only really bad speech, and not attempt to use a censorial power in favor of incumbent officeholders? For example, would an elected district attorney go after a popular local citizen who makes a racist remark in public? Suppose, however, that a Native American leader expresses admiration for Hitler and that there are relatively few Native American citizens in the district attorney's constituency. If you think one prosecution is more likely to move forward than the other, have equality values really been well served? *See* Krotoszynski, *supra*, at 82-87 (discussing prosecution of First Nations leader David Ahenakew for incitement to racial hatred and the differential enforcement of hate speech laws in Canada).

KUNZ v. NEW YORK

340 U.S. 290 (1951)

Mr. Chief Justice VINSON delivered the opinion of the Court.

New York City has adopted an ordinance which makes it unlawful to hold public worship meetings on the streets without first obtaining a permit from the city police commissioner. Appellant, Carl Jacob Kunz, was convicted and fined $10 for violating this ordinance by holding a religious meeting without a permit. The conviction was affirmed by the Appellate Part of the Court of Special Sessions, and by the New York Court of Appeals, three judges dissenting, 300 N.Y. 273, 90 N.E.2d 455 (1950). The case is here on appeal, it having been urged that the ordinance is invalid under the Fourteenth Amendment.

Appellant is an ordained Baptist minister who speaks under the auspices of the "Outdoor Gospel Work," of which he is the director. He has been preaching for about six years, and states that it is his conviction and duty to "go out on the highways and byways and preach the word of God." In 1946, he applied for and received a permit under the ordinance in question, there being no question that appellant comes within the classes of persons entitled to receive permits under the ordinance. This permit, like all others, was good only for the calendar year in which issued. In November, 1946, his permit was revoked after a hearing by the police commissioner. The revocation was based on evidence that he had ridiculed and denounced other religious beliefs in his meetings.

Although the penalties of the ordinance apply to anyone who "ridicules and denounces other religious beliefs," the ordinance does not specify this as a ground for permit revocation. Indeed, there is no mention in the ordinance of any power of revocation. However, appellant did not seek judicial or administrative review of the revocation proceedings, and any question as to the propriety of the revocation is not before us in this case. In any event, the revocation affected appellant's rights to speak in 1946 only. Appellant applied for another permit in 1947, and again in 1948, but was notified each time that his application was "disapproved," with no reason for the disapproval being given. On September 11, 1948, appellant was arrested for speaking at Columbus Circle in New York City without a permit. It is from the conviction which resulted that this appeal has been taken.

Appellant's conviction was thus based upon his failure to possess a permit for 1948. We are here concerned only with the propriety of the action of the police commissioner in refusing to issue that permit. Disapproval of the 1948 permit application by the police commissioner was justified by the New York courts on the ground that a permit had previously been revoked "for good reasons." It is noteworthy that there is no mention in the ordinance of reasons for which such a permit application can be refused. This interpretation allows the police commissioner, an administrative official, to exercise discretion in denying subsequent permit applications on the basis of his interpretation, at that time, of what is deemed to be conduct condemned by the ordinance which gives an administrative official discretionary power to control in advance the right of citizens to speak on religious matters on the streets of New York. As such, the ordinance is clearly invalid as a prior restraint on the exercise of First Amendment rights.

In considering the right of a municipality to control the use of public streets for the expression of religious views, we start with the words of Mr. Justice Roberts that "Wherever the title of streets and parks may rest, they have immemorially been held in trust for the use of the public and, time out of mind, have been used for purposes of assembly, communicating thoughts between citizens, and discussing public questions." *Hague v. C.I.O.*, 307 U.S. 496, 515 (1939). Although this Court has recognized that a statute may be enacted which prevents serious interference with normal usage of streets and parks, *Cox v. New Hampshire*, 312 U.S. 569 (1941), we have consistently condemned licensing systems which vest in an administrative official discretion to grant or withhold a permit upon broad criteria unrelated to proper regulation of public places. . . .

The court below has mistakenly derived support for its conclusion from the evidence produced at the trial that appellant's religious meetings had, in the past, caused some disorder. There are appropriate public remedies to protect the peace and order of the community if appellant's speeches should result in disorder or violence. "In the present case, we have no occasion to inquire as to the permissible scope of subsequent punishment." *Near v. Minnesota*, 283 U.S. 697, 715 (1931). We do not express any opinion on the propriety of punitive remedies which the New York authorities may utilize. We are here concerned with suppression—not punishment. It is sufficient to say that New York cannot vest restraining control over the right to speak on religious subjects in an administrative official where there are no appropriate standards to guide his action.

Reversed.

Mr. Justice JACKSON, dissenting.

Essential freedoms are today threatened from without and within. It may become difficult to preserve here what a large part of the world has lost—the right to speak, even temperately, on matters vital to spirit and body. In such a setting, to blanket hateful and hate-stirring attacks on races and faiths under the protections for freedom of speech may be a noble innovation. On the other hand, it may be a quixotic tilt at windmills which belittles great principles of liberty. Only time can tell. But I incline to the latter view and cannot assent to the decision.

To know what we are doing, we must first locate the point at which rights asserted by Kunz conflict with powers asserted by the organized community. New York City has placed no limitation upon any speech Kunz may choose to make on private property, but it does require a permit to hold religious meetings in its streets. The ordinance, neither by its terms nor as it has been applied, prohibited Kunz, even in street meetings, from preaching his own religion or making any temperate criticism or refutation of other religions; indeed, for the year 1946, he was given a general permit to do so. His meetings, however, brought "a flood of complaints" to city authorities that he was engaging in scurrilous attacks on Catholics and Jews. On notice, he was given a hearing at which eighteen complainants appeared. The Commissioner revoked his permit and applications for 1947 and 1948 were refused. For a time he went on holding meetings without a permit in Columbus Circle, where in September, 1948, he was arrested for violation of the ordinance. He was convicted and fined ten dollars.

At these meetings, Kunz preached, among many other things of like tenor, that "The Catholic Church makes merchandise out of souls," that Catholicism is "a religion of the devil," and that the Pope is "the anti-Christ." The Jews he denounced as "Christ-killers," and he said of them "All the garbage that didn't believe in Christ should have been burnt in the incinerators. It's a shame they all weren't."

These utterances, as one might expect, stirred strife and threatened violence. Testifying in his own behalf, Kunz stated that he "became acquainted with" one of the complaining witnesses, whom he thought to be a Jew, "when he happened to sock one of my Christian boys in the puss." Kunz himself complained to the authorities, charging a woman interrupter with disorderly conduct. He also testified that when an officer is not present at his meetings "I have trouble then," but "with an officer, no trouble."

The contention which Kunz brings here and which this Court sustains is that such speeches on the streets are within his constitutional freedom and therefore New York City has no power to require a permit. He does not deny that this has been and will continue to be his line of talk. He does not claim that he should have been granted a permit; he attacks the whole system of control of street meetings and says the Constitution gives him permission to speak and he needs none from the City.

The speeches which Kunz has made and which he asserts he has a *right* to make in the future were properly held by the courts below to be out of bounds for a street meeting and not constitutionally protected. . . . Of course, if Kunz is only exercising his constitutional *rights*, then New York can neither restrain nor punish him. But I doubt that the Court's assumption will survive analysis.

This Court today initiates the doctrine that language such as this, in the environment of the street meeting, is immune from prior municipal control. We would have a very different question if New York had presumed to say that Kunz could not speak his piece in his own pulpit or hall. But it has undertaken to restrain him only if he chooses to speak at street meetings. There is a world of difference.

The street preacher takes advantage of people's presence on the streets to impose his message upon what, in a sense, is a captive audience. A meeting on private property is made up of an audience that has volunteered to listen. The question, therefore, is not whether New York could, if it tried, silence Kunz, but whether it must place its streets at his service to hurl insults at the passer-by.

What Mr. Justice Holmes said for a unanimous Court in *Schenck v. United States*, 249 U.S. 47, 52, has become an axiom: "The most stringent protection of free speech would not protect a man in falsely shouting fire in a theatre and causing a panic." This concept was applied in one of its few unanimous decisions in recent years when, through Mr. Justice Murphy, the Court said: "There are certain well-defined and narrowly limited classes of speech, *the prevention and punishment* of which *have never been thought to raise any Constitutional problem.* These include the lewd and obscene, the profane, the libelous, and *the insulting or 'fighting' words*—those which by their very utterance inflict injury or *tend to incite* an immediate breach of the peace. . . ." (Emphasis supplied.) *Chaplinsky v. New Hampshire*, 315 U.S. 568, 571-572.

There held to be "insulting or 'fighting' words" were calling one a "God damned racketeer" and a "damned Fascist." Equally inciting and more clearly "fighting words," when thrown at Catholics and Jews who are rightfully on the streets of New York, are statements that "The Pope is the anti-Christ" and the Jews are "Christ-killers." These terse epithets come down to our generation weighted with hatreds accumulated through centuries of bloodshed. They are recognized words of art in the profession of defamation. They are not the kind of insult that men bandy and laugh off when the spirits are high and the flagons are low. They are not in that class of epithets whose literal sting will be drawn if the speaker smiles when he uses them. They are always, and in every context, insults which do not spring from reason and can be answered by none. Their historical associations with violence are well understood, both by those who hurl and those who are struck by these missiles. Jews, many of whose families perished in extermination furnaces of Dachau and Auschwitz, are more than tolerant if they pass off lightly the suggestion that unbelievers in Christ should all have been burned. Of course, people might pass this speaker by as a mental case, and so they might file out of a theatre in good order at the cry of "fire." But in both cases there is genuine likelihood that someone will get hurt. . . .

The question remains whether the Constitution prohibits a city from control of its streets by a permit system which takes into account dangers to public peace and order. I am persuaded that it does not do so, provided of course, that the city does not so discriminate as to deny equal protection of the law or undertake a censorship of utterances that are not so defamatory, insulting, inciting, or provocative as to be reasonably likely to cause disorder and violence. . . .

NOTES AND QUESTIONS

1. *Reconciling* Beauharnais *and* Kunz. The Supreme Court actually decided *Beauharnais* a year *after Kunz*. Even so, the *Kunz* approach better reflects the modern rule than does *Beauharnais*. Still, given that the cases are decided within a year of each other, how does one square the disparate results? Could it be that even with respect to subject matter that might fall outside the scope of the First Amendment, the rule against prior restraints makes a permissive permitting

scheme more objectionable than criminal punishment after the fact? Note that Chief Justice Vinson emphasizes that "[w]e are here concerned with suppression—not punishment." Moreover, the *Kunz* majority did not "express any opinion on the propriety of punitive remedies which the New York authorities may utilize." Thus, is the result in *Kunz* really a function of prior restraint, rather than the notion that speakers have a right to bandy about racial or religious epithets on the public streets?

2. *No protection against highly offensive and insulting speech?* Is New York City (and any other government) powerless to protect random passersby from racist, sexist, or homophobic speech? Why does (or should) the First Amendment protect uncivil discourse? Does a serious commitment to freedom of expression require protection if someone calls another person a "kike," "faggot," "nigger," or "cunt" on a public street? In theory, words of this sort might be excluded from constitutional protection under the doctrine of "fighting words," as mentioned by Justice Jackson in his dissenting opinion in *Kunz*. For better or worse, however, the modern Supreme Court, in a series of cases in the 1970s, significantly limited the potential scope of the fighting-words doctrine. See *infra* pages 82-89.

3. *The potential lessons of history.* Justice Jackson argues that the harms associated with hate speech are sufficiently serious to warrant suspending general free speech principles in order to permit government to regulate (or proscribe) such language. The standard response to this argument is that counter speech, rather than government regulation, presents a better approach. Is this realistic? If a large group of men standing on a street corner calls a lone woman walking by "a fucking dyke cunt," is it really reasonable to expect her to attempt to engage her verbal assailants in some sort of repartee? Consider too that this case, decided in 1951, comes only six years after the liberation of the Nazi death camps for Jews (and other persons deemed unworthy to live by Hitler and his minions). In other words, in all probability, Holocaust survivors, their relatives, and their friends might well have been subjected to Kunz's ravings. Should this matter in evaluating the validity of the New York City policy? Germany, to this day, maintains and enforces strict laws against anti-Semitic speech, as well as a criminal law ban on pro-Nazi speech. *See* Krotoszynski, *supra* page 510, at 118-130.

4. *A different (better) rationale for protecting low value hate speech?* Perhaps a better argument in favor of permitting Kunz to speak isn't that counter speech is an effective defense for those he victimizes but rather that the greater danger to society lies in permitting government to decide what words can, and cannot, be spoken in public. *See* Lyrissa Barnett Lidsky, *Where's the Harm: Free Speech and the Regulation of Lies*, 65 Wash. & Lee L. Rev. 1091, 1097 (2008) ("Yet even if First Amendment theory's faith in the fundamental rationality of public discourse is misplaced, distrust of government still may be a strong enough basis, standing alone, to warrant declaring any attempt to punish Holocaust denial unconstitutional."). As Justice Harlan explains in *Cohen* (*infra* page 523), the ability to control the expression of an idea ultimately implies the ability to control the idea itself. If this is so, perhaps a free society must tolerate evil boors like Kunz because a government empowered to ban words, and hence ideas, is a greater net threat to liberty and happiness than religious bigots screaming on street corners. Even if one finds this argument persuasive, however, it does not

provide much consolation to those persons that people like Kunz verbally assault.

5. *The current precedential status of* Beauharnais. *Beauharnais*, although never formally reversed, has been effectively superseded by later cases, notably including New York Times Co. v. Sullivan, 376 U.S. 254 (1964), and Brandenburg v. Ohio, 395 U.S. 444 (1969). Thus, in *R.A.V.*, decided in 1992, the Supreme Court invalidated on free speech grounds a local St. Paul, Minnesota, ordinance that prohibited speech causing fear or alarm based on race, sex, or religion because the ordinance constituted a form of impermissible content and viewpoint discrimination. *See* R.A.V. v. City of St. Paul, 505 U.S. 377 (1992). [*R.A.V.* appears *infra* page 540.] Under the modern rule, only speech that conveys a true threat may be criminally punished. *See* Virginia v. Black, 538 U.S. 343, 359-361 (2003). Nevertheless, vestiges of *Beauharnais* remain in contemporary free speech law. Even if direct regulations of hate speech transgress the First Amendment, the Supreme Court has sustained more nuanced efforts to punish hate speech.

AN EXTENDED NOTE ON TERRY JONES AND TARGETED INCITEMENT: THE EXAMPLE OF KORAN BURNING

Pastor Terry Jones, a fundamentalist pastor based in Gainesville, Florida, has engaged in targeted burnings of the Koran, both in Florida and elsewhere. He is the author of a self-published book, *Islam Is of the Devil* (Creation House 2010), and his church, the Dove World Outreach Center (once based in Gainesville, but now based in Tampa) sells coffee mugs and t-shirts emblazoned with this offensive slogan. Donna Koehn, *Opinions of Islam Worsen*, Tampa Trib., Sept. 10, 2010, at B1. Jones regularly conducts mass Koran burnings and also encourages others to stage similar events. Keith Morelli, *Preacher Plans to Burn Korans in Polk*, Tampa Trib., July 26, 2013, at B1.

Jones actively seeks to provoke angry reactions to his Koran burnings—presumably in order to garner media attention. For example, he attempted to burn a Koran outside the Arab International Festival in Dearborn, Michigan, but he was met with angry counterprotestors who confronted him and "hemmed him in as he tried to walk down Schaefer Road." *See* Oralandar Brand-Williams, Josh Katzenstein & Mike Wilkinson, *Dearborn Cops Pull Pastor from Crowd*, Detroit News, June 18, 2011, at A3. Jones said that "[i]t got really, really nasty" and that "[t]hey had us completely surrounded, pushing on us and blocking us." Did the police act lawfully in removing Jones and his supporters from the angry crowd?

Jones has made multiple attempts to burn a Koran in Dearborn, a community with a large percentage of residents who adhere to the Islamic faith. He was permitted to stage a rally outside Dearborn City Hall (although he did not burn a Koran at this event). Earlier, in April 2011, he attempted to stage a protest and a Koran burning outside the Islamic Center of Dearborn, but he was prevented from doing so after a jury "ruled he would likely breach the peace" and issued an injunction against the protest. Niraj Warikoo, *Florida Pastor Returning to Dearborn to Protest Islam*, Detroit Free Press, June 17, 2011, at A10. Jones refused to post a security bond after the jury's verdict and was briefly jailed until he posted the bond.

Was the Michigan state court's restraining order against Jones consistent with the First Amendment? Or did Dearborn have an obligation to permit Jones to go forward with his proposed protest and Koran burning outside the Islamic Center, despite a very high probability of violence? Moreover, should the potential effects of Jones's proposed actions worldwide be a potential basis for legal action against him? Senior U.S. government officials have argued that Jones's proposed actions create a serious security risk for U.S. military and diplomatic personnel stationed abroad. *See* Kevin Sieff, *Florida Pastor Terry Jones's Koran Burning Has Far-Reaching Effect*, Wash. Post, Apr. 2, 2011. Would speech restrictions against Jones designed to avoid harm to U.S. troops and diplomatic personnel constitute civility norms? Or something else?

In April 2012, a federal district judge issued a preliminary injunction ordering the city of Dearborn to allow Terry Jones and his followers to protest on public property adjacent to the Islamic Center of America; in August 2013 the court entered a final summary judgment order and permanent injunction in favor of Jones. Stand Up America Now v. City of Dearborn, 969 F. Supp. 2d 843 (E.D. Mich. 2013). The district court's decision does not discuss (at all) the city's claim that social unrest, including the outbreak of violence, could result from the proposed protest at the Islamic Center. Instead, Judge Denise Page Hood explains that "[i]t is well recognized that an ordinance which grants an administrative body or government official unfettered discretion to regulate the licensing of activities protected by the First Amendment is unconstitutional." *Id.* at 847. In addition, "courts have held that a clause requiring the permitee to hold the city harmless from any liability caused by the conduct of the event is unconstitutional." *Id.* Accordingly, the city's demand for an indemnification agreement was also void. Does this outcome surprise you?

On April 7, 2012, the proposed protest, under the protection of the federal district court's injunction, took place on a city-owned grassy area across the street from the Islamic Center of America—peaceably and without any arrests or other problems. *See* Niraj Warikoo, *Florida Pastor at Dearborn Protest*, Detroit Free Press, Apr. 7, 2012, available at *http://www.freep.com/article/20120407/NEWS02/120407023 /Terry-Jones-Dearborn-Quran-Islam*. Does this outcome change your thinking about whether the district judge properly applied the First Amendment? On the other hand, however, in virtually all of the larger democratic world, Jones would face criminal prosecution and imprisonment for attempting to incite religious hatred. *See* Lara Marlowe, *Pastor Feels No Shame, Nor Has He Any Remorse*, Irish Times (Dublin), Apr. 6, 2011, at 11 (noting that "[i]n a different country, Pastor Terry Jones might have been arrested" and explaining that "[i]n the US, where the First Amendment guarantee of free speech is sacrosanct, Jones enjoys police protection").

B.   A CONTEMPORARY EXAMPLE OF REGULATIONS AIMED AT PROMOTING SOCIAL EQUALITY: TITLE VII AS A LIMIT ON FREE SPEECH

Antidiscrimination laws, such as Title VII, obviously have effects on the exercise of free speech. For example, the question of a "hostile work environment" could turn entirely on speech in a workplace. Even so, the Supreme Court has not been sympathetic to arguments that federal and state employment nondiscrimination laws violate the First Amendment.

HISHON v. KING & SPALDING

467 U.S. 69 (1984)

Chief Justice BURGER delivered the opinion of the Court.

We granted certiorari to determine whether the District Court properly dismissed a Title VII complaint alleging that a law partnership discriminated against petitioner, a woman lawyer employed as an associate, when it failed to invite her to become a partner.

In 1972 petitioner Elizabeth Anderson Hishon accepted a position as an associate with respondent, a large Atlanta law firm established as a general partnership. When this suit was filed in 1980, the firm had more than 50 partners and employed approximately 50 attorneys as associates. Up to that time, no woman had ever served as a partner at the firm. [In May 1978, King & Spalding denied Hishon a partnership; in December 1979, following proceedings before the EEOC, Hishon commenced a Title VII action in federal district court.]

The District Court dismissed the complaint on the ground that Title VII was inapplicable to the selection of partners by a partnership. 24 FEP Cases 1303 (1980). A divided panel of the United States Court of Appeals for the Eleventh Circuit affirmed. 678 F.2d 1022 (1982). We granted certiorari, 459 U.S. 1169 (1983), and we reverse. . . .

Several allegations in petitioner's complaint would support the conclusion that the opportunity to become a partner was part and parcel of an associate's status as an employee at respondent's firm, independent of any allegation that such an opportunity was included in associates' employment contracts. Petitioner alleges that respondent's associates could regularly expect to be considered for partnership at the end of their "apprenticeships," and it appears that lawyers outside the firm were not routinely so considered. Thus, the benefit of partnership consideration was allegedly linked directly with an associate's status as an employee, and this linkage was far more than coincidental: petitioner alleges that respondent explicitly used the prospect of ultimate partnership to induce young lawyers to join the firm. Indeed, the importance of the partnership decision to a lawyer's status as an associate is underscored by the allegation that associates' employment is terminated if they are not elected to become partners. These allegations, if proved at trial, would suffice to show that partnership consideration was a term, condition, or privilege of an associate's employment at respondent's firm, and accordingly that partnership consideration must be without regard to sex. . . .

[R]espondent argues that application of Title VII in this case would infringe constitutional rights of expression or association. Although we have recognized that the activities of lawyers may make a "distinctive contribution . . . to the ideas and beliefs of our society," *NAACP v. Button*, 371 U.S. 415, 431 (1963), respondent has not shown how its ability to fulfill such a function would be inhibited by a requirement that it consider petitioner for partnership on her merits. Moreover, as we have held in another context, "[i]nvidious private discrimination may be characterized as a form of exercising freedom of association protected by the First Amendment, but it has never been accorded affirmative constitutional protections." *Norwood v. Harrison*, 413 U.S. 455, 470 (1973). There is no constitutional right, for example, to discriminate in the selection of who may attend a private school or join a labor union. *Runyon v. McCrary*, 427 U.S. 160 (1976); *Railway Mail Assn. v. Corsi*, 326 U.S. 88, 93-94 (1945).

We conclude that petitioner's complaint states a claim cognizable under Title VII. Petitioner therefore is entitled to her day in court to prove her allegations. The judgment of the Court of Appeals is reversed, and the case is remanded for further proceedings consistent with this opinion.

It is so ordered.

[Justice POWELL'S concurring opinion is omitted.]

NOTES AND QUESTIONS

1. *No serious First Amendment implications?* Is the question of First Amendment protection of "invidious private discrimination" as open and shut as Chief Justice Burger suggests? Could the Ku Klux Klan, for example, be required to admit gay men of color to its ranks? Or could a federal or state civil rights law require a religious organization that prohibits female ordination to modify its theological rules and ordain women? In the context of a large, corporate law firm, the claim of a core associational commitment to discriminate on the basis of sex does not wash. If one of King & Spalding's core organizational purposes included promoting gender discrimination, the outcome of the free association claim would probably be different. For the relevant doctrinal analysis, see *Boy Scouts v. Dale* (*supra* p. 227).

2. *Should the nature of the enterprise or organization make a difference?* Even if one can draw a clear distinction between a major corporate law firm, on the one hand, and the Ku Klux Klan or the Aryan Brotherhood, on the other, why shouldn't a major corporate law firm be able to claim the benefit of the First Amendment? If gender discrimination is something that King & Spalding wishes to promote in its hiring and promotion practices, why should the fact that it is a general partnership created to provide legal services to paying clients make any difference? Moreover, in other contexts, *e.g.*, *Bellotti*, *supra* page 350 and *Citizens United*, *supra* pages 289 and 355, the Supreme Court has rejected the idea that corporations and partnerships are not entitled to the protection of the First Amendment. Thus, if corporations and partnerships *do* enjoy First Amendment rights, why don't those rights extend to maintaining gender discriminatory or racially discriminatory workplaces?

3. *The hostile workplace theory and Title VII.* Professor Catharine MacKinnon's book, *The Sexual Harassment of Working Women* (1979), forcefully argued that the federal courts should interpret Title VII to prohibit pervasive, gender-based harassment in the workplace. In 1986, in the following case, the Supreme Court appeared to adopt MacKinnon's theory.

MERITOR SAVINGS BANK v. VINSON
477 U.S. 57 (1986)

Justice REHNQUIST delivered the opinion of the Court.

This case presents important questions concerning claims of workplace "sexual harassment" brought under Title VII of the Civil Rights Act of 1964, 78 Stat. 253, as amended, 42 U.S.C. § 2000e *et seq.*

In 1974, respondent Mechelle Vinson met Sidney Taylor, a vice president of what is now petitioner Meritor Savings Bank (bank) and manager of one of its branch offices. When respondent asked whether she might obtain employment at the bank, Taylor gave her an application, which she completed and returned the next day; later that same day Taylor called her to say that she had been hired. With Taylor as her supervisor, respondent started as a teller-trainee, and thereafter was promoted to teller, head teller, and assistant branch manager. She worked at the same branch for four years, and it is undisputed that her advancement there was based on merit alone. In September 1978, respondent notified Taylor that she was taking sick leave for an indefinite period. On November 1, 1978, the bank discharged her for excessive use of that leave.

Respondent brought this action against Taylor and the bank, claiming that during her four years at the bank she had "constantly been subjected to sexual harassment" by Taylor in violation of Title VII. She sought injunctive relief, compensatory and punitive damages against Taylor and the bank, and attorney's fees. . . .

The District Court denied relief, but did not resolve the conflicting testimony about the existence of a sexual relationship between respondent and Taylor. . . . The court ultimately found that the respondent "was not the victim of sexual harassment and was not the victim of sexual discrimination" while employed at the bank. . . .

The Court of Appeals for the District of Columbia Circuit reversed. Relying on its earlier holding in *Bundy v. Jackson* . . . [t]he court stated that a violation of Title VII may be predicated on either of two types of sexual harassment: harassment that involves the conditioning of concrete employment benefits on sexual favors, and harassment that, while not affecting economic benefits, creates a hostile or offensive working environment. . . .

In accordance with the foregoing, the Court of Appeals reversed the judgment of the District Court and remanded the case for further proceedings. A subsequent suggestion for rehearing en banc was denied, with three judges dissenting. We granted certiorari, 474 U.S. 1047 (1985), and now affirm but for different reasons.

Title VII of the Civil Rights Act of 1964 makes it "an unlawful employment practice for an employer . . . to discriminate against any individual with respect to his compensation, terms, conditions, or privileges of employment, because of such individual's race, color, religion, sex or national origin." 42 U.S.C. § 2000e-2(a)(1). The prohibition against discrimination based on sex was added to Title VII at the last minute on the floor of the House of Representatives. 110 Cong. Rec. 2577-2584 (1964). . . .

Respondent argues, and the Court of Appeals held, that unwelcome sexual advances that create an offensive or hostile working environment violate Title VII. Without question, when a supervisor sexually harasses a subordinate because of the subordinate's sex, that supervisor "discriminate[s]" on the basis of sex. Petitioner apparently does not challenge this proposition. It contends instead that in prohibiting discrimination with respect to "compensation, terms, conditions, or privileges" of employment, Congress was concerned with what petitioner describes as "tangible loss" of "an economic character," not "purely psychological aspects of the workplace environment." In support of this claim petitioner observes that in both the legislative history of Title VII and this Court's Title VII decisions, the focus has been on tangible, economic barriers erected by discrimination.

We reject petitioner's view. First, the language of Title VII is not limited to "economic" or "tangible" discrimination. The phrase "terms, conditions, or privileges of employment" evinces a congressional intent "'to strike at the entire spectrum of disparate treatment of men and women'" in employment. *Los Angeles Dept. of Water and Power v. Manhart*, 435 U.S. 702, 707 n.13 (1978), quoting *Sprogis v. United Air Lines, Inc.*, 444 F.2d 1194, 1198 (CA7 1971). Petitioner has pointed to nothing in the Act to suggest that Congress contemplated the limitation urged here. . . .

Since the [EEOC's] Guidelines were issued, courts have uniformly held, and we agree, that a plaintiff may establish a violation of Title VII by proving that discrimination based on sex has created a hostile or abusive work environment. As the Court of Appeals for the Eleventh Circuit wrote in *Henson v. Dundee*, 682 F.2d 897, 902 (1982):

> "Sexual harassment which creates a hostile or offensive environment for members of one sex is every bit the arbitrary barrier to sexual equality at the workplace that racial harassment is to racial equality. Surely, a requirement that a man or woman run a gauntlet of sexual abuse in return for the privilege of being allowed to work and make a living can be as demeaning and disconcerting as the harshest of racial epithets." . . .

Of course, as the courts in both *Rogers* and *Henson* recognized, not all workplace conduct that may be described as "harassment" affects a "term, condition, or privilege" of employment within the meaning of Title VII. See *Rogers v. EEOC, supra,* at 238 ("mere utterance of an ethnic or racial epithet which engenders offensive feelings in an employee" would not affect the conditions of employment to sufficiently significant degree to violate Title VII); *Henson,* 682 F.2d, at 904 (quoting same). For sexual harassment to be actionable, it must be sufficiently severe or pervasive "to alter the conditions of [the victim's] employment and create an abusive working environment." *Ibid.* Respondent's allegations in this case—which include not only pervasive harassment but also criminal conduct of the most serious nature—are plainly sufficient to state a claim for "hostile environment" sexual harassment. . . .

In sum, we hold that a claim of "hostile environment" sex discrimination is actionable under Title VII, that the District Court's findings were insufficient to dispose of respondent's hostile environment claim, and that the District Court did not err in admitting testimony about respondent's sexually provocative speech and dress.

. . .

Justice MARSHALL, with whom Justice BRENNAN, Justice BLACKMUN, AND Justice STEVENS join, concurring in the judgment. [Opinion omitted.]

NOTES AND QUESTIONS

1. *Private employers and harassing workplace speech.* Why do free speech concerns receive such short shrift in *Hishon* and *Meritor Savings Bank*? If the owner of a garage decorates the place of employment with images of hard-core pornography, why shouldn't the Free Speech Clause provide some measure of protection for this decision? Provided that men and women receive equal pay and benefits, should the First Amendment protect a business owner's idiosyncratic decorating concepts?

2. *Does free speech potentially limit the government's ability to promote workplace equality?* Clearly, if Congress (or a state legislature) wishes to advance equal

employment at the cost of free speech, the Supreme Court will not apply the First Amendment inflexibly as an absolute bar to such legislation. Precisely why does promoting equality trump speech in this context but not in other contexts? Are places of employment different from a home, a rally on private land, or a street march? If so, how are they different?

3. *College and university campuses.* If Congress can prohibit hostile work environments, can a state university or college prohibit hostile learning environments by enacting a campus speech code? How does a campus speech code differ (or does it?) from Title VII? Every lower federal court to consider the constitutional status of a campus speech code has invalidated the campus free speech code on free speech grounds. Why is this so? What is the difference between preventing a hostile work environment in a place of employment and punishing racist, sexist, or homophobic speech on campus? Clearly it cannot be a difference in kind but rather must rest on a difference in the scope of the regulation. Would more narrowly tailored campus speech restrictions survive First Amendment scrutiny? Is it permissible to restrict speech only at the point that another person is forced to choose between a livelihood (or education) and another person's free speech rights? Or is pervasive harassment in a hostile environment more closely akin to a true threat? (Recall that "true threats" enjoy no First Amendment protection. See *supra* pages 70-82.)

4. *Free speech as an absolute value?* As noted in the Introduction to this chapter, a small but vocal group of First Amendment scholars have attacked *Hishon* and *Meritor Savings Bank* as being inconsistent with basic free speech principles, including both content and viewpoint neutrality. *See, e.g.,* Eugene Volokh, *How Harassment Law Restricts Free Speech,* 47 Rutgers L. Rev. 563, 574-579 (1995). These critiques have not proven persuasive to the federal courts or within the larger legal academy.

THEORY-APPLIED PROBLEM

In July 2017, Mississippi State University (MSU) enacts a campus speech code that prohibits "speech creating a hostile learning environment based on race, sex, religion, national origin, or sexual orientation such that no reasonable person within a protected classification would reasonably be expected to remain enrolled as a full time student on campus if regularly subjected to the harassment at issue." MSU general counsel intentionally drafted language that tracks the language of the relevant hostile work environment precedents, which require an environment so toxic that no reasonable woman (in the case of gender) or no reasonable person of color (in the case of race) would tolerate the environment.

In October 2017, the MSU chapter of Kappa Beta Alpha, an undergraduate fraternity, charges its pledge class with sorting out the "bitches" from the "whores" on campus as part of the organization's mandatory pledge activities. As part of their pledge duties, the would-be KBA brothers must, on a 24-hour basis, declare any woman that they encounter to be either a "bitch" or a "whore." Cindy Who, enrolled in advanced organic chemistry, has a term paper due in 48 hours and needs to use the university library to complete the assignment. As she approaches the university library's entrance, a group of around six KBA pledges begins shouting "whore" at her. Startled, she flees the library. Who returns four hours later and is met with chants of "bitch" from a different group of equally fervent KBA pledges. She again flees and does not return. Moreover, she receives a "D" mark on her paper because she is afraid to return to the library, for fear of a third altercation with the KBA pledges. Who files a formal complaint with campus security following the second altercation. After conducting an investigation, campus security finds that more than three dozen women had been subjected to verbal abuse by the KBA pledges during the prior week at various locations on campus, including the library, the student center, the main gymnasium, and classroom buildings.

The Faculty/Student Review Board initiates formal proceedings against the KBA pledges and recommends that they be suspended from campus for at least one academic semester. MSU's provost accepts the Faculty/Student Review Board's recommendation and immediately suspends 11 freshman students from the university for one semester. The KBA pledges secure a lawyer and file a section 1983 action against the university, alleging a violation of their free speech and free association rights. The university defends the action by claiming that the students were not suspended because of their speech but because of the harassing actions. How should the district court rule? Is the MSU policy consistent with the First Amendment?

C. GOVERNMENT EFFORTS TO PROMOTE CIVILITY AND THE FIRST AMENDMENT

Governments at all levels (federal, state, and local), responding to the wishes of voters, have attempted to enact and enforce civility norms. The modern Supreme Court has consistently rebuffed these efforts (save in the context of Title VII). Should a commitment to freedom of expression imply an absolute rule against mandatory civility norms in public places, like a local courthouse, or at public meetings, like a school board meeting?

If one believes that a meaningful commitment to freedom of expression should not imply an absolute ban on mandatory civility regulations, a serious question remains about the ability of government (and perhaps the willingness of government) to enforce such norms consistently. For example, Vice President Dick Cheney, on the floor of the United States Senate, told Senator Patrick Leahy, to "go fuck yourself." Sidney Blumenthal, *When Cheney's Mask Slips, It Reveals Bush*, The Guardian, July 1, 2004, at 25. If a federal civility law existed that prohibited use of profanity in government buildings during regular business hours, is it at all realistic to expect the Department of Justice to prosecute the Vice President? And, if it is not, would it be fair to prosecute an angry veteran who tells a local Veteran's Administration functionary in Jacksonville, Florida, to do the same thing? Even if one agrees in principle that civility norms would enhance, rather than degrade, the marketplace of ideas, how could one ensure that such rules are deployed in a content- and viewpoint-neutral fashion?

COHEN v. CALIFORNIA

403 U.S. 15 (1971)

Mr. Justice HARLAN delivered the opinion of the Court.

This case may seem at first blush too inconsequential to find its way into our books, but the issue it presents is of no small constitutional significance.

Appellant Paul Robert Cohen was convicted in the Los Angeles Municipal Court of violating that part of California Penal Code § 415 which prohibits "maliciously and willfully disturb[ing] the peace or quiet of any neighborhood or person . . . by . . . offensive conduct. . . ." He was given 30 days' imprisonment. The facts upon which his conviction rests are detailed in the opinion of the Court of Appeal of California, Second Appellate District, as follows:

> "On April 26, 1968, the defendant was observed in the Los Angeles County Courthouse in the corridor outside of division 20 of the municipal court wearing a jacket bearing the words 'Fuck the Draft' which were plainly visible. There were women and children present in the corridor. The defendant was arrested. The defendant testified that he wore the jacket knowing that the words were on the jacket as a means of informing the public of the depth of his feelings against the Vietnam War and the draft.
>
> "The defendant did not engage in, nor threaten to engage in, nor did anyone as the result of his conduct in fact commit or threaten to commit any act of violence. The defendant did not make any loud or unusual noise, nor was there any evidence that he uttered any sound prior to his arrest." 1 Cal. App. 3d 94, 97-98, 81 Cal. Rptr. 503, 505 (1969).

In affirming the conviction the Court of Appeal held that "offensive conduct" means "behavior which has a tendency to provoke *others* to acts of violence or to in turn disturb the peace," and that the State had proved this element because, on the facts of this case, "[i]t was certainly reasonably foreseeable that such conduct might cause others to rise up to commit a violent act against the person of the defendant or attempt to forceably remove his jacket." The California Supreme Court declined review by a divided vote. We brought the case here, postponing the consideration of the question of our jurisdiction over this appeal to a hearing of the case on the merits. We now reverse. . . .

In order to lay hands on the precise issue which this case involves, it is useful first to canvass various matters which this record does *not* present.

The conviction quite clearly rests upon the asserted offensiveness of the *words* Cohen used to convey his message to the public. The only "conduct" which the State sought to punish is the fact of communication. Thus, we deal here with a conviction resting solely upon "speech," cf. *Stromberg v. California*, 283 U.S. 359 (1931), not upon any separately identifiable conduct which allegedly was intended by Cohen to be perceived by others as expressive of particular views but which, on its face, does not necessarily convey any message and hence arguably could be regulated without effectively repressing Cohen's ability to express himself. Cf. *United States v. O'Brien*, 391 U.S. 367 (1968). Further, the State certainly lacks power to punish Cohen for the underlying content of the message the inscription conveyed. At least so long as there is no showing of an intent to incite disobedience to or disruption of the draft, Cohen could not, consistently with the First and Fourteenth Amendments, be punished for asserting the evident position on the inutility or immorality of the draft his jacket reflected. *Yates v. United States*, 354 U.S. 298 (1957).

Appellant's conviction, then, rests squarely upon his exercise of the "freedom of speech" protected from arbitrary governmental interference by the Constitution and can be justified, if at all, only as a valid regulation of the manner in which he exercised that freedom, not as a permissible prohibition on the substantive message it conveys. . . .

In the first place, Cohen was tried under a statute applicable throughout the entire State. Any attempt to support this conviction on the ground that the statute seeks to preserve an appropriately decorous atmosphere in the courthouse where Cohen was arrested must fail in the absence of any language in the statute that would have put appellant on notice that certain kinds of otherwise permissible speech or conduct would nevertheless, under California law, not be tolerated in certain places. See *Edwards v. South Carolina*, 372 U.S. 229, 236-237, and n.11 (1963). Cf. *Adderley v. Florida*, 385 U.S. 39 (1966). No fair reading of the phrase "offensive conduct" can be said sufficiently to inform the ordinary person that distinctions between certain locations are thereby created.[3]

In the second place, as it comes to us, this case cannot be said to fall within those relatively few categories of instances where prior decisions have established the power of government to deal more comprehensively with certain forms of individual expression simply upon a showing that such a form was employed. This is not, for example, an obscenity case. . . .

There is, as noted above, no showing that anyone who saw Cohen was in fact violently aroused or that appellant intended such a result. [Accordingly, the fighting-words doctrine does not apply on these facts.]

Finally, in arguments before this Court much has been made of the claim that Cohen's distasteful mode of expression was thrust upon unwilling or unsuspecting viewers, and that the State might therefore legitimately act as it did in order to protect the sensitive from otherwise unavoidable exposure to appellant's crude form of protest. . . . The ability of government, consonant with the Constitution, to shut off discourse solely to protect others from hearing it is, in other words, dependent upon a showing that substantial privacy interests are being invaded in an essentially intolerable manner. Any broader view of this authority would effectively empower a majority to silence dissidents simply as a matter of personal predilections.

In this regard, persons confronted with Cohen's jacket were in a quite different posture than, say, those subjected to the raucous emissions of sound trucks blaring outside their residences. Those in the Los Angeles courthouse could effectively avoid further bombardment of their sensibilities simply by averting their eyes. . . .

Against this background, the issue flushed by this case stands out in bold relief. It is whether California can excise, as "offensive conduct," one particular scurrilous epithet from the public discourse, either upon the theory of the court below that its use is inherently likely to cause violent reaction or upon a more general assertion that the States, acting as guardians of public morality, may properly remove this offensive word from the public vocabulary.

---

[3] It is illuminating to note what transpired when Cohen entered a courtroom in the building. He removed his jacket and stood with it folded over his arm. Meanwhile, a policeman sent the presiding judge a note suggesting that Cohen be held in contempt of court. The judge declined to do so and Cohen was arrested by the officer only after he emerged from the courtroom. App. 18-19.

The rationale of the California court is plainly untenable. At most it reflects an "undifferentiated fear or apprehension of disturbance [which] is not enough to overcome the right to freedom of expression." *Tinker v. Des Moines Indep. Community School Dist.*, 393 U.S. 503, 508 (1969). . . .

Admittedly, it is not so obvious that the First and Fourteenth Amendments must be taken to disable the States from punishing public utterance of this unseemly expletive in order to maintain what they regard as a suitable level of discourse within the body politic. We think, however, that examination and reflection will reveal the shortcomings of a contrary viewpoint.

At the outset, we cannot overemphasize that, in our judgment, most situations where the State has a justifiable interest in regulating speech will fall within one or more of the various established exceptions, discussed above but not applicable here, to the usual rule that governmental bodies may not prescribe the form or content of individual expression. Equally important to our conclusion is the constitutional backdrop against which our decision must be made. The constitutional right of free expression is powerful medicine in a society as diverse and populous as ours. It is designed and intended to remove governmental restraints from the arena of public discussion, putting the decision as to what views shall be voiced largely into the hands of each of us, in the hope that use of such freedom will ultimately produce a more capable citizenry and more perfect polity and in the belief that no other approach would comport with the premise of individual dignity and choice upon which our political system rests. See *Whitney v. California*, 274 U.S. 357, 375-377 (1927) (Brandeis, J., concurring).

To many, the immediate consequence of this freedom may often appear to be only verbal tumult, discord, and even offensive utterance. These are, however, within established limits, in truth necessary side effects of the broader enduring values which the process of open debate permits us to achieve. That the air may at times seem filled with verbal cacophony is, in this sense not a sign of weakness but of strength. We cannot lose sight of the fact that, in what otherwise might seem a trifling and annoying instance of individual distasteful abuse of a privilege, these fundamental societal values are truly implicated. . . .

Against this perception of the constitutional policies involved, we discern certain more particularized considerations that peculiarly call for reversal of this conviction. First, the principle contended for by the State seems inherently boundless. How is one to distinguish this from any other offensive word? Surely the state has no right to cleanse public debate to the point where it is grammatically palatable to the most squeamish among us. Yet no readily ascertainable general principle exists for stopping short of that result were we to affirm the judgment below. For, while the particular four-letter word being litigated here is perhaps more distasteful than most others of its genre, it is nevertheless often true that one man's vulgarity is another's lyric. Indeed, we think it is largely because governmental officials cannot make principled distinctions in this area that the Constitution leaves matters of taste and style so largely to the individual.

Additionally, we cannot overlook the fact, because it is well illustrated by the episode involved here, that much linguistic expression serves a dual communicative function: it conveys not only ideas capable of relatively precise, detached explication, but otherwise inexpressible emotions as well. In fact, words are often chosen as much for their emotive as their cognitive force. We cannot sanction the view that the Constitution, while solicitous of the cognitive content of individual speech, has little or no regard for that emotive function which practically speaking, may often be the more important element of the overall message sought to be communicated. . . .

Finally, and in the same vein, we cannot indulge the facile assumption that one can forbid particular words without also running a substantial risk of suppressing ideas in the process. Indeed, governments might soon seize upon the censorship of particular words as a convenient guise for banning the expression of unpopular views. We have been able, as noted above, to discern little social benefit that might result from running the risk of opening the door to such grave results.

It is, in sum, our judgment that, absent a more particularized and compelling reason for its actions, the State may not, consistently with the First and Fourteenth Amendments, make the simple public display here involved of this single four-letter expletive a criminal offense. Because that is the only arguably sustainable rationale for the conviction here at issue, the judgment below must be

Reversed.

Mr. Justice BLACKMUN, with whom THE CHIEF JUSTICE and Mr. Justice BLACK join.

I dissent, and I do so for two reasons:

1. Cohen's absurd and immature antic, in my view was mainly conduct and little speech. And I cannot characterize it otherwise. Further, the case appears to me to be well within the sphere of *Chaplinsky v. New Hampshire*, 315 U.S. 568 (1942), where Mr. Justice Murphy, a known champion of First Amendment freedoms, wrote for a unanimous bench. As a consequence, this Court's agonizing over First Amendment values seems misplaced and unnecessary.

2. I am not at all certain that the California Court of Appeal's construction of § 415 is now the authoritative California construction. . . . Inasmuch as this Court does not dismiss this case, it ought to be remanded to the California Court of Appeal for reconsideration in the light of the subsequently rendered decision by the State's highest tribunal in *Bushman.*

Mr. Justice WHITE concurs in Paragraph 2 of Mr. Justice BLACKMUN'S dissenting opinion.

NOTES AND QUESTIONS

1. *A binary choice?* Is Justice Harlan correct to suggest that the power to suppress a single curse word from public discourse necessarily leads down the road to more generalized forms of government censorship? Is this a false choice? Could government attempt to maintain civility norms without engaging in broader efforts to censor the entire culture?

2. *The emotive impact of speech.* Justice Harlan's suggestion that the emotive content of communication can be more important than its cognitive content seems persuasive, does it not? To use the facts at issue in *Cohen*, would a jacket with "Down with the Draft" or "I Oppose the Draft" or "The Draft Is Bad, M'Kay?" convey the same message as Cohen's actual jacket? And should Cohen be prevented from communicating his message in public because his preferred means of communication will likely offend at least some other citizens?

3. *A contrary approach.* Contrary to Justice Harlan's thesis, could government create and enforce civility norms in public places and at public meetings without squelching the ability of a speaker to express herself fully? Should Cohen's

interest in expressing himself trump the interest of an unwilling audience in avoiding his expression? If one has unavoidable business in the local courthouse, is an admonition to "avert one's eyes" really a satisfactory response? On the other hand, the federal courts consistently have held that an adverse public reaction is *not* a permissible basis for squelching speech. Viewed from the perspective of that rule, Justice Harlan seems to have the better of the argument.

4. *The* Cohen *rule retains strong precedential force.* The Supreme Court has given absolutely no indication that it is inclined to resile from either the baseline holding or the underlying reasoning of *Cohen*. For example, in Snyder v. Phelps, 562 U.S. 443 (2011) (excerpted *supra* at p. 487) the Supreme Court held protected, on First Amendment grounds, a targeted funeral protest of a marine killed while on active duty in Iraq. Brandishing signs with slogans like "God Hates the USA/Thank God for 9/11," "God Hates Fags," and "Thank God for Dead Soldiers," the protest took place contemporaneously with, and proximate to, Marine Corporal Matthew Snyder's funeral services in Westminster, Maryland. Writing for the 8-1 majority, Chief Justice Roberts held that the First Amendment essentially immunizes speech in a public forum, related to a matter of public concern, from serving as the basis for tort liability—even if the speech at issue badly transgresses baseline and widely held notions of civility and personal dignity. In particular, Roberts squarely rejected the idea that the highly targeted and intentionally offensive nature of the protest removed, or even reduced, the scope of protection the protest activity enjoyed under the First Amendment:

> Given that Westboro's speech was at a public place on a matter of public concern, that speech is entitled to "special protection" under the First Amendment. Such speech cannot be restricted simply because it is upsetting or arouses contempt. "If there is a bedrock principle underlying the First Amendment, it is that government may not prohibit the expression of an idea simply because society finds the idea itself offensive or disagreeable." Texas v. Johnson, 491 U.S. 397, 414 (1989).

Id. at 1219. Moreover, the gravamen of both the intentional infliction of emotional distress and privacy tort claims relates to the *outrageousness* of the speech or the grossly offensive nature of the intrusion upon privacy. Chief Justice Roberts specifically rejected this legal standard, at least in this context, because "'[o]utrageousness,' however, is a highly malleable standard with 'an inherent subjectiveness about it which would allow a jury to impose liability on the basis of the jurors' tastes or views, or perhaps on the basis of their dislike of a particular expression.' *Hustler* [v. Falwell, 485 U.S. 46, 55 (1988)]." *Id.* That a civil jury might take such a step by imposing civil liability on an unpopular speaker or group constitutes an "unacceptable" risk and, accordingly, "the jury verdict imposing tort liability on Westboro for intentional infliction of emotional distress must be set aside." Thus, *Phelps* both applies and extends the general rule against the creation and enforcement of mandatory civility norms, whether through the criminal law (as in *Cohen*) or via civil law rules (as in *Phelps*).

5. *The dissent not written.* What does one make of the Blackmun dissent? Is it at all persuasive to characterize Cohen's wearing the jacket as "conduct" and not "speech"? Was there a better argument to be made in response to Justice Harlan's majority opinion? How about this: Does a commitment to free speech

mean that a society must hold itself absolutely barred from establishing and enforcing any meaningful civility norms in public places? In other words, if a modern day Al Swearengen (the Ian McShane bar proprietor in *Deadwood*) wishes to go about the Los Angeles County courthouse cheerfully greeting passersby as "cocksuckers," may the community disallow this particular form of communication in a public building filled with a captive audience? States maintain laws against public indecency, for example—if one cannot appear nude in public, why should one be permitted to use highly offensive language in public? Both laws aim at protecting essentially aesthetic interests that reflect long-standing cultural norms.

6. *Extending the* Cohen *rationale?* Justice Harlan wrote a thoughtful, but carefully limited, majority opinion in *Cohen*. Subsequent opinions in the *Cohen* line were far less circumscribed about the state's power to limit the use of profanity or other offensive language in public places. Consider the following cases.

GOODING v. WILSON

405 U.S. 518 (1972)

Mr. Justice BRENNAN delivered the opinion of the Court.

Appellee was convicted in Superior Court, Fulton County, Georgia, on two counts of using opprobrious words and abusive language in violation of Georgia Code Ann. § 26-6303, which provides: "Any person who shall, without provocation, use to or of another, and in his presence . . . opprobrious words or abusive language, tending to cause a breach of the peace . . . shall be guilty of a misdemeanor." Appellee appealed the conviction to the Supreme Court of Georgia on the ground, among others, that the statute violated the First and Fourteenth Amendments because vague and overbroad. The Georgia Supreme Court rejected that contention and sustained the conviction. . . .

Section 26-6303 punishes only spoken words. It can therefore withstand appellee's attack upon its facial constitutionality only if, as authoritatively construed by the Georgia courts, it is not susceptible of application to speech, although vulgar or offensive, that is protected by the First and Fourteenth Amendments, *Cohen v. California*, 403 U.S. 15, 18-22 (1971); *Terminiello v. Chicago*, 337 U.S. 1, 4-5 (1949). . . .

The constitutional guarantees of freedom of speech forbid the States to punish the use of words or language not within "narrowly limited classes of speech." *Chaplinsky v. New Hampshire*, 315 U.S. 568, 571 (1942). Even as to such a class, however, because "the line between speech unconditionally guaranteed and speech which may legitimately be regulated, suppressed, or punished is finely drawn," *Speiser v. Randall*, 357 U.S. 513, 525 (1958), "[i]n every case the power to regulate must be so exercised as not, in attaining a permissible end, unduly to infringe the protected freedom," *Cantwell v. Connecticut*, 310 U.S. 296, 304 (1940). In other words, the statute must be carefully drawn or be authoritatively construed to punish only unprotected speech and not be susceptible of application to protected expression. "Because First Amendment freedoms need breathing space to survive, government may regulate in the area only with narrow specificity." *NAACP v. Button, supra*, at 433. . . .

We conclude that "[t]he separation of legitimate from illegitimate speech calls for more sensitive tools than [Georgia] has supplied." *Speiser v. Randall*, 357 U.S. at

525. The most recent decision of the Georgia Supreme Court, *Wilson v. State, supra*, in rejecting appellee's attack on the constitutionality of § 26-6303, stated that the statute "conveys a definite meaning as to the conduct forbidden, measured by common understanding and practice." Because earlier appellate decisions applied § 26-6303 to utterances where there was no likelihood that the person addressed would make an immediate violent response, it is clear that the standard allowing juries to determine guilt "measured by common understanding and practice" does not limit the application of § 26-6303 to "fighting" words defined by *Chaplinsky*. Rather, that broad standard effectively "licenses the jury to create its own standard in each case." *Herndon v. Lowry*, 301 U.S. 242, 263 (1937). Accordingly, we agree with the conclusion of the [lower court], "[t]he fault of the statute is that it leaves wide open the standard of responsibility, so that it is easily susceptible to improper application." Unlike the construction of the New Hampshire statute by the New Hampshire Supreme Court, the Georgia appellate courts have not construed § 26-6303 "so as to avoid all constitutional difficulties." *United States v. Thirty-seven Photographs*, 402 U.S., at 369.

Affirmed.

Mr. Chief Justice BURGER, dissenting.

I fully join in Mr. Justice Blackmun's dissent against the bizarre result reached by the Court. It is not merely odd, it is nothing less than remarkable that a court can find a state statute void on its face, not because of its language—which is the traditional test—but because of the way courts of the state have applied the statute in a few isolated cases, decided as long ago as 1905 and generally long before this Court's decision in *Chaplinsky v. New Hampshire*, 315 U.S. 568 (1942). Even if all of those cases had been decided yesterday, they do nothing to demonstrate that the narrow language of the Georgia statute has any significant potential for sweeping application to suppress or deter important protected speech. . . .

Mr. Justice BLACKMUN, with whom THE CHIEF JUSTICE joins, dissenting.

It seems strange, indeed, that in this day a man may say to a police officer, who is attempting to restore access to a public building, "White son of a bitch, I'll kill you" and "You son of a bitch, I'll choke you to death," and say to an accompanying officer, "You son of a bitch, if you ever put your hands on me again, I'll cut you all to pieces," and yet constitutionally cannot be prosecuted and convicted under a state statute that makes it a misdemeanor to "use to or of another and in his presence...opprobrious words or abusive language, tending to cause a breach of the peace. . . ." This, however, is precisely what the Court pronounces as the law today...

ROSENFELD v. NEW JERSEY

408 U.S. 901 (1972)

PER CURIAM.

Judgment vacated and case remanded for reconsideration in light of *Cohen v. California*, 403 U.S. 15 (1971), and *Gooding v. Wilson*, 405 U.S. 518 (1972).

Mr. Chief Justice BURGER, with whom Mr. Justice BLACKMUN and Mr. Justice REHNQUIST join, dissenting.

I am constrained to express my profound disagreement with what the Court does in these three cases on the basis of *Gooding v. Wilson*, 405 U.S. 518 (1972).

The important underlying aspect of these cases goes really to the function of law in preserving ordered liberty. Civilized people refrain from "taking the law into their own hands" because of a belief that the government, as their agent, will take care of the problem in an organized orderly way with as nearly a uniform response as human skills can manage. History is replete with evidence of what happens when the law cannot or does not provide a collective response for conduct so widely regarded as impermissible and intolerable.

It is barely a century since men in parts of this country carried guns constantly because the law did not afford protection. In that setting, the words used in these cases, if directed toward such an armed civilian, could well have led to death or serious bodily injury. When we undermine the general belief that the law will give protection against fighting words and profane and abusive language such as the utterances involved in these cases, we take steps to return to the law of the jungle. These three cases, like *Gooding*, are small but symptomatic steps. If continued, this permissiveness will tend further to erode public confidence in the law—that subtle but indispensable ingredient of ordered liberty.

In Rosenfeld's case, for example, civilized people attending such a meeting with wives and children would not likely have an instantaneous, violent response, but it does not unduly tax the imagination to think that some justifiably outraged parent whose family were exposed to the foul mouthings of the speaker would "meet him outside" and, either alone or with others, resort to the 19th century's vigorous modes of dealing with such people. I cannot see these holdings as an "advance" in human liberty but rather a retrogression to what men have struggled to escape for a long time.

Mr. Justice POWELL, with whom THE CHIEF JUSTICE and Mr. Justice BLACKMUN join, dissenting.

It has long been established that the First and Fourteenth Amendments prohibit the States from punishing all but the most "narrowly limited classes of speech." *Chaplinsky v. New Hampshire*, 315 U.S. 568, 571 (1942). The right of free speech, however, has never been held to be absolute at all times and under all circumstances. To so hold would sanction invasion of cherished personal rights and would deny the states the power to deal with threats to public order. . . .

This case presents an example of gross abuse of the respected privilege in this country of allowing every citizen to speak his mind. Appellant addressed a public school board meeting attended by about 150 people, approximately 40 of whom were children and 25 of whom were women. In the course of his remarks he used the adjective "m _____ f _____" on four occasions, to describe the teachers, the school board, the town and his own country. . . .

[A] verbal assault on an unwilling audience may be so grossly offensive and emotionally disturbing as to be the proper subject of criminal proscription, whether under a statute denominating it disorderly conduct, or, more accurately, a public nuisance. . . .

The line between such rights and the type of conduct proscribed by the New Jersey statute is difficult to draw. The preservation of the right to free and robust speech is accorded high priority in our society and under the Constitution. Yet, there are other significant values. One of the hallmarks of a civilized society is the level and quality of discourse. We have witnessed in recent years a disquieting deterioration in standards of taste and civility in speech. For the increasing number of persons who derive satisfaction from vocabularies dependent upon filth and obscenities, there are abundant opportunities to gratify their debased tastes. But our free society must be flexible enough to tolerate even such a debasement provided it occurs without subjecting unwilling audiences to the type of verbal nuisance committed in this case. The shock and sense of affront, and sometimes the injury to mind and spirit, can be as great from words as from some physical attacks.

I conclude in this case that appellant's utterances fall within the proscription of the New Jersey statute, and are not protected by the First Amendment. Accordingly, I would dismiss the appeal for want of a substantial federal question.

Mr. Justice REHNQUIST, with whom THE CHIEF JUSTICE and Mr. Justice BLACKMUN join, dissenting.

In *Lewis*, the police were engaged in making an arrest of appellant's son on grounds not challenged here. While the police were engaged in the performance of their duty, appellant intervened and ultimately addressed the police officers as "g- - d - - - m - - - - - f - - - - - - police." . . .

Appellant in *Brown* spoke to a large group of men and women gathered in the University of Tulsa chapel. During a question and answer period he referred to some policemen as "m - - - - - f - - - - - fascist pig cops" and to a particular Tulsa police officer as that "black m - - - - f- - - - - pig. . . ." Brown was convicted of violating an Oklahoma statute that prohibited the utterance of "any obscene or lascivious language or word in any public place, or in the presence of females. . . ." Okla. Stat. Ann., Tit. 21, § 906 (1958). . . .

Insofar as the Court's remand is based on *Cohen, supra*, for the reasons stated in Mr. Justice Blackmun's dissenting opinion in that case, *id.*, at 27, I would not deny to these States the power to punish language of the sort used here by appropriate legislation. Appellant Lewis' words to the police officers were "fighting words," and those of appellants Rosenfeld and Brown were "lewd and obscene" and "profane" as those terms are used in *Chaplinsky v. New Hampshire*, 315 U.S. 568 (1942), the leading case in the field. . . .

The language used by these appellants therefore clearly falls within the class of punishable utterances described in *Chaplinsky*. . . .

I would dismiss these appeals for lack of a substantial federal question.

NOTES AND QUESTIONS

1. *No civility norms in public places?* Is it absolutely necessary to protect the use of the "f-bomb" at a school board meeting to ensure that an Orwellian thought control project does not advance? Or is the *Cohen-Gooding* doctrine best understood as a kind of prophylactic rule that overprotects marginal speech in order to ensure adequate breathing room for intemperate core political speech of a dissenting cast?

2. *Broad protection for offensive and insulting speech.* Notwithstanding *Cohen's* insistence that the holding was limited to the specific context of a generic breach of the peace statute, *Gooding* and *Rosenfeld* make clear that *Cohen* has a broader effect than Justice Harlan's carefully limited opinion would suggest. Along similar lines is Hess v. Indiana, 414 U.S. 105, 107-109 (1973) (holding protected, on free speech grounds, statement to local sheriff that antiwar

protestors would "take the fucking street later" or "take the fucking street again").

3. *Civility norms in the public schools.* Do the public schools present a special case for the creation of mandatory civility norms? Given highly publicized incidents of bullying and mistreatment of students perceived to be "different" in some material respect, many school districts have responded by adopting codes of conduct that require students to treat each other respectfully during school hours and at school events. These codes of conduct commonly prohibit the use of offensive or degrading language (for example, typically a student may not call another student "fag" or "too gay," or otherwise use racist, sexist, homophobic, or religiously offensive language). Although students do not check their First Amendment rights at the schoolhouse door, Tinker v. Des Moines Indep. Cmty. Sch. Dist. (excerpted *infra* p. 674), the Supreme Court has sustained restrictions against vulgar speech at curricular events, Bethel School Dist. No. 403 v. Fraser (excerpted *infra* p. 678), and also restrictions against speech arguably advocating the use of illegal drugs, Morse v. Frederick (excerpted *infra* p. 687). These precedents would seem to support the creation and enforcement of civility codes designed to avoid disruption of the educational mission of the public schools. Although such rules are decidedly content-based (if not *viewpoint*-based), they arguably advance a compelling interest, and the speech itself is the evil to be avoided (given that the speech creates a high probability of disruption).

    What about mandatory civility norms applicable to student speech that takes place off-campus but which is plainly directed at an audience of students, teachers, and administrators, which also has discernable adverse effects within the public schools? The lower federal courts haves split on this question, with some permitting public school officials to establish and enforce civility norms for off-campus student speech that targets an audience consisting of current students, including, for example, students' use of social media outlets such as Facebook and Twitter. Others, however, have held that local school officials may not attempt to regulate expression that takes place off-campus. *Compare* Layshock v. Hermitage School Dist., 650 F.3d 205 (3d Cir. 2011) (disallowing student discipline for a parody of a school administrator where no disruption actually occurred within the school itself as a result), *cert. denied sub nom.*, 565 U.S. 1156 (2012), *with* Doninger v. Niehoff, 527 F.3d 41 (2d Cir. 2008) (permitting regulation of off-campus internet postings where the author intended to reach a school-based audience and disruption occurred in the public school) and Wisniewski v. Bd. of Educ., 494 F.3d 34 (2d Cir. 2007) (same). The Supreme Court has not yet squarely ruled on these questions. For a thoughtful discussion of these issues, see Barry P. McDonald, *Regulating Student Cyberspeech*, 77 Mo. L. Rev. 727 (2012); Mary-Rose Papandrea, *Student Speech Rights in the Digital Age*, 60 Fla. L. Rev. 1027 (2008); Nancy Willard, *School Response to Cyberbullying and Sexting: The Legal Challenges*, 2011 BYU Edu. & L.J. 75.

4. *A different (better?) approach?* Should a more targeted ban on particularly socially harmful kinds of uncivil communications be sustained as a justifiable limit on freedom of expression? Consider Canada's answer to this question, provided in the following case.

R. v. KEEGSTRA

[1990] 3 S.C.R. 697 (Can.)

DICKSON, C.J.

This appeal...raises a delicate and highly controversial issue as to the constitutional validity of s. 319(2) of the Criminal Code, R.S.C. 1985, c. C-46, a legislative provision which prohibits the wilful promotion of hatred, other than in private conversation, towards any section of the public distinguished by colour, race, religion or ethnic origin. In particular, the court must decide whether this section infringes the guarantee of freedom of expression found in s. 2(*b*) of the Canadian Charter of Rights and Freedoms in a manner that cannot be justified under s. 1 of the Charter. A secondary issue arises as to whether the presumption of innocence protected in the Charter's s. 11(*d*) is unjustifiably breached by reason of s. 319(3)(a) of the Code, which affords a defense of "truth" to the wilful promotion of hatred, but only where the accused proves the truth of the communicated statements on the balance of probabilities.

Mr. James Keegstra was a high school teacher in Eckville, Alberta, from the early 1970s until his dismissal in 1982. In 1984 Mr. Keegstra was charged under s. 319(2) (then s. 281.2(2)) of the Criminal Code with unlawfully promoting hatred against an identifiable group by communicating anti-semitic statements to his students. He was convicted by a jury in a trial before McKenzie J. of the Alberta Court of the Queen's Bench.

Mr. Keegstra's teachings attributed various evil qualities to Jews. He thus described Jews to his pupils as "treacherous," "subversive," "sadistic," "money-loving," "power hungry" and "child killers." He taught his classes that Jewish people seek to destroy Christianity and are responsible for depressions, anarchy, chaos, wars and revolution. According to Mr. Keegstra, Jews "created the Holocaust to gain sympathy" and, in contrast to the open and honest Christians, were said to be deceptive, secretive and inherently evil. Mr. Keegstra expected his students to reproduce his teachings in class and on exams. If they failed to do so, their marks suffered. . . .

[After a trial, Keegstra was convicted of violating § 319(2). On appeal, however, the Alberta Court of Appeal unanimously voted to reverse Keesgra's conviction and invalidated § 319(2) on free speech grounds.]

[In relevant part, § 319(2) provides that:]

Every one who, by communicating statements, other than in private conversation, wilfully promotes hatred against any identifiable group is guilty of an indictable offence and is liable to imprisonment for a term not exceeding two years; or an offence punishable on summary conviction.

No person shall be convicted of an offence under subsection (2) if he establishes that the statements communicated were true; if, in good faith, he expressed or attempted to establish by argument an opinion on a religious subject; if the statements were relevant to any subject of public interest, the discussion of which was for the public benefit, and if on reasonable grounds he believed them to be true; or if, in good faith, he intended to point out, for the purpose of removal, matters producing or tending to produce feelings of hatred toward an identifiable group in Canada. No proceedings for an offence under subsection (2) shall be instituted without the consent of the Attorney General. . . .

In my view, through s. 319(2) Parliament seeks to prohibit communications which convey meaning, namely, those communications which are intended to promote hatred against identifiable groups. I thus find s. 319(2) to constitute an infringement of the freedom of expression guaranteed by s. 2(*b*) of the Charter. . . .

Though the language of s. 1 appears earlier in these reasons, it is appropriate to repeat its words:

> The Canadian Charter of Rights and Freedoms guarantees the rights and freedoms set out in it subject only to such reasonable limits prescribed by law as can be demonstrably justified in a free and democratic society. . . .

Having discussed the unique and unifying role of s. 1, I think it appropriate to address a tangential matter, yet one nonetheless crucial to the disposition of this appeal: the relationship between Canadian and American approaches to the constitutional protection of free expression, most notably in the realm of hate propaganda. Those who attack the constitutionality of s. 319(2) draw heavily on the tenor of First Amendment jurisprudence in weighing the competing freedoms and interests in this appeal, a reliance which is understandable given the prevalent opinion that the criminalization of hate propaganda violates the Bill of Rights (see, e.g., L. Tribe, American Constitutional Law, 2nd ed. (1988), at p. 861, n. 2; K. Greenawalt, "Insults and Epithets: Are They Protected Speech?" (1990), 42 Rutgers L. Rev. 287, at p. 304). In response to the emphasis placed upon this jurisprudence, I find it helpful to summarize the American position and to determine the extent to which it should influence the s. 1 analysis in the circumstances of this appeal.

A myriad of sources—both judicial and academic—offer reviews of First Amendment jurisprudence as it pertains to hate propaganda. Central to most discussions is the 1952 case of *Beauharnais v. Illinois*, 343 U.S. 250, where the Supreme Court of the United States upheld as constitutional a criminal statute forbidding certain types of group defamation. Though never overruled, *Beauharnais* appears to have been weakened by later pronouncements of the Supreme Court (see, e.g., *Garrison v. Louisiana*, 379 U.S. 64 (1964); *Ashton v. Kentucky*, 384 U.S. 195 (1966); *New York Times Co. v. Sullivan*, 376 U.S. 254 (1964); *Brandenburg v. Ohio*, 395 U.S. 444 (1969); and *Cohen v. California*, 403 U.S. 15 (1971)). The trend reflected in many of these pronouncements is to protect offensive, public invective as long as the speaker has not knowingly lied and there exists no clear and present danger of violence or insurrection. . . .

Canada and the United States are not alike in every way, nor have the documents entrenching human rights in our two countries arisen in the same context. It is only common sense to recognize that, just as similarities will justify borrowing from the American experience, differences may require that Canada's constitutional vision depart from that endorsed in the United States.

Having examined the American cases relevant to First Amendment jurisprudence and legislation criminalizing hate propaganda, I would be adverse to following too closely the line of argument that would overrule *Beauharnais* on the ground that incursions placed upon free expression are only justified where there is a clear and present danger of imminent breach of peace. Equally, I am unwilling to embrace various categorizations and guiding rules generated by American law without careful consideration of their appropriateness to Canadian constitutional theory. Though I have found the American experience tremendously helpful in coming to my own conclusions regarding this appeal, and by no means reject the whole of the First

Amendment doctrine, in a number of respects I am thus dubious as to the applicability of this doctrine in the context of a challenge to hate propaganda legislation.

First, it is not entirely clear that *Beauharnais* must conflict with existing First Amendment doctrine. Credible arguments have been made that later Supreme Court cases do not necessarily erode its legitimacy (see, e.g., Kenneth Lasson, "Racial Defamation as Free Speech: Abusing the First Amendment" (1985), 17 Colum. Human Rights L. Rev. 11). Indeed, there exists a growing body of academic writing in the United States which evinces a stronger focus upon the way in which hate propaganda can undermine the very values which free speech is said to protect. . . .

Second, the aspect of First Amendment doctrine most incompatible with s. 319(2), at least as that doctrine is described by those who would strike down the legislation, is its strong aversion to content-based regulation of expression. I am somewhat skeptical, however, as to whether this view of free speech in the United States is entirely accurate. Rather, in rejecting the extreme position that would provide an absolute guarantee of free speech in the Bill of Rights, the Supreme Court has developed a number of tests and theories by which protected speech can be identified and the legitimacy of government regulation assessed. Often required is a content-based categorization of the expression under examination. . . .

Third, applying the Charter to the legislation challenged in this appeal reveals important differences between Canadian and American constitutional perspectives. I have already discussed in some detail the special role of s. 1 in determining the protective scope of Charter rights and freedoms. Section 1 has no equivalent in the United States, a fact previously alluded to by this court in selectively utilizing American constitutional jurisprudence. Of course, American experience should never be rejected simply because the Charter contains a balancing provision, for it is well known that American courts have fashioned compromises between conflicting interests despite what appears to be the absolute guarantee of constitutional rights. Where s. 1 operates to accentuate a uniquely Canadian vision of a free and democratic society, however, we must not hesitate to depart from the path taken in the United States. Far from requiring a less solicitous protection of Charter rights and freedoms, such independence of vision protects these rights and freedoms in a different way. As will be seen below, in my view the international commitment to eradicate hate propaganda and, most importantly, the special role given equality and multiculturalism in the Canadian Constitution necessitate a departure from the view, reasonably prevalent in America at present, that the suppression of hate propaganda is incompatible with the guarantee of free expression (in support of this view, see the comments of Professors Kathleen Mahoney and Jamie Cameron in "The James McCormick Mitchell Lecture—Language as Violence v. Freedom of Expression: Canadian and American Perspectives on Group Defamation" (1988-89), 37 Buffalo L. Rev. 337, beginning at pp. 344 and 353 respectively).

In sum, there is much to be learned from First Amendment jurisprudence with regard to freedom of expression and hate propaganda. It would be rash, however, to see First Amendment doctrine as demanding the striking down of s. 319(2). Not only are the precedents somewhat mixed, but the relaxation of the prohibition against content-based regulation of expression in certain areas indicates that American courts are not loath to permit the suppression of ideas in some circumstances. Most importantly, the nature of the s. 1 test as applied in the context of a challenge to s. 319(2) may well demand a perspective particular to Canadian constitutional jurisprudence when weighing competing interests. If values fundamental to the

Canadian conception of a free and democratic society suggest an approach that denies hate propaganda the highest degree of constitutional protection, it is this approach which must be employed. . . .

In my opinion, it would be impossible to deny that Parliament's objective in enacting s. 319(2) is of the utmost importance. Parliament has recognized the substantial harm that can flow from hate propaganda, and in trying to prevent the pain suffered by target group members and to reduce racial, ethnic and religious tension in Canada has decided to suppress the wilful promotion of hatred against identifiable groups. The nature of Parliament's objective is supported not only by the work of numerous study groups but also by our collective historical knowledge of the potentially catastrophic effects of the promotion of hatred (*Jones*, [R. v. Jones, [1986] 2 S.C.R. 284], per La Forest J., at pp. 299-300). Additionally, the international commitment to eradicate hate propaganda and the stress placed upon equality and multiculturalism in the Charter strongly buttress the importance of this objective. I consequently find that the first part of the test under s. 1 of the Charter is easily satisfied and that a powerfully convincing legislative objective exists such as to justify some limit on freedom of expression. . . .

The suppression of hate propaganda undeniably muzzles the participation of a few individuals in the democratic process, and hence detracts somewhat from free expression values, but the degree of this limitation is not substantial. I am aware that the use of strong language in political and social debate—indeed, perhaps even language intended to promote hatred—is an unavoidable part of the democratic process. Moreover, I recognize that hate propaganda is expression of a type which would generally be categorized as "political," thus putatively placing it at the very heart of the principle extolling freedom of expression as vital to the democratic process. Nonetheless, expression can work to undermine our commitment to democracy where employed to propagate ideas anathemic to democratic values. Hate propaganda works in just such a way, arguing as it does for a society in which the democratic process is subverted and individuals are denied respect and dignity simply because of racial or religious characteristics. This brand of expressive activity is thus wholly inimical to the democratic aspirations of the free expression guarantee.

Indeed, one may quite plausibly contend that it is through rejecting hate propaganda that the state can best encourage the protection of values central to freedom of expression, while simultaneously demonstrating dislike for the vision forwarded by hate-mongers. In this regard, the reaction to various types of expression by a democratic government may be perceived as meaningful expression on behalf of the vast majority of citizens. I do not wish to be construed as saying that an infringement of s. 2(*b*) can be justified under s. 1 merely because it is the product of a democratic process; the Charter will not permit even the democratically elected legislature to restrict the rights and freedoms crucial to a free and democratic society. What I do wish to emphasize, however, is that one must be careful not to accept blindly that the suppression of expression must always and unremittingly detract from values central to freedom of expression (Lee C. Bollinger, The Tolerant Society: Freedom of Speech and Extremist Speech in America (1986), at pp. 87-93).

I am very reluctant to attach anything but the highest importance to expression relevant to political matters. But given the unparalleled vigour with which hate propaganda repudiates and undermines democratic values, and in particular its condemnation of the view that all citizens need be treated with equal respect and dignity so as to make participation in the political process meaningful, I am unable to see the protection of such expression as integral to the democratic ideal so central to the s. 2(*b*) rationale. Together with my comments as to the tenuous link between communications covered by s. 319(2) and other values at the core of the free expression guarantee, this conclusion leads me to disagree with the opinion of McLachlin J. that the expression at stake in this appeal mandates the most solicitous degree of constitutional protection. In my view, hate propaganda should not be accorded the greatest of weight in the s. 1 analysis.

[Chief Justice Dickson concludes that all of Section 1's requirements have been met and that Section 1 therefore saves § 319(2) from judicial invalidation on Charter grounds.]

I find that the infringement of the respondent's freedom of expression as guaranteed by s. 2(*b*) should be upheld as a reasonable limit prescribed by law in a free and democratic society. Furthering an immensely important objective and directed at expression distant from the core of free expression values, s. 319(2) satisfies each of the components of the proportionality inquiry. I thus disagree with the Alberta Court of Appeal's conclusion that this criminal prohibition of hate propaganda violates the Charter, and would allow the appeal in this respect. . . .

Insofar as its purpose is to prohibit the expression of certain meanings, s. 319(2) of the Criminal Code infringes the guarantee of freedom of expression found in s. 2(*b*) of the Charter. Given the importance of Parliament's purpose in preventing the dissemination of hate propaganda and the tenuous connection such expression has with s. 2(*b*) values, however, I have found the narrowly drawn parameters of s. 319(2) to be justifiable under s. 1. . . .

McLACHLIN, J. (dissenting):

The issue on this appeal is whether s. 319(2) and (3) of the Criminal Code, R.S.C. 1985, c. C-46, creating the offence of unlawfully promoting hatred, should be struck down on the ground that they infringe the guarantees of free expression and the presumption of innocence embodied in the Canadian Charter of Rights and Freedoms.

The framers of the Charter recognized both the fundamental nature of freedom of expression and the necessity of sometimes limiting it where the risks it poses are too great for society to tolerate. Its importance is reflected in the broad and untrammeled definition of expression embodied in s. 2(*b*). The guarantee of free expression is not internally limited as are certain other Charter rights (e.g., s. 8 of the Charter) or as are the equivalent guarantees in the European Convention for the Protection of Human Rights and Fundamental Freedoms, 213 U.N.T.S. 221 (1950), and the International Covenant on Civil and Political Rights, 999 U.N.T.S. 171 (1966). The guarantees of free expression in those documents explicitly permit a wide variety of limitations on free expression—limitations which the person asserting the right of free expression must observe. By contrast, the Canadian guarantee of free expression is more comprehensive. The provision is a very broad guarantee, and all expression is prima facie protected. Any infringement must be justified by the state under s. 1. Moreover, as will be observed *infra*, freedom of expression had achieved a near-constitutional status in Canada long before its specific entrenchment by the Charter. All this suggests that the framers of the Charter envisaged freedom of expression as a comprehensive, fundamental right of great importance.

At the same time, the Charter permits freedom of speech to be restricted by law where this is justified by the need to protect more important countervailing values. Thus the broad guarantee of freedom of expression in s. 2(*b*) of the Charter is made subject to s. 1 which permits such reasonable limitations on the right as may be justified in a free and democratic society. . . .

The objective of s. 319(2) of the Criminal Code is to prevent the promotion of hatred toward identifiable groups within our society. As the Attorney General of Canada puts it, the objective of the legislation is, "among other things, to protect racial, religious and other groups from the wilful promotion of hatred against them, to prevent the spread of hatred and the breakdown of racial and social harmony," and "to prevent the destruction of our multicultural society." These aims are subsumed in the twin values of social harmony and individual dignity. . . .

Given the problem of racial and religious prejudice in this country, I am satisfied that the objective of the legislation is of sufficient gravity to be capable of justifying limitations on constitutionally protected rights and freedoms. . . .

[Even so, Justice McLachlin found that Section 1 did not save § 319(2) because the provision] catches a broad range of speech and prohibits it in a broad manner, allowing only private conversations to escape scrutiny. Moreover, the process by which the prohibition is effected—the criminal law—is the severest our society can impose and is arguably unnecessary given the availability of alternative remedies. I conclude that the criminalization of hate statements does not impair free speech to the minimum extent permitted by its objectives.

. . . Viewed from the perspective of our society as a whole, the infringement of the guarantee of freedom of expression before this court is a serious one. Section 319(2) of the Criminal Code does not merely regulate the form or tone of expression—it strikes directly at its content and at the viewpoints of individuals. It strikes, moreover, at viewpoints in widely diverse domains, whether artistic, social or political. It is capable of catching not only statements like those at issue in this case, but works of art and the intemperate statement made in the heat of social controversy. While few may actually be prosecuted to conviction under s. 319(2), many fall within the shadow of its broad prohibition. These dangers are exacerbated by the fact that s. 319(2) applies to all public expression. In short, the limitation on freedom of expression created by s. 319(2) of the Criminal Code invokes all of the values upon which s. 2(*b*) of the Charter rests—the value of fostering a vibrant and creative society through the marketplace of ideas; the value of the vigorous and open debate essential to democratic government and preservation of our rights and freedoms; and the value of a society which fosters the self-actualization and freedom of its members. . . .

I turn then to the other side of the scale and the benefit to be gained by maintenance of the limitation on freedom of expression effected by s. 319(2) of the Criminal Code. As indicated earlier, there is no question but that the objectives which underlie this legislation are of a most worthy nature. Unfortunately, the claims of gains to be achieved at the cost of the infringement of free speech represented by s. 319(2) are tenuous. It is far from clear that the legislation does not promote the cause of hate-mongering extremists and hinder the possibility of voluntary amendment of conduct more than it discourages the spread of hate propaganda. Accepting the importance to our society of the goals of social harmony and individual dignity, of multiculturalism and equality, it remains difficult to see how s. 319(2) fosters them.

In my opinion, the result is clear. Any questionable benefit of the legislation is outweighed by the significant infringement on the constitutional guarantee of free expression effected by s. 319(2) of the Criminal Code. . . .

NOTES AND QUESTIONS

1. *Judicial deference to legislative judgments about the need to regulate hate speech.* The Supreme Court of Canada does not exclude hate speech from protection under section 2(b) of the Charter but appears more willing than the Supreme Court of the United States to credit legislative judgments that some speech imposes unreasonable social costs and, accordingly, may be suppressed. Of course, *Keegstra* could be seen as nothing more than a more permissive iteration of the approach reflected in *Hishon.* If advocacy or incitement to racial hatred is itself a social harm, like telemarketing fraud, gender discrimination in the workplace, or a true threat, why shouldn't government be permitted to regulate that harm?

2. *Rejecting the First Amendment's protection of hate speech.* Does the Supreme Court of Canada properly understand U.S. free speech law? If so, why does it reject the U.S. approach? In what respect is the U.S. approach found to be wanting?

3. *The U.S. approach to Keegstra's bad behavior.* Would Keegstra's behavior be lawful in the United States? Would he have kept his job as a public school teacher? Is the real question whether, in addition to losing his job, he should also go to jail? And, if Keegstra goes to jail, is he guilty of a thought crime, or rather some sort of misappropriation of a government trust?

4. *Speech versus conduct.* In the United States, although Keegstra could not be punished directly for his anti-Semitic speech activity, if he committed an independent criminal act, his sentence could be enhanced because of his ideological motivation for the criminal act. Consider the following case and then consider whether the U.S. and Canadian approaches are fundamentally inconsistent.

AN INTRODUCTORY NOTE TO MITCHELL *AND* BLACK

In R.A.V. v. City of St. Paul, 505 U.S. 377 (1992), the Supreme Court invalidated a local St. Paul, Minnesota, ordinance that prohibited verbal assaults based on, among other things, racial animus. Writing for a 5-4 majority, Justice Scalia explained that although fighting words were outside the scope of the Free Speech Clause's protection, and the Minnesota Supreme Court had limited the scope of the ordinance to fighting words, St. Paul nevertheless could not punish fighting words selectively based on the content or viewpoint of the message being conveyed. Justice Scalia found that limiting a prohibition on fighting words to those fighting words that cause alarm or resentment based on race constituted an impermissible form of both content and viewpoint discrimination. A broad reading of *R.A.V.* would seem to preclude similar policies that make adverse legal consequences turn on the expression of racist, sexist, homophobic, or religiously bigoted viewpoints. However, the Supreme Court has declined to extend *R.A.V.*'s reasoning to disallow enhanced penalties for otherwise unlawful behavior based on the identity of the victim and the defendant's intentional selection of the victim because of a characteristic such as race, gender, religion, or sexual orientation. *R.A.V.*, if read broadly, could have prohibited sentencing enhancements based on the victim's identity, if one viewed the victim's identity as a de facto proxy for particular ideological or political commitments. Under this view, the underlying crime constitutes a kind of expressive conduct, and the enhancement, by targeting the ideological or political motivation, punishes speech based on content and viewpoint. The argument, simply enough, would be that although government can punish an assault, it cannot punish a racist assault more severely because the enhanced penalty constitutes a kind of thought crime. On the other hand, the use of motive to enhance punishment is commonplace in the criminal law, and the punishment itself flows from the underlying crime, not from the ideology that gave rise to it. Moreover, the social effects of a hate crime might well be more severe on both the community and the victim than those of a random mugging. *Mitchell* addresses the scope of *R.A.V.*'s holding and, in an opinion authored by Chief Justice Rehnquist (who was part of the *R.A.V.* majority), distinguishes sentencing enhancements from crimes based directly on uttering racial threats. So, too, the Supreme Court has permitted punishment for expressive conduct that conveys a true threat—despite the potential chilling effect that permitting such prosecutions might create.

R.A.V. v. CITY OF ST. PAUL, MINNESOTA

505 U.S. 377 (1992)

Justice SCALIA delivered the opinion of the Court.

In the predawn hours of June 21, 1990, petitioner and several other teenagers allegedly assembled a crudely made cross by taping together broken chair legs. They then allegedly burned the cross inside the fenced yard of a black family that lived across the street from the house where petitioner was staying. Although this conduct could have been punished under any of a number of laws, one of the two provisions under which respondent city of St. Paul chose to charge petitioner (then a juvenile) was the St. Paul Bias-Motivated Crime Ordinance, St. Paul, Minn., Legis. Code § 292.02 (1990), which provides:

> Whoever places on public or private property a symbol, object, appellation, characterization or graffiti, including, but not limited to, a burning cross or Nazi swastika, which one knows or has reasonable grounds to know arouses anger, alarm or resentment in others on the basis of race, color, creed, religion or gender commits disorderly conduct and shall be guilty of a misdemeanor.

Petitioner moved to dismiss this count on the ground that the St. Paul ordinance was substantially overbroad and impermissibly content based and therefore facially invalid under the First Amendment. The trial court granted this motion, but the Minnesota Supreme Court reversed. That court rejected petitioner's overbreadth claim because, as construed in prior Minnesota cases, the modifying phrase "arouses anger, alarm or resentment in others" limited the reach of the ordinance to conduct that amounts to "fighting words," *i.e.,* "conduct that itself inflicts injury or tends to incite immediate violence . . . ," . . . and therefore the ordinance reached only expression "that the first amendment does not protect." The court also concluded that the ordinance was not impermissibly content based because, in its view, "the ordinance is a narrowly tailored means toward accomplishing the compelling governmental interest in protecting the community against bias-motivated threats to public safety and order." . . .

I

. . . [W]e accept the Minnesota Supreme Court's authoritative statement that the ordinance reaches only those expressions that constitute "fighting words" within the meaning of *Chaplinsky*. Petitioner and his *amici* urge us to modify the scope of the *Chaplinsky* formulation, thereby invalidating the ordinance as "substantially overbroad[.]" We find it unnecessary to consider this issue. Assuming, *arguendo*, that all of the expression reached by the ordinance is proscribable under the "fighting words" doctrine, we nonetheless conclude that the ordinance is facially unconstitutional in that it prohibits otherwise permitted speech solely on the basis of the subjects the speech addresses.

The First Amendment generally prevents government from proscribing speech . . . . because of disapproval of the ideas expressed. Content-based regulations are presumptively invalid. . . . From 1791 to the present, however, our society, like other free but civilized societies, has permitted restrictions upon the content of speech in a few limited areas, which are "of such slight social value as a step to truth that any benefit that may be derived from them is clearly outweighed by the social interest in order and morality." *Chaplinsky*. . . .

We have sometimes said that these categories of expression are "not within the area of constitutionally protected speech[.]". . . . Such statements must be taken in context, however[.]. . . . What they mean is that these areas of speech can, consistently with the First Amendment, be regulated *because of their constitutionally proscribable content* (obscenity, defamation, etc.)—not that they are categories of speech entirely invisible to the Constitution, so that they may be made the vehicles for content discrimination unrelated to their distinctively proscribable content. Thus, the government may proscribe libel; but it may not make the further content discrimination of proscribing *only* libel critical of the government. . . .

Our cases surely do not establish the proposition that the First Amendment imposes no obstacle whatsoever to regulation of particular instances of such proscribable expression, so that the government "may regulate [them] freely." . . . That would mean that a city council could enact an ordinance prohibiting only those legally obscene works that contain criticism of the city government or, indeed, that do not include endorsement of the city government. Such a simplistic, all-or-nothing-at-all approach to First Amendment protection is at odds with common sense and with our jurisprudence as well. It is not true that "fighting words" have at most a "*de minimis* " expressive content, or that their content is *in all respects* "worthless and undeserving of constitutional protection"; sometimes they are quite expressive indeed. We have not said that they constitute "*no* part of the expression of ideas," but only that they constitute "no *essential* part of any exposition of ideas." *Chaplinsky*. . . .

[T]he exclusion of "fighting words" from the scope of the First Amendment simply means that, for purposes of that Amendment, the unprotected features of the words are, despite their verbal character, essentially a "nonspeech" element of communication. Fighting words are thus analogous to a noisy sound truck. . . . [B]oth can be used to convey an idea; but neither has, in and of itself, a claim upon the First Amendment. As with the sound truck, however, so also with fighting words: The government may not regulate use based on hostility—or favoritism—towards the underlying message expressed.

Even the prohibition against content discrimination . . . is not absolute. It applies differently in the context of proscribable speech than in the area of fully protected speech. The rationale of the general prohibition, after all, is that content discrimination "raises the specter that the Government may effectively drive certain ideas or viewpoints from the marketplace." . . . But content discrimination among various instances of a class of proscribable speech often does not pose this threat.

When the basis for the content discrimination consists entirely of the very reason the entire class of speech at issue is proscribable, no significant danger of idea or viewpoint discrimination exists. Such a reason, having been adjudged neutral enough to support exclusion of the entire class of speech from First Amendment protection, is also neutral enough to form the basis of distinction within the class. . . . [T]he Federal Government can criminalize only those threats of violence that are directed against the President . . . since the reasons why threats of violence are outside the First Amendment (protecting individuals from the fear of violence, from the disruption that fear engenders, and from the possibility that the threatened violence will occur) have special force when applied to the person of the President. . . . But the Federal Government may not criminalize only those threats against the President that mention his policy on aid to inner cities. . . .

II

Applying these principles to the St. Paul ordinance, we conclude that, even as narrowly construed by the Minnesota Supreme Court, the ordinance is facially unconstitutional. Although the phrase in the ordinance, "arouses anger, alarm or resentment in others," has been limited by the Minnesota Supreme Court's construction to reach only those symbols or displays that amount to "fighting words," the remaining, unmodified terms make clear that the ordinance applies only to "fighting words" that insult, or provoke violence, "on the basis of race, color, creed, religion or gender." Displays containing abusive invective, no matter how vicious or severe, are permissible unless they are addressed to one of the specified disfavored topics. Those who wish to use "fighting words" in connection with other ideas—to express hostility, for example, on the basis of political affiliation, union membership, or homosexuality—are not covered. The First Amendment does not permit St. Paul to impose special prohibitions on those speakers who express views on disfavored subjects. . . .

In its practical operation, moreover, the ordinance goes even beyond mere content discrimination, to actual viewpoint discrimination. Displays containing some words—odious racial epithets, for example—would be prohibited to proponents of all views. But "fighting words" that do not themselves invoke race, color, creed, religion, or gender—aspersions upon a person's mother, for example—would seemingly be usable *ad libitum* in the placards of those arguing *in favor* of racial, color, etc., tolerance and equality, but could not be used by those speakers' opponents. One could hold up a sign saying, for example, that all "anti-Catholic bigots" are misbegotten; but not that all "papists" are, for that would insult and provoke violence "on the basis of religion." St. Paul has no such authority to license one side of a debate to fight freestyle, while requiring the other to follow Marquis of Queensberry rules. . . .

The content-based discrimination reflected in the St. Paul ordinance . . . does not fall within the exception for content discrimination based on the very reasons why the particular class of speech at issue (here, fighting words) is proscribable. . . . [T]he reason why fighting words are categorically excluded from the protection of the First Amendment is not that their content communicates any particular idea, but that their content embodies a particularly intolerable (and socially unnecessary) *mode* of expressing *whatever* idea the speaker wishes to convey. St. Paul has not singled out an especially offensive mode of expression—it has not, for example, selected for prohibition only those fighting words that communicate ideas in a threatening (as opposed to a merely obnoxious) manner. Rather, it has proscribed fighting words of whatever manner that communicate messages of racial, gender, or religious intolerance. Selectivity of this sort creates the possibility that the city is seeking to handicap the expression of particular ideas. That possibility would alone be enough to render the ordinance presumptively invalid, but St. Paul's comments and concessions in this case elevate the possibility to a certainty. . . .

Finally, . . . even if the ordinance regulates expression based on hostility towards its protected ideological content, [St. Paul asserts that] this discrimination is nonetheless justified because it is narrowly tailored to serve compelling state interests. Specifically, [it asserts] that the ordinance helps to ensure the basic human rights of members of groups that have historically been subjected to discrimination, including the right of such group members to live in peace where they wish. We do not doubt that these interests are compelling, and that the ordinance can be said to promote them. But the "danger of censorship" presented by a facially content-based statute . . . requires that that weapon be employed only where it is "*necessary* to serve the asserted [compelling] interest." . . .

The existence of adequate content-neutral alternatives thus "undercut[s] significantly" any defense of such a statute, . . . casting considerable doubt on the government's protestations that "the asserted justification is in fact an accurate description of the purpose and effect of the law." . . . The dispositive question in this case, therefore, is whether content discrimination is reasonably necessary to achieve St. Paul's compelling interests; it plainly is not. An ordinance not limited to the favored topics, for example, would have precisely the same beneficial effect. In fact the only interest distinctively served by the content limitation is that of displaying the city council's special hostility towards the particular biases thus singled out. That is precisely what the First Amendment forbids. . . .

Let there be no mistake about our belief that burning a cross in someone's front yard is reprehensible. But St. Paul has sufficient means at its disposal to prevent such behavior without adding the First Amendment to the fire.

The judgment of the Minnesota Supreme Court is reversed, and the case is remanded for proceedings not inconsistent with this opinion.

It is so ordered.

Justice WHITE, with whom Justice BLACKMUN and Justice O'CONNOR join, and with whom Justice STEVENS joins . . . concurring in the judgment.

I agree with the majority that the judgment of the Minnesota Supreme Court should be reversed. However, our agreement ends there. . . .

Although I disagree with the Court's analysis, I do agree with its conclusion: The St. Paul ordinance is unconstitutional. However, I would decide the case on overbreadth grounds. . . .   Although the ordinance reaches conduct that is unprotected, it also makes criminal expressive conduct that causes only hurt feelings, offense, or resentment, and is protected by the First Amendment. . . . The ordinance is therefore fatally overbroad and invalid on its face . . .

[Justice BLACKMUN'S opinion concurring in the judgment is omitted.]

Justice STEVENS, with whom Justice WHITE and Justice BLACKMUN join . . . concurring in the judgment.

. . . I am . . . troubled by . . . [the Court's] conclusion that the St. Paul ordinance is an unconstitutional content-based regulation of speech. Drawing on broadly worded dicta, the Court establishes a near-absolute ban on content-based regulations of expression and holds that the First Amendment prohibits the regulation of fighting words by subject matter. Thus, while the Court rejects the "all-or-nothing-at-all" nature of [its earlier categorical approach to low value speech], it promptly embraces an absolutism of its own: Within a particular "proscribable" category of expression, the Court holds, a government must either proscribe *all* speech or no speech at all. This aspect of the Court's ruling fundamentally misunderstands the role and constitutional status of content-based regulations on speech, conflicts with the very nature of First Amendment jurisprudence, and disrupts well-settled principles of First Amendment law. . . .

. . . [I] believe our decisions establish a more complex and subtle analysis, one that considers the content and context of the regulated speech, and the nature and scope of the restriction on speech. Applying this analysis and assuming, *arguendo*, (as the Court does) that the St. Paul ordinance is *not* overbroad, I conclude that such a selective, subject-matter regulation on proscribable speech is constitutional. . . .

Contrary to the suggestion of the majority, the St. Paul ordinance does *not* regulate expression based on viewpoint. . . . The St. Paul ordinance is evenhanded. In a battle between advocates of tolerance and advocates of intolerance, the ordinance does not prevent either side from hurling fighting words at the other on the basis of their conflicting ideas, but it does bar *both* sides from hurling such words on the basis of the target's "race, color, creed, religion or gender." To extend the Court's pugilistic metaphor, the St. Paul ordinance simply bans punches "below the belt"— *by either party*. It does not, therefore, favor one side of any debate. . . .

Taken together, these several considerations persuade me that the St. Paul ordinance is not an unconstitutional content-based regulation of speech. Thus, were the ordinance not overbroad, I would vote to uphold it.

NOTES AND QUESTIONS

1. *Targeted versus generic proscriptions against fighting words.* Is it ironic that the logic of Justice Scalia's position would require St. Paul to ban *more* speech rather than less speech? An ordinance that banned fighting words generically would be a permissible form of content discrimination. Justice Scalia, however, views the government's motive in banning only *some* fighting words as constitutionally problematic—a form of both content and viewpoint discrimination. Justice Stevens, on the other hand, seems to believe that banning only those fighting words that constitute a form of hate speech is not inconsistent with the First Amendment. Who has the better view? Why?

2. *Content discrimination within a category of unprotected speech.* What purpose does the Court's prohibition against content discrimination within categories of unprotected speech serve? Does it protect against distortion of public debate or possible illegitimate government purposes? Did the St. Paul ordinance pose either of these dangers? *See* Elena Kagan, *Private Speech, Public Purpose: The Role of Governmental Motive in First Amendment Doctrine*, 63 U. Chi. L. Rev. 413, 418-423 (1996).

3. *Justice Stevens's "harm" rationale.* Justice Stevens suggests that the *R.A.V.* "ordinance regulate[d] speech not on the basis of its subject matter or the viewpoint expressed, but rather on the basis of the *harm* the speech causes." Does he present a viable alternative to the current approach to content-based regulations? Do racist, sexist, homophobic, or religiously-bigoted fighting words cause more social harm than other kinds of fighting words? If this is true, does it justify permitting government to regulate fighting words selectively? Consider carefully the Supreme Court's approach in the next principal case and whether there is a principled distinction between criminalizing speech directly or enhancing a defendant's sentence if he commits a crime motivated by a form of social bias.

4. *Viewpoint versus subject-matter?* Was the *R.A.V.* ordinance viewpoint-based as Justice Scalia claimed, or was it merely subject-matter based, as Justice Stevens claimed? Consider the following arguments:

> [The *R.A.V.* ordinance did] not draw a line between prohibited and permitted points of view. . . . [Rather,] antiwhite and antiblack statements are [treated alike]. In this respect, the law is content-based but viewpoint-neutral. [It] has regulated on the basis of subjects for discussion but not on the basis of viewpoint. . . . As a class, subject-matter restrictions [occupy] a point somewhere between viewpoint-based restrictions and content-neutral ones. [A] subject-matter restriction on unprotected speech should probably be upheld if the legislature can plausibly argue that it is counteracting harms rather than ideas. [This standard is easily satisfied in *R.A.V.* because racially hateful fighting words have] especially severe social consequences, [and there] is nothing partisan or illegitimate in recognizing that distinctive harms are produced by this unusual class of fighting words.

Cass R. Sunstein, *Democracy and the Problem of Free Speech* 188-193 (1993).

> Viewed purely on its face, the St. Paul ordinance, as construed by the Minnesota Supreme Court, appears to discriminate only on the basis of subject matter. . . . Beyond the question of facial discrimination, however, lurked another issue: Did the statute discriminate in its operation on the basis of viewpoint? . . . The St. Paul ordinance, it is true, handicaps both sides (and therefore neither side) when Jews and Catholics, whites and blacks scream slurs based on religion or race at each other. But surely race-based fighting words occur . . . in something other than this double-barreled context. In most instances, racists use race-based fighting words, and racists usually do not assail only each other. When the dispute is of this kind, the government effectively favors a side in barring only race-based fighting words.

See Elena Kagan, *The Changing Faces of First Amendment Neutrality: R.A.V. v. St. Paul, Rust v. Sullivan, and the Problem of Content-Based Underinclusion,* 1992 Sup. Ct. Rev. 29, 70-71.

WISCONSIN v. MITCHELL

508 U.S. 476 (1993)

Chief Justice REHNQUIST delivered the opinion of the Court.

Respondent Todd Mitchell's sentence for aggravated battery was enhanced because he intentionally selected his victim on account of the victim's race. The question presented in this case is whether this penalty enhancement is prohibited by the First and Fourteenth Amendments. We hold that it is not.

On the evening of October 7, 1989, a group of young black men and boys, including Mitchell, gathered at an apartment complex in Kenosha, Wisconsin. Several members of the group discussed a scene from the motion picture "Mississippi Burning," in which a white man beat a young black boy who was praying. The group moved outside and Mitchell asked them: "'Do you all feel hyped up to move on some white people?'" Shortly thereafter, a young white boy approached the group on the opposite side of the street where they were standing. As the boy walked by, Mitchell said: "'You all want to fuck somebody up? There goes a white boy; go get him.'" Mitchell counted to three and pointed in the boy's direction. The group ran toward the boy, beat him severely, and stole his tennis shoes. The boy was rendered unconscious and remained in a coma for four days.

After a jury trial in the Circuit Court for Kenosha County, Mitchell was convicted of aggravated battery. That offense ordinarily carries a maximum sentence of two years' imprisonment. But because the jury found that Mitchell had intentionally selected his victim because of the boy's race, the maximum sentence for Mitchell's offense was increased to seven years under § 939.645. That provision enhances the maximum penalty for an offense whenever the defendant "[i]ntentionally selects the person against whom the crime . . . is committed . . . because of the race, religion, color, disability, sexual orientation, national origin or ancestry of that person. . . ." § 939.645(1)(b). The Circuit Court sentenced Mitchell to four years' imprisonment for the aggravated battery.

Mitchell unsuccessfully sought postconviction relief in the Circuit Court. Then he appealed his conviction and sentence, challenging the constitutionality of Wisconsin's penalty-enhancement provision on First Amendment grounds. The Wisconsin Court of Appeals rejected Mitchell's challenge, but the Wisconsin Supreme Court reversed. The Supreme Court held that the statute "violates the First Amendment directly by punishing what the legislature has deemed to be offensive thought." It rejected the State's contention "that the statute punishes only the 'conduct' of intentional selection of a victim." . . . [The Wisconsin Supreme Court reasoned that] under *R.A.V. v. St. Paul*, 505 U.S. 377 (1992), "the Wisconsin legislature cannot criminalize bigoted thought with which it disagrees." . . .

We granted certiorari because of the importance of the question presented and the existence of a conflict of authority among state high courts on the constitutionality of statutes similar to Wisconsin's penalty-enhancement provision, 506 U.S. 1033 (1992). We reverse. . . .

The State argues that the statute does not punish bigoted thought, as the Supreme Court of Wisconsin said, but instead punishes only conduct. While this argument is literally correct, it does not dispose of Mitchell's First Amendment challenge. To be sure, our cases reject the "view that an apparently limitless variety of conduct can be labeled 'speech' whenever the person engaging in the conduct intends thereby to express an idea." *United States v. O'Brien*, 391 U.S. 367, 376 (1968). Thus a physical assault is not by any stretch of the imagination expressive conduct protected by the First Amendment. See *Roberts v. United States Jaycees*, 468 U.S. 609, 628 (1984) ("[V]iolence or other types of potentially expressive activities that produce special harms distinct from their communicative impact . . . are entitled to no constitutional protection"); *NAACP v. Claiborne Hardware Co.*, 458 U.S. 886, 916 (1982) ("The First Amendment does not protect violence").

But the fact remains that under the Wisconsin statute the same criminal conduct may be more heavily punished if the victim is selected because of his race or other protected status than if no such motive obtained. Thus, although the statute punishes criminal conduct, it enhances the maximum penalty for conduct motivated by a discriminatory point of view more severely than the same conduct engaged in for some other reason or for no reason at all. Because the only reason for the enhancement is the defendant's discriminatory motive for selecting his victim, Mitchell argues (and the Wisconsin Supreme Court held) that the statute violates the First Amendment by punishing offenders' bigoted beliefs.

Traditionally, sentencing judges have considered a wide variety of factors in addition to evidence bearing on guilt in determining what sentence to impose on a convicted defendant. The defendant's motive for committing the offense is one important factor. Thus, in many states the commission of a murder, or other capital offense, for pecuniary gain is a separate aggravating circumstance under the capital sentencing statute. But it is equally true that a defendant's abstract beliefs, however obnoxious to most people, may not be taken into consideration by a sentencing judge. *Dawson v. Delaware*, 503 U.S. 159 (1992). In *Dawson*, the State introduced evidence at a capital sentencing hearing that the defendant was a member of a white supremacist prison gang. Because "the evidence proved nothing more than [the defendant's] abstract beliefs," we held that its admission violated the defendant's First Amendment rights. *Id.*, at 167. In so holding, however, we emphasized that "the Constitution does not erect a *per se* barrier to the admission of evidence concerning one's beliefs and associations at sentencing simply because those beliefs and associations are protected by the First Amendment." *Id.* at 165. Thus, in *Barclay v. Florida*, 463 U.S. 939 (1983) (plurality opinion), we allowed the sentencing judge to take into account the defendant's racial animus towards his victim. The evidence in that case showed that the defendant's membership in the Black Liberation Army and desire to provoke a "race war" were related to the murder of a white man for which he was convicted. See *id.*, at 942-944. Because "the elements of racial hatred in [the] murder" were relevant to several aggravating factors, we held the trial judge permissibly took this evidence into account in sentencing the defendant to death. *Id.*, at 949, and n.7. . . .

Mitchell argues that the Wisconsin penalty-enhancement statute is invalid because it punishes the defendant's discriminatory motive, or reason, for acting. But motive plays the same role under the Wisconsin statute as it does under federal and state antidiscrimination laws, which we have previously upheld against constitutional challenge. . . .

Nothing in our decision last Term in *R.A.V.* compels a different result here. That case involved a First Amendment challenge to a municipal ordinance prohibiting the use of "'fighting words' that insult, or provoke violence, 'on the basis of race, color, creed, religion or gender.'" 505 U.S., at 391 (quoting St. Paul Bias-Motivated Crime Ordinance, St. Paul, Minn., Legis. Code § 292.02 (1990)). Because the ordinance only proscribed a class of "fighting words" deemed particularly offensive by the city—*i.e.*, those "that contain . . . messages of 'bias-motivated' hatred," 505 U.S. at 392—we held that it violated the rule against content-based discrimination. See *id.*, at 392-394. But whereas the ordinance struck down in *R. A. V.* was explicitly directed at expression (*i.e.*, "speech" or "messages"), *id.*, at 392, the statute in this case is aimed at conduct unprotected by the First Amendment.

Moreover, the Wisconsin statute singles out for enhancement bias-inspired conduct because this conduct is thought to inflict greater individual and societal harm. For example, according to the State and its *amici*, bias-motivated crimes are more likely to provoke retaliatory crimes, inflict distinct emotional harms on their victims, and incite community unrest. The State's desire to redress these perceived harms provides an adequate explanation for its penalty-enhancement provision over and above mere disagreement with offenders' beliefs or biases. . . .

For the foregoing reasons, we hold that Mitchell's First Amendment rights were not violated by the application of the Wisconsin penalty-enhancement provision in sentencing him. The judgment of the Supreme Court of Wisconsin is therefore reversed, and the case is remanded for further proceedings not inconsistent with this opinion.

It is so ordered.

NOTES AND QUESTIONS

1. *Reconciling* Mitchell *and* R.A.V. When one reads *Mitchell* in conjunction with *R.A.V.*, the resulting rule appears to be that although government cannot punish hate speech directly (as was the case in *Keegstra*), government may punish otherwise unlawful conduct more severely when the subjective motive for the crime involves animus based on race, gender, religion, or sexual orientation (that is, viewpoint-based considerations). This approach seems to track a widely shared cultural belief that some motives are more blameworthy than others because they impose higher social costs. For example, the *Washington Post* has opined that "crimes that target someone because of his or her race or sexual orientation are more than an offense against that individual. They are crimes that terrorize whole communities." *Protection from Hate*, WASH. POST, May 14, 2007, at A14.

2. *Sentencing and judicial discretion to consider myriad factors.* Speaking for a unanimous court, Chief Justice Rehnquist justifies this rule under the theory that sentencing, as an historical matter, has always taken into account a wide variety of factors, including the social significance of the crime. Is this a sufficient response to the objection that punishing one crime more harshly because of an ideological or political motive violates the otherwise categorical rule against viewpoint discrimination? If person A physically attacks person B because he hates minorities and person B is a minority, then an enhanced sentence could apply. If person A attacks person B because person B is a racist, no enhanced sentence would apply (because the crime would not have been motivated by racial bias but rather on ideological antipathy). Should the intervening cause of a criminal act disable the rule against viewpoint discrimination? Representative Doc Hastings (R-Washington), an opponent of expanding federal hate crime laws, has stated that "[i]f someone commits a crime, they should be punished for that crime. Period." Perhaps, though, the intervening cause should be considered if some motivations in fact impose greater social costs on the community.

3. *A speech versus conduct dichotomy?* If one considers *Mitchell* in conjunction with *Hishon* and *Meritor Savings Bank*, the proposition that *Beauharnais* is an entirely dead letter becomes highly questionable. Rather, the Supreme Court's approach seems to be more nuanced: Although government cannot adopt direct civility regulations, it can enforce civility norms indirectly incident to other (constitutional) regulatory objectives. Government cannot criminalize or create tort liability for the expression of sexist sentiments, but it can take the expression of those sentiments into account in assessing whether an employer maintains a workplace open to both men and women. Similarly, even if government cannot create civil or criminal liability for the expression of racist, sexist, or homophobic viewpoints, it may consider animus based on race, gender, or sexual orientation when determining an appropriate punishment for a crime. It would, therefore, be an overstatement to suggest that the Free Speech Clause categorically disables government from attempting to establish and enforce civility norms; rather, it would be more accurate to say that government cannot use speech regulations as a proxy for conduct regulations aimed at creating a free and equal society.

VIRGINIA v. BLACK

538 U.S. 343 (2003)

Justice O'CONNOR announced the judgment of the Court and delivered the opinion of the Court with respect to Parts I, II, and III, and an opinion with respect to Parts IV and V, in which THE CHIEF JUSTICE, Justice STEVENS, and Justice BREYER join.

I

[Barry Black, Richard Elliott, and Jonathan O'Mara were convicted of violating a Virginia statute, § 18.2-423, which provides: "It shall be unlawful for any person or persons, with the intent of intimidating any person or group of persons, to burn, or cause to be burned, a cross on the property of another, a highway or other public place. . . . Any such burning of a cross shall be prima facie evidence of an intent to intimidate a person or group of persons."

On August 22, 1998, Barry Black led a Ku Klux Klan rally on private property. During the rally, about 40 to 50 cars passed the site, and eight to ten houses were located in the vicinity of the rally. Witnesses claimed the speakers "talked real bad about the blacks and the Mexicans," and one speaker said that "he would love to take a .30/.30 and just randomly shoot the blacks." When the rally ended, the crowd circled around a 25-30 foot cross, which then was engulfed in flames. Black was charged with burning a cross with the intent of intimidating a person or group of persons, in violation of § 18.2-423. The trial court instructed the jury that "the burning of a cross by itself is sufficient evidence from which you may infer the required intent." The jury found Black guilty.

On May 2, 1998, Richard Elliott and Jonathan O'Mara attempted to burn a cross on the yard of James Jubilee, an African-American, who was Elliott's next-door neighbor. Elliott and O'Mara planted a cross on Jubilee's property and set it on fire. Their apparent motive was retaliation for Jubilee's complaints about their shooting in the backyard. Jubilee discovered the partially burned cross the next morning while pulling his car out of the driveway. After seeing the cross, Jubilee was "very nervous" because he "didn't know what would be the next phase," and because "a cross burned in your yard . . . tells you that it's just the first round." Prosecutors charged Elliott and O'Mara with attempted cross burning and conspiracy to commit cross burning. O'Mara pleaded guilty after reserving the right to challenge the constitutionality of the cross-burning statute. At Elliott's trial, . . . the court instructed the jury that the Commonwealth must prove that "the defendant intended to commit cross burning," that "the defendant did a direct act toward the commission of the cross burning," and that "the defendant had the intent of intimidating any person or group of persons." The court did not instruct the jury on the meaning of the word "intimidate," or on the prima facie evidence provision of § 18.2-423. The jury found Elliott guilty. After consolidating the cases, the Supreme Court of Virginia held the statute unconstitutional on its face because the statute was "analytically indistinguishable from the ordinance found unconstitutional in *R.A.V.*"]

II

[The Court examined at length the history of cross-burning, noting especially that "[b]urning a cross in the United States is inextricably intertwined with the history of the Ku Klux Klan" and had "been used to communicate both threats of violence and messages of shared ideology." The Klan often used such burnings as messages of intimidation or threats of impending violence. In effect, "[t]he burning cross became a symbol of the Klan itself and a central feature of Klan gatherings. . . . To this day, regardless of whether the message is a political one or whether the message is also meant to intimidate, the burning of the cross is a 'symbol of hate.'" The majority concluded this discussion noting that: "While cross burning sometimes carries no intimidating message, at other times the intimidating message is the *only* message conveyed. For example, when a cross burning is directed at a particular person not affiliated with the Klan, the burning cross often serves as a message of intimidation, designed to inspire in the victim a fear of bodily harm. . . . Indeed, as the cases of respondents Elliott and O'Mara indicate, individuals without Klan affiliation who wish to threaten or menace another person sometimes use cross burning because of this association between a burning cross and violence. In sum, while a burning cross does not inevitably convey a message of intimidation, often the cross burner intends that the recipients of the message fear for their lives. And when a cross burning is used to intimidate, few if any messages are more powerful."]

III

. . . [T]he First Amendment . . . permits a State to ban a "true threat." . . . "True threats" encompass those statements where the speaker means to communicate a serious expression of an intent to commit an act of unlawful violence to a particular individual or group of individuals. *See Watts; R.A.V.* The speaker need not actually intend to carry out the threat. Rather, a prohibition on true threats "protect[s] individuals from the fear of violence" and "from the disruption that fear engenders," in addition to protecting people "from the possibility that the threatened violence will occur." Intimidation in the constitutionally proscribable sense of the word is a type of true threat, where a speaker directs a threat to a person or group of persons with the intent of placing the victim in fear of bodily harm or death. . . .

. . . The First Amendment permits Virginia to outlaw cross burnings done with the intent to intimidate because burning a cross is a particularly virulent form of intimidation. Instead of prohibiting all intimidating messages, Virginia may choose to regulate this subset of intimidating messages in light of cross burning's long and pernicious history as a signal of impending violence. Thus, just as a State may regulate only that obscenity which is the most obscene due to its prurient content, so too may a State choose to prohibit only those forms of intimidation that are most likely to inspire fear of bodily harm. A ban on cross burning carried out with the intent to intimidate is fully consistent with our holding in *R.A.V.* and is proscribable under the First Amendment. . . .

IV

. . . The Supreme Court of Virginia has not ruled on the meaning of the prima facie evidence provision. It has, however, stated that "the act of burning a cross alone, with no evidence of intent to intimidate, will nonetheless suffice for arrest and prosecution and will insulate the Commonwealth from a motion to strike the evidence at the end of its case-in-chief." . . . The court in Barry Black's case instructed the jury that the provision means: "The burning of a cross, by itself, is sufficient evidence from which you may infer the required intent." . . .

The prima facie evidence provision, as interpreted by the jury instruction, renders the statute unconstitutional. . . . *Terminiello* (striking down an ambiguous statute on facial grounds based upon the instruction given to the jury). . . . As construed by the jury instruction, the prima facie provision strips away the very reason why a State may ban cross burning with the intent to intimidate. The prima facie evidence provision permits a jury to convict in every cross-burning case in which defendants exercise their constitutional right not to put on a defense. And even where a defendant like Black presents a defense, the prima facie evidence provision makes it more likely that the jury will find an intent to intimidate regardless of the particular facts of the case. The provision permits the Commonwealth to arrest, prosecute, and convict a person based solely on the fact of cross burning itself.

It is apparent that the provision as so interpreted "'would create an unacceptable risk of the suppression of ideas.'" . . . The act of burning a cross may mean that a person is engaging in constitutionally proscribable intimidation. But that same act may mean only that the person is engaged in core political speech. The prima facie evidence provision in this statute blurs the line between these two meanings of a burning cross. As interpreted by the jury instruction, the provision chills constitutionally protected political speech because of the possibility that the Commonwealth will prosecute—and potentially convict—somebody engaging only in lawful political speech at the core of what the First Amendment is designed to protect.

As the history of cross burning indicates, a burning cross is not always intended to intimidate. Rather, sometimes the cross burning is a statement of ideology, a symbol of group solidarity. It is a ritual used at Klan gatherings, and it is used to represent the Klan itself. Thus, "[b]urning a cross at a political rally would almost certainly be protected expression." . . . Cross burnings have appeared in movies such as Mississippi Burning, and in plays such as the stage adaptation of Sir Walter Scott's The Lady of the Lake.

The prima facie provision makes no effort to distinguish...between a cross burning done with the purpose of creating anger or resentment and a cross burning done with the purpose of threatening or intimidating a victim. . . . It may be true that a cross burning, even at a political rally, arouses a sense of anger or hatred among the vast majority of citizens who see a burning cross. But this sense of anger or hatred is not sufficient to ban all cross burnings. . . . The prima facie evidence provision in this case ignores all of the contextual factors that are necessary to decide whether a particular cross burning is intended to intimidate. The First Amendment does not permit such a shortcut. . . .

V

With respect to Barry Black, we agree with the Supreme Court of Virginia that his conviction cannot stand, and we affirm the judgment of the Supreme Court of Virginia. With respect to Elliott and O'Mara, we vacate the judgment of the Supreme Court of Virginia, and remand the case for further proceedings.

It is so ordered.

Justice SOUTER, with whom Justice KENNEDY and Justice GINSBURG join, concurring in the judgment in part and dissenting in part.

I agree with the majority that the Virginia statute makes a content-based distinction within the category of punishable intimidating or threatening expression, the very type of distinction we considered in *R.A.V.* I disagree that any exception should save Virginia's law from unconstitutionality under the holding in *R.A.V.* or any acceptable variation of it.

. . . . Because of the burning cross's extraordinary force as a method of intimidation, the *R.A.V.* exception most likely to cover the statute is the first of the three mentioned there, which the *R.A.V.* opinion called an exception for content discrimination on a basis that "consists entirely of the very reason the entire class of speech at issue is proscribable." This is the exception the majority speaks of here as covering statutes prohibiting "particularly virulent" proscribable expression. . . . The Court explained that when the subcategory is confined to the most obviously proscribable instances, "no significant danger of idea or viewpoint discrimination exists" and the explanation was rounded out with some illustrative examples. None of them, however, resembles the case before us.

. . . [W]hether or not the Court should conceive of exceptions to *R.A.V.*'s general rule in a more practical way, no content-based statute should survive even under a pragmatic recasting of *R.A.V.* without a high probability that no "official suppression of ideas is afoot," 505 U.S., at 390. I believe the prima facie evidence provision stands in the way of any finding of such a high probability here. . . .

[That provision's] primary effect is to skew jury deliberations toward conviction in cases where the evidence of intent to intimidate is relatively weak and arguably consistent with a solely ideological reason for burning. . . . One can tell the intimidating instance from the wholly ideological one only by reference to some further circumstance. In the real world . . . there will always be further circumstances, and the factfinder will always learn something more than the isolated fact of cross burning. Sometimes those circumstances will show an intent to intimidate, but sometimes they will be at least equivocal, as in cases where a white supremacist group burns a cross at an initiation ceremony or political rally visible to the public. In such a case, if the factfinder is aware of the prima facie evidence provision, as the jury was in respondent Black's case, the provision will have the practical effect of tilting the jury's thinking in favor of the prosecution. . . . The provision will thus tend to draw nonthreatening ideological expression within the ambit of the prohibition of intimidating expression. . . .

It is difficult to conceive of an intimidation case that could be easier to prove than one with cross burning, assuming any circumstances suggesting intimidation are present. The provision, apparently so unnecessary to legitimate prosecution of intimidation, is therefore quite enough to raise the question whether Virginia's content-based statute seeks more than mere protection against a virulent form of intimidation. . . .

I conclude that the statute under which all three of the respondents were prosecuted violates the First Amendment, since the statute's content-based distinction was invalid at the time of the charged activities, regardless of whether the prima facie evidence provision was given any effect in any respondent's individual case. . . . I would therefore affirm the judgment of the Supreme Court of Virginia vacating the respondents' convictions and dismissing the indictments. Accordingly, I concur in the Court's judgment as to respondent Black and dissent as to respondents Elliott and O'Mara.

Justice THOMAS, dissenting.

Although I agree with the majority's conclusion that it is constitutionally permissible to "ban . . . cross burning carried out with the intent to intimidate," . . . I believe that the majority errs in imputing an expressive component to the activity in question. . . . In my view, whatever expressive value cross burning has, the legislature simply wrote it out by banning only intimidating conduct undertaken by a particular means. A conclusion that the statute prohibiting cross burning with intent to intimidate sweeps beyond a prohibition on certain conduct into the zone of expression overlooks not only the words of the statute but also reality. . . .

Even assuming that the statute implicates the First Amendment, in my view, the fact that the statute permits a jury to draw an inference of intent to intimidate from the cross burning itself presents no constitutional problems. . . . The plurality fears the chill on expression because . . . the inference permits "the Commonwealth to arrest, prosecute and convict a person based solely on the fact of cross burning itself." . . . [But] Virginia law still requires the jury to find the existence of each element, including intent to intimidate, beyond a reasonable doubt. . . .

Because I would uphold the validity of this statute, I respectfully dissent.

[Justice Stevens's opinion concurring in the judgment is omitted.]

[Justice Scalia's concurring in part and dissenting in part of the judgment is omitted.]

NOTES AND QUESTIONS

1. *Is cross burning a per se threat?* Should the government, consistent with the First Amendment, be permitted to presume that *all* cross burnings convey an intent to intimidate or a "true threat? Even in the absence of any evidence—much less proof beyond a reasonable doubt—that a particular act of cross

burning was directed at a particular person or group? How do the Justices divide on this important question?

2. *True threats and offensive expressive conduct.* Is Justice O'Connor correct to observe (in dicta) that a state law applicable only to cross burnings intended to intimidate or threaten a specific person or group of persons would be consistent with the First Amendment? Or does Justice Ginsburg have the better view? Namely, that a generic criminal proscription against threats of violence is all that is required to punish cross burnings that constitute true threats? And that a targeted statute simply invites juries to engage in viewpoint discrimination? Justice Thomas, by way of contrast, argues that cross burnings are always and inherently threatening by their very nature—and are therefore specifically proscribable without violating the First Amendment. Which of these three approaches best accommodates the relevant social interests? Does the answer to this question depend on how one weighs the relative importance of the social interests at stake?

3. *Distinguishing between true threats and political beliefs.* Recall that under *United States v. Watts* (*supra* p. 70), a "true threat" is not protected speech and may be criminalized. On the other hand, ideologies that include abstract calls to violent revolution, such as Soviet-style communism, constitute protected speech—unless a specific call to violent action presents a clear and present danger of unlawful activity. *See* Brandenburg v. Ohio, *supra* p. 56.

4. *Reconciling* R.A.V., Mitchell, *and* Black. How do these three cases fit together? How far may the government go in using an ideological or political belief as a basis for imposing civil or criminal liability? Is the rule that although bigoted ideologies cannot themselves be directly proscribed, they may be *indirectly* punished when conjoined with otherwise constitutionally proscribable conduct? Notwithstanding any potential chilling effect on pure speech that might result? Is this a sensible accommodation of the relevant values? Beliefs as such are protected absolutely—but when actions are motivated by beliefs, and cause cognizable and particularized social harms because of the motivation, government may take the motive into account? Either by enhancing the punishment for a crime or creating a law targeted at a particular kind of true threat?

5. *The U.S. approach to mandatory civility rules is not widely shared.* U.S. constitutional law routinely privileges the protection of freedom of speech over other important human rights values—such as equality and multiculturalism. In so doing, the United States stands virtually alone among major western democracies with constitutional free speech protections in its categorical rejection of direct bans on hate speech. In other nations, including Canada, Germany, South Africa, and the United Kingdom, statutes prohibiting speech that advocates racial or religious hatred exist, and the local domestic courts view these enactments as fully consistent with a meaningful commitment to the freedom of expression. *See* Ronald J. Krotoszynski, Jr., *Privacy Revisited: A Global Perspective on the Right to Be Left Alone* 25-30, 151-160 (2016). What risks do these nations necessarily accept as a consequence of this approach? Conversely, what risks, if any, does the Supreme Court of the United States accept as a consequence of protecting hate speech?

THEORY-APPLIED PROBLEM

Consider the following three hypotheticals, and determine whether a state appellate court should overturn the conviction if the defendant raises a First Amendment argument on appeal. In particular, what specific facts and circumstances might lead a court to sustain, or reject, free speech objections to sanctions for the offensive speech?

1. While testifying in a criminal trial for fraud and forgery in a Missouri state trial court, defendant Robert Holman repeatedly drops the "f-bomb," in statements such as "Mother fuckin' fact—I want my mother fuckin' 40 acres. This is bullshit. You know you can't have me keep this man up there and shit like that. 12 mother fuckin' jurors and stuff." The trial judge instructs Holman to cease using unnecessary profanity in court and tells the court reporter to "cease transcribing Mr. Holman's expletives." The court warns Holman to stop using profanity while testifying, on pain of being found in contempt of court, removed from the stand, and jailed (for contempt, independent of the pending criminal charges against him). Holman says he understands, then continues using the f-bomb as if it were a punctuation mark. The trial judge finds Holman in contempt of court, orders him removed from the witness stand by the bailiff, and orders him jailed for 48 hours or until such time as he will cease using gratuitous profanity in his testimony. Holman appeals the contempt citation to the Missouri Court of Appeals, alleging a violation of his free speech rights. How should the appellate court rule?

2. Timothy Boomer, after his canoe capsizes on the Rifle River, in rural Arenac County, Michigan, unleashes a fusillade of profanity, including words such as "fucking faggots," "dirty motherfuckers," and "goddamn cocksuckers." Other nearby users of the Rifle River included Tammy Smith, her husband, and her five- and two-year-old children. In addition, two sheriff's deputies also hear the tirade and issue a citation to Boomer under a Michigan law that prohibits "any person" from using "any indecent, immoral, obscene, vulgar, or insulting language in the presence or hearing of any woman or child." Violations of section 337 of the Michigan Criminal Code constitute a simple misdemeanor, punishable by a jail term of up to 90 days and a fine up to $100. After a jury trial, Boomer is convicted of the violation, and the trial judge sentences Boomer to four days of community service and orders him to pay a fine of $75. Boomer files an appeal with the Michigan Court of Appeals. How should the appellate court rule?

3. In Rockbridge County High School, in Lexington, Virginia, Fred Jones (a white, eleventh-grade student) calls Michael Smith (a black, tenth-grade student) "a dirty, stupid nigger" during the public high school's lunch period. Smith does not immediately react to the slur and simply walks away from Jones. Immediately thereafter, Smith complains about the incident to the vice principal, Gladys Miller. Later that afternoon, Miller calls Jones into her office and asks whether he used the offensive language in question. When Jones confirms that he used the language, Miller immediately suspends Jones for ten school days under the Rockbridge County School Board's policy prohibiting the use of "offensive, degrading, or harassing language" on school property or at any school-sponsored events. Jones files a section 1983 action in the local federal district court,

challenging both his suspension and the Rockbridge County School Board's policy, at least as applied on these facts. How should the federal district court rule?

CHAPTER
11

The Regulation of Sexually Explicit Speech

TABLE OF CONTENTS

It is doubtful that James Madison, author of the Bill of Rights, would have anticipated the Free Speech Clause applying to pornographic videos featuring Pamela Lee Anderson or nude photographs of Burt Reynolds. Sexually explicit speech lacks any obvious nexus with the project of democratic self-government. Indeed, even if one broadens the democratic self-government theory to encompass scientific, artistic, or literary speech, it is difficult to see how dial-a-porn services fit within the expanded universe of speech necessary to enable citizens to be self-governing.

On the other hand, the Supreme Court's move toward a marketplace paradigm for protecting free speech raises a serious issue for targeted regulations of erotica. If commercial advertising has a strong First Amendment claim to be largely free of government regulation, why shouldn't the same be true for sexually graphic forms of art or literature? If the Free Speech Clause exists to facilitate and protect a free market for speech, how can one justify government regulations aimed at suppressing or proscribing porn? Moreover, if free speech is about facilitating personal autonomy, one could easily imagine a person having a stronger interest in pornography than in President Barack Obama's proposals for cap-and-trade legislation.

Should government have the ability to suppress speech that some within the community deem immoral or wicked? Some advocates of equal rights for women believe that pornography creates social conditions that make securing true equality with respect to gender a difficult, if not impossible, task. Even if community moral norms are not a sufficient basis for regulating erotica, are equality norms a more persuasive rationale for limiting or banning porn?

Even if one accepts the idea that sexually explicit speech has "low value" for First Amendment purposes, serious definitional difficulties exist in sorting out low-value "obscenity" from high-value "art." If *Harry Potter* star Daniel Radcliffe appears nude on stage and simulates sex in the play *Equus*, the probability of government efforts to suppress the performance is quite low. On the other hand, if Bambi grinds her hips while stark naked at the Kitty Kat Club, the probability of government efforts to suppress, if not ban, the performance is quite high. "[W]hile the entertainment afforded by a nude ballet at Lincoln Center to those who can pay the price may differ vastly in content (as viewed by judges) or in quality (as viewed by critics), it may not differ in substance from the dance viewed by the person who . . . wants some 'entertainment' with his beer or shot of rye." Salem Inn, Inc. v. Frank, 501 F.2d 18, 21 n.3 (2d Cir. 1974), *aff'd in part sub nom.* Doran v. Salem Inn, Inc., 422 U.S. 922 (1975).

Traditionally, "obscene" materials, like fighting words and libels, stood completely outside the scope of the Free Speech Clause. *See* Chaplinsky v. New Hampshire, 315 U.S. 568, 571-572 (1942). Over time, however, bans enforced against serious literary and artistic works with sexual themes (for example, D.H. Lawrence's *Lady Chatterley's Lover*) raised serious definitional questions for the Supreme Court. *See, e.g.,* Kingsley Intl. Pictures Corp. v. Regents, 360 U.S. 684 (1959) (holding protected a film version of *Lady Chatterley's Lover* and noting that the First Amendment "protects advocacy of the opinion that adultery may sometimes be proper, no less than advocacy of socialism or the single tax"). Would a passage or two in a novel, or a single scene in a movie, justify the complete criminalization of a film? How could judges properly determine when a particular book, magazine, or film crossed the line from the merely indecent to the shadowlands of the obscene?

In the nineteenth century, the British case Regina v. Hicklin, [1868] L.R. 3 Q.B. 360, influenced the development of U.S. obscenity law with its highly deferential standard for measuring government efforts to suppress erotica. Under the *Hicklin* test, government could proscribe material that "depraves and corrupts those whose minds are open to such immoral influences and into whose hands a publication of this sort might fall"—children, for example. *Id.* at 371. The test asked "whether the tendency of the matter charged as obscenity is to deprave and corrupt those whose minds are open to such immoral influences." *Id.* Materials meeting this standard could be regulated—even banned—as obscenity. The *Hicklin* test "came to stand for the double proposition that obscenity was to be measured by its effect on the most susceptible, and that obscenity of the work as a whole was to be judged by the effect of isolated passages." Laurence Tribe, *American Constitutional Law* § 12-16, at 906 (2d ed. 1988).

The Supreme Court rejected the *Hicklin* standard in Roth v. United States, 354 U.S. 476 (1957). *Roth* adopted as a standard for obscenity the following test:

> [S]ex and obscenity are not synonymous. Obscene material is material which deals with sex in a manner appealing to the prurient interest. The portrayal of sex, e.g., in art, literature, and scientific works, is not itself sufficient reason to deny material the constitutional protection of freedom of speech and press.

Id. at 487-488. Although the *Roth* Court held that "obscenity is not within the protection of constitutionally protected speech or press," *id.* at 485, it also held that "[a]ll ideas having even the slightest redeeming social importance—unorthodox ideas, controversial ideas, even ideas hateful to the prevailing climate of opinion— have the full protection of the guaranties, unless excludable because they encroach upon the limited area of more important interests," *id.* at 484.

Roth thus established a tension in the governing legal doctrine: Obscene materials lie outside the scope of the First Amendment, but ideas with "the slightest redeeming social importance" enjoy protection. How then should a court evaluate a pornographic film that opens with the tasteful recitation of a sonnet by Shakespeare?

Attempting to address this conflict nine years later in Memoirs v. Massachusetts, 383 U.S. 413, 418 (1966), the Supreme Court fashioned a three-part test for defining obscenity:

> [I]t must be established that (a) the dominant theme of the material taken as a whole appeals to the prurient interest in sex; (b) the material is patently offensive because it affronts contemporary community standards relating to the description or representation of sexual matters; and (c) the material is utterly without redeeming social value.

The problem with the *Memoirs* test, obviously enough, is the ease with which a commercial pornographer could meet the third prong of the test—the material had to be "utterly without redeeming social value" to constitute obscenity—which the addition of a sonnet or bit of free verse would defeat. Writing seven years later, Chief Justice Burger described this burden as "virtually impossible to discharge under our criminal standards of proof." Miller v. California, 413 U.S. 15, 22 (1973).

Following the effort to establish a standard in *Memoirs*, a year later the Supreme Court gave up its efforts to tinker with the test and simply reverted to issuing very short opinions summarily reversing certain obscenity convictions. The first of this line, Redrup v. New York, 386 U.S. 767, 770-771 (1967), made no attempt to articulate a standard of review and instead announced that a majority of the Justices did not find particular materials to be obscene (under whatever standard that each member of the majority felt should govern). From 1967 to 1973, the Supreme Court "Redrupped" obscenity convictions without attempting to articulate a governing standard of review for obscenity. Generally, the Justices and their clerks would gather in the Supreme Court basement to view the films under review, a process that several members of the Court felt undignified. For an amusing account of this practice, see Bob Woodward & Scott Armstrong, *The Brethren: Inside the Supreme Court* 192-194 (1979). Finally, in 1973, a working majority of the Court coalesced around a "new and improved" standard for defining "obscenity." As you read through these materials, you should consider whether *Miller* sufficiently resolves the conflicting objectives of protecting ideas absolutely while not protecting prurient content at all.

Even today, serious scholars question the ability of law enforcement officers and judges to discern "obscene" materials from legitimate works of art. Thus, *Miller* did not really solve the definitional problem that has plagued obscenity doctrine for decades. Moreover, even if one could define obscenity with perfect clarity, a serious question would exist about the legitimacy of the censorial project itself. Both content and viewpoint neutrality are central components of the Supreme Court's more general free speech jurisprudence—restrictions on obscenity are both content- and viewpoint-based. Moreover, to the extent that one believes in a free, relatively unregulated marketplace of ideas, why should government have the power to exorcise one particular set of wares from the market? The evidence that sexually explicit speech imposes greater social costs than other kinds of high-risk, low-value speech (for example, public calls for race wars or the extermination of persons belonging to a particular religion) is utterly lacking. Obscenity seems to have particular cultural importance (at least for the Supreme Court), but the notion that it presents specialized risks that justify regulations up to and including complete proscription is highly contestable.

A. LIMITATIONS ON THE TARGETED REGULATION OF SEXUALLY EXPLICIT MATERIALS

Miller provides the standard citation for the proposition that the federal and state governments may criminalize the distribution of obscene materials. *Miller* relies on a public morals theory of justification for suppressing sexually explicit speech. This is not the only basis on which one might attempt to support regulations of erotica: In Canada, the constitutional commitment to gender equality, rather than a concern about the debasing effects of smut, supports the regulation and proscription of "degrading" and "dehumanizing" forms of erotica. *See Butler, infra* page 571.

MILLER v. CALIFORNIA
413 U.S. 15 (1973)

BURGER, C.J., delivered the opinion of the Court.

This is one of a group of "obscenity-pornography" cases being reviewed by the Court in a re-examination of standards enunciated in earlier cases involving what Mr. Justice Harlan called "the intractable obscenity problem." *Interstate Circuit, Inc. v. Dallas*, 390 U.S. 676, 704 (1968) (concurring and dissenting).

Appellant conducted a mass mailing campaign to advertise the sale of illustrated books, euphemistically called "adult" material. After a jury trial, he was convicted of violating California Penal Code § 311.2(a), a misdemeanor, by knowingly distributing obscene matter, and the Appellate Department, Superior Court of California, County of Orange, summarily affirmed the judgment without opinion. Appellant's conviction was specifically based on his conduct in causing five unsolicited advertising brochures to be sent through the mail in an envelope addressed to a restaurant in Newport Beach, California. The envelope was opened by the manager of the restaurant and his mother. They had not requested the brochures; they complained to the police.

The brochures advertise four books entitled "Intercourse," "Man-Woman," "Sex Orgies Illustrated," and "An Illustrated History of Pornography," and a film entitled "Marital Intercourse." While the brochures contain some descriptive printed material, primarily they consist of pictures and drawings very explicitly depicting men and women in groups of two or more engaging in a variety of sexual activities, with genitals often prominently displayed.

This case involves the application of a State's criminal obscenity statute to a situation in which sexually explicit materials have been thrust by aggressive sales action upon unwilling recipients who had in no way indicated any desire to receive such materials. This Court has recognized that the States have a legitimate interest in prohibiting dissemination or exhibition of obscene material[2] when the mode of

---

[2] This Court has defined "obscene material" as "material which deals with sex in a manner appealing to prurient interest," but the *Roth* definition does not reflect the precise meaning of "obscene" as traditionally used in the English language. Derived from the Latin *obscaenus, ob*, to, plus *caenum*, filth, "obscene" is defined in the Webster's Third New International Dictionary (Unabridged 1969) as "1a: disgusting to the senses . . . b: grossly repugnant to the generally accepted notions of what is appropriate . . . 2: offensive or revolting as countering or violating some ideal or principle." The Oxford English Dictionary (1933 ed.) gives a similar definition,

dissemination carries with it a significant danger of offending the sensibilities of unwilling recipients or of exposure to juveniles. It is in this context that we are called on to define the standards which must be used to identify obscene material that a State may regulate without infringing on the First Amendment as applicable to the States through the Fourteenth Amendment. . . .

Apart from the initial formulation in the *Roth* case [requiring the government to show that erotica was "utterly without redeeming social importance" in order to prohibit distribution or possession of it], no majority of the Court has at any given time been able to agree on a standard to determine what constitutes obscene, pornographic material subject to regulation under the States' police power. [] We have seen "a variety of views among the members of the Court unmatched in any other course of constitutional adjudication." *Interstate Circuit, Inc. v. Dallas,* [*supra,*] (Harlan, J., concurring and dissenting).[3] This is not remarkable, for in the area of freedom of speech and press the courts must always remain sensitive to any infringement on genuinely serious literary, artistic, political, or scientific expression. This is an area in which there are few eternal verities.

The case we now review was tried on the theory that the California Penal Code § 311 approximately incorporates the three-stage *Memoirs* test. But now the *Memoirs* test has been abandoned as unworkable by its author, and no Member of the Court today supports the *Memoirs* formulation.

This much has been categorically settled by the court, that obscene material is unprotected by the First Amendment. . . . We acknowledge, however, the inherent dangers of undertaking to regulate any form of expression. State statutes designed to regulate obscene materials must be carefully limited. See *Interstate Circuit, Inc. v. Dallas, supra,* at 682-685. As a result, we now confine the permissible scope of such regulation to works which depict or describe sexual conduct. That conduct must be specifically defined by the applicable state law, as written or authoritatively construed. A state offense must also be limited to works which, taken as a whole, appeal to the prurient interest in sex, which portray sexual conduct in a patently

---

"[o]ffensive to the senses, or to taste or refinement; disgusting, repulsive, filthy, foul, abominable, loathsome."

The material we are discussing in this case is more accurately defined as "pornography" or "pornographic material." "Pornography" derives from the Greek (*porné,* harlot, and *graphos,* writing). The word now means "1: a description of prostitutes or prostitution 2: a depiction (as in writing or painting) of licentiousness or lewdness: a portrayal of erotic behavior designed to cause sexual excitement." Webster's Third New International Dictionary, *supra.* Pornographic material which is obscene forms a sub-group of all "obscene" expression, but not the whole, at least as the word "obscene" is now used in our language. We note, therefore, that the words "obscene material" as used in this case, have a specific judicial meaning which derives from the *Roth* case, *i.e.,* obscene material "which deals with sex." *Roth, supra,* at 487. See also ALI Model Penal Code § 251.4(1) "Obscene Defined." (Official Draft 1962.)

[3] In the absence of a majority view, this Court was compelled to embark on the practice of summarily reversing convictions for the dissemination of materials that at least five members of the Court, applying their separate tests, found to be protected by the First Amendment. *Redrup v. New York,* 386 U.S. 767 (1967). Thirty-one cases have been decided in this manner. Beyond the necessity of circumstances, however, no justification has ever been offered in support of the *Redrup* "policy." See *Walker v. Ohio,* 398 U.S. 434-435 (1970) (dissenting opinion of Burger, C.J., and Harlan, J.). The *Redrup* procedure has cast us in the role of an unreviewable board of censorship for the 50 States, subjectively judging each piece of material brought before us.

offensive way, and which, taken as a whole, do not have serious literary, artistic, political, or scientific value.

The basic guidelines for the trier of fact must be: (a) whether "the average person, applying contemporary community standards" would find that the work, taken as a whole, appeals to the prurient interest, *Kois v. Wisconsin, supra*, at 230, quoting *Roth v. United States, supra*, at 489; (b) whether the work depicts or describes, in a patently offensive way, sexual conduct specifically defined by the applicable state law; and (c) whether the work, taken as a whole, lacks serious literary, artistic, political, or scientific value. We do not adopt as a constitutional standard the "*utterly without redeeming social value*" test of *Memoirs v. Massachusetts*, 383 U.S., at 419; that concept has never commanded the adherence of more than three Justices at one time.[7] If a state law that regulates obscene material is thus limited, as written or construed, the First Amendment values applicable to the States through the Fourteenth Amendment are adequately protected by the ultimate power of appellate courts to conduct an independent review of constitutional claims when necessary.

We emphasize that it is not our function to propose regulatory schemes for the States. That must await their concrete legislative efforts. It is possible, however, to give a few plain examples of what a state statute could define for regulation under part (b) of the standard announced in this opinion: (a) Patently offensive representations or descriptions of ultimate sexual acts, normal or perverted, actual or simulated; (b) Patently offensive representations or descriptions of masturbation, excretory functions, and lewd exhibition of the genitals.

Sex and nudity may not be exploited without limit by films or pictures exhibited or sold in places of public accommodation any more than live sex and nudity can be exhibited or sold without limit in such public places.[8] At a minimum, prurient, patently offensive depiction or description of sexual conduct must have serious literary, artistic, political, or scientific value to merit First Amendment protection. For example, medical books for the education of physicians and related personnel necessarily use graphic illustrations and descriptions of human anatomy. In resolving the inevitably sensitive questions of fact and law, we must continue to rely on the jury system, accompanied by the safeguards that judges, rules of evidence, presumption of innocence, and other protective features provide, as we do with rape, murder, and a host of other offenses against society and its individual members. . . .

Under the holdings announced today, no one will be subject to prosecution for the sale or exposure of obscene materials unless these materials depict or describe patently offensive "hard core" sexual conduct specifically defined by the regulating state law, as written or construed. We are satisfied that these specific prerequisites

---

[7] "A quotation from Voltaire in the flyleaf of a book will not constitutionally redeem an otherwise obscene publication. . . ." *Kois v. Wisconsin*, 408 U.S. 229, 231 (1972). See *Memoirs v. Massachusetts*, 383 U.S. 413, 461 (1966) (White, J., dissenting). We also reject, as a constitutional standard, the ambiguous concept of "social importance." See *id.*, at 462 (White, J., dissenting).

[8] Although we are not presented here with the problem of regulating lewd public conduct itself, the States have greater power to regulate nonverbal, physical conduct than to suppress depictions or descriptions of the same behavior. In *United States v. O'Brien*, 391 U.S. 367, 377 (1968), a case not dealing with obscenity, the Court held a State regulation of conduct which itself embodies both speech and nonspeech elements to be "sufficiently justified if . . . it furthers an important or substantial governmental interest; if the governmental interest is unrelated to the suppression of free expression; and if the incidental restriction on alleged First Amendment freedoms is no greater than is essential to the furtherance of that interest." See *California v. LaRue*, 409 U.S. 109, 117-118 (1972).

will provide fair notice to a dealer in such materials that his public and commercial activities may bring prosecution. . . .

Under a National Constitution, fundamental First Amendment limitations on the powers of the States do not vary from community to community, but this does not mean that there are, or should or can be, fixed, uniform national standards of precisely what appeals to the "prurient interest" or is "patently offensive." These are essentially questions of fact, and our Nation is simply too big and too diverse for this Court to reasonably expect that such standards could be articulated for all 50 States in a single formulation, even assuming the prerequisite consensus exists. When triers of fact are asked to decide whether "the average person, applying contemporary community standards" would consider certain materials "prurient," it would be unrealistic to require that the answer be based on some abstract formulation. The adversary system, with lay jurors as the usual ultimate factfinders in criminal prosecutions, has historically permitted triers of fact to draw on the standards of their community, guided always by limiting instructions on the law. To require a State to structure obscenity proceedings around evidence of a *national* "community standard" would be an exercise in futility. . . .

We conclude that neither the State's alleged failure to offer evidence of "national standards," nor the trial court's charge that the jury consider state community standards, were constitutional errors. Nothing in the First Amendment requires that a jury must consider hypothetical and unascertainable "national standards" when attempting to determine whether certain materials are obscene as a matter of fact. . . .

It is neither realistic nor constitutionally sound to read the First Amendment as requiring that the people of Maine or Mississippi accept public depiction of conduct found tolerable in Las Vegas, or New York City.

People in different States vary in their tastes and attitudes, and this diversity is not to be strangled by the absolutism of imposed uniformity. As the Court made clear in *Mishkin v. New York*, 383 U.S., at 508-509, the primary concern with requiring a jury to apply the standard of "the average person, applying contemporary community standards" is to be certain that, so far as material is not aimed at a deviant group, it will be judged by its impact on an average person, rather than a particularly susceptible or sensitive person—or indeed a totally insensitive one. See *Roth v. United States, supra*, at 489. Cf. the now discredited test in *Regina v. Hicklin*, [1868] L.R. 3 Q.B. 360. We hold that the requirement that the jury evaluate the materials with reference to "contemporary standards of the State of California" serves this protective purpose and is constitutionally adequate. . . .

In sum, we (a) reaffirm the *Roth* holding that obscene material is not protected by the First Amendment; (b) hold that such material can be regulated by the States, subject to the specific safeguards enunciated above, without a showing that the material is "*utterly* without redeeming social value"; and (c) hold that obscenity is to be determined by applying "contemporary community standards," [] not "national standards." The judgment of the Appellate Department of the Superior Court, Orange County, California, is vacated and the case remanded to that court for further proceedings not inconsistent with the First Amendment standards established by this opinion.

Vacated and remanded.

DOUGLAS, J., dissenting.

Today we leave open the way for California to send a man to prison for distributing brochures that advertise books and a movie under freshly written standards defining obscenity which until today's decision were never the part of any law.

The Court has worked hard to define obscenity and concededly has failed. In *Roth v. United States*, 354 U.S. 476, it ruled that "[o]bscene material is material which deals with sex in a manner appealing to prurient interest." Obscenity, it was said, was rejected by the First Amendment because it is "utterly without redeeming social importance." The presence of a "prurient interest" was to be determined by "contemporary community standards." That test, it has been said, could not be determined by one standard here and another standard there, *Jacobellis v. Ohio*, 378 U.S. 184, 194, but "on the basis of a national standard." My Brother Stewart in *Jacobellis* commented that the difficulty of the Court in giving content to obscenity was that it was "faced with the task of trying to define what may be indefinable." . . .

Today the Court retreats from the earlier formulations of the constitutional test and undertakes to make new definitions. This effort, like the earlier ones, is earnest and well intentioned. The difficulty is that we do not deal with constitutional terms, since "obscenity" is not mentioned in the Constitution or Bill of Rights. And the First Amendment makes no such exception from "the press" which it undertakes to protect nor, as I have said on other occasions, is an exception necessarily implied, for there was no recognized exception to the free press at the time the Bill of Rights was adopted which treated "obscene" publications differently from other types of papers, magazines, and books. So there are no constitutional guidelines for deciding what is and what is not "obscene." The Court is at large because we deal with tastes and standards of literature. What shocks me may be sustenance for my neighbor. What causes one person to boil up in rage over one pamphlet or movie may reflect only his neurosis, not shared by others. We deal here with a regime of censorship which, if adopted, should be done by constitutional amendment after full debate by the people. . . .

BRENNAN, J., with whom STEWART, J., and MARSHALL, J., join, dissenting.

In my dissent in *Paris Adult Theatre I v. Slaton*, [413 U.S. 49 (1973),] I noted that I had no occasion to consider the extent of state power to regulate the distribution of sexually oriented material to juveniles or the offensive exposure of such material to unconsenting adults. In the case before us, appellant was convicted of distributing obscene matter in violation of California Penal Code § 311.2, on the basis of evidence that he had caused to be mailed unsolicited brochures advertising various books and a movie. I need not now decide whether a statute might be drawn to impose, within the requirements of the First Amendment, criminal penalties for the precise conduct at issue here. For it is clear that under my dissent in *Paris Adult Theatre I*, the statute under which the prosecution was brought is unconstitutionally overbroad, and therefore invalid on its face. "[T]he transcendent value to all society of constitutionally protected expression is deemed to justify allowing 'attacks on overly broad statutes with no requirement that the person making the attack demonstrate that his own conduct could not be regulated by a statute drawn with the requisite narrow specificity.'" *Gooding v. Wilson*, 405 U.S. 518, 521 (1972), quoting from *Dombrowski v. Pfister*, 380 U.S. 479, 486 (1965).

NOTES AND QUESTIONS

1. *Does the* Miller *test bring clarity?* Did Justice Burger succeed in articulating a bright-line test that will permit state and lower federal courts to define "obscenity" with precision? Or is the *Miller* test simply a reworking of the *Roth* test, with the addition of a "taken as a whole" requirement for "literary, artistic, political, or scientific" value? Is there a way to come up with a bright-line test for something so inherently subjective?

2. *Privacy versus public morals as rationale for regulation.* Justice Brennan, the author of the *Roth* test, dissents in *Miller.* After almost two decades of trying to articulate a viable test for obscenity, Justice Brennan concluded that this was an impossible task. Would the Supreme Court have done better to abandon the effort to define obscenity and instead focus on the problems of protecting both minors and a captive audience from sexually explicit materials? Even if government should not be permitted to ban sexually explicit materials outright, does government have a legitimate interest in protecting citizens against unwanted exposure to such materials? In other words, on the facts in *Miller,* would a privacy rationale be more persuasive than a public morals rationale?

3. *The variable obscenity standard.* The Supreme Court has endorsed a different, less protective, standard of obscenity for materials made available to minors. *See* Ginsberg v. New York, 390 U.S. 629, 637-639 (1968). Thus, materials that are not constitutionally obscene as to adults may be obscene with respect to minors. Even though the state and federal governments may enact laws to protect minors from exposure to sexually explicit materials, such regulations may not have the effect of blocking adults from accessing materials that are not legally obscene as to an adult audience. *See* Butler v. Michigan, 352 U.S. 380, 382-383 (1957).

4. *Local community standards in the internet era.* The viability of the local community standard approach for ascertaining prurience and patent offensiveness has been in serious doubt since the Supreme Court decided Ashcroft v. ACLU, 535 U.S. 564 (2002) ("Ashcroft I"), which dealt with the constitutionality of the Child Online Protection Act (COPA), 47 U.S.C. § 231(a), federal legislation aimed at protection children from indecency online. Although no opinion in the case garnered the unqualified support of five Justices, multiple opinions, representing the views of a majority of the Supreme Court, all expressed serious concerns about the viability of a local community standard as applied to the internet. *See id.* at 576-579 (plurality opinion by Justice Thomas); *id.* at 584, 587-588 (O'Connor, J., concurring); *id.* at 591 (Breyer, J., concurring); *id.* at 593-594 (Kennedy, J., concurring). In consequence, the continuing viability of this aspect of the *Miller* test is open to serious question. In Ashcroft v. ACLU, 542 U.S. 656 (2004) ("Ashcroft II"), Justices Stevens and Ginsburg wrote a concurrence in which they emphasized that the application of community standards to define prohibited speech would "penalize speakers for making available to the general World Wide Web audience that which the least tolerant communities in America deem unfit for their children's consumption, and consider that principle a sufficient basis for deciding this case." For more on the opinions in *Ashcroft I* and *Ashcroft II* and the curious saga of the COPA, which was ultimately deemed unconstitutional, see *supra* Chapter 8.

5. *What about highly graphic depictions of violence?* Can extremely graphic depictions of violence constitute "obscenity"? The Supreme Court's answer is an

emphatic "no." *See* Brown v. Entertainment Merchants Ass'n, 564 U.S. 786 (2011). One of California's principal arguments in favor of a state law banning the sale of violent video games to minors involved characterizing such games as a form of obscenity. *See id.* at 792-94. Justice Antonin Scalia, writing for the majority, squarely rejected California's "attempt to shoehorn speech about violence into obscenity." Justice Scalia explained that "[o]ur cases have been clear that the obscenity exception to the First Amendment does not cover whatever a legislature finds shocking, but only depictions of 'sexual conduct,' *Miller, supra*, at 24." *Id.* at 792-93. Thus, "[b]ecause speech about violence is not obscene, it is of no consequence that California's statute mimics the New York statute regulating obscenity for minors that we upheld in *Ginsberg v. New York*, 390 U.S. 629 (1968)." *Id.* at 793. Should violent or gruesome speech be subject to content-based regulation because of its repulsiveness? For an argument that it should not, except in very limited contexts involving government-owned property, see Eugene Volokh, *Gruesome Speech*, 100 Cornell L. Rev. 901 (2015).

AMERICAN BOOKSELLERS ASS'N, INC. v. HUDNUT

771 F.2d 323 (7th Cir. 1985), *aff'd mem.*, 475 U.S. 1001 (1986)

EASTERBROOK, Circuit Judge.

Indianapolis enacted an ordinance defining "pornography" as a practice that discriminates against women. "Pornography" is to be redressed through the administrative and judicial methods used for other discrimination. The City's definition of "pornography" is considerably different from "obscenity," which the Supreme Court has held is not protected by the First Amendment.

To be "obscene" under *Miller v. California*, 413 U.S. 15 (1973), "a publication must, taken as a whole, appeal to the prurient interest, must contain patently offensive depictions or descriptions of specified sexual conduct, and on the whole have no serious literary, artistic, political, or scientific value." . . .

"Pornography" under the ordinance is "the graphic sexually explicit subordination of women, whether in pictures or in words, that also includes one or more of the following:

(1) Women are presented as sexual objects who enjoy pain or humiliation; or

(2) Women are presented as sexual objects who experience sexual pleasure in being raped; or

(3) Women are presented as sexual objects tied up or cut up or mutilated or bruised or physically hurt, or as dismembered or truncated or fragmented or severed into body parts; or

(4) Women are presented as being penetrated by objects or animals; or

(5) Women are presented in scenarios of degradation, injury, abasement, torture, shown as filthy or inferior, bleeding, bruised, or hurt in a context that makes these conditions sexual; or

(6) Women are presented as sexual objects for domination, conquest, violation, exploitation, possession, or use, or through postures or positions of servility or submission or display."

Indianapolis Code § 16-3(q). The statute provides that the "use of men, children, or transsexuals in the place of women in paragraphs (1) through (6) above shall also constitute pornography under this section." The ordinance as passed in April 1984 defined "sexually explicit" to mean actual or simulated intercourse or the uncovered exhibition of the genitals, buttocks or anus. An amendment in June 1984 deleted this provision, leaving the terms undefined.

The Indianapolis ordinance does not refer to the prurient interest, to offensiveness, or to the standards of the community. It demands attention to particular depictions, not to the work judged as a whole. It is irrelevant under the ordinance whether the work has literary, artistic, political, or scientific value. The City and many amici point to these omissions as virtues. They maintain that pornography influences attitudes, and the statute is a way to alter the socialization of men and women rather than to vindicate community standards of offensiveness. And as one of the principal drafters of the ordinance has asserted, "if a woman is subjected, why should it matter that the work has other value?" Catharine A. MacKinnon, *Pornography, Civil Rights, and Speech*, 20 Harv. Civ. Rts.-Civ. Lib. L. Rev. 1, 21 (1985).

Civil rights groups and feminists have entered this case as amici on both sides. Those supporting the ordinance say that it will play an important role in reducing the tendency of men to view women as sexual objects, a tendency that leads to both unacceptable attitudes and discrimination in the workplace and violence away from it. Those opposing the ordinance point out that much radical feminist literature is explicit and depicts women in ways forbidden by the ordinance and that the ordinance would reopen old battles. It is unclear how Indianapolis would treat works from James Joyce's *Ulysses* to Homer's *Iliad*; both depict women as submissive objects for conquest and domination.

We do not try to balance the arguments for and against an ordinance such as this. The ordinance discriminates on the ground of the content of the speech. Speech treating women in the approved way—in sexual encounters "premised on equality" (MacKinnon, *supra*, at 22)—is lawful no matter how sexually explicit. Speech treating women in the disapproved way—as submissive in matters sexual or as enjoying humiliation—is unlawful no matter how significant the literary, artistic, or political qualities of the work taken as a whole. The state may not ordain preferred viewpoints in this way. The Constitution forbids the state to declare one perspective right and silence opponents. . . .

The district court held the ordinance unconstitutional. 598 F. Supp. 1316 (S.D. Ind. 1984). The court concluded that the ordinance regulates speech rather than the conduct involved in making pornography. The regulation of speech could be justified, the court thought, only by a compelling interest in reducing sex discrimination, an interest Indianapolis had not established. The ordinance is also vague and overbroad, the court believed, and establishes a prior restraint of speech. . . .

"If there is any fixed star in our constitutional constellation, it is that no official, high or petty, can prescribe what shall be orthodox in politics, nationalism, religion, or other matters of opinion or force citizens to confess by word or act their faith therein." *West Virginia State Board of Education v. Barnette*, 319 U.S. 624, 642 (1943). Under the First Amendment the government must leave to the people the evaluation of ideas. Bald or subtle, an idea is as powerful as the audience allows it to be. A belief may be pernicious—the beliefs of Nazis led to the death of millions, those of the Klan to the repression of millions. A pernicious belief may prevail. Totalitarian governments today rule much of the planet, practicing suppression of billions and spreading dogma that may enslave others. One of the things that separates our society from theirs is our absolute right to propagate opinions that the government finds wrong or even hateful.

. . . Under the ordinance graphic sexually explicit speech is "pornography" or not depending on the perspective the author adopts. Speech that "subordinates" women and also, for example, presents women as enjoying pain, humiliation, or rape, or even simply presents women in "positions of servility or submission or display" is forbidden, no matter how great the literary or political value of the work taken as a whole. Speech that portrays women in positions of equality is lawful, no matter how graphic the sexual content. This is thought control. It establishes an "approved" view of women, of how they may react to sexual encounters, of how the sexes may relate to each other. Those who espouse the approved view may use sexual images; those who do not, may not.

Indianapolis justifies the ordinance on the ground that pornography affects thoughts. Men who see women depicted as subordinate are more likely to treat them so. Pornography is an aspect of dominance. It does not persuade people so much as change them. It works by socializing, by establishing the expected and the permissible. In this view pornography is not an idea; pornography is the injury.

There is much to this perspective. Beliefs are also facts. People often act in accordance with the images and patterns they find around them. People raised in a religion tend to accept the tenets of that religion, often without independent examination. People taught from birth that black people are fit only for slavery rarely rebelled against that creed; beliefs coupled with the self-interest of the masters established a social structure that inflicted great harm while enduring for centuries. Words and images act at the level of the subconscious before they persuade at the level of the conscious. Even the truth has little chance unless a statement fits within the framework of beliefs that may never have been subjected to rational study.

Therefore we accept the premises of this legislation. Depictions of subordination tend to perpetuate subordination. The subordinate status of women in turn leads to affront and lower pay at work, insult and injury at home, battery and rape on the streets. . . . Pornography is a systematic practice of exploitation and subordination based on sex which differentially harms women. . . .

Yet this simply demonstrates the power of pornography as speech. All of these unhappy effects depend on mental intermediation. Pornography affects how people see the world, their fellows, and social relations. If pornography is what pornography does, so is other speech. Hitler's orations affected how some Germans saw Jews. Communism is a world view, not simply a *Manifesto* by Marx and Engels or a set of speeches. . . .

Racial bigotry, anti-semitism, violence on television, reporters' biases—these and many more influence the culture and shape our socialization. None is directly answerable by more speech, unless that speech too finds its place in the popular culture. Yet all is protected as speech, however insidious. Any other answer leaves the government in control of all of the institutions of culture, the great censor and director of which thoughts are good for us. . . .

Much of Indianapolis's argument rests on the belief that when speech is "unanswerable," and the metaphor that there is a "marketplace of ideas" does not apply, the First Amendment does not apply either. The metaphor is honored; Milton's *Areopagitica* and John Stewart Mill's *On Liberty* defend freedom of speech on the ground that the truth will prevail, and many of the most important cases under the First Amendment recite this position. The Framers undoubtedly believed it. As a general matter it is true. But the Constitution does not make the dominance of truth a necessary condition of freedom of speech. To say that it does would be to confuse an outcome of free speech with a necessary condition for the application of the amendment.

A power to limit speech on the ground that truth has not yet prevailed and is not likely to prevail implies the power to declare truth. At some point the government must be able to say (as Indianapolis has said): "We know what the truth is, yet a free exchange of speech has not driven out falsity, so that we must now prohibit falsity." If the government may declare the truth, why wait for the failure of speech? Under the First Amendment, however, there is no such thing as a false idea, *Gertz v. Robert Welch, Inc.*, 418 U.S. 323, 339 (1974), so the government may not restrict speech on the ground that in a free exchange truth is not yet dominant.

At any time, some speech is ahead in the game; the more numerous speakers prevail. Supporters of minority candidates may be forever "excluded" from the political process because their candidates never win, because few people believe their positions. This does not mean that freedom of speech has failed.

The Supreme Court has rejected the position that speech must be "effectively answerable" to be protected by the Constitution. . . .

Any rationale we could imagine in support of this ordinance could not be limited to sex discrimination. Free speech has been on balance an ally of those seeking change. Governments that want stasis start by restricting speech. Culture is a powerful force of continuity; Indianapolis paints pornography as part of the culture of power. Change in any complex system ultimately depends on the ability of outsiders to challenge accepted views and the reigning institutions. Without a strong guarantee of freedom of speech, there is no effective right to challenge what is.

The definition of "pornography" is unconstitutional. No construction or excision of particular terms could save it. The offense of trafficking in pornography necessarily falls with the definition. We express no view on the district court's conclusions that the ordinance is vague and that it establishes a prior restraint. Neither is necessary to our judgment. We also express no view on the argument presented by several amici that the ordinance is itself a form of discrimination on account of sex. . . .

No amount of struggle with particular words and phrases in this ordinance can leave anything in effect. The district court came to the same conclusion. Its judgment is therefore

Affirmed.

NOTES AND QUESTIONS

1. *Obscenity regulation as content-based regulation.* Pornography undoubtedly imposes social costs, something that Judge Easterbrook cheerfully acknowledges in *Hudnut*. At the same time, however, graphic forms of erotica also present (often controversial) ideas about sex, human sexuality, and gender norms. The conflict first recognized in *Roth* persists to this day: Regulation of erotica reflects, to some extent, strong content and viewpoint discrimination against the ideas erotica advances. If the regulation of erotica exists because of strong hostility to its message, should the Supreme Court simply invalidate efforts to regulate it? The Supreme Court of Oregon has done so; incident to the Oregon state constitution, Article I, § 8 ("No law shall be passed restraining the free

expression of opinion, or restricting the right to speak, write, or print freely on any subject whatever; but every person shall be responsible for the abuse of this right."), it has held that sexually explicit materials are fully protected speech activity and that government may not regulate such material because it disapproves of the content or views the content as "immoral." *See* Oregon v. Henry, 732 P.2d 9, 17 (Or. 1987) ("We hold that characterizing expression as "obscenity" under any definition, be it *Roth, Miller*, or otherwise, does not deprive it of protection under the Oregon Constitution."). Nevertheless, the Supreme Court of Oregon also held that the state may regulate sexually explicit materials to protect the interests of "unwilling viewers, captive audiences, minors and beleaguered neighbors." *Id.* at 18. As recently as 2005, the Supreme Court of Oregon strongly reaffirmed *Henry*'s approach to the regulation of pornography. *See* State v. Ciancanelli, 121 P.3d 613, 618-620, 633-635 (Or. 2005); City of Nyssa v. Dufloth, 121 P.3d 639, 643-644 (Or. 2005). Is this a more sensible approach than *Miller*? If Judge Easterbrook is correct is positing that erotica has a strong communicative function, how can any regulations of erotica be sustained? Aren't all bans on pornography a reflection of public offense at the content? If so, how can such a regime of regulation be squared with the baseline rule that whatever else the government may do, it cannot regulate speech based on its content or viewpoint?

2. *Articulating the value (or lack thereof) of sexually explicit speech.* Before rejecting Chief Justice Burger's efforts in *Miller*, one should consider the countervailing point of view: What value does sexually explicit speech have? If free speech enjoys protection for instrumental reasons, such as advancing democratic self-government, it is difficult to see why legislatures should not be free to regulate erotica, just as they can regulate the size of shopping malls or establish deposit rules for soda cans. *See* Robert H. Bork, *Neutral Principles and Some First Amendment Problems*, 47 Ind. L.J. 1, 27-29 (1971) (arguing that "art and pornography are on a par with industry and smoke pollution" in terms of the proper scope of a legislature's regulatory powers and that "[f]reedom of non-political speech rests, as does freedom for other valuable forms of behavior, upon the enlightenment of society and its elected representatives"). *But cf.* Steven G. Gey, *The Apologetics of Suppression: The Regulation of Pornography as Act and Idea*, 86 Mich. L. Rev. 1564, 1582-1586 (1988) (offering a trenchant critique of the Bork objection to affording protection to sexually explicit speech and noting that the "disarming honesty of Bork's rendition of the morality principle has never found favor with the [Supreme] Court"). On this view, however, how could one justify protecting commercial speech but not erotica from legislative infringements?

Not all nations committed to free speech find unpersuasive the gender equality rationale for regulating at least some forms of sexually explicit speech. Consider the following landmark case from Canada.

R. v. BUTLER

[1992] 1 S.C.R. 452 (Can.)

SOPINKA, J.

This appeal calls into question the constitutionality of the obscenity provisions of the Criminal Code, R.S.C., 1985, c. C-46, s. 163.[1] They are attacked on the ground that they contravene s. 2(b) of the Canadian Charter of Rights and Freedoms. The case requires the Court to address one of the most difficult and controversial of contemporary issues, that of determining whether, and to what extent, Parliament may legitimately criminalize obscenity. . . .

In August 1987, the appellant, Donald Victor Butler, opened the Avenue Video Boutique located in Winnipeg, Manitoba. The shop sells and rents "hard core" videotapes and magazines as well as sexual paraphernalia. . . .

On August 21, 1987, the City of Winnipeg Police entered the appellant's store with a search warrant and seized all the inventory. The appellant was charged with 173 counts in the first indictment: three counts of selling obscene material contrary to s. 159(2)(a) of the Criminal Code, R.S.C. 1970, c. C-34 (now s. 163(2)(a)), 41 counts

---

[1] Criminal Code, R.S.C., 1985, c. C-46 § 163.

(a) Every one commits an offence who (a) makes, prints, publishes, distributes, circulates, or has in his possession for the purpose of publication, distribution or circulation any obscene written matter, picture, model, phonograph record or other thing whatever; or (b) makes, prints, publishes, distributes, sells or has in his possession for the purpose of publication, distribution or circulation a crime comic.

(b) Every one commits an offence who knowingly, without lawful justification or excuse, (a) sells, exposes to public view or has in his possession for such a purpose any obscene written matter, picture, model, phonograph record or other thing whatever, (b) publicly exhibits a disgusting object or an indecent show, (c) offers to sell, advertises or publishes an advertisement of, or has for sale or disposal, any means, instructions, medicine, drug or article intended or represented as a method of causing abortion or miscarriage, or (d) advertises or publishes an advertisement of any means, instructions, medicine, drug or article intended or represented as a method for restoring sexual virility or curing venereal diseases or diseases of the generative organs.

(c) No person shall be convicted of an offence under this section if he establishes that the public good was served by the acts that are alleged to constitute the offence and that the acts alleged did not extend beyond what served the public good.

(d) For the purposes of this section, it is a question of law whether an act served the public good and whether there is evidence that the act alleged went beyond what served the public good, but it is a question of fact whether the acts did or did not extend beyond what served the public good.

(e) For the purposes of this section, the motives of an accused are irrelevant.

(f) Where an accused is charged with an offence under the subsection (1), the fact that the accused was ignorant of the nature or presence of the matter, picture, model, phonograph record, crime comic or other thing by means of or in relation to which the offence was committed is not a defense to the charge.

(g) In this section, "crime comic" means a magazine, periodical or book that exclusively or substantially comprises matter depicting pictorially (a) the commission of crimes, real or fictitious, or (b) events connected with the commission of crimes, real or fictitious, whether occurring before or after the commission of the crime.

(h) For the purposes of this Act, any publication a dominant characteristic of which is the undue exploitation of sex, or of sex and any one or more of the following subjects, namely, crime, horror, cruelty and violence shall be deemed to be obscene.

of possessing obscene material for the purpose of distribution contrary to s. 159(1)(a) (now s. 163(1)(a)) of the Criminal Code, 128 counts of possessing obscene material for the purpose of sale contrary to s. 159(2)(a) of the Criminal Code and one count of exposing obscene material to public view contrary to s. 159(2)(a) of the Criminal Code.

On October 19, 1987, the appellant reopened the store at the same location. As a result of a police operation a search warrant was executed on October 29, 1987, resulting in the arrest of an employee, Norma McCord. The appellant was arrested at a later date.

A joint indictment was laid against the appellant doing business as Avenue Video boutique and Norma McCord. The joint indictment contains 77 counts under s. 159 (now s. 163) of the Criminal Code: two counts of selling obscene material contrary to s. 159(2)(a), 73 counts of possessing obscene material for the purpose of distribution contrary to s. 159(1)(a), one count of possessing obscene material for the purpose of sale contrary to s. 159(2)(a) and one count of exposing obscene material to public view contrary to s. 159(2)(a).

The trial judge convicted the appellant on eight counts relating to eight films. Convictions were entered against the co-accused McCord with respect to two counts relating to two of the films. Fines of $1,000 per offence were imposed on the appellant. Acquittals were entered on the remaining charges.

The Crown appealed the 242 acquittals with respect to the appellant and the appellant cross-appealed the convictions. The majority of the Manitoba Court of Appeal allowed the appeal of the Crown and entered convictions for the appellant with respect to all of the counts. . . .

. . .

The constitutional questions, as stated, bring under scrutiny the entirety of s. 163. However, both lower courts as well as the parties have focused almost exclusively on the definition of obscenity found in s. 163(8). Other portions of the impugned provision, such as the reverse onus provision envisaged in s. 163(3) as well as the absolute liability offence created by s. 163(6), raise substantial Charter issues which should be left to be dealt with in proceedings specifically directed to these issues. In my view, in the circumstances, this appeal should be confined to the examination of the constitutional validity of s. 163(8) only.

Before proceeding to consider the constitutional question, it will be helpful to review the legislative history of the provision as well as the extensive judicial interpretation and analysis which have infused meaning into the bare words of the statute. . . .

In order for the work or material to qualify as "obscene", the exploitation of sex must not only be its dominant characteristic, but such exploitation must be "undue". In determining when the exploitation of sex will be considered "undue", the courts have attempted to formulate workable tests. The most important of these is the "community standard of tolerance" test.

"COMMUNITY STANDARD OF TOLERANCE" TEST

Our Court was called upon to elaborate the community standards test in *Towne Cinema Theatres Ltd. v. The Queen*, [1985] 1 S.C.R. 494. Dickson C.J. reviewed the case law and found (at pp. 508-9):

"The cases all emphasize that it is a standard of *tolerance* not taste, that is relevant. What matters is not what Canadians think is right for themselves to see. What matters is what Canadians would not abide other Canadians seeing because it would be beyond the contemporary Canadian standard of tolerance to allow them to see it.

Since the standard is tolerance, I think the audience to which the allegedly obscene material is targeted must be relevant. The operative standards are those of the Canadian community as a whole, but since what matters is what other people may see, it is quite conceivable that the Canadian community would tolerate varying degrees of explicitness depending upon the audience and the circumstances." [Emphasis in original.]

Therefore, the community standards test is concerned not with what Canadians would not tolerate being exposed to themselves, but what they would not tolerate other Canadians being exposed to. . . .

"Degradation or Dehumanization" Test

There has been a growing recognition in recent cases that material which may be said to exploit sex in a "degrading or dehumanizing" manner will necessarily fail the community standards test. . . .

[F]ilms which consist substantially or partially of scenes which portray violence and cruelty in conjunction with sex, particularly where the performance of indignities degrade and dehumanize the people upon whom they are performed, exceed the level of community tolerance.

Subsequent decisions…held that material that "degraded" or "dehumanized" any of the participants would exceed community standards even in the absence of cruelty and violence. . . .

This type of material would, apparently, fail the community standards test not because it offends against morals but because it is perceived by public opinion to be harmful to society, particularly to women. While the accuracy of this perception is not susceptible of exact proof, there is a substantial body of opinion that holds that the portrayal of persons being subjected to degrading or dehumanizing sexual treatment results in harm, particularly to women and therefore to society as a whole. [] It would be reasonable to conclude that there is an appreciable risk of harm to society in the portrayal of such material. . . .

"Internal Necessities Test" or "Artistic Defence"

[A third test] or what has been referred to as the "artistic defence" has been interpreted to assess whether the exploitation of sex has a justifiable role in advancing the plot or the theme, and in considering the work as a whole, does not merely represent "dirt for dirt's sake" but has a legitimate role when measured by the internal necessities of the work itself. . . .

Pornography can be usefully divided into three categories: (1) explicit sex with violence, (2) explicit sex without violence but which subjects people to treatment that is degrading or dehumanizing and (3) explicit sex without violence that is neither degrading nor dehumanizing. Violence in this context includes both actual physical violence and threats of physical violence. . . .

Some segments of society would consider that all three categories of pornography cause harm to society because they tend to undermine its moral fibre. Others would contend that none of the categories cause harm. Furthermore there is a range of opinion as to what is degrading or dehumanizing. See Pornography and Prostitution in Canada: Report of the Special Committee on Pornography and Prostitution (1985) (the Fraser Report), vol. 1, at p. 51. Because this is not a matter that is susceptible of proof in the traditional way and because we do not wish to leave it to the individual tastes of judges, we must have a norm that will serve as an arbiter in determining what amounts to an undue exploitation of sex. That arbiter is the community as a whole.

The courts must determine as best they can what the community would tolerate others being exposed to on the basis of the degree of harm that may flow from such exposure. . . . In making this determination with respect to the three categories of pornography referred to above, the portrayal of sex coupled with violence will almost always constitute the undue exploitation of sex. Explicit sex which is degrading or dehumanizing may be undue if the risk of harm is substantial. Finally, explicit sex that is not violent and neither degrading nor dehumanizing is generally tolerated in our society and will not qualify as the undue exploitation of sex unless it employs children in its production.

If material is not obscene under this framework, it does not become so by reason of the person to whom it is or may be shown or exposed nor by reason of the place or manner in which it is shown. The availability of sexually explicit materials in theatres and other public places is subject to regulation by competent provincial legislation. Typically such legislation implies restrictions on the material available to children. See Nova Scotia Board of Censors v. McNeil, [1978] 2 S.C.R. 662.

The foregoing deals with the interrelationship of the "community standards test" and "the degrading or dehumanizing" test. How does the "internal necessities" test fit into this scheme? The need to apply this test only arises if a work contains sexually explicit material that by itself would constitute the undue exploitation of sex. The portrayal of sex must then be viewed in context to determine whether that is the dominant theme of the work as a whole. Put another way, is undue exploitation of sex the main object of the work or is this portrayal of sex essential to a wider artistic, literary or other similar purpose? Since the threshold determination must be made on the basis of community standards, that is, whether the sexually explicit aspect is undue, its impact when considered in context must be determined on the same basis. The court must determine whether the sexually explicit material when viewed in the context of the whole work would be tolerated by the community as a whole. Artistic expression rests at the heart of freedom of expression values and any doubt in this regard must be resolved in favor of freedom of expression. . . .

In light of our recent decision in R. v. Keegstra, [1990] 3 S.C.R. 697, the respondent, and most of the parties intervening in support of the respondent, do not take issue with the proposition that s. 163 of the Criminal Code violates s. 2(b) of the Charter. In Keegstra, we were unanimous in advocating a generous approach to the protection afforded by s. 2(b) of the Charter. . . .

In this case, both the purpose and effect of s. 163 are specifically to restrict the communication of certain types of materials based on their content. In my view, there is no doubt that s. 163 seeks to prohibit certain types of expressive activity and thereby infringes s. 2(b) of the Charter.

Does the prevention of the harm associated with the dissemination of certain obscene materials constitute a sufficiently pressing and substantial concern to warrant restriction on the freedom of expression? In this regard, it should be recalled that in *Keegstra*, this Court unanimously accepted that the prevention of the influence of hate propaganda on society at large was a legitimate objective. . . .

This court has thus recognized that the harm caused by the proliferation of materials which seriously offend the values fundamental to our society is a substantial concern which justifies restricting the otherwise full exercise of the freedom of expression. In my view, the harm sought to be avoided in the case of the dissemination of obscene materials is similar. In the words of Nemetz C.J.B.C. in *R. v. Red Hot Video Ltd.* (1985), 45 C.R. (3d) 36 (B.C.C.A.), there is a growing concern that the exploitation of women and children, depicted in publications and films, can, in certain circumstances, lead to "abject and servile victimization" (at pp. 43-44). As Anderson J.A. also noted in the same case, if true equality between male and female persons is to be achieved, we cannot ignore the threat to equality resulting from exposure to audiences of certain types of violent and degrading material. Material portraying women as a class as objects for sexual exploitation and abuse have a negative impact on "the individual's sense of self-worth and acceptance".

In reaching the conclusion that legislation proscribing obscenity is a valid objective which justifies some encroachment on the right to freedom of expression, I am persuaded in part that such legislation may be found in most free and democratic societies. As Nemetz C.J.B.C. aptly pointed out in *R. v. Red Hot Video, supra*, for centuries democratic societies have set certain limits to freedom of expression. He cited (at p. 40) the following passage of Dickson J.A. (As he then was) in *R. v. Great West News Ltd., supra*, [[1970] 4 C.C.C. 307] at p. 309.

". . . all organized societies have sought in one manner or another to suppress obscenity. The right of the state to legislate to protect its moral fibre and well-being has long been recognized, with roots deep in history. It is within this frame that the Courts and Judges must work." . . .

The enactment of the impugned provision is also consistent with Canada's international obligations (Agreement for the Suppression of the Circulation of Obscene Publications and the Convention for the Suppression of the Circulation of and Traffic in Obscene Publications).

Finally, it should be noted that the burgeoning pornography industry renders the concern even more pressing and substantial than when the impugned provisions were first enacted. I would therefore conclude that the objective of avoiding the harm associated with the dissemination of pornography in this case is sufficiently pressing and substantial to warrant some restriction on full exercise of the right to freedom of expression. The analysis of whether the measure is proportional to the objective must, in my view, be undertaken in light of the conclusion that the objective of the impugned section is valid only in so far as it relates to the harm to society associated with obscene materials. Indeed, the section as interpreted in previous decisions and in these reasons is fully consistent with that objective. The objective of maintaining conventional standards of propriety, independently of any harm to society, is no longer justified in light of the values of individual liberty which underlie the Charter. This, then being the objective of s. 163, which I have found to be pressing and substantial, I must now determine whether the section is rationally connected and proportional to this objective. As outlined above, s. 163(8) criminalizes the exploitation of sex and sex and violence, when, on the basis of the community test, it is undue. The determination of when such exploitation is undue is directly related to the immediacy of a risk of harm to society which is reasonably perceived as arising from its dissemination. . . .

. . . .

While a direct link between obscenity and harm to society may be difficult, if not impossible, to establish, it is reasonable to presume that exposure to images bears a causal relationship to changes in attitudes and beliefs. The Meese Commission Report, supra, concluded in respect of sexually violent material (vol. 1, at p. 326):

> . . .the available evidence strongly supports the hypothesis that substantial exposure to sexually violent materials as described here bears a causal relationship to anti-social acts of sexual violence and, for some subgroups, possibly to unlawful acts of sexual violence.

Although we rely for this conclusion on significant scientific empirical evidence, we feel it worthwhile to note the underlying logic of the conclusion. The evidence says simply that the images that people are exposed to bear a causal relationship to their behavior. This is hardly surprising. What would be surprising would be to find otherwise, and we have not so found. We have not, of course, found that the images people are exposed to are a greater cause of sexual violence than all or even many other possible causes the investigation of which has been beyond our mandate. Nevertheless, it would be strange indeed if graphic representations of a form of behavior, especially in a form that almost exclusively portrays such behavior as desirable, did not have at least some effect on patterns of behavior." . . .

Accordingly, I am of the view that there is a sufficiently rational link between the criminal sanction which demonstrates our community's disapproval of the dissemination of materials which potentially victimize women and which restricts the negative influence which such materials have on changes in attitudes and behavior, and the objective. . . .

There are several factors which contribute to the finding that the provision minimally impairs the freedom which is infringed.

First, the impugned provision does not proscribe sexually explicit erotica without violence that is not degrading or dehumanizing. It is designed to catch material that creates a risk of harm to society. It might be suggested that proof of actual harm should be required. It is apparent from what I have said above that it is sufficient in this regard for Parliament to have a reasonable basis for concluding that harm will result and this requirement does not demand actual proof of harm.

Second, materials which have scientific, artistic or literary merit are not captured by the provision. As discussed above, the court must be generous in its application of the "artistic defense". For example, in certain cases, materials such as photographs, prints, books and films which may undoubtedly be produced with some motive for economic profit, may nonetheless claim the protection of the Charter in so far as their defining characteristic is that of aesthetic expression, and thus represent the artist's attempt at individual fulfilment. The existence of an accompanying economic motive does not, of itself, deprive a work of significance as an example of individual artistic or self-fulfilment.

Third, in considering whether the provision minimally impairs the freedom in question, it is legitimate for the court to take into account Parliament's past abortive attempts to replace the definition with one that is more explicit. In *Irwin Toy*, our Court recognized that it is legitimate to take into account the fact that earlier laws and proposed alternatives were thought to be less effective than the legislation that is presently being challenged. The attempt to provide exhaustive instances of obscenity has been shown to be destined to fail (Bill C-54, 2nd Sess., 33rd Parl.). It seems that the only practicable alternative is to strive towards a more abstract definition of obscenity which is contextually sensitive and responsive to progress in the knowledge and understanding to the phenomenon to which the legislation is directed. In my view, the standard of "undue exploitation" is therefore appropriate. The intractable nature of the problem and the impossibility of precisely defining a notion which is inherently elusive makes the possibility of a more explicit provision remote. In this light, it is appropriate to question whether and at what cost, greater legislative precision can be demanded.

Fourth, while the discussion in this appeal has been limited to the definition portion of s. 163, I would note that the impugned section, with the possible exception of subs. 1, which is not in issue here has been held by this Court not to extend its reach to the private use of viewing of obscene materials. . . .

I conclude that while s. 163(8) infringes s. 2(b) of the Charter, freedom of expression, it constitutes a reasonable limit and is saved by virtue of the provisions of s. 1. [Because neither of the lower courts applied the proper definition of obscenity, the Supreme Court of Canada remanded the case back to the trial court and directed a new trial on all charges.]

NOTES AND QUESTIONS

1. *The gender equality rationale.* Does gender equality represent a more persuasive basis for regulating erotica than generalized concerns about public morality? Does the Supreme Court of Canada make a persuasive case that erotica undermines the government's goal of creating and maintaining a truly egalitarian society? Indianapolis, Indiana, made the same arguments in favor of regulating erotica in *Hudnut* that the Supreme Court of Canada endorses in *Butler.* Is content or viewpoint discrimination in regulating erotica justifiable on equality grounds? Is some pornography more socially harmful than other pornography, because of how it presents women as a class? If you think Judge Easterbrook's argument against this position is persuasive, how can you justify special burdens on erotica in the first place, in that these restrictions rest on viewpoint hostility (whether on generic morals or equality grounds)? *See* Nadine Strossen, *Hate Speech and Pornography: Do We Have to Choose Between Freedom of Speech and Equality?*, 46 Case W. Res. L. Rev. 449, 458-477 (1996) (arguing that restrictions on sexually explicit speech actually undermine efforts to promote gender equality between the sexes).

2. *Degrading and dehumanizing defined.* What kind of pornography is "dehumanizing" and "degrading"? You might be interested to know that the Canadian Customs Service found that gay and lesbian erotica is the epitome of obscenity under section 163. Little Sisters Book & Art Emporium v. Commissioner, [2000] 2 S.C.R. 1120 (Can.). Is a culturally contingent standard, such as whether material is "degrading," capable of even-handed enforcement? For arguments that it is not, see Ronald J. Krotoszynski, Jr., *The First Amendment in Cross-Cultural Perspective: A Comparative Legal Analysis* 69-79, 82-87 (2006) (discussing problems associated with highly targeted enforcement of both obscenity and hate speech laws in Canada); Steven G. Gey, *Postmodern Censorship Revisited: A Reply to Richard Delgado*, 146 U. Pa. L.

Rev. 1077, 1089-1090 (1998) (noting problem of differential enforcement of obscenity laws, and other laws permitting government to restrict speech, to silence unpopular minorities).

3. *Medium-specific regulation and zoning of indecent speech.* Unlike obscene speech, indecent speech is not an unprotected category of speech. As we saw in Chapter 8, however, the Supreme Court has interpreted the First Amendment to permit more restrictions on nonobscene but "indecent" speech in the broadcast medium than in print, on cable television, or the internet. We also saw in Chapter 3 that the Supreme Court upheld a zoning ordinance restricting locations of "adult businesses" by treating it as if it were a content-neutral time, place, and manner restriction rather than a restriction based on the sexual content of the expression offered by these businesses. See City of Renton v. Playtime Theatres, 475 U.S. 41 (1986).

THEORY-APPLIED PROBLEM

The Contemporary Arts Center (CAC), in Cincinnati, Ohio, hosts a traveling exhibition of photographs by Robert Mapplethorpe, entitled *Robert Mapplethorpe: The Perfect Moment.* Mapplethorpe's oeuvre largely consists of graphic depictions of "homoerotic" art, including photographs of hard-core sex acts associated with images of sadomasochism, bondage, domination, and affiliated sex practices. Mapplethorpe's photographs, mostly in black and white, received very positive critical commentary and, in fact, hang on the walls of some of the nation's most well-respected art museums. For a long period of time, Cincinnati has maintained vigilant efforts to maintain its community standards of decency, and has vigorously enforced state and local laws regulating obscenity. When the local district attorney learns of the planned exhibition, he sues Dennis Barrie, the CAC's director, in a local state court, seeking an injunction against the exhibition of the Mapplethorpe photographs to the public. The district attorney argues that the pictures are patently offensive and offend community standards; he also alleges the photographs present sex and excretory functions in a prurient fashion (again applying contemporary community standards). Finally, the district attorney says that promotional materials for the show "pander" by emphasizing the salacious quality of the photographs and that, regardless of whether the photographs are legally obscene under *Miller*, they may be suppressed on the basis of this pandering. At the hearing on the preliminary injunction, the director offers into evidence five affidavits from recognized art experts stating that the Mapplethorpe photographs possess "significant artistic merit." Applying the *Miller* standard, how should the trial court rule? Should an injunction issue prohibiting the display of photographs in advance of the actual exhibit opening to the public? If the promotional materials for the exhibit emphasized the sexual content, would this be a basis for declaring the materials obscene, regardless of whether the prosecution meets the *Miller* standard?

B. CHILDREN AND PORNOGRAPHY

The Supreme Court has signaled that protecting children from sexual exploitation constitutes a compelling government interest that justifies substantially broader regulation of child pornography featuring real children than would be permissible under the *Miller* standard. The following cases set forth the special rules that govern materials featuring nude depictions of children (whether pornographic in nature or not).

NEW YORK v. FERBER

458 U.S. 747 (1982)

WHITE, J., delivered the opinion of the Court.

At issue in this case is the constitutionality of a New York criminal statute which prohibits persons from knowingly promoting sexual performances by children under the age of 16 by distributing material which depicts such performances.

In recent years, the exploitive use of children in the production of pornography has become a serious national problem. The Federal Government and 47 States have sought to combat the problem with statutes specifically directed at the production of child pornography. At least half of such statutes do not require that the materials produced be legally obscene. Thirty-five States and the United States Congress have also passed legislation prohibiting the distribution of such materials; 20 States prohibit the distribution of material depicting children engaged in sexual conduct without requiring that the material be legally obscene. New York is one of the 20. In 1977, the New York Legislature enacted Article 263 of its Penal Law. N.Y. Penal Law, Art. 263 (McKinney 1980). Section 263.05 criminalizes as a class C felony the use of a child in a sexual performance:

> A person is guilty of the use of a child in a sexual performance if knowing the character and content thereof he employs, authorizes or induces a child less than sixteen years of age to engage in a sexual performance or being a parent, legal guardian or custodian of such child, he consents to the participation by such child in a sexual performance.

A "[s]exual performance" is defined as "any performance or part thereof which includes sexual conduct by a child less than sixteen years of age." § 263.00(1). "Sexual conduct" is in turn defined in § 263.00(3):

> Sexual conduct' means actual or simulated sexual intercourse, deviate sexual intercourse, sexual bestiality, masturbation, sado-masochistic abuse, or lewd exhibition of the genitals.

A "performance" is defined as "any play, motion picture, photograph or dance" or "any other visual representation exhibited before an audience." § 263.00(4). . . .

This case arose when Paul Ferber, the proprietor of a Manhattan bookstore specializing in sexually oriented products, sold two films to an undercover police officer. The films are devoted almost exclusively to depicting young boys masturbating. Ferber was indicted on two counts of violating § 263.10 and two counts of violating § 263.15, the two New York laws controlling dissemination of child pornography. After a jury trial, Ferber was acquitted of the two counts of promoting an obscene sexual performance, but found guilty of the two counts under § 263.15, which did not require proof that the films were obscene. Ferber's convictions were affirmed without opinion by the Appellate Division of the New York State Supreme Court.

The New York Court of Appeals reversed, holding that § 263.15 violated the First Amendment. . . .

The Court of Appeals proceeded on the assumption that the standard of obscenity incorporated in § 263.10, which follows the guidelines enunciated in *Miller v. California*, 413 U.S. 15 (1973), constitutes the appropriate line dividing protected from unprotected expression by which to measure a regulation directed at child pornography. It was on the premise that "nonobscene adolescent sex" could not be singled out for special treatment that the court found § 263.15 "strikingly underinclusive." Moreover, the assumption that the constitutionally permissible regulation of pornography could not be more extensive with respect to the distribution of material depicting children may also have led the court to conclude that a narrowing construction of § 263.15 was unavailable.

The Court of Appeals' assumption was not unreasonable in light of our decisions. This case, however, constitutes our first examination of a statute directed at and limited to depictions of sexual activity involving children. We believe our inquiry should begin with the question of whether a State has somewhat more freedom in proscribing works which portray sexual acts or lewd exhibitions of genitalia by children. . . .

The *Miller* standard, like its predecessors, was an accommodation between the State's interests in protecting the "sensibilities of the unwilling recipients" from exposure to pornographic material and the dangers of censorship inherent in unabashedly content-based laws. Like obscenity statutes, laws directed at the dissemination of child pornography run the risk of suppressing protected expression by allowing the hand of the censor to become unduly heavy. For the following reasons, however, we are persuaded that the States are entitled to greater leeway in the regulation of pornographic depictions of children.

First. It is evident beyond the need for elaboration that a State's interest in "safeguarding the physical and psychological well-being of a minor" is "compelling." *Globe Newspaper Co. v. Superior Court*, 457 U.S. 596, 607 (1982). "A democratic society rests, for its continuance, upon the healthy, well-rounded growth of young people into full maturity as citizens." *Prince v. Massachusetts*, 321 U.S. 158, 168 (1944). Accordingly, we have sustained legislation aimed at protecting the physical and emotional well-being of youth even when the laws have operated in the sensitive area of constitutionally protected rights. In *Prince v. Massachusetts, supra*, the Court held that a statute prohibiting use of a child to distribute literature on the street was valid notwithstanding the statute's effect on a First Amendment activity. In *Ginsberg v. New York, supra*, we sustained a New York law protecting children from exposure to nonobscene literature. Most recently, we held that the Government's interest in the "well-being of its youth" justified special treatment of indecent broadcasting received by adults as well as children. *FCC v. Pacifica Foundation*, 438 U.S. 726 (1978).

The prevention of sexual exploitation and abuse of children constitutes a government objective of surpassing importance. [Justice White found that the creation of child pornography causes "physiological, emotional and mental health" harms to children involved in its production.]

Second. The distribution of photographs and films depicting sexual activity by juveniles is intrinsically related to the sexual abuse of children in at least two ways. First, the materials produced are a permanent record of the children's participation and the harm to the child is exacerbated by their circulation. Second, the distribution network for child pornography must be closed if the production of material which requires the sexual exploitation of children is to be effectively controlled. Indeed, there is not serious contention that the legislature was unjustified in believing that it is difficult, if not impossible, to halt the exploitation of children by pursuing only those who produce the photographs and movies. . . .

Third. The advertising and selling of child pornography provide an economic motive for and are thus an integral part of the production of such materials, an activity illegal throughout the Nation. "It rarely has been suggested that the constitutional freedom for speech and press extends its immunity to speech or writing used as an integral part of conduct in violation of a valid criminal statute." *Giboney v. Empire Storage & Ice Co.*, 336 U.S. 490, 498 (1949). . . .

Fourth. The value of permitting live performances and photographic reproductions of children engaged in lewd sexual conduct is exceedingly modest, if not *de minimis.* We consider it unlikely that visual depictions of children performing sexual acts or lewdly exhibiting their genitals would often constitute an important and necessary part of a literary performance or scientific or educational work. As a state judge in this case observed, if it were necessary for literary or artistic value, a person over the statutory age who perhaps looked younger could be utilized. Simulation outside of the prohibition of the statute could provide another alternative. Nor is there any question here of censoring a particular literary theme or portrayal of sexual activity. The First Amendment interest is limited to that of rendering the portrayal somewhat more "realistic" by utilizing or photographing children.

Fifth. Recognizing and classifying child pornography as a category of material outside the protection of the First Amendment is not incompatible with our earlier decisions. . . .

There are, of course, limits on the category of child pornography which, like obscenity, is unprotected by the First Amendment. As with all legislation in this sensitive area, the conduct to be prohibited must be adequately defined by the applicable state law, as written or authoritatively construed. Here the nature of the harm to be combated requires that the state offense be limited to works that *visually* depict sexual conduct by children below a specified age. The category of "sexual conduct" proscribed must also be suitably limited and described.

The test for child pornography is separate from the obscenity standard enunciated in *Miller,* but may be compared to it for the purpose of clarity. The *Miller* formulation is adjusted in the following respects: A trier of fact need not find that the material appeals to the prurient interest of the average person; it is not required that sexual conduct portrayed be done so in a patently offensive manner; and the material at issue need not be considered as whole. We note that the distribution of descriptions or other depictions of sexual conduct, not otherwise obscene, which do not involve live performance or photographic or other visual reproduction of live performances retains First Amendment protection. As with obscenity laws, criminal responsibility may not be imposed without some element of scienter on the part of the defendant. *Smith v. California,* 361 U.S. 147 (1959); *Hamling v. United States,* 418 U.S. 87 (1974).

Section 263.15's prohibition incorporates a definition of sexual conduct that comports with the above-stated principles. The forbidden acts to be depicted are listed with sufficient precision and represent the kind of conduct that, if it were the theme of a work, could render it legally obscene: "actual or simulated sexual intercourse, deviate sexual intercourse, sexual bestiality, masturbation, sado-masochistic abuse, or lewd exhibition of the genitals." § 263.00(3). The term "lewd exhibition of the genitals" is not unknown in this area and, indeed, was given in *Miller* as an example of a permissible regulation. 413 U.S., at 25. A performance is defined only to include live or visual depictions: "any play, motion picture, photograph or dance . . . [or] other visual representation exhibited before an audience." § 263.00(4). Section 263.15 expressly includes a scienter requirement.

We hold that § 263.15 sufficiently describes a category of material the production and distribution of which is not entitled to First Amendment protection. It is therefore clear that there is nothing unconstitutionally "underinclusive" about a statute that singles out this category of material for proscription. It also follows that the State is not barred by the First Amendment from prohibiting the distribution of unprotected materials produced outside the State.

It remains to address the claim that the New York statute is unconstitutionally overbroad because it would forbid the distribution of material with serious literary, scientific, or educational value or material which does not threaten the harms sought to be combated by the State. Respondent prevailed on that ground below, and it is to that issue that we now turn. [The majority concluded that § 263.15 was not substantially overbroad.]

Because § 263.15 is not substantially overbroad, it is unnecessary to consider its application to material that does not depict sexual conduct of a type that New York may restrict consistent with the First Amendment. As applied to Paul Ferber and to others who distribute similar material, the statute does not violate the First Amendment as applied to the States through the Fourteenth. The judgment of the New York Court of Appeals is reversed, and the case is remanded to that court for further proceedings not inconsistent with this opinion.

So ordered.

O'CONNOR, J., concurring.

Although I join the court's opinion, I write separately to stress that the Court does not hold that New York must except "material with serious literary, scientific, or educational value," from its statute. The Court merely holds that, even if the First Amendment shelters such material, New York's current statute is not sufficiently overbroad to support respondent's facial attack. The compelling interests identified in today's opinion, suggest that the Constitution might in fact permit New York to ban knowing distribution of works depicting minors engaged in explicit sexual conduct, regardless of the social value of the depictions. For example, a 12-year-old child photographed while masturbating surely suffers the same psychological harm whether the community labels the photograph "edifying" or "tasteless." The audience's appreciation of the depiction is simply irrelevant to New York's asserted interest in protecting children from psychological, emotional, and mental harm. . . .

BRENNAN, J., with whom MARSHALL, J., joins, concurring in the judgment.

I agree with much of what is said in the Court's opinion. As I made clear in the opinion I delivered for the Court in *Ginsburg v. New York*, 390 U.S. 629 (1968), the State has a special interest in protecting the well-being of its youth. [] This special and compelling interest, and the particular vulnerability of children, afford the State the leeway to regulate pornographic material, the promotion of which is harmful to children, even though the State does not have such leeway when it seeks only to protect consenting adults from exposure to such material. *Ginsburg v. New York*. [] I also agree with the Court that the "tiny fraction," *ante*, at 773, of material of serious artistic, scientific, or educational value that could conceivably fall within the reach of the statute is insufficient to justify striking the statute on the grounds of overbreadth. See *Broadrick v. Oklahoma*, 413 U.S. 601, 630 (1973) (Brennan, J., dissenting).

But in my view application of § 263.15 or any similar statute to depictions of children that in themselves do have serious literary, artistic, scientific, or medical value, would violate the First Amendment. As the Court recognizes, the limited classes of speech, the suppression of which does not raise serious First Amendment concerns, have two attributes. They are of exceedingly "slight social value," and the State has a compelling interest in their regulation. See *Chaplinsky v. New Hampshire*, 315 U.S. 568, 571-572 (1942). The First Amendment value of depictions of children that are in themselves serious contributions to art, literature or science, is, by definition, simply not "*de minimis.* "At the same time, the State's interest in suppression of such materials is likely to be far less compelling. For the Court's assumption of harm to the child resulting from the "permanent record" and "circulation" of the child's "participation," [] lacks much of its force where the depiction is a serious contribution to art or science. The production of materials of serious value is not the "low-profile, clandestine industry" that according to the court produces purely pornographic materials. [] In short, it is inconceivable how a depiction of a child that is itself a serious contribution to the world of art or literature or science can be deemed "material outside the protection of the First Amendment."

I, of course, adhere to my view that, in the absence of exposure, or particular harm, to juveniles or unconsenting adults, the State lacks power to suppress sexually oriented materials. See, *e.g., Paris Adult Theatre I v. Slaton*, 413 U.S. 49, 73 (1973) (Brennan, J., dissenting). With this understanding, I concur in the Court's judgment in this case.

[Justice STEVENS'S concurring opinion is omitted.]

NOTES AND QUESTIONS

1. *Child pornography made without children.* Why does Justice White emphasize, repeatedly, that *Ferber*'s holding is limited to "visual" depictions of real children? Couldn't a book, like Vladimir Nabokov's *Lolita*, although in a purely written form, also help to contribute to a market for child pornography by increasing demand for such wares?
2. *Naked children in artworks.* Should serious works of art be proscribable solely because they depict naked children? For example, photographer Sally Mann created a series of black-and-white posed nudes of her children, Emmett, Jessie, and Virginia, in a series inspired by various classical myths. *See* Sally Mann, *Immediate Family* (1992). Art critics deemed the works to possess significant merit. Should this factor into the First Amendment analysis at all? For an argument that *Ferber* understates the potential loss of serious artistic work, see Amy Adler, *The Perverse Law of Child Pornography*, 101 Colum. L. Rev. 209, 253-256 (2001) (discussing Mann's work and work of other art photographers

that feature nude depictions of children and suggesting that harm of such depictions is largely a function of cultural factors, rather than intrinsic to the creation of such materials); *see also* Connie Samaras, *Feminism, Photography, Censorship, and Sexually Transgressive Imagery: The Work of Robert Mapplethorpe, Joel-Peter Witkin, Jacqueline Livingston, Sally Mann, and Catherine Opie,* 38 N.Y.L. Sch. L. Rev. 75 (1993).

3. *Devaluing child pornography.* Justice Brennan seems to disagree with Justice O'Connor, and perhaps Justice White, that the First Amendment would tolerate suppression of materials that in any way depict real nude children. Instead, his agreement seems to stem from the fact that the materials in question, taken as a whole, possessed meager social value, even if they were not legally obscene in New York City. What are the potential benefits and costs of adopting Brennan's approach to the problem of nude depictions of real children?

4. *Family photos of naked children.* Does *Ferber* mean that a parent could face a felony conviction for taking pictures of his child in the bath or on a training "potty"? Such pictures are relatively common in contemporary U.S. culture (much to the horror of teenage and adult children who find such photographs enormously embarrassing). On the other hand, should the question be whether materials could be used for a prurient purpose, as opposed to whether the possessor actually made or possessed the materials with a prurient intent?

5. *Is violent speech directed at children an unprotected category of speech, akin to obscenity?* Brown v. Entertainment Merchants Ass'n, 564 U.S. 786 (2011), involved a constitutional challenge to a state prohibiting sale or rental of "violent video games" to minors. The state of California argued that the "interactive" nature of violent video games justified restricting them from minors and provided media effects research purportedly showing that interactive or immersive media experiences can lead to harm. The Court rejected the argument that medium-specific characteristics of video games justified relaxing First Amendment prohibitions on content-based regulation or creating a new category of unprotected speech. Although the Court believed that video games serve First Amendment purposes only fitfully, if at all, it nonetheless gave them full protection, observing that "we have long recognized that it is difficult to distinguish politics from entertainment, and dangerous to try." *Id.* at 790. Video games "communicate ideas—and even social messages—through many familiar literary devices" as well as "through features distinctive to the medium (such as the player's interaction with the virtual world)." *Id.* The Court acknowledged "the challenges of applying the Constitution to ever-advancing technology," but affirmed the "most basic First Amendment principle, namely that government may not impose content-based limitations except in "well-defined and narrowly limited classes of speech, the prevention and punishment of which has never been thought to raise any Constitutional problem." *Id.* at 790-91. The Court rejected the invitation to expand the categories of unprotected speech simply because the violent video games were "directed at children." *Id.* at 794. Ultimately, the Court declared the video game legislation unconstitutional because California failed to "show a direct causal link between violent video games and harm to minors." *Brown,* 564 U.S. at 799. The media effects research on which California relied was methodologically unsound. The Court also found the legislation particularly unnecessary in light of the evidence on the record that the video game industry already performed a great deal of self-policing by

voluntarily refusing to sell to minors video games (voluntarily) labeled as appropriate only for mature audiences. *See id.* at 802-803. The legislation was overinclusive because, in attempting to assist parents in controlling their children's access to violent fare, it prevented access even by those children whose parents did not care whether they purchased such fare. *Id.* at 804-05. For a strong argument that violent material aimed at children should not be protected by the First Amendment, see Kevin W. Saunders, *Violence as Obscenity: Limiting the Media's First Amendment Protection* (1996).

In Stanley v. Georgia, 394 U.S. 557 (1969), the Supreme Court held that although government may proscribe obscene materials, adults have a right to possess and review obscene materials in the home as a matter of protected freedom of speech. *Ferber* raised a follow-up question: Does the rule of *Stanley* apply to child pornography? The following case provides the Supreme Court's (unsurprising) answer.

OSBORNE v. OHIO

495 U.S. 103 (1990)

WHITE, J., delivered the opinion of the Court.

In order to combat child pornography, Ohio enacted Rev. Code Ann. § 2907.323(A)(3) (Supp. 1989), which provides in pertinent part:

(A) No person shall do any of the following:

(3) Possess or view any material or performance that shows a minor who is not the person's child or ward in a state of nudity, unless one of the following applies:

(a) The material or performance is sold, disseminated, displayed, possessed, controlled, brought or caused to be brought into this state, or presented for a bona fide artistic, medical, scientific, educational, religious, governmental, judicial, or other proper purpose, by or to a physician, psychologist, sociologist, scientist, teacher, person pursuing bona fide studies or research, librarian, clergyman, prosecutor, judge, or other person having a proper interest in the material or performance.

(b) The person knows that the parents, guardian, or custodian has consented in writing to the photographing or use of the minor in a state of nudity and to the manner in which the material or performance is used or transferred.

Petitioner, Clyde Osborne, was convicted of violating this statute and sentenced to six months in prison, after the Columbus, Ohio, police, pursuant to a valid search, found four photographs in Osborne's home. Each photograph depicts a nude male adolescent posed in a sexually explicit position.[1]

---

[1] Osborne contends that the subject in all of the pictures is the same boy; Osborne testified at trial that he was told that the youth was 14 at the time that the photographs were taken. The government maintains that three of the pictures are of one boy and one of the pictures is of another. Three photographs depict the same boy in different positions: sitting with his legs over his head and his anus exposed; lying down with an erect penis and with an electrical object in his hand; and lying down with a plastic object which appears to be inserted in his anus. The fourth photograph

The Ohio Supreme Court affirmed Osborne's conviction, after an intermediate appellate court did the same. Relying on one of its earlier decisions, the court first rejected Osborne's contention that the First Amendment prohibits the States from proscribing the private possession of child pornography.

Next, the court found that § 2907.323(A)(3) is not unconstitutionally overbroad. In so doing, the court, relying on the statutory exceptions, read § 2907.323(A)(3) as only applying to depictions of nudity involving a lewd exhibition or graphic focus on a minor's genitals. The court also found that scienter is an essential element of a § 2907.323(A) offense. . . .

The threshold question in this case is whether Ohio may constitutionally proscribe the possession and viewing of child pornography or whether, as Osborne argues, our decision in *Stanley v. Georgia*, 394 U.S. 557 (1969), compels the contrary result. In *Stanley*, we struck down a Georgia law outlawing the private possession of obscene material. We recognized that the statute impinged upon Stanley's right to receive information in the privacy of his home, and we found Georgia's justifications for its law inadequate.

Stanley should not be read too broadly. We have previously noted that *Stanley* was a narrow holding, see *United States v. 12 200-ft. Reels of Film*, 413 U.S. 123, 127 (1973), and, since the decision in that case, the value of permitting child pornography has been characterized as "exceedingly modest, if not *de minimis*." *New York v. Ferber*, 458 U.S. 747, 762 (1982). But assuming, for the sake of argument, that Osborne has a First Amendment interest in viewing and possessing child pornography, we nonetheless find this case distinct from *Stanley* because the interests underlying child pornography prohibitions far exceed the interests justifying the Georgia law at issue in *Stanley*. Every court to address the issue has so concluded.

In *Stanley*, Georgia primarily sought to proscribe the private possession of obscenity because it was concerned that obscenity would poison the minds of its viewers. 394 U.S., at 565. We responded that "[w]hatever the power of the state to control public dissemination of ideas inimical to the public morality, it cannot constitutionally premise legislation on the desirability of controlling a person's private thoughts." [] The difference here is obvious: The State does not rely on a paternalistic interest in regulating Osborne's mind. Rather, Ohio has enacted § 2907.323(A)(3) in order to protect the victims of child pornography; it hopes to destroy a market for the exploitative use of children.

> It is evident beyond the need for elaboration that a State's interest in 'safeguarding the physical and psychological wellbeing of a minor' is 'compelling.' . . . The legislative judgment, as well as the judgment found in relevant literature, is that the use of children as subjects of pornographic materials is harmful to the physiological, emotional, and mental health of the child. That judgment, we think, easily passes muster under the First Amendment.

Ferber, 458 U.S., at 756-758 (citations omitted). It is also surely reasonable for the State to conclude that it will decrease the production of child pornography if it penalizes those who possess and view the product, thereby decreasing demand. . . .

Osborne contends that the State should use other measures, besides penalizing possession, to dry up the child pornography market. Osborne points out that in

---

depicts a nude standing boy; it is unclear whether this subject is the same boy photographed in the other pictures because the photograph only depicts the boy's torso.

Stanley we rejected Georgia's argument that its prohibition on obscenity possession was a necessary incident to its proscription on obscenity distribution. 394 U.S., at 567-568. This holding, however, must be viewed in light of the weak interests asserted by the State in that case. *Stanley* itself emphasized that we did not "mean to express any opinion on statutes making criminal possession of other types of printed, filmed, or recorded materials. In such cases, compelling reasons may exist for overriding the right of the individual to possess those materials." []

Given the importance of the State's interest in protecting the victims of child pornography, we cannot fault Ohio for attempting to stamp out this vice at all levels in the distribution chain. According to the State, since the time of our decision in *Ferber*, much of the child pornography market has been driven underground; as a result, it is now difficult, if not impossible, to solve the child pornography problem by only attacking production and distribution. Indeed, 19 States have found it necessary to proscribe the possession of this material.

Other interests also support the Ohio law. First, as *Ferber* recognized, the materials produced by child pornographers permanently record the victim's abuse. The pornography's continued existence causes the child victims continuing harm by haunting the children in years to come. 458 U.S., at 759. The State's ban on possession and viewing encourages the possessors of these materials to destroy them. Second, encouraging the destruction of these materials is also desirable because evidence suggests that pedophiles use child pornography to seduce other children into sexual activity.

Given the gravity of the State's interests in this context, we find that Ohio may constitutionally proscribe the possession and viewing of child pornography.

Osborne next argues that even if the State may constitutionally ban the possession of child pornography, his conviction is invalid because § 2907.323(A)(3) is unconstitutionally overbroad in that it criminalizes an intolerable range of constitutionally protected conduct.[8] In our previous decisions discussing the First Amendment overbreadth doctrine, we have repeatedly emphasized that where a statute regulates expressive conduct, the scope of the statute does not render it unconstitutional unless its overbreadth is not only "real, but substantial as well, judged in relation to the statute's plainly legitimate sweep." *Broadrick v. Oklahoma*, 413 U.S. 601, 615 (1973). Even where a statute at its margins infringes on protected expression, "facial invalidation is inappropriate if the 'remainder of the statute . . . covers a whole range of easily identifiable and constitutionally proscribable . . . conduct. . . .'" *New York v. Ferber*, 458 U.S., at 770, n. 25.

The Ohio statute, on its face, purports to prohibit the possession of "nude" photographs of minors. We have stated that depictions of nudity, without more, constitute protected expression. See *Ferber, supra*, at 765, n. 18. Relying on this observation, Osborne argues that the statute as written is substantially overbroad. We are skeptical of this claim because, in light of the statute's exemptions and "proper purposes" provisions, the statute may not be substantially overbroad under our

---

[8] In the First Amendment context, we permit defendants to challenge statutes on overbreadth grounds, regardless of whether the individual defendant's conduct is constitutionally protected. "The First Amendment doctrine of substantial overbreadth is an exception to the general rule that a person to whom a statute may be constitutionally applied cannot challenge the statute on the ground that it may be unconstitutionally applied to others." Massachusetts v. Oakes, 491 U.S. 576, 581 (1989).

cases.[9] However that may be, Osborne's overbreadth challenge, in any event, fails because the statute, as construed by the Ohio Supreme Court on Osborne's direct appeal, plainly survives overbreadth scrutiny. Under the Ohio Supreme Court reading, the statute prohibits "the possession or viewing of material or performance of a minor who is in a state of nudity, where such nudity constitutes a lewd exhibition or involves a graphic focus on the genitals, and where the person depicted is neither the child nor the ward of the person charged. By limiting the statute's operation in this manner, the Ohio Supreme Court avoided penalizing persons for viewing or possessing innocuous photographs of naked children. We have upheld similar language against overbreadth challenges in the past. . . .

Like the petitioners [in a number of other overbreadth cases], Osborne had notice that his conduct was proscribed. It is obvious from the face of § 2907.323(A)(3) that the goal of the statute is to eradicate child pornography. The provision criminalizes the viewing and possessing of material depicting children in a state of nudity for other than "proper purposes." The provision appears in the "Sex Offenses" chapter of the Ohio Code. Section 2907.323 is preceded by § 2907.322, which proscribes "[p]andering sexually oriented matter involving a minor," and followed by § 2907.33, which proscribes "[d]eception to obtain matter harmful to juveniles." That Osborne's photographs of adolescent boys in sexually explicit situations constitute child pornography hardly needs elaboration. Therefore, although § 2907.323(A)(3) as written may have been imprecise at its fringes, someone in Osborne's position would not be surprised to learn that his possession of the four photographs at issue in this case constituted a crime. . . .

Having rejected Osborne's *Stanley* and overbreadth arguments, we now reach Osborne's final objection to his conviction: his contention that he was denied due process because it is unclear that his conviction was based on a finding that each of the elements of § 2907.323(A)(3) was present. [Justice White found that this argument possessed merit. Because the Ohio trial court used incomplete jury instructions, the Supreme Court granted Osborne a new trial.]

To conclude, although we find Osborne's First Amendment arguments unpersuasive, we reverse his conviction and remand for a new trial in order to ensure that Osborne's conviction stemmed from a finding that the State had proved each of the elements of § 2907.323(A)(3).

---

[9] The statute applies only where an individual possesses or views the depiction of a minor "who is not the person's child or ward." The State, moreover, does not impose criminal liability if either "[t]he material or performance is sold, disseminated, displayed, possessed, controlled, brought or caused to be brought into this state, or presented for a bona fide artistic, medical, scientific, educational, religious, governmental, judicial, or other proper purpose, by or to a physician, psychologist, sociologist, scientist, teacher, person pursuing bona fide studies or research, librarian, clergyman, prosecutor, judge, or other person having a proper interest in the material or performance," or "[t]he person knows that the parents, guardian, or custodian has consented in writing to the photographing or use of the minor in a state of nudity and to the manner in which the material or performance is used or transferred." It is true that, despite the statutory exceptions, one might imagine circumstances in which the statute, by its terms, criminalizes constitutionally protected conduct. If, for example, a parent gave a family friend a picture of the parent's infant taken while the infant was unclothed, the statute would apply. But, given the broad statutory exceptions and the prevalence of child pornography, it is far from clear that the instances where the statute applies to constitutionally protected conduct are significant enough to warrant a finding that the statute is overbroad. . . .

[Justice BLACKMUN'S concurring opinion is omitted.]

BRENNAN, J., with whom MARSHALL, J., and STEVENS, J., join, dissenting.

I agree with the Court that appellant's conviction must be reversed. I do not agree, however, that Ohio is free on remand to retry him under Ohio Rev. Code Ann. § 2907.323(A)(3) (Supp. 1989) as it currently exists. In my view, the state law, even as construed authoritatively by the Ohio Supreme Court, is still fatally overbroad, and our decision in *Stanley v. Georgia*, 394 U.S. 557 (1969), prevents the State from criminalizing appellant's possession of the photographs at issue in this case. I therefore respectfully dissent. . . .

NOTES AND QUESTIONS

1. *Competing principles.* Given that *Ferber* held that suppressing demand for the creation of child pornography was a legitimate government objective, is *Osborne* a logical extension of *Ferber*? Or should the general notion that one's home implicates a zone of privacy justify the application of *Stanley* to these materials? Does Justice White or Justice Brennan have the better view of which principle should be controlling on these facts?

2. *Canada, compared.* Although the Supreme Court of Canada nominally upheld Canada's federal anti–child pornography statute, it engrafted a host of limits and exemptions, including an exemption for any work that possesses even the *slightest* artistic merit. Unlike the United States Supreme Court, Canada's Supreme Court has recognized that even child pornography has some expressive value, which is consistent with its tendency to interpret its Charter as protecting any communicative effort, other than acts of violence. *See* R. v. Sharpe, [2001] 1 S.C.R. 45 (Can.). In *The First Amendment in Cross-Cultural Perspective: A Comparative Legal Analysis of the Freedom of Speech* (2006), Professor Ron Krotoszynski, Jr. details the differences between U.S. and Canadian approaches to regulating child pornography.

3. *Overbreadth.* Osborne attacked the Ohio law as "overbroad," but the majority rejected this claim. The overbreadth doctrine permits a defendant in an obscenity (or other) civil or criminal case to argue that although the government could have written a constitutionally permissible law that regulated his conduct, the law *actually on the books* regulates both unlawful *and* constitutionally protected activity. Such a law will discourage people from exercising First Amendment rights for fear of being subject to civil or criminal sanctions. Because of the "chilling effect" of overbroad laws, the federal courts will permit a defendant to seek invalidation of a law even though the materials at issue could be regulated under a more narrowly tailored law. Thus, if a state legislature enacted a statute that purported to ban "dirty books," a defendant selling legally obscene materials could seek invalidation of the law banning "dirty books" in a criminal prosecution under the "dirty books" statute because the law is overbroad (many books not legally obscene could be deemed "dirty"). A separate, but related, doctrine disallows laws regulating speech if they are vague—this is the so-called void for vagueness doctrine. This doctrine permits a person guilty of behavior that could be criminalized to avoid punishment if the law is written so broadly that it does not give reasonable notice of its coverage. Once again, concerns about a "chilling effect" support this doctrine—if people do not know whether

speech might be lawful or unlawful, they might choose not to speak, rather than speak and run a risk of criminal punishment. Thus, the overbreadth and vagueness doctrines work to protect persons not parties to the actual litigation at bar, on the theory that a good many would-be plaintiffs, being risk-averse, will simply not test the limits of the law (even though the speech in question would be fully protected constitutionally).

To what extent should speech featuring erotic themes enjoy protection if it presents unlawful conduct or seems to advocate such conduct (for example, teens under the age of consent or children as objects of sexual gratification or as sexual actors)? Should a commitment to free speech extend to such materials? Before you answer this question, consider the following case.

ASHCROFT v. FREE SPEECH COALITION

535 U.S. 234 (2002)

KENNEDY, J., delivered the opinion of the Court.

We consider in this case whether the Child Pornography Prevention Act of 1996 (CPPA), 18 U.S.C. § 2251 *et seq.*, abridges the freedom of speech. The CPPA extends the federal prohibition against child pornography to sexually explicit images that appear to depict minors but were produced without using any real children. The statute prohibits, in specific circumstances, possessing or distributing these images which may be created by using adults who look like minors or by using computer imaging. The new technology, according to Congress, makes it possible to create realistic images of children who do not exist.

By prohibiting child pornography that does not depict an actual child, the statute goes beyond *New York v. Ferber*, 458 U.S. 747 (1982), which distinguished child pornography from other sexually explicit speech because of the State's interest in protecting the child exploited by the production process. As a general rule, pornography can be banned only if obscene, but under *Ferber*, pornography showing minors can be proscribed whether or not the images are obscene under the definition set forth in *Miller v. California*, 413 U.S. 15 (1973). *Ferber* recognized that "[t]he *Miller* standard, like all general definitions of what may be banned as obscene, does not reflect the State's particular and more compelling interest in prosecuting those who promote the sexual exploitation of children." 458 U.S., at 761.

While we have not had occasion to consider the question, we may assume that the apparent age of persons engaged in sexual conduct is relevant to whether a depiction offends community standards. Pictures of young children engaged in certain acts might be obscene where similar depictions of adults, or perhaps even older adolescents, would not. The CPPA, however, is not directed at speech that is obscene; Congress has proscribed those materials through a separate statute. 18 U.S.C. §§ 1460-1466. Like the law in *Ferber*, the CPPA seeks to reach beyond obscenity, and it makes no attempt to conform to the *Miller* standard. For instance, the statute would reach visual depictions, such as movies, even if they have redeeming social value.

The principal question to be resolved, then, is whether the CPPA is constitutional where it proscribes a significant universe of speech that is neither obscene under *Miller* nor child pornography under *Ferber*.

Before 1996, Congress defined child pornography as the type of depictions at issue in *Ferber*, images made using actual minors. 18 U.S.C. § 2252 (1994 ed.). The CPPA retains that prohibition at 18 U.S.C. § 2256(8)(A) and adds three other prohibited categories of speech, of which the first, § 2256(8)(B), and the third, § 2256(8)(D), are at issue in this case. Section 2256(8)(B) prohibits "any visual depiction, including any photograph, film, video, picture, or computer or computer-generated image or picture," that "is, or appears to be, of a minor engaging in sexually explicit conduct." The prohibition on "any visual depiction" does not depend at all on how the image is produced. The section captures a range of depictions, sometimes called "virtual child pornography," which include computer-generated images, as well as images produced by more traditional means. For instance, the literal terms of the statute embrace a Renaissance painting depicting a scene from classical mythology, a "picture" that "appears to be, of a minor engaging in sexually explicit conduct." The statute also prohibits Hollywood movies, filmed without any child actors, if a jury believes an actor "appears to be" a minor engaging in "actual or simulated . . . sexual intercourse." § 2256(2).

These images do not involve, let alone harm, any children in the production process; but Congress decided the materials threaten children in other, less direct, ways. Pedophiles might use the materials to encourage children to participate in sexual activity. . . .

In addition, Congress identified another problem created by computer-generated images: Their existence can make it harder to prosecute pornographers who do use real minors. As imaging technology improves, Congress found, it becomes more difficult to prove that a particular picture was produced using actual children. To ensure that defendants possessing child pornography using real minors cannot evade prosecution, Congress extended the ban to virtual child pornography.

Section 2256(8)(C) prohibits a more common and lower tech means of creating virtual images, known as computer morphing. Rather than creating original images, pornographers can alter innocent pictures of real children so that the children appear to be engaged in sexual activity. Although morphed images may fall within the definition of virtual child pornography, they implicate the interests of real children and are in that sense closer to the images in *Ferber*. Respondents do not challenge this provision, and we do not consider it.

Respondents do challenge § 2256(8)(D). Like the text of the "appears to be" provision, the sweep of this provision is quite broad. Section 2256(8)(D) defines child pornography to include any sexually explicit image that was "advertised, promoted, presented, described, or distributed in such a manner that conveys the impression" it depicts "a minor engaging in sexually explicit conduct." One Committee Report identified the provision as directed at sexually explicit images pandered as child pornography. *See* S. Rep. No. 104-358, p. 22 (1996) ("This provision prevents child pornographers and pedophiles from exploiting prurient interests in child sexuality and sexual activity through the production or distribution of pornographic material which is intentionally pandered as child pornography"). The statute is not so limited in its reach, however, as it punishes even those possessors who took no part in pandering. Once a work has been described as child pornography, the taint remains on the speech in the hands of subsequent possessors, making possession unlawful even though the content otherwise would not be objectionable.

Fearing that the CPPA threatened the activities of its members, respondent Free Speech Coalition and others challenged the statute in the United States District Court for the Northern District of California. The Coalition, a California trade association for the adult-entertainment industry, alleged that its members did not use minors in their sexually explicit works, but they believed some of these materials might fall within the CPPA's expanded definition of child pornography. . . . The District Court disagreed [with the plaintiffs' First Amendment objections to the CPPA] and granted summary judgment to the Government. . . .

The Court of Appeals for the Ninth Circuit reversed. The court reasoned that the Government could not prohibit speech because of its tendency to persuade viewers to commit illegal acts. The court held the CPPA to be substantially overbroad because it bans materials that are neither obscene nor produced by the exploitation of real children as in *New York v. Ferber*, 458 U.S. 747 (1982).

While the Ninth Circuit found the CPPA invalid on its face, four other Courts of Appeals have sustained it. . . . We granted certiorari.

The First Amendment commands, "Congress shall make no law abridging the freedom of speech." The government may violate this mandate in many ways, *e.g.*, *Rosenberger v. Rector and Visitors of Univ. of Va.*, 515 U.S. 819 (1995); *Keller v. State Bar of Cal.*, 496 U.S. 1 (1990), but a law imposing criminal penalties on protected speech is a stark example of speech suppression. The CPPA's penalties are indeed severe. A first offender may be imprisoned for 15 years. § 2252A(b)(1). A repeat offender faces a prison sentence of not less than 5 years and not more than 30 years in prison. *Ibid.* While even minor punishments can chill protected speech, see *Wooley v. Maynard*, 430 U.S. 705 (1977), this case provides a textbook example of why we permit facial challenges to statutes that burden expression. With these severe penalties in force, few legitimate movie producers or book publishers, or few other speakers in any capacity, would risk distributing images in or near the uncertain reach of this law. The Constitution gives significant protection from overbroad laws that chill speech within the First Amendment's vast and privileged sphere. Under this principle, the CPPA is unconstitutional on its face if it prohibits a substantial amount of protected expression. See *Broadrick v. Oklahoma*, 413 U.S. 601, 612 (1973). . . .

Congress may pass valid laws to protect children from abuse, and it has. *E.g.*, 18 U.S.C. §§ 2241, 2251. The prospect of crime, however, by itself does not justify laws suppressing protected speech. See *Kingsley Int'l Pictures Corp. v. Regents of Univ. of N.Y.*, 360 U.S. 684, 689 (1959) ("Among free men, the deterrents ordinarily to be applied to prevent crime are education and punishment for violations of the law, not abridgment of the rights of free speech" (internal quotation marks and citation omitted)). It is also well established that speech may not be prohibited because it concerns subjects offending our sensibilities.

As a general principle, the First Amendment bars the government from dictating what we see or read or speak or hear. The freedom of speech has its limits; it does not embrace certain categories of speech, including defamation, incitement, obscenity, and pornography produced with real children. See *Simon & Schuster, Inc. v. Members of N.Y. State Crime Victims Bd.*, 502 U.S. 105, 127 (1991) (Kennedy, J., concurring). While these categories may be prohibited without violating the First Amendment, none of them includes the speech prohibited by the CPPA. In his dissent from the opinion of the Court of Appeals, Judge Ferguson recognized this to be the law and proposed that virtual child pornography should be regarded as an additional category of unprotected speech. [] It would be necessary for us to take this step to uphold the statute.

As we have noted, the CPPA is much more than a supplement to the existing federal prohibition on obscenity. Under *Miller v. California*, 413 U.S. 15 (1973), the

Government must prove that the work, taken as a whole, appeals to the prurient interest, is patently offensive in light of community standards, and lacks serious literary, artistic, political, or scientific value. [] The CPPA, however, extends to images that appear to depict a minor engaging in sexually explicit activity without regard to the *Miller* requirements. The materials need not appeal to the prurient interest. Any depiction of sexually explicit activity, no matter how it is presented, is proscribed. The CPPA applies to a picture in a psychology manual, as well as a movie depicting the horrors of sexual abuse. It is not necessary, moreover, that the image be patently offensive. Pictures of what appear to be 17-year-olds engaging in sexually explicit activity do not in every case contravene community standards.

The CPPA prohibits speech despite its serious literary, artistic, political, or scientific value. The statute proscribes the visual depiction of an idea—that of teenagers engaging in sexual activity—that is a fact of modern society and has been a theme in art and literature throughout the ages. Under the CPPA, images are prohibited so long as the persons appear to be under 18 years of age. 18 U.S.C. § 2256(1). This is higher than the legal age for marriage in many States, as well as the age at which persons may consent to sexual relations. It is, of course, undeniable that some youths engage in sexual activity before the legal age, either on their own inclination or because they are victims of sexual abuse.

Both themes—teenage sexual activity and the sexual abuse of children—have inspired countless literary works. William Shakespeare created the most famous pair of teenage lovers, one of whom is just 13 years of age. See Romeo and Juliet, act I, sc. 2, l. 9 ("She hath not seen the change of fourteen years"). In the drama, Shakespeare portrays the relationship as something splendid and innocent, but not juvenile. The work has inspired no less than 40 motion pictures, some of which suggest that the teenagers consummated their relationship. *E.g.*, Romeo and Juliet (B. Luhrmann director, 1996). Shakespeare may not have written sexually explicit scenes for the Elizabethan audience, but were modern directors to adopt a less conventional approach, that fact alone would not compel the conclusion that the work was obscene.

Contemporary movies pursue similar themes. Last year's Academy Awards featured the movie, Traffic, which was nominated for Best Picture. See Predictable and Less So, the Academy Award Contenders, N.Y. Times, Feb. 14, 2001, p. E11. The film portrays a teenager, identified as a 16-year-old, who becomes addicted to drugs. The viewer sees the degradation of her addiction, which in the end leads her to a filthy room to trade sex for drugs. The year before, American Beauty won the Academy Award for Best Picture. See "American Beauty" Tops the Oscars, N.Y. Times, Mar. 27, 2000, p. E1. In the course of the movie, a teenage girl engages in sexual relations with her teenage boyfriend, and another yields herself to the gratification of a middle-aged man. The film also contains a scene where, although the movie audience understands the act is not taking place, one character believes he is watching a teenage boy performing a sexual act on an older man.

Our society, like other cultures, has empathy and enduring fascination with the lives and destinies of the young. Art and literature express the vital interest we all have in the formative years we ourselves once knew, when wounds can be so grievous, disappointment so profound, and mistaken choices so tragic, but when moral acts and self-fulfillment are still in reach. Whether or not the films we mention violate the CPPA, they explore themes within the wide sweep of the statute's prohibitions. If these films, or hundreds of others of lesser note that explore those subjects, contain a single graphic depiction of sexual activity within the statutory definition, the possessor of the film would be subject to severe punishment without inquiry into the work's redeeming value. This is inconsistent with an essential First Amendment rule: The artistic merit of a work does not depend on the presence of a single explicit scene. See *Book Named "John Cleland's Memoirs of a Woman of Pleasure" v. Attorney General of Mass.*, 383 U.S. 413, 419 (1966) (plurality opinion) ("[T]he social value of the book can neither be weighed against nor canceled by its prurient appeal or patent offensiveness"). Under *Miller,* the First Amendment requires that redeeming value be judged by considering the work as a whole. Where the scene is part of the narrative, the work itself does not for this reason become obscene, even though the scene in isolation might be offensive. See *Kois v. Wisconsin,* 408 U.S. 229, 231 (1972) (*per curiam*). For this reason, and the others we have noted, the CPPA cannot be read to prohibit obscenity, because it lacks the required link between its prohibitions and the affront to community standards prohibited by the definition of obscenity.

In contrast to the speech in *Ferber,* speech that itself is the record of sexual abuse, the CPPA prohibits speech that records no crime and creates no victims by its production. Virtual child pornography is not "intrinsically related" to the sexual abuse of children, as were the materials in *Ferber.* 458 U.S. at 759. While the government asserts that the images can lead to actual instances of child abuse, see *infra,* at 251-254, the causal link is contingent and indirect. The harm does not necessarily follow from the speech, but depends upon some unquantified potential for subsequent criminal acts. . . .

The CPPA, for reasons we have explored, is inconsistent with *Miller* and finds no support in *Ferber.* The Government seeks to justify its prohibitions in other ways. It argues that the CPPA is necessary because pedophiles may use virtual child pornography to seduce children. There are many things innocent in themselves, however, such as cartoons, video games, and candy, that might be used for immoral purposes, yet we would not expect those to be prohibited because they can be misused. The Government, of course, may punish adults who provide unsuitable materials to children, see *Ginsberg v. New York,* 390 U.S. 629 (1968), and it may enforce criminal penalties for unlawful solicitation. The precedents establish, however, that speech within the rights of adults to hear may not be silenced completely in an attempt to shield children from it. . . .

Here, the Government wants to keep speech from children not to protect them from its content but to protect them from those who would commit other crimes. The principle, however, remains the same: The Government cannot ban speech fit for adults simply because it may fall into the hands of children. The evil in question depends upon the actor's unlawful conduct, conduct defined as criminal quite apart from any link to the speech in question. This establishes that the speech ban is not narrowly drawn. The objective is to prohibit illegal conduct, but this restriction goes well beyond that interest by restricting the speech available to law-abiding adults.

The Government submits further that virtual child pornography whets the appetites of pedophiles and encourages them to engage in illegal conduct. This rationale cannot sustain the provision in question. The mere tendency of speech to encourage unlawful acts is not a sufficient reason for banning it. The government "cannot constitutionally premise legislation on the desirability of controlling a person's private thoughts." *Stanley v. Georgia,* 394 U.S. 557, 566 (1969). First Amendment freedoms are most in danger when the government seeks to control thought or to justify its laws for that impermissible end. The right to think is the beginning of freedom, and speech must be protected from the government because speech is the beginning of thought.

To preserve these freedoms, and to protect speech for its own sake, the Court's First Amendment cases draw vital distinctions between words and deeds, between ideas and conduct. The government may not prohibit speech because it increases the chance an unlawful act will be committed "at some indefinite future time." *Hess v. Indiana*, 414 U.S. 105, 108 (1973) (*per curiam*). The government may suppress speech for advocating the use of force or a violation of law only if "such advocacy is directed to inciting or producing imminent lawless action and is likely to incite or produce such action." *Brandenburg v. Ohio*, 395 U.S. 444, 447 (1969) (*per curiam*). There is here no attempt, incitement, solicitation, or conspiracy. The Government has shown no more than a remote connection between speech that might encourage thoughts or impulses and any resulting child abuse. Without a significantly stronger, more direct connection, the Government may not prohibit speech on the ground that it may encourage pedophiles to engage in illegal conduct.

The Government next argues that its objective of eliminating the market for pornography produced using real children necessitates a prohibition on virtual images as well. Virtual images, the Government contends, are indistinguishable from real ones; they are part of the same market and are often exchanged. In this way, it is said, virtual images promote the trafficking in works produced through the exploitation of real children. The hypothesis is somewhat implausible. If virtual images were identical to illegal child pornography, the illegal images would be driven from the market by the indistinguishable substitutes. Few pornographers would risk prosecution by abusing real children if fictional, computerized images would suffice.

In the case of the material covered by *Ferber*, the creation of the speech is itself the crime of child abuse; the prohibition deters the crime by removing the profit motive. See *Osborne*, 495 U.S., at 109-110. Even where there is an underlying crime, however, the Court has not allowed the suppression of speech in all cases. *E.g.*, *Bartnicki, supra* [Bartnicki v. Vopper, 532 U.S. 514,] 529 [(2001)] (market deterrence would not justify law prohibiting a radio commentator from distributing speech that had been unlawfully intercepted). We need not consider where to strike the balance in this case, because here, there is no underlying crime at all. Even if the Government's market deterrence theory were persuasive in some contexts, it would not justify this statute.

Finally, the Government says that the possibility of producing images by using computer imaging makes it very difficult for it to prosecute those who produce pornography by using real children. Experts, we are told, may have difficulty in saying whether the pictures were made by using real children or by using computer imaging. The necessary solution, the argument runs, is to prohibit both kinds of images. The argument, in essence, is that protected speech may be banned as a means to ban unprotected speech. This analysis turns the First Amendment upside down.

The Government may not suppress lawful speech as the means to suppress unlawful speech. Protected speech does not become unprotected merely because it resembles the latter. The Constitution requires the reverse. "[T]he possible harm to society in permitting some unprotected speech to go unpunished is outweighed by the possibility that protected speech of others may be muted. . . ." *Broadrick v. Oklahoma*, 413 U.S., at 612. The overbreadth doctrine prohibits the Government from banning unprotected speech if a substantial amount of protected speech is prohibited or chilled in the process. . . .

In sum, § 2256(8)(B) covers materials beyond the categories recognized in *Ferber* and *Miller*, and the reasons the Government offers in support of limiting the freedom of speech have no justification in our precedents or in the law of the First Amendment. The provision abridges the freedom to engage in a substantial amount of lawful speech. For this reason, it is overbroad and unconstitutional.

Respondents challenge § 2256(8)(D) as well. This provision bans depictions of sexually explicit conduct that are "advertised, promoted, presented, described, or distributed in such a manner that conveys the impression that the material is or contains a visual depiction of a minor engaging in sexually explicit conduct." The parties treat the section as nearly identical to the provision prohibiting materials that appear to be child pornography. In the Government's view, the difference between the two is that "the 'conveys the impression' provision requires the jury to assess the material at issue in light of the manner in which it is promoted." Brief for Petitioners 18, n.3. The Government's assumption, however, is that the determination would still depend principally upon the content of the prohibited work.

We disagree with this view. The CPPA prohibits sexually explicit materials that "conve[y] the impression" they depict minors. While that phrase may sound like the "appears to be" prohibition in § 2256(8)(B), it requires little judgment about the content of the image. Under § 2256(8)(D), the work must be sexually explicit, but otherwise the content is irrelevant. Even if a film contains no sexually explicit scenes involving minors, it could be treated as child pornography if the title and trailers convey the impression that the scenes would be found in the movie. The determination turns on how the speech is presented, not on what is depicted. While the legislative findings address at length the problems posed by materials that look like child pornography, they are silent on the evils posed by images simply pandered that way.

The Government does not offer a serious defense of this provision, and the other arguments it makes in support of the CPPA do not bear on § 2256(8)(D). The materials, for instance, are not likely to be confused for child pornography in a criminal trial. The Court has recognized that pandering may be relevant, as an evidentiary matter, to the question whether particular materials are obscene. See *Ginzburg v. United States*, 383 U.S. 463, 474 (1966) ("[I]n close cases evidence of pandering may be probative with respect to the nature of the material in question and thus satisfy the [obscenity] test"). Where a defendant engages in the "commercial exploitation of erotica solely for the sake of their prurient appeal," *id.*, at 466, the context he or she creates may itself be relevant to the evaluation of the materials.

Section 2256(8)(D), however, prohibits a substantial amount of speech that falls outside *Ginzburg*'s rationale. Materials falling within the proscription are tainted and unlawful in the hands of all who receive it, though they bear no responsibility for how it was marketed, sold, or described. The statute, furthermore, does not require that the context be part of an effort at "commercial exploitation." *Ibid.* As a consequence, the CPPA does more than prohibit pandering. It prohibits possession of material described, or pandered, as child pornography by someone earlier in the distribution chain. The provision prohibits a sexually explicit film containing no youthful actors, just because it is placed in a box suggesting a prohibited movie. Possession is a crime even when the possessor knows the movie was mislabeled. The First Amendment requires a more precise restriction. For this reason, § 2256(8)(D) is substantially overbroad and in violation of the First Amendment.

For the reasons we have set forth, the prohibitions of § 2256(8)(B) and 2256(8)(D) are overbroad and unconstitutional. Having reached this conclusion, we need not address respondents' further contention that the provisions are unconstitutional because of vague statutory language.

The judgment of the Court of Appeals is

Affirmed.

THOMAS, J., concurring in the judgment.

In my view, the Government's most persuasive asserted interest in support of the Child Pornography Prevention Act of 1996 (CPPA), 18 U.S.C. § 2251 *et seq.*, is the prosecution rationale—that persons who possess and disseminate pornographic images of real children may escape conviction by claiming that the images are computer generated, thereby raising a reasonable doubt as to their guilt. At this time, however, the Government asserts only that defendants *raise* such defenses, not that they have done so successfully. In fact, the Government points to no case in which a defendant has been acquitted based on a "computer-generated images" defense. While this speculative interest cannot support the broad reach of the CPPA, technology may evolve to the point where it becomes impossible to enforce actual child pornography laws because the Government cannot prove that certain pornographic images are of real children. In the event this occurs, the Government should not be foreclosed from enacting a regulation of virtual child pornography that contains an appropriate affirmative defense or some other narrowly drawn restriction.

O'CONNOR, J., with whom THE CHIEF JUSTICE and SCALIA, J., join as to Part II, concurring in the judgment in part and dissenting in part.

This litigation involves a facial challenge to the CPPA's prohibitions of pornographic images that "appea[r] to be of a minor" and of material that "conveys the impression" that it contains pornographic images of minors. While I agree with the Court's judgment that the First Amendment requires that the latter prohibition be struck down, I disagree with its decision to strike down the former prohibition in its entirety. The "appears to be of a minor" language in § 2256(8)(B) covers two categories of speech: pornographic images of adults that look like children ("youthful adult pornography") and pornographic images of children created wholly on a computer, without using any actual children ("virtual child pornography"). The Court concludes, correctly, that the CPPA's ban on youthful adult pornography is overbroad. In my view, however, respondents fail to present sufficient evidence to demonstrate that the ban on virtual child pornography is overbroad. Because invalidation due to overbreadth is such "strong medicine," *Broadrick v. Oklahoma*, 413 U.S. 601, 613 (1973), I would strike down the prohibition of pornography that "appears to be" of minors only insofar as it is applied to the class of youthful adult pornography. . . .

REHNQUIST, C.J., with whom SCALIA, J., joins in part, dissenting.

Congress has a compelling interest in ensuring the ability to enforce prohibitions of actual child pornography, and we should defer to its findings that rapidly advancing technology soon will make it all but impossible to do so. *Turner Broadcasting System, Inc. v. FCC*, 520 U.S. 180, 195 (1997) (we "'accord substantial deference to the predictive judgments of Congress'" in First Amendment cases). . . .

NOTES AND QUESTIONS

1. *Balancing the interest in preventing the exploitation of children.* The free speech interest of adults in access to materials suitable for adults, but not children, evidently prohibits Congress from attempting to protect minors from sexual exploitation by banning "virtual" pornography or material featuring "youthful"-looking actors. Should government be permitted to favor the protection of minors from sexual exploitation over the speech interests of adults?

2. *Romeo and Juliet as child photography?* On the other hand, Justice Kennedy has a point, doesn't he? Should *Romeo and Juliet*, whether in print or film format, be banned as child pornography if it doesn't feature any real children in its production? In other words, should governmental efforts to protect minors from sexual exploitation be limited to direct regulation of unlawful sex acts, as opposed to regulating speech that might trigger such acts?

3. *Self-created sexually explicit images of minors or "sexting."* Should the law distinguish between self-created images of minors engaged in lawful sexual activity and images created by adults for an adult audience? Or does the existence of a sexually explicit photograph of a minor, even if self-created, help to sustain an unlawful, and inherently exploitative, media market in such images? Some state prosecutors have brought child pornography charges against minors who send their peers sexually explicit photographs or "sexts." Erik Eckholm, *Prosecutors Weigh Teenage Sexting: Folly or Felony?*, N.Y. Times, Nov. 14, 2015, at A13 (reporting on a North Carolina case in which local prosecutors "charged the two teenagers with the felony of 'exploiting a minor,' which could have brought them years in prison and decades on the sex offender registry, for privately sharing images of themselves"); *see* Deborah Ahrens, *Schools, Cyberbullies, and the Surveillance State*, 49 Am. Crim. L. Rev. 1669, 1692 (2012) ("While such behavior [sexting] has possible poor outcomes for adults, including public embarrassment and humiliation, minors who transmit sexually-explicit images to one another, including nude pictures of themselves, may face criminal prosecution for offenses such as disseminating child pornography."). Around 20 states have adopted laws regulating sexting by minors among their peers. However, virtually all 50 states maintain and enforce child pornography laws that could be applied to peer-to-peer sexting. For a relevant discussion and comparative law treatment of teen sexting, see Joanne Sweeney, *Sexting and Freedom of Expression: A Comparative Approach*, 102 Ky. L.J. 103 (2013). For an extended argument that sexting between consenting teens should not be subject to criminal sanctions and should instead constitute protected speech activity, see Joanna R. Lampe, Note, *A Victimless Sex Crime: The Case for Decriminalizing Consensual Teen Sexting*, 46 U. Mich. J.L. Reform 703 (2013).

4. *Sexting as protected speech activity.* The Supreme Court of Canada, in *R. v. Sharpe*, [2001] 1 S.C.R. 45 (Can.), narrowly construed a federal statute proscribing child pornography to exclude self-created images not intended for commercial distribution. Writing for the majority, Chief Justice Beverley McLachlin explained that:

> Private journals, diaries, writings, drawings and other works of the imagination, created by oneself exclusively for oneself, may all trigger the s.

163.1(4) offence. The law, in its prohibition on the possession of such materials, reaches into a realm of exceedingly private expression, where s. 2(b) values may be particularly implicated and state intervention may be markedly more intrusive. Further, the risk of harm arising from the private creation and possession of such materials, while not eliminated altogether, is low.

Id. at para. 75. Moreover, "[p]ossession of such materials may implicate the values of self-fulfilment and self-actualization. and therefore . . . reside near the heart of the s. 2(b) guarantee." *Id.* at para. 77. The *Sharpe* Court invalidated section 163.1 insofar as it applied to "self-created expressive material" and "private recordings of lawful sexual activity." *Id.* at para. 115. Thus, Canadian free speech law reflects the view that if minors are old enough lawfully to engage in sexual activity, they are also entitled to create and possess records, including visual records, of such activity.

THEORY-APPLIED PROBLEM

In the motion picture *Apt Pupil* (1998), starring Ian McKellen and Brad Renfro, director Bryan Singer (*The Usual Suspects* (1995); *Superman Returns* (2006)) tells the highly disturbing story of a high school student (played by Renfro) obsessed with a former Nazi death camp officer (played by McKellen) and his past; a Stephen King novella inspired the film. In a controversial high school shower scene, director Singer required several young male actors to appear nude; the actors (including Renfro) were, at the time, under 18 years of age. The scene follows a basketball practice and features a fantasy sequence in which Renfro's character imagines himself to be in the showers at a Nazi death camp, surrounded by victims of the Holocaust. The MPAA rated the film "R" for brief nudity, bad language, and violence.

Video Connection is a video rental store in Oklahoma City, Oklahoma, specializing in art, foreign, and "avant-garde" films, including the repertoire of directors such as Fellini and John Waters. Video Connection owns and rents two copies of *Apt Pupil*. On July 1, 2013, a customer presents *Apt Pupil* for rental; when the clerk proceeds to rent the title, she is immediately arrested for "distribution of child pornography," a class B felony under Oklahoma state law. In relevant part, the applicable Oklahoma law prohibits "possession or distribution of any nude photographic or cinematic depiction of a person under 18 years of age, including depiction of the buttocks, genitals, anus, or female breasts." (This statute operates entirely independently of Oklahoma's state law criminalizing obscene materials.) Both the clerk and Video Connection's owners are indicted, tried, and convicted of violating Oklahoma's ban on child pornography. On an appeal of their convictions to the Supreme Court of Oklahoma, the defendants argue that the conviction must be reversed on free speech grounds. The defendants assert that *Free Speech Coalition* plainly protects serious films from proscription as child pornography. The local district attorney, in her brief, counters that under *Ferber* and *Osborne*, any nude depiction of a real minor may be criminalized. How should the Supreme Court of Oklahoma rule on the appeal?

THEORY-APPLIED PROBLEM—SEXTING AND CYBERSTALKING

"Sexting" describes the practice of sending sexually explicit materials, images, or videos as a text message over a mobile phone. In 2011, two teen girls created a photo, purportedly of a classmate, by pasting a picture of the classmate's head on the picture of a nude body. They posted the "fake" nude photo of their classmate on a Facebook page accessible to most of their high school friends. A prosecutor charged the teens with aggravated stalking, or cyberstalking. See Nina Mandell, *Florida Girls in Trouble with Police After Creating Lewd Fake Facebook Profile for Classmate*, N.Y. Daily News, available at *http://articles.nydailynews.com/2011-01-14/news/ 27087490_1_facebook-page-illinois-mother-florida-girls*. "Cyberstalking," defined by state statute as the use of e-mail or other electronic channels to communicate words, images, or language to a specific person, repeatedly, to serve no legitimate purpose, and that causes the person "substantial emotional distress" Fla. Stat. § 784.048 (2010). When one "willfully, maliciously, and repeatedly" cyberstalks another, he or she can be charged with a misdemeanor offense, though the offense becomes a felony when the target is under age 16. If the harassment includes a threat intended to create reasonable fear of bodily injury to the victim or to the victim's family, the crime becomes aggravated stalking. Does this law, as applied to the two teens who created the fake nude photo, violate the First Amendment? See also Miller v. Mitchell, 598 F.3d 139 (3d Cir. 2010), a case in which prosecutors threatened to charge teens with distributing child pornography after they texted explicit images of themselves to "consenting" minors. Does this violate the First Amendment?

C. NUDE DANCING, DIAL-A-PORN, AND THE INTERNET

The cases that follow consider the ability of government to regulate (or even proscribe) live nude dancing. In addition, the materials examine the constitutional status of dial-a-porn service providers, one of the first mass-audience pornographic information services. The chapter also considers the growing phenomenon of "revenge porn" and legal efforts to prevent it. Finally, the chapter closes with a note on the problem of childproofing the internet. Note that the decision in *Barnes v. Glen Theatre*, below, is a plurality opinion.

BARNES v. GLEN THEATRE
501 U.S. 560 (1991)

REHNQUIST, C.J., announced the judgment of the Court and delivered an opinion, in which O'CONNOR, J., and KENNEDY, J., join.

Respondents are two establishments in South Bend, Indiana, that wish to provide totally nude dancing as entertainment, and individual dancers who are employed at these establishments. They claim that the First Amendment's guarantee of freedom of expression prevents the State of Indiana from enforcing its public indecency law to prevent this form of dancing. We reject their claim.

The facts appear from the pleadings and findings of the District Court and are uncontested here. The Kitty Kat Lounge, Inc. (Kitty Kat), is located in the city of

South Bend. It sells alcoholic beverages and presents "go-go dancing." Its proprietor desires to present "totally nude dancing," but an applicable Indiana statute regulating public nudity requires that the dancers wear "pasties" and "G-strings" when they dance. The dancers are not paid an hourly wage, but work on commission. They receive a 100 percent commission on the first $60 in drink sales during their performances. Darlene Miller, one of the respondents in the action, had worked at the Kitty Kat for about two years at the time this action was brought. Miller wishes to dance nude because she believes she would make more money doing so.

Respondent Glen Theatre, Inc., is an Indiana corporation with a place of business in South Bend. Its primary business is supplying so-called adult entertainment through written and printed materials, movie showings, and live entertainment at an enclosed "bookstore." The live entertainment at the "bookstore" consists of nude and seminude performances and showings of the female body through glass panels. Customers sit in a booth and insert coins into a timing mechanism that permits them to observe the live nude and seminude dancers for a period of time. One of Glen Theatre's dancers, Gayle Ann Marie Sutro, has danced, modeled, and acted professionally for more than 15 years, and in addition to her performances at the Glen Theatre, can be seen in a pornographic movie at a nearby theater.

Respondents sued in the United States District Court for the Northern District of Indiana to enjoin the enforcement of the Indiana public indecency statute, Ind. Code § 35-45-4-1 (1988), asserting that its prohibition against complete nudity in public places violated the First Amendment. . . .

[T]he District Court concluded that "the type of dancing these plaintiffs wish to perform is not expressive activity protected by the Constitution of the United States," and rendered judgment in favor of the defendants. . . . [A] panel of [the Seventh Circuit] reversed the District Court, holding that the nude dancing involved here was expressive conduct protected by the First Amendment. The Court of Appeals then heard the case en banc and rendered a series of comprehensive and thoughtful opinions. . . . The majority concluded that nonobscene nude dancing performed for entertainment is expression protected by the First Amendment, and that the public indecency statute was an improper infringement of that expressive activity because its purpose was to prevent the message of eroticism and sexuality conveyed by the dancers. We granted certiorari, 498 U.S. 807 (1990), and now hold that the Indiana statutory requirement that the dancers in the establishments involved in this case must wear pasties and G-strings does not violate the First Amendment.

Several of our cases contain language suggesting that nude dancing of the kind involved here is expressive conduct protected by the First Amendment. . . . These statements support the conclusion of the Court of Appeals that nude dancing of the kind sought to be performed here is expressive conduct within the outer perimeters of the First Amendment, though we view it as only marginally so. This, of course, does not end our inquiry. We must determine the level of protection to be afforded to the expressive conduct at issue, and must determine whether the Indiana statute is an impermissible infringement of that protected activity.

Indiana, of course, has not banned nude dancing as such, but has proscribed public nudity across the board. The Supreme Court of Indiana has construed the Indiana statute to preclude nudity in what are essentially places of public accommodation such as the Glen Theatre and the Kitty Kat Lounge. In such places, respondents point out, minors are excluded and there are no nonconsenting viewers. Respondents contend that while the State may license establishments such as the ones involved here, and limit the geographical area in which they do business, it may not in any way limit the performance of the dances within them without violating the First Amendment. The petitioners contend, on the other hand, that Indiana's restriction on nude dancing is a valid "time, place, or manner" restriction under cases such as *Clark v. Community for Creative Non-Violence*, 468 U.S. 288 (1984).

The "time, place, or manner" test was developed for evaluating restrictions on expression taking place on public property which had been dedicated as a "public forum," *Ward v. Rock Against Racism*, 491 U.S. 781, 791 (1989), although we have on at least one occasion applied it to conduct occurring on private property. See *Renton v. Playtime Theatres, Inc.*, 475 U.S. 41 (1986). In *Clark* we observed that this test has been interpreted to embody much the same standards as those set forth in *United States v. O'Brien*, 391 U.S. 367 (1968), and we turn, therefore, to the rule enunciated in *O'Brien*. . . .

Applying the four-part *O'Brien* test...we find that Indiana's public indecency statute is justified despite its incidental limitations on some expressive activity. The public indecency statute is clearly within the constitutional power of the State and furthers substantial governmental interests. It is impossible to discern, other than from the text of the statute, exactly what governmental interest the Indiana legislators had in mind when they enacted this statute, for Indiana does not record legislative history, and the State's highest court has not shed additional light on the statute's purpose. Nonetheless, the statute's purpose of protecting societal order and morality is clear from its text and history. Public indecency statutes of this sort are of ancient origin and presently exist in at least 47 States. Public indecency, including nudity, was a criminal offense at common law, and this Court recognized the common-law roots of the offense of "gross and open indecency" in *Winters v. New York*, 333 U.S. 507, 515 (1948). Public nudity was considered an act *malum in se*. *Le Roy v. Sidley*, 1 Sid. 168, 82 Eng. Rep. 1036 (K.B. 1664). Public indecency statutes such as the one before us reflect moral disapproval of people appearing in the nude among strangers in public places. . . .

This and other public indecency statutes were designed to protect morals and public order. The traditional police power of the States is defined as the authority to provide for the public health, safety, and morals, and we have upheld such a basis for legislation. . . .

Thus, the public indecency statute furthers a substantial government interest in protecting order and morality.

This interest is unrelated to the suppression of free expression. Some may view restricting nudity on moral grounds as necessarily related to expression. We disagree. . . .

Respondents contend that even though prohibiting nudity in public generally may not be related to suppressing expression, prohibiting the performance of nude dancing is related to expression because the State seeks to prevent its erotic message. Therefore, they reason that the application of the Indiana statute to the nude dancing in this case violates the First Amendment, because it fails the third part of the *O'Brien* test, viz: the governmental interest must be unrelated to the suppression of free expression.

But we do not think that when Indiana applies its statute to the nude dancing in these nightclubs it is proscribing nudity because of the erotic message conveyed by the dancers. Presumably numerous other erotic performances are presented at these establishments and similar clubs without any interference from the State, so long as the performers wear a scant amount of clothing. Likewise, the requirement that the dancers don pasties and G-strings does not deprive the dance of whatever erotic message it conveys; it simply makes the message slightly less graphic. The perceived evil that Indiana seeks to address is not erotic dancing, but public nudity. The appearance of people of all shapes, sizes and ages in the nude at a beach, for example, would convey little if any erotic message, yet the State still seeks to prevent it. Public nudity is the evil the State seeks to prevent, whether or not it is combined with expressive activity.

The fourth part of the *O'Brien* test requires that the incidental restriction on First Amendment freedom be no greater than is essential to the furtherance of the governmental interest. As indicated in the discussion above, the governmental interest served by the text of the prohibition is societal disapproval of nudity in public places and among strangers. The statutory prohibition is not a means to some greater end, but an end in itself. It is without cavil that the public indecency statute is "narrowly tailored"; Indiana's requirement that the dancers wear at least pasties and G-strings is modest, and the bare minimum necessary to achieve the State's purpose.

The judgment of the Court of Appeals accordingly is

Reversed.

SCALIA, J., concurring in the judgment.

I agree that the judgment of the Court of Appeals must be reversed. In my view, however, the challenged regulation must be upheld, not because it survives some lower level of First Amendment scrutiny, but because, as a general law regulating conduct and not specifically directed at expression, it is not subject to First Amendment scrutiny at all. . . .

Indiana's statute is in the line of a long tradition of laws against public nudity, which have never been thought to run afoul of traditional understanding of "the freedom of speech." Public indecency—including public nudity—has long been an offense at common law. Indiana's first public nudity statute, Rev. Laws of Ind., ch. 26, § 60 (1831), predated by many years the appearance of nude barroom dancing. It was general in scope, directed at all public nudity, and not just at public nude expression; and all succeeding statutes, down to the present one, have been the same. Were it the case that Indiana *in practice* targeted only expressive nudity, while turning a blind eye to nude beaches and unclothed purveyors of hot dogs and machine tools, see *Miller*, 904 F.2d, at 1120, 1121, it might be said that what posed as a regulation of conduct in general was in reality a regulation of only communicative conduct. Respondents have adduced no evidence of that. Indiana officials have brought many public indecency prosecutions for activities having no communicative element. . . .

The purpose of Indiana's nudity law would be violated, I think, if 60,000 fully consenting adults crowded into the Hoosier Dome to display their genitals to one another, even if there were not an offended innocent in the crowd. Our society prohibits, and all human societies have prohibited, certain activities not because they harm others but because they are considered, in the traditional phrase, "*contra bonos mores*," *i.e.*, immoral. In American society, such prohibitions have included, for example, sadomasochism, cockfighting, bestiality, suicide, drug use, prostitution, and sodomy. While there may be great diversity of view on whether various of these prohibitions should exist (though I have found few ready to abandon, in principle, all of them), there is no doubt that, absent specific constitutional protection for the conduct involved, the Constitution does not prohibit them simply because they regulate "morality." See *Bowers v. Hardwick*, 478 U.S. 186, 196 (1986) (upholding prohibition of private homosexual sodomy enacted solely on "the presumed belief of a majority of the electorate in [the jurisdiction] that homosexual sodomy is immoral and unacceptable"). The purpose of the Indiana statute, as both its text and the manner of its enforcement demonstrate, is to enforce the traditional moral belief that people should not expose their private parts indiscriminately, regardless of whether those who see them are disedified. Since that is so, the dissent has no basis for positing that, where only thoroughly edified adults are present, the purpose must be repression of communication.

Since the Indiana regulation is a general law not specifically targeted at expressive conduct, its application to such conduct does not in my view implicate the First Amendment. . . .

All our holdings (though admittedly not some of our discussion) support the conclusion that "the only First Amendment analysis applicable to laws that do not directly or indirectly impede speech is the threshold inquiry of whether the purpose of the law is to suppress communication. If not, that is the end of the matter so far as First Amendment guarantees are concerned; if so, the court then proceeds to determine whether there is substantial justification for the proscription." Such a regime ensures that the government does not act to suppress communication, without requiring that all conduct-restricting regulation (which means in effect all regulation) survive an enhanced level of scrutiny. . . .

Indiana may constitutionally enforce its prohibition of public nudity even against those who choose to use public nudity as a means of communication. The State is regulating conduct, not expression, and those who choose to employ conduct as a means of expression must make sure that the conduct they select is not generally forbidden. For these reasons, I agree that the judgment should be reversed.

SOUTER, J., concurring in the judgment.

Because the State's interest in banning nude dancing results from a simple correlation of such dancing with other evils, rather than from a relationship between the other evils and the expressive component of the dancing, the interest is unrelated to the suppression of free expression. . . .

White, J., with whom Marshall, J., Blackmun, J., and Stevens, J., join, dissenting.

The first question presented to us in this case is whether nonobscene nude dancing performed as entertainment is expressive conduct protected by the First Amendment. The Court of Appeals held that it is, observing that our prior decisions permit no other conclusion. Not surprisingly, then, the plurality now concedes that "nude dancing of the kind sought to be performed here is expressive conduct within the outer perimeters of the First Amendment. . . ." *Ante*, at 566. This is no more than recognizing, as the Seventh Circuit observed, that dancing is an ancient art form and "inherently embodies the expression and communication of ideas and emotions." *Miller v. Civil City of South Bend*, 904 F.2d 1081, 1087 (1990) (en banc). . . .

The plurality's analysis is erroneous in several respects. Both the plurality and Justice Scalia in his opinion concurring in the judgment overlook a fundamental and critical aspect of our cases upholding the States' exercise of their police powers. None of the cases they rely upon, including *O'Brien* and *Bowers v. Hardwick*, 478 U.S. 186 (1986), involved anything less than truly *general* proscriptions on individual conduct. . . . By contrast, in this case Indiana does not suggest that its statute applies to, or could be applied to, nudity wherever it occurs, including the home. We do not understand the plurality or Justice Scalia to be suggesting that Indiana could constitutionally enact such an intrusive prohibition, nor do we think such a suggestion would be tenable in light of our decision in *Stanley v. Georgia*, 394 U.S. 557 (1969), in which we held that States could not punish the mere possession of obscenity in the privacy of one's own home.

We are told by the attorney general of Indiana that, in *State v. Baysinger*, 272 Ind. 236, 397 N.E.2d 580 (1979), the Indiana Supreme Court held that the statute at issue here cannot and does not prohibit nudity as a part of some larger form of expression meriting protection when the communication of ideas is involved. Petitioners also state that the evils sought to be avoided by applying the statute in this case would not obtain in the case of theatrical productions, such as "Salome" or "Hair." Neither is there any evidence that the State has attempted to apply the statute to nudity in performances such as plays, ballets, or operas. "No arrests have ever been made for nudity as part of a play or ballet."

Thus, the Indiana statute is not a *general* prohibition of the type we have upheld in prior cases. As a result, the plurality and Justice Scalia's simple references to the State's general interest in promoting societal order and morality are not sufficient justification for a statute which concededly reaches a significant amount of protected expressive activity. Instead, in applying the *O'Brien* test, we are obligated to carefully examine the reasons the State has chosen to regulate this expressive conduct in a less than general statute. In other words, when the State enacts a law that draws a line between expressive conduct which is regulated and non-expressive conduct of the same type which is not regulated, *O'Brien* places the burden on the State to justify the distinctions it has made. Closer inquiry as to the purpose of the statute is surely appropriate. . . .

That the performances in the Kitty Kat Lounge may not be high art, to say the least, and may not appeal to the Court, is hardly an excuse for distorting and ignoring settled doctrine. The Court's assessment of the artistic merits of nude dancing performances should not be the determining factor in deciding this case. In the words of Justice Harlan: "[I]t is largely because governmental officials cannot make principled decisions in this area that the Constitution leaves matters of taste and style so largely to the individual." *Cohen v. California*, 403 U.S. 15, 25 (1971). . . .

NOTES AND QUESTIONS

1. *A divided Court.* The *Barnes* Court was unable to muster a majority for any particular result. Clearly, however, a majority of the Justices were not prepared to protect nude dancing in absolute terms. Instead, a state interest in public decency would justify denying a liquor license to an all-nude club or prohibiting completely such an establishment in South Bend (or elsewhere in Indiana).

2. *Content-neutral regulation of erotica?* If, as Justice Harlan famously once quipped, "one man's vulgarity is another's lyric," why should courts permit local or state governments to regulate erotica more aggressively than other kinds of speech? Should a production of the musical *Hair*, which often features full frontal nudity, enjoy greater protection than dancers at the Kitty Kat Klub because of the aesthetic norms of the ruling caste in South Bend (or, more generally, in Indiana)? If not, how can you square the result in *Barnes* with a meaningful commitment to protect erotica without regard to its content or viewpoint?

3. *Speech/conduct and nude dancing.* Is nude dancing speech? Or is it conduct akin to prostitution? If nude dancing is really conduct, rather than speech, should this imply that the government has a lower burden to meet in regulating it?

4. *Secondary effects doctrine.* Justice Souter's concurring opinions in *Barnes* uses an analytical device that usually provides little traction to state and local governments in First Amendment cases: the doctrine of secondary effects. Under the doctrine of secondary effects, speech may be regulated, even if the speech itself is not intrinsically harmful, because it produces harmful effects. For example, leafleting produces litter on the streets and sidewalks; governments have, from time to time, attempted to regulate or ban leafleting because of its secondary effect of causing increased litter. In contexts other than "adult entertainment," federal courts, including the Supreme Court, mostly have rejected such arguments out of hand, essentially telling local and state governments to punish those who litter, rather than silence those seeking to distribute pamphlets. Yet, in the area of adult entertainment or erotica (including both fixed media, like books or films, and live performance art), the Supreme Court has permitted local governments to establish special, restrictive zoning regimes for adult businesses because of the "secondary effects" associated with such businesses, presumed to include the sale of illegal drugs, alcohol abuse, prostitution, and breaches of the peace, as well as general concerns about neighborhood "blight." *See, e.g.,* City of Renton v. Playtime Theaters, Inc., 475 U.S. 41, 46, 48-52 (1986). Thus, the Supreme Court has sustained restrictive zoning ordinances that limit adult businesses to within "1,000 feet of another regulated use" or "500 feet of a residential use." Young v. American Mini Theatres, Inc., 427 U.S. 50, 72-73 (1976). The factual predicate for the decision to regulate the purveyors of "adult" entertainments, through restrictive zoning and licensing regulations, need not be empirically rigorous—a study conducted 20 years ago or longer can be sufficient to support regulations aimed at reducing the "blight and crime" associated with adult businesses. *See* City of Los Angeles v. Alameda Books, Inc., 535 U.S. 425, 435-441 (2002). This is perhaps the *only* area in which the Supreme Court has permitted the regulation of expressive activity, not because the expression itself causes a harm, but because other social harms tend to follow from it. *Cf.* Brandenburg v. Ohio, 395 U.S. 444, 447 (1969) (holding protected calls for race wars absent a clear and present danger of imminent lawlessness, even though such calls probably correlate with secondary effects, such as race-based assaults, that the government has the power to proscribe). The net effect of these regulations can make large portions of a city essentially "off limits" to adult businesses—and city officials establish regulatory regimes designed to have just that effect. Although these cases remain good law, with the advent of the internet and the ability to download pornographic materials from the privacy of one's own home, the actual burden that restrictive zoning schemes place on adult access to fixed forms of erotica is certainly decreasing. For further discussion, see Alan C. Weinstein & Richard McCleary, *The Association of Adult Businesses with Secondary Effects: Legal Doctrine, Social Theory, and Empirical Evidence,* 20 Cardozo Arts & Ent. L.J. 101 (2011) (documenting secondary effects).

5. *Licensing requirements.* A local government, incident to its comprehensive zoning rules, may adopt a mandatory licensing scheme for "adult" businesses to ensure full compliance with those regulations. *See* City of Littlejohn v. Z.J. Gifts

D-4, L.L.C., 541 U.S. 774 (2004). If a local government denies or revokes a license to operate an adult business, however, the government must ensure the availability of prompt judicial review of the adverse decision and a prompt judicial determination of the merits. *Id.* at 778-781, 783-784. In addition, the licensing scheme must use "reasonably objective, nondiscretionary criteria unrelated to the content of the expressive materials that an adult business may sell or display." *Id.* at 783.

The Supreme Court was unable to produce a single majority opinion in *Barnes*, leaving the area more unsettled than some Justices thought wise. Almost ten years later, the Supreme Court agreed to review another ban on nude dancing.

CITY OF ERIE v. PAP'S A.M.

529 U.S. 277 (2000)

O'CONNOR, J., announced the judgment of the Court and delivered the opinion of the Court with respect to Parts I and II, and an opinion with respect to Parts III and IV, in which THE CHIEF JUSTICE, KENNEDY, J., and BREYER, J., join.

The city of Erie, Pennsylvania, enacted an ordinance banning public nudity. Respondent Pap's A.M. (hereinafter Pap's), which operated a nude dancing establishment in Erie, challenged the constitutionality of the ordinance and sought a permanent injunction against its enforcement. The Pennsylvania Supreme Court, although noting that this Court in *Barnes v. Glen Theatre, Inc.*, 501 U.S. 560 (1991), had upheld an Indiana ordinance that was "strikingly similar" to Erie's, found that the public nudity sections of the ordinance violated respondent's right to freedom of expression under the United States Constitution. This case raises the question whether the Pennsylvania Supreme Court properly evaluated the ordinance's constitutionality under the First Amendment. We hold that Erie's ordinance is a content-neutral regulation that satisfies the four-part test of *United States v. O'Brien*, 391 U.S. 367 (1968). Accordingly, we reverse the decision of the Pennsylvania Supreme Court and remand for the consideration of any remaining issues.

On September 28, 1994, the city council for the city of Erie, Pennsylvania, enacted Ordinance 75-1994, a public indecency ordinance that makes it a summary offense to knowingly or intentionally appear in public in a "state of nudity." Respondent Pap's, a Pennsylvania corporation, operated an establishment in Erie known as "Kandyland" that featured totally nude erotic dancing performed by women. To comply with the ordinance, these dancers must wear, at a minimum, "pasties" and a "G-string." On October 14, 1994, two days after the ordinance went into effect, Pap's filed a complaint against the city of Erie, the mayor of the city, and members of the city council, seeking declaratory relief and a permanent injunction against the enforcement of the ordinance.

The Court of Common Pleas of Erie County granted the permanent injunction and struck down the ordinance as unconstitutional. On cross appeals, the Commonwealth Court reversed the trial court's order.

The Pennsylvania Supreme Court granted review and reversed, concluding that the public nudity provisions of the ordinance violated respondent's rights to freedom of expression as protected by the First and Fourteenth Amendments. . . .

The city of Erie petitioned for a writ of certiorari, which we granted. . . .

Being "in a state of nudity" is not an inherently expressive condition. As we explained in *Barnes*, however, nude dancing of the type at issue here is expressive conduct, although we think that it falls only within the outer ambit of the First Amendment's protection. See *Barnes v. Glen Theatre, Inc.*, 501 U.S. at 565-566 (plurality opinion); *Schad v. Mount Ephraim*, 452 U.S. 61, 66 (1981).

To determine what level of scrutiny applies to the ordinance at issue here, we must decide "whether the State's regulation is related to the suppression of expression." *Texas v. Johnson*, 491 U.S. 397, 403 (1989); see also *United States v. O'Brien*, 391 U.S., at 377. If the governmental purpose in enacting the regulation is unrelated to the suppression of expression, then the regulation need only satisfy the "less stringent" standard from *O'Brien* for evaluating restrictions on symbolic speech. *Texas v. Johnson, supra*, at 403; *United States v. O'Brien, supra*, at 377. If the government interest is related to the content of the expression, however, then the regulation falls outside the scope of the *O'Brien* test and must be justified under a more demanding standard. *Texas v. Johnson, supra*, at 403. . . .

Even if we had not already rejected the view that a ban on public nudity is necessarily related to the suppression of the erotic message of nude dancing, we would do so now because the premise of such a view is flawed. The State's interest in preventing harmful secondary effects is not related to the suppression of expression. In trying to control the secondary effects of nude dancing, the ordinance seeks to deter crime and the other deleterious effects caused by the presence of such an establishment in the neighborhood. . . .

Similarly, even if Erie's public nudity ban has some minimal effect on the erotic message by muting that portion of the expression that occurs when the last stitch is dropped, the dancers at Kandyland and other such establishments are free to perform wearing pasties and G-strings. Any effect on the overall expression is *de minimis*. And as Justice Stevens eloquently stated for the plurality in *Young v. American Mimi Theatres, Inc.*, 427 U.S. 50, 70 (1976), "even though we recognize that the First Amendment will not tolerate the total suppression of erotic materials that have some arguably artistic value, it is manifest that society's interest in protecting this type of expression is of a wholly different, and lesser, magnitude than the interest in untrammeled political debate," and "few of us would march our sons and daughters off to war to preserve the citizen's right to see" specified anatomical areas exhibited at establishments like Kandyland. If States are to be able to regulate secondary effects, the *de minimis* intrusions on expression such as those at issue here cannot be sufficient to render the ordinance content based.

This case is, in fact, similar to *O'Brien, Community for Creative Non-Violence*, and *Ward*. The justification for the government regulation in each case prevents harmful "secondary" effects that are unrelated to the suppression of expression. . . . While the doctrinal theories behind "incidental burdens" and "secondary effects" are, of course, not identical, there is nothing objectionable about a city passing a general ordinance to ban public nudity (even though such a ban may place incidental burdens on some protected speech) and at the same time recognizing that one specific occurrence of public nudity—nude erotic dancing—is particularly problematic because it produces harmful secondary effects. . . .

We conclude that Erie's asserted interest in combating the negative secondary effects associated with adult entertainment establishments like Kandyland is unrelated to the suppression of the erotic message conveyed by nude dancing. The ordinance prohibiting public nudity is therefore valid if it satisfies the four-factor test from *O'Brien* for evaluating restrictions on symbolic speech.

Applying that standard here, we conclude that Erie's ordinance is justified under *O'Brien*. . . .

We hold, therefore, that Erie's ordinance is a content-neutral regulation that is valid under *O'Brien*. Accordingly, the judgment of the Pennsylvania Supreme Court is reversed, and the case is remanded for further proceedings.

It is so ordered.

[Justice Scalia's concurring opinion joined by Justice Thomas is omitted.]

SOUTER, J., concurring in part and dissenting in part.

I join Parts I and II of the Court's opinion and agree with the analytical approach that the plurality employs in deciding this case. Erie's stated interest in combating the secondary effects associated with nude dancing establishments is an interest unrelated to the suppression of expression under *United States v. O'Brien*, 391 U.S. 367 (1968), and the city's regulation is thus properly considered under the *O'Brien* standards. I do not believe, however, that the current record allows us to say that the city has made a sufficient evidentiary showing to sustain its regulation, and I would therefore vacate the decision of the Pennsylvania Supreme Court and remand the case for further proceedings. . . .

The record before us now does not permit the conclusion that Erie's ordinance is reasonably designed to mitigate real harms. This does not mean that the required showing cannot be made, only that, on this record, Erie has not made it. I would remand to give it the opportunity to do so. Accordingly, although I join with the plurality in adopting the *O'Brien* test, I respectfully dissent from the Court's disposition of the case.

STEVENS, J., with whom GINSBURG, J., joins, dissenting.

Far more important than the question whether nude dancing is entitled to protection of the First Amendment are the dramatic changes in legal doctrine that the Court endorses today. Until now, the "secondary effects" of commercial enterprises featuring indecent entertainment have justified only the regulation of their location. For the first time, the Court has now held that such effects may justify the total suppression of protected speech. Indeed, the plurality opinion concludes that admittedly trivial advancements of a State's interests may provide the basis for censorship. The Court's commendable attempt to replace the fractured decision in *Barnes v. Glen Theatre, Inc.*, 501 U.S. 560 (1991), with a single coherent rationale is strikingly unsuccessful; it is supported neither by precedent nor by persuasive reasoning. . . .

The plurality relies on the so-called "secondary effects" test to defend the ordinance. The present use of that rationale, however, finds no support whatsoever in our precedents. Never before have we approved the use of that doctrine to justify a total ban on protected First Amendment expression. On the contrary, we have been quite clear that the doctrine would not support that end. . . .

The reason we have limited our secondary effects cases to zoning and declined to extend their reasoning to total bans is clear and straightforward: A dispersal that simply limits the places where speech may occur is a minimal imposition, whereas a total ban is the most exacting of restrictions. The State's interest in fighting presumed secondary effects is sufficiently strong to justify the former, but far too weak to support the latter, more severe burden. Yet it is perfectly clear that in the present case—to use Justice Powell's metaphor in *American Mini Theatres*—the city of Erie has totally silenced a message the dancers at Kandyland want to convey. The fact that this censorship may have a laudable ulterior purpose cannot mean that censorship is not censorship. For these reasons, the Court's holding rejects the explicit reasoning in *American Mini Theatres* and *Renton* and the express holding in *Schad.*

The Court's use of the secondary effects rationale to permit a total ban has grave implications for basic free speech principles. Ordinarily, laws regulating the primary effects of speech, *i.e.*, the intended persuasive effects caused by the speech, are presumptively invalid. Under today's opinion, a State may totally ban speech based on its secondary effects—which are defined as those effects that "happen to be associated" with speech, *Boos v. Barry*, 485 U.S. 312, 320-321 (1988); see *ante*, at 291—yet the regulation is not presumptively invalid. Because the category of effects that "happen to be associated" with speech includes the narrower subset of effects caused by speech, today's holding has the effect of swallowing whole a most fundamental principle of First Amendment jurisprudence.

The plurality's mishandling of our secondary effects cases is not limited to its approval of a total ban. It compounds that error by dramatically reducing the degree to which the State's interest must be furthered by the restriction imposed on speech, and by ignoring the critical difference between secondary effects caused by speech and the incidental effects on speech that may be caused by a regulation of conduct.

In what can most delicately be characterized as an enormous understatement, the plurality concedes that "requiring dancers to wear pasties and G-strings may not greatly reduce these secondary effects." To believe that the mandatory addition of pasties and a G-string will have *any* kind of noticeable impact on secondary effects requires nothing short of a titanic surrender to the implausible. It would be more accurate to acknowledge, as Justice Scalia does, that there is no reason to believe that such a requirement "will at all reduce the tendency of establishments such as Kandyland to attract crime and prostitution, and hence to foster sexually transmitted disease." Nevertheless, the plurality concludes that the "less stringent" test announced in *United States v. O'Brien*, 391 U.S. 367 (1968), "requires only that the regulation further the interest in combating such effects." It is one thing to say, however, that *O'Brien* is more lenient that the "more demanding standard" we have imposed in cases such as *Texas v. Johnson*, 491 U.S. 397 (1989). See *ante*, at 289. It is quite another to say that the test can be satisfied by nothing more than the mere possibility of *de minimis* effects on the neighborhood. . . .

This narrow aim [of suppressing only erotic dancing and not other forms of nudity in public places] is confirmed by the expressed views of the Erie City Councilmembers who voted for the ordinance. The four city councilmembers who approved the measure (of the six total councilmembers) each stated his or her view that the ordinance was aimed specifically at nude adult entertainment, and not at more mainstream forms of entertainment that include total nudity, nor even at nudity in general. One lawmaker observed: "We're not talking about nudity. We're not talking about the theater or art. . . . We're talking about what is indecent and immoral. . . . We're not prohibiting nudity, we're prohibiting nudity when it's used in a lewd and immoral fashion." Though not quite as succinct, the other councilmembers expressed similar convictions. For example, one member illustrated his understanding of the aim of the law by contrasting it with his recollection about high school students swimming in the nude in the school's pool. The ordinance was not intended to cover those incidents of nudity: "But what I'm getting at is [the swimming] wasn't indecent, it wasn't an immoral thing, and yet there was nudity."

The same lawmaker then disfavorably compared the nude swimming incident to the activities that occur in "some of these clubs" that exist in Erie—clubs that would be covered by the law. *Ibid*. Though such comments could be consistent with an interest in a general prohibition of nudity, the complete absence of commentary on that broader interest, and the councilmembers' exclusive focus on adult entertainment, is evidence of the ordinance's aim. In my view, we need not strain to find consistency with more general purposes when the most natural reading of the record reflects a near obsessive preoccupation with a single target of the law. . . .

It is clear beyond a shadow of a doubt that the Erie ordinance was a response to a more specific concern than nudity in general, namely, nude dancing of the sort found in Kandyland. Given that the Court has not even tried to defend the ordinance's total ban on the ground that its censorship of protected speech might be justified by an overriding state interest, it should conclude that the ordinance is patently invalid. For these reasons, as well as the reasons set forth in Justice White's dissent in *Barnes*, I respectfully dissent.

NOTES AND QUESTIONS

1. *Secondary effects revisited.* Even after a second bite at the apple, the Supreme Court could not muster a clean majority in favor of a single rationale for permitting the regulation of nude dancing. As in *Barnes*, however, a plurality of the Supreme Court invokes the secondary effects of nude dancing as a basis for prohibiting the speech. And, as was the case in *Barnes*, the Court's decision to sustain a speech ban in order to avoid secondary effects associated with the speech fails to observe the generally applicable rule that government cannot ban speech in order to regulate the downstream effects of speech (such as litter on a public sidewalk associated with leafletting).

2. *Are secondary effects real?* Even if one were prepared to credit the secondary effects argument, did the City of Erie present any concrete data showing that the totally nude dancing presented a greater risk of causing serious social harms than the operation of a bowling alley, a McDonald's restaurant, or an Elk's Club? If the empirical basis for regulating "secondary effects" is far from clear, why does the Supreme Court sustain the regulation? Note that in both *Alameda Books* and *Playtime Theatres*, the Supreme Court did not require the local government to document empirically that zoning requirements would actually reduce the "blight and crime" that adult businesses attracted. *See, e.g.,* City of Los Angeles v. Alameda Books, 535 U.S. 425, 435-442 (2002); City of Renton v. Playtime Theatres, Inc., 475 U.S. 41, 50-52 (1986). On the other hand, however, both of these cases—unlike *Pap's A.M.*—did not involve a total ban on the speech activity but rather efforts to limit the locations where such speech activity could take place.

3. *Seminude versus fully nude.* Is the message of an almost nude dancer the same as that of a totally nude dancer? If not, is the difference really a function of the secondary effects of dancers with g-strings and pasties versus dancers without these accouterments? Did Erie (or the Supreme Court) make a persuasive case that the risk of fights, prostitution, and drug dealing correlates positively with the absence of pasties and g-strings and that the use of pasties and g-strings by erotic dancers directly lowers these undesirable secondary effects?

4. *Content discrimination and nude dancing.* Is this really just a simple case of
    either content or viewpoint discrimination? Is nudity dispreferred because of its
    message of unbridled eroticism and sexuality? Public nudity exists in a variety of
    public accommodations in Erie—presumably including country clubs, high
    school and college locker rooms, and health spas. If nudity, per se, were the
    issue, why doesn't Erie regulate nudity in other places of public
    accommodation? Doesn't this selective regulation strongly suggest that the
    government's concern isn't really related to the hypothetical secondary effects
    caused by nude dancing? Note, too, on the question of content or viewpoint
    discrimination, that nudity incident to a major Broadway play or musical, such as
    Equus or *Hair*, does not seem to trigger the same censorial impulse either on the
    part of local officials or the courts.

SABLE COMMUNICATIONS, INC. v. FCC

492 U.S. 115 (1989)

WHITE, J., delivered the opinion of the Court.

The issue before us is the constitutionality of § 223(b) of the Communications
Act of 1934. 47 U.S.C. § 223(b) (1982 ed., Supp. V). The statute, as amended in
1988, imposes an outright ban on indecent as well as obscene interstate commercial
telephone messages. The District Court upheld the prohibition against obscene
interstate telephone communications for commercial purposes, but enjoined the
enforcement of the statute insofar as it applied to indecent messages. We affirm the
District Court in both respects.

In 1983, Sable Communications, Inc., a Los Angeles-based affiliate of Carlin
Communications, Inc., began offering sexually oriented prerecorded telephone
messages (popularly known as "dial-a-porn") through the Pacific Bell telephone
network. In order to provide the messages, Sable arranged with Pacific Bell to use
special telephone lines, designed to handle large volumes of calls simultaneously.
Those who called the adult message number were charged a special fee. The fee was
collected by Pacific Bell and divided between the phone company and the message
provider. Callers outside the Los Angeles metropolitan area could reach the number
by means of a long-distance toll call to the Los Angeles area code.

In 1988, Sable brought suit in District Court seeking declaratory and injunctive
relief against enforcement of the recently amended § 223(b). The 1988 amendments
to the statute imposed a blanket prohibition on indecent as well as obscene interstate
commercial telephone messages. Sable brought this action to enjoin the Federal
Communications Commission (FCC) and the Justice Department from initiating any
criminal investigation or prosecution, civil action or administrative proceeding under
the statute. Sable also sought a declaratory judgment, challenging the indecency and
the obscenity provisions of the amended § 223(b) as unconstitutional, chiefly under
the First and Fourteenth Amendments to the Constitution.

The District Court . . . struck down the "indecent speech" provision of § 223(b),
holding that in this respect the statute was overbroad and unconstitutional and that
this result was consistent with *FCC v. Pacifica Foundation*, 438 U.S. 726 (1978). . . .

While dial-a-porn services are a creature of this decade, the medium, in its brief history, has been the subject of much litigation and the object of a series of attempts at regulation.[3]

[I]n April 1988, Congress amended § 223(b) of the Communications Act to prohibit indecent as well as obscene interstate commercial telephone communications directed to any person regardless of age. The amended statute, which took effect on July 1, 1988, also eliminated the requirement that the FCC promulgate regulations for restricting access to minors since a total ban was imposed on dial-a-porn, making it illegal for adults, as well as children, to have access to the sexually explicit messages, Pub. L. 100-297, 102 Stat. 424. It was this version of the statute that was in effect when Sable commenced this action.

In the ruling at issue in No. 88-515, the District Court upheld § 223(b)'s prohibition of obscene telephone messages as constitutional. We agree with that judgment. In contrast to the prohibition on indecent communications, there is no constitutional barrier to the ban on obscene dial-a-porn recordings. We have repeatedly held that the protection of the First Amendment does not extend to obscene speech. See, e.g., *Paris Adult Theatre I v. Slaton*, 413 U.S. 49, 69 (1973). . . .

In No. 88-525, the District Court concluded that while the Government has a legitimate interest in protecting children from exposure to indecent dial-a-porn messages, § 223(b) was not sufficiently narrowly drawn to serve that purpose and thus violated the First Amendment. We agree.

Sexual expression which is indecent but not obscene is protected by the First Amendment; and the federal parties do not submit that the sale of such materials to adults could be criminalized solely because they are indecent. The Government may, however, regulate the content of constitutionally protected speech in order to promote a compelling interest if it chooses the least restrictive means to further the articulated interest. We have recognized that there is a compelling interest in protecting the physical and psychological well-being of minors. This interest extends to shielding minors from the influence of literature that is not obscene by adult standards. *Ginsberg v. New York*, 390 U.S. 629, 639-640 (1968); *New York v. Ferber*, 458 U.S. 747, 756-757 (1982). The Government may serve this legitimate interest, but to withstand constitutional scrutiny, "it must do so by narrowly drawn regulations designed to serve those interests without unnecessarily interfering with First Amendment freedoms. [] It is not enough to show that the Government's ends are compelling; the means must be carefully tailored to achieve those ends.

In *Butler v. Michigan*, 352 U.S. 380 (1957), a unanimous Court reversed a conviction under a statute which made it an offense to make available to the general public materials found to have a potentially harmful influence on minors. The Court found the law to be insufficiently tailored since it denied adults their free speech rights by allowing them to read only what was acceptable for children. As Justice Frankfurter said in that case, "[s]urely this is to burn the house to roast the pig." *Id.*, at 383. In our judgment, this case, like *Butler*, presents us with "legislation not reasonably restricted to the evil with which it is said to deal."

In attempting to justify the complete ban and criminalization of the indecent commercial telephone communications with adults as well as minors, the federal

---

[3] Dial-a-porn is big business. The dial-a-porn service in New York City alone received six to seven million calls a month for the 6-month period ending in April 1985. *Carlin Communications, Inc. v. FCC*, 787 F.2d 846, 848 (CA 2 1986).

parties rely on *FCC v. Pacifica Foundation*, 438 U.S. 726 (1978), a case in which the Court considered whether the FCC has the power to regulate a radio broadcast that is indecent but not obscene. In an emphatically narrow holding, the *Pacifica* Court concluded that special treatment of indecent broadcasting was justified.

Pacifica is readily distinguishable from these cases, most obviously because it did not involve a total ban on broadcasting indecent material. The FCC rule was not "'intended to place an absolute prohibition on the broadcast of this type of language, but rather sought to channel it to times of day when children most likely would not be exposed to it.'" *Pacifica*, []. The issue of a total ban was not before the Court.

The *Pacifica* opinion also relied on the "unique" attributes of broadcasting, noting that broadcasting is "uniquely pervasive," can intrude on the privacy of the home without prior warning as to program content, and is "uniquely accessible to children, even those too young to read." [] The private commercial telephone communications at issue here are substantially different from the public radio broadcast at issue in *Pacifica*. In contrast to public displays, unsolicited mailings and other means of expression which the recipient has no meaningful opportunity to avoid, the dial-in medium requires the listener to take affirmative steps to receive the communication. There is no "captive audience" problem here; callers will generally not be unwilling listeners. The context of dial-in services, where a caller seeks and is willing to pay for the communication, is manifestly different from a situation in which a listener does not want the received message. Placing a telephone call is not the same as turning on a radio and being taken by surprise by an indecent message. Unlike an unexpected outburst on a radio broadcast, the message received by one who places a call to a dial-a-porn service is not so invasive or surprising that it prevents an unwilling listener from avoiding exposure to it. . . .

The federal parties nevertheless argue that the total ban on indecent commercial telephone communications is justified because nothing less could prevent children from gaining access to such messages. We find the argument quite unpersuasive. The FCC, after lengthy proceedings, determined that its credit card, access code, and scrambling rules were a satisfactory solution to the problem of keeping indecent dial-a-porn messages out of the reach of minors. The Court of Appeals, after careful consideration, agreed that these rules represented a "feasible and effective" way to serve the Government's compelling interest in protecting children. 837 F.2d, at 555.

The federal parties now insist that the rules would not be effective enough—that enterprising youngsters could and would evade the rules and gain access to communications from which they should be shielded. There is no evidence in the record before us to that effect, nor could there be since the FCC's implementation of § 223(b) prior to its 1988 amendment has never been tested over time. In this respect, the federal parties assert that in amending § 223(b) in 1988, Congress expressed its view that there was not a sufficiently effective way to protect minors short of the total ban that it enacted. The federal parties claim that we must give deference to that judgment.

To the extent that the federal parties suggest that we should defer to Congress' conclusion about an issue of constitutional law, our answer is that while we do not ignore it, it is our task in the end to decide whether Congress has violated the Constitution. This is particularly true where the Legislature has concluded that its product does not violate the First Amendment. . . .

For all we know from this record, the FCC's technological approach to restricting dial-a-porn messages to adults who seek them would be extremely effective, and only a few of the most enterprising and disobedient young people would manage to secure access to such messages. If this is the case, it seems to us that § 223(b) is not a narrowly tailored effort to serve the compelling interest of preventing minors from being exposed to indecent telephone messages. Under our precedents, § 223(b), in its present form, has the invalid effect of limiting the content of adult telephone conversations to that which is suitable for children to hear. It is another case of "burn[ing] the house to roast the pig." *Butler v. Michigan*, 352 U.S., at 383.

Because the statute's denial of adult access to telephone messages which are indecent but not obscene far exceeds that which is necessary to limit the access of minors to such messages, we hold that the ban does not survive constitutional scrutiny.

Accordingly, we affirm the judgment of the District Court in Nos. 88-515 and 88-525.

It is so ordered.

SCALIA, J., concurring.

I join the opinion of the Court, but add a few words. It should not be missed that we are making a value judgment with respect to the indecency portion of the statute. . . .

I join the Court's opinion because I think it correct that a wholesale prohibition upon adult access to indecent speech cannot be adopted merely because the FCC's alternate proposal could be circumvented by as few children as the evidence suggests. But where a reasonable person draws the line in this balancing process— that is, how few children render the risk unacceptable—depends in part upon what mere "indecency" (as opposed to "obscenity") includes. The more narrow the understanding of what is "obscene," and hence the more pornographic what is embraced within the residual category of "indecency," the more reasonable it becomes to insist upon greater assurance of insulation from minors. So while the Court is unanimous on the reasoning of Part IV, I am not sure it is unanimous on the assumptions underlying that reasoning. I do not believe, for example, that any sort of sexual activity portrayed or enacted over the phone lines would fall outside of the obscenity portion of the statute that we uphold, and within the indecency portion that we strike down, so long as it appeals only to "normal, healthy sexual desires" as opposed to "shameful or morbid" ones. *Brockett v. Spokane Arcades, Inc.*, 472 U.S. 491, 498 (1985). . . .

Finally, I note that while we hold the Constitution prevents Congress from banning indecent speech in this fashion, we do not hold that the Constitution requires public utilities to carry it.

BRENNAN, J., with whom MARSHALL, J., and STEVENS, J., join, concurring in part and dissenting in part.

I agree that a statute imposing criminal penalties for making, or for allowing other to use a telephone under one's control to make, any indecent telephonic communication for a commercial purpose is patently unconstitutional. I therefore join Parts I, II, and IV of the Court's opinion.

In my view, however, 47 U.S.C. § 223(b)(1)(A)'s parallel criminal prohibition with regard to obscene commercial communications likewise violates the First Amendment. I have long been convinced that the exaction of criminal penalties for the distribution of obscene materials to consenting adults is constitutionally intolerable. In my judgment, "the concept of 'obscenity' cannot be defined with sufficient specificity and clarity to provide fair notice to persons who create and distribute sexually oriented materials, to prevent substantial erosion of protected speech as a byproduct of the attempt to suppress unprotected speech, and to avoid very costly institutional harms." Paris Adult Theatre I v. Slaton, 413 U.S. 49, 103 (1973) (Brennan, J., dissenting). To be sure, the Government has a strong interest in protecting children against exposure to pornographic material that might be harmful to them. New York v. Ferber, 458 U.S. 747, 775-777 (1982) (Brennan, J., concurring in judgment); Ginsberg v. New York, 390 U.S. 629 (1968). But a complete criminal ban on obscene telephonic messages for profit is "unconstitutionally overbroad, and therefore invalid on its face," as a means for achieving this end. Miller v. California, 413 U.S. 15, 47 (1973) (Brennan, J., dissenting). . . .

NOTES AND QUESTIONS

1. *The value of dial-a-porn.* What possible value does dial-a-porn have in terms of the traditional values thought to be associated with protecting the freedom of speech? For example, how do dial-a-porn services facilitate the process of democratic deliberation (the Meiklejohn theory)? In fact, does the majority make any serious effort to defend dial-a-porn with reference to a purposive reading of the Free Speech Clause? Is the Free Speech Clause, at least as construed in *Sable*, essentially a guarantor of an unregulated marketplace of ideas?

2. *The slippery slope problem.* Note that by 1989, Justice Brennan—who authored the *Roth* test in 1957—had completely given up on judicial efforts to define obscenity as an unprotected form of expression. Why did Justice Brennan abandon efforts to sift wheat from chaff in the area of erotica? Is any effort to characterize or classify erotica doomed to rest on purely subjective aesthetic values? In this regard, consider Canada's effort to reorient limitations on erotica in terms of advancing gender equality rather than as an effort to create and enforce standards of public morality. Is Canada's approach more or less consistent with an appropriate understanding of the scope of the freedom of expression?

3. *Scalia's approach.* Moving in exactly the opposite direction as Justice Brennan, Justice Scalia seems to be suggesting that the universe of obscene telephonic communications might be sufficiently broad to permit a fairly comprehensive proscription of erotic telephone messages. What would the net effects be of permitting government to define "obscene" materials broadly? Would this approach enhance or degrade the protection of important political, literary, scientific, and artistic speech? Would the chilling effect of the obscenity doctrine be enhanced or reduced if, as Justice Scalia suggests, the federal courts were to define obscenity relatively broadly?

AN EXTENDED NOTE ON THE PROBLEM OF "REVENGE PORN"

Should the First Amendment preclude state governments, or the federal government, from adopting criminal laws aimed at preventing the online distribution of embarrassing intimate photographs by vengeful ex-spouses or former boyfriends/girlfriends? Several websites, such as yougotposted.com, godaddy.com, and texxxan.com, exist for the primary purpose of facilitating the distribution of embarrassing, explicit photographs of former intimate partners. Usually, but not always, men post these images of their former wives or girlfriends. *See* Erica Goode, *Once Scorned, But on Revenge Sites, Twice Hurt*, N.Y. Times, Sept. 24, 2013, at A11 (noting that "[r]evenge porn sites feature explicit photos posted by ex-boyfriends, ex-husbands and ex-lovers, often accompanied by disparaging descriptions and identifying details, like where the women live and work, as well as links to their Facebook pages").

Utah, for example, has enacted a statute that criminally punishes the unauthorized distribution of "intimate images" via social media. *See* Utah Code Ann. § 76-5b-203 (2016). In relevant part, the statute, which is typical of enactments in about a dozen other states, proscribes the "distribution of intimate images if the actor, with the intent to cause emotional distress or harm, knowingly or intentionally distributes to any third party any intimate image of an individual who is 18 years of age or older, if: (a) the actor knows that the depicted individual has not given consent to the actor to distribute the intimate image; (b) the intimate image was created by or provided to the actor under circumstances in which the individual has a reasonable expectation of privacy; and (c) actual emotional distress or harm is caused to the person as a result of the distribution under this section." *Id.* at § 76-5b-203(2). Under the statute, "intimate images" encompass "any visual depiction, photograph, film, video, recording, picture, or computer or computer-generated image or picture, whether made or produced by electronic, mechanical, or other means" depicting human genitals, female breasts, or "sexually explicit conduct." *Id.* at § 76-5b-203(1)(b). In turn, "sexually explicit conduct" includes images featuring "partial nudity" or "simulated sexually explicit conduct" that does not depict actual sexual conduct (but seems to do so). *See id.* at § 76-5b-203(1)(b) & (c).

Is this statute constitutional as against a First Amendment challenge? Does simulated sexual activity or partial nudity meet the *Miller* test for obscenity? On the other hand, must a revenge porn statute be limited in scope to materials that are legally obscene? If a statute simply provided specific civil and criminal remedies for legally obscene revenge porn, would it be constitutional? Or would such a narrowly drafted law be subject to an *R.A.V.* objection? (See *R.A.V., supra* p. 540.) On the other hand, would a statute that criminally prohibits posting merely "unflattering" or "upsetting" images be consistent with the First Amendment? For an argument that narrowly drawn anti-revenge porn criminal laws are consistent with the First Amendment, see Danielle Keats Citron & Mary Anne Franks, *Criminalizing Revenge Porn*, 49 Wake Forest L. Rev. 345 (2014). For more skeptical points of view on the need for such laws and their consistency with the First Amendment, see Clay Calvert, *Revenge Porn and Freedom of Expression: Legislative Pushback to an Online Weapon of Emotional and Reputational Destruction*, 24 Fordham Intell. Prop. Media & Ent. L.J. 673, 683-701 (2014) and John A. Humbach, *Privacy and the Right of Free Expression*, 11 First Amend. L. Rev. 16 (2012).

Finally, would the Supreme Court's *New York Times Co. v. Sullivan (supra, p. 457)* line of precedent present an obstacle to the application of revenge porn statutes in circumstances involving a public official, a public figure, or someone involved in a matter of public concern? Could government seek to protect a persons's interest in privacy if, in context, the intimate images related to a public official, a public figure, or a matter of public concern? It bears noting that in much of the wider world, a law prohibiting the unauthorized distribution of a nude or even a merely embarrassing personal photograph would be viewed as fully consistent with a strong and meaningful commitment to the freedom of speech. *See* Krotoszynski, *supra* p. 589, at 16-21, 143-44, 156-173. Of course, the First Amendment, as defined and applied by the U.S. federal courts, often compels results that other democratic nations with constitutional free speech guarantees would not embrace.

THEORY-APPLIED PROBLEM

The actor Daniel Radcliffe, a-k-a "Harry Potter," starred in a very successful production of the play *Equus* on London's West End during the 2007-2008 theater season. At the time, Radcliffe was only 17 years old. The play, as originally written and blocked by author Peter Shaffer, and as performed by Radcliffe, requires Radcliffe's character, mentally disturbed stable boy Alan Strang, to appear nude for extended periods on stage, to simulate sex with an actress, and to mutilate six horses with a hoof pick in a state of psychosexual ecstasy. The play, since its debut in London in 1973, has received very favorable critical notices (it won the Tony for "Best New Play" after it opened in New York City), and the new production was no exception.

In July 2008, Radcliffe comes to the United States to perform *Equus*. (At this point, he is 18 years old.) To prepare for its Broadway run, the producers book the Taft Theater, in downtown Cincinnati, Ohio, presumably unaware of the local district attorney's long-standing efforts to keep Cincinnati as smut-free as possible. Ohio, like Indiana, maintains a generic statute that prohibits public nudity. *See* Ohio Rev. Code § 2907.09. In relevant part, the law prohibits public "expos[ure] of one's private parts" or "engag[ing] in conduct that to an ordinary observer would appear to be sexual conduct or masturbation." In the production of *Equus*, Radcliffe does both things, causing the district attorney great anxiety. After the play's opening night, the district attorney seeks an injunction ordering the production closed, and indicts Radcliffe for a second-degree misdemeanor. After learning that persons under 18 had attended the performance, the district attorney initiates a felony prosecution against Radcliffe for public nudity. (The law punishes public nudity in front of minors more severely.) Lawyers for the play's producers and Radcliffe file a motion to dismiss, arguing that the injunction and prosecution violate the Free Speech Clause of the First Amendment. How should the Ohio trial court rule? For bonus points, consider whether Radcliffe could lawfully have performed the role of Alan Strang while under the age of 18. Moreover, if a video recording of the 2007 West End production of *Equus* were available commercially, could one legally sell or possess it in the United States?

AN EXTENDED NOTE ON "CHILDPROOFING" THE INTERNET

As a general matter, government efforts to protect children from age-inappropriate materials on the internet cannot encompass regulations that effectively silence speech appropriate for adults. To be sure, obscene communications do not enjoy any special legal privilege simply because many such communications happen to occur over the Web. Similarly, laws against presenting nude pictures of minors apply with full force to the internet. Even so, the Supreme Court has been vigilant in protecting the rights of adults to access noncommercial internet sites, even if those sites contain materials that are inappropriate (perhaps even obscene) as to minors. Thus, legislators may not restrict internet content solely to material fit for children. Reno v. American Civil Liberties Union, 542 U.S. 656 (1997); Ashcroft v. ACLU,

535 U.S. 564 (2002) ("Ashcroft I"); Ashcroft v. ACLU ("Ashcroft II"), 542 U.S. 656 (2004). For further discussion, see *supra* Chapter 8.

Even though the Supreme Court will not accept blanket efforts to childproof the internet, *see Ashcroft*, 542 U.S. at 670-673; *Reno*, 521 U.S. at 867-870, 874-879, there is good cause to believe that a majority of the Justices might accept narrowly tailored, carefully drawn statutes that require good-faith efforts by Webmasters to limit or block access by minors, at least when and if technologies facilitating such blocking can be deployed without significant cost or technical difficulty. Thus, a statute requiring a site visitor to check a box indicating that she is 18 or older would likely pass constitutional muster—implementing an age check box would impose little cost and might have some deterrent effect. For a discussion of these issues and the relevant Supreme Court cases addressing them, see Ronald J. Krotoszynski, Jr., *Childproofing the Internet*, 41 Brandeis L.J. 447 (2003).

CHAPTER
12

The Government as Speaker, Employer, and Educator

TABLE OF CONTENTS

Previous chapters have dealt with First Amendment principles triggered by government regulations of private speech. This chapter addresses the First Amendment principles that apply when the government subsidizes or finances speech, restricts the speech of its employees or contractors, or imposes regulations on expression in government institutions such as public schools or libraries.

For many years courts took the position that the First Amendment offers no protection to a speaker who violates a condition on the receipt of government funds. When Oliver Wendell Holmes was a Justice on the Massachusetts Supreme Judicial Court in the late nineteenth century, for example, he wrote a famous opinion in which he upheld the firing of a policeman who had violated limitations on political activity in his contract. McAuliffe v. Mayor of New Bedford, 29 N.E. 517 (Mass. 1892). "The petitioner may have a constitutional right to talk politics," Holmes wrote, "but he has no constitutional right to be a policeman." Holmes noted that in the public sphere, as in private employment, the employee "takes the employment on the terms which are offered him." Prior to the twentieth century, the courts' tendency to equate public and private authority to restrict the speech of employees coincided with similarly broad assumptions about the ability of both public and private entities to restrict speech on the property they controlled. *See* Commonwealth v. Davis, 39 N.E. 113, 113 (Mass. 1895), *aff'd*, 167 U.S. 43 (1897) ("For the Legislature absolutely or conditionally to forbid public speaking in a highway or public park is no more an infringement of the rights of a member of the public than for the owner of a private house to forbid it in his house.").

As we saw in Chapter 4, the Supreme Court long ago abandoned the notion that the government has the same authority as a private entity to prohibit speech on its property. *See* Hague v. CIO, *supra* p. 120. As the materials in this chapter will illustrate, the Court has also abandoned the notion that the government has unfettered authority to restrict speech in other contexts involving government financing, including public employment. Unfortunately, the Court has been both less consistent and less clear about the rules constraining the government in these contexts than it has in the public forum area. This chapter attempts to provide some structure to these cases by subdividing the cases into three broad categories: general government subsidies of expression, limitations on the expression of government employees, and restrictions on expression in public schools and libraries. Keep in mind, however, that these categories are somewhat arbitrary, and many cases have elements that fall into several different categories. The Court's jurisprudence in this area is very much a work in progress, and the only definitive statement that can be made is that the First Amendment now limits the extent to which the government can control the content of a speaker's expression, even if the government has paid the speaker.

A.   GOVERNMENT-SUBSIDIZED SPEECH AND GOVERNMENT SPEECH

RUST v. SULLIVAN

500 U.S. 173 (1991)

REHNQUIST, C.J., delivered the opinion of the Court.

In 1970, Congress enacted Title X of the Public Health Service Act (Act), which provides federal funding for family planning services. The Act authorizes the Secretary to "make grants to and enter into contracts with public or nonprofit private entities to assist in the establishment and operation of voluntary family planning projects which shall offer a broad range of acceptable and effective family planning methods and services." Grants and contracts under Title X must "be made in accordance with such regulations as the Secretary may promulgate."

In 1988, the Secretary promulgated new regulations designed to provide "'clear and operational guidance' to grantees about how to preserve the distinction between Title X programs and abortion as a method of family planning." The regulations attach three principal conditions on the grant of federal funds for Title X projects. First, the regulations specify that a "Title X project may not provide counseling concerning the use of abortion as a method of family planning or provide referral for abortion as a method of family planning." The Title X project is expressly prohibited from referring a pregnant woman to an abortion provider, even upon specific request. One permissible response to such an inquiry is that "the project does not consider abortion an appropriate method of family planning, and therefore does not counsel or refer for abortion." Second, the regulations broadly prohibit a Title X project from engaging in activities that "encourage, promote or advocate abortion as a method of family planning." Forbidden activities include lobbying for legislation that would increase the availability of abortion as a method of family planning, developing or disseminating materials advocating abortion as a method of family planning, providing speakers to promote abortion as a method of family planning, using legal action to make abortion available in any way as a method of family planning, and paying dues to any group that advocates abortion as a method of family planning as a substantial part of its activities. Third, the regulations require that Title X projects be organized so that they are "physically and financially separate" from prohibited abortion activities.

Petitioners are Title X grantees and doctors who supervise Title X funds suing on behalf of themselves and their patients. Petitioners contend that the regulations violate the First Amendment by impermissibly discriminating based on viewpoint because they prohibit "all discussion about abortion as a lawful option—including counseling, referral, and the provision of neutral and accurate information about ending a pregnancy—while compelling the clinic or counselor to provide information that promotes continuing a pregnancy to term."

There is no question but that the statutory prohibition [on speech favoring abortion] is constitutional. The Government can, without violating the Constitution, selectively fund a program to encourage certain activities it believes to be in the public interest, without at the same time funding an alternate program which seeks to deal with the problem in another way. In so doing, the Government has not discriminated on the basis of viewpoint; it has merely chosen to fund one activity to the exclusion of the other. "[A] legislature's decision not to subsidize the exercise of a fundamental right does not infringe the right."

The challenged regulations implement the statutory prohibition by prohibiting counseling, referral, and the provision of information regarding abortion as a method of family planning. They are designed to ensure that the limits of the federal program are observed. The Title X program is designed not for prenatal care, but to encourage family planning. A doctor who wished to offer prenatal care to a project patient who became pregnant could properly be prohibited from doing so because such service is outside the scope of the federally funded program. The regulations prohibiting abortion counseling and referral are of the same ilk; "no funds appropriated for the project may be used in programs where abortion is a method of family planning," and a doctor employed by the project may be prohibited in the course of his project duties from counseling abortion or referring for abortion. This is not a case of the Government "suppressing a dangerous idea," but of a prohibition on a project grantee or its employees from engaging in activities outside of the project's scope.

By requiring that the Title X grantee engage in abortion-related activity separately from activity receiving federal funding, Congress has, consistent with our teachings in *League of Women Voters* and *Regan*, not denied it the right to engage in abortion-related activities. Congress has merely refused to fund such activities out of the public fisc, and the Secretary has simply required a certain degree of separation from the Title X project in order to ensure the integrity of the federally funded program.

The same principles apply to petitioners' claim that the regulations abridge the free speech rights of the grantee's staff. Individuals who are voluntarily employed for a Title X project must perform their duties in accordance with the regulation's restrictions on abortion counseling and referral. The employees remain free, however, to pursue abortion-related activities when they are not acting under the auspices of the Title X project. The regulations, which govern solely the scope of the Title X project's activities, do not in any way restrict the activities of those persons acting as private individuals. The employees' freedom of expression is limited during the time that they actually work for the project; but this limitation is a consequence of their decision to accept employment in a project, the scope of which is permissibly restricted by the funding authority.

This is not to suggest that funding by the Government, even when coupled with the freedom of the fund recipients to speak outside the scope of the Government-funded project, is invariably sufficient to justify government control over the content of expression. For example, this Court has recognized that the existence of a Government "subsidy," in the form of Government-owned property, does not justify the restriction of speech in areas that have "been traditionally open to the public for expressive activity," or have been "expressly dedicated to speech activity." Similarly, we have recognized that the university is a traditional sphere of free expression so fundamental to the functioning of our society that the Government's ability to control speech within that sphere by means of conditions attached to the expenditure of Government funds is restricted by the vagueness and overbreadth doctrines of the First Amendment. It could be argued by analogy that traditional relationships such as that between doctor and patient should enjoy protection under the First Amendment from government regulation, even when subsidized by the Government. We need not resolve that question here, however, because the Title X program regulations do not significantly impinge upon the doctor-patient relationship. Nothing in them requires a doctor to represent as his own any opinion that he does not in fact hold. Nor is the doctor-patient relationship established by the Title X program sufficiently all-encompassing so as to justify an expectation on the part of the patient of comprehensive medical advice. The program does not provide postconception medical care, and therefore a doctor's silence with regard to abortion cannot reasonably be thought to mislead a client into thinking that the doctor does not consider abortion an appropriate option for her. The doctor is always free to make clear that advice regarding abortion is simply beyond the scope of the program. In these circumstances, the general rule that the Government may choose not to subsidize speech applies with full force.

BLACKMUN, J., dissenting, with whom MARSHALL, J., joins, and with whom STEVENS, J., and O'CONNOR, J., join in part.

It cannot seriously be disputed that the counseling and referral provisions at issue in the present cases constitute content-based regulation of speech. Title X grantees may provide counseling and referral regarding any of a wide range of family planning and other topics, save abortion.

The Regulations are also clearly viewpoint-based. While suppressing speech favorable to abortion with one hand, the Secretary compels anti-abortion speech with the other. For example, the Department of Health and Human Services' own description of the Regulations makes plain that "Title X projects are required to facilitate access to prenatal care and social services, including adoption services, that might be needed by the pregnant client to promote her wellbeing and that of her child, while making it abundantly clear that the project is not permitted to promote abortion by facilitating access to abortion through the referral process."

Moreover, the Regulations command that a project refer for prenatal care each woman diagnosed as pregnant, irrespective of the woman's expressed desire to continue or terminate her pregnancy. If a client asks directly about abortion, a Title X physician or counselor is required to say, in essence, that the project does not consider abortion to be an appropriate method of family planning. Both requirements are antithetical to the First Amendment.

The Regulations pertaining to "advocacy" are even more explicitly viewpoint-based. These provide: "A Title X project may not encourage, promote or advocate abortion as a method of family planning." They explain: "This requirement prohibits actions to assist women to obtain abortions or increase the availability or accessibility of abortion for family planning purposes." The Regulations do not, however, proscribe or even regulate antiabortion advocacy. These are clearly restrictions aimed at the suppression of "dangerous ideas."

Remarkably, the majority concludes that "the Government has not discriminated on the basis of viewpoint; it has merely chosen to fund one activity to the exclusion of another." But the majority's claim that the Regulations merely limit a Title X project's speech to preventive or preconceptional services rings hollow in light of the broad range of non-preventive services that the Regulations authorize Title X projects to provide. By refusing to fund those family planning projects that advocate abortion because they advocate abortion, the Government plainly has targeted a particular viewpoint.

NOTES AND QUESTIONS

1. *Can the government treat the professionals it funds merely as means to its ends?* *Rust* held that the First Amendment does not prohibit the government from heavily restricting the speech of health care workers whose employment is financed by government funds. The Court's theory is that workers in this situation are merely mouthpieces for the government itself; therefore, the government may demand that the workers say only what the government wants them to say. Should the simple fact that the government is hiring someone to speak on its behalf settle the question whether the worker's speech is protected by the First Amendment or should we assess the nature of the government's relationship with the speaker? Dean Robert Post argues that the government should be allowed to regulate the speech of individuals receiving government funds within what he calls "managerial domains," which he defines as domains in which "the state organizes its resources so as to achieve specified ends." Robert C. Post, *Subsidized Speech*, 106 Yale L.J. 151, 164 (1996). Government may regulate the speech of workers within managerial domains because they conceptualize "persons as means to an end rather than as autonomous agents." Nevertheless, Post contends that the government should not be allowed to regulate the speech of health care professionals in cases such as *Rust* because the workers' professional obligations require that they "always qualify their loyalty and commitment to the vertical hierarchy of an organization by their horizontal commitment to general professional norms and standards." *Id.* at 172. *See also* Christina E. Wells, *Abortion Counseling as Vice Activity: The Free Speech Implications of* Rust v. Sullivan *and* Planned Parenthood v. Casey, 95 Colum. L. Rev.1724, 1725-26 (1995) (arguing that federal courts tend to treat regulatory burdens on medical professionals as regulations of activity, rather than speech, even when the regulations directly restrict professional speech); Timothy Zick, *Professional Rights Speech*, 47 Ariz. State L.J. 1289, 1292 (2015) ("State regulations of professional speech have become more prevalent, more politically tinged, and more likely to structure and dictate the specific content of professional-client interactions."); Claudia E. Haupt, *Professional Speech*, 125 Yale L.J. 1238, 1240 (2016) (arguing that the federal courts have failed to develop and apply an adequate First Amendment framework to safeguard professional speech).

2. *Can government demand that professionals provide false, misleading, or incomplete information?* Should individuals receiving government financing have a First Amendment right to inform members of the public that the government is intentionally misleading them? A controversy arose when South African President Thabo Mbeki expressed the opinion that the HIV virus did not cause AIDS—a point of view widely rejected by the medical and scientific community. Suppose an American government agency adopted this position, and then inserted in the contracts of private scientists receiving government grants

from that agency a prohibition on asserting publicly the mainstream scientific position that the HIV virus causes AIDS. Would scientists receiving grants from the agency have a First Amendment right to disobey the contractual directive and espouse publicly the mainstream scientific view?

LEGAL SERVICES CORP. v. VELAZQUEZ
531 U.S. 522 (2001)

KENNEDY, J., delivered the opinion of the Court.

In 1974, Congress enacted the Legal Services Corporation Act. The Act establishes the Legal Services Corporation (LSC) as a District of Columbia nonprofit corporation. LSC's mission is to distribute funds appropriated by Congress to eligible local grantee organizations "for the purpose of providing financial support for legal assistance in noncriminal proceedings or matters to persons financially unable to afford legal assistance."

The grantee organizations hire and supervise lawyers to provide free legal assistance to indigent clients. Each year LSC appropriates funds to grantees or recipients that hire and supervise lawyers for various professional activities, including representation of indigent clients seeking welfare benefits.

This suit requires us to decide whether one of the conditions imposed by Congress on the use of LSC funds violates the First Amendment rights of LSC grantees and their clients. For purposes of our decision, the restriction prohibits legal representation funded by recipients of LSC moneys if the representation involves an effort to amend or otherwise challenge existing welfare law. As interpreted by the LSC and by the Government, the restriction prevents an attorney from arguing to a court that a state statute conflicts with a federal statute or that either a state or federal statute by its terms or in its application is violative of the United States Constitution.

The United States and LSC rely on *Rust* v. *Sullivan* as support for the LSC program restrictions. The Court in *Rust* did not place explicit reliance on the rationale that the counseling activities of the doctors under Title X amounted to governmental speech; when interpreting the holding in later cases, however, we have explained *Rust* on this understanding. As we said in *Rosenberger* [*v. Rector & Visitors of the University of Virginia*, excerpted in this chapter], "[w]hen the government disburses public funds to private entities to convey a governmental message, it may take legitimate and appropriate steps to ensure that its message is neither garbled nor distorted by the grantee."

Neither the latitude for government speech nor its rationale applies to subsidies for private speech in every instance, however. . . . [T]he salient point is that . . . the LSC program was designed to facilitate private speech, not to promote a governmental message. Congress funded LSC grantees to provide attorneys to represent the interests of indigent clients. In the specific context of suits for benefits, an LSC-funded attorney speaks on the behalf of the client in a claim against the government for welfare benefits. The lawyer is not the government's speaker. The attorney defending the decision to deny benefits will deliver the government's message in the litigation. The LSC lawyer, however, speaks on the behalf of his or her private, indigent client.

The Government has designed this program to use the legal profession and the established Judiciary of the States and the Federal Government to accomplish its end of assisting welfare claimants in determination or receipt of their benefits. The advice from the attorney to the client and the advocacy by the attorney to the courts cannot be classified as governmental speech even under a generous understanding of the concept. In this vital respect this suit is distinguishable from *Rust*.

By providing subsidies to LSC, the Government seeks to facilitate suits for benefits by using the State and Federal courts and the independent bar on which those courts depend for the proper performance of their duties and responsibilities. Restricting LSC attorneys in advising their clients and in presenting arguments and analyses to the courts distorts the legal system by altering the traditional role of the attorneys.

Interpretation of the law and the Constitution is the primary mission of the judiciary when it acts within the sphere of its authority to resolve a case or controversy. *Marbury v. Madison*. An informed, independent judiciary presumes an informed, independent bar. The disability [imposed on attorneys by the LSC funding restriction] is inconsistent with the proposition that attorneys should present all the reasonable and well-grounded arguments necessary for proper resolution of the case. By seeking to prohibit the analysis of certain legal issues and to truncate presentation to the courts, the enactment under review prohibits speech and expression upon which courts must depend for the proper exercise of the judicial power. Congress cannot wrest the law from the Constitution which is its source.

The restriction imposed by the statute here threatens severe impairment of the judicial function. [The LSC funding statute] sifts out cases presenting constitutional challenges in order to insulate the Government's laws from judicial inquiry. If the restriction on speech and legal advice were to stand, the result would be two tiers of cases. In cases where LSC counsel were attorneys of record, there would be lingering doubt whether the truncated representation had resulted in complete analysis of the case, full advice to the client, and proper presentation to the court. The courts and the public would come to question the adequacy and fairness of professional representations when the attorney, either consciously to comply with this statute or unconsciously to continue the representation despite the statute, avoided all reference to questions of statutory validity and constitutional authority. A scheme so inconsistent with accepted separation-of-powers principles is an insufficient basis to sustain or uphold the restriction on speech.

SCALIA, J., with whom THE CHIEF JUSTICE, O'CONNOR, J., and THOMAS, J., join, dissenting.

The LSC Act is a federal subsidy program, not a federal regulatory program, and "[t]here is a basic difference between [the two]." *Maher v. Roe*. Regulations directly restrict speech; subsidies do not. Subsidies, it is true, may *indirectly* abridge speech, but only if the funding scheme is "'manipulated' to have a 'coercive effect'" on those who do not hold the subsidized position. *Finley* (Scalia, J., dissenting).

In *Rust v. Sullivan*, the Court applied these principles to a statutory scheme that is in all relevant respects indistinguishable from [the LSC funding restriction challenged here]. . . .

The LSC Act, like the scheme in *Rust*, does not create a public forum. Far from encouraging a diversity of views, it has always, as the Court accurately states, "placed restrictions on its use of funds." Nor does [the LSC funding restriction] discriminate on the basis of viewpoint, since it funds neither challenges to nor defenses of existing welfare law. The provision simply declines to subsidize a certain class of litigation, and under *Rust* that decision "does not infringe the right" to bring such litigation. The Court's repeated claims that [the restriction] "restricts" and "prohibits" speech, and "insulates" laws from judicial review, are simply baseless. No litigant who, in the absence of LSC funding, would bring a suit challenging existing welfare law is deterred from doing so [by the funding restriction]. *Rust* thus controls these cases and compels the conclusion that [the restriction] is constitutional.

The Court contends that *Rust* is different because the program at issue subsidized government speech, while the LSC funds private speech. This is so unpersuasive it hardly needs response. If the private doctors' confidential advice to their patients at issue in *Rust* constituted "government speech," it is hard to imagine what subsidized speech would *not* be government speech. Moreover, the majority's contention that the subsidized speech in these cases is not government speech because the lawyers have a professional obligation to represent the interests of their clients founders on the reality that the doctors in *Rust* had a professional obligation to serve the interests of their patients—which at the time of *Rust* we had held to be highly relevant to the permissible scope of federal regulation. Even respondents agree that "the true speaker in *Rust* was not the government, but a doctor."

ROSENBERGER v.
RECTOR & VISITORS OF THE UNIVERSITY OF VIRGINIA
515 U.S. 819 (1995)

KENNEDY, J., delivered the opinion of the Court.

[The University of Virginia maintains a Student Activity Fund (SAF), which is designed] to support a broad range of extracurricular student activities that "are related to the educational purpose of the University." The SAF is based on the University's "recogni[tion] that the availability of a wide range of opportunities" for its students "tends to enhance the University environment." The Guidelines require that it be administered "in a manner consistent with the educational purpose of the University as well as with state and federal law." The SAF receives its money from a mandatory fee of $14 per semester assessed to each full-time student. The Student Council, elected by the students, has the initial authority to disburse the funds, but its actions are subject to review by a faculty body chaired by a designee of the Vice President for Student Affairs.

Guidelines [for the SAF] recognize 11 categories of student groups that may seek payment to third-party contractors because they "are related to the educational purpose of the University of Virginia." One of these is "student news, information, opinion, entertainment, or academic communications media groups." The Guidelines also specify, however, that the costs of certain activities that are otherwise eligible for funding will not be reimbursed by the SAF. The student activities which are excluded from SAF support are religious activities, philanthropic contributions and activities, political activities, activities that would jeopardize the University's tax-exempt status, those which involve payment of honoraria or similar fees, or social entertainment or related expenses. The prohibition on "political activities" is defined so that it is limited to electioneering and lobbying. The Guidelines provide that "[t]hese restrictions on funding political activities are not intended to preclude funding of any otherwise eligible student organization which . . . espouses particular positions or ideological viewpoints, including those that may be unpopular or are not generally accepted." A "religious activity," by contrast, is defined as any activity that "primarily promotes or manifests a particular belie[f] in or about a deity or an ultimate reality."

Petitioners' organization, Wide Awake Productions (WAP) was established "[t]o publish a magazine of philosophical and religious expression," "[t]o facilitate discussion which fosters an atmosphere of sensitivity to and tolerance of Christian viewpoints," and "[t]o provide a unifying focus for Christians of multicultural backgrounds." WAP publishes Wide Awake: A Christian Perspective at the University of Virginia. The paper's Christian viewpoint was evident from the first issue, in which its editors wrote that the journal "offers a Christian perspective on both personal and community issues, especially those relevant to college students at the University of Virginia." The editors committed the paper to a two-fold mission: "to challenge Christians to live, in word and deed, according to the faith they proclaim and to encourage students to consider what a personal relationship with Jesus Christ means." The first issue had articles about racism, crisis pregnancy, stress, prayer, C. S. Lewis' ideas about evil and free will, and reviews of religious music. In the next two issues, Wide Awake featured stories about homosexuality, Christian missionary work, and eating disorders, as well as music reviews and interviews with University professors. Each page of Wide Awake, and the end of each article or review, is marked by a cross. The advertisements carried in Wide Awake also reveal the Christian perspective of the journal. For the most part, the advertisers are churches, centers for Christian study, or Christian bookstores. By June 1992, WAP had distributed about 5,000 copies of Wide Awake to University students, free of charge. WAP requested the SAF to pay its printer $5,862 for the costs of printing its newspaper. The Appropriations Committee of the Student Council denied WAP's request on the ground that Wide Awake was a "religious activity" within the meaning of the Guidelines, i.e., that the newspaper "promote[d] or manifest[ed] a particular belie[f] in or about a deity or an ultimate reality."

It is axiomatic that the government may not regulate speech based on its substantive content or the message it conveys. Other principles follow from this precept. In the realm of private speech or expression, government regulation may not favor one speaker over another. Discrimination against speech because of its message is presumed to be unconstitutional. These rules informed our determination that the government offends the First Amendment when it imposes financial burdens on certain speakers based on the content of their expression. When the government targets not subject matter but particular views taken by speakers on a subject, the violation of the First Amendment is all the more blatant. Viewpoint discrimination is thus an egregious form of content discrimination. The government must abstain from regulating speech when the specific motivating ideology or the opinion or perspective of the speaker is the rationale for the restriction.

These principles provide the framework forbidding the State from exercising viewpoint discrimination, even when the limited public forum is one of its own creation. In a case involving a school district's provision of school facilities for private uses, we declared that "[t]here is no question that the District, like the private owner of property, may legally preserve the property under its control for the use to which it is dedicated." The necessities of confining a forum to the limited and legitimate purposes for which it was created may justify the State in reserving it for certain groups or for the discussion of certain topics. Once it has opened a limited forum, however, the State must respect the lawful boundaries it has itself set. The State may not exclude speech where its distinction is not "reasonable in light of the purpose served by the forum," nor may it discriminate against speech on the basis of its viewpoint. Thus, in determining whether the State is acting to preserve the limits of the forum it has created so that the exclusion of a class of speech is legitimate, we have observed a distinction between, on the one hand, content discrimination, which may be permissible if it preserves the purposes of that limited forum, and, on the other hand, viewpoint discrimination, which is presumed impermissible when directed against speech otherwise within the forum's limitations.

The SAF is a forum more in a metaphysical than in a spatial or geographic sense, but the same principles are applicable.

The University does acknowledge (as it must in light of our precedents) that "ideologically driven attempts to suppress a particular point of view are presumptively unconstitutional in funding, as in other contexts," but insists that this case does not present that issue because the Guidelines draw lines based on content, not viewpoint. [I]t must be acknowledged, the distinction is not a precise one. It is, in a sense, something of an understatement to speak of religious thought and discussion as just a viewpoint, as distinct from a comprehensive body of thought. The nature of our origins and destiny and their dependence upon the existence of a divine being have been subjects of philosophic inquiry throughout human history. We conclude, nonetheless, that viewpoint discrimination is the proper way to interpret the University's objections to Wide Awake. By the very terms of the SAF prohibition, the University does not exclude religion as a subject matter but selects for disfavored treatment those student journalistic efforts with religious editorial viewpoints. Religion may be a vast area of inquiry, but it also provides, as it did here, a specific premise, a perspective, a standpoint from which a variety of subjects may be discussed and considered. The prohibited perspective, not the general subject matter, resulted in the refusal to make third-party payments, for the subjects discussed were otherwise within the approved category of publications.

The University begins with the unremarkable proposition that the State must have substantial discretion in determining how to allocate scarce resources to accomplish its educational mission. Citing [our decision in *Rust*,] the University argues that content-based funding decisions are both inevitable and lawful. Were the reasoning of [our public forum cases] to apply to funding decisions as well as to those involving access to facilities, it is urged, [the holdings of these cases] "would become a judicial juggernaut, constitutionalizing the ubiquitous content-based decisions that schools, colleges, and other government entities routinely make in the allocation of public funds."

. . . [I]n *Rust v. Sullivan* . . . the government did not create a program to encourage private speech but instead used private speakers to transmit specific information pertaining to its own program. We recognized that when the government appropriates public funds to promote a particular policy of its own it is entitled to say what it wishes. When the government disburses public funds to private entities to convey a governmental message, it may take legitimate and appropriate steps to ensure that its message is neither garbled nor distorted by the grantee.

It does not follow, however, that viewpoint-based restrictions are proper when the University does not itself speak or subsidize transmittal of a message it favors but instead expends funds to encourage a diversity of views from private speakers. A holding that the University may not discriminate based on the viewpoint of private persons whose speech it facilitates does not restrict the University's own speech, which is controlled by different principles.

The distinction between the University's own favored message and the private speech of students is evident in the case before us. The University itself has taken steps to ensure the distinction in the agreement each [student organization] must sign. The University declares that the student groups eligible for SAF support are not the

University's agents, are not subject to its control, and are not its responsibility. Having offered to pay the third-party contractors on behalf of private speakers who convey their own messages, the University may not silence the expression of selected viewpoints.

[The Court also rejected the University's argument that financing the religious newspaper would violate the Establishment Clause.]

SOUTER, J., with whom STEVENS, J., GINSBURG, J., and BREYER, J., join, dissenting.

The Court today, for the first time, approves direct funding of core religious activities by an arm of the State. . . . Because there is no warrant for distinguishing among public funding sources for purposes of applying the First Amendment's prohibition of religious establishment, I would hold that the University's refusal to support petitioners' religious activities is compelled by the Establishment Clause.

[Justice O'Connor's and Justice Thomas's concurring opinions are omitted.]

NOTES AND QUESTIONS

1. *Forums, subsidies, and exclusivity.* Like *Rosenberger*, Cornelius v. NAACP Legal Defense & Educ. Fund, 473 U.S. 788 (1985), also involved a metaphysical forum. In contrast to *Rosenberger*, however, the *Cornelius* Court upheld the government restrictions, permitting the government to exclude legal defense and political advocacy organizations from the Combined Federal Campaign, a charity drive aimed at federal employees. The Court held that the Combined Federal Campaign was a nonpublic forum, and emphasized that "[c]ontrol over access to a nonpublic forum can be based on subject matter and speaker identity so long as the distinctions drawn are reasonable in light of the purpose served by the forum and are viewpoint neutral." *Id.* at 806. What distinguishes the program in *Cornelius* from the program in *Rosenberger*? In both cases the government intended to exclude entire categories of participants from the forums, and in both cases the government argued that the exclusion was based on the government's desire to avoid disruption and conflict. Could the paradoxical outcome of the Supreme Court's decision in *Rosenberger* be to encourage public universities and other government funders of private expression to require that speakers receiving government funds express only ideas endorsed by the government? Presumably, if the university officially declared at the program's outset that recipients of student activity funds were speaking on behalf of the university, then the university would be allowed to limit the speech of those recipients, either under the government speech rationale of *Rust* or the nonpublic forum theory of *Cornelius.*

2. *Content versus viewpoint neutrality.* Does the Court's decision in *Rosenberger* "blur the line between viewpoint and content neutrality, suggesting the Court might scrutinize a government's establishment or application of content parameters in a limited public forum more strictly than the 'reasonableness' language [of the constitutional standard] might at first suggest"? *See* Lyrissa Barnett Lidsky, *Public Forum 2.0*, 91 B. U. L. Rev. 1975, 1988 (2011). How do you reconcile *Rosenberger* with Christian Legal Society v. Martinez, *supra* p. 185, where the Court found the university's all-comers policy to be reasonable

and viewpoint-neutral, even though it had a greater effect on religious student organizations than on secular ones?

NATIONAL ENDOWMENT FOR THE ARTS v. FINLEY

524 U.S. 569 (1998)

O'CONNOR, J., delivered the opinion of the Court.

The National Foundation on the Arts and Humanities Act, as amended in 1990, requires the Chairperson of the National Endowment for the Arts (NEA) to ensure that "artistic excellence and artistic merit are the criteria by which [grant] applications are judged, taking into consideration general standards of decency and respect for the diverse beliefs and values of the American public."

[The four individual respondents in this case, Karen Finley, John Fleck, Holly Hughes, and Tim Miller, are performance artists who applied for NEA grants before the "decency and respect" provision was enacted. An advisory panel recommended approval of respondents' projects, both initially and after receiving the NEA Chairman's request to reconsider three of the applications. A majority of the National Council on the Arts subsequently recommended disapproval, and in June 1990, the NEA informed respondents that they had been denied funding. Respondents filed suit, alleging that the NEA had violated their First Amendment rights. A footnote in Justice Souter's dissent describes the art of the three respondents:]

> [The oeuvres d'art for which the four individual plaintiffs in this case sought funding have been described as follows: "Finley's controversial show, 'We Keep Our Victims Ready,' contains three segments. In the second segment, Finley visually recounts a sexual assault by stripping to the waist and smearing chocolate on her breasts and by using profanity to describe the assault. Holly Hughes' monologue 'World Without End' is a somewhat graphic recollection of the artist's realization of her lesbianism and reminiscence of her mother's sexuality. John Fleck, in his stage performance 'Blessed Are All the Little Fishes,' confronts alcoholism and Catholicism. During the course of the performance, Fleck appears dressed as a mermaid, urinates on the stage and creates an altar out of a toilet bowl by putting a photograph of Jesus Christ on the lid. Tim Miller derives his performance 'Some Golden States' from childhood experiences, from his life as a homosexual, and from the constant threat of AIDS. Miller uses vegetables in his performances to represent sexual symbols." Note, 48 Wash. & Lee L. Rev. 1545, 1546, n. 2 (1991) (citations omitted).]

In this case, we review the Court of Appeals' determination that [the "decency and respect" clause] on its face, impermissibly discriminates on the basis of viewpoint and is void for vagueness under the First and Fifth Amendments. We conclude that [the clause] is facially valid, as it neither inherently interferes with First Amendment rights nor violates constitutional vagueness principles.

Since 1965, the NEA has distributed over $3 billion in grants to individuals and organizations, funding that has served as a catalyst for increased state, corporate, and foundation support for the arts. Throughout the NEA's history, only a handful of the agency's roughly 100,000 awards have generated formal complaints about misapplied funds or abuse of the public's trust. Two provocative works, however, prompted public controversy in 1989 and led to congressional revaluation of the NEA's funding priorities and efforts to increase oversight of its grant-making procedures. The Institute of Contemporary Art at the University of Pennsylvania had used $30,000 of a visual arts grant it received from the NEA to fund a 1989 retrospective of photographer Robert Mapplethorpe's work. The exhibit, entitled The Perfect Moment, included homoerotic photographs that several Members of Congress condemned as pornographic. Members also denounced artist Andres Serrano's work Piss Christ, a photograph of a crucifix immersed in urine. Serrano had been awarded a $15,000 grant from the Southeast Center for Contemporary Art, an organization that received NEA support. [Congress responded to the controversy surrounding the Mapplethorpe and Serrano photographs by eliminating $45,000 from the agency's budget, the precise amount contributed to the two exhibits by NEA grant recipients, and enacting a series of limitations on the discretion of the NEA's grant-making authority. Some of the initial restrictions on the NEA's authority were struck down by lower courts, which led Congress to adopt the "decency and respect" provision at issue here.]

Respondents argue that the provision is a paradigmatic example of viewpoint discrimination because it rejects any artistic speech that either fails to respect mainstream values or offends standards of decency. The premise of respondents' claim is that [the "decency and respect" provision] constrains the agency's ability to fund certain categories of artistic expression. The NEA, however, reads the provision as merely hortatory, and contends that it stops well short of an absolute restriction. The [contested provision] adds "considerations" to the grant-making process; it does not preclude awards to projects that might be deemed "indecent" or "disrespectful," nor place conditions on grants, or even specify that those factors must be given any particular weight in reviewing an application. Indeed, the agency asserts that it has adequately implemented [the provision] merely by ensuring the representation of various backgrounds and points of view on the advisory panels that analyze grant applications. We do not decide whether the NEA's view—that the formulation of diverse advisory panels is sufficient to comply with Congress' command—is in fact a reasonable reading of the statute. It is clear, however, that the text of [the "decency and respect" provision] imposes no categorical requirement. The advisory language stands in sharp contrast to congressional efforts to prohibit the funding of certain classes of speech. When Congress has in fact intended to affirmatively constrain the NEA's grant-making authority, it has done so in no uncertain terms. [See, for example, another statutory provision relating to NEA funding stating that "[O]bscenity is without artistic merit, is not protected speech, and shall not be funded".]

Respondent's reliance on our decision in *Rosenberger v. Rector and Visitors of Univ. of Va.* is misplaced. In *Rosenberger*, a public university declined to authorize disbursements from its Student Activities Fund to finance the printing of a Christian student newspaper. We held that by subsidizing the Student Activities Fund, the University had created a limited public forum, from which it impermissibly excluded all publications with religious editorial viewpoints. Although the scarcity of NEA funding does not distinguish this case from *Rosenberger*, the competitive process according to which the grants are allocated does. In the context of arts funding, in contrast to many other subsidies, the Government does not indiscriminately "encourage a diversity of views from private speakers." The NEA's mandate is to make aesthetic judgments, and the inherently content-based "excellence" threshold for NEA support sets it apart from the subsidy at issue in *Rosenberger*—which was available to all student organizations that were "'related to the educational purpose of the University'"—and from comparably objective decisions on allocating public benefits, such as access to a school auditorium or a municipal theater.

Finally, although the First Amendment certainly has application in the subsidy context, we note that the Government may allocate competitive funding according to criteria that would be impermissible were direct regulation of speech or a criminal penalty at stake. So long as legislation does not infringe on other constitutionally protected rights, Congress has wide latitude to set spending priorities. [A]s we held in *Rust*, Congress may "selectively fund a program to encourage certain activities it believes to be in the public interest, without at the same time funding an alternative program which seeks to deal with the problem in another way." *Rust*. In doing so, "the Government has not discriminated on the basis of viewpoint; it has merely chosen to fund one activity to the exclusion of the other." *Ibid.*; *see also Maher v. Roe* ("There is a basic difference between direct state interference with a protected activity and state encouragement of an alternative activity consonant with legislative policy").

[The Court also rejected a vagueness challenge to the "decency and respect" provision, on the grounds that "[i]n the context of selective subsidies, it is not always feasible for Congress to legislate with clarity. Indeed, if this statute is unconstitutionally vague, then so too are all government programs awarding scholarships and grants on the basis of subjective criteria such as 'excellence.'"]

SCALIA, J., with whom THOMAS, J., joins, concurring in the judgment.

"The operation was a success, but the patient died." What such a procedure is to medicine, the Court's opinion in this case is to law. It sustains the constitutionality of [the "decency and respect" provision] by gutting it. The most avid congressional opponents of the provision could not have asked for more. I write separately because, unlike the Court, I think that [the provision] must be evaluated as written, rather than as distorted by the agency it was meant to control. By its terms, it establishes content and viewpoint-based criteria upon which grant applications are to be evaluated. And that is perfectly constitutional.

The Court devotes so much of its opinion to explaining why this statute means something other than what it says that it neglects to cite the constitutional text governing our analysis. The First Amendment reads: "Congress shall make no law . . . *abridging* the freedom of speech." To abridge is "to contract, to diminish; to deprive of." T. Sheridan, A Complete Dictionary of the English Language (6th ed. 1796). With the enactment of [the "decency and respect" provision] Congress did not *abridge* the speech of those who disdain the beliefs and values of the American public, nor did it *abridge* indecent speech. Those who wish to create indecent and disrespectful art are as unconstrained now as they were before the enactment of this statute. *Avant-garde artistes* such as respondents remain entirely free to *epater les bourgeois*; they are merely deprived of the additional satisfaction of having the bourgeoisie taxed to pay for it. It is preposterous to equate the denial of taxpayer subsidy with measures "aimed at the *suppression* of dangerous ideas."

SOUTER, J., dissenting.

The decency and respect proviso mandates viewpoint-based decisions in the disbursement of government subsidies, and the Government has wholly failed to explain why the statute should be afforded an exemption from the fundamental rule of the First Amendment that viewpoint discrimination in the exercise of public authority over expressive activity is unconstitutional. The Court's conclusions that the proviso is not viewpoint based, that it is not a regulation, and that the NEA may permissibly engage in viewpoint-based discrimination, are all patently mistaken. . . .

Scarce money demands choices, of course, but choices "on some acceptable [viewpoint] neutral principle," *Rosenberger,* like artistic excellence and artistic merit; "nothing in our decision[s] indicate[s] that scarcity would give the State the right to exercise viewpoint discrimination that is otherwise impermissible." If the student activities fund at issue in *Rosenberger* had awarded competitive, merit-based grants to only 50%, or even 5%, of the applicants, on the basis of "journalistic merit taking into consideration the message of the newspaper," it is obvious beyond peradventure that the Court would not have come out differently, leaving the University free to refuse funding after considering a publication's Christian perspective.

NOTES AND QUESTIONS

1. *Protecting the government's editorial and artistic judgments.* While the Court eventually avoided the difficult constitutional issues in *Finley* by holding that the statute in question did not impose viewpoint restrictions on NEA staff decisions, a background theme of the Court's opinion is that the NEA had the right to make content-based funding decisions because it was exercising professional expertise about the artistic excellence of applicants for government grants. For another variation on the theme of editorial judgments and professional expertise by government decision makers, *see* Arkansas Educational Television Commission v. Forbes, 523 U.S. 666 (1998).

2. *Editorial discretion and viewpoint discrimination.* In *Forbes,* the Court rejected a First Amendment claim by a political candidate who was excluded from a televised debate by the producers of a state-owned public television station. The Court held that the producers' editorial discretion insulated them from a First Amendment challenge. "As a general rule, the nature of editorial discretion counsels against subjecting broadcasters to claims of viewpoint discrimination. Programming decisions would be particularly vulnerable to claims of this type because even principled exclusions rooted in sound journalistic judgment can often be characterized as viewpoint-based. To comply with their obligation to air programming that serves the public interest, broadcasters must often choose among speakers expressing different viewpoints."

PLEASANT GROVE CITY, UTAH v. SUMMUM

555 U.S. 460 (2009)

ALITO, J., delivered the opinion of the Court.

This case presents the question whether the Free Speech Clause of the First Amendment entitles a private group to insist that a municipality permit it to place a permanent monument in a city park in which other donated monuments were previously erected. The Court of Appeals held that the municipality was required to accept the monument because a public park is a traditional public forum. We conclude, however, that although a park is a traditional public forum for speeches and other transitory expressive acts, the display of a permanent monument in a public park is not a form of expression to which forum analysis applies. Instead, the placement of a permanent monument in a public park is best viewed as a form of government speech and is therefore not subject to scrutiny under the Free Speech Clause.

I.

. . . Respondent Summum is a religious organization founded in 1975 and headquartered in Salt Lake City, Utah. [Summum asked Pleasant Grove City for] permission to erect a "stone monument" [containing the "aphorisms" of Summum in its 2.5-acre "Pioneer Park." The Park contained 15 monuments at the time, most donated by private groups or individuals. The monuments included "a wishing well," a "September 11 monument," and a "Ten Commandments monument donated by the Fraternal Order of Eagles in 1971."] The City denied the requests and explained that its practice was to limit monuments in the Park to those that "either (1) directly relate to the history of Pleasant Grove, or (2) were donated by groups with longstanding ties to the Pleasant Grove community." The following year, the City passed a resolution putting this policy into writing [and rejected Summum's subsequent request to erect its monument].

In 2005, respondent filed this action against the City and various local officials (petitioners), asserting, among other claims, that petitioners had violated the Free Speech Clause of the First Amendment by accepting the Ten Commandments monument but rejecting the proposed Seven Aphorisms monument. . . .

II.

No prior decision of this Court has addressed the application of the Free Speech Clause to a government entity's acceptance of privately donated, permanent monuments for installation in a public park. . . . Petitioners contend that the pertinent cases are those concerning government speech. Respondent, on the other hand, agrees with the Court of Appeals panel that the applicable cases are those that analyze private speech in a public forum. The parties' fundamental disagreement thus centers on the nature of petitioners' conduct when they permitted privately donated monuments to be erected in Pioneer Park. Were petitioners engaging in their own expressive conduct? Or were they providing a forum for private speech?

If petitioners were engaging in their own expressive conduct, then the Free Speech Clause has no application. The Free Speech Clause restricts government regulation of private speech; it does not regulate government speech. See *Johanns* [*supra* Chapter 6], ("[T]he Government's own speech . . . is exempt from First Amendment scrutiny"). A government entity has the right to "speak for itself." "[I]t is entitled to say what it wishes," *Rosenberger,* and to select the views that it wants to express. See *Rust; Finley.*

Indeed, it is not easy to imagine how government could function if it lacked this freedom. "If every citizen were to have a right to insist that no one paid by public funds express a view with which he disagreed, debate over issues of great concern to the public would be limited to those in the private sector, and the process of government as we know it radically transformed." *Keller v. State Bar of Cal.* [*supra,* Chapter 6].

A government entity may exercise this same freedom to express its views when it receives assistance from private sources for the purpose of delivering a government-controlled message. . . .

This does not mean that there are no restraints on government speech. For example, government speech must comport with the Establishment Clause. The involvement of public officials in advocacy may be limited by law, regulation, or practice. And of course, a government entity is ultimately "accountable to the electorate and the political process for its advocacy."

While government speech is not restricted by the Free Speech Clause, the government does not have a free hand to regulate private speech on government property. [Here the court briefly summarizes the types of public forums and the constitutional standards applicable to them.]

III.

There may be situations in which it is difficult to tell whether a government entity is speaking on its own behalf or is providing a forum for private speech, but this case does not present such a situation. Permanent monuments displayed on public property typically represent government speech.

Governments have long used monuments to speak to the public. Since ancient times, kings, emperors, and other rulers have erected statues of themselves to remind their subjects of their authority and power. . . . A monument, by definition, is a structure that is designed as a means of expression. When a government entity arranges for the construction of a monument, it does so because it wishes to convey some thought or instill some feeling in those who see the structure. Neither the Court of Appeals nor respondent disputes the obvious proposition that a monument that is commissioned and financed by a government body for placement on public land constitutes government speech.

Just as government-commissioned and government-financed monuments speak for the government, so do privately financed and donated monuments that the government accepts and displays to the public on government land. [P]ersons who observe donated monuments routinely—and reasonably—interpret them as conveying some message on the property owner's behalf. In this context, there is little chance that observers will fail to appreciate the identity of the speaker. This is true whether the monument is located on private property or on public property, such as national, state, or city park land.

We think it is fair to say that throughout our Nation's history, the general government practice with respect to donated monuments has been one of selective receptivity. A great many of the monuments that adorn the Nation's public parks were financed with private funds or donated by private parties, including the Statue of Liberty, the Marine Corps War Memorial (the Iwo Jima monument), and the Vietnam Veterans Memorial. . . . By accepting monuments that are privately funded or donated, government entities save tax dollars and are able to acquire monuments that they could not have afforded to fund on their own.

. . . Public parks are often closely identified in the public mind with the government unit that owns the land. City parks . . . commonly play an important role in defining the identity that a city projects to its own residents and to the outside world. . . . Government decision makers select the monuments that portray what they view as appropriate for the place in question, taking into account such content-based factors as esthetics, history, and local culture. The monuments that are accepted, therefore, are meant to convey and have the effect of conveying a government message, and they thus constitute government speech.

IV.

In this case, it is clear that the monuments in Pleasant Grove's Pioneer Park represent government speech. Although many of the monuments were not designed or built by the City and were donated in completed form by private entities, the City decided to accept those donations and to display them in the Park. The City has "effectively controlled" the messages sent by the monuments in the Park by exercising "final approval authority" over their selection. The City has selected those monuments that it wants to display for the purpose of presenting the image of the City that it wishes to project to all who frequent the Park; it has taken ownership of most of the monuments in the Park, including the Ten Commandments monument that is the focus of respondent's concern; and the City has now expressly set forth the criteria it will use in making future selections.

Respondent voices the legitimate concern that the government speech doctrine not be used as a subterfuge for favoring certain private speakers over others based on viewpoint. Respondent's suggested solution is to require a government entity accepting a privately donated monument to go through a formal process of adopting a resolution publicly embracing "the message" that the monument conveys.

We see no reason for imposing a requirement of this sort. The parks of this country contain thousands of donated monuments that government entities have used for their own expressive purposes, usually without producing the sort of formal documentation that respondent now says is required to escape Free Speech Clause restrictions. Requiring all of these jurisdictions to go back and proclaim formally that they adopt all of these monuments as their own expressive vehicles would be a pointless exercise that the Constitution does not mandate.

. . . [The Court rejects the argument that that the City must explicitly "adopt" the monument's "message" for it to be government speech.] Even when a monument features the written word, the monument may be intended to be interpreted, and may in fact be interpreted by different observers, in a variety of ways.

. . . [I]t frequently is not possible to identify a single "message" that is conveyed by an object or structure, and consequently, the thoughts or sentiments expressed by a government entity that accepts and displays such an object may be quite different from those of either its creator or its donor. By accepting a privately donated monument and placing it on city property, a city engages in expressive conduct, but the intended and perceived significance of that conduct may not coincide with the thinking of the monument's donor or creator. . . .

The message that a government entity conveys by allowing a monument to remain on its property may also be altered by the subsequent addition of other monuments in the same vicinity. For example, following controversy over the original design of the Vietnam Veterans Memorial, a compromise was reached that called for the nearby addition of a flagstaff and bronze Three Soldiers statue, which many believed changed the overall effect of the memorial. See, *e.g.*, J. Mayo, War Memorials as Political Landscape: The American Experience and Beyond.

The "message" conveyed by a monument may change over time. A study of war memorials found that "people reinterpret" the meaning of these memorials as "historical interpretations" and "the society around them changes."

A striking example of how the interpretation of a monument can evolve is provided by one of the most famous and beloved public monuments in the United States, the Statue of Liberty. The statue was given to this country by the Third French Republic to express republican solidarity and friendship between the two countries. At the inaugural ceremony, President Cleveland saw the statue as an emblem of international friendship and the widespread influence of American ideals. Only later did the statue come to be viewed as a beacon welcoming immigrants to a land of freedom.

Respondent and the Court of Appeals analogize the installation of permanent monuments in a public park to the delivery of speeches and the holding of marches and demonstrations, and they thus invoke the rule that a public park is a traditional public forum for these activities. But "public forum principles . . . are out of place in the context of this case." *United States v. American Library Assn., Inc.* [*infra,* Chapter 12]. The forum doctrine has been applied in situations in which government-owned property or a government program was capable of accommodating a large number of public speakers without defeating the essential function of the land or the program.

By contrast, public parks can accommodate only a limited number of permanent monuments. . . . [I]t is hard to imagine how a public park could be opened up for the installation of permanent monuments by every person or group wishing to engage in that form of expression.

. . .

To be sure, there are limited circumstances in which the forum doctrine might properly be applied to a permanent monument—for example, if a town created a monument on which all of its residents (or all those meeting some other criterion) could place the name of a person to be honored or some other private message. But as a general matter, forum analysis simply does not apply to the installation of permanent monuments on public property.

In sum, we hold that the City's decision to accept certain privately donated monuments while rejecting respondent's is best viewed as a form of government speech. As a result, the City's decision is not subject to the Free Speech Clause, and the Court of Appeals erred in holding otherwise. We therefore reverse.

STEVENS, J., with whom GINSBURG, J., joins, concurring. . . .

Unlike other decisions relying on the government speech doctrine, our decision in this case excuses no retaliation for, or coercion of, private speech. Nor is it likely, given the near certainty that observers will associate permanent displays with the governmental property owner, that the government will be able to avoid political accountability for the views that it endorses or expresses through this means. Finally, recognizing permanent displays on public property as government speech will not give the government free license to communicate offensive or partisan messages. For even if the Free Speech Clause neither restricts nor protects government speech, government speakers are bound by the Constitution's other proscriptions, including those supplied by the Establishment and Equal Protection Clauses. Together with the checks imposed by our democratic processes, these constitutional safeguards ensure that the effect of today's decision will be limited.

SCALIA, J., with whom THOMAS, J., joins, concurring.

. . . The city ought not fear that today's victory propelled it from the free speech clause frying pan into the establishment clause fire. . . .

NOTES AND QUESTIONS

1. *Distinguishing government speech from private speech.* What qualities or characteristics help us know that the government is speaking? In Salazar v. Buono, 559 U.S. 700 (2010) *infra* p. 945, the government tried to disclaim ownership of a cross erected in 1934 by the Veterans of Foreign Wars (VFW) on a hill (Sunrise Rock) in the Mojave National Preserve. A Buddhist asked to erect a religious monument in the same spot, and the Park Service said no, stating it was trying to get rid of the cross, which never had government permission to be there. After the Buddhist sued, Congress transferred ownership of the land on which the cross stood to the VFW. There is, of course, no Establishment Clause problem when a private individual erects a religious symbol on his or her own property. However, the government's attempt to convey the monument to private owners turned it into a mirror image of *Summum.* As Professor RonNell Andersen Jones has pointed out, *Summum* involved arguably *private* speech that the government endeavored to characterize as *government* speech in order to avoid a First Amendment Speech Clause problem; in so doing, it potentially created for itself a First Amendment Establishment Clause problem. Conversely, *Buono* involved arguably *government* speech that the government endeavored to characterize as *private* speech in order to avoid a First Amendment Establishment Clause problem; in so doing, it potentially created for itself a First Amendment Speech Clause problem. RonNell Andersen Jones, *Pick Your Poisons: Private Speech, Government Speech, and the Special Problem of Religious Displays,* 2010 BYU L. Rev. 2045 (2010).

2. *Temporary versus permanent displays on government property.* Suppose the Court had held that state actors must maintain viewpoint neutrality in choosing which donated monuments to place on government property. Should temporary displays placed on government property be governed by different constitutional standards than permanent displays? *See* Capitol Square Review and Advisory Bd. v. Pinette, 515 U.S. 753 (1995) (holding that the Ku Klux Klan had a free speech right to erect a cross on a statehouse plaza—a public forum—during Christmas season on the same terms as other groups).

WALKER v.
TEXAS DIVISION, SONS OF CONFEDERATE VETERANS, INC.
135 S. Ct. 2239 (2015)

Justice BREYER delivered the opinion of the Court. . . .

I

[In Texas, all motor vehicles operating on the State's roads must display valid license plates. Drivers may display the State's general-issue license plates, which contain the word "Texas," a license plate number, a silhouette of the State, a graphic of the Lone Star, and the slogan "The Lone Star State." Or drivers may choose a specialty license plate, which contains the word "Texas," a license plate number, and one of a selection of designs prepared by the State. Texas offers a variety of specialty plates for an annual fee. There are three processes for selecting the specialty plates. First, the state legislature may call for the development of a specialty license plate. Second, the Department of Motor Vehicles Board ("Board") may approve a specialty plate design that a state-designated private vendor has created at the request of an individual or organization. Third, the Board "may create new specialty license plates on its own initiative or on receipt of an application from a" nonprofit entity seeking to sponsor a specialty plate. A nonprofit must include in its application "a draft design of the specialty license plate." Texas law vests authority in the Board to approve or disapprove an application. The relevant statute says that the Board "may refuse to create a new specialty license plate" for many reasons, including "if the design might be offensive to any member of the public . . . or for any other reason established by rule." . . .

In 2010, the Texas division of the Sons of Confederate Veterans (SCV), a nonprofit organization, applied to sponsor a specialty license plate. SCV's draft plate design included the words "SONS OF CONFEDERATE VETERANS" at the bottom, the organization's logo at the side, and a square Confederate battle flag framed by the words "Sons of Confederate Veterans 1896." A faint Confederate battle flag appeared in the background. The license plate number appeared in the middle of the plate with the State's name and silhouette at the top. After public hearing asking for comments on its website and at an open meeting, the Board explained that it found "it necessary to deny th[e] plate design application, specifically the confederate flag portion of the design, because public comments ha[d] shown that many members of the general public find the design offensive, and because such comments are reasonable." The Board added "that a significant portion of the public associate the confederate flag with organizations advocating expressions of hate directed toward people or groups that is demeaning to those people or groups." In 2012, SCV sued the Board, arguing that its decision violated the First Amendment. SCV sought an injunction requiring the Board to approve the proposed plate design. The District Court entered judgment for the Board. A divided panel of the Court of Appeals for the Fifth Circuit reversed.]

II

When government speaks, it is not barred by the Free Speech Clause from determining the content of what it says. *Pleasant Grove City v. Summum*, 555 U.S. 460, 467–468 (2009). That freedom in part reflects the fact that it is the democratic electoral process that first and foremost provides a check on government speech. Thus, government statements (and government actions and programs that take the form of speech) do not normally trigger the First Amendment rules designed to protect the marketplace of ideas. . . .

Were the Free Speech Clause interpreted otherwise, government would not work. . . . "[I]t is not easy to imagine how government could function if it lacked th[e] freedom" to select the messages it wishes to convey. *Summum.* . . .

That is not to say that a government's ability to express itself is without restriction. Constitutional and statutory provisions outside of the Free Speech Clause may limit government speech. And the Free Speech Clause itself may constrain the government's speech if, for example, the government seeks to compel private persons to convey the government's speech. But, as a general matter, when the government speaks it is entitled to promote a program, to espouse a policy, or to take a position. In doing so, it represents its citizens and it carries out its duties on their behalf.

III

In our view, specialty license plates issued pursuant to Texas's statutory scheme convey government speech. Our reasoning rests primarily on our analysis in *Summum,* a recent case that presented a similar problem. . . .

A

In *Summum,* we considered a religious organization's request to erect in a 2.5–acre city park a monument setting forth the organization's religious tenets. In the park were 15 other permanent displays. At least 11 of these . . . had been donated to the city by private entities. . . .

This Court . . . held that the city had not "provid[ed] a forum for private speech" with respect to monuments. Rather, the city, even when "accepting a privately donated monument and placing it on city property," had "engage[d] in expressive conduct." The speech at issue, this Court decided, was "best viewed as a form of government speech" and "therefore [was] not subject to scrutiny under the Free Speech Clause."

We based our conclusion on several factors. First, history shows that "[g]overnments have long used monuments to speak to the public." . . .

Second, we noted that it "is not common for property owners to open up their property for the installation of permanent monuments that convey a message with which they do not wish to be associated." As a result, "persons who observe donated monuments routinely—and reasonably—interpret them as conveying some message on the property owner's behalf." . . .

Third, . . . we observed that the city government in *Summum* "'effectively controlled' the messages sent by the monuments in the [p]ark by exercising 'final approval authority' over their selection."

In light of these and a few other relevant considerations, the Court concluded that the expression at issue was government speech. And, in reaching that conclusion, the Court rejected the premise that the involvement of private parties in designing the monuments was sufficient to prevent the government from controlling which monuments it placed in its own public park.

B

Our analysis in *Summum* leads us to the conclusion that here, too, government speech is at issue. First, the history of license plates shows that, insofar as license plates have conveyed more than state names and vehicle identification numbers, they long have communicated messages from the States. . . .

Texas . . . has selected various messages to communicate through its license plate designs. By 1919, Texas had begun to display the Lone Star emblem on its plates. . . .

In 1977, Texas replaced the Lone Star with a small silhouette of the State. And in 1995, Texas plates celebrated "150 Years of Statehood." Additionally, the Texas Legislature has specifically authorized specialty plate designs stating, among other things, "Read to Succeed," "Houston Livestock Show and Rodeo," "Texans Conquer Cancer," and "Girl Scouts." This kind of state speech has appeared on Texas plates for decades.

Second, Texas license plate designs "are often closely identified in the public mind with the [State]." Each Texas license plate is a government article serving the governmental purposes of vehicle registration and identification. . . .

Texas license plates are, essentially, government IDs. And issuers of ID "typically do not permit" the placement on their IDs of "message[s] with which they do not wish to be associated." Consequently, "persons who observe" designs on IDs "routinely—and reasonably—interpret them as conveying some message on the [issuer's] behalf."

Indeed, a person who displays a message on a Texas license plate likely intends to convey to the public that the State has endorsed that message. If not, the individual could simply display the message in question in larger letters on a bumper sticker right next to the plate. But the individual prefers a license plate design to the purely private speech expressed through bumper stickers. That may well be because Texas's license plate designs convey government agreement with the message displayed.

Third, Texas maintains direct control over the messages conveyed on its specialty plates. Texas law provides that the State "has sole control over the design, typeface, color, and alphanumeric pattern for all license plates." The Board must approve every specialty plate design proposal before the design can appear on a Texas plate. And the Board and its predecessor have actively exercised this authority. Texas asserts, and SCV concedes, that the State has rejected at least a dozen proposed designs. . . .

These considerations, taken together, convince us that the specialty plates here in question are similar enough to the monuments in *Summum* to call for the same result. That is not to say that every element of our discussion in *Summum* is relevant here. For instance, in *Summum* we . . . believed that the speech at issue was government speech rather than private speech in part because we found it "hard to imagine how a public park could be opened up for the installation of permanent monuments by every person or group wishing to engage in that form of expression." Here, a State could theoretically offer a much larger number of license plate designs, and those designs need not be available for time immemorial.

But those characteristics of the speech at issue in *Summum* were particularly important because the government speech at issue occurred in public parks, which are traditional public forums for "the delivery of speeches and the holding of marches and demonstrations" by private citizens. By contrast, license plates are not traditional public forums for private speech. . . .

C

SCV believes . . . the State does not engage in expressive activity through [the] slogans and graphics [on its specialty license plates], but rather provides a forum for private speech by making license plates available to display the private parties' designs. We cannot agree.

. . . [F]orum analysis is misplaced here. Because the State is speaking on its own behalf, the First Amendment strictures that attend the various types of government-established forums do not apply.

The parties agree that Texas's specialty license plates are not a "traditional public forum," such as a street or a park[.]. . . .

It is equally clear that Texas's specialty plates are neither a "'designated public forum,'" which exists where "government property that has not traditionally been regarded as a public forum is intentionally opened up for that purpose," nor a "limited public forum," which exists where a government has "reserv[ed a forum] for certain groups or for the discussion of certain topics[.]". . . . [I]n order "to ascertain whether [a government] intended to designate a place not traditionally open to assembly and debate as a public forum," this Court "has looked to the policy and practice of the government" and to "the nature of the property and its compatibility with expressive activity."

Texas's policies and the nature of its license plates indicate that the State did not intend its specialty license plates to serve as either a designated public forum or a limited public forum. First, the State exercises final authority over each specialty license plate design. This authority militates against a determination that Texas has created a public forum. Second, Texas takes ownership of each specialty plate design, making it particularly untenable that the State intended specialty plates to serve as a forum for public discourse. Finally, Texas license plates have traditionally been used for government speech, are primarily used as a form of government ID, and bear the State's name. These features of Texas license plates indicate that Texas explicitly associates itself with the speech on its plates.

For similar reasons, we conclude that Texas's specialty license plates are not a "nonpublic for[um]," which exists "[w]here the government is acting as a proprietor, managing its internal operations." With respect to specialty license plate designs, Texas is not simply managing government property, but instead is engaging in expressive conduct. . . . Texas's specialty license plate designs "are meant to convey and have the effect of conveying a government message." They "constitute government speech."

The fact that private parties take part in the design and propagation of a message does not extinguish the governmental nature of the message or transform the government's role into that of a mere forum-provider. In *Summum*, private entities "financed and donated monuments that the government accept[ed] and display[ed] to the public." Here, similarly, private parties propose designs that Texas may accept and display on its license plates. In this case, as in *Summum*, the "government entity may exercise [its] freedom to express its views" even "when it receives assistance from private sources for the purpose of delivering a government-controlled message." And in this case, as in *Summum*, forum analysis is inapposite.

Of course, Texas allows many more license plate designs than the city in *Summum* allowed monuments. But our holding in *Summum* was not dependent on the precise number of monuments found within the park. . . . Further, there may well be many more messages that Texas wishes to convey through its license plates than there were messages that the city in *Summum* wished to convey through its monuments. Texas's desire to communicate numerous messages does not mean that the messages conveyed are not Texas's own. . . .

For the reasons stated, we hold that Texas's specialty license plate designs constitute government speech and that Texas was consequently entitled to refuse to issue plates featuring SCV's proposed design. Accordingly, the judgment of the United States Court of Appeals for the Fifth Circuit is

Reversed.

Justice ALITO, with whom THE CHIEF JUSTICE, Justice SCALIA, and Justice KENNEDY join, dissenting.

. . .

Unfortunately, the Court's decision categorizes private speech as government speech and thus strips it of all First Amendment protection. The Court holds that all the privately created messages on the many specialty plates issued by the State of Texas convey a government message rather than the message of the motorist displaying the plate. Can this possibly be correct?

Here is a test. Suppose you sat by the side of a Texas highway and studied the license plates on the vehicles passing by. You would see, in addition to the standard Texas plates, an impressive array of specialty plates. (There are now more than 350 varieties.) You would likely observe plates that honor numerous colleges and universities. You might see plates bearing the name of a high school, a fraternity or sorority, the Masons, the Knights of Columbus, the Daughters of the American Revolution, a realty company, a favorite soft drink, a favorite burger restaurant, and a favorite NASCAR driver.

As you sat there watching these plates speed by, would you really think that the sentiments reflected in these specialty plates are the views of the State of Texas and not those of the owners of the cars? If a car with a plate that says "Rather Be Golfing" passed by at 8:30 am on a Monday morning, would you think: "This is the official policy of the State—better to golf than to work?" . . .

The Court says that all of these messages are government speech. It is essential that government be able to express its own viewpoint, the Court reminds us, because otherwise, how would it promote its programs, like recycling and vaccinations? So when Texas issues a "Rather Be Golfing" plate, but not a "Rather Be Playing Tennis" or "Rather Be Bowling" plate, it is furthering a state policy to promote golf but not tennis or bowling. And when Texas allows motorists to obtain a Notre Dame license plate but not a University of Southern California plate, it is taking sides in that long-time rivalry.

This capacious understanding of government speech takes a large and painful bite out of the First Amendment. Specialty plates may seem innocuous. They make motorists happy, and they put money in a State's coffers. But the precedent this case sets is dangerous. While all license plates unquestionably contain *some* government speech (*e.g.,* the name of the State and the numbers and/or letters identifying the vehicle), the State of Texas has converted the remaining space on its specialty plates into little mobile billboards on which motorists can display their own messages. And what Texas did here was to reject one of the messages that members of a private group wanted to post on some of these little billboards because the State thought that many of its citizens would find the message offensive. That is blatant viewpoint discrimination.

If the State can do this with its little mobile billboards, could it do the same with big, stationary billboards? Suppose that a State erected electronic billboards along its highways. Suppose that the State posted some government messages on these billboards and then, to raise money, allowed private entities and individuals to purchase the right to post their own messages. And suppose that the State allowed only those messages that it liked or found not too controversial. Would that be constitutional?

What if a state college or university did the same thing with a similar billboard or a campus bulletin board or dorm list serve? What if it allowed private messages that are consistent with prevailing views on campus but banned those that disturbed some students or faculty? Can there be any doubt that these examples of viewpoint discrimination would violate the First Amendment? I hope not, but the future uses of today's precedent remain to be seen. . . .

II

The Court badly misunderstands *Summum.* . . .

The[] characteristics [that] rendered public monuments government speech in *Summum,* are not present in Texas's specialty plate program.

I begin with history. As we said in *Summum,* governments have used monuments since time immemorial to express important government messages, and there is no history of governments giving equal space to those wishing to express dissenting views. . . .

The history of messages on license plates is quite different. After the beginning of motor vehicle registration in 1917, more than 70 years passed before the proliferation of specialty plates in Texas. It was not until the 1990's that motorists were allowed to choose from among 10 messages, such as "Read to Succeed" and "Keep Texas Beautiful."

Up to this point, the words on the Texas plates can be considered government speech. The messages were created by the State, and they plausibly promoted state programs. But when, at some point within the last 20 years or so, the State began to allow private entities to secure plates conveying their own messages, Texas crossed the line. . . .

The Texas specialty plate program also does not exhibit the "selective receptivity" present in *Summum*. To the contrary, Texas's program is *not* selective by design. The Board's chairman, who is charged with approving designs, explained that the program's purpose is "to encourage private plates" in order to "generate additional revenue for the state." And most of the time, the Board "base[s] [its] decisions on rules that primarily deal with reflectivity and readability." . . .

The Court believes that messages on privately created plates are government speech because motorists want a seal of state approval for their messages and therefore prefer plates over bumper stickers. This is dangerous reasoning. There is a big difference between government speech (that is, speech by the government in furtherance of its programs) and governmental blessing (or condemnation) of private speech. Many private speakers in a forum would welcome a sign of government approval. But in the realm of private speech, government regulation may not favor one viewpoint over another.

A final factor that was important in *Summum* was space. A park can accommodate only so many permanent monuments. Often large and made of stone, monuments can last for centuries and are difficult to move. License plates, on the other hand, are small, light, mobile, and designed to last for only a relatively brief time. The only absolute limit on the number of specialty plates that a State could issue is the number of registered vehicles. The variety of available plates is limitless, too. Today Texas offers more than 350 varieties. In 10 years, might it be 3,500?

In sum, the Texas specialty plate program has none of the factors that were critical in *Summum,* and the Texas program exhibits a very important characteristic that was missing in that case: Individuals who want to display a Texas specialty plate, instead of the standard plate, must pay an increased annual registration fee. How many groups or individuals would clamor to pay $8,000 (the cost of the deposit required to create a new plate) in order to broadcast the government's message as opposed to their own? And if Texas really wants to speak out in support of, say, Iowa State University (but not the University of Iowa) or "Young Lawyers" (but not old ones), why must it be paid to say things that it really wants to say? . . .

States have not adopted specialty license plate programs like Texas's because they are now bursting with things they want to say on their license plates. Those programs were adopted because they bring in money. . . .

III

What Texas has done by selling space on its license plates is to create what we have called a limited public forum. It has allowed state property (*i.e.,* motor vehicle license plates) to be used by private speakers according to rules that the State prescribes. Under the First Amendment, however, those rules cannot discriminate on the basis of viewpoint. But that is exactly what Texas did here. The Board rejected Texas SCV's design, "specifically the confederate flag portion of the design, because public comments have shown that many members of the general public find the design offensive, and because such comments are reasonable." These statements indisputably demonstrate that the Board denied Texas SCV's design because of its viewpoint.

The Confederate battle flag is a controversial symbol. To the Texas Sons of Confederate Veterans, it is said to evoke the memory of their ancestors and other soldiers who fought for the South in the Civil War. To others, it symbolizes slavery, segregation, and hatred. Whatever it means to motorists who display that symbol and to those who see it, the flag expresses a viewpoint. The Board rejected the plate design because it concluded that many Texans would find the flag symbol offensive. That was pure viewpoint discrimination. . . .

The Board's decision cannot be saved by its suggestion that the plate, if allowed, "could distract or disturb some drivers to the point of being unreasonably dangerous." This rationale cannot withstand strict scrutiny. Other States allow specialty plates with the Confederate Battle Flag, and Texas has not pointed to evidence that these plates have led to incidents of road rage or accidents. Texas does not ban bumper stickers bearing the image of the Confederate battle flag. Nor does it ban any of the many other bumper stickers that convey political messages and other messages that are capable of exciting the ire of those who loathe the ideas they express.

Messages that are proposed by private parties and placed on Texas specialty plates are private speech, not government speech. Texas cannot forbid private speech based on its viewpoint. That is what it did here. Because the Court approves this violation of the First Amendment, I respectfully dissent.

NOTES AND QUESTIONS

1. SCV*'s lasting effects.* Is Justice Scalia right that the majority opinion in *SCV* "takes a large and painful bite out of the First Amendment?"
2. *Which precedents to use?* Which opinion has the better argument about the appropriate line of applicable precedent (government speech versus public forum doctrine)?
3. *Mixed speech.* Is the problem in SCV that the speech involved is really "mixed"—i.e., both government speech and private speech? How could the Court craft rules if it explicitly recognized that fact? For discussion, *see*, Caroline Mala Corbin, *Mixed Speech: When Speech is Both Private and Governmental*, 83 NYU L. Rev. 605 (2008). For a discussion of First Amendment principles applicable to government-sponsored social media sites, *see* Lyrissa Barnett Lidsky, *Public Forum 2.0*, 91 B. U. L. Rev. 1975 (2011).
4. *Personalized license plates.* Should the majority's or the dissent's reasoning apply to personalized license plates—i.e., standard state plates that individuals seek to have made with specific personalized messages)?

AN EXTENDED NOTE ON GOVERNMENT AS SPEAKER AND SPEECH SUBSIDIZER

Reconciling the cases in this section is not an easy task. Several of these opinions seem to point in different directions, and the factual backgrounds of the cases are often not immediately distinguishable. Consider the following thumbnail sketch of the holdings of these cases. On the one hand, the government is allowed to strictly regulate the content of the speech of individuals that the government hires to speak on its behalf (*Rust*); distinguish among speakers based on the content of speech when the government agent is exercising professional expertise (*Finley*); distinguish among speakers when the government agent is serving an editorial function (*Forbes*); choose which private monuments to "adopt" to convey its own message (*Summum*); and choose which specialty license plates to "adopt" when proposed by private organizations (*SCV*). On the other hand, the government is not allowed to make content-based distinctions among speakers where government funds are used to create a forum that is intended to encourage a diversity of views from private speakers (*Rosenberger*), or where the professional responsibilities of the person or entity hired by the government require that person or entity to express opposition to the government (*Velazquez*). Although this schematic rendering of the Court's holdings may initially seem to draw logical distinctions between the cases, fitting new facts into the various categories will often be difficult. Even in the cases already decided by the Court, it is not immediately evident why one case fits on one side of the line and another case fits on the other side of the line. For example, as Justice Scalia notes in *Velazquez*, it is difficult to distinguish between the lawyer in that case—whom the Court deemed independent of government control—and the doctors and other health professionals in *Rust*—whose speech the Court subjected to virtually complete government control. Nor is it clear why the specialty license plate rules in *SCV* favor a finding of government speech rather than creation of a public forum. The situation becomes even more complicated in the next section, in which the Court creates an entirely different framework for considering constitutional protections for the speech of government employees. Keep in mind that there is substantial overlap between various categories of government speech or government-funded speech, and many factual scenarios could logically be treated under several different categories.

THEORY-APPLIED PROBLEM—THE MEN'S CLUB

The University of Exum is a public university. A group of students at the university wish to become an accredited university group so they can apply for the University's student activities fund and use the University's electronic mailing lists to recruit members and announce group events. This new student group calls itself the "Men's Club" and has as its stated purpose "preventing male decline as women enroll in higher education institutions at greater rates than men and increasingly become the breadwinners for their families." Accreditation of student groups at the University of Exum is granted by a joint faculty-student committee whose assigned task is to grant accreditation to "educationally appropriate student groups that further the educational mission of the University of Exum." Examples of previously accredited groups include the Debate Club, the Art Appreciation Society, and the University Choral Group. The accreditation committee denies accreditation to the Men's Club, stating that it is not an "educationally appropriate student group." The Men's Club is the first student group ever denied accreditation by the University. The Men's Club approaches you for legal advice. What legal strategy do you recommend?

THEORY-APPLIED PROBLEM—DANCING AT THE MEMORIAL

Mary Beth Smith and 17 members of her dance troupe were recently ticketed and fined by police for demonstrating without a permit after engaging in a "flashmob" dance performance at the Lincoln Memorial in Washington, D.C. The dancers each had their own headphones and were dancing alone up the steps and into the memorial at a time of day when there were very few tourists or visitors there. A National Park Service regulation prohibits demonstrations at public memorials in Washington, D.C., without a permit; demonstrations are defined as "picketing, speechmaking, marching, holding vigils or religious services and all other like forms of conduct which involve the communication or expression of views, engaged in by one or more persons, the conduct of which has the effect, intent, or propensity to draw a crowd of onlookers." This regulation is designed to preserve a "solemn atmosphere" at all public memorials in the District of Columbia and to maintain them as places for "quiet reflection." A different provision of the regulations states that no permits for demonstrations can be granted for the space inside of the Lincoln Memorial. However, the government is allowed to hold an annual birthday celebration in honor of Abraham Lincoln inside of the Memorial. Mary Beth Smith contends that the regulations, as applied to her, violate the First Amendment. Is she correct, or can the government credibly argue that its control of the interior of the Memorial is government speech? This problem is based loosely on Oberwetter v. Hillard, 639 F.3d 545 (D.C. Cir. 2011), discussed *supra* p. 184.

THEORY-APPLIED PROBLEM–PUBLIC SCHOOL BANNERS

Since 2010, the Palm Beach County School District ("District") has used a banner program to recognize business sponsors of its school programs, such as athletics or academic programs. Sponsors have been valuable in giving monetary donations to these programs and the District views these banners, which are hung on fences and gym walls, as a means of recognizing the sponsors' support. The donations are not considered to be payment for advertising. Furthermore, the District's Policy Manual specifically notes that "by permitting the recognition of business sponsors on school campuses, it is not the intent of the District to create or open any school, school property, or facility as a forum for expressive activity or to create a forum for expression that is inconsistent with the educational mission of the District or which could be perceived as bearing the imprimatur or endorsement of the District." David Mech provides a tutoring service in Palm Beach County under the name the "Happy/Fun Math Tutor." He has bachelor's and master's degrees in math. He is also a retired porn star and producer of pornographic films. Beginning in 2013, Mech's business hung a banner with his company's name, location and phone number (after giving a donation of $500) at several local middle and high schools. In 2015, the schools removed the banners after several parents complained upon learning of Mech's past career and current production company. Mech sued the District claiming that the removal of the banners violated his First Amendment rights. The District argued that the banner program amounted to government speech. Can the District credibly argue that the banner program is government speech. This problem is somewhat based on Mech v. School Board of Palm Beach County, 806 F.3d 1070 (11th Cir. 2015).

B. SPEECH BY GOVERNMENT EMPLOYEES

PICKERING v. BOARD OF EDUCATION

391 U.S. 563 (1968)

MARSHALL, J., delivered the opinion of the Court.

Appellant Marvin L. Pickering, a teacher in Township High School District 205, Will County, Illinois, was dismissed from his position by the appellee Board of Education for sending a letter to a local newspaper in connection with a recently proposed tax increase that was critical of the way in which the Board and the district superintendent of schools had handled past proposals to raise new revenue for the schools. Appellant's dismissal resulted from a determination by the Board, after a full hearing, that the publication of the letter was "detrimental to the efficient operation and administration of the schools of the district" and hence, under the relevant Illinois statute that "interests of the school require[d] [his dismissal]."

The letter constituted, basically, an attack on the School Board's handling of the [proposed tax increase] and its subsequent allocation of financial resources between the schools' educational and athletic programs. It also charged the superintendent of schools with attempting to prevent teachers in the district from opposing or criticizing the proposed bond issue.

. . . [T]he Board charged that numerous statements in the letter were false and that the publication of the statements unjustifiably impugned the "motives, honesty, integrity, truthfulness, responsibility and competence" of both the Board and the school administration. The Board also charged that the false statements damaged the professional reputations of its members and of the school administrators, would be disruptive of faculty discipline, and would tend to foment "controversy, conflict and dissension" among teachers, administrators, the Board of Education, and the residents of the district.

[The Illinois Supreme Court rejected Pickering's claim that the First Amendment prohibited the Board from firing him. The Illinois Court rested its decision] on the ground that [Pickering's] acceptance of a teaching position in the public schools obliged him to refrain from making statements about the operation of the schools "which in the absence of such position he would have an undoubted right to engage in."

To the extent that the Illinois Supreme Court's opinion may be read to suggest that teachers may constitutionally be compelled to relinquish the First Amendment rights they would otherwise enjoy as citizens to comment on matters of public interest in connection with the operation of the public schools in which they work, it proceeds on a premise that has been unequivocally rejected in numerous prior decisions of this Court. At the same time it cannot be gainsaid that the State has interests as an employer in regulating the speech of its employees that differ significantly from those it possesses in connection with regulation of the speech of the citizenry in general. The problem in any case is to arrive at a balance between the interests of the teacher, as a citizen, in commenting upon matters of public concern and the interest of the State, as an employer, in promoting the efficiency of the public services it performs through its employees.

Because of the enormous variety of fact situations in which critical statements by teachers and other public employees may be thought by their superiors, against whom the statements are directed, to furnish grounds for dismissal, we do not deem it either appropriate or feasible to attempt to lay down a general standard against which all such statements may be judged. However, in the course of evaluating the conflicting claims of First Amendment protection and the need for orderly school administration in the context of this case, we shall indicate some of the general lines along which an analysis of the controlling interests should run.

An examination of the statements in appellant's letter objected to by the Board reveals that they, like the letter as a whole, consist essentially of criticism of the Board's allocation of school funds between educational and athletic programs, and of both the Board's and the superintendent's methods of informing, or preventing the informing of, the district's taxpayers of the real reasons why additional tax revenues were being sought for the schools. The statements are in no way directed towards any person with whom appellant would normally be in contact in the course of his daily work as a teacher. Thus no question of maintaining either discipline by immediate superiors or harmony among coworkers is presented here. Appellant's employment relationships with the Board and, to a somewhat lesser extent, with the superintendent are not the kind of close working relationships for which it can persuasively be claimed that personal loyalty and confidence are necessary to their proper functioning. Accordingly, to the extent that the Board's position here can be taken to suggest that even comments on matters of public concern that are substantially correct furnish grounds for dismissal if they are sufficiently critical in tone, we unequivocally reject it.

[The Court then discussed several factually inaccurate statements in Pickering's letter.] What we do have before us is a case in which a teacher has made erroneous public statements upon issues then currently the subject of public attention, which are critical of his ultimate employer but which are neither shown nor can be presumed to have in any way either impeded the teacher's proper performance of his daily duties in the classroom or to have interfered with the regular operation of the schools generally. In these circumstances we conclude that the interest of the school administration in limiting teachers' opportunities to contribute to public debate is not significantly greater than its interest in limiting a similar contribution by any member of the general public.

While criminal sanctions and damage awards have a somewhat different impact on the exercise of the right to freedom of speech from dismissal from employment, it is apparent that the threat of dismissal from public employment is nonetheless a potent means of inhibiting speech. We have already noted our disinclination to make an across-the-board equation of dismissal from public employment for remarks critical of superiors with awarding damages in a libel suit by a public official for similar criticism. However, in a case such as the present one, in which the fact of employment is only tangentially and insubstantially involved in the subject matter of the public communication made by a teacher, we conclude that it is necessary to regard the teacher as the member of the general public he seeks to be.

[Justice White's separate opinion is omitted.]

CONNICK v. MYERS
461 U.S. 138 (1983)

WHITE, J., delivered the opinion of the Court.

In *Pickering v. Board of Education*, we stated that a public employee does not relinquish First Amendment rights to comment on matters of public interest by virtue of government employment. We also recognized that the State's interests as an employer in regulating the speech of its employees "differ significantly from those it possesses in connection with regulation of the speech of the citizenry in general." The problem, we thought, was arriving "at a balance between the interests of the [employee], as a citizen, in commenting upon matters of public concern and the interest of the State, as an employer, in promoting the efficiency of the public services it performs through its employees." We return to this problem today and consider whether the First and Fourteenth Amendments prevent the discharge of a state employee for circulating a questionnaire concerning internal office affairs.

The respondent, Sheila Myers, was employed as an Assistant District Attorney in New Orleans for five and a half years. She served at the pleasure of petitioner Harry Connick, the District Attorney for Orleans Parish. During this period Myers competently performed her responsibilities of trying criminal cases.

In the early part of October 1980, Myers was informed that she would be transferred to prosecute cases in a different section of the criminal court. Myers was strongly opposed to the proposed transfer and expressed her view to several of her supervisors, including Connick. A number of other office matters were discussed and Myers later testified that, in response to [her supervisor's] suggestion that her concerns were not shared by others in the office, she informed him that she would do some research on the matter.

That night Myers prepared a questionnaire soliciting the views of her fellow staff members concerning office transfer policy, office morale, the need for a grievance committee, the level of confidence in supervisors, and whether employees felt pressured to work in political campaigns. [The next day,] Myers distributed the questionnaire to 15 Assistant District Attorneys. Shortly after noon, [one of her supervisors] learned that Myers was distributing the survey. He immediately phoned Connick and informed him that Myers was creating a "mini-insurrection" within the office. Connick returned to the office and told Myers that she was being terminated because of her refusal to accept the transfer. She was also told that her distribution of the questionnaire was considered an act of insubordination. Connick particularly objected to the question which inquired whether employees "had confidence in and would rely on the word" of various superiors in the office, and to a question concerning pressure to work in political campaigns which he felt would be damaging if discovered by the press.

For at least 15 years, it has been settled that a State cannot condition public employment on a basis that infringes the employee's constitutionally protected interest in freedom of expression. Our task, as we defined it in *Pickering*, is to seek "a balance between the interests of the [employee], as a citizen, in commenting upon matters of public concern and the interest of the State, as an employer, in promoting the efficiency of the public services it performs through its employees." The District Court [and Court of Appeals] misapplied our decision in *Pickering* and consequently, in our view, erred in striking the balance for respondent.

The District Court got off on the wrong foot in this case by initially finding that, "[t]aken as a whole, the issues presented in the questionnaire relate to the effective functioning of the District Attorney's Office and are matters of public importance and concern." Connick contends at the outset that no balancing of interests is required in this case because Myers' questionnaire concerned only internal office matters and that such speech is not upon a matter of "public concern," as the term was used in *Pickering*. Although we do not agree that Myers' communication in this case was wholly without First Amendment protection, there is much force to Connick's submission. The repeated emphasis in *Pickering* on the right of a public employee "as a citizen, in commenting upon matters of public concern," was not accidental. This language, reiterated in all of *Pickering*'s progeny, reflects both the historical evolvement of the rights of public employees, and the common-sense realization that government offices could not function if every employment decision became a constitutional matter.

In the precedents in which *Pickering* is rooted, the invalidated statutes and actions sought to suppress the rights of public employees to participate in public affairs. The issue was whether government employees could be prevented or "chilled" by the fear of discharge from joining political parties and other associations that certain public officials might find "subversive."

Pickering v. Board of Education followed from this understanding of the First Amendment. Pickering's subject was "a matter of legitimate public concern" upon which "free and open debate is vital to informed decision-making by the electorate."

Pickering, its antecedents, and its progeny lead us to conclude that if Myers' questionnaire cannot be fairly characterized as constituting speech on a matter of public concern, it is unnecessary for us to scrutinize the reasons for her discharge. When employee expression cannot be fairly considered as relating to any matter of political, social, or other concern to the community, government officials should enjoy wide latitude in managing their offices, without intrusive oversight by the judiciary in the name of the First Amendment. Perhaps the government employer's dismissal of the worker may not be fair, but ordinary dismissals from government service which violate no fixed tenure or applicable statute or regulation are not subject to judicial review even if the reasons for the dismissal are alleged to be mistaken or unreasonable.

We do not suggest, however, that Myers' speech, even if not touching upon a matter of public concern, is totally beyond the protection of the First Amendment. "[T]he First Amendment does not protect speech and assembly only to the extent it can be characterized as political. 'Great secular causes, with smaller ones, are guarded.'" We hold only that when a public employee speaks not as a citizen upon matters of public concern, but instead as an employee upon matters only of personal interest, absent the most unusual circumstances, a federal court is not the appropriate forum in which to review the wisdom of a personnel decision taken by a public agency allegedly in reaction to the employee's behavior.

Whether an employee's speech addresses a matter of public concern must be determined by the content, form, and context of a given statement, as revealed by the whole record. In this case, with but one exception, the questions posed by Myers to her co-workers do not fall under the rubric of matters of "public concern." We view the questions pertaining to the confidence and trust that Myers' co-workers possess in various supervisors, the level of office morale, and the need for a grievance committee as mere extensions of Myers' dispute over her transfer to another section of the criminal court. Unlike the dissent, we do not believe these questions are of public import in evaluating the performance of the District Attorney as an elected official. Myers did not seek to inform the public that the District Attorney's Office was not discharging its governmental responsibilities in the investigation and prosecution of criminal cases. Nor did Myers seek to bring to light actual or potential wrongdoing or breach of public trust on the part of Connick and others. Indeed, the questionnaire, if released to the public, would convey no information at all other than the fact that a single employee is upset with the status quo. While discipline and morale in the workplace are related to an agency's efficient performance of its duties, the focus of Myers' questions is not to evaluate the performance of the office but rather to gather ammunition for another round of controversy with her superiors. These questions reflect one employee's dissatisfaction with a transfer and an attempt to turn that displeasure into a cause celebre.

To presume that all matters which transpire within a government office are of public concern would mean that virtually every remark—and certainly every criticism directed at a public official—would plant the seed of a constitutional case. While as a matter of good judgment, public officials should be receptive to constructive criticism offered by their employees, the First Amendment does not require a public office to be run as a roundtable for employee complaints over internal office affairs.

One question in Myers' questionnaire, however, does touch upon a matter of public concern. Question 11 inquires if assistant district attorneys "ever feel pressured to work in political campaigns on behalf of office supported candidates." We have recently noted that official pressure upon employees to work for political candidates not of the worker's own choice constitutes a coercion of belief in violation of fundamental constitutional rights. Given this history, we believe it apparent that the issue of whether assistant district attorneys are pressured to work in political campaigns is a matter of interest to the community upon which it is essential that public employees be able to speak out freely without fear of retaliatory dismissal.

Because one of the questions in Myers' survey touched upon a matter of public concern and contributed to her discharge, we must determine whether Connick was justified in discharging Myers.

The *Pickering* balance requires full consideration of the government's interest in the effective and efficient fulfillment of its responsibilities to the public. One hundred years ago, the Court noted the government's legitimate purpose in "promot[ing] efficiency and integrity in the discharge of official duties, and [in] maintain[ing] proper discipline in the public service."

We agree with the District Court that there is no demonstration here that the questionnaire impeded Myers' ability to perform her responsibilities. The District Court was also correct to recognize that "it is important to the efficient and successful operation of the District Attorney's office for Assistants to maintain close working relationships with their superiors." Connick's judgment, and apparently also that of his first assistant Dennis Waldron, who characterized Myers' actions as causing a "mini-insurrection," was that Myers' questionnaire was an act of insubordination which interfered with working relationships. When close working relationships are essential to fulfilling public responsibilities, a wide degree of deference to the employer's judgment is appropriate. Furthermore, we do not see the necessity for an employer to allow events to unfold to the extent that the disruption of the office and the destruction of working relationships is [sic] manifest before taking action. We caution that a stronger showing may be necessary if the employee's speech more substantially involved matters of public concern.

Also relevant is the manner, time, and place in which the questionnaire was distributed. Here the questionnaire was prepared and distributed at the office; the manner of distribution required not only Myers to leave her work but others to do the same in order that the questionnaire be completed. Although some latitude in when official work is performed is to be allowed when professional employees are involved, and Myers did not violate announced office policy, the fact that Myers, unlike Pickering, exercised her rights to speech at the office supports Connick's fears that the functioning of his office was endangered.

Finally, the context in which the dispute arose is also significant. This is not a case where an employee, out of purely academic interest, circulated a questionnaire so as to obtain useful research. Myers acknowledges that it is no coincidence that the questionnaire followed upon the heels of the transfer notice. When employee speech concerning office policy arises from an employment dispute concerning the very application of that policy to the speaker, additional weight must be given to the supervisor's view that the employee has threatened the authority of the employer to run the office.

BRENNAN, J., with whom MARSHALL, J., BLACKMUN, J., and STEVENS, J., join, dissenting.

The balancing test articulated in *Pickering* comes into play only when a public employee's speech implicates the government's interests as an employer. When public employees engage in expression unrelated to their employment while away from the workplace, their First Amendment rights are, of course, no different from those of the general public. Thus, whether a public employee's speech addresses a matter of public concern is relevant to the constitutional inquiry only when the statements at issue—by virtue of their content or the context in which they were made—may have an adverse impact on the government's ability to perform its duties efficiently.

The Court's decision today is flawed in three respects. First, the Court distorts the balancing analysis required under *Pickering* by suggesting that one factor, the context in which a statement is made, is to be weighed *twice*—first in determining whether an employee's speech addresses a matter of public concern and then in deciding whether the statement adversely affected the government's interest as an employer. Second, in concluding that the effect of respondent's personnel policies on employee morale and the work performance of the District Attorney's Office is not a matter of public concern, the Court impermissibly narrows the class of subjects on which public employees may speak out without fear of retaliatory dismissal. Third, the Court misapplies the *Pickering* balancing test in holding that Myers could constitutionally be dismissed for circulating a questionnaire addressed to at least one subject that *was* "a matter of interest to the community," in the absence of evidence that her conduct disrupted the efficient functioning of the District Attorney's Office.

The Court's decision today inevitably will deter public employees from making critical statements about the manner in which government agencies are operated for fear that doing so will provoke their dismissal. As a result, the public will be deprived of valuable information with which to evaluate the performance of elected officials. Because protecting the dissemination of such information is an essential function of the First Amendment, I dissent.

GARCETTI v. CEBALLOS

547 U.S. 410 (2006)

KENNEDY, J., delivered the opinion of the Court.

Respondent Richard Ceballos has been employed since 1989 as a deputy district attorney for the Los Angeles County District Attorney's Office. During the period relevant to this case, Ceballos was a calendar deputy in the office's Pomona branch, and in this capacity he exercised certain supervisory responsibilities over other lawyers. In February 2000, a defense attorney contacted Ceballos about a pending criminal case. The defense attorney said there were inaccuracies in an affidavit used to obtain a critical search warrant. The attorney informed Ceballos that he had filed a motion to traverse, or challenge, the warrant, but he also wanted Ceballos to review the case.

After examining the affidavit and visiting the location it described, Ceballos determined the affidavit contained serious misrepresentations. The affidavit called a long driveway what Ceballos thought should have been referred to as a separate roadway. Ceballos also questioned the affidavit's statement that tire tracks led from a stripped-down truck to the premises covered by the warrant. His doubts arose from his conclusion that the roadway's composition in some places made it difficult or impossible to leave visible tire tracks.

Ceballos spoke on the telephone to the warrant affiant, a deputy sheriff from the Los Angeles County Sheriff's Department, but he did not receive a satisfactory explanation for the perceived inaccuracies. He relayed his findings to his supervisors, petitioners Carol Najera and Frank Sundstedt, and followed up by preparing a disposition memorandum. The memo explained Ceballos' concerns and recommended dismissal of the case.

Based on Ceballos' statements, a meeting was held to discuss the affidavit. Attendees included Ceballos, Sundstedt, and Najera, as well as the warrant affiant and other employees from the sheriff's department. The meeting allegedly became heated, with one lieutenant sharply criticizing Ceballos for his handling of the case.

Despite Ceballos' concerns, Sundstedt decided to proceed with the prosecution, pending disposition of the defense motion to traverse. The trial court held a hearing on the motion. Ceballos was called by the defense and recounted his observations about the affidavit, but the trial court rejected the challenge to the warrant.

Ceballos claims that in the aftermath of these events he was subjected to a series of retaliatory employment actions. The actions included reassignment from his calendar deputy position to a trial deputy position, transfer to another courthouse, and denial of a promotion. He alleged petitioners violated the First and Fourteenth Amendments by retaliating against him based on his memo.

As the Court's decisions have noted, for many years "the unchallenged dogma was that a public employee had no right to object to conditions placed upon the terms of employment—including those which restricted the exercise of constitutional rights." *Connick.* That dogma has been qualified in important respects. The Court has made clear that public employees do not surrender all their First Amendment rights by reason of their employment. Rather, the First Amendment protects a public employee's right, in certain circumstances, to speak as a citizen addressing matters of public concern. The Court's decisions have sought both to promote the individual and societal interests that are served when employees speak as citizens on matters of public concern and to respect the needs of government employers attempting to perform their important public functions. Underlying our cases has been the premise that while the First Amendment invests public employees with certain rights, it does not empower them to "constitutionalize the employee grievance." *Connick.*

With these principles in mind we turn to the instant case. Respondent Ceballos believed the affidavit used to obtain a search warrant contained serious misrepresentations. He conveyed his opinion and recommendation in a memo to his supervisor. That Ceballos expressed his views inside his office, rather than publicly, is not dispositive. Employees in some cases may receive First Amendment protection for expressions made at work. Many citizens do much of their talking inside their respective workplaces, and it would not serve the goal of treating public employees like "any member of the general public," *Pickering,* to hold that all speech within the office is automatically exposed to restriction.

The memo concerned the subject matter of Ceballos' employment, but this, too, is nondispositive. The First Amendment protects some expressions related to the speaker's job. As the Court noted in *Pickering:* "Teachers are, as a class, the members of a community most likely to have informed and definite opinions as to how funds allotted to the operation of the schools should be spent. Accordingly, it is essential that they be able to speak out freely on such questions without fear of retaliatory dismissal." The same is true of many other categories of public employees.

The controlling factor in Ceballos' case is that his expressions were made pursuant to his duties as a calendar deputy. That consideration—the fact that Ceballos spoke as a prosecutor fulfilling a responsibility to advise his supervisor about how best to proceed with a pending case—distinguishes Ceballos' case from those in which the First Amendment provides protection against discipline. We hold that when public employees make statements pursuant to their official duties, the employees are not speaking as citizens for First Amendment purposes, and the Constitution does not insulate their communications from employer discipline.

Ceballos wrote his disposition memo because that is part of what he, as a calendar deputy, was employed to do. The significant point is that the memo was written pursuant to Ceballos' official duties. Restricting speech that owes its existence to a public employee's professional responsibilities does not infringe any liberties the employee might have enjoyed as a private citizen. It simply reflects the exercise of employer control over what the employer itself has commissioned or created. Contrast, for example, the expressions made by the speaker in *Pickering*, whose letter to the newspaper had no official significance and bore similarities to letters submitted by numerous citizens every day.

Ceballos did not act as a citizen when he went about conducting his daily professional activities, such as supervising attorneys, investigating charges, and preparing filings. In the same way he did not speak as a citizen by writing a memo that addressed the proper disposition of a pending criminal case. When he went to work and performed the tasks he was paid to perform, Ceballos acted as a government employee. The fact that his duties sometimes required him to speak or write does not mean his supervisors were prohibited from evaluating his performance.

Employers have heightened interests in controlling speech made by an employee in his or her professional capacity. Official communications have official consequences, creating a need for substantive consistency and clarity. Supervisors must ensure that their employees' official communications are accurate, demonstrate sound judgment, and promote the employer's mission. Ceballos' memo is illustrative. It demanded the attention of his supervisors and led to a heated meeting with employees from the sheriff's department. If Ceballos' superiors thought his memo was inflammatory or misguided, they had the authority to take proper corrective action.

The Court of Appeals based its holding in part on what it perceived as a doctrinal anomaly. The court suggested it would be inconsistent to compel public employers to tolerate certain employee speech made publicly but not speech made pursuant to an employee's assigned duties. This objection misconceives the theoretical underpinnings of our decisions. Employees who make public statements outside the course of performing their official duties retain some possibility of First Amendment protection because that is the kind of activity engaged in by citizens who do not work for the government. The same goes for writing a letter to a local newspaper, see *Pickering*, or discussing politics with a co-worker, see *Rankin* [*v. MacPherson*, 483 U.S. 378 (1987)]. When a public employee speaks pursuant to employment responsibilities, however, there is no relevant analogue to speech by citizens who are not government employees.

The Court of Appeals' concern also is unfounded as a practical matter. The perceived anomaly, it should be noted, is limited in scope: It relates only to the expressions an employee makes pursuant to his or her official responsibilities, not to statements or complaints (such as those at issue in cases like *Pickering* and *Connick*) that are made outside the duties of employment. If, moreover, a government employer is troubled by the perceived anomaly, it has the means at hand to avoid it. A public employer that wishes to encourage its employees to voice concerns privately retains the option of instituting internal policies and procedures that are receptive to employee criticism. Giving employees an internal forum for their speech will discourage them from concluding that the safest avenue of expression is to state their views in public.

Two final points warrant mentioning. First, as indicated above, the parties in this case do not dispute that Ceballos wrote his disposition memo pursuant to his employment duties. We thus have no occasion to articulate a comprehensive framework for defining the scope of an employee's duties in cases where there is room for serious debate. We reject, however, the suggestion that employers can restrict employees' rights by creating excessively broad job descriptions. The proper inquiry is a practical one. Formal job descriptions often bear little resemblance to the duties an employee actually is expected to perform, and the listing of a given task in an employee's written job description is neither necessary nor sufficient to demonstrate that conducting the task is within the scope of the employee's professional duties for First Amendment purposes.

Second, Justice Souter suggests today's decision may have important ramifications for academic freedom, at least as a constitutional value. There is some argument that expression related to academic scholarship or classroom instruction implicates additional constitutional interests that are not fully accounted for by this Court's customary employee-speech jurisprudence. We need not, and for that reason do not, decide whether the analysis we conduct today would apply in the same manner to a case involving speech related to scholarship or teaching.

Exposing governmental inefficiency and misconduct is a matter of considerable significance. As the Court noted in *Connick*, public employers should, "as a matter of good judgment," be "receptive to constructive criticism offered by their employees." The dictates of sound judgment are reinforced by the powerful network of legislative enactments—such as whistle-blower protection laws and labor codes—available to those who seek to expose wrongdoing. Cases involving government attorneys implicate additional safeguards in the form of, for example, rules of conduct and constitutional obligations apart from the First Amendment. See, *e.g.*, Cal. Rule Prof. Conduct 5-110 (2005) ("A member in government service shall not institute or cause to be instituted criminal charges when the member knows or should know that the charges are not supported by probable cause"); *Brady v. Maryland*, 373 U.S. 83 (1963). These imperatives, as well as obligations arising from any other applicable constitutional provisions and mandates of the criminal and civil laws, protect employees and provide checks on supervisors who would order unlawful or otherwise inappropriate actions.

We reject, however, the notion that the First Amendment shields from discipline the expressions employees make pursuant to their professional duties. Our precedents do not support the existence of a constitutional cause of action behind every statement a public employee makes in the course of doing his or her job.

SOUTER, J., with whom STEVENS, J., and GINSBURG, J., join, dissenting.

The Court holds that "when public employees make statements pursuant to their official duties, the employees are not speaking as citizens for First Amendment purposes, and the Constitution does not insulate their communications from employer discipline." I respectfully dissent. I agree with the majority that a government employer has substantial interests in effectuating its chosen policy and objectives, and in demanding competence, honesty, and judgment from employees who speak for it in doing their work. But I would hold that private and public interests in addressing official wrongdoing and threats to health and safety can outweigh the government's stake in the efficient implementation of policy, and when they do public employees who speak on these matters in the course of their duties should be eligible to claim First Amendment protection.

Up to a point, then, the majority makes good points: government needs civility in the workplace, consistency in policy, and honesty and competence in public service. But why do the majority's concerns, which we all share, require categorical exclusion of First Amendment protection against any official retaliation for things said on the job? Is it not possible to respect the unchallenged individual and public interests in the speech through a *Pickering* balance? This is, to be sure, a matter of judgment, but the judgment has to account for the undoubted value of speech to those, and by those, whose specific public job responsibilities bring them face to face with wrongdoing and incompetence in government, who refuse to avert their eyes and shut their mouths. And it has to account for the need actually to disrupt government if its officials are corrupt or dangerously incompetent. It is thus no adequate justification for the suppression of potentially valuable information simply to recognize that the government has a huge interest in managing its employees and preventing the occasionally irresponsible one from turning his job into a bully pulpit. Even there, the lesson of *Pickering* (and the object of most constitutional adjudication) is still to the point: when constitutionally significant interests clash, resist the demand for winner-take-all; try to make adjustments that serve all of the values at stake.

Two reasons in particular make me think an adjustment using the basic *Pickering* balancing scheme is perfectly feasible here. First, the extent of the government's legitimate authority over subjects of speech required by a public job can be recognized in advance by setting in effect a minimum heft for comments with any claim to outweigh it. Thus, the risks to the government are great enough for us to hold from the outset that an employee commenting on subjects in the course of duties should not prevail on balance unless he speaks on a matter of unusual importance and satisfies high standards of responsibility in the way he does it. The examples I have already given indicate the eligible subject matter, and it is fair to say that only comment on official dishonesty, deliberately unconstitutional action, other serious wrongdoing, or threats to health and safety can weigh out in an employee's favor.

My second reason for adapting *Pickering* to the circumstances at hand is the experience in Circuits that have recognized claims like Ceballos's here. First Amendment protection less circumscribed than what I would recognize has been available in the Ninth Circuit for over 17 years, and neither there nor in other Circuits that accept claims like this one has there been a debilitating flood of litigation. There has indeed been some: as represented by Ceballos's lawyer at oral argument, each year over the last five years, approximately 70 cases in the different Courts of Appeals and approximately 100 in the various District Courts. But even these figures reflect a readiness to litigate that might well have been cooled by my view about the importance required before *Pickering* treatment is in order.

The majority accepts the fallacy propounded by the county petitioners and the Federal Government as *amicus* that any statement made within the scope of public employment is (or should be treated as) the government's own speech, and should thus be differentiated as a matter of law from the personal statements the First Amendment protects. The majority invokes the interpretation set out in *Rosenberger* of *Rust*, which held there was no infringement of the speech rights of Title X funds recipients and their staffs when the Government forbade any on-the-job counseling in favor of abortion as a method of family planning. We have read *Rust* to mean that "when the government appropriates public funds to promote a particular policy of its own it is entitled to say what it wishes." *Rosenberger.*

The key to understanding the difference between this case and *Rust* lies in the terms of the respective employees' jobs and, in particular, the extent to which those terms require espousal of a substantive position prescribed by the government in advance. Some public employees are hired to "promote a particular policy" by broadcasting a particular message set by the government, but not everyone working for the government, after all, is hired to speak from a government manifesto. See *Legal Services Corporation v. Velazquez.* There is no claim or indication that Ceballos was hired to perform such a speaking assignment. He was paid to enforce the law by constitutional action: to exercise the county government's prosecutorial power by acting honestly, competently, and constitutionally. The only sense in which his position apparently required him to hew to a substantive message was at the relatively abstract point of favoring respect for law and its evenhanded enforcement, subjects that are not at the level of controversy in this case and were not in *Rust.* Unlike the doctors in *Rust*, Ceballos was not paid to advance one specific policy among those legitimately available, defined by a specific message or limited by a particular message forbidden. The county government's interest in his speech cannot therefore be equated with the terms of a specific, prescribed, or forbidden substantive position comparable to the Federal Government's interest in *Rust*, and *Rust* is no authority for the notion that government may exercise plenary control over every comment made by a public employee in doing his job.
[Citations omitted.]

[Justices Stevens's and Breyer's dissenting opinions are omitted.]

NOTES AND QUESTIONS

1. *Applying the* Connick *standard.* The *Connick* standard is very favorable to public employers seeking to limit the speech of their employees. Under *Connick*, the employee has no First Amendment right whatsoever if the employee's expression does not relate to a matter of public concern, and even if the employee's expression is about a matter of public concern, the employer may still restrict the expression if it would disrupt the workplace in any significant way. In several other decisions involving the free speech rights of government employees, the Court has described the details of the First Amendment analysis in ways that make the standard for assessing free speech rights in this context even more employer-friendly. For example, the Court places the initial burden on the employee to demonstrate "that his conduct was constitutionally protected, and that this conduct was a 'substantial factor'—or, to put it in other words, that it was a 'motivating factor'" in the decision to fire or sanction the employee. Mt. Healthy City Sch. Dist. Bd. of Educ. v. Doyle, 429 U.S. 274, 287 (1977). Once the employee has met that burden, the government employer must then show "by a preponderance of the evidence that it would have reached the same decision as to [the employee's] re-employment even in the absence of the protected conduct." The employer thus has three chances to avoid liability when an employee has been sanctioned for expression that the employer disfavors. First, the employer may argue that the speech does not pertain to a matter of public concern; second, the employer may argue that the speech disrupts the workplace;

and third, the employer may argue that it would have sanctioned the employee regardless of the employee's protected speech.

2. *Defining disruption of the workplace.* In assessing whether an employee's speech has disrupted the workplace, the Court has held that employers must be given substantial deference in quelling potential disruption. This deference is so substantial that courts must even defer to an employer's mistaken impression of what the employee said. In Waters v. Churchill, 511 U.S. 661 (1994), for example, a plurality of the Court held that a public employer may punish an employee in reliance on the employer's reasonable belief that an employee engaged in constitutionally unprotected speech—even if it turns out that the employee's actual remarks were constitutionally protected. The case involved a conversation between two nurses who worked at a public hospital. The first nurse was thinking of transferring to the hospital's obstetrics department, in which the second nurse worked. Three other employees overhead this conversation, and later told their supervisor that the second nurse had made several derogatory comments about the department and one of her supervisors. When the supervisor confronted her, the second nurse denied that she had made some of the negative comments attributed to her. The supervisor nevertheless fired her. Subsequent investigation indicated that the supervisor apparently misunderstood the full context and content of the second nurse's comments. The nurse sued, alleging a violation of her First Amendment rights. Writing for a plurality of the Supreme Court, Justice O'Connor concluded that, unlike First Amendment contexts involving government regulation of private speech, in cases involving government employment "the government's interest in achieving its goals as effectively and efficiently as possible is elevated from a relatively subordinate interest . . . to a significant one." Thus, while the government may not regulate private speech in the interest of efficiency alone, "where the government is employing someone for the very purpose of effectively achieving its goals, such restrictions may well be appropriate." Justice O'Connor specifically recognized that in making the decision to sanction employees based on their speech, government employers may rely "on hearsay, on past similar conduct, on their personal knowledge of people's credibility, and on other factors that the judicial process ignores." The only limit on the employer is that the employer's assessment of the situation must be reasonable. "We think employer decisionmaking will not be unduly burdened by having courts look to the facts as the employer reasonably found them to be." The employee will prevail under this standard only if the employer acts on the basis of no evidence or very weak evidence of what the employee said. The employer will prevail in a claim governed by the *Connick* standard, however, if the employer merely makes a reasonable mistake about the content of the employee's speech. Is the plurality insufficiently protective of government employees' speech rights? Would it give a government employer free rein to fire an employee based on a false rumor that she had criticized her supervisor's management style? How about a false rumor that she had voted for a Democrat?

3. *Employee or citizen? On-duty or off?* After *Garcetti*, an employee speaking as an employee receives no protection for her speech, but the line

between speaking as an employee and speaking as a citizen is by no means always clear. Garcetti suggests that when an employer "commission[s] or create[s]" the employee's speech, the speech is subject to the control of the government. In what other circumstances can the government punish or control employee speech in order to further its own message? How critical is the distinction between off-duty speech and on-duty speech? Does it depend on the job? For example, may an assistant attorney general be fired for creating a blog calling a gay student body president a "racist" and a "liar" promoting a "radical homosexual agenda"? *See* Mary-Rose Papandrea, *The Free Speech Rights of "Off-Duty" Government Employees*, 2010 BYU L. Rev. 2117, 2120 (2010) (arguing that "the *Connick/ Pickering* framework should not apply in cases involving off-duty, non-work-related government-employee speech" because it "is not appropriately tailored to address a government employer's legitimate interests").

LANE v. FRANKS

134 S. Ct. 2369 (2014)

SOTOMAYOR, J., delivered the opinion of the Court.

. . . Today, we consider whether the First Amendment [ ] protects a public employee who provided truthful sworn testimony, compelled by subpoena, outside the course of his ordinary job responsibilities. We hold that it does.

In 2006, Central Alabama Community College (CACC) hired petitioner Edward Lane to be the Director of Community Intensive Training for Youth (CITY), a statewide program for underprivileged youth. . . .

At the time of Lane's appointment, CITY faced significant financial difficulties. That prompted Lane to conduct a comprehensive audit of the program's expenses. The audit revealed that Suzanne Schmitz, an Alabama State Representative on CITY's payroll, had not been reporting to her CITY office. . . .

Lane [ ] contacted Schmitz again and instructed her to show up to the Huntsville office to serve as a counselor. Schmitz refused; she responded that she wished to "'continue to serve the CITY program in the same manner as [she had] in the past.'" Lane fired her shortly thereafter. Schmitz told another CITY employee, Charles Foley, that she intended to "'get [Lane] back'" for firing her.

Schmitz' termination drew the attention of many, including agents of the Federal Bureau of Investigation, which initiated an investigation into Schmitz' employment with CITY. In November 2006, Lane testified before a federal grand jury about his reasons for firing Schmitz. In January 2008, the grand jury indicted Schmitz on four counts of mail fraud and four counts of theft concerning a program receiving federal funds. The indictment alleged that Schmitz had collected $177,251.82 in federal funds even though she performed "'virtually no services,'" "'generated virtually no work product,'" and "'rarely even appeared for work at the CITY Program offices.'" [ ]

[Schmitz was tried twice. The first jury hung, and the second convicted Schmitz of mail fraud and theft. Lane testified under subpoena at both trials.]

Meanwhile, CITY continued to experience considerable budget shortfalls. [Steve Franks, president of CACC laid off 29 probationary employees, and then hired all back except for Lane and one other.] Franks claims that he "did not rescind Lane's termination . . . because he believed that Lane was in a fundamentally different category than the other employees: he was the director of the entire CITY program, and not simply an employee." In September 2009, CACC eliminated the CITY program and terminated the program's remaining employees. Franks later retired, and respondent Susan Burrow, the current Acting President of CACC, replaced him while this case was pending before the Eleventh Circuit.

In January 2011, Lane sued Franks in his individual and official capacities under Rev. Stat. § 1979, 42 U.S.C. § 1983, alleging that Franks had violated the First Amendment by firing him in retaliation for his testimony against Schmitz. . . .

The District Court granted Franks' motion for summary judgment [on the grounds that Franks was entitled to qualified immunity because a reasonable official in his position had reason to believe, based on Garcetti, that Lane's speech was not protected because he learned the information about which the testified while working as a Director and thus his speech was part of his official job duties. The Eleventh Circuit affirmed.]

We granted certiorari to resolve discord among the Courts of Appeals as to whether public employees may be fired—or suffer other adverse employment consequences—for providing truthful subpoenaed testimony outside the course of their ordinary job responsibilities.

II

Speech by citizens on matters of public concern lies at the heart of the First Amendment, which "was fashioned to assure unfettered interchange of ideas for the bringing about of political and social changes desired by the people," *Roth v. United States*, 354 U.S. 476, 484 (1957). This remains true when speech concerns information related to or learned through public employment. After all, public employees do not renounce their citizenship when they accept employment, and this Court has cautioned time and again that public employers may not condition employment on the relinquishment of constitutional rights. . . . "The interest at stake is as much the public's interest in receiving informed opinion as it is the employee's own right to disseminate it." *San Diego v. Roe*, 543 U.S. 77, 82, 125 S. Ct. 521, 160 L.Ed.2d 410 (2004) (*per curiam*).

Our precedents have also acknowledged the government's countervailing interest in controlling the operation of its workplaces. "Government employers, like private employers, need a significant degree of control over their employees' words and actions; without it, there would be little chance for the efficient provision of public services." Garcetti.

Pickering provides the framework for analyzing whether the employee's interest or the government's interest should prevail in cases where the government seeks to curtail the speech of its employees. It requires "balanc[ing] . . . the interests of the [public employee], as a citizen, in commenting upon matters of public concern and the interest of the State, as an employer, in promoting the efficiency of the public services it performs through its employees." . . .

In *Garcetti*, we described a two-step inquiry into whether a public employee's speech is entitled to protection:

> "The first requires determining whether the employee spoke as a citizen on a matter of public concern. If the answer is no, the employee has no First Amendment cause of action based on his or her employer's reaction to the speech. If the answer is yes, then the possibility of a First Amendment claim arises. The question becomes whether the relevant government entity had an adequate

justification for treating the employee differently from any other member of the general public."

In describing the first step in this inquiry, *Garcetti* distinguished between employee speech and citizen speech. Whereas speech as a citizen may trigger protection, the Court held that "when public employees make statements pursuant to their official duties, the employees are not speaking as citizens for First Amendment purposes, and the Constitution does not insulate their communications from employer discipline." Applying that rule to the facts before it, the Court found that an internal memorandum prepared by a prosecutor in the course of his ordinary job responsibilities constituted unprotected employee speech.

III

Against this backdrop, we turn to the question presented: whether the First Amendment protects a public employee who provides truthful sworn testimony, compelled by subpoena, outside the scope of his ordinary job responsibilities. We hold that it does.

The first inquiry is whether the speech in question—Lane's testimony at Schmitz' trials—is speech as a citizen on a matter of public concern. It clearly is.

Truthful testimony under oath by a public employee outside the scope of his ordinary job duties is speech as a citizen for First Amendment purposes. That is so even when the testimony relates to his public employment or concerns information learned during that employment.

In rejecting Lane's argument that his testimony was speech as a citizen, the Eleventh Circuit gave short shrift to the nature of sworn judicial statements and ignored the obligation borne by all witnesses testifying under oath. Sworn testimony in judicial proceedings is a quintessential example of speech as a citizen for a simple reason: Anyone who testifies in court bears an obligation, to the court and society at large, to tell the truth. [ ].

When the person testifying is a public employee, he may bear separate obligations to his employer—for example, an obligation not to show up to court dressed in an unprofessional manner. But any such obligations as an employee are distinct and independent from the obligation, as a citizen, to speak the truth. That independent obligation renders sworn testimony speech as a citizen and sets it apart from speech made purely in the capacity of an employee.

In holding that Lane did not speak as a citizen when he testified, the Eleventh Circuit read *Garcetti* far too broadly. It reasoned that, because Lane learned of the subject matter of his testimony in the course of his employment with CITY, *Garcetti* requires that his testimony be treated as the speech of an employee rather than that of a citizen. It does not.

The sworn testimony in this case is far removed from the speech at issue in Garcetti—an internal memorandum prepared by a deputy district attorney for his supervisors recommending dismissal of a particular prosecution. The Garcetti Court held that such speech was made pursuant to the employee's "official responsibilities" because "[w]hen [the employee] went to work and performed the tasks he was paid to perform, [he] acted as a government employee. The fact that his duties sometimes required him to speak or write does not mean that his supervisors were prohibited from evaluating his performance."

But *Garcetti* said nothing about speech that simply relates to public employment or concerns information learned in the course of public employment. The *Garcetti* Court made explicit that its holding did not turn on the fact that the memo at issue "concerned the subject matter of [the prosecutor's] employment," because "[t]he First Amendment protects some expressions related to the speaker's job." In other words, the mere fact that a citizen's speech concerns information acquired by virtue of his public employment does not transform that speech into employee—rather than citizen—speech. The critical question under *Garcetti* is whether the speech at issue is itself ordinarily within the scope of an employee's duties, not whether it merely concerns those duties.

It bears emphasis that our precedents dating back to *Pickering* have recognized that speech by public employees on subject matter related to their employment holds special value precisely because those employees gain knowledge of matters of public concern through their employment. [ ].

The importance of public employee speech is especially evident in the context of this case: a public corruption scandal. The United States, for example, represents that because "[t]he more than 1000 prosecutions for federal corruption offenses that are brought in a typical year . . . often depend on evidence about activities that government officials undertook while in office," those prosecutions often "require testimony from other government employees." It would be antithetical to our jurisprudence to conclude that the very kind of speech necessary to prosecute corruption by public officials—speech by public employees regarding information learned through their employment—may never form the basis for a First Amendment retaliation claim. Such a rule would place public employees who witness corruption in an impossible position, torn between the obligation to testify truthfully and the desire to avoid retaliation and keep their jobs.

Applying these principles, it is clear that Lane's sworn testimony is speech as a citizen.

Lane's testimony is also speech on a matter of public concern. Speech involves matters of public concern "when it can 'be fairly considered as relating to any matter of political, social, or other concern to the community,' or when it 'is a subject of legitimate news interest; that is, a subject of general interest and of value and concern to the public.'" Snyder v. Phelps [ ]. The inquiry turns on the "content, form, and context" of the speech. *Connick.*

The content of Lane's testimony—corruption in a public program and misuse of state funds—obviously involves a matter of significant public concern. [ ]. And the form and context of the speech—sworn testimony in a judicial proceeding—fortify that conclusion. "Unlike speech in other contexts, testimony under oath has the formality and gravity necessary to remind the witness that his or her statements will be the basis for official governmental action, action that often affects the rights and liberties of others." *United States v. Alvarez,* 567 U.S. ___, ___, 132 S. Ct. 2537, 2546 (2012) (plurality opinion).

. . . Under *Pickering,* if an employee speaks as a citizen on a matter of public concern, the next question is whether the government had "an adequate justification for treating the employee differently from any other member of the public" based on the government's needs as an employer.

As discussed previously, we have recognized that government employers often have legitimate "interest[s] in the effective and efficient fulfillment of [their] responsibilities to the public," including "'promot[ing] efficiency and integrity in the discharge of official duties,'" and "'maintain[ing] proper discipline in public service.'" We have also cautioned, however, that "a stronger showing [of government interests] may be necessary if the employee's speech more substantially involve[s] matters of public concern." *Connick*.

Here, the employer's side of the *Pickering* scale is entirely empty: Respondents do not assert, and cannot demonstrate, any government interest that tips the balance in their favor. There is no evidence, for example, that Lane's testimony at Schmitz' trials was false or erroneous or that Lane unnecessarily disclosed any sensitive, confidential, or privileged information while testifying. In these circumstances, we conclude that Lane's speech is entitled to protection under the First Amendment.

[The Court held that even though Lane's speech was protected by the First Amendment, the Eleventh Circuit correctly held that Respondent Franks could reasonably have believed that a government employer could fire an employee under these circumstances. Therefore, Franks was entitled to qualified immunity.]

THOMAS, J., with whom SCALIA, J., and ALITO, J., join, concurring.

. . . The petitioner in this case did not speak "pursuant to" his ordinary job duties because his responsibilities did not include testifying in court proceedings, and no party has suggested that he was subpoenaed as a representative of his employer. Because petitioner did not testify to "fulfil[l] a [work] responsibility," *Garcetti*, he spoke "as a citizen," not as an employee.

We accordingly have no occasion to address the quite different question whether a public employee speaks "as a citizen" when he testifies in the course of his ordinary job responsibilities. For some public employees—such as police officers, crime scene technicians, and laboratory analysts—testifying is a routine and critical part of their employment duties. Others may be called to testify in the context of particular litigation as the designated representatives of their employers. The Court properly leaves the constitutional questions raised by these scenarios for another day.

NOTES AND QUESTIONS

1. *Protecting federal functions?* Would a dismissal of a state employee based on his truthful testimony in federal court be an "unconstitutional state interference with legitimate federal functions"? For analysis, Marty Lederman, *Commentary: The fundamental constitutional principle not discussed in Lane v. Franks,* SCOTUSBLOG (Jun. 20, 2014, 2:53 PM), http://www.scotusblog.com/2014/06/commentary-the-fundamental-constitutional-principle-not-discussed-in-lane-v-franks/.

2. *The interplay of the government financing and government employee decisions.* Many of the holdings in the Court's government financing and government employee cases are difficult to reconcile. Consider four cases in particular: First, in *Connick* the Court allowed a District Attorney to sanction a staff attorney for distributing a questionnaire concerning the internal operations of the office. The Court held that questions concerning internal staff morale and staff attorney confidence in supervising attorneys were not matters of public concern, but that questions concerning internal coercion to work in political campaigns were matters of public concern. Second, in *Rust* the Court allowed government-funded agencies to prohibit doctors who receive government funds from informing their patients about particular forms of care that were relevant to the patients' medical conditions. Third, in *Velazquez* the Court prohibited Congress from imposing

restrictions on the ability of government-funded attorneys to raise certain kinds of claims on behalf of their clients. The rationale of this decision was that the funding agency cannot override the attorneys' professional obligations to the courts and their clients. Fourth, in *Garcetti* the Court allowed supervising attorneys in a District Attorney's office to sanction a staff attorney for expressing concerns about the prosecution of a case—even though the staff attorney's concerns arguably may have involved fraud on the court. How can these decisions be reconciled? *Rust* seems to treat government-funded speakers as having no First Amendment protection against government constraints that impinge on the funded employee's professional obligations, yet *Velazquez* seems to hold that the First Amendment provides absolute protection of speech undertaken as part of a speaker's professional obligations. Likewise, *Velazquez* seems to hold that the First Amendment protects the government-funded speaker in raising claims that the government specifically forbids the speaker to raise, yet *Garcetti* holds that the government may sanction a government employee for raising claims that the government has specifically forbidden the speaker to raise. Can these seemingly inconsistent results be reconciled by focusing on whether the speech in question occurred within the government office rather than being directed to outsiders? In *Velazquez*, for example, the Court protected the government-funded speakers' ability to speak to an outside body (the courts), and in *Garcetti* the Court noted the "anomaly" that the government would have to tolerate employee speech made to outsiders, but could sanction speech on the same subject made within the workplace as a part of the employee's "professional responsibilities." But if this "insider/outsider" dichotomy is the key to understanding the Court's decisions in this area, then why in *Rust* does the Court uphold restrictions on the doctors' conversations with outsiders (patients), and in *Garcetti* uphold restrictions on speech that is intended to be presented to outsiders (the courts)?

3. *Constitutional protection of internal complaints.* After *Garcetti*, the availability of First Amendment protection under *Pickering* and *Connick* for complaints expressed by an employee to his or her government employer rather than the public at large depends on the employee's precise job description and an assessment of whether the subject matter of the employee's complaint falls within the description of the employee's professional duties. Under the *Garcetti* holding, the employee's speech is not protected if it is within the scope of the employee's job, but it is protected if the speech falls outside the scope of the employee's job description. In *Garcetti*, the Court limited the scope of Givhan v. Western Line Consolidated School District, 439 U.S. 410 (1979). *Givhan* involved a junior high school English teacher, who was fired from her job with a public school system because she had complained about the racially discriminatory hiring practices of the school district as a whole and at the school where she was assigned. The Supreme Court held that her speech was protected by *Pickering*, and noted that "[n]either the [First] Amendment itself nor our decisions indicate that [the employee's] freedom [of speech] is lost to the public employee who arranges to communicate privately with his employer rather than to spread his views before the public." In *Garcetti*, the Court reaffirmed *Givhan*'s holding that the First Amendment protects some speech by employees at the workplace, but held that *Givhan* does not apply in situations in which the employee was speaking "pursuant to his duties." "We hold that when public

employees make statements pursuant to their official duties, the employees are not speaking as citizens for First Amendment purposes, and the Constitution does not insulate their communications from employer discipline." Dissenting in *Garcetti*, Justice criticized the majority's distinction between expression that falls within a public employee's official duties and expression that falls outside the scope of those duties: The difference between a case like *Givhan* and this one is that the subject of Ceballos's speech fell within the scope of his job responsibilities, whereas choosing personnel was not what the teacher was hired to do. The effect of the majority drawing a constitutional line between these two cases, then, is that a schoolteacher is protected when complaining to the principal about hiring policy, but a school personnel officer would not be protected if he protested that the principal disapproved of hiring minority job applicants. What is the justification for denying protection to a government employee's speech uttered pursuant to official duties?

4. *The scope of official duties of faculty at public universities.* What implications does *Garcetti* have for faculty at public universities? Assume a law professor at a state university writes on a blog that his law school admits students whose LSAT scores are so low that they are "unqualified to be lawyers"? His employer seeks to discipline him after his speech triggers student protests and a decline in the law school's ability to recruit students. May the law school discipline him? Would the result be different if a high school teacher wrote on her Facebook page that her students "are all too dumb to learn what I'm trying to teach"? Does the concept of academic freedom in the university setting affect the outcome of the first scenario?

U.S. CIVIL SERVICE COMMISSION v. NATIONAL ASS'N OF LETTER CARRIERS
413 U.S. 548 (1973)

WHITE, J., delivered the opinion of the Court.

[The] single question [in this case is] whether the prohibition in 9(a) of the Hatch Act, against federal employees taking "an active part in political management or in political campaigns," is unconstitutional on its face. [This section provides:]

> An employee in an Executive agency or an individual employed by the government of the District of Columbia may not
> (1) use his official authority or influence for the purpose of interfering with or affecting the result of an election; or
> (2) take an active part in political management or in political campaigns.

A divided three-judge court sitting in the District of Columbia had held the section unconstitutional. We reverse the judgment of the District Court.

Each of the plaintiffs alleged that the Civil Service Commission was enforcing, or threatening to enforce, the Hatch Act's prohibition against active participation in political management or political campaigns with respect to certain defined activity in which that plaintiff desired to engage.[3] The Union, for example, stated among

---

[3] The Union alleged that its members were desirous of "a. Running in local elections for such offices as school board member, city council member or mayor. b. Writing letters on political

other things that its members desired to campaign for candidates for public office. The Democratic and Republican Committees complained of not being able to get federal employees to run for state and local offices.

We unhesitatingly reaffirm [our earlier holding] that Congress had, and has, the power to prevent [government employees] from holding a party office, working at the polls, and acting as party paymaster for other party workers. An Act of Congress going no farther would in our view unquestionably be valid. So would it be if, in plain and understandable language, the statute forbade activities such as organizing a political party or club; actively participating in fund-raising activities for a partisan candidate or political party; becoming a partisan candidate for, or campaigning for, an elective public office; actively managing the campaign of a partisan candidate for public office; initiating or circulating a partisan nominating petition or soliciting votes for a partisan candidate for public office; or serving as a delegate, alternate or proxy to a political party convention. Our judgment is that neither the First Amendment nor any other provision of the Constitution invalidates a law barring this kind of partisan political conduct by federal employees.

It seems fundamental in the first place that employees in the Executive Branch of the Government, or those working for any of its agencies, should administer the law in accordance with the will of Congress, rather than in accordance with their own or the will of a political party. They are expected to enforce the law and execute the programs of the Government without bias or favoritism for or against any political party or group or the members thereof. A major thesis of the Hatch Act is that to serve this great end of Government—the impartial execution of the laws—it is essential that federal employees, for example, not take formal positions in political parties, not undertake to play substantial roles in partisan political campaigns, and not run for office on partisan political tickets. Forbidding activities like these will reduce the hazards to fair and effective government.

There is another consideration in this judgment: it is not only important that the Government and its employees in fact avoid practicing political justice, but it is also critical that they appear to the public to be avoiding it, if confidence in the system of representative Government is not to be eroded to a disastrous extent.

Another major concern of the restriction against partisan activities by federal employees was perhaps the immediate occasion for enactment of the Hatch Act in 1939. That was the conviction that the rapidly expanding Government work force should not be employed to build a powerful, invincible, and perhaps corrupt political machine. The experience of the 1936 and 1938 campaigns convinced Congress that these dangers were sufficiently real that substantial barriers should be raised against the party in power—or the party out of power, for that matter—using the thousands

---

subjects to newspapers. c. Participating as a delegate in a political convention and running for office in a political party. d. Campaigning for candidates for political office." The Democratic and Republican Committees complained that they had been deterred "from seeking desirable candidates who are Federal or state employees covered by the Hatch Act to run on the Democratic or Republican ticket for state and local offices. In addition, numerous individuals who would otherwise desire and be available to become members of Plaintiff Committees have been and continue to be deterred from doing so by said provisions of the Hatch Act." Plaintiff Hummel alleged that he desired to engage in a wide variety of political activities including "(1) participation as a delegate in conventions of a political party; (2) public endorsement of candidates of a political party for local, state and national office; (3) work at polling places on behalf of a political party during elections; (4) holding office in a political club."

or hundreds of thousands of federal employees, paid for at public expense, to man its political structure and political campaigns.

A related concern, and this remains as important as any other, was to further serve the goal that employment and advancement in the Government service not depend on political performance, and at the same time to make sure that Government employees would be free from pressure and from express or tacit invitation to vote in a certain way or perform political chores in order to curry favor with their superiors rather than to act out their own beliefs. It may be urged that prohibitions against coercion are sufficient protection; but for many years the joint judgment of the Executive and Congress has been that to protect the rights of federal employees with respect to their jobs and their political acts and beliefs it is not enough merely to forbid one employee to attempt to influence or coerce another. For example, at the hearings in 1972 on proposed legislation for liberalizing the prohibition against political activity, the Chairman of the Civil Service Commission stated that "the prohibitions against active participation in partisan political management and partisan political campaigns constitute the most significant safeguards against coercion. . . ." Perhaps Congress at some time will come to a different view of the realities of political life and Government service; but that is its current view of the matter, and we are not now in any position to dispute it. Nor, in our view, does the Constitution forbid it.

. . . . [T]he District Court's judgment was that [the Hatch Act] was both unconstitutionally vague and fatally overbroad. Appellees make the same contentions here, but we cannot agree that the section is unconstitutional on its face for either reason.

Whatever might be the difficulty with a provision against taking "active part in political management or in political campaigns," the Act specifically provides that the employee retains the right to vote as he chooses and to express his opinion on political subjects and candidates. [T]he plain import of the 1940 amendment to the Hatch Act is that the proscription against taking an active part in the proscribed activities is not open-ended but is limited to those rules and proscriptions that had been developed under Civil Service Rule I up to the date of the passage of the 1940 Act. Those rules, as refined by further adjudications within the outer limits of the 1940 rules, were restated by the Commission in 1970 in the form of regulations specifying the conduct that would be prohibited or permitted by [the Act].

There might be quibbles about the meaning of taking an "active part in managing" or about "actively participating in... fund-raising" or about the meaning of becoming a "partisan" candidate for office; but there are limitations in the English language with respect to being both specific and manageably brief, and it seems to us that although the prohibitions may not satisfy those intent on finding fault at any cost, they are set out in terms that the ordinary person exercising ordinary common sense can sufficiently understand and comply with, without sacrifice to the public interest.

DOUGLAS, J., with whom BRENNAN, J., and MARSHALL, J., concur, dissenting.

There is no definition of what "an active part . . . in political campaigns" means. The Act incorporates over 3,000 rulings of the Civil Service Commission between 1886 and 1940 and many hundreds of rulings since 1940. But even with that gloss on the Act, the critical phrases lack precision. . . .

The present Act cannot be appropriately narrowed to meet the need for narrowly drawn language not embracing First Amendment speech or writing without substantial revision. That rewriting cannot be done by the Commission because Congress refused to delegate to it authority to regulate First Amendment rights.

I would strike this provision of the law down as unconstitutional so that a new start may be made on this old problem that confuses and restricts nearly five million federal, state, and local public employees today that live under the present Act.

AN EXTENDED NOTE ON LOYALTY OATHS AND POLITICAL PATRONAGE

From the perspective of the politically engaged government employee, the Supreme Court's First Amendment jurisprudence presents some good news and some bad news. The bad news is that in decisions like *National Ass'n of Letter Carriers*, the Court has been willing to uphold some very restrictive sets of rules, which strictly limit even mundane forms of political participation by government employees. On the other hand, the good news is that the Court has ruled that the First Amendment prohibits the government from imposing on employees ideological litmus tests, and also prohibits the government from enforcing on its employees a mandate of political conformity as a condition of their employment.

Some of the earliest cases in this area dealt with governmental attempts to exclude political leftists from government employment. In Wieman v. Updegraff, 344 U.S. 183 (1952), for example, the Court struck down an Oklahoma statute that required all state employees to sign a "loyalty oath" stating that during the previous five years the employee had not been a member of any organization listed by the Attorney General of the United States as "communist front" or "subversive." The Court struck down the statute because it did not distinguish between general membership in a political organization and membership driven by the specific intent to aid the organization in the illegal overthrow of the government by force or violence. The Court noted that "[t]here can be no dispute about the consequences visited upon a person excluded from public employment on disloyalty grounds. In the view of the community, the stain is a deep one; indeed, it has become a badge of infamy. Especially is this so in time of cold war and hot emotions when 'each man begins to eye his neighbor as a possible enemy.'"

As the Court moved into the 1960s and beyond, the Court shifted its focus from anti-Communist loyalty oaths to more mainstream forms of political patronage. In Elrod v. Burns, 427 U.S. 347 (1976), the Court took up the issue of political patronage in the context of the old Cook County Democratic Party machine of Mayor Richard Daley. In late 1970 the Republican Sheriff of Cook County was replaced by a Democrat, who upon taking office followed the local political tradition by replacing all non-civil-service employees of the Sheriff's Office with members of his own party. After noting the long history of political patronage in this country, Justice Brennan's plurality opinion turned to the costs the practice imposed on public employees. "In order to maintain their jobs, respondents were required to pledge their political allegiance to the Democratic Party, work for the election of other candidates of the Democratic Party, contribute a portion of their wages to the Party, or obtain the sponsorship of a member of the Party, usually at the price of one of the first three alternatives." The plurality concluded that these costs violated the protections the Court had already provided for public employees in the loyalty oath cases. "[I]f the government could deny a benefit to a person because of his constitutionally protected speech or associations, his exercise of those freedoms would in effect be penalized and inhibited. This would allow the government to 'produce a result which [it] could not command directly.'" Having established that the patronage requirement infringed on First Amendment rights of employees, the plurality then rejected all of the interests that the government offered to justify this infringement. These interests included "the need to insure effective government and the efficiency of public employees," "giving the employees of an incumbent party the incentive to perform well in order to insure their party's incumbency and thereby their jobs," and "the need for political loyalty of employees." The plurality held that limiting patronage dismissals to policymaking positions was sufficient to satisfy the government's legitimate interests. In Justice Stewart's concurring opinion, he agreed with the plurality opinion that a "nonpolicymaking, nonconfidential government employee" could not be "discharged or threatened with discharge from a job that he is satisfactorily performing upon the sole ground of his political beliefs."

Four years after it decided *Elrod*, the Court returned to the issue of political patronage to clarify the scope of the First Amendment defense to politically motivated firings of public employees. In Branti v. Finkel, 445 U.S. 507 (1980), the Court considered a case involving the firing of two assistant public defenders, who had been discharged based solely on their political affiliation. According to the Court, "[b]oth opinions in *Elrod* recognize that party affiliation may be an acceptable requirement for some types of government employment. Thus, if an employee's private political beliefs would interfere with the discharge of his public duties, his First Amendment rights may be required to yield to the State's vital interest in maintaining governmental effectiveness and efficiency." The Court went on to note, however, that it is not always easy to determine when an employee's political beliefs are relevant to that employee's job. The key to that determination, the Court held, was not whether someone is a "nonpolicymaking, nonconfidential government employee," but rather whether political affiliation is "an appropriate requirement for the effective performance of the public office involved." In *Branti* itself, the Court held, "it is manifest that the continued employment of an assistant public defender cannot properly be conditioned upon his allegiance to the political party in control of the county government. The primary, if not the only, responsibility of an assistant public defender is to represent individual citizens in controversy with the State. . . . Thus, whatever policymaking occurs in the public defender's office must relate to the needs of individual clients and not to any partisan political interests."

Both *Elrod* and *Branti* involved politically motivated discharges. In Rutan v. Republican Party of Illinois, 497 U.S. 62 (1990), the Court extended the rationale of those cases to cover politically motivated decisions to hire, promote, and transfer an employee. With regard to promotions and transfers, the Court held that *Elrod* and *Branti* must apply because otherwise employees "will feel a significant obligation to support political positions held by their superiors, and to refrain from acting on the political views they actually hold, in order to progress up the career ladder." With regard to hiring decisions, the Court held that applying the principles of *Elrod* and *Branti* was a logical extension of the long-standing axiom that the government "may not enact a regulation providing that no Republican . . . shall be appointed to federal office." Public Workers v. Mitchell, 330 U.S. 75, 100 (1947).

In O'Hare Truck Service, Inc. v. City of Northlake, 518 U.S. 712 (1996), the Court held that the same First Amendment principles that protect public employees against being discharged for refusing to support a political party or its candidates also extend to independent contractors. The plaintiff in *O'Hare* was a tow truck company that had worked under contract to the city of Northlake, Illinois, for 24 years. When the city's mayor ran for reelection, the plaintiff supported the mayor's opponent. After the mayor won reelection, the plaintiff's company was dropped from the list of tow truck companies used by the city. The Court noted that "[r]ecognizing the distinction [between employees and independent contractors] in these circumstances would invite manipulation by government, which could avoid constitutional liability simply by attaching different labels to particular jobs." The Court recognized that there were a wide range of permissible reasons for the government to exercise its discretion to retain or terminate independent contractors, including the need to "maintain stability, reward good performance, deal with known and reliable persons, or ensure the uninterrupted supply of goods or services." The Court went on to hold, however, that "it does not follow that this discretion can be exercised to impose conditions on expressing, or not expressing, specific political views."

In another application, the Court in Heffernan v. City of Paterson, 136 S. Ct. 1412 (2016), ruled it unconstitutional to demote a government employee based on the *mistaken* belief that the officer had engaged in political activity. The plaintiff in *Heffernan* was a police officer in Paterson, New Jersey, who was demoted after other police officers saw him with a sign for a mayoral candidate, leaving the impression that he supported the candidate. In fact, Heffernan was merely picking up the sign at the request of his bedridden mother. Justice Stephen G. Breyer, writing for the Court, recognized that "[w]hen an employer demotes an employee out of a desire to prevent the employee from engaging in political activity that the First Amendment protects, the employee is entitled to challenge that unlawful action under the First Amendment." That is true "even if, as here, the employer makes a factual mistake about the employee's behavior."

Do decisions such as *Elrod* and *Branti* in effect use the First Amendment to create a national civil service system? In his dissent to *Branti*, Justice Powell argued that "[t]he benefits of political patronage and the freedom of voters to structure their representative government are substantial governmental interests that justify the selection of the assistant public defenders of Rockland County on the basis of political affiliation. The decision to place certain governmental positions within a civil service system is a sensitive political judgment that should be left to the voters and to elected representatives of the people." What are the benefits of political patronage? Is it a sufficient response to this objection that state and local governments can continue to hire and fire employees without proving "cause" so long as they do not do so on the basis of a narrow range of constitutional criteria such as political affiliation, religion, or race? As Justice Brennan summed up the Court's position in *Rutan*: "To the victor belongs only those spoils that may be constitutionally obtained."

C. PUBLIC SCHOOLS AND LIBRARIES

TINKER v.
DES MOINES INDEPENDENT COMMUNITY SCHOOL DISTRICT
393 U.S. 503 (1969)

FORTAS, J., delivered the opinion of the Court.

Petitioner John F. Tinker, 15 years old, and petitioner Christopher Eckhardt, 16 years old, attended high schools in Des Moines, Iowa. Petitioner Mary Beth Tinker, John's sister, was a 13-year-old student in junior high school.

In December 1965, a group of adults and students in Des Moines held a meeting at the Eckhardt home. The group determined to publicize their objections to the hostilities in Vietnam and their support for a truce by wearing black armbands during the holiday season and by fasting on December 16 and New Year's Eve. Petitioners and their parents had previously engaged in similar activities, and they decided to participate in the program.

The principals of the Des Moines schools became aware of the plan to wear armbands. On December 14, 1965, they met and adopted a policy that any student wearing an armband to school would be asked to remove it, and if he refused he would be suspended until he returned without the armband. Petitioners were aware of the regulation that the school authorities adopted.

On December 16, Mary Beth and Christopher wore black armbands to their schools. John Tinker wore his armband the next day. They were all sent home and suspended from school until they would come back without their armbands. They did not return to school until after the planned period for wearing armbands had expired—that is, until after New Year's Day.

[Petitioners then filed suit in federal court, seeking] an injunction restraining the respondent school officials and the respondent members of the board of directors of the school district from disciplining the petitioners.

[T]he wearing of armbands in the circumstances of this case was entirely divorced from actually or potentially disruptive conduct by those participating in it. It was closely akin to "pure speech" which, we have repeatedly held, is entitled to comprehensive protection under the First Amendment.

First Amendment rights, applied in light of the special characteristics of the school environment, are available to teachers and students. It can hardly be argued that either students or teachers shed their constitutional rights to freedom of speech or expression at the schoolhouse gate.

On the other hand, the Court has repeatedly emphasized the need for affirming the comprehensive authority of the States and of school officials, consistent with fundamental constitutional safeguards, to prescribe and control conduct in the schools. Our problem lies in the area where students in the exercise of First Amendment rights collide with the rules of the school authorities.

The school officials banned and sought to punish petitioners for a silent, passive expression of opinion, unaccompanied by any disorder or disturbance on the part of petitioners. There is here no evidence whatever of petitioners' interference, actual or nascent, with the schools' work or of collision with the rights of other students to be secure and to be let alone. Accordingly, this case does not concern speech or action that intrudes upon the work of the schools or the rights of other students.

Only a few of the 18,000 students in the school system wore the black armbands. Only five students were suspended for wearing them. There is no indication that the work of the schools or any class was disrupted. Outside the classrooms, a few students made hostile remarks to the children wearing armbands, but there were no threats or acts of violence on school premises.

The District Court concluded that the action of the school authorities was reasonable because it was based upon their fear of a disturbance from the wearing of the armbands. But, in our system, undifferentiated fear or apprehension of disturbance is not enough to overcome the right to freedom of expression. Any departure from absolute regimentation may cause trouble. Any variation from the majority's opinion may inspire fear. Any word spoken, in class, in the lunchroom, or on the campus, that deviates from the views of another person may start an argument or cause a disturbance. But our Constitution says we must take this risk, and our history says that it is this sort of hazardous freedom—this kind of openness—that is the basis of our national strength and of the independence and vigor of Americans who grow up and live in this relatively permissive, often disputatious, society.

In order for the State in the person of school officials to justify prohibition of a particular expression of opinion, it must be able to show that its action was caused by something more than a mere desire to avoid the discomfort and unpleasantness that always accompany an unpopular viewpoint. Certainly where there is no finding and no showing that engaging in the forbidden conduct would "materially and substantially interfere with the requirements of appropriate discipline in the operation of the school," the prohibition cannot be sustained.

It is also relevant that the school authorities did not purport to prohibit the wearing of all symbols of political or controversial significance. The record shows that students in some of the schools wore buttons relating to national political campaigns, and some even wore the Iron Cross, traditionally a symbol of Nazism. The order prohibiting the wearing of armbands did not extend to these. Instead, a particular symbol—black armbands worn to exhibit opposition to this Nation's involvement in Vietnam—was singled out for prohibition. Clearly, the prohibition of expression of one particular opinion, at least without evidence that it is necessary to avoid material and substantial interference with schoolwork or discipline, is not constitutionally permissible.

In our system, state-operated schools may not be enclaves of totalitarianism. School officials do not possess absolute authority over their students. Students in school as well as out of school are "persons" under our Constitution. They are possessed of fundamental rights which the State must respect, just as they themselves must respect their obligations to the State. In our system, students may not be regarded as closed-circuit recipients of only that which the State chooses to communicate. They may not be confined to the expression of those sentiments that are officially approved. In the absence of a specific showing of constitutionally valid reasons to regulate their speech, students are entitled to freedom of expression of their views. As Judge Gewin, speaking for the Fifth Circuit, said, school officials cannot suppress "expressions of feelings with which they do not wish to contend."

Under our Constitution, free speech is not a right that is given only to be so circumscribed that it exists in principle but not in fact. Freedom of expression would not truly exist if the right could be exercised only in an area that a benevolent government has provided as a safe haven for crackpots. The Constitution says that Congress (and the States) may not abridge the right to free speech. This provision means what it says. We properly read it to permit reasonable regulation of speech-connected activities in carefully restricted circumstances. But we do not confine the permissible exercise of First Amendment rights to a telephone booth or the four corners of a pamphlet, or to supervised and ordained discussion in a school classroom.

BLACK, J., dissenting.

The Court's holding in this case ushers in what I deem to be an entirely new era in which the power to control pupils by the elected "officials of state supported public schools . . ." in the United States is in ultimate effect transferred to the Supreme Court.

    . . . The original idea of schools, which I do not believe is yet abandoned as worthless or out of date, was that children had not yet reached the point of experience and wisdom which enabled them to teach all of their elders. It may be that the Nation has outworn the old-fashioned slogan that "children are to be seen not heard," but one may, I hope, be permitted to harbor the thought that taxpayers send children to school on the premise that at their age they need to learn, not teach.

[The concurring opinions of Justices Stewart and White, and the dissenting opinion of Harlan, J., are omitted.]

NOTES AND QUESTIONS

1. *The general themes of* Tinker. *Tinker* is the foundation of the Court's student-speech cases, and in many ways *Tinker* simply involves the application of long-standing First Amendment principles to the school context. One aspect of *Tinker*, for example, prohibits school authorities from engaging in content or viewpoint regulation of student speech. *See* R.A.V. v. St. Paul, *supra* p. 540. Another aspect of *Tinker* focuses on the compatibility of student speech with the pedagogical requirements of an educational institution. *See* Grayned v. Rockford, 408 U.S. 104 (1972). Still another aspect of *Tinker* emphasizes the need for time, place, and manner restrictions on disruptive speech. *See* Ward v. Rock Against Racism, 491 U.S. 781 (1989). The overriding theme of the case, however, is that students have many of the same First Amendment rights as adults to express opinions that the government may not like. When reading the next three student-speech cases, reflect on the extent to which the Court has subsequently abandoned this last proposition, in favor of the contrary notion that students generally can be viewed as wards of the state while at school, and in that context should not expect to be afforded anything approaching the same First Amendment rights as adults.

2. *The pragmatics of* Tinker: *The parameters of "disruption."* The linchpin of *Tinker* is its holding that students have First Amendment rights of free speech except when the student speech would "materially and substantially disrupt the work and discipline of the school." The key to enforcing *Tinker*, therefore, is determining when a student's speech becomes so disruptive that it interferes with the educational functions of the school. The subsequent cases applying *Tinker* have given school officials a fair amount of leeway in applying this disruption standard. The lower court cases consistently have held that school officials do not have to wait to silence potentially disruptive speech until the disruption actually occurs, nor do school officials have to produce definitive evidence that disruption will occur. Moreover, the cases routinely apply the disruption analysis to an overall context that includes the hostile responses of listeners to the student speech. Note that this is somewhat inconsistent with the rule the Court applies outside the school context, where the Court generally does not permit governments to regulate potentially disruptive speech based on hostile listeners' response to that speech. *See* Boos v. Barry, 485 U.S. 312, 321 (1988) (striking down a statute regulating signs bringing foreign governments into "public odium" or "public disrepute" within 500 feet of foreign embassies, and holding

that the statute was impermissibly content-based because the statute regulated "the content of the speech and the direct impact that speech has on its listeners. The emotive impact of speech on its audience is not a 'secondary effect.'"). Does the consideration of antagonistic listener responses as part of the assessment of "disruption" in the school context invite the "heckler's veto"? Does this consideration also raise the possibility that speakers who are engaged in the most unpopular speech, or who are in an extreme minority in a particular school, will be protected less vigorously under *Tinker* than more moderate or more popular speakers (because speech by less popular or less numerous speakers will be more likely to engender disruptive responses from hostile listeners)?

BETHEL SCHOOL DISTRICT NO. 403 v. FRASER

478 U.S. 675 (1986)

BURGER, C.J., delivered the opinion of the Court

On April 26, 1983, respondent Matthew N. Fraser, a student at Bethel High School in Pierce County, Washington, delivered a speech nominating a fellow student for student elective office. Approximately 600 high school students, many of whom were 14-year-olds, attended the assembly. Students were required to attend the assembly or to report to the study hall. The assembly was part of a school-sponsored educational program in self-government. Students who elected not to attend the assembly were required to report to study hall. During the entire speech, Fraser referred to his candidate in terms of an elaborate, graphic, and explicit sexual metaphor.

[*Editor's note*: Chief Justice Burger does not quote the speech in his majority opinion. Justice Brennan does quote the speech in his concurring opinion, however. This is the full text of the speech Fraser gave to the assembly:

I know a man who is firm—he's firm in his pants, he's firm in his shirt, his character is firm—but most . . . of all, his belief in you, the students of Bethel, is firm.

Jeff Kuhlman is a man who takes his point and pounds it in. If necessary, he'll take an issue and nail it to the wall. He doesn't attack things in spurts—he drives hard, pushing and pushing until finally—he succeeds.

Jeff is a man who will go to the very end—even the climax, for each and every one of you.

So vote for Jeff for A.S.B. vice-president—he'll never come between you and the best our high school can be.]

Two of Fraser's teachers, with whom he discussed the contents of his speech in advance, informed him that the speech was "inappropriate and that he probably should not deliver it," and that his delivery of the speech might have "severe consequences."

During Fraser's delivery of the speech, a school counselor observed the reaction of students to the speech. Some students hooted and yelled; some by gestures graphically simulated the sexual activities pointedly alluded to in respondent's speech. Other students appeared to be bewildered and embarrassed by the speech. One teacher reported that on the day following the speech, she found it necessary to forgo a portion of the scheduled class lesson in order to discuss the speech with the class.

A Bethel High School disciplinary rule prohibiting the use of obscene language in the school provides: "Conduct which materially and substantially interferes with the educational process is prohibited, including the use of obscene, profane language or gestures."

The morning after the assembly, the Assistant Principal called Fraser into her office and notified him that the school considered his speech to have been a violation of this rule. Fraser was presented with copies of five letters submitted by teachers, describing his conduct at the assembly; he was given a chance to explain his conduct, and he admitted to having given the speech described and that he deliberately used sexual innuendo in the speech. Fraser was then informed that he would be suspended for three days, and that his name would be removed from the list of candidates for graduation speaker at the school's commencement exercises.

[The school board's hearing officer affirmed the suspension, and Fraser sued in federal court, claiming a violation of his First Amendment right to free speech. The district court ruled in Fraser's favor, and the United States Court of Appeals for the Ninth Circuit affirmed, holding that Fraser's speech was indistinguishable from the speech at issue in *Tinker*. The Supreme Court reversed.]

The marked distinction between the political "message" of the armbands in Tinker and the sexual content of respondent's speech in this case seems to have been given little weight by the Court of Appeals. In upholding the students' right to engage in a nondisruptive, passive expression of a political viewpoint in *Tinker*, this Court was careful to note that the case did "not concern speech or action that intrudes upon the work of the schools or the rights of other students."

The role and purpose of the American public school system were well described by two historians, who stated: "[P]ublic education must prepare pupils for citizenship in the Republic. . . . It must inculcate the habits and manners of civility as values in themselves conducive to happiness and as indispensable to the practice of self-government in the community and the nation." C. Beard & M. Beard, New Basic History of the United States 228 (1968). In *Ambach v. Norwick*, 441 U.S. 68, 76-77 (1979), we echoed the essence of this statement of the objectives of public education as the "inculcat[ion of] fundamental values necessary to the maintenance of a democratic political system."

These fundamental values of "habits and manners of civility" essential to a democratic society must, of course, include tolerance of divergent political and religious views, even when the views expressed may be unpopular. But these "fundamental values" must also take into account consideration of the sensibilities of others, and, in the case of a school, the sensibilities of fellow students. The undoubted freedom to advocate unpopular and controversial views in schools and classrooms must be balanced against the society's countervailing interest in teaching students the boundaries of socially appropriate behavior. Even the most heated political discourse in a democratic society requires consideration for the personal sensibilities of the other participants and audiences.

The First Amendment guarantees wide freedom in matters of adult public discourse. A sharply divided Court upheld the right to express an antidraft viewpoint in a public place, albeit in terms highly offensive to most citizens. See *Cohen v. California*, [*supra* p. 523]. It does not follow, however, that simply because the use of an offensive form of expression may not be prohibited to adults making what the speaker considers a political point, the same latitude must be permitted to children in a public school. [T]he constitutional rights of students in public school are not automatically coextensive with the rights of adults in other settings. As cogently expressed by Judge Newman, "the First Amendment gives a high school student the classroom right to wear Tinker's armband, but not Cohen's jacket." *Thomas v. Board of Education, Granville Central School Dist.*, 607 F.2d 1043, 1057 (CA2 1979) (opinion concurring in result).

The process of educating our youth for citizenship in public schools is not confined to books, the curriculum, and the civics class; schools must teach by example the shared values of a civilized social order. Consciously or otherwise, teachers—and indeed the older students—demonstrate the appropriate form of civil discourse and political expression by their conduct and deportment in and out of class. Inescapably, like parents, they are role models. The schools, as instruments of the state, may determine that the essential lessons of civil, mature conduct cannot be conveyed in a school that tolerates lewd, indecent, or offensive speech and conduct such as that indulged in by this confused boy.

The pervasive sexual innuendo in Fraser's speech was plainly offensive to both teachers and students—indeed to any mature person. By glorifying male sexuality, and in its verbal content, the speech was acutely insulting to teenage girl students. The speech could well be seriously damaging to its less mature audience, many of whom were only 14 years old and on the threshold of awareness of human sexuality. Some students were reported as bewildered by the speech and the reaction of mimicry it provoked.

We hold that petitioner School District acted entirely within its permissible authority in imposing sanctions upon Fraser in response to his offensively lewd and indecent speech. Unlike the sanctions imposed on the students wearing armbands in *Tinker*, the penalties imposed in this case were unrelated to any political viewpoint. The First Amendment does not prevent the school officials from determining that to permit a vulgar and lewd speech such as respondent's would undermine the school's basic educational mission.

STEVENS, J., dissenting.

"Frankly, my dear, I don't give a damn."

When I was a high school student, the use of those words in a public forum shocked the Nation. Today Clark Gable's four-letter expletive is less offensive than it was then. Nevertheless, I assume that high school administrators may prohibit the use of that word in classroom discussion and even in extracurricular activities that are sponsored by the school and held on school premises. For I believe a school faculty must regulate the content as well as the style of student speech in carrying out its educational mission. It does seem to me, however, that if a student is to be punished for using offensive speech, he is entitled to fair notice of the scope of the prohibition and the consequences of its violation. The interest in free speech protected by the First Amendment and the interest in fair procedure protected by the Due Process Clause of the Fourteenth Amendment combine to require this conclusion.

. . . At the time the discipline was imposed, as well as in its defense of this lawsuit, the school took the position that respondent violated [a rule prohibiting "disruptive conduct"—that is, "conduct which materially and substantially interferes with the educational process . . ., including the use of obscene, profane language or gestures."]

. . . [T]he evidence in the record, as interpreted by the District Court and the Court of Appeals, makes it perfectly clear that respondent's speech was not "conduct" prohibited by the disciplinary rule. . . .

It seems fairly obvious that respondent's speech would be inappropriate in certain classroom and formal social settings. On the other hand, in a locker room or perhaps in a school corridor the metaphor in the speech might be regarded as rather routine comment. If this be true, and if respondent's audience consisted almost entirely of young people with whom he conversed on a daily basis, can we—at this distance—confidently assert that he must have known that the school administration would punish him for delivering it?

For three reasons, I think not. First, it seems highly unlikely that he would have decided to deliver the speech if he had known that it would result in his suspension and disqualification from delivering the school commencement address. Second, I believe a strong presumption in favor of free expression should apply whenever an issue of this kind is arguable. Third, because the Court has adopted the policy of applying contemporary community standards in evaluating expression with sexual connotations, this Court should defer to the views of the district and circuit judges who are in a much better position to evaluate this speech than we are.

AN EXTENDED NOTE ON THE "VULGARITY" EXCEPTION

Fraser is commonly interpreted as introducing a "vulgarity" exception to the protection of student speech described in *Tinker*, and in fact Chief Justice Burger's majority opinion in *Fraser* focuses on the sexual innuendo in Fraser's speech. Note that in *Fraser* the Court applies this vulgarity exception to a student engaged in the most highly protected form of free speech—a campaign speech on behalf of a political candidate. The significant question in *Fraser* is: When is student speech so "vulgar" that it loses First Amendment protection even when uttered in what would otherwise be one of the most highly protected free speech circumstances? In answering this question, recall Chief Justice Burger's broad rationale for giving the Bethel school officials authority to regulate Fraser's speech: "The undoubted freedom to advocate unpopular and controversial views in schools and classrooms must be balanced against the society's countervailing interest in teaching students the boundaries of socially appropriate behavior. Even the most heated political discourse in a democratic society requires consideration for the personal sensibilities of the other participants and audiences." Many lower courts have taken this rationale to heart, and have interpreted the concept of "vulgarity" to include general concepts of social decorum that have nothing to do with sex or sexuality.

Consider the following scenario. A student running for president of the student council at a public high school gives a speech at an election campaign assembly for all the candidates. His speech includes the following passage:

> The administration plays tricks with your mind and they hope you won't notice. For example, why does Mr. Davidson stutter while he is on the intercom? He doesn't have a speech impediment. If you want to break the iron grip of this school, vote for me for president. I can try to bring back student rights that you have missed and maybe get things that you have always wanted. All you have to do is vote for me, Dean Poling.

At the conclusion of this speech, "many of the students jumped up at the reference to Mr. Davidson (the assistant principal in charge of discipline at the school), clapped their hands, and yelled things like 'way to go, Dean,' and 'we don't like him either.'" The school principal on the other hand, was "quite upset," adding that "I thought that the content of this speech was inappropriate, disruptive of school discipline, and in bad taste." The other candidates on the ballot for student council president were also displeased. They approached a guidance counselor "and complained that Dean Poling had gained an unfair advantage in the election by saying what he had said about Mr. Davidson." School officials responded to these complaints by announcing that Mr. Poling would not be allowed to run for student council president, and that any votes cast for him would not be counted.

Does this scenario seem to fit the model of "vulgarity" set forth in *Fraser*? The Sixth Circuit Court of Appeals thought so. In Poling v. Murphy, 872 F.2d 757 (6th Cir. 1989), *cert. denied*, 493 U.S. 1021 (1990), a divided panel of the Sixth Circuit rejected Mr. Poling's claim that school officials violated his First Amendment rights when they excluded him from the election. The court held that this case was controlled by the rules of *Fraser* and *Kuhlmeier*, rather than *Tinker*. With regard to *Fraser*, the court referred to the school's legitimate concern with teaching its students the "shared values of the civilized social order." According to the court, "these 'shared values' [sometimes] come in conflict with one another; independence of thought and frankness of expression occupy a high place on our scale of values, or ought to, but so too do discipline, courtesy, and respect for authority. Judgments on how best to balance such values may well vary from school to school. Television has not yet so thoroughly homogenized us that conduct deemed unexceptionable in New York City, for example, will necessarily be considered acceptable in rural Tennessee." *Id.* at 762.

Might a geographical dichotomy in attitudes toward profanity or sexual mores explain cases such as B.H. v. Easton Area School District, 725 F.3d 293 (2013)? There, the Third Circuit Court of Appeals, sitting in Philadelphia, ruled in favor of two students who were punished for wearing "I Heart Boobies (Keep A Breast)" bracelets to promote breast cancer awareness at their school. Relying on *Fraser*, the school board argued that the breast cancer bracelets could be misinterpreted as "lewd, vulgar, profane, or plainly offensive student speech." But an *en banc* panel of the Third Circuit clarified that schools, under *Fraser*, "may restrict ambiguously lewd speech only if it cannot plausibly be interpreted as commenting on a social or political matter." The court said the school district could not categorically ban the bracelets because they "are not plainly lewd and express support for . . . [an] unquestionably . . . important social issue." *Id.* at 302.

HAZELWOOD SCHOOL DISTRICT v. KUHLMEIER

484 U.S. 260 (1988)

WHITE, J., delivered the opinion of the Court.

Respondents are three former Hazelwood East students who were staff members of Spectrum, the school newspaper. They contend that school officials violated their First Amendment rights by deleting two pages of articles from the May 13, 1983, issue of Spectrum.

Spectrum was written and edited by the Journalism II class at Hazelwood East. The newspaper was published every three weeks or so during the 1982-1983 school year. More than 4,500 copies of the newspaper were distributed during that year to students, school personnel, and members of the community.

The costs associated with the newspaper—such as supplies, textbooks, and a portion of the journalism teacher's salary—were borne entirely by the Board.

The practice at Hazelwood East during the spring 1983 semester was for the journalism teacher to submit page proofs of each Spectrum issue to Principal Reynolds for his review prior to publication. On May 10, Emerson delivered the proofs of the May 13 edition to Reynolds, who objected to two of the articles scheduled to appear in that edition. One of the stories described three Hazelwood East students' experiences with pregnancy; the other discussed the impact of divorce on students at the school.

Reynolds was concerned that, although the pregnancy story used false names "to keep the identity of these girls a secret," the pregnant students still might be identifiable from the text. He also believed that the article's references to sexual activity and birth control were inappropriate for some of the younger students at the school. In addition, Reynolds was concerned that a student identified by name in the divorce story had complained that her father "wasn't spending enough time with my mom, my sister and I" prior to the divorce, "was always out of town on business or out late playing cards with the guys," and "always argued about everything" with her mother. Reynolds believed that the student's parents should have been given an opportunity to respond to these remarks or to consent to their publication. He was unaware that Emerson had deleted the student's name from the final version of the article.

Reynolds believed that there was no time to make the necessary changes in the stories before the scheduled press run and that the newspaper would not appear before the end of the school year if printing were delayed to any significant extent. He concluded that his only options under the circumstances were to publish a four-page newspaper instead of the planned six-page newspaper, eliminating the two pages on which the offending stories appeared, or to publish no newspaper at all. Accordingly, he directed Emerson to withhold from publication the two pages containing the stories on pregnancy and divorce.

[The students sued, claiming that the Principal's decision not to publish the two stories violated the students' First Amendment rights.]

We deal first with the question whether Spectrum may appropriately be characterized as a forum for public expression.

The policy of school officials toward Spectrum was reflected in Hazelwood School Board Policy 348.51 and the Hazelwood East Curriculum Guide. Board Policy 348.51 provided that "[s]chool sponsored publications are developed within the adopted curriculum and its educational implications in regular classroom activities." The Hazelwood East Curriculum Guide described the Journalism II course as a "laboratory situation in which the students publish the school newspaper applying skills they have learned in Journalism I." The lessons that were to be learned from the Journalism II course, according to the Curriculum Guide, included development of journalistic skills under deadline pressure, "the legal, moral, and ethical restrictions imposed upon journalists within the school community," and "responsibility and acceptance of criticism for articles of opinion." Journalism II was taught by a faculty member during regular class hours. Students received grades and academic credit for their performance in the course.

One might reasonably infer from the full text of Policy 348.51 that school officials retained ultimate control over what constituted "responsible journalism" in a school-sponsored newspaper. Although the Statement of Policy published in the September 14, 1982, issue of *Spectrum* declared that "*Spectrum*, as a student-press publication, accepts all rights implied by the First Amendment," this statement, understood in the context of the paper's role in the school's curriculum, suggests at most that the administration will not interfere with the students' exercise of those First Amendment rights that attend the publication of a school-sponsored newspaper. It does not reflect an intent to expand those rights by converting a curricular newspaper into a public forum. School officials did not evince either "by policy or by practice," any intent to open the pages of Spectrum to "indiscriminate use," by its student reporters and editors, or by the student body generally. Instead, they "reserve[d] the forum for its intended purpos[e]," as a supervised learning experience for journalism students. Accordingly, school officials were entitled to regulate the contents of Spectrum in any reasonable manner. It is this standard, rather than our decision in *Tinker*, that governs this case.

The question whether the First Amendment requires a school to tolerate particular student speech—the question that we addressed in *Tinker*—is different from the question whether the First Amendment requires a school affirmatively to promote particular student speech. The former question addresses educators' ability to silence a student's personal expression that happens to occur on the school premises. The latter question concerns educators' authority over school-sponsored publications, theatrical productions, and other expressive activities that students, parents, and members of the public might reasonably perceive to bear the imprimatur of the school. These activities may fairly be characterized as part of the school curriculum, whether or not they occur in a traditional classroom setting, so long as they are supervised by faculty members and designed to impart particular knowledge or skills to student participants and audiences.

Educators are entitled to exercise greater control over this second form of student expression to assure that participants learn whatever lessons the activity is designed to teach, that readers or listeners are not exposed to material that may be inappropriate for their level of maturity, and that the views of the individual speaker are not erroneously attributed to the school. Hence, a school may in its capacity as publisher of a school newspaper or producer of a school play "disassociate itself," *Fraser*, not only from speech that would "substantially interfere with [its] work . . . or impinge upon the rights of other students," *Tinker*, but also from speech that is, for example, ungrammatical, poorly written, inadequately researched, biased or prejudiced, vulgar or profane, or unsuitable for immature audiences. A school must be able to set high standards for the student speech that is disseminated under its auspices—standards that may be higher than those demanded by some newspaper publishers or theatrical producers in the "real" world—and may refuse to disseminate student speech that does not meet those standards. In addition, a school must be able to take into account the emotional maturity of the intended audience in determining whether to disseminate student speech on potentially sensitive topics, which might range from the existence of Santa Claus in an elementary school setting to the particulars of teenage sexual activity in a high school setting. A school must also retain the authority to refuse to sponsor student speech that might reasonably be perceived to advocate drug or alcohol use, irresponsible sex, or conduct otherwise inconsistent with "the shared values of a civilized social order," *Fraser*, or to associate the school with any position other than neutrality on matters of political controversy.

Accordingly, we conclude that the standard articulated in *Tinker* for determining when a school may punish student expression need not also be the standard for determining when a school may refuse to lend its name and resources to the dissemination of student expression. Instead, we hold that educators do not offend the First Amendment by exercising editorial control over the style and content of student speech in school-sponsored expressive activities so long as their actions are reasonably related to legitimate pedagogical concerns.

It is only when the decision to censor a school-sponsored publication, theatrical production, or other vehicle of student expression has no valid educational purpose that the First Amendment is so "directly and sharply implicate[d]," [*Epperson v. Arkansas, infra* p. 910], as to require judicial intervention to protect students' constitutional rights.

BRENNAN, J., with whom MARSHALL, J., and BLACKMUN, J., join, dissenting.

When the young men and women of Hazelwood East High School registered for Journalism II, they expected a civics lesson. Spectrum, the newspaper they were to publish, "was not just a class exercise in which students learned to prepare papers and hone writing skills, it was a . . . forum established to give students an opportunity to express their views while gaining an appreciation of their rights and responsibilities under the First Amendment to the United States Constitution. . . ." 795 F.2d 1368, 1373 (CA8 1986). "[A]t the beginning of each school year," the student journalists published a Statement of Policy—tacitly approved each year by school authorities—announcing their expectation that "*Spectrum*, as a student-press publication, accepts all rights implied by the First Amendment. . . . Only speech that 'materially and substantially interferes with the requirements of appropriate discipline' can be found unacceptable and therefore prohibited." ([Q]uoting *Tinker.*) The school board itself affirmatively guaranteed the students of Journalism II an atmosphere conducive to fostering such an appreciation and exercising the full panoply of rights associated with a free student press. "School sponsored student publications," it vowed, "will not restrict free expression or diverse viewpoints within the rules of responsible journalism."

This case arose when the Hazelwood East administration breached its own promise, dashing its students' expectations. The school principal, without prior consultation or explanation, excised six articles—comprising two full pages—of the May 13, 1983, issue of Spectrum. He did so not because any of the articles would "materially and substantially interfere with the requirements of appropriate discipline," but simply because he considered two of the six "inappropriate, personal, sensitive, and unsuitable" for student consumption.

In my view the principal broke more than just a promise. He violated the First Amendment's prohibitions against censorship of any student expression that neither disrupts classwork nor invades the rights of others, and against any censorship that is not narrowly tailored to serve its purpose.

Free student expression undoubtedly sometimes interferes with the effectiveness of the school's pedagogical functions. Some brands of student expression do so by directly preventing the school from pursuing its pedagogical mission: The young polemic who stands on a soapbox during calculus class to deliver an eloquent political diatribe interferes with the legitimate teaching of calculus. And the student who delivers a lewd endorsement of a student-government candidate might so extremely distract an impressionable high school audience as to interfere with the orderly operation of the school. See *Bethel.* Other student speech, however, frustrates the school's legitimate pedagogical purposes merely by expressing a message that conflicts with the school's, without directly interfering with the school's expression of its message: A student who responds to a political science teacher's question with the retort, "socialism is good," subverts the school's inculcation of the message that capitalism is better. Even the maverick who sits in class passively sporting a symbol of protest against a government policy, cf. *Tinker*, or the gossip who sits in the student commons swapping stories of sexual escapade could readily muddle a clear official message condoning the government policy or condemning teenage sex. Likewise, the student newspaper that, like Spectrum, conveys a moral position at odds with the school's official stance might subvert the administration's legitimate inculcation of its own perception of community values.

If mere incompatibility with the school's pedagogical message were a constitutionally sufficient justification for the suppression of student speech, school officials could censor each of the students or student organizations in the foregoing hypotheticals, converting our public schools into "enclaves of totalitarianism," *id.*, that "strangle the free mind at its source," *West Virginia Board of Education v. Barnette*. The First Amendment permits no such blanket censorship authority.

NOTES AND QUESTIONS

1. *What is curricular?* Each of the Supreme Court's student-speech cases has one main concept that is central to that case's application. In *Tinker*, that concept is "disruption." In *Fraser*, that concept is "vulgarity." In *Kuhlmeier*, the key concept is "curricular." The crucial language in *Kuhlmeier* grants school officials the authority to regulate or proscribe student speech with regard to "activities [that] may fairly be characterized as part of the school curriculum, whether or not they occur in a traditional classroom setting, so long as they are supervised by faculty members and designed to impart particular knowledge or skills to student participants and audiences." As with the central concepts of the Court's other student-speech cases, the lower courts have tended to interpret the *Kuhlmeier* concept of "curricular activities" very broadly. Language in one Tenth Circuit Court of Appeals opinion is typical. According to that court, *Kuhlmeier* applies not just to activities that are directly integrated into the school's classroom instruction but also to "activities that might reasonably be perceived to bear the imprimatur of the school and that involve pedagogical concerns." Fleming v. Jefferson County Sch. Dist. R1, 298 F.3d 918, 923 (10th Cir. 2002). Under this broad reading, lower courts have applied the *Kuhlmeier* analysis to several different aspects of the educational experience outside the traditional classroom setting. *See id.* (decorative tiles placed outside a high school); Planned Parenthood of S. Nev., Inc. v. Clark County Sch. Dist., 941 F.2d 817 (9th Cir. 1991) (advertisements in programs distributed at athletic events); Poling v. Murphy, 872 F.2d 757 (6th Cir. 1989) (student government elections); Crosby v. Holsinger, 852 F.2d 801 (4th Cir. 1988) (school mascot); Brody v. Spang, 957 F.2d 1108 (3d Cir. 1992) (commencement exercises); Lundberg v. West Monona Cmty. Sch. Dist., 731 F. Supp. 331 (N.D. Iowa 1989) (same); Golden v. Rossford Exempted Vill. Sch. Dist., 445 F. Supp. 2d 820 (N.D. Ohio 2006) (student assemblies).

2. *College Students and Professionalism as Basis for Discipline*: In Tatro v. Univ. of Minn., 816 N.W.2d 509 (Minn. 2012), the Minnesota Supreme Court upheld a state university's right to discipline a student in a Mortuary Science Program who discussed her human cadaver in an irreverent way using social media, in violation of university policies governing mortuary science students that the court found to be narrowly tailored to achieve professionalism objectives. Can a state university discipline a student in its M.B.A program for posting on

Facebook that "my professor is so boring I want to gouge my eyes out with pencils during her class"? What if the student posts: "The girl who sits next to me in Accounting is a 10"? Does it matter whether the Facebook posts are set to be public or not?

3. Kuhlmeier *and teachers' rights.* The Supreme Court has never addressed the issue of whether teachers below the university level have academic freedom rights protected by the First Amendment. Several lower courts, however, have cited *Kuhlmeier* for the proposition that a school board's control of the curriculum gives it virtually complete authority to dictate how teachers conduct their class and what they teach. *See, e.g.,* Boring v. Buncombe County Bd. of Educ., 136 F.3d 364 (4th Cir.), *cert. denied,* 525 U.S. 813 (1998) (citing *Kuhlmeier* in upholding the transfer of a teacher after the teacher used a controversial play in her theater class); Kirkland v. Northside Indep. Sch. Dist., 890 F.2d 794 (5th Cir. 1989), *cert. denied,* 496 U.S. 926 (1990) (citing *Kuhlmeier* in upholding the nonrenewal of a teacher who used an unapproved supplemental reading list in his class). For extended discussion of the speech rights of public school teachers, *see* Mary-Rose Papandrea, *Social Media, Public School Teachers, and the First Amendment,* 90 N.C. L. Rev. 1597 (2012).

MORSE v. FREDERICK

551 U.S. 393 (2007)

ROBERTS, C.J., delivered the opinion of the Court.

On January 24, 2002, the Olympic Torch Relay passed through Juneau, Alaska, on its way to the winter games in Salt Lake City, Utah. The torchbearers were to proceed along a street in front of Juneau-Douglas High School (JDHS) while school was in session. Petitioner Deborah Morse, the school principal, decided to permit staff and students to participate in the Torch Relay as an approved social event or class trip. Students were allowed to leave class to observe the relay from either side of the street. Teachers and administrative officials monitored the students' actions.

Respondent Joseph Frederick, a JDHS senior, was late to school that day. When he arrived, he joined his friends (all but one of whom were JDHS students) across the street from the school to watch the event. Not all the students waited patiently. Some became rambunctious, throwing plastic cola bottles and snowballs and scuffling with their classmates. As the torchbearers and camera crews passed by, Frederick and his friends unfurled a 14-foot banner bearing the phrase: "BONG HiTS 4 JESUS." The large banner was easily readable by the students on the other side of the street.

Principal Morse immediately crossed the street and demanded that the banner be taken down. Everyone but Frederick complied. Morse confiscated the banner and told Frederick to report to her office, where she suspended him for 10 days. Morse later explained that she told Frederick to take the banner down because she thought it encouraged illegal drug use, in violation of established school policy. Juneau School Board Policy No. 5520 states: "The Board specifically prohibits any assembly or public expression that . . . advocates the use of substances that are illegal to minors. . . ."

Frederick administratively appealed his suspension, but the Juneau School District Superintendent upheld it, limiting it to time served (8 days). In a memorandum setting forth his reasons, the superintendent determined that Frederick had displayed his banner "in the midst of his fellow students, during school hours, at a school-sanctioned activity." He further explained that Frederick "was not disciplined because the principal of the school 'disagreed' with his message, but because his speech appeared to advocate the use of illegal drugs."

The superintendent continued:

> "The common-sense understanding of the phrase 'bong hits' is that it is a reference to a means of smoking marijuana. Given [Frederick's] inability or unwillingness to express any other credible meaning for the phrase, I can only agree with the principal and countless others who saw the banner as advocating the use of illegal drugs. [Frederick's] speech was not political. He was not advocating the legalization of marijuana or promoting a religious belief. He was displaying a fairly silly message promoting illegal drug usage in the midst of a school activity, for the benefit of television cameras covering the Torch Relay. [Frederick's] speech was potentially disruptive to the event and clearly disruptive of and inconsistent with the school's educational mission to educate students about the dangers of illegal drugs and to discourage their use."

II.

At the outset, we reject Frederick's argument that this is not a school speech case—as has every other authority to address the question. The event occurred during normal school hours. It was sanctioned by Principal Morse "as an approved social event or class trip," and the school district's rules expressly provide that pupils in "approved social events and class trips are subject to district rules for student conduct." Teachers and administrators were interspersed among the students and charged with supervising them. The high school band and cheerleaders performed. Frederick, standing among other JDHS students across the street from the school, directed his banner toward the school, making it plainly visible to most students. Under these circumstances, we agree with the superintendent that Frederick cannot "stand in the midst of his fellow students, during school hours, at a school-sanctioned activity and claim he is not at school." There is some uncertainty at the outer boundaries as to when courts should apply school-speech precedents, see *Porter v. Ascension Parish School Bd.*, 393 F.3d 608, 615, n. 22 (CA5 2004), but not on these facts.

III.

The message on Frederick's banner is cryptic. It is no doubt offensive to some, perhaps amusing to others. To still others, it probably means nothing at all. Frederick himself claimed "that the words were just nonsense meant to attract television cameras." But Principal Morse thought the banner would be interpreted by those viewing it as promoting illegal drug use, and that interpretation is plainly a reasonable one.

We agree with Morse. At least two interpretations of the words on the banner demonstrate that the sign advocated the use of illegal drugs. First, the phrase could be interpreted as an imperative: "[Take] bong hits . . ."—a message equivalent, as Morse explained in her declaration, to "smoke marijuana" or "use an illegal drug." Alternatively, the phrase could be viewed as celebrating drug use—"bong hits [are a good thing]," or "[we take] bong hits"—and we discern no meaningful distinction between celebrating illegal drug use in the midst of fellow students and outright advocacy or promotion.

The pro-drug interpretation of the banner gains further plausibility given the paucity of alternative meanings the banner might bear. The best Frederick can come up with is that the banner is "meaningless and funny." Gibberish is surely a possible interpretation of the words on the banner, but it is not the only one, and dismissing the banner as meaningless ignores its undeniable reference to illegal drugs.

. . . [T]he dissent emphasizes the importance of political speech and the need to foster "national debate about a serious issue," as if to suggest that the banner is political speech. But not even Frederick argues that the banner conveys any sort of political or religious message. Contrary to the dissent's suggestion, this is plainly not a case about political debate over the criminalization of drug use or possession.

IV.

The question thus becomes whether a principal may, consistent with the First Amendment, restrict student speech at a school event, when that speech is reasonably viewed as promoting illegal drug use. We hold that she may.

Kuhlmeier does not control this case because no one would reasonably believe that Frederick's banner bore the school's imprimatur. The case is nevertheless instructive because it confirms both principles cited above. *Kuhlmeier* acknowledged that schools may regulate some speech "even though the government could not censor similar speech outside the school." And, like *Fraser*, it confirms that the rule of *Tinker* is not the only basis for restricting student speech.

Drawing on the principles applied in our student speech cases, we have held in the Fourth Amendment context that "while children assuredly do not 'shed their constitutional rights...at the schoolhouse gate,' . . . the nature of those rights is what is appropriate for children in school." *Vernonia School Dist. 47J v. Acton*, 515 U.S. 646, 655-656 (1995) (quoting *Tinker, supra*, at 506). Even more to the point, these cases also recognize that deterring drug use by schoolchildren is an "important—indeed, perhaps compelling" interest. Drug abuse can cause severe and permanent damage to the health and well-being of young people[.]

Just five years ago, we wrote: "The drug abuse problem among our Nation's youth has hardly abated since *Vernonia* was decided in 1995. In fact, evidence suggests that it has only grown worse."

Congress has declared that part of a school's job is educating students about the dangers of illegal drug use. It has provided billions of dollars to support state and local drug-prevention programs. . . . Thousands of school boards throughout the country—including JDHS—have adopted policies aimed at effectuating this message. Those school boards know that peer pressure is perhaps "the single most important factor leading schoolchildren to take drugs," and that students are more likely to use drugs when the norms in school appear to tolerate such behavior. Student speech celebrating illegal drug use at a school event, in the presence of school administrators and teachers, thus poses a particular challenge for school officials working to protect those entrusted to their care from the dangers of drug abuse.

Tinker warned that schools may not prohibit student speech because of "undifferentiated fear or apprehension of disturbance" or "a mere desire to avoid the discomfort and unpleasantness that always accompany an unpopular viewpoint." The danger here is far more serious and palpable. The particular concern to prevent student drug abuse at issue here, embodied in established school policy, extends well beyond an abstract desire to avoid controversy.

Petitioners urge us to adopt the broader rule that Frederick's speech is proscribable because it is plainly "offensive" as that term is used in *Fraser*. We think this stretches *Fraser* too far; that case should not be read to encompass any speech that could fit under some definition of "offensive." After all, much political and religious speech might be perceived as offensive to some. The concern here is not that Frederick's speech was offensive, but that it was reasonably viewed as promoting illegal drug use.

THOMAS, J., concurring.

The Court today decides that a public school may prohibit speech advocating illegal drug use. I agree and therefore join its opinion in full. I write separately to state my view that the standard set forth in *Tinker v. Des Moines Independent Community School Dist.*, is without basis in the Constitution.

In my view, the history of public education suggests that the First Amendment, as originally understood, does not protect student speech in public schools. Although colonial schools were exclusively private, public education proliferated in the early 1800's. By the time the States ratified the Fourteenth Amendment, public schools had become relatively common. If students in public schools were originally understood as having free-speech rights, one would have expected 19th-century public schools to have respected those rights and courts to have enforced them. They did not.

Because public schools were initially created as substitutes for private schools, when States developed public education systems in the early 1800's, no one doubted the government's ability to educate and discipline children as private schools did. Like their private counterparts, early public schools were not places for freewheeling debates or exploration of competing ideas. Rather, teachers instilled "a core of common values" in students and taught them self-control.

In short, in the earliest public schools, teachers taught, and students listened. Teachers commanded, and students obeyed. Teachers did not rely solely on the power of ideas to persuade; they relied on discipline to maintain order.

Tinker's reasoning conflicted with the traditional understanding of the judiciary's role in relation to public schooling, a role limited by *in loco parentis*. Perhaps for that reason, the Court has since scaled back *Tinker*'s standard, or rather set the standard aside on an ad hoc basis. [Discussing *Fraser* and *Kuhlmeier*.]

Today, the Court creates another exception. In doing so, we continue to distance ourselves from *Tinker*, but we neither overrule it nor offer an explanation of when it operates and when it does not. I am afraid that our jurisprudence now says that students have a right to speak in schools except when they don't—a standard continuously developed through litigation against local schools and their administrators. In my view, petitioners could prevail for a much simpler reason: As originally understood, the Constitution does not afford students a right to free speech in public schools.

ALITO, J., with whom KENNEDY, J., joins, concurring.

I join the opinion of the Court on the understanding that (a) it goes no further than to hold that a public school may restrict speech that a reasonable observer would interpret as advocating illegal drug use and (b) it provides no support for any restriction of speech that can plausibly be interpreted as commenting on any political or social issue, including speech on issues such as "the wisdom of the war on drugs or of legalizing marijuana for medicinal use."

I do not read the opinion to mean that there are necessarily any grounds for such regulation that are not already recognized in the holdings of this Court. In addition to *Tinker*, the decision in the present case allows the restriction of speech advocating illegal drug use; *Bethel*, permits the regulation of speech that is delivered in a lewd or vulgar manner as part of a middle school program; and *Hazelwood*, allows a school to regulate what is in essence the school's own speech, that is, articles that appear in a publication that is an official school organ. I join the opinion of the Court on the understanding that the opinion does not hold that the special characteristics of the public schools necessarily justify any other speech restrictions.

The opinion of the Court does not endorse the broad argument advanced by petitioners and the United States that the First Amendment permits public school officials to censor any student speech that interferes with a school's "educational mission." This argument can easily be manipulated in dangerous ways, and I would reject it before such abuse occurs. The "educational mission" of the public schools is defined by the elected and appointed public officials with authority over the schools and by the school administrators and faculty. As a result, some public schools have defined their educational missions as including the inculcation of whatever political and social views are held by the members of these groups.

The public schools are invaluable and beneficent institutions, but they are, after all, organs of the State. When public school authorities regulate student speech, they act as agents of the State; they do not stand in the shoes of the students' parents. It is a dangerous fiction to pretend that parents simply delegate their authority—including their authority to determine what their children may say and hear—to public school authorities.

For these reasons, any argument for altering the usual free speech rules in the public schools cannot rest on a theory of delegation but must instead be based on some special characteristic of the school setting. The special characteristic that is relevant in this case is the threat to the physical safety of students.

In most settings, the First Amendment strongly limits the government's ability to suppress speech on the ground that it presents a threat of violence. See *Brandenburg v. Ohio*. But due to the special features of the school environment, school officials must have greater authority to intervene before speech leads to violence. And, in most cases, *Tinker*'s "substantial disruption" standard permits school officials to step in before actual violence erupts.

Speech advocating illegal drug use poses a threat to student safety that is just as serious, if not always as immediately obvious. As we have recognized in the past and as the opinion of the Court today details, illegal drug use presents a grave and in many ways unique threat to the physical safety of students. I therefore conclude that the public schools may ban speech advocating illegal drug use. But I regard such regulation as standing at the far reaches of what the First Amendment permits. I join the opinion of the Court with the understanding that the opinion does not endorse any further extension.

STEVENS, J., with whom SOUTER, J., and GINSBURG, J., join, dissenting.

I would hold . . . that the school's interest in protecting its students from exposure to speech "reasonably regarded as promoting illegal drug use" cannot justify disciplining Frederick for his attempt to make an ambiguous statement to a television audience simply because it contained an oblique reference to drugs. The First Amendment demands more, indeed, much more.

The Court holds otherwise only after laboring to establish two uncontroversial propositions: first, that the constitutional rights of students in school settings are not coextensive with the rights of adults; and second, that deterring drug use by schoolchildren is a valid and terribly important interest. As to the first, I take the Court's point that the message on Frederick's banner is not *necessarily* protected speech, even though it unquestionably would have been had the banner been unfurled elsewhere. As to the second, I am willing to assume that the Court is correct that the pressing need to deter drug use supports JDHS's rule prohibiting willful conduct that expressly "advocates the use of substances that are illegal to minors." But it is a gross non sequitur to draw from these two unremarkable propositions the remarkable conclusion that the school may suppress student speech that was never meant to persuade anyone to do anything.

In my judgment, the First Amendment protects student speech if the message itself neither violates a permissible rule nor expressly advocates conduct that is illegal and harmful to students. This nonsense banner does neither, and the Court does serious violence to the First Amendment in upholding—indeed, lauding—a school's decision to punish Frederick for expressing a view with which it disagreed.

. . . [T]oday the Court fashions a test that trivializes the two cardinal principles upon which *Tinker* rests. See *ante* ("[S]chools [may] restrict student expression that they reasonably regard as promoting illegal drug use"). The Court's test invites stark viewpoint discrimination. In this case, for example, the principal has unabashedly acknowledged that she disciplined Frederick because she disagreed with the pro-drug viewpoint she ascribed to the message on the banner.

It is also perfectly clear that "promoting illegal drug use" comes nowhere close to proscribable "incitement to imminent lawless action." *Brandenburg.* Encouraging drug use might well increase the likelihood that a listener will try an illegal drug, but that hardly justifies censorship.

No one seriously maintains that drug advocacy (much less Frederick's ridiculous sign) comes within the vanishingly small category of speech that can be prohibited because of its feared consequences. Such advocacy, to borrow from Justice Holmes, "ha[s] no chance of starting a present conflagration." *Gitlow v. New York.*

[I]t takes real imagination to read a "cryptic" message (the Court's characterization, not mine) with a slanting drug reference as an incitement to drug use. . . . The notion that the message on this banner would actually persuade either the average student or even the dumbest one to change his or her behavior is most implausible. That the Court believes such a silly message can be proscribed as advocacy underscores the novelty of its position, and suggests that the principle it articulates has no stopping point.

Among other things, the Court's ham-handed, categorical approach is deaf to the constitutional imperative to permit unfettered debate, even among high-school students, about the wisdom of the war on drugs or of legalizing marijuana for medicinal use. See *Tinker* ("[Students] may not be confined to the expression of those sentiments that are officially approved"). If Frederick's stupid reference to marijuana can in the Court's view justify censorship, then high school students everywhere could be forgiven for zipping their mouths about drugs at school lest some "reasonable" observer censor and then punish them for promoting drugs.

Consider, too, that the school district's rule draws no distinction between alcohol and marijuana, but applies evenhandedly to all "substances that are illegal to minors." []. Given the tragic consequences of teenage alcohol consumption—drinking causes far more fatal accidents than the misuse of marijuana—the school district's interest in deterring teenage alcohol use is at least comparable to its interest in preventing marijuana use. Under the Court's reasoning, must the First Amendment give way whenever a school seeks to punish a student for any speech mentioning beer, or indeed anything else that might be deemed risky to teenagers? While I find it hard to believe the Court would support punishing Frederick for flying a "WINE SiPS 4 JESUS" banner—which could quite reasonably be construed either as a protected religious message or as a pro-alcohol message—the breathtaking sweep of its opinion suggests it would.

. . . [T]he current dominant opinion supporting the war on drugs in general, and our antimarijuana laws in particular, is reminiscent of the opinion that supported the nationwide ban on alcohol consumption when I was a student. While alcoholic beverages are now regarded as ordinary articles of commerce, their use was then condemned with the same moral fervor that now supports the war on drugs. The ensuing change in public opinion occurred much more slowly than the relatively rapid shift in Americans' views on the Vietnam War, and progressed on a state-by-state basis over a period of many years. But just as prohibition in the 1920's and early 1930's was secretly questioned by thousands of otherwise law-abiding patrons of bootleggers and speakeasies, today the actions of literally millions of otherwise law-abiding users of marijuana, and of the majority of voters in each of the several States that tolerate medicinal uses of the product, lead me to wonder whether the fear of disapproval by those in the majority is silencing opponents of the war on drugs. Surely our national experience with alcohol should make us wary of dampening speech suggesting—however inarticulately—that it would be better to tax and regulate marijuana than to persevere in a futile effort to ban its use entirely.

Even in high school, a rule that permits only one point of view to be expressed is less likely to produce correct answers than the open discussion of countervailing views. In the national debate about a serious issue, it is the expression of the minority's viewpoint that most demands the protection of the First Amendment. Whatever the better policy may be, a full and frank discussion of the costs and benefits of the attempt to prohibit the use of marijuana is far wiser than suppression of speech because it is unpopular.

Justice BREYER, concurring in the judgment in part and dissenting in part.

This Court need not and should not decide this difficult First Amendment issue on the merits. Rather, I believe that it should simply hold that qualified immunity bars the student's claim for monetary damages and say no more.

NOTES AND QUESTIONS

1. *What are the rules for student speech that disagrees with the state's official anti-drug message?* The majority in *Morse* does not hold that all student speech disagreeing with the state's official anti-drug message is unprotected by the First Amendment. But the Court fails to clearly describe when that speech is protected and when it is not. On the one hand, the Court says that student speech "promoting illegal drug use" may be sanctioned by the school authorities. On the other hand, the Court also suggests that students have a First Amendment right to say favorable things about drugs in the context of "political debate over the

criminalization of drug use or possession." How likely is it that this distinction will survive the onslaught of clever students seeking to push the boundaries of what is permissible? Suppose the student in *Morse* changed his posters slightly to say "BONG HITS 4 LEGALIZATION." Would this poster be protected under Chief Justice Roberts's plurality opinion in *Morse*? This modified poster promotes illegal drug use to the same extent as the original poster, but its message is also clearly political. How would Chief Justice Roberts's distinction apply to speech advocating civil disobedience? The entire point of such speech is to advocate illegal behavior, but at the same time such speech carries obvious political messages and ramifications. Would such speech therefore be characterized as unprotected "promotional" speech or as protected "political" speech? Suppose on the day after the Supreme Court issued its *Morse* decision, some of the plaintiff's classmates decided to support his right to free speech by holding up outside the school replica "BONG HiTS 4 JESUS" signs. Would their act of protest be protected under *Morse*? Suppose the principal interpreted their actions as promoting the first student's promotion of illegal drugs. Would the fact that this speech was indirectly pro-drug justify the principal in suspending those students as well?

2. *The applicability of* Tinker *and other student-speech cases to student speech that occurs off-campus.* Although the speech in *Morse* occurred outside the school, on a public sidewalk, and in a crowd that included several members of the general public, the Court treated the case as subject to the same regulatory rules that would have applied if the speech had occurred within the schoolhouse. In Chief Justice Roberts's plurality opinion, he notes that "[t]here is some uncertainty at the outer boundaries as to when courts should apply school-speech precedents." The case Chief Justice Roberts cites for this proposition is Porter v. Ascension Parish School Board, 393 F.3d 608 (5th Cir. 2004), in which the Fifth Circuit declined to apply the Court's student-speech decisions to a case involving sanctions imposed on a 16-year-old student who had composed a violent drawing off-campus. The court held that "[b]ecause Adam's drawing was composed off-campus, displayed only to members of his own household, stored off-campus, and not purposefully taken by him to [his high school] or publicized in a way certain to result in its appearance at [the school], we have found that the drawing is protected by the First Amendment. Furthermore, we have found that it is neither speech directed at the campus nor a purposefully communicated true threat." *Id.* at 620. Note, however, that other lower courts have applied the student-speech decisions to off-campus student speech, including cases involving off-campus newspapers and Web sites. *See* Wynar v. Douglas County Sch. Dist., 728 F.3d 1062 (9th Cir. 2013) (off-campus Web site); Doninger v. Niehoff, 642 F.3d 334, 339-43 (2d Cir. 2011) (off-campus email and blog post); Boucher v. School Bd. of Sch. Dist. of Greenfield, 134 F.3d 821 (7th Cir. 1998) (off-campus newspaper); Bystrom v. Fridley High Sch., 686 F. Supp. 1387 (D. Minn. 1987) (off-campus newspaper); Killion v. Franklin Reg'l Sch. Dist., 136 F. Supp. 2d 446 (W.D. Pa. 2001) (off-campus e-mail); Emmett v. Kent Sch. Dist. No. 415, 92 F. Supp. 2d 1088 (W.D. Wash. 2000) (off-campus Web site); Beussink v. Woodland R-IV Sch. Dist., 30 F. Supp. 2d 1175 (E.D. Mo. 1998) (off-campus Web site). *But see* Doninger v. Niehoff, 642 F.3d 334 (2d Cir. 2011) (holding in favor of student for off-campus parody website). If schools can discipline students for speech that occurs off-campus, does this undercut the

original purpose of the Court's student-speech jurisprudence, which rests on the proposition that schools must be able to limit student speech in order to protect the decorum in the classroom that is necessary to carry out the school's educational functions?

3. Professor Clay Calvert has shown that some courts of appeals have interpreted the concurrences of Justices Alito and Kennedy in *Morse* to permit schools to censor homophobic and violent expression without applying *Tinker*'s substantial disruption standard. Clay Calvert, *Misuse and Abuse of* Morse v. Frederick *by Lower Courts*, 32 Seattle U. L. Rev. 1 (2008). He points, for example, to the Fifth Circuit's decision in Ponce v. Socorro Independent Sch. Dist., 508 F.3d 765 (5th Cir. 2007), in which the court interpreted *Morse* as standing for the principle that "speech advocating a harm that is demonstrably grave and that derives that gravity from the 'special danger' to the physical safety of students arising from the school environment is unprotected." In other words, the court concluded that "some harms are in fact so great in the school setting that requiring a school administrator to evaluate their disruptive potential is unnecessary."

THEORY-APPLIED PROBLEMS

In order to understand and attempt to reconcile the various strains of the Court's four major student-speech cases, try applying them in the following scenarios:

1. A middle school student draws a Confederate flag on a piece of paper during class and is suspended for three days. *See* West v. Derby Unified Sch. Dist. No. 260, 206 F.3d 1358 (10th Cir.), *cert. denied*, 531 U.S. 825 (2000).

2. A middle school student is suspended for wearing a T-shirt that contains large print reading "George W. Bush," below which is the text, "Chicken-Hawk-in-Chief." Directly below these words is a large picture of the President's face, wearing a helmet, superimposed on the body of a chicken. Surrounding the President are images of oil rigs and dollar symbols. To one side of the President, three lines of cocaine and a razor blade appear. In the "chicken wing" of the President nearest the cocaine, there is a straw. In the other "wing" the President is holding a martini glass with an olive in it. Directly below all these depictions is printed, "1st Chicken Hawk Wing," and below that is text reading "World Domination Tour." *See* Guiles ex rel. Guiles v. Marineau, 461 F.3d 320 (2d Cir. 2006).

3. A school adopts a policy that prohibits all handouts containing "political, religious or organizational symbols." *See* Heinkel ex rel. Heinkel v. School Bd. of Lee County, Fla., 194 Fed. Appx. 604 (11th Cir. 2006).

4. Members of a high school basketball team are suspended from the team after they sign a letter requesting their coach's resignation. *See* Pinard v. Clatskanie Sch. Dist. 6J, 467 F.3d 755 (9th Cir. 2006).

5. School officials punish a student for remaining silent and raising a clenched fist in the air during the class's daily recitation of the Pledge of Allegiance. *See* Holloman ex rel. Holloman v. Harland, 370 F.3d 1252 (11th Cir. 2004).

6. A student is suspended for wearing to school a Marilyn Manson T-shirt depicting a three-headed Jesus accompanied by the words "See No Truth. Hear No Truth.

Speak No Truth." *See* Boroff v. Van Wert City Bd. of Educ., 220 F.3d 465 (6th Cir. 2000), *cert. denied,* 532 U.S. 920 (2001).

7. A student is expelled from school after he shows a teacher a poem that includes several examples of violent imagery. *See* LaVine v. Blaine Sch. Dist., 257 F.3d 981 (9th Cir. 2001), *cert. denied,* 536 U.S. 959 (2002).

8. Students who believe that homosexuality is a sin are prohibited by a school anti-harassment policy from expressing their views on the subject. *See* Saxe v. State Coll. Area Sch. Dist., 240 F.3d 200 (3d Cir. 2001).

9. Students are suspended for wearing to school various T-shirts printed with phrases such as "See Dick Drink. See Dick Drive. See Dick Die. Don't Be a Dick," "Coed Naked Band: Do It to the Rhythm," and "Coed Naked Gerbils: Some People Will Censor Anything." *See* Pyle ex rel. Pyle v. South Hadley Sch. Comm., 861 F. Supp. 157 (D. Mass. 1994).

10. A student and his friend created "Satan's web page" which listed "people I wish would die" as well as "people that are cool." It urged viewers, in a hyperbolic fashion, to "Stab someone for no reason..." but also included a disclaimer stating "PS: NOW THAT YOU'VE READ MY WEB PAGE PLEASE DON'T GO KILLING PEOPLE AND STUFF THEN BLAMING IT ON ME. OK?" *See* Mahaffey v. Aldrich, 236 F. Supp. 2d 779 (E.D. Mich. 2002).

11. A West Virginia high school student created a MySpace page alleging that a fellow student was infected with a sexually transmitted disease and inviting comments from other students, some of whom posted to MySpace from school computers. The father of the targeted girl complained to the school, and the principal investigated and suspended the student for violating the school's anti-bullying policy. *See* Kowalski v. Berkeley County Schools, 652 F.3d 565 (4th Cir. 2011), *cert. denied,* 132 S. Ct. 1095 (2012).

12. A school district suspended a student for creating, off campus, a vulgar and "outrageous" parody MySpace profile of her middle school principal making fun of, among other things, his appearance and the size of his penis. The student limited access to the site. The parody was not accessible on campus because the school district blocked access to MySpace. In addition, MySpace removed the profile at the principal's request. The student sued, alleging that the suspension violated the First Amendment. The district court granted summary judgment for the school district on the basis that vulgar and lewd speech that affects campus can be disciplined even without "substantial disruption" as defined by *Tinker.* ex rel. Snyder v. Blue Mountain Sch. Dist., 650 F.3d 915 (3d Cir. 2011) (en banc), *cert. denied,* 132 S. Ct. 1097 (2012).

BOARD OF EDUCATION v. PICO

457 U.S. 853 (1982)

BRENNAN, J., announced the judgment of the Court and delivered an opinion, in which MARSHALL, J., and STEVENS, J., joined, and in which BLACKMUN, J., joined [in part].

In September 1975, petitioners Ahrens, Martin, and Hughes attended a conference sponsored by Parents of New York United (PONYU), a politically conservative organization of parents concerned about education legislation in the State of New York. At the conference these petitioners obtained lists of books described by Ahrens as "objectionable," and by Martin as "improper fare for school students." It was later determined that the [Island Trees] High School library contained nine of the listed books, and that another listed book was in the [Island Trees Memorial] Junior High School library.[3] In February 1976, at a meeting with the Superintendent of Schools and the Principals of the High School and Junior High School, the Board gave an "unofficial direction" that the listed books be removed from the library shelves and delivered to the Board's offices, so that Board members could read them. When this directive was carried out, it became publicized, and the Board issued a press release justifying its action. It characterized the removed books as "anti-American, anti-Christian, anti-Sem[i]tic, and just plain filthy," and concluded that "[i]t is our duty, our moral obligation, to protect the children in our schools from this moral danger as surely as from physical and medical dangers."

A short time later, the Board appointed a "Book Review Committee," consisting of four Island Trees parents and four members of the Island Trees schools staff, to read the listed books and to recommend to the Board whether the books should be retained, taking into account the books' "educational suitability," "good taste," "relevance," and "appropriateness to age and grade level." In July, the Committee made its final report to the Board, recommending that five of the listed books be retained and that two others be removed from the school libraries. As for the remaining four books, the Committee could not agree on two, took no position on one, and recommended that the last book be made available to students only with parental approval. The Board substantially rejected the Committee's report later that month, deciding that only one book should be returned to the High School library without restriction, that another should be made available subject to parental approval, but that the remaining nine books should "be removed from elementary and secondary libraries and [from] use in the curriculum." The Board gave no reasons for rejecting the recommendations of the Committee that it had appointed. [Respondents then sued, claiming a violation of their First Amendment rights.]

We emphasize at the outset the limited nature of the substantive question presented by the case before us. For as this case is presented to us, it does not involve textbooks, or indeed any books that Island Trees students would be required to read. Respondents do not seek in this Court to impose limitations upon their school Board's discretion to prescribe the curricula of the Island Trees schools. On the contrary, the only books at issue in this case are *library* books, books that by their nature are optional rather than required reading. Our adjudication of the present case thus does not intrude into the classroom, or into the compulsory courses taught there. Furthermore, even as to library books, the action before us does not involve the *acquisition* of books. Respondents have not sought to compel their school Board to add to the school library shelves any books that students desire to read. Rather, the only action challenged in this case is the *removal* from school libraries of books originally placed there by the school authorities, or without objection from them.

---

[3] The nine books in the High School library were: Slaughter House Five, by Kurt Vonnegut, Jr.; The Naked Ape, by Desmond Morris; Down These Mean Streets, by Piri Thomas; Best Short Stories of Negro Writers, edited by Langston Hughes; Go Ask Alice, of anonymous authorship; Laughing Boy, by Oliver LaFarge; Black Boy, by Richard Wright; A Hero Ain't Nothin' But A Sandwich, by Alice Childress; and Soul On Ice, by Eldridge Cleaver. The book in the Junior High School library was A Reader for Writers, edited by Jerome Archer. Still another listed book, The Fixer, by Bernard Malamud, was found to be included in the curriculum of a 12th-grade literature course.

The Court has long recognized that local school boards have broad discretion in the management of school affairs. We are therefore in full agreement with petitioners that local school boards must be permitted "to establish and apply their curriculum in such a way as to transmit community values," and that "there is a legitimate and substantial community interest in promoting respect for authority and traditional values be they social, moral, or political."

At the same time, however, we have necessarily recognized that the discretion of the States and local school boards in matters of education must be exercised in a manner that comports with the transcendent imperatives of the First Amendment.

Of course, courts should not "intervene in the resolution of conflicts which arise in the daily operation of school systems" unless "basic constitutional values" are "directly and sharply implicate[d]" in those conflicts. *Epperson v. Arkansas*, [*infra* p. 910]. But we think that the First Amendment rights of students may be directly and sharply implicated by the removal of books from the shelves of a school library. Our precedents have focused "not only on the role of the First Amendment in fostering individual self-expression but also on its role in affording the public access to discussion, debate, and the dissemination of information and ideas." And we have recognized that "the State may not, consistently with the spirit of the First Amendment, contract the spectrum of available knowledge." *Griswold v. Connecticut.* In keeping with this principle, we have held that in a variety of contexts "the Constitution protects the right to receive information and ideas." *Stanley v. Georgia*, [*supra* Chapter 11].

In sum, just as access to ideas makes it possible for citizens generally to exercise their rights of free speech and press in a meaningful manner, such access prepares students for active and effective participation in the pluralistic, often contentious society in which they will soon be adult members. Of course all First Amendment rights accorded to students must be construed "in light of the special characteristics of the school environment." *Tinker.* But the special characteristics of the school *library* make that environment especially appropriate for the recognition of the First Amendment rights of students.

A school library, no less than any other public library, is "a place dedicated to quiet, to knowledge, and to beauty." *Brown v. Louisiana* (opinion of Fortas, J.). *Keyishian v. Board of Regents* observed that "'students must always remain free to inquire, to study and to evaluate, to gain new maturity and understanding.'" The school library is the principal locus of such freedom.

Petitioners emphasize the inculcative function of secondary education, and argue that they must be allowed *unfettered* discretion to "transmit community values" through the Island Trees schools. But that sweeping claim overlooks the unique role of the school library. It appears from the record that use of the Island Trees school libraries is completely voluntary on the part of students. Their selection of books from these libraries is entirely a matter of free choice; the libraries afford them an opportunity at self-education and individual enrichment that is wholly optional. Petitioners might well defend their claim of absolute discretion in matters of *curriculum* by reliance upon their duty to inculcate community values. But we think that petitioners' reliance upon that duty is misplaced where, as here, they attempt to extend their claim of absolute discretion beyond the compulsory environment of the classroom, into the school library and the regime of voluntary inquiry that there holds sway.

In rejecting petitioners' claim of absolute discretion to remove books from their school libraries, we do not deny that local school boards have a substantial legitimate role to play in the determination of school library content. We thus must turn to the question of the extent to which the First Amendment places limitations upon the discretion of petitioners to remove books from their libraries.

. . . [T]he message of [our] precedents is clear. Petitioners rightly possess significant discretion to determine the content of their school libraries. But that discretion may not be exercised in a narrowly partisan or political manner. If a Democratic school board, motivated by party affiliation, ordered the removal of all books written by or in favor of Republicans, few would doubt that the order violated the constitutional rights of the students denied access to those books. The same conclusion would surely apply if an all-white school board, motivated by racial animus, decided to remove all books authored by blacks or advocating racial equality and integration. Our Constitution does not permit the official suppression of *ideas*. Thus whether petitioners' removal of books from their school libraries denied respondents their First Amendment rights depends upon the motivation behind petitioners' actions. If petitioners *intended* by their removal decision to deny respondents access to ideas with which petitioners disagreed, and if this intent was the decisive factor in petitioners' decision, then petitioners have exercised their discretion in violation of the Constitution. To permit such intentions to control official actions would be to encourage the precise sort of officially prescribed orthodoxy unequivocally condemned in *Barnette*. On the other hand, respondents implicitly concede that an unconstitutional motivation would *not* be demonstrated if it were shown that petitioners had decided to remove the books at issue because those books were pervasively vulgar. And again, respondents concede that if it were demonstrated that the removal decision was based solely upon the "educational suitability" of the books in question, then their removal would be "perfectly permissible." In other words, in respondents' view such motivations, if decisive of petitioners' actions, would not carry the danger of an official suppression of ideas, and thus would not violate respondents' First Amendment rights.

As noted earlier, nothing in our decision today affects in any way the discretion of a local school board to choose books to *add* to the libraries of their schools. Because we are concerned in this case with the suppression of ideas, our holding today affects only the discretion to *remove* books. In brief, we hold that local school boards may not remove books from school library shelves simply because they dislike the ideas contained in those books and seek by their removal to "prescribe what shall be orthodox in politics, nationalism, religion, or other matters of opinion." *West Virginia Board of Education v. Barnette*. Such purposes stand inescapably condemned by our precedents.

[The Court then remanded the case to the District Court for a determination of whether] petitioners' decision to remove the books rested decisively upon disagreement with constitutionally protected ideas in those books, or upon a desire on petitioners' part to impose upon the students of the Island Trees High School and Junior High School a political orthodoxy to which petitioners and their constituents adhered.

BLACKMUN, J., concurring in part and concurring in the judgment.

In my view, then, the principle involved here is both narrower and more basic than the "right to receive information" identified by the plurality. I do not suggest that the State has any affirmative obligation to provide students with information or ideas, something that may well be associated with a "right to receive." And I do not believe, as the plurality suggests, that the right at issue here is somehow associated with the peculiar nature of the school library; if schools may be used to inculcate ideas, surely libraries may play a role in that process. Instead, I suggest that certain forms of state discrimination *between* ideas are improper. In particular, our precedents command the conclusion that the State may not act to deny access to an idea simply because state officials disapprove of that idea for partisan or political reasons.

In my view, we strike a proper balance here by holding that school officials may not remove books for the *purpose* of restricting access to the political ideas or social perspectives discussed in them, when that action is motivated simply by the officials' disapproval of the ideas involved. It does not seem radical to suggest that state action calculated to suppress novel ideas or concepts is fundamentally antithetical to the values of the First Amendment. At a minimum, allowing a school board to engage in such conduct hardly teaches children to respect the diversity of ideas that is fundamental to the American system. In this context, then, the school board must "be able to show that its action was caused by something more than a mere desire to avoid the discomfort and unpleasantness that always accompany an unpopular viewpoint," *Tinker*, and that the board had something in mind in addition to the suppression of partisan or political views it did not share.

WHITE, J., concurring in the judgment.

The District Court found that the books were removed from the school library because the school board believed them "to be, in essence, vulgar." Both Court of Appeals judges in the majority concluded, however, that there was a material issue of fact that precluded summary judgment sought by petitioners. The unresolved factual issue, as I understand it, is the reason or reasons underlying the school board's removal of the books. I am not inclined to disagree with the Court of Appeals on such a fact-bound issue and hence concur in the judgment of affirmance. Presumably this will result in a trial and the making of a full record and findings on the critical issues.

The plurality seems compelled to go further and issue a dissertation on the extent to which the First Amendment limits the discretion of the school board to remove books from the school library. I see no necessity for doing so at this point. When findings of fact and conclusions of law are made by the District Court, that may end the case. If, for example, the District Court concludes after a trial that the books were removed for their vulgarity, there may be no appeal. In any event, if there is an appeal, if there is dissatisfaction with the subsequent Court of Appeals' judgment, and if certiorari is sought and granted, there will be time enough to address the First Amendment issues that may then be presented.

BURGER, C.J., with whom POWELL, J., REHNQUIST, J., and O'CONNOR, J., join, dissenting.

Stripped to its essentials, the issue comes down to two important propositions: *first*, whether local schools are to be administered by elected school boards, or by federal judges and teenage pupils; and *second*, whether the values of morality, good taste, and relevance to education are valid reasons for school board decisions concerning the contents of a school library. In an attempt to place this case within the protection of the First Amendment, the plurality suggests a new "right" that, when shorn of the plurality's rhetoric, allows this Court to impose its own views about what books must be made available to students.

The plurality concludes that under the Constitution school boards cannot choose to retain or dispense with books if their discretion is exercised in a "narrowly partisan or political manner." The plurality concedes that permissible factors are whether the books are "pervasively vulgar," or educationally unsuitable. "Educational suitability," however, is a standardless phrase. This conclusion will undoubtedly be drawn in many—if not most—instances because of the decisionmaker's content-based judgment that the ideas contained in the book or the idea expressed from the author's method of communication are inappropriate for teenage pupils.

The plurality also tells us that a book may be removed from a school library if it is "pervasively vulgar." But why must the vulgarity be "pervasive" to be offensive? Vulgarity might be concentrated in a single poem or a single chapter or a single page, yet still be inappropriate. Or a school board might reasonably conclude that even "random" vulgarity is inappropriate for teenage school students. A school board might also reasonably conclude that the school board's retention of such books gives those volumes an implicit endorsement.

Further, there is no guidance whatsoever as to what constitutes "political" factors. This Court has previously recognized that public education involves an area of broad public policy and "'go[es] to the heart of representative government.'" As such, virtually all educational decisions necessarily involve "political" determinations.

We can all agree that as a matter of *educational policy* students should have wide access to information and ideas. But the people elect school boards, who in turn select administrators, who select the teachers, and these are the individuals best able to determine the substance of that policy. The plurality fails to recognize the fact that local control of education involves democracy in a microcosm. In most public schools in the United States the *parents* have a large voice in running the school. Through participation in the election of school board members, the parents influence, if not control, the direction of their children's education. A school board is not a giant bureaucracy far removed from accountability for its actions; it is truly "of the people and by the people." A school board reflects its constituency in a very real sense and thus could not long exercise unchecked discretion in its choice to acquire or remove books. If the parents disagree with the educational decisions of the school board, they can take steps to remove the board members from office. Finally, even if parents and students cannot convince the school board that book removal is inappropriate, they have alternative sources to the same end. Books may be acquired from bookstores, public libraries, or other alternative sources unconnected with the unique environment of the local public schools.

No amount of "limiting" language could rein in the sweeping "right" the plurality would create. The plurality distinguishes library books from textbooks because library books "by their nature are optional rather than required reading." It is not clear, however, why this distinction requires *greater* scrutiny before "optional" reading materials may be removed. It would appear that required reading and textbooks have a greater likelihood of imposing a "'pall of orthodoxy'" over the educational process than do optional reading. In essence, the plurality's view transforms the availability of this "optional" reading into a "right" to have this "optional" reading maintained at the demand of teenagers.

The plurality also limits the new right by finding it applicable only to the *removal* of books once acquired. Yet if the First Amendment commands that certain books cannot be removed, does it not equally require that the same books be *acquired*? Why does the coincidence of timing become the basis of a constitutional holding? According to the plurality, the evil to be avoided is the "official suppression of ideas." It does not follow that the decision to *remove* a book is less "official suppression" than the decision not to acquire a book desired by someone. Similarly, a decision to eliminate certain material from the curriculum, history for example, would carry an equal—probably greater—prospect of "official suppression." Would the decision be subject to our review?

POWELL, J., dissenting.

The plurality opinion today rejects a basic concept of public school education in our country: that the States and locally elected school boards should have the responsibility for determining the educational policy of the public schools. After today's decision any junior high school student, by instituting a suit against a school board or teacher, may invite a judge to overrule an educational decision by the official body designated by the people to operate the schools.

A school board's attempt to instill in its students the ideas and values on which a democratic system depends is viewed [by the plurality] as an impermissible suppression of other ideas and values on which other systems of government and other societies thrive. Books may not be removed because they are indecent; extol violence, intolerance, and racism; or degrade the dignity of the individual. Human history, not the least that of the 20th century, records the power and political life of these very ideas. But they are not our ideas or values. Although I would leave this educational decision to the duly constituted board, I certainly would not require a school board to promote ideas and values repugnant to a democratic society or to teach such values to children.

[Judge Rehnquist's dissenting opinion is omitted.]

NOTES AND QUESTIONS

In *Morse v. Frederick*, the Supreme Court allowed a high school principal to suspend a student for holding up what the Court called a "cryptic" banner that the principal interpreted as promoting illegal drug use. The Court justified upholding the principal's actions on ground that "deterring drug use by schoolchildren is an 'important—indeed, perhaps compelling' interest. Drug abuse can cause severe and permanent damage to the health and well-being of young people." In *Pico*, the school board removed from a high school library nine books, arguing that "[i]t is our duty, our moral obligation, to protect the children in our schools from this moral danger as surely as from physical and medical dangers." Approximately half of these books dealt extensively with drugs, in ways that could be characterized as promoting illegal drug use. In *Pico*, the plurality overturned the school board's decision on the ground that their action constituted the unconstitutional suppression of unpopular ideas. Does *Morse* cast into doubt the holding of *Pico*? How far does the *Morse* majority seem to go in permitting the censorship of school speech that can be interpreted by school authorities as "promoting illegal drug use"? The *Morse* majority seems to exempt from its new rule permitting school authorities to censor pro-drug speech any speech promoting illegal drug use that is embodied in statements of political advocacy or critiques of drug policy. Should art and literature that promote illegal drug use fall within the same exemption? If so, would the student in *Morse* be constitutionally protected in writing a short story or painting a painting depicting someone contentedly smoking marijuana? Suppose a student presented to a classroom of students in a high school English class a very favorable book review of Hunter S. Thompson's *Fear and Loathing in Las Vegas*? Could the student be sanctioned by the teacher, or does the First Amendment protect the student's inclusion of a pro-drug message in otherwise legitimate school activities?

UNITED STATES v. AMERICAN LIBRARY ASS'N

539 U.S. 194 (2003)

REHNQUIST, C.J., announced the judgment of the Court and delivered an opinion, in which O'CONNOR, J., SCALIA, J., and THOMAS, J., joined.

To address the problems associated with the availability of Internet pornography in public libraries, Congress enacted the Children's Internet Protection Act (CIPA). Under CIPA, a public library may not receive federal assistance to provide Internet access unless it installs software to block images that constitute obscenity or child pornography, and to prevent minors from obtaining access to material that is harmful to them. The District Court held these provisions facially invalid on the ground that they induce public libraries to violate patrons' First Amendment rights. We now reverse.

Public libraries pursue the worthy missions of facilitating learning and cultural enrichment. Appellee ALA's Library Bill of Rights states that libraries should provide "[b]ooks and other . . . resources . . . for the interest, information, and enlightenment of all people of the community the library serves." To fulfill their traditional missions, public libraries must have broad discretion to decide what material to provide to their patrons. Although they seek to provide a wide array of information, their goal has never been to provide "universal coverage." Instead, public libraries seek to provide materials "that would be of the greatest direct benefit or interest to the community." To this end, libraries collect only those materials deemed to have "requisite and appropriate quality." See W. Katz, Collection Development: The Selection of Materials for Libraries 6 (1980) ("The librarian's responsibility . . . is to separate out the gold from the garbage, not to preserve everything"); F. Drury, Book Selection xi (1930) ("[I]t is the aim of the selector to give the public, not everything it wants, but the best that it will read or use to advantage"); App. 636 (Rebuttal Expert Report of Donald G. Davis, Jr.) ("A hypothetical collection of everything that has been produced is not only of dubious value, but actually detrimental to users trying to find what they want to find and really need").

We have held in two analogous contexts that the government has broad discretion to make content-based judgments in deciding what private speech to make available to the public. [The Court then discussed Arkansas Educational Television Commission v. Forbes and National Endowment for Arts v. Finley.]

The principles underlying *Forbes* and *Finley* also apply to a public library's exercise of judgment in selecting the material it provides to its patrons. Just as forum analysis and heightened judicial scrutiny are incompatible with the role of public television stations and the role of the NEA, they are also incompatible with the discretion that public libraries must have to fulfill their traditional missions. Public library staffs necessarily consider content in making collection decisions and enjoy broad discretion in making them.

A public library does not acquire Internet terminals in order to create a public forum for Web publishers to express themselves, any more than it collects books in order to provide a public forum for the authors of books to speak. It provides Internet access, not to "encourage a diversity of views from private speakers," *Rosenberger*, but for the same reasons it offers other library resources: to facilitate research, learning, and recreational pursuits by furnishing materials of requisite and appropriate quality.

The District Court disagreed because, whereas a library reviews and affirmatively chooses to acquire every book in its collection, it does not review every Web site that it makes available. Based on this distinction, the court reasoned that a public library enjoys less discretion in deciding which Internet materials to make available than in making book selections. We do not find this distinction constitutionally relevant. A library's failure to make quality-based judgments about all the material it furnishes from the Web does not somehow taint the judgments it does make. A library's need to exercise judgment in making collection decisions depends on its traditional role in identifying suitable and worthwhile material; it is no less entitled to play that role when it collects material from the Internet than when it collects material from any other source. Most libraries already exclude pornography from their print collections because they deem it inappropriate for inclusion. We do not subject these decisions to heightened scrutiny; it would make little sense to treat libraries' judgments to block online pornography any differently, when these judgments are made for just the same reason.

Like the District Court, the dissents fault the tendency of filtering software to "overblock"—that is, to erroneously block access to constitutionally protected speech that falls outside the categories that software users intend to block. Due to the software's limitations, "[m]any erroneously blocked [Web] pages contain content that is completely innocuous for both adults and minors, and that no rational person could conclude matches the filtering companies' category definitions, such as 'pornography' or 'sex.'" Assuming that such erroneous blocking presents constitutional difficulties, any such concerns are dispelled by the ease with which patrons may have the filtering software disabled. When a patron encounters a blocked site, he need only ask a librarian to unblock it or (at least in the case of adults) disable the filter. As the District Court found, libraries have the capacity to permanently unblock any erroneously blocked site, and the Solicitor General stated at oral argument that a "library may . . . eliminate the filtering with respect to specific sites . . . at the request of a patron." With respect to adults, CIPA also expressly authorizes library officials to "disable" a filter altogether "to enable access for bona fide research or other lawful purposes." The Solicitor General confirmed that a "librarian can, in response to a request from a patron, unblock the filtering mechanism altogether," and further explained that a patron would not "have to explain . . . why he was asking a site to be unblocked or the filtering to be disabled." The District Court viewed unblocking and disabling as inadequate because some patrons may be too embarrassed to request them. But the Constitution does not guarantee the right to acquire information at a public library without any risk of embarrassment.

[The Court also rejected the Appellees' claim that CIPA imposes an unconstitutional condition on the receipt of federal assistance.] We need not decide this question because, even assuming that appellees may assert an "unconstitutional conditions" claim, this claim would fail on the merits. Within broad limits, "when the Government appropriates public funds to establish a program it is entitled to define the limits of that program." *Rust v. Sullivan.*

The same is true here. The E-rate and LSTA programs were intended to help public libraries fulfill their traditional role of obtaining material of requisite and appropriate quality for educational and informational purposes. Congress may certainly insist that these "public funds be spent for the purposes for which they were authorized." *Id.* Especially because public libraries have traditionally excluded pornographic material from their other collections, Congress could reasonably impose a parallel limitation on its Internet assistance programs. As the use of filtering software helps to carry out these programs, it is a permissible condition under *Rust.*

Appellees mistakenly contend, in reliance on *Legal Services Corporation v. Velazquez,* that CIPA's filtering conditions "[d]istor[t] the [u]sual [f]unctioning of [p]ublic [l]ibraries." In *Velazquez,* the Court concluded that a Government program of furnishing legal aid to the indigent differed from the program in *Rust* "[i]n th[e] vital respect" that the role of lawyers who represent clients in welfare disputes is to advocate *against* the Government, and there was thus an assumption that counsel would be free of state control. The Court concluded that the restriction on advocacy in such welfare disputes would distort the usual functioning of the legal profession and the federal and state courts before which the lawyers appeared. Public libraries, by contrast, have no comparable role that pits them against the Government, and there is no comparable assumption that they must be free of any conditions that their benefactors might attach to the use of donated funds or other assistance.

KENNEDY, J., concurring in the judgment.

If, on the request of an adult user, a librarian will unblock filtered material or disable the Internet software filter without significant delay, there is little to this case.

If some libraries do not have the capacity to unblock specific Web sites or to disable the filter or if it is shown that an adult user's election to view constitutionally protected Internet material is burdened in some other substantial way, that would be the subject for an as-applied challenge, not the facial challenge made in this case.

There are, of course, substantial Government interests at stake here. The interest in protecting young library users from material inappropriate for minors is legitimate, and even compelling, as all Members of the Court appear to agree. Given this interest, and the failure to show that the ability of adult library users to have access to the material is burdened in any significant degree, the statute is not unconstitutional on its face. For these reasons, I concur in the judgment of the Court.

BREYER, J., concurring in the judgment.

I reach the plurality's ultimate conclusion in a different way.

In ascertaining whether the statutory provisions are constitutional, I would apply a form of heightened scrutiny, examining the statutory requirements in question with special care. The Act directly restricts the public's receipt of information. And it does so through limitations imposed by outside bodies (here Congress) upon two critically important sources of information—the Internet as accessed via public libraries. For that reason, we should not examine the statute's constitutionality as if it raised no special First Amendment concern—as if, like tax or economic regulation, the First Amendment demanded only a "rational basis" for imposing a restriction. Nor should we accept the Government's suggestion that a presumption in favor of the statute's constitutionality applies.

At the same time, in my view, the First Amendment does not here demand application of the most limiting constitutional approach—that of "strict scrutiny." The statutory restriction in question is, in essence, a kind of "selection" restriction (a kind of editing). It affects the kinds and amount of materials that the library can present to its patrons. And libraries often properly engage in the selection of materials, either as a matter of necessity (*i.e.*, due to the scarcity of resources) or by design (*i.e.*, in accordance with collection development policies). To apply "strict scrutiny" to the "selection" of a library's collection (whether carried out by public libraries themselves or by other community bodies with a traditional legal right to engage in that function) would unreasonably interfere with the discretion necessary to create, maintain, or select a library's "collection" (broadly defined to include all the information the library makes available).

Instead, I would examine the constitutionality of the Act's restrictions here as the Court has examined speech-related restrictions in other contexts where circumstances call for heightened, but not "strict," scrutiny—where, for example, complex, competing constitutional interests are potentially at issue or speech-related harm is potentially justified by unusually strong governmental interests. Typically the key question in such instances is one of proper fit.

In such cases the Court has asked whether the harm to speech-related interests is disproportionate in light of both the justifications and the potential alternatives. It has considered the legitimacy of the statute's objective, the extent to which the statute will tend to achieve that objective, whether there are other, less restrictive ways of achieving that objective, and ultimately whether the statute works speech-related harm that, in relation to that objective, is out of proportion.

The Act's restrictions satisfy these constitutional demands. The Act seeks to restrict access to obscenity, child pornography, and, in respect to access by minors, material that is comparably harmful. These objectives are "legitimate," and indeed often "compelling."

At the same time, the Act contains an important exception that limits the speech-related harm that "overblocking" might cause. As the plurality points out, the Act allows libraries to permit any adult patron access to an "overblocked" Web site; the adult patron need only ask a librarian to unblock the specific Web site or, alternatively, ask the librarian, "Please disable the entire filter."

Given the comparatively small burden that the Act imposes upon the library patron seeking legitimate Internet materials, I cannot say that any speech-related harm that the Act may cause is disproportionate when considered in relation to the Act's legitimate objectives.

STEVENS, J., dissenting.

A federal statute penalizing a library for failing to install filtering software on every one of its Internet-accessible computers would unquestionably violate that Amendment. I think it equally clear that the First Amendment protects libraries from being denied funds for refusing to comply with an identical rule. An abridgment of speech by means of a threatened denial of benefits can be just as pernicious as an abridgment by means of a threatened penalty.

The issue in this case does not involve governmental attempts to control the speech or views of its employees. It involves the use of its treasury to impose controls on an important medium of expression. In an analogous situation, we specifically held that when "the Government seeks to use an existing medium of expression and to control it, in a class of cases, in ways which distort its usual functioning," the distorting restriction must be struck down under the First Amendment. *Legal Services Corporation v. Velazquez.* The question, then, is whether requiring the filtering software on all Internet-accessible computers distorts that medium. . . . [T]he over- and underblocking of the software does just that.

The plurality argues that the controversial decision in *Rust v. Sullivan* requires rejection of appellees' unconstitutional conditions claim. But, as subsequent cases have explained, *Rust* only involved and only applies to instances of governmental speech—that is, situations in which the government seeks to communicate a specific message. The discounts under the E-rate program and funding under the Library Services and Technology Act program involved in this case do not subsidize any message favored by the Government. As Congress made clear, these programs were designed "[t]o help public libraries provide their patrons with Internet access," which in turn "provide[s] patrons with a vast amount of valuable information." These programs thus are designed to provide access, particularly for individuals in low-income communities, to a vast amount and wide variety of private speech. They are not designed to foster or transmit any particular governmental message.

The plurality's reliance on *National Endowment for Arts v. Finley* is also misplaced. That case involved a challenge to a statute setting forth the criteria used by a federal panel of experts administering a federal grant program. Unlike this case, the Federal Government was not seeking to impose restrictions on the administration of a nonfederal program.

Also unlike *Finley*, the Government does not merely seek to control a library's discretion with respect to computers purchased with Government funds or those computers with Government-discounted Internet access. CIPA requires libraries to install filtering software on *every* computer with Internet access if the library receives *any* discount from the E-rate program or *any* funds from the LSTA program. If a library has 10 computers paid for by nonfederal funds and has Internet service for those computers also paid for by nonfederal funds, the library may choose not to put filtering software on any of those 10 computers. Or a library may decide to put filtering software on the 5 computers in its children's section. Or a library in an elementary school might choose to put filters on every single one of its 10 computers. But under this statute, if a library attempts to provide Internet service for even *one* computer through an E-rate discount, that library must put filtering software on *all* of its computers with Internet access, not just the one computer with E-rate discount.

This Court should not permit federal funds to be used to enforce this kind of broad restriction of First Amendment rights, particularly when such a restriction is unnecessary to accomplish Congress' stated goal.

SOUTER, J., with whom GINSBURG, J., joins, dissenting.

[We] have to take the statute on the understanding that adults will be denied access to a substantial amount of nonobscene material harmful to children but lawful for adult examination, and a substantial quantity of text and pictures harmful to no one. As the plurality concedes, this is the inevitable consequence of the indiscriminate behavior of current filtering mechanisms, which screen out material to an extent known only by the manufacturers of the blocking software.

The question for me, then, is whether a local library could itself constitutionally impose these restrictions on the content otherwise available to an adult patron through an Internet connection, at a library terminal provided for public use. The answer is no. A library that chose to block an adult's Internet access to material harmful to children (and whatever else the undiscriminating filter might interrupt) would be imposing a content-based restriction on communication of material in the library's control that an adult could otherwise lawfully see. This would simply be censorship. True, the censorship would not necessarily extend to every adult, for an intending Internet user might convince a librarian that he was a true researcher or had a "lawful purpose" to obtain everything the library's terminal could provide. But as to those who did not qualify for discretionary unblocking, the censorship would be complete and, like all censorship by an agency of the Government, presumptively invalid owing to strict scrutiny in implementing the Free Speech Clause of the First Amendment. "The policy of the First Amendment favors dissemination of information and opinion, and the guarantees of freedom of speech and press were not designed to prevent the censorship of the press merely, but any action of the government by means of which it might prevent such free and general discussion of public matters as seems absolutely essential." *Bigelow v. Virginia*, 421 U.S. 809, 829 (1975) (internal quotation marks and brackets omitted).

Public libraries are indeed selective in what they acquire to place in their stacks, as they must be. There is only so much money and so much shelf space, and the necessity to choose some material and reject the rest justifies the effort to be selective with an eye to demand, quality, and the object of maintaining the library as a place of civilized enquiry by widely different sorts of people. Selectivity is thus necessary and complex, and these two characteristics explain why review of a library's selection decisions must be limited: the decisions are made all the time, and only in extreme cases could one expect particular choices to reveal impermissible reasons (reasons even the plurality would consider to be illegitimate), like excluding books because their authors are Democrats or their critiques of organized Christianity are unsympathetic. See *Pico*. Review for rational basis is probably the most that any court could conduct, owing to the myriad particular selections that might be attacked by someone, and the difficulty of untangling the play of factors behind a particular decision.

At every significant point, however, the Internet blocking here defies comparison to the process of acquisition. Whereas traditional scarcity of money and space require a library to make choices about what to acquire, and the choice to be made is whether or not to spend the money to acquire something, blocking is the subject of a choice made after the money for Internet access has been spent or committed. Since it makes no difference to the cost of Internet access whether an adult calls up material harmful for children or the Articles of Confederation, blocking (on facts like these) is not necessitated by scarcity of either money or space. In the instance of the Internet, what the library acquires is electronic access, and the choice to block is a choice to limit access that has already been acquired. Thus, deciding against buying a book means there is no book (unless a loan can be obtained), but blocking the Internet is merely blocking access purchased in its entirety and subject to unblocking if the librarian agrees. The proper analogy therefore is not to passing up a book that might have been bought; it is either to buying a book and then keeping it from adults lacking an acceptable "purpose," or to buying an encyclopedia and then cutting out pages with anything thought to be unsuitable for all adults.

Thus, there is no preacquisition scarcity rationale to save library Internet blocking from treatment as censorship, and no support for it in the historical development of library practice. To these two reasons to treat blocking differently from a decision declining to buy a book, a third must be added. Quite simply, we can smell a rat when a library blocks material already in its control, just as we do when a library removes books from its shelves for reasons having nothing to do with wear and tear, obsolescence, or lack of demand. Content-based blocking and removal tell us something that mere absence from the shelves does not.

NOTES AND QUESTIONS

1. *Undervaluing anonymity?* In *American Library Association,* the Court does little to resolve definitively the question of how the First Amendment applies to the rights of public librarians and public library patrons. To the Justices who provided the key votes for the majority, the fact that library patrons could get unfettered access to the Internet simply by making a request to a librarian essentially eliminated the First Amendment issue from the case. Were these Justices correct in assuming that making such a request is not a significant First Amendment burden? In cases such as McIntyre v. Ohio Elections Commission, 514 U.S. 334 (1995), *supra* p. 275, the Court has held that the right to speak anonymously is protected by the First Amendment. Should the same interest in anonymity apply to library patrons seeking access to certain information or expressive materials? Does the fact that a library patron has to publicly announce a desire to access certain materials on the Internet inhibit expression in the same way that identifying the speaker was found to unconstitutionally inhibit speech in *McIntyre?* Does it matter that the expressive materials in question in *American Library Ass'n* were sexual in nature? For example, could the government require that all libraries require patrons to identify themselves before checking out radical political or religious materials?

2. *Striking the balance between government control and free speech. American Library Ass'n* is an example of the Court attempting to identify some midpoint between government claims of complete authority to control speech it funds and efforts by speakers to communicate information freely. On one hand, the Court rejected attempts by the plaintiffs to characterize libraries as public forums and refused to grant librarians complete editorial freedom from their government employers in deciding which materials to put in their collections and which materials to leave out. On the other hand, the Court also refused to accept the government's attempt to analogize the case to *Rust.* Several Justices noted that the statute's restriction on the public's receipt of information raised serious First Amendment concerns, which prevented the Court from affording the government the same degree of authority over speech that the Court had granted in *Rust* with regard to government spokespersons. In the end, a majority of the Court rejected both extremes regarding First Amendment rights in public libraries, but its opinion does not strike a clear or precise balance between them.

PART II

The Religion Clauses

CHAPTER
13

Introduction to the Religion Clauses

TABLE OF CONTENTS

A. THE RELIGION CLAUSES

The First Amendment states that "Congress shall make no law respecting an establishment of religion, or prohibiting the free exercise thereof." This sentence has been read as containing two clauses: The Free Exercise Clause ("Congress shall make no law . . . prohibiting the free exercise [of religion].") and the Establishment Clause ("Congress shall make no law respecting an establishment of religion.").

The Free Exercise Clause facilitates people's practice of religion, and is therefore triggered when the government impedes religious practices. Laws that target religion for disfavor might be struck down altogether under the Free Exercise Clause. The Free Exercise Clause might also require exemptions from otherwise applicable laws. Thanks to the Free Exercise Clause, the government cannot ban religious beliefs. It cannot outlaw Judaism, or Islam, or Sikhism. Nor can it generally target religious practices, such as banning Sabbath observances. The question becomes a bit trickier, however, when a law that does not target religion nonetheless makes religious practices like Saturday Sabbath observances more difficult, such as a law that requires subpoenaed witnesses to come to court even if it is Saturday, or a law that mandates all stores close on Sunday. Must Saturday Sabbath observers comply, or does the Free Exercise Clause provide them with a religious exemption?

The Establishment Clause, which is popularly described as mandating "separation of church and state," limits the government from establishing, funding, or practicing religion, or declaring what is religiously true. The Establishment Clause also bars the government from favoring one or some religions over others. Thus, the state cannot grant tax exempt status to Jewish and Buddhist temples but not Muslim mosques and Christian churches. The Establishment Clause has also been interpreted as forbidding the government from favoring religion over its secular counterpart, such as by granting a tax break to religious nonprofit publications but not to secular nonprofit publications, or favoring religion at the expense of others. And yet the limits are unclear: "In God We Trust," after all, has been the national motto since 1956.

How the two clauses interact is also an ongoing question. Are they in tension, where the Free Exercise Clause encourages government accommodation of religion while the Establishment Clause puts limits on such encouragement? Or do they both work together to ensure freedom of religion for all, including religious minorities?

The following cases are merely an introduction to these questions. The chapters that follow address each clause in depth.

B.   SATURDAY SABBATH AND SUNDAY CLOSING LAWS

BRAUNFELD v. BROWN
366 U.S. 599 (1961)

Mr. Chief Justice WARREN announced the judgment of the Court and an opinion in which Mr. Justice BLACK, Mr. Justice CLARK, and Mr. Justice WHITTAKER concur.

This case concerns the constitutional validity of the application to appellants of the Pennsylvania criminal statute, enacted in 1959, which proscribes the Sunday retail sale of certain enumerated commodities. Among the questions presented are whether the statute is a law respecting an establishment of religion and whether the statute violates equal protection. Since both of these questions, in reference to this very statute, have already been answered in the negative, *Two Guys from Harrison-Allentown, Inc. v. McGinley,* . . . and since appellants present nothing new regarding them, they need not be considered here. Thus, the only question for consideration is whether the statute interferes with the free exercise of appellants' religion.

Appellants are merchants in Philadelphia who engage in the retail sale of clothing and home furnishings within the proscription of the statute in issue. Each of the appellants is a member of the Orthodox Jewish faith, which requires the closing of their places of business and a total abstention from all manner of work from nightfall each Friday until nightfall each Saturday. . . .

Appellants contend that the enforcement against them of the Pennsylvania statute will prohibit the free exercise of their religion because, due to the statute's compulsion to close on Sunday, appellants will suffer substantial economic loss, to the benefit of their non-Sabbatarian competitors, if appellants also continue their Sabbath observance by closing their businesses on Saturday; that this result will either compel appellants to give up their Sabbath observance, a basic tenet of the Orthodox Jewish faith, or will put appellants at a serious economic disadvantage if they continue to adhere to their Sabbath. . . .

Concededly, appellants and all other persons who wish to work on Sunday will be burdened economically by the State's day of rest mandate; and appellants point out that their religion requires them to refrain from work on Saturday as well. Our inquiry then is whether, in these circumstances, the First and Fourteenth Amendments forbid application of the Sunday Closing Law to appellants.

Certain aspects of religious exercise cannot, in any way, be restricted or burdened by either federal or state legislation. Compulsion by law of the acceptance of any creed or the practice of any form of worship is strictly forbidden. The freedom to hold religious beliefs and opinions is absolute. . . . But this is not the case at bar; the statute before us does not make criminal the holding of any religious belief or opinion, nor does it force anyone to embrace any religious belief or to say or believe anything in conflict with his religious tenets.

However, the freedom to act, even when the action is in accord with one's religious convictions, is not totally free from legislative restrictions. . . . Thus, in *Reynolds v. United States*, this Court upheld the polygamy conviction of a member of the Mormon faith despite the fact that an accepted doctrine of his church then imposed upon its male members the *duty* to practice polygamy. And, in *Prince v. Massachusetts*, this Court upheld a statute making it a crime for a girl under eighteen years of age to sell any newspapers, periodicals or merchandise in public places despite the fact that a child of the Jehovah's Witnesses faith believed that it was her religious *duty* to perform this work.

But, again, this is not the case before us because the statute at bar does not make unlawful any religious practices of appellants; the Sunday law simply regulates a secular activity and, as applied to appellants, operates so as to make the practice of their religious beliefs more expensive. Furthermore, the law's effect does not inconvenience all members of the Orthodox Jewish faith but only those who believe it necessary to work on Sunday. And even these are not faced with as serious a choice as forsaking their religious practices or subjecting themselves to criminal prosecution. Fully recognizing that the alternatives open to appellants and others similarly situated—retaining their present occupations and incurring economic disadvantage or engaging in some other commercial activity which does not call for either Saturday or Sunday labor—may well result in some financial sacrifice in order to observe their religious beliefs, still the option is wholly different than when the legislation attempts to make a religious practice itself unlawful.

To strike down, without the most critical scrutiny, legislation which imposes only an indirect burden on the exercise of religion, *i.e.*, legislation which does not make unlawful the religious practice itself, would radically restrict the operating latitude of the legislature. Statutes which tax income and limit the amount which may be deducted for religious contributions impose an indirect economic burden on the observance of the religion of the citizen whose religion requires him to donate a greater amount to his church; statutes which require the courts to be closed on Saturday and Sunday impose a similar indirect burden on the observance of the religion of the trial lawyer whose religion requires him to rest on a weekday. The list of legislation of this nature is nearly limitless. . . .

Of course, to hold unassailable all legislation regulating conduct which imposes solely an indirect burden on the observance of religion would be a gross oversimplification. If the purpose or effect of a law is to impede the observance of one or all religions or is to discriminate invidiously between religions, that law is constitutionally invalid even though the burden may be characterized as being only indirect. But if the State regulates conduct by enacting a general law within its power, the purpose and effect of which is to advance the State's secular goals, the statute is valid despite its indirect burden on religious observance unless the State may accomplish its purpose by means which do not impose such a burden. . . .

However, appellants advance yet another means at the State's disposal which they would find unobjectionable. They contend that the State should cut an exception from the Sunday labor proscription for those people who, because of religious conviction, observe a day of rest other than Sunday. By such regulation, appellants contend, the economic disadvantages imposed by the present system would be removed and the State's interest in having all people rest one day would be satisfied.

A number of States provide such an exemption and this may well be the wiser solution to the problem. But our concern is not with the wisdom of legislation but with its constitutional limitation. Thus, reason and experience teach that to permit the exemption might well undermine the State's goal of providing a day that, as best possible, eliminates the atmosphere of commercial noise and activity. Although not dispositive of the issue, enforcement problems would be more difficult since there would be two or more days to police rather than one and it would be more difficult to observe whether violations were occurring.

Additional problems might also be presented by a regulation of this sort. To allow only people who rest on a day other than Sunday to keep their businesses open on that day might well provide these people with an economic advantage over their competitors who must remain closed on that day; this might cause the Sunday-observers to complain that their religions are being discriminated against. With this competitive advantage existing, there could well be the temptation for some, in order to keep their businesses open on Sunday, to assert that they have religious convictions which compel them to close their businesses on what had formerly been their least profitable day. This might make necessary a state-conducted inquiry into the sincerity of the individual's religious beliefs, a practice which a State might believe would itself run afoul of the spirit of constitutionally protected religious guarantees. Finally, in order to keep the disruption of the day at a minimum, exempted employers would probably have to hire employees who themselves qualified for the exemption because of their own religious beliefs, a practice which a State might feel to be opposed to its general policy prohibiting religious discrimination in hiring. For all of these reasons, we cannot say that the Pennsylvania statute before us is invalid, either on its face or as applied.

Mr. Justice Harlan concurs in the judgment. Mr. Justice Brennan and Mr. Justice Stewart concur in our disposition of appellants' claims under the Establishment Clause and the Equal Protection Clause. Mr. Justice Frankfurter and Mr. Justice Harlan have rejected appellants' claim under the Free Exercise Clause in a separate opinion.

Accordingly, the decision is

Affirmed.

Mr. Justice BRENNAN, concurring and dissenting.

I agree with the Chief Justice that there is no merit in appellants' establishment and equal-protection claims. I dissent, however, as to the claim that Pennsylvania has prohibited the free exercise of appellants' religion. . . .

Mr. Justice STEWART, dissenting.

I agree with substantially all that Mr. Justice Brennan has written. Pennsylvania has passed a law which compels an Orthodox Jew to choose between his religious faith and his economic survival. That is a cruel choice. It is a choice which I think no State can constitutionally demand. For me this is not something that can be swept under the rug and forgotten in the interest of enforced Sunday togetherness. I think the impact of this law upon these appellants grossly violates their constitutional right to the free exercise of their religion.

NOTES AND QUESTIONS

1. *Burden on religion.* How heavy was the religious burden on Braunfeld and his fellow shopkeepers? The Court pointed out that the Sunday closing law did not directly punish Braunfeld from observing his Saturday Sabbath, rather it made it much more expensive for him to do so. Would it matter to Braunfeld if the law directly or indirectly burdened his practice of religion? Should laws that directly burden Sabbath observance be accommodated? For example, what if someone subpoenaed to testify has a Sabbath during the workweek? What if the witness's religion mandated a two-day Sabbath? Three-day Sabbath?

2. *Government's interests.* A law that burdens religious exercise might nonetheless be enforced if the government's interests are sufficiently important. Laws prohibiting murder still apply even if child sacrifice is a religion's central tenet. What are the government's interests in the Sunday closing law? What were the government's interests in *Reynolds* (banning polygamy) and *Prince* (banning child labor)? How do these government interests compare?

3. *Limitless exemptions.* Should the government have to accommodate every religious practice burdened by laws that do not target religion? What about the Court's observation that the "[t]he list of legislation of this nature [i.e., laws that impose an indirect burden on religion] is nearly limitless"?

4. *Accommodation creating burdens for others.* Would allowing Saturday Sabbath observers to close their shops on Saturday rather than Sunday impose any hardships on others? The Court suggests that accommodating Orthodox Jewish shopkeepers would give them a competitive advantage over those who close on Sunday. How does this potential advantage compare to the Orthodox Jewish shopkeepers' economic disadvantage?

5. *Find another job or profession?* What should one make of Chief Justice Warren's suggestion that if closing two days a week makes it economically impossible for people like Braunfeld to operate a viable clothing or furniture store, such persons should "engag[e] in some other commercial activity which does not call for either Saturday or Sunday labor"?

6. *Lurking Establishment Clause issues.* Are Sunday Sabbath observers faced with the same choice: abandon your religious beliefs or possibly lose your business? Why not? Is it fair that some religions are spared this dilemma while others are not? McGowan v. Maryland, below, addresses an Establishment Clause challenge to a Sunday closing law—a law which had its roots in enforcing the Fourth Commandment ("Keep Holy the Sabbath").

7. *Secular counterpart.* What if Saturday was the only day someone had to spend with their children or sick parent? Should they be entitled to an exemption? Is it fair that they are not? Does it depend on whether time with family is considered a secular counterpart to Sabbath observance?

McGOWAN v. MARYLAND

366 U.S. 420 (1961)

Mr. Chief Justice WARREN delivered the opinion of the Court.

The issues in this case concern the constitutional validity of Maryland criminal statutes, commonly known as Sunday Closing Laws or Sunday Blue Laws. These statutes, with exceptions to be noted hereafter, generally proscribe all labor, business and other commercial activities on Sunday. The questions presented are whether the classifications within the statutes bring about a denial of equal protection of the law, . . . and whether the statutes are laws respecting an establishment of religion or prohibiting the free exercise thereof.

Appellants are seven employees of a large discount department store located on a highway in Anne Arundel County, Maryland. They were indicted for the Sunday sale of a three-ring loose-leaf binder, a can of floor wax, a stapler and staples, and a toy submarine in violation of Md. Ann. Code, Art. 27, § 521. Generally, this section prohibited, throughout the State, the Sunday sale of all merchandise except the retail sale of tobacco products, confectioneries, milk, bread, fruits, gasoline, oils, greases, drugs and medicines, and newspapers and periodicals. Recently amended, this section also now excepts from the general prohibition the retail sale in Anne Arundel County of all foodstuffs, automobile and boating accessories, flowers, toilet goods, hospital supplies and souvenirs. It now further provides that any retail establishment in Anne Arundel County which does not employ more than one person other than the owner may operate on Sunday. . . .

Among other things, appellants contended at the trial that the Maryland statutes under which they were charged were contrary to the Fourteenth Amendment for the reasons stated at the outset of this opinion. Appellants were convicted and each was fined five dollars and costs. The Maryland Court of Appeals affirmed, 220 Md. 117, 151 A.2d 156; on appeal brought under 28 U.S.C. § 1257 (2), we noted probable jurisdiction. 362 U.S. 959.

[Chief Justice Warren considered and rejected an equal protection challenge to the Sunday closing laws.]

. . . .

[A]ppellants contend that the statutes violate the guarantee of separation of church and state in that the statutes are laws respecting an establishment of religion contrary to the First Amendment, made applicable to the States by the Fourteenth Amendment.

The essence of appellants' "establishment" argument is that Sunday is the Sabbath day of the predominant Christian sects; that the purpose of the enforced stoppage of labor on that day is to facilitate and encourage church attendance; that the purpose of setting Sunday as a day of universal rest is to induce people with no religion or people with marginal religious beliefs to join the predominant Christian sects; that the purpose of the atmosphere of tranquility created by Sunday closing is to aid the conduct of church services and religious observance of the sacred day. In substantiating their "establishment" argument, appellants rely on the wording of the present Maryland statutes, on earlier versions of the current Sunday laws and on prior judicial characterizations of these laws by the Maryland Court of Appeals. . . .

In light of the evolution of our Sunday Closing Laws through the centuries, and of their more or less recent emphasis upon secular considerations, it is not difficult to discern that as presently written and administered, most of them, at least, are of a secular rather than of a religious character, and that presently they bear no relationship to establishment of religion as those words are used in the Constitution of the United States.

Throughout this century and longer, both the federal and state governments have oriented their activities very largely toward improvement of the health, safety, recreation and general well-being of our citizens. Numerous laws affecting public health, safety factors in industry, laws affecting hours and conditions of labor of women and children, week-end diversion at parks and beaches, and cultural activities of various kinds, now point the way toward the good life for all. Sunday Closing Laws, like those before us, have become part and parcel of this great governmental concern wholly apart from their original purposes or connotations. The present purpose and effect of most of them is to provide a uniform day of rest for all citizens; the fact that this day is Sunday, a day of particular significance for the dominant Christian sects, does not bar the State from achieving its secular goals. To say that the States cannot prescribe Sunday as a day of rest for these purposes solely because centuries ago such laws had their genesis in religion would give a constitutional interpretation of hostility to the public welfare rather than one of mere separation of church and State.

Finally, we should make clear that this case deals only with the constitutionality of § 521 of the Maryland statute before us. We do not hold that Sunday legislation may not be a violation of the "Establishment" Clause if it can be demonstrated that its purpose—evidenced either on the face of the legislation, in conjunction with its legislative history, or in its operative effect—is to use the State's coercive power to aid religion.

Accordingly, the decision is

Affirmed.

Separate opinion of Mr. Justice FRANKFURTER, whom Mr. Justice HARLAN joins.

Mr. Justice DOUGLAS, dissenting.

The question is not whether one day out of seven can be imposed by a State as a day of rest. The question is not whether Sunday can by force of custom and habit be retained as a day of rest. The question is whether a State can impose criminal sanctions on those who, unlike the Christian majority that makes up our society, worship on a different day or do not share the religious scruples of the majority.

If the "free exercise" of religion were subject to reasonable regulations, as it is under some constitutions, or if all laws "respecting the establishment of religion" were not proscribed, I could understand how rational men, representing a predominantly Christian civilization, might think these Sunday laws did not unreasonably interfere with anyone's free exercise of religion and took no step toward a burdensome establishment of any religion. . . .

With that as my starting point I do not see how a State can make protesting citizens refrain from doing innocent acts on Sunday because the doing of those acts offends sentiments of their Christian neighbors. . . .

The Court picks and chooses language from various decisions to bolster its conclusion that these Sunday laws in the modern setting are "civil regulations." No matter how much is written, no matter what is said, the parentage of these laws is the Fourth Commandment; and they serve and satisfy the religious predispositions of our Christian communities. After all, the labels a State places on its laws are not binding on us when we are confronted with a constitutional decision. We reach our own conclusion as to the character, effect, and practical operation of the regulation in determining its constitutionality.

It seems to me plain that by these laws the States compel one, under sanction of law, to refrain from work or recreation on Sunday because of the majority's religious views about that day. The State by law makes Sunday a symbol of respect or adherence. Refraining from work or recreation in deference to the majority's religious feelings about Sunday is within every person's choice. By what authority can government compel it? . . .

These laws are sustained because, it is said, the First Amendment is concerned with religious convictions or opinion, not with conduct. But it is a strange Bill of Rights that makes it possible for the dominant religious group to bring the minority to heel because the minority, in the doing of acts which intrinsically are wholesome are not antisocial, does not defer to the majority's religious beliefs. . . .

The reverse side of an "establishment" is a burden on the "free exercise" of religion. Receipt of funds from the State benefits the established church directly; laying an extra tax on nonmembers benefits the established church indirectly. Certainly the present Sunday laws place Orthodox Jews and Sabbatarians under extra burdens because of their religious opinions or beliefs. Requiring them to abstain from their trade or business on Sunday reduces their work-week to five days, unless they violate their religious scruples. This places them at a competitive disadvantage and penalizes them for adhering to their religious beliefs. . . .

[T]he special protection which Sunday laws give the dominant religious groups and the penalty they place on minorities whose holy day is Saturday constitute, in my view, state interference with the "free exercise" of religion.

NOTES AND QUESTIONS

1. *Religious establishment.* If Maryland had enacted its Sunday closing laws in order to encourage people to attend Christian church and to respect it as a sacred day, as the plaintiffs alleged, then it would violate the Establishment Clause. The government would be favoring Christianity over other religions. In what way, if any, would this establishment also affect people's practice of their religion?

2. *The "evolving purpose" stratagem.* Is Chief Justice Warren's "evolving purpose" theory persuasive? If mandatory Sunday closing laws have a legislative history associated with enforcing the Fourth Commandment ("Keep Holy the Sabbath"), does a *post hoc* rationalization of the Blue Laws as mere labor regulations serve to sever any religious meaning from such enactments?

3. *A legislative accommodation?* One way of viewing *McGowan* is as a kind of legislative effort to ensure that Sunday worshippers are not faced with a conflict between workplace duties and religious duties. Would this be a more honest rationale for sustaining the Maryland law? Should Maryland's legislature, as a matter of free exercise principles, be permitted to enact a statute that facilitates religious observance by reducing otherwise probable conflicts?

4. *Narrow tailoring?* Even if one might imagine a mandatory accommodation measure, is the Maryland law well crafted to that purpose? If a more limited law would serve this purpose, why doesn't the Supreme Court require Maryland to use more narrowly tailored means?

5. *Accommodations for all?* If a state creates a statutory exemption for one group— most likely the dominant religious group or groups—does it have an obligation to accommodate minority religionists?

ESTATE OF THORNTON v. CALDOR, INC.

472 U.S. 703 (1985)

Chief Justice BURGER delivered the opinion of the Court.

We granted certiorari to decide whether a state statute that provides employees with the absolute right not to work on their chosen Sabbath violates the Establishment Clause of the First Amendment.

In early 1975, petitioner's decedent Donald E. Thornton[1] began working for respondent Caldor, Inc., a chain of New England retail stores; he managed the men's and boys' clothing department in respondent's Waterbury, Connecticut, store. At that time, respondent's Connecticut stores were closed on Sundays pursuant to state law. Conn.Gen.Stat. §§ 53-300 to 53-303 (1958).

In 1977, following the state legislature's revision of the Sunday-closing laws, respondent opened its Connecticut stores for Sunday business. In order to handle the expanded store hours, respondent required its managerial employees to work every third or fourth Sunday. Thornton, a Presbyterian who observed Sunday as his Sabbath, initially complied with respondent's demand and worked a total of 31 Sundays in 1977 and 1978. In October 1978, Thornton was transferred to a management position in respondent's Torrington store; he continued to work on Sundays during the first part of 1979. In November 1979, however, Thornton informed respondent that he would no longer work on Sundays because he observed that day as his Sabbath; he invoked the protection of Conn.Gen.Stat. § 53-303e(b) (1985), which provides:

"No person who states that a particular day of the week is observed as his Sabbath may be required by his employer to work on such day. An employee's refusal to work on his Sabbath shall not constitute grounds for his dismissal."

Thornton rejected respondent's offer either to transfer him to a management job in a Massachusetts store that was closed on Sundays, or to transfer him to a nonsupervisory position in the Torrington store at a lower salary. In March 1980, respondent transferred Thornton to a clerical position in the Torrington store; Thornton resigned two days later and filed a grievance with the State Board of Mediation and Arbitration alleging that he was discharged from his manager's position in violation of Conn.Gen.Stat. § 53-303e(b) (1985).

Respondent defended its action on the ground that Thornton had not been "discharged" within the meaning of the statute; respondent also urged the Board to find that the statute violated Article 7 of the Connecticut Constitution as well as the Establishment Clause of the First Amendment. . .

Under the Religion Clauses, government must guard against activity that impinges on religious freedom, and must take pains not to compel people to act in the name of any religion. In setting the appropriate boundaries in Establishment Clause cases, the Court has frequently relied on our holding in *Lemon* for guidance, and we do so here. To pass constitutional muster under *Lemon* a statute must not only have a secular purpose and not foster excessive entanglement of government with religion, its primary effect must not advance or inhibit religion.

---

[1] Thornton died on February 4, 1982, while his appeal was pending before the Supreme Court of Connecticut. The administrator of Thornton's estate has continued the suit on behalf of the decedent's estate.

The Connecticut statute challenged here guarantees every employee, who "states that a particular day of the week is observed as his Sabbath," the right not to work on his chosen day. Conn.Gen.Stat. § 53-303e(b) (1985). The State has thus decreed that those who observe a Sabbath any day of the week as a matter of religious conviction must be relieved of the duty to work on that day, no matter what burden or inconvenience this imposes on the employer or fellow workers. The statute arms Sabbath observers with an absolute and unqualified right not to work on whatever day they designate as their Sabbath.

In essence, the Connecticut statute imposes on employers and employees an absolute duty to conform their business practices to the particular religious practices of the employee by enforcing observance of the Sabbath the employee unilaterally designates. The State thus commands that Sabbath religious concerns automatically control over all secular interests at the workplace; the statute takes no account of the convenience or interests of the employer or those of other employees who do not observe a Sabbath. The employer and others must adjust their affairs to the command of the State whenever the statute is invoked by an employee.

There is no exception under the statute for special circumstances, such as the Friday Sabbath observer employed in an occupation with a Monday through Friday schedule—a school teacher, for example; the statute provides for no special consideration if a high percentage of an employer's work force asserts rights to the same Sabbath. Moreover, there is no exception when honoring the dictates of Sabbath observers would cause the employer substantial economic burdens or when the employer's compliance would require the imposition of significant burdens on other employees required to work in place of the Sabbath observers. Finally, the statute allows for no consideration as to whether the employer has made reasonable accommodation proposals.

This unyielding weighting in favor of Sabbath observers over all other interests contravenes a fundamental principle of the Religion Clauses, so well articulated by Judge Learned Hand:

"The First Amendment . . . gives no one the right to insist that in pursuit of their own interests others must conform their conduct to his own religious necessities." Otten v. Baltimore & Ohio R. Co., 205 F.2d 58, 61 (CA2 1953). As such, the statute goes beyond having an incidental or remote effect of advancing religion. The statute has a primary effect that impermissibly advances a particular religious practice.

We hold that the Connecticut statute, which provides Sabbath observers with an absolute and unqualified right not to work on their Sabbath, violates the Establishment Clause of the First Amendment. Accordingly, the judgment of the Supreme Court of Connecticut is

Affirmed.

Justice REHNQUIST dissents.

Justice O'CONNOR, with whom Justice MARSHALL joins, concurring.

The Court applies the test enunciated in Lemon v. Kurtzman, 403 U.S. 602, 612-613 (1971), and concludes that Conn.Gen.Stat. § 53-303e(b) (1985) has a primary effect that impermissibly advances religion. I agree, and I join the Court's opinion and judgment. In my view, the Connecticut Sabbath law has an impermissible effect because it conveys a message of endorsement of the Sabbath observance.

All employees, regardless of their religious orientation, would value the benefit which the statute bestows on Sabbath observers—the right to select the day of the week in which to refrain from labor. Yet Connecticut requires private employers to confer this valued and desirable benefit only on those employees who adhere to a particular religious belief. The statute singles out Sabbath observers for special and, as the Court concludes, absolute protection without according similar accommodation to ethical and religious beliefs and practices of other private employees. There can be little doubt that an objective observer or the public at large would perceive this statutory scheme precisely as the Court does today. The message conveyed is one of endorsement of a particular religious belief, to the detriment of those who do not share it. As such, the Connecticut statute has the effect of advancing religion, and cannot withstand Establishment Clause scrutiny.

I do not read the Court's opinion as suggesting that the religious accommodation provisions of Title VII of the Civil Rights Act of 1964 are similarly invalid. These provisions preclude employment discrimination based on a person's religion and require private employers to reasonably accommodate the religious practices of employees unless to do so would cause undue hardship to the employer's business. 42 U.S.C. §§ 2000e(j) and 2000e-2(a)(1). Like the Connecticut Sabbath law, Title VII attempts to lift a burden on religious practice that is imposed by private employers, and hence it is not the sort of accommodation statute specifically contemplated by the Free Exercise Clause. The provisions of Title VII must therefore manifest a valid secular purpose and effect to be valid under the Establishment Clause. In my view, a statute outlawing employment discrimination based on race, color, religion, sex, or national origin has the valid secular purpose of assuring employment opportunity to all groups in our pluralistic society. Since Title VII calls for reasonable rather than absolute accommodation and extends that requirement to all religious beliefs and practices rather than protecting only the Sabbath observance, I believe an objective observer would perceive it as an anti-discrimination law rather than an endorsement of religion or a particular religious practice.

NOTES AND QUESTIONS

1. *Sunday closing law.* This case arose because Connecticut eliminated its Sunday closing law. As a result, Sunday Sabbath observers like Thornton found themselves facing the dilemma that had previously confronted Saturday Sabbath observers: choosing between their employment and their Sabbath observance. Do the burdens on Sabbath observance differ for Thornton compared to Braunfeld?

2. *Favoring religion.* Does the Connecticut law protecting all Sabbath observers favor one religion over others? Does it favor some religions over others? Does it favor religion over its secular counterpart? Is there a secular counterpart to Sabbath observance?

3. *Burden on others.* The Court held that the absolute nature of the law's protection violated the Establishment Clause because it imposed on employers and employees. In what way? How do these burdens compare to burdens that would have been created had Braunfeld been accommodated?

4. *Proposed alternative.* Justice O'Connor maintains that it is possible to accommodate Sabbath observers without violating the Establishment Clause and points to the religious accommodations offered by Title VII of the Civil Rights Act as a model. How does Title VII differ from the Connecticut law in terms of

which religious practices are accommodated? How does it differ from the Connecticut law in terms of what burden on others is tolerated?

CHAPTER
14

Free Exercise of Religion:
Individual Exemptions

TABLE OF CONTENTS

The Supreme Court's initial response to Free Exercise Clause challenges, reflected in cases like *Reynolds* and *Beason*, was to reject categorically the judicial imposition of religious exemptions from generally applicable laws that did not target a particular sect for punishment. In other words, even though religious belief was free from any and all government regulation, conduct of any sort could be the subject of neutral laws of general application. (Note, however, that cases like *Ballard* could be seen as raising a question about the Court's commitment to safeguarding even mere religious belief.) Thus, one of the first doctrinal dichotomies in the Supreme Court's free exercise jurisprudence is the belief/conduct dichotomy: The Free Exercise Clause protects all religious beliefs, but not necessarily all conduct mandated by religious belief.

The Warren Court questioned and ultimately rejected the belief/conduct dichotomy. Writing for the Supreme Court in *Sherbert*, Justice William J. Brennan, Jr., instead suggested that neutral laws of general applicability should be subject to strict judicial scrutiny when such laws impeded religiously motivated conduct. For a period of years from 1963 to 1990, the Supreme Court sometimes applied strict scrutiny, but sometimes did not, to test the constitutionality, as applied, of general laws that substantially burdened religiously motivated conduct. The new dichotomy contrasted "direct" versus "indirect" burdens on religious practice. The Free Exercise Clause generally protected against "direct" burdens but not against "indirect" burdens (for example, the economic losses that would result from closing on Saturday, as well as Sunday, for observant Jews in a state with mandatory Sunday store-closing laws). Moreover, the "strictness" of the strict scrutiny was very much open to doubt. Preferred religions, such as the Old Order Amish, were able to obtain exemptions from generally applicable state laws. On the other hand, new religious movements, like the Scientologists, did not fare so well. And even the Old Order Amish found that the strictness of strict scrutiny waned in the face of a general government welfare program, like Social Security.

In 1990, in *Smith*, the Supreme Court seemed to return its free exercise jurisprudence to the pre-*Sherbert* regime, finding that neutral laws of general applicability did not violate the Free Exercise Clause.

In thinking about the merits of *Smith* versus *Sherbert*, one should consider the overall purpose that the Free Exercise Clause exists to serve. If religious autonomy is the primary rationale for the clause, then the *Sherbert* approach arguably advances free exercise values more effectively than does *Smith*. A focus on equality, however, would not necessarily entail the judicial creation and enforcement of autonomy-enhancing religious exemptions. Instead, judicial scrutiny should focus on overt and covert efforts to impede or punish unpopular religions and religionists. An equalitarian theory of the Free Exercise Clause would also reduce the tension with the Establishment Clause: Just as the Establishment Clause prevents government from preferring or advancing one particular religious sect, the Free Exercise Clause prevents government from *discouraging* any particular religious sect—both clauses exist to prevent government from either proselytizing or proscribing particular religions or religious beliefs.

Although an equality-based theory of the Free Exercise Clause is plausible, most contemporary scholars strongly embrace the autonomy rationale and accordingly are very skeptical of *Smith*. As you read these materials, consider whether the rules that the Court provides are capable of neutral and consistent enforcement, regardless of whether the religion at bar is the Roman Catholic Church or the Unification Church (that is, the "Moonies").

A. THE BELIEF/CONDUCT DICHOTOMY

The earliest Free Exercise Clause cases involve efforts to suppress the Mormon practice of plural marriage. The federal, state, and territorial governments engaged in a concerted effort to prevent polygamy. Efforts at suppression of the practice led to criminal enforcement actions. Members of the Mormon Church defended against these prosecutions by invoking the Free Exercise Clause (which, even in the 1870s, clearly applied against the federal and territorial governments). As you will see, these efforts did not prove successful. The Supreme Court construed the Free Exercise Clause narrowly to protect only religious belief, and not actions mandated by religious belief.

REYNOLDS v. UNITED STATES
98 U.S. (8 Otto) 145 (1879)

ERROR to the Supreme Court of the Territory of Utah. This is an indictment found in the District Court for the third judicial district of the Territory of Utah, charging George Reynolds with bigamy, in violation of sect. 5352 of the Revised Statutes, which, omitting its exceptions, is as follows:—

"Every person having a husband or wife living, who marries another, whether married or single, in a Territory, or other place over which the United States have exclusive jurisdiction, is guilty of bigamy, and shall be punished by a fine of not more than $500, and by imprisonment for a term of not more than five years.

[Reynolds was tried and convicted of violating the Utah territory's proscription against bigamy. He appealed his conviction, in part, on a free exercise claim.]

Mr. Chief Justice WAITE delivered the opinion of the court.

The assignments of error, when grouped, present the following questions:—

. . .

Should the accused have been acquitted if he married the second time, because he believed it to be his religious duty? . . .

As to the defence of religious belief or duty.

On the trial, the plaintiff in error, the accused, proved that at the time of his alleged second marriage he was, and for may years before had been, a member of the Church of Jesus Christ of Latter-Day Saints, commonly called the Mormon Church, and a believer in its doctrines; that it was an accepted doctrine of that church "that it was the duty of male members of said church, circumstances permitting, to practise polygamy; . . . that this duty was enjoined by different books which the members of said church believed to be of divine origin, and among others the Holy Bible, and also that the members of the church believed that the practice of polygamy was directly enjoined upon the male members thereof by the Almighty God, in a revelation to Joseph Smith, the founder and prophet of said church; that the failing or refusing to practise polygamy by such male members of said church, when circumstances would admit, would be punished, and that the penalty for such failure and refusal would be damnation in the life to come." He also proved "that he had received permission from the recognized authorities in said church to enter into polygamous marriage."

Upon this proof he asked the court to instruct the jury that if they found from the evidence that he "was married as charged—if he was married—in pursuance of and in conformity with what he believed at the time to be a religious duty, that the verdict must be 'not guilty.'" . . .

Congress cannot pass a law for the government of the Territories which shall prohibit the free exercise of religion. The first amendment to the Constitution expressly forbids such legislation. Religious freedom is guaranteed everywhere throughout the United States, so far as congressional interference is concerned. The question to be determined is, whether the law now under consideration comes within this prohibition.

The word "religion" is not defined in the Constitution. We must go elsewhere, therefore, to ascertain its meaning, and nowhere more appropriately, we think, than to the history of the times in the midst of which the provision was adopted. The precise point of the inquiry is, what is the religious freedom which has been guaranteed.

Before the adoption of the Constitution, attempts were made in some of the colonies and States to legislate not only in respect to the establishment of religion, but in respect to its doctrines and precepts as well. The people were taxed, against their will, for the support of religion, and sometimes for the support of particular sects to whose tenets they could not and did not subscribe. Punishments were prescribed for a failure to attend upon public worship, and sometimes for entertaining heretical opinions. The controversy upon this general subject was animated in many of the States, but seemed at last to culminate in Virginia. In 1784, the House of Delegates of that State having under consideration "a bill establishing provision for teachers of the Christian religion," postponed it until the next session, and directed that the bill should be published and distributed, and that the people be requested "to signify their opinion respecting the adoption of such bill at the next session of assembly."

This brought out a determined opposition. Amongst others, Mr. Madison prepared a "Memorial and Remonstrance," which was widely circulated and signed, and in which he demonstrated "that religion, or the duty we owe the Creator," was not within the cognizance of civil government. . . . At the next session the proposed bill was not only defeated, but another, 'for establishing religious freedom,' drafted by Mr. Jefferson, was passed. . . .

In a little more than a year after the passage of this statute the convention met which prepared the Constitution of the United States. . . . Five of the States, while adopting the Constitution, proposed amendments. Three—New Hampshire, New York, and Virginia—included in one form or another a declaration of religious freedom in the changes they desired to have made, as did also North Carolina, where the convention at first declined to ratify the Constitution until the proposed amendments were acted upon. Accordingly, at the first session of the first Congress the amendment now under consideration was proposed with others by Mr. Madison. It met the view of the advocates of religious freedom, and was adopted. Mr. Jefferson afterwards, in reply to an address to him by a committee of the Danbury Baptist Association, took occasion to say: "Believing with you that religion is a matter which lies solely between man and his God; that he owes account to none other for his faith or his worship; that the legislative powers of the government reach actions only, and not opinions, I contemplate with sovereign reverence that act of the whole American people which declared that their legislature should 'make no law respecting an establishment of religion or prohibiting the free exercise thereof,' thus building a wall of separation between church and State. Adhering to this expression of the supreme will of the nation in behalf of the rights of conscience, I shall see with sincere satisfaction the progress of those sentiments which tend to restore man to all his natural rights, convinced he has no natural right in opposition to his social duties." Coming as this does from an acknowledged leader of the advocates of the measure, it may be accepted almost as an authoritative declaration of the scope and effect of the amendment thus secured. Congress was deprived of all legislative power over mere opinion, but was left free to reach actions which were in violation of social duties or subversive of good order.

Polygamy has always been odious among the northern and western nations of Europe, and, until the establishment of the Mormon Church, was almost exclusively a feature of the life of Asiatic and of African people. At common law, the second marriage was always void (2 Kent, Com. 79), and from the earliest history of England polygamy has been treated as an offence against society. . . . .

By the statute of 1 James I. (c. 11), the offence, if committed in England or Wales, was made punishable in the civil courts, and the penalty was death. As this statute was limited in its operation to England and Wales, it was at a very early period re-enacted, generally with some modifications, in all the colonies. In connection with the case we are now considering, it is a significant fact that on the 8th of December, 1788, after the passage of the act establishing religious freedom, and after the convention of Virginia had recommended as an amendment to the Constitution of the United States the declaration in a bill of rights that 'all men have an equal, natural, and unalienable right to the free exercise of religion, according to the dictates of conscience,' the legislature of that State substantially enacted the statute of James I., death penalty included, because, as recited in the preamble, 'it hath been doubted whether bigamy or poligamy be punishable by the laws of this

Commonwealth.' From that day to this we think it may safely be said there never has been a time in any State of the Union when polygamy has not been an offence against society, cognizable by the civil courts and punishable with more or less severity. In the face of all this evidence, it is impossible to believe that the constitutional guaranty of religious freedom was intended to prohibit legislation in respect to this most important feature of social life. Marriage, while from its very nature a sacred obligation, is nevertheless, in most civilized nations, a civil contract, and usually regulated by law. Upon it society may be said to be built, and out of its fruits spring social relations and social obligations and duties, with which government is necessarily required to deal. In fact, according as monogamous or polygamous marriages are allowed, do we find the principles on which the government of the people, to a greater or less extent, rests. . . .

In our opinion, the statute immediately under consideration is within the legislative power of Congress. It is constitutional and valid as prescribing a rule of action for all those residing in the Territories, and in places over which the United States have exclusive control. This being so, the only question which remains is, whether those who make polygamy a part of their religion are excepted from the operation of the statute. If they are, then those who do not make polygamy a part of their religious belief may be found guilty and punished, while those who do, must be acquitted and go free. This would be introducing a new element into criminal law. Laws are made for the government of actions, and while they cannot interfere with mere religious belief and opinions, they may with practices. Suppose one believed that human sacrifices were a necessary part of religious worship, would it be seriously contended that the civil government under which he lived could not interfere to prevent a sacrifice? Or if a wife religiously believed it was her duty to burn herself upon the funeral pile of her dead husband, would it be beyond the power of the civil government to prevent her carrying her belief into practice?

So here, as a law of the organization of society under the exclusive dominion of the United States, it is provided that plural marriages shall not be allowed. Can a man excuse his practices to the contrary because of his religious belief? To permit this would be to make the professed doctrines of religious belief superior to the law of the land, and in effect to permit every citizen to become a law unto himself. Government could exist only in name under such circumstances.

Upon a careful consideration of the whole case, we are satisfied that no error was committed by the court below.

Judgment affirmed.

DAVIS v. BEASON

133 U.S. 333 (1890)

[Davis was indicted for conspiracy to commit voting fraud. The Idaho territory conditioned voting on an oath that stated:

> I do further swear that I am not a bigamist or polygamist, that I am not a member of any order, organization or association which teaches, advises, counsels or encourages its members, devotees or any other person to commit the crime of bigamy or polygamy, or any other crime defined by law, as a duty arising or resulting from membership in such order, organization or association, or which practises bigamy, polygamy or plural or celestial marriage as a doctrinal rite of

such organization, that I do not and will not, publicly or privately, or in any manner whatever teach, advise, counsel or encourage any person to commit the crime of bigamy or polygamy, or any other crime defined by law, either as a religious duty or otherwise.

The defendants, members of the Mormon Church, "demurred to the indictment, and the demurrer being overruled they pleaded separately not guilty. On the trial which followed on the 12th of September, 1889, the jury found the defendant, Samuel D. Davis, guilty as charged in the indictment. The defendant was thereupon sentenced to pay of fine of $500, and in default of its payment to be confined in the county jail of Oneida County for a term not exceeding 250 days, and was remanded to the custody of the sheriff until the judgment should be satisfied."]

Mr. Justice FIELD, after stating the case, delivered the opinion of the court.

On this appeal, our only inquiry is whether the District Court of the Territory had jurisdiction of the offence charged in the indictment of which the defendant was found guilty. . . .

On this hearing we can only consider whether, these allegations being taken as true, an offence was committed of which the territorial court had jurisdiction to try the defendant. And on this point there can be no serious discussion or difference of opinion. Bigamy and polygamy are crimes by the laws of all civilized and Christian countries. They are crimes by the laws of the United States, and they are crimes by the laws of Idaho. They tend to destroy the purity of the marriage relation, to disturb the peace of families, to degrade woman and to debase man. Few crimes are more pernicious to the best interests of society and receive more general or more deserved punishment. To extend exemption from punishment for such crimes would be to shock the moral judgment of the community. If they are crimes, then to teach, advise and counsel their practice is to aid in their commission, and such teaching and counselling are themselves criminal and proper subjects of punishment, as aiding and abetting crime are in all other cases.

The term "religion" has reference to one's views of his relations to his Creator, and to the obligations they impose of reverence for his being and character, and of obedience to his will. It is often confounded with the *cultus* or form of worship of a particular sect, but is distinguishable from the latter. The first amendment to the Constitution, in declaring that Congress shall make no law respecting the establishment of religion, or forbidding the free exercise thereof, was intended to allow every one under the jurisdiction of the United States to entertain such notions respecting his relations to his Maker and the duties they impose as may be approved by his judgment and conscience, and to exhibit his sentiments in such form of worship as he may think proper, not injurious to the equal rights of others, and to prohibit legislation for the support of any religious tenets, or the modes of worship of any sect. The oppressive measures adopted, and the cruelties and punishments inflicted by the governments of Europe for many ages, to compel parties to conform, in their religious beliefs and modes of worship, to the views of the most numerous sect, and the folly of attempting in that way to control the mental operations of persons, and enforce an outward conformity to a prescribed standard, led to the adoption of the amendment in question. It was never intended or supposed that the amendment could be invoked as a protection against legislation for the punishment of acts inimical to the peace, good order and morals of society. With man's relations to his Maker and the obligations he may think they impose, and the manner in which an expression shall be made by him of his belief on those subjects, no interference can be permitted, provided always the laws of society, designed to secure its peace and prosperity, and the morals of its people, are not interfered with. However free the exercise of religion may be, it must be subordinate to the criminal laws of the country, passed with reference to actions regarded by general consent as properly the subjects of punitive legislation. There have been sects which denied as a part of their religious tenets that there should be any marriage tie, and advocated promiscuous intercourse of the sexes as prompted by the passions of its members. And history discloses the fact that the necessity of human sacrifices, on special occasions, has been a tenet of many sects. Should a sect of either of these kinds ever find its way into this country, swift punishment would follow the carrying into effect of its doctrines, and no heed would be given to the pretence that, as religious beliefs, their supporters could be protected in their exercise by the Constitution of the United States. Probably never before in the history of this country has it been seriously contended that the whole punitive power of the government for acts, recognized by the general consent of the Christian world in modern times as proper matters for prohibitory legislation, must be suspended in order that the tenets of a religious sect encouraging crime may be carried out without hindrance. . . .

It is assumed by counsel of the petitioner, that because no mode of worship can be established or religious tenets enforced in this country, therefore any form of worship may be followed and any tenets, however destructive of society, may be held and advocated, if asserted to be a part of the religious doctrines of those advocating and practising them. But nothing is further from the truth. Whilst legislation for the establishment of a religion is forbidden, and its free exercise permitted, it does not follow that everything which may be so called can be tolerated. Crime is not the less odious because sanctioned by what any particular sect may designate as religion.

It only remains to refer to the laws which authorized the legislature of the Territory of Idaho to prescribe the qualifications of voters and the oath they were required to take.

[Justice Field concluded that the territorial legislature possessed the power to enact the law and that it had properly enacted the Statute.]

The judgment of the court below is therefore affirmed.

NOTES AND QUESTIONS

1. *The belief/conduct dichotomy.* Both *Reynolds* and *Beason* strongly endorse the belief/conduct dichotomy. Was the rationale persuasive? Should the Free Exercise Clause protect only belief, and not action? What about drinking sacramental wine incident to the Catholic Mass? Or ingesting peyote incident to the rites of the Native American Church? Is "belief" really free if a religion cannot practice its liturgy? Would your answer change if the religion at issue was Rastafarianism? If it does, what does that say about the importance of culture in theorizing free exercise?

2. *Neutral laws?* Even if the Free Exercise Clause does not provide judicially recognized exemptions from neutral laws of general applicability, were the laws in *Reynolds* and *Beason* really "neutral"? Could Idaho fine a person $20 for spitting in public, but $40 if the person spits in public and advocates plural marriage? Does the linkage of voting rights to an oath to oppose plural marriage

constitute a regulation of conduct? Or of belief? Does the Supreme Court seem to care?

3. *Ethnocentrism.* Is polygamy subversive of good order? According to whom? What should one make of the Supreme Court's overt racial language in *Reynolds* (describing polygamy as "almost exclusively a feature of the life of Asiatic and of African people")?

4. *A "Christian nation" and the Establishment Clause.* What should one make of the Supreme Court's rhetoric regarding the United States being a European, Christian nation? How does such a declaration square with the Establishment Clause? Does this suggest that the Supreme Court is bringing a skeptical eye to bear on the beliefs of the defendants? Should the Supreme Court declare particular religious beliefs unacceptable?

5. *The limits of autonomy.* Even if the anti-Mormon rhetoric is problematic, was the Supreme Court correct to assert that it simply is not possible to make every person "a law unto himself"? Or would it be possible to grant at least some religious exemptions from neutral laws of general applicability without making the business of government impossible?

UNITED STATES v. BALLARD

322 U.S. 78 (1944)

Mr. Justice DOUGLAS delivered the opinion of the Court.

Respondents were indicted and convicted for using, and conspiring to use, the mails to defraud. § 215 Criminal Code, 18 U.S.C. § 338; § 37 Criminal Code, 18 U.S.C. § 88. The indictment was in twelve counts. It charged a scheme to defraud by organizing and promoting the I Am movement through the use of the mails. The charge was that certain designated corporations were formed, literature distributed and sold, funds solicited, and memberships in the I Am movement sought "by means of false and fraudulent representations, pretenses and promises." . . .

The following are representative:

> that Guy W. Ballard, now deceased, alias Saint Germain, Jesus, George Washington, and Godfre Ray King, had been selected and thereby designated by the alleged "ascertained masters," Saint Germain, as a divine messenger; and that the words of "ascended masters" and the words of the alleged divine entity, Saint Germain, would be transmitted to mankind through the medium of the said Guy W. Ballard;
>
> that Guy W. Ballard, during his lifetime, and Edna W. Ballard, and Donald Ballard, by reason of their alleged high spiritual attainments and righteous conduct, had been selected as divine messengers through which the words of the alleged "ascended masters," including the alleged Saint Germain, would be communicated to mankind under the teachings commonly known as the "I Am" movement;
>
> that Guy W. Ballard, during his lifetime, and Edna W. Ballard and Donald Ballard had, by reason of supernatural attainments, the power to heal persons of ailments and diseases and to make well persons afflicted with any diseases, injuries, or ailments, and did falsely represent to persons intended to be defrauded that the three designated persons had the ability and power to cure persons of those diseases normally classified as curable and also of diseases which are ordinarily classified by the medical profession as being incurable diseases; and did

further represent that the three designated persons had in fact cured either by the activity of one, either, or all of said persons, hundreds of persons afflicted with diseases and ailments;

Each of the representations enumerated in the indictment was followed by the charge that respondents "well knew" it was false. . . .

Early in the trial, however, objections were raised to the admission of certain evidence concerning respondents' religious beliefs. The court conferred with counsel in absence of the jury and with the acquiescence of counsel for the United States and for respondents confined the issues on this phase of the case to the question of the good faith of respondents. [The district court instructed the jury not to consider the ultimate truth of the Ballards' theology, but rather whether "these defendants honestly and in good faith believe[d] those things."]

The Circuit Court of Appeals reversed the judgment of conviction and granted a new trial, one judge dissenting. 138 F.2d 540. In its view the restriction of the issue in question to that of good faith was error.

The case is here on a petition for a writ of certiorari which we granted because of the importance of the question presented.

As we have noted, the Circuit Court of Appeals held that the question of the truth of the representations concerning respondents' religious doctrines or beliefs should have been submitted to the jury. . . . [W]e do not agree that the truth or verity of respondents' religious doctrines or beliefs should have been submitted to the jury. Whatever this particular indictment might require, the First Amendment precludes such a course, as the United States seems to concede. "The law knows no heresy, and is committed to the support of no dogma, the establishment of no sect." *Watson v. Jones*, 13 Wall. 679, 728. The First Amendment has a dual aspect. It not only "forestalls compulsion by law of the acceptance of any creed or the practice of any form of worship" but also "safeguards the free exercise of the chosen form of religion." *Cantwell v. Connecticut*, 310 U.S. 296, 303. "Thus the Amendment embraces two concepts—freedom to believe and freedom to act. The first is absolute but, in the nature of things, the second cannot be." *Id.*, pp. 303-304. Freedom of thought, which includes freedom of religious belief, is basic in a society of free men. *Board of Education v. Barnette*, 319 U.S. 624. It embraces the right to maintain theories of life and of death and of the hereafter which are rank heresy to followers of the orthodox faiths. Heresy trials are foreign to our Constitution. Men may believe what they cannot prove. They may not be put to the proof of their religious doctrines or beliefs. Religious experiences which are as real as life to some may be incomprehensible to others. Yet the fact that they may be beyond the ken of mortals does not mean that they can be made suspect before the law. Many take their gospel from the New Testament. But it would hardly be supposed that they could be tried before a jury charged with the duty of determining whether those teachings contained false representations. The miracles of the New Testament, the Divinity of Christ, life after death, the power of prayer are deep in the religious convictions of many. If one could be sent to jail because a jury in a hostile environment found those teachings false, little indeed would be left of religious freedom. The Fathers of the Constitution were not unaware of the varied and extreme views of religious sects, of the violence of disagreement among them, and of the lack of any one religious creed on which all men would agree. They fashioned a charter of government which envisaged the widest possible toleration of conflicting views. Man's relation to his God was made no concern of the state. He was granted the right to worship as he pleased and to answer to no man for the verity of his religious views. The religious views espoused by respondents might seem incredible, if not preposterous, to most people. But if those doctrines are subject to trial before a jury charged with finding their truth or falsity, then the same can be done with the religious beliefs of any sect. When the triers of fact undertake that task, they enter a forbidden domain. The First Amendment does not select any one group or any one type of religion for preferred treatment. . . . So we conclude that the District Court ruled properly when it withheld from the jury all questions concerning the truth or falsity of the religious beliefs or doctrines of respondents. . . .

The judgment is reversed and the cause is remanded to the Circuit Court of Appeals for further proceedings in conformity to this opinion.

Reversed.

Mr. Justice JACKSON, dissenting:

I should say the defendants have done just that for which they are indicted. If I might agree to their conviction without creating a precedent, I cheerfully would do so. I can see in their teachings nothing but humbug, untainted by any trace of truth. But that does not dispose of the constitutional question whether misrepresentation of religious experience or belief is prosecutable; it rather emphasizes the danger of such prosecutions.

The Ballard family claimed miraculous communication with the spirit world and supernatural power to heal the sick. They were brought to trial for mail fraud on an indictment which charged that their representations were false and that they "well knew" they were false. The trial judge, obviously troubled, ruled that the court could not try whether the statements were untrue, but could inquire whether the defendants knew them to be untrue; and, if so, they could be convicted.

I find it difficult to reconcile this conclusion with our traditional religious freedoms.

In the first place, as a matter of either practice or philosophy I do not see how we can separate an issue as to what is believed from considerations as to what is believable. The most convincing proof that one believes his statements is to show that they have been true in his experience. Likewise, that one knowingly falsified is best proved by showing that what he said happened never did happen. How can the Government prove these persons knew something to be false which it cannot prove to be false? If we try religious sincerity severed from religious verity, we isolate the dispute from the very considerations which in common experience provide its most reliable answer. . . .

Belief in what one may demonstrate to the senses is not faith. All schools of religious thought make enormous assumptions, generally on the basis of revelations authenticated by some sign or miracle. The appeal in such matters is to a very different plane of credulity than is invoked by representations of secular fact in commerce. Some who profess belief in the Bible read literally what others read as allegory or metaphor, as they read Aesop's fables. Religious symbolism is even used by some with the same mental reservations one has in teaching of Santa Claus or Uncle Sam or Easter bunnies or dispassionate judges. It is hard in matters so mystical to say how literally one is bound to believe the doctrine he teaches and even more difficult to say how far it is reliance upon a teacher's literal belief which induces followers to give him money.

There appear to be persons—let us hope not many—who find refreshment and courage in the teachings of the "I Am" cult. If the members of the sect get comfort from the celestial guidance of their "Saint Germain," however doubtful it seems to me, it is hard to say that they do not get what they pay for. Scores of sects flourish in this country by teaching what to me are queer notions. It is plain that there is wide variety in American religious taste. The Ballards are not alone in catering to it with a pretty dubious product.

The chief wrong which false prophets do to their following is not financial. The collections aggregate a tempting total, but individual payments are not ruinous. I doubt if the vigilance of the law is equal to making money stick by over-credulous people. But the real harm is on the mental and spiritual plane. There are those who hunger and thirst after higher values which they feel wanting in their humdrum lives. They live in mental confusion or moral anarchy and seek vaguely for truth and beauty and moral support. When they are deluded and then disillusioned, cynicism and confusion follow. The wrong of these things, as I see it, is not in the money the victims part with half so much as in the mental and spiritual poison they get. But that is precisely the thing the Constitution put beyond the reach of the prosecutor, for the price of freedom of religion or of speech or of the press is that we must put up with, and even pay for, a good deal of rubbish.

Prosecutions of this character easily could degenerate into religious persecution. I do not doubt that religious leaders may be convicted of fraud for making false representations on matters other than faith or experience, as for example if one represents that funds are being used to construct a church when in fact they are being used for personal purposes. But that is not this case, which reaches into wholly dangerous ground. When does less than full belief in a professed credo become actionable fraud if one is soliciting gifts or legacies? Such inquiries may discomfort orthodox as well as unconventional religious teachers, for even the most regular of them are sometimes accused of taking their orthodoxy with a grain of salt.

I would dismiss the indictment and have done with this business of judicially examining other people's faiths.

NOTES AND QUESTIONS

1. *Examining the validity of religious beliefs.* Justice Douglas, writing for the *Ballard* majority, holds that the federal fraud statutes may be applied with respect to the Ballards' subjective beliefs; accordingly, a jury may inquire into whether the Ballards subjectively believed the tenets of the "I Am" religion, but *not* into whether those tenets are objectively true. Justice Stone (whose dissent is omitted) would have permitted inquiry into both subjective belief and objective truth of "I Am." Justice Jackson, however, believed that protecting freedom of religious belief requires a judicially created exemption for all fraud claims based on representations of matters of faith or belief. Who has the best view? Why?

2. *Evaluating sincerity.* How does a court determine whether someone is sincere or not? For those seeking to avoid work on Saturday, one could look to whether their religion has a Saturday Sabbath or whether they regularly observe it. But not everyone belongs to a familiar religion, or necessarily agrees with all its tenets.

3. *Belief versus believability.* Is it possible to distinguish between the plausibility of religious beliefs and whether a person subjectively believes the doctrine to be true? The Church of I Am certainly maintained some highly improbable doctrines. Yet, was Justice Jackson correct in suggesting that there cannot be any

such thing as "religious fraud" with respect to matters of theology and faith? Of course, even Justice Jackson would permit a prosecution if monies collected for a school or theme park were diverted to some other purpose (like personal use). Should the Free Exercise Clause be read to prohibit prosecutions of the sort at issue in *Ballard*, as de facto efforts to regulate religious beliefs?

4. *Just another kind of fraud?* On the other hand, if someone makes a false representation to extract money, why should the criminal law turn a blind eye because the representation happened to relate to the medical healing powers of a sacred amulet, rather than a pill or potion? Are fraud prosecutions for intentional false claims really the first step toward government-enforced limits on religious beliefs?

B.   THE FREE EXERCISE CLAUSE AND PROTECTION OF RELIGIOUS CONDUCT

The Warren Court rejected, at least in part, the belief/conduct dichotomy. In a series of cases starting in the 1960s, the Supreme Court required the government to provide exemptions from neutral laws of general applicability that conflicted with religiously motivated conduct. Even in these cases, however, religionists did not always win judicially crafted exemptions from neutral laws of general applicability. As you read the following cases, consider whether they reflect any general patterns regarding who wins, and who loses, free exercise cases.

SHERBERT v. VERNER

374 U.S. 398 (1963)

Mr. Justice BRENNAN delivered the opinion of the Court.

Appellant, a member of the Seventh-day Adventist church, was discharged by her South Carolina employer because she would not work on Saturday, the Sabbath Day of her faith. [1] When she was unable to obtain other employment because from conscientious scruples she would not take Saturday work, she filed a claim for unemployment compensation benefits under the South Carolina Unemployment Compensation Act. That law provides that, to be eligible for benefits, a claimant must be "able to work . . . available for work"; and further, that a claimant is ineligible for benefits "[i]f . . . he has failed, without good cause . . . to accept available suitable work when offered him by the employment office or the employer. . . ." The appellee Employment Security Commission, in administrative proceedings under the statute, found that appellant's restriction upon her availability for Saturday work brought her within the provision disqualifying for benefits insured workers who

---

[1] Appellant became a member of the Seventh-day Adventist Church in 1957, at a time when her employer, a textile-mill operator, permitted her to work a five-day week. It was not until 1959 that the work week was changed to six days, including Saturday, for all three shifts in the employer's mill. No question has been raised in this case concerning the sincerity of appellant's religious beliefs. Nor is there any doubt that the prohibition against Saturday labor is a basic tenet of the Seventh-day Adventist creed, based upon that religion's interpretation of the Holy Bible.

fail, without good cause, to accept "suitable work when offered... by the employment office or the employer. . . ."

[The South Carolina state courts affirmed the agency's findings and held Sherbert ineligible for benefits.]

We reverse the judgment of the South Carolina Supreme Court and remand for further proceedings not inconsistent with this opinion.

The door of the Free Exercise Clause stands tightly closed against any governmental regulation of religious *beliefs* as such, *Cantwell v. Connecticut*, 310 U.S. 296, 303. Government may neither compel affirmation of a repugnant belief, *Torcaso v. Watkins*, 367 U.S. 488; nor penalize or discriminate against individuals or groups because they hold religious views abhorrent to the authorities, *Fowler v. Rhode Island*, 345 U.S. 67; nor employ the taxing power to inhibit the dissemination of particular religious views, *Murdock v. Pennsylvania*, 319 U.S. 105; *Follett v. McCormick*, 321 U.S. 573; cf. *Grosjean v. American Press Co.*, 297 U.S. 233. On the other hand, the Court has rejected challenges under the Free Exercise Clause to governmental regulation of certain overt acts prompted by religious beliefs or principles, for "even when the action is in accord with one's religious convictions, [it] is not totally free from legislative restrictions." *Braunfeld v. Brown*, 366 U.S. 599, 603. The conduct or actions so regulated have invariably posed some substantial threat to public safety, peace or order. See, *e. g., Reynolds v. United States*, 98 U.S. 145; *Jacobson v. Massachusetts*, 197 U.S. 11; *Prince v. Massachusetts*, 321 U.S. 158; *Cleveland v. United States*, 329 U.S. 14.

Plainly enough, appellant's conscientious objection to Saturday work constitutes no conduct prompted by religious principles of a kind within the reach of state legislation. If, therefore, the decision of the South Carolina Supreme Court is to withstand appellant's constitutional challenge, it must be either because her disqualification as a beneficiary represents no infringement by the State of her constitutional rights of free exercise, or because any incidental burden on the free exercise of appellant's religion may be justified by a "compelling state interest in the regulation of a subject within the State's constitutional power to regulate. . . ." *NAACP v. Button*, 371 U.S. 415, 438.

We turn first to the question whether the disqualification for benefits imposes any burden on the free exercise of appellant's religion. We think it is clear that it does. . . . Here not only is it apparent that appellant's declared ineligibility for benefits derives solely from the practice of her religion, but the pressure upon her to forego that practice is unmistakable. The ruling forces her to choose between following the precepts of her religion and forfeiting benefits, on the one hand, and abandoning one of the precepts of her religion in order to accept work, on the other hand. Governmental imposition of such a choice puts the same kind of burden upon the free exercise of religion as would a fine imposed against appellant for her Saturday worship. . . .

Significantly South Carolina expressly saves the Sunday worshipper from having to make the kind of choice which we here hold infringes the Sabbatarian's religious liberty. When in times of "national emergency" the textile plants are authorized by the State Commissioner of Labor to operate on Sunday, "no employee shall be required to work on Sunday . . . who is conscientiously opposed to Sunday work; and if any employee should refuse to work on Sunday on account of conscientious . . . objections he or she shall not jeopardize his or her seniority by such refusal or be discriminated against in any other manner." S. C. Code, § 64-4. No question of the disqualification of a Sunday worshipper for benefits is likely to arise, since we cannot suppose that an employer will discharge him in violation of this statute. The unconstitutionality of the disqualification of the Sabbatarian is thus compounded by the religious discrimination which South Carolina's general statutory scheme necessarily effects.

We must next consider whether some compelling state interest enforced in the eligibility provisions of the South Carolina statute justifies the substantial infringement of appellant's First Amendment right. It is basic that no showing merely of a rational relationship to some colorable state interest would suffice; in this highly sensitive constitutional area, "[o]nly the gravest abuses, endangering paramount interests, give occasion for permissible limitation," *Thomas v. Collins*, 323 U.S. 516, 530. No such abuse or danger has been advanced in the present case. The appellees suggest no more than a possibility that the filing of fraudulent claims by unscrupulous claimants feigning religious objections to Saturday work might not only dilute the unemployment compensation fund but also hinder the scheduling by employers of necessary Saturday work. But that possibility is not apposite here because no such objection appears to have been made before the South Carolina Supreme Court, and we are unwilling to assess the importance of an asserted state interest without the views of the state court. . . .

In these respects, then, the state interest asserted in the present case is wholly dissimilar to the interests which were found to justify the less direct burden upon religious practices in *Braunfeld v. Brown, supra.* The Court recognized that the Sunday closing law which that decision sustained undoubtedly served "to make the practice of [the Orthodox Jewish merchants'] . . . religious beliefs more expensive," 366 U.S., at 605. But the statute was nevertheless saved by a countervailing factor which finds no equivalent in the instant case—a strong state interest in providing one uniform day of rest for all workers. That secular objective could be achieved, the Court found, only by declaring Sunday to be that day of rest. Requiring exemptions for Sabbatarians, while theoretically possible, appeared to present an administrative problem of such magnitude, or to afford the exempted class so great a competitive advantage, that such a requirement would have rendered the entire statutory scheme unworkable. In the present case no such justifications underlie the determination of the state court that appellant's religion makes her ineligible to receive benefits.

In holding as we do, plainly we are not fostering the "establishment" of the Seventh-day Adventist religion in South Carolina, for the extension of unemployment benefits to Sabbatarians in common with Sunday worshippers reflects nothing more than the governmental obligation of neutrality in the face of religious differences, and does not represent that involvement of religious with secular institutions which it is the object of the Establishment Clause to forestall. Nor does the recognition of the appellant's right to unemployment benefits under the state statute serve to abridge any other person's religious liberties. Nor do we, by our decision today, declare the existence of a constitutional right to unemployment benefits on the part of all persons whose religious convictions are the cause of their unemployment. This is not a case in which an employee's religious convictions serve to make him a nonproductive member of society. Finally, nothing we say today constrains the States to adopt any particular form or scheme of unemployment compensation. Our holding today is only that South Carolina may not constitutionally apply the eligibility provisions so as to constrain a worker to abandon his religious convictions respecting the day of rest.

The judgment of the South Carolina Supreme Court is reversed and the case is remanded for further proceedings not inconsistent with this opinion.

It is so ordered.

Mr. Justice STEWART, concurring in the result.

[Justice Stewart's concurring opinion is omitted.]

Mr. Justice HARLAN, whom Mr. Justice WHITE joins, dissenting.

Today's decision is disturbing both in its rejection of existing precedent and in its implications for the future. . . .

The South Carolina Supreme Court has uniformly applied this law in conformity with its clearly expressed purpose. It has consistently held that one is not 'available for work' if his unemployment has resulted not from the inability of industry to provide a job but rather from personal circumstances, no matter how compelling. . . . Thus in no proper sense can it be said that the State discriminated against the appellant on the basis of her religious beliefs or that she was denied benefits because she was a Seventh-day Adventist. She was denied benefits just as any other claimant would be denied benefits who was not 'available for work' for personal reasons.

With this background, this Court's decision comes into clearer focus. What the Court is holding is that if the State chooses to condition unemployment compensation on the applicant's availability for work, it is constitutionally compelled to *carve out an exception*—and to provide benefits—for those whose unavailability is due to their religious convictions. Such a holding has particular significance in two respects.

First, despite the Court's protestations to the contrary, the decision necessarily overrules *Braunfeld v. Brown*, 366 U.S. 599, which held that it did not offend the "Free Exercise" Clause of the Constitution for a State to forbid a Sabbatarian to do business on Sunday. . . . [T]he indirect financial burden of the present law is far less than that involved in Braunfeld. Forcing a store owner to close his business on Sunday may well have the effect of depriving him of a satisfactory livelihood if his religious convictions require him to close on Saturday as well. Here we are dealing only with temporary benefits, amounting to a fraction of regular weekly wages and running for not more than 22 weeks. Clearly, any differences between this case and Braunfeld cut against the present appellant.

Second, the implications of the present decision are far more troublesome than its apparently narrow dimensions would indicate at first glance. The meaning of today's holding, as already noted, is that the State must furnish unemployment benefits to one who is unavailable for work if the unavailability stems from the exercise of religious convictions. The State, in other words, must *single out* for financial assistance those whose behavior is religiously motivated, even though it denies such assistance to others whose identical behavior (in this case, inability to work on Saturdays) is not religiously motivated.

It has been suggested that such singling out of religious conduct for special treatment may violate the constitutional limitations on state action. See Kurland, Of Church and State and The Supreme Court, 29 U. of Chi. L. Rev. 1; cf. *Cammarano v. United States*, 358 U.S. 498, 515 (concurring opinion). My own view, however, is that at least under the circumstances of this case it would be a permissible accommodation of religion for the State, if it *chose* to do so, to create an exception to its eligibility requirements for persons like the appellant. . . . [T]here is, I believe, enough flexibility in the Constitution to permit a legislative judgment accommodating an unemployment compensation law to the exercise of religious beliefs such as appellant's.

For very much the same reasons, however, I cannot subscribe to the conclusion that the State is constitutionally *compelled* to carve out an exception to its general rule of eligibility in the present case. Those situations in which the Constitution may require special treatment on account of religion are, in my view, few and far between, and this view is amply supported by the course of constitutional litigation in this area.

For these reasons I respectfully dissent from the opinion and judgment of the Court.

NOTES AND QUESTIONS

1. *A direct or indirect burden?* Was the burden on *Sherbert* direct, and the equivalent of a fine? Or was it indirect, as in *Braunfeld*, because the state did not require her to work Saturday but made it more expensive to observe a Saturday Sabbath?

2. *The problem of differential treatment.* Is *Sherbert* really about indirect burdens, or is it better conceptualized as a differential treatment case? Justice Brennan notes that South Carolina would not force a Sunday worshipper to choose between "keeping holy the Sabbath" and maintaining eligibility for state unemployment benefits. If South Carolina creates an exemption for Sunday worshippers, can it withhold an exemption from others? Should it matter that a Sunday exemption benefits the dominant religious groups in South Carolina (mainline Protestants and evangelical Christians)?

3. *Penalizing or privileging religiously motivated objections.* Is it unfairly penalizing religion if South Carolina provides unemployment benefits to people who refused jobs that were too far away or outside their field, but not to people who refuse for religious reasons? Is it unfairly privileging religion to recognize deeply held *religious* moral commitments like Sabbath observance as "good cause" to reject Saturday work, but not deeply held *secular* moral commitments such as needing Saturdays off to take care of a sick parent or spend time with one's children?

4. *A broader availability for work requirement.* Suppose South Carolina had a firm rule, without any exceptions or individualized review, that required all persons seeking unemployment benefits to be available any time, any place, for any available work (including work that might give rise to religious objections, such as a distillery or a munitions factory). Would *Sherbert* require South Carolina to recognize religious exemptions for those seeking benefits because religious duty prevents them from meeting the "any job, any time, any place" rule?

5. *The formal neutrality approach.* Professor Phillip C. Kurland famously argued that the best reading of the Establishment and Free Exercise Clauses would be to require "formal neutrality" from the government. Under this approach, religious motivations or purposes could serve neither as the basis for an exemption nor as a basis for imposing a burden. Under this approach, a targeted property tax exemption for property owned by religious organizations, but not other charitable entities, would not be permissible. But neither would a statute that provided property tax exemptions to all charitable entities except religiously affiliated ones. *See* Phillip C. Kurland, *Of Church and State and the Supreme*

Court, 29 U. Chi. L. Rev. 1, 6-7 (1961). Although this theory received a great deal of scholarly and judicial attention, it never gained much traction, perhaps because it would have disallowed a great many targeted accommodations of religion. Indeed, Kurland himself acknowledged that his neutrality theory met with "almost uniform rejection." Phillip C. Kurland, *The Irrelevance of the Constitution: The Religion Clauses of the First Amendment and the Supreme Court*, 24 Vill. L. Rev. 3, 24 (1978).

WISCONSIN v. YODER

406 U.S. 205 (1972)

Mr. Chief Justice BURGER delivered the opinion of the Court.

On petition of the State of Wisconsin, we granted the writ of certiorari in this case to review a decision of the Wisconsin Supreme Court holding that respondents' convictions of violating the State's compulsory school-attendance law were invalid under the Free Exercise Clause of the First Amendment to the United States Constitution made applicable to the States by the Fourteenth Amendment. For the reasons hereafter stated we affirm the judgment of the Supreme Court of Wisconsin.

Respondents Jonas Yoder and Wallace Miller are members of the Old Order Amish religion, and respondent Adin Yutzy is a member of the Conservative Amish Mennonite Church. Wisconsin's compulsory school-attendance law required them to cause their children to attend public or private school until reaching age 16 but the respondents declined to send their children, ages 14 and 15, to public school after they completed the eighth grade. . . .

On complaint of the school district administrator for the public schools, respondents were charged, tried, and convicted of violating the compulsory-attendance law in Green County Court and were fined the sum of $5 each. Respondents defended on the ground that the application of the compulsory-attendance law violated their rights under the First and Fourteenth Amendments. The trial testimony showed that respondents believed, in accordance with the tenets of Old Order Amish communities generally, that their children's attendance at high school, public or private, was contrary to the Amish religion and way of life. They believed that by sending their children to high school, they would not only expose themselves to the danger of the censure of the church community, but, as found by the county court, also endanger their own salvation and that of their children. The State stipulated that respondents' religious beliefs were sincere. . . .

. . . [I]n order for Wisconsin to compel school attendance beyond the eighth grade against a claim that such attendance interferes with the practice of a legitimate religious belief, it must appear either that the State does not deny the free exercise of religious belief by its requirement, or that there is a state interest of sufficient magnitude to override the interest claiming protection under the Free Exercise Clause. . . .

We come then to the quality of the claims of the respondents concerning the alleged encroachment of Wisconsin's compulsory school-attendance statute on their rights and the rights of their children to the free exercise of the religious beliefs they and their forebears have adhered to for almost three centuries. In evaluating those claims we must be careful to determine whether the Amish religious faith and their mode of life are, as they claim, inseparable and interdependent. A way of life, however virtuous and admirable, may not be interposed as a barrier to reasonable state regulation of education if it is based on purely secular considerations; to have the protection of the Religion Clauses, the claims must be rooted in religious belief. Although a determination of what is a "religious" belief or practice entitled to constitutional protection may present a most delicate question, the very concept of ordered liberty precludes allowing every person to make his own standards on matters of conduct in which society as a whole has important interests. Thus, if the Amish asserted their claims because of their subjective evaluation and rejection of the contemporary secular values accepted by the majority, much as Thoreau rejected the social values of his time and isolated himself at Walden Pond, their claims would not rest on a religious basis. Thoreau's choice was philosophical and personal rather than religious, and such belief does not rise to the demands of the Religion Clauses.

Giving no weight to such secular considerations, however, we see that the record in this case abundantly supports the claim that the traditional way of life of the Amish is not merely a matter of personal preference, but one of deep religious conviction, shared by an organized group, and intimately related to daily living. . . .

The impact of the compulsory-attendance law on respondents' practice of the Amish religion is not only severe, but inescapable, for the Wisconsin law affirmatively compels them, under threat of criminal sanction, to perform acts undeniably at odds with fundamental tenets of their religious beliefs. See *Braunfeld v. Brown*, 366 U.S. 599, 605 (1961). Nor is the impact of the compulsory-attendance law confined to grave interference with important Amish religious tenets from a subjective point of view. It carries with it precisely the kind of objective danger to the free exercise of religion that the First Amendment was designed to prevent. As the record shows, compulsory school attendance to age 16 for Amish children carries with it a very real threat of undermining the Amish community and religious practice as they exist today; they must either abandon belief and be assimilated into society at large, or be forced to migrate to some other and more tolerant region.

In sum, the unchallenged testimony of acknowledged experts in education and religious history, almost 300 years of consistent practice, and strong evidence of a sustained faith pervading and regulating respondents' entire mode of life support the claim that enforcement of the State's requirement of compulsory formal education after the eighth grade would gravely endanger if not destroy the free exercise of respondents' religious beliefs. . . .

Wisconsin concedes that under the Religion Clauses religious beliefs are absolutely free from the State's control, but it argues that "actions," even though religiously grounded, are outside the protection of the First Amendment. But our decisions have rejected the idea that religiously grounded conduct is always outside the protection of the Free Exercise Clause. It is true that activities of individuals, even when religiously based, are often subject to regulation by the States in the exercise of their undoubted power to promote the health, safety, and general welfare, or the Federal Government in the exercise of its delegated powers. . . . But to agree that religiously grounded conduct must often be subject to the broad police power of the State is not to deny that there are areas of conduct protected by the Free Exercise Clause of the First Amendment and thus beyond the power of the State to control, even under regulations of general applicability. . . . This case, therefore, does not become easier because respondents were convicted for their "actions" in refusing to send their children to the public high school; in this context belief and action cannot be neatly confined in logic-tight compartments.

Nor can this case be disposed of on the grounds that Wisconsin's requirement for school attendance to age 16 applies uniformly to all citizens of the State and does not, on its face, discriminate against religions or a particular religion, or that it is motivated by legitimate secular concerns. . . .

The Court must not ignore the danger that an exception from a general obligation of citizenship on religious grounds may run afoul of the Establishment Clause, but that danger cannot be allowed to prevent any exception no matter how vital it may be to the protection of values promoted by the right of free exercise.

The State advances two primary arguments in support of its system of compulsory education. It notes, as Thomas Jefferson pointed out early in our history, that some degree of education is necessary to prepare citizens to participate effectively and intelligently in our open political system if we are to preserve freedom and independence. Further, education prepares individuals to be self-reliant and self-sufficient participants in society. We accept these propositions.

However, the evidence adduced by the Amish in this case is persuasively to the effect that an additional one or two years of formal high school for Amish children in place of their long-established program of informal vocational education would do little to serve those interests. Respondents' experts testified at trial, without challenge, that the value of all education must be assessed in terms of its capacity to prepare the child for life. It is one thing to say that compulsory education for a year or two beyond the eighth grade may be necessary when its goal is the preparation of the child for life in modern society as the majority live, but it is quite another if the goal of education be viewed as the preparation of the child for life in the separated agrarian community that is the keystone of the Amish faith. See *Meyer v. Nebraska*, 262 U.S., at 400.

The State attacks respondents' position as one fostering "ignorance" from which the child must be protected by the State. No one can question the State's duty to protect children from ignorance but this argument does not square with the facts disclosed in the record. Whatever their idiosyncrasies as seen by the majority, this record strongly shows that the Amish community has been a highly successful social unit within our society, even if apart from the conventional "mainstream." Its members are productive and very law-abiding members of society; they reject public welfare in any of its usual modern forms. The Congress itself recognized their self-sufficiency by authorizing exemption of such groups as the Amish from the obligation to pay social security taxes. . . .

The State, however, supports its interest in providing an additional one or two years of compulsory high school education to Amish children because of the possibility that some such children will choose to leave the Amish community, and that if this occurs they will be ill-equipped for life. . . .

There is nothing in this record to suggest that the Amish qualities of reliability, self-reliance, and dedication to work would fail to find ready markets in today's society. Absent some contrary evidence supporting the State's position, we are unwilling to assume that persons possessing such valuable vocational skills and habits are doomed to become burdens on society should they determine to leave the Amish faith, nor is there any basis in the record to warrant a finding that an additional one or two years of formal school education beyond the eighth grade would serve to eliminate any such problem that might exist.

Insofar as the State's claim rests on the view that a brief additional period of formal education is imperative to enable the Amish to participate effectively and intelligently in our democratic process, it must fall. The Amish alternative to formal secondary school education has enabled them to function effectively in their day-to-day life under self-imposed limitations on relations with the world, and to survive and prosper in contemporary society as a separate, sharply identifiable and highly self-sufficient community for more than 200 years in this country. In itself this is strong evidence that they are capable of fulfilling the social and political responsibilities of citizenship without compelled attendance beyond the eighth grade at the price of jeopardizing their free exercise of religious belief. . . .

The independence and successful social functioning of the Amish community for a period approaching almost three centuries and more than 200 years in this country are strong evidence that there is at best a speculative gain, in terms of meeting the duties of citizenship, from an additional one or two years of compulsory formal education. Against this background it would require a more particularized showing from the State on this point to justify the severe interference with religious freedom . . .

Our holding in no way determines the proper resolution of possible competing interests of parents, children, and the State in an appropriate state court proceeding in which the power of the State is asserted on the theory that Amish parents are preventing their minor children from attending high school despite their expressed desires to the contrary. Recognition of the claim of the State in such a proceeding would, of course, call into question traditional concepts of parental control over the religious upbringing and education of their minor children recognized in this Court's past decisions. It is clear that such an intrusion by a State into family decisions in the area of religious training would give rise to grave questions of religious freedom comparable to those raised here and those presented in *Pierce v. Society of Sisters*, 268 U.S. 510 (1925). On this record we neither reach nor decide those issues. . . .

Aided by a history of three centuries as an identifiable religious sect and a long history as a successful and self-sufficient segment of American society, the Amish in this case have convincingly demonstrated the sincerity of their religious beliefs, the interrelationship of belief with their mode of life, the vital role that belief and daily conduct play in the continued survival of Old Order Amish communities and their religious organization, and the hazards presented by the State's enforcement of a statute generally valid as to others. Beyond this, they have carried the even more difficult burden of demonstrating the adequacy of their alternative mode of continuing informal vocational education in terms of precisely those overall interests that the State advances in support of its program of compulsory high school education. In light of this convincing showing, one that probably few other religious groups or sects could make, and weighing the minimal difference between what the State would require and what the Amish already accept, it was incumbent on the State to show with more particularity how its admittedly strong interest in compulsory education would be adversely affected by granting an exemption to the Amish. *Sherbert v. Verner, supra.*

Mr. Justice POWELL and Mr. Justice REHNQUIST took no part in the consideration or decision of this case.

Mr. Justice WHITE, with whom Mr. Justice BRENNAN and Mr. Justice STEWART join, concurring.

Cases such as this one inevitably call for a delicate balancing of important but conflicting interests. I join the opinion and judgment of the Court because I cannot say that the State's interest in requiring two more years of compulsory education in the ninth and tenth grades outweighs the importance of the concededly sincere Amish religious practice to the survival of that sect. . . .

I join the Court because the sincerity of the Amish religious policy here is uncontested, because the potentially adverse impact of the state requirement is great, and because the State's valid interest in education has already been largely satisfied by the eight years the children have already spent in school.

Mr. Justice DOUGLAS, dissenting in part.

I agree with the Court that the religious scruples of the Amish are opposed to the education of their children beyond the grade schools, yet I disagree with the Court's conclusion that the matter is within the dispensation of parents alone. The Court's analysis assumes that the only interests at stake in the case are those of the Amish parents on the one hand, and those of the State on the other. The difficulty with this approach is that, despite the Court's claim, the parents are seeking to vindicate not only their own free exercise claims, but also those of their high-school-age children. .

. . I think the emphasis of the Court on the "law and order" record of this Amish group of people is quite irrelevant. A religion is a religion irrespective of what the misdemeanor or felony records of its members might be. I am not at all sure how the Catholics, Episcopalians, the Baptists, Jehovah's Witnesses, the Unitarians, and my own Presbyterians would make out if subjected to such a test. It is, of course, true that if a group or society was organized to perpetuate crime and if that is its motive, we would have rather startling problems akin to those that were raised when some years back a particular sect was challenged here as operating on a fraudulent basis. *United States v. Ballard*, 322 U.S. 78. But no such factors are present here, and the Amish, whether with a high or low criminal record, certainly qualify by all historic standards as a religion within the meaning of the First Amendment.

The Court rightly rejects the notion that actions, even though religiously grounded, are always outside the protection of the Free Exercise Clause of the First Amendment. In so ruling, the court departs from the teaching of *Reynolds v. United States*, 98 U.S. 145, 164, where it was said concerning the reach of the Free Exercise Clause of the First Amendment, "Congress was deprived of all legislative power over mere opinion, but was left free to reach actions which were in violation of social duties or subversive of good order." In that case it was conceded that polygamy was a part of the religion of the Mormons. Yet the Court said, "It matters not that his belief [in polygamy] was a part of his professed religion: it was still belief, and belief only." *Id.*, at 167.

Action, which the Court deemed to be antisocial, could be punished even though it was grounded on deeply held and sincere religious convictions. What we do today, at least in this respect, opens the way to give organized religion a broader base than it has ever enjoyed; and it even promises that in time *Reynolds* will be overruled. . . .

NOTES AND QUESTIONS

1. *The continuing relevance of the belief/conduct dichotomy.* After *Yoder*, does anything remain of the *Reynolds* and *Davis* belief/conduct dichotomy? Suppose that a sect requires the ceremonial ingestion of marijuana smoke. Will courts analyze their claim to an exemption from drug laws as seriously as the Old Order Amish claim to an exemption from mandatory school-attendance laws?

2. *The problem of discrimination against unfamiliar religious groups.* In very real ways, such as by repeatedly invoking the 300-year success of the Old Order Amish in the United States, Chief Justice Burger seems to be declaring the

Amish to be a "good" religion meriting special considerations. What is the risk that courts will take some claims, and some religions, more seriously than others? Should groups like the Moonies or the Hare Krishnas have the same free exercise rights as the Old Order Amish? Should the federal courts decide which are "good" religions and which are "bad" religions? Which groups need more protection from the courts: older, well-established, well-liked groups or newer, less well-known groups? For a critical commentary, *see* Mark Tushnet, *"Of Church and State and the Supreme Court Revisited": Kurland Revisited,* 1989 Sup. Ct. Rev. 373, 380-382.

3. *A targeted or general exemption?* Chief Justice Burger plainly weighs the state's interest in enforcing a mandatory school-attendance law only against an exemption for the Old Order Amish, rather than against an exemption for any group that might seek an exemption from truancy laws on a religious basis. Is this the correct numerator? Surprising as it might seem, in later cases, the Supreme Court regularly weighs the state's burden against a universal exemption from a general law, rather than a limited exemption.

4. *Viewpoint of Amish children.* Would the Court still have granted the exemption if the Amish children had wanted to continue their public school education? The majority notes that there was no evidence that Amish vocational training would disadvantage them in today's society. Do you agree? Does it matter if boys and girls are taught different skills?

AN EXTENDED NOTE ON "STRICT IN THEORY BUT FEEBLE IN FACT"

The standard enunciated by Sherbert v. Verner and Wisconsin v. Yoder provided for strict scrutiny for laws that imposed a substantial religious burden. This reflected the view that the Free Exercise Clause ought to mean more than an absence of religious discrimination. Instead, free exercise principles should protect religiously motivated conduct, at least when the government could not proffer a really important reason for applying its general law on the facts presented. In actual practice, however, the Court regularly rejected Free Exercise Clause claims. The one exception was a series of unemployment benefit cases that followed in the footsteps of Sherbert v. Verner.

United States v. Lee, 455 U.S. 252 (1982). Lee, an Old Order Amish employer, objected to withholding his employees' social security taxes and to paying his share of his employees' social security taxes on the grounds that "the Amish believe it sinful not to provide for their own elderly and needy and therefore are religiously opposed to the national social security system." Lee unsuccessfully sought a religious exemption from the insurance program. The Supreme Court first held that "[b]ecause the payment of the taxes or receipt of benefits violates Amish religious beliefs, compulsory participation in the social security system interferes with their free exercise rights." Nevertheless, the government's interests were compelling, and the means narrowly tailored: "The design of the system requires support by mandatory contributions from covered employers and employees. This mandatory participation is indispensable to the fiscal vitality of the social security system. . . . [A] comprehensive national social security system providing for voluntary participation would be almost a contradiction in terms and difficult, if not impossible, to administer." Moreover, "Unlike the situation presented in Wisconsin v. Yoder, it would be difficult to accommodate the comprehensive social security system with myriad exceptions flowing from a wide variety of religious beliefs." In short, "To maintain an organized society that guarantees religious freedom to a great variety of faiths requires that some religious practices yield to the common good. Religious beliefs can be accommodated, but there is a point at which accommodation would 'radically restrict the operating latitude of the legislature.'"

Bob Jones University v. United States, 461 U.S. 574 (1983). Two private schools lost their tax-exempt status because of their racially discriminatory policies. Based on their interpretation of the Bible, Goldsboro Christian Schools refused to admit African-Americans and Bob Jones University banned interracial dating and marriage among its students. The Supreme Court rejected their request for a free exercise exemption. After observing that "Denial of tax benefits will inevitably have a substantial impact on the operation of private religious schools, but will not prevent those schools from observing their religious tenets," the Court held that the government had a compelling interest in eradicating racial discrimination in education. "The governmental interest at stake here is compelling. As discussed [earlier], the Government has a fundamental, overriding interest in eradicating racial discrimination in education—discrimination that prevailed, with official approval, for the first 165 years of this Nation's history. That governmental interest substantially outweighs whatever burden denial of tax benefits places on petitioners' exercise of their religious beliefs. The interests asserted by petitioners cannot be accommodated with that compelling governmental interest and no 'less restrictive means,' are available to achieve the governmental interest."

Goldman v. Weinberger, 475 U.S. 503 (1986). Goldman was an Orthodox Jew in the United States Air Force. As the dissent noted, "one of the traditional religious obligations of a male Orthodox Jew [is] to cover his head before an omnipresent God." Military dress code prohibited Goldman from wearing his yarmulke while on duty and in uniform. In rejecting Goldman's free exercise claim, the Supreme Court emphasized the deference owed to the military: "[T]o accomplish its mission the military must foster instinctive obedience, unity, commitment, and esprit de corps. The essence of military service 'is the subordination of the desires and interests of the individual to the needs of the service.' . . . In the context of the present case, when evaluating whether military needs justify a particular restriction on religiously motivated conduct, courts must give great deference to the professional judgment of military authorities concerning the relative importance of a particular military interest." The Court then accepted the military's claims: "The considered professional judgment of the Air Force is that the traditional outfitting of personnel in standardized uniforms encourages the subordination of personal preferences and identities in favor of the overall group mission. Uniforms encourage a sense of hierarchical unity by tending to eliminate outward individual distinctions except for those of rank. The Air Force considers them as vital during peacetime as during war . . . . The Air Force has drawn the line essentially between religious apparel that is visible and that which is not, and we hold that those portions of the regulations challenged here reasonably and evenhandedly regulate dress in the interest of the military's perceived need for uniformity."

Bowen v. Roy, 476 U.S. 693 (1986). Parents applied for welfare and food stamp benefits. As a condition of receiving benefits, applicants were required to provide the Social Security number of all household members. The parents refused because using a Social Security number for their 2-year-old daughter, Little Bird of the Snow, would violate their Native American religious beliefs. The Supreme Court rejected their Free Exercise Clause claim, holding that "Never to our knowledge has the Court interpreted the First Amendment to require the Government itself to behave in ways that the individual believes will further his or her spiritual development or that of his or her family. The Free Exercise Clause simply cannot be understood to require the Government to conduct its own internal affairs in ways that comport with the religious beliefs of particular citizens. Just as the Government may not insist that appellees engage in any set form of religious observance, so appellees may not demand that the Government join in their chosen religious practices by refraining from using a number to identify their daughter. . . . The Free Exercise Clause affords an individual protection from certain forms of governmental compulsion; it does not afford an individual a right to dictate the conduct of the Government's internal procedures."

Lyng v. Northwest Indian Cemetery Protection Ass'n, 485 U.S. 439 (1988). In order to finish a road project linking two California towns, the United States Forest Service planned a six-mile paved road through a section of Six Rivers National Forest. The road, however, "would cause serious and irreparable damage to the sacred areas which are an integral and necessary part of the belief systems and lifeway of Northwest California Indian peoples." The Supreme Court rejected a challenge brought by members of three American Indian tribes. First the Court argued that, as in *Roy*, the government was not forcing anyone to violate their faith but merely conducting its own internal operations. "In both cases, the challenged Government action would interfere significantly with private persons' ability to pursue spiritual fulfillment according to their own religious beliefs. In neither case, however, would the affected individuals be coerced by the Government's action into violating their religious beliefs; nor would either governmental action penalize religious activity by denying any person an equal share of the rights, benefits, and privileges enjoyed by other citizens." Next, the Court argued that the government could not function were it to accommodate every religious belief. "However much we might wish that it were otherwise, government simply could not operate if it were required to satisfy every citizen's religious needs and desires. A broad range of government activities—from social welfare programs to foreign aid to conservation projects—will always be considered essential to the spiritual well-being of some citizens, often on the basis of sincerely held religious beliefs. Others will find the very same activities deeply offensive, and perhaps incompatible with their own search for spiritual fulfillment and with the tenets of their religion. The First Amendment must apply to all citizens alike, and it can give to none of them a veto over public programs that do not prohibit the free exercise of religion." The dissent took issue with the majority's determination that there was no substantial religious burden because "even where the Government uses federal land in a manner that threatens the very existence of a Native American religion, the Government is simply not 'doing' anything to the practitioners of that faith." The dissent concluded, "Because the Court today refuses even to acknowledge the constitutional injury respondents will suffer, and because this refusal essentially leaves Native Americans with absolutely no constitutional protection against perhaps the gravest threat to their religious practices, I dissent. . . ."

Thomas v. Review Bd. of Ind. Emp't Sec. Div., 450 U.S. 707 (1981). In contrast to most cases, the Supreme Court did grant religious exemptions in three unemployment benefits cases, including Thomas v. Review Board of The Indiana Employment Security Division. Thomas, a Jehovah's Witness, left his job in a foundry to avoid manufacturing parts for military tanks, claiming that "his religious beliefs prevented him from participating in the production of war materials." He brought a free exercise claim after being denied unemployment benefits. Although the Indiana Supreme Court had questioned the religious basis for his belief, the Supreme Court found that "the guarantee of free exercise is not limited to beliefs which are shared by all the members of a religious sect." It then held that "[u]nless we are prepared to overrule *Sherbert*, Thomas cannot be denied the benefits due him."

NOTES AND QUESTIONS

1. *Denied benefits and substantial burdens.* Why was denying unemployment compensation a substantial religious burden in *Sherbert* but denying tax exemptions in *Bob Jones University* was not? Perhaps the results could be reconciled if one views *Sherbert* (its broader language notwithstanding) as being a case about religious discrimination. Recall that South Carolina structured its unemployment program so as to protect the rights of Sunday worshippers—they would never face the hard choice of violating their religious duties or forgoing unemployment benefits. If South Carolina's decision to accommodate, de facto, one group of religionists but not another is the key to the outcome, then *Sherbert* can be reconciled with *Bob Jones University*. If this distinction seems persuasive, however, how then to explain *Braunfeld*?

2. *The applicable standard of review.* Although *Sherbert* and *Yoder* ostensibly established strict scrutiny review for all free exercise claims, *Goldman* suggests that the rule was not quite so categorical. As it turns out, Congress did not think much of the *Goldman* majority's reasoning and was not inclined to defer to the military's judgment regarding the need for uniform appearance. It immediately enacted legislation that permits members of the armed forces to wear religious garb that does not detract from a service member's "neat and conservative" appearance. *See* 10 U.S.C. § 774 (2006); *see also* National Defense Authorization Act for Fiscal Year 1988 and 1989, Pub. L. No. 100-180, 101 Stat. 1019 (1987).

3. *Control over its own internal operations.* *Lyng* attempts to establish a distinction between the government "coercing" violations of religious beliefs or "penalizing" religious beliefs, on the one hand, and government "merely conducting its own internal operations," on the other. The former trigger the Free Exercise Clause, whereas the latter does not. Did *Sherbert* or the other unemployment benefits cases feature either "coercion" or targeted "penalties"? If not, why isn't the government free to use "*its* [money]" just as freely as the *Lyng* Court holds it may use "*its* land"?

C. THE MODERN FREE EXERCISE STANDARD

In 1990, the Supreme Court changed course and appeared to reorient its Free Exercise Clause jurisprudence. This turn did not enjoy unanimous support, and it is clear that some members of the Supreme Court would like to return to the *Sherbert/Yoder* standard. Moreover, Congress responded to *Smith* by enacting the Religious Freedom Restoration Act (RFRA). RFRA represented a legislative effort to overturn *Smith* and restore the *Sherbert/Yoder* standard of review (that is, heightened scrutiny for laws that impose substantial religious burdens). The legislative history and substantive effects of RFRA appear in *City of Boerne, infra* Part D.

EMPLOYMENT DIVISION, DEPARTMENT OF HUMAN RESOURCES v. SMITH

494 U.S. 872 (1990)

Justice SCALIA delivered the opinion of the Court.

This case requires us to decide whether the Free Exercise Clause of the First Amendment permits the State of Oregon to include religiously inspired peyote use within the reach of its general criminal prohibition on use of that drug, and thus permits the State to deny unemployment benefits to persons dismissed from their jobs because of such religiously inspired use.

Oregon law prohibits the knowing or intentional possession of a "controlled substance" unless the substance has been prescribed by a medical practitioner. Schedule I contains the drug peyote, a hallucinogen derived from the plant *Lophophora williamsii Lemaire....*

Respondents Alfred Smith and Galen Black (hereinafter respondents) were fired from their jobs with a private drug rehabilitation organization because they ingested peyote for sacramental purposes at a ceremony of the Native American Church, of which both are members. When respondents applied to petitioner Employment Division (hereinafter petitioner) for unemployment compensation, they were determined to be ineligible for benefits because they had been discharged for work-related "misconduct." The Oregon Court of Appeals reversed that determination, holding that the denial of benefits violated respondents' free exercise rights under the First Amendment.

. . . [T]he Oregon Supreme Court held that respondents' religiously inspired use of peyote fell within the prohibition of the Oregon statute, which "makes no exception for the sacramental use" of the drug. It then considered whether that prohibition was valid under the Free Exercise Clause, and concluded that it was not. [It] ruled that the State could not deny unemployment benefits to respondents for having engaged in that practice. . . .

The Free Exercise Clause of the First Amendment, which has been made applicable to the States by incorporation into the Fourteenth Amendment, see *Cantwell v. Connecticut*, 310 U.S. 296, 303 (1940), provides that "Congress shall make no law respecting an establishment of religion, or *prohibiting the free exercise thereof. . . .*" U.S. Const., Amdt. 1 (emphasis added). The free exercise of religion means, first and foremost, the right to believe and profess whatever religious doctrine one desires. Thus, the First Amendment obviously excludes all "governmental regulation of religious *beliefs* as such." *Sherbert v. Verner, supra,* at 402.

But the "exercise of religion" often involves not only belief and profession but the performance of (or abstention from) physical acts: assembling with others for a worship service, participating in sacramental use of bread and wine, proselytizing, abstaining from certain foods or certain modes of transportation. It would be true, we think (though no case of ours has involved the point), that a State would be "prohibiting the free exercise [of religion]" if it sought to ban such acts or abstentions only when they are engaged in for religious reasons, or only because of the religious belief that they display. It would doubtless be unconstitutional, for example, to ban the casting of "statues that are to be used for worship purposes," or to prohibit bowing down before a golden calf.

Respondents in the present case, however, seek to carry the meaning of "prohibiting the free exercise [of religion]" one large step further. They contend that their religious motivation for using peyote places them beyond the reach of a criminal law that is not specifically directed at their religious practice, and that is concededly constitutional as applied to those who use the drug for other reasons. . . . As a textual matter, we do not think the words must be given that meaning. It is no more necessary to regard the collection of a general tax, for example, as "prohibiting the free exercise [of religion]" by those citizens who believe support of organized government to be sinful, than it is to regard the same tax as "abridging the freedom . . . of the press" of those publishing companies that must pay the tax as a condition of staying in business. It is a permissible reading of the text, in the one case as in the other, to say that if prohibiting the exercise of religion (or burdening the activity of printing) is not the object of the tax but merely the incidental effect of a generally applicable and otherwise valid provision, the First Amendment has not been offended. Compare *Citizen Publishing Co. v. United States*, 394 U.S. 131, 139 (1969) (upholding application of antitrust laws to press), with *Grosjean v. American Press Co.*, 297 U.S. 233, 250-251 (1936) (striking down license tax applied only to newspapers with weekly circulation above a specified level).

Our decisions reveal that the latter reading is the correct one. We have never held that an individual's religious beliefs excuse him from compliance with an otherwise valid law prohibiting conduct that the State is free to regulate. On the contrary, the record of more than a century of our free exercise jurisprudence contradicts that proposition. . . . We first had occasion to assert that principle in *Reynolds v. United States*, 98 U.S. 145 (1878), where we rejected the claim that criminal laws against polygamy could not be constitutionally applied to those whose religion commanded the practice. "Laws," we said, "are made for the government of actions, and while they cannot interfere with mere religious belief and opinions, they may with practices. . . . Can a man excuse his practices to the contrary because of his religious belief? To permit this would be to make the professed doctrines of religious belief superior to the law of the land, and in effect to permit every citizen to become a law unto himself." *Id.* at 166-167. Subsequent decisions have consistently held that the right of free exercise does not relieve an individual of the obligation to comply with a "valid and neutral law of general applicability on the ground that the law proscribes (or prescribes) conduct that his religion prescribes (or proscribes)." . . .

The only decisions in which we have held that the First Amendment bars application of a neutral, generally applicable law to religiously motivated action have involved not the Free Exercise Clause alone, but the Free Exercise Clause in conjunction with other constitutional protections, such as freedom of speech and of the press, see *Cantwell v. Connecticut, Murdock v. Pennsylvania,* or the right of parents, acknowledged in *Pierce v. Society of Sisters*, 268 U.S. 510 (1925), to direct the education of their children, see *Wisconsin v. Yoder*, 406 U.S. 205 (1972) (invalidating compulsory school-attendance laws as applied to Amish parents who refused on religious grounds to send their children to school). Some of our cases prohibiting compelled expression, decided exclusively upon free speech grounds, have also involved freedom of religion, cf. *Wooley v. Maynard*, 430 U.S. 705 (1977) (invalidating compelled display of a license plate slogan that offended individual religious beliefs); *West Virginia Bd. of Education v. Barnette.*

The present case does not present such a hybrid situation, but a free exercise claim unconnected with any communicative activity or parental right. Respondents urge us to hold, quite simply, that when otherwise prohibitable conduct is accompanied by religious convictions, not only the convictions but the conduct itself must be free from governmental regulation. We have never held that, and decline to do so now. There being no contention that Oregon's drug law represents an attempt to regulate religious beliefs, the communication of religious beliefs, or the raising of one's children in those beliefs, the rule to which we have adhered ever since *Reynolds* plainly controls. "Our cases do not at their farthest reach support the proposition that a stance of conscientious opposition relieves an objector from any colliding duty fixed by a democratic government." *Gillette v. United States, supra,* at 461. . . .

Respondents argue that even though exemption from generally applicable criminal laws need not automatically be extended to religiously motivated actors, at least the claim for a religious exemption must be evaluated under the balancing test set forth in *Sherbert v. Verner.* Under the Sherbert test, governmental actions that substantially burden a religious practice must be justified by a compelling governmental interest. . . . We have never invalidated any governmental action on the basis of the *Sherbert* test except the denial of unemployment compensation. Although we have sometimes purported to apply the *Sherbert* test in contexts other than that, we have always found the test satisfied. In recent years we have abstained from applying the *Sherbert* test (outside the unemployment compensation field) at all.

Even if we were inclined to breathe into *Sherbert* some life beyond the unemployment compensation field, we would not apply it to require exemptions from a generally applicable criminal law. The *Sherbert* test, it must be recalled, was developed in a context that lent itself to individualized governmental assessment of the reasons for the relevant conduct. As a plurality of the Court noted in *Roy*, a distinctive feature of unemployment compensation programs is that their eligibility criteria invite consideration of the particular circumstances behind an applicant's unemployment: "The statutory conditions [in *Sherbert* and *Thomas*] provided that a person was not eligible for unemployment compensation benefits if, 'without good cause,' he had quit work or refused available work. The 'good cause' standard created a mechanism for individualized exemptions." . . . As the plurality pointed out in *Roy*, our decisions in the unemployment cases stand for the proposition that where the State has in place a system of individual exemptions, it may not refuse to extend that system to cases of "religious hardship" without compelling reason. *Bowen v. Roy, supra,* at 708. . . .

Although, as noted earlier, we have sometimes used the Sherbert test to analyze free exercise challenges to such laws, *see United States v. Lee, Gillette v. United States,* we have never applied the test to invalidate one. We conclude today that the sounder approach, and the approach in accord with the vast majority of our precedents, is to hold the test inapplicable to such challenges. The government's ability to enforce generally applicable prohibitions of socially harmful conduct, like its ability to carry out other aspects of public policy, "cannot depend on measuring the effects of a governmental action on a religious objector's spiritual development." To make an individual's obligation to obey such a law contingent upon the law's coincidence with his religious beliefs, except where the State's interest is "compelling"—permitting him, by virtue of his beliefs, "to become a law unto himself," *Reynolds v. United States*, contradicts both constitutional tradition and common sense.

The "compelling government interest" requirement seems benign, because it is familiar from other fields. But using it as the standard that must be met before the government may accord different treatment on the basis of race, see, *e.g.*, *Palmore v. Sidoti*, 466 U.S. 429, 432 (1984), or before the government may regulate the content of speech, see, *e.g.*, *Sable Communications of California v. FCC*, 492 U.S. 115, 126 (1989), is not remotely comparable to using it for the purpose asserted here. What it produces in those other fields—equality of treatment and an unrestricted flow of contending speech—are constitutional norms; what it would produce here—a private right to ignore generally applicable laws—is a constitutional anomaly.

Nor is it possible to limit the impact of respondents' proposal by requiring a "compelling state interest" only when the conduct prohibited is "central" to the individual's religion. Cf. *Lyng v. Northwest Indian Cemetery Protective Assn.*, 485 U.S. at 474-476 (Brennan, J., dissenting). It is no more appropriate for judges to determine the "centrality" of religious beliefs before applying a "compelling interest" test in the free exercise field, than it would be for them to determine the "importance" of ideas before applying the "compelling interest" test in the free speech field. What principle of law or logic can be brought to bear to contradict a believer's assertion that a particular act is "central" to his personal faith? Judging the centrality of different religious practices is akin to the unacceptable "business of evaluating the relative merits of differing religious claims." . . . Repeatedly and in many different contexts, we have warned that courts must not presume to determine the place of a particular belief in a religion or the plausibility of a religious claim.

If the "compelling interest" test is to be applied at all, then, it must be applied across the board, to all actions thought to be religiously commanded. Moreover, if "compelling interest" really means what it says (and watering it down here would subvert its rigor in the other fields where it is applied), many laws will not meet the test. Any society adopting such a system would be courting anarchy, but that danger increases in direct proportion to the society's diversity of religious beliefs, and its determination to coerce or suppress none of them. Precisely because "we are a cosmopolitan nation made up of people of almost every conceivable religious preference," *Braunfeld v. Brown*, 366 U.S. at 606, and precisely because we value and protect that religious divergence, we cannot afford the luxury of deeming presumptively invalid, as applied to the religious objector, every regulation of conduct that does not protect an interest of the highest order. The rule respondents favor would open the prospect of constitutionally required religious exemptions from civic obligations of almost every conceivable kind-ranging from compulsory military service, see, e.g., *Gillette v. United States*, to the payment of taxes, see, e.g., *United States v. Lee*; to health and safety regulation such as manslaughter and child neglect laws, compulsory vaccination laws, drug laws, and traffic laws, see *Cox v. New Hampshire*; to social welfare legislation such as minimum wage laws, see *Tony and Susan Alamo Foundation v. Secretary of Labor*, child labor laws, see, e.g., *Prince v. Massachusetts*, . . . and laws providing for equality of opportunity for the races, see, e.g., *Bob Jones University v. United States*. The First Amendment's protection of religious liberty does not require this.

Values that are protected against government interference through enshrinement in the Bill of Rights are not thereby banished from the political process. Just as a society that believes in the negative protection accorded to the press by the First Amendment is likely to enact laws that affirmatively foster the dissemination of the printed word, so also a society that believes in the negative protection accorded to religious belief can be expected to be solicitous of that value in its legislation as well. It is therefore not surprising that a number of States have made an exception to their drug laws for sacramental peyote use. But to say that a nondiscriminatory religious-practice exemption is permitted, or even that it is desirable, is not to say that it is constitutionally required, and that the appropriate occasions for its creation can be discerned by the courts. It may fairly be said that leaving accommodation to the political process will place at a relative disadvantage those religious practices that are not widely engaged in; but that unavoidable consequence of democratic government must be preferred to a system in which each conscience is a law unto itself or in which judges weigh the social importance of all laws against the centrality of all religious beliefs.

Because respondents' ingestion of peyote was prohibited under Oregon law, and because that prohibition is constitutional, Oregon may, consistent with the Free Exercise Clause, deny respondents unemployment compensation when their dismissal results from use of the drug. The decision of the Oregon Supreme Court is accordingly reversed.

It is so ordered.

Justice O'CONNOR, with whom Justice BRENNAN, Justice MARSHALL, and Justice BLACKMUN join as to Parts I and II, concurring in the judgment.

Although I agree with the result the Court reaches in this case, I cannot join its opinion. In my view, today's holding dramatically departs from well-settled First Amendment jurisprudence, appears unnecessary to resolve the question presented, and is incompatible with our Nation's fundamental commitment to individual religious liberty. . . .

The Court today extracts from our long history of free exercise precedents the single categorical rule that "if prohibiting the exercise of religion . . . is . . . merely the incidental effect of a generally applicable and otherwise valid provision, the First Amendment has not been offended." *Ante*, at 878 (citations omitted). Indeed, the Court holds that where the law is a generally applicable criminal prohibition, our usual free exercise jurisprudence does not even apply. *Ante*, at 884. To reach this sweeping result, however, the Court must not only give a strained reading of the First Amendment but must also disregard our consistent application of free exercise doctrine to cases involving generally applicable regulations that burden religious conduct. . . .

The Court today, however, interprets the Clause to permit the government to prohibit, without justification, conduct mandated by an individual's religious beliefs, so long as that prohibition is generally applicable. *Ante*, at 878. But a law that prohibits certain conduct—conduct that happens to be an act of worship for someone—manifestly does prohibit that person's free exercise of his religion. A person who is barred from engaging in religiously motivated conduct is barred from freely exercising his religion. Moreover, that person is barred from freely exercising his religion regardless of whether the law prohibits the conduct only when engaged in for religious reasons, only by members of that religion, or by all persons. It is difficult to deny that a law that prohibits religiously motivated conduct, even if the law is generally applicable, does not at least implicate First Amendment concerns. . . .

Under our established First Amendment jurisprudence, we have recognized that the freedom to act, unlike the freedom to believe, cannot be absolute. See, *e.g.*, *Cantwell, supra*, at 304; *Reynolds v. United States*, 98 U.S. 145, 161-167 (1879).

Instead, we have respected both the First Amendment's express textual mandate and the governmental interest in regulation of conduct by requiring the government to justify any substantial burden on religiously motivated conduct by a compelling state interest and by means narrowly tailored to achieve that interest. . . . The compelling interest test effectuates the First Amendment's command that religious liberty is an independent liberty, that it occupies a preferred position, and that the Court will not permit encroachments upon this liberty, whether direct or indirect, unless required by clear and compelling governmental interests "of the highest order," *Yoder, supra*, at 215. "Only an especially important governmental interest pursued by narrowly tailored means can justify exacting a sacrifice of First Amendment freedoms as the price for an equal share of the rights, benefits, and privileges enjoyed by other citizens." *Roy, supra*, at 728 (opinion concurring in part and dissenting in part). . . .

In my view, however, the essence of a free exercise claim is relief from a burden imposed by government on religious practices or beliefs, whether the burden is imposed directly through laws that prohibit or compel specific religious practices, or indirectly through laws that, in effect, make abandonment of one's own religion or conformity to the religious beliefs of others the price of an equal place in the civil community. . . .

Finally, the Court today suggests that the disfavoring of minority religions is an "unavoidable consequence" under our system of government and that accommodation of such religions must be left to the political process. *Ante*, at 890. In my view, however, the First Amendment was enacted precisely to protect the rights of those whose religious practices are not shared by the majority and may be viewed with hostility. The history of our free exercise doctrine amply demonstrates the harsh impact majoritarian rule has had on unpopular or emerging religious groups such as the Jehovah's Witnesses and the Amish. . . .

[T]he critical question in this case is whether exempting respondents from the State's general criminal prohibition "will unduly interfere with fulfillment of the governmental interest." . . . Although the question is close, I would conclude that uniform application of Oregon's criminal prohibition is "essential to accomplish," *Lee, supra*, at 257, its overriding interest in preventing the physical harm caused by the use of a Schedule I controlled substance. Oregon's criminal prohibition represents that State's judgment that the possession and use of controlled substances, even by only one person, is inherently harmful and dangerous. Because the health effects caused by the use of controlled substances exist regardless of the motivation of the user, the use of such substances, even for religious purposes, violates the very purpose of the laws that prohibit them. Moreover, in view of the societal interest in preventing trafficking in controlled substances, uniform application of the criminal prohibition at issue is essential to the effectiveness of Oregon's stated interest in preventing any possession of peyote.

For these reasons, I believe that granting a selective exemption in this case would seriously impair Oregon's compelling interest in prohibiting possession of peyote by its citizens. Under such circumstances, the Free Exercise Clause does not require the State to accommodate respondents' religiously motivated conduct. . . . I would therefore adhere to our established free exercise jurisprudence and hold that the State in this case has a compelling interest in regulating peyote use by its citizens and that accommodating respondents' religiously motivated conduct "will unduly interfere with fulfillment of the governmental interest." *Lee, supra*, at 259. Accordingly, I concur in the judgment of the Court.

Justice BLACKMUN, with whom Justice BRENNAN and Justice MARSHALL join, dissenting.

[Justice Blackmun agreed with Justice O'Connor that strict scrutiny should apply but, unlike Justice O'Connor, found that Oregon's interest in suppressing the peyote market did not satisfy strict scrutiny.]

NOTES AND QUESTIONS

1. *The same approach or a new approach?* Was Justice Scalia intellectually honest in suggesting that the Supreme Court had never ordered exemptions from neutral laws of general applicability? What about *Yoder*? Why didn't Justice Scalia simply overrule *Sherbert* and *Yoder*, if that is what he really has in mind?

2. *Exceptions to new* Smith *rule.* Actually, *Smith* did not overrule *Sherbert* and *Yoder.* The new *Smith* rule does not apply to cases like *Sherbert* in which a state is making an individualized determination, nor to "hybrid" rights cases like *Yoder* which implicate free exercise as well as another constitutional right (in *Yoder*'s case, the substantive due process right to control the upbringing of one's children). Many scholars have argued that the exceptions were created expressly to avoid overruling *Sherbert* and *Yoder. See, e.g.,* Michael W. McConnell, *Free Exercise Revisionism and the* Smith *Decision,* 57 U. Chi. L. Rev. 1109 (1990) (arguing that the exceptions "have one function only: to enable the Court to reach the conclusion it desired without openly overruling any prior decisions"). Justice Souter's concurrence in Church of the Lukumi Babalu Aye, Inc. v. City of Hialeah criticizes the hybrid right claim: "If a hybrid claim is simply one in which another constitutional right is implicated, then the hybrid exception would probably be so vast as to swallow the *Smith* rule, and, indeed, the hybrid exception would cover the situation exemplified by *Smith,* since free speech and associational rights are certainly implicated in the peyote ritual. But if a hybrid claim is one in which a litigant would actually obtain an exemption from a formally neutral, generally applicable law under another constitutional provision, then there would have been no reason for the Court in what *Smith* calls the hybrid cases to have mentioned the Free Exercise Clause at all."

3. *Judicial competence and balancing.* Do you agree with Justice Scalia that federal judges should not engage in ad hoc reviews of general laws and balance those laws against religious objections? Why can't judges evaluate the centrality of religious beliefs? Must they decide on the centrality of religious beliefs in order to determine whether a religious burden is substantial?

4. *Courting anarchy?* Justice Scalia suggests that requiring religious exemptions from neutral laws of general applicability will lead to legal anarchy and that religious individuals will become a law unto themselves. Do you agree? Has his "parade of horribles" come to pass?

5. *The problem of discrimination against unpopular religious groups.* Under *Sherbert,* Christians had better luck than members of minority religions in obtaining exemptions. *See, e.g.,* Ronald J. Krotoszynski, Jr., *If Judges Were Angels: Religious Equality, Free Exercise, and the (Underappreciated) Merits of* Smith, 102 Nw. U.L. Rev. 1189 (2008). Under *Smith,* members of minority religions will now have to appeal to legislatures. Is the problem of religious discrimination likely to be greater in the courts or in politically elected and accountable legislative bodies?

6. *An unpopular decision.* Most, but not all, scholarly commentary has been highly
   critical of *Smith*, with preeminent scholars of the Religion Clauses describing it
   as having "eviscerated" the Free Exercise Clause, *see* Kent Greenawalt, *Religion
   and the Rehnquist Court,* 99 Nw. U.L. Rev. 145, 149-151 (2004), and another
   critic describing *Smith* as "produc[ing] widespread disbelief and anger," Douglas
   Laycock, *The Remnants of Free Exercise,* 1990 S. Ct. Rev. 1, 2-3. *See also*
   Michael W. McConnell, *Free Exercise Revisionism and the* Smith *Decision,* 57
   U. Chi. L. Rev. 1109 (1990). Notwithstanding these strong critiques, *Smith* does
   have defenders. *See, e.g.,* William P. Marshall, *In Defense of* Smith *and Free
   Exercise Revisionism,* 58 U. Chi. L. Rev. 308 (1991). Which regime do you
   prefer: *Sherbert* or *Smith*?

CHURCH OF THE LUKUMI BABALU AYE, INC. v. CITY OF HIALEAH

508 U.S. 520 (1993)

Justice KENNEDY delivered the opinion of the Court, except as to Part II-A-2.

The principle that government may not enact laws that suppress religious belief or
practice is so well understood that few violations are recorded in our opinions. Cf.
McDaniel v. Paty, 435 U.S. 618 (1978); *Fowler v. Rhode Island,* 345 U.S. 67 (1953).
Concerned that this fundamental nonpersecution principle of the First Amendment
was implicated here, however, we granted certiorari. 503 U.S. 935 (1992).

Our review confirms that the laws in question were enacted by officials who did
not understand, failed to perceive, or chose to ignore the fact that their official
actions violated the Nation's essential commitment to religious freedom. The
challenged laws had an impermissible object; and in all events the principle of
general applicability was violated because the secular ends asserted in defense of the
laws were pursued only with respect to conduct motivated by religious beliefs. We
invalidate the challenged enactments and reverse the judgment of the Court of
Appeals.

This case involves practices of the Santeria religion, which originated in the 19th
century. When hundreds of thousands of members of the Yoruba people were
brought as slaves from western Africa to Cuba, their traditional African religion
absorbed significant elements of Roman Catholicism. The resulting syncretion, or
fusion, is Santeria, "the way of the saints." The Cuban Yoruba express their devotion
to spirits, called *orishas,* through the iconography of Catholic saints, Catholic
symbols are often present at Santeria rites, and Santeria devotees attend the Catholic
sacraments.

The Santeria faith teaches that every individual has a destiny from God, a destiny
fulfilled with the aid and energy of the *orishas.* The basis of the Santeria religion is
the nurture of a personal relation with the *orishas,* and one of the principal forms of
devotion is an animal sacrifice. . . .

According to Santeria teaching, the *orishas* are powerful but not immortal. They
depend for survival on the sacrifice. Sacrifices are performed at birth, marriage, and
death rites, for the cure of the sick, for the initiation of new members and priests and
during an annual celebration. Animals sacrificed in Santeria rituals include chickens,
pigeons, doves, ducks, guinea pigs, goats, sheep, and turtles. The animals are killed
by the cutting of the carotid arteries in the neck. The sacrificed animal is cooked and
eaten, except after healing and death rituals. . . .

Petitioner Church of the Lukumi Babalu Aye, Inc. (Church), is a not-for-profit corporation organized under Florida law in 1973. The Church and its congregants practice the Santeria religion. . . . In April 1987, the Church leased land in the city of Hialeah, Florida, and announced plans to establish a house of worship as well as a school, cultural center, and museum. [T]he Church's goal was to bring the practice of the Santeria faith, including its ritual of animal sacrifice, into the open. The Church began the process of obtaining utility service and receiving the necessary licensing, inspection, and zoning approvals. . . .

The prospect of a Santeria church in their midst was distressing to many members of the Hialeah community, and the announcement of the plans to open a Santeria church in Hialeah prompted the city council to hold an emergency public session on June 9, 1987. The resolutions and ordinances passed at that and later meetings [effectively and intentionally prevented the Santerians from observing their religious rites, which involved the ritual sacrifice of live animals]. . . .

In September 1987, the city council adopted three substantive ordinances addressing the issue of religious animal sacrifice. Ordinance 87-52 defined "sacrifice" as "to unnecessarily kill, torment, torture, or mutilate an animal in a public or private ritual or ceremony not for the primary purpose of food consumption," and prohibited owning or possessing an animal "intending to use such animal for food purposes." It restricted application of this prohibition, however, to any individual or group that "kills, slaughters or sacrifices animals for any type of ritual, regardless of whether or not the flesh or blood of the animal is to be consumed." The ordinance contained an exemption for slaughtering by "licensed establishment[s]" of animals "specifically raised for food purposes." Declaring, moreover, that the city council "has determined that the sacrificing of animals within the city limits is contrary to the public health, safety, welfare and morals of the community," the city council adopted Ordinance 87-71. That ordinance defined "sacrifice" as had Ordinance 87-52, and then provided that "[i]t shall be unlawful for any person, persons, corporations or associations to sacrifice any animal within the corporate limits of the City of Hialeah, Florida." The final Ordinance, 87-72, defined "slaughter" as "the killing of animals for food" and prohibited slaughter outside of areas zoned for slaughterhouse use. The ordinance provided an exemption, however, for the slaughter or processing for sale of "small numbers of hogs and/or cattle per week in accordance with an exemption provided by state law." All ordinances and resolutions passed the city council by unanimous vote. Violations of each of the four ordinances were punishable by fines not exceeding $500 or imprisonment not exceeding 60 days, or both.

Following enactment of these ordinances, the Church and Pichardo [the church's priest and leader] filed this action pursuant to 42 U.S.C. § 1983 in the United States District Court for the Southern District of Florida. Named as defendants were the city of Hialeah and its mayor and members of its city council in their individual capacities. Alleging violations of petitioners' rights under, *inter alia*, the Free Exercise Clause, the complaint sought a declaratory judgment and injunctive and monetary relief. . . .

. . . . In addressing the constitutional protection for free exercise of religion, our cases establish the general proposition that a law that is neutral and of general applicability need not be justified by a compelling governmental interest even if the law has the incidental effect of burdening a particular religious practice. *Employment Div., Dept. of Human Resources of Ore. v. Smith, supra.* Neutrality and general applicability are interrelated, and, as becomes apparent in this case, failure to satisfy one requirement is a likely indication that the other has not been satisfied. A law falling to satisfy these requirements must be justified by a compelling governmental interest and must be narrowly tailored to advance that interest. These ordinances fail to satisfy the *Smith* requirements. We begin by discussing neutrality. . . . At a minimum, the protections of the Free Exercise Clause pertain if the law at issue discriminates against some or all religious beliefs or regulates or prohibits conduct because it is undertaken for religious reasons. . . .

Although a law targeting religious beliefs as such is never permissible, if the object of a law is to infringe upon or restrict practices because of their religious motivation, the law is not neutral, see *Employment Div., Dept. of Human Resources of Ore. v. Smith*, and it is invalid unless it is justified by a compelling interest and is narrowly tailored to advance that interest. There are, of course, many ways of demonstrating that the object or purpose of a law is the suppression of religion or religious conduct. To determine the object of a law, we must begin with its text, for the minimum requirement of neutrality is that a law not discriminate on its face. A law lacks facial neutrality if it refers to a religious practice without a secular meaning discernible from the language or context. Petitioners contend that three of the ordinances fail this test of facial neutrality because they use the words "sacrifice" and "ritual," words with strong religious connotations. We agree that these words are consistent with the claim of facial discrimination, but the argument is not conclusive. The words "sacrifice" and "ritual" have a religious origin, but current use admits also of secular meanings. The ordinances, furthermore, define "sacrifice" in secular terms, without referring to religious practices.

We reject the contention advanced by the city, see Brief for Respondent 15, that our inquiry must end with the text of the laws at issue. Facial neutrality is not determinative. The Free Exercise Clause, like the Establishment Clause, extends beyond facial discrimination. . . . Official action that targets religious conduct for distinctive treatment cannot be shielded by mere compliance with the requirement of facial neutrality. The Free Exercise Clause protects against governmental hostility which is masked as well as overt. . . .

The record in this case compels the conclusion that suppression of the central element of the Santeria worship service was the object of the ordinances. First, though use of the words "sacrifice" and "ritual" does not compel a finding of improper targeting of the Santeria religion, the choice of these words is support for our conclusion. There are further respects in which the text of the city council's enactments discloses the improper attempt to target Santeria.

It becomes evident that these ordinances target Santeria sacrifice when the ordinances' operation is considered. Apart from the text, the effect of a law in its real operation is strong evidence of its object. To be sure, adverse impact will not always lead to a finding of impermissible targeting. . . . [F]ew if any killings of animals are prohibited other than Santeria sacrifice, which is proscribed because it occurs during a ritual or ceremony and its primary purpose is to make an offering to the *orishas*, not food consumption. Indeed, careful drafting ensured that, although Santeria sacrifice is prohibited, killings that are no more necessary or humane in almost all other circumstances are unpunished. . . .

The ordinance exempts . . . "any licensed [food] establishment" with regard to "any animals which are specifically raised for food purposes," if the activity is permitted by zoning and other laws. This exception, too, seems intended to cover kosher slaughter. Again, the burden of the ordinance, in practical terms, falls on Santeria adherents but almost no others: If the killing is—unlike most Santeria sacrifices—unaccompanied by the intent to use the animal for food, then it is not prohibited by Ordinance 87-52; if the killing is specifically for food but does not occur during the course of "any type of ritual," it again falls outside the prohibition; and if the killing is for food and occurs during the course of a ritual, it is still exempted if it occurs in a properly zoned and licensed establishment and involves animals "specifically raised for food purposes." A pattern of exemptions parallels the pattern of narrow prohibitions. Each contributes to the gerrymander. . . .

We also find significant evidence of the ordinances' improper targeting of Santeria sacrifice in the fact that they proscribe more religious conduct than is necessary to achieve their stated ends. It is not unreasonable to infer, at least when there are no persuasive indications to the contrary, that a law which visits "gratuitous restrictions" on religious conduct, seeks not to effectuate the stated governmental interests, but to suppress the conduct because of its religious motivation. The legitimate governmental interests in protecting the public health and preventing cruelty to animals could be addressed by restrictions stopping far short of a flat prohibition of all Santeria sacrificial practice. If improper disposal, not the sacrifice itself, is the harm to be prevented, the city could have imposed a general regulation on the disposal of organic garbage. It did not do so.

In determining if the object of a law is a neutral one under the Free Exercise Clause, we can also find guidance in our equal protection cases. . . .

Here, as in equal protection cases, we may determine the city council's object from both direct and circumstantial evidence. *Arlington Heights v. Metropolitan Housing Development Corp.*, 429 U.S. 252, 266 (1977). Relevant evidence includes, among other things, the historical background of the decision under challenge, the specific series of events leading to the enactment or official policy in question, and the legislative or administrative history, including contemporaneous statements made by members of the decisionmaking body. *Id.*, at 267-268. These objective factors bear on the question of discriminatory object. *Personnel Administrator of Mass. v. Feeney*, 442 U.S. 256, 279, n.24 (1979).

That the ordinances were enacted "'because of,' not merely 'in spite of,'" their suppression of Santeria religious practice, *id.*, at 279, is revealed by the events preceding their enactment. Although respondent claimed at oral argument that it had experienced significant problems resulting from the sacrifice of animals within the city before the announced opening of the Church, Tr. of Oral Arg. 27, 46, the city council made no attempt to address the supposed problem before its meeting in June 1987, just weeks after the Church announced plans to open. The minutes and taped excerpts of the June 9 session, both of which are in the record, evidence significant hostility exhibited by residents, members of the city council, and other city officials toward the Santeria religion and its practice of animal sacrifice. The public crowd that attended the June 9 meetings interrupted statements by council members critical of Santeria with cheers and the brief comments of Pichardo with taunts. When Councilman Martinez, a supporter of the ordinances, stated that in pre-revolution Cuba "people were put in jail for practicing this religion," the audience applauded. Taped excerpts of Hialeah City Council Meeting, June 9, 1987.

Other statements by members of the city council were in a similar vein. For example, Councilman Martinez, after noting his belief that Santeria was outlawed in Cuba, questioned: "[I]f we could not practice this [religion] in our homeland [Cuba], why bring it to this country?" Councilman Cardoso said that Santeria devotees at the Church "are in violation of everything this country stands for." Councilman Mejides indicated that he was "totally against the sacrificing of animals" and distinguished kosher slaughter because it had a "real purpose." The "Bible says we are allowed to sacrifice an animal for consumption," he continued, "but for any other purposes, I don't believe that the Bible allows that." The president of the city council, Councilman Echevarria, asked: "What can we do to prevent the Church from opening?"

Various Hialeah city officials made comparable comments. The chaplain of the Hialeah Police Department told the city council that Santeria was a sin, "foolishness," "an abomination to the Lord," and the worship of "demons." He advised the city council: "We need to be helping people and sharing with them the truth that is found in Jesus Christ." He concluded: "I would exhort you . . . not to permit this Church to exist." The city attorney commented that Resolution 87-66 indicated: "This community will not tolerate religious practices which are abhorrent to its citizens. . . ." *Ibid.* Similar comments were made by the deputy city attorney. This history discloses the object of the ordinances to target animal sacrifice by Santeria worshippers because of its religious motivation.

In sum, the neutrality inquiry leads to one conclusion: The ordinances had as their object the suppression of religion. The pattern we have recited discloses animosity to Santeria adherents and their religious practices; the ordinances by their own terms target this religious exercise; the texts of the ordinances were gerrymandered with care to proscribe religious killings of animals but to exclude almost all secular killings; and the ordinances suppress much more religious conduct than is necessary in order to achieve the legitimate ends asserted in their defense. These ordinances are not neutral, and the court below committed clear error in failing to reach this conclusion.

We turn next to a second requirement of the Free Exercise Clause, the rule that laws burdening religious practice must be of general applicability. *Employment Div., Dept. of Human Resources of Ore. v. Smith*, 494 U.S., at 879-881. All laws are selective to some extent, but categories of selection are of paramount concern when a law has the incidental effect of burdening religious practice. . . .

Respondent claims that Ordinances 87–40, 87–52, and 87–71 advance two interests: protecting the public health and preventing cruelty to animals. The ordinances are underinclusive for those ends. They fail to prohibit nonreligious conduct that endangers these interests in a similar or greater degree than Santeria sacrifice does. The underinclusion is substantial, not inconsequential. Despite the city's proffered interest in preventing cruelty to animals, the ordinances are drafted with care to forbid few killings but those occasioned by religious sacrifice. Many types of animal deaths or kills for nonreligious reasons are either not prohibited or approved by express provision. For example, fishing is legal. Extermination of mice and rats within a home is also permitted. Florida law incorporated by Ordinance 87–40 sanctions euthanasia of "stray, neglected, abandoned, or unwanted animals," Fla.Stat. § 828.058 (1987); destruction of animals judicially removed from their owners "for humanitarian reasons" or when the animal "is of no commercial value," § 828.073(4)(c)(2); the infliction of pain or suffering "in the interest of medical science," § 828.02; the placing of poison in one's yard or enclosure, § 828.08; and the use of a live animal "to pursue or take wildlife or to participate in any hunting," § 828.122(6)(b), and "to hunt wild hogs," § 828.122(6)(e). . . .

The ordinances are also underinclusive with regard to the city's interest in public health, which is threatened by the disposal of animal carcasses in open public places and the consumption of uninspected meat. Neither interest is pursued by respondent with regard to conduct that is not motivated by religious conviction. The health risks posed by the improper disposal of animal carcasses are the same whether Santeria sacrifice or some nonreligious killing preceded it. The city does not, however, prohibit hunters from bringing their kill to their houses, nor does it regulate disposal after their activity.

We conclude, in sum, that each of Hialeah's ordinances pursues the city's governmental interests only against conduct motivated by religious belief. The ordinances "ha[ve] every appearance of a prohibition that society is prepared to impose upon [adherents of Santeria] but not upon itself." This precise evil is what the requirement of general applicability is designed to prevent.

A law burdening religious practice that is not neutral or not of general application must undergo the most rigorous of scrutiny. To satisfy the commands of the First Amendment, a law restrictive of religious practice must advance "interests of the highest order" and must be narrowly tailored in pursuit of those interests. The compelling interest standard that we apply once a law fails to meet the *Smith* requirements is not "water[ed] . . . down" but "really means what it says." *Employment Div., Dept. of Human Resources of Ore. v. Smith*, 494 U.S., at 888. A law that targets religious conduct for distinctive treatment or advances legitimate governmental interests only against conduct with a religious motivation will survive strict scrutiny only in rare cases. It follows from what we have already said that these ordinances cannot withstand this scrutiny.

As we have discussed, all four ordinances are overbroad or underinclusive in substantial respects. The proffered objectives are not pursued with respect to analogous nonreligious conduct, and those interests could be achieved by narrower ordinances that burdened religion to a far lesser degree. The absence of narrow tailoring suffices to establish the invalidity of the ordinances. . . .

Reversed.

Justice SCALIA, with whom THE CHIEF JUSTICE joins, concurring in part and concurring in the judgment.

The Court analyzes the "neutrality" and the "general applicability" of the Hialeah ordinances in separate sections (Parts II-A and II-B, respectively), and allocates various invalidating factors to one or the other of those sections. If it were necessary to make a clear distinction between the two terms, I would draw a line somewhat different from the Court's. But I think it is not necessary, and would frankly acknowledge that the terms are not only "interrelated," *ante*, at 531, but substantially overlap.

I do not join that section because it departs from the opinion's general focus on the object of the *laws* at issue to consider the subjective motivation of the *lawmakers*, *i.e.*, whether the Hialeah City Council actually *intended* to disfavor the religion of Santeria. As I have noted elsewhere, it is virtually impossible to determine the singular "motive" of a collective legislative body, see, *e.g.*, *Edwards v. Aguillard*, 482 U.S. 578, 636-639 (1987) (dissenting opinion), and this Court has a long tradition of refraining from such inquiries. . . .

Justice BLACKMUN, with whom Justice O'CONNOR joins, concurring in the judgment.

The Court holds today that the city of Hialeah violated the First and Fourteenth Amendments when it passed a set of restrictive ordinances explicitly directed at petitioners' religious practice. With this holding I agree. I write separately to emphasize that the First Amendment's protection of religion extends beyond those rare occasions on which the government explicitly targets religion (or a particular religion) for disfavored treatment, as is done in this case. In my view, a statute that burdens the free exercise of religion "may stand only if the law in general, and the State's refusal to allow a religious exemption in particular, are justified by a compelling interest that cannot be served by less restrictive means." *Employment Div., Dept. of Human Resources of Ore. v. Smith*, 494 U.S. 872, 907 (1990) (dissenting opinion). . . . I continue to believe that *Smith* was wrongly decided, because it ignored the value of religious freedom as an affirmative individual liberty and treated the Free Exercise Clause as no more than an antidiscrimination principle. See 494 U.S., at 908-909. Thus, while I agree with the result the Court reaches in this case, I arrive at that result by a different route.

NOTES AND QUESTIONS

1. *Equality and free exercise.* If one adopts an equalitarian approach to interpreting the Free Exercise Clause, do *Smith* and *Lukumi Babalu Aye* sufficiently protect against religious discrimination? Virtually everyone agrees that, whatever else the Free Exercise Clause might mean, it prohibits government from targeting religion for unfavorable treatment. How effectively will the rules announced and applied in *Lukumi Babalu Aye* protect minority religionists from both overt and covert forms of discrimination?

2. *Neutrality.* There was an abundance of proof that the ordinances targeted the Santeria practice of ritual animal sacrifice: the text, the timing of the emergency session, and the hostile comments, for a start. But even without those, when laws are as grossly overinclusive and underinclusive as the Hialeah ordinances, it gives rise to the suspicion that the state's proffered motive is not the actual motive. In other words, the extreme mismatch between the means and ends suggests something else, such as animus, was at play.

3. *General applicability.* Laws that are riddled with exceptions, as these ordinances were, are obviously not generally applicable. But what about a law that has only one or two exceptions—is it generally applicable? For example, if a police dress code bans beards except for medically necessary beards (required by some skin conditions), is that policy generally applicable? *See* Fraternal Order of Police v. City of Newark, 170 F.3d 359 (3d Cir. 1999). Is it a question of numbers, intent, or something else?

4. *Reliance on equal protection jurisprudence. Smith* made clear that laws neutral on their face are not necessarily neutral under the Free Exercise Clause. The same is true for the Equal Protection Clause, which Justice Kennedy explicitly references. At the same time, in equal protection doctrine, disparate impact alone is not enough to trigger the Equal Protection Clause. Instead, laws neutral on their face that have a discriminatory impact must also have a discriminatory purpose in order to merit heightened scrutiny under the Equal Protection Clause. See generally Washington v. Davis, 426 U.S. 229 (1976). Does the Supreme Court mean to import the same requirement of disparate impact plus discriminatory intent into free exercise doctrine when it writes that the ordinances were passed "because of" rather than "in spite of" their disparate impact on the Santeria religious practice?

THEORY-APPLIED PROBLEM

In May 2017, the City of Hialeah adopts an animal cruelty ordinance prohibiting "cruelty towards animals, including the intentional infliction of serious pain and torture, including but not limited to the cutting, mutilation, or maiming of an animal." At the time of adoption, no anti-Santerian statements issue from local government officials. Instead, generic statements about the need to protect "innocent creatures" pepper the legislative record. On May 15, 2017, the day the ordinance takes effect, a local city policeman cites the chief priest of the local Santerian church for violating the anti-animal-cruelty ordinance after observing a Santerian rite involving the intentional killing of a small goat. The police officer's report states, in relevant part, that "the goat appeared to be terrified, was bleating loudly, and attempted to escape, but could not." If the Santerian priest challenged the citation on free exercise grounds, what would be the likely outcome of the claim in the federal courts? If you believe that the citation would probably withstand a Free Exercise Clause challenge, how much protection does *Lukumi Babalu Aye* really provide to minority religionists? Is benign neglect any less harmful to minority religionists than overt forms of discrimination? Or is discrimination qualitatively different from benign neglect?

D. STATUTORY ACCOMMODATIONS OF RELIGION: THE RELIGIOUS FREEDOM RESTORATION ACT AND THE RELIGIOUS LAND USE AND INSTITUTIONALIZED PERSONS ACT

After *Smith*, Congress passed, almost unanimously, the Religious Freedom Restoration Act (RFRA), which attempted to restore the *Sherbert* standard to religious liberty claims. As explained in City of Boerne v. Flores, 521 U.S. 507 (1997):

> Congress enacted RFRA in direct response to the Court's decision in Employment Div., Dept. of Human Resources of Ore. v. Smith, 494 U.S. 872 (1990). . . . The application of the *Sherbert* test, the *Smith* decision explained, would have produced an anomaly in the law, a constitutional right to ignore neutral laws of general applicability. The anomaly would have been accentuated, the Court reasoned, by the difficulty of determining whether a particular practice was central to an individual's religion. We explained, moreover, that it "is not within the judicial ken to question the centrality of particular beliefs or practices to a faith, or the validity of particular litigants' interpretations of those creeds." . . .

These points of constitutional interpretation were debated by Members of Congress in hearings and floor debates. Many criticized the Court's reasoning, and this disagreement resulted in the passage of RFRA. Congress announced:

> "(1) [T]he framers of the Constitution, recognizing free exercise of religion as an unalienable right, secured its protection in the First Amendment to the Constitution;

"(2) laws 'neutral' toward religion may burden religious exercise as surely as laws intended to interfere with religious exercise;

"(3) governments should not substantially burden religious exercise without compelling justification;

"(4) in Employment Division v. Smith, 494 U.S. 872 (1990), the Supreme Court virtually eliminated the requirement that the government justify burdens on religious exercise imposed by laws neutral toward religion; and

"(5) the compelling interest test as set forth in prior Federal court rulings is a workable test for striking sensible balances between religious liberty and competing prior governmental interests." 42 U.S.C. § 2000bb(a).

The Act's stated purposes are:

"(1) to restore the compelling interest test as set forth in Sherbert v. Verner, 374 U.S. 398 (1963) and Wisconsin v. Yoder, 406 U.S. 205 (1972) and to guarantee its application in all cases where free exercise of religion is substantially burdened; and

"(2) to provide a claim or defense to persons whose religious exercise is substantially burdened by government." § 2000bb(b).

RFRA prohibits "[g]overnment" from "substantially burden[ing] a person's exercise of religion even if the burden results from a rule of general applicability unless the government can demonstrate the burden "(1) is in furtherance of a compelling governmental interest; and (2) is the least restrictive means of furthering that compelling governmental interest." § 2000bb-1.

By its terms, RFRA "applies to all Federal and State law, and the implementation of that law, whether statutory or otherwise, and whether adopted before or after [RFRA's enactment]." The Supreme Court held in *Boerne* that Congress had exceeded its authority in passing RFRA. Under its Fourteenth Amendment enforcement power, Congress may enact prophylactic laws to "remedy or prevent unconstitutional actions." However, "There must be a congruence and proportionality between the injury to be prevented or remedied and the means adopted to that end. Lacking such a connection, legislation may become substantive in operation and effect." In other words, Congress rather than the Supreme Court would be dictating the substance of the Free Exercise Clause. "Congress' power under § 5, however, extends only to 'enforc[ing]' the provisions of the Fourteenth Amendment. . . . Legislation which alters the meaning of the Free Exercise Clause cannot be said to be enforcing the Clause. Congress does not enforce a constitutional right by changing what the right is. It has been given the power 'to enforce,' not the power to determine what constitutes a constitutional violation." According to the Court, RFRA was not congruent and proportional: "RFRA is so out of proportion to a supposed remedial or preventive object that it cannot be understood as responsive to, or designed to prevent, unconstitutional behavior. It appears, instead, to attempt a substantive change in constitutional protections." As a consequence, RFRA is unconstitutional as applied to the states. However, as later cases confirmed, including Gonzales v. O Centro Espirita Beneficente Uniao Do Vegetal and Burwell v. Hobby Lobby Stores, Inc., RFRA does apply to federal laws. Moreover, since *Boerne*, roughly half of the states have passed their own version of RFRA, and these state RFRAs apply to their state laws.

Congress also enacted the Religious Land Use and Institutionalized Persons Act (RLUIPA). Like RFRA, it reintroduced the *Sherbert* test for religious liberty claims. Unlike RFRA, RLUIPA applies to only two types of cases: those involving land use (such as zoning regulations) and those involving institutionalized persons (such as prisoners). In addition, rather than rely on the Fourteenth Amendment, Congress enacted RLUIPA pursuant to its power to regulate interstate commerce and to condition federal spending.

GONZALES v.
O CENTRO ESPIRITA BENEFICENTE UNIAO DO VEGETAL

546 U.S. 418 (2006)

Chief Justice ROBERTS delivered the opinion of the Court.

A religious sect with origins in the Amazon Rainforest receives communion by drinking a sacramental tea, brewed from plants unique to the region, that contains a hallucinogen regulated under the Controlled Substances Act by the Federal Government. The Government concedes that this practice is a sincere exercise of religion, but nonetheless sought to prohibit the small American branch of the sect from engaging in the practice, on the ground that the Controlled Substances Act bars all use of the hallucinogen. The sect sued to block enforcement against it of the ban on the sacramental tea, and moved for a preliminary injunction. It relied on the Religious Freedom Restoration Act of 1993. . . .

O Centro Espírita Beneficente União do Vegetal (UDV) is a Christian Spiritist sect based in Brazil, with an American branch of approximately 130 individuals. Central to the UDV's faith is receiving communion through hoasca (pronounced "wass-ca"), a sacramental tea made from two plants unique to the Amazon region. One of the plants, psychotria viridis, contains dimethyltryptamine (DMT), a hallucinogen . . . listed in Schedule I of the Controlled Substances Act. . . .

The Government contends that the Act's description of Schedule I substances as having "a high potential for abuse," "no currently accepted medical use in treatment in the United States," and "a lack of accepted safety for use . . . under medical supervision," 21 U.S.C. § 812(b)(1), by itself precludes any consideration of individualized exceptions such as that sought by the UDV. The Government goes on to argue that the regulatory regime established by the Act—a "closed" system that prohibits all use of controlled substances except as authorized by the Act itself— "cannot function with its necessary rigor and comprehensiveness if subjected to judicial exemptions." Brief for Petitioners 18. According to the Government, there would be no way to cabin religious exceptions once recognized, and "the public will misread" such exceptions as signaling that the substance at issue is not harmful after all. *Id.* at 23. Under the Government's view, there is no need to assess the particulars of the UDV's use or weigh the impact of an exemption for that specific use, because the Controlled Substances Act serves a compelling purpose and simply admits of no exceptions.

RFRA, and the strict scrutiny test it adopted, contemplate an inquiry more focused than the Government's categorical approach. . . . Under the more focused inquiry required by RFRA and the compelling interest test, the Government's mere invocation of the general characteristics of Schedule I substances, as set forth in the Controlled Substances Act, cannot carry the day. It is true, of course, that Schedule I substances such as DMT are exceptionally dangerous. Nevertheless, there is no indication that Congress, in classifying DMT, considered the harms posed by the particular use at issue here—the circumscribed, sacramental use of hoasca by the UDV. . . . Schedule I simply does not provide a categorical answer that relieves the Government of the obligation to shoulder its burden under RFRA.

This conclusion is reinforced by the Controlled Substances Act itself. The Act contains a provision authorizing the Attorney General to "waive the requirement for registration of certain manufacturers, distributors, or dispensers if he finds it consistent with the public health and safety." 21 U.S.C. § 822(d). The fact that the Act itself contemplates that exempting certain people from its requirements would be "consistent with the public health and safety" indicates that congressional findings with respect to Schedule I substances should not carry the determinative weight, for RFRA purposes, that the Government would ascribe to them.

And in fact an exception has been made to the Schedule I ban for religious use. For the past 35 years, there has been a regulatory exemption for use of peyote—a Schedule I substance—by the Native American Church. See 21 CFR § 1307.31 (2005). In 1994, Congress extended that exemption to all members of every recognized Indian Tribe. See 42 U.S.C. § 1996a(b)(1). Everything the Government says about the DMT in hoasca—that, as a Schedule I substance, Congress has determined that it "has a high potential for abuse," "has no currently accepted medical use," and has "a lack of accepted safety for use . . . under medical supervision," 21 U.S.C. § 812(b)(1)—applies in equal measure to the mescaline in peyote, yet both the Executive and Congress itself have decreed an exception from the Controlled Substances Act for Native American religious use of peyote. If such use is permitted in the face of the congressional findings in § 812(b)(1) for hundreds of thousands of Native Americans practicing their faith, it is difficult to see how those same findings alone can preclude any consideration of a similar exception for the 130 or so American members of the UDV who want to practice theirs. . . .

The well-established peyote exception also fatally undermines the Government's broader contention that the Controlled Substances Act establishes a closed regulatory system that admits of no exceptions under RFRA. The Government argues that the effectiveness of the Controlled Substances Act will be "necessarily . . . undercut" if the Act is not uniformly applied, without regard to burdens on religious exercise. Brief for Petitioners 18. The peyote exception, however, has been in place since the outset of the Controlled Substances Act, and there is no evidence that it has "undercut" the Government's ability to enforce the ban on peyote use by non-Indians.

NOTES AND QUESTIONS

1. *Equal protection for minority religions.* Does *O Centro Espirita* provide an important counterweight to *Smith* and a pointed rejoinder to those who posit that courts are incapable of providing full and equal protection to unfamiliar religions and religious practices under either the Free Exercise Clause itself or civil rights statutes that protect religiously mandated conduct from the impact of generally applicable laws? Or is the outcome better explained by the fact that Congress had already granted an exemption for religious use of peyote?

2. *One exemption vs. all exemptions.* The Court emphasized the very small size of the sect in the United States ("approximately 130 individuals") and the fact that the practical effect of granting the UDV an exemption was quite minimal.

Should courts focus on only the requested exemption, or should they consider all possible exemptions? After all, just as the Court pointed to the peyote exemption, won't future challenges point the *hoasca* exemption?

3. *Broad or highly targeted exemptions from general laws?* Is it possible to limit the scope of a religious exemption as narrowly as Chief Justice Roberts posits in *O Centro Espirita*? Suppose a group of college students interested in experimenting with *hoasca* establish the "Church of the Sacred Visions" and attempt to import the drug for their "sacred rites"? Could the Customs Service apply the Controlled Substances Act against them? Or would the exemption have to be broadly construed to encompass any other "religious" groups that seek to consume the hallucinogenic *hoasca* tea?

4. *Religion v. secular counterpart.* Although RFRA could potentially provide a religious exemption for those who wanted to consume sacred *ganja* (that is marijuana), it would not reach a cancer patient who wanted to use marijuana for medical reasons in a state that had not yet legalized medical marijuana. Does RFRA unfairly privilege religious uses over secular uses? Wasn't that the point?

BURWELL v. HOBBY LOBBY STORES, INC.
___ U.S. ___, 134 S. Ct. 2751 (2014)

[Under the Affordable Care Act, employer-sponsored health insurance plans must cover basic preventive care without any cost-sharing from employees. Pursuant to a Department of Health and Human Services regulation that went into effect in 2012, preventive care included all FDA-approved contraception, including morning-after pills and IUDs. Religious employers such as churches, synagogues, mosques, temples and their auxiliaries were automatically exempt from this "contraception mandate," while religiously affiliated non-profit employers became exempt once they notified the Department of Health and Human Services of their religious objections. For-profit corporations, however, were required to comply. Hobby Lobby Stores, Inc. and Conestoga Wood Specialties Corp., both closely held for-profit corporations, brought suit. The owners of these companies were religiously opposed to abortion, and believed that morning-after pills and IUDs caused abortions. They argued that forcing their corporations to include these contraceptives in their health care plan violated the companies' RFRA rights.]

Justice ALITO delivered the opinion of the Court.

We must decide in these cases whether the Religious Freedom Restoration Act of 1993 (RFRA), 107 Stat. 1488, 42 U.S.C. § 2000bb et seq., permits the United States Department of Health and Human Services (HHS) to demand that three closely held corporations provide health-insurance coverage for methods of contraception that violate the sincerely held religious beliefs of the companies' owners. We hold that the regulations that impose this obligation violate RFRA, which prohibits the Federal Government from taking any action that substantially burdens the exercise of religion unless that action constitutes the least restrictive means of serving a compelling government interest.

In holding that the HHS mandate is unlawful, we reject HHS's argument that the owners of the companies forfeited all RFRA protection when they decided to organize their businesses as corporations rather than sole proprietorships or general partnerships. The plain terms of RFRA make it perfectly clear that Congress did not discriminate in this way against men and women who wish to run their businesses as for-profit corporations in the manner required by their religious beliefs.

Since RFRA applies in these cases, we must decide whether the challenged HHS regulations substantially burden the exercise of religion, and we hold that they do. The owners of the businesses have religious objections to abortion, and according to their religious beliefs the four contraceptive methods at issue are abortifacients. If the owners comply with the HHS mandate, they believe they will be facilitating abortions, and if they do not comply, they will pay a very heavy price—as much as $1.3 million per day, or about $475 million per year, in the case of one of the companies. If these consequences do not amount to a substantial burden, it is hard to see what would.

Under RFRA, a Government action that imposes a substantial burden on religious exercise must serve a compelling government interest, and we assume that the HHS regulations satisfy this requirement. But in order for the HHS mandate to be sustained, it must also constitute the least restrictive means of serving that interest, and the mandate plainly fails that test. There are other ways in which Congress or HHS could equally ensure that every woman has cost-free access to the particular contraceptives at issue here and, indeed, to all FDA-approved contraceptives.

In fact, HHS has already devised and implemented a system that seeks to respect the religious liberty of religious nonprofit corporations while ensuring that the employees of these entities have precisely the same access to all FDA-approved contraceptives as employees of companies whose owners have no religious objections to providing such coverage. The employees of these religious nonprofit corporations still have access to insurance coverage without cost sharing for all FDA-approved contraceptives; and according to HHS, this system imposes no net economic burden on the insurance companies that are required to provide or secure the coverage.

Although HHS has made this system available to religious nonprofits that have religious objections to the contraceptive mandate, HHS has provided no reason why the same system cannot be made available when the owners of for-profit corporations have similar religious objections. We therefore conclude that this system constitutes an alternative that achieves all of the Government's aims while providing greater respect for religious liberty. And under RFRA, that conclusion means that enforcement of the HHS contraceptive mandate against the objecting parties in these cases is unlawful.

As this description of our reasoning shows, our holding is very specific. We do not hold, as the principal dissent alleges, that for-profit corporations and other commercial enterprises can "opt out of any law (saving only tax laws) they judge incompatible with their sincerely held religious beliefs." Nor do we hold, as the dissent implies, that such corporations have free rein to take steps that impose "disadvantages . . . on others" or that require "the general public [to] pick up the tab." And we certainly do not hold or suggest that "RFRA demands accommodation of a for-profit corporation's religious beliefs no matter the impact that accommodation may have on . . . thousands of women employed by Hobby Lobby." The effect of the HHS-created accommodation on the women employed by Hobby Lobby and the other companies involved in these cases would be precisely zero. Under that accommodation, these women would still be entitled to all FDA-approved contraceptives without cost sharing. . . .

III

RFRA prohibits the "Government [from] substantially burden[ing] a person's exercise of religion even if the burden results from a rule of general applicability" unless the Government "demonstrates that application of the burden to the person— (1) is in furtherance of a compelling governmental interest; and (2) is the least restrictive means of furthering that compelling governmental interest." 42 U.S.C. §§ 2000bb–1(a), (b) (emphasis added). The first question that we must address is whether this provision applies to regulations that govern the activities of for-profit corporations like Hobby Lobby, Conestoga, and Mardel.

HHS contends that neither these companies nor their owners can even be heard under RFRA. . . . In holding that . . . a "secular, for-profit corporation," lacks RFRA protection, the Third Circuit wrote as follows: "General business corporations do not, separate and apart from the actions or belief systems of their individual owners or employees, exercise religion. They do not pray, worship, observe sacraments or take other religiously-motivated actions separate and apart from the intention and direction of their individual actors." 724 F.3d, at 385 (emphasis added). . . .

As we noted above, RFRA applies to "a person's" exercise of religion, 42 U.S.C. §§ 2000bb–1(a), (b), and RFRA itself does not define the term "person." We therefore look to the Dictionary Act, which we must consult "[i]n determining the meaning of any Act of Congress, unless the context indicates otherwise." 1 U.S.C. § 1. Under the Dictionary Act, "the wor[d] 'person' . . . include[s] corporations, companies, associations, firms, partnerships, societies, and joint stock companies, as well as individuals." . . .

The principal argument advanced by HHS and the principal dissent regarding RFRA protection for Hobby Lobby, Conestoga, and Mardel focuses not on the statutory term "person," but on the phrase "exercise of religion." According to HHS and the dissent, these corporations are not protected by RFRA because they cannot exercise religion. . . .

Is it because of the corporate form? The corporate form alone cannot provide the explanation because, as we have pointed out, HHS concedes that nonprofit corporations can be protected by RFRA . . . If the corporate form is not enough, what about the profit-making objective? . . . If, as Braunfeld recognized, a sole proprietorship that seeks to make a profit may assert a free-exercise claim, why can't Hobby Lobby, Conestoga, and Mardel do the same? Some lower court judges have suggested that RFRA does not protect for-profit corporations because the purpose of such corporations is simply to make money. . . . While it is certainly true that a central objective of for-profit corporations is to make money, modern corporate law does not require for-profit corporations to pursue profit at the expense of everything else, and many do not do so.

For all these reasons, we hold that a federal regulation's restriction on the activities of a for-profit closely held corporation must comply with RFRA.

IV

Because RFRA applies in these cases, we must next ask whether the HHS contraceptive mandate "substantially burden[s]" the exercise of religion. 42 U.S.C. § 2000bb–1(a). We have little trouble concluding that it does.

As we have noted, the Hahns and Greens have a sincere religious belief that life begins at conception. They therefore object on religious grounds to providing health insurance that covers methods of birth control that, as HHS acknowledges, may result in the destruction of an embryo. By requiring the Hahns and Greens and their companies to arrange for such coverage, the HHS mandate demands that they engage in conduct that seriously violates their religious beliefs. . . .

It is true that the plaintiffs could avoid these assessments by dropping insurance coverage altogether and thus forcing their employees to obtain health insurance on one of the exchanges established under ACA. But if at least one of their full-time employees were to qualify for a subsidy on one of the government-run exchanges, this course would also entail substantial economic consequences. The companies could face penalties of $2,000 per employee each year. . . .

[A]mici supporting HHS have suggested that the $2,000 per-employee penalty is actually less than the average cost of providing health insurance, see Brief for Religious Organizations 22, and therefore, they claim, the companies could readily eliminate any substantial burden by forcing their employees to obtain insurance in the government exchanges. We do not generally entertain arguments that were not raised below and are not advanced in this Court by any party . . .

Even if we were to reach this argument, we would find it unpersuasive. As an initial matter, it entirely ignores the fact that the Hahns and Greens and their companies have religious reasons for providing health-insurance coverage for their employees. Before the advent of ACA, they were not legally compelled to provide insurance, but they nevertheless did so—in part, no doubt, for conventional business reasons, but also in part because their religious beliefs govern their relations with their employees. . . .

In taking the position that the HHS mandate does not impose a substantial burden on the exercise of religion, HHS's main argument (echoed by the principal dissent) is basically that the connection between what the objecting parties must do (provide health-insurance coverage for four methods of contraception that may operate after the fertilization of an egg) and the end that they find to be morally wrong (destruction of an embryo) is simply too attenuated. HHS and the dissent note that providing the coverage would not itself result in the destruction of an embryo; that would occur only if an employee chose to take advantage of the coverage and to use one of the four methods at issue.

This argument dodges the question that RFRA presents (whether the HHS mandate imposes a substantial burden on the ability of the objecting parties to conduct business in accordance with their religious beliefs) and instead addresses a very different question that the federal courts have no business addressing (whether the religious belief asserted in a RFRA case is reasonable). The Hahns and Greens believe that providing the coverage demanded by the HHS regulations is connected to the destruction of an embryo in a way that is sufficient to make it immoral for them to provide the coverage. This belief implicates a difficult and important question of religion and moral philosophy, namely, the circumstances under which it is wrong for a person to perform an act that is innocent in itself but that has the effect of enabling or facilitating the commission of an immoral act by another. Arrogating the authority to provide a binding national answer to this religious and philosophical question, HHS and the principal dissent in effect tell the plaintiffs that their beliefs are flawed. For good reason, we have repeatedly refused to take such a step. See, e.g., *Smith*, 494 U.S., at 887 ("Repeatedly and in many different contexts, we have warned that courts must not presume to determine ... the plausibility of a religious claim"). . . .

Moreover, in *Thomas v. Review Bd. of Indiana Employment Security Div.*, 450 U.S. 707 (1981), we considered and rejected an argument that is nearly identical to the one now urged by HHS and the dissent. In Thomas, a Jehovah's Witness was initially employed making sheet steel for a variety of industrial uses, but he was later transferred to a job making turrets for tanks. Because he objected on religious grounds to participating in the manufacture of weapons, he lost his job and sought unemployment compensation. Ruling against the employee, the state court had difficulty with the line that the employee drew between work that he found to be consistent with his religious beliefs (helping to manufacture steel that was used in making weapons) and work that he found morally objectionable (helping to make the weapons themselves). This Court, however, held that "it is not for us to say that the line he drew was an unreasonable one." Id. at 715. . . .

V

Since the HHS contraceptive mandate imposes a substantial burden on the exercise of religion, we must move on and decide whether HHS has shown that the mandate both "(1) is in furtherance of a compelling governmental interest; and (2) is the least restrictive means of furthering that compelling governmental interest." 42 U.S.C. § 2000bb–1(b).

A

. . . The objecting parties contend that HHS has not shown that the mandate serves a compelling government interest, and it is arguable that there are features of ACA that support that view. As we have noted, many employees—those covered by grandfathered plans and those who work for employers with fewer than 50 employees—may have no contraceptive coverage without cost sharing at all. HHS responds that many legal requirements have exceptions and the existence of exceptions does not in itself indicate that the principal interest served by a law is not compelling. . . .

We find it unnecessary to adjudicate this issue. We will assume that the interest in guaranteeing cost-free access to the four challenged contraceptive methods is compelling within the meaning of RFRA, and we will proceed to consider the final prong of the RFRA test, i.e., whether HHS has shown that the contraceptive mandate is "the least restrictive means of furthering that compelling governmental interest." § 2000bb–1(b)(2).

B

The least-restrictive-means standard is exceptionally demanding, see *City of Boerne*, 521 U.S., at 532, and it is not satisfied here. HHS has not shown that it lacks other means of achieving its desired goal without imposing a substantial burden on the exercise of religion by the objecting parties in these cases. . . .

The most straightforward way of doing this would be for the Government to assume the cost of providing the four contraceptives at issue to any women who are unable to obtain them under their health-insurance policies due to their employers' religious objections. This would certainly be less restrictive of the plaintiffs' religious liberty, and HHS has not shown, see § 2000bb–1(b)(2), that this is not a viable alternative. . . .

In the end, however, we need not rely on the option of a new, government-funded program in order to conclude that the HHS regulations fail the least-restrictive-means test. HHS itself has demonstrated that it has at its disposal an approach that is less restrictive than requiring employers to fund contraceptive methods that violate their religious beliefs. As we explained above, HHS has already established an accommodation for nonprofit organizations with religious objections. Under that accommodation, the organization can self-certify that it opposes providing coverage for particular contraceptive services. If the organization makes such a certification, the organization's insurance issuer or third-party administrator must "[e]xpressly exclude contraceptive coverage from the group health insurance coverage provided in connection with the group health plan" and "[p]rovide separate payments for any contraceptive services required to be covered" without imposing "any cost-sharing requirements . . . on the eligible organization, the group health plan, or plan participants or beneficiaries." 45 CFR § 147.131(c)(2); 26 CFR § 54.9815–2713A(c)(2).

We do not decide today whether an approach of this type complies with RFRA for purposes of all religious claims. At a minimum, however, it does not impinge on the plaintiffs' religious belief that providing insurance coverage for the contraceptives at issue here violates their religion, and it serves HHS's stated interests equally well.

The principal dissent identifies no reason why this accommodation would fail to protect the asserted needs of women as effectively as the contraceptive mandate, and there is none. . . .

C

HHS and the principal dissent argue that a ruling in favor of the objecting parties in these cases will lead to a flood of religious objections regarding a wide variety of medical procedures and drugs, such as vaccinations and blood transfusions, but HHS has made no effort to substantiate this prediction. . . .

It is HHS's apparent belief that no insurance-coverage mandate would violate RFRA—no matter how significantly it impinges on the religious liberties of employers—that would lead to intolerable consequences. Under HHS's view, RFRA would permit the Government to require all employers to provide coverage for any medical procedure allowed by law in the jurisdiction in question—for instance, third-trimester abortions or assisted suicide.

The owners of many closely held corporations could not in good conscience provide such coverage, and thus HHS would effectively exclude these people from full participation in the economic life of the Nation. RFRA was enacted to prevent such an outcome.

In any event, our decision in these cases is concerned solely with the contraceptive mandate. Our decision should not be understood to hold that an insurance-coverage mandate must necessarily fall if it conflicts with an employer's religious beliefs. Other coverage requirements, such as immunizations, may be supported by different interests (for example, the need to combat the spread of infectious diseases) and may involve different arguments about the least restrictive means of providing them.

The principal dissent raises the possibility that discrimination in hiring, for example on the basis of race, might be cloaked as religious practice to escape legal sanction. Our decision today provides no such shield. The Government has a compelling interest in providing an equal opportunity to participate in the workforce without regard to race, and prohibitions on racial discrimination are precisely tailored to achieve that critical goal. . . .

It is so ordered.

Justice KENNEDY, concurring.

As to RFRA's first requirement, the Department of Health and Human Services (HHS) makes the case that the mandate serves the Government's compelling interest in providing insurance coverage that is necessary to protect the health of female employees, coverage that is significantly more costly than for a male employee. There are many medical conditions for which pregnancy is contraindicated. It is important to confirm that a premise of the Court's opinion is its assumption that the HHS regulation here at issue furthers a legitimate and compelling interest in the health of female employees.

Justice GINSBURG, with whom Justice Sotomayor joins, and with whom Justice BREYER and Justice KAGAN join as to all but Part III–C–1, dissenting.

In a decision of startling breadth, the Court holds that commercial enterprises, including corporations, along with partnerships and sole proprietorships, can opt out of any law (saving only tax laws) they judge incompatible with their sincerely held religious beliefs. Compelling governmental interests in uniform compliance with the law, and disadvantages that religion-based opt-outs impose on others, hold no sway, the Court decides, at least when there is a "less restrictive alternative." And such an alternative, the Court suggests, there always will be whenever, in lieu of tolling an enterprise claiming a religion-based exemption, the government, i.e., the general public, can pick up the tab.

The Court does not pretend that the First Amendment's Free Exercise Clause demands religion-based accommodations so extreme, for our decisions leave no doubt on that score. Instead, the Court holds that Congress, in the Religious Freedom Restoration Act of 1993 (RFRA), 42 U.S.C. § 2000bb et seq., dictated the extraordinary religion-based exemptions today's decision endorses. In the Court's view, RFRA demands accommodation of a for-profit corporation's religious beliefs no matter the impact that accommodation may have on third parties who do not share the corporation owners' religious faith—in these cases, thousands of women employed by Hobby Lobby and Conestoga or dependents of persons those corporations employ. Persuaded that Congress enacted RFRA to serve a far less radical purpose, and mindful of the havoc the Court's judgment can introduce, I dissent.

III

A

RFRA's purpose is specific and written into the statute itself. The Act was crafted to "restore the compelling interest test as set forth in *Sherbert v. Verner,* 374 U.S. 398, 83 S.Ct. 1790, 10 L.Ed.2d 965 (1963) and *Wisconsin v. Yoder,* 406 U.S. 205, 92

S.Ct. 1526, 32 L.Ed.2d 15 (1972) and to guarantee its application in all cases where free exercise of religion is substantially burdened." § 2000bb(b)(1). . . .

The legislative history is correspondingly emphatic on RFRA's aim. See, e.g., S. Rep. No. 103–111, p. 12 (1993) (hereinafter Senate Report) (RFRA's purpose was "only to overturn the Supreme Court's decision in *Smith*," not to "unsettle other areas of the law."); 139 Cong. Rec. 26178 (1993) (statement of Sen. Kennedy) (RFRA was "designed to restore the compelling interest test for deciding free exercise claims."). In line with this restorative purpose, Congress expected courts considering RFRA claims to "look to free exercise cases decided prior to *Smith* for guidance." Senate Report 8. See also H.R.Rep. No. 103–88, pp. 6–7 (1993) (hereinafter House Report) (same). In short, the Act reinstates the law as it was prior to *Smith*, without "creat[ing] ... new rights for any religious practice or for any potential litigant." 139 Cong. Rec. 26178 (statement of Sen. Kennedy). Given the Act's moderate purpose, it is hardly surprising that RFRA's enactment in 1993 provoked little controversy. See Brief for Senator Murray et al. as Amici Curiae 8 (hereinafter Senators Brief) (RFRA was approved by a 97–to–3 vote in the Senate and a voice vote in the House of Representatives).

B

Despite these authoritative indications, the Court sees RFRA as a bold initiative departing from, rather than restoring, pre-*Smith* jurisprudence. . . .

[T]he Court highlights RFRA's requirement that the government, if its action substantially burdens a person's religious observance, must demonstrate that it chose the least restrictive means for furthering a compelling interest. "[B]y imposing a least-restrictive-means test," the Court suggests, RFRA "went beyond what was required by our pre-*Smith* decisions." But as RFRA's statements of purpose and legislative history make clear, Congress intended only to restore, not to scrap or alter, the balancing test as this Court had applied it pre-*Smith*. . . .

C

With RFRA's restorative purpose in mind, I turn to the Act's application to the instant lawsuits. That task, in view of the positions taken by the Court, requires consideration of several questions, each potentially dispositive of Hobby Lobby's and Conestoga's claims: Do for-profit corporations rank among "person[s]" who "exercise . . . religion"? Assuming that they do, does the contraceptive coverage requirement "substantially burden" their religious exercise? If so, is the requirement "in furtherance of a compelling government interest"? And last, does the requirement represent the least restrictive means for furthering that interest?

Misguided by its errant premise that RFRA moved beyond the pre-*Smith* case law, the Court falters at each step of its analysis.

1

RFRA's compelling interest test, as noted, applies to government actions that "substantially burden a person's exercise of religion." 42 U.S.C. § 2000bb-1(a) (emphasis added). This reference, the Court submits, incorporates the definition of "person" found in the Dictionary Act, 1 U.S.C. § 1, which extends to "corporations, companies, associations, firms, partnerships, societies, and joint stock companies, as well as individuals." The Dictionary Act's definition, however, controls only where "context" does not "indicat[e] otherwise." § 1. Here, context does so indicate. RFRA speaks of "a person's exercise of religion." 42 U.S.C. § 2000bb–1(a) (emphasis added). See also §§ 2000bb–2(4), 2000cc–5(7)(a). Whether a corporation qualifies as a "person" capable of exercising religion is an inquiry one cannot answer without reference to the "full body" of pre-*Smith* "free-exercise caselaw." *Gilardi*, 733 F.3d, at 1212. There is in that case law no support for the notion that free exercise rights pertain to for-profit corporations.

Until this litigation, no decision of this Court recognized a for-profit corporation's qualification for a religious exemption from a generally applicable law, whether under the Free Exercise Clause or RFRA. The absence of such precedent is just what one would expect, for the exercise of religion is characteristic of natural persons, not artificial legal entities. As Chief Justice Marshall observed nearly two centuries ago, a corporation is "an artificial being, invisible, intangible, and existing only in contemplation of law." *Trustees of Dartmouth College v. Woodward*, 4 Wheat. 518, 636, 4 L.Ed. 629 (1819). Corporations, Justice Stevens more recently reminded, "have no consciences, no beliefs, no feelings, no thoughts, no desires." *Citizens United v. Federal Election Comm'n*, 558 U.S. 310, 466 (2010) (opinion concurring in part and dissenting in part).

The First Amendment's free exercise protections, the Court has indeed recognized, shelter churches and other nonprofit religion-based organizations. . . . The Court's "special solicitude to the rights of religious organizations," *Hosanna–Tabor Evangelical Lutheran Church and School v. EEOC,*132 S.Ct. 694, 706 (2012), however, is just that. No such solicitude is traditional for commercial organizations. Indeed, until today, religious exemptions had never been extended to any entity operating in "the commercial, profit-making world." *Amos*, 483 U.S., at 337.

The reason why is hardly obscure. Religious organizations exist to foster the interests of persons subscribing to the same religious faith. Not so of for-profit corporations. Workers who sustain the operations of those corporations commonly are not drawn from one religious community. Indeed, by law, no religion-based criterion can restrict the work force of for-profit corporations. . . . The distinction between a community made up of believers in the same religion and one embracing persons of diverse beliefs, clear as it is, constantly escapes the Court's attention. One can only wonder why the Court shuts this key difference from sight.

Reading RFRA, as the Court does, to require extension of religion-based exemptions to for-profit corporations surely is not grounded in the pre-*Smith* precedent Congress sought to preserve. Had Congress intended RFRA to initiate a change so huge, a clarion statement to that effect likely would have been made in the legislation. . . .

Citing *Braunfeld v. Brown*, 366 U.S. 599 (1961), the Court questions why, if "a sole proprietorship that seeks to make a profit may assert a free-exercise claim, [Hobby Lobby and Conestoga] can't . . . do the same?" But even accepting, arguendo, the premise that unincorporated business enterprises may gain religious accommodations under the Free Exercise Clause, the Court's conclusion is unsound. In a sole proprietorship, the business and its owner are one and the same. By incorporating a business, however, an individual separates herself from the entity and escapes personal responsibility for the entity's obligations. One might ask why the separation should hold only when it serves the interest of those who control the corporation. . . .

The Court's determination that RFRA extends to for-profit corporations is bound to have untoward effects. Although the Court attempts to cabin its language to closely held corporations, its logic extends to corporations of any size, public or private. . . .

2

Even if Hobby Lobby and Conestoga were deemed RFRA "person[s]," to gain an exemption, they must demonstrate that the contraceptive coverage requirement "substantially burden[s] [their] exercise of religion." 42 U.S.C. § 2000bb–1(a). Congress no doubt meant the modifier "substantially" to carry weight. In the original draft of RFRA, the word "burden" appeared unmodified. The word "substantially" was inserted pursuant to a clarifying amendment offered by Senators Kennedy and Hatch. See 139 Cong. Rec. 26180. In proposing the amendment, Senator Kennedy stated that RFRA, in accord with the Court's pre-*Smith* case law, "does not require the Government to justify every action that has some effect on religious exercise." Ibid.

The Court barely pauses to inquire whether any burden imposed by the contraceptive coverage requirement is substantial. . . . I agree with the Court that the Green and Hahn families' religious convictions regarding contraception are sincerely held. . . . But those beliefs, however deeply held, do not suffice to sustain a RFRA claim. RFRA, properly understood, distinguishes between "factual allegations that [plaintiffs'] beliefs are sincere and of a religious nature," which a court must accept as true, and the "legal conclusion ... that [plaintiffs'] religious exercise is substantially burdened," an inquiry the court must undertake.

That distinction is a facet of the pre-*Smith* jurisprudence RFRA incorporates. *Bowen v. Roy*, 476 U.S. 693 (1986), is instructive. There, the Court rejected a free exercise challenge to the Government's use of a Native American child's Social Security number for purposes of administering benefit programs. Without questioning the sincerity of the father's religious belief that "use of [his daughter's Social Security] number may harm [her] spirit," the Court concluded that the Government's internal uses of that number "place[d] [no] restriction on what [the father] may believe or what he may do." Id., at 699. Recognizing that the father's "religious views may not accept" the position that the challenged uses concerned only the Government's internal affairs, the Court explained that "for the adjudication of a constitutional claim, the Constitution, rather than an individual's religion, must supply the frame of reference." Id., at 700–701, n. 6. . . . Inattentive to this guidance, today's decision elides entirely the distinction between the sincerity of a challenger's religious belief and the substantiality of the burden placed on the challenger.

Undertaking the inquiry that the Court forgoes, I would conclude that the connection between the families' religious objections and the contraceptive coverage requirement is too attenuated to rank as substantial. The requirement carries no command that Hobby Lobby or Conestoga purchase or provide the contraceptives they find objectionable. Instead, it calls on the companies covered by the requirement to direct money into undifferentiated funds that finance a wide variety of benefits under comprehensive health plans. . . .

Importantly, the decisions whether to claim benefits under the plans are made not by Hobby Lobby or Conestoga, but by the covered employees and dependents, in consultation with their health care providers. . . . It is doubtful that Congress, when it specified that burdens must be "substantia[l]," had in mind a linkage thus interrupted by independent decisionmakers (the woman and her health counselor) standing between the challenged government action and the religious exercise claimed to be infringed. . . .

3

Even if one were to conclude that Hobby Lobby and Conestoga meet the substantial burden requirement, the Government has shown that the contraceptive coverage for which the ACA provides furthers compelling interests in public health and women's well being. Those interests are concrete, specific, and demonstrated by a wealth of empirical evidence. To recapitulate, the mandated contraception coverage enables women to avoid the health problems unintended pregnancies may visit on them and their children. The coverage helps safeguard the health of women for whom pregnancy may be hazardous, even life threatening. And the mandate secures benefits wholly unrelated to pregnancy, preventing certain cancers, menstrual disorders, and pelvic pain. . . .

4

After assuming the existence of compelling government interests, the Court holds that the contraceptive coverage requirement fails to satisfy RFRA's least restrictive means test. . . . A "least restrictive means" cannot require employees to relinquish benefits accorded them by federal law in order to ensure that their commercial employers can adhere unreservedly to their religious tenets.

Then let the government pay (rather than the employees who do not share their employer's faith), the Court suggests. . . . The ACA, however, requires coverage of preventive services through the existing employer-based system of health insurance "so that [employees] face minimal logistical and administrative obstacles." 78 Fed.Reg. 39888. Impeding women's receipt of benefits "by requiring them to take steps to learn about, and to sign up for, a new [government funded and administered] health benefit" was scarcely what Congress contemplated. . . .

And where is the stopping point to the "let the government pay" alternative? Suppose an employer's sincerely held religious belief is offended by health coverage of vaccines, or paying the minimum wage, see *Tony and Susan Alamo Foundation v. Secretary of Labor*, 471 U.S. 290, 303 (1985), or according women equal pay for substantially similar work, see *Dole v. Shenandoah Baptist Church*, 899 F.2d 1389, 1392 (C.A.4 1990)? Does it rank as a less restrictive alternative to require the government to provide the money or benefit to which the employer has a religion-based objection?

Because the Court cannot easily answer that question, it proposes something else: Extension to commercial enterprises of the accommodation already afforded to nonprofit religion-based organizations. . . . Ultimately, the Court hedges on its proposal to align for-profit enterprises with nonprofit religion-based organizations. "We do not decide today whether [the] approach [the opinion advances] complies with RFRA for purposes of all religious claims." Counsel for Hobby Lobby was similarly noncommittal. Asked at oral argument whether the Court-proposed alternative was acceptable, counsel responded: "We haven't been offered that accommodation, so we haven't had to decide what kind of objection, if any, we would make to that." Tr. of Oral Arg. 86–87. . . .

In sum, in view of what Congress sought to accomplish, i.e., comprehensive preventive care for women furnished through employer-based health plans, none of the proffered alternatives would satisfactorily serve the compelling interests to which Congress responded.

IV

Among the pathmarking pre-Smith decisions RFRA preserved is *United States v. Lee*, 455 U.S. 252 (1982). Lee, a sole proprietor engaged in farming and carpentry, was a member of the Old Order Amish. He sincerely believed that withholding Social Security taxes from his employees or paying the employer's share of such taxes would violate the Amish faith. This Court held that, although the obligations imposed by the Social Security system conflicted with Lee's religious beliefs, the burden was not unconstitutional. . . . [T]oday's Court dismisses Lee as a tax case. But the *Lee* Court made two key points one cannot confine to tax cases. "When followers of a particular sect enter into commercial activity as a matter of choice," the Court observed, "the limits they accept on their own conduct as a matter of conscience and faith are not to be superimposed on statutory schemes which are binding on others in that activity." . . . Further, the Court recognized in *Lee* that allowing a religion-based exemption to a commercial employer would "operat[e] to impose the employer's religious faith on the employees." . . . Working for Hobby Lobby or Conestoga, in other words, should not deprive employees of the preventive care available to workers at the shop next door, at least in the absence of directions from the Legislature or Administration to do so. . . .

For the reasons stated, I would reverse the judgment of the Court of Appeals for the Tenth Circuit and affirm the judgment of the Court of Appeals for the Third Circuit.

NOTES AND QUESTIONS

1. *RFRA vs. Free Exercise Clause.* The majority and dissent disagree over whether RFRA was meant to restore pre-*Smith* religious liberty protection or exceed it. Who do you think has the better argument?

2. *Corporations as religious rights holders.* This was the first Supreme Court decision that held that for-profit corporations were entitled to religious exemptions. The majority argued that the owners of closely held for-profit corporations should not have to give up their religious rights just because they decide to incorporate. What was the dissent's response? Why do people form corporations? *See generally* Caroline Mala Corbin, *Corporate Religious Liberty*, 30 Const. Commentary 277 (2015).

3. *Substantial burden.* The claim in *Hobby Lobby* was that facilitating someone else's sinful conduct was a substantial religious burden. How does this burden compare to the religious burdens articulated in the free exercise cases you have read so far? Should the courts independently evaluate whether a religious burden is substantial? If they do, would they be passing judgement on religious beliefs? If they do not, would they be reading out the requirement that the burden be "substantial"? How deferential should the courts be to claims of substantial burden? What if the plaintiffs make a factual error, such as thinking morning-

after pills cause abortions when the scientific consensus is that they do not;
should the courts still be deferential?

4. *Compelling state interest.* Although the plurality assumed without deciding that
the government had a compelling interest, Justice Kennedy's controlling
concurrence contributes the fifth vote for holding that the state's "interest in
providing insurance coverage that is necessary to protect the health of female
employees" was in fact compelling. Why does the Court maintain that
exceptions undermine the government's compelling interests? Would exceptions
to the Civil Rights Act undermine the state's compelling interest in ending
discrimination? Is grandfathering insurance plans an exception or a means of
gradually implementing major changes? Is excluding small employers an
exception or a question of scope?

5. *Narrowly tailored means.* The Court held that the contraception mandate was not
narrowly tailored because the government could provide the contraception itself
instead. Does this reasoning work for religious objections to other laws as well,
such as laws mandating social security taxes, minimum wage, or equal pay, or is
there something unique about the law mandating contraception coverage? Is a
proposed alternative a less restrictive alternative if it is much less effective in
accomplishing the government's goals? What if it is just slightly less effective?

6. *Challenge of nonprofits.* The Court also pointed to the accommodation made for
religiously affiliated nonprofits as evidence that the mandate was not narrowly
tailored. However, even though these nonprofits could opt-out of contraception
coverage by notifying either their insurance carriers or the Department of Health
and Human Services of their religious objections, they argued that the
accommodation itself violated their rights under RFRA: filing the paperwork in
order to receive this accommodation still made them complicit in sin and
therefore imposed a substantial religious burden. Although the Supreme Court
heard arguments in the lawsuit, its decision in Zubik v. Burwell, 136 S. Ct. 1557
(2016), dodged the issue by sending the case back to the lower courts with
instructions to work out a compromise. "[T]he parties on remand should be
afforded an opportunity to arrive at an approach going forward that
accommodates petitioners' religious exercise while at the same time ensuring
that women covered by petitioners' health plans 'receive full and equal health
coverage, including contraceptive coverage.' We anticipate that the Courts of
Appeals will allow the parties sufficient time to resolve any outstanding issues
between them."

HOLT v. HOBBS
___ U.S. ___, 135 S. Ct. 853 (2015)

Justice ALITO delivered the opinion of the Court.

Petitioner Gregory Holt, also known as Abdul Maalik Muhammad, is an Arkansas
inmate and a devout Muslim who wishes to grow a ½-inch beard in accordance with
his religious beliefs. Petitioner's objection to shaving his beard clashes with the
Arkansas Department of Correction's grooming policy, which prohibits inmates from
growing beards unless they have a particular dermatological condition. We hold that
the Department's policy, as applied in this case, violates the Religious Land Use and
Institutionalized Persons Act of 2000 (RLUIPA). . . .

Following our decision in *Smith*, Congress enacted RFRA in order to provide greater protection for religious exercise than is available under the First Amendment. . . . In making RFRA applicable to the States and their subdivisions, Congress relied on Section 5 of the Fourteenth Amendment, but in [City of Boerne], this Court held that RFRA exceeded Congress' powers under that provision. Congress responded to *City of Boerne* by enacting RLUIPA, which applies to the States and their subdivisions and invokes congressional authority under the Spending and Commerce Clauses. See § 2000cc–1(b). RLUIPA concerns two areas of government activity: Section 2 governs land-use regulation, § 2000cc; and Section 3—the provision at issue in this case—governs religious exercise by institutionalized persons, § 2000cc–1. Section 3 mirrors RFRA . . .

Petitioner, as noted, is in the custody of the Arkansas Department of Correction and he objects on religious grounds to the Department's grooming policy, which provides that "[n]o inmates will be permitted to wear facial hair other than a neatly trimmed mustache that does not extend beyond the corner of the mouth or over the lip." App. to Brief for Petitioner 11a. The policy makes no exception for inmates who object on religious grounds, but it does contain an exemption for prisoners with medical needs. . . .

Petitioner sought permission to grow a beard and, although he believes that his faith requires him not to trim his beard at all, he proposed a "compromise" under which he would grow only a ½–inch beard. App. 164. Prison officials denied his request . . .

In addition to showing that the relevant exercise of religion is grounded in a sincerely held religious belief, petitioner also bore the burden of proving that the Department's grooming policy substantially burdened that exercise of religion. Petitioner easily satisfied that obligation. The Department's grooming policy requires petitioner to shave his beard and thus to "engage in conduct that seriously violates [his] religious beliefs." *Hobby Lobby*, 134 S.Ct., at 2775. If petitioner contravenes that policy and grows his beard, he will face serious disciplinary action. Because the grooming policy puts petitioner to this choice, it substantially burdens his religious exercise. Indeed, the Department does not argue otherwise.

Since petitioner met his burden of showing that the Department's grooming policy substantially burdened his exercise of religion, the burden shifted to the Department to show that its refusal to allow petitioner to grow a ½–inch beard "(1) [was] in furtherance of a compelling governmental interest; and (2) [was] the least restrictive means of furthering that compelling governmental interest." § 2000cc–1(a). . . .

The Department contends that enforcing this prohibition is the least restrictive means of furthering prison safety and security in two specific ways. The Department first claims that the no-beard policy prevents prisoners from hiding contraband. The Department worries that prisoners may use their beards to conceal all manner of prohibited items, including razors, needles, drugs, and cellular phone subscriber identity module (SIM) cards. We readily agree that the Department has a compelling interest in staunching the flow of contraband into and within its facilities, but the argument that this interest would be seriously compromised by allowing an inmate to grow a ½–inch beard is hard to take seriously. . . .

[Moreover], the Department cannot show that forbidding very short beards is the least restrictive means of preventing the concealment of contraband. "The least-restrictive-means standard is exceptionally demanding," and it requires the government to "sho[w] that it lacks other means of achieving its desired goal without imposing a substantial burden on the exercise of religion by the objecting part[y]." *Hobby Lobby,* 134 S.Ct., at 2780. The Department failed to establish that it could not satisfy its security concerns by simply searching petitioner's beard. The Department already searches prisoners' hair and clothing, and it presumably examines the ¼–inch beards of inmates with dermatological conditions. It has offered no sound reason why hair, clothing, and ¼–inch beards can be searched but ½–inch beards cannot. . . .

The Department contends that its grooming policy is necessary to further an additional compelling interest, *i.e.,* preventing prisoners from disguising their identities. The Department tells us that the no-beard policy allows security officers to identify prisoners quickly and accurately. It claims that bearded inmates could shave their beards and change their appearance in order to enter restricted areas within the prison, to escape, and to evade apprehension after escaping.

We agree that prisons have a compelling interest in the quick and reliable identification of prisoners, and we acknowledge that any alteration in a prisoner's appearance, such as by shaving a beard, might, in the absence of effective countermeasures, have at least some effect on the ability of guards or others to make a quick identification. But even if we assume for present purposes that the Department's grooming policy sufficiently furthers its interest in the identification of prisoners, that policy still violates RLUIPA as applied in the circumstances present here. The Department contends that a prisoner who has a beard when he is photographed for identification purposes might confuse guards by shaving his beard. But as petitioner has argued, the Department could largely solve this problem by requiring that all inmates be photographed without beards when first admitted to the facility and, if necessary, periodically thereafter. . . .

We emphasize that although RLUIPA provides substantial protection for the religious exercise of institutionalized persons, it also affords prison officials ample ability to maintain security. We highlight three ways in which this is so. First, in applying RLUIPA's statutory standard, courts should not blind themselves to the fact that the analysis is conducted in the prison setting. Second, if an institution suspects that an inmate is using religious activity to cloak illicit conduct, "prison officials may appropriately question whether a prisoner's religiosity, asserted as the basis for a requested accommodation, is authentic." *Cutter v. Wilkinson,* 544 U.S. 709, 725, n. 13 (2005). See also *Hobby Lobby,* 134 S.Ct., at 2774, n. 28. Third, even if a claimant's religious belief is sincere, an institution might be entitled to withdraw an accommodation if the claimant abuses the exemption in a manner that undermines the prison's compelling interests.

In sum, we hold that the Department's grooming policy violates RLUIPA insofar as it prevents petitioner from growing a ½–inch beard in accordance with his religious beliefs. . . .

It is so ordered.

Justice GINSBURG, with whom Justice SOTOMAYOR joins, concurring.

Unlike the exemption this Court approved in *Burwell v. Hobby Lobby Stores, Inc.,* 134 S.Ct. 2751 (2014), accommodating petitioner's religious belief in this case would not detrimentally affect others who do not share petitioner's belief. See 134 S.Ct., at 2787-2788, 2790-2791, and n. 8, 2801 (GINSBURG, J., dissenting). On that understanding, I join the Court's opinion.

NOTES AND QUESTIONS

1. Holt v. Hobby Lobby. In what way do the religious burdens created by the challenged regulations differ in *Holt* and *Hobby Lobby*? In what way do the burdens on others created by granting an exemption differ?

2. *A less restrictive alternative?* Do you agree that regular beard searches and periodic identification photographs were less restrictive alternatives? How much less effective may the alternatives be and still count as a less restrictive alternative?

3. *How much deference?* How deferential was the Supreme Court to prison officials? What does the Court mean when it says that courts should not be blind to the prison setting?

THEORY-APPLIED PROBLEM

Two cashiers work at a small local pharmacy with two cash registers. Both are religiously opposed to contraception and refuse to ring up any purchase of contraception on the grounds that such conduct makes them complicit in sin. Their state has enacted the Equal Access to Medicine Act that requires pharmacies to fill and sell all safe and legal prescriptions. While the law provides an exemption for pharmacists with religious objections, the exemption does not extend to other pharmacy employees. The cashiers file suit, arguing that the law violates their rights under their state's Religious Freedom Restoration Act, which is modeled on the federal law. Not only does the law substantially burden their religious conscience, the cashiers argue, but the state has a less restrictive alternative: let someone else ring up the purchase instead. Will they win? Should they win?

THEORY-APPLIED PROBLEM

Pennsylvania's state legislature, concerned about the quality of the state's public schools, creates a new "choice" program in 2017. The choice program includes a variety of incentives to improve public schools, to create new "magnet" and "charter" schools, and to provide vouchers to assist parents with the expenses associated with private and parochial schools. In addition, Pennsylvania creates a new tax deduction for educational expenses incurred for primary, middle, or secondary education. All of these benefits, however, are limited to "accredited institutions that do not practice discrimination on the basis of race, sex, religion, national origin, ethnicity, or sexual orientation in any policies related to admissions, employment, or any other school-sponsored program." The legislature is anxious to avoid subsidizing schools that practice invidious forms of discrimination that, if adopted by the public schools, would violate the Fourteenth Amendment's Equal Protection Clause. The legislative history of the statute does not reflect any targeted animus toward any particular religion or group of religionists.

The Al Said Madrassa (ASM) is located in Philadelphia, Pennsylvania, and is affiliated with a mosque operated by the Brothers of Islam. ASM enjoys state accreditation and offers instruction for grades K-12. The curriculum is "consistent with the teachings and requirements of Shar'ia" and the school "seeks to foster a comprehensively Islamic environment." The school will admit persons of any race, sex, religion, national origin, ethnicity, or sexual orientation. However, the school features completely sex-segregated dual programs, with entirely separate facilities and faculties, and gender-appropriate dress codes and curricula. Girls must wear full dresses and head scarves at all times, and adult women teaching or visiting in the school must wear burkas (full body coverings, with small eye slits). In addition, only men are permitted to teach in the boys program, and only women are permitted to teach in the girls program. Although both programs meet state curricular mandates, significant differences exist in the programs for boys and girls, with the boys' program enjoying broader academic offerings and college preparatory AP courses not available in the girls' school. ASM argues that it prepares women for "gender-appropriate" vocations and that the curriculum reflects religious beliefs about the proper, but quite different, roles of men and women in a well-ordered and godly society. It notes that its practices have deep roots, stretching back for hundreds of years within the Islamic world.

The Pennsylvania State Department of Revenue (Department) holds that ASM is not eligible to receive state-funded school vouchers because it practices pervasive gender discrimination. It alleges that the educational programs, although separate, are far from being equal. The Department also objects to the differential gender-based dress codes that apply to girls and women. In addition, the Department disallows state income tax deductions for educational expenses associated with attending ASM on the grounds that ASM violates the state's nondiscrimination policies. The parents of ASM students respond by bringing a class action suit against the Department, alleging a violation of their Free Exercise Clause rights, as well as their rights under the state Religious Freedom Restoration Act. The parents claim that, as designed and implemented, the Pennsylvania voucher and tax deduction programs discriminate against traditional Islamic schools that observe religiously mandated gender rules, noting that single-sex parochial (Catholic) schools routinely receive vouchers and that the Department allowed parents of parochial school students to claim deductions for educational expenses associated with attending single-sex parochial schools. (The Department says that the parochial schools are different because they provide "fully equivalent" educational opportunities, albeit in a gender-segregated environment, and do not practice comprehensive sex discrimination in staffing single-sex schools.) The plaintiffs allege that, in cultural context, the rules do not constitute gender discrimination. How should the district court rule?

CHAPTER
15

Free Exercise of Religion:
Church Exemptions

TABLE OF CONTENTS

One final matter that requires attention involves the problem of disputes within congregations. If a religious organization has a falling out, with the congregation dividing into two (or more) camps, who gets to keep the church building and the fellowship hall? If a dispute arises regarding leadership within the church, what role (if any) may the government play in resolving the dispute? What if a minister brings an employment discrimination claim? In other words, in what ways can government act to resolve disputes within religious organizations without transgressing the Free Exercise Clause?

The problem implicates both religion clauses. It may constitute a free exercise issue if, by interfering in the internal affairs of a religious organization, the court ends up regulating religious beliefs. It may constitute an establishment issue if, by resolving disputes, the court finds itself deciding theological controversies or otherwise favoring one claim to religious truth over another. For example, British law once permitted civil courts to determine whether a church had substantially departed from the tenets of the faith; if it had, the trust creating or funding the church might revert to some other entity or person. Obviously, deciding whether a church has abandoned the essential tenets of its faith requires a court to, at a minimum, define those tenets in the first place. Accordingly, courts in the United States have struggled to establish neutral rules to resolve intra-church disputes that will not require government theology lessons. As you read the following cases, consider whether the categorical approach of *Watson* and *Hosanna-Tabor*, or the "neutral principles" approach of *Jones*, better serves the goal of government neutrality in matters of theology.

A. CHURCH PROPERTY DISPUTES

WATSON v. JONES
80 (13 Wall) U.S. 679 (1872)

[This litigation grew out of certain disturbances in what is known as the "Third or Walnut Street Presbyterian Church," of Louisville, Kentucky, and which resulted in a division of its members into two distinct bodies, each claiming the exclusive use of the property held and owned by that local church.]

Mr. Justice MILLER now delivered the opinion of the Court.

This case belongs to a class, happily rare in our courts, in which one of the parties to a controversy, essentially ecclesiastical, resorts to the judicial tribunals of the State for the maintenance of rights which the church has refused to acknowledge, or found itself unable to protect. Much as such dissensions among the members of a religious society should be regretted, a regret which is increased when passing from the control of the judicial and legislative bodies of the entire organization to which the society belongs, an appeal is made to the secular authority; the courts when so called on must perform their functions as in other cases.

Religious organizations come before us in the same attitude as other voluntary associations for benevolent or charitable purposes, and their rights of property, or of contract, are equally under the protection of the law, and the actions of their members subject to its restraints. . . .

The questions which have come before the civil courts concerning the rights to property held by ecclesiastical bodies, may, so far as we have been able to examine them, be profitably classified under three general heads, which of course do not include cases governed by considerations applicable to a church established and supported by law as the religion of the state.

1. The first of these is when the property which is the subject of controversy has been, by the deed or will of the donor, or other instrument by which the property is held, by the express terms of the instrument devoted to the teaching, support, or spread of some specific form of religious doctrine or belief.

2. The second is when the property is held by a religious congregation which, by the nature of its organization, is strictly independent of other ecclesiastical associations, and so far as church government is concerned, owes no fealty or obligation to any higher authority.

3. The third is where the religious congregation or ecclesiastical body holding the property is but a subordinate member of some general church organization in which there are superior ecclesiastical tribunals with a general and ultimate power of control more or less complete, in some supreme judicatory over the whole membership of that general organization.

In regard to the first of these classes it seems hardly to admit of a rational doubt that an individual or an association of individuals may dedicate property by way of trust to the purpose of sustaining, supporting, and propagating definite religious doctrines or principles, provided that in doing so they violate no law of morality, and give to the instrument by which their purpose is evidenced, the formalities which the laws require. And it would seem also to be the obvious duty of the court, in a case properly made, to see that the property so dedicated is not diverted from the trust which is thus attached to its use. So long as there are persons qualified within the meaning of the original dedication, and who are also willing to teach the doctrines or principles prescribed in the act of dedication, and so long as there is any one so interested in the execution of the trust as to have a standing in court, it must be that they can prevent the diversion of the property or fund to other and different uses. This is the general doctrine of courts of equity as to charities, and it seems equally applicable to ecclesiastical matters.

In such case, if the trust is confided to a religious congregation of the independent or congregational form of church government, it is not in the power of the majority of that congregation, however preponderant, by reason of a change of views on religious subjects, to carry the property so confided to them to the support of new and conflicting doctrine. A pious man building and dedicating a house of worship to the sole and exclusive use of those who believe in the doctrine of the Holy Trinity, and placing it under the control of a congregation which at the time holds the same belief, has a right to expect that the law will prevent that property from being used as a means of support and dissemination of the Unitarian doctrine, and as a place of Unitarian worship. Nor is the principle varied when the organization to which the trust is confided is of the second or associated form of church government. The protection which the law throws around the trust is the same. And though the task may be a delicate one and a difficult one, it will be the duty of the court in such cases, when the doctrine to be taught or the form of worship to be used is definitely and clearly laid down, to inquire whether the party accused of violating the trust is holding or teaching a different doctrine, or using a form of worship which is so far variant as to defeat the declared objects of the trust.

The second class of cases which we have described has reference to the case of a church of a strictly congregational or independent organization, governed solely within itself, either by a majority of its members or by such other local organism as it may have instituted for the purpose of ecclesiastical government; and to property held by such a church, either by way of purchase or donation, with no other specific trust attached to it in the hands of the church than that it is for the use of that congregation as a religious society.

In such cases where there is a schism which leads to a separation into distinct and conflicting bodies, the rights of such bodies to the use of the property must be determined by the ordinary principles which govern voluntary associations. If the principle of government in such cases is that the majority rules, then the numerical majority of members must control the right to the use of the property. If there be within the congregation officers in whom are vested the powers of such control, then those who adhere to the acknowledged organism by which the body is governed are entitled to the use of the property. The minority in choosing to separate themselves into a distinct body, and refusing to recognize the authority of the governing body, can claim no rights in the property from the fact that they had once been members of the church or congregation. This ruling admits of no inquiry into the existing religious opinions of those who comprise the legal or regular organization; for, if such was permitted, a very small minority, without any officers of the church among them, might be found to be the only faithful supporters of the religious dogmas of the founders of the church. There being no such trust imposed upon the property when purchased or given, the court will not imply one for the purpose of expelling from its use those who by regular succession and order constitute the church, because they may have changed in some respect their views of religious truth. . . .

But the third of these classes of cases is the one which is oftenest found in the courts, and which, with reference to the number and difficulty of the questions involved, and to other considerations, is every way the most important.

It is the case of property acquired in any of the usual modes for the general use of a religious congregation which is itself part of a large and general organization of some religious denomination, with which it is more or less intimately connected by religious views and ecclesiastical government.

The case before us is one of this class, growing out of a schism which has divided the congregation and its officers, and the presbytery and synod, and which appeals to the courts to determine the right to the use of the property so acquired. Here is no case of property devoted forever by the instrument which conveyed it, or by any specific declaration of its owner, to the support of any special religious dogmas, or any peculiar form of worship, but of property purchased for the use of a religious congregation, and so long as any existing religious congregation can be ascertained to be that congregation, or its regular and legitimate successor, it is entitled to the use of the property. In the case of an independent congregation we have pointed out how this identity, or succession, is to be ascertained, but in cases of this character we are bound to look at the fact that the local congregation is itself but a member of a much larger and more important religious organization, and is under its government and control, and is bound by its orders and judgments. There are in the Presbyterian system of ecclesiastical government, in regular succession, the presbytery over the session or local church, the synod over the presbytery, and the General Assembly over all. These are called, in the language of the church organs, "judicatories," and they entertain appeals from the decisions of those below, and prescribe corrective measures in other cases.

In this class of cases we think the rule of action which should govern the civil courts, founded in a broad and sound view of the relations of church and state under our system of laws, and supported by a preponderating weight of judicial authority is, that, whenever the questions of discipline, or of faith, or ecclesiastical rule, custom, or law have been decided by the highest of these church judicatories to which the matter has been carried, the legal tribunals must accept such decisions as final, and as binding on them, in their application to the case before them.

In this country the full and free right to entertain any religious belief, to practice any religious principle, and to teach any religious doctrine which does not violate the laws of morality and property, and which does not infringe personal rights, is conceded to all. The law knows no heresy, and is committed to the support of no dogma, the establishment of no sect. The right to organize voluntary religious associations to assist in the expression and dissemination of any religious doctrine, and to create tribunals for the decision of controverted questions of faith within the association, and for the ecclesiastical government of all the individual members, congregations, and officers within the general association, is unquestioned. All who unite themselves to such a body do so with an implied consent to this government, and are bound to submit to it. But it would be a vain consent and would lead to the total subversion of such religious bodies, if any one aggrieved by one of their decisions could appeal to the secular courts and have them reversed. It is of the essence of these religious unions, and of their right to establish tribunals for the decision of questions arising among themselves, that those decisions should be binding in all cases of ecclesiastical cognizance, subject only to such appeals as the organism itself provides for.

Nor do we see that justice would be likely to be promoted by submitting those decisions to review in the ordinary judicial tribunals. Each of these large and influential bodies (to mention no others, let reference be had to the Protestant Episcopal, the Methodist Episcopal, and the Presbyterian churches), has a body of constitutional and ecclesiastical law of its own, to be found in their written organic laws, their books of discipline, in their collections of precedents, in their usage and customs, which as to each constitute a system of ecclesiastical law and religious faith that tasks the ablest minds to become familiar with. It is not to be supposed that the judges of the civil courts can be as competent in the ecclesiastical law and religious faith of all these bodies as the ablest men in each are in reference to their own. It would therefore be an appeal from the more learned tribunal in the law which should decide the case, to one which is less so. . . .

Under cover of inquiries into the jurisdiction of the synod and presbytery over the congregation, and of the General Assembly over all, [the Kentucky Court of Appeals] went into an elaborate examination of the principles of Presbyterian church government, and ended by overruling the decision of the highest judicatory of that church in the United States, both on the jurisdiction and the merits; and, substituting its own judgment for that of the ecclesiastical court, decides that ruling elders, declared to be such by that tribunal, are not such, and must not be recognized by the congregation, though four-fifths of its members believe in the judgment of the Assembly and desired to conform to its decree.

But we need pursue this subject no further. Whatever may have been the case before the Kentucky court, the appellants in the case presented to us have separated themselves wholly from the church organization to which they belonged when this controversy commenced. They now deny its authority, denounce its action, and refuse to abide by its judgments. They have first erected themselves into a new organization, and have since joined themselves to another totally different, if not hostile, to the one to which they belonged when the difficulty first began. Under any of the decisions which we have examined, the appellants, in their present position, have no right to the property, or to the use of it, which is the subject of this suit.

The novelty of the questions presented to this court for the first time, their intrinsic importance and far-reaching influence, and the knowledge that the schism in which the case originated has divided the Presbyterian churches throughout Kentucky and Missouri, have seemed to us to justify the careful and laborious examination and discussion which we have made of the principles which should govern the case. For the same reasons we have held it under advisement for a year; not uninfluenced by the hope, that since the civil commotion, which evidently lay at the foundation of the trouble, has passed away, that charity, which is so large an element in the faith of both parties, and which, by one of the apostles of that religion, is said to be the greatest of all the Christian virtues, would have brought about a reconciliation. But we have been disappointed. It is not for us to determine or apportion the moral responsibility which attaches to the parties for this result. We can only pronounce the judgment of the law as applicable to the case presented to us, and that requires us to affirm the decree of the Circuit Court as it stands.

Decree affirmed.

NOTES AND QUESTIONS

1. *The rules applicable to resolving disputes regarding church property. Watson* recognizes three distinct classes of church property ownership: (1) church property given in trust for the teaching of a particular faith or doctrine; (2) church property owned by a free-standing and independent congregation; and (3) church property owned by a unit of a hierarchical church. With respect to the second and third categories, the Supreme Court establishes fairly clear rules. A court should ascertain the governing rules for a congregational church and enforce the decision of the entity that has a right to control the property under the charter. For a hierarchical church, the court should enforce the decision of the highest entity with the hierarchy. The first category, however, is potentially problematic because church property held in trust for the teaching of a particular doctrine might require a court to determine whether a church had in fact modified its doctrines.

2. *The difficulty of applying the* Watson *rules.* Even though the rule governing control of property held by a local unit of a hierarchical church is straightforward, in practice its application can be remarkably unpopular. Local courts are unlikely to want to strip local community members of their church in deference to an out-of-state person or entity. In part because of these pressures, state courts have attempted to avoid applying the *Watson* rule with respect to hierarchical churches (with some success—*see Jones, infra*).

3. *Identifying the highest authority within a hierarchical church.* Under *Watson,* if a church is hierarchical in nature, then the decision of the highest official or entity within the hierarchy controls. This approach provides a categorical rule that should, in theory, permit courts to settle property disputes without delving into matters of theology. But is this really the case? Suppose that two persons claim to be Bishop of Rome (or the Supreme Pontiff of the Roman Catholic Church). Historically, during the Great Schism, two popes both claimed to be "The" pope—one in Rome and the other in Avignon, France. How should the courts determine which pope speaks for the hierarchy?

PRESBYTERIAN CHURCH IN THE UNITED STATES v. MARY ELIZABETH BLUE HULL MEMORIAL PRESBYTERIAN CHURCH

393 U.S. 440 (1969)

Mr. Justice BRENNAN delivered the opinion of the Court.

This is a church property dispute which arose when two local churches withdrew from a hierarchical general church organization. Under Georgia law the right to the property previously used by the local churches was made to turn on a civil court jury decision as to whether the general church abandoned or departed from the tenets of faith and practice it held at the time the local churches affiliated with it. The question presented is whether the restraints of the First Amendment, as applied to the States through the Fourteenth Amendment, permit a civil court to award church property on the basis of the interpretation and significance the civil court assigns to aspects of church doctrine.

Petitioner, Presbyterian Church in the United States, is an association of local Presbyterian churches governed by a hierarchical structure of tribunals which consists of, in ascending order, (1) the Church Session, composed of the elders of the local church; (2) the Presbytery, composed of several churches in a geographical area; (3) the Synod, generally composed of all Presbyteries within a State; and (4) the General Assembly, the highest governing body.

A dispute arose between petitioner, the general church, and two local churches in Savannah, Georgia—the respondents, Hull Memorial Presbyterian Church and Eastern Heights Presbyterian Church—over control of the properties used until they by the local churches. In 1966, the membership of the local churches, in the belief that certain actions and pronouncements of the general church were violations of that organization's constitution and departures from the doctrine and practice in force at the time of affiliation, voted to withdraw from the general church and to reconstitute the local churches as an autonomous Presbyterian organization. The ministers of the two churches renounced the general church's jurisdiction and authority over them, as did all but two of the ruling elders. In response, the general church, through the Presbytery of Savannah, established an Administrative Commission to seek a conciliation. The dissident local churchmen remained steadfast; consequently, the Commission acknowledged the withdrawal of the local leadership and proceeded to take over the local churches' property on behalf of the general church until new local leadership could be appointed.

The local churchmen made no effort to appeal the Commission's action to higher church tribunals—the Synod of Georgia or the General Assembly. Instead, the churches filed separate suits in the Superior Court of Chatham County to enjoin the general church from trespassing on the disputed property, title to which was in the local churches. The cases were consolidated for trial. The general church moved to dismiss the actions and cross-claimed for injunctive relief in its own behalf on the ground that civil courts were without power to determine whether the general church had departed from its tenets of faith and practice. . . .

It is of course true that the State has a legitimate interest in resolving property disputes, and that a civil court is a proper forum for that resolution. Special problems arise, however, when these disputes implicate controversies over church doctrine and practice. The approach of this Court in such cases was originally developed in *Watson v. Jones*, 13 Wall. 679 (1872), a pre-*Erie R. Co. v. Tompkins* diversity decision decided before the application of the First Amendment to the States but nonetheless informed by First Amendment considerations. There, as here, civil courts were asked to resolve a property dispute between a national Presbyterian organization and local churches of that organization. There, as here, the disputes arose out of a controversy over church doctrine. There, as here, the Court was asked to decree the termination of an implied trust because of departures from doctrine by the national organization. The Watson Court refused pointing out that it was wholly inconsistent with the American concept of the relationship between church and state to permit civil courts to determine ecclesiastical questions. In language which has a clear constitutional ring, the Court said

'In this country the full and free right to entertain any religious belief, to practice any religious principle, and to teach any religious doctrine which does not violate the laws of morality and property, and which does not infringe personal rights, is conceded to all. The law knows no heresy, and is committed to the support of no dogma, the establishment of no sect. . . . All who unite themselves to such a body (the general church) do so with an implied consent to (its) government, and are bound to submit to it. But it would be a vain consent and would lead to the total subversion of such religious bodies, if any one aggrieved by one of their decisions could appeal to the secular courts and have them (sic) reversed. It is of the essence of these religious unions, and of their right to establish tribunals for the decision of questions arising among themselves, that those decisions should be binding in all cases of ecclesiastical cognizance, subject only to such appeals as the organism itself provides for.' 13 Wall., at 728-729.

The logic of this language leaves the civil courts no role in determining ecclesiastical questions in the process of resolving property disputes.

Later cases, however, also decided on nonconstitutional grounds, recognized that there might be some circumstances in which marginal civil court review of ecclesiastical determinations would be appropriate. The scope of this review was delineated in *Gonzalez v. Roman Catholic Archbishop of Manila*, 280 U.S. 1 (1929). There, Gonzalez claimed the right to be appointed to a chaplaincy in the Roman Catholic Church under a will which provided that a member of his family receive that appointment. The Roman Catholic Archbishop of Manila, Philippine Islands, refused to appoint Gonzalez on the ground that he did not satisfy the qualifications established by Canon Law for that office. Gonzalez brought suit in the Court of First Instance of Manila for a judgment directing the Archbishop, among other things, to appoint him chaplain. The trial court entered such an order, but the Supreme Court of the Philippine Islands reversed and 'absolved the Archbishop from the complaint.' This Court affirmed. Mr. Justice Brandeis, speaking for the Court, defined the civil court role in the following words: 'In the absence of fraud, collusion, or arbitrariness, the decisions of the proper church tribunals on matters purely ecclesiastical, although affecting civil rights, are accepted in litigation before the secular courts as conclusive, because the parties in interest made them so by contract or otherwise.' 280 U.S., at 16.

In *Kedroff v. St. Nicholas Cathedral of Russian Orthodox Church in North America*, 344 U.S. 94 (1952), the Court converted the principle of *Watson* as qualified by *Gonzalez* into a constitutional rule. *Kedroff* grew out of a dispute between the Moscow-based general Russian Orthodox Church and the Russian Orthodox churches located in North America over an appointment to St. Nicholas Cathedral in New York City. The North American churches declared their independence from the general church, and the New York Legislature enacted a statute recognizing their administrative autonomy. The New York courts sustained the constitutionality of the statute and held that the North American churches' elected hierarch had the right to use the cathedral. This Court reversed, finding that the Moscow church had not acknowledged the schism, and holding the statute unconstitutional. The Court said:

'The opinion (in *Watson v. Jones*) radiates . . . a spirit of freedom for religious organizations, an independence from secular control or manipulation—in short, power to decide for themselves, free from state interference, matters of church government as well as those of faith and doctrine. Freedom to select the clergy, where no improper methods of choice are proven, we think, must now be said to have federal constitutional protection as a part of the free exercise of religion against state interference.' (Italics supplied.)

. . . This holding invalidating legislative action was extended to judicial action in *Kreshik v. St. Nicholas Cathedral*, 363 U.S. 190 (1960), where the Court held that the constitutional guarantees of religious liberty required the reversal of a judgment of the New York courts which transferred control of St. Nicholas Cathedral from the central governing authority of the Russian Orthodox Church to the independent Russian Church of America.

Thus, the First Amendment severely circumscribes the role that civil courts may play in resolving church property disputes. It is obvious, however, that not every civil court decision as to property claimed by a religious organization jeopardizes values protected by the First Amendment. Civil courts do not inhibit free exercise of religion merely by opening their doors to disputes involving church property. And there are neutral principles of law, developed for use in all property disputes, which can be applied without 'establishing' churches to which property is awarded. But First Amendment values are plainly jeopardized when church property litigation is made to turn on the resolution by civil courts of controversies over religious doctrine and practice. If civil courts undertake to resolve such controversies in order to adjudicate the property dispute, the hazards are ever present of inhibiting the free development of religious doctrine and of implicating secular interests in matters of purely ecclesiastical concern. . . . [The First] Amendment therefore commands civil courts to decide church property disputes without resolving underlying controversies over religious doctrine. Hence, States, religious organizations, and individuals must structure relationships involving church property so as not to require the civil courts to resolve ecclesiastical questions.

The Georgia courts have violated the command of the First Amendment. The departure-from-doctrine element of the implied trust theory which they applied requires the civil judiciary to determine whether actions of the general church constitute such a 'substantial departure' from the tenets of faith and practice existing at the time of the local churches' affiliation that the trust in favor of the general church must be declared to have terminated. This determination has two parts. The civil court must first decide whether the challenged actions of the general church depart substantially from prior doctrine. In reaching such a decision, the court must of necessity make its own interpretation of the meaning of church doctrines. If the court should decide that a substantial departure has occurred, it must then go on to determine whether the issue on which the general church has departed holds a place of such importance in the traditional theology as to require that the trust be terminated. A civil court can make this determination only after assessing the relative significance to the religion of the tenets from which departure was found. Thus, the departure-from-doctrine element of the Georgia implied trust theory requires the civil court to determine matters at the very core of a religion—the interpretation of particular church doctrines and the importance of those doctrines to the religion. Plainly, the First Amendment forbids civil courts from playing such a role. . . .

The judgment of the Supreme Court of Georgia is reversed, and the case is remanded for further proceedings not inconsistent with this opinion.

It is so ordered.

Mr. Justice HARLAN, concurring.

I am in entire agreement with the Court's rejection of the 'departure-from-doctrine' approach taken by the Georgia courts, as that approach necessarily requires the civilian courts to weigh the significance and the meaning of disputed religious doctrine. I do not, however, read the Court's opinion to go further to hold that the Fourteenth Amendment forbids civilian courts from enforcing a deed or will which expressly and clearly lays down conditions limiting a religious organization's use of the property which is granted. If, for example, the donor expressly gives his church some money on the condition that the church never ordain a woman as a minister or elder, or never amend certain specified articles of the Confession of Faith, he is entitled to his money back if the condition is not fulfilled. In such a case, the church should not be permitted to keep the property simply because church authorities have determined that the doctrinal innovation is justified by the faith's basic principles. Cf. *Watson v. Jones*, 13 Wall. 679, 722-724 (1872).

On this understanding, I join the Court's opinion.

NOTES AND QUESTIONS

1. *Departure-from-doctrine approach.* Is the main problem with the departure-from-doctrine approach a Free Exercise Clause problem or an Establishment Clause problem? In what way do the concerns overlap?

2. *Congregational vs. hierarchical structures.* Watson v. Jones dictated that different approaches were to apply to congregational vs. hierarchical religious bodies. The Presbyterian Church is an example of a hierarchical structure. Do churches, temples, mosques, and other houses of worship always fall neatly into one category or another? If not, how is a court to decide? Does a court risk answering theological questions beyond its competence in making this determination?

3. *Absolute deference.* For disputes in hierarchical structures, must a court always defer to the highest church authority? Note that the Court quotes with approval the following limitation: "In the absence of fraud, collusion, or arbitrariness, the decisions of the proper church tribunals on matters purely ecclesiastical, although affecting civil rights, are accepted in litigation before the secular courts as conclusive, because the parties in interest made them so by contract or otherwise." What counts as fraud, collusion, or arbitrariness?

4. *Alternative approaches?* What if a reviewing court really does not like the decision of the hierarchy? Does it have any options other than enforcing that decision? Consider this question in light of the following case.

JONES v. WOLF

443 U.S. 595 (1979)

Mr. Justice BLACKMUN delivered the opinion of the Court.

This case involves a dispute over the ownership of church property following a schism in a local church affiliated with a hierarchical church organization. The question for decision is whether civil courts, consistent with the First and Fourteenth Amendments to the Constitution, may resolve the dispute on the basis of "neutral principles of law," or whether they must defer to the resolution of an authoritative tribunal of the hierarchical church.

The Vineville Presbyterian Church of Macon, Ga., was organized in 1904, and first incorporated in 1915. Its corporate charter lapsed in 1935, but was revived and renewed in 1939, and continues in effect at the present time. [The property was deeded to the trustees of the Vineville Presbyterian Church, and local congregants provided funds for the construction and maintenance of the church.]

In the same year it was organized, the Vineville church was established as a member church of the Augusta-Macon Presbytery of the Presbyterian Church in the

United States (PCUS). The PCUS has a generally hierarchical or connectional form of government, as contrasted with a congregational form.

Under the polity of the PCUS, the government of the local church is committed to its Session in the first instance, but the actions of this assembly or "court" are subject to the review and control of the higher church courts, the Presbytery, Synod, and General Assembly, respectively. The powers and duties of each level of the hierarchy are set forth in the constitution of the PCUS, the Book of Church Order, which is part of the record in the present case.

On May 27, 1973, at a congregational meeting of the Vineville church attended by a quorum of its duly enrolled members, 164 of them, including the pastor, voted to separate from the PCUS. Ninety-four members opposed the resolution. The majority immediately informed the PCUS of the action, and then united with another denomination, the Presbyterian Church in America. Although the minority remained on the church rolls for three years, they ceased to participate in the affairs of the Vineville church and conducted their religious activities elsewhere.

In response to the schism within the Vineville congregation, the Augusta-Macon Presbytery appointed a commission to investigate the dispute and, if possible, to resolve it. The commission eventually issued a written ruling declaring that the minority faction constituted "the true congregation of Vineville Presbyterian Church," and withdrawing from the majority faction "all authority to exercise office derived from the [PCUS]." The majority took no part in the commission's inquiry, and did not appeal its ruling to a higher PCUS tribunal.

Representatives of the minority faction sought relief in federal court, but their complaint was dismissed for want of jurisdiction. *Lucas v. Hope*, 515 F.2d 234 (CA5 1975), *cert. denied*, 424 U. S. 967 (1976). They then brought this class action in state court, seeking declaratory and injunctive orders establishing their right to exclusive possession and use of the Vineville church property as a member congregation of the PCUS. The trial court, purporting to apply Georgia's "neutral principles of law" approach to church property disputes, granted judgment for the majority. The Supreme Court of Georgia, holding that the trial court had correctly stated and applied Georgia law, and rejecting the minority's challenge based on the First and Fourteenth Amendments, affirmed. We granted certiorari.

Georgia's approach to church property litigation has evolved in response to *Presbyterian Church v. Hull Church*, 393 U.S. 440 (1969) (*Presbyterian Church I*), *rev'g Presbyterian Church v. Eastern Heights Church*, 224 Ga. 61, 159 S.E.2d 690 (1968). That case was a property dispute between the PCUS and two local Georgia churches that had withdrawn from the PCUS. The Georgia Supreme Court resolved the controversy by applying a theory of implied trust, whereby the property of a local church affiliated with a hierarchical church organization was deemed to be held in trust for the general church, provided the general church had not "substantially abandoned" the tenets of faith and practice as they existed at the time of affiliation. This Court reversed, holding that Georgia would have to find some other way of resolving church property disputes that did not draw the state courts into religious controversies. The court did not specify what that method should be, although it noted in passing that "there are neutral principles of law, developed for use in all property disputes, which can be applied without 'establishing' churches to which property is awarded."

On remand, the Georgia Supreme Court concluded that, without the departure-from-doctrine element, the implied trust theory would have to be abandoned in its entirety. In its place, the court adopted what is now known as the "neutral principles of law" method for resolving church property disputes. The court examined the deeds to the properties, the state statutes dealing with implied trusts, Ga. Code §§ 108-106, 108-107 (1978), and the Book of Church Order to determine whether there was any basis for a trust in favor of the general church. Finding nothing that would give rise to a trust in any of these documents, the court awarded the property on the basis of legal title, which was in the local church, or in the names of trustees for the local church. . . .

The only question presented by this case is which faction of the formerly united Vineville congregation is entitled to possess and enjoy the property located at 2193 Vineville Avenue in Macon, Ga. There can be little doubt about the general authority of civil courts to resolve this question. The State has an obvious and legitimate interest in the peaceful resolution of property disputes, and in providing a civil forum where the ownership of church property can be determined conclusively.

It is also clear, however, that "the First Amendment severely circumscribes the role that civil courts may play in resolving church property disputes." Most importantly, the First Amendment prohibits civil courts from resolving church property disputes on the basis of religious doctrine and practice. As a corollary to this commandment, the Amendment requires that civil courts defer to the resolution of issues of religious doctrine or polity by the highest court of a hierarchical church organization. Subject to these limitations, however, the First Amendment does not dictate that a State must follow a particular method of resolving church property disputes. Indeed, "a State may adopt *any* one of various approaches for settling church property disputes so long as it involves no consideration of doctrinal matters, whether the ritual and liturgy of worship or the tenets of faith."

At least in general outline, we think the "neutral principles of law" approach is consistent with the foregoing constitutional principles. . . .

The primary advantages of the neutral-principles approach are that it is completely secular in operation, and yet flexible enough to accommodate all forms of religious organization and polity. The method relies exclusively on objective, well-established concepts of trust and property law familiar to lawyers and judges. It thereby promises to free civil courts completely from entanglement in questions of religious doctrine, polity, and practice. Furthermore, the neutral-principles analysis shares the peculiar genius of private-law systems in general—flexibility in ordering private rights and obligations to reflect the intentions of the parties. Through appropriate reversionary clauses and trust provisions, religious societies can specify what is to happen to church property in the event of a particular contingency, or what religious body will determine the ownership in the event of a schism or doctrinal controversy. In this manner, a religious organization can ensure that a dispute over the ownership of church property will be resolved in accord with the desires of the members.

This is not to say that the application of the neutral-principles approach is wholly free of difficulty. The neutral-principles method, at least as it has evolved in Georgia, requires a civil court to examine certain religious documents, such as a church constitution, for language of trust in favor of the general church. In undertaking such an examination, a civil court must take special care to scrutinize the document in purely secular terms, and not to rely on religious precepts in determining whether the document indicates that the parties have intended to create a trust. In addition, there may be cases where the deed, the corporate charter, or the constitution of the general church incorporates religious concepts in the provisions relating to the ownership of property. If in such a case the interpretation of the instruments of ownership would require the civil court to resolve a religious controversy, then the court must defer to the resolution of the doctrinal issue by the authoritative ecclesiastical body. *Serbian Orthodox Diocese*, 426 U.S., at 709.

On balance, however, the promise of nonentanglement and neutrality inherent in the neutral-principles approach more than compensates for what will be occasional problems in application. These problems, in addition, should be gradually eliminated as recognition is given to the obligation of "States, religious organizations, and individuals [to] structure relationships involving church property so as not to require the civil courts to resolve ecclesiastical questions." *Presbyterian Church I*, 393 U.S., at 449. We therefore hold that a State is constitutionally entitled to adopt neutral principles of law as a means of adjudicating a church property dispute. . . .

The neutral-principles approach cannot be said to "inhibit" the free exercise of religion, any more than do other neutral provisions of state law governing the manner in which churches own property, hire employees, or purchase goods. Under the neutral-principles approach, the outcome of a church property dispute is not foreordained. At any time before the dispute erupts, the parties can ensure, if they so desire, that the faction loyal to the hierarchical church will retain the church property. They can modify the deeds or the corporate charter to include a right of reversion or trust in favor of the general church. Alternatively, the constitution of the general church can be made to recite an express trust in favor of the denominational church. The burden involved in taking such steps will be minimal. And the civil courts will be bound to give effect to the result indicated by the parties, provided it is embodied in some legally cognizable form.

It remains to be determined whether the Georgia neutral-principles analysis was constitutionally applied on the facts of this case. . . .

If in fact Georgia has adopted a presumptive rule of majority representation, defeasible upon a showing that the identity of the local church is to be determined by some other means, we think this would be consistent with both the neutral-principles analysis and the First Amendment. Majority rule is generally employed in the governance of religious societies. See *Bouldin v. Alexander*, 15 Wall. 131 (1872). Furthermore, the majority faction generally can be identified without resolving any question of religious doctrine or polity. Certainly, there was no dispute in the present case about the identity of the duly enrolled members of the Vineville church when the dispute arose, or about the fact that a quorum was present, or about the final vote. Most importantly, any rule of majority representation can always be overcome, under the neutral-principles approach, either by providing, in the corporate charter or the constitution of the general church, that the identity of the local church is to be established in some other way, or by providing that the church property is held in trust for the general church and those who remain loyal to it. Indeed, the State may adopt any method of overcoming the majoritarian presumption, so long as the use of that method does not impair free-exercise rights or entangle the civil courts in matters of religious controversy.

Neither the trial court nor the Supreme Court of Georgia, however, explicitly stated that it was adopting a presumptive rule of majority representation. Moreover, there are at least some indications that under Georgia law the process of identifying the faction that represents the Vineville church involves considerations of religious doctrine and polity. Georgia law requires that "church property be held according to the terms of the church government," and provides that a local church affiliated with a hierarchical religious association "is part of the whole body of the general church and is subject to the higher authority of the organization and its laws and regulations." All this may suggest that the identity of the "Vineville Presbyterian Church" named in the deeds must be determined according to terms of the Book of Church Order, which sets out the laws and regulations of churches affiliated with the PCUS. Such a determination, however, would appear to require a civil court to pass on questions of religious doctrine, and to usurp the function of the commission appointed by the Presbytery, which already has determined that petitioners represent the "true congregation" of the Vineville church. Therefore, if Georgia law provides that the identity of the Vineville church is to be determined according to the "laws and regulations" of the PCUS, then the First Amendment requires that the Georgia courts give deference to the presbyterial commission's determination of that church's identity.

This Court, of course, does not declare what the law of Georgia is. Since the grounds for the decision that respondents represent the Vineville church remain unarticulated, the judgment of the Supreme Court of Georgia is vacated, and the case is remanded for further proceedings not inconsistent with this opinion.

It is so ordered.

Mr. Justice POWELL, with whom THE CHIEF JUSTICE, Mr. Justice STEWART, and Mr. Justice WHITE join, dissenting.

This case presents again a dispute among church members over the control of a local church's property. Although the Court appears to accept established principles that I have thought would resolve this case, it superimposes on these principles a new structure of rules that will make the decision of these cases by civil courts more difficult. The new analysis also is more likely to invite intrusion into church polity forbidden by the First Amendment.

The Court begins by stating that "[t]his case involves a dispute over the ownership of church property," suggesting that the concern is with legal or equitable ownership in the real property sense. But the ownership of the property of the Vineville church is not at issue. The deeds place title in the Vineville Presbyterian Church, or in trustees of that church, and none of the parties has questioned the validity of those deeds. The question actually presented is which of the factions within the local congregation has the right to control the actions of the titleholder, and thereby to control the use of the property, as the Court later acknowledges.

Since 1872, disputes over control of church property usually have been resolved under principles established by *Watson v. Jones*, 13 Wall. 679 (1872). Under the new and complex, two-stage analysis approved today, a court instead first must apply newly defined "neutral principles of law" to determine whether property titled to the local church is held in trust for the general church organization with which the local church is affiliated. If it is, then the court will grant control of the property to the councils of the general church. If not, then control by the local congregation will be recognized. In the latter situation, if there is a schism in the local congregation, as in this case, the second stage of the new analysis becomes applicable. Again, the Court fragments the analysis into two substeps for the purpose of determining which of the factions should control the property.

As this new approach inevitably will increase the involvement of civil courts in church controversies, and as it departs from long-established precedents, I dissent. . . .

When civil courts step in to resolve intrachurch disputes over control of church property, they will either support or overturn the authoritative resolution of the dispute within the church itself. The new analysis, under the attractive banner of "neutral principles," actually invites the civil courts to do the latter. The proper rule of decision, that I thought had been settled until today, requires a court to give effect in all cases to the decisions of the church government agreed upon by the members before the dispute arose. . . .

The Court acknowledges that the church law of the Presbyterian Church in the United States (PCUS), of which the Vineville church is a part, provides for the authoritative resolution of this question by the Presbytery. Indeed, the Court indicates that Georgia, consistently with the First Amendment, may adopt the *Watson v. Jones* rule of adherence to the resolution of the dispute according to church law—a rule that would necessitate reversal of the judgment for the respondents. But instead of requiring the state courts to take this approach, the Court approves as well an alternative rule of state law: the Georgia courts are said to be free to "adop[t] a presumptive rule of majority representation, defeasible upon a showing that the identity of the local church is to be determined by some other means." This showing may be made by proving that the church has "provid[ed], in the corporate charter or the constitution of the general church, that the identity of the local church is to be established in some other way."

On its face, this rebuttable presumption also requires reversal of the state court's judgment in favor of the schismatic faction. The polity of the PCUS commits to the Presbytery the resolution of the dispute within the local church. Having shown this structure of church government for the determination of the identity of the local congregation, the petitioners have rebutted any presumption that this question has been left to a majority vote of the local congregation.

The Court nevertheless declines to order reversal. Rather than decide the case here in accordance with established First Amendment principles, the Court leaves open the possibility that the state courts might adopt some restrictive evidentiary rule that would render the petitioners' evidence inadequate to overcome the presumption of majority control. But, aside from a passing reference to the use of the neutral-principles approach developed earlier in its opinion, the Court affords no guidance as to the constitutional limitations on such an evidentiary rule; the state courts, it says, are free to adopt any rule that is constitutional.

> "Indeed, the state may adopt any method of overcoming the majoritarian presumption, so long as the use of that method does not impair free-exercise rights or entangle the civil courts in matters of religious controversy."

In essence, the Court's instructions on remand therefore allow the state courts the choice of following the long-settled rule of *Watson v. Jones* or of adopting some other rule—unspecified by the Court—that the state courts view as consistent with the First Amendment. Not only questions of state law but also important issues of federal constitutional law thus are left to the state courts for their decision, and, if they depart from *Watson v. Jones*, they will travel a course left totally uncharted by this Court.

Disputes among church members over the control of church property arise almost invariably out of disagreements regarding doctrine and practice. Because of the religious nature of these disputes, civil courts should decide them according to principles that do not interfere with the free exercise of religion in accordance with church polity and doctrine.

The only course that achieves this constitutional requirement is acceptance by civil courts of the decisions reached within the polity chosen by the church members themselves. . . .

Accordingly, in each case involving an intrachurch dispute—including disputes over church property—the civil court must focus directly on ascertaining, and then following, the decision made within the structure of church governance. By doing so, the court avoids two equally unacceptable departures from the genuine neutrality mandated by the First Amendment. First, it refrains from direct review and revision of decisions of the church on matters of religious doctrine and practice that underlie the church's determination of intrachurch controversies, including those that relate to control of church property. Equally important, by recognizing the authoritative resolution reached within the religious association, the civil court avoids interfering indirectly with the religious governance of those who have formed the association and submitted themselves to its authority. . . .

The principles developed in prior decisions thus afford clear guidance in the case before us. The Vineville church is presbyterian, a part of the PCUS. The presbyterian form of church government, adopted by the PCUS, is "a hierarchical structure of tribunals which consists of, in ascending order, (1) the Church Session, composed of the elders of the local church; (2) the Presbytery, composed of several churches in a geographical area; (3) the Synod, generally composed of all Presbyteries within a State; and (4) the General Assembly, the highest governing body." The Book of Church Order subjects the Session to "review and control" by the Presbytery in all matters, even authorizing the Presbytery to replace the leadership of the local congregation, to winnow its membership, and to take control of it. No provision of the Book of Church Order gives the Session the authority to withdraw the local church, removing the dissidents from church office, asserting direct control over the government of the church, and recognizing the petitioners as the legitimate congregation and Session of the church.

NOTES AND QUESTIONS

1. *The neutral principles of law alternative.* What do you make of the *Jones* "neutral principles" approach? Is Justice Powell persuasive when he argues that it cannot be applied without getting into matters of church doctrine? Can *Watson*'s deference approach always be applied without entanglement in religious controversies? Which approach, the *Jones* "neutral principles" approach or the *Watson* deference approach, advances the values of "nonentanglement and neutrality" more effectively? Is one approach generally easier for courts to apply?

2. *Choice of test.* At one point, the Supreme Court holds that courts have a choice of which test to apply: "[A] State may adopt *any* one of various approaches for settling church property disputes so long as it involves no consideration of doctrinal matters, whether the ritual and liturgy of worship or the tenets of faith." What principle should guide courts in choosing which should apply? Is there a risk in giving courts this choice?

3. *Advance planning.* Perhaps the lesson of *Jones* is that, if hierarchal churches wish to retain ownership of local church properties in the event of a schism, they must require all affiliated member churches to record new property deeds with clear statements of trust in favor of the mother church. Should the mother church have the burden of revising land records to protect its interests? Is it more difficult for religious associations compared to other associations to specify what is to happen to its property in the event of a dispute?

B. EMPLOYMENT DISPUTES

AN EXTENDED NOTE ON SERBIAN EASTERN ORTHODOX DIOCESE V. MILIVOJEVICH

In Serbian Eastern Orthodox Diocese v. Milivojevich, 426 U.S. 696 (1976), the Supreme Court faced a case in which Bishop Dionisije Milivojevich alleged that his removal as Bishop of the American-Canadian Diocese did not comply with church procedures or rules and was therefore void under the *Gonzalez* "fraud, collusion, or arbitrariness" exception to the rule that civil courts must enforce the decision of the highest body in a hierarchical dispute. *Id.* at 698. The highest bodies of the Serbian Eastern Orthodox Church, the Holy Assembly and Holy Synod, removed Milivojevich in 1964 incident to defrockment proceedings. Milivojevich sued in the Illinois state courts, alleging that the church's proceedings were both substantively and procedurally deficient. The proceedings commenced in state trial court in 1963 and continued over a 13-year period. After a "lengthy trial, the trial court filed [an opinion] which concluded that 'no substantial evidence was produced . . . that fraud, collusion, or arbitrariness existed in any of the actions or decisions preliminary to or during the final proceedings of the decision to defrock Bishop Dionisije made by the highest Hierarchical bodies of the Mother Church.'" *Id.* at 707.

On appeal, however, the Illinois Supreme Court ruled for Milivojevich, holding that the church failed to follow its own rules and official procedures in removing him; accordingly, the court declined to give legal effect to the actions of the Holy Assembly and the Holy Synod because the church's decision was "arbitrary." *Id.* at 708. In order to reach the merits of Bishop Milivojevich's claims, the Illinois Supreme Court reviewed and applied various church documents, including its constitution and bylaws. *Id.* at 698-699, 707-709. The Illinois Supreme Court essentially ordered the church to reinstate Milivojevich to his post as bishop. The Supreme Court of the United States granted a writ of certiorari to review the case.

Writing for an eight-justice majority, Justice Brennan rejected the state supreme court's reasoning in the case. "The fallacy fatal to the judgment of the Illinois Supreme Court is that it rests upon an impermissible rejection of the decisions of the highest ecclesiastical tribunals of this hierarchical church upon the issues in dispute, and impermissibly substitutes its own inquiry into church polity and resolutions based thereon of those disputes." *Id.* at 708. He explained that "where resolution of the disputes cannot be made without extensive inquiry by civil courts into religious law and polity, the First and Fourteenth Amendments mandate that civil courts shall not disturb the decisions of the highest ecclesiastical tribunal within a church of hierarchical polity, but must accept such decisions as binding on them, in the application to the religious issues of doctrine or polity before them." *Id.* at 709.

With respect to the question of "fraud, collusion, or arbitrariness," Justice Brennan found that "[n]o issue of 'fraud' or 'collusion' is involved in this case." *Id.* at 713 n.7. With respect to the "arbitrariness" exception, invoked by the state supreme court, Justice Brennan found that "no 'arbitrariness' exception—in the sense of an inquiry whether the decisions of the highest ecclesiastical tribunal of a hierarchical church complied with church laws and regulations—is consistent with the constitutional mandate that civil courts are bound to accept the decisions of the highest judicatories of a religious organization of hierarchical polity on matters of discipline, faith, internal organization, or ecclesiastical rule, custom, or law." *Id.* Because such inquiries entrain courts into matters of religious doctrine, "a civil court must accept the ecclesiastical decisions of church tribunals as it finds them." *Id.* Applying the rules of the Serbian Eastern Orthodox Church, Justice Brennan held the Holy Assembly of Bishops rested at the top of the church hierarchy and, accordingly, that its decision—however reached—was binding on the civil courts. *See id.* at 716-719. Although the Court did not formally abolish the "fraud, collusion, or arbitrariness" exceptions recognized in the *Gonzalez* dicta, the majority very narrowly construed these exemptions to exclude claims that a church failed to follow its own internal procedures properly. Civil courts do not sit to judge whether a church tribunal has observed its own rules, but with respect to a hierarchical church, instead sit only to identify the person or body that possesses final decisional authority.

Dissenting, then-Justice Rehnquist argued that Illinois state courts faced both the necessity and duty "to ask the real Bishop of the American-Canadian Diocese [to] please stand up." *Id.* at 726 (Rehnquist, J., dissenting). "If civil courts, consistently with the First Amendment, may do that much, the question arises why they may not do what the Illinois courts did here regarding the defrockment of Bishop Dionisije [Milivojevich], and conclude, on the basis of testimony from experts on the canon law at issue, that the decision of the religious tribunal involved was rendered in violation of its own stated rules of procedure." *Id.* at 727. He objected that "[i]f the civil courts are to be bound by any sheet of parchment bearing the ecclesiastical seal and purporting to be a decree of a church court, they can easily be converted into the handmaidens of arbitrary lawlessness." *Id.* A state court may simply enforce a religious organization's own procedural rules, without becoming enmeshed in any questions of religious doctrine, because "an application of neutral principles of law [is] consistent with the decisions of this Court." *Id.* at 734. For Justice Rehnquist, the only relevant First Amendment consideration consists of ascertaining whether the civil courts "remain neutral on matters of religious doctrine." *Id.* at 735.

NOTES AND QUESTIONS

1. *Resolving disputes within hierarchical churches. Milivojevich* represents a strong application of a mandatory rule of near-absolute deference to the decision of the highest authority within a hierarchical church—a position seriously undermined a few years later in *Jones.* The Brennan approach in *Milivojevich* has the virtue of limiting, to the maximum extent possible, the potential for civil courts to become enmeshed in questions of religious dogma—even at the cost of enforcing dubious decisions tainted by arbitrary decision making within the church hierarchy. Is the risk of government imposed religious doctrine so great as to justify a near-complete abdication of judicial review of decisions reached by hierarchical church authorities?

2. *The "fraud, collusion, or arbitrariness" exceptions revisited.* Suppose that a member of the Holy Assembly of Bishops admitted, in a deposition, that he took a bribe to vote to remove Milivojevich. Would that be a sufficient basis for voiding the decision, if one were to apply the substance of Justice Brennan's reasoning in *Milivojevich?*

3. *Enforcing internal church procedural rules.* Is Justice Rehnquist persuasive when he argues that holding a church to its own stated procedures does not (and

cannot) seriously implicate the substance of church doctrines? On the other hand, if the dichotomy between substance and procedure is vague, isn't Justice Brennan right to worry that the government may end up imposing its view of religious doctrine on church entities? For example, if a church rule calls for trial by ordeal, but the body sua sponte declares that the divine will, as ascertained by the assembly, strongly prefers a game of paper, rock, scissors, should the trial courts of Illinois force trial by ordeal?

How do the rules regarding government involvement in internal religious disputes apply in the context of personnel decisions that allegedly violate otherwise applicable civil rights statutes, such at Title VII (which prohibits entities that employ more than 15 persons from engaging in discrimination based on race or sex)? *See* 42 U.S.C. § 2000e-2 (declaring it unlawful to "fail or refuse to hire or to discharge any individual, or otherwise to discriminate against any individual with respect to his compensation, terms, conditions, or privileges of employment, because of such individual's race, color, religion, sex, or national origin"). Or other federal or state antidiscrimination laws, such as the Americans with Disabilities Act, 42 U.S.C. §§ 12101 *et seq.*, or the Age Discrimination Act, 29 U.S.C. §§ 621 *et seq.*? May Congress, a state legislature, or a city council apply such laws to religious organizations and institutions? Or does the Free Exercise Clause and Establishment Clause require that religious organizations enjoy the freedom to choose their employees as they think best?

HOSANNA-TABOR EVANGELICAL LUTHERAN CHURCH AND SCHOOL v. EQUAL EMPLOYMENT OPPORTUNITY COMMISSION

565 U.S. 171 (2012)

Chief Justice ROBERTS delivered the opinion of the Court.

Certain employment discrimination laws authorize employees who have been wrongfully terminated to sue their employers for reinstatement and damages. The question presented is whether the Establishment and Free Exercise Clauses of the First Amendment bar such an action when the employer is a religious group and the employee is one of the group's ministers. . . .

[Cheryl Perich worked at a religiously affiliated school in Redford, Michigan. She was classified as a "called teacher," that is a teacher "called to their vocation by God through a congregation." She held the title "Minister of Religion, Commissioned" within the church and also at her school. Perich's teaching duties included both academic subjects and religion classes. "Perich taught kindergarten during her first four years at Hosanna-Tabor and fourth grade during the 2003-2004 school year. She taught math, language arts, social studies, science, gym, art, and music. She also taught a religion class four days a week [and] led the students in prayer and devotional exercises each day." Perich claimed that the school retaliated against her in violation of the Americans with Disability Act (ADA). After a medical leave and narcolepsy diagnosis, Perich informed the school principal that her doctor had cleared her to return to work. In response, the principal expressed concerns about the safety of Perich's students. The school board requested that Perich resign but she declined. After Perich told the principal that she would sue for disability discrimination, she was fired. Correspondence from the school indicated that she lost her job because she was insubordinate and threatened to take legal action. Under the

ADA, it is illegal for an employer to retaliate against an employee for bringing or threatening to bring a disability discrimination suit. Hosanna-Tabor Evangelical Lutheran Church and School (Hosanna-Tabor) responded to this lawsuit by filing a motion to dismiss, invoking a First Amendment-grounded "ministerial exception" to the ADA. "According to the Church, Perich was a minister, and she had been fired for a religious reason—namely, that her threat to sue the Church violated the Synod's belief that Christians should resolve their disputes internally." The district court agreed with the Church's ministerial exception claim, at least as applied on these facts, and accordingly granted summary judgment in Hosanna-Tabor's favor. The U.S. Court of Appeals, however, reversed the grant of summary judgment, 597 F.3d 769, 777 (6th Cir. 2012). It found that although a ministerial exception applied under the ADA, it did not apply in this instance because Perich was not, in fact, a "minister." *Id.* at 778-781. The Supreme Court granted review.]

The First Amendment provides, in part, that "Congress shall make no law respecting an establishment of religion, or prohibiting the free exercise thereof." We have said that these two Clauses "often exert conflicting pressures," *Cutter v. Wilkinson,* 544 U.S. 709, 719 (2005), and that there can be "internal tension . . . between the Establishment Clause and the Free Exercise Clause," *Tilton v. Richardson,* 403 U.S. 672, 677 (1971) (plurality opinion). Not so here. Both Religion Clauses bar the government from interfering with the decision of a religious group to fire one of its ministers. . . .

[Chief Justice Roberts provides an extended history of religious establishments in the colonial, revolutionary, and framing eras, including President James Madison's veto of a bill that could have chartered the "Protestant Episcopal Church in the town of Alexandria in what was then the District of Columbia." Chief Justice Roberts places particular emphasis on the fact that the Framers, including Madison, did not believe that the federal government could select or remove ministers consistently with the Religion Clauses.]

Given this understanding of the Religion Clauses—and the absence of government employment regulation generally—it was some time before questions about government interference with a church's ability to select its own ministers came before the courts. This Court touched upon the issue indirectly, however, in the context of disputes over church property. Our decisions in that area confirm that it is impermissible for the government to contradict a church's determination of who can act as its ministers. . . .

Until today, we have not had occasion to consider whether this freedom of a religious organization to select its ministers is implicated by a suit alleging discrimination in employment. The Courts of Appeals, in contrast, have had extensive experience with this issue. Since the passage of Title VII of the Civil Rights Act of 1964, 42 U.S.C. § 2000e *et seq.,* and other employment discrimination laws, the Courts of Appeals have uniformly recognized the existence of a "ministerial exception," grounded in the First Amendment, that precludes application of such legislation to claims concerning the employment relationship between a religious institution and its ministers.

We agree that there is such a ministerial exception. The members of a religious group put their faith in the hands of their ministers. Requiring a church to accept or retain an unwanted minister, or punishing a church for failing to do so, intrudes upon more than a mere employment decision. Such action interferes with the internal governance of the church, depriving the church of control over the selection of those who will personify its beliefs. By imposing an unwanted minister, the state infringes the Free Exercise Clause, which protects a religious group's right to shape its own faith and mission through its appointments. According the state the power to determine which individuals will minister to the faithful also violates the Establishment Clause, which prohibits government involvement in such ecclesiastical decisions. . . .

The EEOC and Perich [] contend that our decision in *Employment Div., Dept. of Human Resources of Ore. v. Smith,* 494 U.S. 872 (1990), precludes recognition of a ministerial exception. In *Smith,* two members of the Native American Church were denied state unemployment benefits after it was determined that they had been fired from their jobs for ingesting peyote, a crime under Oregon law. We held that this did not violate the Free Exercise Clause, even though the peyote had been ingested for sacramental purposes, because the "right of free exercise does not relieve an individual of the obligation to comply with a valid and neutral law of general applicability on the ground that the law proscribes (or prescribes) conduct that his religion prescribes (or proscribes)." *Id.,* at 879 (internal quotation marks omitted).

It is true that the ADA's prohibition on retaliation, like Oregon's prohibition on peyote use, is a valid and neutral law of general applicability. But a church's selection of its ministers is unlike an individual's ingestion of peyote. *Smith* involved government regulation of only outward physical acts. The present case, in contrast, concerns government interference with an internal church decision that affects the faith and mission of the church itself. See *id.,* at 877 (distinguishing the government's regulation of "physical acts" from its "lend[ing] its power to one or the other side in controversies over religious authority or dogma"). The contention that *Smith* forecloses recognition of a ministerial exception rooted in the Religion Clauses has no merit.

Having concluded that there is a ministerial exception grounded in the Religion Clauses of the First Amendment, we consider whether the exception applies in this case. We hold that it does. . . .

Because Perich was a minister within the meaning of the exception, the First Amendment requires dismissal of this employment discrimination suit against her religious employer. The EEOC and Perich originally sought an order reinstating Perich to her former position as a called teacher. By requiring the Church to accept a minister it did not want, such an order would have plainly violated the Church's freedom under the Religion Clauses to select its own ministers. . . .

The case before us is an employment discrimination suit brought on behalf of a minister, challenging her church's decision to fire her. Today we hold only that the ministerial exception bars such a suit. We express no view on whether the exception bars other types of suits, including actions by employees alleging breach of contract or tortious conduct by their religious employers. There will be time enough to address the applicability of the exception to other circumstances if and when they arise.

. . . The interest of society in the enforcement of employment discrimination statutes is undoubtedly important. But so too is the interest of religious groups in choosing who will preach their beliefs, teach their faith, and carry out their mission. When a minister who has been fired sues her church alleging that her termination was discriminatory, the First Amendment has struck the balance for us. The church must be free to choose those who will guide it on its way.

The judgment of the Court of Appeals for the Sixth Circuit is reversed.

It is so ordered.

Justice THOMAS, concurring.

I join the Court's opinion. I write separately to note that, in my view, the Religion Clauses require civil courts to apply the ministerial exception and to defer to a religious organization's good-faith understanding of who qualifies as its minister. As the Court explains, the Religion Clauses guarantee religious organizations autonomy in matters of internal governance, including the selection of those who will minister the faith. A religious organization's right to choose its ministers would be hollow, however, if secular courts could second-guess the organization's sincere determination that a given employee is a "minister" under the organization's theological tenets. . . .

[Justice Alito's concurring opinion, with whom Justice Kagan joins, is omitted.]

NOTES AND QUESTIONS

1. *Application of* Smith. The Court concedes that the American with Disabilities Act was a neutral law of general applicability. Nonetheless, it distinguished *Smith* on the grounds that "*Smith* involved government regulation of only outward physical acts. The present case, in contrast, concerns government interference with an internal church decision that affects the faith and mission of the church itself." Is this distinction persuasive? How should a court categorize a church decision that ingesting peyote is a sacrament?

2. *Neutral principles of law.* In order to win her retaliation suit, Perich would have had to prove that (1) she engaged in activity protected by the ADA; (2) she suffered a materially adverse action; and (3) there was a causal link between the protected activity and the adverse action. Would it be possible to resolve Perich's ADA claim without delving into questions of religious doctrine? What did the Court have to say about the Jones v. Wolf approach?

3. *Absolute nature of exemption.* Under the ministerial exemption, religious institutions do not need to offer a religious justification for their employment decisions. Both churches whose doctrine requires that their clergy be male as well as churches whose doctrine espouses equality between the sexes are exempt from sex discrimination suits brought by ministers.

4. *What suits are barred by the ministerial exemption?* The Court expressed "no view on whether the exception bars other types of suits, including actions by employees alleging breach of contract or tortious conduct by their religious employers." Are those claims different? If they are different, what explains why a sex discrimination or sexual harassment claim is barred but not a breach of contract claim? If they are not different, does this mean that those who qualify as ministers are stripped of all legal protections vis-à-vis their employer?

5. *Who counts as a "minister."* What kinds of jobs might plausibly fall within the "ministerial exception" recognized in *Hosanna-Tabor*? Clearly someone with direct clerical responsibilities falls within the category—but what other kinds of employments qualify for the exemption? Would a choir director, for example, qualify? What about a person working in a church-related day care center? A janitor? Does *Hosanna-Tabor* provide a workable test for deciding precisely who counts as a "minister"?

6. *Entanglement in religious doctrine.* What causes greater entanglement in religious doctrine: deciding whether Hosanna-Tabor retaliated against Perich for

threatening to bring an ADA suit or deciding whether Perich qualifies as a minister for purposes of the ministerial exemption?

THEORY-APPLIED PROBLEM

After the Episcopal Church (USA) approves the ordination of women as well as gay and lesbian priests and bishops, the congregation of St. John's Episcopal Church, in Pascagoula, Mississippi, becomes embroiled in a bitter dispute. The Board of Vestry votes to remain part of the Episcopal Church. The congregation, enraged at this outcome, votes by a margin of 174-33 to break with the Episcopal Church (USA) and align instead with the Congregation of Anglicans in North America (CANA), which has denounced the ordination of gays and lesbians.

The deed in question, properly recorded in 1909, simply states that the property "shall be used in perpetuity for an Episcopal church and shall always observe the true doctrines of the Anglican Communion of Churches." The church's charter provides for the regular election of vestrymen by popular vote at regular intervals, corresponding to annual terms of office; the rules do not provide any means of recalling a vestry member once elected. The Episcopal Diocese of Mississippi finds that the minority group of 33 represents the bona fide congregation, endorses the authority of the local Board of Vestry, and claims ownership on the Board's behalf of the St. John's church, buildings, and assets. The dissenting majority faction also claims ownership on the grounds that they are the ones that an "Episcopal" church.

The Jackson County Chancery Court, applying neutral principles of state law, rules in favor of the dissident majority, holding that the deed established a trust in favor of the Anglican theological doctrines as they existed in 1909. Because the Episcopal Church did not ordain women, gays, or lesbians as either priests or bishops in 1909, the state court judge rules that because of departure from true Anglican doctrine, the trust failed.

The Episcopal Diocese of Mississippi appeals the chancery court decision to the Mississippi Court of Appeals. How should the appellate state court rule? May it affirm the lower court ruling without violating the Free Exercise Clause? Is the trial court ruling consistent with Jones? With Watson?

CHAPTER 16

Defining and Enforcing the Establishment Clause

TABLE OF CONTENTS

The Establishment Clause is one of the most controversial and frequently litigated components of the First Amendment. Although disputes about the proper relationship between church and state have been a feature of this country's history since the earliest settlements by Western Europeans, it may surprise many students to learn that the Supreme Court has only been actively interpreting and applying the Establishment Clause since 1947. As if to make up for lost time, the Court has generated a huge body of case law in that 70-year period, covering virtually every aspect of life in which government action intersects with religious belief and practice.

As in every other area of the First Amendment, there are endless debates about both the history and the theory of the constitutional law that governs the relationship between church and state. These debates inform the actual holdings of the cases and the doctrine on which those holdings are based. This chapter begins with a brief discussion of the history of religious establishment in the United States, before turning to a discussion of various different standards being used by different members of the Supreme Court to enforce the Establishment Clause. Many observers of the Court's church/state jurisprudence have been frustrated in recent years because the Justices on the Supreme Court have failed to coalesce around one Establishment Clause standard.

One explanation for the Court's failure to articulate a single standard is that the Court continues to be sharply divided about the underlying theory of the Establishment Clause. In brief, there are two broad schools of thought about the meaning of the Establishment Clause. The basic differences between these schools of thought can be illustrated by their contrasting attitudes toward the concept of separation of church and state. The concept of church/state separation was advanced early in the country's history by Thomas Jefferson. While serving as President, Jefferson wrote a letter to the Danbury Baptist Association, in which he argued that when the citizens of the United States adopted the First Amendment they intended to build "a wall of separation between Church & State." Thomas Jefferson, "A Bill for Establishing Religious Freedom," in *The Portable Thomas Jefferson* 303 (Merrill D. Peterson ed., 1975). Jefferson borrowed the "wall of separation" metaphor from Roger Williams, who founded the first Baptist Church in the United States and was also one of the founders of the state of Rhode Island, which from its origins was unusual in welcoming into the state members of every religious denomination. Williams once wrote that "when they have opened a gap in the hedge or wall of Separation between the Garden of the Church and the Wilderness of the world, God hath ever broke down the wall itself, removed the Candlestick, and made his Garden a Wilderness." Roger Williams, *Mr. Cotton's Letter Examined and Answered* (1644), reprinted in 1 *The Complete Writings of Roger Williams* 313, 392 (Russel & Russel, Inc., 1963).

Modern supporters of the "wall of separation" between church and state tend to argue that in order to preserve the purity and independence of both church and state the government should be a secular entity that is neutral with regard to any one sect and to religion in general. In other words, the government should neither support nor oppose any religious doctrine or institution.

From this perspective, religion is an intensely private matter that should not be subject to either pressure or manipulation by the government. As indicated by the excerpts in Section A below, this was the position of Jefferson's good friend James Madison (who wrote the First Amendment), and also the stance adopted by the Supreme Court in its first modern Establishment Clause decision, Everson v. Board of Education.

Until very recently, most members of the Court have continued to express support for the separation of church and state, although the Court's enforcement of this theory has often been deeply inconsistent. These inconsistencies have been accentuated in recent years because several members of the Court have begun expressing strong disagreement with the very goal of separating church and state. They argue that the United States is (and always has been) a deeply religious country, and that the government should reflect this fact. Thus, in his dissent in Wallace v. Jaffree (excerpted in this chapter and in Chapter 19), then-Justice Rehnquist argued that the Establishment Clause should be interpreted to permit the government to endorse and finance religion in general, as long as it refrains from endorsing or financing only particular religious sects favored by the government. Another variation on this theme is Justice Scalia's argument in McCreary County v. ACLU (excerpted in Chapter 20) that the Establishment Clause should be interpreted to permit the government to favor those who belong to monotheistic faiths and should also be allowed to "disregard" atheists, agnostics, and those who belong to polytheistic faiths. The limitations of space do not permit a full survey of the theoretical materials in this casebook, but the basic theoretical dispute between those who support and those who oppose the separation of church and state lies just below the surface of virtually every decision included in the next four chapters.

After discussing the history and doctrine of the Establishment Clause in this chapter, Chapter 17 focuses on an area of tension between free exercise and establishment: government attempts to facilitate religious practice that may or may not go too far and violate the Establishment Clause. Chapter 18 addresses decisions involving government efforts to finance religious activities or institutions. Chapter 19 discusses religion in the public school context, and Chapter 20 addresses government-sponsored prayers and religious symbols outside the public school context.

A. EARLY EFFORTS TO DEFINE THE SEPARATION OF CHURCH AND STATE

The history of religious freedom in the United States is not always enlightening or encouraging. In pre-revolutionary times, when religious groups who came to this country seeking religious freedom for themselves became the dominant religious group in their new home, they often fell into the habit of oppressing members of other faiths. The history of the American colonies is riddled with examples of religious oppression, and that oppression did not end with the American Revolution. When John Jay, the first Chief Justice of the Supreme Court, was governor of New York, for example, he proposed to ban Catholics from that state. *See* Thomas J. Curry, *The First Freedoms: Church and State in America to the Passage of the First Amendment* 162 (1986). Similarly, Massachusetts proposed to banish Anabaptists and to execute Catholic priests who strayed back into Massachusetts after having been excluded from that state. *See* Alexis de Tocqueville, *Democracy in America* 42-43 & nn. 26-27 (George Lawrence trans., Perennial Classics 1969) (1848).

Religious oppression in the young Republic took many different forms. Five states refused to grant full rights to Catholics. *See* 1 Anson Stokes, *Church and State in the United States* 402 (1950) (North Carolina); *id.* at 406 (New York); *id.* at 430 (New Hampshire); *id.* at 435 (New Jersey); *id.* at 441 (Vermont). Other states, such as Virginia, mandated that all persons be married in the Anglican Church. *See* Sanford H. Cobb, *The Rise of Religious Liberty in America: A History* 494 (Burt Franklin 1970) (1902). More commonly, religious oppression took the form of Protestant financial establishments in states such as Massachusetts, whose constitution required towns in the state "to make suitable provision, at their own expense, for the institutions of the public worship of God, and for the support and maintenance of public Protestant teachers of piety, religion and morality. . . ." *See* Declaration of Rights in the 1780 Massachusetts Constitution, in 3 Francis Newton Thorpe, ed., *The Federal and State Constitutions, Colonial Charters, and Other Organic Laws* 1890 (1909).

On the other hand, the political landscape of the early Republic also included more hopeful examples such as Rhode Island, which never had an established church and from the outset granted full liberty of conscience to members of all faiths. And many of the most influential leaders of the new country were freethinkers, including rationalists like Ethan Allen and Thomas Paine and Deists like James Madison, Thomas Jefferson, and (most likely) George Washington. The religious and political context in which the First Amendment was written was complicated and fluid, and although several broad trends and themes can be discerned in the historical data, many of these trends and themes have led observers to contradictory conclusions about the meaning of the Establishment Clause.

At the time the First Amendment was written, some states still maintained official religious establishments, mostly in the form of mandatory tax collections for the financial support of churches. All of the states that continued to maintain religious establishments, however, had moved from the establishment of a single church to so-called multiple establishments, which permitted the taxpayer to designate the church that the taxpayer's taxes would support.

It is common practice to cluster the states into three groups: The New England states, with political regimes derived from traditional Puritan establishments, maintained official establishments that lasted well into the first decades of the nineteenth century. The Southern states, which started out with Anglican establishments, soon pursued disestablishment to accommodate both the surge of Protestant dissenters and the hostility toward an Anglican church that was closely associated with the former colonial ruler. The Middle Atlantic states tended to have weak establishments or no establishments at all. Indeed, four states, all in the middle of the country, never maintained official establishments: Rhode Island, Pennsylvania, Delaware, and New Jersey. By 1791, 8 of the original 13 states had eliminated their official religious establishments. The other five states would eliminate their official establishments soon thereafter, culminating with Massachusetts, which would be the last state to eliminate its official establishment in 1833.

What is one to make of this history? It does not represent a consistent story of religious liberty and disestablishment. The one clear message of this history, however, is that at the time the Bill of Rights was drafted the trend throughout the country was towards eliminating all religious establishments.

Perhaps the best illustration of the disestablishment trend in the United States during this period is the dispute in Virginia over Governor Patrick Henry's proposal to revive Virginia's religious establishment, in the form of a "Bill establishing a provision for Teachers of the Christian Religion." This proposed Bill was a fairly benign form of religious establishment compared to previous versions, in the sense that it did not favor any Christian sect (although it did favor Christianity generally), establish any articles of faith, or speak in terms of an explicit establishment of an official religion for the state of Virginia. Nevertheless, James Madison vigorously opposed the Bill, and in the course of his opposition produced the Memorial and Remonstrance Against Religious Assessments, one of the primary documents expounding on the peculiarly American form of religious liberty. Madison's rhetorical and political skills were instrumental in mustering substantial opposition to Henry's bill, not only among the usual opponents such as Baptists, Quakers, and secularists, but also among many Presbyterians, Episcopalians, and Methodists, who had originally supported the bill. Upon defeat of the assessment bill, Madison then proposed and the Virginia legislature passed Thomas Jefferson's Statute for Religious Freedom, which in many ways provides a model for the theory of the Establishment Clause that has dominated the Supreme Court's jurisprudence for the last 70 years.

EVERSON v. BOARD OF EDUCATION

330 U.S. 1 (1947)

Mr. Justice BLACK delivered the opinion of the Court.

[*Everson* involved a challenge to a state statute that authorized the reimbursement of bus fares paid for transporting children to private schools, most of which were Catholic. After holding that the Establishment Clause was incorporated into the Fourteenth Amendment and therefore applicable to the states, the Court considered the history of the adoption of the Clause.]

A large proportion of the early settlers of this country came here from Europe to escape the bondage of laws which compelled them to support and attend government-favored churches. The centuries immediately before and contemporaneous with the colonization of America had been filled with turmoil, civil strife, and persecutions, generated in large part by established sects determined to maintain their absolute political and religious supremacy. With the power of government supporting them, at various times and places, Catholics had persecuted Protestants, Protestants had persecuted Catholics, Protestant sects had persecuted other Protestant sects, Catholics of one shade of belief had persecuted Catholics of another shade of belief, and all of these had from time to time persecuted Jews. In efforts to force loyalty to whatever religious group happened to be on top and in league with the government of a particular time and place, men and women had been fined, cast in jail, cruelly tortured, and killed. Among the offenses for which these punishments had been inflicted were such things as speaking disrespectfully of the views of ministers of government-established churches, non-attendance at those churches, expressions of non-belief in their doctrines, and failure to pay taxes and tithes to support them.

These practices of the Old World were transplanted to and began to thrive in the soil of the new America. The very charters granted by the English Crown to the individuals and companies designated to make the laws which would control the destinies of the colonials authorized these individuals and companies to erect religious establishments which all, whether believers or non-believers, would be required to support and attend. An exercise of this authority was accompanied by a repetition of many of the Old-World practices and persecutions. Catholics found themselves hounded and proscribed because of their faith; Quakers who followed their conscience went to jail; Baptists were peculiarly obnoxious to certain dominant Protestant sects; men and women of varied faiths who happened to be in a minority in a particular locality were persecuted because they steadfastly persisted in worshipping God only as their own consciences dictated. And all of these dissenters were compelled to pay tithes and taxes to support government-sponsored churches whose ministers preached inflammatory sermons designed to strengthen and consolidate the established faith by generating a burning hatred against dissenters.

These practices became so commonplace as to shock the freedom-loving colonials into a feeling of abhorrence. . . . But Virginia, where the established church had achieved a dominant influence in political affairs and where many excesses attracted wide public attention, provided a great stimulus and able leadership for the movement. The people there, as elsewhere, reached the conviction that individual religious liberty could be achieved best under a government which was stripped of all power to tax, to support, or otherwise to assist any or all religions, or to interfere with the beliefs of any religious individual or group.

The movement toward this end reached its dramatic climax in Virginia in 1785-86 when the Virginia legislative body was about to renew Virginia's tax levy for the support of the established church. Thomas Jefferson and James Madison led the fight against this tax. Madison wrote his great Memorial and Remonstrance against the law. In it, he eloquently argued that a true religion did not need the support of law; that no person, either believer or non-believer, should be taxed to support a religious institution of any kind; that the best interest of a society required that the minds of men always be wholly free; and that cruel persecutions were the inevitable result of government-established religions. Madison's Remonstrance received strong support throughout Virginia, and the Assembly postponed consideration of the proposed tax measure until its next session. When the proposal came up for consideration at that session, it not only died in committee, but the Assembly enacted the famous "Virginia Bill for Religious Liberty" originally written by Thomas Jefferson. The preamble to that Bill stated among other things that

> "Almighty God hath created the mind free; that all attempts to influence it by temporal punishments or burthens, or by civil incapacitations, tend only to beget habits of hypocrisy and meanness, and are a departure from the plan of the Holy author of our religion, who being Lord both of body and mind, yet chose not to propagate it by coercions on either . . . ; that to compel a man to furnish contributions of money for the propagation of opinions which he disbelieves, is sinful and tyrannical; that even the forcing him to support this or that teacher of his own religious persuasion, is depriving him of the comfortable liberty of giving his contributions to the particular pastor, whose morals he would make his pattern. . . ."

And the statute itself enacted

> "That no man shall be compelled to frequent or support any religious worship, place, or ministry whatsoever, nor shall be enforced, restrained, molested, or burthened in his body or goods, nor shall otherwise suffer on account of his religious opinions or belief. . . ."

This Court has previously recognized that the provisions of the First Amendment, in the drafting and adoption of which Madison and Jefferson played such leading roles, had the same objective and were intended to provide the same protection against governmental intrusion on religious liberty as the Virginia statute. Prior to the adoption of the Fourteenth Amendment, the First Amendment did not apply as a restraint against the states. Most of them did soon provide similar constitutional protections for religious liberty. But some states persisted for about half a century in imposing restraints upon the free exercise of religion and in discriminating against particular religious groups. . . .

The "establishment of religion" clause of the First Amendment means at least this: Neither a state nor the Federal Government can set up a church. Neither can pass laws which aid one religion, aid all religions, or prefer one religion over another. Neither can force nor influence a person to go to or to remain away from church against his will or force him to profess a belief or disbelief in any religion. No person can be punished for entertaining or professing religious beliefs or disbeliefs, for church attendance or non-attendance. No tax in any amount, large or small, can be levied to support any religious activities or institutions, whatever they may be called, or whatever form they may adopt to teach or practice religion. Neither a state nor the Federal Government can, openly or secretly, participate in the affairs of any religious organizations or groups and vice versa. In the words of Jefferson, the clause against establishment of religion by law was intended to erect "a wall of separation between church and State." *Reynolds v. United States*, 98 U.S. at 164.

[Although all nine members of the *Everson* Court agreed with Justice Black's separationist account of the Establishment Clause, they disagreed about the application of the Clause to the facts of *Everson* itself. Five Justices voted to uphold the New Jersey program using government funds to transport children to private religious schools, and four Justices dissented.]

JAMES MADISON,
MEMORIAL AND REMONSTRANCE AGAINST RELIGIOUS ASSESSMENTS

(1785)

We, the subscribers, citizens of the said Commonwealth, ... remonstrate against the ["Bill establishing a provision for Teachers of the Christian Religion,"]

1. Because we hold it for a fundamental and undeniable truth, "that Religion or the duty which we owe to our Creator and the Manner of discharging it, can be directed only by reason and conviction, not by force or violence." The Religion then of every man must be left to the conviction and conscience of every man; and it is the right of every man to exercise it as these may dictate. This right is in its nature an unalienable right. It is unalienable; because the opinions of men, depending only on the evidence contemplated by their own minds, cannot follow the dictates of other men: It is unalienable also; because what is here a right towards men, is a duty towards the Creator. It is the duty of every man to render to the Creator such homage, and such only, as he believes to be acceptable to him. This duty is precedent both in order of time and degree of obligation, to the claims of Civil Society. Before any man can be considered as a member of Civil Society, he must be considered as a subject of the Governor of the Universe: And if a member of Civil Society, who enters into any subordinate Association, must always do it with a reservation of his duty to the general authority; much more must every man who becomes a member of any particular Civil Society, do it with a saving of his allegiance to the Universal Sovereign. We maintain therefore that in matters of Religion, no man's right is abridged by the institution of Civil Society, and that Religion is wholly exempt from its cognizance. True it is, that no other rule exists, by which any question which may divide a Society, can ultimately be determined, but the will of the majority; but it is also true, that the majority may trespass on the rights of the minority. . . .

3. Because, it is proper to take alarm at the first experiment on our liberties. We hold this prudent jealousy to be the first duty of citizens, and one of [the] noblest characteristics of the late Revolution. The freemen of America did not wait till usurped power had strengthened itself by exercise, and entangled the question in precedents. They saw all the consequences in the principle, and they avoided the consequences by denying the principle. We revere this lesson too much, soon to forget it. Who does not see that the same authority which can establish Christianity, in exclusion of all other Religions, may establish with the same ease any particular sect of Christians, in exclusion of all other Sects? That the same authority which can force a citizen to contribute three pence only of his property for the support of any one establishment, may force him to conform to any other establishment in all cases whatsoever? . . .

5. Because the bill implies either that the Civil Magistrate is a competent Judge of Religious truth; or that he may employ Religion as an engine of Civil policy. The first is an arrogant pretension falsified by the contradictory opinions of Rulers in all ages, and throughout the world: The second an unhallowed perversion of the means of salvation.

6. Because the establishment proposed by the Bill is not requisite for the support of the Christian Religion. To say that it is, is a contradiction to the Christian Religion itself; for every page of it disavows a dependence on the powers of this world: it is a contradiction to fact; for it is known that this Religion both existed and flourished, not only without the support of human laws, but in spite of every opposition from

them; and not only during the period of miraculous aid, but long after it had been left to its own evidence, and the ordinary care of Providence: Nay, it is a contradiction in terms; for a Religion not invented by human policy, must have pre-existed and been supported, before it was established by human policy. It is moreover to weaken in those who profess this Religion a pious confidence in its innate excellence, and the patronage of its Author; and to foster in those who still reject it, a suspicion that its friends are too conscious of its fallacies, to trust it to its own merits.

7. Because experience witnesseth that ecclesiastical establishments, instead of maintaining the purity and efficacy of Religion, have had a contrary operation. During almost fifteen centuries, has the legal establishment of Christianity been on trial. What have been its fruits? More or less in all places, pride and indolence in the Clergy; ignorance and servility in the laity; in both, superstition, bigotry and persecution. Enquire of the Teachers of Christianity for the ages in which it appeared in its greatest lustre; those of every sect, point to the ages prior to its incorporation with Civil policy. Propose a restoration of this primitive state in which its Teachers depended on the voluntary rewards of their flocks; many of them predict its downfall. On which side ought their testimony to have greatest weight, when for or when against their interest?

8. Because the establishment in question is not necessary for the support of Civil Government. If it be urged as necessary for the support of Civil Government only as it is a means of supporting Religion, and it be not necessary for the latter purpose, it cannot be necessary for the former. If Religion be not within [the] cognizance of Civil Government, how can its legal establishment be said to be necessary to civil Government? What influence in fact have ecclesiastical establishments had on Civil Society? In some instances they have been seen to erect a spiritual tyranny on the ruins of Civil authority; in many instances they have been seen upholding the thrones of political tyranny; in no instance have they been seen the guardians of the liberties of the people. Rulers who wished to subvert the public liberty, may have found an established clergy convenient auxiliaries. A just government, instituted to secure & perpetuate it, needs them not. Such a government will be best supported by protecting every citizen in the enjoyment of his Religion with the same equal hand which protects his person and his property; by neither invading the equal rights of any Sect, nor suffering any Sect to invade those of another.

9. Because the proposed establishment is a departure from that generous policy, which, offering an asylum to the persecuted and oppressed of every Nation and Religion, promised a lustre to our country, and an accession to the number of its citizens. What a melancholy mark is the Bill of sudden degeneracy? Instead of holding forth an asylum to the persecuted, it is itself a signal of persecution. It degrades from the equal rank of Citizens all those whose opinions in Religion do not bend to those of the Legislative authority. Distant as it may be, in its present form, from the Inquisition it differs from it only in degree. The one is the first step, the other the last in the career of intolerance. The magnanimous sufferer under this cruel scourge in foreign Regions, must view the Bill as a Beacon on our Coast, warning him to seek some other haven, where liberty and philanthrophy in their due extent may offer a more certain repose from his troubles. . . .

11. Because, it will destroy that moderation and harmony which the forbearance of our laws to intermeddle with Religion, has produced amongst its several sects. Torrents of blood have been spilt in the old world, by vain attempts of the secular arm to extinguish Religious discord, by proscribing all difference in Religious opinions. Time has at length revealed the true remedy. Every relaxation of narrow

and rigorous policy, wherever it has been tried, has been found to assuage the disease. The American Theatre has exhibited proofs, that equal and complete liberty, if it does not wholly eradicate it, sufficiently destroys its malignant influence on the health and prosperity of the State. If with the salutary effects of this system under our own eyes, we begin to contract the bonds of Religious freedom, we know no name that will too severely reproach our folly. At least let warning be taken at the first fruits of the threatened innovation. The very appearance of the Bill has transformed that "Christian forbearance, love and charity," which of late mutually prevailed, into animosities and jealousies, which may not soon be appeased. What mischiefs may not be dreaded should this enemy to the public quiet be armed with the force of a law?

NOTES AND QUESTIONS

1. *Madison's views.* James Madison is known as the Chief Architect of the First Amendment. His Memorial & Remonstrance presents several arguments as to why it is beneficial for church and state to remain separate.

2. *Establishment harms civil peace.* According to paragraph 11, separation of church and state leads to "moderation and harmony." In contrast, attempts to establish religion led to "torrents of blood" in the Old World. Indeed, how has the "public quiet" been affected by Virginia's proposed "Bill establishing a provision for Teachers of the Christian Religion"?

3. *Establishment harms religious minorities.* According to paragraph 9, establishment is the first step to what? Even if state-established religion does not lead to persecution of religious minorities, it creates second-class citizens: "It degrades from the equal rank of Citizens all those whose opinions do not bend to those of the Legislative authority."

4. *Establishment harms favored religion.* A close relationship with the government or support from the government is not always beneficial to the favored religion either. According to paragraph 6, what does establishment do to a church's reputation? According to paragraph 7, what does history reveal about established churches and their clergy?

B.   MODERN TESTS FOR IMPERMISSIBLE RELIGIOUS ESTABLISHMENTS

1.   The "Lemon *Test*"

One of the oldest Establishment Clause doctrinal tests is the three-part *Lemon* test: "Three such tests may be gleaned from our cases. First, the statute must have a secular legislative purpose; second, its principal or primary effect must be one that neither advances nor inhibits religion; finally, the statute must not foster 'an excessive government entanglement with religion.'" Lemon v. Kurtzman, 403 U.S. 602, 612-13 (1971). Although some components of the three-part *Lemon* test have been part of the Court's Establishment Clause jurisprudence since the early 1960s, the *Lemon* test became the subject of controversy almost from the moment it was

818 16. Defining and Enforcing the Establishment Clause

articulated. Some of the attacks on *Lemon* are quite vivid. Justice Scalia, for example, once likened *Lemon* to "some ghoul in a late-night horror movie that repeatedly sits up in its grave and shuffles abroad, after being repeatedly killed and buried." Lamb's Chapel v. Center Moriches Union Free Sch. Dist. (Scalia, J., concurring in the judgment). The *Lemon* test's continued vitality is in question. Although a clear majority has never squarely rejected the *Lemon* framework, the Supreme Court does not routinely and reliably apply it in major Establishment Clause cases. Thus, even if *Lemon* has not been officially repudiated, its continuing precedential force has been open to serious doubts.

2. *The Endorsement Analysis*

The endorsement test was developed by Justice O'Connor, but later adopted by the Court in cases involving government-sponsored religious displays. She introduced her views in a concurrence, writing, "The Establishment Clause prohibits government from making adherence to a religion relevant in any way to a person's standing in the political community. . . . Endorsement sends a message to nonadherents that they are outsiders, not full members of the political community, and an accompanying message to adherents that they are insiders, favored members of the political community. Disapproval sends the opposite message." For Justice O'Connor, the question was whether a "reasonable person" would conclude that the government had the purpose or effect of endorsing religion. Moreover, "the reasonable observer in the endorsement inquiry must be deemed aware of the history and context of the community and forum in which the religious display appears. Nor can the knowledge attributed to the reasonable observer be limited to the information gleaned simply from viewing the challenged display." County of Allegheny v. ACLU, 492 U.S. 573 (1989) (O'Connor, J., concurring). Some lower courts have treated the endorsement test as distinct from the *Lemon* test. Others view it as a refinement of the *Lemon* test: instead of asking whether the government's challenged action had the purpose or effect of advancing religion, the question is whether a reasonable person would find that the challenged government action had the purpose or effect of endorsing religion.

3. *The Coercion Analysis*

A few Justices have argued that the Establishment Clause has not been violated by government-sponsored religious displays or practices unless the state has coerced someone into participating in a religious exercise. Others had steadfastly maintained that while coercion is sufficient it is not necessary to violate the Establishment Clause. For example, Justice Blackmun in concurrence wrote: "The Court repeatedly has recognized that a violation of the Establishment Clause is not predicated on coercion." Lee v. Weisman, 505 U.S. 577, 604 (1992). Adding to the confusion is that not all Justices define coercion in the same way. Justice Scalia, for example, had a very narrow definition. A supporter of the coercion requirement, he argued that only those actions that entail the coercion of religious belief or practice "by force of law and threat of penalty" were unconstitutional. In contrast, Justice Kennedy, writing for the majority in a case challenging short prayers at a public middle school graduation, took a broader view of coercion. "[T]here are heightened concerns with protecting freedom of conscience from subtle coercive pressure in the elementary and secondary public schools. . . . The undeniable fact is that the school district's supervision and control of a high school graduation ceremony places public pressure, as well as peer pressure, on attending students to stand as a group or, at least, maintain respectful silence during the invocation and benediction. This pressure, though subtle and indirect, can be as real as any overt compulsion." Lee v. Weisman, 505 U.S. 577 (1992). Notably, Justice Kennedy did not opine on whether coercion is a prerequisite, and the Supreme Court has not yet explicitly held that coercion is necessary for an Establishment Clause violation.

4. The Historical Analysis

In Marsh v. Chambers, 463 U.S. 783 (1983), the Supreme Court debuted yet another approach to Establishment Clause cases. Marsh was challenging Nebraska's practice of opening its legislative sessions with a prayer delivered by a state-funded chaplain. The Court upheld the prayer practice, emphasizing the long history of legislative prayers. "The opening of sessions of legislative and other deliberative public bodies with prayer is deeply embedded in the history and tradition of this country." The Court also pointed out that the same Congress that approved the First Amendment also approved Congressional chaplains. "On September 25, 1789, three days after Congress authorized the appointment of paid chaplains, final agreement was reached on the language of the Bill of Rights. Clearly the men who wrote the First Amendment Religion Clause did not view paid legislative chaplains and opening prayers as a violation of that Amendment, for the practice of opening sessions with prayer has continued without interruption ever since that early session of Congress." It is not clear whether this historical approach will be confined to longstanding practices dating to the founding era or will bleed into other types of cases.

THEORY-APPLIED PROBLEMS

Even a cursory perusal of the Establishment Clause standards summarized in this chapter will indicate the conflicting outcomes that are possible under the various standards. To further clarify what these standards mean, and how they may lead to different results in specific cases, consider how each of these standards would apply to the following five church/state disputes based on cases that have been litigated under the Establishment Clause. Do not worry for the moment about how the Court has actually resolved these disputes; the next four chapters will discuss the outcomes of the specific cases. For the moment, focus on what each standard means, how the cases would be resolved if each standard were applied consistently to different types of church/state disputes, and what each standard implies about a comprehensive theory of the proper relationship between church and state.

1. The government passes a statute that obligates private employers to accommodate the religious activities of their employees in situations in which a religious obligation of an employee conflicts with a requirement of the job. The statute is challenged by a nonreligious employee who has been forced by her employer to work on Sundays because a religious employee with less seniority is given that day off because of the employee's religious obligations.

2. The government operates a program that provides supplemental educational resources to private schools within the school district, almost all of which are religious. Under this program, the government supplies to the private schools publicly funded teachers for classes in art, music, calculus, and other elective subjects. The publicly funded teachers teach these subjects on the premises of the religious schools to classes comprised entirely of the religious school students. This program is challenged by a local taxpayer who objects to spending tax money to finance a portion of the religious schools' curriculums.

3. The administration at a public high school invites a local minister to give a brief, nondenominational prayer at the school's graduation ceremony. This invitation is challenged by a graduating senior who does not want to sit through the prayer.

4. A state statute requires schoolchildren to recite the Pledge of Allegiance every morning in public school classrooms, including the words "one nation under God." This statute is challenged by a parent who does not want his child exposed to the religious portion of the Pledge.

5. A city erects a holiday display every year in a public park. The display includes secular holiday symbols such as a Santa Claus, candy canes, and sleighs, but also includes a manger scene that depicts the baby Jesus, Mary and Joseph, and the wise men. The display is challenged by a local citizen who objects to the religious component of the display.

CHAPTER
17

The Establishment Clause and Voluntary
Religious Accommodations

GENERAL OVERVIEW

The Supreme Court's Establishment Clause decisions can be grouped into three broad categories. The first category, which is the subject of this chapter, involves cases where the government's voluntary religious accommodation risks violating the Establishment Clause. The second category includes cases involving government financing of religious activities and institutions. They are covered in Chapter 18. The third category, covered in Chapters 19 and 20, includes cases in which the government practices or endorses religion.

PLAY BETWEEN THE JOINTS

It does not necessarily violate the Establishment Clause for the legislature to provide religious accommodations that are not required by the Free Exercise Clause. Thus, there is "play between the joints" of the two religion clauses. At the same time, some religious accommodations, like the absolute protection for Sabbath observance struck down in Estate of Thornton v. Caldor do violate the Establishment Clause. Some of the factors the Supreme Court has considered in deciding which side of the line an accommodation falls include: the burden on religious exercise the accommodation relieves; the burden the accommodation imposes on nonbeneficiaries; and whether the accommodation favors one religion over others or religion over secular counterparts that might also benefit from a similar accommodation.

TEXAS MONTHLY, INC. v. BULLOCK
489 U.S. 1 (1989)

Justice BRENNAN announced the judgment of the Court and delivered an opinion, in which Justice MARSHALL and Justice STEVENS join.

Texas exempts from its sales tax "[p]eriodicals that are published or distributed by a religious faith and that consist wholly of writings promulgating the teaching of the faith and books that consist wholly of writings sacred to a religious faith." Tex.Tax Code Ann. § 151.312 (1982). The question presented is whether this exemption violates the Establishment Clause or the Free Press Clause of the First

Amendment when the State denies a like exemption for other publications. We hold that, when confined exclusively to publications advancing the tenets of a religious faith, the exemption runs afoul of the Establishment Clause; accordingly, we need not reach the question whether it contravenes the Free Press Clause as well. . . .

In proscribing all laws "respecting an establishment of religion," the Constitution prohibits, at the very least, legislation that constitutes an endorsement of one or another set of religious beliefs or of religion generally. It is part of our settled jurisprudence that "the Establishment Clause prohibits government from abandoning secular purposes in order to put an imprimatur on one religion, or on religion as such, or to favor the adherents of any sect or religious organization." Gillette v. United States, 401 U.S. 437, 450 (1971). The core notion animating the requirement that a statute possess "a secular legislative purpose" and that "its principal or primary effect . . . be one that neither advances nor inhibits religion," Lemon v. Kurtzman, 403 U.S., at 612, is not only that government may not be overtly hostile to religion but also that it may not place its prestige, coercive authority, or resources behind a single religious faith or behind religious belief in general, compelling nonadherents to support the practices or proselytizing of favored religious organizations and conveying the message that those who do not contribute gladly are less than full members of the community.

It does not follow, of course, that government policies with secular objectives may not incidentally benefit religion. The nonsectarian aims of government and the interests of religious groups often overlap, and this Court has never required that public authorities refrain from implementing reasonable measures to advance legitimate secular goals merely because they would thereby relieve religious groups of costs they would otherwise incur. . . . [I]n the case most nearly on point, Walz v. Tax Comm'n of New York City, 397 U.S. 664 (1970), we sustained a property tax exemption that applied to religious properties no less than to real estate owned by a wide array of nonprofit organizations, despite the sizable tax savings it accorded religious groups.

In all of these cases, however, we emphasized that the benefits derived by religious organizations flowed to a large number of nonreligious groups as well. Indeed, were those benefits confined to religious organizations, they could not have appeared other than as state sponsorship of religion; if that were so, we would not have hesitated to strike them down for lacking a secular purpose and effect. See, e.g., Estate of Thornton v. Caldor, Inc., 472 U.S. 703 (1985) (finding violative of the Establishment Clause a statute providing Sabbath observers with an unconditional right not to work on their chosen Sabbath). . . .

Finally, we emphasized in Walz that in granting a property tax deduction, the State "has not singled out one particular church or religious group or even churches as such; rather, it has granted exemption to all houses of religious worship within a broad class of property owned by nonprofit, quasi-public corporations which include hospitals, libraries, playgrounds, scientific, professional, historical, and patriotic groups." 397 U.S., at 673. The breadth of New York's property tax exemption was essential to our holding that it was "not aimed at establishing, sponsoring, or supporting religion," id., at 674, but rather possessed the legitimate secular purpose and effect of contributing to the community's moral and intellectual diversity and encouraging private groups to undertake projects that advanced the community's well-being and that would otherwise have to be funded by tax revenues or left undone. . . .

Texas' sales tax exemption for periodicals published or distributed by a religious faith and consisting wholly of writings promulgating the teaching of the faith lacks sufficient breadth to pass scrutiny under the Establishment Clause. . . . [W]hen government directs a subsidy exclusively to religious organizations that is not required by the Free Exercise Clause and that either burdens nonbeneficiaries markedly or cannot reasonably be seen as removing a significant state-imposed deterrent to the free exercise of religion, as Texas has done, see infra, at 901-902, it "provide[s] unjustifiable awards of assistance to religious organizations" and cannot but "conve[y] a message of endorsement" to slighted members of the community. Corporation of Presiding Bishop of Church of Jesus Christ of Latter-day Saints v. Amos, 483 U.S. 327, 348 (1987) (O'CONNOR, J., concurring in judgment). This is particularly true where, as here, the subsidy is targeted at writings that promulgate the teachings of religious faiths. It is difficult to view Texas' narrow exemption as anything but state sponsorship of religious belief, regardless of whether one adopts the perspective of beneficiaries or of uncompensated contributors.

How expansive the class of exempt organizations or activities must be to withstand constitutional assault depends upon the State's secular aim in granting a tax exemption. If the State chose to subsidize, by means of a tax exemption, all groups that contributed to the community's cultural, intellectual, and moral betterment, then the exemption for religious publications could be retained, provided that the exemption swept as widely as the property tax exemption we upheld in Walz. By contrast, if Texas sought to promote reflection and discussion about questions of ultimate value and the contours of a good or meaningful life, then a tax exemption would have to be available to an extended range of associations whose publications were substantially devoted to such matters; the exemption could not be reserved for publications dealing solely with religious issues, let alone restricted to publications advocating rather than criticizing religious belief or activity, without signaling an endorsement of religion that is offensive to the principles informing the Establishment Clause. See Estate of Thornton v. Caldor, Inc., 472 U.S., at 711 (O'CONNOR, J., concurring) (because the statute bestows an advantage on Sabbath observers "without according similar accommodation to ethical and religious beliefs and practices of other private employees," "[t]he message conveyed is one of endorsement of a particular religious belief, to the detriment of those who do not share it"; the statute therefore "has the effect of advancing religion, and cannot withstand Establishment Clause scrutiny"); Welsh v. United States, 398 U.S., at 356-361 (Harlan, J., concurring in result) (conscientious objector status cannot be limited to those whose opposition to war has religious roots, but must extend to those whose convictions have purely moral or philosophical sources). . . .

Because Texas' sales tax exemption for periodicals promulgating the teaching of any religious sect lacks a secular objective that would justify this preference along with similar benefits for nonreligious publications or groups, and because it effectively endorses religious belief, the exemption manifestly fails this test. . . . We conclude that Texas' sales tax exemption for religious publications violates the First Amendment, as made applicable to the States by the Fourteenth Amendment. Accordingly, the judgment of the Texas Court of Appeals is reversed, and the case is remanded for further proceedings.

It is so ordered.

Justice WHITE, concurring in the judgment.

Justice BLACKMUN, with whom Justice O'CONNOR joins, concurring in the judgment. . . .

Perhaps it is a vain desire, but I would like to decide the present case without necessarily sacrificing either the Free Exercise Clause value or the Establishment Clause value. It is possible for a State to write a tax-exemption statute consistent with both values: for example, a state statute might exempt the sale not only of religious literature distributed by a religious organization but also of philosophical literature distributed by nonreligious organizations devoted to such matters of conscience as life and death, good and evil, being and nonbeing, right and wrong. Such a statute, moreover, should survive Press Clause scrutiny because its exemption would be narrowly tailored to meet the compelling interests that underlie both the Free Exercise and Establishment Clauses. . . .

In this case, by confining the tax exemption exclusively to the sale of religious publications, Texas engaged in preferential support for the communication of religious messages. Although some forms of accommodating religion are constitutionally permissible, see Corporation of Presiding Bishop of Church of Jesus Christ of Latter-day Saints v. Amos, 483 U.S. 327 (1987), this one surely is not. A statutory preference for the dissemination of religious ideas offends our most basic understanding of what the Establishment Clause is all about and hence is constitutionally intolerable.

Justice SCALIA, with whom THE CHIEF JUSTICE and Justice KENNEDY join, dissenting.

Where accommodation of religion is the justification, by definition religion is being singled out. . . . It is not always easy to determine when accommodation slides over into promotion, and neutrality into favoritism, but the withholding of a tax upon the dissemination of religious materials is not even a close case. The subjects of the exemption before us consist exclusively of "writings promulgating the teaching of the faith" and "writings sacred to a religious faith." If there is any close question, it is not whether the exemption is permitted, but whether it is constitutionally compelled in order to avoid "interference with the dissemination of religious ideas." Gillette, 401 U.S., at 462.

NOTES AND QUESTIONS

1. *Which Establishment test(s) did the Court rely on?* The opinion alludes to both the *Lemon* test and the endorsement test. What prong of the *Lemon* test did the Court focus on? Did the decision clarify the relationship between the two tests?
2. *Lack of burden on religious exercise.* The Court writes that the government violates the Establishment Clause "when government directs a subsidy exclusively to religious organizations that is not required by the Free Exercise Clause and . . . cannot reasonably be seen as removing a significant state-imposed deterrent to the free exercise of religion." Did the tax exemption for religious periodicals remove a significant religious burden?
3. *Significant burden on nonbeneficiaries.* The Court also writes that a government accommodation not required by free exercise run afoul of the Establishment Clause if the accommodation "burdens nonbeneficiaries markedly." Was that the case here?

4. *Favoring religion over secular counterparts.* The majority and concurrence both emphasize that the state may not provide a benefit to religious periodicals and not secular periodicals. What if there were no secular counterpart? Would it still violate the Establishment Clause to single out religion?

5. *What exemption would pass muster?* The majority and concurrence both suggest that a broader tax exemption, that also included secular periodicals, would have passed constitutional muster. In what way would that change a reasonable observer's view of the tax benefit?

CORPORATION OF THE PRESIDING BISHOP OF THE CHURCH OF JESUS CHRIST OF LATTER-DAY SAINTS v. AMOS

483 U.S. 327 (1987)

Justice WHITE delivered the opinion of the Court.

Section 702 of the Civil Rights Act of 1964, 78 Stat. 255, as amended, 42 U.S.C. § 2000e-1, exempts religious organizations from Title VII's prohibition against discrimination in employment on the basis of religion. The question presented is whether applying the § 702 exemption to the secular nonprofit activities of religious organizations violates the Establishment Clause of the First Amendment. The District Court held that it does, and these cases are here on direct appeal pursuant to 28 U.S.C. § 1252.2. We reverse.

The Deseret Gymnasium (Gymnasium) in Salt Lake City, Utah, is a nonprofit facility, open to the public, run by the Corporation of the Presiding Bishop of The Church of Jesus Christ of Latter-day Saints (CPB), and the Corporation of the President of The Church of Jesus Christ of Latter-day Saints (COP). The CPB and the COP are religious entities associated with The Church of Jesus Christ of Latter-day Saints (Church), an unincorporated religious association sometimes called the Mormon or LDS Church.

Appellee Mayson worked at the Gymnasium for some 16 years as an assistant building engineer and then as building engineer. He was discharged in 1981 because he failed to qualify for a temple recommend, that is, a certificate that he is a member of the Church and eligible to attend its temples.

Mayson and others purporting to represent a class of plaintiffs brought an action against the CPB and the COP alleging, among other things, discrimination on the basis of religion in violation of § 703 of the Civil Rights Act of 1964, 42 U.S.C. § 2000e-2.5. The defendants moved to dismiss this claim on the ground that § 702 shields them from liability. The plaintiffs contended that if construed to allow religious employers to discriminate on religious grounds in hiring for nonreligious jobs, § 702 violates the Establishment Clause. . . .

"This Court has long recognized that the government may (and sometimes must) accommodate religious practices and that it may do so without violating the Establishment Clause." Hobbie v. Unemployment Appeals Comm'n of Fla., 480 U.S. 136, 144-145 (1987) (footnote omitted). It is well established, too, that "[t]he limits of permissible state accommodation to religion are by no means co-extensive with the noninterference mandated by the Free Exercise Clause." Walz v. Tax Comm'n, 397 U.S. 664, 673 (1970). . . . At some point, accommodation may devolve into "an unlawful fostering of religion," Hobbie, supra, ___ U.S., at 145, but these are not such cases, in our view.

The private appellants contend that we should not apply the three-part *Lemon* approach, which is assertedly unsuited to judging the constitutionality of exemption statutes such as § 702. Brief for Appellants in No. 86-179, pp. 24-26. The argument is that an exemption statute will always have the effect of advancing religion and hence be invalid under the second (effects) part of the *Lemon* test. [W]e need not reexamine Lemon as applied in this context, for the exemption involved here is in no way questionable under the Lemon analysis.

Lemon requires first that the law at issue serve a "secular legislative purpose." Id., at 612. This does not mean that the law's purpose must be unrelated to religion—that would amount to a requirement "that the government show a callous indifference to religious groups," Zorach v. Clauson, 343 U.S. 306, 314 (1952), and the Establishment Clause has never been so interpreted. Rather, *Lemon*'s "purpose" requirement aims at preventing the relevant governmental decisionmaker—in this case, Congress-from abandoning neutrality and acting with the intent of promoting a particular point of view in religious matters.

Under the *Lemon* analysis, it is a permissible legislative purpose to alleviate significant governmental interference with the ability of religious organizations to define and carry out their religious missions. Appellees argue that there is no such purpose here because § 702 provided adequate protection for religious employers prior to the 1972 amendment, when it exempted only the religious activities of such employers from the statutory ban on religious discrimination. We may assume for the sake of argument that the pre-1972 exemption was adequate in the sense that the Free Exercise Clause required no more. Nonetheless, it is a significant burden on a religious organization to require it, on pain of substantial liability, to predict which of its activities a secular court will consider religious. The line is hardly a bright one, and an organization might understandably be concerned that a judge would not understand its religious tenets and sense of mission. Fear of potential liability might affect the way an organization carried out what it understood to be its religious mission.

After a detailed examination of the legislative history of the 1972 amendment, the District Court concluded that Congress' purpose was to minimize governmental "interfer[ence] with the decision-making process in religions." 594 F. Supp., at 812. We agree with the District Court that this purpose does not violate the Establishment Clause.

The second requirement under Lemon is that the law in question have "a principal or primary effect . . . that neither advances nor inhibits religion." 403 U.S. at 612. Undoubtedly, religious organizations are better able now to advance their purposes than they were prior to the 1972 amendment to § 702. But religious groups have been better able to advance their purposes on account of many laws that have passed constitutional muster. . . . A law is not unconstitutional simply because it allows churches to advance religion, which is their very purpose. For a law to have forbidden "effects" under *Lemon*, it must be fair to say that the government itself has advanced religion through its own activities and influence. . . .

We find unpersuasive the District Court's reliance on the fact that § 702 singles out religious entities for a benefit. Although the Court has given weight to this consideration in its past decisions, it has never indicated that statutes that give special consideration to religious groups are per se invalid. That would run contrary to the teaching of our cases that there is ample room for accommodation of religion under the Establishment Clause. Where, as here, government acts with the proper purpose of lifting a regulation that burdens the exercise of religion, we see no reason to require that the exemption comes packaged with benefits to secular entities. . . .

It cannot be seriously contended that § 702 impermissibly entangles church and state; the statute effectuates a more complete separation of the two and avoids the kind of intrusive inquiry into religious belief that the District Court engaged in in this case. The statute easily passes muster under the third part of the *Lemon* test.

The judgment of the District Court is reversed, and the cases are remanded for further proceedings consistent with this opinion.

It is so ordered.

Justice BRENNAN, with whom Justice MARSHALL joins, concurring in the judgment.

I write separately to emphasize that my concurrence in the judgment rests on the fact that these cases involve a challenge to the application of § 702's categorical exemption to the activities of a nonprofit organization. I believe that the particular character of nonprofit activity makes inappropriate a case-by-case determination whether its nature is religious or secular.

These cases present a confrontation between the rights of religious organizations and those of individuals. Any exemption from Title VII's proscription on religious discrimination necessarily has the effect of burdening the religious liberty of prospective and current employees. An exemption says that a person may be put to the choice of either conforming to certain religious tenets or losing a job opportunity, a promotion, or, as in these cases, employment itself. The potential for coercion created by such a provision is in serious tension with our commitment to individual freedom of conscience in matters of religious belief.

At the same time, religious organizations have an interest in autonomy in ordering their internal affairs, so that they may be free to: "select their own leaders, define their own doctrines, resolve their own disputes, and run their own institutions. Religion includes important communal elements for most believers. They exercise their religion through religious organizations, and these organizations must be protected by the [Free Exercise] [C]lause." Laycock, Towards a General Theory of the Religion Clauses: The Case of Church Labor Relations and the Right to Church Autonomy, 81 Colum. L. Rev. 1373, 1389 (1981).

. . . For many individuals, religious activity derives meaning in large measure from participation in a larger religious community. Such a community represents an ongoing tradition of shared beliefs, an organic entity not reducible to a mere aggregation of individuals. Determining that certain activities are in furtherance of an organization's religious mission, and that only those committed to that mission should conduct them, is thus a means by which a religious community defines itself. Solicitude for a church's ability to do so reflects the idea that furtherance of the autonomy of religious organizations often furthers individual religious freedom as well.

The authority to engage in this process of self-definition inevitably involves what we normally regard as infringement on free exercise rights, since a religious organization is able to condition employment in certain activities on subscription to particular religious tenets. We are willing to countenance the imposition of such a condition because we deem it vital that, if certain activities constitute part of a religious community's practice, then a religious organization should be able to require that only members of its community perform those activities.

This rationale suggests that, ideally, religious organizations should be able to discriminate on the basis of religion only with respect to religious activities, so that a determination should be made in each case whether an activity is religious or secular. This is because the infringement on religious liberty that results from conditioning performance of secular activity upon religious belief cannot be defended as necessary for the community's self-definition. . . .

What makes the application of a religious-secular distinction difficult is that the character of an activity is not self-evident. As a result, determining whether an activity is religious or secular requires a searching case-by-case analysis. This results in considerable ongoing government entanglement in religious affairs. Furthermore, this prospect of government intrusion raises concern that a religious organization may be chilled in its free exercise activity. While a church may regard the conduct of certain functions as integral to its mission, a court may disagree. A religious organization therefore would have an incentive to characterize as religious only those activities about which there likely would be no dispute, even if it genuinely believed that religious commitment was important in performing other tasks as well. As a result, the community's process of self-definition would be shaped in part by the prospects of litigation. A case-by-case analysis for all activities therefore would both produce excessive government entanglement with religion and create the danger of chilling religious activity.

The risk of chilling religious organizations is most likely to arise with respect to nonprofit activities. The fact that an operation is not organized as a profit-making commercial enterprise makes colorable a claim that it is not purely secular in orientation. . . . Nonprofit activities therefore are most likely to present cases in which characterization of the activity as religious or secular will be a close question. If there is a danger that a religious organization will be deterred from classifying as religious those activities it actually regards as religious, it is likely to be in this domain. . . .

Sensitivity to individual religious freedom dictates that religious discrimination be permitted only with respect to employment in religious activities. Concern for the autonomy of religious organizations demands that we avoid the entanglement and the chill on religious expression that a case-by-case determination would produce. We cannot escape the fact that these aims are in tension. Because of the nature of nonprofit activities, I believe that a categorical exemption for such enterprises appropriately balances these competing concerns. As a result, I concur in the Court's judgment that the nonprofit Deseret Gymnasium may avail itself of an automatic exemption from Title VII's proscription on religious discrimination.

[Justice BLACKMUN, concurred in the judgment.]

Justice O'CONNOR, concurring in the judgment.

Although I agree with the judgment of the Court, I write separately to note that this action once again illustrates certain difficulties inherent in the Court's use of the test articulated in *Lemon v. Kurtzman*, 403 U.S. 602, 612-613 (1971). . . . [T]he Court seems to suggest that the "effects" prong of the *Lemon* test is not at all implicated as long as the government action can be characterized as "allowing" religious organizations to advance religion, in contrast to government action directly advancing religion. This distinction seems to me to obscure far more than to enlighten. Almost any government benefit to religion could be recharacterized as simply "allowing" a religion to better advance itself, unless perhaps it involved actual proselytization by government agents. . . . It is for this same reason that there is little significance to the Court's observation that it was the Church rather than the

Government that penalized Mayson's refusal to adhere to Church doctrine. The Church had the power to put Mayson to a choice of qualifying for a temple recommend or losing his job because the Government had lifted from religious organizations the general regulatory burden imposed by § 702.

The necessary first step in evaluating an Establishment Clause challenge to a government action lifting from religious organizations a generally applicable regulatory burden is to recognize that such government action does have the effect of advancing religion. The necessary second step is to separate those benefits to religion that constitutionally accommodate the free exercise of religion from those that provide unjustifiable awards of assistance to religious organizations. As I have suggested in earlier opinions, the inquiry framed by the *Lemon* test should be "whether government's purpose is to endorse religion and whether the statute actually conveys a message of endorsement." Wallace, 472 U.S., at 69. To ascertain whether the statute conveys a message of endorsement, the relevant issue is how it would be perceived by an objective observer, acquainted with the text, legislative history, and implementation of the statute. Id., at 76. Of course, in order to perceive the government action as a permissible accommodation of religion, there must in fact be an identifiable burden on the exercise of religion that can be said to be lifted by the government action . . .

The above framework, I believe, helps clarify why the amended § 702 raises different questions as it is applied to nonprofit and for-profit organizations. As Justice BRENNAN observes in his concurrence: "The fact that an operation is not organized as a profit-making commercial enterprise makes colorable a claim that it is not purely secular in orientation." These cases involve a Government decision to lift from a nonprofit activity of a religious organization the burden of demonstrating that the particular nonprofit activity is religious as well as the burden of refraining from discriminating on the basis of religion. Because there is a probability that a nonprofit activity of a religious organization will itself be involved in the organization's religious mission, in my view the objective observer should perceive the Government action as an accommodation of the exercise of religion rather than as a Government endorsement of religion.

It is not clear, however, that activities conducted by religious organizations solely as profit-making enterprises will be as likely to be directly involved in the religious mission of the organization. While I express no opinion on the issue, I emphasize that under the holding of the Court, and under my view of the appropriate Establishment Clause analysis, the question of the constitutionality of the § 702 exemption as applied to for-profit activities of religious organizations remains open.

NOTES AND QUESTIONS

1. *Title VII exemption.* Title VII of the Civil Rights Act bans discrimination in employment on the basis of religion; however, § 702 exempts religious organizations from this prohibition. The exemption was originally limited to religious positions, thereby allowing a Jewish day school to discriminate on the basis of religion when hiring a Judaic studies teacher, for example. The exemption was expanded in 1972 to cover to all positions, including janitors.

2. Lemon *and secular purpose & effect.* According to the majority, how can granting a religious accommodation advance a secular purpose or have a secular effect? How does Justice O'Connor's endorsement analysis change the question?

3. *Burden on religious exercise.* Both the majority and Justice O'Connor's concurrence emphasize that in order to comply with the Establishment Clause, an accommodation must relieve an identifiable burden on religious practice. What burden does Title VII impose on religious organizations vis-à-vis nonreligious jobs? The argument is not that the organization needs people who adhere to their beliefs to fill those positions, as might be the case with religious positions.

4. *Burden on nonbeneficiaries.* Exempting religious organizations from Title VII allows them to discriminate on the basis of religion. This discrimination imposes significant costs on people like Mayson who are not hired or who are fired because of their religion. In Estate of Thornton v. Caldor, an accommodation that significantly burdened nonbeneficiaries was found unconstitutional (see *supra* p. 721). Why wasn't the § 702 accommodation also unconstitutional?

5. *Favoring religion.* On the one hand, § 702 grants a benefit to religious groups— the right to discriminate on the basis of religion—without granting the same benefit to secular groups. On the other hand, if an environmental group is allowed to hire only those people who identify as environmentalists, why shouldn't a religious group be able to hire only those people who share its beliefs?

6. *Nonprofits vs. for-profits.* The holding applies to the nonprofit activities of religious organizations. Justice Brennan argues it is limited to nonprofits while Justice O'Connor leaves the question open. Do you think the reasoning applies to the for-profit activities of religious organizations? What about for-profit corporations?

CUTTER v. WILKINSON

544 U.S. 709 (2005)

Justice GINSBURG delivered the opinion of the Court.

Section 3 of the Religious Land Use and Institutionalized Persons Act of 2000 (RLUIPA), 114 Stat. 804, 42 U.S.C. § 2000cc-1(a)(1) [to] (2), provides in part: "No government shall impose a substantial burden on the religious exercise of a person residing in or confined to an institution," unless the burden furthers "a compelling governmental interest," and does so by "the least restrictive means." Plaintiffs below, petitioners here, are current and former inmates of institutions operated by the Ohio Department of Rehabilitation and Correction and assert that they are adherents of "nonmainstream" religions: The Satanist, Wicca, and Asatru religions, and the Church of Jesus Christ Christian. They complain that Ohio prison officials (respondents here), in violation of RLUIPA, have failed to accommodate their religious exercise. . . .

In response to petitioners' complaints, respondent prison officials have mounted a facial challenge to the institutionalized-persons provision of RLUIPA; respondents contend, inter alia, that the Act improperly advances religion in violation of the First Amendment's Establishment Clause. The District Court denied respondents' motion to dismiss petitioners' complaints, but the Court of Appeals reversed that determination. The appeals court held, as the prison officials urged, that the portion of RLUIPA applicable to institutionalized persons, 42 U.S.C. § 2000cc-1, violates the Establishment Clause. We reverse the Court of Appeals' judgment.

"This Court has long recognized that the government may . . . accommodate religious practices . . . without violating the Establishment Clause." *Hobbie v. Unemployment Appeals Comm'n of Fla.*, 480 U.S. 136, 144-145 (1987). Just last term, in *Locke v. Davey*, 540 U.S. 712 (2004) the Court reaffirmed that "there is room for play in the joints between" the Free Exercise and Establishment Clauses, allowing the government to accommodate religion beyond free exercise requirements, without offense to the Establishment Clause. *Id.*, at 718 (quoting *Walz v. Tax Comm'n of City of New York*, 397 U.S. 664, 669 (1970)). "At some point, accommodation may devolve into 'an unlawful fostering of religion.'" But § 3 of RLUIPA, we hold, does not, on its face, exceed the limits of permissible government accommodation of religious practices. . . .

RLUIPA is the latest of long-running congressional efforts to accord religious exercise heightened protection from government-imposed burdens, consistent with this Court's precedents. Ten years before RLUIPA's enactment, the Court held, in *Employment Div., Dept. of Human Resources of Ore. v. Smith*, 494 U.S. 872, 878-882 (1990), that the First Amendment's Free Exercise Clause does not inhibit enforcement of otherwise valid laws of general application that incidentally burden religious conduct. In particular, we ruled that the Free Exercise Clause did not bar Oregon from enforcing its blanket ban on peyote possession with no allowance for sacramental use of the drug. Accordingly, the State could deny unemployment benefits to persons dismissed from their jobs because of their religiously inspired peyote use.

Responding to *Smith*, Congress enacted the Religious Freedom Restoration Act of 1993 (RFRA), 107 Stat. 1488, 42 U.S.C. § 2000bb *et seq.* RFRA "prohibits '[g]overnment' from 'substantially burden[ing]' a person's exercise of religion even if the burden results from a rule of general applicability unless the government can demonstrate the burden '(1) is in furtherance of a compelling governmental interest; and (2) is the least restrictive means of furthering that compelling governmental interest.'" City of Boerne v. Flores, 521 U.S. 507, 515-516 (1997) (brackets in original) (quoting § 2000bb-1). "[U]niversal" in its coverage, RFRA "applie[d] to all Federal and State law," *id.*, at 516 (quoting former § 2000bb-3 (a)), but notably lacked a Commerce Clause underpinning or a Spending Clause limitation to recipients of federal funds. In *City of Boerne*, this Court invalidated RFRA as applied to States and their subdivisions, holding that the Act exceeded Congress' remedial powers under the Fourteenth Amendment. *Id.*, at 532-536.

Congress again responded, this time by enacting RLUIPA. Less sweeping than RFRA, and invoking federal authority under the Spending and Commerce Clauses, RLUIPA targets two areas: Section 2 of the Act concerns land-use regulation, 42 U.S.C. § 2000cc; § 3 relates to religious exercise by institutionalized persons, § 2000cc-1. Section 3, at issue here, provides that "[n]o [state or local] government shall impose a substantial burden on the religious exercise of a person residing in or confined to an institution," unless the government shows that the burden furthers "a compelling governmental interest" and does so by "the least restrictive means." § 2000cc-1(a)(1)-(2). The Act defines "religious exercise" to include "any exercise of religion, whether or not compelled by, or central to, a system of religious belief." § 2000cc-5(7)(A). Section 3 applies when "the substantial burden [on religious exercise] is imposed in a program or activity that receives Federal financial assistance," or "the substantial burden affects, or removal of that substantial burden would affect, commerce with foreign nations, among the several States, or with Indian tribes." § 2000cc-1(b)(1)-(2). "A person may assert a violation of [RLUIPA] as a claim or defense in a judicial proceeding and obtain appropriate relief against a government." § 2000cc-2(a). . . .

The Religion Clauses of the First Amendment provide: "Congress shall make no law respecting an establishment of religion, or prohibiting the free exercise thereof." The first of the two Clauses, commonly called the Establishment Clause, commands a separation of church and state. The second, the Free Exercise Clause, requires government respect for, and noninterference with, the religious beliefs and practices of our Nation's people. While the two Clauses express complementary values, they often exert conflicting pressures. See *Locke*, 540 U.S. at 718 ("These two Clauses . . . are frequently in tension."); *Walz*, 397 U.S., at 668-669 ("The court has struggled to find a neutral course between the two Religion Clauses, both of which are cast in absolute terms, and either of which, if expanded to a logical extreme, would tend to clash with the other.")

Our decisions recognize that "there is room for play in the joints" between the Clauses, *id.*, at 669, some space for legislative action neither compelled by the Free Exercise Clause nor prohibited by the Establishment Clause. . . . In accord with the majority of Courts of Appeals that have ruled on the question, we hold that § 3 of RLUIPA fits within the corridor between the Religion Clauses: On its face, the Act qualifies as a permissible legislative accommodation of religion that is not barred by the Establishment Clause.

Foremost, we find RLUIPA's institutionalized-persons provision compatible with the Establishment Clause because it alleviates exceptional government-created burdens on private religious exercise. . . . Furthermore, the Act on its face does not founder on shoals our prior decisions have identified: Properly applying RLUIPA, courts must take adequate account of the burdens a requested accommodation may impose on nonbeneficiaries, see *Estate of Thornton v. Caldor, Inc.*, 472 U.S. 703 (1985); and they must be satisfied that the Act's prescriptions are and will be administered neutrally among different faiths, see *Kiryas Joel*, 512 U.S. 687. . . .

We do not read RLUIPA to elevate accommodation of religious observances over an institution's need to maintain order and safety. Our decisions indicate that an accommodation must be measured so that it does not override other significant interests. In *Caldor*, the Court struck down a Connecticut law that "arm[ed] Sabbath observers with an absolute and unqualified right not to work on whatever day they designate[d] as their Sabbath." 472 U.S., at 709. We held the law invalid under the Establishment Clause because it "unyielding[ly] weigh[ted]" the interests of Sabbatarians "over all other interests." *Id.*, at 710.

We have no cause to believe that RLUIPA would not be applied in an appropriately balanced way, with particular sensitivity to security concerns. While the Act adopts a "compelling governmental interest" standard, see *supra*, at 2118, "[c]ontext matters" in the application of that standard. See Grutter v. Bollinger, 539 U.S. 306, 327 (2003). Lawmakers supporting RLUIPA were mindful of the urgency of discipline, order, safety, and security in penal institutions. See, e.g., 139 Cong. Rec. 26190 (1993) (remarks of Senator Hatch). They anticipated that courts would apply the Act's standard with "due deference to the experience and expertise of prison and jail administrators in establishing necessary regulations and procedures to maintain good order, security and discipline, consistent with consideration of costs and limited resources." Joint Statement S7775 (quoting S. Rep. No. 103-111, p. 10 (1993), U.S. Code Cong. & Admin. News 1993, pp. 1892, 1899, 1900).

Finally RLUIPA does not differentiate among bona fide faiths. In *Kiryas Joel*, we invalidated a state law that carved out a separate school district to serve exclusively a community of highly religious Jews, the Satmar Hasidim. We held that the law violated the Establishment Clause, 512 U.S., at 690, in part because it "single[d] out a particular religious sect for special treatment," *id.*, at 706 (footnote omitted). RLUIPA presents no such defect. In confers no privileged status on any particular religious sect, and singles out no bona fide faith for disadvantageous treatment.

The Sixth Circuit misread our precedents to require invalidation of RLUIPA as "impermissibly advancing religion by giving greater protection to religious rights than to other constitutionally protected rights." 349 F.3d, at 264. Our decision in *Amos* counsels otherwise. There, we upheld against an Establishment Clause challenge a provision exempting "religious organizations from Title VII's prohibition against discrimination in employment on the basis of religion." 483 U.S., at 329. The District Court in *Amos*, reasoning in part that the exemption improperly "single[d] out religious entities for a benefit," *id.*, at 338, had "declared the statute unconstitutional as applied to secular activity," *id.*, at 333. Religious accommodations, we held, need not "come packaged with benefits to secular entities." *Id.*, at 338; see *Madison*, 355 F.3d, at 318 ("There is no requirement that legislative protections for fundamental rights march in lockstep.").

Were the Court of Appeals' view the correct reading of our decisions, all manner of religious accommodations would fall. Congressional permission for members of the military to wear religious apparel while in uniform would fail, see 10 U.S.C. § 774, as would accommodations Ohio itself makes. Ohio could not, as it now does, accommodate "traditionally recognized" religions, 221 F. Supp. 2d, at 832: The State provides inmates with chaplains "but not with publicists or political consultants," and allows "prisoners to assemble for worship, but not for political rallies." Reply Brief for United States 5.

In upholding RLUIPA's institutionalized-persons provision, we emphasize that respondents "have raised a facial challenge to [the Act's] constitutionality, and have not contended that under the facts of any of [petitioners'] specific cases . . . [that] applying RLUIPA would produce unconstitutional results." 221 F. Supp. 2d, at 831. The District Court, noting the underdeveloped state of the record, concluded: A finding "that it is factually impossible to provide the kind of accommodations that RLUIPA will require without significantly compromising prison security or the levels of service provided to other inmates" cannot be made at this juncture. *Id.*, at 848 (emphasis added). We agree. . . .

We see no reason to anticipate that abusive prisoner litigation will overburden the operations of state and local institutions. The procedures mandated by the Prison Litigation Reform Act of 1995, we note, are designed to inhibit frivolous filings.

Should inmate requests for religious accommodations become excessive, impose unjustified burdens on other institutionalized persons, or jeopardize the effective functioning of an institution, the facility would be free to resist the imposition. In that event, adjudication in as-applied challenges would be in order.

For the reasons stated, the judgment of the United States Court of Appeals for the Sixth Circuit is reversed, and the case is remanded for further proceedings consistent with this opinion.

It is so ordered.

NOTES AND QUESTIONS

1. *Facial challenge to RLUIPA.* Congress passed RLUIPA after the Supreme Court struck down the Religious Freedom Restoration Act's application to the states in *Boerne* (see *supra* pp. 764-66). While RFRA was passed pursuant to Congress's Fourteenth Amendment enforcement power, RLUIPA was passed pursuant to its spending and commerce clause powers. Note that the challenge in *Cutter* was a facial rather than an as-applied challenge. *Cutter* demonstrates that, if Congress acts pursuant to a valid constitutional power, it can enact civil rights legislation that mandates accommodation of religious practices.

2. *Burdens on religion.* The Court does not describe the "exceptional government-created burdens on private religious exercise," but it ought not be difficult to imagine how incarceration might severely impair prisoners' ability to practice their religion.

3. *Burdens on nonbeneficiaries.* The Court emphasized that accommodating prisoners' religious practices would not impose on others by compromising order or safety in prison. In fact, the Court essentially advises that RLUIPA be applied with "due deference to the experience and expertise of prison and jail administrators in establishing necessary regulations and procedures to maintain good order, security and discipline, consistent with consideration of costs and limited resources." But if courts defer to prison officials, would they really be applying strict scrutiny as RLUIPA requires? Is the decision's suggestion that strict scrutiny is not always as strict in some cases as in others limited to the prison context? Should strict scrutiny vary with the perceived importance of the government's interests? Of the popularity of the plaintiff religious group? Both? Neither?

4. *Favoring religion.* RLUIPA does not favor some religions over others, as it "does not differentiate among bona fide faiths." At the same time, the Court acknowledged that the "play in the joints" is sufficient to permit legislatively enacted accommodations for only religiously motivated conduct. In other words, the law requires that a refusal to provide a prisoner a Bible be scrutinized in a way that a refusal to provide a family photograph will not. Is this result consistent with *Texas Monthly*? How else are the two cases distinguishable?

5. *Play between the joints.* The "play between the joints" that exists between the two religion clauses not only allows the government to provide accommodations that are not required by the Free Exercise Clause, but also allows the government to curtail aid to religion that is not required by the Establishment Clause. In Locke v. Davey, 540 U.S. 712 (2004), "The State of Washington established the Promise Scholarship Program to assist academically gifted students with postsecondary education expenses. In accordance with the State Constitution, students may not use the scholarship at an institution where they are pursuing a degree in devotional theology." Joshua Davey won a Promise Scholarship, and sued when he was not allowed to use it towards a degree in pastoral ministries. The Supreme Court rejected his Free Exercise Clause claim. After finding that it would not violate the Establishment Clause for the state to fund Davey's studies, it held that ban was allowed by the "play in the joints." "Even though the differently worded Washington Constitution draws a more stringent line than that drawn by the United States Constitution, the interest it seeks to further is scarcely novel. In fact, we can think of few areas in which a State's

antiestablishment interests come more into play. Since the founding of our country, there have been popular uprisings against procuring taxpayer funds to support church leaders, which was one of the hallmarks of an 'established' religion. . . . Most States that sought to avoid an establishment of religion around the time of the founding placed in their constitutions formal prohibitions against using tax funds to support the ministry." The Court held that "Given the historic and substantial state interest at issue, we therefore cannot conclude that the denial of funding for vocational religious instruction alone is inherently constitutionally suspect" and that "If any room exists between the two Religion Clauses, it must be here."

AN EXTENDED NOTE ON THE VIETNAM-ERA CONSCIENTIOUS OBJECTOR CASES SEEGER AND WELSH

The conscientious objector cases provide additional insight into the question of whether the government may provide an exemption for some religionists but not others. The federal government had, from time to time, maintained a national system of compulsory military service from the Civil War until the conclusion of the Vietnam War. Congress, by statute, ended involuntary military conscription in June 1973 and put the nation's armed forces on an all-volunteer basis. However, when the policy of a mandatory draft was in effect, Congress consistently provided an exemption for those persons who held a conscientious religiously based objection to military service predicated on opposition to all forms of war. Among the faith communities categorically opposed to war, and whose adherents were accordingly eligible to claim conscientious objector status, were Quakers, Mennonites, Moravian Brethren, and some Seventh Day Adventists and Jehovah's Witnesses.

During the Vietnam War period, the relevant statutory language granted conscientious objector status to any person "who, by reason of religious training and belief, is conscientiously opposed to participation in war in any form. Religious training and belief in this connection means an individual's belief in a relation to a Supreme Being involving duties superior to those arising from any human relation, but does not include essentially political, sociological, or philosophical views or a merely personal moral code." Universal Military Training and Service Act of 1948, § 6(j), 62 Stat. 612, 50 U.S.C. App. § 456(j). Thus, Congress expressly tried to exclude philosophical or abstract moral objections to war as a basis for securing conscientious objector status.

The federal government applied the exemption narrowly and routinely rejected applications for conscientious objector status when an applicant disclaimed a traditional belief in God. In United States v. Seeger, 380 U.S. 163 (1965) and Welsh v. United States, 398 U.S. 333 (1970), defendants had unsuccessfully sought to claim conscientious objector status while emphatically and overtly disclaiming any theistic or formal religious basis for their opposition to war. Notwithstanding the clear language of the statute, however, the Supreme Court held that both Seeger and Welsh qualified for conscientious objector status under Section 456(j). In both cases, the Supreme Court read the statute broadly in order to avoid Establishment Clause problems.

In *Seeger*, Daniel Seeger had "declared that he was conscientiously opposed to participation in war in any form by reason of his 'religious' belief; that he preferred to leave the question as to his belief in a Supreme Being open, 'rather than answer 'yes' or 'no'; that his 'skepticism or disbelief in the existence of God' did 'not necessarily mean lack of faith in anything whatsoever'; that his was a 'belief in and devotion to goodness and virtue for their own sakes, and a religious faith in a purely ethical creed.' R. 69-70, 73. He cited such personages as Plato, Aristotle and Spinoza for support of his ethical belief in intellectual and moral integrity 'without belief in God, except in the remotest sense.'" *Id.* at 166. Plainly, Seeger lacked a belief premised on a "Supreme Being," as required by the statute.   The statute, by exempting only members of religions that believed in a Supreme Being (as opposed to religions such as Buddhism, Taoism and Ethical Culture that do not necessary center around a Supreme Being), appeared to violate the Establishment Clause prohibition on favoring some religions over others.

The Court held that Seeger was covered by the statute. Writing for the *Seeger* majority, Justice Tom C. Clark explained:

> We have concluded that Congress, in using the expression "Supreme Being" rather than the designation "God," was merely clarifying the meaning of religious training and belief so as to embrace all religions and to exclude essentially political, sociological, or philosophical views. We believe that under this construction, the test of belief "in a relation to a Supreme Being" is whether a given belief that is sincere and meaningful occupies a place in the life of its possessor parallel to that filled by the orthodox belief in God of one who clearly qualifies for the exemption. Where such beliefs have parallel positions in the lives of their respective holders we cannot say that one is "in a relation to a Supreme Being" and the other is not. We have concluded that the beliefs of the objectors in these cases [including Seeger] meet these criteria. . . .

Id. at 165-166.

Thus, to avoid striking down the entire statute as unconstitutional, the Supreme Court found Seeger to be eligible for conscientious objector status, holding that the governing test was "essentially an objective one, namely, does the claimed belief occupy the same place in the life of the objector as an orthodox belief in God holds in the life of one clearly qualified for exemption?" *Id.* at 184; *see also id.* at 187 ("We think it clear that the beliefs which prompted [Seeger's] objection occupy the same place in his life as the belief in a traditional deity holds in the lives of his friends, the Quakers."). Justice Clark cautioned that "it must be remembered that in resolving these exemption problems one deals with the beliefs of different individuals who will articulate them in a multitude of ways" and that "[i]n such an intensely personal area, of course, the claim of the registrant that his belief is an essential part of a religious faith must be given great weight." *Id.* at 184.

Elliott Welsh presented an even harder case than did Daniel Seeger. Although the statute had been amended to eliminate language about a Supreme Being, it still limited conscientious objectors status to those "who, by reason of religious training and belief, is conscientiously opposed to participation in war in any form."   The Selective Service denied Welsh conscientious objector status because "Welsh could sign [the required affirmation] only after striking the words "my religious training and." *Welsh*, 398 U.S. at 336. Thus, Welsh expressly disclaimed an overtly religious basis for his objection to war and participation in the military services. If the Court held that the statute did not cover Welsh, it would likely face the question of whether it violated the Establishment Clause to grant exemptions to those with deeply held religious objections to war but refuse exemptions to those with deeply held nonreligious objections to war. In other words, may the government favor religion over its secular counterpart?

To avoid answering this difficult Establishment Clause question, the Supreme Court held that Welsh was entitled to claim conscientious objector status even though Welsh's objection to military service was, at least in part, based on political, sociological, and philosophical beliefs. *See id.* at 342-344. The Court reasoned that as long as the moral beliefs in question hold the same place and importance as traditional religious beliefs as a form of compelled and binding moral commitment, a person may claim the benefit of the conscientious objector policy. Accordingly, Justice Hugo L. Black, writing for the *Welsh* majority, concluded that Section 456(j) "exempts from military service all those whose consciences, spurred by deeply held moral, ethical, or religious beliefs, would give them no rest or peace if they allowed themselves to become a part of an instrument of war." *Id.* at 344.

In sum, in order to avoid Establishment Clause problems that arguably would have required the complete invalidation of the conscientious objector exemption from conscription, the Supreme Court instead interpreted the exemption broadly to provide an exemption to anyone who held a "moral, ethical, or religious" objection to war under any and all circumstances. *But cf.* Gillette v. United States, 401 U.S. 437, 454-462 (1971) (holding that Congress could constitutionally limit eligibility for conscientious objector status to persons who "oppose participation in war in any form" and that this restriction on eligibility does not violate either the Establishment Clause or Free Exercise Clause). The logic of *Welsh* and *Seeger* suggests that when Congress provides statutory exemptions for religious organizations and their adherents, it cannot do so on a highly selective basis. So long as Congress crafts an exemption broadly, making it available to all persons who hold a religious belief or the material equivalent of such a belief, such exemptions may constitutionally help to advance Free Exercise Clause values without running afoul of the Establishment Clause.

THEORY-APPLIED PROBLEM

Maryland's legislature is considering revisions to the official state holiday calendar, which provides all state workers (including local public school teachers) with certain automatic vacation days, in addition to individualized vacation benefits. The Senate Government Affairs Committee commissions a survey of possible new holidays; the survey asks state and local government employees to list the top five holidays that they would like to have off as a matter of course. Of the respondents, 93 percent list "Good Friday" as one of the "top five" most desired holidays. In addition, the State Personnel Manager reports that state agencies have a larger number of requests for vacation time on Good Friday, as well as very high rates of absenteeism from those workers unable to obtain approved vacation. In light of this information, Maryland adds "Good Friday" to the official list of state holidays. The chief sponsor of the bill in the state Senate, when introducing the measure, says that "[w]e need to recognize the needs of our workforce, and Maryland's employees want to observe Good Friday." The Maryland ACLU promptly files a federal lawsuit seeking to invalidate the creation of the Good Friday state holiday. Maryland defends the law by arguing that it is a permissible accommodation of the dominant religious groups in the state. The ACLU argues that the state cannot enshrine an overtly Christian holy day as a secular holiday, and that a more generic accommodation of religious practices should be required (that is, a "floating holiday" approach). How should the district court rule?

CHAPTER
18

The Establishment Clause and Government Financing of Religion

TABLE OF CONTENTS

This chapter deals with the area of church/state relations that first instigated the movement against religious establishments in this country. Most of the early battles over religious establishments involved disputes over the collection of state taxes to finance religious institutions. By the time the Bill of Rights was ratified, most states had eliminated their financial establishments, and by 1833 all states had done so. In the modern era, disputes over government financial support for religion usually arise over tax exemption programs, government financial support to church-related social services providers, and government grants to private religious education.

The Court's rhetoric in the financing cases has tended to describe a system of strict separation between church and state. Recall the phrase from *Everson* to the effect that "[n]o tax in any amount, large or small, can be levied to support any religious activities or institutions, whatever they may be called, or whatever form they may adopt to teach or practice religion." The Court's implementation of this principle has been far less strict. In *Everson* itself, for example, the Court voted 5-4 to uphold a New Jersey statute that provided free transportation of students to parochial schools.

As for aid to religious schools, subsequent decisions during the next 50 years following the Court's *Everson* decision did little to clarify the situation. During the last decade, a new majority on the Supreme Court has fundamentally revamped Establishment Clause jurisprudence to make it far easier for the government to finance private religious institutions—especially schools.

Mitchell v. Helms overruled decades of precedent barring direct governmental subsidies to religious schools in the form of educational materials. Justice O'Connor provided the fifth vote in *Mitchell* to uphold the direct subsidy program but continued to insist that the Constitution prohibits religious schools from diverting government financial support to explicitly religious activities. Four Justices in *Mitchell* would permit such diversions, and it is not clear whether a current Supreme Court majority would subscribe to the non-diversion requirement.

In Mueller v. Allen, the Court developed the theory that government funds can be filtered to religious schools through the parents of students at those schools. In the tax deduction scheme of *Mueller*, parents serve as a kind of constitutional circuit-breaker, insulating the government from Establishment Clause challenges despite the fact that the program in question provided a large portion of its financial benefits to private religious education. In Zelman v. Simmons-Harris, the *Mueller* majority once again used the private-choice logic to justify a multi-million-dollar voucher program of subsidies to parents sending children to private schools, virtually all of which were religious. The only limits on the parental-subsidy model that remains after *Zelman* is that the subsidies formally be available on a neutral basis, such that secular schools could also apply for a subsidy, and that the parents' decision to direct the subsidy to a religious school be the result of a genuine and independent choice.

A.   SEPARATION VERSUS NEUTRALITY: EVERSON v. BOARD OF EDUCATION

Everson v. Board of Education marked both the beginning of the Supreme Court's modern Establishment Clause era generally and its modern jurisprudence regarding government financial aid to religion. As noted above, the Court unanimously agreed on a broad statement of principles regarding the Establishment Clause, including the proposition that "[n]o tax in any amount, large or small, can be levied to support any religious activities or institutions, whatever they may be called, or whatever form they may adopt to teach or practice religion." But having agreed on this absolutist principle, the Court then split 5-4 on the application of that principle to a New Jersey statute providing publicly funded K-12 school transportation for students attending private religious schools. Writing on behalf of the majority, Justice Black found no constitutional problem with the program.

EVERSON v. BOARD OF EDUCATION OF EWING TP. et al.

330 U.S. 1 (1947)

Mr. Justice BLACK delivered the opinion of the Court.

A New Jersey statute authorizes its local school districts to make rules and contracts for the transportation of children to and from schools. The appellee, a township board of education, acting pursuant to this statute authorized reimbursement to parents of money expended by them for the bus transportation of their children on regular busses operated by the public transportation system. Part of this money was for the payment of transportation of some children in the community to Catholic parochial schools. These church schools give their students, in addition to secular education, regular religious instruction conforming to the religious tenets and modes of worship of the Catholic Faith. The superintendent of these schools is a Catholic priest.

The appellant, in his capacity as a district taxpayer, filed suit in a State court challenging the right of the Board to reimburse parents of parochial school students. . . . The New Jersey statute is challenged as a 'law respecting an establishment of religion.' The First Amendment, as made applicable to the states by the Fourteenth,

Murdock v. Commonwealth of Pennsylvania, 319 U.S. 105 (1943), commands that a state 'shall make no law respecting an establishment of religion, or prohibiting the free exercise thereof.' These words of the First Amendment reflected in the minds of early Americans a vivid mental picture of conditions and practices which they fervently wished to stamp out in order to preserve liberty for themselves and for their posterity. Doubtless their goal has not been entirely reached; but so far has the Nation moved toward it that the expression 'law respecting an establishment of religion,' probably does not so vividly remind present-day Americans of the evils, fears, and political problems that caused that expression to be written into our Bill of Rights. Whether this New Jersey law is one respecting the 'establishment of religion' requires an understanding of the meaning of that language, particularly with respect to the imposition of taxes. Once again, therefore, it is not inappropriate briefly to review the background and environment of the period in which that constitutional language was fashioned and adopted. . . .

The 'establishment of religion' clause of the First Amendment means at least this: Neither a state nor the Federal Government can set up a church. Neither can pass laws which aid one religion, aid all religions, or prefer one religion over another. Neither can force nor influence a person to go to or to remain away from church against his will or force him to profess a belief or disbelief in any religion. No person can be punished for entertaining or professing religious beliefs or disbeliefs, for church attendance or non-attendance. No tax in any amount, large or small, can be levied to support any religious activities or institutions, whatever they may be called, or whatever form they may adopt to teach or practice religion. Neither a state nor the Federal Government can, openly or secretly, participate in the affairs of any religious organizations or groups and vice versa. In the words of Jefferson, the clause against establishment of religion by law was intended to erect 'a wall of separation between Church and State.' Reynolds v. United States, supra, 98 U.S. at 164.

We must consider the New Jersey statute in accordance with the foregoing limitations imposed by the First Amendment. But we must not strike that state statute down if it is within the state's constitutional power even though it approaches the verge of that power. New Jersey cannot consistently with the 'establishment of religion' clause of the First Amendment contribute tax-raised funds to the support of an institution which teaches the tenets and faith of any church. On the other hand, other language of the amendment commands that New Jersey cannot hamper its citizens in the free exercise of their own religion. Consequently, it cannot exclude individual Catholics, Lutherans, Mohammedans, Baptists, Jews, Methodists, Non-believers, Presbyterians, or the members of any other faith, because of their faith, or lack of it, from receiving the benefits of public welfare legislation. While we do not mean to intimate that a state could not provide transportation only to children attending public schools, we must be careful, in protecting the citizens of New Jersey against state-established churches, to be sure that we do not inadvertently prohibit New Jersey from extending its general State law benefits to all its citizens without regard to their religious belief.

Measured by these standards, we cannot say that the First Amendment prohibits New Jersey from spending tax raised funds to pay the bus fares of parochial school pupils as a part of a general program under which it pays the fares of pupils attending public and other schools. It is undoubtedly true that children are helped to get to church schools. There is even a possibility that some of the children might not be sent to the church schools if the parents were compelled to pay their children's bus fares out of their own pockets when transportation to a public school would have been paid for by the State. The same possibility exists where the state requires a local transit company to provide reduced fares to school children including those attending parochial schools, or where a municipally owned transportation system undertakes to carry all school children free of charge. Moreover, state-paid policemen, detailed to protect children going to and from church schools from the very real hazards of traffic, would serve much the same purpose and accomplish much the same result as state provisions intended to guarantee free transportation of a kind which the state deems to be best for the school children's welfare. And parents might refuse to risk their children to the serious danger of traffic accidents going to and from parochial schools, the approaches to which were not protected by policemen. Similarly, parents might be reluctant to permit their children to attend schools which the state had cut off from such general government services as ordinary police and fire protection, connections for sewage disposal, public highways and sidewalks. Of course, cutting off church schools from these services, so separate and so indisputably marked off from the religious function, would make it far more difficult for the schools to operate. But such is obviously not the purpose of the First Amendment. That Amendment requires the state to be a neutral in its relations with groups of religious believers and non-believers; it does not require the state to be their adversary. State power is no more to be used so as to handicap religions, than it is to favor them.

This Court has said that parents may, in the discharge of their duty under state compulsory education laws, send their children to a religious rather than a public school if the school meets the secular educational requirements which the state has power to impose. See Pierce v. Society of Sisters, 268 U.S. 510 (1925). It appears that these parochial schools meet New Jersey's requirements. The State contributes no money to the schools. It does not support them. Its legislation, as applied, does no more than provide a general program to help parents get their children, regardless of their religion, safely and expeditiously to and from accredited schools.

The First Amendment has erected a wall between church and state. That wall must be kept high and impregnable. We could not approve the slightest breach. New Jersey has not breached it here.

Affirmed.

Mr. Justice JACKSON, dissenting.

. . . The Township of Ewing is not furnishing transportation to the children in any form; it is not operating school busses itself or contracting for their operation; and it is not performing any public service of any kind with this taxpayer's money. All school children are left to ride as ordinary paying passengers on the regular busses operated by the public transportation system. What the Township does, and what the taxpayer complains of, is at stated intervals to reimburse parents for the fares paid, provided the children attend either public schools or Catholic Church schools. This expenditure of tax funds has no possible effect on the child's safety or expedition in transit. As passengers on the public busses they travel as fast and no faster, and are as safe and no safer, since their parents are reimbursed as before. . . .

It is of no importance in this situation whether the beneficiary of this expenditure of tax-raised funds is primarily the parochial school and incidentally the pupil, or whether the aid is directly bestowed on the pupil with indirect benefits to the school. The state cannot maintain a Church and it can no more tax its citizens to furnish free carriage to those who attend a Church. The prohibition against establishment of religion cannot be circumvented by a subsidy, bonus or reimbursement of expense to individuals for receiving religious instruction and indoctrination. . . .

[The state] may socialize utilities and economic enterprises and make taxpayers' business out of what conventionally had been private business. It may make public business of individual welfare, health, education, entertainment or security. But it cannot make public business of religious worship or instruction, or of attendance at religious institutions of any character. There is no answer to the proposition more fully expounded by Mr. Justice RUTLEDGE that the effect of the religious freedom Amendment to our Constitution was to take every form of propagation of religion out of the realm of things which could directly or indirectly be made public business and thereby be supported in whole or in part at taxpayers' expense. That is a difference which the Constitution sets up between religion and almost every other subject matter of legislation, a difference which goes to the very root of religious freedom and which the Court is overlooking today. This freedom was first in the Bill of Rights because it was first in the forefathers' minds; it was set forth in absolute terms, and its strength is its rigidity. It was intended not only to keep the states' hands out of religion, but to keep religion's hands off the state, and above all, to keep bitter religious controversy out of public life by denying to every denomination any advantage from getting control of public policy or the public purse. Those great ends I cannot but think are immeasurably compromised by today's decision.

This policy of our Federal Constitution has never been wholly pleasing to most religious groups. They all are quick to invoke its protections; they all are irked when they feel its restraints. . . . But we cannot have it both ways. Religious teaching cannot be a private affair when the state seeks to impose regulations which infringe on it indirectly, and a public affair when it comes to taxing citizens of one faith to aid another, or those of no faith to aid all. If these principles seem harsh in prohibiting aid to Catholic education, it must not be forgotten that it is the same Constitution that alone assures Catholics the right to maintain these schools at all when predominant local sentiment would forbid them. Pierce v. Society of Sisters, 268 U.S. 510. Nor should I think that those who have done so well without this aid would want to see this separation between Church and State broken down. If the state may aid these religious schools, it may therefore regulate them. Many groups have sought aid from tax funds only to find that it carried political controls with it. Indeed this Court has declared that 'It is hardly lack of due process for the Government to regulate that which it subsidizes.' Wickard v. Filburn, 317 U.S. 111. . . .

Mr. Justice RUTLEDGE, with whom Mr. Justice FRANKFURTER, Mr. Justice JACKSON and Mr. Justice BURTON agree, dissenting.

'Congress shall make no law respecting an establishment of religion, or prohibiting the free exercise thereof. . . .' U.S.Const.Am. Art. I.

'Well aware that Almighty God hath created the mind free; . . . that to compel a man to furnish contributions of money for the propagation of opinions which he disbelieves, is sinful and tyrannical; . . .

'We, the General Assembly, do enact, That no man shall be compelled to frequent or support any religious worship, place, or ministry whatsoever, nor shall be enforced, restrained, molested, or burthened in his body or goods, nor shall otherwise suffer on account of his religious opinions or belief. . . .

I cannot believe that the great author of those words, or the men who made them law, could have joined in this decision. Neither so high nor so impregnable today as yesterday is the wall raised between church and state by Virginia's great statute of religious freedom and the First Amendment, now made applicable to all the states by the Fourteenth. New Jersey's statute sustained is the first, if indeed it is not the second breach to be made by this Court's action. That a third, and a fourth, and still others will be attempted, we may be sure. . . .

Not simply an established church, but any law respecting an establishment of religion is forbidden. The Amendment was broadly but not loosely phrase . . . The Amendment's purpose was not to strike merely at the official establishment of a single sect, creed or religion, outlawing only a formal relation such as had prevailed in England and some of the colonies. Necessarily it was to uproot all such relationships. But the object was broader than separating church and state in this narrow sense. It was to create a complete and permanent separation of the spheres of religious activity and civil authority by comprehensively forbidding every form of public aid or support for religion. . . . The prohibition broadly forbids state support, financial or other, of religion in any guise, form or degree. It outlaws all use of public funds for religious purposes. . . .

As the Remonstrance discloses throughout, Madison opposed every form and degree of official relation between religion and civil authority. For him religion was a wholly private matter beyond the scope of civil power either to restrain or to support. Denial or abridgment of religious freedom was a violation of rights both of conscience and of natural equality. State aid was no less obnoxious or destructive to freedom and to religion itself than other forms of state interference. 'Establishment' and 'free exercise' were correlative and coextensive ideas, representing only different facets of the single great and fundamental freedom. The Remonstrance, following the Virginia statute's example, referred to the history of religious conflicts and the effects of all sorts of establishments, current and historical, to suppress religion's free exercise. With Jefferson, Madison believed that to tolerate any fragment of establishment would be by so much to perpetuate restraint upon that freedom. Hence he sought to tear out the institution not partially but root and branch, and to bar its return forever.

In no phase was he more unrelentingly absolute than in opposing state support or aid by taxation. Not even 'three pence' contribution was thus to be exacted from any citizen for such a purpose. Remonstrance, Par. 3. . . .

Here parents pay money to send their children to parochial schools and funds raised by taxation are used to reimburse them. This not only helps the children to get to school and the parents to send them. It aids them in a substantial way to get the very thing which they are sent to the particular school to secure, namely, religious training and teaching. . . . New Jersey's action therefore exactly fits the type of exaction and the kind of evil at which Madison and Jefferson struck. . . .

This is not therefore just a little case over bus fares. In paraphrase of Madison, distant as it may be in its present form from a complete establishment of religion, it differs from it only in degree; and is the first step in that direction. Id., Par. 9.53

No one conscious of religious values can by unsympathetic toward the burden which our constitutional separation puts on parents who desire religious instruction mixed with secular for their children. They pay taxes for others' children's education, at the same time the added cost of instruction for their own. Nor can one happily see benefits denied to children which others receive, because in conscience they or their parents for them desire a different kind of training others do not demand.

But if those feelings should prevail, there would be an end to our historic constitutional policy and command. No more unjust or discriminatory in fact is it to deny attendants at religious schools the cost of their transportation than it is to deny them tuitions, sustenance for their teachers, or any other educational expense which others receive at public cost. Hardship in fact there is which none can blink. But, for assuring to those who undergo it the greater, the most comprehensive freedom, it is one written by design and firm intent into our basic law.

Of course discrimination in the legal sense does not exist. The child attending the religious school has the same right as any other to attend the public school. But he foregoes exercising it because the same guaranty which assures this freedom forbids the public school or any agency of the state to give or aid him in securing the religious instruction he seeks.

Were he to accept the common school, he would be the first to protest the teaching there of any creed or faith not his own. And it is precisely for the reason that their atmosphere is wholly secular that children are not sent to public schools under the Pierce doctrine. But that is a constitutional necessity, because we have staked the very existence of our country on the faith that complete separation between the state and religion is best for the state and best for religion. Remonstrance, Par. 8, 12.

That policy necessarily entails hardship upon persons who forego the right to educational advantages the state can supply in order to secure others it is precluded from giving. Indeed this may hamper the parent and the child forced by conscience to that choice. But it does not make the state unneutral to withhold what the Constitution forbids it to give. . . .

Two great drives are constantly in motion to abridge, in the name of education, the complete division of religion and civil authority which our forefathers made. One is to introduce religious education and observances into the public schools. The other, to obtain public funds for the aid and support of various private religious schools. In my opinion both avenues were closed by the Constitution. Neither should be opened by this Court. . . .

The judgment should be reversed.

NOTES AND QUESTIONS

1. *Separation or neutrality.* The decision presents two approaches to government funding of religion. The first is strict separation, holding that no taxpayer money whatsoever be directed towards religion. Certainly much of the majority opinion's language supports this approach. Yet the holding itself suggests an alternate: If the government's goal is secular, and the money is made available on a neutral basis, why shouldn't religious organizations also participate? Which approach do you favor?

2. *Funding for police and fire protection.* If you believe in a strict separation between church and state, should this preclude funding for fire and police protection of religious schools? How do you distinguish this aid to religion from the aid in *Everson*?

3. *Funding for math and ethics education.* If you support a more neutral approach to government funding, would you also support government subsidies to math teachers in religious schools in order to improve state math achievement? What about government subsidies to religious schools as part of a state-wide effort to improve ethics?

4. *Direct vs. indirect funding.* In *Everson*, the government reimbursed the parents of schoolchildren in parochial schools rather than the parochial schools themselves. Do you think this makes any difference?

5. For 50 years after *Everson* the Court's religious financing cases were characterized by similarly sharp disputes within the Court about particular

programs under which government money was given to religious enterprises. Subsequent decisions during the next 50 years following the Court's *Everson* decision did little to clarify the situation. *Compare* Zobrest v. Catalina Foothills Sch. Dist., 509 U.S. 1 (1993) (upholding the provision of a government-funded interpreter to a deaf student attending a Catholic high school), Mueller v. Allen, 463 U.S. 388 (1983) (upholding a state program providing tax deductions for private and public school students, most of which went to religious school students), Hunt v. McNair, 413 U.S. 734 (1973) (upholding the issuance of state revenue bonds to benefit Baptist colleges), Tilton v. Richardson, 403 U.S. 672 (1971) (upholding federal construction grants for religious colleges and universities), Roemer v. Board of Pub. Works, 426 U.S. 736 (1976) (upholding a general state subsidy to religious colleges and universities), *and* Board of Educ. v. Allen, 392 U.S. 236 (1968) (upholding a state program loaning secular textbooks to students at private religious schools), *with* School Dist. of the City of Grand Rapids v. Ball, 473 U.S. 373 (prohibiting a city from sending public school teachers into private religious schools to teach remedial education classes), Wolman v. Walter, 433 U.S. 229 (1977) (striking down a state program providing instructional materials other than books to private religious schools), Meek v. Pittenger, 421 U.S. 349 (1975) (same), Committee for Pub. Educ. v. Nyquist, 413 U.S. 756 (1973) (striking down state maintenance, repair, and tuition reimbursement grants to private religious schools), *and* Lemon v. Kurtzman, 403 U.S. 602 (1971) (striking down state programs providing reimbursement to religious schools for teacher salaries, textbooks, and instructional aids).

B.   TAX DEDUCTIONS FOR RELIGIOUS ORGANIZATIONS

WALZ v. TAX COMMISSION OF THE CITY OF NEW YORK

397 U.S. 664 (1970)

Mr. Chief Justice BURGER delivered the opinion of the Court.

Appellant, owner of real estate in Richmond County, New York, sought an injunction in the New York courts to prevent the New York City Tax Commission from granting property tax exemptions to religious organizations for religious properties used solely for religious worship. The exemption from state taxes provides in relevant part:

> "Exemptions from taxation may be granted only by general laws. Exemptions may be altered or repealed except those exempting real or personal property used exclusively for religious, educational or charitable purposes as defined by law and owned by any corporation or association organized or conducted exclusively for one or more of such purposes and not operating for profit."

The essence of appellant's contention was that the New York City Tax Commission's grant of an exemption to church property indirectly requires the appellant to make a contribution to religious bodies and thereby violates provisions prohibiting establishment of religion under the First Amendment which under the Fourteenth Amendment is binding on the States.

The course of constitutional neutrality in this area cannot be an absolutely straight line; rigidity could well defeat the basic purpose of these provisions, which is to insure that no religion be sponsored or favored, none commanded, and none inhibited. The general principle deducible from the First Amendment and all that has been said by the Court is this: that we will not tolerate either governmentally established religion or governmental interference with religion. Short of those expressly proscribed governmental acts there is room for play in the joints productive of a benevolent neutrality which will permit religious exercise to exist without sponsorship and without interference.

The legislative purpose of a property tax exemption is neither the advancement nor the inhibition of religion; it is neither sponsorship nor hostility. New York, in common with the other States, has determined that certain entities that exist in a harmonious relationship to the community at large, and that foster its "moral or mental improvement," should not be inhibited in their activities by property taxation or the hazard of loss of those properties for nonpayment of taxes. It has not singled out one particular church or religious group or even churches as such; rather, it has granted exemption to all houses of religious worship within a broad class of property owned by nonprofit, quasi-public corporations which include hospitals, libraries, playgrounds, scientific, professional, historical, and patriotic groups. The State has an affirmative policy that considers these groups as beneficial and stabilizing influences in community life and finds this classification useful, desirable, and in the public interest. Qualification for tax exemption is not perpetual or immutable; some tax-exempt groups lose that status when their activities take them outside the classification and new entities can come into being and qualify for exemption.

We find it unnecessary to justify the tax exemption on the social welfare services or "good works" that some churches perform for parishioners and others—family counseling, aid to the elderly and the infirm, and to children. Churches vary substantially in the scope of such services; programs expand or contract according to resources and need. As public-sponsored programs enlarge, private aid from the church sector may diminish. The extent of social services may vary, depending on whether the church serves an urban or rural, a rich or poor constituency. To give emphasis to so variable an aspect of the work of religious bodies would introduce an element of governmental evaluation and standards as to the worth of particular social welfare programs, thus producing a kind of continuing day-to-day relationship which the policy of neutrality seeks to minimize. Hence, the use of a social welfare yardstick as a significant element to qualify for tax exemption could conceivably give rise to confrontations that could escalate to constitutional dimensions.

Granting tax exemptions to churches necessarily operates to afford an indirect economic benefit and also gives rise to some, but yet a lesser, involvement than taxing them. In analyzing either alternative the questions are whether the involvement is excessive, and whether it is a continuing one calling for official and continuing surveillance leading to an impermissible degree of entanglement. Obviously a direct money subsidy would be a relationship pregnant with involvement and, as with most governmental grant programs, could encompass sustained and detailed administrative relationships for enforcement of statutory or administrative standards, but that is not this case. The hazards of churches supporting government are hardly less in their potential than the hazards of government supporting churches; each relationship carries some involvement rather than the desired insulation and separation. We cannot ignore the instances in history when church support of government led to the kind of involvement we seek to avoid.

Mr. Justice BRENNAN, concurring.

Government has two basic secular purposes for granting real property tax exemptions to religious organizations. First, these organizations are exempted because they, among a range of other private, nonprofit organizations contribute to the well-being of the community in a variety of nonreligious ways, and thereby bear burdens that would otherwise either have to be met by general taxation, or be left undone, to the detriment of the community. Thus, New York exempts "[r]eal property owned by a corporation or association organized exclusively for the moral or mental improvement of men and women, or for religious, bible, tract, charitable, benevolent, missionary, hospital, infirmary, educational, public playground, scientific, literary, bar association, medical society, library, patriotic, historical or cemetery purposes, for the enforcement of laws relating to children or animals, or for two or more such purposes. . . ."

Appellant seeks to avoid the force of this secular purpose of the exemptions by limiting his challenge to "exemptions from real property taxation to religious organizations on real property used exclusively for religious purposes." Appellant assumes, apparently, that church-owned property is used for exclusively religious purposes if it does not house a hospital, orphanage, weekday school, or the like. Any assumption that a church building itself is used for exclusively religious activities, however, rests on a simplistic view of ordinary church operations. As the appellee's brief cogently observes, "the public welfare activities and the sectarian activities of religious institutions are . . . intertwined. . . . Often a particular church will use the same personnel, facilities and source of funds to carry out both its secular and religious activities." Thus, the same people who gather in church facilities for religious worship and study may return to these facilities to participate in Boy Scout activities, to promote antipoverty causes, to discuss public issues, or to listen to chamber music. Accordingly, the funds used to maintain the facilities as a place for religious worship and study also maintain them as a place for secular activities beneficial to the community as a whole. Even during formal worship services, churches frequently collect the funds used to finance their secular operations and make decisions regarding their nature.

Second, government grants exemptions to religious organizations because they uniquely contribute to the pluralism of American society by their religious activities. Government may properly include religious institutions among the variety of private, nonprofit groups that receive tax exemptions, for each group contributes to the diversity of association, viewpoint, and enterprise essential to a vigorous, pluralistic society. To this end, New York extends its exemptions not only to religious and social service organizations but also to scientific, literary, bar, library, patriotic, and historical groups, and generally to institutions "organized exclusively for the moral or mental improvement of men and women." The very breadth of this scheme of exemptions negates any suggestion that the State intends to single out religious organizations for special preference. The scheme is not designed to inject any religious activity into a nonreligious context, as was the case with school prayers. No particular activity of a religious organization—for example, the propagation of its beliefs—is specially promoted by the exemptions. They merely facilitate the existence of a broad range of private, non-profit organizations, among them religious groups, by leaving each free to come into existence, then to flourish or wither, without being burdened by real property taxes.

Although governmental purposes for granting religious exemptions may be wholly secular, exemptions can nonetheless violate the Establishment Clause if they result in extensive state involvement with religion. Accordingly, those who urge the exemptions' unconstitutionality argue that exemptions are the equivalent of governmental subsidy of churches. General subsidies of religious activities would, of course, constitute impermissible state involvement with religion. Tax exemptions and general subsidies, however, are qualitatively different. Though both provide economic assistance, they do so in fundamentally different ways. A subsidy involves the direct transfer of public monies to the subsidized enterprise and uses resources exacted from taxpayers as a whole. An exemption, on the other hand, involves no such transfer. It assists the exempted enterprise only passively, by relieving a privately funded venture of the burden of paying taxes. In other words, '(i)n the case of direct subsidy, the state forcibly diverts the income of both believers and nonbelievers to churches,' while '(i)n the case of an exemption, the state merely refrains from diverting to its own uses income independently generated by the churches through voluntary contributions.' Giannella, Religious Liberty, Nonestablishment, and Doctrinal Development, pt. II, 81 Harv. L. Rev. 513, 553 (1968). Thus, 'the symbolism of tax exemption is significant as a manifestation that organized religion is not expected to support the state; by the same token the state is not expected to support the church.' Freund, Public Aid to Parochial Schools, 82 Harv. L. Rev. 1680, 1687 n. 16 (1969). Tax exemptions, accordingly, constitute mere passive state involvement with religion and not the affirmative involvement characteristic of outright governmental subsidy.

Mr. Justice DOUGLAS, dissenting.

There is a line between what a State may do in encouraging "religious" activities, and what a State may not do by using its resources to promote "religious" activities, or bestowing benefits because of them. Yet that line may not always be clear. Closing public schools on Sunday is in the former category; subsidizing churches, in my view, is in the latter. Indeed I would suppose that in common understanding one of the best ways to "establish" one or more religions is to subsidize them, which a tax exemption does.

State aid to places of worship, whether in the form of direct grants or tax exemption, takes us back to the Assessment Bill and the Remonstrance. The church *qua* church would not be entitled to that support from believers and from nonbelievers alike. Yet the church *qua* nonprofit, charitable institution is one of many that receive a form of subsidy through tax exemption.

Churches perform some functions that a State would constitutionally be empowered to perform. I refer to nonsectarian social welfare operations such as the care of orphaned children and the destitute and people who are sick. A tax exemption to agencies performing those functions would therefore be as constitutionally proper as the grant of direct subsidies to them. Under the First Amendment a State may not, however, provide worship if private groups fail to do so.

That is a major difference between churches on the one hand and the rest of the nonprofit organizations on the other. Government could provide or finance operas, hospitals, historical societies, and all the rest because they represent social welfare programs within the reach of the police power. In contrast, government may not provide or finance worship because of the Establishment Clause any more than it

may single out "atheistic" or "agnostic" centers or groups and create or finance them.
. . .

TEXAS MONTHLY, INC. v. BULLOCK
489 U.S. 1 (1989)

[See *supra* p. 821.]

NOTES AND QUESTIONS

1. *General or targeted tax benefits?* There is a key difference between *Walz*'s and *Texas Monthly*'s approaches to tax deductions for religious organizations. In *Walz*, tax deductions to religious organizations were incorporated into programs granting deductions to a broad range of secular and religious organizations. *Texas Monthly*, in contrast, involved a tax deduction program that explicitly provided benefits to religious organizations alone.
2. *State support for associations.* Justice Brennan's concurrence in *Walz* noted two secular reasons to support nonprofit organizations like churches. First, they "contribute to the well-being of the community in a variety of nonreligious ways, and thereby bear burdens that would otherwise either have to be met by general taxation, or be left undone, to the detriment of the community." Second, they "contribute to the pluralism of American society." What if, however, the former were not true. Is the latter sufficient justification for government financial aid?
3. *Tax deductions.* Are tax deductions better characterized as direct financial aid or indirect financial aid? Justice Brennan's *Walz* concurrence suggests the latter: "A subsidy involves the direct transfer of public monies to the subsidized enterprise and uses resources exacted from taxpayers as a whole. An exemption, on the other hand, involves no such transfer." Do you agree? Does it make a difference? The Court has not always been consistent in how it characterizes tax deductions.

C. DIRECT AID

There have been several proposals in recent years to allocate public funds to religious groups that provide various social services to members of the public. These proposals are generally referred to by the term "charitable choice," a term coined in the 1990s by John Ashcroft, then a United States Senator from Missouri. Before leaving the Senate, Senator Ashcroft succeeded in adding charitable choice provisions to two pieces of federal legislation: the Welfare Reform Act of 1996 and the Health and Human Services Reauthorization Act of 1998.

The language of the Welfare Reform Act provision is typical of charitable choice statutes. The purpose of the provision, according to the statute, is to "allow states to contract with religious organizations" to disburse welfare assistance "without impairing the religious character of such organizations." 42 U.S.C. §604a(b). The provision generally prohibits both state and federal governments from refusing to use religious organizations to distribute aid, and guarantees the independence of religious organizations that want to participate in government aid programs. Certain types of government control over these organizations are specifically prohibited. The government is prohibited from regulating the internal governance of the organizations participating in public aid programs and is also prohibited from interfering with the organizations' religious expression or their use of religious symbols or scripture. Although federal money cannot be used to pay for the religious aspects of church operations, the religious organizations distributing the funds can be overwhelmingly religious in nature.

In addition to these statutes, the George W. Bush Administration implemented through a series of executive orders a much more aggressive plan to encourage religious organizations to participate in federally funded social service programs. This is how the Supreme Court described the Administration's "Faith-Based Initiatives":

> In 2001, the President issued an executive order creating the White House Office of Faith-Based and Community Initiatives within the Executive Office of the President. Exec. Order No. 13199, 3 CFR 752 (2001 Comp.). The purpose of this new office was to ensure that "private and charitable community groups, including religious ones . . . have the fullest opportunity permitted by law to compete on a level playing field, so long as they achieve valid public purposes" and adhere to "the bedrock principles of pluralism, nondiscrimination, evenhandedness, and neutrality." Ibid. The office was specifically charged with the task of eliminating unnecessary bureaucratic, legislative, and regulatory barriers that could impede such organizations' effectiveness and ability to compete equally for federal assistance. Id., at 752-753.
>
> By separate executive orders, the President also created Executive Department Centers for Faith-Based and Community Initiatives within several federal agencies and departments. These centers were given the job of ensuring that faith-based community groups would be eligible to compete for federal financial support without impairing their independence or autonomy, as long as they did "not use direct Federal financial assistance to support any inherently religious activities, such as worship, religious instruction, or proselytization." Exec. Order No. 13279, 3 CFR §2(f), p. 260 (2002 Comp.). To this end, the President directed that "[n]o organization should be discriminated against on the basis of religion or religious belief in the administration or distribution of Federal financial assistance under social service programs," id., §2(c), at 260, and that "[a]ll organizations that receive Federal financial assistance under social services programs should be prohibited from discriminating against beneficiaries or potential beneficiaries of the social services programs on the basis of religion or religious belief," id., §2(d), at 260.

Hein v. Freedom from Religion Found., 551 U.S. 587, 593-594 (2007).

Although renamed the Office of Faith-Based and Neighborhood Partnerships, President Obama did not significantly alter the program. Faith-based organizations may still compete on equal footing for federal social service grants without having to change their religious identity or cease offering (privately funded) religious activities to social service beneficiaries. President Obama even left intact the ability of faith-based organizations that receive federal grants to discriminate on the basis of religion in hiring. The newest regulations do require that social service beneficiaries get a written notice of their rights, which include the right not to be discriminated against on account of their religious beliefs, the right not to participate in any religious activities, and the right to request an alternate nonreligious provider.

It is still too early to know in what direction the new Administration will take faith-based funding.

The Supreme Court has not yet ruled on the constitutionality of modern "charitable choice" statutes or the Faith-Based Initiatives, but during the late 1980s the Court considered a facial challenge to an earlier social service program that specifically encouraged the participation of religious groups in the provision of government services.

BOWEN, SECRETARY OF HEALTH & HUMAN SERVICES v. KENDRICK
487 U.S. 589 (1988)

Chief Justice REHNQUIST delivered the opinion of the Court.

I.

The Adolescent Family Life Act (AFLA or Act) was passed by Congress in 1981 in response to the "severe adverse health, social, and economic consequences" that often follow pregnancy and childbirth among unmarried adolescents.

In pertinent part, grant recipients are to provide two types of services: "care services," for the provision of care to pregnant adolescents and adolescent parents, § 300z-1(a)(7), and "prevention services," for the prevention of adolescent sexual relations, § 300z-1(a)(8).

In drawing up the AFLA and determining what services to provide under the Act, Congress was well aware that "the problems of adolescent premarital sexual relations, pregnancy, and parenthood are multiple and complex." Indeed, Congress expressly recognized that legislative or governmental action alone would be insufficient:

> "[S]uch problems are best approached through a variety of integrated and essential services provided to adolescents and their families by other family members, religious and charitable organizations, voluntary associations, and other groups in the private sector as well as services provided by publicly sponsored initiatives." § 300z(a)(8)(B).

Accordingly, the AFLA expressly states that federally provided services in this area should promote the involvement of parents, and should "emphasize the provision of support by other family members, religious and charitable organizations, voluntary associations, and other groups."

In addition, AFLA requires grant applicants, among other things, to describe how they will, "as appropriate in the provision of services[,] involve families of adolescents[, and] involve religious and charitable organizations, voluntary associations, and other groups in the private sector as well as services provided by publicly sponsored initiatives." This broad-based involvement of groups outside of the government was intended by Congress to "establish better coordination, integration, and linkages" among existing programs in the community to aid in the development of "strong family values and close family ties," and to "help adolescents and their families deal with complex issues of adolescent premarital sexual relations and the consequences of such relations."

Since 1981, when the AFLA was adopted, the Secretary has received 1,088 grant applications and awarded 141 grants. It is undisputed that a number of grantees or subgrantees were organizations with institutional ties to religious denominations.

II.

The District Court in this lawsuit held the AFLA unconstitutional both on its face and as applied. Few of our cases in the Establishment Clause area have explicitly distinguished between facial challenges to a statute and attacks on the statute as applied. Several cases have clearly involved challenges to a statute "on its face." For example, in *Edwards v. Aguillard* we considered the validity of the Louisiana "Creationism Act," finding the Act "facially invalid." Indeed, in that case it was clear that only a facial challenge could have been considered, as the Act had not been implemented. Other cases, as well, have considered the validity of statutes without the benefit of a record as to how the statute had actually been applied.

There is, then, precedent in this area of constitutional law for distinguishing between the validity of the statute on its face and its validity in particular applications. This said, we turn to consider whether the District Court was correct in concluding that the AFLA was unconstitutional on its face.

As we see it, it is clear from the face of the statute that the AFLA was motivated primarily, if not entirely, by a legitimate secular purpose—the elimination or reduction of social and economic problems caused by teenage sexuality, pregnancy, and parenthood. Appellees cannot, and do not, dispute that, on the whole, religious concerns were not the sole motivation behind the Act, nor can it be said that the AFLA lacks a legitimate secular purpose.

As usual in Establishment Clause cases, the more difficult question is whether the primary effect of the challenged statute is impermissible.

Given [the] statutory framework, there are two ways in which the statute, considered "on its face," might be said to have the impermissible primary effect of advancing religion. First, it can be argued that the AFLA advances religion by expressly recognizing that "religious organizations have a role to play" in addressing the problems associated with teenage sexuality. In this view, even if no religious institution receives aid or funding pursuant to the AFLA, the statute is invalid under the Establishment Clause because, among other things, it expressly enlists the involvement of religiously affiliated organizations in the federally subsidized programs, it endorses religious solutions to the problems addressed by the Act, or it creates symbolic ties between church and state. Secondly, it can be argued that the AFLA is invalid on its face because it allows religiously affiliated organizations to participate as grantees or subgrantees in AFLA programs. From this standpoint, the Act is invalid because it authorizes direct federal funding of religious organizations which, given the AFLA's educational function and the fact that the AFLA's "viewpoint" may coincide with the grantee's "viewpoint" on sexual matters, will result unavoidably in the impermissible "inculcation" of religious beliefs in the context of a federally funded program.

We consider the former objection first. Putting aside for the moment the possible role of religious organizations as grantees, these provisions of the statute reflect at most Congress' considered judgment that religious organizations can help solve the problems to which the AFLA is addressed. Nothing in our previous cases prevents Congress from making such a judgment or from recognizing the important part that religion or religious organizations may play in resolving certain secular problems. Particularly when, as Congress found, "prevention of adolescent sexual activity and adolescent pregnancy depends primarily upon developing strong family values and close family ties," it seems quite sensible for Congress to recognize that religious organizations can influence values and can have some influence on family life, including parents' relations with their adolescent children. To the extent that this congressional recognition has any effect of advancing religion, the effect is at most "incidental and remote." In addition, although the AFLA does require potential grantees to describe how they will involve religious organizations in the provision of services under the Act, it also requires grantees to describe the involvement of "charitable organizations, voluntary associations, and other groups in the private sector." In our view, this reflects the statute's successful maintenance of "a course of neutrality among religions, and between religion and non-religion."

This brings us to the second ground for objecting to the AFLA: the fact that it allows religious institutions to participate as recipients of federal funds. The AFLA defines an "eligible grant recipient" as a "public or nonprofit private organization or agency" which demonstrates the capability of providing the requisite services. As this provision would indicate, a fairly wide spectrum of organizations is eligible to apply for and receive funding under the Act, and nothing on the face of the Act suggests it is anything but neutral with respect to the grantee's status as a sectarian or purely secular institution. In this regard, then, the AFLA is similar to other statutes that this Court has upheld against Establishment Clause challenges in the past.

Of course, even when the challenged statute appears to be neutral on its face, we have always been careful to ensure that direct government aid to religiously affiliated institutions does not have the primary effect of advancing religion. One way in which direct government aid might have that effect is if the aid flows to institutions that are "pervasively sectarian." We stated in *Hunt* that

> "[a]id normally may be thought to have a primary effect of advancing religion when it flows to an institution in which religion is so pervasive that a substantial portion of its functions are subsumed in the religious mission. . . ."

The reason for this is that there is a risk that direct government funding, even if it is designated for specific secular purposes, may nonetheless advance the pervasively sectarian institution's "religious mission." Accordingly, a relevant factor in deciding whether a particular statute on its face can be said to have the improper effect of advancing religion is the determination of whether, and to what extent, the statute directs government aid to pervasively sectarian institutions.

In this lawsuit, nothing on the face of the AFLA indicates that a significant proportion of the federal funds will be disbursed to "pervasively sectarian" institutions. Indeed, the contention that there is a substantial risk of such institutions receiving direct aid is undercut by the AFLA's facially neutral grant requirements, the wide spectrum of public and private organizations which are capable of meeting the AFLA's requirements, and the fact that, of the eligible religious institutions, many will not deserve the label of "pervasively sectarian."

[We] disagree with the District Court's conclusion that the AFLA is invalid because it authorizes "teaching" by religious grant recipients on "matters [that] are fundamental elements of religious doctrine," such as the harm of premarital sex and the reasons for choosing adoption over abortion. On an issue as sensitive and important as teenage sexuality, it is not surprising that the Government's secular concerns would either coincide or conflict with those of religious institutions. But the possibility or even the likelihood that some of the religious institutions who receive AFLA funding will agree with the message that Congress intended to deliver to adolescents through the AFLA is insufficient to warrant a finding that the statute on its face has the primary effect of advancing religion. Nor does the alignment of the statute and the religious views of the grantees run afoul of our proscription against "fund[ing] a specifically religious activity in an otherwise substantially secular setting." *Hunt*, 413 U.S., at 743.

As yet another reason for invalidating parts of the AFLA, the District Court found that the involvement of religious organizations in the Act has the impermissible effect of creating a "crucial symbolic link" between government and religion. If we were to adopt the District Court's reasoning, it could be argued that any time a government aid program provides funding to religious organizations in an area in which the organization also has an interest, an impermissible "symbolic link" could be created, no matter whether the aid was to be used solely for secular purposes. This would jeopardize government aid to religiously affiliated hospitals, for example, on the ground that patients would perceive a "symbolic link" between the hospital—part of whose "religious mission" might be to save lives—and whatever government entity is subsidizing the purely secular medical services provided to the patient. We decline to adopt the District Court's reasoning and conclude that, in this litigation, whatever "symbolic link" might in fact be created by the AFLA's disbursement of funds to religious institutions is not sufficient to justify striking down the statute on its face.

This, of course, brings us to the third prong of the *Lemon* Establishment Clause "test"—the question whether the AFLA leads to "'an excessive government entanglement with religion.'" There is no doubt that the monitoring of AFLA grants is necessary if the Secretary is to ensure that public money is to be spent in the way that Congress intended and in a way that comports with the Establishment Clause. Accordingly, this litigation presents us with yet another "Catch-22" argument: the very supervision of the aid to assure that it does not further religion renders the statute invalid.

[Here there is] no reason to fear that... monitoring involved here will cause the Government to intrude unduly in the day-to-day operation of the religiously affiliated AFLA grantees. Unquestionably, the Secretary will review the programs set up and run by the AFLA grantees, and undoubtedly this will involve a review of, for example, the educational materials that a grantee proposes to use. The Secretary may also wish to have Government employees visit the clinics or offices where AFLA programs are being carried out to see whether they are in fact being administered in accordance with statutory and constitutional requirements. But in our view, this type of grant monitoring does not amount to "excessive entanglement," at least in the context of a statute authorizing grants to religiously affiliated organizations that are not necessarily "pervasively sectarian."

For the foregoing reasons we conclude that the AFLA does not violate the Establishment Clause "on its face."

III.

We turn now to consider whether the District Court correctly ruled that the AFLA was unconstitutional as applied. [A]lthough there is no dispute that the record contains evidence of specific incidents of impermissible behavior by AFLA grantees, we feel that this lawsuit should be remanded to the District Court for consideration of the evidence presented by appellees insofar as it sheds light on the manner in which the statute is presently being administered.

Justice BLACKMUN, with whom Justice BRENNAN, Justice MARSHALL, and Justice STEVENS join, dissenting.

In 1981, Congress enacted the Adolescent Family Life Act (AFLA), thereby "involv[ing] families[,]. . . . religious and charitable organizations, voluntary associations, and other groups," in a broad-scale effort to alleviate some of the problems associated with teenage pregnancy. It is unclear whether Congress ever envisioned that public funds would pay for a program during a session of which parents and teenagers would be instructed:

> "You want to know the church teachings on sexuality. . . . You are the church. You people sitting here are the body of Christ. The teachings of you and the things you value are, in fact, the values of the Catholic Church."

Or of curricula that taught:

> "The Church has always taught that the marriage act, or intercourse, seals the union of husband and wife, (and is a representation of their union on all levels.) [sic] Christ commits Himself to us when we come to ask for the sacrament of marriage. We ask Him to be active in our life. God is love. We ask Him to share His love in ours, and God procreates with us, He enters into our physical union with Him, and we begin new life."

Or the teaching of a method of family planning described on the grant application as "not only a method of birth regulation but also a philosophy of procreation," and promoted as helping "spouses who are striving . . . to transform their married life into testimony[,]. . . to cultivate their matrimonial spirituality[, and] to make themselves better instruments in God's plan," and as "facilitat[ing] the evangelization of homes."

Whatever Congress had in mind, however, it enacted a statute that facilitated and, indeed, encouraged the use of public funds for such instruction, by giving religious groups a central pedagogical and counseling role without imposing any restraints on the sectarian quality of the participation. As the record developed thus far in this litigation makes all too clear, federal tax dollars appropriated for AFLA purposes have been used, with Government approval, to support religious teaching. Today the majority upholds the facial validity of this statute and remands the action to the District Court for further proceedings concerning appellees' challenge to the manner in which the statute has been applied. Because I am firmly convinced that our cases require invalidating this statutory scheme, I dissent. . . .

Notwithstanding the fact that Government funds are paying for religious organizations to teach and counsel impressionable adolescents on a highly sensitive subject of considerable religious significance, often on the premises of a church or parochial school and without any effort to remove religious symbols from the sites,

657 F. Supp., at 1565-1566, the majority concludes that the AFLA is not facially invalid. The majority acknowledges the constitutional proscription on government-sponsored religious indoctrination but, on the basis of little more than an indefensible assumption that AFLA recipients are not pervasively sectarian and consequently are presumed likely to comply with statutory and constitutional mandates, dismisses as insubstantial the risk that indoctrination will enter counseling. Similarly, the majority rejects the District Court's conclusion that the subject matter renders the risk of indoctrination unacceptable, and does so, it says, because "the likelihood that some of the religious institutions who receive AFLA funding will agree with the message that Congress intended to deliver to adolescents through the AFLA" does not amount to the advancement of religion. I do not think the statute can be so easily and conveniently saved.

The District Court concluded that asking religious organizations to teach and counsel youngsters on matters of deep religious significance, yet expect them to refrain from making reference to religion is both foolhardy and unconstitutional. The majority's rejection of this view is illustrative of its doctrinal misstep in relying so heavily on the college-funding cases. The District Court reasoned:

"To presume that AFLA counselors from religious organizations can put their beliefs aside when counseling an adolescent on matters that are part of religious doctrine is simply unrealistic. . . Moreover, the statutory scheme is fraught with the possibility that religious beliefs might infuse instruction and never be detected by the impressionable and unlearned adolescent to whom the instruction is directed" (emphasis in original). 657 F. Supp., at 1563.

The majority rejects the District Court's assumptions as unwarranted outside the context of a pervasively sectarian institution. In doing so, the majority places inordinate weight on the nature of the institution receiving the funds, and ignores altogether the targets of the funded message and the nature of its content. . . .

The AFLA, unlike any statute this Court has upheld, pays for teachers and counselors, employed by and subject to the direction of religious authorities, to educate impressionable young minds on issues of religious moment. Time and again we have recognized the difficulties inherent in asking even the best-intentioned individuals in such positions to make "a total separation between secular teaching and religious doctrine." Lemon v. Kurtzman, 403 U.S., at 619. . . . Where the targeted audience is composed of children, of course, the Court's insistence on adequate safeguards has always been greatest. . . .

Whereas there may be secular values promoted by the AFLA, including the encouragement of adoption and premarital chastity and the discouragement of abortion, it can hardly be doubted that when promoted in theological terms by religious figures, those values take on a religious nature. Not surprisingly, the record is replete with observations to that effect. It should be undeniable by now that religious dogma may not be employed by government even to accomplish laudable secular purposes such as "the promotion of moral values, the contradiction to the materialistic trends of our times, the perpetuation of our institutions and the teaching of literature." Abington School District v. Schempp, 374 U.S. 203, 223 (1963) (holding unconstitutional daily reading of Bible verses and recitation of the Lord's Prayer in public schools); Stone v. Graham, 449 U.S. 39 (1980) (holding unconstitutional posting of Ten Commandments despite notation explaining secular application thereof).[10] It is true, of course, that the Court has recognized that the Constitution does not prohibit the government from supporting secular social-welfare services solely because they are provided by a religiously affiliated organization. But such recognition has been closely tied to the nature of the subsidized social service: "the State may send a cleric, indeed even a clerical order, to perform a *wholly secular task*." There is a very real and important difference between running a soup kitchen or a hospital, and counseling pregnant teenagers on how to make the difficult decisions facing them. The risk of advancing religion at public expense, and of creating an appearance that the government is endorsing the medium and the message, is much greater when the religious organization is directly engaged in pedagogy, with the express intent of shaping belief and changing behavior, than where it is neutrally dispensing medication, food, or shelter. . . .

For some religious organizations, the answer to a teenager's question "Why shouldn't I have an abortion?" or "Why shouldn't I use barrier contraceptives?" will undoubtedly be different from an answer based solely on secular considerations. Public funds may not be used to endorse the religious message.

NOTES AND QUESTIONS

1. *Symbolic link.* The majority argues that government financial aid in the form of direct social service grants to religiously affiliated organizations does not automatically create an unconstitutional symbolic link between church and state. Is this always the case? What features makes this true for AFLA?
2. *Pervasively sectarian.* The majority also held that direct financial aid to a pervasively sectarian organization would violate the Establishment Clause. What characterizes a pervasively sectarian organization? According to *Bowen*, why would directly funding a pervasively sectarian organization inevitably advance religion? Does the rule still hold after Mitchell v. Helms?
3. *Alignment of government and religious values.* According to the majority, the fact that the government's message on premarital sex coincides with religious beliefs does not necessarily mean it advances religion. After all, there may be secular reasons for the message as well. For example, avoiding teen pregnancies is a secular reason to advocate for teen abstinence. What is the secular value underlying the government's opposition to abortion?
4. *Teaching abstinence vs. providing food.* The dissent argues that "There is a very real and important difference between running a soup kitchen or a hospital" and counseling teenagers on sexual abstinence. In particular, the majority and dissent disagree about the ability of people of faith to teach "highly sensitive subject[s] of considerable religious significance" without interjecting their religious beliefs

---

[10] Religion plays an important role to many in our society. By enlisting its aid in combating certain social ills, while imposing the restrictions required by the First Amendment on the use of public funds to promote religion, we risk secularizing and demeaning the sacred enterprise. Whereas there is undoubtedly a role for churches of all denominations in helping prevent the problems often associated with early sexual activity and unplanned pregnancies, any attempt to confine that role within the strictures of a government-sponsored secular program can only taint the religious mission with a "corrosive secularism." Grand Rapids School District v. Ball, 473 U.S. 373, 385 (1985). The First Amendment protects not only the State from being captured by the Church, but also protects the Church from being corrupted by the State and adopted for its purposes.

into the lessons. Who do you think is more likely to be correct about the risk of religious indoctrination?

5. *Faith-based initiatives and the problem of religiously motivated discrimination.* If government funds faith-based providers that supply social services to the public, may such entities discriminate with respect to hiring and employment? What if the discrimination is not just favoring co-religionists? For example, could a religiously affiliated foster home for abused and neglected children that receives placements from the state's Department of Social Services refuse to employ openly gay or lesbian persons? Or could it refuse to place children with gay or lesbian foster parents? If the state itself could not directly adopt and enforce such policies for a state-run foster home, can it achieve the same results through the expedient of contracting out these services to faith-based service providers?

6. *The risk of undue dependence on government funds.* How might government money affect how a religiously affiliated entity undertakes its mission more generally? Independent of the constitutional permissibility of using faith-based providers of social services, is such a close relationship between church and state good for religious organizations? If a religious organization relies heavily on government funds to maintain and support its social outreach programs, how likely will it be to stick to its theological and doctrinal guns when the state conditions its largesse on a practice or policy offensive to the tenets of the faith?

MITCHELL v. HELMS

530 U.S. 793 (2000)

Justice THOMAS announced the judgment of the Court and delivered an opinion, in which THE CHIEF JUSTICE, Justice SCALIA, and Justice KENNEDY join.

As part of a longstanding school-aid program known as Chapter 2, the Federal Government distributes funds to state and local governmental agencies, which in turn lend educational materials and equipment to public and private schools, with the enrollment of each participating school determining the amount of aid that it receives. The question is whether Chapter 2, as applied in Jefferson Parish, Louisiana, is a law respecting an establishment of religion, because many of the private schools receiving Chapter 2 aid in that parish are religiously affiliated. We hold that Chapter 2 is not such a law.

I

Several restrictions apply to aid to private schools. Most significantly, the "services, materials, and equipment" provided to private schools must be "secular, neutral, and nonideological." In addition, private schools may not acquire control of Chapter 2 funds or title to Chapter 2 materials, equipment, or property. A private school receives the materials and equipment listed in [the federal statute] by submitting to the LEA [Local Educational Authorities] an application detailing which items the school seeks and how it will use them; the LEA, if it approves the application, purchases those items from the school's allocation of funds, and then lends them to that school.

In Jefferson Parish (the Louisiana governmental unit at issue in this case), as in Louisiana as a whole, private schools have primarily used their allocations for nonrecurring expenses, usually materials and equipment. In the 1986-1987 fiscal year, for example, 44% of the money budgeted for private schools in Jefferson Parish was spent by LEA's for acquiring library and media materials, and 48% for instructional equipment. Among the materials and equipment provided have been library books, computers, and computer software, and also slide and movie projectors, overhead projectors, television sets, tape recorders, VCR's, projection screens, laboratory equipment, maps, globes, filmstrips, slides, and cassette recordings.

It appears that, in an average year, about 30% of Chapter 2 funds spent in Jefferson Parish are allocated for private schools. For the 1985-1986 fiscal year, 41 private schools participated in Chapter 2. For the following year, 46 participated, and the participation level has remained relatively constant since then. Of these 46, 34 were Roman Catholic; 7 were otherwise religiously affiliated; and 5 were not religiously affiliated.

II

A

[T]he question whether governmental aid to religious schools results in governmental indoctrination is ultimately a question whether any religious indoctrination that occurs in those schools could reasonably be attributed to governmental action. We have also indicated that the answer to the question of indoctrination will resolve the question whether a program of educational aid "subsidizes" religion, as our religion cases use that term.

In distinguishing between indoctrination that is attributable to the State and indoctrination that is not, we have consistently turned to the principle of neutrality, upholding aid that is offered to a broad range of groups or persons without regard to their religion. If the religious, irreligious, and areligious are all alike eligible for governmental aid, no one would conclude that any indoctrination that any particular recipient conducts has been done at the behest of the government. For attribution of indoctrination is a relative question. If the government is offering assistance to recipients who provide, so to speak, a broad range of indoctrination, the government itself is not thought responsible for any particular indoctrination. To put the point differently, if the government, seeking to further some legitimate secular purpose, offers aid on the same terms, without regard to religion, to all who adequately further that purpose, then it is fair to say that any aid going to a religious recipient only has the effect of furthering that secular purpose. The government, in crafting such an aid program, has had to conclude that a given level of aid is necessary to further that purpose among secular recipients and has provided no more than that same level to religious recipients. . . .

B

Respondents . . . offer two rules that they contend should govern our determination of whether Chapter 2 has the effect of advancing religion. They argue first, and chiefly, that "direct, nonincidental" aid to the primary educational mission of religious schools is always impermissible. Second, they argue that provision to religious schools of aid that is divertible to religious use is similarly impermissible. Respondents' arguments are inconsistent with our more recent case law . . . and we therefore reject them.

Although some of our earlier cases, particularly [*Grand Rapids v.*] *Ball*, did emphasize the distinction between direct and indirect aid, the purpose of this distinction was merely to prevent "subsidization" of religion. Of course, we have seen "special Establishment Clause dangers" when *money* is given to religious schools or entities directly rather than . . . indirectly. But direct payments of money are not at issue in this case, and we refuse to allow a "special" case to create a rule for all cases.

Respondents also contend that the Establishment Clause requires that aid to religious schools not be impermissibly religious in nature or be divertible to religious use. We agree with the first part of this argument but not the second. Respondents' "no divertibility" rule is inconsistent with our more recent case law and is unworkable. So long as the governmental aid is not itself "unsuitable for use in the public schools because of religious content," and eligibility for aid is determined in a constitutionally permissible manner, any use of that aid to indoctrinate cannot be attributed to the government and is thus not of constitutional concern.

Our recent precedents, particularly *Zobrest*, require us to reject respondents' argument. . . . [In these earlier cases] we did not, as respondents do, think that the *use* of governmental aid to further religious indoctrination was synonymous with religious indoctrination *by* the government or that such use of aid created any improper incentives.

The issue is not divertibility of aid but rather whether the aid itself has an impermissible content. Where the aid would be suitable for use in a public school, it is also suitable for use in any private school. Similarly, the prohibition against the government providing impermissible content resolves the Establishment Clause concerns that exist if aid is actually diverted to religious uses. . . . [J]ust as a government [sign-language] interpreter [as in *Zobrest*] does not herself inculcate a religious message—even when she is conveying one—so also a government computer or overhead projector does not itself inculcate a religious message, even when it is conveying one.

A concern for divertibility, as opposed to improper content, is misplaced not only because it fails to explain why the sort of aid that we have allowed is permissible, but also because it is boundless—enveloping all aid, no matter how trivial—and thus has only the most attenuated (if any) link to any realistic concern for preventing an "establishment of religion." Presumably, for example, government-provided lecterns, chalk, crayons, pens, paper, and paintbrushes would have to be excluded from religious schools under respondents' proposed rule. But we fail to see how indoctrination by means of (*i.e.*, diversion of) such aid could be attributed to the government. In fact, the risk of improper attribution is *less* when the aid lacks content, for there is no risk (as there is with books), of the government inadvertently providing improper content.

C

The dissent serves up a smorgasbord of 11 factors that, depending on the facts of each case "in all its particularity," could be relevant to the constitutionality of a school-aid program. One of the dissent's factors deserves special mention: whether a school that receives aid (or whose students receive aid) is pervasively sectarian. The dissent is correct that there was a period when this factor mattered, particularly if the pervasively sectarian school was a primary or secondary school. But that period is one that the Court should regret, and it is thankfully long past.

There are numerous reasons to formally dispense with this factor. First, its relevance in our precedents is in sharp decline. Although our case law has consistently mentioned it even in recent years, we have not struck down an aid program in reliance on this factor since 1985.

Second, the religious nature of a recipient should not matter to the constitutional analysis, so long as the recipient adequately furthers the government's secular purpose. If a program offers permissible aid to the religious (including the pervasively sectarian), the areligious, and the irreligious, it is a mystery which view of religion the government has established, and thus a mystery what the constitutional violation would be. The pervasively sectarian recipient has not received any special favor, and it is most bizarre that the Court would, as the dissent seemingly does, reserve special hostility for those who take their religion seriously, who think that their religion should affect the whole of their lives, or who make the mistake of being effective in transmitting their views to children.

Third, the inquiry into the recipient's religious views required by a focus on whether a school is pervasively sectarian is not only unnecessary but also offensive. It is well established, in numerous other contexts, that courts should refrain from trolling through a person's or institution's religious beliefs. Yet that is just what this factor requires, as was evident before the District Court. Although the dissent welcomes such probing, we find it profoundly troubling. In addition, and related, the application of the "pervasively sectarian" factor collides with our decisions that have prohibited governments from discriminating in the distribution of public benefits based upon religious status or sincerity.

Finally, hostility to aid to pervasively sectarian schools has a shameful pedigree that we do not hesitate to disavow. Although the dissent professes concern for "the implied exclusion of the less favored," the exclusion of pervasively sectarian schools from government-aid programs is just that, particularly given the history of such exclusion. Opposition to aid to "sectarian" schools acquired prominence in the 1870's with Congress' consideration (and near passage) of the Blaine Amendment, which would have amended the Constitution to bar any aid to sectarian institutions. Consideration of the amendment arose at a time of pervasive hostility to the Catholic Church and to Catholics in general, and it was an open secret that "sectarian" was code for "Catholic." See generally Green, The Blaine Amendment Reconsidered, 36 Am. J. Legal Hist. 38 (1992). Notwithstanding its history, of course, "sectarian" could, on its face, describe the school of any religious sect, but the Court eliminated this possibility of confusion when, in *Hunt v. McNair*, 413 U.S., at 743, it coined the term "pervasively sectarian"—a term which, at that time, could be applied almost exclusively to Catholic parochial schools and which even today's dissent exemplifies chiefly by reference to such schools.

In short, nothing in the Establishment Clause requires the exclusion of pervasively sectarian schools from otherwise permissible aid programs, and other doctrines of this Court bar it. This doctrine, born of bigotry, should be buried now.

Justice O'CONNOR, with whom Justice BREYER joins, concurring in the judgment.

I write separately because, in my view, the plurality announces a rule of unprecedented breadth for the evaluation of Establishment Clause challenges to government school-aid programs. Reduced to its essentials, the plurality's rule states that government aid to religious schools does not have the effect of advancing religion so long as the aid is offered on a neutral basis and the aid is secular in content. The plurality also rejects the distinction between direct and indirect aid, and holds that the actual diversion of secular aid by a religious school to the advancement of its religious mission is permissible. Although the expansive scope of the plurality's rule is troubling, two specific aspects of the opinion compel me to write separately. First, the plurality's treatment of neutrality comes close to assigning that factor singular importance in the future adjudication of Establishment Clause challenges to government school-aid programs. Second, the plurality's approval of actual diversion of government aid to religious indoctrination is in tension with our precedents and, in any event, unnecessary to decide the instant case.

I do not quarrel with the plurality's recognition that neutrality is an important reason for upholding government-aid programs against Establishment Clause challenges. Our cases have described neutrality in precisely this manner, and we have emphasized a program's neutrality repeatedly in our decisions approving various forms of school aid. Nevertheless, we have never held that a government-aid program passes constitutional muster *solely* because of the neutral criteria it employs as a basis for distributing aid.

I also disagree with the plurality's conclusion that actual diversion of government aid to religious indoctrination is consistent with the Establishment Clause. Although "[o]ur cases have permitted some government funding of secular functions performed by sectarian organizations," our decisions "provide no precedent for the use of public funds to finance religious activities." [W]e have long been concerned that secular government aid not be diverted to the advancement of religion.

Like Justice Souter, I do not believe that we should treat a per-capita-aid program the same as . . . true private-choice programs. . . . . I believe the distinction between a per-capita school-aid program and a true private-choice program is significant for purposes of endorsement. In terms of public perception, a government program of direct aid to religious schools based on the number of students attending each school differs meaningfully from the government distributing aid directly to individual students who, in turn, decide to use the aid at the same religious schools. In the former example, if the religious school uses the aid to inculcate religion in its students, it is reasonable to say that the government has communicated a message of endorsement. Because the religious indoctrination is supported by government assistance, the reasonable observer would naturally perceive the aid program as *government* support for the advancement of religion.

Finally, the distinction between a per-capita-aid program and a true private-choice program is important when considering aid that consists of direct monetary subsidies. This Court has "recognized special Establishment Clause dangers where the government makes direct money payments to sectarian institutions." If, as the plurality contends, a per-capita-aid program is identical in relevant constitutional respects to a true private-choice program, then there is no reason that, under the plurality's reasoning, the government should be precluded from providing direct money payments to religious organizations (including churches) based on the number of persons belonging to each organization. And, because actual diversion is permissible under the plurality's holding, the participating religious organizations (including churches) could use that aid to support religious indoctrination. To be sure, the plurality does not actually hold that its theory extends to direct money payments. That omission, however, is of little comfort. In its logic—as well as its specific advisory language—the plurality opinion foreshadows the approval of direct monetary subsidies to religious organizations, even when they use the money to advance their religious objectives.

[Having rejected the plurality's approach, Justice O'Connor upholds the program: "The Chapter 2 aid is allocated on the basis of neutral, secular criteria; the aid must be supplementary and cannot supplant non-Federal funds; no Chapter 2 funds ever reach the coffers of religious schools; the aid must be secular; any evidence of actual diversion is *de minimis*; and the program includes adequate safeguards. Regardless of whether these factors are constitutional requirements, they are surely sufficient to find that the program at issue here does not have the impermissible effect of advancing religion. For the same reasons, 'this carefully constrained program also cannot reasonably be viewed as an endorsement of religion.' Accordingly, I concur in the judgment."]

Justice SOUTER, with whom Justice STEVENS and Justice GINSBURG join, dissenting.

The establishment prohibition of government religious funding serves more than one end. It is meant to guarantee the right of individual conscience against compulsion, to protect the integrity of religion against the corrosion of secular support, and to preserve the unity of political society against the implied exclusion of the less favored and the antagonism of controversy over public support for religious causes.

These objectives are always in some jeopardy since the substantive principle of no aid to religion is not the only limitation on government action toward religion. Because the First Amendment also bars any prohibition of individual free exercise of religion, and because religious organizations cannot be isolated from the basic government functions that create the civil environment, it is as much necessary as it is difficult to draw lines between forbidden aid and lawful benefit. For more than 50 years, this Court has been attempting to draw these lines. Owing to the variety of factual circumstances in which the lines must be drawn, not all of the points creating the boundary have enjoyed self-evidence.

The insufficiency of evenhandedness neutrality as a stand-alone criterion of constitutional intent or effect has been clear from the beginning of our interpretative efforts, for an obvious reason. . . . .

[I]f we looked no further than evenhandedness, and failed to ask what activities the aid might support, or in fact did support, religious schools could be blessed with government funding as massive as expenditures made for the benefit of their public school counterparts, and religious missions would thrive on public money. This is why the consideration of less than universal neutrality has never been recognized as dispositive and has always been teamed with attention to other facts bearing on the substantive prohibition of support for a school's religious objective.

At least three main lines of enquiry addressed particularly to school aid have emerged to complement evenhandedness neutrality. First, we have noted that two types of aid recipients heighten Establishment Clause concern: pervasively religious schools and primary and secondary religious schools. Second, we have identified two important characteristics of the method of distributing aid: directness or indirectness of distribution and distribution by genuinely independent choice. Third, we have found relevance in at least five characteristics of the aid itself: its religious content; its cash form; its divertibility or actually diversion to religious support; its supplantation of traditional items of religious school expense; and its substantiality.

1

Two types of school aid recipients have raised special concern. First, we have recognized the fact that the overriding religious mission of certain schools, those sometimes called "pervasively sectarian," is not confined to a discrete element of the curriculum. Based on record evidence and long experience, we have concluded that religious teaching in such schools is at the core of the instructors' individual and personal obligations, cf. Canon 803, §2, Text & Commentary 568 ("It is necessary that the formation and education given in a Catholic school be based upon the principles of Catholic doctrine; teachers are to be outstanding for their correct doctrine and integrity of life"), and that individual religious teachers will teach religiously. As religious teaching cannot be separated from secular education in such schools or by such teachers, we have concluded that direct government subsidies to such schools are prohibited because they will inevitably and impermissibly support religious indoctrination.

Second, we have expressed special concern about aid to primary and secondary religious schools. On the one hand, we have understood how the youth of the students in such schools makes them highly susceptible to religious indoctrination. On the other, we have recognized that the religious element in the education offered in most sectarian primary and secondary schools is far more intertwined with the secular than in university teaching, where the natural and academic skepticism of most older students may separate the two. Thus, government benefits accruing to these pervasively religious primary and secondary schools raise special dangers of diversion into support for the religious indoctrination of children and the involvement of government in religious training and practice.

2

We have also evaluated the portent of support to an organization's religious mission that may be inherent in the method by which aid is granted, finding pertinence in at least two characteristics of distribution. First, we have asked whether aid is direct or indirect, observing distinctions between government schemes with individual beneficiaries and those whose beneficiaries in the first instance might be religious schools. Direct aid obviously raises greater risks, although recent cases have discounted this risk factor, looking to other features of the distribution mechanism.

Second, we have distinguished between indirect aid that reaches religious schools only incidentally as a result of numerous individual choices and aid that is in reality directed to religious schools by the government or in practical terms selected by religious schools themselves. In these cases, we have declared the constitutionality of programs providing aid directly to parents or students as tax deductions or scholarship money, where such aid may pay for education at some sectarian institutions, but only as the result of "genuinely independent and private choices of aid recipients."

3

In addition to the character of the school to which the benefit accrues, and its path from government to school, a number of features of the aid itself have figured in the classifications we have made. First, we have barred aid with actual religious content, which would obviously run afoul of the ban on the government's participation in religion. In cases where we have permitted aid, we have regularly characterized it as "neutral" in the sense of being without religious content.

Second, we have long held government aid invalid when circumstances would allow its diversion to religious education. The risk of diversion is obviously high when aid in the form of government funds makes its way into the coffers of religious organizations, and so from the start we have understood the Constitution to bar outright money grants of aid to religion.

Divertibility is not, of course, a characteristic of cash alone, and when examining provisions for ostensibly secular supplies we have considered their susceptibility to the service of religious ends. In upholding a scheme to provide students with secular textbooks, we emphasized that "each book loaned must be approved by the public school authorities; only secular books may receive approval."

With the same point in mind, we held that buildings constructed with government grants to universities with religious affiliation must be barred from religious use indefinitely to prevent the diversion of government funds to religious objectives. We were accordingly constrained to strike down aid for repairing buildings of nonpublic schools because they could be used for religious education.

Third, our cases have recognized the distinction, adopted by statute in the Chapter 2 legislation, between aid that merely supplements and aid that supplants expenditures for offerings at religious schools, the latter being barred. Although we have never adopted the position that any benefit that flows to a religious school is impermissible because it frees up resources for the school to engage in religious indoctrination, from our first decision holding it permissible to provide textbooks for religious schools we have repeatedly explained the unconstitutionality of aid that supplants an item of the school's traditional expense.

Finally, we have recognized what is obvious (however imprecise), in holding "substantial" amounts of aid to be unconstitutional whether or not a plaintiff can show that it supplants a specific item of expense a religious school would have borne....

The plurality's mistaken assumptions explain and underscore its sharp break with the Framers' understanding of establishment and this Court's consistent interpretative course. Under the plurality's regime, little would be left of the right of conscience against compelled support for religion; the more massive the aid the more potent would be the influence of the government on the teaching mission; the more generous the support, the more divisive would be the resentments of those resisting religious support, and those religions without school systems ready to claim their fair share.

[T]here is no mistaking the abandonment of doctrine that would occur if the plurality were to become a majority. It is beyond question that the plurality's notion of evenhandedness neutrality as a practical guarantee of the validity of aid to sectarian schools would be the end of the principle of no aid to the schools' religious mission. And if that were not so obvious it would become so after reflecting on the plurality's thoughts about diversion and about giving attention to the pervasiveness of a school's sectarian teaching.

The plurality is candid in pointing out the extent of actual diversion of Chapter 2 aid to religious use in the case before us, and equally candid in saying it does not matter. To the plurality there is nothing wrong with aiding a school's religious mission; the only question is whether religious teaching obtains its tax support under a formally evenhanded criterion of distribution. The principle of no aid to religious teaching has no independent significance.

And if this were not enough to prove that no aid in religious school aid is dead under the plurality's First Amendment, the point is nailed down in the plurality's attack on the legitimacy of considering a school's pervasively sectarian character when judging whether aid to the school is likely to aid its religious mission. The relevance of this consideration is simply a matter of common sense: where religious indoctrination pervades school activities of children and adolescents, it takes great care to be able to aid the school without supporting the doctrinal effort. This is obvious. The plurality nonetheless condemns any enquiry into the pervasiveness of doctrinal content as a remnant of anti-Catholic bigotry (as if evangelical Protestant schools and Orthodox Jewish yeshivas were never pervasively sectarian), and it equates a refusal to aid religious schools with hostility to religion (as if aid to religious teaching were not opposed in this very case by at least one religious respondent and numerous religious *amici curiae* in a tradition claiming descent from Roger Williams). My concern with these arguments goes not so much to their details as it does to the fact that the plurality's choice to employ imputations of bigotry and irreligion as terms in the Court's debate makes one point clear: that in rejecting the principle of no aid to a school's religious mission the plurality is attacking the most fundamental assumption underlying the Establishment Clause, that government can in fact operate with neutrality in its relation to religion. I believe that it can, and so respectfully dissent.

NOTES AND QUESTIONS

1. *Earlier cases on direct aid.* Earlier cases, decided during the primacy of *Lemon,* generally disallowed the provision of any instructional materials, equipment, or funding that provided generalized support to pervasively sectarian schools or that could be "diverted" to support a pervasively sectarian school's religious mission. *See* Wolman v. Walters, 433 U.S. 229 (1977) (permitting Ohio to provide textbooks, testing services, and diagnostic services to students enrolled in pervasively sectarian K-12 schools, but invalidating on Establishment Clause grounds Ohio's provision of "instructional materials and equipment" and financial support for field trips, because such government assistance "necessarily results in aid to the sectarian school enterprise as a whole"); Meek v. Pittenger, 421 U.S. 349 (1975) (allowing state-supplied "auxiliary services" and textbooks in secular subjects to students in pervasively sectarian K-12 schools, but disallowing the provision of "instructional material and equipment," including audiovisual equipment, maps, and laboratory equipment, to such schools because "[s]ubstantial aid to the educational function of such schools . . . necessarily results in aid to the sectarian school enterprise as a whole").

2. *Defining government neutrality.* The theme of government neutrality has been repeatedly used by the Court over the years to describe the central mandate of the Establishment Clause, but the term *neutrality* seems to have meant very different things to different Justices and commentators. The most prominent early proponent of the neutrality theory of the Establishment Clause was Philip Kurland. His version of neutrality—sometimes referred to as "strict neutrality"—also can be found in Justice Black's famous early description of the Establishment Clause standard in *Everson,* which is quoted earlier in this

chapter. Under the more recent version of "formal neutrality," on the other hand, government programs that provide benefits to religious individuals or organizations would not violate the Establishment Clause as long as they offer the same aid under the same conditions to both religious and nonreligious recipients. Thus, according to the *Mitchell* plurality, the government can provide (noncash) aid directly to private religious schools, as long as the aid is not "impermissibly religious in nature" and the program that authorizes the aid is formally open to secular as well as sectarian schools. It does not matter that all or most of the funds go to religious schools. Nor does it matter, according to the plurality, if the schools are pervasively sectarian in the sense that religion permeates every aspect of the school's curriculum or if the pervasively sectarian schools divert government aid to explicitly religious uses. However, Justice O'Connor's concurrence rather than the plurality controls. Why is that?

3. *"Diversion" as a limit on direct government support.* Justice O'Connor "disagree[s] with the plurality's conclusion that actual diversion of government aid to religious indoctrination is consistent with the Establishment Clause." What other limits on direct government aid does Justice O'Connor list? One thing Justice O'Connor does not disallow is direct aid to pervasively sectarian schools. But won't aid to pervasively sectarian schools always be diverted to explicitly religious uses?

4. *Blaine Amendment.* In 1875, Congress considered but ultimately did not pass an amendment known as the "Blaine Amendment" that would have explicitly barred directing any public funds to religious organizations. However, 37 states have some form of constitutional prohibition on aid to religious education. Supporters of government funding for religious institutions have recently attacked the legacy of the Blaine Amendment as evidence of (to use Justice Thomas's characterization from *Mitchell*) "pervasive hostility to the Catholic Church and to Catholics in general." The history of the state constitutional provisions barring state aid to religious institutions is actually a much more complicated affair. It is true that many state provisions (and their federal analogue) were motivated partly by anti-Catholic bias. But it is not true that state no-aid provisions were exclusively motivated by anti-Catholic animus. As is evident from the Virginia experience in 1785-1786, there is a long history of anti-establishment sentiment in this country.

5. *Neutrality as the only limit on government support of religious education.* Does the simple (and easily satisfied) requirement that all government aid programs be formally neutral adequately protect against whatever concerns about establishment remain in the modern era?

D. VOUCHER PROGRAMS

In Mueller v. Allen, the Court upheld a tax exemption program that extended benefits to parents of students attending private religious schools. In this case the Court relied heavily on the fact that the deductions went to parents who independently decided where to send their children to school. Thus, the Court reasoned, this system of private choice could not be attributable to the government and therefore could not possibly violate the Establishment Clause. In Zelman v. Simmons-Harris, the Court combined this notion of private choice with a theory of formal neutrality and produced the model for the new era of government financing decisions under the Establishment Clause. In this new era, the government is allowed to fund religious institutions (including schools) so long as it allows secular institutions to apply for funds from the same programs and so long as it configures the financing program in a way that funnels the money to religious institutions through parents or other private individuals. In reading these decisions, consider whether these two formal limitations are effective in enforcing the spirit of the First Amendment's prohibition on religious establishments.

MUELLER v. ALLEN

463 U.S. 388 (1983)

Justice REHNQUIST delivered the opinion of the Court.

Minnesota allows taxpayers, in computing their state income tax, to deduct certain expenses incurred in providing for the education of their children. The United States Court of Appeals for the Eighth Circuit held that the Establishment Clause of the First and Fourteenth Amendments was not offended by this arrangement. We now affirm.

Minnesota, like every other state, provides its citizens with free elementary and secondary schooling. It seems to be agreed that about 820,000 students attended this school system in the most recent school year. During the same year, approximately 91,000 elementary and secondary students attended some 500 privately supported schools located in Minnesota, and about 95% of these students attended schools considering themselves to be sectarian.

Minnesota, by a law originally enacted in 1955 and revised in 1976 and again in 1978, permits state taxpayers to claim a deduction from gross income for certain expenses incurred in educating their children. The deduction is limited to actual expenses incurred for the "tuition, textbooks and transportation" of dependents attending elementary or secondary schools. A deduction may not exceed $500 per dependent in grades K through six and $700 per dependent in grades seven through twelve.

A State's decision to defray the cost of educational expenses incurred by parents—regardless of the type of schools their children attend—evidences a purpose that is both secular and understandable. An educated populace is essential to the political and economic health of any community, and a state's efforts to assist parents in meeting the rising cost of educational expenses plainly serves this secular purpose of ensuring that the state's citizenry is well-educated. Similarly, Minnesota, like other states, could conclude that there is a strong public interest in assuring the continued financial health of private schools, both sectarian and non-sectarian. By educating a substantial number of students such schools relieve public schools of a correspondingly great burden—to the benefit of all taxpayers. In addition, private schools may serve as a benchmark for public schools, in a manner analogous to the "TVA yardstick" for private power companies.

We turn therefore to the more difficult but related question whether the Minnesota statute has "the primary effect of advancing the sectarian aims of the nonpublic schools." *Lemon v. Kurtzman*. . . . Most importantly, the deduction is available for educational expenses incurred by all parents, including those whose children attend public schools and those whose children attend non-sectarian private schools or sectarian private schools. Just as in *Widmar v. Vincent*, [*infra* p. 919,] where we concluded that the state's provision of a forum neutrally "open to a broad class of nonreligious as well as religious speakers" does not "confer any imprimatur of State approval," so here: "the provision of benefits to so broad a spectrum of groups is an important index of secular effect."

We also agree with the Court of Appeals that, by channeling whatever assistance it may provide to parochial schools through individual parents, Minnesota has reduced the Establishment Clause objections to which its action is subject. It is true, of course, that financial assistance provided to parents ultimately has an economic effect comparable to that of aid given directly to the schools attended by their children. It is also true, however, that under Minnesota's arrangement public funds become available only as a result of numerous, private choices of individual parents of school-age children. It is noteworthy that all but one of our recent cases invalidating state aid to parochial schools have involved the direct transmission of assistance from the state to the schools themselves. Where, as here, aid to parochial schools is available only as a result of decisions of individual parents no "imprimatur of State approval" can be deemed to have been conferred on any particular religion, or on religion generally.

Petitioners argue that, notwithstanding the facial neutrality of [the tax deduction], in application the statute primarily benefits religious institutions. Petitioners rely, as they did below, on a statistical analysis of the type of persons claiming the tax deduction. They contend that most parents of public school children incur no tuition expenses, and that other [deductible] expenses are negligible in value; moreover, they claim that 96% of the children in private schools in 1978-1979 attended religiously affiliated institutions. Because of all this, they reason, the bulk of deductions will be claimed by parents of children in sectarian schools. Respondents reply that petitioners have failed to consider the impact of deductions for items such as transportation, summer school tuition, tuition paid by parents whose children attended schools outside the school districts in which they resided, rental or purchase costs for a variety of equipment, and tuition for certain types of instruction not ordinarily provided in public schools.

We need not consider these contentions in detail. We would be loath to adopt a rule grounding the constitutionality of a facially neutral law on annual reports reciting the extent to which various classes of private citizens claimed benefits under the law. Such an approach would scarcely provide the certainty that this field stands in need of, nor can we perceive principled standards by which such statistical evidence might be evaluated. Moreover, the fact that private persons fail in a particular year to claim the tax relief to which they are entitled—under a facially neutral statute—should be of little importance in determining the constitutionality of the statute permitting such relief.

Justice MARSHALL, with whom Justice BRENNAN, Justice BLACKMUN, and Justice STEVENS join, dissenting.

That the Minnesota statute makes some small benefit available to all parents cannot alter the fact that the most substantial benefit provided by the statute is available only to those parents who send their children to schools that charge tuition. It is simply undeniable that the single largest expense that may be deducted under the Minnesota statute is tuition. The statute is little more than a subsidy of tuition masquerading as a subsidy of general educational expenses. The other deductible expenses are *de minimis* in comparison to tuition expenses.

Contrary to the majority's suggestion, the bulk of the tax benefits afforded by the Minnesota scheme are enjoyed by parents of parochial school children not because parents of public school children fail to claim deductions to which they are entitled, but because the latter are simply *unable* to claim the largest tax deduction that Minnesota authorizes. Fewer than 100 of more than 900,000 school-age children in Minnesota attend public schools that charge a general tuition. Of the total number of taxpayers who are eligible for the tuition deduction, approximately 96% send their children to religious schools. Parents who send their children to free public schools are simply ineligible to obtain the full benefit of the deduction except in the unlikely event that they buy $700 worth of pencils, notebooks, and bus rides for their school-age children. Yet parents who pay at least $700 in tuition to nonpublic, sectarian schools can claim the full deduction even if they incur no other educational expenses.

In this case, it is undisputed that well over 90% of the children attending tuition-charging schools in Minnesota are enrolled in sectarian schools. History and experience likewise instruct us that any generally available financial assistance for elementary and secondary school tuition expenses mainly will further religious education because the majority of the schools which charge tuition are sectarian. Because Minnesota, like every other State, is committed to providing free public education, tax assistance for tuition payments inevitably redounds to the benefit of nonpublic, sectarian schools and parents who send their children to those schools.

In my view, Minnesota's tax deduction for the cost of textbooks and other instructional materials is also constitutionally infirm. The majority is simply mistaken in concluding that a tax deduction, unlike a tax credit or a direct grant to parents, promotes religious education in a manner that is only "attenuated." A tax deduction has a primary effect that advances religion if it is provided to offset expenditures which are not restricted to the secular activities of parochial schools.

The instructional materials which are subsidized by the Minnesota tax deduction plainly may be used to inculcate religious values and belief. In *Meek v. Pittenger*, 421 U.S., at 366, we held that even the use of "wholly neutral, secular instructional material and equipment" by church-related schools contributes to religious instruction because "'[t]he secular education those schools provide goes hand in hand with the religious mission that is the only reason for the schools' existence.'" It follows that a tax deduction to offset the cost of purchasing instructional materials for use in sectarian schools, like a loan of such materials to parents, "necessarily results in aid to the sectarian school enterprise as a whole" and is therefore a "substantial advancement of religious activity" that "constitutes an impermissible establishment of religion." *Meek*.

For the first time, the Court has upheld financial support for religious schools without any reason at all to assume that the support will be restricted to the secular functions of those schools and will not be used to support religious instruction. This result is flatly at odds with the fundamental principle that a State may provide no financial support whatsoever to promote religion.

ZELMAN, SUPERINTENDENT OF PUBLIC INSTRUCTION OF OHIO v. SIMMONS-HARRIS

536 U.S. 639 (2002)

Chief Justice REHNQUIST delivered the opinion of the Court.

The State of Ohio has established a pilot program designed to provide educational choices to families with children who reside in the Cleveland City School District. The question presented is whether this program offends the Establishment Clause of the United States Constitution. We hold that it does not.

There are more than 75,000 children enrolled in the Cleveland City School District. The majority of these children are from low-income and minority families. Few of these families enjoy the means to send their children to any school other than an inner-city public school. For more than a generation, however, Cleveland's public schools have been among the worst performing public schools in the Nation. In 1995, a Federal District Court declared a crisis of magnitude and placed the entire Cleveland school district under state control. Shortly thereafter, the state auditor found that Cleveland's public schools were in the midst of a crisis that is perhaps unprecedented in the history of American education. Cleveland City School District Performance Audit 21 (Mar. 1996). The district had failed to meet any of the 18 state standards for minimal acceptable performance. Only 1 in 10 ninth graders could pass a basic proficiency examination, and students at all levels performed at a dismal rate compared with students in other Ohio public schools. More than two-thirds of high school students either dropped or failed out before graduation. Of those students who managed to reach their senior year, one of every four still failed to graduate. Of those students who did graduate, few could read, write, or compute at levels comparable to their counterparts in other cities.

It is against this backdrop that Ohio enacted, among other initiatives, its Pilot Project Scholarship Program. The program provides financial assistance to families in any Ohio school district that is or has been under federal court order requiring supervision and operational management of the district by the state superintendent. Cleveland is the only Ohio school district to fall within that category.

The program provides two basic kinds of assistance to parents of children in a covered district. First, the program provides tuition aid for students in kindergarten through third grade, expanding each year through eighth grade, to attend a participating public or private school of their parent's choosing. Second, the program provides tutorial aid for students who choose to remain enrolled in public school.

The tuition aid portion of the program is designed to provide educational choices to parents who reside in a covered district. Any private school, whether religious or nonreligious, may participate in the program and accept program students so long as the school is located within the boundaries of a covered district and meets statewide educational standards. Participating private schools must agree not to discriminate on the basis of race, religion, or ethnic background, or to "advocate or foster unlawful behavior or teach hatred of any person or group on the basis of race, ethnicity, national origin, or religion." Any public school located in a school district adjacent to the covered district may also participate in the program. Adjacent public schools are eligible to receive a $2,250 tuition grant for each program student accepted in addition to the full amount of per-pupil state funding attributable to each additional student. All participating schools, whether public or private, are required to accept students in accordance with rules and procedures established by the state superintendent.

Tuition aid is distributed to parents according to financial need. Families with incomes below 200% of the poverty line are given priority and are eligible to receive 90% of private school tuition up to $2,250. For these lowest-income families, participating private schools may not charge a parental co-payment greater than $250. For all other families, the program pays 75% of tuition costs, up to $1,875, with no co-payment cap. These families receive tuition aid only if the number of available scholarships exceeds the number of low-income children who choose to participate. Where tuition aid is spent depends solely upon where parents who receive tuition aid choose to enroll their child. If parents choose a private school, checks are made payable to the parents who then endorse the checks over to the chosen school.

The program has been in operation within the Cleveland City School District since the 1996-1997 school year. In the 1999-2000 school year, 56 private schools participated in the program, 46 (or 82%) of which had a religious affiliation. None of the public schools in districts adjacent to Cleveland have elected to participate. More than 3,700 students participated in the scholarship program, most of whom (96%) enrolled in religiously affiliated schools. Sixty percent of these students were from families at or below the poverty line. In the 1998-1999 school year, approximately 1,400 Cleveland public school students received tutorial aid. This number was expected to double during the 1999-2000 school year.

There is no dispute that the program challenged here was enacted for the valid secular purpose of providing educational assistance to poor children in a demonstrably failing public school system. Thus, the question presented is whether the Ohio program nonetheless has the forbidden effect of advancing or inhibiting religion.

To answer that question, our decisions have drawn a consistent distinction between government programs that provide aid directly to religious schools, and programs of true private choice, in which government aid reaches religious schools only as a result of the genuine and independent choices of private individuals.

[Our previous cases] make clear that where a government aid program is neutral with respect to religion, and provides assistance directly to a broad class of citizens who, in turn, direct government aid to religious schools wholly as a result of their own genuine and independent private choice, the program is not readily subject to challenge under the Establishment Clause. A program that shares these features permits government aid to reach religious institutions only by way of the deliberate choices of numerous individual recipients. The incidental advancement of a religious mission, or the perceived endorsement of a religious message, is reasonably attributable to the individual recipient, not to the government, whose role ends with the disbursement of benefits.

Respondents suggest that even without a financial incentive for parents to choose a religious school, the program creates a public perception that the State is endorsing religious practices and beliefs. But we have repeatedly recognized that no reasonable observer would think a neutral program of private choice, where state aid reaches religious schools solely as a result of the numerous independent decisions of private individuals, carries with it the *imprimatur* of government endorsement. The argument is particularly misplaced here since the reasonable observer in the endorsement inquiry must be deemed aware of the history and context underlying a challenged program. Any objective observer familiar with the full history and context of the

Ohio program would reasonably view it as one aspect of a broader undertaking to assist poor children in failed schools, not as an endorsement of religious schooling in general.

Justice Souter speculates that because more private religious schools currently participate in the program, the program itself must somehow discourage the participation of private nonreligious schools. But Cleveland's preponderance of religiously affiliated private schools certainly did not arise as a result of the program; it is a phenomenon common to many American cities. Indeed, by all accounts the program has captured a remarkable cross-section of private schools, religious and nonreligious. It is true that 82% of Cleveland's participating private schools are religious schools, but it is also true that 81% of private schools in Ohio are religious schools. To attribute constitutional significance to this figure, moreover, would lead to the absurd result that a neutral school-choice program might be permissible in some parts of Ohio, such as Columbus, where a lower percentage of private schools are religious schools, but not in inner-city Cleveland, where Ohio has deemed such programs most sorely needed, but where the preponderance of religious schools happens to be greater. Cf. Brief for State of Florida et al. as *Amici Curiae* 17 ("[T]he percentages of sectarian to nonsectarian private schools within Florida's 67 school districts vary from zero to 100 percent[.]"). Likewise, an identical private choice program might be constitutional in some States, such as Maine or Utah, where less than 45% of private schools are religious schools, but not in other States, such as Nebraska or Kansas, where over 90% of private schools are religious schools.

Respondents and Justice Souter claim that even if we do not focus on the number of participating schools that are religious schools, we should attach constitutional significance to the fact that 96% of scholarship recipients have enrolled in religious schools. They claim that this alone proves parents lack genuine choice, even if no parent has ever said so. We need not consider this argument in detail, since it was flatly rejected in *Mueller*, where we found it irrelevant that 96% of parents taking deductions for tuition expenses paid tuition at religious schools. Indeed, we have recently found it irrelevant even to the constitutionality of a direct aid program that a vast majority of program benefits went to religious schools. The constitutionality of a neutral educational aid program simply does not turn on whether and why, in a particular area, at a particular time, most private schools are run by religious organizations, or most recipients choose to use the aid at a religious school. As we said in *Mueller*, "[s]uch an approach would scarcely provide the certainty that this field stands in need of, nor can we perceive principled standards by which such statistical evidence might be evaluated."

Justice O'CONNOR, concurring.

These cases are different from prior indirect aid cases in part because a significant portion of the funds appropriated for the voucher program reach religious schools without restrictions on the use of these funds. The share of public resources that reach religious schools is not, however, as significant as respondents suggest. Data from the 1999-2000 school year indicate that 82 percent of schools participating in the voucher program were religious and that 96 percent of participating students enrolled in religious schools, but these data are incomplete. These statistics do not take into account all of the reasonable educational choices that may be available to students in Cleveland public schools. When one considers the option to attend community schools, the percentage of students enrolled in religious schools falls to

62.1 percent. If magnet schools are included in the mix, this percentage falls to 16.5 percent.

Even these numbers do not paint a complete picture. The Cleveland program provides voucher applicants from low-income families with up to $2,250 in tuition assistance and provides the remaining applicants with up to $1,875 in tuition assistance. In contrast, the State provides community schools $4,518 per pupil and magnet schools, on average, $7,097 per pupil. Even if one assumes that all voucher students came from low-income families and that each voucher student used up the entire $2,250 voucher, at most $8.2 million of public funds flowed to religious schools under the voucher program in 1999-2000. Although just over one-half as many students attended community schools as religious private schools on the state fisc, the State spent over $1 million more on students in community schools than on students in religious private schools because per-pupil aid to community schools is more than double the per-pupil aid to private schools under the voucher program. Moreover, the amount spent on religious private schools is minor compared to the $114.8 million the State spent on students in the Cleveland magnet schools.

Although $8.2 million is no small sum, it pales in comparison to the amount of funds that federal, state, and local governments already provide religious institutions. Religious organizations may qualify for exemptions from the federal corporate income tax; the corporate income tax in many States; and property taxes in all 50 States; and clergy qualify for a federal tax break on income used for housing expenses. In addition, the Federal Government provides individuals, corporations, trusts, and estates a tax deduction for charitable contributions to qualified religious groups. Finally, the Federal Government and certain state governments provide tax credits for educational expenses, many of which are spent on education at religious schools.

These tax exemptions, which have "much the same effect as [cash grants] . . . of the amount of tax [avoided]," are just part of the picture. Federal dollars also reach religiously affiliated organizations through public health programs such as Medicare and Medicaid, through educational programs such as the Pell Grant program, and the G.I. Bill of Rights, and through child care programs such as the Child Care and Development Block Grant Program (CCDBG). These programs are well-established parts of our social welfare system, and can be quite substantial.

Against this background, the support that the Cleveland voucher program provides religious institutions is neither substantial nor atypical of existing government programs. While this observation is not intended to justify the Cleveland voucher program under the Establishment Clause, it places in broader perspective alarmist claims about implications of the Cleveland program and the Court's decision in these cases.

Justice STEVENS, dissenting.

Is a law that authorizes the use of public funds to pay for the indoctrination of thousands of grammar school children in particular religious faiths a "law respecting an establishment of religion" within the meaning of the First Amendment? In answering that question, I think we should ignore three factual matters that are discussed at length by my colleagues.

First, the severe educational crisis that confronted the Cleveland City School District when Ohio enacted its voucher program is not a matter that should affect our appraisal of its constitutionality. In the 1999-2000 school year, that program provided relief to less than five percent of the students enrolled in the district's schools. The solution to the disastrous conditions that prevented over 90 percent of the student body from meeting basic proficiency standards obviously required massive improvements unrelated to the voucher program. Of course, the emergency may have given some families a powerful motivation to leave the public school system and accept religious indoctrination that they would otherwise have avoided, but that is not a valid reason for upholding the program.

Second, the wide range of choices that have been made available to students *within the public school system* has no bearing on the question whether the State may pay the tuition for students who wish to reject public education entirely and attend private schools that will provide them with a sectarian education. The fact that the vast majority of the voucher recipients who have entirely rejected public education receive religious indoctrination at state expense does, however, support the claim that the law is one "respecting an establishment of religion." The State may choose to divide up its public schools into a dozen different options and label them magnet schools, community schools, or whatever else it decides to call them, but the State is still required to provide a public education and it is the State's decision to fund private school education over and above its traditional obligation that is at issue in these cases.

Third, the voluntary character of the private choice to prefer a parochial education over an education in the public school system seems to me quite irrelevant to the question whether the government's choice to pay for religious indoctrination is constitutionally permissible. Today, however, the Court seems to have decided that the mere fact that a family that cannot afford a private education wants its children educated in a parochial school is a sufficient justification for this use of public funds.

For the reasons stated by Justice Souter and Justice Breyer, I am convinced that the Court's decision is profoundly misguided. Admittedly, in reaching that conclusion I have been influenced by my understanding of the impact of religious strife on the decisions of our forbears to migrate to this continent, and on the decisions of neighbors in the Balkans, Northern Ireland, and the Middle East to mistrust one another. Whenever we remove a brick from the wall that was designed to separate religion and government, we increase the risk of religious strife and weaken the foundation of our democracy.

Justice SOUTER, with whom Justice STEVENS, Justice GINSBURG, and Justice BREYER join, dissenting.

The Court's majority holds that the Establishment Clause is no bar to Ohio's payment of tuition at private religious elementary and middle schools under a scheme that systematically provides tax money to support the schools' religious missions. The occasion for the legislation thus upheld is the condition of public education in the city of Cleveland. The record indicates that the schools are failing to serve their objective, and the vouchers in issue here are said to be needed to provide adequate alternatives to them. If there were an excuse for giving short shrift to the Establishment Clause, it would probably apply here. But there is no excuse. Constitutional limitations are placed on government to preserve constitutional values in hard cases, like these.

Today, however, the majority holds that the Establishment Clause is not offended by Ohio's Pilot Project Scholarship Program, under which students may be eligible to receive as much as $2,250 in the form of tuition vouchers transferable to religious schools. In the city of Cleveland the overwhelming proportion of large appropriations for voucher money must be spent on religious schools if it is to be spent at all, and will be spent in amounts that cover almost all of tuition. The money will thus pay for eligible students' instruction not only in secular subjects but in religion as well, in schools that can fairly be characterized as founded to teach religious doctrine and to imbue teaching in all subjects with a religious dimension. Public tax money will pay at a systemic level for teaching the covenant with Israel and Mosaic law in Jewish schools, the primacy of the Apostle Peter and the Papacy in Catholic schools, the truth of reformed Christianity in Protestant schools, and the revelation to the Prophet in Muslim schools, to speak only of major religious groupings in the Republic.

How can a Court consistently leave *Everson* on the books and approve the Ohio vouchers? The answer is that it cannot. It is only by ignoring *Everson* that the majority can claim to rest on traditional law in its invocation of neutral aid provisions and private choice to sanction the Ohio law. It is, moreover, only by ignoring the meaning of neutrality and private choice themselves that the majority can even pretend to rest today's decision on those criteria.

II.

A.

Consider first the criterion of neutrality. As recently as two Terms ago, a majority of the Court recognized that neutrality conceived of as evenhandedness toward aid recipients had never been treated as alone sufficient to satisfy the Establishment Clause, *Mitchell*. But at least in its limited significance, formal neutrality seemed to serve some purpose. Today, however, the majority employs the neutrality criterion in a way that renders it impossible to understand.

In order to apply the neutrality test, it makes sense to focus on a category of aid that may be directed to religious as well as secular schools, and ask whether the scheme favors a religious direction. Here, one would ask whether the voucher provisions, allowing for as much as $2,250 toward private school tuition (or a grant to a public school in an adjacent district), were written in a way that skewed the scheme toward benefiting religious schools.

This, however, is not what the majority asks. The majority looks not to the provisions for tuition vouchers, but to every provision for educational opportunity: "The program permits the participation of *all* schools within the district, [as well as public schools in adjacent districts], religious or nonreligious." The majority then finds confirmation that "participation of *all* schools" satisfies neutrality by noting that the better part of total state educational expenditure goes to public schools, thus showing there is no favor of religion.

The illogic is patent. If regular, public schools (which can get no voucher payments) "participate" in a voucher scheme with schools that can, and public expenditure is still predominantly on public schools, then the majority's reasoning would find neutrality in a scheme of vouchers available for private tuition in districts with no secular private schools at all. Neutrality as the majority employs the term is, literally, verbal and nothing more. This, indeed, is the only way the majority can gloss over the very nonneutral feature of the total scheme covering "*all* schools": public tutors may receive from the State no more than $324 per child to support extra tutoring (that is, the State's 90% of a total amount of $360), whereas the tuition voucher schools (which turn out to be mostly religious) can receive up to $2,250.

Why the majority does not simply accept the fact that the challenge here is to the more generous voucher scheme and judge its neutrality in relation to religious use of voucher money seems very odd. It seems odd, that is, until one recognizes that comparable schools for applying the criterion of neutrality are also the comparable schools for applying the other majority criterion, whether the immediate recipients of voucher aid have a genuinely free choice of religious and secular schools to receive the voucher money. And in applying this second criterion, the consideration of "*all* schools" is ostensibly helpful to the majority position.

B.

The majority addresses the issue of choice the same way it addresses neutrality, by asking whether recipients or potential recipients of voucher aid have a choice of public schools among secular alternatives to religious schools. Again, however, the majority asks the wrong question and misapplies the criterion. The majority has confused choice in spending scholarships with choice from the entire menu of possible educational placements, most of them open to anyone willing to attend a public school. I say "confused" because the majority's new use of the choice criterion, which it frames negatively as "whether Ohio is coercing parents into sending their children to religious schools," ignores the reason for having a private choice enquiry in the first place. Cases since *Mueller* have found private choice relevant under a rule that aid to religious schools can be permissible so long as it first passes through the hands of students or parents. The majority's view that all educational choices are comparable for purposes of choice thus ignores the whole point of the choice test: it is a criterion for deciding whether indirect aid to a religious school is legitimate because it passes through private hands that can spend or use the aid in a secular school. The question is whether the private hand is genuinely free to send the money in either a secular direction or a religious one. The majority now has transformed this question about private choice in channeling aid into a question about selecting from examples of state spending (on education) including direct spending on magnet and community public schools that goes through no private hands and could never reach a religious school under any circumstance. When the choice test is transformed from where to spend the money to where to go to school, it is cut loose from its very purpose.

Defining choice as choice in spending the money or channeling the aid is, moreover, necessary if the choice criterion is to function as a limiting principle at all. If "choice" is present whenever there is any educational alternative to the religious school to which vouchers can be endorsed, then there will always be a choice and the voucher can always be constitutional, even in a system in which there is not a single private secular school as an alternative to the religious school. And because it is unlikely that any participating private religious school will enroll more pupils than the generally available public system, it will be easy to generate numbers suggesting that aid to religion is not the significant intent or effect of the voucher scheme.

That is, in fact, just the kind of rhetorical argument that the majority accepts in these cases. In addition to secular private schools (129 students), the majority considers public schools with tuition assistance (roughly 1,400 students), magnet schools (13,000 students), and community schools (1,900 students), and concludes that fewer than 20% of pupils receive state vouchers to attend religious schools. (In fact, the numbers would seem even more favorable to the majority's argument if enrollment in traditional public schools without tutoring were considered, an alternative the majority thinks relevant to the private choice enquiry.) Justice O'Connor focuses on how much money is spent on each educational option and notes that at most $8.2 million is spent on vouchers for students attending religious schools, which is only 6% of the State's expenditure if one includes separate funding for Cleveland's community ($9.4 million) and magnet ($114.8 million) public schools. The variations show how results may shift when a judge can pick and choose the alternatives to use in the comparisons, and they also show what dependably comfortable results the choice criterion will yield if the identification of relevant choices is wide open. If the choice of relevant alternatives is an open one, proponents of voucher aid will always win, because they will always be able to find a "choice" somewhere that will show the bulk of public spending to be secular. The choice enquiry will be diluted to the point that it can screen out nothing, and the result will always be determined by selecting the alternatives to be treated as choices.

If, contrary to the majority, we ask the right question about genuine choice to use the vouchers, the answer shows that something is influencing choices in a way that aims the money in a religious direction: of 56 private schools in the district participating in the voucher program (only 53 of which accepted voucher students in 1999-2000), 46 of them are religious; 96.6% of all voucher recipients go to religious schools, only 3.4% to nonreligious ones. Unfortunately for the majority position, there is no explanation for this that suggests the religious direction results simply from free choices by parents. One answer to these statistics, for example, which would be consistent with the genuine choice claimed to be operating, might be that 96.6% of families choosing to avail themselves of vouchers choose to educate their children in schools of their own religion. This would not, in my view, render the scheme constitutional, but it would speak to the majority's choice criterion. Evidence shows, however, that almost two out of three families using vouchers to send their children to religious schools did not embrace the religion of those schools. The families made it clear they had not chosen the schools because they wished their children to be proselytized in a religion not their own, or in any religion, but because of educational opportunity. . . . There is, in any case, no way to interpret the 96.6% of current voucher money going to religious schools as reflecting a free and genuine choice by the families that apply for vouchers. The 96.6% reflects, instead, the fact that too few nonreligious school desks are available and few but religious schools can afford to accept more than a handful of voucher students. And contrary to the majority's assertion, public schools in adjacent districts hardly have a financial incentive to participate in the Ohio voucher program, and none has. For the overwhelming number of children in the voucher scheme, the only alternative to the public schools is religious. And it is entirely irrelevant that the State did not deliberately design the network of private schools for the sake of channeling money into religious institutions. The criterion is one of genuinely free choice on the part of the private individuals who choose, and a Hobson's choice is not a choice, whatever the reason for being Hobsonian. . . .

Justice BREYER, with whom Justice STEVENS and Justice SOUTER join, dissenting.

The First Amendment begins with a prohibition, that "Congress shall make no law respecting an establishment of religion," and a guarantee, that the government shall not prohibit "the free exercise thereof." These Clauses embody an understanding, reached in the 17th century after decades of religious war, that liberty and social stability demand a religious tolerance that respects the religious views of all citizens, permits those citizens to "worship God in their own way," and allows all families to "teach their children and to form their characters" as they wish. The Clauses reflect the Framers vision of an American Nation free of the religious strife that had long plagued the nations of Europe. Whatever the Framers might have thought about particular 18th century school funding practices, they undeniably intended an interpretation of the Religion Clauses that would implement this basic First Amendment objective.

In part for this reason, the Court's 20th-century Establishment Clause cases—both those limiting the practice of religion in public schools and those limiting the public funding of private religious education—focused directly upon social conflict, potentially created when government becomes involved in religious education.

When it decided these 20th-century Establishment Clause cases, the Court did not deny that an earlier American society might have found a less clear-cut church/state separation compatible with social tranquility. Indeed, historians point out that during the early years of the Republic, American schools—including the first public schools—were Protestant in character. Their students recited Protestant prayers, read the King James version of the Bible, and learned Protestant religious ideals. Those practices may have wrongly discriminated against members of minority religions, but given the small number of such individuals, the teaching of Protestant religions in schools did not threaten serious social conflict.

The 20th-century Court was fully aware, however, that immigration and growth had changed American society dramatically since its early years. By 1850, 1.6 million Catholics lived in America, and by 1900 that number rose to 12 million. There were similar percentage increases in the Jewish population. Not surprisingly, with this increase in numbers, members of non-Protestant religions, particularly Catholics, began to resist the Protestant domination of the public schools. Scholars report that by the mid-19th century religious conflict over matters such as Bible reading grew intense, as Catholics resisted and Protestants fought back to preserve their domination. Dreading Catholic domination, native Protestants terrorized Catholics. In some States "Catholic students suffered beatings or expulsions for refusing to read from the Protestant Bible, and crowds . . . rioted over whether Catholic children could be released from the classroom during Bible reading."

The principle underlying these cases—avoiding religiously based social conflict—remains of great concern. As religiously diverse as America had become when the Court decided its major 20th-century Establishment Clause cases, we are exponentially more diverse today. America boasts more than 55 different religious groups and subgroups with a significant number of members. Major religions include, among others, Protestants, Catholics, Jews, Muslims, Buddhists, Hindus, and Sikhs. And several of these major religions contain different subsidiary sects with different religious beliefs. Newer Christian immigrant groups are "expressing their Christianity in languages, customs, and independent churches that are barely recognizable, and often controversial, for European-ancestry Catholics and Protestants." . . .

In a society as religiously diverse as ours, the Court has recognized that we must rely on the Religion Clauses of the First Amendment to protect against religious strife, particularly when what is at issue is an area as central to religious belief as the shaping, through primary education, of the next generation's minds and spirits.

I concede that the Establishment Clause currently permits States to channel various forms of assistance to religious schools, for example, transportation costs for students, computers, and secular texts.

School voucher programs differ, however, in both *kind* and *degree* from aid programs upheld in the past. They differ in kind because they direct financing to a core function of the church: the teaching of religious truths to young children. For that reason the constitutional demand for "separation" is of particular constitutional concern.

Vouchers also differ in *degree*. The aid programs recently upheld by the Court involved limited amounts of aid to religion. But the majority's analysis here appears to permit a considerable shift of taxpayer dollars from public secular schools to private religious schools. That fact, combined with the use to which these dollars will be put, exacerbates the conflict problem. State aid that takes the form of peripheral secular items, with prohibitions against diversion of funds to religious teaching, holds significantly less potential for social division. In this respect as well, the secular aid upheld in *Mitchell* differs dramatically from the present case.

The Court, in effect, turns the clock back. It adopts, under the name of "neutrality," an interpretation of the Establishment Clause that this Court rejected more than half a century ago. In its view, the parental choice that offers each religious group a kind of equal opportunity to secure government funding overcomes the Establishment Clause concern for social concord. An earlier Court found that "equal opportunity" principle insufficient; it read the Clause as insisting upon greater separation of church and state, at least in respect to primary education. In a society composed of many different religious creeds, I fear that this present departure from the Court's earlier understanding risks creating a form of religiously based conflict potentially harmful to the Nation's social fabric. Because I believe the Establishment Clause was written in part to avoid this kind of conflict, and for reasons set forth by Justice Souter and Justice Stevens, I respectfully dissent.

NOTES AND QUESTIONS

1. *Constitutional requirements for vouchers.* In order to comply with the Establishment Clause, school vouchers must be available on a neutral basis (which is also the case for direct aid), and they must end up at religious institutions as the result of the "genuine and independent choice" of private individuals. Unlike direct aid, voucher aid may be used for religious purposes. What do each of these, "neutrality" and "genuine and independent choice," actually require?

2. *Neutrality.* Does *Zelman* require more than formal neutrality? In other words, as long as the funding program is formally open to any educational institution, does it matter that as a practical matter only religious schools apply for the government funds? When analyzing what percentage of the financial aid is directed to religious as opposed to secular schools, whose analysis is more persuasive, Justice O'Connor's, who considers all educational options, or Justice Souter's, who considers only the voucher program?

3. *Neutrality among religions.* Is Ohio's program neutral in terms of various religions? In other words, does the voucher program favor some religions over others?

4. *Genuine and independent choice.* Justice Souter points out that for most parents, the only alternative to the failing public schools is a religious school. In addition, "almost two out of three families using vouchers to send their children to religious schools did not embrace the religion of those schools." In other words,

most parents chose a private religious school not because of the religious education but in spite of it. Does this affect the genuineness and independence of their choice?

5. *Endorsement.* The majority argues that no reasonable person would conclude that Ohio was endorsing religion in part because "where the tuition aid is spent depends solely upon where parents who receive tuition aid choose to enroll their child." That is, "no reasonable observer would think a neutral program of private choice, where state aid reaches religious schools solely as the result of the numerous independent decisions of private individuals, carries with it the imprimatur of government endorsement." Do you agree?

6. *Conditions on aid.* Private schools that accept voucher money may not discriminate on the basis of race, religion, or ethnic background, nor may they "advocate or foster unlawful behavior or teach hatred of any person or group" on those bases. Participating schools are not barred from discriminating on the basis of sex or sexual orientation or teaching hatred on the basis of sex or sexual orientation. Should schools have to compromise their religious beliefs in order to participate in the voucher program? Should taxpayers have to help fund schools that compromise the nation's commitment to equality?

7. *Memorial and Remonstrance.* If we view these recent disputes over government funding of religion as a replay of the political battle between Patrick Henry and James Madison over religious assessments in Virginia in 1785-1786, then have the latter-day Patrick Henry forces won this round? What are the significant differences (if any) between a modern voucher program that allocates virtually all of its funding to finance religious education and a Virginia-style statute explicitly providing for the funding of religious education? Does the fact that the modern Supreme Court has never come close to enforcing Madison's strict injunction against granting even "three pence" of government money to religious organizations mean that this was always an unrealistic objective? Are the arguments Madison raised in Virginia in 1785 still compelling today, or does the modern political and social context diminish the importance of many of his concerns?

8. *Do voucher programs advance neutrality?* Could supporters of the voucher program argue that a school system with vouchers would actually be more substantively neutral than a school system without vouchers because the vouchers would provide alternatives for religious parents who objected to the secular orientation of the public schools? On the other hand, could opponents of the voucher system argue that vouchers are inherently nonneutral in the sense that they subsidize religious education, thereby encouraging religious belief and practice?

AN EXTENDED NOTE ON STANDING TO CHALLENGE GOVERNMENT FINANCING OF RELIGION

In *Bowen*, the plaintiffs were granted standing to challenge the AFLA based on their status as taxpayers. In general, taxpayer standing has not been recognized as sufficient to establish a case or controversy under Article III's grant of jurisdiction to federal courts. *See* Frothingham v. Mellon, 262 U.S. 447 (1923). In Flast v. Cohen, 392 U.S. 83 (1968), however, the Supreme Court created an exception to this general rule in cases in which plaintiffs were challenging the use of tax funds for religious activities in violation of the Establishment Clause. In *Flast*, the Court held that plaintiffs would be granted standing to pursue a lawsuit in federal court if they could establish a nexus between their taxpayer status and the nature of the claims in the lawsuit:

> The nexus demanded of federal taxpayers has two aspects to it. First, the taxpayer must establish a logical link between that status and the type of legislative enactment attacked. Thus, a taxpayer will be a proper party to allege the unconstitutionality only of exercises of congressional power under the taxing and spending clause of Art. I, 8, of the Constitution. It will not be sufficient to allege an incidental expenditure of tax funds in the administration of an essentially regulatory statute. Secondly, the taxpayer must establish a nexus between that status and the precise nature of the constitutional infringement alleged. Under this requirement, the taxpayer must show that the challenged enactment exceeds specific constitutional limitations imposed upon the exercise of the congressional taxing and spending power and not simply that the enactment is generally beyond the powers delegated to Congress by Art. I, 8. When both nexuses are established, the litigant will have shown a taxpayer's stake in the outcome of the controversy and will be a proper and appropriate party to invoke a federal court's jurisdiction.

The Court noted that claims under the Establishment Clause would satisfy the second taxpayer standing nexus because opposition to the use of tax funds for religious purposes was at the heart of Establishment Clause history.

> Our history vividly illustrates that one of the specific evils feared by those who drafted the Establishment Clause and fought for its adoption was that the taxing and spending power would be used to favor one religion over another or to support religion in general. James Madison, who is generally recognized as the leading architect of the religion clauses of the First Amendment, observed in his famous Memorial and Remonstrance Against Religious Assessments that "the same authority which can force a citizen to contribute three pence only of his property for the support of any one establishment, may force him to conform to any other establishment in all cases whatsoever." Writings of James Madison 183, 186 (Hunt ed. 1901). The concern of Madison and his supporters was quite clearly that religious liberty ultimately would be the victim if government could employ its taxing and spending powers to aid one religion over another or to aid religion in general. The Establishment Clause was designed as a specific bulwark against such potential abuses of governmental power, and that clause of the First Amendment operates as a specific constitutional limitation upon the exercise by Congress of the taxing and spending power conferred by Art. I, 8.

In *Bowen*, the government argued that plaintiffs should not be allowed to raise "as-applied" challenges to particular grants under the AFLA because such claims would really be challenges "to executive action, not to an exercise of congressional authority under the Taxing and Spending Clause." The Court rejected this argument, and granted the plaintiffs taxpayer-standing status to pursue "as-applied" challenges to grants under the statute:

> We do not think that appellees' claim that AFLA funds are being used improperly by individual grantees is any less a challenge to congressional taxing and spending power simply because the funding authorized by Congress has flowed through and been administered by the Secretary. Indeed, *Flast* itself was a suit against the Secretary of HEW, who had been given the authority under the challenged statute

to administer the spending program that Congress had created. In subsequent cases, most notably *Tilton* [*v. Richardson*, 403 U.S. 672 (1971)], we have not questioned the standing of taxpayer plaintiffs to raise Establishment Clause challenges, even when their claims raised questions about the administratively made grants. . . . The AFLA is at heart a program of disbursement of funds pursuant to Congress' taxing and spending powers, and appellees' claims call into question how the funds authorized by Congress are being disbursed pursuant to the AFLA's statutory mandate. In this litigation there is thus a sufficient nexus between the taxpayer's standing as a taxpayer and the congressional exercise of taxing and spending power, notwithstanding the role the Secretary plays in administering the statute.

In recent years, the Court has limited the scope of the Flast v. Cohen taxpayer standing rule, most recently in a decision that seems to retract some of what the Court said in *Bowen*.

The first major limitation of *Flast* occurred before the Court decided *Bowen*. In Valley Forge Christian College v. Americans United for Separation of Church & State, Inc., 454 U.S. 464 (1982), the Court held that *Flast* did not give taxpayers standing to challenge transfers of public property to religious organizations under the Constitution's Property Clause, art. IV, §3, cl. 2. Thus, the Court held that taxpayers had no standing to challenge a decision of the Secretary of Health, Education, and Welfare to convey to a Christian college a 77-acre tract of government-owned land, which was worth approximately $577,500.

The second major limitation of *Flast* was imposed by Hein v. Freedom from Religion Foundation, 551 U.S. 587 (2007), where the Court denied taxpayer standing to a challenge to the actions of executive branch officials in carrying out the Bush Administration's Faith-Based and Community Initiatives program. The plaintiffs in *Hein* challenged specific grants under the Initiative, and also challenged the constitutionality of several conferences held by government officials to encourage religious organizations to participate in the Initiative. The challenges to specific grants were settled at the summary judgment stage of the proceedings in the District Court, and not appealed. With regard to the remaining issue in the lawsuit, the District Court held that the plaintiffs did not have taxpayer standing status to challenge the conferences. The Court of Appeals reversed this holding, and in a split decision the Supreme Court reversed the Court of Appeals.

There is no majority opinion for the Supreme Court in *Hein*. The court split three ways. Three Justices (Chief Justice Roberts, and Justices Alito and Kennedy) ruled that Flast v. Cohen does not apply to lawsuits challenging expenditures of government funds that were not specifically earmarked by Congress. The plurality held that the plaintiffs in *Hein* could not rely on *Flast* because "the expenditures at issue here were not made pursuant to any Act of Congress. Rather, Congress provided general appropriations to the Executive Branch to fund its day-to-day activities. These appropriations did not expressly authorize, direct, or even mention the expenditures of which respondents complain. Those expenditures resulted from executive discretion, not congressional action." The other six Justices rejected the plurality's distinction between executive allocations of generally appropriated funds and specific congressional authorizations of expenditures, but the other six justices split on the viability of *Flast* itself. Justices Scalia and Thomas argued that *Flast* should be overruled. The other four Justices (Souter, Stevens, Breyer, and Ginsburg) dissented. They argued that *Flast* should apply to all expenditures of funds that violate the Establishment Clause, regardless of whether the ultimate determination to allocate funds illegally was made by executive officials or under the specific terms of a statute. The dissenters noted that this had been the Court's practice in cases such as *Bowen*, and concluded that "if the Executive could accomplish through the exercise of discretion exactly what Congress cannot do through legislation, Establishment Clause protection would melt away."

The Supreme Court once again considered the continuing precedential value of *Flast* in Arizona Christian School Tuition Organization v. Winn, 563 U.S. 125 (2011). Writing for a 5-4 majority, Justice Kennedy held that taxpayer standing under *Flast* does not exist to challenge tax expenditures that benefit religiously affiliated schools. Arizona "provides tax credits for contributions to school tuition organizations, or STOs" and the STOs, in turn, "use these contributions to provide scholarships to students attending private schools, many of which are religious." *Id.* at 129. "Respondents are a group of Arizona taxpayers who challenge the STO tax credit as a violation of the First and Fourteenth Amendments." *Id.* The plaintiffs who challenged Arizona's STO program invoked *Flast* to establish standing as taxpayers seeking to litigate an Establishment Clause claim.

Justice Kennedy rejected the application of *Flast* to tax expenditure programs, such as Arizona's STO program, even though he acknowledged that "[i]t is easy to see that tax credits and governmental expenditures can have similar economic consequences, at least for beneficiaries whose tax liability is sufficiently large to take full advantage of the credit. Yet tax credits and governmental expenditures do not both implicate individual taxpayers in sectarian activities." *Id.* at 141-42. The majority found that tax expenditures are less direct and particularized than direct affirmative subsidies to religious organizations using government funds. This "distinction between governmental expeditures and tax credits refutes respondents' assertion of standing" because "[w]hen Arizona taxpayers choose to contribute to STO's, they spend their own money, not money the state has collected from respondents or other taxpayers." *Id.* at 142. Thus, "[t]he STO tax credit is not tantamount to a religious tax or to a tithe and does not visit the injury identified in *Flast.*" *Id.* at 142-43. "It follows that respondents have neither alleged an injury for standing purposes under general rules nor met the *Flast* exception." *Id.*

Justice Scalia, joined by Justice Thomas, wrote a concurring opinion, arguing that *Flast* should be squarely overruled: "*Flast* is an anomaly in our jurisprudence, irreconcilable with the Article III restrictions on federal judicial power that our opinions have established. I would repudiate that misguided decision and enforce the Constitution." *Id.* at 146-47 (Scalia, J., dissenting). Justice Scalia nevertheless joined the "Court's opinion because it finds respondents lack standing by applying *Flast* rather than distinguishing it away on unprincipled grounds." *Id.* at 147.

In dissent, Justice Kagan, joined by Justices Ginsburg, Breyer, and Sotomayor, squarely rejected Justice Kennedy's attempt to distinguish between direct appropriations and tax expenditures for purposes of applying *Flast*:

> This novel distinction in standing law between appropriations and tax expenditures has as little basis in principle as it has in our precedent. Cash grants and targeted tax breaks are means of accomplishing the same government objective—to provide financial support to select individuals or organizations. Taxpayers who oppose state aid of religion have equal reason to protest whether that aid flows from the one form of subsidy or the other. Either way, the government has financed the religious activity. And so either way, taxpayers should be able to challenge the subsidy.

Still worse, the Court's arbitrary distinction threatens to eliminate *all* occasions for a taxpayer to contest the government's monetary support of religion. Precisely because appropriations and tax breaks can achieve identical objectives, the government can easily substitute one for the other. Today's opinion thus enables the government to end-run *Flast*'s guarantee of access to the Judiciary. From now on, the government need follow just one simple rule—subsidize through the tax system—to preclude taxpayer challenges to state funding of religion.

Id. at 148 (Kagan, J., dissenting).

In sum, although at least four current justices favor applying *Flast* broadly to recognize taxpayer standing for both direct and indirect forms of government financial support for religious entities (Justices Ginsburg, Breyer, Sotomayor, and Kagan), for the time being, *Flast* seems limited essentially to its specific facts: taxpayer standing will be available only for challenges to specific congressional or state legislative appropriations that violate the Establishment Clause.

THEORY-APPLIED PROBLEM

You work on a pro bono basis as a lawyer for the Mississippi Chapter of the American Civil Liberties Union (ACLU), based in Jackson, Mississippi. The ACLU's staff director forwards you an e-mail from Ms. Janet Givens, an inmate at the Central Mississippi Correctional Facility (CMCF), in Pearl, Missisisippi, seeking the ACLU's assistance. Ms. Givens was convicted of possession of heroin and sentenced to serve five to seven years in the CMCF. Under the applicable statute and regulations, however, she should be eligible for parole after serving three years of her sentence. The state parole board's regulations provide that "for persons convicted of drug offenses, clear and convincing evidence of successful substance abuse treatment shall be required as a condition of favorable action on an inmate's application for parole." The explanatory notes add: "Normally, evidence of successful substance abuse treatment would include successful completion of a state-approved drug rehabilitation program, such as Narcotics Anonymous or a similarly successful program."

Ms. Givens has served just over two years of her sentence, but she has not yet participated in a state-approved drug rehabilitation program. The only such free program at CMCF is sponsored by a local evangelical church and is called "InnerTruth" (IT). IT offers "freedom from addiction through the healing power of Christ." Unfortunately, Givens is an avowed and somewhat evangelical atheist. However, in order to be eligible for parole, she enrolled in IT. Alas, things did not go very well. At her first IT meeting, she strongly objected to "dragging God's name into this messy business of addictions" and expressed vehement disagreement with the "vengeance obsessed, hypercontrolling, and just plain mean" depiction of Jesus propounded at the session. Givens regards IT's fundamentalist view of Jesus, and God for that matter, as entirely irreconcilable with her own beliefs about free will; more generally, she has found the program's religious content to be profoundly offensive to her personal religious beliefs. Givens subsequently asks CMCF officials to permit her to enroll in a nonsectarian drug abuse treatment program. Responding to this request, the CMCF's chief staff counselor tells Givens that "the budget is real tight at the moment" and that "no funding exists for an alternative program to

InnerTruth." The counselor urges Givens to reconsider participating in IT—at least if she wants to be eligible for early release through parole.

Givens has asked the ACLU to sue the Mississippi Department of Corrections on her behalf, arguing that the state's parole program for convicted drug offenders, at least as currently implemented, violates the Establishment Clause. How do you advise her regarding the merits of her claim? Is Givens likely to prevail? Why or why not? For bonus points: What test will a federal court likely apply to resolve the merits of the Establishment Clause claim?

CHAPTER
19

The Establishment Clause and Public Schools

TABLE OF CONTENTS

Government endorsement of religion can take various forms, ranging from officially sanctioned government prayer, to the use of religious symbols such as crosses on government property, to the granting of special privileges to religious entities. The category of government endorsement cases can be further subdivided into two subcategories: cases involving government endorsement of religion in the public schools, and cases involving government endorsement of religion in the adult world. The school cases should be considered separately from other cases because the Court has consistently recognized that "there are heightened concerns with protecting freedom of conscience from subtle coercive pressure in the elementary and secondary public schools." Lee v. Weisman, 505 U.S. 577, 592 (1992).

Thus, although the Court may say that it applies the same constitutional standard to alleged Establishment Clause violations in every context, that standard may take on additional rigor when the alleged violations take place in public schools. This phenomenon is evident from the basic holdings of the cases excerpted below.

The materials in this chapter start with the Court's school prayer decisions. Note how uncharacteristically uniform the Court's conclusions are in this segment of Establishment Clause jurisprudence. The Supreme Court has issued five full opinions on the subject of school prayer or school Bible reading over a 40-year period, and in every case a large majority of the Court has held the religious exercise unconstitutional. The same consistency is evident in the Court's decisions regarding government attempts to limit on religious grounds the teaching of mainstream science. Once we turn in the next chapter to the Court's decisions regarding religious endorsement outside the public school context, however, this consistency breaks down, and it is often difficult to discern any coherent pattern to the Court's decisions.

A. GOVERNMENT ENDORSEMENT OF RELIGION IN THE PUBLIC SCHOOLS: SCHOOL PRAYER

ENGEL v. VITALE
370 U.S. 421 (1962)

[Public schools in New York directed teachers to lead students in the following prayer, which was composed by the New York Board of Regents:

> Almighty God, we acknowledge our dependence upon Thee, and we beg Thy blessings upon us, our parents, our teachers and our Country.

The New York courts upheld the prayer but also required school systems to accommodate students who objected to the prayer, either by allowing the students to remain silent or excusing them altogether from the religious exercise. Objecting students and parents appealed to the United States Supreme Court, which held the prayer exercise unconstitutional.]

Mr. Justice BLACK delivered the opinion of the Court.

We think that by using its public school system to encourage recitation of the Regents' prayer, the State of New York has adopted a practice wholly inconsistent with the Establishment Clause. There can, of course, be no doubt that New York's program of daily classroom invocation of God's blessings as prescribed in the Regents' prayer is a religious activity. It is a solemn avowal of divine faith and supplication for the blessings of the Almighty. The nature of such a prayer has always been religious, none of the respondents has denied this and the trial court expressly so found.

The petitioners contend among other things that the state laws requiring or permitting use of the Regents' prayer must be struck down as a violation of the Establishment Clause because that prayer was composed by governmental officials as a part of a governmental program to further religious beliefs. For this reason, petitioners argue, the State's use of the Regents' prayer in its public school system breaches the constitutional wall of separation between Church and State. We agree with that contention since we think that the constitutional prohibition against laws respecting an establishment of religion must at least mean that in this country it is no part of the business of government to compose official prayers for any group of the American people to recite as a part of a religious program carried on by government.

. . .

By the time of the adoption of the Constitution, our history shows that there was a widespread awareness among many Americans of the dangers of a union of Church and State. These people knew, some of them from bitter personal experience, that one of the greatest dangers to the freedom of the individual to worship in his own way lay in the Government's placing its official stamp of approval upon one particular kind of prayer or one particular form of religious services. They knew the anguish, hardship and bitter strife that could come when zealous religious groups struggled with one another to obtain the Government's stamp of approval from each King, Queen, or Protector that came to temporary power. The Constitution was intended to avert a part of this danger by leaving the government of this country in the hands of the people rather than in the hands of any monarch. But this safeguard was not enough. Our Founders were no more willing to let the content of their prayers and their privilege of praying whenever they pleased be influenced by the ballot box than they were to let these vital matters of personal conscience depend upon the succession of monarchs. The First Amendment was added to the Constitution to stand as a guarantee that neither the power nor the prestige of the Federal Government would be used to control, support or influence the kinds of prayer the American people can say—that the people's religions must not be subjected to the pressures of government for change each time a new political administration is elected to office. Under that Amendment's prohibition against governmental establishment of religion, as reinforced by the provisions of the Fourteenth Amendment, government in this country, be it state or federal, is without power to prescribe by law any particular form of prayer which is to be used as an official prayer in carrying on any program of governmentally sponsored religious activity.

There can be no doubt that New York's state prayer program officially establishes the religious beliefs embodied in the Regents' prayer. The respondents' argument to the contrary, which is largely based upon the contention that the Regents' prayer is "nondenominational" and the fact that the program, as modified and approved by state courts, does not require all pupils to recite the prayer but permits those who wish to do so to remain silent or be excused from the room, ignores the essential nature of the program's constitutional defects. Neither the fact that the prayer may be denominationally neutral nor the fact that its observance on the part of the students is voluntary can serve to free it from the limitations of the Establishment Clause, as it might from the Free Exercise Clause, of the First Amendment, both of which are operative against the States by virtue of the Fourteenth Amendment. Although these two clauses may in certain instances overlap, they forbid two quite different kinds of governmental encroachment upon religious freedom. The Establishment Clause, unlike the Free Exercise Clause, does not depend upon any showing of direct governmental compulsion and is violated by the enactment of laws which establish an official religion whether those laws operate directly to coerce nonobserving individuals or not. This is not to say, of course, that laws officially prescribing a particular form of religious worship do not involve coercion of such individuals. When the power, prestige and financial support of government is placed behind a particular religious belief, the indirect coercive pressure upon religious minorities to conform to the prevailing officially approved religion is plain. But the purposes underlying the Establishment Clause go much further than that. Its first and most immediate purpose rested on the belief that a union of government and religion tends to destroy government and to degrade religion. The history of governmentally established religion, both in England and in this country, showed that whenever government had allied itself with one particular form of religion, the inevitable result had been that it had incurred the hatred, disrespect and even contempt of those who held contrary beliefs. That same history showed that many people had lost their respect for any religion that had relied upon the support for government to spread its faith. The Establishment Clause thus stands as an expression of principle on the part of the Founders of our Constitution that religion is too personal, too sacred, too holy, to permit its "unhallowed perversion" by a civil magistrate. Another purpose of the Establishment Clause rested upon an awareness of the historical fact that governmentally established religions and religious persecutions go hand in hand. The Founders knew that only a few years after the Book of Common Prayer became the only accepted form of religious services in the established Church of England, an Act of Uniformity was passed to compel all Englishmen to attend those services and to make it a criminal offense to conduct or attend religious gatherings of any other kind—a law which was consistently flouted by dissenting religious groups in England and which contributed to widespread persecutions of people like John Bunyan who persisted in holding "unlawful (religious) meetings . . . to the great disturbance and distraction of the good subjects of this kingdom. . . ." And they knew that similar persecutions had received the sanction of law in several of the colonies in this country soon after the establishment of official religions in those colonies. It was in large part to get completely away from this sort of systematic religious persecution that the Founders brought into being our Nation, our Constitution, and our Bill of Rights with its prohibition against any governmental establishment of religion. The New York laws officially prescribing the Regents' prayer are inconsistent both with the purposes of the Establishment Clause and with the Establishment Clause itself.

It has been argued that to apply the Constitution in such a way as to prohibit state laws respecting an establishment of religious services in public schools is to indicate a hostility toward religion or toward prayer. Nothing, of course, could be more wrong. The history of man is inseparable from the history of religion. And perhaps it is not too much to say that since the beginning of that history many people have devoutly believed that "More things are wrought by prayer than this world dreams of." It was doubtless largely due to men who believed this that there grew up a sentiment that caused men to leave the cross-currents of officially established state religions and religious persecution in Europe and come to this country filled with the hope that they could find a place in which they could pray when they pleased to the God of their faith in the language they chose. And there were men of this same faith in the power of prayer who led the fight for adoption of our Constitution and also for our Bill of Rights with the very guarantees of religious freedom that forbid the sort of governmental activity which New York has attempted here. These men knew that the First Amendment, which tried to put an end to governmental control of religion and of prayer, was not written to destroy either. They knew rather that it was written to quiet well-justified fears which nearly all of them felt arising out of an awareness that governments of the past had shackled men's tongues to make them speak only the religious thoughts that government wanted them to speak and to pray only to the God that government wanted them to pray to. It is neither sacrilegious nor antireligious to say that each separate government in this country should stay out of the business of writing or sanctioning official prayers and leave that purely religious function to the people themselves and to those the people choose to look to for religious guidance.[21]

Mr. Justice STEWART, dissenting.

A local school board in New York has provided that those pupils who wish to do so may join in a brief prayer at the beginning of each school day, acknowledging their dependence upon God and asking His blessing upon them and upon their

---

[21] There is of course nothing in the decision reached here that is inconsistent with the fact that school children and others are officially encouraged to express love for our country by reciting historical documents such as the Declaration of Independence which contain references to the Deity or by singing officially espoused anthems which include the composer's professions of faith in a Supreme Being, or with the fact that there are many manifestations in our public life of belief in God. Such patriotic or ceremonial occasions bear no true resemblance to the unquestioned religious exercise that the State of New York has sponsored in this instance.

parents, their teachers, and their country. The Court today decides that in permitting this brief non-denominational prayer the school board has violated the Constitution of the United States. I think this decision is wrong.

The Court does not hold, nor could it, that New York has interfered with the free exercise of anybody's religion. For the state courts have made clear that those who object to reciting the prayer must be entirely free of any compulsion to do so, including any "embarrassments and pressures." *Cf. West Virginia State Board of Education v. Barnette*, 319 U.S. 624. But the Court says that in permitting school children to say this simple prayer, the New York authorities have established "an official religion."

With all respect, I think the Court has misapplied a great constitutional principle. I cannot see how an "official religion" is established by letting those who want to say a prayer say it. On the contrary, I think that to deny the wish of these school children to join in reciting this prayer is to deny them the opportunity of sharing in the spiritual heritage of our Nation.

The Court's historical review of the quarrels over the Book of Common Prayer in England throws no light for me on the issue before us in this case. England had then and has now an established church. Equally unenlightening, I think, is the history of the early establishment and later rejection of an official church in our own States. For we deal here not with the establishment of a state church, which would, of course, be constitutionally impermissible, but with whether school children who want to begin their day by joining in prayer must be prohibited from doing so. Moreover, I think that the Court's task, in this as in all areas of constitutional adjudication, is not responsibly aided by the uncritical invocation of metaphors like the "wall of separation," a phrase nowhere to be found in the Constitution. What is relevant to the issue here is not the history of an established church in sixteenth century England or in eighteenth century America, but the history of the religious traditions of our people, reflected in countless practices of the institutions and officials of our government.

At the opening of each day's Session of this Court we stand, while one of our officials invokes the protection of God. Since the days of John Marshall our Crier has said, "God save the United States and this Honorable Court." Both the Senate and the House of Representatives open their daily Sessions with prayer. Each of our Presidents, from George Washington to John F. Kennedy, has upon assuming his Office asked the protection and help of God.

Countless similar examples could be listed, but there is no need to belabor the obvious. It was all summed up by this Court just ten years ago in a single sentence: "We are a religious people whose institutions presuppose a Supreme Being." *Zorach v. Clauson*, 343 U.S. 306, 313.

SCHOOL DISTRICT OF ABINGTON TOWNSHIP v. SCHEMPP

374 U.S. 203 (1963)

Mr. Justice CLARK delivered the opinion of the Court.

[A Pennsylvania statute] requires that "At least ten verses from the Holy Bible shall be read, without comment, at the opening of each public school on each school day. Any child shall be excused from such Bible reading, or attending such Bible reading, upon the written request of his parent or guardian." The Schempp family, husband and wife and two of their three children, brought suit to enjoin enforcement of the statute. [The Schempps] are members of the Unitarian Church in Germantown, Philadelphia, Pennsylvania, where they, as well as another son, Ellory, regularly attend religious services.

On each school day at the Abington Senior High School between 8:15 and 8:30 a.m., while the pupils are attending their home rooms or advisory sections, opening exercises are conducted pursuant to the statute. The exercises are broadcast into each room in the school building through an intercommunications system and are conducted under the supervision of a teacher by students attending the school's radio and television workshop. Selected students from this course gather each morning in the school's workshop studio for the exercises, which include readings by one of the students of 10 verses of the Holy Bible, broadcast to each room in the building. This is followed by the recitation of the Lord's Prayer, likewise over the intercommunications system, but also by the students in the various classrooms, who are asked to stand and join in repeating the prayer in unison. The exercises are closed with the flag salute and such pertinent announcements as are of interest to the students. Participation in the opening exercises, as directed by the statute, is voluntary. The student reading the verses from the Bible may select the passages and read from any version he chooses, although the only copies furnished by the school are the King James version, copies of which were circulated to each teacher by the school district. During the period in which the exercises have been conducted the King James, the Douay and the Revised Standard versions of the Bible have been used, as well as the Jewish Holy Scriptures. There are no prefatory statements, no questions asked or solicited, no comments or explanations made and no interpretations given at or during the exercises. The students and parents are advised that the student may absent himself from the classroom or, should he elect to remain, not participate in the exercises.

At the first trial Edward Schempp and the children testified as to specific religious doctrines purveyed by a literal reading of the Bible "which were contrary to the religious beliefs which they held and to their familial teaching." Edward Schempp testified at the second trial that he had considered having Roger and Donna excused from attendance at the exercises but decided against it for several reasons, including his belief that the children's relationships with their teachers and classmates would be adversely affected.

Applying the Establishment Clause principles to the cases at bar we find that the States are requiring the selection and reading at the opening of the school day of verses from the Holy Bible and the recitation of the Lord's Prayer by the students in unison. These exercises are prescribed as part of the curricular activities of students who are required by law to attend school. They are held in the school buildings under the supervision and with the participation of teachers employed in those schools. The trial court has found that such an opening exercise is a religious ceremony and was intended by the State to be so. We agree with the trial court's finding as to the religious character of the exercises. Given that finding, the exercises and the law requiring them are in violation of the Establishment Clause.

[T]he State contends that the program is an effort to extend its benefits to all public school children without regard to their religious belief. Included within its secular purposes, it says, are the promotion of moral values, the contradiction to the materialistic trends of our times, the perpetuation of our institutions and the teaching of literature. The case came up on demurrer, of course, to a petition which alleged that the uniform practice under the rule had been to read from the King James version of the Bible and that the exercise was sectarian. The short answer, therefore, is that the religious character of the exercise was admitted by the State. But even if its purpose is not strictly religious, it is sought to be accomplished through readings, without comment, from the Bible. Surely the place of the Bible as an instrument of religion cannot be gainsaid, and the State's recognition of the pervading religious character of the ceremony is evident from the rule's specific permission of the alternative use of the Catholic Douay version as well as the recent amendment permitting nonattendance at the exercises. None of these factors is consistent with the contention that the Bible is here used either as an instrument for nonreligious moral inspiration or as a reference for the teaching of secular subjects.

It is insisted that unless these religious exercises are permitted a "religion of secularism" is established in the schools. We agree of course that the State may not establish a "religion of secularism" in the sense of affirmatively opposing or showing hostility to religion, thus "preferring those who believe in no religion over those who do believe." We do not agree, however, that this decision in any sense has that effect. In addition, it might well be said that one's education is not complete without a study of comparative religion or the history of religion and its relationship to the advancement of civilization. It certainly may be said that the Bible is worthy of study for its literary and historic qualities. Nothing we have said here indicates that such study of the Bible or of religion, when presented objectively as part of a secular program of education, may not be effected consistently with the First Amendment. But the exercises here do not fall into those categories. They are religious exercises, required by the States in violation of the command of the First Amendment that the Government maintain strict neutrality, neither aiding nor opposing religion.

Mr. Justice BRENNAN, concurring.

The secular purposes which devotional exercises are said to serve fall into two categories—those which depend upon an immediately religious experience shared by the participating children; and those which appear sufficiently divorced from the religious content of the devotional material that they can be served equally by nonreligious materials. With respect to the first objective, much has been written about the moral and spiritual values of infusing some religious influence or instruction into the public school classroom. To the extent that only *religious* materials will serve this purpose, it seems to me that the purpose as well as the means is so plainly religious that the exercise is necessarily forbidden by the Establishment Clause. The fact that purely secular benefits may eventually result does not seem to me to justify the exercises, for similar indirect nonreligious benefits could no doubt have been claimed for the released time program invalidated in [*Illinois ex rel. McCollum v. Board of Education*, 333 U.S. 203 (1948)].

The second justification assumes that religious exercises at the start of the school day may directly serve solely secular ends—for example, by fostering harmony and tolerance among the pupils, enhancing the authority of the teacher, and inspiring better discipline. To the extent that such benefits result not from the content of the readings and recitation, but simply from the holding of such a solemn exercise at the opening assembly or the first class of the day, it would seem that less sensitive materials might equally well serve the same purpose. I have previously suggested that [our earlier precedents] forbid the use of religious means to achieve secular ends where nonreligious means will suffice. That principle is readily applied to these cases. It has not been shown that readings from the speeches and messages of great Americans, for example, or from the documents of our heritage of liberty, daily recitation of the Pledge of Allegiance, or even the observance of a moment of reverent silence at the opening of class, may not adequately serve the solely secular purposes of the devotional activities without jeopardizing either the religious liberties of any members of the community or the proper degree of separation between the spheres of religion and government. Such substitutes would, I think, be unsatisfactory or inadequate only to the extent that the present activities do in fact serve religious goals. While I do not question the judgment of experienced educators that the challenged practices may well achieve valuable secular ends, it seems to me that the State acts unconstitutionally if it either sets about to attain even indirectly religious ends by religious means, or if it uses religious means to serve secular ends where secular means would suffice.

It has been suggested that a tentative solution to these problems may lie in the fashioning of a "common core" of theology tolerable to all creeds but preferential to none. But as one commentator has recently observed, "[h]istory is not encouraging to" those who hope to fashion a "common denominator of religion detached from its manifestation in any organized church." Sutherland, *Establishment According to Engel*, 76 HARV. L. REV. 25, 51 (1962). Thus, the notion of a "common core" litany or supplication offends many deeply devout worshippers who do not find clearly sectarian practices objectionable. Father Gustave Weigel has recently expressed a widely shared view: "The moral code held by each separate religious community can reductively be unified, but the consistent particular believer wants no such reduction." And, as the American Council on Education warned several years ago, "The notion of a common core suggests a watering down of the several faiths to the point where common essentials appear. This might easily lead to a new sect—a public school sect—which would take its place alongside the existing faiths and compete with them." *Engel* is surely authority that nonsectarian religious practices, equally with sectarian exercises, violate the Establishment Clause. Moreover, even if the Establishment Clause were oblivious to nonsectarian religious practices, I think it quite likely that the "common core" approach would be sufficiently objectionable to many groups to be foreclosed by the prohibitions of the Free Exercise Clause.

STONE v. GRAHAM

449 U.S. 39 (1992)

PER CURIAM.

A Kentucky statute requires the posting of a copy of the Ten Commandments, purchased with private contributions, on the wall of each public classroom in the State. Petitioners, claiming that this statute violates the Establishment and Free Exercise Clauses of the First Amendment, sought an injunction against its enforcement. The state trial court upheld the statute, finding that its "avowed purpose" was "secular and not religious," and that the statute would "neither advance nor inhibit any religion or religious group" nor involve the State excessively in religious matters. The Supreme Court of the Commonwealth of Kentucky affirmed by an equally divided court. We reverse.

The Commonwealth insists that the statute in question serves a secular legislative purpose, observing that the legislature required the following notation in small print at the bottom of each display of the Ten Commandments: "The secular application of the Ten Commandments is clearly seen in its adoption as the fundamental legal code of Western Civilization and the Common Law of the United States."

The pre-eminent purpose for posting the Ten Commandments on schoolroom walls is plainly religious in nature. The Ten Commandments are undeniably a sacred text in the Jewish and Christian faiths, and no legislative recitation of a supposed secular purpose can blind us to that fact. The Commandments do not confine themselves to arguably secular matters, such as honoring one's parents, killing or murder, adultery, stealing, false witness, and covetousness. *See* Exodus 20: 12-17; Deuteronomy 5: 16-21. Rather, the first part of the Commandments concerns the religious duties of believers: worshipping the Lord God alone, avoiding idolatry, not using the Lord's name in vain, and observing the Sabbath Day. See Exodus 20: 1-11; Deuteronomy 5: 6-15.

This is not a case in which the Ten Commandments are integrated into the school curriculum, where the Bible may constitutionally be used in an appropriate study of history, civilization, ethics, comparative religion, or the like. Posting of religious texts on the wall serves no such educational function. If the posted copies of the Ten Commandments are to have any effect at all, it will be to induce the schoolchildren to read, meditate upon, perhaps to venerate and obey, the Commandments. However desirable this might be as a matter of private devotion, it is not a permissible state objective under the Establishment Clause.

It does not matter that the posted copies of the Ten Commandments are financed by voluntary private contributions, for the mere posting of the copies under the auspices of the legislature provides the "official support of the State... Government" that the Establishment Clause prohibits. Nor is it significant that the Bible verses involved in this case are merely posted on the wall, rather than read aloud as in *Schempp* and *Engel*, for "it is no defense to urge that the religious practices here may be relatively minor encroachments on the First Amendment."

NOTES AND QUESTIONS

1. *Religious purpose.* Does the state always have a religious purpose when it sponsors prayers or posts the Ten Commandments, both of which are inherently religious texts? What about Justice Brennan's argument that the government's true goals are religious when "it uses religious means to serve secular ends when secular means would suffice." Do you agree? If so, may the government ever use religious symbols?

2. *Religion not completely barred.* Americans often misunderstand the Establishment Clause limits on religion in school. One poll showed that 23% thought that public school teachers cannot read from the Bible as an example of literature. Pew Research Center, U.S. Religious Knowledge Survey (2010). *Abington*, however, notes that "Nothing we have said here indicates that such study of the Bible or of religion, when presented objectively as part of a secular program of education" is unconstitutional. Stone v. Graham reiterates this sentiment, noting that "the Bible may be constitutionally used in an appropriate study of history, civilization, ethics, comparative religion, or the like."

3. *Coercion. Engel* is the first of many cases to hold that coercion is sufficient but not necessary for an Establishment Clause violation. Assuming every child were a willing and eager participant, in what way(s) would school-sponsored prayers still violate the Establishment Clause?

4. *Prayers as indirectly coercive.   Engel* also concludes that, even though participation was optional, the recitation of the Regent's Prayer exerted "indirect

coercive pressure" on students. What form does that pressure take? Is it fair to attribute that pressure to the government? Why did Schempp in *Abington* have his children participate in the religious exercises despite the fact that those exercises clashed with the family's religious beliefs?

5. *Hostility to religion?* Does barring school-sponsored recitation of the Regent's prayer or the Lord's Prayer indicate hostility to religion? Does it not favor nonreligion over religion, and endorse "a religion of secularism"? What might a devout Buddhist say? What type of prayer would avoid the problem of favoring some religions over others?

AN EXTENDED NOTE ON THE CONSTITUTIONAL STATUS OF "MOMENT OF SILENCE" REQUIREMENTS IN THE PUBLIC SCHOOLS

Both *Engel* and *Schempp* involved spoken and explicitly religious exercises in the public school classroom. In *Engel*, the state actually wrote the prayer; in *Schempp*, students chose the prayers, but the state assembled the captive audience of students to listen to the prayers. What would be the result, however, if the state did nothing more than assemble the students in a classroom and require them to remain silent for a brief period, during which many of the students individually decided to pray? In Wallace v. Jaffree, 472 U.S. 38 (1985), the Supreme Court struck down an Alabama statute that authorized teachers in public school classrooms to announce "that a period of silence not to exceed one minute in duration shall be observed for meditation or voluntary prayer." The ground for the Court's decision, however, was fairly narrow. The Court ruled that the Alabama Legislature passed the statute in question with impermissible religious motives, thereby violating the first part of the three-part *Lemon* test, which requires that all statutes must have a secular purpose. When Alabama passed the statute in question, it already had on its books another statute requiring that in every public school classroom "a period of silence, not to exceed one minute in duration, shall be observed for meditation." (This earlier statute was not challenged by the plaintiffs in *Wallace*, and the Court did not rule on its constitutionality.) The Court held that the only plausible reason the legislature passed a second statute requiring a moment of silent meditation and mentioning "voluntary prayer" was "for the sole purpose of expressing the State's endorsement of prayer activities for one minute at the beginning of each school day."

The open question after *Wallace* is whether a "clean" silent meditation statute—that is, one that did not implicitly or explicitly endorse prayer—would pass constitutional muster. In her concurring opinion to *Wallace*, Justice O'Connor asserted that it would:

> A state-sponsored moment of silence in the public schools is different from state-sponsored vocal prayer or Bible reading. First, a moment of silence is not inherently religious. Silence, unlike prayer or Bible reading, need not be associated with a religious exercise. Second, a pupil who participates in a moment of silence need not compromise his or her beliefs. During a moment of silence, a student who objects to prayer is left to his or her own thoughts, and is not compelled to listen to the prayers or thoughts of others. For these simple reasons, a moment of silence statute does not stand or fall under the Establishment Clause according to how the Court regards vocal prayer or Bible reading. . . . It is difficult to discern a serious threat to religious liberty from a room of silent, thoughtful schoolchildren.

The lower courts that have considered the matter have tended to agree with Justice O'Connor's assessment. *See* Brown v. Gilmore, 258 F.3d 265 (4th Cir.), *cert. denied*, 534 U.S. 996 (2001) (upholding a Virginia statute mandating a "minute of silence" in the state's public schools); Bown v. Gwinnett County Sch. Dist., 112 F.3d 1464 (11th Cir. 1997) (upholding a Georgia state statute requiring one minute of silent reflection in the state's public school classrooms). *But see* May v. Cooperman, 780 F.2d 240 (3d Cir. 1985) (holding that a New Jersey statute requiring students in public schools to observe a one-minute period of silence at the beginning of each school day lacked a secular purpose and was therefore unconstitutional). *See also* Holloman v. Harland, 370 F.3d 1252 (11th Cir. 2004) (holding unconstitutional an individual public school teacher's practice of enforcing a moment of silence at the beginning of the school day and soliciting prayer requests from students as a means of indicating that the moment of silence was regarded as a religious activity).

In the absence of "smoking gun" evidence that a state legislature or local school board has adopted a moment of silence policy to encourage or facilitate school prayer, should this practice be deemed invalid on Establishment Clause grounds? Or is the Establishment Clause objection primarily related to the practice of organized, official religious observances in the public schools? For one perspective, see Eric J. Segall, *Mired in the* Marsh: *Legislative Prayers, Moments of Silence, and the Establishment Clause*, 63 U. Miami L. Rev. 713, 738 (2009) (arguing that "starting each day with a moment of silent reflection allows each person to use that time in a way that most benefits his or her conscience without infringing on the rights of others" and that "unlike the case with school prayer, even if the intent behind the moment is to encourage prayer, as long as there was no direct coercion, there probably would not be a constitutional violation").

On the other hand, could a public school district purport to ban all voluntary prayer or religious observances on school property? Would such a policy be consistent with general free speech principles? Moreover, what bearing might the Free Exercise Clause, addressed *supra* in Chapter 14, have on this question? Do these considerations suggest that a moment of silence—without the presence of organized prayer by school officials or teachers—should be no more objectionable than recess periods, lunch breaks, and study halls (that is, times during the school day when students presumably can and sometimes do pray)? Or is a moment of silence clearly distinguishable, on its face, from a recess period, a lunch break, or a study hall?

LEE v. WEISMAN

505 U.S. 577 (1992)

Justice KENNEDY delivered the opinion of the Court.

School principals in the public school system of the city of Providence, Rhode Island, are permitted to invite members of the clergy to offer invocation and benediction prayers as part of the formal graduation ceremonies for middle schools and for high schools. The question before us is whether including clerical members who offer prayers as part of the official school graduation ceremony is consistent with the Religion Clauses of the First Amendment, provisions the Fourteenth Amendment makes applicable with full force to the States and their school districts.

Deborah Weisman graduated from Nathan Bishop Middle School, a public school in Providence, at a formal ceremony in June 1989. She was about 14 years old. For many years it has been the policy of the Providence School Committee and the Superintendent of Schools to permit principals to invite members of the clergy to give invocations and benedictions at middle school and high school graduations.

It has been the custom of Providence school officials to provide invited clergy with a pamphlet entitled "Guidelines for Civic Occasions," prepared by the National Conference of Christians and Jews. The Guidelines recommend that public prayers at nonsectarian civic ceremonies be composed with "inclusiveness and sensitivity." . . . The principal gave Rabbi Gutterman the pamphlet before the graduation and advised him the invocation and benediction should be nonsectarian. Agreed Statement of Facts ¶ 17, *id.*, at 13. . . .

. . . It is beyond dispute that, at a minimum, the Constitution guarantees that government may not coerce anyone to support or participate in religion or its exercise, or otherwise act in a way which "establishes a [state] religion or religious faith, or tends to do so." *Lynch, supra,* at 678. The State's involvement in the school prayers challenged today violates these central principles.

That involvement is as troubling as it is undenied. A school official, the principal, decided that an invocation and a benediction should be given; this is a choice attributable to the State, and from a constitutional perspective it is as if a state statute decreed that the prayers must occur. The principal chose the religious participant, here a rabbi, and that choice is also attributable to the State.

The State's role did not end with the decision to include a prayer and with the choice of a clergyman. Principal Lee provided Rabbi Gutterman with a copy of the "Guidelines for Civic Occasions," and advised him that his prayers should be nonsectarian. Through these means the principal directed and controlled the content of the prayers. Even if the only sanction for ignoring the instructions were that the rabbi would not be invited back, we think no religious representative who valued his or her continued reputation and effectiveness in the community would incur the State's displeasure in this regard. It is a cornerstone principle of our Establishment Clause jurisprudence that "it is no part of the business of government to compose official prayers for any group of the American people to recite as a part of a religious program carried on by government," *Engel v. Vitale,* 370 U.S. 421, 425 (1962), and that is what the school officials attempted to do.

Petitioners argue, and we find nothing in the case to refute it, that the directions for the content of the prayers were a good-faith attempt by the school to ensure that the sectarianism which is so often the flashpoint for religious animosity be removed from the graduation ceremony.

It must not be forgotten then, that while concern must be given to define the protection granted to an objector or a dissenting nonbeliever, these same Clauses exist to protect religion from government interference. James Madison, the principal author of the Bill of Rights, did not rest his opposition to a religious establishment on the sole ground of its effect on the minority. A principal ground for his view was: "[E]xperience witnesseth that ecclesiastical establishments, instead of maintaining the purity and efficacy of Religion, have had a contrary operation." Memorial and Remonstrance Against Religious Assessments (1785).

. . . The degree of school involvement here made it clear that the graduation prayers bore the imprint of the State and thus put school-age children who objected in an untenable position. We turn our attention now to consider the position of the students, both those who desired the prayer and she who did not. . . .

The lessons of the First Amendment are as urgent in the modern world as in the 18th century when it was written. One timeless lesson is that if citizens are subjected to state-sponsored religious exercises, the State disavows its own duty to guard and respect that sphere of inviolable conscience and belief which is the mark of a free people. To compromise that principle today would be to deny our own tradition and forfeit our standing to urge others to secure the protections of that tradition for themselves.

As we have observed before, there are heightened concerns with protecting freedom of conscience from subtle coercive pressure in the elementary and secondary public schools. Our decisions in *Engel v. Vitale*, 370 U.S. 421 (1962), and *School Dist. of Abington, supra,* recognize, among other things, that prayer exercises in public schools carry a particular risk of indirect coercion. The concern may not be limited to the context of schools, but it is most pronounced there. What to most believers may seem nothing more than a reasonable request that the nonbeliever respect their religious practices, in a school context may appear to the nonbeliever or dissenter to be an attempt to employ the machinery of the State to enforce a religious orthodoxy.

We need not look beyond the circumstances of this case to see the phenomenon at work. The undeniable fact is that the school district's supervision and control of a high school graduation ceremony places public pressure, as well as peer pressure, on attending students to stand as a group or, at least, maintain respectful silence during the invocation and benediction. This pressure, though subtle and indirect, can be as real as any overt compulsion. Of course, in our culture standing or remaining silent can signify adherence to a view or simple respect for the views of others. And no doubt some persons who have no desire to join a prayer have little objection to standing as a sign of respect for those who do. But for the dissenter of high school age, who has a reasonable perception that she is being forced by the State to pray in a manner her conscience will not allow, the injury is no less real. There can be no doubt that for many, if not most, of the students at the graduation, the act of standing or remaining silent was an expression of participation in the rabbi's prayer. That was the very point of the religious exercise. It is of little comfort to a dissenter, then, to be told that for her the act of standing or remaining in silence signifies mere respect, rather than participation. What matters is that, given our social conventions, a reasonable dissenter in this milieu could believe that the group exercise signified her own participation or approval of it.

Finding no violation under these circumstances would place objectors in the dilemma of participating, with all that implies, or protesting. We do not address whether that choice is acceptable if the affected citizens are mature adults, but we think the State may not, consistent with the Establishment Clause, place primary and secondary school children in this position. Research in psychology supports the common assumption that adolescents are often susceptible to pressure from their peers towards conformity, and that the influence is strongest in matters of social convention. To recognize that the choice imposed by the State constitutes an unacceptable constraint only acknowledges that the government may no more use social pressure to enforce orthodoxy than it may use more direct means.

The injury caused by the government's action, and the reason why Daniel and Deborah Weisman object to it, is that the State, in a school setting, in effect required participation in a religious exercise. It is, we concede, a brief exercise during which the individual can concentrate on joining its message, meditate on her own religion, or let her mind wander. But the embarrassment and the intrusion of the religious exercise cannot be refuted by arguing that these prayers, and similar ones to be said in the future, are of a *de minimis* character. To do so would be an affront to the rabbi who offered them and to all those for whom the prayers were an essential and profound recognition of divine authority. And for the same reason, we think that the intrusion is greater than the two minutes or so of time consumed for prayers like these. Assuming, as we must, that the prayers were offensive to the student and the parent who now object, the intrusion was both real and, in the context of a secondary school, a violation of the objectors' rights. That the intrusion was in the course of promulgating religion that sought to be civic or nonsectarian rather than pertaining to one sect does not lessen the offense or isolation to the objectors. At best it narrows their number, at worst increases their sense of isolation and affront. See *supra,* at 2658.

There was a stipulation in the District Court that attendance at graduation and promotional ceremonies is voluntary. Petitioners and the United States, as *amicus,* made this a center point of the case, arguing that the option of not attending the graduation excuses any inducement or coercion in the ceremony itself. The argument lacks all persuasion. Law reaches past formalism. And to say a teenage student has a real choice not to attend her high school graduation is formalistic in the extreme. True, Deborah could elect not to attend commencement without renouncing her diploma; but we shall not allow the case to turn on this point. Everyone knows that in our society and in our culture high school graduation is one of life's most significant occasions. . . .

The importance of the event is the point the school district and the United States rely upon to argue that a formal prayer ought to be permitted, but it becomes one of the principal reasons why their argument must fail. Their contention, one of considerable force were it not for the constitutional constraints applied to state action, is that the prayers are an essential part of these ceremonies because for many persons an occasion of this significance lacks meaning if there is no recognition, however brief, that human achievements cannot be understood apart from their spiritual essence. We think the Government's position that this interest suffices to force students to choose between compliance or forfeiture demonstrates fundamental inconsistency in its argumentation. It fails to acknowledge that what for many of Deborah's classmates and their parents was a spiritual imperative was for Daniel and Deborah Weisman religious conformance compelled by the State. While in some societies the wishes of the majority might prevail, the Establishment Clause of the First Amendment is addressed to this contingency and rejects the balance urged upon us. The Constitution forbids the State to exact religious conformity from a student as the price of attending her own high school graduation. This is the calculus the Constitution commands. . . . It is a tenet of the First Amendment that the State cannot require one of its citizens to forfeit his or her rights and benefits as the price of resisting conformance to state-sponsored religious practice. . . .

We do not hold that every state action implicating religion is invalid if one or a few citizens find it offensive. People may take offense at all manner of religious as well as nonreligious messages, but offense alone does not in every case show a violation. We know too that sometimes to endure social isolation or even anger may be the price of conscience or nonconformity. But, by any reading of our cases, the conformity required of the student in this case was too high an exaction to withstand the test of the Establishment Clause. The prayer exercises in this case are especially improper because the State has in every practical sense compelled attendance and participation in an explicit religious exercise at an event of singular importance to every student, one the objecting student had no real alternative to avoid.

For the reasons we have stated, the judgment of the Court of Appeals is

Affirmed.

Justice BLACKMUN, with whom Justices STEVENS and O'CONNOR join, concurring.

[I]t is not enough that the government restrain from compelling religious practices: It must not engage in them either. The Court repeatedly has recognized that a violation of the Establishment Clause is not predicated on coercion. The Establishment Clause proscribes public schools from "conveying or attempting to convey a message that religion or a particular religious belief is favored or preferred," even if the schools do not actually "impos[e] pressure upon a student to participate in a religious activity."

When the government puts its imprimatur on a particular religion, it conveys a message of exclusion to all those who do not adhere to the favored beliefs. A government cannot be premised on the belief that all persons are created equal when it asserts that God prefers some.

Justice SOUTER, with whom Justice STEVENS and O'CONNOR join, concurring.

Over the years, this Court has declared the invalidity of many noncoercive state laws and practices conveying a message of religious endorsement. For example, in *County of Allegheny, supra,* we forbade the prominent display of a nativity scene on public property; without contesting the dissent's observation that the crèche coerced no one into accepting or supporting whatever message it proclaimed, five Members of the Court found its display unconstitutional as a state endorsement of Christianity. Likewise, in *Wallace v. Jaffree,* 472 U.S. 38 (1985), we struck down a state law requiring a moment of silence in public classrooms not because the statute coerced students to participate in prayer (for it did not), but because the manner of its enactment "convey[ed] a message of state approval of prayer activities in the public schools." *Id.,* at 61. In *Epperson v. Arkansas,* 393 U.S. 97 (1968), we invalidated a state law that barred the teaching of Darwin's theory of evolution because, even though the statute obviously did not coerce anyone to support religion or participate in any religious practice, it was enacted for a singularly religious purpose. See also *Edwards v. Aguillard,* 482 U.S. 578, 593 (1987). Our precedents may not always have drawn perfectly straight lines. They simply cannot, however, support the position that a showing of coercion is necessary to a successful Establishment Clause claim.

 . . . While petitioners insist that the prohibition extends only to the "coercive" features and incidents of establishment, they cannot easily square that claim with the constitutional text. The First Amendment forbids not just laws "respecting an establishment of religion," but also those "prohibiting the free exercise thereof." Yet laws that coerce nonadherents to "support or participate in any religion or its exercise," would virtually by definition violate their right to religious free exercise. Thus, a literal application of the coercion test would render the Establishment Clause a virtual nullity.

Justice SCALIA, with whom THE CHIEF JUSTICE, Justice WHITE, and Justice THOMAS, join, dissenting.

In holding that the Establishment Clause prohibits invocations and benedictions at public-school graduation ceremonies, the Court—with nary a mention that it is doing so—lays waste a tradition that is as old as public-school graduation ceremonies themselves, and that is a component of an even more longstanding American tradition of nonsectarian prayer to God at public celebrations generally. As its instrument of destruction, the bulldozer of its social engineering, the Court invents a boundless, and boundlessly manipulable, test of psychological coercion. Today's opinion shows more forcefully than volumes of argumentation why our Nation's protection, that fortress which is our Constitution, cannot possibly rest upon the changeable philosophical predilections of the Justices of this Court, but must have deep foundations in the historic practices of our people.

The Court presumably would separate graduation invocations and benedictions from other instances of public "preservation and transmission of religious beliefs" on the ground that they involve "psychological coercion." I find it a sufficient embarrassment that our Establishment Clause jurisprudence regarding holiday displays, see *County of Allegheny,* has come to "requir[e] scrutiny more commonly associated with interior decorators than with the judiciary." *American Jewish Congress* v. *Chicago,* 827 F.2d 120, 129 (CA7 1987) (Easterbrook, J., dissenting). But interior decorating is a rock-hard science compared to psychology practiced by amateurs. A few citations of "[r]esearch in psychology" that have no particular bearing upon the precise issue here cannot disguise the fact that the Court has gone beyond the realm where judges know what they are doing. The Court's argument that state officials have "coerced" students to take part in the invocation and benediction at graduation ceremonies is, not to put too fine a point on it, incoherent.

The Court declares that students' "attendance and participation in the [invocation and benediction] are in a fair and real sense obligatory." But what exactly is this "fair and real sense"? According to the Court, students at graduation who want "to avoid the fact or appearance of participation" in the invocation and benediction are *psychologically* obligated by "public pressure, as well as peer pressure. . . . to stand as a group or, at least, maintain respectful silence" during those prayers. This assertion—*the very linchpin of the Court's opinion—* is almost as intriguing for what it does not say as for what it says. It does not say, for example, that students are psychologically coerced to bow their heads, place their hands in a Dürer-like prayer position, pay attention to the prayers, utter "Amen," or in fact pray. (Perhaps further intensive psychological research remains to be done on these matters.) It claims only that students are psychologically coerced "to stand . . . *or,* at least, maintain respectful silence." . . .

The deeper flaw in the Court's opinion does not lie in its wrong answer to the question whether there was state-induced "peer-pressure" coercion; it lies, rather, in the Court's making violation of the Establishment Clause hinge on such a precious question. The coercion that was a hallmark of historical establishments of religion was coercion of religious orthodoxy and of financial support *by force of law and threat of penalty.* Typically, attendance at the state church was required; only clergy of the official church could lawfully perform sacraments; and dissenters, if tolerated, faced an array of civil disabilities. Thus, for example, in the Colony of Virginia, where the Church of England had been established, ministers were required by law to conform to the doctrine and rites of the Church of England; and all persons were required to attend church and observe the Sabbath, were tithed for the public support of Anglican ministers, and were taxed for the costs of building and repairing churches.

The Establishment Clause was adopted to prohibit such an establishment of religion at the federal level (and to protect state establishments of religion from federal interference). I will further acknowledge for the sake of argument that, as some scholars have argued, by 1790 the term "establishment" had acquired an additional meaning—"financial support of religion generally, by public taxation"—

that reflected the development of "general or multiple" establishments, not limited to a single church. But that would still be an establishment coerced *by force of law*. And I will further concede that our constitutional tradition, from the Declaration of Independence and the first inaugural address of Washington, quoted earlier, down to the present day, has, with a few aberrations, ruled out of order government-sponsored endorsement of religion—even when no legal coercion is present, and indeed even when no ersatz, "peer-pressure" psycho-coercion is present—where the endorsement is sectarian, in the sense of specifying details upon which men and women who believe in a benevolent, omnipotent Creator and Ruler of the world are known to differ (for example, the divinity of Christ). But there is simply no support for the proposition that the officially sponsored nondenominational invocation and benediction read by Rabbi Gutterman—with no one legally coerced to recite them— violated the Constitution of the United States. To the contrary, they are so characteristically American they could have come from the pen of George Washington or Abraham Lincoln himself.

The reader has been told much in this case about the personal interest of Mr. Weisman and his daughter, and very little about the personal interests on the other side. They are not inconsequential. Church and state would not be such a difficult subject if religion were, as the Court apparently thinks it to be, some purely personal avocation that can be indulged entirely in secret, like pornography, in the privacy of one's room. For most believers it is *not* that, and has never been. Religious men and women of almost all denominations have felt it necessary to acknowledge and beseech the blessing of God as a people, and not just as individuals, because they believe in the "protection of divine Providence," as the Declaration of Independence put it, not just for individuals but for societies; because they believe God to be, as Washington's first Thanksgiving Proclamation put it, the "Great Lord and Ruler of Nations." One can believe in the effectiveness of such public worship, or one can deprecate and deride it. But the longstanding American tradition of prayer at official ceremonies displays with unmistakable clarity that the Establishment Clause does not forbid the government to accommodate it.

The narrow context of the present case involves a community's celebration of one of the milestones in its young citizens' lives, and it is a bold step for this Court to seek to banish from that occasion, and from thousands of similar celebrations throughout this land, the expression of gratitude to God that a majority of the community wishes to make. The issue before us today is not the abstract philosophical question whether the alternative of frustrating this desire of a religious majority is to be preferred over the alternative of imposing "psychological coercion," or a feeling of exclusion, upon nonbelievers. Rather, the question is *whether a mandatory choice in favor of the former has been imposed by the United States Constitution*. As the age-old practices of our people show, the answer to that question is not at all in doubt.

I must add one final observation: The Founders of our Republic knew the fearsome potential of sectarian religious belief to generate civil dissension and civil strife. And they also knew that nothing, absolutely nothing, is so inclined to foster among religious believers of various faiths a toleration—no, an affection—for one another than voluntarily joining in prayer together, to the God whom they all worship and seek. Needless to say, no one should be compelled to do that, but it is a shame to deprive our public culture of the opportunity, and indeed the encouragement, for people to do it voluntarily. The Baptist or Catholic who heard and joined in the simple and inspiring prayers of Rabbi Gutterman on this official and patriotic occasion was inoculated from religious bigotry and prejudice in a manner that cannot be replicated. To deprive our society of that important unifying mechanism, in order to spare the nonbeliever what seems to me the minimal inconvenience of standing or even sitting in respectful nonparticipation, is as senseless in policy as it is unsupported in law.

For the foregoing reasons, I dissent.

SANTA FE INDEPENDENT SCHOOL DISTRICT v. DOE
530 U.S. 290 (2000)

Justice STEVENS delivered the opinion of the Court.

[Prior to 1995, the Santa Fe High School student who occupied the school's elective office of student council chaplain delivered a prayer over the public address system before each varsity football game for the entire season. This practice, along with others, was challenged in District Court as a violation of the Establishment Clause of the First Amendment. Because of their fear of retaliation, the plaintiffs sued under a "John Doe" pseudonym. (This practice is not uncommon in Establishment Clause cases, and is discussed in more detail in the notes after this case.) While proceedings against the original prayer policy were pending in the District Court, the school district adopted a different policy that permitted, but did not require, prayer initiated and led by a student at all home games. The District Court entered an order modifying that policy to permit only nonsectarian, nonproselytizing prayer. The Court of Appeals held that, even as modified by the District Court, the football prayer policy was invalid.]

We granted the District's petition for certiorari, limited to the following question: "Whether petitioner's policy permitting student-led, student-initiated prayer at football games violates the Establishment Clause." We conclude, as did the Court of Appeals, that it does. . . .

The actual or perceived endorsement of the message . . . is established by factors beyond just the text of the policy. Once the student speaker is selected and the message composed, the invocation is then delivered to a large audience assembled as part of a regularly scheduled, school-sponsored function conducted on school property. The message is broadcast over the school's public address system, which remains subject to the control of school officials. It is fair to assume that the pregame ceremony is clothed in the traditional indicia of school sporting events, which generally include not just the team, but also cheerleaders and band members dressed in uniforms sporting the school name and mascot. The school's name is likely written in large print across the field and on banners and flags. The crowd will certainly include many who display the school colors and insignia on their school T-shirts, jackets, or hats and who may also be waving signs displaying the school name. It is in a setting such as this that "[t]he board has chosen to permit" the elected student to rise and give the "statement or invocation."

Regardless of the listener's support for, or objection to, the message, an objective Santa Fe High School student will unquestionably perceive the inevitable pregame prayer as stamped with her school's seal of approval.

The text and history of this policy, moreover, reinforce our objective student's perception that the prayer is, in actuality, encouraged by the school. When a governmental entity professes a secular purpose for an arguably religious policy, the government's characterization is, of course, entitled to some deference. But it is nonetheless the duty of the courts to "distinguis[h] a sham secular purpose from a sincere one."

According to the District, the secular purposes of the policy are to "foste[r] free expression of private persons . . . as well [as to] solemniz[e] sporting events, promot[e] good sportsmanship and student safety, and establis[h] an appropriate environment for competition." We note, however, that the District's approval of only one specific kind of message, an "invocation," is not necessary to further any of these purposes. Additionally, the fact that only one student is permitted to give a content-limited message suggests that this policy does little to "foste[r] free expression." Furthermore, regardless of whether one considers a sporting event an appropriate occasion for solemnity, the use of an invocation to foster such solemnity is impermissible when, in actuality, it constitutes prayer sponsored by the school. And it is unclear what type of message would be both appropriately "solemnizing" under the District's policy and yet nonreligious.

Most striking to us is the evolution of the current policy from the long-sanctioned office of "Student Chaplain" to the candidly titled "Prayer at Football Games" regulation. This history indicates that the District intended to preserve the practice of prayer before football games.

The District further argues that attendance at the commencement ceremonies at issue in *Lee* "differs dramatically" from attendance at high school football games, which it contends "are of no more than passing interest to many students" and are "decidedly extracurricular," thus dissipating any coercion. Attendance at a high school football game, unlike showing up for class, is certainly not required in order to receive a diploma. Moreover, we may assume that the District is correct in arguing that the informal pressure to attend an athletic event is not as strong as a senior's desire to attend her own graduation ceremony.

There are some students, however, such as cheerleaders, members of the band, and, of course, the team members themselves, for whom seasonal commitments mandate their attendance, sometimes for class credit. The District also minimizes the importance to many students of attending and participating in extracurricular activities as part of a complete educational experience. As we noted in *Lee*, "[l]aw reaches past formalism." To assert that high school students do not feel immense social pressure, or have a truly genuine desire, to be involved in the extracurricular event that is American high school football is "formalistic in the extreme." We stressed in *Lee* the obvious observation that "adolescents are often susceptible to pressure from their peers towards conformity, and that the influence is strongest in matters of social convention." High school home football games are traditional gatherings of a school community; they bring together students and faculty as well as friends and family from years present and past to root for a common cause. Undoubtedly, the games are not important to some students, and they voluntarily choose not to attend. For many others, however, the choice between whether to attend these games or to risk facing a personally offensive religious ritual is in no practical sense an easy one. The Constitution, moreover, demands that the school may not force this difficult choice upon these students for "[i]t is a tenet of the First Amendment that the State cannot require one of its citizens to forfeit his or her rights and benefits as the price of resisting conformance to state-sponsored religious practice."

Chief Justice REHNQUIST, with whom Justice SCALIA and Justice THOMAS join, dissenting.

The Court distorts existing precedent to conclude that the school district's student-message program is invalid on its face under the Establishment Clause. But even more disturbing than its holding is the tone of the Court's opinion; it bristles with hostility to all things religious in public life. Neither the holding nor the tone of the opinion is faithful to the meaning of the Establishment Clause, when it is recalled that George Washington himself, at the request of the very Congress which passed the Bill of Rights, proclaimed a day of "public thanksgiving and prayer, to be observed by acknowledging with grateful hearts the many and signal favors of Almighty God." [The Chief Justice then devoted much of his dissent to the argument that the majority should not have permitted a facial challenge to the policy, but rather should have waited until the policy was put into practice.] Had the policy been put into practice, the students may have chosen a speaker according to wholly secular criteria—like good public speaking skills or social popularity—and the student speaker may have chosen, on her own accord, to deliver a religious message. Such an application of the policy would likely pass constitutional muster.

NOTES AND QUESTIONS

1. *Attributable to the state.* Unlike the earlier school prayers cases, the prayers in *Lee* and *Santa Fe* were given by private individuals. Nonetheless, in both cases the Court held that the prayers were still attributable to the government. What features allowed the Court to reach this conclusion?

2. *Religious purpose.* Do you agree with the Court in *Santa Fe* that the purpose of the school's policy allowing a student speaker at football games was to encourage prayers? Why or why not?

3. *Coercion: mandatory attendance.* According to the *Lee* decision, one factor contributing to the coerciveness of graduation prayers was that students' presence at graduation was not voluntary. While strictly speaking students were not required to attend, "law reaches beyond formalism." Is it more accurate to describe attendance as valued rather than mandatory, so that the issue is not so much that students must attend but that student should not have to forgo attendance? Would the prayers be constitutional if attendance were purely voluntary? Also, how would you characterize attendance at school football games?

4. *Coercion: social pressure.* Justice Kennedy held that the social and peer pressure at school graduation, "though subtle and indirect, can be as real as any overt compulsion." Are these types of subtle and indirect pressures as coercive as those backed by the force of law? Whether as real or not, they are surely harder to measure. Is the test "incoherent," as Justice Scalia accuses?

5. *Necessary and legal coercion.* Justice Scalia suggests that legal coercion is necessary to violate the Establishment Clause, at least in this case. Would this interpretation render the Establishment Clause a "virtual nullity" as Justice Souter contends? If this narrow version of the Establishment Clause controlled, what would it actually prevent the government from doing? Could the government require public school teachers to lead their classes in officially sanctioned daily prayers, so long as dissenting students are not sanctioned for refusing to participate? See Engel v. Vitale. Could a state declare that

Christianity, or the Abrahamic tradition, was the official state religion? How would such a proclamation differ from the state declaring that the cello was the official state musical instrument or that Caucasian was the official state race?

6.   *Anonymous litigation in Establishment Clause cases.* Cases involving school prayer raise passions like few other Establishment Clause disputes. The risks of retaliation against Establishment Clause plaintiffs in these cases are often quite serious—especially in religiously homogeneous communities in which the plaintiffs are in a distinct minority. Two families litigated *Santa Fe.* One family was Mormon and the other was Catholic. Note that they litigated the case under a "John Doe" alias. In Justice Stevens's majority opinion in *Santa Fe,* he notes that the District Court entered the anonymity order to protect the Does from intimidation and harassment. The fear of harassment was well founded. Stevens quotes the Fifth Circuit's conclusion that the decision to permit the plaintiffs to litigate anonymously was one that the school officials "apparently neither agreed with nor particularly respected." Stevens also quotes the order that the District Court was forced to enter a month after the complaint was filed:

> [A]ny further attempt on the part of District or school administration, officials, counsellors, teachers, employees or servants of the School District, parents, students or anyone else, overtly or covertly to ferret out the identities of the Plaintiffs in this cause, by means of bogus petitions, questionnaires, individual interrogation, or downright "snooping," will cease immediately. ANYONE TAKING ANY ACTION ON SCHOOL PROPERTY, DURING SCHOOL HOURS, OR WITH SCHOOL RESOURCES OR APPROVAL FOR PURPOSES OF ATTEMPTING TO ELICIT THE NAMES OR IDENTITIES OF THE PLAINTIFFS IN THIS CAUSE OF ACTION, BY OR ON BEHALF OF ANY OF THESE INDIVIDUALS, WILL FACE THE HARSHEST POSSIBLE CONTEMPT SANCTIONS FROM THIS COURT, AND MAY ADDITIONALLY FACE CRIMINAL LIABILITY. The Court wants these proceedings addressed on their merits, and not on the basis of intimidation or harassment of the participants on either side.

Santa Fe, 530 U.S. at 294 n.1 (emphasis in original). For other cases discussing the need to sue pseudonymously in religious rights cases, see Doe v. Stegall, 653 F.2d 180 (5th Cir. 1981); Doe v. Harlan County Sch. Dist., 96 F. Supp. 2d 667 (E.D. Ky. 2000).

7.   *School prayer in the university context.* All of the school prayer cases considered by the Supreme Court have involved public schools below the university level. At the lower court level, courts have been equally vigilant in restricting the direct infusion of religion into public university classrooms, although a few courts have been somewhat more lenient with regard to religious exercises at university graduation ceremonies. Should there be a distinction between college and university students, on the one hand, and K-12 students, on the other?

B.   GOVERNMENT ENDORSEMENT OF RELIGION IN THE PUBLIC SCHOOLS: RELIGION IN THE PUBLIC SCHOOL CURRICULUM

EPPERSON v. ARKANSAS
393 U.S. 97 (1968)

Mr. Justice FORTAS delivered the opinion of the Court.

This appeal challenges the constitutionality of the "anti-evolution" statute which the State of Arkansas adopted in 1928 to prohibit the teaching in its public schools and universities of the theory that man evolved from other species of life. The statute was a product of the upsurge of "fundamentalist" religious fervor of the twenties. The Arkansas statute was an adaptation of the famous Tennessee "monkey law" which that State adopted in 1925. The constitutionality of the Tennessee law was upheld by the Tennessee Supreme Court in the celebrated *Scopes* case in 1927.[2]

The Arkansas law makes it unlawful for a teacher in any state-supported school or university "to teach the theory or doctrine that mankind ascended or descended from a lower order of animals," or "to adopt or use in any such institution a textbook that teaches" this theory. Violation is a misdemeanor and subjects the violator to dismissal from his position.

The present case concerns the teaching of biology in a high school in Little Rock. According to the testimony, until the events here in litigation, the official textbook furnished for the high school biology course did not have a section on the Darwinian Theory. Then, for the academic year 1965-1966, the school administration, on recommendation of the teachers of biology in the school system, adopted and prescribed a textbook which contained a chapter setting forth "the theory about the origin . . . of man from a lower form of animal."

Susan Epperson, a young woman who graduated from Arkansas' school system and then obtained her master's degree in zoology at the University of Illinois, was employed by the Little Rock school system in the fall of 1964 to teach 10th grade biology at Central High School. At the start of the next academic year, 1965, she was confronted by the new textbook (which one surmises from the record was not unwelcome to her). She faced at least a literal dilemma because she was supposed to use the new textbook for classroom instruction and presumably to teach the statutorily condemned chapter; but to do so would be a criminal offense and subject her to dismissal.

She instituted the present action in the Chancery Court of the State, seeking a declaration that the Arkansas statute is void and enjoining the State and the defendant officials of the Little Rock school system from dismissing her for violation of the statute's provisions. H. H. Blanchard, a parent of children attending the public schools, intervened in support of the action.

---

[2] *Scopes v. State*, 154 Tenn. 105, 289 S.W. 363 (1927). The Tennessee court, however, reversed Scopes' conviction on the ground that the jury and not the judge should have assessed the fine of $100. Since Scopes was no longer in the State's employ, it saw "nothing to be gained by prolonging the life of this bizarre case." It directed that a *nolle prosequi* be entered, in the interests of "the peace and dignity of the state." 154 Tenn., at 121, 289 S.W., at 367.

[The Chancery Court held that the statute violated the Fourteenth Amendment to the United States Constitution. On appeal, the Supreme Court of Arkansas reversed. In a two-sentence opinion, it sustained the statute as an exercise of the State's power to specify the curriculum in public schools. It did not address itself to the competing constitutional considerations.]

We do not rest our decision upon the asserted vagueness of the statute. On either interpretation of its language, Arkansas' statute cannot stand. It is of no moment whether the law is deemed to prohibit mention of Darwin's theory, or to forbid any or all of the infinite varieties of communication embraced within the term "teaching." Under either interpretation, the law must be stricken because of its conflict with the constitutional prohibition of state laws respecting an establishment of religion or prohibiting the free exercise thereof. The overriding fact is that Arkansas' law selects from the body of knowledge a particular segment which it proscribes for the sole reason that it is deemed to conflict with a particular religious doctrine; that is, with a particular interpretation of the Book of Genesis by a particular religious group.

Government in our democracy, state and national, must be neutral in matters of religious theory, doctrine, and practice.

As early as 1872, this Court said: "The law knows no heresy, and is committed to the support of no dogma, the establishment of no sect." *Watson v. Jones*, 13 Wall. 679, 728. There is and can be no doubt that the First Amendment does not permit the State to require that teaching and learning must be tailored to the principles or prohibitions of any religious sect or dogma.

In the present case, there can be no doubt that Arkansas has sought to prevent its teachers from discussing the theory of evolution because it is contrary to the belief of some that the Book of Genesis must be the exclusive source of doctrine as to the origin of man. No suggestion has been made that Arkansas' law may be justified by considerations of state policy other than the religious views of some of its citizens. It is clear that fundamentalist sectarian conviction was and is the law's reason for existence.[16]

Its antecedent, Tennessee's "monkey law," candidly stated its purpose: to make it unlawful "to teach any theory that denies the story of the Divine Creation of man as taught in the Bible, and to teach instead that man has descended from a lower order

---

[16] The following advertisement is typical of the public appeal which was used in the campaign to secure adoption of the statute:

"THE BIBLE OR ATHEISM, WHICH?

"All atheists favor evolution. If you agree with atheism vote against Act No. 1. If you agree with the Bible vote for Act No. 1. . . . Shall conscientious church members be forced to pay taxes to support teachers to teach evolution which will undermine the faith of their children? The Gazette said Russian Bolshevists laughed at Tennessee. True, and that sort will laugh at Arkansas. Who cares? Vote FOR ACT NO. 1." The Arkansas Gazette, Little Rock, Nov. 4, 1928, p. 12, cols. 4-5.

Letters from the public expressed the fear that teaching of evolution would be "subversive of Christianity," *id.*, Oct. 24, 1928, p. 7, col. 2; see also *id.*, Nov. 4, 1928, p. 19, col. 4; and that it would cause school children "to disrespect the Bible," *id.*, Oct. 27, 1928, p. 15, col. 5. One letter read: "The cosmogony taught by (evolution) runs contrary to that of Moses and Jesus, and as such is nothing, if anything at all, but atheism. . . . Now let the mothers and fathers of our state that are trying to raise their children in the Christian faith arise in their might and vote for this anti-evolution bill that will take it out of our tax supported schools. When they have saved the children, they have saved the state." *Id.*, at cols. 4-5.

of animals."[17] Perhaps the sensational publicity attendant upon the *Scopes* trial induced Arkansas to adopt less explicit language.[18] It eliminated Tennessee's reference to "the story of the Divine Creation of man" as taught in the Bible, but there is no doubt that the motivation for the law was the same: to suppress the teaching of a theory which, it was thought, "denied" the divine creation of man.

Arkansas' law cannot be defended as an act of religious neutrality. Arkansas did not seek to excise from the curricula of its schools and universities all discussion of the origin of man. The law's effort was confined to an attempt to blot out a particular theory because of its supposed conflict with the Biblical account, literally read. Plainly, the law is contrary to the mandate of the First, and in violation of the Fourteenth, Amendment to the Constitution.

AN EXTENDED NOTE ON THE SCOPES TRIAL

For much of the last century, certain religious groups have resisted the exclusion of biblical theories of creation from public school science curricula. This resistance generated one of the more colorful and well-known constitutional battles: the Tennessee "monkey trial" of John Scopes, which is noted in a footnote to the *Epperson* decision. Scopes was a public school teacher in a small Tennessee town who was convicted of violating the Tennessee anti-evolution statute by teaching the theory of evolution in his high school science class. The Tennessee statute made it "unlawful for any teacher in any of the Universitis [*sic*], Normals and all other public schools of the State which are supported in whole or in part by the public school funds of the State, to teach any theory that denies the story of the Divine Creation of man as taught in the Bible, and to teach instead that man has descended from a lower order of animals." Act of Mar. 13, 1925, ch. 27, 1925 Tenn. Pub. Acts 50.

The Scopes trial brought the dispute between science and religion to center stage, complete with appearances by larger-than-life characters such as Clarence Darrow and William Jennings Bryan, and a running commentary by a third outsized figure in the form of H.L. Mencken. The popular memory of this battle is that science and sophisticated rationalism defeated ignorance and parochial sophistry. Much of this popular understanding is probably attributable to the Jerome Lawrence and Robert E. Lee play about the trial. *See* Jerome Lawrence & Robert E. Lee, *Inherit the Wind* (1955). This play was later made into a famous movie, with Spencer Tracy playing the role of the fictionalized Darrow character. For the background to the actual trial and the story of how the trial gradually achieved near-mythical status, see Edward J. Larson, *Summer for the Gods: The Scopes Trial and America's Continuing Debate Over Science and Religion* (1997). To the chagrin of modern opponents of evolution, Mencken's harsh judgment about Darrow's public humiliation of Bryan probably sums up much of the country's common understanding of the battle between evolution and creationism: "On the one side was bigotry, ignorance, hatred, superstition, every sort of blackness that the human mind is capable of. On the other side was sense. And sense achieved a great victory." H.L. Mencken, "Aftermath," in

---

[17] Arkansas' law was adopted by popular initiative in 1928, three years after Tennessee's law was enacted and one year after the Tennessee Supreme Court's decision in the *Scopes* case, *supra*.

[18] In its brief, the State says that the Arkansas statute was passed with the holding of the *Scopes* case in mind. Brief for Appellee 1.

The Impossible H.L. Mencken: A Selection of His Best Newspaper Stories 611 (Marion Elizabeth Rodgers ed., 1991).

Contrary to popular perception, no federal court ever ruled on the constitutionality of the Scopes conviction. Scopes was convicted and fined $100 in state court for violating the Tennessee anti-evolution statute, and the Tennessee Supreme Court overturned this verdict on the ground that the jury, rather than the judge, had imposed the fine. Although the Tennessee Supreme Court reversed the verdict, it also expressed the view that the Tennessee statute did not constitute an establishment of religion in violation of either the federal or the state constitution. *See* Scopes v. State, 289 S.W. 363, 367 (Tenn. 1927) ("We are not able to see how the prohibition of teaching the theory that man has descended from a lower order of animals gives preference to any religious establishment or mode of worship. So far as we know, there is no religious establishment or organized body that has in its creed or confession of faith any article denying or affirming such a theory."). But having asserted the constitutionality of the Tennessee statute, the court avoided further embarrassment to the state by noting that "[w]e see nothing to be gained by prolonging the life of this bizarre case" and "suggested" that the Attorney General enter a nolle prosequi in the case. *Id.* Thus, in *Scopes* the constitutional issues were addressed only in dicta in the state court, and never even reached the United States Supreme Court. It would be another 40 years before the Supreme Court would finally review a Scopes-style creationism statute in *Epperson* and announce its determination that, contrary to the Tennessee court's dicta, the Establishment Clause of the United States Constitution does not permit states to prohibit the teaching of evolution in public schools.

EDWARDS v. AGUILLARD

482 U.S. 578 (1987)

Justice BRENNAN delivered the opinion of the Court.

The question for decision is whether Louisiana's "Balanced Treatment for Creation-Science and Evolution-Science in Public School Instruction" Act (Creationism Act) is facially invalid as violative of the Establishment Clause of the First Amendment.

The Creationism Act forbids the teaching of the theory of evolution in public schools unless accompanied by instruction in "creation science." No school is required to teach evolution or creation science. If either is taught, however, the other must also be taught. The theories of evolution and creation science are statutorily defined as "the scientific evidences for [creation or evolution] and inferences from those scientific evidences."

[T]he Act's stated purpose is to protect academic freedom. This phrase might, in common parlance, be understood as referring to enhancing the freedom of teachers to teach what they will. The Court of Appeals, however, correctly concluded that the Act was not designed to further that goal.[6] We find no merit in the State's argument that the "legislature may not [have] use[d] the terms 'academic freedom' in the correct legal sense. They might have [had] in mind, instead, a basic concept of

---

[6] The Act actually serves to diminish academic freedom by removing the flexibility to teach evolution without also teaching creation science, even if teachers determine that such curriculum results in less effective and comprehensive science instruction.

fairness; teaching all of the evidence." Even if "academic freedom" is read to mean "teaching all of the evidence" with respect to the origin of human beings, the Act does not further this purpose. The goal of providing a more comprehensive science curriculum is not furthered either by outlawing the teaching of evolution or by requiring the teaching of creation science.

While the Court is normally deferential to a State's articulation of a secular purpose, it is required that the statement of such purpose be sincere and not a sham.

It is clear from the legislative history that the purpose of the legislative sponsor, Senator Bill Keith, was to narrow the science curriculum. During the legislative hearings, Senator Keith stated: "My preference would be that neither [creationism nor evolution] be taught." Such a ban on teaching does not promote—indeed, it undermines—the provision of a comprehensive scientific education.

It is equally clear that requiring schools to teach creation science with evolution does not advance academic freedom. The Act does not grant teachers a flexibility that they did not already possess to supplant the present science curriculum with the presentation of theories, besides evolution, about the origin of life. Indeed, the Court of Appeals found that no law prohibited Louisiana public school teachers from teaching any scientific theory. As the president of the Louisiana Science Teachers Association testified, "[a]ny scientific concept that's based on established fact can be included in our curriculum already, and no legislation allowing this is necessary." The Act provides Louisiana school teachers with no new authority. Thus the stated purpose is not furthered by it.

Thus we agree with the Court of Appeals' conclusion that the Act does not serve to protect academic freedom, but has the distinctly different purpose of discrediting "evolution by counterbalancing its teaching at every turn with the teaching of creationism. . . ."

As in *Stone* [*v. Graham*] and *Abington* [*v. Schempp*], we need not be blind in this case to the legislature's preeminent religious purpose in enacting this statute. There is a historic and contemporaneous link between the teachings of certain religious denominations and the teaching of evolution. It was this link that concerned the Court in *Epperson v. Arkansas*, which also involved a facial challenge to a statute regulating the teaching of evolution. These same historic and contemporaneous antagonisms between the teachings of certain religious denominations and the teaching of evolution are present in this case. The preeminent purpose of the Louisiana Legislature was clearly to advance the religious viewpoint that a supernatural being created humankind.

In this case, the purpose of the Creationism Act was to restructure the science curriculum to conform with a particular religious viewpoint. Out of many possible science subjects taught in the public schools, the legislature chose to affect the teaching of the one scientific theory that historically has been opposed by certain religious sects. As in *Epperson*, the legislature passed the Act to give preference to those religious groups which have as one of their tenets the creation of humankind by a divine creator. The "overriding fact" that confronted the Court in *Epperson* was "that Arkansas' law selects from the body of knowledge a particular segment which it proscribes for the sole reason that it is deemed to conflict with . . . a particular interpretation of the Book of Genesis by a particular religious group." The Establishment Clause, however, "forbids *alike* the preference of a religious doctrine *or* the prohibition of theory which is deemed antagonistic to a particular dogma." *Epperson*. Because the primary purpose of the Creationism Act is to advance a particular religious belief, the Act endorses religion in violation of the First Amendment.

Justice SCALIA, with whom THE CHIEF JUSTICE joins, dissenting.

We have relatively little information upon which to judge the motives of those who supported the Act. About the only direct evidence is the statute itself and transcripts of the seven committee hearings at which it was considered. Unfortunately, several of those hearings were sparsely attended, and the legislators who were present revealed little about their motives. We have no committee reports, no floor debates, no remarks inserted into the legislative history, no statement from the Governor, and no postenactment statements or testimony from the bill's sponsor or any other legislators. Nevertheless, there is ample evidence that the majority is wrong in holding that the Balanced Treatment Act is without secular purpose.

The Act had its genesis (so to speak) in legislation introduced by Senator Bill Keith in June 1980.

Before summarizing the testimony of Senator Keith and his supporters, I wish to make clear that I by no means intend to endorse its accuracy. But my views (and the views of this Court) about creation science and evolution are (or should be) beside the point. Our task is not to judge the debate about teaching the origins of life, but to ascertain what the members of the Louisiana Legislature believed. The vast majority of them voted to approve a bill which explicitly stated a secular purpose; what is crucial is not their *wisdom* in believing that purpose would be achieved by the bill, but their *sincerity* in believing it would be. . . .

It is undoubtedly true that what prompted the legislature to direct its attention to the misrepresentation of evolution in the schools (rather than the inaccurate presentation of other topics) was its awareness of the tension between evolution and the religious beliefs of many children. But even appellees concede that a valid secular purpose is not rendered impermissible simply because its pursuit is prompted by concern for religious sensitivities. If a history teacher falsely told her students that the bones of Jesus Christ had been discovered, or a physics teacher that the Shroud of Turin had been conclusively established to be inexplicable on the basis of natural causes, I cannot believe (despite the majority's implication to the contrary) that legislators or school board members would be constitutionally prohibited from taking corrective action, simply because that action was prompted by concern for the religious beliefs of the misinstructed students.

In sum, even if one concedes, for the sake of argument, that a majority of the Louisiana Legislature voted for the Balanced Treatment Act partly in order to foster (rather than merely eliminate discrimination against) Christian fundamentalist beliefs, our cases establish that that alone would not suffice to invalidate the Act, so long as there was a genuine secular purpose as well. We have, moreover, no adequate basis for disbelieving the secular purpose set forth in the Act itself, or for concluding that it is a sham enacted to conceal the legislators' violation of their oaths of office. I am astonished by the Court's unprecedented readiness to reach such a conclusion, which I can only attribute to an intellectual predisposition created by the facts and the legend of *Scopes v. State*—an instinctive reaction that any governmentally imposed requirements bearing upon the teaching of evolution must be a manifestation of Christian fundamentalist repression. In this case, however, it seems to me the Court's position is the repressive one. The people of Louisiana, including those who are Christian fundamentalists, are quite entitled, as a secular matter, to have whatever scientific evidence there may be against evolution presented in their schools, just as

Mr. Scopes was entitled to present whatever scientific evidence there was for it. Perhaps what the Louisiana Legislature has done is unconstitutional because there is no such evidence, and the scheme they have established will amount to no more than a presentation of the Book of Genesis. But we cannot say that on the evidence before us in this summary judgment context, which includes ample uncontradicted testimony that "creation science" is a body of scientific knowledge rather than revealed belief. *Infinitely less* can we say (or should we say) that the scientific evidence for evolution is so conclusive that no one could be gullible enough to believe that there is any real scientific evidence to the contrary, so that the legislation's stated purpose must be a lie. Yet that illiberal judgment, that *Scopes*-in-reverse, is ultimately the basis on which the Court's facile rejection of the Louisiana Legislature's purpose must rest.

NOTES AND QUESTIONS

1. *Secular purpose.* In order to satisfy the *Lemon* test, is it enough that a statute have a secular purpose, or must the primary purpose be secular? Must it be the latter because it is always possible to come up with a secular justification? Is the answer different for the endorsement test? What if the Arkansas law or the Creationism Act was motivated in part by a desire to avoid controversy in the public schools?

2. *Some definitions.* The National Academy of Sciences and Institute of Medicine define "science" as "the use of evidence to construct testable explanation and prediction of natural phenomena, as well as the knowledge generated through this process." National Academy of Sciences and Institute of Medicine, *Science, Evolution, and Creationism (2008).* Does creationism meet that criteria? Note too that "theory" has a special meaning in science. According to the National Academy of Sciences and the Institute of Medicine: "The formal scientific definition of theory is quite different from the everyday meaning of the word. It refers to a comprehensive explanation of some aspect of nature that is supported by a vast body of evidence." *Id.* In addition to the theory of evolution, other scientific theories include the heliocentric theory (the earth revolves around the sun), cell theory (living things are made up of cells), and the theory of plate tectonics. *Id.*

3. *The scientific community's response to Justice Scalia.* Justice Scalia's *Edwards* dissent did not fare very well with the scientific community. "[T]hough it may form only part of his rationale, Scalia's argument relies crucially upon a false concept of science. . . . I regret to say that Justice Scalia does not understand the subject matter of evolutionary biology. He has simply adopted the creationists' definition and thereby repeated their willful mistake. . . . He equates creation and evolution because creationists can't explain life's beginning while evolutionists can't resolve the ultimate origin of the inorganic components that later aggregate to life. But this inability is the very heart of creationist logic and the central reason why their doctrine is not science, while science's inability to specify the ultimate origin of matter is irrelevant because we are not trying to do any such thing. We know that we can't, and we do not even consider such a question as part of science." Stephen Jay Gould, *Justice Scalia's Misunderstanding*, 5 Const. Commentary 1, 8, 10 (1988).

4. *Favoring one religion over others.* Doesn't a school favor one religion over others if it teaches Biblical creationism? After all, other Christian denominations and other religions have different origin stories. Indeed, evolution does not necessarily clash with religious belief. While it describes how species change and develop, it does not address the ultimate origins of life. Moreover, someone could, for example, believe that God chose natural selection as the means to create new species.

5. *Neutrality.* When evolution and religious belief do clash, is the state acting neutrally when it offers the secular view without acknowledging the religious view? Consider Stephen Carter's critique of the *Edwards* holding as an example of the conflict between two completely different ways of viewing the world: the empirical, rationalist outlook that forms the heart of the French Enlightenment worldview, and the religious worldview that is defined by faith and a belief in the primacy of an essentially unknowable supernatural power. *See* Stephen L. Carter, *Evolution, Creationism, and Treating Religion as a Hobby,* 1987 Duke L.J. 977. Carter criticizes the Supreme Court for its *Edwards* decision, and suggests that the larger problem with the decision is the inability of the secular legal and political structure to come to terms with the basic attributes of religion. According to Carter, "The liberal critic may be right to say that creationism is bad science. But why should that issue be the crucial one? Creationists are not irrational merely because they are unscientific. Creationism was not created from thin air; creation theory developed as a consequence of the preferred hermeneutical method of many Christian fundamentalists for understanding the world." *Id.* at 980. The hermeneutical assumptions to which Carter refers are derived from the assumption of biblical inerrancy. If one assumes that the Bible is the literally true, received word of God, Carter argues, "what chance is there that the theory of evolution is correct? Virtually none." *Id.* Carter argues that the root of the conflict is the "reliance of liberalism on dialogue and rationality as indispensable components of its political theory, and the often unstated premise of many liberal theorists that reasoning and religious belief are mutually exclusive means for understanding the world." *Id.* at 986. Is Carter right? Is the reliance on "dialogue and rationality" itself an Establishment Clause violation? Do the scientific method and its essential requisites of empiricism and rationality form a sufficiently comprehensive worldview to fall within the ambit of the term "religion"?

6. *The third generation of creationism: Intelligent Design.* Creationism has, perhaps ironically, evolved since the Scopes "Monkey Trial" in the 1920s. The theory has gone through two major transformations in response to the legal decisions summarized above. The first generation of creationism statutes barred the teaching of evolution altogether. These statutes were the basis of the *Scopes* trial in 1927 and were finally held unconstitutional by the 1968 Supreme Court decision, Epperson v. Arkansas. The second generation of creationism statutes no longer challenged the teaching of evolution, but required public school teachers who taught evolution to give creationist theory equal time. These so-called balanced treatment statutes were held unconstitutional in 1987 in Edwards v. Aguillard. Both of the first two generations of creationism statutes relied heavily on so-called young-earth creationist doctrine, which suggests that the earth is only approximately 6,000 years old, all geological phenomena can be

explained by catastrophism (a flood), and diverse new species do not evolve from common ancestors.

In response to *Edwards*, a third generation of creationism has developed in the form of so-called Intelligent Design doctrine. There are two main distinctions between Intelligent Design creationism and its predecessors. First, unlike earlier versions of creationism, Intelligent Design doctrine does not attempt to make an affirmative case for supernatural creation but instead relies mostly on the claim that evolutionary theory is flawed. (Intelligent Design proponents do continue to advance the most important claim made by previous generations of creationists, however, which is the contention that higher species have not evolved from common ancestors.) Second, unlike earlier versions of creationism, which explicitly asserted that God created the world in essentially its present form, Intelligent Design does not identify the "intelligent designer" by the name "God." Intelligent Design hopes to escape the Establishment Clause restrictions imposed by *Epperson* and *Edwards* by avoiding mentioning the religious concept of God by name. Intelligent Design proposals come in various forms, including efforts to have school boards directly advance the theory in science classes in addition to the traditional scientific renditions of evolution theory, the incorporation of Intelligent Design precepts in state science standards, and the placement of disclaimers in science textbooks. Thus far, these proposals have failed to survive judicial scrutiny in the lower courts.

The most important decision involving a school board's attempt to incorporate Intelligent Design precepts into a public school curriculum is Kitzmiller v. Dover Area School District, 400 F. Supp. 2d 707 (M.D. Pa. 2005). In *Kitzmiller*, a Dover, Pennsylvania, school board attempted to interject Intelligent Design into the curriculum by reading to students official disclaimers implying that evolutionary theory might be flawed. The school board also placed Intelligent Design textbooks in the school library. The judge ruled that the Dover policy was unconstitutional both on secular purpose and secular effect grounds as an impermissible endorsement of religion. The judge concluded "that the religious nature of ID [the common abbreviation for Intelligent Design] would be readily apparent to an objective observer, adult or child." *Id.* at 718. The decision is important not only for its basic holding but also because the court ruled on the merits of the scientific claims made by Intelligent Design proponents. After hearing extensive expert testimony on the subject, the judge ruled that

> ID is not science. We find that ID fails on three different levels, any one of which is sufficient to preclude a determination that ID is science. They are: (1) ID violates the centuries-old ground rules of science by invoking and permitting supernatural causation; (2) the argument of irreducible complexity, central to ID, employs the same flawed and illogical contrived dualism [between religion and science] that doomed creation science in the 1980's; and (3) ID's negative attacks on evolution have been refuted by the scientific community. . . . [I]t is additionally important to note that ID has failed to gain acceptance in the scientific community, it has not generated peer-reviewed publications, nor has it been the subject of testing and research.

Id. at 735; *see also id.* at 738 ("ID fails to meet the essential ground rules that limit science to testable, natural explanations."). In November 2005, the citizens of Dover voted to turn out of office all eight members of the Dover school board who had supported the anti-evolution policy. The new school board decided not to appeal the *Kitzmiller* decision.

7. *Disavowal of evolution on public school science textbooks.* The Cobb County, Georgia, public schools, facing objections from parents over the inclusion of Darwin's theory of evolution in new science textbooks being used in local public schools, adopted a policy of placing stickers on the books. The stickers stated: "This textbook contains material on evolution. Evolution is a theory, not a fact, regarding the origin of living things. This material should be approached with an open mind, studied carefully, and critically considered." Selman v. Cobb Cnty. Sch. Dist., 390 F. Supp. 1286, 1292 (N.D. Ga. 2005), *rev'd*, 449 F.3d 1320 (11th Cir. 2006). In subsequent litigation, a federal district court ordered removal of the stickers because they constituted an endorsement of religion. *See id.* at 1306-1312. On appeal, however, the Eleventh Circuit found the record inadequate and vacated and remanded the district court's decision. On remand, the school district elected to settle the case. May a school district distance itself from Darwin's theory of evolution in this way? Or is the effort to disavow evolution itself objectionable on Establishment Clause grounds?

C. RELIGIOUS SPEECH IN PUBLIC SCHOOLS

WIDMAR v. VINCENT

454 U.S. 263 (1981)

Justice POWELL delivered the opinion of the Court.

This case presents the question whether a state university [the University of Missouri at Kansas City], which makes its facilities generally available for the activities of registered student groups, may close its facilities to a registered student group desiring to use the facilities for religious worship and religious discussion.

From 1973 until 1977 a registered religious group named Cornerstone regularly sought and received permission to conduct its meetings in University facilities.[2] In 1977, however, the University informed the group that it could no longer meet in University buildings. The exclusion was based on a regulation, adopted by the Board of Curators in 1972, that prohibits the use of University buildings or grounds "for purposes of religious worship or religious teaching."

The University first argues that it cannot offer its facilities to religious groups and speakers on the terms available to other groups without violating the Establishment Clause of the Constitution of the United States. We agree that the interest of the University in complying with its constitutional obligations may be characterized as compelling. It does not follow, however, that an "equal access" policy would be incompatible with this Court's Establishment Clause cases.

---

[2] Cornerstone is an organization of evangelical Christian students from various denominational backgrounds. . . . A typical Cornerstone meeting included prayer, hymns, Bible commentary, and discussion of religious views and experiences.

In this case two prongs of the [*Lemon*] test are clearly met. Both the District Court and the Court of Appeals held that an open-forum policy, including nondiscrimination against religious speech, would have a secular purpose and would avoid entanglement with religion. But the District Court concluded, and the University argues here, that allowing religious groups to share the limited public forum would have the "primary effect" of advancing religion.

The University's argument misconceives the nature of this case. The question is not whether the creation of a religious forum would violate the Establishment Clause. The University has opened its facilities for use by student groups, and the question is whether it can now exclude groups because of the content of their speech. In this context we are unpersuaded that the primary effect of the public forum, open to all forms of discourse, would be to advance religion.

We are not oblivious to the range of an open forum's likely effects. It is possible—perhaps even foreseeable—that religious groups will benefit from access to University facilities. But this Court has explained that a religious organization's enjoyment of merely "incidental" benefits does not violate the prohibition against the "primary advancement" of religion.

We are satisfied that any religious benefits of an open forum at UMKC would be "incidental" within the meaning of our cases. Two factors are especially relevant.

First, an open forum in a public university does not confer any imprimatur of state approval on religious sects or practices. As the Court of Appeals quite aptly stated, such a policy "would no more commit the University . . . to religious goals" than it is "now committed to the goals of the Students for a Democratic Society, the Young Socialist Alliance," or any other group eligible to use its facilities.

Second, the forum is available to a broad class of nonreligious as well as religious speakers; there are over 100 recognized student groups at UMKC. The provision of benefits to so broad a spectrum of groups is an important index of secular effect. If the Establishment Clause barred the extension of general benefits to religious groups, "a church could not be protected by the police and fire departments, or have its public sidewalk kept in repair." At least in the absence of empirical evidence that religious groups will dominate UMKC's open forum, we agree with the Court of Appeals that the advancement of religion would not be the forum's "primary effect."

LAMB'S CHAPEL v.
CENTER MORICHES UNION FREE SCHOOL DISTRICT
508 U.S. 384 (1993)

Justice WHITE delivered the opinion of the Court.

New York [Education Law] authorizes local school boards to adopt reasonable regulations for the use of school property for 10 specified purposes when the property is not in use for school purposes. Among the permitted uses is the holding of "social, civic and recreational meetings and entertainments, and other uses pertaining to the welfare of the community; but such meetings, entertainment and uses shall be non-exclusive and shall be open to the general public." The list of permitted uses does not include meetings for religious purposes, and a New York appellate court ruled that local boards could not allow student bible clubs to meet on school property because "[r]eligious purposes are not included in the enumerated purposes for which a school may be used under section 414."

Pursuant to [the state law], the Board of Center Moriches Union Free School District (District) has issued rules and regulations with respect to the use of school property when not in use for school purposes. The rules allow only 2 of the 10 purposes authorized by [state law]: social, civic, or recreational uses (Rule 10) and use by political organizations if [properly authorized] (Rule 8). Rule 7, however, consistent with the judicial interpretation of state law, provides that "[t]he school premises shall not be used by any group for religious purposes."

The issue in this case is whether, against this background of state law, it violates the Free Speech Clause of the First Amendment, made applicable to the States by the Fourteenth Amendment, to deny a church access to school premises to exhibit for public viewing and for assertedly religious purposes, a film series dealing with family and child-rearing issues faced by parents today.[2]

The District, as a respondent, would save its judgment below on the ground that to permit its property to be used for religious purposes would be an establishment of religion forbidden by the First Amendment. This Court suggested in *Widmar v. Vincent*, that the interest of the State in avoiding an Establishment Clause violation "may be [a] compelling" one justifying an abridgment of free speech otherwise protected by the First Amendment; but the Court went on to hold that permitting use of university property for religious purposes under the open access policy involved there would not be incompatible with the Court's Establishment Clause cases.

We have no more trouble than did the *Widmar* Court in disposing of the claimed defense on the ground that the posited fears of an Establishment Clause violation are unfounded. The showing of this film series would not have been during school hours, would not have been sponsored by the school, and would have been open to the public, not just to church members. The District property had repeatedly been used by a wide variety of private organizations. Under these circumstances, as in *Widmar*, there would have been no realistic danger that the community would think that the District was endorsing religion or any particular creed, and any benefit to religion or to the Church would have been no more than incidental.

NOTES AND QUESTIONS

1. *If religion dominated.* What if the empirical evidence in *Widmar* reveals that religious groups dominate the open forum? Would that change the Establishment Clause analysis? Is it possible for a religious group to "so dominate a public forum that a formal policy of equal access is transformed into a demonstration of approval"? *Pinette* (O'Connor, J., concurring).

2. *Religion as a subject or viewpoint.* Free Speech Clause forum doctrine does not always treat subject matter regulations and viewpoint regulations in the same way. In nonpublic forums, the government may restrict the forum to certain subjects as long as the limit is reasonable. However, any attempt to exclude

---

[2] [*Editor's Note: Relocated Footnote*] Shortly before the first of these requests, the Church had applied for permission to use school rooms for its Sunday morning services and for Sunday School. The hours specified were 9 a.m. to 1 p.m. and the time period one year beginning in the next month. 959 F.2d 381, 383 (CA2 1992). Within a few days the District wrote petitioner that the application "requesting use of the high school for your Sunday services" was denied, citing both N.Y. Educ. Law §414 and the District's Rule 7 barring uses for religious purposes. The Church did not challenge this denial in the courts and the validity of this denial is not before us.

viewpoints triggers strict scrutiny. See *supra* Chapter 3. *Lamb's Chapel* holds that the regulation barring access for "religious purposes" was a viewpoint restriction that could not survive strict scrutiny. Is religion better characterized as a subject matter or a viewpoint? What if the exclusion were limited to religious worship? In other words, is a regulation allowing Lamb's Chapel to screen a religious film about childrearing but not hold religious worship services a subject matter or viewpoint regulation?

3. *May (must) government distance itself from sectarian proselytizing?* Suppose a religious group seeks to use a government public forum at a school to proselytize. Suppose that the speech takes the form of an attack against unbelievers; for example, the cover of a student-edited, university-supported publication proclaims in large, bold letters: "Why Papists Will Surely Burn in Hell." Does a public university have an obligation to distance itself from such overtly sectarian speech? Cf. *Pinette* (Justice O'Connor, concurring) ("The [Establishment] Clause is more than a negative prohibition against certain narrowly defined forms of government favoritism; it also imposes affirmative obligations that may require a State, in some situations, to take steps to avoid being perceived as supporting or endorsing a private religious message.").

4. *Extension in* Rosenberger. The reasoning of *Widmar* and *Lamb's Chapel*, which involved access to physical spaces, was extended to access to funding in *Rosenberger v. Rector & Visitors of the University of Virginia*, where the school allowed its student activity fund to subsidize student extracurricular activities yet declined to subsidize an evangelical student newspaper. The Court held that when the university created the student activity fund, it had essentially designated a public forum, albeit a public forum "more in a metaphysical than in a spatial or geographic sense," but in which the same rules applied. *Id.* at 830. The Court held that denying funds to religious speakers would constitute unconstitutional viewpoint discrimination under the Free Speech Clause of the First Amendment. The Court rejected the university's theory that the Establishment Clause prohibited the university from providing government funds to the religious magazine on the ground that the program was neutral with regard to the perspective of speakers receiving funds. "The neutrality of the program distinguishes the student fees from a tax levied for the direct support of a church or group of churches." *Id.* at 840. Should the same reasoning apply to funding as to facilities? To after-school access as opposed to school extracurriculars?

5. *The difficulty in fashioning a truly neutral policy.* If the government attempts to advance Establishment Clause values by excluding religious speakers from a limited-purpose public forum, it engages in a form of content/viewpoint discrimination. On the other hand, if it permits religious activities and even services to take place on public property, it is directly subsidizing overtly sectarian activities. This Scylla and Charybdis does not admit of an obvious or easy solution; the framing device completely prefigures the constitutional outcome.

6. *Free speech and religion.* Note that these cases brought by religious plaintiffs rely on the Free Speech Clause rather than the Free Exercise Clause. What are the advantages and disadvantages of viewing religious liberty rights through the lens of free speech rather than free exercise?

AN EXTENDED NOTE ON OPEN ACCESS REQUIREMENTS

In Board of Education v. Mergens, 496 U.S. 226 (1990), the Supreme Court upheld the federal Equal Access Act, 20 U.S.C. §§4071-4074 (1994), which makes it "unlawful for any public secondary school which receives Federal financial assistance and which has a limited open forum to deny equal access or a fair opportunity to, or discriminate against, any students who wish to conduct a meeting within that limited open forum on the basis of the religious, political, philosophical, or other content of the speech at such meetings." A "limited open forum" exists "whenever such school grants an offering to or opportunity for one or more noncurriculum related student groups to meet on school premises during noninstructional time." The Court emphasized several factors that were important considerations in upholding the statute: (1) the meetings were held in noninstructional time; (2) the meetings did not interfere with the educational program of the school; (3) the meetings were not endorsed by the school; (4) school officials did not participate in the meetings; (5) the religious club was merely one of many different student-initiated voluntary clubs, including many secular clubs; and (6) unwilling students were not coerced into attending the religious meetings.

Should a "neutral" access policy of this sort be seen as consistent with the purposes and objectives of the Establishment Clause? Alternatively, if a government entity, such as a local public library, makes meeting space generally available to the public, can it *exclude* those with religious viewpoints from the meeting space? Wouldn't such an exclusion constitute content, if not viewpoint, discrimination? To exclude such viewpoints appears to reflect hostility toward religion and religiously motivated points of view. On the other hand, does a policy of mandatory neutrality toward religious groups seeking to meet on public property have the effect of promoting religion? Or should equal treatment be viewed as a genuinely neutral policy that facially neither advances nor inhibits religion? Does the Free Exercise Clause have any bearing on the constitutional validity of such policies? (For the answer to this question, *see infra* Chapter 16.)

THEORY-APPLIED PROBLEMS

Litigants have raised Establishment Clause claims against a diverse array of religious exercises in public schools, and the Court has used a variety of theoretical approaches to resolve these challenges. One recurrent consideration in the cases is whether private religious exercise or expression should be attributed to the government and therefore limited by the Establishment Clause. In many cases the Court has found it easy to attribute the religious exercise to the government because government officials wrote the prayer (*Engel*), mandated the Bible reading by students (*Schempp*), legally required the posting of religious materials (*Stone*), officially invited the clergyman who recited the offending prayer (*Lee*), or formally organized the vote at which students were allowed to choose to include prayer at an official school function (*Santa Fe*). In other cases the Court has decided that the religious expression in question was not attributable to the government because the expression took place in a context in which many other varieties of expression also occurred (*Widmar, Lamb's Chapel*), or the government put in place certain institutional impediments to prevent official participation or encouragement of the private religious exercise (*Mergens*). Another recurring consideration is whether young impressionable students would feel pressure to participate in a religious exercise. For example, in *Schempp*, *Lee*, and *Santa Fe*, the Court expressed great concern that permitting private religious speech at a public school or at an official public school function would exert pressure on religious minorities, especially in communities where one or a few religious faiths predominated. The Court also expressed concern that dissenting students in the audience essentially would be captive to the private religious expression. Therefore, the students' Bible readings in *Schempp*, the rabbi's prayer in *Lee*, and the student prayers in *Santa Fe* were all deemed constitutionally impermissible, even though the religious speech in question was that of private individuals. Consider the following variations on the theme of religious expression in public school, and ask yourself on which side of the constitutional line they should fall.

1. A student reads aloud a paper on "Why I Love Jesus" in a public high school English class. (*See* C.H. ex rel. Z.H. v. Oliva, 195 F.3d 167 (3d Cir.), *vacated and reh'g en banc granted by* 197 F.3d 63 (3d Cir. 1999), *on reh'g en banc*, 226 F.3d 198 (3d Cir. 2000); Denooyer v. Merinelli, No. 92-2080, 1993 WL 477030 (6th Cir. Nov. 18, 1993) (per curiam).)

2. At a public high school graduation ceremony, a student elected as valedictorian of the graduating class bows her head during the valedictory address and recites a short prayer. (*See* Lassonde v. Pleasanton Unified Sch. Dist., 320 F.3d 979 (9th Cir. 2003); Cole v. Oroville Union High Sch. Dist., 228 F.3d 1092 (9th Cir. 2000).)

3. A state-mandated moment of silence is observed in a public high school classroom in which 95 percent of students bow and quietly pray.

4. A moment of silence is observed at a public high school graduation ceremony, at which numerous members of the audience spontaneously recite the Lord's Prayer, then applaud after "amen." (*See* Chaudhuri v. Tennessee, 130 F.3d 232 (6th Cir. 1997), *cert. denied*, 523 U.S. 1024 (1998).)

5. The incident described in example 4 occurs repeatedly over a period of several years, and school officials do nothing in response.

6. Every morning before the school day starts, a large group of students at a public high school gather to pray around the flagpole in front of the school (which all students have to pass by before entering the school).

7. Several teachers participate (before the school day starts) in the flagpole prayer described in example 6. (*See* Daugherty v. Vanguard Charter Sch. Acad., 116 F. Supp. 2d 897 (W.D. Mich. 2000).)

8. Most of the students on a public high school basketball team pray together on center court immediately before each game. (*See* Doe v. Duncanville Indep. Sch. Dist., 70 F.3d 402 (5th Cir. 1995).)

9. Most of the students on a public high school basketball team pray together in the locker room immediately before each game.

10. Several public school teachers wear "We Are One in Christ" T-shirts to class during a school spirit day. (*See* Harper v. Poway Unified Sch. Dist., 445 F.3d 1166 (9th Cir. 2006), *dismissed as moot*, 485 F.3d 1052 (9th Cir. 2007).)

11. An overwhelming majority of the students at a public school wear "We Are One in Christ" T-shirts to class during a school spirit day.

12. Several female Muslim students wear the hijab to class in a public high school. (*See* Isaacs ex rel. Isaacs v. Board of Educ. of Howard County, Md., 40 F. Supp. 2d 335 (D. Md. 1999).)

13. A Muslim teacher wears the hijab to teach her class in a public high school. (*See* United States v. Board of Educ., 911 F.2d 882 (3d Cir. 1990).)

14. A teacher places a large Bible on the corner of his desk, where the class is likely to notice it. (*See* Roberts v. Madigan, 921 F.2d 1047 (10th Cir. 1990), *cert. denied*, 505 U.S. 1218 (1992).)

15. A teacher invites her class at a public elementary school to decorate the classroom for Christmas, and permits the inclusion of religious elements among the decorations.

16. A choir at a public school performs a repertoire that includes mostly religious music. (*See* Bauchman v. West High Sch., 132 F.3d 542 (10th Cir. 1997), *cert. denied*, 524 U.S. 953 (1998).)

CHAPTER
20

The Establishment Clause and Government Endorsement of Religion

TABLE OF CONTENTS

A. GOVERNMENT-SPONSORED RELIGIOUS DISPLAYS

LYNCH v. DONNELLY

465 U.S. 668 (1984)

Chief Justice BURGER delivered the opinion of the Court.

We granted certiorari to decide whether the Establishment Clause of the First Amendment prohibits a municipality from including a crèche, or Nativity scene, in its annual Christmas display.

Each year, in cooperation with the downtown retail merchants' association, the city of Pawtucket, R. I., erects a Christmas display as part of its observance of the Christmas holiday season. The display is situated in a park owned by a nonprofit organization and located in the heart of the shopping district. The display is essentially like those to be found in hundreds of towns or cities across the Nation—often on public grounds—during the Christmas season. The Pawtucket display comprises many of the figures and decorations traditionally associated with Christmas, including, among other things, a Santa Claus house, reindeer pulling Santa's sleigh, candy-striped poles, a Christmas tree, carolers, cutout figures representing such characters as a clown, an elephant, and a teddy bear, hundreds of colored lights, a large banner that reads "SEASONS GREETINGS," and the crèche at issue here. All components of this display are owned by the City.

The crèche, which has been included in the display for 40 or more years, consists of the traditional figures, including the Infant Jesus, Mary and Joseph, angels, shepherds, kings, and animals, all ranging in height from 5″ to 5′. In 1973, when the present crèche was acquired, it cost the City $1,365; it now is valued at $200. The erection and dismantling of the crèche costs the City about $20 per year; nominal expenses are incurred in lighting the crèche. No money has been expended on its maintenance for the past 10 years.

There is an unbroken history of official acknowledgment by all three branches of government of the role of religion in American life from at least 1789. . . . Our history is replete with official references to the value and invocation of Divine guidance in deliberations and pronouncements of the Founding Fathers and contemporary leaders. Beginning in the early colonial period long before Independence, a day of Thanksgiving was celebrated as a religious holiday to give thanks for the bounties of Nature as gifts from God. President Washington and his successors proclaimed Thanksgiving, with all its religious overtones, a day of national celebration and Congress made it a National Holiday more than a century ago. Ch. 167, 16 Stat. 168 (1870). That holiday has not lost its theme of expressing thanks for Divine aid any more than has Christmas lost its religious significance.

Executive Orders and other official announcements of Presidents and of the Congress have proclaimed both Christmas and Thanksgiving National Holidays in religious terms. And, by Acts of Congress, it has long been the practice that federal employees are released from duties on these National Holidays, while being paid from the same public revenues that provide the compensation of the Chaplains of the Senate and the House and the military services. See J. Res. 5, 23 Stat. 516 (1885). Thus, it is clear that Government has long recognized—indeed it has subsidized—holidays with religious significance.

Other examples of reference to our religious heritage are found in the statutorily prescribed national motto "In God We Trust," 36 U.S.C. § 186, which Congress and the President mandated for our currency, see 31 U.S.C. § 324, and in the language "One nation under God," as part of the Pledge of Allegiance to the American flag. That pledge is recited by thousands of public school children—and adults—every year.

Art galleries supported by public revenues display religious paintings of the 15th and 16th centuries, predominantly inspired by one religious faith. The National Gallery in Washington, maintained with Government support, for example, has long exhibited masterpieces with religious messages, notably the Last Supper, and paintings depicting the Birth of Christ, the Crucifixion, and the Resurrection, among many others with explicit Christian themes and messages. The very chamber in which oral arguments on this case were heard is decorated with a notable and permanent—not seasonal—symbol of religion: Moses with Ten Commandments. Congress has long provided chapels in the Capitol for religious worship and meditation. There are countless other illustrations of the Government's acknowledgment of our religious heritage and governmental sponsorship of graphic manifestations of that heritage. . . .

This history may help explain why the Court consistently has declined to take a rigid, absolutist view of the Establishment Clause. . . .

In the line-drawing process we have often found it useful to inquire whether the challenged law or conduct has a secular purpose, whether its principal or primary effect is to advance or inhibit religion, and whether it creates an excessive entanglement of government with religion. *Lemon, supra.* But, we have repeatedly emphasized our unwillingness to be confined to any single test or criterion in this sensitive area.

The District Court inferred from the religious nature of the crèche that the City has no secular purpose for the display. In so doing, it rejected the City's claim that its reasons for including the crèche are essentially the same as its reasons for sponsoring the display as a whole. The District Court plainly erred by focusing almost exclusively on the crèche. When viewed in the proper context of the Christmas Holiday season, it is apparent that, on this record, there is insufficient evidence to establish that the inclusion of the crèche is a purposeful or surreptitious effort to express some kind of subtle governmental advocacy of a particular religious message. In a pluralistic society a variety of motives and purposes are implicated. The City, like the Congresses and Presidents, however, has principally taken note of a significant historical religious event long celebrated in the Western World. The crèche in the display depicts the historical origins of this traditional event long recognized as a National Holiday.

The narrow question is whether there is a secular purpose for Pawtucket's display of the crèche. The display is sponsored by the City to celebrate the Holiday and to depict the origins of that Holiday. These are legitimate secular purposes. The District Court's inference, drawn from the religious nature of the crèche, that the City has no secular purpose was, on this record, clearly erroneous.

The District Court found that the primary effect of including the crèche is to confer a substantial and impermissible benefit on religion in general and on the Christian faith in particular. Comparisons of the relative benefits to religion of different forms of governmental support are elusive and difficult to make. But to conclude that the primary effect of including the crèche is to advance religion in violation of the Establishment Clause would require that we view it as more beneficial to and more an endorsement of religion than, for example, expenditure of public funds for transportation of students to church-sponsored schools, *Everson v. Board of Education, supra*; and the tax exemptions for church properties sanctioned in *Walz, supra*. It would also require that we view it as more of an endorsement of religion than the Sunday Closing Laws upheld in *McGowan v. Maryland*, 366 U.S. 420 (1961). We are unable to discern a greater aid to religion deriving from inclusion of the crèche than from these benefits and endorsements previously held not violative of the Establishment Clause. . . .

The dissent asserts some observers may perceive that the City has aligned itself with the Christian faith by including a Christian symbol in its display and that this serves to advance religion. We can assume, *arguendo*, that the display advances religion in a sense; but our precedents plainly contemplate that on occasion some advancement of religion will result from governmental action. The Court has made it abundantly clear, however, that "not every law that confers an 'indirect,' 'remote,' or 'incidental' benefit upon [religion] is, for that reason alone, constitutionally invalid." *Nyquist, supra*, 413 U.S., at 771. Here, whatever benefit to one faith or religion or to all religions, is indirect, remote and incidental; display of the crèche is no more an advancement or endorsement of religion than the Congressional and Executive recognition of the origins of the Holiday itself as "Christ's Mass," or the exhibition of literally hundreds of religious paintings in governmentally supported museums.

. . . We hold that, notwithstanding the religious significance of the crèche, the City of Pawtucket has not violated the Establishment Clause of the First Amendment. Accordingly, the judgment of the Court of Appeals is reversed.

It is so ordered.

Justice O'CONNOR, concurring

The Establishment Clause prohibits government from making adherence to a religion relevant in any way to a person's standing in the political community. . . . Endorsement sends a message to nonadherents that they are outsiders, not full members of the political community, and an accompanying message to adherents that they are insiders, favored members of the political community. Disapproval sends the opposite message. See generally *Abington School District v. Schempp*, 374 U.S. 203 (1963). . . .

The central issue in this case is whether Pawtucket has endorsed Christianity by its display of the crèche. To answer that question, we must examine both what Pawtucket intended to communicate in displaying the crèche and what message the City's display actually conveyed. The purpose and effect prongs of the Lemon test represent these two aspects of the meaning of the City's action. . . .

The purpose prong of the Lemon test requires that a government activity have a secular purpose. That requirement is not satisfied, however, by the mere existence of some secular purpose, however dominated by religious purposes. In Stone v. Graham, 449 U.S. 39 (1980), for example, the Court held that posting copies of the Ten Commandments in schools violated the purpose prong of the Lemon test, yet the State plainly had some secular objectives, such as instilling most of the values of the Ten Commandments and illustrating their connection to our legal system . . .

The evident purpose of including the crèche in the larger display was not promotion of the religious content of the crèche but celebration of the public holiday through its traditional symbols. Celebration of public holidays, which have cultural significance even if they also have religious aspects, is a legitimate secular purpose.

The District Court's finding that the display of the crèche had no secular purpose was based on erroneous reasoning. The District Court believed that it should ascertain the City's purpose in displaying the creche separate and apart from the general purpose in setting up the display. . . .

Pawtucket's display of its crèche, I believe, does not communicate a message that the government intends to endorse the Christian beliefs represented by the crèche. Although the religious and indeed sectarian significance of the crèche, as the district court found, is not neutralized by the setting, the overall holiday setting changes what viewers may fairly understand to be the purpose of the display—as a typical museum setting, though not neutralizing the religious content of a religious painting, negates any message of endorsement of that content. The display celebrates a public holiday, and no one contends that declaration of that holiday is understood to be an endorsement of religion. The holiday itself has very strong secular components and traditions. Government celebration of the holiday, which is extremely common, generally is not understood to endorse the religious content of the holiday, just as government celebration of Thanksgiving is not so understood. The crèche is a traditional symbol of the holiday that is very commonly displayed along with purely secular symbols, as it was in Pawtucket.

These features combine to make the government's display of the crèche in this particular physical setting no more an endorsement of religion than such governmental "acknowledgments" of religion as legislative prayers of the type approved in *Marsh v. Chambers*, 463 U.S. 783 (1983), government declaration of Thanksgiving as a public holiday, printing of "In God We Trust" on coins, and opening court sessions with "God save the United States and this honorable court." Those government acknowledgments of religion serve, in the only ways reasonably possible in our culture, the legitimate secular purposes of solemnizing public occasions, expressing confidence in the future, and encouraging the recognition of what is worthy of appreciation in society. For that reason, and because of their history and ubiquity, those practices are not understood as conveying government approval of particular religious beliefs. The display of the crèche likewise serves a secular purpose—celebration of a public holiday with traditional symbols. It cannot fairly be understood to convey a message of government endorsement of religion. . . .

Giving the challenged practice the careful scrutiny it deserves, I cannot say that the particular crèche display at issue in this case was intended to endorse or had the effect of endorsing Christianity. I agree with the Court that the judgment below must be reversed.

Justice BRENNAN, with whom Justice MARSHALL, Justice BLACKMUN, and Justice STEVENS join, dissenting.

The Court advances two principal arguments to support its conclusion that the Pawtucket crèche satisfies the *Lemon* test. Neither is persuasive.

First. The Court, by focusing on the holiday "context" in which the nativity scene appeared, seeks to explain away the clear religious import of the crèche and the findings of the District Court that most observers understood the crèche as both a symbol of Christian beliefs and a symbol of the city's support for those beliefs. Thus, although the Court concedes that the city's inclusion of the nativity scene plainly serves "to depict the origins" of Christmas as a "significant historical religious event," and that the crèche "is identified with one religious faith," we are nevertheless expected to believe that Pawtucket's use of the crèche does not signal the city's support for the sectarian symbolism that the nativity scene evokes. The effect of the crèche, of course, must be gauged not only by its inherent religious significance but also by the overall setting in which it appears. But it blinks reality to claim, as the Court does, that by including such a distinctively religious object as the crèche in its Christmas display, Pawtucket has done no more than make use of a "traditional" symbol of the holiday, and has thereby purged the crèche of its religious content and conferred only an "incidental and indirect" benefit on religion.

[E]ven in the context of Pawtucket's seasonal celebration, the crèche retains a specifically Christian religious meaning. I refuse to accept the notion implicit in today's decision that non-Christians would find that the religious content of the crèche is eliminated by the fact that it appears as part of the City's otherwise secular celebration of the Christmas holiday. The nativity scene is clearly distinct in its purpose and effect from the rest of the Hodgson Park display for the simple reason that it is the only one rooted in a biblical account of Christ's birth. It is the chief symbol of the characteristically Christian belief that a divine Savior was brought into the world and that the purpose of this miraculous birth was to illuminate a path toward salvation and redemption. For Christians, that path is exclusive, precious and holy. But for those who do not share these beliefs, the symbolic re-enactment of the birth of a divine being who has been miraculously incarnated as a man stands as a dramatic reminder of their differences with Christian faith.[14]

---

[14] For Christians, of course, the essential message of the nativity is that God became incarnate in the person of Christ. But just as fundamental to Jewish thought is the belief in the "non-incarnation of God, . . . [t]he God in whom [Jews] believe, to whom [Jews] are pledged, does not unite with human substance on earth." M. Buber, Israel and the World (1948) (reprinted in F. Talmage, Disputation and Dialogue: Readings in the Jewish-Christian Encounter 281-282 (1975)) (emphasis deleted). This distinction, according to Buber, "constitute[s] the ultimate division between Judaism and Christianity." *Id.,* at 281. See also R. Reuther, Faith and Fratricide 246 (1974).

Similarly, those who follow the tenets of Unitarianism might well find Pawtucket's support for the symbolism of the crèche, which highlights the trinitarian tradition in Christian faith, to be an affront to their belief in a single divine being. See J. Williams, What Americans Believe and How

When government appears to sponsor such religiously inspired views, we cannot say that the practice is "'so separate and so indisputably marked off from the religious function,' . . . that [it] may fairly be viewed as reflect[ing] a neutral posture toward religious institutions." To be so excluded on religious grounds by one's elected government is an insult and an injury that, until today, could not be countenanced by the Establishment Clause.

Second. The Court also attempts to justify the crèche by entertaining a beguilingly simple, yet faulty syllogism. The Court begins by noting that government may recognize Christmas day as a public holiday; the Court then asserts that the crèche is nothing more than a traditional element of Christmas celebrations; and it concludes that the inclusion of a crèche as part of a government's annual Christmas celebration is constitutionally permissible. The Court apparently believes that once it finds that the designation of Christmas as a public holiday is constitutionally acceptable, it is then free to conclude that virtually every form of governmental association with the celebration of the holiday is also constitutional. The vice of this dangerously superficial argument is that it overlooks the fact that the Christmas holiday in our national culture contains both secular and sectarian elements. To say that government may recognize the holiday's traditional, secular elements of gift-giving, public festivities and community spirit, does not mean that government may indiscriminately embrace the distinctively sectarian aspects of the holiday. Indeed, in its eagerness to approve the crèche, the Court has advanced a rationale so simplistic that it would appear to allow the Mayor of Pawtucket to participate in the celebration of a Christmas Mass, since this would be just another unobjectionable way for the City to "celebrate the holiday." As is demonstrated below, the Court's logic is fundamentally flawed both because it obscures the reason why public designation of Christmas Day as a holiday is constitutionally acceptable, and blurs the distinction between the secular aspects of Christmas and its distinctively religious character, as exemplified by the crèche.

When government decides to recognize Christmas Day as a public holiday, it does no more than accommodate the calendar of public activities to the plain fact that many Americans will expect on that day to spend time visiting with their families, attending religious services, and perhaps enjoying some respite from preholiday activities. The Free Exercise Clause, of course, does not necessarily compel the government to provide this accommodation, but neither is the Establishment Clause offended by such a step. Because it is clear that the celebration of Christmas has both secular and sectarian elements, it may well be that by taking note of the holiday, the government is simply seeking to serve the same kinds of wholly secular goals—for instance, promoting goodwill and a common day of rest—that were found to justify Sunday Closing Laws in *McGowan* [*v. Maryland*]. If public officials go further and participate in the *secular* celebration of Christmas—by, for example, decorating public places with such secular images as wreaths, garlands or Santa Claus figures—they move closer to the limits of their constitutional power but nevertheless remain within the boundaries set by the Establishment Clause. But when those officials participate in or appear to endorse the distinctively religious elements of this otherwise secular event, they encroach upon First Amendment freedoms. For it is at that point that the government brings to the forefront the theological content of the

---

They Worship 316-317 (3d ed. 1969). See also C. Olmstead, History of Religion in the United States 296-299 (1960).

holiday, and places the prestige, power, and financial support of a civil authority in the service of a particular faith.

The inclusion of a crèche in Pawtucket's otherwise secular celebration of Christmas clearly violates these principles. Unlike such secular figures as Santa Claus, reindeer and carolers, a nativity scene represents far more than a mere "traditional" symbol of Christmas. The essence of the crèche's symbolic purpose and effect is to prompt the observer to experience a sense of simple awe and wonder appropriate to the contemplation of one of the central elements of Christian dogma—that God sent His son into the world to be a Messiah. Contrary to the Court's suggestion, the crèche is far from a mere representation of a "particular historic religious event." It is, instead, best understood as a mystical re-creation of an event that lies at the heart of Christian faith. To suggest, as the Court does, that such a symbol is merely "traditional" and therefore no different from Santa's house or reindeer is not only offensive to those for whom the crèche has profound significance, but insulting to those who insist for religious or personal reasons that the story of Christ is in no sense a part of "history" nor an unavoidable element of our national "heritage."

For these reasons, the crèche in this context simply cannot be viewed as playing the same role that an ordinary museum display does. The Court seems to assume that prohibiting Pawtucket from displaying a crèche would be tantamount to forbidding a state college from including the Bible or Milton's Paradise Lost in a course on English literature. But in those cases the religiously-inspired materials are being considered solely as literature. The purpose is plainly not to single out the particular religious beliefs that may have inspired the authors, but to see in these writings the outlines of a larger imaginative universe shared with other forms of literary expression. The same may be said of a course devoted to the study of art; when the course turns to Gothic architecture, the emphasis is not on the religious beliefs which the cathedrals exalt, but rather upon the "aesthetic consequences of [such religious] thought."

AN EXTENDED NOTE ON GOVERNMENT-SPONSORED SEASONAL HOLIDAY DISPLAYS

Litigation over the constitutionality of holiday displays is now almost as much of a traditional feature of the holiday season as the displays themselves. One of the major reasons that litigation is so frequent is that the standard used by the Supreme Court to adjudicate holiday displays is so contextual and indefinite. A good illustration of how problematic these cases have been for the Court can be found in the Court's other main holiday display case, County of Allegheny v. ACLU, 492 U.S. 573 (1989). The case involved Establishment Clause challenges to two holiday displays on Allegheny County property. One display included a crèche, which contained a traditional representation of the manger scene in Bethlehem surrounded by poinsettias and topped with an angel bearing a banner that proclaimed "Gloria in Excelsis Deo!" The crèche was placed on the Grand Staircase inside the county courthouse. The second display was under an arch outside the city-county building, another government property located a block away from the county courthouse. The second display contained an 18-foot menorah, placed alongside a 45-foot Christmas tree and a sign entitled "Salute to Liberty."

The Court split into three groups on the issue of whether these displays were constitutional. Justice Kennedy, joined by the Chief Justice and Justices Scalia and White, asserted that both displays were constitutional. Justices Brennan, Marshall, and Stevens argued that both displays were unconstitutional. Justices Blackmun and O'Connor, who both relied on Justice O'Connor's endorsement test, distinguished the crèche from the menorah. They held that the crèche display was an unconstitutional endorsement of religion, but the menorah display was "simply a recognition of cultural diversity." *Id.* at 619. Justices Blackmun and O'Connor were therefore the only two Justices to agree on the result in the case, but even they could not get their respective objective observers to see the same religious significance in the menorah display. Although Justice Blackmun recognized that the menorah is a religious symbol, he also asserted that a menorah has secular symbolic value. Blackmun argued that by placing the menorah beside a disclaimer sign and a Christmas tree, which he viewed as a wholly secular symbol, the city had brought the menorah's secular symbolism to the fore and had conveyed only the "city's secular recognition of different traditions for celebrating the winter-holiday season." *Id.* at 620. Justice O'Connor disagreed, noting that she did not "strain to argue that the menorah has a 'secular dimension.'" *Id.* at 634 (O'Connor, J., concurring). Instead, O'Connor recognized that the menorah is a religious symbol and Chanukah is a religious holiday. But this acknowledgment of the religious nature of the symbol did not keep O'Connor from finding that this particular use of an admittedly religious symbol celebrating an admittedly religious holiday conveyed a purely secular message to an objective observer. O'Connor concluded that the city's placement of the admittedly religious symbol beside the tree and the sign was merely an "effort to acknowledge the cultural diversity of our country and to convey tolerance of different choices in matters of religious belief or nonbelief by recognizing that the winter holiday season is celebrated in diverse ways by our citizens." *Id.* at 636 (O'Connor, J., concurring).

As this brief description indicates, there is no precise standard for distinguishing the permissible use of overtly religious symbols to acknowledge the society's religious diversity from the impermissible use of the same symbols to endorse religion. The lack of a precise standard, coupled with the different factual contexts raised in every display case, means that the likelihood of litigation over new displays ranges from high to inevitable. The likelihood that lower courts will produce inconsistent rulings in these cases is equally high.

NOTES AND QUESTIONS

1. *Secular purpose.* Is it possible to depict the origins of Christmas without displaying a crèche? Is it necessary to depict the origins of Christmas in order to celebrate it? Do we generally celebrate holidays by depicting their origins?
2. *Effect and Context.* The effect of a government-sponsored religious display may turn on the context in which it appears. Most reasonable people would not conclude that art museums were endorsing or promoting religion by displaying images of the birth of Jesus. Does the same hold true for including the birth of Jesus in a state-sponsored holiday display? Why was the holiday crèche in *Lynch* constitutional but the one in *Allegheny* was not? Does displaying a crèche surrounded by secular items always serve to neutralize any message of

endorsement? What if the crèche were displayed with only one other secular item?

3. *Christmas as national holiday.* Both the majority and the dissent in *Lynch* agree that the government does not violate the Establishment Clause by designating Christmas as a national holiday. Why not? Would declaring Good Friday a national holiday also be constitutional? Is the difference that everyone celebrates Christmas? Does everyone celebrate Christmas? How does Christmas compare to Thanksgiving?

4. *Crèche vs. menorah.* When comparing the display of a crèche to the display of a menorah, does it matter that 70.6% of Americans identify as Christian compared to 1.9% who identify as Jewish? Pew Research Center, Public & Religious Life, Religious Landscape Study, http://www.pewforum.org/religious-landscape-study/. In what way?

5. *Ceremonial deism.* The majority suggests that displaying a crèche is merely an acknowledgment of our religious heritage on par with mentioning God in our national motto ("In God We Trust"). Are the two comparable? In any event, is including God in our national motto problematic? The official national motto used to be "E Pluribus Unum" (Out of Many, One). It was changed in 1956, during the Cold War, in order to differentiate the United States from the atheistic USSR. Does this history change your answer? The Cold War era also saw the addition of "under God" to the Pledge of Allegiance. Although the Pledge's constitutionality was challenged in *Elk Grove Unified School District v. Newdow*, 542 U.S. 1 (2004), the Court found that Newdow lacked standing and therefore did not reach the Establishment Clause question.

6. *Reasonable person.* The endorsement test asks whether a reasonable person would conclude that the government's display had the purpose or effect of endorsing religion. Does the reasonable person have a religion? Would a reasonable Christian view the crèche or "In God We Trust" differently from a reasonable Muslim, Buddhist, or atheist? How would you feel if instead of the crèche surrounded by secular objects, the town of Pawtucket displayed a five foot menorah or a five foot Buddha surrounded by toys?

7. *Protecting religion.* Among its other goals, the Establishment Clause was designed to protect the sponsored religion from degradation. Has Christianity been tarnished or insulted by a government sponsored holiday display that pairs a crèche with Santa's house, festive reindeer, and a clown?

McCREARY COUNTY, KENTUCKY v. AMERICAN CIVIL LIBERTIES UNION OF KENTUCKY

545 U.S. 844 (2005)

[In the initial action that eventually led to this lawsuit, two Kentucky Counties posted large copies of the Ten Commandments in their courthouses. The ACLU sued to enjoin the displays on the ground that they violated the First Amendment's Establishment Clause. In response, the Counties adopted nearly identical resolutions calling for a more extensive exhibit meant to show that the Commandments are Kentucky's "precedent legal code." The resolutions noted several grounds for taking that position, including the state legislature's acknowledgment of Christ as the "Prince of Ethics." The displays around the Commandments were modified to include eight smaller, historical documents containing religious references as their sole common element, for example, the Declaration of Independence's "endowed by their Creator" passage. The District Court held that the new display lacked a secular purpose under *Lemon*. After changing counsel, the Counties revised the exhibits again. The new exhibit, entitled "The Foundations of American Law and Government Display," consisted of nine framed documents of equal size. One set out the Commandments explicitly identified as the "King James Version," quoted them at greater length, and explained that they have profoundly influenced the formation of Western legal thought and this Nation. Along with the Commandments, the counties posted framed copies of, among other things, the Star Spangled Banner's lyrics and the Declaration of Independence, accompanied by statements about their historical and legal significance. Both the District Court and the Court of Appeals held the third display unconstitutional under the *Lemon* secular purpose analysis, and the Supreme Court affirmed.]

Justice SOUTER delivered the opinion of the Court.

Ever since *Lemon v. Kurtzman* summarized the three familiar considerations for evaluating Establishment Clause claims, looking to whether government action has "a secular legislative purpose" has been a common, albeit seldom dispositive, element of our cases. Though we have found government action motivated by an illegitimate purpose only four times since *Lemon*, and "the secular purpose requirement alone may rarely be determinative . . ., it nevertheless serves an important function."

We take *Stone* [v. *Graham*] as the initial legal benchmark, our only case dealing with the constitutionality of displaying the Commandments. *Stone* recognized that the Commandments are an "instrument of religion" and that, at least on the facts before it, the display of their text could presumptively be understood as meant to advance religion: although state law specifically required their posting in public school classrooms, their isolated exhibition did not leave room even for an argument that secular education explained their being there. But *Stone* did not purport to decide the constitutionality of every possible way the Commandments might be set out by the government, and under the Establishment Clause detail is key. Hence, we look to the record of evidence showing the progression leading up to the third display of the Commandments.

The display rejected in *Stone* had two obvious similarities to the first one in the sequence here: both set out a text of the Commandments as distinct from any traditionally symbolic representation, and each stood alone, not part of an arguably secular display. *Stone* stressed the significance of integrating the Commandments into a secular scheme to forestall the broadcast of an otherwise clearly religious message, and for good reason, the Commandments being a central point of reference in the religious and moral history of Jews and Christians. They proclaim the existence of a monotheistic god (no other gods). They regulate details of religious obligation (no graven images, no sabbath breaking, no vain oath swearing). And they unmistakably rest even the universally accepted prohibitions (as against murder, theft, and the like) on the sanction of the divinity proclaimed at the beginning of the text. Displaying that text is thus different from a symbolic depiction, like tablets with 10 roman numerals, which could be seen as alluding to a general notion of law, not a sectarian conception of faith. Where the text is set out, the insistence of the religious message is hard to avoid in the absence of a context plausibly suggesting a message going beyond an excuse to promote the religious point of view. The display in *Stone* had no context that might have indicated an object beyond the religious character of the text, and the Counties' solo exhibit here did nothing more to counter the sectarian implication than the postings at issue in *Stone*. Actually, the posting by the Counties lacked even the *Stone* display's implausible disclaimer that the Commandments were set out to show their effect on the civil law. What is more, at the ceremony for posting the framed Commandments in Pulaski County, the county executive was accompanied by his pastor, who testified to the certainty of the existence of God. The reasonable observer could only think that the Counties meant to emphasize and celebrate the Commandments' religious message.

This is not to deny that the Commandments have had influence on civil or secular law; a major text of a majority religion is bound to be felt. The point is simply that the original text viewed in its entirety is an unmistakably religious statement dealing with religious obligations and with morality subject to religious sanction. When the government initiates an effort to place this statement alone in public view, a religious object is unmistakable.

[The Court then discussed the history of the three displays.] These new statements of purpose [issued in conjunction with the third display] were presented only as a litigating position, there being no further authorizing action by the Counties' governing boards. And although repeal of the earlier county authorizations would not have erased them from the record of evidence bearing on current purpose, the extraordinary resolutions for the second display passed just months earlier were not repealed or otherwise repudiated. Indeed, the sectarian spirit of the common resolution found enhanced expression in the third display, which quoted more of the purely religious language of the Commandments than the first two displays had done; ("I the LORD thy God am a jealous God") (text of Second Commandment in third display); ("the LORD will not hold him guiltless that taketh his name in vain") (from text of Third Commandment); and ("that thy days may be long upon the land which the LORD thy God giveth thee") (text of Fifth Commandment). No reasonable observer could swallow the claim that the Counties had cast off the objective so unmistakable in the earlier displays.

Nor did the selection of posted material suggest a clear theme that might prevail over evidence of the continuing religious object. In a collection of documents said to be "foundational" to American government, it is at least odd to include a patriotic anthem, but to omit the Fourteenth Amendment, the most significant structural provision adopted since the original Framing. And it is no less baffling to leave out the original Constitution of 1787 while quoting the 1215 Magna Carta even to the point of its declaration that "fish-weirs shall be removed from the Thames." If an observer found these choices and omissions perplexing in isolation, he would be puzzled for a different reason when he read the Declaration of Independence seeking confirmation for the Counties' posted explanation that the "Ten Commandments . . . influence is clearly seen in the Declaration"; in fact the observer would find that the Commandments are sanctioned as divine imperatives, while the Declaration of Independence holds that the authority of government to enforce the law derives "from the consent of the governed." If the observer had not thrown up his hands, he would probably suspect that the Counties were simply reaching for any way to keep a religious document on the walls of courthouses constitutionally required to embody religious neutrality.

In holding the preliminary injunction adequately supported by evidence that the Counties' purpose had not changed at the third stage, we do not decide that the Counties' past actions forever taint any effort on their part to deal with the subject matter. We hold only that purpose needs to be taken seriously under the

Establishment Clause and needs to be understood in light of context; an implausible claim that governmental purpose has changed should not carry the day in a court of law any more than in a head with common sense. It is enough to say here that district courts are fully capable of adjusting preliminary relief to take account of genuine changes in constitutionally significant conditions.

[Justice O'Connor's concurring opinion is omitted.]

Justice SCALIA, with whom THE CHIEF JUSTICE and Justice THOMAS join and with whom Justice KENNEDY joins, dissenting.

Besides appealing to the demonstrably false principle that the government cannot favor religion over irreligion, today's opinion suggests that the posting of the Ten Commandments violates the principle that the government cannot favor one religion over another. That is indeed a valid principle where public aid or assistance to religion is concerned or where the free exercise of religion is at issue, but it necessarily applies in a more limited sense to public acknowledgment of the Creator. If religion in the public forum had to be entirely nondenominational, there could be no religion in the public forum at all. One cannot say the word "God," or "the Almighty," one cannot offer public supplication or thanksgiving, without contradicting the beliefs of some people that there are many gods, or that God or the gods pay no attention to human affairs. With respect to public acknowledgment of religious belief, it is entirely clear from our Nation's historical practices that the Establishment Clause permits this disregard of polytheists and believers in unconcerned deities, just as it permits the disregard of devout atheists. The Thanksgiving Proclamation issued by George Washington at the instance of the First Congress was scrupulously nondenominational—but it was monotheistic.

Perhaps in recognition of the centrality of the Ten Commandments as a widely recognized symbol of religion in public life, the Court is at pains to dispel the impression that its decision will require governments across the country to sandblast the Ten Commandments from the public square. The constitutional problem, the Court says, is with the Counties' *purpose* in erecting the Foundations Displays, not the displays themselves. The Court adds in a footnote: "One consequence of taking account of the purpose underlying past actions is that the same government action may be constitutional if taken in the first instance and unconstitutional if it has a sectarian heritage."

This inconsistency may be explicable in theory, but I suspect that the "objective observer" with whom the Court is so concerned will recognize its absurdity in practice. By virtue of details familiar only to the parties to litigation and their lawyers, McCreary and Pulaski Counties, Kentucky, and Rutherford County, Tennessee, have been ordered to remove the same display that appears in courthouses from Mercer County, Kentucky to Elkhart County, Indiana. Displays erected in silence (and under the direction of good legal advice) are permissible, while those hung after discussion and debate are deemed unconstitutional. Reduction of the Establishment Clause to such minutiae trivializes the Clause's protection against religious establishment; indeed, it may inflame religious passions by making the passing comments of every government official the subject of endless litigation.

VAN ORDEN v. PERRY

545 U.S. 677 (2005)

[Among the 21 historical markers and 17 monuments surrounding the Texas State Capitol is a 6-foot-high monolith inscribed with the Ten Commandments. The monolith stands 6 feet high and 31/2 feet wide. It is located to the north of the Capitol building, between the Capitol and the Supreme Court building. Its primary content is the text of the Ten Commandments. An eagle grasping the American flag, an eye inside of a pyramid, and two small tablets with what appears to be an ancient script are carved above the text of the Ten Commandments. Below the text are two Stars of David and the superimposed Greek letters Chi and Rho, which represent Christ. The bottom of the monument bears the inscription "PRESENTED TO THE PEOPLE AND YOUTH OF TEXAS BY THE FRATERNAL ORDER OF EAGLES OF TEXAS 1961." The legislative record surrounding the State's acceptance of the monument is limited to legislative journal entries. After the monument was accepted, the State selected a site for the monument based on the recommendation of the state organization responsible for maintaining the Capitol grounds. The Eagles paid the cost of erecting the monument, the dedication of which was presided over by two state legislators.]

Chief Justice REHNQUIST announced the judgment of the Court and delivered an opinion, in which Justice SCALIA, Justice KENNEDY, and Justice THOMAS join.

Our cases, Januslike, point in two directions in applying the Establishment Clause. One face looks toward the strong role played by religion and religious traditions throughout our Nation's history. The other face looks toward the principle that governmental intervention in religious matters can itself endanger religious freedom.

This case, like all Establishment Clause challenges, presents us with the difficulty of respecting both faces. Our institutions presuppose a Supreme Being, yet these institutions must not press religious observances upon their citizens. One face looks to the past in acknowledgment of our Nation's heritage, while the other looks to the present in demanding a separation between church and state. Reconciling these two faces requires that we neither abdicate our responsibility to maintain a division between church and state nor evince a hostility to religion by disabling the government from in some ways recognizing our religious heritage.

Whatever may be the fate of the *Lemon* test in the larger scheme of Establishment Clause jurisprudence, we think it not useful in dealing with the sort of passive monument that Texas has erected on its Capitol grounds. Instead, our analysis is driven both by the nature of the monument and by our Nation's history.

In this case we are faced with a display of the Ten Commandments on government property outside the Texas State Capitol. Such acknowledgments of the role played by the Ten Commandments in our Nation's heritage are common throughout America. We need only look within our own Courtroom. Since 1935, Moses has stood, holding two tablets that reveal portions of the Ten Commandments written in Hebrew, among other lawgivers in the south frieze. Representations of the Ten Commandments adorn the metal gates lining the north and south sides of the Courtroom as well as the doors leading into the Courtroom. Moses also sits on the exterior east facade of the building holding the Ten Commandments tablets.

Of course, the Ten Commandments are religious—they were so viewed at their inception and so remain. The monument, therefore, has religious significance. According to Judeo-Christian belief, the Ten Commandments were given to Moses by God on Mt. Sinai. But Moses was a lawgiver as well as a religious leader. And the Ten Commandments have an undeniable historical meaning, as the foregoing examples demonstrate. Simply having religious content or promoting a message consistent with a religious doctrine does not run afoul of the Establishment Clause.

There are, of course, limits to the display of religious messages or symbols. For example, we held unconstitutional a Kentucky statute requiring the posting of the Ten Commandments in every public schoolroom. *Stone v. Graham*, 449 U.S. 39 (1980) (*per curiam*). In the classroom context, we found that the Kentucky statute had an improper and plainly religious purpose. As evidenced by *Stone*'s almost exclusive reliance upon two of our school prayer cases, it stands as an example of the fact that we have "been particularly vigilant in monitoring compliance with the Establishment Clause in elementary and secondary schools." Neither *Stone* itself nor subsequent opinions have indicated that *Stone*'s holding would extend to a legislative chamber, or to capitol grounds.[11]

[Justices Scalia's and Thomas's concurring opinions are omitted.]

Justice BREYER, concurring in the judgment.

In *School Dist. of Abington Township v. Schempp*, Justice Goldberg, joined by Justice Harlan, wrote, in respect to the First Amendment's Religion Clauses, that there is "no simple and clear measure which by precise application can readily and invariably demark the permissible from the impermissible." One must refer instead to the basic purposes of those Clauses. They seek to "assure the fullest possible scope of religious liberty and tolerance for all." They seek to avoid that divisiveness based upon religion that promotes social conflict, sapping the strength of government and religion alike. They seek to maintain that "separation of church and state" that has long been critical to the "peaceful dominion that religion exercises in [this] country," where the "spirit of religion" and the "spirit of freedom" are productively "united," "reign[ing] together" but in separate spheres "on the same soil." A. de Tocqueville, Democracy in America 282-283 (1835) (H. Mansfield & D. Winthrop transls. and eds. 2000).

The Court has made clear, as Justices Goldberg and Harlan noted, that the realization of these goals means that government must "neither engage in nor compel religious practices," that it must "effect no favoritism among sects or between religion and nonreligion," and that it must "work deterrence of no religious belief." The government must avoid excessive interference with, or promotion of, religion. But the Establishment Clause does not compel the government to purge from the public sphere all that in any way partakes of the religious. Such absolutism is not

---

[11] Nor does anything suggest that *Stone* would extend to displays of the Ten Commandments that lack a "plainly religious," "pre-eminent purpose," [*Stone v. Graham*,] at 41. See *Edwards v. Aguillard*, . . . ("[*Stone*] did not mean that no use could ever be made of the Ten Commandments, or that the Ten Commandments played an exclusively religious role in the history of Western Civilization"). Indeed, we need not decide in this case the extent to which a primarily religious purpose would affect our analysis because it is clear from the record that there is no evidence of such a purpose in this case.

only inconsistent with our national traditions, but would also tend to promote the kind of social conflict the Establishment Clause seeks to avoid. . . .

If the relation between government and religion is one of separation, but not of mutual hostility and suspicion, one will inevitably find difficult borderline cases. And in such cases, I see no test-related substitute for the exercise of legal judgment. That judgment is not a personal judgment. Rather, as in all constitutional cases, it must reflect and remain faithful to the underlying purposes of the Clauses, and it must take account of context and consequences measured in light of those purposes. While the Court's prior tests provide useful guideposts—and might well lead to the same result the Court reaches today, no exact formula can dictate a resolution to such fact-intensive cases.

The case before us is a borderline case. It concerns a large granite monument bearing the text of the Ten Commandments located on the grounds of the Texas State Capitol. On the one hand, the Commandments' text undeniably has a religious message, invoking, indeed emphasizing, the Deity. On the other hand, focusing on the text of the Commandments alone cannot conclusively resolve this case. Rather, to determine the message that the text here conveys, we must examine how the text is *used.* And that inquiry requires us to consider the context of the display.

In certain contexts, a display of the tablets of the Ten Commandments can convey not simply a religious message but also a secular moral message (about proper standards of social conduct). And in certain contexts, a display of the tablets can also convey a historical message (about a historic relation between those standards and the law)—a fact that helps to explain the display of those tablets in dozens of courthouses throughout the Nation, including the Supreme Court of the United States.

Here the tablets have been used as part of a display that communicates not simply a religious message, but a secular message as well. The circumstances surrounding the display's placement on the capitol grounds and its physical setting suggest that the State itself intended the latter, nonreligious aspects of the tablets' message to predominate. And the monument's 40-year history on the Texas state grounds indicates that that has been its effect. . . .

The physical setting of the monument, moreover, suggests little or nothing of the sacred. The monument sits in a large park containing 17 monuments and 21 historical markers, all designed to illustrate the "ideals" of those who settled in Texas and of those who have lived there since that time. The setting does not readily lend itself to meditation or any other religious activity. But it does provide a context of history and moral ideals. It (together with the display's inscription about its origin) communicates to visitors that the State sought to reflect moral principles, illustrating a relation between ethics and law that the State's citizens, historically speaking, have endorsed. That is to say, the context suggests that the State intended the display's moral message—an illustrative message reflecting the historical "ideals" of Texans—to predominate.

If these factors provide a strong, but not conclusive, indication that the Commandments' text on this monument conveys a predominantly secular message, a further factor is determinative here. As far as I can tell, 40 years passed in which the presence of this monument, legally speaking, went unchallenged (until the single legal objection raised by petitioner). And I am not aware of any evidence suggesting that this was due to a climate of intimidation. Hence, those 40 years suggest more strongly than can any set of formulaic tests that few individuals, whatever their system of beliefs, are likely to have understood the monument as amounting, in any significantly detrimental way, to a government effort to favor a particular religious sect, primarily to promote religion over nonreligion, to "engage in" any "religious practice," to "compel" any "religious practice," or to "work deterrence" of any "religious belief." Those 40 years suggest that the public visiting the capitol grounds has considered the religious aspect of the tablets' message as part of what is a broader moral and historical message reflective of a cultural heritage. . . .

Justice STEVENS, with whom Justice GINSBURG joins, dissenting.

The sole function of the monument on the grounds of Texas' State Capitol is to display the full text of one version of the Ten Commandments. The monument is not a work of art and does not refer to any event in the history of the State. It is significant because, and only because, it communicates the following message:

"I AM the LORD thy God.

"Thou shalt have no other gods before me.

"Thou shalt not make to thyself any graven images.

"Thou shalt not take the Name of the Lord thy God in vain.

"Remember the Sabbath day, to keep it holy.

"Honor thy father and thy mother, that thy days may be long upon the land which the Lord thy God giveth thee.

"Thou shalt not kill.

"Thou shalt not commit adultery.

"Thou shalt not steal.

"Thou shalt not bear false witness against thy neighbor.

"Thou shalt not covet thy neighbor's house.

"Thou shalt not covet thy neighbor's wife, nor his manservant, nor his maidservant, nor his cattle, nor anything that is thy neighbor's.

Viewed on its face, Texas' display has no purported connection to God's role in the formation of Texas or the founding of our Nation; nor does it provide the reasonable observer with any basis to guess that it was erected to honor any individual or organization. The message transmitted by Texas' chosen display is quite plain: This State endorses the divine code of the "Judeo-Christian" God.

For those of us who learned to recite the King James version of the text long before we understood the meaning of some of its words, God's Commandments may seem like wise counsel. The question before this Court, however, is whether it is counsel that the State of Texas may proclaim without violating the Establishment Clause of the Constitution. If any fragment of Jefferson's metaphorical "wall of separation between church and State" is to be preserved—if there remains any meaning to the "wholesome 'neutrality' of which this Court's [Establishment Clause] cases speak,"—a negative answer to that question is mandatory.

The reason this message stands apart is that the Decalogue is a venerable religious text. As we held 25 years ago, it is beyond dispute that "[t]he Ten Commandments are undeniably a sacred text in the Jewish and Christian faiths." *Stone v. Graham.* For many followers, the Commandments represent the literal word of God as spoken to Moses and repeated to his followers after descending from Mount Sinai. The message conveyed by the Ten Commandments thus cannot be analogized to an appendage to a common article of commerce ("In God we Trust") or an incidental part of a familiar recital ("God save the United States and this honorable Court"). Thankfully, the plurality does not attempt to minimize the religious significance of the Ten Commandments. Attempts to secularize what is unquestionably a sacred text defy credibility and disserve people of faith.

[D]espite the Eagles' best efforts to choose a benign nondenominational text,[15] the Ten Commandments display projects not just a religious, but an inherently sectarian message. There are many distinctive versions of the Decalogue, ascribed to by different religions and even different denominations within a particular faith; to a pious and learned observer, these differences may be of enormous religious significance.[16] See Lubet, *The Ten Commandments in Alabama*, 15 Constitutional Commentary 471, 474-476 (Fall 1998). In choosing to display this version of the Commandments, Texas tells the observer that the State supports this side of the doctrinal religious debate. The reasonable observer, after all, has no way of knowing that this text was the product of a compromise, or that there is a rationale of any kind for the text's selection.

The Establishment Clause, if nothing else, forbids government from "specifying details upon which men and women who believe in a benevolent, omnipotent Creator and Ruler of the world are known to differ." Given that the chosen text inscribed on the Ten Commandments monument invariably places the State at the center of a serious sectarian dispute, the display is unquestionably unconstitutional under our case law.

Even if, however, the message of the monument, despite the inscribed text, fairly could be said to represent the belief system of all Judeo-Christians, it would still run afoul of the Establishment Clause by prescribing a compelled code of conduct from one God, namely a Judeo-Christian God, that is rejected by prominent polytheistic

---

[15] Despite the Eagles' efforts, not all of the monuments they donated in fact conform to a "universally-accepted" text. Compare, *e.g.*, Appendix, *infra* (including the command that "Thou shalt not make to thyself any graven images"), with *Freedom from Religion Foundation*, 898 P.2d at 1016 (omitting that command altogether). The distinction represents a critical divide between the Protestant and Catholic faiths. During the Reformation, Protestants destroyed images of the Virgin Mary and of Jesus Christ that were venerated in Catholic churches. Even today there is a notable difference between the imagery in different churches, a difference that may in part be attributable to differing understandings of the meaning of what is the Second Commandment in the King James Bible translation and a portion of the First Commandment in the Catholic translation. See Finkelman, The Ten Commandments on the Courthouse Lawn and Elsewhere, 73 Ford. L. Rev. 1477, 1493-1494 (2005).

[16] For example, in the Jewish version of the Sixth Commandment God commands: "You shall not murder"; whereas, the King James interpretation of the same command is: "Thou shalt not kill." Compare W. Plaut, The Torah: A Modern Commentary 534 (1981), with Appendix, *infra*. The difference between the two versions is not merely semantic; rather, it is but one example of a deep theological dispute. See Finkelman, *supra*, at 1481-1500; P. Maier, Enumerating the Decalogue; Do We Number the Ten Commandments Correctly? 16 Concordia J. 18, 18-26 (1990). Varying interpretations of this Commandment explain the actions of vegetarians who refuse to eat meat, pacifists who refuse to work for munitions makers, prison officials who refuse to administer lethal injections to death row inmates, and pharmacists who refuse to sell morning-after pills to women. See Finkelman, *supra*, at 1494-1496; Brief for American Jewish Congress et al. as *Amici Curiae* 22-23. Although the command is ambiguous, its power to motivate likeminded interpreters of its message cannot be denied.

sects, such as Hinduism, as well as nontheistic religions, such as Buddhism. And, at the very least, the text of the Ten Commandments impermissibly commands a preference for religion over irreligion. Any of those bases, in my judgment, would be sufficient to conclude that the message should not be proclaimed by the State of Texas on a permanent monument at the seat of its government.

[Justice Souter's and Justice O'Connor's dissenting opinions are omitted.]

NOTES AND QUESTIONS

1. *A principled distinction or ad hoc decision making?* In light of the different outcomes of *McCreary County* and *Van Orden*, how should an attorney advise a city or county regarding a plaque or monument depicting the Ten Commandments? Is the key factor the existence of an explicit and plausible disavowal by the government officials of any intent to endorse the religious message of the Commandments? Or is what surrounds the plaque or monument the key? Might the age of the monument be the deciding factor? Is the divisiveness caused by the placement of a particular display crucial?

2. *Religion in the public square.* Dissenting from *McCreary County*, Justice Scalia writes that "if religion in the public forum has to be entirely nondenominational there could be no religion in the public forum at all." Of course, his point is limited to government-sponsored religion. We know from the equal access cases, see *supra* pp. 921-22, that the Free Speech Clause protects private religious speech in any forum open to the public. Justice Scalia concludes that because nondenominational religion is impossible, the Establishment Clause does not bar the government from favoring some religions over others, and favoring those that center around God in particular. If Justice Scalia is correct about the impossibility of nondenominational religion, what other conclusion might you draw about government-sponsored religion?

3. *Context.* Justice Rehnquist wrote for the four Justices in *Van Orden v. Perry*, with Justice Breyer providing the fifth vote. Justice Breyer emphasizes the importance of context. Context might include the background to enactment, which informed the decision in *McCreary*. Context might refer to the setting, such as a museum, school, or grounds of the State Capitol. Context might also encompass what is physically around the display. What else might context include?

4. *Divisiveness.* Justice Breyer's *Van Orden* concurrence also highlights the issue of divisiveness. According to Justice Breyer, the lack of complaints about the Ten Commandments monument for forty years showed that it conveyed a secular message and not a divisive religious one. What, if anything, does the apparent need to permit Establishment Clause plaintiffs to sue anonymously say about the viability of Justice Breyer's proposed "divisiveness" test for Establishment Clause violations? Should religious minorities be required to seek out public confrontations in order to establish a viable Establishment Clause claim?

5. *May government favor one sect's version of a religious text?* As Justice Stevens explains in dissent, different faith traditions have different Ten Commandments, with the variations reflecting theological differences. Is the existence of multiple versions of the Ten Commandments relevant? In his *McCreary County* dissent,

Justice Scalia thought not: "I doubt that most religious adherents are even aware that there are competing versions with doctrinal consequences (I certainly was not)." Suppose a municipality is considering posting a Ten Commandments plaque or monument, and both Protestant and Catholic residents seek to have their version of the Commandments engraved on the display; would the simple fact that the municipality chooses one and rejects the other be evidence of an impermissible Establishment Clause violation?

6. *Source of law.* Are the Ten Commandments an important source for American law? Are all the commandments incorporated into our laws? Is murder, theft, and perjury also forbidden in countries that do not rely on the Ten Commandments for their laws? Does the United States Constitution refer to the Ten Commandments? What about the fact that the Declaration of Independence refers to a "Creator"?

7. *Other examples of government appropriation of religious symbols.* In addition to the Ten Commandments, several other examples of official government references to religion or religious symbols have been the subject of lower court rulings. *See* O'Hair v. Murray, 588 F.2d 1144 (5th Cir. 1979) (upholding a federal statute requiring the motto "In God We Trust" to be inscribed on coins and currency); Murray v. Austin, 947 F.2d 147 (5th Cir. 1991) (holding that Establishment Clause is not violated by the use of Christian cross in city insignia); Harris v. Zion, 927 F.2d 1401 (7th Cir. 1991), *cert. denied,* 505 U.S. 1229 (1992) (holding unconstitutional the use of a Latin cross in city insignias); ACLU v. Capitol Square Review & Advisory Bd., 243 F.3d 289 (6th Cir. 2001) (upholding the constitutionality of Ohio's state motto "With God All Things Are Possible" on the grounds that (1) no reasonable observer would perceive motto to be an endorsement of Christianity, (2) the motto serves a secular legislative purpose by boosting morale and serving as a symbol of a common identity, and (3) the motto has a secular effect because it "merely pays lip service to the puissance of God").

8. *Does government appropriation potentially degrade religious symbols?* Finally, consider one of the points made in Judge Boyce's dissenting opinion in *Capitol Square*: "When Jesus' key to eternal salvation is lumped in the Ohio statutes with the Buckeye tree and tomato juice, the signal sent is that religion is no more important than those two nice but ultimately inconsequential things. To many, religion is much more important, perhaps the most important force in their lives. I fear that Ohio has given Christianity a crutch it is better left without." *Id.* at 312. Does Judge Boyce have a valid point here? Does government appropriation of religious symbols have the effect of repurposing them for secular ends? And, if so, does this process of reinterpretation do more to debase than to edify religious iconography?

AN EXTENDED NOTE ON THE ENDORSEMENT TEST AND THE PLACEMENT OF OVERTLY RELIGIOUS SYMBOLS ON PUBLIC PROPERTY

Can any symbol, no matter how intrinsically religious, nevertheless pass the "reasonable observer" endorsement test? For example, can a cross prominently displayed on federal park land pass constitutional muster? In Salazar v. Buono, 559 U.S. 700 (2010), Justice Kennedy, writing for a plurality of the Supreme Court, upheld against an Establishment Clause challenge a federal land transfer statute designed to protect a cross placed in a federal park. In 1934, the Veterans of Foreign Wars (VFW) erected a seven-foot-tall Latin cross on Sunrise Rock, a rocky outcrop located in the Mojave National Preserve; private citizens subsequently maintained the cross using nongovernment funds. Frank Buono, a retired National Park Service employee, initiated litigation challenging the continued placement of the cross on federal lands. After Buono prevailed in the lower federal courts, Congress enacted a statute that transferred the park land on which the cross was located to the VFW, in hopes of preventing its removal from Sunrise Rock, but the federal district court enjoined the land transfer on Establishment Clause grounds.

Justice Kennedy, writing for a plurality, found that the cross was not an impermissible government endorsement of Christianity but rather a symbol with a "complex meaning beyond the expression of religious views." *Id.* at 717. He explained that "[t]he goal of avoiding government endorsement does not require eradication of all religious symbols in the public realm." *Id.* at 718. For example, "[a] cross by the side of a public highway marking, for instance, the place where a state trooper perished need not be taken as a statement of governmental support for sectarian beliefs." *Id.* at 718-19; *see also id.* at 715 ("Placement of the cross on Government-owned land was not an attempt to set the *imprimatur* of the state on a particular creed. Rather, those who erected the cross intended simply to honor our Nation's fallen soldiers."). Because the cross, in context, did not constitute an endorsement of Christianity, the district court erred in flatly rejecting the land transfer as a means of curing any possible constitutional defect associated with the cross's location on federal land. *See id.* at 714-22.

The Court splintered badly and could not agree on rationale for deciding the case. Justices Scalia and Thomas, concurred in the judgment to reverse the lower courts but relied entirely on the theory that Buono lacked standing to challenge the land transfer statute. *See id.* at 729-34 (Scalia, J., concurring). Justice Stevens, joined by Justices Ginsburg and Sotomayor, dissented and rejected the notion that a Latin cross placed on public land could be squared with the Establishment Clause. As he explained, "[e]ven though Congress recognized this cross for its military associations, the solitary cross conveys an inescapably sectarian message." *Id.* at 747 (Stevens, J., dissenting). He added that "[t]he reasonable observer 'who knows all of the pertinent facts and circumstances surrounding the symbol and its placement,' would perceive that the Government has endorsed the cross: It prohibited the use of federal funds to take down the cross, designated the cross as a national memorial, and engaged in 'herculean efforts to preserve the Latin cross' following the District Court's initial injunction." *Id.* at 751. Thus, "[c]hanging the ownership status of the underlying land in the manner required by [the land transfer statute] would not change the fact that the cross conveys a message of government endorsement of religion." *Id.* Finally, Justice Breyer also dissented and suggested that the Supreme Court should simply dismiss the case without reaching the merits: Because "[t]he legal principles that answer the question presented are found not in the Constitution but in cases that concern the law of injunctions," he argued that "the Court should now dismiss the writ [of certiorari] as improvidently granted." *Id.* at 764 (Breyer, J., dissenting).

Because the *Buono* Court was unable to muster a majority opinion, it is difficult to predict its precise long-term effect—if any—on the application of the endorsement test to government efforts to preserve the display of religious symbols on publicly owned lands or in government-owned buildings. If Justice Kennedy's approach to the endorsement test enjoys a majority in future cases, however, the underlying *purpose* of a religious display, rather than its *content*, as assessed by a reasonable objective observer, might be the controlling factor. In some respects, and perhaps ironically, reorienting Establishment Clause queries toward a purpose-based approach would reflect a return to the first prong of the *Lemon* test. Moreover, government entities clearly may display intrinsically religious images (for example, a famous Renaissance-era Italian painting of the Madonna and infant Jesus) provided that its purpose for displaying the image is entirely secular (viz., the painting hangs in the National Gallery of Art, in Washington, D.C., because of its objective artistic importance).

The object at issue in the *Buono* litigation ceased to exist when an unknown person or persons stole the Latin cross from Sunrise Ridge, thereby making a transfer of land to preserve the monument arguably moot. *See* Randal C. Archibold, *Cross at Center of Dispute Disappears*, N.Y. Times, May 12, 2010, at A15.

B.   GOVERNMENT-SPONSORED PRAYERS OUTSIDE SCHOOL

MARSH v. CHAMBERS

463 U.S. 783 (1983)

Chief Justice BURGER delivered the opinion of the Court.

The question presented is whether the Nebraska Legislature's practice of opening each legislative day with a prayer by a chaplain paid by the State violates the Establishment Clause of the First Amendment. . . . Robert E. Palmer, a Presbyterian minister, has served as chaplain since 1965 at a salary of $319.75 per month for each month the legislature is in session.

II.

The opening of sessions of legislative and other deliberative public bodies with prayer is deeply embedded in the history and tradition of this country. From colonial times through the founding of the Republic and ever since, the practice of legislative prayer has coexisted with the principles of disestablishment and religious freedom. In the very courtrooms in which the United States District Judge and later three Circuit Judges heard and decided this case, the proceedings opened with an announcement that concluded, "God save the United States and this Honorable Court." The same invocation occurs at all sessions of this Court. . . .

Although prayers were not offered during the Constitutional Convention, the First Congress, as one of its early items of business, adopted the policy of selecting a chaplain to open each session with prayer. . . . On Sept. 25, 1789, three days after Congress authorized the appointment of paid chaplains, final agreement was reached on the language of the Bill of Rights. Clearly the men who wrote the First Amendment Religion Clause did not view paid legislative chaplains and opening prayers as a violation of that Amendment, for the practice of opening sessions with prayer has continued without interruption ever since that early session of

Congress. It has also been followed consistently in most of the states, including Nebraska, where the institution of opening legislative sessions with prayer was adopted even before the State attained statehood.

Standing alone, historical patterns cannot justify contemporary violations of constitutional guarantees, but there is far more here than simply historical patterns. In this context, historical evidence sheds light not only on what the draftsmen intended the Establishment Clause to mean, but also on how they thought that Clause applied to the practice authorized by the First Congress-their actions reveal their intent. . . .

In *Walz v. Tax Comm'n,* 397 U.S. 664, 678 (1970), we considered the weight to be accorded to history: "It is obviously correct that no one acquires a vested or protected right in violation of the Constitution by long use, even when that span of time covers our entire national existence and indeed predates it. Yet an unbroken practice . . . is not something to be lightly cast aside."

No more is Nebraska's practice of over a century, consistent with two centuries of national practice, to be cast aside. It can hardly be thought that in the same week Members of the First Congress voted to appoint and to pay a Chaplain for each House and also voted to approve the draft of the First Amendment for submission to the States, they intended the Establishment Clause of the Amendment to forbid what they had just declared acceptable. . . .

Respondent cites Justice BRENNAN's concurring opinion in Abington School Dist. v. Schempp, 374 U.S. 203, 237 (1963), and argues that we should not rely too heavily on "the advice of the Founding Fathers" because the messages of history often tend to be ambiguous and not relevant to a society far more heterogeneous than that of the Framers, Respondent also points out that John Jay and John Rutledge opposed the motion to begin the first session of the Continental Congress with prayer. Brief for Respondent 60.

We do not agree that evidence of opposition to a measure weakens the force of the historical argument; indeed it infuses it with power by demonstrating that the subject was considered carefully and the action not taken thoughtlessly, by force of long tradition and without regard to the problems posed by a pluralistic society. . . .

In light of the unambiguous and unbroken history of more than 200 years, there can be no doubt that the practice of opening legislative sessions with prayer has become part of the fabric of our society. To invoke Divine guidance on a public body entrusted with making the laws is not, in these circumstances, an "establishment" of religion or a step toward establishment; it is simply a tolerable acknowledgment of beliefs widely held among the people of this country. As Justice Douglas observed, "[w]e are a religious people whose institutions presuppose a Supreme Being." *Zorach v. Clauson,* 343 U.S. 306, 313 (1952).

III.

We turn then to the question of whether any features of the Nebraska practice violate the Establishment Clause. Beyond the bare fact that a prayer is offered, three points have been made: first, that a clergyman of only one denomination-Presbyterian-has been selected for 16 years; second, that the chaplain is paid at public expense; and third, that the prayers are in the Judeo-Christian tradition.[14] Weighed against the historical background, these factors do not serve to invalidate Nebraska's practice.

The Court of Appeals was concerned that Palmer's long tenure has the effect of giving preference to his religious views. . . . To the contrary, the evidence indicates that Palmer was reappointed because his performance and personal qualities were acceptable to the body appointing him. . . . Absent proof that the chaplain's reappointment stemmed from an impermissible motive, we conclude that his long tenure does not in itself conflict with the Establishment Clause.

Nor is the compensation of the chaplain from public funds a reason to invalidate the Nebraska Legislature's chaplaincy; remuneration is grounded in historic practice initiated, as we noted earlier, by the same Congress that adopted the Establishment Clause of the First Amendment. . . .

The content of the prayer is not of concern to judges where, as here, there is no indication that the prayer opportunity has been exploited to proselytize or advance any one, or to disparage any other, faith or belief. That being so, it is not for us to embark on a sensitive evaluation or to parse the content of a particular prayer. . . .

The unbroken practice for two centuries in the National Congress, for more than a century in Nebraska and in many other states, gives abundant assurance that there is no real threat "while this Court sits."

The judgment of the Court of Appeals is

Reversed.

Justice BRENNAN, with whom Justice MARSHALL joins, dissenting.

I

The Court makes no pretense of subjecting Nebraska's practice of legislative prayer to any of the formal "tests" that have traditionally structured our inquiry under the Establishment Clause. That it fails to do so is, in a sense, a good thing, for it simply confirms that the Court is carving out an exception to the Establishment Clause rather than reshaping Establishment Clause doctrine to accommodate legislative prayer. For my purposes, however, I must begin by demonstrating what should be obvious: that, if the Court were to judge legislative prayer through the unsentimental eye of our settled doctrine, it would have to strike it down as a clear violation of the Establishment Clause.

The most commonly cited formulation of prevailing Establishment Clause doctrine is found in *Lemon v. Kurtzman,* 403 U.S. 602 (1971). . . .That the "purpose" of legislative prayer is preeminently religious rather than secular seems to me to be self-evident. "To invoke Divine guidance on a public body entrusted with making the laws," is nothing but a religious act. Moreover, whatever secular functions legislative prayer might play-formally opening the legislative session, getting the members of the body to quiet down, and imbuing them with a sense of seriousness and high purpose-could so plainly be performed in a purely nonreligious fashion that to claim

---

[14] Palmer characterizes his prayers as "nonsectarian," "Judeo Christian," and with "elements of the American civil religion." App. 75 and 87. (Deposition of Robert E. Palmer). Although some of his earlier prayers were often explicitly Christian, Palmer removed all references to Christ after a 1980 complaint from a Jewish legislator. *Id.,* at 49.

a secular purpose for the prayer is an insult to the perfectly honorable individuals who instituted and continue the practice.

The "primary effect" of legislative prayer is also clearly religious. As we said in the context of officially sponsored prayers in the public schools, "prescribing a particular form of religious worship," even if the individuals involved have the choice not to participate, places "indirect coercive pressure upon religious minorities to conform to the prevailing officially approved religion. . . ." *Engel v. Vitale,* 370 U.S. 421, 431 (1962). More importantly, invocations in Nebraska's legislative halls explicitly link religious belief and observance to the power and prestige of the State. . . .

Finally, there can be no doubt that the practice of legislative prayer leads to excessive "entanglement" between the State and religion. . . . In the case of legislative prayer, the process of choosing a "suitable" chaplain, whether on a permanent or rotating basis, and insuring that the chaplain limits himself or herself to "suitable" prayers, involves precisely the sort of supervision that agencies of government should if at all possible avoid.

In sum, I have no doubt that, if any group of law students were asked to apply the principles of *Lemon* to the question of legislative prayer, they would nearly unanimously find the practice to be unconstitutional.

II

The path of formal doctrine, however, can only imperfectly capture the nature and importance of the issues at stake in this case. A more adequate analysis must therefore take into account the underlying function of the Establishment Clause, and the forces that have shaped its doctrine. . . .

Legislative prayer clearly violates the principles of neutrality and separation that are embedded within the Establishment Clause. It is contrary to the fundamental message of *Engel* and *Schempp.* It intrudes on the right to conscience by forcing some legislators either to participate in a "prayer opportunity," with which they are in basic disagreement, or to make their disagreement a matter of public comment by declining to participate. It forces all residents of the State to support a religious exercise that may be contrary to their own beliefs. It requires the State to commit itself on fundamental theological issues. It has the potential for degrading religion by allowing a religious call to worship to be intermeshed with a secular call to order. And it injects religion into the political sphere by creating the potential that each and every selection of a chaplain, or consideration of a particular prayer, or even reconsideration of the practice itself, will provoke a political battle along religious lines and ultimately alienate some religiously identified group of citizens.

We have also recognized that Government cannot, without adopting a decidedly *anti*-religious point of view, be forbidden to recognize the religious beliefs and practices of the American people as an aspect of our history and culture. Certainly, bona fide classes in comparative religion can be offered in the public schools. And certainly, the text of Abraham Lincoln's Second Inaugural Address which is inscribed on a wall of the Lincoln Memorial need not be purged of its profound theological content. The practice of offering invocations at legislative sessions cannot, however, simply be dismissed as "a tolerable *acknowledgment of beliefs* widely held among the people of this country." "Prayer is religion *in act.*" "Praying means to take hold of a word, the end, so to speak, of a line that leads to

God." Reverend Palmer and other members of the clergy who offer invocations at legislative sessions are not museum pieces, put on display once a day for the edification of the legislature. Rather, they are engaged by the legislature to lead it-as a body-in an act of religious worship. If upholding the practice requires denial of this fact, I suspect that many supporters of legislative prayer would feel that they had been handed a pyrrhic victory. . . .

Finally, our cases recognize that, in one important respect, the Constitution is *not* neutral on the subject of religion: Under the Free Exercise Clause, religiously motivated claims of conscience may give rise to constitutional rights that other strongly-held beliefs do not . . . This is not, however, a case in which a State is accommodating individual religious interests. We are not faced here with the right of the legislature to allow its members to offer prayers during the course of general legislative debate. We are certainly not faced with the right of legislators to form voluntary groups for prayer or worship. We are not even faced with the right of the state to employ members of the clergy to minister to the private religious needs of individual legislators. Rather, we are faced here with the regularized practice of conducting official prayers, on behalf of the entire legislature, as part of the order of business constituting the formal opening of every single session of the legislative term. If this is Free Exercise, the Establishment Clause has no meaning whatsoever.

III

The Court's main argument for carving out an exception sustaining legislative prayer is historical. The Court cannot-and does not-purport to find a pattern of "undeviating acceptance," *Walz,* 397 U.S. at 681 (BRENNAN, J., concurring), of legislative prayer. It also disclaims exclusive reliance on the mere longevity of legislative prayer. The Court does, however, point out that, only three days before the First Congress reached agreement on the final wording of the Bill of Rights, it authorized the appointment of paid chaplains for its own proceedings, and the Court argues that in light of this "unique history," the actions of Congress reveal its intent as to the meaning of the Establishment Clause. I agree that historical practice is "of considerable import in the interpretation of abstract constitutional language," *Walz,* 397 U.S. at 681, (BRENNAN, J., concurring). This is a case, however, in which-absent the Court's invocation of history-there would be no question that the practice at issue was unconstitutional.[30] . . .

[T]he Court assumes that the Framers of the Establishment Clause would not have themselves authorized a practice that they thought violated the guarantees contained in the clause. This assumption, however, is questionable. Legislators, influenced by the passions and exigencies of the moment, the pressure of constituents and colleagues, and the press of business, do not always pass sober constitutional judgment on every piece of legislation they enact, and this must be assumed to be as true of the members of the First Congress as any other. Indeed, the fact that James Madison, who voted for the bill authorizing the payment of the first congressional chaplains, later expressed the view that the practice was unconstitutional, is

---

[30] [FN30, slightly moved] Indeed, the sort of historical argument made by the Court should be advanced with some hesitation in light of certain other skeletons in the congressional closet. See, e.g., . . . Act of July 23, 1866, 14 Stat. 216 (reaffirming the racial segregation of the public schools in the District of Columbia; enacted exactly one week after Congress proposed Fourteenth Amendment to the States).

instructive on precisely this point. Madison's later views may not have represented so much a change of *mind* as a change of *role*, from a member of Congress engaged in the hurley-burley of legislative activity to a detached observer engaged in unpressured reflection. Since the latter role is precisely the one with which this Court is charged, I am not at all sure that Madison's later writings should be any less influential in our deliberations than his earlier vote. . . .

[*A*]*ny* practice of legislative prayer, even if it might look "non-sectarian" to nine Justices of the Supreme Court, will inevitably and continuously involve the state in one or another religious debate. Prayer is serious business-serious theological business-and it is not a mere "acknowledgment of beliefs widely held among the people of this country" for the State to immerse itself in that business. Some religious individuals or groups find it theologically problematic to engage in joint religious exercises predominantly influenced by faiths not their own. Some might object even to the attempt to fashion a "non-sectarian" prayer. Some would find it impossible to participate in any "prayer opportunity," marked by Trinitarian references. Some would find a prayer *not* invoking the name of Christ to represent a flawed view of the relationship between human beings and God. . . . And some might object on theological grounds to the Court's requirement that prayer, even though religious, not be proselytizing. But, in this case, we are faced with potential religious objections to an activity at the very center of religious life, and it is simply beyond the competence of government, and inconsistent with our conceptions of liberty, for the state to take upon itself the role of ecclesiastical arbiter.

Justice STEVENS, dissenting.

In a democratically elected legislature, the religious beliefs of the chaplain tend to reflect the faith of the majority of the lawmakers' constituents. Prayers may be said by a Catholic priest in the Massachusetts Legislature and by a Presbyterian minister in the Nebraska Legislature, but I would not expect to find a Jehovah's Witness or a disciple of Mary Baker Eddy or the Reverend Moon serving as the official chaplain in any state legislature. Regardless of the motivation of the majority that exercises the power to appoint the chaplain, it seems plain to me that the designation of a member of one religious faith to serve as the sole official chaplain of a state legislature for a period of 16 years constitutes the preference of one faith over another in violation of the Establishment Clause of the First Amendment.

NOTES AND QUESTIONS

1. *History and tradition.* If the same Congress that approved the Establishment Clause believed that legislative prayers were consistent with the Establishment Clause, why shouldn't we? Moreover, if the practice has existed since the founding of the country, isn't the message communicated more about a deeply embedded tradition than about religion?

2. *Change in nation's religious composition.* The dissent notes that "our religious composition makes us a vastly more diverse people than were our forefathers." In *"Nonpreferential" Aid to Religion: A False Claim about Original Intent*, 27 WM. & MARY L. REV. 875 (1986), Douglas Laycock concludes, "In 1791, almost no one thought that government support of Protestantism was inconsistent with religious liberty, because almost no one could imagine a more broadly

pluralist state." What might the Framers think if confronted with today's diversity?

3. *The (primary) Framer's intent.* If, as Chief Justice Burger's *Marsh* opinion suggests, we should look to the Framers' own words and actions to determine the meaning of the phrase "respecting an establishment of religion," then should we pay special attention to the precise views of the author of the First Amendment? As Justice Brennan points out in his *Marsh* dissent, James Madison had a very specific opinion on the constitutionality of legislative prayers, which can be found in the following passage from Madison's "Detached Memoranda" (abbreviations and punctuation are as in the original):

> Is the appointment of Chaplains to the two Houses of Congress consistent with the Constitution, and with the pure principle of religious freedom?
>
> In strictness the answer on both points must be in the negative. The Constitution of the U.S. forbids everything like an establishment of a national religion. The law appointing Chaplains establishes a religious worship for the national representatives, to be performed by Ministers of religion, elected by a majority of them; and these are to be paid out of the national taxes. Does not this involve the principle of a national establishment, applicable to a provision for a religious worship for the Constituent as well as of the representative Body, approved by the majority, and conducted by Ministers of religion paid by the entire nation.
>
> The establishment of the chaplainship to Congs is a palpable violation of equal rights, as well as of Constitutional principles: The tenets of the chaplains elected [by the majority] shut the door of worship agst the members whose creeds & consciences forbid a participation in that of the majority. To say nothing of other sects, this is the case with that of Roman Catholics & Quakers who have always had members in one or both of the Legislative branches. Could a Catholic clergyman ever hope to be appointed a Chaplain? To say that his religious principles are obnoxious or that his sect is small, is to lift the evil at once and exhibit in its naked deformity the doctrine that religious truth is to be tested by numbers. [O]r that the major sects have a right to govern the minor.

4. *Bound by original understanding?* Should we interpret the Constitution just as the Framers or founding generation did? What about the fact that the same Congress that proposed the Fourteenth Amendment's Equal Protection Clause also approved funding for segregated schools in Washington, D.C.?

5. *Applying the Establishment Clause tests.* How would these state-funded prayers fare under the various Establishment Clause tests? Is it true, as Justice Brennan argues, that if "any groups of law students" were asked to apply *Lemon*, "they would nearly unanimously find the practice to be unconstitutional"? What about the endorsement test? Or the coercion test? If you were a Nebraska representative up for reelection, would you feel pressure to participate?

6. *Exception or new approach?* Is the emphasis on history and tradition approach limited to legislative prayers? To practices that date to the founding? Or does this represent an alternative approach to the Establishment Clause? Looking back over the cases you have read, what role did history and tradition play?

TOWN OF GREECE v. GALLOWAY

___ U.S. ___, 134 S. Ct. 1811 (2014)

Justice KENNEDY delivered the opinion of the Court, except as to Part II–B.

The Court must decide whether the town of Greece, New York, imposes an impermissible establishment of religion by opening its monthly board meetings with a prayer. It must be concluded, consistent with the Court's opinion in *Marsh v. Chambers*, 463 U.S. 783 (1983), that no violation of the Constitution has been shown.

I

Greece, a town with a population of 94,000, is in upstate New York. For some years, it began its monthly town board meetings with a moment of silence. In 1999, the newly elected town supervisor, John Auberger, decided to replicate the prayer practice he had found meaningful while serving in the county legislature. Following the roll call and recitation of the Pledge of Allegiance, Auberger would invite a local clergyman to the front of the room to deliver an invocation. After the prayer, Auberger would thank the minister for serving as the board's "chaplain for the month" and present him with a commemorative plaque. The prayer was intended to place town board members in a solemn and deliberative frame of mind, invoke divine guidance in town affairs, and follow a tradition practiced by Congress and dozens of state legislatures. App. 22a–25a.

The town followed an informal method for selecting prayer givers, all of whom were unpaid volunteers. A town employee would call the congregations listed in a local directory until she found a minister available for that month's meeting. The town eventually compiled a list of willing "board chaplains" who had accepted invitations and agreed to return in the future. The town at no point excluded or denied an opportunity to a would-be prayer giver. Its leaders maintained that a minister or layperson of any persuasion, including an atheist, could give the invocation. But nearly all of the congregations in town were Christian; and from 1999 to 2007, all of the participating ministers were too.

Greece neither reviewed the prayers in advance of the meetings nor provided guidance as to their tone or content, in the belief that exercising any degree of control over the prayers would infringe both the free exercise and speech rights of the ministers. The town instead left the guest clergy free to compose their own devotions. Some of the ministers spoke in a distinctly Christian idiom; and a minority invoked religious holidays, scripture, or doctrine. . . .

Respondents Susan Galloway and Linda Stephens attended town board meetings to speak about issues of local concern, and they objected that the prayers violated their religious or philosophical views. . . .

II

In *Marsh v. Chambers*, 463 U.S. 783 (1983), the Court found no First Amendment violation in the Nebraska Legislature's practice of opening its sessions with a prayer delivered by a chaplain paid from state funds. The decision concluded that legislative prayer, while religious in nature, has long been understood as compatible with the

Establishment Clause. As practiced by Congress since the framing of the Constitution, legislative prayer lends gravity to public business, reminds lawmakers to transcend petty differences in pursuit of a higher purpose, and expresses a common aspiration to a just and peaceful society. . . .

Marsh is sometimes described as "carving out an exception" to the Court's Establishment Clause jurisprudence, because it sustained legislative prayer without subjecting the practice to "any of the formal 'tests' that have traditionally structured" this inquiry. Id., at 796, 813 (Brennan, J., dissenting). The Court in *Marsh* found those tests unnecessary because history supported the conclusion that legislative invocations are compatible with the Establishment Clause. . . .

Marsh stands for the proposition that it is not necessary to define the precise boundary of the Establishment Clause where history shows that the specific practice is permitted. Any test the Court adopts must acknowledge a practice that was accepted by the Framers and has withstood the critical scrutiny of time and political change. . . .

The Court's inquiry, then, must be to determine whether the prayer practice in the town of Greece fits within the tradition long followed in Congress and the state legislatures. Respondents assert that the town's prayer exercise falls outside that tradition and transgresses the Establishment Clause for two independent but mutually reinforcing reasons. First, they argue that *Marsh* did not approve prayers containing sectarian language or themes, such as the prayers offered in Greece that referred to the "death, resurrection, and ascension of the Savior Jesus Christ," App. 129a, and the "saving sacrifice of Jesus Christ on the cross," id., at 88a. Second, they argue that the setting and conduct of the town board meetings create social pressures that force nonadherents to remain in the room or even feign participation in order to avoid offending the representatives who sponsor the prayer and will vote on matters citizens bring before the board. . . .

A

The Congress that drafted the First Amendment would have been accustomed to invocations containing explicitly religious themes of the sort respondents find objectionable. . . . The decidedly Christian nature of these prayers must not be dismissed as the relic of a time when our Nation was less pluralistic than it is today. Congress continues to permit its appointed and visiting chaplains to express themselves in a religious idiom. It acknowledges our growing diversity not by proscribing sectarian content but by welcoming ministers of many creeds. . . .

Marsh nowhere suggested that the constitutionality of legislative prayer turns on the neutrality of its content. . . . To hold that invocations must be nonsectarian would force the legislatures that sponsor prayers and the courts that are asked to decide these cases to act as supervisors and censors of religious speech. . . . Government may not mandate a civic religion that stifles any but the most generic reference to the sacred any more than it may prescribe a religious orthodoxy. . . . Once it invites prayer into the public sphere, government must permit a prayer giver to address his or her own God or gods as conscience dictates, unfettered by what an administrator or judge considers to be nonsectarian.

In rejecting the suggestion that legislative prayer must be nonsectarian, the Court does not imply that no constraints remain on its content. The relevant constraint derives from its place at the opening of legislative sessions, where it is meant to lend gravity to the occasion and reflect values long part of the Nation's heritage. Prayer that is solemn and respectful in tone, that invites lawmakers to reflect upon shared ideals and common ends before they embark on the fractious business of governing, serves that legitimate function. If the course and practice over time shows that the invocations denigrate nonbelievers or religious minorities, threaten damnation, or preach conversion, many present may consider the prayer to fall short of the desire to elevate the purpose of the occasion and to unite lawmakers in their common effort. That circumstance would present a different case than the one presently before the Court. ...

Absent a pattern of prayers that over time denigrate, proselytize, or betray an impermissible government purpose, a challenge based solely on the content of a prayer will not likely establish a constitutional violation. *Marsh*, indeed, requires an inquiry into the prayer opportunity as a whole, rather than into the contents of a single prayer. 463 U.S., at 794-795.

Finally, the Court disagrees with the view taken by the Court of Appeals that the town of Greece contravened the Establishment Clause by inviting a predominantly Christian set of ministers to lead the prayer. The town made reasonable efforts to identify all of the congregations located within its borders and represented that it would welcome a prayer by any minister or layman who wished to give one. That nearly all of the congregations in town turned out to be Christian does not reflect an aversion or bias on the part of town leaders against minority faiths. So long as the town maintains a policy of nondiscrimination, the Constitution does not require it to search beyond its borders for non-Christian prayer givers in an effort to achieve religious balancing. . . .

B

Respondents further seek to distinguish the town's prayer practice from the tradition upheld in *Marsh* on the ground that it coerces participation by nonadherents. They and some amici contend that prayer conducted in the intimate setting of a town board meeting differs in fundamental ways from the invocations delivered in Congress and state legislatures, where the public remains segregated from legislative activity and may not address the body except by occasional invitation. Citizens attend town meetings, on the other hand, to accept awards; speak on matters of local importance; and petition the board for action that may affect their economic interests, such as the granting of permits, business licenses, and zoning variances. Respondents argue that the public may feel subtle pressure to participate in prayers that violate their beliefs in order to please the board members from whom they are about to seek a favorable ruling. In their view the fact that board members in small towns know many of their constituents by name only increases the pressure to conform.

On the record in this case the Court is not persuaded that the town of Greece, through the act of offering a brief, solemn, and respectful prayer to open its monthly meetings, compelled its citizens to engage in a religious observance.

It is presumed that the reasonable observer is acquainted with this tradition and understands that its purposes are to lend gravity to public proceedings and to acknowledge the place religion holds in the lives of many private citizens, not to afford government an opportunity to proselytize or force truant constituents into the pews. . . . Respondents suggest that constituents might feel pressure to join the prayers to avoid irritating the officials who would be ruling on their petitions, but this argument has no evidentiary support. . . . Adults often encounter speech they find disagreeable; and an Establishment Clause violation is not made out any time a person experiences a sense of affront from the expression of contrary religious views in a legislative forum, especially where, as here, any member of the public is welcome in turn to offer an invocation reflecting his or her own convictions.

It is so ordered.

[Justice ALITO, with whom Justice SCALIA joins, concurred.]

[Justice THOMAS, with whom Justice SCALIA joined as to Part II, concurring in part and concurring in the judgment.]

Justice BREYER, dissenting.

As we all recognize, this is a "fact-sensitive" case. . . . I also here emphasize several factors that I believe underlie the conclusion that, on the particular facts of this case, the town's prayer practice violated the Establishment Clause.

First, Greece is a predominantly Christian town, but it is not exclusively so. A map of the town's houses of worship introduced in the District Court shows many Christian churches within the town's limits. It also shows a Buddhist temple within the town and several Jewish synagogues just outside its borders, in the adjacent city of Rochester, New York. Id., at 24. Yet during the more than 120 monthly meetings at which prayers were delivered during the record period (from 1999 to 2010), only four prayers were delivered by non-Christians. And all of these occurred in 2008, shortly after the plaintiffs began complaining about the town's Christian prayer practice and nearly a decade after that practice had commenced.

Second, the town made no significant effort to inform the area's non-Christian houses of worship about the possibility of delivering an opening prayer. . . .

Third, in this context, the fact that nearly all of the prayers given reflected a single denomination takes on significance. That significance would have been the same had all the prayers been Jewish, or Hindu, or Buddhist, or of any other denomination. The significance is that, in a context where religious minorities exist and where more could easily have been done to include their participation, the town chose to do nothing. . . .

Justice KAGAN, with whom Justice GINSBURG, Justice BREYER, and Justice SOTOMAYOR join, dissenting.

For centuries now, people have come to this country from every corner of the world to share in the blessing of religious freedom. Our Constitution promises that they may worship in their own way, without fear of penalty or danger, and that in itself is a momentous offering. Yet our Constitution makes a commitment still more remarkable—that however those individuals worship, they will count as full and equal American citizens. A Christian, a Jew, a Muslim (and so forth)—each stands in the same relationship with her country, with her state and local communities, and with every level and body of government. So that when each person performs the duties or seeks the benefits of citizenship, she does so not as an adherent to one or another religion, but simply as an American.

I respectfully dissent from the Court's opinion because I think the Town of Greece's prayer practices violate that norm of religious equality—the breathtakingly generous constitutional idea that our public institutions belong no less to the Buddhist or Hindu than to the Methodist or Episcopalian. . . . The practice at issue here differs from the one sustained in *Marsh* because Greece's town meetings involve participation by ordinary citizens, and the invocations given—directly to those citizens—were predominantly sectarian in content. Still more, Greece's Board did nothing to recognize religious diversity: In arranging for clergy members to open each meeting, the Town never sought (except briefly when this suit was filed) to involve, accommodate, or in any way reach out to adherents of non-Christian religions. So month in and month out for over a decade, prayers steeped in only one faith, addressed toward members of the public, commenced meetings to discuss local affairs and distribute government benefits. In my view, that practice does not square with the First Amendment's promise that every citizen, irrespective of her religion, owns an equal share in her government.

. . . I agree with the majority that the issue here is "whether the prayer practice in the Town of Greece fits within the tradition long followed in Congress and the state legislatures."

Where I depart from the majority is in my reply to that question. . . . [T]he Board's meetings are also occasions for ordinary citizens to engage with and petition their government, often on highly individualized matters. That feature calls for Board members to exercise special care to ensure that the prayers offered are inclusive— that they respect each and every member of the community as an equal citizen. But the Board, and the clergy members it selected, made no such effort. Instead, the prayers given in Greece, addressed directly to the Town's citizenry, were more sectarian, and less inclusive, than anything this Court sustained in *Marsh*. . . .

Let's count the ways in which these pictures diverge. First, the governmental proceedings at which the prayers occur differ significantly in nature and purpose. The Nebraska Legislature's floor sessions—like those of the U.S. Congress and other state assemblies—are of, by, and for elected lawmakers. Members of the public take no part in those proceedings; any few who attend are spectators only, watching from a high-up visitors' gallery. (In that respect, note that neither the Nebraska Legislature nor the Congress calls for prayer when citizens themselves participate in a hearing— say, by giving testimony relevant to a bill or nomination.) Greece's town meetings, by contrast, revolve around ordinary members of the community. Each and every aspect of those sessions provides opportunities for Town residents to interact with public officials. And the most important parts enable those citizens to petition their government. In the Public Forum, they urge (or oppose) changes in the Board's policies and priorities; and then, in what are essentially adjudicatory hearings, they request the Board to grant (or deny) applications for various permits, licenses, and zoning variances. So the meetings, both by design and in operation, allow citizens to actively participate in the Town's governance—sharing concerns, airing grievances, and both shaping the community's policies and seeking their benefits.

Second (and following from what I just said), the prayers in these two settings have different audiences. In the Nebraska Legislature, the chaplain spoke to, and only to, the elected representatives. . . The very opposite is true in Greece: Contrary to the majority's characterization, the prayers there are directed squarely at the citizens. . . . In essence, the chaplain leads, as the first part of a town meeting, a highly intimate (albeit relatively brief) prayer service, with the public serving as his congregation.

And third, the prayers themselves differ in their content and character. . . . [N]o one can fairly read the prayers from Greece's Town meetings as anything other than explicitly Christian—constantly and exclusively so. . . . About two-thirds of the prayers given over this decade or so invoked "Jesus," "Christ," "Your Son," or "the Holy Spirit"; in the 18 months before the record closed, 85% included those references. See generally id., at 27a–143a. Many prayers contained elaborations of Christian doctrine or recitations of scripture.

Those three differences, taken together, remove this case from the protective ambit of *Marsh* and the history on which it relied. . . .

Let's say that a Muslim citizen of Greece goes before the Board to share her views on policy or request some permit. Maybe she wants the Board to put up a traffic light at a dangerous intersection; or maybe she needs a zoning variance to build an addition on her home. But just before she gets to say her piece, a minister deputized by the Town asks her to pray "in the name of God's only son Jesus Christ." App. 99a. She must think—it is hardly paranoia, but only the truth—that Christian worship has become entwined with local governance. And now she faces a choice—to pray alongside the majority as one of that group or somehow to register her deeply felt difference. She is a strong person, but that is no easy call—especially given that the room is small and her every action (or inaction) will be noticed. She does not wish to be rude to her neighbors, nor does she wish to aggravate the Board members whom she will soon be trying to persuade. And yet she does not want to acknowledge Christ's divinity, any more than many of her neighbors would want to deny that tenet. So assume she declines to participate with the others in the first act of the meeting—or even, as the majority proposes, that she stands up and leaves the room altogether. At the least, she becomes a different kind of citizen, one who will not join in the religious practice that the Town Board has chosen as reflecting its own and the community's most cherished beliefs. And she thus stands at a remove, based solely on religion, from her fellow citizens and her elected representatives.

Everything about that situation, I think, infringes the First Amendment. . . . That the clergy thus put some residents to the unenviable choice of either pretending to pray like the majority or declining to join its communal activity, at the very moment of petitioning their elected leaders. That the practice thus divides the citizenry, creating one class that shares the Board's own evident religious beliefs and another (far smaller) class that does not. And that the practice also alters a dissenting citizen's relationship with her government, making her religious difference salient when she seeks only to engage her elected representatives as would any other citizen.

. . .

In this country, when citizens go before the government, they go not as Christians or Muslims or Jews (or what have you), but just as Americans (or here, as Grecians). That is what it means to be an equal citizen, irrespective of religion. And that is what the Town of Greece precluded by so identifying itself with a single faith. . . .

When the citizens of this country approach their government, they do so only as Americans, not as members of one faith or another. And that means that even in a partly legislative body, they should not confront government-sponsored worship that divides them along religious lines. I believe, for all the reasons I have given, that the Town of Greece betrayed that promise. I therefore respectfully dissent from the Court's decision.

NOTES AND QUESTIONS

1. Marsh *as starting point.* Both the majority and the dissents accepted the constitutionality of legislative prayers, and focused on whether the *Greece* prayers could be considered part of the same tradition as the prayers upheld in

Marsh. What would have been the outcome had they applied the *Lemon* test or endorsement test instead? Have those tests been supplanted?

2. *Sectarian prayers*. Were the prayers in *Marsh* sectarian? Did *Marsh* require that the prayers be nonsectarian? The majority argues that prayers during the Founding era were sectarian, and that "[t]he decidedly Christian nature of these prayers must not be dismissed as the relic of a time when our Nation was less pluralistic than it is today." Why not? Wasn't the Nation much less pluralistic than it is today?

3. *The constitutionality of requiring nonsectarian prayers*. The majority suggests that for Greece to require its prayers be nonsectarian would violate the Free Exercise or Free Speech Clause. A Free Exercise Clause violation requires a substantial religious burden. What is the burden on religious exercise at stake here? Regulating religious viewpoints would indeed violate the Free Speech Clause if Greece has opened up a forum for private speech. Has it? Does Greece, for example, encourage all viewpoints on "the fractious business of governing"?

4. *Any constraints?* The majority notes that not anything goes: "[A] pattern of prayers that over time denigrate, proselytize, or betray an impermissible government purpose" would violate the Establishment Clause. Why is requiring nonproselytizing prayers less problematic than requiring nonsectarian ones?

5. *Discriminatory intent*. For the majority, as long as every religious tradition in theory may be reflected in the prayer, the prayer practice does not violate the Establishment Clause if in fact most of them are Christian. According to the majority, only if the predominance of Christianity was the result of intentional exclusion of non-Christian religions is the Establishment Clause violated. The dissents argue that the Establishment Clause is also violated if the predominance of Christianity was the result of the indifference: Once Greece realized that Christianity dominated, it ought to have done more. Which approach better advances Establishment Clause values? *See generally* Caroline Mala Corbin, *Intentional Discrimination in Establishment Clause Jurisprudence*, 67 ALA. L. REV. 299 (2015).

6. *Coercion*. The majority holds that there is no "evidentiary support" that anyone feels coerced into participating in Greece's prayers. Has the Court required evidence of actual coercion before? Must someone, such as Justice Kagan's hypothetical Muslim petitioner, have actually suffered retaliation for refusing to participate in order to feel pressure to join in?

7. *Harm*. What is the harm, if any, of sectarian prayer? Is it that they are simply offensive to those whose beliefs are different? Or is it something more?

C. GOVERNMENT/RELIGION POWER SHARING

LARKIN v. GRENDEL'S DEN
459 U.S. 116 (1982)

Chief Justice BURGER delivered the opinion of the Court.

Appellee operates a restaurant located in the Harvard Square area of Cambridge, Mass. The Holy Cross Armenian Catholic Parish is located adjacent to the restaurant;

the back walls of the two buildings are 10 feet apart. In 1977, appellee applied to the Cambridge License Commission for approval of an alcoholic beverages license for the restaurant.

[Massachusetts law] provides: "Premises . . . located within a radius of five hundred feet of a church or school shall not be licensed for the sale of alcoholic beverages if the governing body of such church or school files written objection thereto." Holy Cross Church objected to appellee's application, expressing concern over "having so many licenses so near." The License Commission voted to deny the application, citing only the objection of Holy Cross Church and noting that the church "is within 10 feet of the proposed location."

The purpose of [the Massachusetts law giving churches the right to object to the sale of alcoholic beverages] is to "protec[t] spiritual, cultural, and educational centers from the 'hurly-burly' associated with liquor outlets." There can be little doubt that this embraces valid secular legislative purposes. However, these valid secular objectives can be readily accomplished by other means—either through an absolute legislative ban on liquor outlets within reasonable prescribed distances from churches, schools, hospitals, and like institutions, or by ensuring a hearing for the views of affected institutions at licensing proceedings where, without question, such views would be entitled to substantial weight.

[This law] gives churches the right to determine whether a particular applicant will be granted a liquor license, or even which one of several competing applicants will receive a license. The churches' power under the statute is standardless, calling for no reasons, findings, or reasoned conclusions. That power may therefore be used by churches to promote goals beyond insulating the church from undesirable neighbors; it could be employed for explicitly religious goals, for example, favoring liquor licenses for members of that congregation or adherents of that faith. We can assume that churches would act in good faith in their exercise of the statutory power, yet [Massachusetts law] does not by its terms require that churches' power be used in a religiously neutral way. "[T]he potential for conflict inheres in the situation," and appellants have not suggested any "effective means of guaranteeing" that the delegated power "will be used exclusively for secular, neutral, and nonideological purposes." In addition, the mere appearance of a joint exercise of legislative authority by Church and State provides a significant symbolic benefit to religion in the minds of some by reason of the power conferred. It does not strain our prior holdings to say that the statute can be seen as having a "primary" and "principal" effect of advancing religion.

Turning to the third phase of the inquiry called for by Lemon v. Kurtzman, we see that we have not previously had occasion to consider the entanglement implications of a statute vesting significant governmental authority in churches. This statute enmeshes churches in the exercise of substantial governmental powers contrary to our consistent interpretation of the Establishment Clause. Ordinary human experience and a long line of cases teach that few entanglements could be more offensive to the spirit of the Constitution.

[Justice Rehnquist's dissent is omitted.]

AN EXTENDED NOTE ON BOARD OF EDUCATION OF KIRYAS JOEL V. GRUMET

The other major decision raising the issue of government/religion power sharing is Board of Education of Kiryas Joel v. Grumet, 512 U.S. 687 (1994). In *Kiryas Joel*, the Court held unconstitutional a New York statute that created a special school district for the Satmar Hasidim, practitioners of a strict form of Judaism. Members of the sect "interpret the Torah strictly; segregate the sexes outside the home; speak Yiddish as their primary language; eschew television, radio, and English language publications; and dress in distinctive ways that include head coverings and special garments for boys and modest dresses for girls. Children are educated in private religious schools, most boys at the United Talmudic Academy, where they receive a thorough grounding in the Torah and limited exposure to secular subjects, and most girls at Bais Rochel, an affiliated school with a curriculum designed to prepare girls for their roles as wives and mothers." *Id.* at 691. The New York statute created a special school district exclusively to allow members of this sect to obtain services for their handicapped children within their own religious community. Before the statute was enacted, members of the sect who had handicapped children were forced to send their children to schools run by the public school district in which the Satmars lived. The Court held that the New York statute "resembles the issue raised in *Larkin* to the extent that the earlier case teaches that a State may not delegate its civic authority to a group chosen according to a religious criterion." *Id.* at 698.

> The fundamental source of constitutional concern here is that the legislature itself may fail to exercise governmental authority in a religiously neutral way. The anomalously case-specific nature of the legislature's exercise of state authority in creating this district for a religious community leaves the Court without any direct way to review such state action for the purpose of safeguarding a principle at the heart of the Establishment Clause, that government should not prefer one religion to another, or religion to irreligion. . . . Because the religious community of Kiryas Joel did not receive its new governmental authority simply as one of many communities eligible for equal treatment under a general law, we have no assurance that the next similarly situated group seeking a school district of its own will receive one. . . . Nor can the historical context in this case furnish us with any reason to suppose that the Satmars are merely one in a series of communities receiving the benefit of special school district laws. Early on in the development of public education in New York, the State rejected highly localized school districts for New York City when they were promoted as a way to allow separate schooling for Roman Catholic children. And in more recent history, the special Act in this case stands alone.

Id. at 703-704. The Court went on to point out that there were several alternatives to the creation of a special school district to serve the Satmars, including having the broader school district provide special educational services at a neutral site near one of the village's parochial schools.

NOTES AND QUESTIONS

1. *Rajneeshpuram and the problem of a municipality controlled by a religious sect.* Does the fact that a political entity, such as the town of Kiryas Joel, has a

distinctive religious character, mean that it cannot constitutionally exercise government power? Is this the best reading of *Larkin* and *Grumet*? Or is there a difference between empowering a religious group to exercise state power and a simple coincidence that most people within a particular political subdivision happen to share a common faith? *Cf.* Oregon v. City of Rajneeshpuram, 598 F. Supp. 1208, 1216-1217 (D. Ore. 1984) (holding the incorporation of a religiously identified commune invalid on Establishment Clause grounds because "control over the City of Rajneeshpuram by these religious organizations is different enough from the control exercised by the religious leaders in a city of private landowners of one religion as to allow a constitutional distinction to be made between the two situations"). Rajneeshpuram was a religious commune in rural Oregon; only adherents of the faith, followers in good standing of the Bhagwan Shree Rajneesh, were permitted to reside in the community, and all land within the city was owned by the religious organization. *See id.* at 1210-1211. Should the fact that a religious organization owns all of the land within a municipality and uses this ownership to categorically exclude nonbelievers affect the constitutional analysis? For an argument that it should, see *id.* at 1216 (holding that "[t]he provision of services by a municipal government in a city whose residents are private landowners of one religious faith has the direct and primary effect of aiding the individual landowners" whereas when "all of the real property in the City of Rajneeshpuram is owned or controlled by religious organizations, the provision of municipal services by the City of Rajneeshpuram necessarily has the effect of aiding not only the individual residents of the City of Rajneeshpuram, but also of directly, obviously, and immediately benefitting the religious organizations themselves").

2. *Expressly rejecting certain religious beliefs.* May government take the opposite step—that is, go out of its way to *reject* the exercise of government power by members of a particular faith? On November 2, 2010, Oklahoma voters passed the "Save Our State Amendment," a statewide referendum proposition that prohibited the Oklahoma state courts from recognizing or giving any effect to "international law or Sharia law." *See* Awad v. Ziriax, 670 F.3d 1111, 1116-1118 (10th Cir. 2012). The measure passed with the support of over 70 percent of the voters. *Id.* at 1118. Mr. Muneer Awad brought suit in federal district court seeking to block implementation of the state constitutional amendment, alleging that it violated his rights under both the Establishment and Free Exercise Clauses of the First Amendment. Finding that Awad had satisfied all the requirements for a preliminary injunction, the federal district court issued a preliminary injunction that enjoined Oklahoma from enforcing the Save Our State Amendment. *See* Awad v. Ziriax, 754 F. Supp. 2d 1298 (W.D. Okla. 2010), *aff'd*, 670 F.3d 1111 (10th Cir. 2012). The U.S. Court of Appeals for the Tenth Circuit subsequently affirmed the district court, applying the strict scrutiny test set forth in Larson v. Valente, 456 U.S. 228, 255 (1982), and concluding that the state of Oklahoma "failed to assert a compelling interest" and, accordingly, the amendment "failed to satisfy strict scrutiny," as required under *Larson*. *Id.* at 1130. The Tenth Circuit also found that the Save Our State Amendment was not narrowly tailored: "Even if the state could identify and support a reason to single out and restrict Sharia law in its courts, the amendment's complete ban of Sharia law is hardly an exercise of narrow tailoring." *Id.* at 1131. One could see *Larkin* and *Grumet* as the other side of the same coin at issue in *Awad*: Government can

neither attempt to delegate power to a particular religion or group or religionists nor try to prohibit members of a religion from using the law on equal terms to protect their interests (even if religiously motivated or inspired).

3. *May government prohibit religious leaders from holding public office?* Just as government may not prohibit members of a particular religious group from seeking the protection of the state's law and courts, so too a state may not ban persons who hold religious offices from serving in a government office. *See* McDaniel v. Paty, 435 U.S. 618, 626-628 (1978). Strictly speaking, however, the *McDaniel* decision rests on Free Exercise, rather than Establishment Clause, grounds. The fact that the Free Exercise Clause prohibits government from banning religious ministers or priests from serving in public office clearly limits the potential scope of *Larkin* and *Grumet*.

4. *A formal neutrality approach.* In this line of cases, the Supreme Court appears to be saying that, consistent with the imperatives of the Establishment Clause, government may not discriminate in favor of a particular religion or group of religionists in allocating state power and, under the Free Exercise Clause, it may not ban adherents of particular religions from holding government office simply because of their religious beliefs. Is this a sensible approach?

Table of Cases

Table of Authorities

Strossen, Nadine, Hate Speech and Pornography: Do We Have to Choose Between Freedom of Speech and Equality?, 46 Case W. Res. L. Rev. 449, 458-477 (1996), 577

Sullivan, Kathleen, Sex, Money, and Groups, Free Speech, and Association Decisions in the October 1999 Term, 28 Pepp. L. Rev. 723 (2001), 117

Sunstein, Cass, Democracy and the Problem of Free Speech (1993), 253, 545

Sweeney, Joanne, Sexting and Freedom of Expression: A Comparative Approach, 102 Ky. L.J. 103 (2013), 598

Tien, Lee, Who's Afraid of Anonymous Speech? *McIntyre* and the Internet, 75 Or. L. Rev. 117 (1996), 281

Tushnet, Mark, "Of Church and State and the Supreme Court Revisited": Kurland Revisited, 1989 Sup. Ct. Rev. 373, 746

Van Alstyne, William W., The Hazards to the Press of Claiming a "Preferred Position," 28 Hastings L.J. 761 (1977), 374

_____, Remembering Melville Nimmer: Some Cautionary Notes on Commercial Speech, 43 UCLA L. Rev. 1635 (1996), 337

Velvel, Lawrence R., Freedom of Speech and the Draft Card Burning Cases, 16 U. Kan. L. Rev. 149 (1968), 207

Volokh, Eugene, Freedom of Speech and Workplace Harassment, 39 UCLA L. Rev. 1791 (1992), 504

_____, How Harassment Law Restricts Free Speech, 47 Rutgers L. Rev. 563 (1995), 521

_____, Crime-Facilitating Speech, 57 Stan. L. Rev. 1095 (2005), 59

_____, Freedom for the Press as an Industry or the Press as a Technology? From the Framing to Today, 160 U. Pa. L. Rev. 1 (2011),360

_____, Gruesome Speech, 100 Cornell L. Rev. 901 (2015), 450, 566

Waldron, Jeremy, The Harm in Hate Speech (2012), 606

Weinstein, Alan C. & Richard McCleary, The Association of Adult Businesses with Secondary Effects: Legal Doctrine, Social Theory, and Empirical Evidence, 20 Cardozo Arts & Ent. L.J. 101 (2011), 606

Wells, Christina E., Reinvigorating Autonomy: Freedom and Responsibility in the Supreme Court's First Amendment Jurisprudence, 32 Harv. Civ. Rt.-Civ. Lib. L. Rev. 159 (1997), 18

_____, Abortion Counseling as Vice Activity: The Free Speech Implications of *Rust v. Sullivan* and *Planned Parenthood v. Casey*, 95 Colum. L. Rev.1724, 1725-26 (1995), 625

_____, Discussing the First Amendment, 101 Mich. L. Rev. 1566 (2003), 28, 31

_____, Questioning Deference, 69 Mo. L. Rev. 903 (2004), 33, 47

_____, Fear and Loathing in Constitutional Decision-Making, 2005 Wis. L. Rev. 115, 47, 53, 58

_____, Privacy and Funeral Protests, 87 N.C. L. Rev. 151 (2008), 490

_____, Contextualizing Disclosure's Effects: Wikileaks, Balancing and the First Amendment, 97 Iowa L. Rev. Bull. 51 (2012), 404

_____, "The Promise and Peril of Protesting in the Internet Era," in Free Speech in the Internet Era 65 (2013), 156

_____, Protest, Policing and the Petition Clause, 66 Alabama Law Review 1159 (2015), 156

Werbach, Kevin D., Supercommons: Toward A Unified Theory of Wireless Communication, 82 Tx. L. Rev. (2004), 418

West, Sonja, Awakening the Press Clause, 58 UCLA L. Rev. 1025 (2011), 374

White, G. Edward, Justice Holmes and the Modernization of Free Speech Jurisprudence: The Human Dimension, 80 Cal. L. Rev. 391 (1992), 15, 38

Wiecek, William C., The Legal Foundations of Domestic Anti-Communism: The Background of *Dennis v. United States*, 2001 Sup. Ct. Rev. 375, 47

Willard, Nancy, School Response to Cyberbullying and Sexting: The Legal Challenges, 2011 BYU Ed. & L.J. 75, 532

Williams, Roger, Complete Writings of Roger Williams (Russell & Russell, Inc. 1963), 810

Williams, Susan, Content Discrimination and the First Amendment, 139 U. Pa. L. Rev. 615 (1991), 125

INDEX